TERRORISM AND COUNTERTERRORISM TODAY

SOCIOLOGY OF CRIME, LAW AND DEVIANCE

Series Editors: Mathieu Deflem
Jeffrey T. Ulmer (Volumes 1–5)

Recent Volumes:

Volume 8: Police Occupational Culture: New Debates and Directions – Edited by Megan O'Neill, Monique Marks and Anne-Marie Singh, 2007

Volume 9: Crime and Human Rights – Edited by Stephan Paramentier and Elmar Weitekamp, 2007

Volume 10: Surveillance and Governance: Crime Control and Beyond – Edited by Mathieu Deflem, 2008

Volume 11: Restorative Justice: From Theory to Practice – Edited by Holly Ventura Miller, 2008

Volume 12: Access to Justice – Edited by Rebecca Sandefur, 2009

Volume 13: Immigration, Crime and Justice – Edited by William F. McDonald, 2009

Volume 14: Popular Culture, Crime and Social Control – Edited by Mathieu Deflem, 2010

Volume 15: Social Control: Informal, Legal and Medical – Edited by James J. Chriss, 2010

Volume 16: Economic Crisis and Crime – Edited by Mathieu Deflem, 2011

Volume 17: Disasters, Hazards and Law – Edited by Mathieu Deflem, 2012

Volume 18: Music and Law – Edited by Mathieu Deflem, 2013

Volume 19: Punishment and Incarceration: A Global Perspective – Edited by Mathieu Deflem, 2014

SOCIOLOGY OF CRIME, LAW AND DEVIANCE
VOLUME 20

TERRORISM AND COUNTERTERRORISM TODAY

EDITED BY

MATHIEU DEFLEM
University of South Carolina, Columbia, SC, USA

Emerald

United Kingdom – North America – Japan
India – Malaysia – China

Emerald Group Publishing Limited
Howard House, Wagon Lane, Bingley BD16 1WA, UK

First edition 2015

Reprints and permissions service
Contact: permissions@emeraldinsight.com

British Library Cataloguing in Publication Data
A catalogue record for this book is available from the British Library

ISBN: 978-1-78560-191-0
ISSN: 1521-6136 (Series)

Printed and bound by CPI Group (UK) Ltd, Croydon, CR0 4YY

CONTENTS

LIST OF CONTRIBUTORS

Nicole Bigman	Department of Sociology, University of Georgia, Athens, GA, USA
Andreas Braun	Institute of Sociology, RWTH Aachen University, Aachen, Germany
Bradley Campbell	Department of Sociology, California State University, Los Angeles, CA, USA
Mark Cooney	Department of Sociology, University of Georgia, Athens, GA, USA
Kelly R. Damphousse	College of Arts and Sciences, University of Oklahoma, Norman, OK, USA
Willem de Lint	Flinders Law School, Flinders University of South Australia, Adelaide, Australia
Laura Dugan	Department of Criminology and Criminal Justice, University of Maryland, College Park, MD, USA
Gregg W. Etter, Sr.	Department of Criminal Justice, University of Central Missouri, Warrensburg, MO, USA
Jennifer C. Gibbs	School of Public Affairs, Penn State Harrisburg, Middletown, PA, USA
Jeff Gruenewald	Department of Sociology and Criminal Justice, University of Arkansas, Fayetteville, AR, USA
Eva-Maria Heinke	Institute of Sociology, RWTH Aachen University, Aachen, Germany
Cynthia A. Karaffa	Department of Justice Studies, Carlow University, Pittsburgh, PA, USA

Thomas Kron	Institute of Sociology, RWTH Aachen University, Aachen, Germany
Gary LaFree	START Center and Department of Criminology and Criminal Justice, University of Maryland, College Park, MD, USA
Jason Manning	Department of Sociology and Anthropology, West Virginia University, Morgantown, WV, USA
Paxton Roberts	Department of Sociology and Criminal Justice, University of Arkansas, Fayetteville, AR, USA
Christopher A. Shields	Department of Sociology and Criminal Justice, University of Arkansas, Fayetteville, AR, USA
Brent L. Smith	Department of Sociology and Criminal Justice, University of Arkansas, Fayetteville, AR, USA
Michael Welch	Department of Criminal Justice, Rutgers University, Piscataway, NJ, USA

INTRODUCTION: THE STUDY OF TERRORISM AND COUNTERTERRORISM TODAY

There is no rational way to deny the relevance of the tragic events of September 11, 2001, for the world's social and political conditions – and not only with respect to continued concerns over the spread and evolving nature of terrorism. The shock of that day has also been felt in the academic community that was and/or should have been devoted to the study of terrorism and counterterrorism, and it has continued to affect, in varying and variable ways, the course and development of (counter)terrorism studies until this day. This volume seeks to provide a state-of-the-art overview of some of the sociological and criminological dimensions and implications of the contemporary study of terrorism and counterterrorism since 9/11, with a view to the continued relevance of such work well into the future.

A little over a decade ago, a first collection of articles was published in the present series, "Sociology of Crime, Law and Deviance," that dealt with the criminology of terrorism and counterterrorism (Deflem, 2004). That volume grew directly out of the events of 9/11 and was mostly aimed at showing what social scientists interested in crime and social control could contribute to the study of (counter)terrorism, indicating a potential for theory and research that considerably exceeded what scholars actually had already achieved in this area of study. For, indeed, until those years, the most relevant work in the area of terrorism and counterterrorism had been conducted by scholars of political science, international studies, and law. A pertinent book such as *Terrorism Today*, published shortly before September 11, could not have been written by a criminologist (Harmon, 2000). But immediately thereafter, those of us working in the broad field of criminology and criminal justice clearly felt the need to catch up with ongoing relevant developments in the social world (Deflem, 2009).

Over the past 10–15 years, the situation of the study of (counter)terrorism has changed for the better, not least of all because concerns and problems over the terrorist matters have remained at the forefront of social and policy developments. This condition has favorably evolved to the extent that the study of terrorism and counterterrorism has attracted not only more attention from those scholars already well placed to study relevant issues, but has also been steadily developed and applied in those fields where such issues had erstwhile occupied a rather marginal place. Thus, rather than merely arguing for the usefulness of the perspectives and insights of sociology and criminology for the study of terrorism and its control (Savelsberg, 2006), we are now in the fortunate position of having garnered a considerable number of such works that have already made both theoretical and empirical contributions (Forst, Greene & Lynch, 2011; LaFree, 2009; Tracy, 2012). In fact, it is a testimony to the vibrancy of this area of research that some of its manifestations have already been subjected to evaluation and critique (Deflem & McDonough, 2015; Schmidt, 2010; Stampnitzky, 2011). It is within this intellectually exciting context that the contributions of this volume are situated.

The chapters in this volume are presented in three thematic parts. In Part I, selected theoretical and conceptual issues are addressed in the study of terrorism from the viewpoint of crime and/or deviance. Opening up the discussion is a chapter by Gary LaFree and Laura Dugan that head-on addresses the issue of how criminologists have contributed to the study of terrorism. The authors demonstrate that criminologists have indeed, much more than before September 11, turned to the study of terrorism and made contributions in various respects, with the special observation that methodological work has exceeded theoretical criminological writings. Taking up this theoretical challenge, Mark Cooney and Nicole Bigman draw upon the insights of pure sociology, originally developed by Donald Black, to show how ordinary citizens can become radicalized to be attracted to a commitment to terrorist activities. Cooney and Bigman argue that this transition takes place in a specific social geometry that is marked by a social closeness to a powerful organization and a social distance from a constructed enemy. Extending the same broad underlying model of pure sociology, Bradley Campbell argues that terrorism has much in common with genocide, but also that there are differences between the two. The author maintains that the similarities between these two forms of violence include that they constitute forms of conflict between socially distant, unequal groups, while the main difference is the upward orientation of terrorism toward more powerful targets, whereas genocide is usually downward in orientation. Cynthia

A. Karaffa also takes up an important theoretical question by pondering on the reality and the constructed nature of terrorism, an issue that has been at the center of many terrorism studies. Reviewing the history and perceptions of terrorism, Karaffa shows that individuals create their own reality of terrorism in an (inter-subjective) cultural context that exerts great influence on such subjective interpretations.

The chapters of Part II carry on some of the conceptual issues in the study of terrorism to contemplate on various forms and variations of terrorism today. Brent L. Smith and associates focus on the phenomenon of the lone wolf terrorist. Based on systematic data, the authors demonstrate that these type of perpetrators tend to be more educated and socially isolated than group-based actors. They can also better evade arrests because they are able to temporally and geospatially position the planning and preparations of their criminal acts. Discussing the form of the so-called "second order" terrorism, Willem de Lint suggests the construction of a type of terrorism that is seen as a reaction against other, typically state-enacted forms of violence. From this perspective, de Lint sees emerging a complex constellation of terrorism and event, on the one hand, and counterterrorism and interdiction, on the other. Turning to what they label as "terrok," Thomas Kron, Andreas Braun, and Eva-Maria Heinke seek to make sense a new form of hybrid perpetrator merging the qualities of those who commit terror and those who run amok. The authors argue that what is new about such current forms of terrorism is the evolution of individual perpetrators who radicalize without any clear connection to a terrorist organization. Finally, Jason Manning discusses the terrorist form of suicide attacks on the basis of a social-geometric model that focuses on such characteristics as status inferiority, social distance, and large movements of social time. Also arguing that sacrifice is greater among socially marginal individuals, Manning reveals the similarities between suicide attacks and other forms of violence and suicide.

In Part III, various dimensions of law, policy, and law enforcement in connection with counterterrorism are examined. Co-authors Christopher A. Shields, Brent L. Smith, and Kelly R. Damphousse offer an examination of the manner in which terrorism cases have been prosecuted in the United States over the past half century, especially in the years since September 11. The authors show that prosecutorial authority in U.S. terrorism cases has fluctuated in the evolving context of terrorist incidents and the relative success and failure of law enforcement efforts, whereby the most recent years have seen an unprecedented level of terrorism-related prosecutions and convictions. In the next chapter, Michael Welch delves into the presentation of scientific value in the practices of detention and interrogation in the U.S.-led war on terror. The author shows that these practices can actually be questioned in terms of effectiveness and legitimacy and, worse yet, that they constitute torture and human rights abuses. Turning to the policing of terrorism, Gregg W. Etter, Sr. discusses the impact of the events of September 11 on local law enforcement in the United States. The central issue, in the present post-9/11 environment, is how these new terrorism-related tasks co-exist with the traditional mission of police to control other, ordinary crimes. Rounding up the present investigations showing the value of the criminological study of terrorism and its control, Jennifer C. Gibbs attempts to clarify the concept of legitimacy in connection with counterterrorist policies. The author offers a basis to distinguish various counterterrorism policies on the basis of a typology of three categories of legitimacy, based on legality, customs, and consent, respectively.

Taken together, the chapters in this volume make a valid and valuable contribution to the study of terrorism and counterterrorism the world today. As such, they seek to offer an effort in the ongoing project to continue – recalling the now infamous words of Canadian prime minister Stephen Harper (Kaye & Béland, 2014) – to commit sociology and criminology for the benefit of the study of terrorism and counterterrorism.

Mathieu Deflem
Editor

REFERENCES

Deflem, M. (Ed.). (2004). *Terrorism and counter-terrorism: Criminological perspectives* (Vol. 5). Sociology of Crime, Law and Deviance. Amsterdam: Elsevier.

Deflem, M. (2009). Terrorism. In J. M. Miller (Ed.), *21st century criminology: A reference handbook* (pp. 533–540). Thousand Oaks, CA: Sage.

Deflem, M., & McDonough, S. (2015). The fear of counterterrorism: Surveillance and civil liberties since 9/11. *Society*, *52*, 70–79.

Forst, B., Greene, J. R., & Lynch, J. P. (2011). *Criminologists on terrorism and homeland security*. New York, NY: Cambridge University Press.

Harmon, C. C. (2000). *Terrorism today*. London: Frank Cass.

Kaye, J., & Béland, D. (2014). Stephen Harper's dangerous refusal to "commit sociology". *The Toronto Star*. Retrieved from http://www.thestar.com/opinion/commentary/2014/08/22/stephen_harpers_dangerous_refusal_to_commit_sociology.html. Accessed on August 22, 2014.

LaFree, G. (2009). Criminology's third war: Special issue on terrorism and responses to terrorism. *Criminology & Public Policy*, *8*, 431–444.

Savelsberg, J. J. (2006). Underused potentials for criminology: Applying the sociology of knowledge to terrorism. *Crime, Law and Social Change*, *46*, 35–50.

Schmidt, G. J. (2010). Sociology of terrorism following the events of 9/11/2001: A bibliography. *International Journal of Contemporary Sociology*, *47*, 381–391.

Stampnitzky, L. (2011). Disciplining an unruly field: Terrorism experts and theories of scientific/intellectual production. *Qualitative Sociology*, *34*, 1–19.

Tracy, P. E. (2012). Terrorism research in criminology: Current topics and future prospects. *Crime & Delinquency*, *58*, 647–662.

PART I
PERSPECTIVES AND CONCEPTS IN THE STUDY OF TERRORISM

HOW HAS CRIMINOLOGY CONTRIBUTED TO THE STUDY OF TERRORISM SINCE 9/11?

Gary LaFree and Laura Dugan

ABSTRACT

Purpose – *Prior to 9/11 criminologists paid relatively little attention to the study of terrorism. In 2004, the authors argued that criminologists had much to offer to advance our understanding of terrorism and urged scholars to conduct such research. This chapter accounts the theoretical and methodological contributions by the field of criminology to terrorist research.*

Methodology/approach – *This chapter demonstrates how the study of terrorism has begun to get more attention in various professional settings of criminology. It then reviews applications of criminological theory and methodological advances by criminologist to terrorism research. It ends by describing efforts to build terrorism event databases.*

Findings – *Terrorism-related research has become common at both of the major criminological professional association meetings. Funding for research on terrorism, especially a large program on domestic extremism sponsored by the National Institute of Justice, has contributed to a*

Terrorism and Counterterrorism Today
Sociology of Crime, Law and Deviance, Volume 20, 3–23

ISSN: 1521-6136/doi:10.1108/S1521-613620150000020002

growing research literature. Academic courses on terrorism have also been added to criminology programs around the country. While the criminological literature on terrorism has expanded greatly more progress has been made in applying criminological methods than theories to the study of terrorism. To date the most common theoretical perspective from criminology applied to terrorism studies has been rational choice and deterrence.

Originality/value – *This chapter takes inventory on how criminology has contributed to terrorism research. It serves to validate current efforts while encouraging continued progress.*

Keywords: Criminology; terrorism; theory; methodology; terrorism databases

INTRODUCTION

Much has changed in the relationship between terrorism research and the field of criminology in the last ten years. Research on terrorism and bias crime now routinely appears in major criminology outlets, a new generation of criminologists are examining terrorism and bias crimes for class projects, dissertations, and research papers, the National Institute of Justice is funding a major new portfolio on extremist violence and radicalization, the American Society of Criminology (ASC) just added a Division on Terrorism and Bias crime to the organization, and the ASC and the Academy of Criminal Justice Studies now feature several dozen papers and panels on terrorism and counterterrorism each year at their annual meetings.

In an earlier chapter for this series (LaFree & Dugan, 2004), we argued that terrorism is an important part of criminology and that while there are important differences between terrorism and more ordinary forms of crime, terrorism nonetheless falls solidly within the purview of criminology. This argument seems increasingly unnecessary. In this chapter we review some of the ways that criminological approaches to terrorism and bias crime have changed in the years since 9/11. We will begin by considering the evidence that criminologists have changed their attitudes toward research on terrorism and responses to terrorism in recent years. Here we will consider articles in mainstream criminology outlets, activities of the American

Society of Criminology and the American Academy of Criminal Justice Studies and research funding for the criminology of terrorism. Next we will consider the theoretical and methodological contributions to the research literature on terrorism. And finally, we will consider how data on terrorism has evolved since 9/11.

THE GROWING CONNECTION BETWEEN CRIMINOLOGY AND TERRORISM RESEARCH

In order to assess how the role of academic criminology has evolved since 9/11 we began by looking for relevant literature from this period from six of Criminology's most important journals: *Criminology, Criminology and Public Policy, the Journal of Quantitative Criminology, the Journal of Research on Crime and Delinquency, the Law and Society Review* and the *American Sociological Review*. We identified 41 research articles and notes on terrorism and bias crime from these sources from 2001 through the present. Of these, 21 appeared in *Criminology and Public Policy*, 13 in the *Journal of Quantitative Criminology*, 4 in *Criminology*, and 1 each in the *Journal of Research on Crime and Delinquency*, the *Law and Society Review*, and the *American Sociological Review*. So in general, while the numbers are still relatively modest, we have nonetheless seen a major increase in terrorism-related research appearing in mainstream criminology journals in the past decade.[1]

We also see other evidence that terrorism research is gaining traction as a serious specialization among criminologists. Within the American Society of Criminology (ASC) terrorism and responses to terrorism were first added to the annual meetings specialty topics in 2005. Since then, the number of papers on terrorism and responses to terrorism has continued to increase. At the 2014 ASC meetings in San Francisco, there were a total of 40 papers under the theme of terrorism research. These numbers compare very favorably to the number of papers listed under other major subspecializations in criminology represented at the annual meetings, including organized crime (34 papers) and white collar and corporate crime (42 papers). The output of terrorism-related research was very similar for the American Academy of Criminal Justice Studies in Philadelphia in 2014 where a total of 38 papers on terrorism-related topics were listed.

It is more difficult to gather systematic data on the extent to which terrorism courses are being added to the curricula for criminology departments but there is a good deal of indirect evidence for such a shift. For example, criminology programs as varied as those at American University, John Jay College, University of Massachusetts Lowell, Drexel, and Arizona State University all list terrorism courses as part of their curriculum.

Funding for the criminological study of terrorism has also expanded in the past ten years. Although the National Institute of Justice (NIJ) has funded select projects on terrorism for many years, its efforts received a major boost with a large new program on the causes and consequences of domestic radicalization, initiated in 2012. For the past three years NIJ has issued RFPs for research on countering and preventing violent extremists, defined by NIJ "as those who support or commit ideologically motivated violence to further political, social or religious goals." A major long-term goal of NIJ's work on violent extremism is to provide community leaders with evidence-based practices for bolstering resilience and developing community-wide responses that can prevent and mitigate threats posed by violent extremists. More generally, the policy aim of this NIJ program is to develop a better understanding of domestic radicalization to violent extremism and to advance evidence-based strategies for effective intervention and prevention of radicalization in the United States. At the time this chapter was being prepared, NIJ was conducting the third round of RFPs on domestic radicalization in the United States.

The National Consortium for Studies of Terrorism and Responses to Terrorism (START) is a university center of excellence funded initially by the U.S. Department of Homeland Security. Although START is highly interdisciplinary, criminology is one its major areas of research and START has funded a good deal of research by criminologists since it opened its doors in January of 2005. This has included (but is not limited to) large-scale studies of terrorist attacks by Brent Smith, Kelly Damphousse and their colleagues (Smith & Damphousse, 2009; Smith, Damphousse, Jackson, & Sellers, 2002); studies of extremist crime by Josh Freilich, Steve Chermak, and their colleagues (Freilich, Adamczyk, Chermak, Boyd, & Parkin, 2015; Freilich, Chermak, & Caspi, 2009); right-wing extremism by Peter Simi (Simi, Bubolz, & Hardman, 2012); studies of attitudes toward terrorism by Adamczyk and LaFree (2015), studies of responses to terrorism by Dugan and Chenoweth (2012), etiological studies of county-level terrorism by LaFree and Bersani (2014), linkages between crime and terrorism by Gruenewald, Chermak, & Freilich, 2013), quantitative analysis of terrorism by Johnson (2012) and Morris and Slocum (2012), bias crimes by King and Sutton (2013), cybercrime by Maimon,

Alper, Cukier, and Sobesto (2014), terrorist organizations by Miller (2012), radicalization of U.S. prisoners by Bert Useem and Clayton (2009), and terrorism and policing by Weisburd, Hasisi, and Jonathan-Zamir (2014).

THEORETICAL CONTRIBUTIONS BY CRIMINOLOGISTS

In looking over the recent criminology research literature on terrorism and bias crime we can conclude that researchers have begun to apply theoretical perspectives from criminology to help understand terrorism and responses to terrorism. While terrorism research informed by criminology theory is still maturing there have been major advances in the decade since we completed our earlier review. One of the most common theoretical applications from criminology appears to be rational choice/deterrence perspectives. For example, Dugan, LaFree, and Piquero (2005) adopted a rational choice framework to study the trends in worldwide aerial hijackings between 1931 and 2003. They found that enhanced security screening and metal detectors significantly reduced the risk of aerial hijackings but had no significant impact on terrorist-motivated hijacking. Similarly, Carson (2014) recently applied the rational choice framework to study radical eco-groups and counterterrorism. She examined four counterterrorism laws: (1) the Anti-Drug Abuse Act of 1988, (2) the Animal Enterprise Protection Act of 1992, (3) the Anti-Terrorism and Effective Death Penalty Act of 1996, and (4) the Animal Enterprise Terrorism Act of 2006. In a series hazard model based on more than 1 000 terrorist attacks from 1970 to 2011, Carson found significant declines in the risk of new attacks following the legislation.

Closely related to deterrence models are a number of criminological studies that have examined not only the potential for deterrence effects of policy responses to terrorism but have also looked for the possibility of backlash effects. During a wave of anti-abortion violence in the early 1990s, several U.S. states also enacted legislation protecting abortion clinics, staff, and patients. Pridemore and Freilich (2007) compare the possibility that these laws either had a deterrent effect, by reducing future attacks, or a backlash by being followed by increases in attacks. Employing logistic regression and controlling for several potential covariates, they found no support for either hypothesis. LaFree, Dugan, and Korte (2009) examined the impact of deterrence and backlash models for terrorist violence on 2,603 attacks claimed by republican groups from 1969 to 1992 taken from the Global Terrorism Database (GTD). Using models that are described later, the authors found more support for backlash than deterrence models. Specifically, three government interventions were followed by statistically significant increases in the risk of terrorist attacks, one was followed by declines and one showed neither increases nor decreases.

Dugan and Chenoweth (2012) point out that rational choice approaches to reducing terrorist violence typically suggest that states raise the costs of terrorism through punishment, thereby reducing the overall expected utility of terrorism. Alternatively, the authors argue that states should also consider raising the expected utility of abstaining from terrorism through rewards. The researchers test effects of repressive (or punishing) and conciliatory (or rewarding) actions on terrorist behavior in Israel from 1987 to 2004. Their results show that repressive actions were either unrelated to terror or related to subsequent increases in terror, and conciliatory actions were generally related to decreases in terror, depending on the tactical period.

Situational theories of crime can be linked to rational choice theories in that situational theorists usually assume a rationally motivated offender (Hsu & Newman, 2016). Clarke and Newman (2006) develop a detailed explanation of how terrorism can be explained and countered using a situational crime prevention perspective. Their strategy is to focus on what makes targets attractive and what types of weapons and tools are most appropriate for the specific attack planned. Thus, they argue that terrorists will be drawn to targets that are more exposed, more vital and more iconic. They also argue that terrorists, like more ordinary offenders, will be attracted to targets that are within easy reach of their home base. Bouhana and Wikström (2008) develop a related view based on Wikström's (2010) Situational Action theory. They argue that individuals who commit terrorist attacks are motivated by their own moral lexicon, but that the choice to engage in an attack will be defined by the viability of the situational context.

Agnew (2010, 2016) has developed a theory of terrorism based on general strain theory, arguing that collective strains increase the likelihood of terrorism because they increase negative emotions, reduce social and self-controls, reduce the ability to cope through legal and military channels, foster the social learning of terrorism, strengthen group ties, and contribute to the formation of terrorist groups. These strains increase the likelihood of terrorism by leading to negative emotional states and traits such as frustration and humiliation and reducing the effectiveness of social control through legal channels. While Agnew sets out a theoretical framework he does not provide an empirical test.

There have been at least two recent articles in the criminological literature on terrorism that draw on social disorganization perspectives. LaFree and Bersani (2014) develop a set of hypotheses informed by a social disorganization framework and test them on nearly 600 terrorist attacks in U.S. counties from 1990 to 2011. Their results show that terrorist attacks were more common in counties characterized by greater language diversity, a larger proportion of foreign-born residents, greater residential instability, and a higher percentage of urban residents. Contrary to the social disorganization perspective but in keeping with most prior research, terrorist attacks were less common in counties marked by high levels of concentrated disadvantage.

Freilich et al. (forthcoming) examine whether social disorganization theory can explain county-level variation in where far-right extremists live at the time they strike. The authors focus on the American far right, one of the most deadly extremist movements in the United States. Using logistic regression analysis the authors find that social disorganization measures were strong predictors of having a far-right extremist residing in the county. These findings support the idea that social disorganization and related systemic and control models may be useful in the study of terrorism. Conceptually, these results undermine the view that completely differentiates terrorism from regular crime and argues for separate causal models to explain each.

In general, research on terrorism guided by mainstream criminological theories is still relatively uncommon but clearly growing since 9/11. For example, as this chapter was being prepared new theoretical approaches to the study of terrorism grounded in criminology were on the horizon including work applying lifestyle/victimization perspectives (Parkin, 2016), social learning theories (Winfree & Akins, 2016) and situational action theory (Wikstrom & Bouhana, 2016).

METHODOLOGICAL CONTRIBUTIONS BY CRIMINOLOGISTS

As predicted in 2004 by LaFree and Dugan, criminologists have begun to apply sophisticated analytical methods to better understand the problem of terrorism. Because terrorists – like other criminals – operate over space and time, analyses need to account for the dynamic nature of attacks. We have identified three general contributions to the field by criminologists that are flexible enough to capture the nuances of terrorist behavior. The first are methods developed by criminologists that have been applied to terrorism. The second set of contributions includes methods that were developed in other disciplines, but have been introduced to terrorism research by criminologists. The last set includes tried and true methodologies to address terrorist-based research questions that have been used by criminologists and those in other disciplines, such as multi-level modeling, negative binomial regression, and time-series analysis. This section delineates the contributions in the first two sets. The key for all of the research presented here is that the selected methods are the most appropriate for addressing the research question at hand. And, as expected, the pool of analytical tools available to study terrorism has greatly expanded because of criminologists' contributions.

Methods Developed by Criminologists

At least two analytical tools were developed by criminologists and applied to terrorism: series hazard modeling, first used in Dugan et al. (2005) and group-based trajectory analysis (GBTA), developed by Nagin and Land (1993) and Nagin (2005). The series hazard model was developed to model event-based data, like terrorist attacks; and GBTA was developed to model the criminological patterns of individuals over time and has since been applied to geographic units and terrorist organizations.

The series hazard model is an extension of the Cox (1972) proportional hazard model, and is used to estimate the impact of interventions on the hazard of an additional incident (such as a terrorist attack) controlling a set of relevant variables. The key distinction between the series hazard model and the more traditional Cox proportional hazard model is that it estimates the contributions of covariates to the hazard of repeated events (e.g., terrorist attacks) for *one unit* rather than for a single event (e.g., arrest) across *multiple units* (Dugan, 2011). This method is used as an alternative to time-series analysis, which also estimates the effects of covariates on outcomes for a single unit over time. Dugan (2011) lists several advantages of the series hazard model over time-series including its ability to capture variation in the timing between events rather than arbitrarily aggregating the events to one unit of time (e.g., month, quarter, year) and counting their frequency.

Despite being formally named in a 2011 *Journal of Quantitative Criminology* article, the series hazard model was first used in 2005 to estimate the effects of three policies on the hazard of aerial hijacking (Dugan et al., 2005). As the model currently allows for only single series, the authors produced six models to estimate the effects of the policies on different outcomes: (1) all hijackings, (2) only U.S. hijackings, (3) only non-U.S. hijackings, (4) hijackings to Cuba, (5) terrorist-motivated hijackings, and (6) non-terrorist-motivated hijackings. The results showed that the policies that targeted specific types of hijackings were most relevant to those events (e.g., criminalizing hijackings in Cuba on Cuban hijackings). Further, as mentioned above, the findings also revealed that traditional deterrence strategies operationalized through these policies appeared ineffective to terrorist-motivated events. The series hazard model was next used in two of the projects described above: LaFree et al.'s (2009) evaluation of six interventions by the British government on Republican terrorist attacks and Carson's (2014) assessment of the impact of four laws on the activity of radical eco-groups. Finally, the series hazard model has also been used by scholars outside of criminology. Sharvit et al. (2013), a team of mostly social psychologists, used the method to assess the effects of efforts by the Israeli government on different measures of Palestinian terrorism by specific groups and found that the response to Israeli tactics varied across groups. Argomaniz and Vidal-Diez (2015), a political scientist and statistician, respectively, use the series hazard model to test the effects of six major efforts by the Spanish government to reduce the risk of terrorism by the Basque group, Euzkadi Ta Askatasuna (ETA) and found evidence that some of these efforts may have actually increased the risk of continued terror by ETA rather than deter it.

Turning now to one of the most significant methodological innovations in criminology over the past twenty years, group-based trajectory analysis (GBTA; Nagin, 2005; Nagin & Land, 1993) was developed to examine individual patterns of offending beginning early in a person's childhood, extending through adolescence (Nagin & Tremblay, 1999), and on into adulthood (Doherty, 2005). GBTA became popular in the general context of a debate among scholars about whether the well-known age-crime curve described a universal continuum of criminal involvement that changes as individuals age (i.e., criminal propensity: Hirschi & Gottfredson, 1983) or whether it is instead composed of a complex mixture of nonoffenders and offenders with varying durations of criminal careers, marked by constant offending rates. This information contributes to both policy and theory because by understanding why certain groups of individuals follow one pathway instead of another, we can gain important insight into their differing etiologies.

The same sort of advantage can be given in other contexts, as GBTA has been applied to the "life course" of units other than individuals.

LaFree, Yang, and Crenshaw (2009) used GBTA to study the patterns of attack over four decades for the 53 foreign terrorist groups that have been identified by the U.S. Department of State as posing a special threat to the United States. The authors produced two sets of analyses distinguished by whether the attacks targeted U.S. nationals or others; and found that each set produced four distinct groups. These groups followed three primary waves that showed terrorist booms in the 1970s, 1980s, and the early 21st century. Further, the analysis also revealed that despite being labeled as a threat to U.S. nationals these groups had targeted the United States in only 3% of their attacks.

In 2012, Miller expanded the use of GBTA on terrorist organizations by using it to better understand how patterns of onset related to patterns of decline for the 557 terrorist organizations in the GTD that were active for at least 365 days between 1970 and 2008. This study was especially innovative because she used the method to quantitatively contribute to the discussion of how terrorist organizations decline by modeling the period of activity after the organizations' most active year. Her findings reveal that organizations that perpetrate attacks at a rapid pace immediately after onset are two to three times more likely to perpetrate at a high volume throughout their career, and will later decline at a relatively slow rate (Miller, 2012).

Criminologists have also applied GBTA to spatial units in order to discern how countries might have different "life course" patterns of terrorist activity. LaFree, Morris, and Dugan (2010) used GBTA to examine the patterns of terrorist attacks in 206 countries from 1970 through 2006 and found five distinct trajectory groups. Among them was one composed of only five countries, but with an alarming pattern that accounted for close to forty percent of all attacks. The analysis demonstrates that, just like more common crime, terrorist behavior also produces hotspots of activity over time and space. This study was later updated in a methodological paper that compares the results of the GBTA (there referred to as the more general Latent Class Growth Analysis) to general mixture models (Morris & Slocum, 2012). The authors conclude that this method is better suited to identify terrorist hotspots.

Methods Developed by Others, But Applied to Terrorism by Criminologists

The second group of methodologies were developed by scholars in other disciplines but brought to the study of terrorism by criminologists. These include the self-exciting point process models, Knox analysis, and estimating Local Indicators of Spatial Autocorrelation (LISA) statistics.

White, Porter, and Mazerolle (2013) have applied self-exciting point process models to terrorist events. This type of stochastic process, introduced by Hawkes (1971) and currently referred to as the Hawkes process, describe the intensity of event clusters that are partially determined by the timing of previously occurring events. Accordingly, clusters of future events come from either previous events or from similar predictors of previous events. In both cases, the determinants "excite" the process (White et al., 2013). The application of the Hawkes process to terrorism is evident, and White and his colleagues use GTD data of terrorist attacks from Indonesia, the Philippines, and Thailand from 2000 to 2010 to measure and compare the fluctuation of terrorist activity over time. The scholars estimate three theoretically important parameters of terrorism: risk, resilience, and volatility. Risk is measured by increases in the expected number of daily attacks. Resilience is defined as the length of time after the initial attack that it takes risk to return to its pre-event level. Volatility is measured by the total increase in risk caused by a terrorist attack. Their findings show that the patterns of risk, resilience, and volatility differ across countries. The Philippines is the riskiest with the least resilience across all countries. Indonesia, on the other hand, is least risky, least volatile, and has the most resilience. Thailand is the most volatile of the three.

Porter and White (2012) present a variation of this model that jointly estimates the probability of an attack and the number of attacks on a given day in Indonesia as a function of the timing of previous attacks. This self-exciting hurdle model improves the predictability as the model quickly adapted to changing attack behavior. The authors argue that the predictive capabilities of this model can help government more strategically allocate security resources.

Another set of methodological contributions that were developed by others and applied to terrorism by criminologists also identifies hotspots in terrorist activity, but this time by estimating the spatial and temporal clustering of events. The most widely used test for space-time clustering is the Knox test (1964), which uses a 2×2 contingency table to assess pairs of events according to how close they are in space and time. This approach allows researchers to directly analyze the space and time interaction of two events at the micro-level, thus preserving the "richness" of the data. Since the mid-1960s, the Knox test has been used to explore space-time clustering of several cancers. This methodology was applied to terrorism decades later when Braithwaite and Johnson (2012) investigated the space and time clustering of the Improvised Explosive Device (IED) attacks in Iraq and their subsequent trends of decay using data on 3,775 IED events (discoveries and explosions) between January and June 2005.[2] Using Knox analysis to study the local-level interaction of IED attacks and a wide variety of counterinsurgency activities to estimate the spatial and temporal parameters for clusters and decay, the authors found significant evidence that each series of counterinsurgency activities is, indeed, clustered, falling within 5.5 kilometers and one week of each other. The authors found a similar clustering with IED events, as after an initial IED explosion, the others are more likely to occur sooner (within two weeks) and nearby (within 1.5 kilometers) followed by decay in both time and space.

Behlendorf, LaFree, and Legault (2012) use the Knox analysis to identify microcycles, or localized bursts of terrorism, for ETA attacks between 1970 and 2007 and Farabundo Marti National Liberation Front (FMLN) attacks between 1980 and 1992. The authors found significant evidence for space and time interaction for five miles and two weeks from the original event, based on an analysis of 1.5 million pairs of attacks perpetuated by ETA and 3.5 million pairs perpetuated by the FMLN. They then modeled the predictors of attack characteristics that fall into microcycles and found that bombings are the predominant attack mode and that among other things fatal attacks are less likely to be part of microcycles than independent attacks.

Another type of spatial analysis brought to the study of terrorism by criminologists is the use of Local Indicators of Spatial Association (LISA) statistics. LISA statistics were developed by Anselin (1995) to address a weakness found in the Moran's *I* statistic for identifying spatial dependency. The Moran's *I*, the most common metric for identifying spatial dependencies across neighborhoods, is a global measure that ignores heterogeneity in spatial dependency (Cohen & Tita, 1999). On the other hand, LISA statistics are able to identify local hotspots and outlying events (Anselin, 1995). Cohen and Tita (1999) extended the cross-sectional application of LISA statistics to identify patterns of diffusion for youth-gang homicides over time within one city. Their model distinguishes between contagious diffusion, which is diffusion across contiguous units, and hierarchical diffusion that spreads more broadly with common influences.

LaFree, Dugan, Xie, and Singh (2012) apply temporal LISA statistics to terrorist attacks by the Basque group, ETA. ETA was chosen because its campaign between 1970 and 2007 was nearly continuous, allowing for the shifts in spatial patterns to be meaningful. Further, in 1978 the group announced a change in tactic from seeking an outright military victory in the Basque region to undertaking a war of attrition in Spain. The authors interpret this tactical shift as a shift from control attacks that would take place mostly in the Basque region to attrition attacks that would be perpetrated deeper into Spanish territory. LaFree et al. (2012) equate these tactics to contagious and hierarchical diffusion, respectively, as defined by Cohen and Tita (1999). Indeed, the authors found that after 1978 ETA attacks were consistent with hierarchical diffusion.

The research described in this section demonstrates that criminologists have indeed contributed to the sophistication of terrorism research. As most of these articles have been well cited, we expect that new audiences are being exposed to them expanding the "toolbox" for terrorism scholars everywhere.

CHANGES IN DATABASES SINCE 9/11

Finally, we discuss changes in the data that measure terrorism since the September 11th attacks. Of course, the fundamental challenge of collecting data on terrorism that we discussed in our earlier chapter (LaFree & Dugan, 2004) remains. We are unable to collect terrorism data by relying on the three traditional sources of crime data: "official" data collected by legal agents, especially the police; "victimization" data collected from crime victims; and "self-report" data collected from offenders. Data on terrorism collected by government entities are inevitably influenced by political considerations. Of course, to some extent, this is also a problem with official data on common crimes. Police, courts, and correctional officers frequently face political pressure to present their crime data in particular ways. However, the political pressure is likely to be especially acute with regard to terrorism, as both terrorists and politicians are trying to influence public opinion. Moreover, while huge amounts of detailed official data on common crimes are routinely produced by the various branches of the criminal justice system in most nations, this is rarely the case for terrorism. In fact, until recently, most suspected terrorists in the United States were not legally processed for their acts of terrorism, but for other related offenses (Smith & Damphousse, 1996).

Victimization data, which have played an increasingly important role in the study of crime, are almost entirely irrelevant to the study of terrorist activities. Several features of terrorism mean that victimization surveys are unlikely to ever have widespread applicability. To begin with, for most nations and at most points in time, terrorism is much rarer than criminal acts. This means that even with extremely large sample sizes, few individuals in most countries will have been victimized by terrorists. Moreover, because one of the hallmarks of terrorism is that victims are often chosen by convenience, victims of terrorist events frequently have few details to report. Consider, for example, the bombing at the Boston Marathon on April 15, 2013, engineered by two Chechen brothers, Dzhokhar and Tamerlan Tsarnaev. The perpetrators left two pressure cooker bombs about 210 yards apart near the Marathon finish line. When the bombs exploded, about 12 seconds apart, they killed three persons and injured an estimated 264 others (Kotz, 2013). In this case the victims were based on the individuals who just happened to be near the finish line when the bombs exploded and had no prior contact with the Tsarnaev brothers.

Self-report data on terrorists has been more important than victimization data, but it too faces serious limitations. Most active terrorists are unwilling to participate in interviews. And even if they are willing to participate, getting access to known terrorists for research purposes raises obvious challenges. As Merari (1991) has put it, "The clandestine nature of terrorist organizations and the ways and means by which intelligence can be obtained will rarely enable data collection which meets commonly accepted academic standards." Still, we can learn a good deal from direct contact with terrorists or former terrorists. A good example is the work by Horgan (2009) based on interviews with individuals who disengaged from participating in terrorist violence.

Because of the difficulties with the use of official data, victimization data and self-report data, research on terrorism has continued to rely heavily on secondary data sources. Here there has been a fair amount of change in the past decade. At the time of the 9/11 attacks there was a small cottage industry composed of individuals and companies in several countries (especially the United States and the United Kingdom) collecting data on terrorist attacks from unclassified media sources. Many of those collecting data on terrorism had armed forces backgrounds and many had worked for military intelligence before starting new careers as terrorism data collectors in the private sector.

While all of these terrorism event databases had unique individual characteristics, they all shared a reliance on open media accounts of terrorism – collected originally from some combination of news wire services, unclassified government reports such as those issued by the U.S. State Department, and leading international newspapers. Several of these open-source databases started in the late 1960s – at the same time that portable cameras coupled with satellite technology first allowed reporters to send pictures and stories almost instantaneously from anywhere in the world. Over time, the Internet played an increasingly important role in open-source data collection efforts. Among the most important of these event databases in the years since 9/11 have been the RAND-MIPT (Research and Development-Memorial Institute for the Prevention of Terrorism) data, the International Terrorism: Attributes of Terrorist Events (ITERATE) data, the U.S. State Department data, the Worldwide Incidents Tracking System data (WITS) collected by the National Counterterrorism Center (NCTC), and the Global Terrorism Database (GTD).

The situation with regard to these event databases has been extremely fluid over the past ten years (for a review, see LaFree, Dugan, & Miller, 2015). The RAND-MIPT and WITS data were discontinued during this period, the ITERATE data are still available (although they must be purchased) and remain limited to international attacks, and the GTD has greatly evolved during this period. Current collection of the GTD is done by a research team at the START Center. At present, the data collection process begins with a universe of over one million articles published daily worldwide, in order to identify the relatively small subset of articles that describe terrorist attacks. This is accomplished using customized search strings to isolate an initial pool of potentially relevant articles, followed by more sophisticated techniques to further refine the search results. In order to maximize the efficiency of the data collection process, the START team uses natural language processing techniques to automatically identify and remove duplicate source articles by measuring similarities between pairs of documents. In addition, the staff has developed a machine-learning model using feedback from trained GTD staff that classifies the remaining documents as either likely or not likely to be relevant to terrorism. This model is continually refined using input from the research team regarding the accuracy of the classification results. To facilitate this iterative process, the staff has developed a web-based interface that staff use to provide continuous feedback to the system through their review of the source documents and identification of false-positives (source documents that appear to describe terrorist attacks but do not) and false-negatives (source documents that appear to not describe terrorist attacks but actually do).

The GTD team reviews all the source documents that have been classified as relevant by the machine-learning model and generates database entries for individual attacks that satisfy the GTD inclusion criteria. They use the document analysis tools to cluster similar documents together based on key identifying features of the text. In addition, as the set of identified incidents expands they use this information to supply coders with details of already created events or related sources that are potential matches for a given attack under review. At present, approximately 10,000 – 15,000 articles are manually reviewed to identify attacks for each month of data collection. Once the attacks have been identified, domain-specific research teams record data on over 120 variables pertaining to the location, perpetrators, targets, weapons, tactics, casualties, and consequences of each attack.

Three other databases developed by criminologists have had a large and growing impact on terrorism-related research. For many years, a team of researchers headed by Brent Smith and Kelly Damphousse has developed the American Terrorism Study (ATS). These data are based on federal terrorism court cases and incident and antecedent geospatial data. The ATS allows examination of a wide range of variables including characteristics of federal terrorism court cases; the characteristics of persons indicted in each court case or involved in incidents, otherwise referred to as indictees; characteristics of incidents and planned incidents; and antecedent activities that lead up to the incident and are necessary to carry it out and/or achieve the goals of the persons or groups.

The ATS allows researchers to examine detailed characteristics of the terrorism incidents and perpetrators' antecedent activities associated with each of these federal court cases. Since some court cases involved arrests prior to an incident, these cases are not associated with a geocoded incident location unless the conspiracy had progressed to the point of target identification. Other court cases may be associated with multiple incidents. Therefore, the number of cases and number of incidents do not match. In addition to geocoded information on incident or target locations, the ATS includes geocoded information on what are variously referred to as "precursor," "pre-incident," or "antecedent" activities.

Two additional terrorism-related databases since 9/11 are the Extremist Crime Database (ECDB), developed by Josh Freilich, Steve Chermak and their colleagues and the Eco Incidents Database (EID) was developed by Jennifer Carson (Carson, 2014; Carson, LaFree, & Dugan, 2012). The ECDB collects open-source data on non-violent and violent criminal behavior associated with far-right-wing extremist groups, including data on event, perpetrator, and victim. Early work by the team focused on ideologically motivated homicides. The team has identified more than 375 far-right homicide incidents that occurred since 1990. The researchers identified over 50 law-enforcement officers (i.e., federal, state, local police, correctional officers, and private security guards) killed by far-right extremists and 29 far-right suspects that were killed by law enforcement (12 of these far-rightists were killed during one of the 375 far-right homicide incidents and the other 17 were killed in additional incidents where no far-right homicide occurred). In addition, the ECDB team identified 41 far-right suspects who committed suicide (22 of these suspects were linked to one of the 375 homicide incidents, the other 19 committed suicide in additional incidents where no far-right homicide occurred).

The ECDB also includes a wide variety of other illegal acts committed by far-right extremists, including tax refusal, gun charges, land-use violations, false liens and financial schemes, abortion-related crimes, hate-crimes, anti-government attacks, anti-global strikes, preparatory crimes (such as bank robberies, drug dealing, cybercrime, and identity theft), and other crimes that further the group's survival or ideology. The researchers are also exploring the relational ties between extremists and non-extremist associates to understand how financial extremist networks are formed and operate. In addition, they will investigate whether the criminality of political extremists escalate from non-violent financial offenses to violent acts. A number of far-right suspects who committed high profile ideologically motivated attacks during the last 20 years first committed financial crimes.

The EID includes over 1,000 illegal incidents perpetrated by extremist environmental or animal rights groups based on data from the Global Terrorism Database (described above) and data maintained by the Foundation for Biomedical Research. Perhaps the single most striking conclusion from analysis of the EID is that thus far, environmental and animal rights terrorist attacks and crimes in the United States have been aimed overwhelmingly at property damage rather than causing injury or death to humans. Despite the argument that there is considerable overlap between radical environmental and animal rights groups, Carson (2014) finds important differences in the characteristics of the attacks attributed to these two groups: attacks perpetrated in the name of animal rights are more likely to target people while environmental extremists are more likely to choose weapons (e.g., sabotaging equipment) that have less potential for lethality.

Together, these databases have expanded scholars' ability to understand terrorism and other bias crimes.

CONCLUSION

This chapter set forth to take inventory on the contributions by criminologists to the study of terrorism since the attacks on September 11. It uses a

2004 chapter by the same authors as a motivating reference point. In 2004, criminologists needed to be convinced that terrorism was relevant to the field of criminology and that by joining other disciplines in studying it, we could further advance knowledge. Criminology has always been a multidisciplinary field that draws on theories and methodologies from other disciplines to better understand crime. It is with this muscle that the discipline has been able to contribute to the improved understanding of terrorism. While we are still near the advent of the trajectory of scholarly work in this area, patterns suggest that criminologists will continue to study terrorism. We anticipate that the field will help develop a deeper theoretical understanding of its causes and ways to reduce its incidence while strategically applying appropriate methodologies in order to improve estimation.

NOTES

1. Brent Smith and Kelly Damphousse were among the first criminologists to publish terrorism-related research in high profile criminology journals (see Smith & Damphousse, 1996, 1998).
2. The study is based on five data series drawn from Significant Activity (SIGACTS) Reports by the United States Army.

REFERENCES

Adamczyk, A., & LaFree, G. (2015). Religiosity and reactions to terrorism. *Social Science Research*, *51*, 17–29.

Agnew, R. (2010). A general strain theory of terrorism. *Theoretical Criminology*, *14*(2), 131–153.

Agnew, R. (2016). General strain theory and terrorism. In G. LaFree & J. Freilich (Eds.), *The handbook of the criminology of terrorism*. Hoboken, NJ: Wiley.

Anselin, L. (1995). Local indicators of spatial association – LISA. *Geographical Analysis*, *27*, 93–115.

Argomaniz, J., & Vidal-Diez, A. (2015). Examining deterrence and backlash effects in counterterrorism: The case of ETA. *Terrorism and Political Violence*, *27*, 160–181.

Behlendorf, B., LaFree, G., & Legault, R. (2012). Microcycles of violence: Evidence from terrorist attacks by ETA and the FMLN. *Journal of Quantitative Criminology*, *28*, 49–75.

Bouhana, N., & Wikström, P.-O. (2008). *Theorizing terrorism: Terrorism as moral actions*. Research Report. London: Jill Dando Institute, University College of London.

Braithwaite, A., & Johnson, S. D. (2012). Space-time modeling of insurgency and counterinsurgency in Iraq. *Journal of Quantitative Criminology*, *28*, 31–48.

Carson, J. V. (2014). Counterterrorism and radical eco-groups: A context for exploring the series hazard model. *Journal of Quantitative Criminology*, *30*, 485–504.

Carson, J. V., LaFree, G., & Dugan, L. (2012). Terrorist and nonterrorist criminal attacks by radical environmental and animal rights groups in the United States, 1970–2007. *Terrorism and Political Violence*, *24*, 295–315.

Clarke, R. V. G., & Newman, G. (2006). *Outsmarting the terrorists*. Westport, CT: Greenwood Publishing Group.

Cohen, J., & Tita, G. (1999). Diffusion of homicide: Exploring a general method for detecting spatial diffusion processes. *Journal of Quantitative Criminology*, *15*, 451–493.

Cox, D. (1972). Regression models and life-tables. *Journal of the Royal Statistical Society*. Series B (Methodological), *34*, 187–220.

Doherty, E. E. (2005). *Assessing an age-graded theory of informal social control: Are there conditional effects of life events in the desistance process*. Doctoral Dissertation, University of Maryland, College Park, MD.

Dugan, L. (2011). The series hazard model: An alternative to time series for event data. *Journal of Quantitative Criminology*, *27*, 379–402.

Dugan, L., & Chenoweth, E. (2012). Moving beyond deterrence: The effectiveness of raising the expected utility of abstaining from terrorism in Israel. *American Sociological Review*, *77*, 597–624.

Dugan, L., LaFree, G., & Piquero, A. R. (2005). Testing a rational choice model of airline hijackings. *Criminology*, *43*, 1031–1065.

Freilich, J. D., Adamczyk, A., Chermak, S. M., Boyd, K., & Parkin, W. S. (2015). Investigating the applicability of macro-level criminology theory to terrorism: A county-level analysis. *Journal of Quantitative Criminology*. doi: 10.1007/s10940-014-9239-0

Freilich, J. D., Chermak, S. M., & Caspi, D. (2009) Critical events in the life trajectories of domestic extremist white supremacist groups: A case study analysis of four violent organizations. *Criminology and Public Policy*, *8*, 497–530.

Gruenewald, J., Chermak, S., & Freilich, J. D. (2013). Distinguishing "loner" attacks from other domestic extremist violence: A comparison of far-right homicide incident and offender characteristics. *Criminology and Public Policy*, *12*, 65–91.

Hawkes, A. G. (1971). Spectra of some self-exciting and mutually exciting point processes. *Biometrika*, *58*, 83–90.

Hirschi, T., & Gottfredson, M. (1983) Age and the explanation of crime. *American Journal of Sociology*, *89*, 552–584.

Horgan, J. (2009). *Walking away from terrorism: Accounts of disengagement from radical and extremist movements*. London: Routledge.

Hsu, H. Y., & Newman, G. R. (2016). The situational approach to terrorism. In G. LaFree & J. Freilich (Eds.), *Handbook of the criminology of terrorism*. Hoboken, NJ: Wiley.

Johnson, D. B. (2012). Cross-classified multilevel models: An application to the criminal case processing of indicted terrorists *Journal of Quantitative Criminology*, *28*, 163–189.

King, R. D., & Sutton, G. M. (2013). High times for hate crimes: Explaining the temporal clustering of hate-motivated offending. *Criminology*, *51*, 871–894.

Knox, G. (1964). Epidemiology of childhood leukemia in Northumberland and Durham. *British Journal of Prevention and Social Medicine*, *18*, 17–24.

Kotz, D. (2013). Injury toll from Marathon bombs reduced to 264. *The Boston Globe*, April 24. Retrieved from https://www.bostonglobe.com/lifestyle/health-wellness/2013/04/23/number-injured-marathon-bombing-revised-downward/NRpaz5mmvGquP7KMA6XsIK/story.html

LaFree, G., & Bersani, B. (2014). County-level correlates of terrorist attacks in the United States, 1990–2011. *Criminology and Public Policy, 13*, 455–481.

LaFree, G., & Dugan, L. (2004). How does studying terrorism compare to studying crime? In M. Deflem (Ed.), *Terrorism and counter-terrorism: Criminological perspectives* (pp. 53–74). New York, NY: Elsevier.

LaFree, G., Dugan, L., & Korte, R. (2009). The impact of British counterterrorist strategies on political violence in Northern Ireland: Comparing deterrence and backlash models. *Criminology, 47*, 17–45.

LaFree, G., Dugan, L., & Miller, E. (2015). *Putting terrorism into context: Lessons learned from the world's most comprehensive terrorism database*. New York, NY: Routledge.

LaFree, G., Dugan, L., Xie, M., & Singh, P. (2012). Spatial and temporal patterns of terrorist attacks by ETA 1970 to 2007. *Journal of Quantitative Criminology, 28*, 7–29.

LaFree, G., Morris, N. A., & Dugan, L. (2010). Cross-national patterns of terrorism: Comparing trajectories for total, attributed, and fatal attacks, 1970–2006. *British Journal of Criminology, 50*, 622–649.

LaFree, G., Yang, S.-M., & Crenshaw, M. (2009). Trajectories of terrorism: Attack patterns of foreign groups that have targeted the United States, 1970–2004. *Criminology and Public Policy, 8*, 445–473.

Maimon, D., Alper, M., Cukier, M., & Sobesto, B. (2014). Restrictive deterrent effects of a warning banner in an attacked computer system. *Criminology, 52*, 33–59.

Merari, A. (1991). Academic research and government policy on terrorism. *Terrorism and Political Violence, 3*, 88–102.

Miller, E. (2012). Patterns of onset and decline among terrorist organizations. *Journal of Quantitative Criminology, 28*, 77–101.

Morris, N. A., & Slocum, L. A. (2012). Estimating country-level terrorism trends using group-based trajectory analyses: Latent class growth analysis and general mixture modeling. *Journal of Quantitative Criminology, 28*, 103–139.

Nagin, D. S. (2005). *Group-based modeling of development*. Cambridge, MA: Harvard University Press.

Nagin, D. S., & Land, K. C. (1993). Age, criminal careers, and population heterogeneity: Specification and estimation of a nonparametric, mixed Poisson model. *Criminology, 31*, 327–362.

Nagin, D. S., & Tremblay, R. E. (1999). Trajectories of boys' physical aggression, opposition, and hyperactivity on the path to physically violent and nonviolent juvenile delinquency. *Child Development, 70*, 1181–1196.

Parkin, W. S. (2016). Victimization theories and terrorism. In G. LaFree & J. Freilich (Eds.), *The handbook of the criminology of terrorism*. Hoboken, NJ: Wiley.

Porter, M. D., & White., G. (2012). Self-exciting hurdle models for terrorist activity. *The Annals of Applied Statistics, 6*, 106–124.

Pridemore, W. A., & Freilich, J. D. (2007). The impact of state laws protecting abortion clinics and reproductive rights: Deterrence, backlash, or neither? *Law and Human Behavior, 31*, 611–627.

Sharvit, K., Kruglanski, A. W., Wang, M., Chen, X., Boyatzi, L. M., Ganor, B., & Azani, E. (2013). The effects of Israeli use of coercive and conciliatory tactics on Palestinian's use of terrorist tactics: 2000–2006. *Dynamics of Asymmetric Conflict, 6*, 22–44.

Simi, P., Bubolz, B., & Hardman, A. (2012). Military experience, identity discrepancies, and far right terrorism: An exploratory analysis. *Studies in Conflict and Terrorism, 36*, 654–667.

Smith, B. L., & Damphousse, K. R. (1996). Punishing political offenders: The effect of political motive on federal sentencing decisions. *Criminology*, *34*, 289–321.

Smith, B. L., & Damphouse, K. (1998). The prosecution and punishment of international terrorist in federal courts: 1980–1998. *Criminology and Public Policy*, *1*, 311–338.

Smith, B. L., & Damphousse, K. R. (2009). Patterns of precursor behaviors in the life span of a U.S. environmental terrorist group. *Criminology and Public Policy*, *8*, 475–496.

Smith, B. L., Damphousse, K. R., Jackson, F., & Sellers, A. (2002). The prosecution and punishment of international terrorists in federal courts: 1980–1998. *Criminology and Public Policy*, *1*, 311–338.

Useem, B., & Clayton, O. (2009). Radicalization of U.S. prisoners. *Criminology and Public Policy*, *8*, 561–592.

Weisburd, D., Hasisi, B., & Jonathan-Zamir, T. (2014). Trends in Israeli policing: Terrorism, community, victimization and crime control. *Police Practice and Research: An International Journal*, *15*, 97–100.

White, G., Porter, M. D., & Mazerolle, L. (2013). Terrorism risk, resilience and volatility: A comparison of terrorism patterns in three Southeast Asian countries. *Journal of Quantitative Criminology*, *29*, 295–320.

Wikström, P.-O. (2010). *Situational action theory*. Oxford Bibliographies Online. Oxford University Press.

Wikstrom, P.-O., & Bouhana, N. (2016). Explaining terrorism and radicalization: A situational action theory. In G. LaFree & J. Freilich (Eds.), *The handbook of the criminology of terrorism*. Hoboken, NJ: Wiley.

Winfree, L. T., & Akins, J. K. (2016). Social learning theory, terrorism, and terrorists: Exploring the boundaries of a general theory. In G. LaFree & J. Freilich (Eds.), *The handbook of the criminology of terrorism*. Hoboken, NJ: Wiley.

TERRORISM AS GRAVITATIONAL ATTRACTION

Mark Cooney and Nicole Bigman

ABSTRACT

Purpose – *Drawing on the theoretical system known as pure sociology, this chapter presents a theory of the transition from ordinary citizen to dedicated terrorist.*

Methodology/approach – *We support our argument with data drawn from the diverse literature on terrorist affiliation, with particular emphasis on qualitative investigations into the background of individual terrorists.*

Findings – *The transition from citizen to terrorist represents a dramatic increase in commitment to a moral cause, or partisanship. Such commitment is a product of a specific social geometry: social closeness to a powerful organization and social distance from the enemy. That geometry is triggered by a movement of social time entailing loss and proceeds via gravitational attraction. If uninterrupted, the process reverses social time, resulting in a highly partisan geometry that calls forth risky sacrifice for the cause and severe violence toward enemy civilians.*

Originality/value – *Our theory builds upon network explanations of the transition to terrorism but goes beyond them in three ways: (1) it*

Terrorism and Counterterrorism Today
Sociology of Crime, Law and Deviance, Volume 20, 25–46

ISSN: 1521-6136/doi:10.1108/S1521-613620150000020001

provides an explanation of the initial drift into terrorist networks; (2) it does not invoke psychology, purposes or other subjective mental states of the actors; and (3) it situates the transition to terrorism within a general theory of conflict.

Keywords: Terrorism; terrorists; jihadis; social gravitation; social time; pure sociology

INTRODUCTION

Why do people become terrorists? This question has yet to receive a clear answer. One reason is sheer empirical complexity: there are many forms of terrorism and many types of terrorists. Another lies in how the issue is typically approached – as a matter of terrorist motivations or goals. Terrorism experts commonly pronounce on the motives of terrorists for joining organizations and attacking particular targets (see, e.g., Nesser, 2006; Richardson, 2006; compare Horgan, 2014a). The problem is that motives are inscrutable. People have no access to their own motives let alone those of others. Since motives cannot be observed but only imputed, they are forever open to further speculation.

We propose to address the question sociologically, without reference to the unknowable inner psychology of the actor. Employing the theoretical paradigm known as pure sociology, we suggest that the transition to terrorism is a function of the location, direction, and alteration of actors in social space (Black, 1976, 1993, 2011). Individuals who experience particular movements of social time while occupying particular locations in social space are gravitationally attracted to terrorism.

"Terrorists" we define as individuals who are members of, or claim affiliation with, a terrorist organization or movement whether or not they personally engage in violence or some other activity (e.g., fundraising). "Terrorism" we define as mass covert violence by organized civilians against civilians (Black, 2004). Since the protagonists are invariably divided by language, ethnicity, religion, or ideology into groups such as communists or non-communists, Protestants or Catholics, Tamils or Sinhalese, Muslims or non-Muslims, terrorism is, in particular, mass intercultural violence. But terrorism in the strict or pure sense is typically only one form of intercultural violence perpetrated by terrorists (Moghadam, Berger, & Beliakova, 2014). Terrorist groups often engage in guerilla warfare by attacking soldiers, police officers, diplomats, and politicians. If they are powerful, they may control and rule a territory, constituting an insurgency. Our theory extends to terrorists in these broader senses as well. And while it embraces terrorists of every stripe, we primarily apply it here to the dominant form of terrorism across the globe today – that committed in the name of radical Islamism: jihadi terrorism.

Our focus, then, is not the attraction of terrorism for individuals (Cottee & Hayward, 2011). Rather, it is the attraction of individuals to terrorism. After briefly reviewing the multi-disciplinary literature on terrorist affiliation, we lay out our theoretical perspective. We then apply the theory to jihadis, drawing on empirical data generated by scholars and journalists. We make particular use of qualitative research on the lives of terrorists, such as interviews with the relatives of suicide terrorists. The information is inevitably incomplete and unsystematic. However, by piecing together various components it is possible to discern clear patterns in how individuals are attracted to terrorism.

LITERATURE REVIEW

Terrorists engage in violence on behalf of terrorist organizations or movements. Here we address the social causes and conditions by which individuals come to be attracted to such organizations and movements. The important question of why terrorist organizations or movements come into being in the first place is beyond our remit.

Scholars have traced terrorist affiliation to three main sources: psychological characteristics, rational choice, and social networks.

Psychological Characteristics

Early work on terrorists focused on developing and identifying a terrorist personality or psychology. Particular attention was paid to pathological characteristics, but little progress was made. Few terrorists appear to have mental illnesses, suffer from pathological narcissism or childhood traumas, or exhibit paranoid or authoritarian personalities (see, e.g., Sageman, 2004, pp. 81–97). More recently, Lankford (2013) proposes that most jihadi suicide terrorists are actually suicidal and that jihadi ideology allows them to present their destructive tendencies as serving a noble cause. Others remain skeptical, however, and believe that Lankford's evidence is "questionable at best" (Horgan, 2014b, p. 32). Horgan (2009) has argued that psychologists will never work out a "terrorist profile" but ought instead to focus on factors such as temporary emotional states, dissatisfaction with current activity, identifying with victims, and expectation of reward.

Rational Choice

Economists and political scientists have analyzed the transition to terrorism from a rational choice perspective. The model, sometimes explicit and sometimes implicit, is that since terrorism is a risky or high-cost activity, it is more likely to appeal to those who either place high value on excitement and/or have little to lose. A natural line of inquiry, then, is the economic background of terrorists. The data repeatedly show that terrorists are not the poorest or least educated individuals (Krueger, 2007). Indeed, most studies identify the average terrorist as being more educated, wealthier, and more socially privileged than their direct peers (although not necessarily privileged in comparison to western styles of living) (Lee, 2011; Reinares, 2004). Kuznar and Lutz (2007) argue that people are particularly sensitive to potential losses of wealth and status relative to others, and consequently are most open to assume the risks of terrorism either when downturns and misfortunes occur or when their neighbors experience upturns (see also Shahbaz, Shabbir, Malk, & Wolters, 2013). For instance, the benefits of terrorism loom large for Palestinians who have experienced a long period of economic stagnation as the Israeli economy continued to expand. However, low levels of economic activity reduce the utility cost of joining a terrorist movement, thus incentivizing the act. In contrast, Krueger (2007) emphasizes political incentives: a lack of civil liberties prevents people with strong opinions from expressing them, thereby increasing the benefits of violence.

While rational choice theory has many virtues, it suffers a fundamental weakness: testability. Rational choice is based on subjective preferences that vary across individuals. But it is currently impossible to observe a preference. All that can be observed is behavior, verbal and physical. While rational choice theory has many testable implications, the core assertions of the approach, the foundation on which the entire edifice is constructed, cannot be empirically verified or refuted.

Social Networks

A third approach looks to social ties. Della Porta's (1988) analysis of some 1,200 members of leftist Italian terrorist groups during the 1970s found that at least 69% of recruits had at least one tie to a member inside the organization (relative, friend, neighbor), and in 74% of those cases the recruit had more than one than one tie. Sageman (2004) elaborates this line of reasoning and applies it to terrorists involved in jihad against foreign governments and their populations. Analyzing 172 terrorists, Sageman finds that their common feature was having some ties of kinship, friendship, or discipleship to individuals affiliated or about to be affiliated with the jihad. Rarely were they proactively recruited by jihadi groups. They formed self-reinforcing cliques – "a bunch of guys" that eventually made contact with the global movement, often through a chance encounter with an individual who provided a bridge to a terrorist organization. Sageman (2004, pp. 126–130) compares recruitment to conversion to a new religion as specified by Lofland and Stark (1965). Both proceed through networks that ultimately result in the individual joining a group with an unconventional world view and a high degree of internal solidarity.

Sageman (2008) identifies two major global jihadi trajectories. The first consists of Muslim expatriates who are sent to Europe to study. These individuals are from affluent background and usually not devout. Away from home, they seek companionship at mosques where they radicalize as a group over time. The second path is followed by second or third generation immigrants who were raised in Europe, often secularly. Marginalized because of their ethnicity, they reject European culture altogether. These homegrown terrorists groups also form out of family and friendship networks, often supplemented by electronic contacts made in internet forums or chatrooms. Sageman (2008, p. 118) stresses that internet information or propaganda alone does not change minds; again, it is discussion of such material "with one's friends and family and the interactive exchanges in the chat rooms that inspire and radicalize."

The network approach to identifying terrorists is the most thorough and developed. However, it has at least three important limitations: it does not explain the initial drift into terrorist networks; it is not situated within a larger theoretical framework; and it often invokes difficult-to-measure subjective states (e.g., "individual motivations are affected by the activists' social networks": Della Porta, 1992, p. 5). To address these limitations, we draw upon the theoretical system known as pure sociology developed by Black (1976, 1995, 2011).

PURE SOCIOLOGY

Pure sociology explains behavior with its location, direction, and movement in social space. Social space has several dimensions, including the vertical (wealth and its distribution), horizontal (social relationships), organizational (groups), cultural (symbolic life), and normative (social control, or the definition and response to deviance). Social actors (people and groups) occupy different locations within each dimension. For example, an actor might be wealthy but have a criminal record and hence have high vertical but low normative status. Or she might be highly integrated into her community and be a member of a cultural minority and so have high radial but low cultural status. Interaction between social actors therefore has a direction and distance in these dimensions. A lawsuit by a bank against an individual, for instance, takes place downwardly in organizational space; a gift from a child to a wealthier parent has an upward direction and traverses little relational space; and a conversation between a local person and a foreign tourist spans considerable cultural distance. Together, these variables constitute the social geometry of behavior.

Social Geometry

Every behavior has its own social geometry – its location and direction in social space. For example, in his seminal work, *The Behavior of Law*, Black (1976) specifies that the social geometry most conducive to law (governmental social control) is a downward complaint against a socially distant adversary.

Pure sociology can be applied to any form of behavior, though scholars have used it most frequently to address variation in the handling of conflict, violent and non-violent (see Campbell, 2011). However, while social geometry successfully explains the response to conflict it does not explain what triggers the conflict in the first place. Social geometry cannot answer that question because it is a snapshot of the configuration of social space at any given moment. Only change can trigger change – why something transforms from non-being to being. To explain change, a dynamic theory is required. Black's (2011) book, *Moral Time*, provides such a theory.

Black argues that the fundamental cause of conflict is the movement of social time. Just as physical time is change in physical space (e.g., the rotation of the earth), social time is change in social space. Social time can be divided into three main types. Vertical time consists of changes in inequality, both increases such as losing a job (overstratification), and decreases such as challenges to authority (understratification). Relational time is any change in intimacy, either increases such as invading someone's space (overintimacy), or decreases such as death of a loved one (underintimacy).

Cultural time comprises changes in social diversity, whether increases such as contact with foreigners (overdiversity) or decreases such as banning foreigners (underdiversity). Each of these three main forms has sub-types. Black argues that the greater and faster these movements of social time are, the more severe conflict is likely to be.

Social behavior is a function of both social geometry and social time. For instance, Manning (2015) has shown that most suicides are triggered by overstratification (in particular, loss of status such as unemployment, bankruptcy, or disgrace) and underintimacy (in particular, loss of close relationships due to death, divorce, or abandonment). Given such a movement, suicide is more likely among the socially marginal – those who participate less in social life. People who are single, isolated, and uninvolved in social activities are the most likely to commit suicide in response to overstratification and underintimacy.

We argue that becoming a terrorist is, similarly, a combination of social geometry and social time. Consider, first, social geometry. Where in social space are terrorists located? To answer this question, consider the theory of partisanship.

Partisanship

Partisanship is the taking of sides in a conflict by parties other than the principals (third parties). Partisanship is a matter of degree, known by the burden undertaken by the third party. To speak up on behalf of somebody is to lend support but to take up arms on his or her behalf is to provide much greater support. Terrorism, therefore, represents a high degree of partisanship by the individual toward an organization or, more diffusely, a movement or cause. And suicide terrorism, involving the certain sacrifice of one's own life, is an even higher degree (see Pape, 2005, pp. 171–198).

Black (1993) proposes that partisanship is a form of "social gravitation." The principals to a conflict create a gravitational field that attracts third parties. Attraction is a function of the social status and closeness of the parties. Third parties are pulled toward the causes of higher status principals, and the higher the status, the greater the pull. Powerful and wealthy individuals and organizations embroiled in conflict therefore tend to garner considerable support, particularly from lower status third parties. Partisanship likewise increases with the social closeness of third parties to one side and their social distance from the other side. Thus, third parties generally support relatives and friends (relational closeness) and those who share the same religion, language, or ideology (cultural closeness), and their support is all the stronger when they have little or no contact or shared culture with the opposing side. Social superiority and differential social closeness explain why, for instance, in times of war masses of citizens volunteer to fight for their countries. From this perspective, their partisanship is not the result of a series of individual decisions or choices but, rather, the product of a strong attraction to the cause of a socially close, superior actor.

Partisanship varies with a third factor as well: the social closeness of the third parties themselves – their social solidarity (Senechal de la Roche, 2001; see also Cooney, 1998, chapter 4). Third parties who are highly intimate, interdependent, and who share a common culture should provide more wholehearted support than those whose bonds are looser and whose culture is diverse.

The social geometry of strong partisanship describes the social geometry of terrorists (Black, 1993, pp. 131–132). Jihadis, for example, exhibit high degrees of social solidarity – they live, work, and pray together. Since groups and movements have more organizational status than individuals, jihads are attached to a higher status actor. And they are relationally and culturally close to the terrorist group while being relationally and culturally distant from the group's enemies (infidels, Westerners).

In short, the end point of terrorist geometry seems clear. But how do they arrive at that end point? After all, as is often said, "nobody is born a terrorist" (see, e.g., Speckhard, 2012, p. 9). We argue that the attraction to terrorism starts with a sociological predisposition to terrorism. People are predisposed when they belong to the side fighting the terrorist cause and are somewhat distant from the other side. Thus, the vast majority of people who become jihadis are Muslims and many are members of communities that are isolated from those the terrorists define as enemies. Their partisan geometry, however, is insufficiently strong to attract the considerable sacrifice that terrorism entails. To become terrorists they must first experience one or more movements of social time. Movements of social time that involve losses – of status, relationships, or cultural respect – are particularly likely to trigger the gravitational pull of terrorism which reverses the movement of social time. Consider, first, vertical time.

VERTICAL TIME

Vertical time moves when inequality increases or decreases. "Inequality" here refers broadly to differences in social standing based on, for example, wealth, power, or reputation. The most important movement of vertical time for the transformation to terrorism is any increase in inequality, or overstratification.

Overstratification

Overstratification occurs when one actor moves ahead of another (over-superiority) or when one actor falls below another (overinferiority). Overinferiority is a constantly recurring theme in the lives of terrorists prior to affiliation. An analysis of 1,500 individuals who had radicalized within the United States, for example, found that "Individuals who experience a drop in social standing prior to their illegal extremist activity were more likely to use violence" (Jensen, James, & Tinsley, 2015). However, the manner in which status is lost varies considerably.

Escalating personal failure appears to have been central to the evolution of the two Tsarnaev brothers from peaceful immigrants to bombers of the Boston marathon in 2013, in which three people were killed and over 250 were injured. Ethnic Chechens, the Tsarnaev family of two parents and four children immigrated to the United States in 2002 with hopes of upward mobility.[1] However, they found only blue collar jobs and lived in a crowded apartment. The parents' hopes were pinned on their eldest child, Tamerlan, whose praises they were forever singing. Tamerlan dropped out of community college but he had a promising career as an amateur boxer. However, a rule change prohibited non-citizens from competing in high-level amateur boxing, effectively ending his career. Unemployed and lacking a college degree, Tamerlan was supported by his wife Katherine. He spent long hours at home visiting radical Islamic websites. In 2012, he visited the Russian province of Dagestan where he spent time with member of Union of the Just, some of whose members were radical Islamists who seek a global caliphate based on a strict interpretation of Sharia law. He also began to attend a conservative mosque and may have had direct contact with a terrorist organization. With Tamerlan adrift, the family's aspirations then shifted to the younger boy Dzhokhar, deemed by his parents to be the brains of the family and destined to have a professional occupation. But once he entered college, Dzhokhar spiraled downward, becoming a drug dealer, earning poor grades, and acquiring a substantial educational debt (Jacobs, Filipov, & Wen, 2013).

Drastic economic loss can be a spur. A man who was drawn to a Chechen terrorist group was described by his cousin as having been

> a very sociable, cheerful young man. His family lived richly. They had cars, a big house. In general, they had all things. During the first war [with Russia] they lost everything … He became very embittered. (Speckhard & Ahkmedova, 2006, p. 451)

Moving to a new country commonly involves a loss of status, particularly for middle- and upper-income immigrants who quickly go from being a "somebody" at home to being a "nobody" abroad. This drift downward is evident in the biography of several of the men who hijacked planes that killed almost 3,000 people in the United States in September 2001 (9/11). For instance, one of the leaders of the group, Mohammed Atta, was born to a middle class household in Egypt and he moved to Germany to attend graduate school. He experienced several difficulties gaining proper visas and was originally denied admissions to school upon his arrival. While in Germany, he worked several low-paying jobs to make ends meet (McDermott, 2005).

Other forms of downward mobility may be important as well. For women, sexual humiliation may be the trigger. Being sexually abused or raped by civilians or security forces on the opposing side is particularly humiliating for Muslim women who live in communities that adhere to a traditional concept of female honor based on sexual modesty and chastity (Bloom, 2005, chapter 6).

For either gender, arrest, conviction, or incarceration lowers an actor's respectability, or normative status (Black, 1976, p. 111). Some terrorists have such a history of crime and punishment. For instance, the road to terrorism for the Kouachi brothers, Chérif and Said, (who attacked a French satirical magazine in Paris, killing 12 people in January 2015) stretched back many years to when they were part of a

> A group of Parisian friends [who] were all in their early 20s; many had met at a local middle school, most had poor school records and chaotic family lives ... The dozen or so friends, mainly unemployed or in small jobs, were involved in petty crime, theft, drugs, trafficking. (Chrisafis, 2015)

As the hunt for the Kouachi brothers went on, an acquaintance of theirs, Amédy Coulibaly, who claimed affiliation with Al Qaeda, shot four hostages and a policewoman at a kosher supermarket in another part of Paris. All three men had seen their normative status decline to one degree or another. Chérif had been jailed for trying to fly to Syria and Iraq to become a jihadi. Said had been arrested and questioned by police (and had spent several months in Yemen, where he was suspected of having fought for Al Qaeda). Coulibaly had served four terms of imprisonment, including three for armed robbery (Chrisafis, 2015).

Understratification

If terrorist affiliation is often a response to overstratification, the affiliation itself is a form of understratification, in particular underinferiority (the ascent of a lower status actor). For many the first step in affiliation is adoption of the Islamist philosophy that seeks to create a powerful political movement based on conservative Islam. A rebellion against traditional Islam, Islamism is "cool" in many circles, bringing respect and prestige to those who adopt it (see, e.g., Sageman, 2008, pp. 159–160).

Entry into a jihadist group is a greater increase in status. Post (2005, p. 21) notes that "By belonging to a radical group, otherwise powerless people become powerful." Statements by radicals themselves make the same point. "After recruitment my social status was greatly enhanced. I got a lot of respect from my acquaintances and from the young people in the village," a Palestinian man incarcerated in Israel for terrorist activity told a researcher. Another stated that "recruits were treated with great respect. A youngster who belonged to Hamas or Fatah was regarded more highly than one who didn't belong to a group, and got better treatment than unaffiliated kids" (Post, 2005, p. 18). The same is true in European prisons where jihadis "are 'feared and respected by prisoners and prison staff alike'" (Neumann & Rogers, 2007, p. 41). And the higher a person's place in the organization, the greater their status. For jihadis, "Osama Bin Laden" [the former head of Al Qaeda] is a romantic hero" (Post, 2005, p. 25). "Even America is afraid of him" (quoted in Speckhard & Ahkmedova, 2006, p. 463).

Jihadi terrorism brings a particularly sharp rise in status because the affiliation is with the highest status actor of all: God. Previous terrorist movements allied themselves with secular causes, such as nationalism or socialism. Jihadi groups go further, allying themselves with the most powerful being in the universe and, consequently, are more successful in attracting more and more committed members.

CULTURAL TIME

Cultural time moves when cultural diversity changes. Increases in diversity (overdiversity) are important triggers of terrorist affiliation (and of conflict more generally: Black, 2011, p. 102). The increases do not typically occur at the level of the society (e.g., an invasion) but within the society: "in any multicultural society, people are constantly encountering those who are different, increasing the diversity in their lives" (Campbell, 2013, p. 470).

Overdiversity

The path to terrorism often begins with contact across a cultural divide. The interaction may be the result of travel to a foreign country. The 9/11 bombers left their native countries and lived among foreigners in Europe for several years. Or the interaction may take place at home. Many Palestinians in the West Bank primarily encounter Israelis at security checkpoints staffed by the Israeli Defense Forces. These encounters are often a source of considerable friction. A young man interviewed by a researcher was one of 31 students in his high school class; during the Palestinian uprising of 2000–2005 against the Israeli occupation (known as the Second Intifada), 27 of them had become suicide bombers or martyrs ("shaheed") as he preferred to call them. He described his contact with the Israeli military personnel staffing the security checkpoint outside his village thus:

> Let me tell you how it is. When you climb the hill of muddy soil to the tank you sink in it up to your thighs. Many women have to lift their skirts to get up. It's so disgusting. When we get there we have to stand in line for hours waiting to cross. I have stood for hours at the Hawara checkpoint: the Israelis take my ID, always keep me for at least five hours and then free me. Every time, I thought, "Come on get out of your tank, I want to kill you. Come on, come out of your tank, give me your hand, I want to kill you ...." It's not only me that felt this anger – this checkpoint is what has created "shaheeds" in my village. (Speckhard, 2012, p. 107)

On one occasion the researcher approaches the checkpoint with two European students and two Palestinian translators. Armed Jewish settlers taunted the group, describing Palestinians as animals. The Palestinians were furious, one of them muttering "I wish I had a knife. I'd cut them to pieces. Just give me a knife and I'll do it now ... If I had a knife, I'd kill as many of them as I could right now'" (Speckhard, 2012, pp. 142–143).

Cultural conflicts tend to collectivize because of the shared nature of culture (Black, 2011, p. 121). Thus an insult or injury to one member of a cultural group may trigger retaliation by another member, especially if they are relationally close. One young Russian man of Ingush ethnicity who participated in the seizing over 1,100 hostages at a school in Beslen, North Ossieta, Russia in 2004 was radicalized by the rape of his pregnant sister and other women by Ossetians when he was thirteen years old (Speckhard, 2012, p. 576). A Palestinian man who joined the Popular Front for the Liberation of Palestine (and killed a member of the Israeli cabinet) had parents who had been arrested and jailed, a brother who had been shot in the mouth and later jailed (and had himself been jailed) – all by member of the Israeli security forces (Speckhard, 2012, p. 261).

In Europe, contact between ethnic Europeans and Muslims, native or immigrant, can be a flashpoint. Many European Muslims live in ethnic enclaves, isolated from mainstream society. Contact with non-Muslims takes place across a considerable cultural gulf. Their countries of residence do not have a long history of immigration. As Black (2011, pp. 139–140) notes, the more homogenous the group, the more conflict overdiversity will trigger. Interaction across the cultural divide can be fraught with tension. In Belgium, for instance, a person of Moroccan descent approaching a nightclub entrance is a common point of friction. As one young man said,

> I don't try to go to clubs because it's difficult to enter … It's like a tension inside, I ask myself 'Who is the doorkeeper to say to me *Don't Enter*?' He has the power to make me feel I am less. Who do I have to be to enter? We [Moroccans] always have to prove who we are to enter, to be respected … Belgian culture is not open to other people. It's a type of racism. It's in their genes. (Speckhard, 2012, pp. 591–592)

Some European Muslims experience more extreme forms of discrimination. English Muslims might hear taunts of "Pakis, Pakis, F—off back home" (Husain, 2007, p. 2). Or they might be the targets of physical attacks. One Anglo-Pakistani man who became a leading member of a radical Islamist organization recalled growing up in the south of England in the 1980s when a local gang of skinheads known as Combat 18 became active:

> Their favored form of attack was with hammers or screwdrivers, but they also carried clubs and butchers knives. That started a bit of a local arms race, with everyone tooling up in response to everyone else. Suddenly everyone in Essex was carrying in a way people hadn't been fifteen years before. Good friends of mine got badly hurt – Moe had his head smashed with a hammer and was lucky to survive. That was the climate non-whites faced in Southend, and that was why we carried knives. We were being hunted down for sport in our own streets by C18. They even had a name for it: Paki-bashing. Friends were being randomly stabbed, hammered, and clubbed just because of the color of their skin. (Nawaz, 2013, pp. 28–29)

Underdiversity

A common response to overdiversity is underdiversity – the reduction or rejection of diversity. Joining a terrorist movement involves a repudiation of the culture of the enemy group. Thus, jihadis denounce and renounce the "Westoxifiction" of Muslim life:

> The main elements of perceived poisonous "Western" influence include the ascendant of the material over the spiritual life, permissiveness, complacency and comfort valued more than honor or glory and the corrupting influence of the "city" (Babylon) through its cultural intermingling and loss of rootedness. (Change Institute, 2008, p. 45)

The most extreme rejection of Western culture is to adopt a culture that is radically opposed to it: jihadi ideology. The core of the ideology

> Is centered on a narrative, which claims that Islam and Muslims are constantly attacked and humiliated by the West, Israel, and corrupt local regimes in Muslim countries. It claims that in order to return to a society of peace, harmony, and social justice, Muslims need to unite and stand up for their faith. They need to fight the West and other corrupting influences. Violence, including violence against civilians, is a necessary and legitimate means given the superior military power of the West. The fight, which militant Islamism claims is a religiously sanctioned faith, is an individual duty and an emancipatory journey which brings the fighter closer to God. (Dalgaard-Nielsen, 2010, p. 798)

Terrorist groups capitalize on the tendency of cultural conflicts to collectivize. For instance, a common argument used by Islamist groups, from which jihadis are sometimes recruited, is to link local discrimination against Muslims to discrimination against Muslims across the globe (see, e.g., Nawaz, 2013, pp. 49–50). The remedy, according to jihadi ideology, is Islamism – the creation of a powerful, united Islamic superstate free of Western influence, a "caliphate guided by the words and actions of the Prophet including the application of Shari'a law" (Change Institute, 2008, p. 42). In 2014, a jihadi group known as Islamic State effectively ruled large portions of Iraq and Syria and declared a caliphate that they hoped to expand eventually across the entire world (Wood, 2015).

RELATIONAL TIME

Relational time moves when intimacy (participation in the life of another) changes. Decreases of intimacy (underintimacy) are the most fateful for the movement into terrorism.

Underintimacy

Underintimacy occurs when parties either becomes less involved with each other (underinvolvement) or expose less of themselves to each other (underexposure). Underinvolvement is a particularly strong factor in many cases of terrorist affiliation. More concretely, it is the loss of close relationships that drives many into the arms of terrorists. For instance, it was the death of her much-loved aunt that appears to have launched a 15-year-old middle-class Parisian girl on a path to joining a jihadi group in Syria (Ruthven, 2015).

Interviews with family members of 34 suicide terrorists and four potential suicide terrorists from Chechnya found that all had experienced the violent death or near death (through being captured and tortured) of a close family member (Speckhard & Ahkmedova, 2006, p. 454). In one instance, a 17-year-old woman was visited by her brother whom she persuaded to stay the night in order to avoid breaking the curfew. But the Russian forces spot-checked her home that night. They beat and took away her husband and brother. Two weeks later, the corpses of the two men were found on the outskirts of the village bearing marks of torture. Three months later, most likely after having had contact with jihadis, the woman strapped on a bomb and managed to talk her way into a meeting with the officer who had seized her husband and brother. She exploded the bomb, killing the officer, several guards, and herself (2006, p. 456). In another case, after his father and brother were killed when he was 15 years old, a boy became increasingly interested in religion. He grew a beard and allowed his hair to grow long. He joined his uncle in a jihadi training camp. He confided to a cousin that "he dreams to die in Jihad and that life is a burden, that happiness can only be in paradise." He later died in a siege of a Moscow theater (2006, pp. 457–458). A woman who was also killed in the theater had a brother who had been seized by Russian soldiers. They tied explosives to his legs and exploded him. She continued to have contact with her brother's jihadi friends. Telling her parents she was going to Moscow to buy clothes for her dowry, she joined the attack on Russian civilians (2006, p. 458). In general, terrorists are often "those who have suffered traumatic bereavement and have lost important family members in their lives" (Speckhard, 2012, p. 775).

Relational losses need not involve death. The breakup of a romantic relationship is a significant movement of relational time, especially for someone living in a foreign land and has few other contacts. Ziad Jarrah, one the 9/11 bombers, is an example. Shortly after arriving in Germany from Lebanon for school, he met Aysel Segun. They became a couple and eventually married. However their relationship was volatile – a constant cycle of breaking up and rekindling their romance. Aysel eventually noticed that he was behaving differently and seeing her much less frequently. She began to question if he was involved with some kind of radical group (McDermott, 2005).

Terrorists typically experience another form of underintimacy in response to some movement of social time – like Ziad Jarrah they draw away from family members and friends. Parents sometimes describe this process as akin to losing a child to addiction – the child becomes secretive and withdrawn. "You've changed" one former Islamist recalls his mother saying. "You're no longer the son I raised" (Husain, 2007, p. 42). This form of underintimacy is the corollary of a critical component of the transition to terrorism – overintimacy with terrorists.

Overintimacy

Becoming a terrorist is, above all, a movement of relational time – a forging of new relationships. Recall that terrorists are close to each other and to one side of a conflict (while being distant from the other side). That structure does not just suddenly take shape but unfolds over time as the prospective terrorist gradually gets drawn closer to jihadis. This transition is as, Sageman (2004, pp. 126–130) notes, similar to converting to a new religion: both are processes of increasing intimacy. Both only take place when the individual's ties to supporters of terrorists are stronger than to opponents of terrorists. The status of ties is also important, however: developing relations with wealthy, powerful, or highly integrated individuals connected to terrorism exerts an additional pull. With the strengthening of the new ties a set of beliefs that once seemed implausible even ridiculous begin to make perfect sense (Lofland & Stark, 1965).

The journey often starts with existing relationships – with ties the individual has to family members or friends who happen to be already linked to terrorism. Sageman's (2004, p. 112) analysis of 172 global jihadis linked to Al Qaeda found that kinship played a role in the affiliation of 14% and friendship in 68% of the cases. For instance,

> After a few years of a life of petty crime, Meskini asked his childhood friend Haouari to help him join the jihad and fight with Muslim men in Chechnya or Afghanistan. Haouari introduced him to Ressam, who asked Makhulif for a visa. Haouari vouched for his childhood friend and Ressam vouched for Haouari. (Sageman, 2004, p. 110; references omitted)

A study of 242 jihadis involved in terrorist attacks or plots in European countries found that about 35% of the sample had ties of kinship or friendship to terrorists at the time of their recruitment (Bakker, 2006, p. 49). For Europeans, contacts forged with strangers in mosques, book stores, cafes, gyms, universities, and, especially, prisons may be just as important as friendship and kinship (Neumann & Rogers, 2007, pp. 33–47). These contacts may be a matter of chance. Or not: individuals already active in terrorist organizations may "recruit new members into the cell, such as by 'spotting' and 'befriending' people at mosques" (Neumann & Rogers, 2007, p. 62). And some contacts may be merely electronic with the individual self-recruiting through the internet by downloading videos, posting messages, and chatting to other extremists (Neumann & Rogers, 2007, pp. 87–90).

As the individual becomes more intimate with those already committed to jihad, a cell or group may form. Facing common danger from a hostile environment, the group becomes all-enveloping – a substitute family (Speckhard, 2012, p. 594). Group members live, work, and pray together. They enter a spiral of overintimacy with social closeness breeding further closeness. Their ideas align. Such intense closeness exerts a strong gravitational pull of loyalty, especially for those who have suffered a loss of intimacy, felt the sting of discrimination, or fallen on hard times (Abrahms, 2008).[2]

The immediate family of the group may be part of a larger family not just of like-minded fighters but fellow-sufferers across the globe. Terror groups forge "fictive kinship" with larger collectivities, such as social classes, nations, ethnicities, or religions (Atran, 2010). Becoming a terrorist creates a connection to this larger kin group created out of a common struggle. The jihadi in London, Copenhagen, Ramallah, or Islamabad is not just fighting a local fight but is part of a global struggle in support of Muslims everywhere. He serves a greater cause.

MULTIPLE MOVEMENTS

The transition to terrorism, then, is typically triggered by a movement of social time. In particular, it is triggered by some loss – of status, intimacy, or cultural respect. But many people experience such losses and never become terrorists. Other possible responses to loss include suicide, going into exile, joining a non-violent political party, or becoming an isolate. Of the various possibilities, becoming a terrorist is the most hostile toward the enemy. Such hostility is more likely if the third parties are already socially close to one side and distant from the enemy. Nobody is born a terrorist, but some people are born into families and neighborhoods with strong connections to powerful terrorist groups. The journey to jihad from an active conflict zone, such as contemporary Iraq, is shorter than the journey from a middle class European suburb.

A terrorist response becomes, in addition, more likely with the magnitude of the movement of social time. Large effects are generally the product of large causes. Terrorism therefore tends to be triggered by larger (and faster) movement of social time. Many such movements will be multidimensional in nature, such as downward economic mobility combined with arrest and the loss of a close relative. Such indeed is often the case. Many of the Chechen suicide bombers mentioned previously, for example, did not just experience underintimacy through losing a close family member. Rather, the family member was killed by the Russian security forces, sometimes an in extremely violent manner. Violence is a movement of vertical time – a large drop in status that radiates out to those who are close to the victim (Black, 2011, pp. 76–77).

The Tsarnaev brothers provide a concrete example of multidimensionality. Both men lost considerably more than their promising careers. Their father was badly beaten in a bar fight and became unable to work full-time. Their mother was charged with shoplifting and one of their sisters with counterfeiting. Tamerlan, the elder brother, was arrested for domestic violence. He, his wife, and child had to move from the apartment his family had long occupied. Later, he had religious conflicts at his local mosque. In addition, his and Dzhokhar's two sisters separated from their husbands shortly after being married. Their parents, too, divorced, and moved back to Russia separately. In short, their entire world collapsed around them (Jacobs et al., 2013).

CONCLUSION

The origins of individual terrorism are not always easy to discern. Look closely, however, and it becomes apparent that the journey is activated by one or more movements of social time, vertical, cultural, or relational. The larger and faster these movements of social time the more likely they are to lead to terrorism. Once initiated, the transition to terrorism proceeds through gravitational attraction: contact with people involved in the movement, especially those of higher status, pulls the individual toward the terrorist organization. Moreover, affiliation with the movement effectively reverses the movement of social time. Terrorism transforms relational death into relational birth, repression into resistance, powerlessness into power. Loss becomes gain.

Social actors are drawn inwardly and upwardly in social space – toward wealthier and more powerful agents (Black, 1993, p. 127). Since success builds social status, it exerts a powerful gravitational pull. The more success a group enjoys – whether a street gang, corporation, or terrorist group – the more attractive it is to those in its world. Terrorist groups that launch daring and spectacular attacks at the heart of a stronger enemy thus attract more and more ardent supporters – greater numbers of people join up, prepared to lay down their lives for the cause. Among jihadi groups, Hezbollah displayed this ability in the 1980s; Hamas in the 1990s; Al Qaeda in the 2000s, and Islamic State in the 2010s. Over time, the leading groups have become larger and more lethal. They go beyond killing military or even civilian targets. They invade, occupy, and control large swaths of territory. And they do so by attracting more people from more places across the globe. Islamic State is said to have gained some 20,000 recruits from abroad.[3] Success breeds success.

The gravitational process is not inexorable. Should the movement of social time reverse yet again, the probability of becoming a terrorist will decline substantially. Just as religious conversion is unlikely to occur if the potential convert has stronger ties to people outside the religion than inside it so the pull of terrorism will be halted by the development or activation of ties of greater intimacy or of higher status to opponents than proponents of terrorism. Betrayal by the organization is another possibility: A group, terrorist or otherwise, that refuses to stand by the member in times of trouble is likely to lose much of its allure (see, e.g., Nawaz, 2013, pp. 166, 182). A third route is counterterrorist disruption by arrest or death of the recruit before the transition to terrorism is complete. A fourth is the weakening of the terrorist organization itself. Defeat – military, economic, political, or cultural – will make the cause much less attractive. Without some significant movement of social time, however, affiliation tends to proceed relentlessly with intimacy breeding more intimacy. As social closeness intensifies, the individual comes to belong to a group of comrades fiercely dedicated to one another and wholly isolated – relationally, culturally, and organizationally – from the opposing side.

In short, becoming a terrorist is typically the transition from being an undifferentiated member of a cultural group to being a member of a highly intimate and powerful violent organization or movement claiming to represent that cultural group. Set in motion by a movement of social time, the gravitational attraction proceeds via networks: the individual becomes ever closer to those supportive of terrorism and ever less close with those opposed to it resulting in an ever-stronger partisan commitment. These changes reverse the movement of social time and form the geometry of extremism, a geometry that attracts heroic sacrifice for the cause and merciless violence against enemy civilians.

NOTES

1. Zubeidat Tsarnaev, the wife and mother, was actually an Avar, neighbors and historical rivals of the Chechens.

2. Abrahms even argues that social solidarity is the goal of terrorists. Relational not political purposes are what drive them to join and remain in terrorist groups, he contends. The problem is that we have no access to the "real" goals of terrorists or indeed of anyone else (Black, 1995, pp. 861–864). All we can observe is the strength of intimate groups and the strong attraction they have.

3. http://www.cbsnews.com/news/ap-20000-foreign-fighters-flock-to-syria-iraq-to-join-terrorists/

ACKNOWLEDGMENT

For their comments on a prior draft, we thank Zach Bigman, Donald Black, Matthew Greife, and Scott Phillips.

REFERENCES

Abrahms, M. (2008). What terrorists really want: Terrorist motives and counterterrorism strategy. *International Security*, *32*, 78–105.

Atran, S. (2010). *Talking to the enemy: Faith, brotherhood, and the (un)making of terrorists*. New York, NY: HarperCollins.

Bakker, E. (2006). *Jihadi terrorists in Europe: Their characteristics and the circumstances in which they joined the jihad: An exploratory study*. The Hague: Netherlands Institute of International Relations.

Black, D. (1976). *The behavior of law*. New York, NY: Academic press.

Black, D. (1993). Taking sides. In *The social structure of right and wrong*. San Diego, CA: Academic Press.

Black, D. (1995). The epistemology of pure sociology. *Law and Social Inquiry*, *20*, 829–870.

Black, D. (2004). The geometry of terrorism. *Sociological Theory*, *22*(1), 14–25.

Black, D. (2011). *Moral time*. New York, NY: Oxford University Press.

Bloom, M. (2005). *Dying to kill: The allure of suicide terror*. New York, NY: Columbia University Press.

Campbell, B. (2011). Black's theory of law and social control. In R. Rosenfeld (Ed.), *Oxford bibliographies online*. Oxford: Oxford University Press.

Campbell, B. (2013). Genocide and social time. *Dilemas: Revista de Estudos de Conflito e Controle Social*, *6*, 465–488.

Change Institute. (2008). *Studies into violent radicalization: Lot 2. The beliefs, ideologies, and narratives*. London: Change Institute.

Chrisafis, A. (2015). Charlie Hebdo attackers: born, raised and radicalised in France. *The Guardian*, January 15. Retrieved from http://www.theguardian.com/world/2015/jan/12/-sp-charlie-hebdo-attackers-kids-frnaceradicalised-paris. Accessed on February 16, 2015.

Cooney, M. (1998). *Warriors and peacemakers: How third parties shape violence*. New York, NY: New York University Press.

Cottee, S., & Hayward, K. (2011). Terrorist (e)motives: The existential attractions of terrorism. *Studies in Conflict and Terrorism*, *34*, 963–986.

Dalgaard-Nielsen, A. (2010). Violent radicalization in Europe: What we know and what we do not know. *Studies in Conflict and Terrorism*, *33*, 797–814.

Della Porta, D. (1988). Recruitment processes in clandestine political organization: Italian left-wing terrorism. *International Social Movements Research*, *1*, 155–169.

Della Porta, D. (1992). Introduction: On individual motivations in underground political organizations. *International Social Movement Research*, *4*, 3–28.

Horgan, J. (2009). *Walking away from terrorism: Accounts of disengagement from radical and extremist movements*. New York, NY: Routledge.

Horgan, J. (2014a). Don't ask why people join the Islamic State, ask how. *Vice News*, September 10. Retrieved from http://news.vice.com/article/don't-ask-why-people-join-the-islamic-state-ask-how. Accessed on February 22, 2015.

Horgan, J. (2014b). *The psychology of terrorism*. London: Routledge.

Husain, E. (2007). *The Islamist: Why I became an Islamic fundamentalist, what I saw inside, and why I left*. New York, NY: Penguin.

Jacobs, S., Filipov, D., & Wen, P. (2013). The fall of the house of Tsarnaev. *Boston Globe*. Retrieved from http://www.bostonglobe.com/Page/Boston/2011-2020/WebGraphics/Metro/BostonGlobe.com/2013/12/15tsarnaev/tsarnaev.html

Jensen, M., James, P., & Tinsley, H. (2015). *Profiles of individual radicalization in the United States: Preliminary findings*. Retrieved from https://www.start.umd.edu/pubs/PIRUS%20Research%Brief_Jan%202015.pdf

Krueger, A. B. (2007). *What makes a terrorist*. Princeton, NJ: Princeton University Press.

Kuznar, L. A., & Lutz, J. M. (2007). Risk sensitivity and terrorism. *Political Studies*, *55*(2), 341–361.

Lankford, A. (2013). *The myth of martyrdom: What really drives suicide bombers, rampage shooters, and other self-destructive killers*. New York, NY: Palgrave Macmillan.

Lee, A. (2011). Who becomes a terrorist? Poverty, education, and the origins of political violence. *World Politics*, *63*(2), 203–245.

Lofland, J., & Stark, R. (1965). Becoming a world saver: A theory of conversion to a deviant perspective. *American Sociological Review*, *30*(6), 862–875.

Manning, J. (2015). Suicide and social time. *Dilemas: Revista de Estudos de Conflito e Controle Social*, *8*, 97–216.

McDermott, T. (2005). *Perfect soldiers: Who they were, why they did it*. New York, NY: HarperCollins.

Moghadam, A., Berger, R., & Beliakova, P. (2014). Say terrorist, think insurgent: Labeling and analyzing contemporary political actors. *Perspectives on Terrorism*, *8*(5), 2–17.

Nawaz, M. (2013). *Radical: My journey out of Islamist extremism*. Guilford, CT: Lyons Press.

Nesser, P. (2006). Jihadism in western Europe after the invasion of Iraq: Tracing motivational influences from the Iraq war to jihadist terrorism in western Europe. *Studies in Conflict and Terrorism*, *29*, 323–342.

Neumann, P., & Rogers, B. (2007). *Recruitment and mobilization for the Islamist militant movement in Europe*. London: King's College London.

Pape, R. A. (2005). *Dying to win: The strategic logic of suicide terrorism*. New York, NY: Random House.

Post, J. M. (2005). "When hatred is bred in the bone:" The sociocultural underpinnings of terrorist psychology. In J. J. F. Forest (Ed.), *The making of a terrorist* (Vol. 2). Recruitment. Westport, CT: Praeger Security International.

Reinares, F. (2004). Who are the terrorists? Analyzing changes in sociological profile among members of the ETA. *Studies in Conflict and Terrorism*, *27*(6), 465–488.

Richardson, L. (2006). *What terrorists want: Understanding the enemy, containing the threat*. New York, NY: Random House.

Ruthven, M. (2015). Lure of the caliphate. *New York Review of Books Blog*, February 28.

Sageman, M. (2004). *Understanding terror networks*. Philadelphia, PA: University of Pennsylvania Press.

Sageman, M. (2008). *Leaderless jihad: Terror networks in the twenty-first century*. Philadelphia, PA: University of Pennsylvania Press.

Senechal de la Roche, R. (2001). Why is collective violence collective? *Sociological Theory*, *19*(2), 126–144.

Shahbaz, M., Shabbir, M. S., Malk, M. N., & Wolters, M. E. (2013). An analysis of causal relationship between economic growth and terrorism in Pakistan. *Economic Modeling*, *35*, 21–29.

Speckhard, A. (2012). *Talking to terrorists: Understanding the psycho-social motivations of militant jihadi terrorists, mass hostage takers, suicide bombers, and "martyrs"*. McLean, VA: Advances Press.

Speckhard, A., & Ahkmedova, K. (2006). The making of a martyr: Chechen suicide terrorists. *Studies in Conflict and Terrorism*, *29*(5), 429–492.

Wood, G. (2015). What ISIS really wants. *Atlantic Monthly*, March.

TERRORISM AND GENOCIDE

Bradley Campbell

ABSTRACT

Purpose – *Terrorism has much in common with genocide and sometimes may even be a form of genocide. In this chapter I systematically compare these two phenomena.*

Methodology/approach – *Drawing mainly from Donald Black's work on terrorism and my own work on genocide, I examine the conceptual and theoretical overlap between terrorism and genocide.*

Findings – *Terrorism and genocide are similar and sometimes overlapping, and they occur under similar social conditions – in response to conflicts between socially distant and unequal groups. Conceptually they differ mainly in that terrorism is covert and carried out by civilians, and genocide may not be. The main theoretical difference is that terrorism tends to be upward – against more powerful targets – while genocide tends to be downward – against less powerful targets. Terrorism tends to be less effective than extreme genocide, then, and the most extreme cases have death tolls much lower than the most extreme cases of genocide.*

Originality/value – *This analysis draws from previous theories of terrorism, genocide, and social control to better place terrorism in a broader sociological context. In doing so it highlights and explains key features*

Terrorism and Counterterrorism Today
Sociology of Crime, Law and Deviance, Volume 20, 47–65

ISSN: 1521-6136/doi:10.1108/S1521-613620150000020003

of terrorism, and it even helps us to speculate about the future of terrorism. That is, technological advances might in the long run destroy the social conditions conducive to terrorism, thus leading to terrorism's ultimate demise, but in the short run they might allow terrorists to more effectively kill, leading terrorism to resemble extreme genocide in its deadliness.

Keywords: Terrorism; genocide; social control; violence; pure sociology

INTRODUCTION

The most extreme acts of terrorism, those involving the killing of hundreds or thousands of civilians, commonly occur across ethnic lines. This has been true, for example, of the deadliest attacks of recent years, such as on August 14, 2007, when Arab Sunni Muslims associated with Al Qaeda killed more than 700 Kurdish Yazidis – followers of a small, pre-Islamic religion – in suicide truck bomb attacks in the villages of Qahtaniya and Jazeera in Iraq (Al Jazeera, 2010; Cave & Glanz, 2007). It was also true of the 2002 bombings of Indonesian nightclubs frequented by Western tourists, the 2004 bombings of four commuter trains in Madrid, Spain, and the 2006 bombings of commuter trains in Mumbai, India, all by Islamic militants and resulting in about 200 deaths each (BBC News, 2003; Rai & Sengupta, 2006; Wilkinson, 2004). Notably, it was true as well of the deadliest case of terrorism in history, the September 11, 2001 Al Qaeda attacks on the World Trade Center in New York and the Pentagon in Washington, DC (often called the "9/11 attacks"), which resulted in nearly 3,000 deaths. And it was true of many of the deadliest "pre-9/11" terrorist attacks, and even of terrorist campaigns with more limited violence, such as the attacks in Northern Ireland by Irish Catholics against Protestants of English and Scottish descent, the suicide bombings in Israel by Palestinian Muslims, and the suicide bombings by Tamil Hindus against Sinhalese Buddhists in Sri Lanka.

These are terrorist acts, cases of what might be called *ethnic terrorism* (Byman, 1998), but a number of observers point to their similarity to another form of violence – genocide. Commenting on the 2007 bombing of Yazidis in Iraq, Army Major General Benjamin Mixon said, "This is an act of ethnic cleaning, if you will, almost genocide" (quoted in Gamel, 2007). Likewise political scientist Adam Jones asks whether the 9/11 attacks in New York and Washington, DC were "more than terroristic" – whether they were also genocidal – and concludes that there was "a palpable genocidal impetus and intent in 9/11 – one that could yet result in a fully fledged genocide" (2006, p. 27). And political scientist Daniel Jonah Goldhagen, commenting on suicide bombings by Islamic terrorists, says that such acts should actually be called *proto-genocide bombings*, or as he prefers, just *genocide bombings*. The ethnically based targeting conveys the message "that any people in a given country, or adhering to a particular non-Islamic creed are fit to be slaughtered." Each of the bombings, he says, "beyond the actual murder it perpetrates, symbolically mass murders everyone else it could have targeted, and is an installment in an ongoing assault of, if the perpetrators had their way, a stream, perhaps an unending torrent of genocide bombings" (Goldhagen, 2009, p. 496).

Who is right? Should we say that some terrorist acts are "almost genocide," that they contain an impetus that could yet result in genocide, or that they are in fact genocides? Depending on how we define genocide, we may have different answers, but I define it as unilateral, ethnically based mass killing (Campbell, 2015; see also Campbell, 2009, p. 153, 2011, p. 589). Using this definition, all of the terrorist acts mentioned above are genocides, though even the most extreme cases of terrorism – including the 9/11 attacks – are not extreme cases of genocide. Death tolls in the hundreds, or in the one case the thousands, are still nowhere near the 1 million Armenians killed by Turks and Kurds in Turkey during World War I, the 6 million Jews killed by Germans and their allies during World War II, or the 800,000 Tutsis killed by Hutus in 1994 Rwanda.

What we see is some overlap between the two phenomena, but terrorism and genocide are not identical. To better understand cases of genocidal terrorism, let us look first at the conceptual overlap between genocide and terrorism – the similarities and differences in their definitions – and then at the theoretical overlap – the similarities and differences in their social environments. This will help us begin to explain genocidal terrorism and to explain why it takes the form that it does, including why such terrorism has not involved the degree of mass killing seen in the Armenian Genocide, the Holocaust, the Rwandan Genocide, or other major cases of genocide.

THE CONCEPTUAL OVERLAP

Definitions of terrorism and genocide have not always been consistent or clear. Some people use *terrorism* or *genocide* almost as a stand-in for *evil*, and then defining the terms and classifying cases become ways of advancing a political cause. For example, once after I gave a presentation on genocide at an academic conference, an audience member asked me to address the killing of nonhuman animals for food, which he thought should also be called genocide. Political activists might thus label all sorts of behaviors like this, behaviors they object to and want to portray as evil, as terrorism or genocide.[1] Still others, out of sympathy for the causes of those engaging in violence, might resist calling their actions terrorism or genocide, even in cases where civilians are slaughtered en masse. This kind of politicization then leads others to abandon the idea of defining these terms at all. For some, as political scientist Boaz Ganor points out, whether a given act of violence is terrorism "depends entirely on the subjective outlook of the definer." No definition is possible, they might say, since "one man's terrorist is another man's freedom fighter" (Ganor, 2002, p. 287; see also Barak, 2004, p. 37).

Whether or not such ambiguity about the meaning of these terms actually helps in advancing political causes, it is certainly unacceptable in the social sciences. Social science is about describing and explaining human behaviors, not about condemning or praising them (Black, 2013; Campbell, 2014). And if our definitions are to help us in the tasks of description and explanation, they need to be as clear and as easy to apply to actual cases as possible. The definitions of terrorism and genocide I use here – sociologist Donald Black's definition of terrorism and my own definition of genocide – are clear and applicable, but they also have another advantage, we shall see: Black and I have defined these phenomena in a way that allows us to apply a general theory of conflict and violence in explaining them.

Defining Terrorism and Genocide

Genocide, again, is unilateral, ethnically based mass killing, and Black's definition of terrorism is as follows: "Pure terrorism is unilateral self-help by organized civilians who covertly inflict mass violence on other civilians" (2004a, p. 10). Each of these needs some elaboration. To say that genocide is unilateral means that it is one-sided, with the violence flowing mainly in one direction, rather than two-sided like warfare. And to say that the killing is ethnically based just means that the targets are chosen based on their ethnic identity, with an *ethnicity* broadly defined as a people with some notion (accurate or not) that they have a common ancestry. Black says pure terrorism is *self-help*, a term that refers to the use of aggression by aggrieved parties in a conflict, and that it involves civilians *covertly* inflicting mass violence, meaning there is some degree of surprise or secrecy.

To begin with, consider what cases of terrorism and genocide have in common. Both are forms of *social control*. Social control is the handling of conflict, any way of defining or responding to deviant behavior (Black, 1998, p. 4). People might handle conflicts by negotiating with one another, ending relationships, filing lawsuits, gossiping, or even by using violence against those who have offended them. Black says that terrorism is self-help, a form of social control, and though I have not included this in my definition of genocide, given that nearly all cases of genocide can be classified as social control (Campbell, 2009), for the sake of convenience I treat it here as a conceptual requirement. Terrorism and genocide, then, both respond to behavior viewed by the aggressors as deviant; they are ways of pursuing grievances, of seeking justice. Those who planned and carried out the 9/11 attacks, for example, objected to the presence of American troops in the Middle East, to the existence of Israel and the treatment of Palestinian Arabs, to the Crusades and other actions by Christians in the distant past, to the decadence of modern Western societies, and much more. Likewise the Holocaust was a response to the various grievances of the Nazis and other Germans, including the belief that Jews were responsible for Germany's defeat in World War I, that they were responsible for the war with the Soviet Union, and that as part of a worldwide conspiracy they were the secret power behind both communism and capitalism.

Sometimes the grievances that terrorism and genocide respond to are similar or nearly identical. Contemporary Islamic terrorists and their supporters, for example, often sound almost indistinguishable from Nazi propagandists. The charter of the Palestinian terrorist group Hamas, which Goldhagen describes as "a Nazi-like anti-Semitic cascade of accusatory fancy," claims that Jewish fingerprints are on all wars and that "Jews plan to subjugate the entire Middle East as a stepping stone to turning on the world" (Goldhagen, 2009, p. 498). And one Hamas suicide bomber left behind a video message saying, "There is no blood better than the blood of Jews. We will not leave you alone until we have quenched our thirst with your blood" (quoted in Goldhagen, 2009, p. 504). Or listen to Hassan Nasrallah of the Lebanese Islamic group Hezbollah: "If we searched the entire world for a person more cowardly, despicable, weak and feeble in psyche, mind, ideology and religion, we would not find anyone like the Jew" (quoted in Goldhagen, 2009, p. 499). The false accusations, the dehumanizing rhetoric, the conspiratorial thinking, and the open hatred expressed are on par with that associated with the Holocaust and even more extreme than what is seen in many other genocides.

Terrorism and genocide are ways of handling conflict, then, often very similar types of conflict, but they have three characteristics making them similar to one another but different from many other forms of social control. Both are forms of *mass* violence, distinguishing them from lynchings, assassinations, and other forms of violence aimed at individuals. Both are unilateral, distinguishing terrorism from *guerrilla warfare* and genocide from *total warfare*, which each otherwise has much in common with (Black, 2004a, pp. 11–12; Campbell, 2009, p. 154, n. 7). And both employ collective liability, the allocation of responsibility based on social identity rather than individual wrongdoing.

Along with these commonalities, there are three main ways terrorism and genocide may differ. First, terrorists are civilians, but the perpetrators of genocide might not be. Second, pure terrorism is covert, but genocide can be overt. Third, although collective liability is a feature of both, genocide is a narrower concept in this regard. Terrorists handle their grievances by targeting civilians based on some social characteristic, but this can be any characteristic, such as their ethnicity, religion, or political party (Black, 2004a, p. 10). The perpetrators of genocide, though, choose their targets based at least in part on ethnicity, thus employing ethnic liability, a specific form of collective liability (Campbell, 2011, p. 598).

These conceptual differences mean that many cases of mass killing are clearly terrorism or genocide but not both. Thus the Holocaust, planned and carried out by the German government and its agents and allies, was genocide, but it was not terrorism because the killers were not civilians. This was true of other major cases of genocide too. Governments do not have to be involved in genocide, though, and in many less extreme cases they are not. For example, in the Round Valley of Northern California, in the 1850s, white cattle ranchers would massacre nearby Indians when the Indians would kill the ranchers' horses or cattle. As one rancher explained, "These expeditions were formed by gathering together a few white men whenever the Indians committed depredations on their stock. … The result was that we would kill, on an average, fifty or sixty Indians on a trip, and take some prisoners, which we always took to the reserve" (Laycock, 1860, p. 49). Here civilians inflicted mass violence on other civilians, but not covertly. Missing this key feature of Black's definition, this too was genocide but not terrorism. Unlike these genocidal ranchers, terrorist groups operate underground, planning their actions in secret, though they might take credit afterward (Black, 2004a, p. 11; Hawdon & Ryan, 2009, p. 327). And not just the planning but also the carrying out of the violence might require secrecy, as in a suicide bombing, where the moment of violence comes suddenly with the detonation of a bomb. This kind of "clandestine, confrontation-avoiding violence," according to sociologist Randall Collins, is successful "because the attacker is good at pretending that he or she is not threatening at all" (2008).

The Holocaust and the Round Valley Genocide, then, are acts of genocide but not terrorism because the definition of terrorism is more restrictive in that it requires civilian perpetrators and covert activity. On the third divergence in the definitions, though, the issue of liability, it is genocide that is more restrictive, and thus we also see acts of terrorism that are not genocide. An example is the 1995 sarin gas attack on Tokyo's subways by the religious group Aum Shinrikyo (Juergensmeyer, 2000, pp. 102–116). The attackers here employed collective liability, targeting religious outsiders, but these were not ethnic outsiders; both the aggressors and their targets were mostly ethnic Japanese. Often violence between religious groups or political groups has some ethnic component, but here, as in many other cases, it did not, and without any ethnic targeting, the violence was terroristic but not genocidal.

With several points of conceptual convergence, terrorism and genocide are similar phenomena, but with several points of divergence, they are not identical. But note that the similarities refer to matters specified by both definitions, features that terrorism and genocide must have in common, while the differences refer to matters specified by one definition but not the other. These do not refer to features terrorism and genocide *must* differ on, only ones they *may* differ on. What this means is that the definitions are not mutually exclusive; they allow overlap, where some acts of violence can be both terrorism and genocide. Violence cannot be terrorism if the perpetrators are not civilians, but the perpetrators of genocide *can* be civilians. Violence cannot be terrorism if it is not covert, but genocide *can* be covert. And violence cannot be genocide if it does not involve ethnic targeting, but terrorism *can* involve ethnic targeting. Cases of ethnic terrorism such as those featured at the beginning of the chapter – the 9/11 attacks, the 2007 bombings of Yazidis, and others – were genocidal, but remember something else we noticed when considering these cases: They were not *extreme* cases of genocide. The cases of overlap tend to be extreme cases of terrorism but not of genocide, but what does it mean to say that a case of terrorism or genocide is extreme? The thing to keep in mind is that both definitions allow a great deal of variation in what is considered terrorism or genocide, so we can view each phenomenon as a matter of degree.

Terrorism and Genocide as a Matter of Degree

Black's definition is a definition of *pure terrorism*, implying that cases that deviate somewhat might still be terrorism. But even if we just look at the pure cases – where civilians unilaterally and covertly inflict mass violence on other civilians – they can vary in the degree of mass violence and the degree to which they are unilateral and covert. The same is true of genocide: The degree of mass killing, unilateralism, and ethnic liability can vary. As I have argued elsewhere (Campbell, 2011), we should move beyond simply considering whether a case is or is not genocide; if it is genocide, we should ask how genocidal it is. When we do this, we see a range from, at one end of the continuum, what I call *protogenocide*, cases with a low degree of mass killing, unilateralism, and ethnic liability, to, at the other end, what I call *hypergenocide*, where mass killing, unilateralism, and ethnic liability are at a maximum.

The Round Valley Genocide in California in the 1850s was a protogenocide due to its low degree of mass killing and ethnic liability. Mass killing has two dimensions: intensiveness and scale. *Intensiveness* refers to the proportion of the targets killed and *scale* to the time and territory over which the killing occurs. Recall that the rancher's account quoted earlier notes that they would kill some Indians and take others to a nearby reservation, so they were not exterminating all of the targets. And clearly a massacre of nearby Indians in response to theft did not have the same scale as a genocide conducted over months or years and throughout a nation-state or even larger territory. Violence in the Round Valley *was* highly unilateral, since the whites were responding to theft but not violence on the part of the Indians, and since the Indians were seldom capable of resisting. But many similar genocidal attacks against California Indians were not so completely one-sided. Killings of the Yana Indians of Butte County, for example, were often responses to the killings of whites, and the Yana were sometimes able to gain an advantage over groups of whites trying to kill them (Kroeber, 1961). The third element of genocide, ethnic liability, varies in that sometimes ethnicity is a factor but not the only factor in selecting targets. When whites in California attacked Indians, they often spared the women, so in these cases the mass killing was of only a portion of the ethnic group.

As genocides become more extreme on each element – as the intensiveness and scale of the killing increase, and as the unilateralism and ethnic liability increase – they become more genocidal. The Holocaust was the most extreme case of all, extreme even for a hypergenocide, involving the killing of 6 million Jews throughout Europe, without any violent provocation and almost without any resistance, and with little regard to age, sex, or any characteristic of the targets other than their Jewishness.

Terrorist acts look much more like the Round Valley Genocide and other massacres of California Indians than like the Holocaust. The amount of killing is comparable to these kinds of genocides, for one thing, with even the most extreme case of terrorism, the 9/11 attacks, resulting in only 3,000 deaths, and no others coming close to that. As Black notes, "terrorism operates on small scale and employs hit-and-run or possibly suicidal tactics rather than the sustained application of brute power characteristic of conventional military campaigns for territorial domination" (2004a, p. 11). The genocides in California did not employ hit-and-run or suicidal tactics – both examples of covert tactics – but they were small in scale like terrorist acts and certainly did not involve a sustained application of brute power, something characteristic not only of conventional military campaigns, but also of hypergenocides. When terrorism is genocidal, it is protogenocidal. We have been able to see this by examining the conceptual overlap between terrorism and genocide, and now to understand it, let us examine the theoretical overlap.

THE THEORETICAL OVERLAP

Pure sociology is a theoretical strategy Black (2010) developed and used initially to explain law, but he and others have since used it to explain many other forms of social control, including lynchings (Senechal de la Roche, 1996, 2001), suicides (Manning, 2012, 2015), honor killings (Cooney, 2014), homicides (Cooney, 1998), death row apologies (Cooney & Phillips, 2013), and complaints about "microaggressions" (Campbell & Manning, 2014). They have applied it to other forms of behavior too, but when applying pure sociology to social control they point to a social geometry that makes it likely someone handles a conflict a certain way.

Social Geometry and Social Control

Social geometry refers to the characteristics of all who are involved in an instance of human behavior. The social geometry of a conflict – any situation in which at least one person has a grievance against another – includes the social characteristics of the aggrieved parties, those they have grievances against, and anyone else with knowledge of the conflict. These social characteristics include various kinds of social distance and various kinds of social elevation, or status. Black's theory of law, for example, predicts that people will be punished more severely for offenses against strangers – those who are *relationally distant*, one type of social distance – than for offenses against intimates. And it predicts that they will be punished more severely for offenses against the wealthy – wealth is one type of status – than for offenses against the poor (Black, 2010). In this way pure sociologists explain the handling of a conflict with the conflict's social geometry, its location and direction in social space.[2]

In addition to law, another form of social control is gossip, informal evaluative talk in the absence of the offender. Gossip tends to occur among those who are intimate, homogeneous, and equal, and it tends to be about those who are equally and maximally distant from the gossipers (Black, 1995, p. 855, n. 129). Still another form of social control is avoidance, the reduction of interaction with the offender, such as by breaking off a relationship. Avoidance is most common in contexts where hierarchy is absent, relationships are fluid and fragmented, the division of labor is minimal, and social life is highly atomized (Black, 1998, pp. 80–82). In principle any reaction to a conflict can be explained this way. That is, we can identify a particular social geometry associated with every form of social control, not just law, gossip, and avoidance, but also negotiation, therapy, apology, complaint, and forms of violence such as lynching, suicide, feuding, or dueling.

The more similar two forms of social control are, the more similar their social geometries should be. Suicide and lynching, for example, are both unilateral, and they occur in response to conflicts in which the adversaries are unequal – conflicts with social superiors in the case of suicide and with social inferiors in the case of lynching (Manning, 2012; Senechal de la Roche, 1996). Feuding and dueling are both reciprocal forms of violence, on the other hand, with violence flowing similarly in both directions, and both occur between social equals (Black, 1995, p. 855, n. 130). To give one more example, lynching and feuding, though different in that lynching is unilateral and feuding is reciprocal, are similar in that both are forms of collective violence – violence by groups – so both occur under conditions conducive to at least some strong partisan support on behalf of a victim, such as where people who are socially close to the victim – but distant from the offender – mobilize in response to the offense (Black, 1995, p. 855, n. 130; Senechal de la Roche, 2001). A lynching in the American South of the early twentieth century might thus occur in response to the killing of a highly integrated member of the community by an outsider, and a blood feud in a tribal society might begin with the killing of a member of one clan by a member of another.

The Geometry of Terrorism and Genocide

Terrorism and genocide are no different. They each have their own geometries, and their similarities and differences correspond with geometrical similarities and differences. "Pure terrorism," Black tells us, "arises inter-collectively and upwardly across long distances in multidimensional social space" (2004b, p. 19), while genocide, I argue, "is a direct function of social distance and inequality," most likely to occur "when the antagonists are lacking in intimacy, interdependence, cultural similarity, and other forms of closeness, and when the aggressors have more authority, military power, and other forms of status than the targets" (Campbell, 2013, p. 468; see also Campbell, 2009, p. 160, 2010, p. 303). The phrasing and emphases here are different, but the concepts are the same, so we can glean from these two theories the main commonalities and differences in the geometries of terrorism and genocide. Terrorism and genocide both become more likely as social distance and inequality increase, but terrorism more often aims upward, targeting groups that are more powerful than the terrorists, while genocide more often aims downward.

Genocidal terrorism, then, differs from most other cases of genocide, and from all of the extreme cases, in that like other cases of terrorism it is usually a form of what sociologist M. P. Baumgartner (1984) calls "social control from below," the handling of a grievance with a superior. This would seem to make terrorism and genocide near opposites, except that as Baumgartner tells us, upward and downward social control are largely isomorphic, such that there is actually "a greater affinity between the two than between either of these and the forms of social control found among equals" (1984, p. 336). Whether directed against those who are higher or lower in status, social control among those who are unequal is commonly accusatory in its style and authoritarian in its procedure. To say the style is accusatory means that it involves punishment or a demand for compensation, not a working out of disagreements such as is often seen in conflicts between equals. And to say the procedure is authoritarian means the offended party simply *imposes* social control on the offender – without concern for the offender's wishes or for any kind of legal procedures established in advanced (Baumgartner, 1984, pp. 332–336).

Both terrorism and genocide involve the unilateral imposition of punishment on the targets. Inequality thus accounts generally for the severity of both forms of violence, as does social distance, a feature of conflict also associated with a tendency to treat adversaries as enemies (Black, 1998, pp. 144–157). But even though upward and downward social control are isomorphic, they are not exactly the same, as any difference in the social geometry of a conflict leads to differences in the handling of conflict. Unsurprisingly, then, the main difference in the geometries of terrorism and genocide, the upward direction of terrorism and the downward direction of genocide, is connected with one of the main conceptual differences between terrorism and genocide: It explains the covertness of violence.

Counterterrorism and Covertness

Baumgartner says that upward and downward social control differ in one major way: "As people of higher status ordinarily have abundant means of social control at their disposal, subordinates who attempt to sanction those above them incur a substantial risk of retaliation in most cases" (1984, p. 336). Commonly their actions are crimes attracting harsh punishments seldom seen in other contexts. As an illustration of what can happen when people rebel against authority, Black describes the response to an assassination attempt against Louis XV in eighteenth-century France:

> The executioner first ignited sulfur on the hand that held the knife in the attack, then ripped pieces of flesh from his calves, thighs, arms, and breasts with hot pincers and poured molten wax, lead, and boiling oil on his wounds. Next his arms and legs were tied to horses and pulled in four directions until they came apart, leaving only the trunk of his body ("drawing and quartering"), and his remains were burned. His house was also razed to the ground; his father, wife, and daughter were banished from France; and his brothers and sisters were required to change their names, so that his family would effectively cease to exist. (Black, 2011, p. 91)

Punishment by inferiors infuriates the powerful, and infuriating the powerful can be dangerous. For this reason those who still wish to pursue grievances against higher status parties often do so covertly. Think of employees stealing on the job because their employers have mistreated them, slaves sabotaging their work in response to their enslavement, or political dissidents assassinating prominent government officials

(Baumgartner, 1984, pp. 308–312; Tucker, 1989). Without some secrecy in the planning and execution of such actions, the more powerful targets would be able to stop the aggrieved parties beforehand or punish them afterward. This is less often a concern when the powerful have grievances against the powerless, such as when employers reprimand their employees, when slave masters beat their slaves, or when governments imprison dissidents. Social control from above is more overt.

Terrorism, like so many other forms of upward social control, elicits an aggressive response. The social control of terrorism, called *counterterrorism*, is a combination of criminal justice and quasi-warfare, so as Black points out, it goes far beyond treating individual terrorists as criminals: "It prosecutes some but detains others in a condition akin to prisoners of war – particularly noncitizens from the most distant locations in social space" (2004b, p. 23). Another feature of counterterrorism is its concern with the prevention of future acts of terrorism, not just punishing prior acts. This is one reason for the detainment of likely terrorists, and it also accounts for the guarding of possible targets, screenings for weapons at airports and other public places, and for the use of torture to gather information from detainees (Black, 2004b, p. 23). Some of this is successful enough that terrorism, though not eliminated, becomes much more difficult. Shortly after the 9/11 attacks in 2001, for example, many observers expected terrorist attacks on that scale to become commonplace. This has not happened, in part because counterterrorism efforts lessened Al Qaeda's ability to carry out such attacks. Writing in the *New York Times*, journalist Scott Shane says, "Al Qaeda and its ideology of global jihad are in a pronounced decline – with its central leadership thrown off balance as operatives are increasingly picked off by missiles and manhunts and, more important, with its tactics discredited in public opinion across the Muslim world" (2009). Typical of upward violence, terrorism results in efforts to stop it, efforts that might be very effective, and it might be condemned even by those who share grievances with the terrorists. Carrying out terrorism in this environment requires stealth. This aspect of terrorism then explains why terrorist acts have not been more severe.

The Severity of Terrorism

To ask why terrorism is not more severe may seem odd given the extreme violence involved – violence directed at civilians and intended to kill as many as possible. And indeed, like genocide terrorism is extremely violent because it travels across great distances in social space. But we have seen that terrorism, when genocidal, is protogenocide, and even the most extreme acts of terrorism do not compare in severity to the most extreme acts of genocide. And this is because the upwardness and covertness of terrorism limit the violence to some extent. Attacking those who are more powerful can be difficult given the differences in wealth and technology, possibly limiting how many of one's adversaries it is possible to kill. And the need for secrecy and for surprise attacks limits one's ability to carry on a sustained campaign of violence.

On the other hand, the most extreme cases of genocide, the hypergenocides, have all been downward and mostly overt, orchestrated by governments able to mobilize large numbers of participants and to act with impunity. Some secrecy might be employed to hide the violence from outsiders who might intervene, or to help carry out the killing more smoothly, but in these situations the aggressors have little to fear from the targets of the violence – at least not as long as the aggressors remain in power. Any punishment normally comes after the genocide, in situations where power has changed hands.

THE FUTURE OF TERRORISM AND GENOCIDE

So terrorist acts, as violent as they are, have been among the least violent cases of genocide. Will this continue, or will the death toll from terrorism increase? Will terrorism and genocide even last, or will they instead become rarer and finally wither away? These are questions we cannot answer definitively, but our knowledge of the social contexts in which terrorism and genocide occur can inform our speculation.

In speculating about the future of terrorism and genocide, we might first consider the trajectory of violence more generally. What we find when we do so, as psychologist and linguist Steven Pinker has documented, is that "violence has declined over long stretches of time, and today we may be living in the most peaceable era in our species' existence" (2011, p. xxi). First the raiding and feuding characteristic of tribal societies declined. Next homicide rates declined with the development of modern systems of government and law. Then humanitarian movements arose to combat slavery, torture, sadistic punishment, and other previously acceptable forms of violence. Today the trend toward nonviolence continues, and Pinker says that warfare and even genocide and terrorism are now in decline (2011, p. xxiv).

The decline of violence that Pinker describes is large and well documented, but because it has multiple causes, and because it deals with disparate forms of violence that might have very different social geometries, there are a number of complications. Certainly a consistent decline in violence is hard to see given the world wars, genocides, civil wars, and terrorist acts of the twentieth century. Yet it is probably wrong to say, as many have, that the twentieth century was the deadliest century ever, since many of the massacres of the past were likely greater, as a proportion of the world's population, than those of the last century. By one estimate, for instance, the An Lushan Revolt during China's Tang dynasty in the eighth century resulted in 36 million deaths.[3] This would have been two-thirds of the empire's population and one-sixth of the world's. The equivalent percentage of the world's population in the mid-twentieth century would have been 429 million deaths (Pinker, 2011, pp. 194–195). Still, the twentieth century was an incredibly violent, if not the most violent, century, and some forms of violence such as warfare and genocide operated in a manner not seen before then. So did terrorism, and pure terrorism, as defined by Black, hardly existed at all before the twentieth century (2004a, p. 10). Amid an overall worldwide decline in violence, certain extreme forms of violence became more extreme than ever. But Pinker says these will decline too, or already have, and we have reason to think he is right.

The Decline of Terrorism and Genocide

Terrorism and genocide will likely decline and even disappear not because they must follow the trajectory of other forms of violence, but because the social geometries that give rise to them are likely to become less common. Pure terrorism arose in the twentieth century when technological changes made it possible by making physically close those who were socially distant. As Black points out, "Terrorism by and against civilians requires physical contact between enemies separated by huge chasms in social space – a combination of physical and social geometry uncommon in human history" (2004b, p. 23). Rapid transportation and communication brought this about. Black says that these same technologies, though, will ultimately lead to the destruction of the social distances that now divide terrorists and their enemies – and thus to the decline of terrorism. What is true of terrorism is true of genocide as well, due to the similarities in their social geometries. Genocide too will decline as social distances decease, and for an additional reason: Since the most severe genocides are conducted by powerful, highly organized aggressors, usually authoritarian or totalitarian governments, the proliferation of democracy will also inhibit genocide (Campbell, 2013, pp. 479–480).

If current trends continue, the conflicts of the future will not have social geometries conducive to genocide and terrorism, and these two forms of mass violence would appear to be destined for destruction.[4] Because of its downward nature, extreme genocide is already in decline; it surely reached its zenith in the Holocaust. But since the perpetrators of terrorism are by definition civilians rather than governments, the decline of totalitarianism and authoritarianism is less important. Extreme terrorism is likely to continue in the near future, then, before the changes leading to its demise take full effect. And just as technological changes gave rise to pure terrorism and may one day lead to its fall, they may very well, in the near future, lead to terrorism surpassing the 9/11 attacks.

Terrorism and Technology

Recall that what distinguishes terrorism and genocide theoretically is that extreme terrorism is usually upward, against the more powerful, while extreme genocide is usually downward, against the less powerful. One result is that terrorists, who operate covertly to avoid detection and punishment by their powerful enemies, cannot kill on the same scale, and their most successful attacks result in the deaths of hundreds or at most thousands, not hundreds of thousands or millions. What is clear is that this is not because of any hesitancy on the part of terrorists to kill their enemies; the upward nature of the violence just makes it harder. But what if it became easier?

To some extent that has already happened, and it helped give rise to pure terrorism. Technology made killing easier. Better technology would make it easier still, and a nuclear weapon might enable the killing of millions. Of course the obstacles to upward violence still make obtaining and using such a weapon difficult, but if such technologies do fall into the hands of terrorist groups, they could change the nature of terrorism. As Goldhagen says, "Nuclear weapons can be the great mass-murderous and eliminationist equalizer .... Until today, the strong perpetrated mass exterminations and eliminations against the weak. With high technology, the weak finally have an opportunity to mass murder the strong" (2009, p. 511).

Should aggrieved groups of civilians succeed in carrying out such a nuclear attack against their ethnic enemies, the overlap between terrorism and genocide in this instance would be complete: It would be an act of pure terrorism as well as hypergenocide. Technology has the potential to lessen the differences between upward and downward mass violence, so before the demise of terrorism and genocide is complete, terrorism might become much more deadly.

NOTES

1. This applies to other forms of violence as well, and to the term *violence* itself. The tendency among the more politicized scholars of violence, for example, is to create concepts like *economic violence*, which might include "violations of economic and social rights, corruption, and the plunder of natural resources" (Sharp, 2014, p. 2). This way whatever the scholars find most morally objectionable can become a new type of violence.

2. More recently Black (2011) has used the strategy to identify the cause of conflict itself – not just the geometrical features that explain how a conflict is handled. The cause of all conflict, he says, is the movement of *social time*, and movements of social time are simply social changes, changes in the shape of social space, such as increases or decreases in intimacy, stratification, or diversity. I have employed this theory to identify the causes of genocidal conflicts, which are primarily increases or attempts to increase social diversity and decreases or attempts to decrease social stratification (Campbell, 2013). Movements of social time also cause the conflicts that lead to terrorism, and perhaps these movements are similar to those that lead to genocide, but here I do not address the origin of either terroristic or genocidal conflicts. Instead I look at the social features that explain whether and to what extent a given conflict will lead to terrorism or genocide.

3. The number here might be too high, and Pinker acknowledges that the estimated death tolls from ancient massacres should not be taken at face value. Still, as he notes, "history confirms that earlier civilizations were certainly capable of killing in vast numbers" (Pinker, 2011, p. 194). And while the An Lushan Revolt is the deadliest of mass killings by Pinker's reckoning, other events, such as the Mongol conquests of the thirteenth century, the fall of the Ming Dynasty in the seventeenth century, and the fall of Rome between the third and fifth centuries, also led to a vast amount of killing – to millions or tens of millions of deaths each (Pinker, 2011, p. 195).

4. Current trends might not continue, though, so keep in mind the speculative and contingent nature of this prediction. As criminologist Richard Rosenfeld points out in a discussion of the future of terrorism, "we always should be suspicious of theories of historical inevitability" (2004, p. 27). But I only say what will likely happen if social distances keep shrinking it is not inevitable that they will do so.

REFERENCES

Al Jazeera. (2010). How suicide bombings shattered Iraq. *Al Jazeera*. Retrieved from http://www.aljazeera.com/secretiraqfiles/2010/10/20101022161025428625.html. Accessed on October 24.

Barak, G. (2004). A reciprocal approach to terrorism and terrorist-like behavior. In M. Deflem (Ed.), *Terrorism and counter-terrorism: Criminological perspectives* (pp. 33–49). Amsterdam: Elsevier.

Baumgartner, M. P. (1984). Social control from below. In D. Black (Ed.), *Toward a general theory of social control: Fundamentals* (Vol. 1, pp. 203–345). Orlando, FL: Academic Press.

BBC News. (2003). Bali death toll set and 202. *BBC News*, February 19. Retrieved from http://news.bbc.co.uk/2/hi/asia-pacific/2778923.stm

Black, D. (1995). The epistemology of pure sociology. *Law and Social Inquiry*, *20*(3), 829–870.

Black, D. (1998). *The social structure of right and wrong* (Rev. ed.). San Diego, CA: Academic Press.

Black, D. (2004a). Terrorism as social control. In M. Deflem (Ed.), *Terrorism and counter-terrorism: Criminological perspectives* (pp. 9–18). Amsterdam: Elsevier.

Black, D. (2004b). The geometry of terrorism. *Sociological Theory*, *22*(1), 14–25.

Black, D. (2010). *The behavior of law* (special ed.). Bingley, UK: Emerald Group Publishing Limited.

Black, D. (2011). *Moral time*. New York, NY: Oxford University Press.

Black, D. (2013). On the almost inconceivable misunderstandings concerning the subject of value-free social science. *British Journal of Sociology*, *64*(4), 763–780.

Byman, D. (1998). The logic of ethnic terrorism. *Studies in Conflict & Terrorism*, *21*, 149–169.

Campbell, B. (2009). Genocide as social control. *Sociological Theory*, *27*(2), 150–172.

Campbell, B. (2010). Contradictory behavior during genocides. *Sociological Forum*, *25*(2), 296–314.

Campbell, B. (2011). Genocide as a matter of degree. *British Journal of Sociology*, *62*(4), 586–612.

Campbell, B. (2013). Genocide and social time. *Dilemas: Revista de Estudos de Conflito e Controle Social*, *6*(3), 465–488.

Campbell, B. (2014). Anti-minotaur: The myth of a sociological morality. *Society*, *51*(5), 443–451.

Campbell, B. (2015). *The geometry of genocide: A study in pure sociology*. Charlottesville, VA: University of Virginia Press.

Campbell, B., & Manning, J. (2014). Microaggression and moral cultures. *Comparative Sociology*, *13*(6), 692–726.

Cave, D., & Glanz, J. (2007). Toll in Iraq bombings is raised to more than 500. *The New York Times*, August 22. Retrieved from http://www.nytimes.com/2007/08/22/world/middleeast/22iraq-top.html?_r=1&hp&oref=login

Collins, R. (2008). Suicide bombers: Warriors of the middle class. *Foreign Policy*, January 8. Retrieved from http://foreignpolicy.com/2008/01/08/suicide-bombers-warriors-of-the-middle-class/

Cooney, M. (1998). *Warriors and peacemakers: How third parties shape violence*. New York, NY: New York University Press.

Cooney, M. (2014). Death by family: Honor violence as punishment. *Punishment and Society*, *16*(4), 406–427.

Cooney, M., & Phillips, S. (2013). With god on one's side: The social geometry of death row apologies. *Sociological Forum*, *28*(1), 159–178.

Gamel, K. (2007). Death toll in Iraq bomb attack at 250. *The Washington Post*, August 16. Retrieved from http://www.washingtonpost.com/wp-dyn/content/article/2007/08/15/AR2007081500206_pf.html

Ganor, B. (2002). Defining terrorism: Is one man's terrorist another man's freedom fighter? *Police Practice and Research*, *3*(4), 287–304.

Goldhagen, D. J. (2009). *Worse than war: Genocide, eliminationism, and the ongoing assault on humanity*. New York, NY: PublicAffairs.

Hawdon, J., & Ryan, J. (2009). Hiding in plain sight: Community organization, naïve trust and terrorism. *Current Sociology*, *57*(3), 323–343.

Jones, A. (2006). *Genocide: A comprehensive introduction*. New York, NY: Routledge.

Juergensmeyer, M. (2000). *Terror in the mind of God: The global rise of religious violence*. Berkeley, CA: University of California Press.

Kroeber, T. (1961). *Ishi in two worlds: A biography of the last wild Indian in North America*. Berkeley, CA: University of California Press.

Laycock, D. (1860). Deposition of Dryden Laycock. *Majority and minority reports of the special joint committee on the mendocino war*. (pp. 48–51). Appendix to the journals of the eleventh session of the legislature of the state of California. Sacramento: C. T. Botts, State Printer. Micropublished in "Western Americana: Frontier history of the trans-Mississippi west, 1550–1900." New Haven, CT: Yale University Library and Newberry Library.

Manning, J. (2012). Suicide as social control. *Sociological Forum*, *27*(1), 207–227.

Manning, J. (2015). Suicide and social time. *Dilemas: Revista de Estudos de Conflito e Controle Social*, *8*(1), 97–126.

Pinker, S. (2011). *The better angels of our nature: Why violence has declined*. New York, NY: Viking.

Rai, S., & Sengupta, S. (2006). Series of bombs explode on seven trains in India, killing scores. *New York Times*, July 12. Retrieved from http://www.nytimes.com/2006/07/12/world/asia/12india.html?pagewanted=all&_r=0

Rosenfeld, R. (2004). Terrorism and criminology. In M. Deflem (Ed.), *Terrorism and counter-terrorism: Criminological perspectives* (pp. 19–32). Amsterdam: Elsevier.

Senechal de la Roche, R. (1996). Collective violence as social control. *Sociological Forum*, *11*(1), 97–128.

Senechal de la Roche, R. (2001). Why is collective violence collective? *Sociological Theory*, *19*(2), 126–144.

Shane, S. (2009). Rethinking our terrorist fears. *New York Times*, September 26. Retrieved from http://www.nytimes.com/2009/09/27/weekinreview/27shane.html?pagewanted=all

Sharp, D. N. (2014). Introduction: Addressing economic violence in times of transition. In D. N. Sharp (Ed.), *Justice and economic violence in transition* (pp. 1–26). New York, NY: Springer.

Tucker, J. (1989). Employee theft as social control. *Deviant Behavior*, *10*, 319–334.

Wilkinson, T. (2004). Train bombings kill nearly 200 in Spain. *Los Angeles Times*, March 12. Retrieved from http://articles.latimes.com/2004/mar/12/world/fg-spain12

THE SOCIAL CONSTRUCTION OF TERRORISM

Cynthia A. Karaffa

ABSTRACT

Purpose – *This chapter explores the expansion of reality regarding the issue of terrorism. "There are those who argue that there is an empirically verifiable truth as to what constitutes the political" (Easton, D. (1968).* International encyclopaedia of the social sciences *(Vol. 12, pp. 46, 282–298), while others maintain any definition is a contingent social construction, with the disciple of politics dependent upon the nature of the political arena, itself dependent upon socially constructed and historically variable forces. Definitions of "political" are not discoverable in nature, but are rather a legacy or convention (Wolin, S. (1961).* Politics and vision *(p. 5). London: Allan & Unwin).*

Methodology/approach – *Regarding terrorism as an objective reality and subjective interpretation, this chapter reviews the definition, history, and perceptions of terrorism as it relates to the theoretical interpretations of constructivism (the meaning-making activity of the individual mind and unique experiences) and social constructionism (social interpretations of understanding).*

Terrorism and Counterterrorism Today
Sociology of Crime, Law and Deviance, Volume 20, 67–87

ISSN: 1521-6136/doi:10.1108/S1521-613620150000020004

Findings – *The need to comprehend the notion of ontological relativity – that each person has a unique history from which to make sense of and create an individual reality that is valid to the self, while at the same time knowing that culture has an enormous influence on an individual's worldview.*

Originality/value – *Thoughts, ideas, perceptions, and interpretations are important for all nations and especially in the United States because voters in history's most influential, wide- ranging, hegemonic power are helping to shape American policy. Perceptions and interpretations (subjective reality) influence whether or not – and for whom – a person votes, which has long-lasting and far-reaching political implications. Once a vote is cast, that vote becomes an objective reality.*

Keywords: Social construction; terrorism; political; reality

INTRODUCTION

"Terrorism is an objective reality and a subjective interpretation" (Karaffa, 2012, p. 3). The destruction that terrorism leaves behind is observable and quantifiable which is an objective reality, however what constitutes terrorism and who is a terrorist is a matter of subjective interpretation. How reality is constructed and experienced groups may create new possibilities of reality (Karaffa, 2012).

Interpretive social constructionism (ISC) is the "more radical form of constructionism" (Harris, 2008, p. 232). Harris identifies themes from several diverse traditions, such as: pragmatism, symbolic interaction, phenomenology, ethnomethodology, narrative analysis, cognitive sociology, semiotic sociology and postmodernism; which led to the statement that "the core principle of ISC is the idea that *the meaning of things is not inherent*" (p. 232). This applies to everything. Social phenomena are "*interpreted* entities whose existence and qualities are dependent in large part on people's meaning-making practices" (p. 233). Objective social constructionists (OSC) do not focus on the meaning, but on the "real state of affairs" (p. 234) and the creation of "real things" (p. 234). Real things are produced by the "actions of individual actors and groups, by constraining social forces, by the operations of class, race, gender, politics, or religion, and so on" (p. 234). Regarding terrorism as an objective reality and subjective interpretation, this study explores the expansion of reality regarding the issue of terrorism and the interplay between self, society, and the world. As Berger and Luckmann

(1967) suggest, a human being constructs reality on every level: with the self; in one-on-one interactions; in small and large groups; with their own culture; and with other cultures. How do individuals and groups view themselves, other individuals and groups, the actions of governments, and statements of legitimacy and power that are caused by and at the root of terrorism?

"Individuals and groups often are given a heavy dose of ethnocentrism minus the complexities of cultural relativism" (Karaffa, 2012, p. 5). Ethnocentrism is the practice of judging another culture by the standards of one's own culture (Macionis, 2010, p. 78) and cultural relativism is the practice of judging a culture by its own standards (p. 79). "Nations (and cultures) have their own preferred version of the world, and this usually dismisses competing versions. Not only do we construct our realities, we then institutionalize these realities into structures, these structures then subject us to them" (Karaffa, 2012, p. 5). Edmund Husserl, commonly considered the founder of phenomenology (Appelrouth & Desffor-Edles, 2008, p. 539), developed what he called transcendental phenomenology which holds "there is no pure subjective subject or pure objective object" meaning that "all consciousness is consciousness of something, and objects do not have appearances independent of the beings that perceive them" making the world "a world of meaningful objectives and relations" (Appelrouth & Desffor-Edles, 2008, p. 539). Husserl used the word "lifeworld" to refer to the world of "existing assumptions as they are experienced and made meaningful in consciousness" (p. 539). Both Husserl and Alfred Schutz emphasized that "humans do not experience the world as an *objective* reality; rather they experience the world as made of meaningful objects and relations … and for Schutz *reality* then requires paying attention to the meaning structures by and through which individuals perceive the world" (p. 539). However, Schutz states that humans do not merely internalize elements of the lifeworld and that we are simply not just vessels for pre-existing cultural forms, but rather we "experience them, interpret them, thereby reflecting an individual approach to order … the lifeworld possesses a private component" (p. 544).

How we experience and interpret our world has both the individual and cultural dimension. Richard Nisbett in his book *The Geography of Thought: How Asians and Westerns Think Differently and Why* tells the story of working with one of his Chinese graduate students. One day his student said to him:

> you know, the difference between you and me is that I think the world is a circle and you think it's a line. The Chinese believe in constant change, but with things always

> moving back to some prior state. They pay attention to a wide range of events; they search for relationships between things; and they think you can't understand the part without understanding the whole. Westerners live in a simpler, more deterministic world; they focus on salient objects or people instead of the larger picture; and they think they can control events because they know the rules that govern the behavior of objects. (2003, p. xiii)

Nisbett said he was intrigued because as a lifelong believer that all groups perceive and reason the same way; thinking that "indoctrination into distinctive habits of thought from birth could result in very large *cultural* differences in habits of thought ... I found these assertions to be revolutionary in their implications ... human cognition is not everywhere the same" (2003, p. xvii). For Nisbett this insight made important claims about the nature of thought: "first that the members of different cultures differ in their metaphysics or fundamental beliefs about the nature of the world and secondly that the characteristic thought processes of different groups differ greatly" (p. xvii). His contention now is that very different systems of perception and thought have existed for thousands of years and that we need to be aware of the different thought processes utilized by different individuals, cultures and groups (p. xxi). The questions for this investigation are what are interpretations of "terrorism" and "terrorist"?

DEFINING TERRORISM

What is *terrorism*? Who is a *terrorist*? These words have worked their way into the 21st century vocabulary with such ease and voracity "abetted partly by the modern media, whose efforts to communicate an often complex and convoluted message in the briefest amount of airtime or print space possible have led to the promiscuous labeling of a range of violent acts as terrorism" (Hoffman, 2006, p. 1). "We cannot pick up a newspaper or watch or listen to a newscast without seeing or hearing some reference to terrorism" (Ross, 2006, p. 2). Diverse entities ranging from governments to individuals, and actions from genocide, bombings, to "contamination of over- the-counter medication" (Hoffman, 2006, p. 1) are labeled terrorist and terrorism. Pillar (2001) states that the word terrorism is a "catch-all pejorative" (p. 12) and is applied to the use of force, political authority or to someone else's disliked policy agenda. Dekmejian (2007) asserts the scholarly discourse by academics over the use of the words terrorist and terrorism has been "mostly replaced with rhetoric from a motley crew of politicians, pundits, journalists, lobbyists, and intelligence analysts who obfuscated the meaning of terrorism, in keeping with their individual perceptions and political agendas" (p. 15). According to Ross (2006) terrorism has become a value-laden term and phrases such as "one man's terrorist is another man's freedom fighter" (p. 2) are often used to clarify situations or to "muddy" them. Sederberg (1991) would view this as a "relativity definition" which implies that "all attempts to formulate the concept will be hopelessly compromised by essentially arbitrary personal or political bias. Consequently, any analysis based on such dubious conceptual foundations will be distorted and most likely vacuous" (p. 6). A terrorist "will never acknowledge he is a terrorist and moreover will go to great lengths to evade and obscure any such inference or connection" (Hoffman, 2006, p. 22). To the above construction of terrorist, the *real* terrorist is society, the socioeconomic system[1] or the government (Hoffman, 2006). Hoffman quotes the spiritual leader of a Lebanese terrorist group, Sheikh Muhammad Hussein Fadlallah: "we don't see ourselves as terrorists because we don't believe in terrorism and we don't see resisting the occupier as a terrorist action" (p. 23).

Jenkins (1980) from RAND acknowledges that "what is called terrorism thus seems to depend on one's point of view" (p. 23). Hoffman (2006), Pillar (2001), Dekmejian (2007) and Ross (2006) agree that the words terrorism and terrorist lack precision and objectivity, but yet these words are found incessantly in our everyday lives, and that no internationally accepted definition of terrorism exists. Dekmejian (2007) states "in the quest for a scientific study of politics, political scientists have long faced the problem of finding appropriate terminology to describe and classify the actors and actions involved in the political processes within and across countries and cultures" (p. 15). Terrorism is not a new phenomenon. Nor is it simply a religious or political manifestation, but a struggle for power; and in this struggle for power between competing entities or ideologies, the word terrorism "lacks precision and objectivity from a scholarly point of view" (p. 15). Perceptions, misperceptions, interpretations and misinterpretations can be deadly.

Bjorgo (2005) contends that "researchers have identified more than 200 definitions of terrorism but failed to agree on any one" (p. 1). He asserts there is a growing consensus among researchers and governments about the "core meaning of the concept of terrorism" which includes "a set of methods or strategies of combat rather than an identifiable ideology or movement … premeditated use of violence against primarily non-combatants in order to achieve a psychological effect of fear on others than the immediate target" (p. 20). He does acknowledge that there is "heated disagreement" concerning the boundaries of the "phenomenon" of terrorism and which groups or violent acts should or should not be included within the label, "terrorism" (p. 2). For Hoffman (2006) understanding terrorism as a *political* concept is paramount and is inescapably about power: "the pursuit of power, the acquisition of power, and the use of power to achieve political change" (p. 2). Therefore, terrorism is violence and or the threat of violence "used and directed in pursuit of, or in service of, a political aim" (pp. 2–3). Terrorism is "planned, calculated, and indeed systematic act" (p. 3).

Adding to the confusion of defining "terrorism" and "terrorist" is the fact that different departments and agencies within, for example, the United States Government use different definitions reflecting "the priorities and particular interests of the specific agency involved" (Hoffman, 2006, p. 31) referring to the U.S. State Department, Federal Bureau of Investigation, Department of Homeland Security, and the Department of Defense. In his 2004 article "Frameworks for Conceptualizing Terrorism," Alex P. Schmid views terrorism from five different perspectives: crime, politics, warfare, communication and religion. Reich (1998) characterizes terrorism as a "complex problem: its origins are diverse; and those who engage in it, even more so" (p. 1). Retrospectively history may hold the answers to the complexity of defining terrorism and terrorist, and the root causes of social violence.

HISTORY AND TERRORISM

"The assassin's dagger, poison, bullet, or bomb are Roman tribunes, Arab caliphs, ottoman sultans, European monarchs, U.S. presidents, and scores of prime ministers and leading public figures" (Dekmejian, 2007, p. 25) have all been modes and victims of what Dekmejian calls the oldest form of political violence, "the murder of government leaders and officials" (p. 25). All assassinations, even without a political motive, are acts of political violence because they have consequences that alter the present and future (p. 25). "Et tu, Brute?" Shakespeare's famous line from the play Julius Caesar dramatizes one of the first known and most famous ancient political assassinations, March 15, 44 BC, followed by the Emperors Caligula on January 15, 41 BC and Commodus on December 31, 192 AD. Ross (2006) dates "ancient terrorism" from 66 to 1870 AD (p. 32), Dekmejian (2007) from 66 to 1250s, and Hoffman (2006) from 66 to 1250s to the late nineteenth century depending on the type of classification.[2] These three authors cite the mix of politics-challenging Roman power, religious fanatics and extreme nationalists in their description of Jewish

Zealots and the religious sect, the Sicarri 66 to 71 AD.[3] The Zealots[4] "waged a ruthless campaign of assassination, mostly of individuals" (Hoffman, 2006, p. 83) in which these "religious militants sought to achieve freedom from Rome through a mass revolt that required the grassroots mobilization and unity of the Jewish community" (Dekmejian, 2007, p. 30) by using the *sica*, a primitive dagger or short sword (Ross, 2006, p. 33) to kill their opponents "in public places in order to maximize the psychological horror of their grisly deeds" (Dekmejian, 2007, p. 30).

Other ancient terrorist groups included the Thugs and the Assassins. According to Hoffman (2006), the Thugs were a seventh-century "religious cult that terrorized India until its suppression in the mid-nineteenth century" (p. 83). Thugs would engage in ritual killings of "innocent travelers" who would be strangled to honor the Hindu goddess Kali. Over their 1200-year existence, the thugs killed approximately a million people (p. 83). Between 1090 and 1272 AD "a radical offshoot of the Muslim Shi'a Ismali sect, the Assassins,[5] fought to repel the Christian Crusaders attempting to conquer present-day Syria and Iran" (p. 84). Ross (2006) asserts that the Assassins were "defending their way of life against the Seljuqus, a Turkish dynasty, who wanted to suppress them" (p. 33). Dekmejian (2007) dates the Assassins slightly earlier in time than Ross (2006) and Hoffman (2006), to 644 AD after the death of the Prophet Muhammad and the "series of assassinations that generated sectarian and political divisions ... a manifestation of the struggle for power among competing factions at the center of an expanding empire ... the succession to the Prophet Muhammad had become a great chess game" (Dekmejian, 2007, pp. 30–31). These three authors state that the Assassins ended the killings during the mid to late 1200s. However, Dekmejian explains that "beyond the Sunni-Shia divide, the basic social units that have continued to shape the power interactions among the Arabs and some Muslims are tribal and kinship groups which act according to their specific calculations of collective self-interest based on group solidarity" (2007, p. 31) still play an active role in Muslim countries today.

PERCEPTIONS OF THE WESTERN WORLD AND TERRORISM

If the goal is achieving a global world and peaceful society then we must know all sides of an issue and that great powers also use and threaten to use force, although when used by the powerful, threats are called coercive diplomacy, not terrorism (Chomsky, Mitchell, & Schoeffel, 2002, p. 16). Blowback[6] is a metaphor for the unintended consequences of the United States government's international activities that have been kept secret from the American people. False-flag operations[7] are a cause of blowback. False-flag operations are covert operations conducted by government, corporations or other organizations, which are designed to appear like they are being carried out by other entities. In other words, it is an action in which the perpetrator intends for the blame (or credit) to be placed on a different party. The term originally comes from the naval concept of flying another country's flag to deceive and confuse other ships. For example, citizens perceive and interpret events with the information they are given and this information becomes their knowledge of the truth. The individual then acts and reacts within this version of the state-constructed "truth." However, when others have information that we do not possess, this unknown secret does not change our version of the truth, but does render our version inadequate and wrong. Our knowledge is based on a fabrication.

Noam Chomsky has never hidden his linguistic viewpoint on the term "war against terrorism." It is simply "propaganda" (Chomsky & Barsamian, 2001). "Western powers could never abide by their own official definitions of the term [terrorism], as in the U.S. Code[8] or Army manuals, to do so would at once reveal that the United States is a leading terrorist state, as are its clients" (Chomsky, 2001, p. 16). Chomsky believes that U.S. citizens need to know when to accept or when to question the information disseminated to us by the government and media. Citizens need knowledge of self and others, and critical thinking skills to analyze the barrage of information. As Reich (1998) stated, one of the best ways to understand terrorism and the terrorist is through interdisciplinary study, such as history, religion, political science, and psychology. To extend on that thought, Diana Glyer and David L. Weeks in *The Liberal Arts in Higher Education* state:

> [I]f truth is elusive, contingent, and subjective; then value judgments depend wholly on context and perspective. Because the human perspective is ultimately derived from social context, human affairs and the needs of the community become the abiding concern. Practical reason, problem solving, and social progress become the foci of liberal education ... liberal education becomes preparation for the demands of contemporary society ....The social sciences illuminate individual behavior, provide insight into social relations, and help devise a better world. (1998, p. xix)

"Not only do we (as individuals and a nation) need to comprehend our background and knowledge, but also recognize and appreciate others (other individuals and nations) and their viewpoints so that we can distinguish between what we perceive as global reality or what we are asserting to others as a global reality when in fact it is only our viewpoint and not fact" (Karaffa, 2012, pp. 23–24). Shipman (2002) states "whether hailed or hated, globalization is not new, it is the way things always were" (p. 27) "so when globalization strikes, localization is the antidote most instinctively reached for" (p. 18). He also asks if globalization is a "thinly-disguised Americanization" (p. 207) and if the world's last remaining superpower is using globalization as a disguise for its own world domination or "merely trying to hold its own in a world that's still beyond it" (p. 26). Shipman, who is a freelance economist affiliated with Cambridge University believes one of the reasons why the United States of America is so widely resented in the world is that "other nations must assist the United States in maintaining a level of life that they can't aspire to, because their own more modest lifestyle would collapse if the biggest spender were ever to tighten its belt" (Shipman, 2002, p. 207).

Referring to a Pew Research Center Global Attitudes Survey released in 2003, Virginia Straus and Nel Noddings state that there is "a widespread belief among people in most nations that their culture is superior to others …. Among wealthy nations, Americans stand out for their sense of cultural superiority. Six in ten people in the United States agree with the statement: Our people are not perfect, but our culture is superior to others" (Noddings, 2005, p. xiii). The Straus–Nodding statement demonstrates the necessity for more comprehensive global knowledge to be taught in schools and students need to understand that:

> the paradigm of Western thought known as modernity is unraveling … [and] has been unraveling for some time … its dissolution was made inevitable by a flaw attributable to its very core and essence … modernity appears both as a conceit and a coherence: it was sustained from the first by the self-satisfied claim of objective knowledge and systematic understanding that helped place the concept of Western man in charge of the destiny of all humankind …. The cause for failure turns out to be very simple: the *reason* Western man has used since the eighteenth century both to found and legitimate his understanding of reality is increasingly incapable of accounting for the complexity it uncovers and for the causality it purports to explain. (Racevskis, 1993, p. 1)

The core issue in Racevskis' (1993) statement is Western modernity and its' conceit. Whether the vision of Western modernity is explained politically, sociologically, scientifically, or artistically, the modernity vision is not entirely capable of explaining complex realities. Just as in the title of his book *What We Say Goes*, Chomsky and Barsamian (2007) succinctly in four words articulates Western conceit. "The United States is a leading outlaw state, totally unconstrained by international law, and it openly says so" (2007, p. 1).

CONSTRUCTING REALITY: TERROR REALITIES AND INTERPRETATION

Much of the history of "terrorism" literature focuses on Europe and the East during this "ancient period" and is lacking information on any activity, if any, going on in other parts of the world, such as North America. North America has been protected by the distance of oceans, insularity and naïveté that when the tragedy of terrorism hits, reality is shocking for many people; for example, Oklahoma City April 1995[9] and September 11, 2001[10]. Cited are April 1995 and September 2001 for three reasons: (1) current collective memory of these events; (2) because of the differences in the standpoint of each attack, one from the inside by an American Christian White Supremacist and the other from the outside by Muslim Radicals; (3) the confirmation that "terrorism is an extremely complex set of phenomena, covering a great diversity of groups with different origins and causes" (Bjorgo, 2005, p. 1).

Reich (1998) rationalizes that one of the best ways to understand terrorism and the terrorist is through interdisciplinary study, such as history, religion, political science and psychology (p. 2). Croft (2006) views the discourse concerning the "war on terror" via September 11, 2001, develops not only through American politics, but other channels "including the media, the church, music, novels, films, television, jokes and tattoos." Croft creates an understanding of how a social process of crisis is perceived and how that processes creates assumptions and policy-making. Being a professor of international relations, he combines these approaches with insights from cultural studies to "understand the war on terror as a cultural phenomenon … and war as a social construction" (p. 1). In an introduction to a social problems textbook, Robert Nisbett states:

> a social problem cannot be said to exist until it is defined as one. The way of behavior involved may be fixed and may be found among many peoples. But unless the way of behavior is defined as a violation of some norm, unless it is regarded by large number of people as being repugnant to moral consciousness, it cannot be termed a social problem …. We are obliged, as sociologists, to recognize that social problems are inseparably joined to subjective awareness of a particular set of norms …. There is a reciprocal

> relation between moral consciousness in a society and the perceived existence of social problems .... No social problem exists for any people unless it has been defined as a social problem. The subjective element is inescapable. (Merton & Nisbett, 1971, pp. 2–3)

As noted from Hoffman's *Inside Terrorism* the words terrorism and terrorist are difficult to define because much of the definition depends on who is doing the defining. Socially constructing reality can be a decidedly changeable activity based on exposure, definition, and response. Herbert Blumer, basing some of his theoretical outlooks on the insight of George Herbert Mead, explored how individuals understand and negotiate their everyday life and through this process of understanding and negotiating forms his symbolic interactionist approach to social life (Appelrouth & Desffor-Edles, 2008, chapter 12).

"As humans, we act toward things based on the meaning we give to them, that meaning stems from social interaction, these meanings are then interpreted by the individual experiencing the event. So for some a suicide bombing may be an act of cowardice and hate, for others it may be seen as an act of supreme courage and love" (Karaffa, 2012, p. 43). Blumer highlights the "significance of meaning, interaction, and interpretation to the fitting together of individuals' lines of action. Interpretation entails *constructing* the meaning of objects or another's actions, for meaning is not released by or inherent in, things or the actions themselves" (Appelrouth & Desffor-Edles, 2008, p. 476), using Pape's discussion on the social construction of altruistic martyrdom, based on Emil Durkheim's study of suicide as an example: altruistic motives are heavily influenced by social approval. Although one could believe that an action would benefit others even if those others did not agree with the judgment, an individual is more likely to conclude that an act is beneficial if society actually supports and honors it. In fact, social approval is central to the logic of altruistic suicide as Durkheim conceived it (Pape, 2005, p. 187).

"Terrorism is an interpretive social problem" (Karaffa, 2012, p. 44). There are various ways to construct and approach social problems; through the functional and normative definitions, the value-conflict school, and labeling theory to name a few. According to Spector and Kitsuse (1977) the functional etiological approach stresses the idea of social disorganization or dysfunctionality, also called social pathology. At the core of this approach is the "identification of conditions or behaviors that impede the fulfillment of society's goals that interfere with the smooth functioning of society, or throw society into disequilibrium" (p. 23), and once these conditions or behaviors are identified as social problems, "functionalists seek to analyze and explain the origins" (p. 23). Critics of the functional approach contend that value judgments are merely disguised as factual assessments (Spector & Kitsuse, 1977).

Below is a quotation from Martindale (1957) concerning crime rings, in which for the purpose of this investigation, the words crime rings have been replaced by terrorist/terrorism.

> [Terrorist/terrorism], for example, are treated as examples of disorganization. Yet they are often more "organized" than the society in which they appear, and in which they are assumed to represent "disorganization." Clearly normative judgments, in these instances, are being disguised as factual judgments. [Terrorist/terrorism] are not objected to because they are examples of disequilibrium, but because they are normatively objectionable. (p. 358)

For the theorists of the value-conflict school, the most important element that characterizes a social problem is the value judgments of the members of society (Spector & Kitsuse, 1977). For Merton and Nisbett (1971) the value judgments of the members of society would constitute reckless subjectivism and would be a self-deceiving justification. Spector and Kitsuse treat social problems as social constructions – "as products of claims-making and constitutive definitional process" (Holstein & Miller, 2003, p. 1). Proponents of the interpretative paradigm share the belief that "what people know and believe to be true about the world is constructed-or made up-as people interact with one another over time in specific social settings" (LeCompte & Schensul, 1999, p. 48).

The view in Berger and Luckmann's (1967) *The Social Construction of Reality* is that the researcher's aim is to understand this complex and constructed reality from the point of view of those who live in it. "Interpretivists[11] operate from the belief that all constructs are equally important and valid" (LeCompte & Schensul, 1999, p. 49). Ian Hacking (2001) asserts that "social construction" has been used for raising consciousness (p. 6). Our lived experiences and the world in which we inhabit are socially constructed. Hacking opens his book by asking the question, "the social construction of what?" and maintains that these "reality" claims are used to raise consciousness. Berger and Luckmann (1967) claim that there are various realities in this very complex world in which we live; however, they do not claim that *everything* is a social construct, but that our meanings of, experiences of, feelings of, and responsiveness of reality, are socially constructed. We act, react, interpret, and perceive phenomena by how they are conceptualized in our own social milieu; "knowledge is a key feature of societies .... But it is also a key feature of the fragmentation between social groups" (Dant, 1991, p. 1). Knowledge joins us and separates us; if we share the same perceptive, we might agree that this is "truth" and "those with whom we disagree we treat [their knowledge] as ideological as being mere ideas, as not knowledge in the sense of something consistent with our lived reality" (Dant, p. 1). We create our lived reality through cultural communication, such as language, pictures, movies, television, jokes, music, dance, plays, novels, and even tattoos; this cultural communication "knowledge truth" is evident in our major societal institutions (Croft, 2006; Dant, 1991).

Determinism[12] views human action resulting from physical, emotional and environmental factors that are beyond the control of the individual. Conversely, the human mind has the capacity to choose or initiate actions or events, or free-will. What if reality was equally created from all individuals' and groups' conception of self; would deterministic factors (the antecedents of gender, race, age, religion, ethnicity, socio-economics, etc ...) still lead to events or outcomes such as the ones experienced by oppressed groups? Adding to the quandary of determinism and free-will is the matter of power. C. Wright Mills wrote "all politics is a struggle for power" and "the ultimate kind of power is violence" (Mills, 1956, p. 171). For Hoffman, terrorism is where politics and violence intersect in the hope of delivering power (p. 254).

Utilizing Thomas A. Schwandt's examination of interpretivism, hermeneutics, and social constructionism as embracing "different perspectives on the aim and practice of understanding human action, different ethical commitments, and different stances on methodology and epistemological issues of representation, validity, objectivity ..." (2000, p. 190) we may be able to grasp the concept of power and the act of violence from the terrorists' viewpoint. Schwandt poses social inquiry as a practice that transforms and guides the very theory it is trying to understand. The researcher is actively interpreting the data and giving meaning to "what others are doing and saying, then transforming that understanding into public knowledge" (p. 191). Schwandt states that acting, thinking, practice and theory are a "continuous process of critical reflection and transformation" (p. 191). Crotty (1998) views constructionism as an epistemology, "a way of understanding and explaining how we know what we know" (p. 3). Interpretivism and hermeneutics are theoretical perspectives, "the philosophical stance informing the methodology and thus providing a context for the process and grounding its logic and criteria" (p. 3). For Schwandt "acting and thinking, practice and theory, are linked in a continuous process of critical reflection and transformation" (2000, p. 191).

Two earlier thinkers in this field are Wilhelm Dilthey (1833–1911) and Max Weber (1864–1920) and their associations with *Erklären* (explaining) and *Verstehen* (understanding) (Dilthey, 1976; Weber, 1949). Dilthey stated that natural reality and social reality are different kinds of reality and require different methods of investigation (Crotty, 1998; Dilthey, 1976). For Schwandt, interpretivism and positivism are marked by the differentiation between two things by identifying their contrasting qualities, "interpretivism was conceived in reaction to the effort to develop a natural science of the social" (Schwandt, 1994, p. 119). Characteristics of positivism are value-free, detached observation with explanation, control and predictability. Conversely, interpretivism "looks for culturally derived and historically situated interpretations of the social life-world" (Crotty, 1998, p. 67). Human action is inherently meaningful. Schwandt states that to understand a particular social action, we must grasp the meanings that constitute that action which "requires that one interpret in a particular way what the actors are doing" (2000, p. 191).

Schutz (1971) explains *Verstehen* as two-dimensional; primarily it is "the name of a complex process by which all of us in our everyday life interpret the meaning of our own actions and those of others with whom we interact" (Bernstein, 1976, p. 9. 139). Also, *Verstehen* is a method in the social sciences, a "process by which the social scientist seeks to understand the primary process, hence interpretivists aim to reconstruct the self-understanding of actors engaged in particular actions" (Schwandt, 2000, p. 193). Outhwaite (1975) and Schwandt (2000) stated that interpretivist epistemologies can be characterized as hermeneutic "because they emphasize that one must grasp the situation in which human actions make (or acquire) meaning in order to say one has an understanding of the particular action" (Schwandt, 2000, p. 193), therefore, *Verstehen* "considers understanding to be an intellectual process whereby a knower (the inquirer as subject) gains knowledge about an object (the meaning of human action)" (p. 194).

Schwandt defines hermeneutics as "the art, theory, and philosophy of interpreting the meaning of an object" (2001, p. 115) and that there are several varieties of hermeneutics with complex theoretical disputes. Dilthey (1833–1911) expanded on Schleiermacher's (1768–1834) original definition to include the epistemology and methodology of the social sciences, therefore for Dilthey "hermeneutics has meant the theory of interpretation as a particular methodology" (Schwandt, 2001, p. 115). Heidegger (1889–1976) viewed hermeneutics as an existential-phenomenological analysis of *Dasein* (existence or being-in-the-world) and that hermeneutics is a concept of ontology or a basis characteristic of human existence (p. 115). Gadamer further developed Heidegger's ideas to include the "centrality of language and dialogue to understanding" (p. 115). For Gadamer, "understanding is interpretation" and is not "an isolated activity of human beings but a basic structure of our experience of life. We are always taking something *as* something" (Schwandt, 2000, p. 194). Secondly for Gadamer, sociohistorically inherited bias or prejudice is not something the interpreter must get rid of, it is "not something that is external, objective and past ... tradition is a living force that enters into all understanding ... and despite the fact that traditions operate for the most part behind our backs, they are there, ahead of us conditioning our interpretations" (p. 194). Prejudgments are "necessary to make our way, in everyday thought, conversation, and action" and that "meaning is negotiated mutually in the act of interpretation; it is not simply discovered" (p. 195). Nietzsche (1844–1900), Foucault (1926–1984), Derrida, Ricoeur and to some extent Habermas, practiced "hermeneutics of suspicion" (Schwandt, 2001, p. 116), also called radical or deconstructionist hermeneutics: "this practice is profoundly suspicious of whatever purports to be the truth; it argues that all interpretations are false and there is no escape from false consciousness" (p. 116). For the deconstructionist, the goal is to "decipher, decode, or unmask the reality or truth of the meaning of all notions or ideas that we take for granted and show these meanings to be entirely contingent and relative" (p. 116).

Schwandt (2000) contends that "human beings do not find or discover knowledge so much as we construct or make it" (p. 197). Crotty (1998) defines constructivism as the meaning-making activity of the individual mind; the unique experiences of each of us, suggesting that each one's way of making sense of the world is valid and worthy of respect (p. 58).

Crotty uses the term constructionism to mean the collective generation and transmission of meaning, emphasizing that our culture shapes us and shapes the way we see things and feel things and gives us a view of the world. There are two strands of constructivist thought: radical constructivism (or psychological constructivism) and symbolic interaction (resemblance to social constructionism) (Schwandt, 2001, p. 31). Following Hegel and Marx, social constructionism is largely the work of Karl Mannheim (1893–1947) and Berger and Luckmann's *The Social Construction of Reality* (1967). The emphasis here is on "the actor's definition of the situation- seeking to understand how social actors recognize, produce, and reproduce social actions and how they share an intersubjective understanding of specific life circumstances" (Schwandt, 2001, pp. 31–32). There are weak and strong versions of social constructionism (Schwandt, 2000, 2001).

The weak version "does not deny reality in the ordinary commonplace sense of that term … this variety would not hold that *every* object, idea, and indeed *every* aspect of the world is a social construct" (Schwandt, 2001, p. 33). On the contrary, strong social constructionists "do appear to deny any ontology of the real whatsoever" (p. 33).

The postmodernist interpretive viewpoint, such as the one held by Denzin (1997), steadfastly rejects "that accurate representations of the world can be produced, and that these representations truthfully map the worlds of real experience" (p. 265). Denzin supports the point of view "of the historical and culturally situated individual" (Schwandt, 2000, p. 200) or standpoint epistemologies,[13] and also considers the life-world.[14] Schwandt (2000) reminds us that "social inquiry is a practice, not simply a way of knowing. Understanding what others are doing or saying and transforming that knowledge into public form involves moral-political commitments and that moral issues arise from the fact that a theory of knowledge is supported by a particular view of human agency" (p. 203). Our task as researchers is to use these epistemological stances to understand and explain the complexities of a particular phenomenon of global security; terrorism.

CONCLUSIONS

Reich (1998) rationalizes that one of the best ways to understand terrorism and the terrorist is through interdisciplinary study, such as history, religion, political science and psychology (p. 2). Education is not only a foundation for individual security, but also for global security. Christopher Williams' article "Education and Human Survival" (2000) assesses the discipline of international education and the global security framework. The fundamental rationale of global security is the assurance of human survival. Many of the Founders (Washington, Adams, Jefferson, Franklin) of the United States of America believed that an informed citizenry was necessary for the survival of the newly created country. "There has always been a linkage in the United States between the rights and duties of national citizenship and public education" (Thornton, 2005, p. 81). Thornton proceeds to position his case for incorporating Internationalism into the curriculum by stating the world's nations have become "more interdependent … Americans now live in a world in which vital civic concerns routinely cross national boundaries" (pp. 81–82). The Liberal Arts are able to bridge nations by using Objective Social Construction (OSC) and Interpretive Social Construction (ISC), as they can be:

> understood as the key to survival in any field that is subject to change over time. The standard definition of liberal arts education implies a program of study designed to foster capacities of analysis, critical reflection, problem solving, communication, computation and synthesis of knowledge from different disciplines. Its goal is to provide students with an intellectual, historical, and social context for recognizing the continuity between the past and future and for drawing on the human capacity of reason to understand human experience, to question the values dimension of human enterprise, and to articulate the results of this process of thinking. (Nolan, 2010, online)

The origins of the liberal arts education[15] can be traced back to ancient Greece, solidified with the Roman era through the Middle Ages, and then challenged during the Renaissance and early modern period (Glyer & Weeks, 1998, p. xxvii). Historically, the *artes liberales*, which translates as the arts of freedom, were for free men as opposed to slaves (1998, p. 9). The art of war and economics were necessary, but the artes liberales were studied for the "sake of the good life" (p. 9). The liberal arts deal with the mind (or spirit) and this is where our freedom resides; "in and through this essential freedom, the freedom of the mind, our humanity[16] is revealed" (p. 11). For two thousand years Western civilization held the belief of a "final end" and education was oriented to the "highest good" as the central concern for humanity. Modern thought is characterized by science and to "enlarge the power and empire of mankind in general over the universe" and that "knowledge and human power are synonymous" (Francis Bacon quoted in Glyer & Weeks, p. 12). In today's world, the knowledge that is believed to build and sustain power and empire resides in STEM (Science, Technology, Engineering, and Mathematics). However, both the Liberal Arts and the STEM curriculums are needed. The Liberal Arts support the understanding that social phenomena are "interpreted entities whose existence and qualities are dependent in a large part on people's meaning-making practices" (Harris, 2008, p. 233) or interpretive social constructionism (ISC), we need to understand the "other." We need to understand the moral, political, religious, social, and psychological struggles for power between competing entities or ideologies where perceptions, misperceptions, interpretations, and misinterpretations can be deadly.

NOTES

1. Dipak K. Gupta ("Exploring roots of terrorism") and Jitka Maleckova ("Impoverished Terrorists") in Tore Bjorgo's (ed.) *Root Causes of Terrorism* (2005) would disagree stating that the links are weak between terrorism and socioeconomic structural factors, such as poverty and lack of economic opportunity.

2. Both Dekmejian and Hoffman have different "historical stages" from Ross concerning the timeframe of "ancient" turning into "modern" terrorism; classification meaning religious, political, warfare, crime, communication.

3. Dekmejian dates the Jewish Revolt in Judea from 66 to 71 AD and Hoffman uses the date 66–73 AD.

4. Hoffman states the etymology of the word Zealot, meaning "fanatical enthusiast" can be traced back to this Jewish sect. Also, thug now used to describe "a vicious or brutal ruffian."

5. Dekmejian, Hoffman, and Ross identify the word "assassin" to be derived from the Arabic word *Hashashim*, meaning hash eaters. Getting high was a ritual before undertaking their missions of murder.

6. See Chalmer Johnson at http://www.thenation.com/doc/20011015/Johnson and his book, *Blowback: the Cost and Consequences of American Empire*. A Central Intelligence Agency term first used in March 1954 in a recently declassified report on the 1953 operation to overthrow the government of Mohammed Mossadegh in Iran.

7. See http://truthmove.org/content/false-flag-operations/. For False-flag terrorism see truthmove.org and the book, *9/11 and American Empire; Christians, Jews, and Muslims Speak Out* (eds.) Kevin Barrett, John Cobb, Jr., and Sandra Lubarsky. False-flag terrorism is terror by states, organizations, and agencies which is meant to be pinned on others in order to influence policy, public opinion, or military aggression.

8. From Chomsky *9/11*, p. 16; "An act of terrorism, means any activity that (A) involves a violent act or an act dangerous to human life that is a violation of the criminal laws of the United States or any State, or that would be a criminal violation if committed within the jurisdiction of the United States or of any State; and (B) appears to be intended (i) to intimidate or coerce a civilian population; (ii) to influence the policy of a government by assassination or kidnapping." *United States Code Congressional and Administrative News, 98th Congress, Second Session, 1984, Oct. 19, volume 2; par.3077, 98 STAT. 2707 West Publishing Co., 1984*.

9. The bombing of the Alfred P. Murrah Federal office Building in Oklahoma in which 168 people perished at the hands of Timothy McVeigh, U.S. Army veteran and an "indigenous, violent, Christian white supremacist, an antigovernment, right-wing extremist" (Hoffman, 2006, p. 101). Again Hoffman: McVeigh planned the attack with the help of Terry L. Nichols to "commemorate the second anniversary of the FBI's bloody assault on the Branch Davidians' compound in Waco, Texas" (pp. 101–102). McVeigh obsessively believed that the "U.S. government plans to outlaw and seize all privately held firearms. There were other motivations as well-including "vengeance, protest, and armed resistance." These ideas are shared by the members of the "well-armed, militantly antigovernment "citizens" militias with whom McVeigh mixed."

10. From Hoffman: "The terrorist attacks on September 11, 2001, inevitably, redefined "terrorism" yet again. On that day, nineteen terrorists belonging to a group calling itself al Qaeda (or al Qa-ida) hijacked four passenger aircraft soon after they took off from airports in Boston, Newark, New Jersey, and Washington, D.C. Two of the planes were then deliberately flown into the twin towers of New York City's World Trade Center ... a third aircraft smashed into the Pentagon ... the fourth aircraft ... into a field in rural Pennsylvania ... a total of

nearly three thousand people were killed in the attacks … more than twice as many Americans perished on 9/11 that had been killed by terrorists since 1968 – the year acknowledged as marking the advent of modern, international terrorism" (pp. 18–19).

11. Interpretivist or interpretive is a general descriptor for what is regarded as "a loosely coupled family of methodological and philosophical persuasions," from T. A. Schwandt's Constructivist, interpretivist approaches to human inquiry, in Denzin and Lincoln's *Handbook of qualitative research* (1994, p. 118).

12. Existential Determinism states that these antecedents are essential to identity and are integral to "who we are," we cannot choose these factors, but once we are capable of interaction we influence and are influenced by these factors. http://davidjlarkin.com/catalog/titles/the_moral_consensus/es2_2.html

13. Standpoint Epistemologies as defined by Schwandt (2001, p. 238). These are ways of thinking about the nature of knowledge that begin with the assumption that there is no universal from which we can know the world. All efforts to know, and all knowledge, are socially situated. Various kinds of standpoint epistemologies (women, gays, lesbians, people of color, people experiencing colonial oppression, etc.) share the assumption that *knowing* must begin in the experiences, interests, and values of some traditionally excluded group because in this way dominant knowledge claims can be effectively criticized and revised. Standpoint epistemologies are a means of deconstructing what has passed for knowledge so as to expose its exclusions and dominant perspectives (masculine, Eurocentric, racist, straight, etc.). Standpoints are almost always linked to some liberatory, emancipatory, or critical aim. There is an influence from postmodern thought that all views (standpoints) are partial and incomplete – it is impossible to unite them into a single complete or collective view of what knowledge is; knowing is always an act of living within limits and contradictions.

14. Life-World as defined by Schwandt (2001, p. 147). The everyday world or the life-world (*Lebenswelt*) is the intersubjective world of human experience and social action; it is the world of commonsense knowledge of everyday life. It is constituted by the thoughts and acts of individuals and the social expressions of those thoughts and acts (laws, institutions, etc.). For example, Alfred Schutz (1899–1956) developed a descriptive phenomenology of the life-world or a phenomenological sociology. He analyzed the concepts of subjective meaning, action, experience, intentionality, behavior, and intersubjectivity.

15. In the Fifth Century Martianus Capella categorized subjects into two groups: the Trivium, meaning "the three ways," which consisted of grammar, rhetoric, and logic; and the Quadrivium, meaning "the four ways," which consisted of geometry, mathematics, music, and astronomy (Glyer & Weeks, 1998, p. 8).

16. The integrative principle of the liberal arts is this idea, humanitas, which gives us the word for humanities (Glyer & Weeks, 1998).

REFERENCES

Appelrouth, S., & Desffor-Edles, L. (2008). *Classical and contemporary sociological theory*. Los Angeles, CA: Pine Forge Press.

Berger, P. L., & Luckmann, T. (1967). *The social construction of reality*. Garden City, NY: Anchor Books.
Bernstein, R. J. (1976). *The restructuring of social and political theory*. Philadelphia, PA: University of Pennsylvania Press.
Bjorgo, T. (2005). *Root causes of terrorism myths, reality and ways forward*. Abingdon, OX: Routledge.
Chomsky, N. (2001). *9/11*. New York, NY: Seven Stories Press.
Chomsky, N., & Barsamian, D. (2001). *Propaganda and the public mind: Conversations with Noam Chomsky*. Cambridge, MA: South End Press.
Chomsky, N., & Barsamian, D. (2007). *What we say goes: Conversations on U.S. power in a changing world*. New York, NY: Henry Holt.
Chomsky, N., Mitchell, P. R., & Schoeffel, J. (Eds.). (2002). *Understanding power: The indispensable Chomsky*. New York, NY: The New Press.
Croft, S. (2006). *Culture, crisis and America's war on terror*. New York, NY: Cambridge University Press.
Crotty, M. (1998). *The foundations of social research: Meaning and perspective in the research process*. Thousand Oaks, CA: Sage.
Dant, T. (1991). *Knowledge, ideology and discourse a sociological perspective*. New York, NY: Routledge.
Dekmejian, R. H. (2007). *Spectrum of terror*. Washington, DC: CQ Press.
Denzin, N. K. (1997). *Interpretive ethnography: Ethnographic practices for the 21st century*. Thousand Oaks, CA: Sage.
Dilthey, W. (1976). Selected writings *(H. P. Rickman, Trans.)*. Cambridge: CUP.
Glyer, D., & Weeks, D. L. (1998). *The liberal arts in higher education*. Lanham, MD: Azusa Pacific University.
Hacking, I. (2001). *The social construction of what?* Cambridge, MA: Harvard University Press.
Harris, S. R. (2008). Constructionism in sociology. In J. A. Holstein & J. F. Gubrium (Eds.), *Handbook of constructionist research* (pp. 231–247). New York, NY: The Guilford Press.
Hoffman, B. (2006). *Inside terrorism* (rev. and expanded ed.). New York, NY: Columbia University Press.
Holstein, J. A., & Miller, G. (2003). *Challenges and choices constructionist perspectives on social problems*. New York, NY: Aldine De Gruyter.
Jenkins, B. M. (1980). *The study of terrorism: Definitional problems*. Santa Monica, CA: RAND.
Karaffa, C. (2012). *Intellectual courage and the social construction of terrorism: Embodying reality*. Pittsburgh, PA: University of Pittsburgh.
LeCompte, M. D., & Schensul, J. (1999). *Designing and conducting ethnographic research*. Walnut Creek, CA: AltaMire Press.
Macionis, J. (2010). *Sociology* (13th ed.). Boston, MA: Prentice Hall.
Martindale, D. (1957). Social disorganization: The conflict of normative and empirical approahes. In H. Beker & A. Boskoff (Eds.), *Modern sociological theory* (pp. 340–368). New York, NY: Holt, Rinehart and Winston.
Merton, R. K., & Nisbet, R. (1971). *Contemporary social problems*. New York, NY: Harcourt Brace Jovanovich.
Mills, W. C. (1956). *The power elite*. London: Oxford University Press.

Nisbett, R. (2003). *The geography of thought: How Asians and Westerns think differently and why*. New York, NY: The Free Press.

Noddings, N. (2005). *Educating citizens for global awareness*. New York, NY: Teachers College Press.

Nolan, E. I. (2010). The 2010 High School Graduate. Liberal Arts Education: A foundation for success. Retrieved from http://www.thehighschoolgraduate.com/editorial/DE/liberalarts.htm

Outhwaite, W. (1975). *Understanding social life: The method called Verstehen*. London: George Allen & Unwin.

Pape, R. A. (2005). *Dying to win the strategic logic of suicide terrorism*. New York, NY: Random House.

Pillar, P. (2001). *Terrorism and U.S. foreign policy*. Washington, DC: The Brookings Institutue.

Racevskis, K. (1993). *Postmodernism and the search for enlightment*. Charlottesville, VA: University Press of Virginia.

Reich, W. (1998). *Origins of terrorism psychologies, ideologies, theologists, states of mind*. Washington, DC: The Woodrow Wilson Center Press.

Ross, J. I. (2006). *Political terrorism an interdisciplinary approach*. New York, NY: Peter Lang Publishing, Inc.

Schutz, A. (1971). *Collected papers I: The problem of social reality* (M. Natanson, Trans.) (3rd ed.). The Hague: Martinus Nijhoff.

Schwandt, T. A. (1994). Constructivist, interpretivist approaches to human inquiry. In Y. S. Lincoln & N. K. Denzin (Eds.), *Handbook of qualitative research*. Thousand Oaks, CA: Sage.

Schwandt, T. A. (2000). Three epistemological stances for qualitative inquiry. In N. K. Denzin & Y. S. Lincoln (Eds.), *Handbook of qualitative research* (2nd ed., pp. 189–213). Thousand Oaks, CA: Sage.

Schwandt, T. A. (2001). *Dictionary of qualitative inquiry* (2nd ed.). Thousand Oaks, CA: Sage.

Sederberg, P. (1991). Defining terrorism: Contending themes in contemporary research. *Annual review of conflict knowledge*. New York, NY: Garland Publishing.

Shipman, A. (2002). *The globalization myth*. Duxford: Icon Books Ltd.

Spector, M., & Kitsuse, J. I. (1977). *Constructing social problems*. Menlo Park, CA: Cummings Publishing Company Inc.

Thornton, S. (2005). Incorporating internationalism into the social studies curriculum. In N. Noddings (Ed.), *Educating citizens for global awareness*. New York, NY: Teachers College Press.

Weber, M. (1949). *The methodology of the social sciences*. Glencoe: Free Press.

Williams, C. (2000). Education and human survival: The relevance of the global security framework to international education. *International Review of Education*, *46*(3–4), 183–203.

PART II
VARIATIONS AND REALITIES OF CONTEMPORARY TERRORISM

THE EMERGENCE OF LONE WOLF TERRORISM: PATTERNS OF BEHAVIOR AND IMPLICATIONS FOR INTERVENTION

Brent L. Smith, Jeff Gruenewald, Paxton Roberts and Kelly R. Damphousse

ABSTRACT

Purpose – *In this chapter, we examine several attributes of lone wolf terrorists and how their activities are temporally and geospatially patterned. In particular, we demonstrate how precursor behaviors and attack characteristics of lone wolves are similar and different compared to those of group-based terrorists.*

Methodology/approach – *Based on data drawn from the American Terrorism Study (ATS), we examine 268 federal terrorism "indictees" linked to 264 incidents. Three types of loners are identified based on group affiliations and levels of assistance in preparing for and executing terrorist attacks. A series of analyses comparatively examine loners who had no assistance and those actors that did.*

Terrorism and Counterterrorism Today
Sociology of Crime, Law and Deviance, Volume 20, 91–110

ISSN: 1521-6136/doi:10.1108/S1521-613620150000020005

Findings – *The results of this study suggest that lone wolf terrorists are more educated and socially isolated than group-based actors. Lone wolves also engage in less precursor activities than group actors, but are willing to travel greater distances to prepare for and execute attacks. Explanations for why lone wolves are able to "survive" longer than terrorist groups by avoiding arrest may in part stem from their ability to temporally and geospatially position their planning and preparatory activities.*

Originality/value – *Studies on lone wolf terrorism remain few and many are plagued by methodological and conceptual limitations. The current study adds to this growing literature by relying on lone wolf terrorism data recently made available by the American Terrorism Study (ATS). Our findings are valuable for members of the law enforcement and intelligence communities responsible for the early detection and prevention of lone wolf terrorism in the United States.*

Keywords: American terrorism; lone wolf; lone actor; precursor conduct; pre-incident indicators; leaderless resistance

INTRODUCTION

The emergence of lone wolf terrorism is one of the most frequently mentioned issues among those tasked with countering the threat of terrorism in America. Despite this, it is also one of the most frequently misunderstood concepts in the criminological literature, difficult to define conceptually, and even more problematic to measure empirically. When compounded with the notion that lone wolves are especially difficult to detect, more likely to engage in "low expense and high success" targeting (Zierhoffer, 2014), and less likely to be caught using traditional counterintelligence methods than other types of terrorists (Bakker & de Graaf, 2011; Hewitt, 2014), the problem of "lone wolf" terrorism becomes even more exasperating.

Conceptually, "lone wolf" terrorism has gone by a number of different names, such as "lone avengers" (Stern, 2003) or "free-lance terrorists" (Hewitt, 2003). Like the term "terrorism," both those who are responsible for responding to it and those who academically study it, have had a difficult time arriving at a consensus regarding what constitutes a "lone wolf."

Consequently, efforts to operationalize the concept of "lone wolf" have resulted in a wide variety of names or variables and multiple ways of measuring them. Not surprisingly, the resulting literature reflects an impressive array of conflicting patterns and demographic traits that supposedly reveal the characteristics of "lone wolves." Unfortunately, this growing body of literature is so absent of a consensus on defining the term that we have few methodologically rigorous pieces from which to even identify the nature and extent of the problem.

In the sections that follow, we will examine why the "lone wolf" strategy emerged, the origins of the concept of the "lone wolf," and efforts to further refine the definition. We will also review recent empirical efforts to study the phenomenon and how these varying definitions of "lone wolf" have resulted in somewhat contradictory findings and patterns of behavior. We will also enter into this fray by analyzing data from a different source, the American Terrorism Study (ATS) to assess the nature and extent of "lone actor" terrorism in America as measured through the use of FBI "officially designated" acts of terrorism over the past 30 years or so. Finally, we hope that our findings will provide some clarity to the often-confusing body of literature on "lone wolf" terrorism.

BACKGROUND ON THE ORIGINS OF LONE ACTOR TERRORISM

Although "lone wolf" or lone actor terrorism by Al Qaeda adherents is thought to be one of the greatest threats to American security, and some may believe that this is a uniquely Al Qaeda phenomenon, the evolution of "lone wolf" or lone actor terrorism has an extensive history in the United States. In fact, it is difficult to fully appreciate the use of this tactic without understanding its evolution in American terrorism. The story begins several decades before the 9/11 attacks.

In the late 1950s, Fidel Castro instigated revolt in Cuba by employing a *rural revolutionary* model. Inspired by the Arab revolt against French rule in Algeria in 1954, Castro modeled his strategy from the rural movement employed initially by the National Liberation Front in Algeria. Castro's rural revolutionary model had four major characteristics. First, it utilized a traditional military hierarchical structure composed of a traditional command and control structure. Second, this conventional guerilla army focused on the traditional military efforts to capture and hold terrain. In

Castro's case, this involved extortion and terrorism in addition to traditional military operations as his army obtained control of rural Cuba, while isolating the urban areas surrounding Havana. Third, as part of the effort to capture and hold terrain, Castro created "fixed compounds" such as military hospitals and training camps as he advanced on Havana. Finally, he took advantage of a system of national and international networking to finance, arm, and feed his growing military component.

With the successful overthrow of the Batista regime in 1959, Castro sought to import the model to other countries, primarily through what became known as the Tri-Continental Conferences (Sterling, 1981). However, when Che Guevara tried to implement the rural revolutionary model in Bolivia in 1967, he was quickly captured and his army disintegrated. The intelligence gathering capabilities of targeted governments had improved dramatically since the late 1950s and the use of fixed compounds and a hierarchical military structure resulted in abysmal failure. The extreme left adapted almost overnight with the introduction of an *urban cellular* model. In the Western Hemisphere, the publication of Carlos Marighella's *Mini-Manual of the Urban Guerilla* in 1969 led to the wholesale adoption of the cellular approach by a wide range of American leftist extremists. Throughout the 1970s and 1980s, the strategy was employed by the United Freedom Front, the Weather Underground, the SLA, the May 19th Communist Organization, and scores of other violent leftist groups.

Extreme right wing groups in America, however, failed to learn the lessons of Che Guevara's defeat in Bolivia. When they turned violent in the early 1980s, they immediately adopted a strategy similar to Castro's old rural revolutionary model. Almost all of the right wing terrorist groups indicted under the FBI's Counterterrorism Program in the 1980s employed fixed compounds, national networking, and a hierarchical structure to some extent (Smith, 1994). From the anti-tax groups like the Arizona Patriots and the Sheriff's Posse Commitatus to Christian Identity groups like the Aryan Nations and Covenant, Sword and Arm of the Lord, all sought to "capture and hold terrain" by initially creating local compounds, staking out townships, or mapping the boundaries of their proposed new "sovereign states."

Similar to Guevara's demise, within three years, the FBI had identified the locations of violent right wing compounds in the United States, indicted, and captured or killed the leading members of over half a dozen groups. The so-called "war in '84" merely led to "arrests in '85" as the FBI had one of its most productive counterterrorism efforts of all time. All but three of the leading figures of the extreme right had been convicted on various federal charges by 1987. To complete the campaign, U.S. Attorneys indicted Louis Beam, Richard Butler, and eight others associated with the Order, Aryan Nations, and the Covenant, Sword, and Arm of the Lord on seditious conspiracy charges in federal district court in Fort Smith, Arkansas. All 11 indictees were acquitted of all charges in 1988. While the case itself is worthy of additional comment, for the purposes of this chapter, the lessons learned, particularly by Beam, are of particular interest.

Over the next four years, Beam concentrated on developing a strategy to minimize the civil and criminal liability of group leaders (Damphousse & Smith, 2004). The siege at Ruby Ridge, Idaho in 1992 provided the catalyst for Beam to advance his strategy (Kaplan, 1997). At a hastily called meeting of extreme right group leaders in Estes Park, Colorado that summer, he publicly called for the implementation of "leaderless resistance" (Beam, 1992), an uncoordinated violence model that essentially bypassed the cellular approach adopted by leftists. Although some scholars have suggested that the "lone wolf" concept began in the post-9/11 era and is largely a byproduct of the emergence of Al Qaeda (e.g., Barnes, 2012), the term "lone wolf" emerged in the mid-1990s and was used to describe the threat of right wing terrorism in the United States. It became particularly prominent among counterterrorism officials soon after the Oklahoma City bombing in 1995, as many came to believe that McVeigh's actions may have represented an early example of leaderless resistance and lone wolf behavior.[1] Although leaderless resistance is the most famous of these uncoordinated violence models, it is not the only one.

The mid-1990s proved to be a turning point in the strategic planning of terrorist groups worldwide. In addition to the advocacy of leaderless resistance by the extreme right, environmental groups began using the newly created World Wide Web as both a recruiting tool and as a way to disseminate information about strategic targets (Joosse, 2007). Both the Earth Liberation Front and the Animal Liberation Front produced some of the most advanced websites on the Internet in the mid-1990s. The structure of the movement and their use of the Web allowed leading movement figures to indirectly identify potential targets to other members through articles and posts, while recording the successful "direct actions" made by members for supposedly informational purposes only.

Similarly, Islamic extremists, particularly those associated with Bin Laden's Al Qaeda movement, used "fatwas" as a call to action that would make establishing criminal liability extremely difficult solely on the basis of the issued proclamation. Bin Laden's famous 1998 fatwa to "kill the Americans" is the classic example:

> On that basis, and in compliance with God's order, we issue the following fatwa to all Muslims: The ruling to kill the Americans and their allies – civilians and military – is an individual duty for every Muslim who can do it in any country in which it is possible to do it .... [E]very Muslim who believes in God and wishes to be rewarded to comply with God's order to kill the Americans and plunder their money wherever and whenever they find it. (as cited in Ranstorp, 1998, p. 329)

Although Al Qaeda and subsequent Sunni extremist groups like ISIL represent a hybrid model in which components of the rural revolutionary model (creating an Islamic State through the holding of terrain), the cellular model (e.g., the 9/11 attackers), and an uncoordinated violence model featuring lone wolves (e.g., the 2009 Nidal Hasan attack at Fort Hood, TX), the greatest concern among homeland security experts here is the United States in the last of these strategic and tactical approaches (Borum, Fein, & Vossekuil, 2012; Gruenewald, Chermak, & Freilich, 2013; Zierhoffer, 2014).

While our consideration of the origins of the "lone wolf" concept may be broader than other relevant studies, we believed it necessary to place the use of the term in the historical context of American terrorism. Doing so seems especially important, as a significant body of literature on lone actor terrorism has begun to emerge over the past decade. Although all of this literature has surely contributed to our understanding of the concept, the term nevertheless remains conceptually confusing and, consequently, difficult to measure with any degree of accuracy (Spaaij & Hamm, 2015). In the following section, we review highlights of some of this burgeoning literature.

REVIEW OF THE LITERATURE

In a recent review of research on lone wolf terrorism, Spaaij and Hamm (2015) recounted 16 different monikers used for the term "lone wolf." Some scholars have used these terms interchangeably though these seemingly synonymous terms may actually refer to conceptually unique forms of terrorist offending. A consensus definition of lone wolf terrorism continues to elude researchers; however, several conceptual dimensions of this phenomenon have begun to emerge. The first, and arguably least problematic, dimension of lone wolf terrorism is motivation. While Simon (2013) suggested that conventional (or non-ideological) criminals be included as one type of lone wolf (Simon, 2013), most other lone wolf definitions necessitate offenders to have political, social, or other ideological objectives. A second fuzzier conceptual dimension involves terrorists' affiliations with groups that are organized by hierarchical command and control organizational structures. Past studies have varied in subtle but important ways in regards to how group affiliation is measured. For example, Gruenewald et al. (2013) and Pantucci (2011) conceptualize group affiliation as direct (or first-hand) interaction with other like-minded extremists, while others consider group influence in terms of autonomous decision-making, or the extent to which terrorists receive direction from group leaders (Borum et al., 2012). According to Hewitt (2003) and other terrorism experts, lone wolves can be members of terrorist groups as long as they are not acting under the orders of terrorist leaders. The third key definitional dimension of lone wolf terrorism refers to the extent that terrorists operate alone. While measuring the "aloneness" of terrorists may seem straightforward, empirical considerations of offending arrangements can quickly become muddled. For instance, some definitional schema allow for multiple "lone actors" to be categorized as lone wolf "packs" or "isolated dyads" (Gill, Horgan, & Deckert, 2014; Gruenewald et al., 2013; Pantucci, 2011), while other researchers draw a harder line on the necessity of aloneness (Spaaij & Hamm, 2015). Relatedly, there remains conceptual ambiguity in regards to the specific activities terrorists must engage in alone to be considered a lone wolf. Borum et al. (2012) refer to offenders who initiate, plan, prepare for, and execute an attack without direct assistance from any other person as "solo" offenders, while those who receive direct assistance from one or two others in accomplishing these activities are considered "lone" offenders. It is possible, however, that terrorists may receive direct assistance in some stages of the terrorist cycle, while receiving no assistance in other stages. It remains unclear as to whether or not a terrorist who executes an attack by himself can be considered a lone wolf if he had assistance in building the bomb. Addressing this question is an important next step in sorting through the conceptual ambiguities of lone wolf definitions.

Though the number of empirical studies of lone wolf terrorism remain relatively few, conceptual and methodological dilemmas have not kept all researchers from studying this important topic. Just as the number of academic studies of terrorism has grown exponentially, the number of lone wolf studies has also increased in the past few years. It is from this small but growing literature that offender and incident patterns of lone wolf terrorism begin to emerge. Below, we review some of these patterns, and then suggest how the current study fills some remaining gaps in the extant literature.

Several studies have concluded that lone wolf offending is on the rise. A study by Spaaij (2010), for instance, concluded that while lone wolf offending has remained stable in Europe, this type of terrorism had increased dramatically in the United States. Another earlier study found that unaffiliated individuals killed one in six terrorism victims in the United States, and when including the Oklahoma City bombing, the majority of terrorism-related deaths between 1978 and 2001 were attacks committed by "unaffiliated" individuals (Hewitt, 2003). Still other studies have shown that trends in lone wolf offending may be terrorism movement specific. Though lone wolf terrorism by Islamic extremists may be increasing after 9/11, far-right lone wolf terrorism may have peaked during the 1990s (Gruenewald et al., 2013; see also Hewitt, 2003; Spaaij, 2010).

A social and demographic "profile" of lone wolves has also begun to emerge from recent studies. In regards to age, studies have found that lone wolves are typically in their mid to late 30s (Gill et al., 2014). Ages of offenders may vary, however, by the "type" of lone wolf. For example, far-right lone wolves who operate in small cells, or "wolf packs," have been shown to be, on average, much younger (in their early 20s) (Gruenewald et al., 2013). The disproportionate number of male offenders is generally one of the most consistent findings across terrorism studies and extends to lone wolves as well. In fact, Gill et al. (2014) found that nearly 97% of the 119 lone wolves they examined were male. Though few studies have measured terrorists' educational attainment statuses, recent evidence indicates that approximately 75% of lone wolves have at least some college experience. Fourteen percent of lone wolves actually earned graduate degrees. Despite their relatively privileged social positions, lone wolves have often been described as socially "isolated," "withdrawn," "awkward," and "inept" (Moskalenko & McCauley, 2011; Nijboer, 2012; Spaaij, 2010). As evidence, Gruenewald et al. (2013) found that far-right "loners" were more likely to be divorced, separated, or widowed than other types of far-right terrorists. In addition, one study found that less than 25% of lone wolves had been married, relatively less compared to other types of terrorists operating around the world (Gill et al., 2014).

In addition to offenders' background characteristics, we suggest that observing how terrorism event "cycles" are geospatially and temporally patterned is an important next step in research on lone wolf terrorism. This involves not only examining completed terrorist acts, but also the pre-incident activities of lone wolves and those planned but failed or foiled plots that never come to fruition. Gill et al. (2014) have already begun to examine several of these questions, which have important implications for the law enforcement communities responsible for preventing and investigating terrorism. Based on open-source data that they collected, Gill et al. (2014) observed several types of pre-incident activities that occurred within the planning and preparatory stages of terrorist cycles, such as recruitment and the assembly of explosive devices. They found that over half of these pre-incident activities occurred within one year of the attacks. Though they suggested that lone wolves were not necessarily impulsive, there was often very little time between the lone wolves' choices to use violence and the commission of attacks (Gill et al., 2014).

Much has been learned about lone wolves in the last several years, but limitations of available terrorism data continue to plague researchers (Silke, 2001). While the American Terrorism Study has maintained data on key terrorism activities for over 25 years, it has only been recently that adequate data have become available to conceptually distinguish between different forms of lone wolf terrorism. Based on these data, the remainder of this essay seeks to contribute to the growing lone wolf literature in several ways. First, a categorization scheme of lone wolf offending is offered that considers the extent to which offenders received assistance for planning and preparing for attacks separately from assistance received in the execution of attacks. Second, the ATS provides us access to the only known source of information on thousands of pre-incident activities associated with U.S. federal terrorism cases. Increasing our understanding of these precursor activities can potentially aid law enforcement in preventing seemingly elusive forms of terrorist offending. Finally, this study extends the work of Gill et al. (2014) by exploring temporal and geospatial patterns of lone wolf terrorists in comparison to group-based terrorist actors. In particular, the extent that lone wolves travel to commit their acts, engage in preparatory behaviors, and "survive" before being detected by law enforcement is examined.

METHODOLOGY

Data for our analysis of lone actor terrorism in the United States was drawn from the American Terrorism Study (ATS). The ATS was created in 1987 in collaboration with the FBI's Terrorist Research and Analytical Center. At that time, the FBI provided the names and case numbers of persons indicted in federal district courts from 1980 to 1987 as a result of an official FBI investigation for "terrorism or terrorism-related activities." For the period 1988–2004, the FBI provided the names of terrorism defendants through sponsorship with either the U.S. House of Representatives Judiciary Subcommittee on Crime or the Senate Judiciary Committee. Since 2004, the name of terrorism defendants and their respective court case numbers have been provided by requests through Congressional representatives in the State of Arkansas.

Court documents for each case are retrieved through the federal Public Access to Court Electronic Records (PACER) system. If the information is not available on PACER, ATS personnel visit the district courts where the cases were filed, extract the needed documents, and copy them into the ATS Oracle relational database. Once the court documents are obtained, they are read and quantifiable variables are extracted and coded for entry into the database. ATS program managers then review the coded data for accuracy before final entry. Quantitative data on each case includes primarily: (1) demographic individual and group information, (2) legal information about each count/case and its outcome, and (3) any information related to the precursor conduct of the terrorists prior to commission of a terrorist incident. Information on the precursor data includes "time-stamping" the dates of these events as well as geo-coding the addresses where these events took place.

For the current analysis, we examined 267 discrete "indictees" who were linked to 264 prevented or completed acts of terrorism from 1980 to present. These persons were indicted for over 3,000 federal counts and were associated with 1,788 known precursor behaviors at over 1,100 addresses. Building on the work of Pantucci (2011), Borum et al. (2012), and Gruenewald et al. (2013), we chose to examine the patterns of behavior of these indictees by creating a *participatory typology* based on three basic elements: (1) was the person affiliated with a group or movement; (2) did the individual have help committing any of the known precursor behaviors identified in court records; and (3) did the person have help committing the planned or completed incident. While we recognize that this is a rather simple approach to examining the issue of lone wolf behavior, we chose to do so because the three categories may be operationalized and readily quantified. As such, we hoped to avoid some of the methodological problems identified by Spaaij and Hamm (2015).

As seen in Fig. 1, the terrorists were categorized in the typology based on the extent to which they scored positive on each of these three operationalized variables. Persons who were not affiliated with a known terrorist group, had no help committing any of the precursor acts, and who had no help committing the terrorist incident were categorized as *loners*. An

	LONERS		CELLS/GROUPS	
	Loners	Affiliated Loners	Lone Conspirators	Cells/ Groups
Had Help Committing Incident	✗	✗	✗	✓
Had Help Committing Precursor Acts	✗	✗	✓	✓
Movement/Group Affiliation	✗	✓	✓	✓

Fig. 1. Participatory Typology.

example in our sample would be Ted Kaczynski, the Unabomber. Persons where were affiliated with a group known to have been involved in terrorism in the United States, but who had no help in either preparing or carrying out the terrorism incident for which they were indicted were labeled as *affiliated loners*. Buford Furrow, the Aryan Nations affiliate who opened fire in a Los Angeles Jewish community center in 1999, is one example from our dataset who fits this categorization.

Those who were affiliated with a group and who had help preparing for the incident, but who carried out the terrorism incident by themselves were categorized as *lone conspirators*. While the term lone conspirator seems like an oxymoron (a conspiracy requires more than one person, otherwise it cannot meet the essential element for the legal requirements under this particular inchoate crime). In our situation, however, the term is quite appropriate when placed in the context of the typology. Timothy McVeigh, the Oklahoma City bomber who enlisted the aid of Terry Nichols, but who carried out the attack alone, fits this category. Finally, those who exhibited all of the characteristics (group affiliation, precursor help, and help committing the incident) were identified as *cells/groups*. Although all of the 9/11 participants who actually carried out the attack died in the incident and were therefore never indicted, they serve as a good example of a cell/group.

Sample size has been a serious methodological problem in previous examinations of lone wolf terrorism. Therefore, for the current analysis, we have chosen to collapse our typology into two simple categories – those who had help and those who did not. *Loners* and *affiliated loners* fall into the first category, while *lone conspirators* and *cells/groups* fall into the category in which the participant(s) had help. We compared these two groups (*those who had help* and *those who did not*) on five major issues: (1) successful completion of the terrorist incident, (2) volume of precursor activity, (3) length of the planning cycle, (4) spatial variances, and (5) length of the individual terrorist's "life cycle."

RESULTS

Before presenting the results of our analyses on the issues above, some discussion of the characteristics of the sample is appropriate. As noted earlier, the sample includes 267 discrete individuals who were involved in 264 "officially designated" terrorism incidents in the United States. Only one of these individuals was involved in multiple terrorism incidents as both a "loner" and as part of a "cell/group." Consequently, for our analysis, this person is counted more than once, rendering an analysis of the behavior of 268 individuals. As previous scholars have noted, lone wolf activity is relatively rare, even among terrorists. Only 6% ($n = 17$) of the 268 persons committed terrorism incidents without any help in planning, preparing, or carrying out the incident (Table 1).

On average, loners were slightly older than cell/group participants, 38 years compared to 34 years of age, respectively. However, our measure of age was "age at indictment" and as we shall later see, loners participate in terrorism for much longer periods of time before arrest and indictment

Table 1. Demographics of Loners versus Cells/Groups.

	Loners	Cells/Groups
Perpetrators	6% $n = 17$	94% $n = 251$
Gender	0% female** $n = 17$	13% female** $n = 251$
Average age	38 years old $n = 17$	34 years old $n = 250$
College education	91% attended college*** $n = 11$	63% attended college*** $n = 197$
Marital status	29% had been married*** $n = 14$	57% had been married*** $n = 191$

$^{**}p < .01$, $^{***}p < .001$.

than do cell/group participants. If we had used “age at first preparatory conduct,” loners probably would have been slightly younger than cell/group participants. This finding is generally consistent with other scholars (Gill et al., 2014; Gruenewald et al., 2013). We then compared loners to cell/group members on three other demographic traits: gender, education, and marital status. Loners were significantly different from cell/group participants on each of these variables. Loners were much less likely to be married (29% compared to 57%), a finding that is consistent with most of the lone wolf literature and which supports the notion that loners tend to be socially isolated (Nijboer, 2012). They also tended to be much better educated than cell/group participants. Approximately nine out of ten (91%) of the loners had attended college to some extent compared with 63% of cell/group members. Our findings were also consistent with other scholars who had found that lone terrorists tended to be overwhelmingly male (Gill et al, 2014). Although females constituted some 13% of our sample of American terrorists, none of the 17 loners in our sample were female (Table 2).

We examined whether the incident was successfully completed by comparing incidents where the attack was carried out and known objectives were met with those in which the incident failed and/or was foiled. Although we found a slight difference between the failure rates of loners and cells/groups, these differences were not significant. This is in contrast to the recent work of Gill et al. (2014) who found that terrorists operating “without command and control links” were significantly more likely to successfully execute an attack than those operating under some form of command and control. It should be noted, however, that Gill and his colleagues’ sample includes both American and European terrorists, while our sample is limited to American terrorism.

Next, we examined the volume of precursor conduct specifically associated with the planning and preparation of an incident (Table 3). As one might expect, we found a significant difference between loners and cells/groups on this measure. Members of cells/groups engaged in over

Table 2. Incident Completions by Loners versus Cells/Groups.

	Attack Completed Successfully	Attack Not Completed Successfully
Loner incidents, $n = 65$	34%	66%
Cell/group incidents, $n = 199$	44%	56%
All incidents, $n = 264$	42%	58%

$p < .10$.

three times as many preparatory behaviors per incident than loners (8.4 compared to 2.5, respectively). For law enforcement planning, the lesser volume of activity prior to an incident is one of the major reasons lone wolf tactics have become of such concern (Hewitt, 2014). To our knowledge, however, this is the first empirical evidence confirming this pattern. Also of particular note in Table 3 is the ratio of incidents to group size. Although not calculated explicitly, loners (who comprise only 8% of the sample) accounted for one-fourth of the terrorism incidents (65 of 264). This disproportionate number of incidents should be substantial cause for concern to counterterrorism officials. However, it should also be noted, that the fewer the number of precursor activities, the greater the likelihood that the planned incident is of lesser magnitude. This postulate is being tested currently with funding from the National Institute of Justice.[2]

We were also interested in assessing whether incidents involving loners required a shorter planning cycle. Since our earlier finding indicated that they engaged in substantially fewer precursor activities in preparation for an incident, it was logical to hypothesize that their planning cycle would be shortened. Interestingly, this was not the case. Using increments of "less than three months," "three months to one year," and "longer than one year," Table 4 demonstrates the almost identical patterns among the two groups relative to the overall temporal dimensions of the planning process.

Table 3. Precursor Activities per Incident.

	Precursor Acts	Incidents	Precursor Acts per Incident
Loner incidents	162	65	2.49
Cell/group incidents	1,675	199	8.42
All incidents	1,837	264	6.96

$p < .001$.

Table 4. Length of Planning Cycle for Attacks.

	Time Span from First Precursor Act to Incident		
	Less than 3 months	3 months to 1 year	Longer than 1 year
Loner incidents, $n = 30$	33%	33%	33%
Cell/group incidents, $n = 154$	33%	31%	36%
All incidents, $n = 184$	33%	31%	36%

p = not significant.

Since temporal patterns may be shaped by spatial limitations or constraints, we wanted to compare the behavior of loners and cells/groups on two issues: (1) how far they lived from where they committed their preparatory activities, and (2) how far they lived from the selected terrorism incident location. These analyses were conducted through a series of "rose diagrams" in which the residences of the terrorists are placed in the center of a series of concentric circles representing distances from the residence. Then the location of either the precursor conduct or the terrorist incident location (depending on what is being analyzed) is located on the rose diagram using both a distance measurement and an azimuth. This strategy renders a visual depiction of both the distances and direction from the independent to the dependent variable, in this case, residence locations to either the locations of precursor activities or locations of the incidents.[3]

For the current analysis, the patterns are demonstrated numerically in Tables 5 and 6. To avoid the impact of outliers, the use of "median distances" are the most meaningful. Median distances indicate that half of the behaviors occurred closer than the median, while the other half occurred farther than the median distance. Table 5 reveals that loners, on average, committed their precursor conduct over twice as far from their places of residence than did members of cells/groups (170 and 79 miles, respectively). Over two-fifths (41%) of the preparatory behavior committed by cell/group members occurred within thirty miles of their residences; less than one-fourth (23%) of loners committed preparatory acts within the same thirty-mile radius (table not shown).

The same pattern emerges when examining the distances between residence of the terrorist and incident location (see Table 6). Loners traveled, on average, almost three times further from their places of residence to strike targets than did the members of cells/groups (328 miles compared to 118 miles, respectively). An analysis of the concentric patterns associated with this data revealed that over one-third (37%) of cell/group

Table 5. Linear Distances from Residences to Precursor Activities.

	Loners	Cells/Groups	All Perpetrators
Average distance	454 miles	444 miles	445 miles
Median distance	*170 miles*	*79 miles*	*88 miles*
Standard deviation	638	669	666
Minimum distance	0 miles	0 miles	0 miles
Maximum distance	2,571 miles	2,596 miles	2,696 miles

Table 6. Linear Distances from Residences to Incidents.

	Loners	Cells/Groups	All Perpetrators
Average distance	604 miles	374 miles	403 miles
Median distance	*328 miles*	*118 miles*	*132 miles*
Standard deviation	685	543	567
Minimum distance	0.57 miles	0.32 miles	0.32 miles
Maximum distance	2,563 miles	2,696 miles	2,696 miles

members lived within thirty miles of the incident location compared with less than one-fifth (18%) of loners who lived that close to the target. Fifty-five percent of loners resided greater than 270 miles from the incident location compared with only 38% of cell/group members (table not shown). All of these patterns suggest that loners go to much greater lengths to disguise their activities and avoid detection than do members of cells or groups. In some ways, they defy the logic of time and space that suggests that greater distances require longer periods of time for planning, preparation, and execution. While that general premise appears to be true of cell/group affiliated terrorists, the pattern is not evidenced in the behavior of loners – they travel greater distances to prepare for an incident and they live substantially greater distances from their chosen target locations, yet they exhibit a planning process that is of essentially the same length as terrorists operating under a command and control structure with multiple members. These behaviors, combined with their relative isolation (as evidenced by their lower marriage rates) and other indicators suggested by recent scholarship (Becker, 2014; Gill et al., 2014; Hewitt, 2014) all suggest that loners do indeed pose a difficult task for law enforcement early intervention.

Given these findings, we wondered if the behaviors of loners enabled them to survive longer than members of cells/groups before being arrested or killed. The differences, reported in Table 7, were highly significant. Proportionally, nearly three times as many cell/group members were arrested within three months of their first precursor activity compared to loners (22% and 8%, respectively). Similarly, three-fifths (60%) of cell/group members in the dataset were arrested within one year of their first known precursor activity. In contrast, only about one-fifth (21%) of loners were arrested during the first year following engagement in precursor conduct. An analysis of "longevity" measured as a continuous variable ranging from date of first known precursor act to date of indictment revealed even more astounding results. On average, cell/group

Table 7. Length of Terrorist's Life Cycle.

	Percent of Terrorist Precursor Acts by Time Period		
	Less than 3 months	3 months to 1 year	Longer than 1 year
Loners, $n = 24$	8%	13%	79%
Cells/groups, $n = 279$	22%	28%	50%
All perpetrators, $n = 303$	21%	26%	53%

$p < .001$.

participants "survived" about one year (median of 370 days) before being indicted, while loners had an average "lifespan" from first precursor to indictment (or arrest, if not captured prior to indictment) of over 1,900 days – a period of over five years. While some of these loners, exemplified by terrorists like Olympic Park and abortion clinic bomber Eric Rudolph, desisted from terrorists and lived "underground" for years after committing their last act of terrorism (Vollers, 2006), their ability to avoid capture fuels the imagination of individuals radicalizing toward violence.

CONCLUSIONS

Despite a lack of consensus about what constitutes a "lone wolf," our understanding of terrorism committed by loners has increased in the past several years. Like others, we suggest that a shared terminology needs to consider three key conceptual dimensions of lone actor terrorism, including ideological motive, group affiliation, and the degree to which terrorists receive assistance in preparing and executing terrorist attacks. It was based on these dimensions that this study sought to extend previous categorization schemes by distinguishing between lone actor terrorists who had no help preparing for attacks and executed them alone from those loners who received assistance preparing for attacks but executed them alone. As is often the case with terrorism research, our limited sample size precluded us from making statistical comparisons across each of our three types of lone wolf terrorism in relation to group-based terrorism. We did, however, statistically examine how cases involving lone wolves, which included both "loners" and "unaffiliated loners" who had no help in preparing for or executing attacks, compared to all other terrorism cases involving multiple conspirators. The results of our study suggested that the majority of lone wolves were predominately male, slightly older, and significantly more educated than group-based terrorists. Our analysis also supported previous research by finding that lone wolves were, on average, more socially isolated than group-based actors. Unfortunately, the increased isolation of these terrorists is one of the most problematic symptoms of the lone wolf "syndrome" for law enforcement to counter. Fewer social ties conceivably reduce the opportunities for family, friends, employers, and others known to terrorists to detect suspicious behaviors, and opportunities for the public to "see something, say something" are reduced.

Also perplexing to the law enforcement and intelligence community is the assumption that that lone wolves engage in fewer precursor, or planning and preparatory, activities that also reduce opportunities for interdiction by law enforcement. With the exceptions of Gill et al. (2014) and the current study, there has been a lack of empirical research on the differences in precursor behaviors of lone wolves and group-based terrorists. Based on data made available by the American Terrorism Study, we not only confirmed conventional wisdom that lone wolves engage in less detectable precursor activities but we also found that these activities are similarly temporally spaced and increasingly geospatially distanced compared to group-based terrorism cases. As each precursor activity represents a potential opportunity for criminal and suspicious behaviors to be detected, lone wolves provide fewer and more distanced "dots" that can be connected by officials prior to terrorism attacks.

Although our findings support the emerging narrative that depicts lone wolves as a formidable challenge and significant threat to homeland security, it is also important to remember that no terrorist operates within a social vacuum. Lone wolves are unique from group-based terrorists in several ways; however, they do plan, prepare, and may even solicit direct and virtual forms of assistance prior to committing their crimes. It is clear that lone wolves tend to be more isolated than other terrorists in regards to personal and intimate relationships, but these individuals are often employed, attending classes, members of the military, or members of online (or Internet) communities. It is up to terrorism researchers to learn more about the patterned nature of criminal and non-criminal precursor activities of lone wolves, while also being careful not to assume homogeneity in precursor activities across loners, unaffiliated loners, lone conspirators, and group-based actors. Ideally, members of the law enforcement and intelligence communities will ultimately be able to use evidence-based findings such as the ones presented in this study to inform terrorism prevention policies and practices.

NOTES

1. Personal conversations and meetings in 1995–1996 with members of JTTF's in different FBI field offices following the bombing of the Murrah Federal Building. One of the authors of this article was criticized extensively in an article by William Pierce on his website following the author's testimony before the House Judiciary Subcommittee on Crime after the Oklahoma City Bombing. Concerns that mention of the author by name might be suggestive of a target for a lone wolf resulted in increased security by law enforcement – the point being that the term "lone wolf" was used extensively even prior to Al Qaeda's emergence as a global threat.
2. Sequencing Terrorists' Precursor Behaviors: A Crime-Specific Analysis. National Institute of Justice, Grant # 2013-ZA-BX-0001.
3. The rose diagrams are not show here, but examples may be seen in some of our preliminary work published in Smith (2009).

REFERENCES

Bakker, E., & de Graaf, B. (2011). Preventing lone wolf terrorism: Some CT approaches. *Perspectives on Terrorism*, *5*(5–6). Retrieved from http://www.terrorismanalysts.com/pt/index.php/pot/article/view/preventing-lone-wolf/html

Barnes, B. (2012). Confronting the one-man wolf pack: Adapting law enforcement and prosecution responses to the threat of lone wolf terrorism. *Boston University Law Review*, *92*, 1613–1662.

Beam, L. (1992). Leaderless resistance. *The Seditionist*, *12*. Retrieved from http://www.louisbeam.com/leaderless.htm

Becker, M. (2014). Explaining lone wolf target selection in the United States. *Studies in Conflict & Terrorism*, *37*(11), 959–978.

Borum, R., Fein, R., & Vossekuil, B. (2012). A dimensional approach to analyzing lone offender terrorism. *Aggression and Violent Behavior*, *17*, 389–396.

Damphousse, K., & Smith, B. (2004). Terrorism and empirical testing: Using indictment data to assess changes in terrorist conduct. In M. Deflem (Ed.), *Terrorism and counterterrorism: Criminological perspectives* (pp. 75–90). New York, NY: Elsevier.

Gill, P., Horgan, J., & Deckert, P. (2014). Bombing alone: Tracing the motivations and antecedent behaviors of lone-actor terrorists. *Journal of Forensic Sciences*, *59*(2), 425–435.

Gruenewald, J., Chermak, S., & Freilich, J. D. (2013). Distinguishing "loner" attacks from other domestic extremist violence: A comparison of homicide incident and offender characteristics. *Criminology & Public Policy*, *12*(1), 65–91.

Hewitt, C. (2003). *Understanding terrorism in America: From the Klan to Al Qaeda*. New York, NY: Routledge.

Hewitt, C. (2014). Law enforcement tactics and their effectiveness in dealing with American terrorism: Organizations, autonomous cells, and lone wolves. *Terrorism & Political Violence*, *26*(1), 58–68.

Joosse, P. (2007). Leaderless resistance and ideological inclusion: The case of the Earth Liberation Front. *Terrorism & Political Violence*, *19*(3), 351–368.

Kaplan, J. (1997). Leaderless resistance. *Terrorism and Political Violence*, *9*, 80–95.

Moskalenko, S., & McCauley, C. (2011). The psychology of lone-wolf terrorism. *Counseling Psychology Quarterly*, *24*, 115–126.

Nijboer, M. (2012). A review of lone wolf terrorism: The need for a different approach. *Social Cosmos*, *3*. Retrieved from http://socialcosmos.%20library.uu.nl/index.php/sc/article/viewFile/43/38

Pantucci, R. (2011). *A typology of lone wolves: Preliminary analysis of lone Islamist terrorists*. London: The International Centre for the Study of Radicalisation and Political Violence. Retrieved from http://www.trackingterrorism.org/sites/default/files/chatter/1302002992ICSRPaper_ATypologyofLoneWolves_Pantucci.pdf

Ranstorp, M. (1998). Interpreting the broader context and meaning of Bin-Laden's fatwa. *Studies in Conflict & Terrorism*, *21*(4), 321–330.

Silke, A. (2001). The devil you know: Continuing problems with research on terrorism. *Terrorism & Political Violence*, *13*(4), 1–14.

Simon, J. D. (2013). *Lone wolf terrorism: Understanding the growing threat*. Amherst, NY: Prometheus Books.

Smith, B. (1994). *Terrorism in America: Pipe bombs and pipe dreams*. Albany, NY: State University of New York Press.

Smith, B. (2009). A look at terrorist behavior: How they prepare, where they strike. *National Institute of Justice Journal*, *260*, 2–6.

Spaaij, R. (2010). The enigma of lone wolf terrorism: An assessment. *Studies in Conflict & Terrorism*, *33*, 854–870.

Spaaij, R., & Hamm, M. S. (2015). Key issues and research agendas in lone wolf terrorism. *Studies in Conflict & Terrorism*, *38*(3), 167–178.

Sterling, C. (1981). *The terror network: The secret war of international terrorism*. New York, NY: Holt, Rinehart, and Winston.

Stern, J. (2003). *Terror in the name of God: Why religious militants kill*. New York, NY: Harper Collins.

Vollers, M. (2006). *Lone wolf: Eric Rudolph and the legacy of American terror*. New York, NY: Harper Perennial.

Zierhoffer, D. M. (2014). Threat assessment: Do lone terrorists differ from other lone offenders? *Journal of Strategic Security*, *7*(3), 48–62.

SECOND ORDER TERRORISM[☆]

Willem de Lint

ABSTRACT

Purpose – *Post-9/11 a first order terrorism narrative has been widely asserted. In this chapter, I explore the development of second order terrorism narrative or ideal-type.*

Methodology/approach – *The chapter begins by providing a brief synopsis of three highly mediated Australian counter-terrorism operations and of shortcomings in incident counting. It also relies on some U.S. research on counter-terrorism prosecutions in support.*

Findings – *In first order terrorism, crime appears as a spectacular irruption or original sin on a tabula rasa of innocence and there is a clean division between us and them, non-state and state, victim and offender. In the second order terrorism narrative there is a contrasting claim that 9/11 is blowback, in kind, for U.S.-led interventions and does not offer a clean division between how we and they behave, blurs non-state and state culpability in big crimes, and sees victims and offenders trading places over time. As we adjust our perspective from the presumptive first order*

[☆]This chapter borrows from arguments and examples made in de Lint and Kassa (2015). It is also indebted to Wondwossen Kassa for research assistance and has benefitted from an Australian Research Council grant, DP 120100191.

Terrorism and Counterterrorism Today
Sociology of Crime, Law and Deviance, Volume 20, 111–130

ISSN: 1521-6136/doi:10.1108/S1521-613620150000020006

to second order event-acts, terrorism and counter-terrorism, event-act and interdiction, is merged as one.

Originality/value – *The concept may be useful in accounting for assumptions pertaining to this category of crime, including its relation with precaution and security.*

Keywords: Constructive terrorism; spectacular crime; terrorism prosecutions; positivist terrorism

INTRODUCTION

In the gulf between the editorial "We are all Americans" in *Le Monde* on September 12, 2001 and the opinion column "We are no longer Americans" in the *Guardian* on September 8, 2006 U.S. moral capital was squandered and the public imaginary of terrorism began to change. After Abu Gharib, rendition, black sites, and a CIA-led torture program – and as precautionary, networked operations produce a regular dribble of "terrorists" – the straightforward binary division on which depends "our" innocence falls away.

The narrative should be familiar to criminologists. From Cesare Beccaria's *Treatise on Crimes and Punishments*, which famously railed against the homicidal impulsivity of the magistrates of the Old Regime through Howard S. Becker's, *Outsiders: Studies in the Sociology of Deviance*, which upset conventional understandings of inclusivity and presumptive inside-outside subjectivities, to David Garland's, *The Culture of Control*, which accounts for a rising punitiveness in contemporary Western nations by exploring the conditions in which a cultural identification with criminals (rehabilitation) becomes a culture identified in its rejection of the criminal other (control), the best criminology has striven to hold a mirror on the relation between the imagery and the imaginary of crime in a variety of cultural, institutional or societal contexts. Currently, and following Garland's (2001) point that governments succeed not by mitigating the underlying criminogenic condition but by appearing to manage its effects, it is the contention in this chapter that a first order terrorism, which innocently counts up the numbers of terrorists and interdicts against them as permanent exiles from civilization, is being supplanted by a second order terrorism, which does much the same work, but without the innocence of motive or objective.

Governments finesse terrorism as a significant opportunity to demonstrate their subservience to the priorities of regional and global security alliances. National security draws from a conception of security both as a basic condition of freedom and as an existential, or ultimate and overriding human value (Berki, 1986, p. 20). But it should also be understood as a form or technique of governmental power. As such, national security tests the strength of the state not only against external forces, but also against internal institutions, and configurations of law, as is seen in precautionary crime. As a form of power (Burke, 2007, p. 5), security is "a political technology that mobilises two linked techniques of social production and regulation." As we shall argue, the apparent connection between national security as a policy implying secret state actors and a necessary condition of government or life itself, while mostly unremarkable, is exploited to, in a word, demonstrate government efficacy, increasingly without an overture that plays to underlying factors. In so doing, it provides what we would call a meta-frame (Bateson, 1952), or *ordering principle* to clarify and stipulate meta-governance, on the one hand, and the proper alignment of individual attitudes or subjectivities to this "totalizing power" (Burke, 2007, p. 5), on the other.

Taking terrorism in Australia as a point of departure this chapter explores how, as we adjust our perspective from the presumptive first order to second order event-acts, terrorism and counter-terrorism, event-act and interdiction, is merged as one. The chapter begins by providing a brief synopsis of three highly mediated Australian counter-terrorism operations and of shortcomings in incident counting. The argument then relies on some U.S. research on counter-terrorism prosecutions in support.

FIRST ORDER TERRORISM IN AUSTRALIA

Terrorism presents researchers, policymakers, and the public at large with what is almost an unbridgeable impasse: knowledge of terrorism depends upon and reinforces political assumption orthodoxies, which set the contours of the knowledge field (Foucault, 1972; Fuchs & Ward, 1994). For the government faithful, including most liberals and conservatives toward the middle of the political spectrum, it represents a challenge to a political and social solidarity that requires the fine-tuning and re-assertion of its disciplining instruments. This may perhaps even strengthen liberal democratic institutions; at least this is an argument among the faithful. For the skeptical, on the contrary, the event and its redress through security intelligence maneuvers is an expression of the neo-authoritarian impulse that will eclipse the rule of law; it also suggests the erasure of context, antecedent or history from policy, as the event-act announced is then exploited to distinguish whole cultures, civilizations, regimes, etc. (see, e.g., Ranstorp, 2009, p. 23).

Irruptive Spectacle or Existential Challenge?

Between November 1 and 8, 2005, 107 articles appeared in the *Herald Sun*, *Canberra Times*, *The Age*, and *The Australian* to divide public attention between the pending (and need for) terrorism legislation and the possibility of a terrorist attack.[1] On November 2, a draft to amend the anti-terrorism provisions of the criminal law was introduced to the federal parliament. At same time ASIO (Australian Security Intelligence Organisation) and the AFP (Australian Federal Police) were busy massaging the media with strategic media leaks. For example, *The Australian* claimed that home-grown terrorist suspects in Melbourne and Sydney were believed to be building the capability to mount an attack.[2] Prime Minister John Howard made appearances to warn that the legislation was crucial, influenced by security and law enforcement emergency, and the need to develop adequate capacity to criminally prosecute "home-grown terrorists." Mr. Howard's announcement also came *a day after* ASIO warned in its annual general report to parliament of a threat of home-grown terrorists (BBC News, 2005a). Suggesting the role of ASIO in influencing the amendment, *BBC News* reported that it was *based on specific intelligence of a possible attack* that John Howard announced an amendment to existing laws (BBC News, 2005b). He said the amendment he proposed would make it easier to prosecute suspects believed to be involved in the early stages of planning attacks, since it allowed arrest even when the exact nature and target of a terrorist act could not yet be identified (Corera, 2005).

One week after the law was amended, the raid to arrest occurred. On November 8, hundreds of police backed by helicopters launched pre-dawn raids in 20 homes in Sydney and Melbourne in what was then the biggest counter-terrorism strike in Australian history. The accused were charged under the anti-terrorism law as amended. Referring to the changes made by the amendment, Victoria Police Commissioner Christine Nixon said that "[t]he men were detained after the Australian government passed new anti-terrorism legislation making it easier to prosecute suspects allegedly involved in the early stages of planning an attack."[3] John Howard said that swift passage of federal laws had contributed to the arrests which utilized these new powers and that the need for passage of new powers to law enforcement agencies was *vindicated* by them (Corera, 2005).

In sum, those caught up in this sweep were announced to be not prosecutable as terrorists without the passage of the amended bill, and the amended bill's passage was cleared of roadblocks by alarmist, partial, and to some extent erroneous information passed to media and parliamentary actors. These leaks included, as Greg Barns notes, reports about Melbourne landmarks such as the Westgate Bridge, Flinders Street railway station and the MCG being targets for terrorist activity by this group of men.

> The evidence in the lengthy court proceedings that culminated in a Supreme Court trial in 2008 showed nothing of the sort. The reference to the Westgate Bridge had been taken out of context and was completely innocent. There was simply no evidence of a plot to blow up Flinders Street station, and the reference to the MCG was in the context of a vague conversation between two of the accused. (Barns, 2014)

A second "terror wave" was witnessed in 2014. In front page news all over Australia, the National Public Alert System raised the "terror threat level" from medium to high on September 12. This occurred *just hours in advance of a coordinated arrest* of "terror suspects" in Sydney and Brisbane. Public officials claimed at the same instant that there could be a "Bali-style attack," (Irvine, 2014) that it would mean more security at airports and large public events, but that agencies "had not detected any particular plots," that "it would not make a difference to daily life for a vast majority of Australians" (Abbott, 2014), and "we certainly want people to enjoy the football if their teams are lucky enough to be in the grand final" (Abbott, 2014). The announcement that no particular plots had been detected came at precisely the moment a massive operation was being organized and the threat level was being raised and another terrorism amendment was introduced to parliament. As reported in the *Sydney Morning Herald* (September 18, 2014), "[t]he morning for Mr Azari began with a shock – a shock shared by millions of Australians as 800 police mounted what has been billed as Australia's largest counterterrorism operation." Prime Minister Tony Abbott seized upon the occasion to announce the need for Australians "shift" the balance between freedom and security. As Ben Eltham commented in the *New Matilda* (September 23, 2014), "the speed with which Australia's national conversation has turned from the normal stuff of budget measures and social policy to an overwhelming atmosphere of fear and insecurity has been breathtaking.

It is all the more disturbing because the terrorist threat facing Australia is so negligible."

Early in 2015, another terror splash occurred. This time, details of the alleged plot were provided by Prime Minister Tony Abbott, who said in parliament that the two accused men, arrested in a highly publicized raid, were keen to "stab kidneys" and "strike necks."

> Kneeling before the death cult flag with a knife in his hand and a machete before him, one of those arrested said this: "I swear to almighty Allah we will carry out the first operation for the soldiers of the caliphate in Australia." He went on to say, "I swear to almighty Allah, blonde people, there is no room for blame between you and us. We only owe you, stabbing the kidneys and striking the necks." I don't think it would be possible to witness uglier fanaticism than this – more monstrous fanaticism and extremism than this – and I regret to say it is now present in our country. (ABC News, February 13, 2015)

Criminal lawyers as well as Jane Needham, President of the New South Wales Bar Association, said such public commentary about a suspect (presumed innocent until proven guilty by a jury) could undermine the adversarial system, given that jurors are to come to their task without prior prejudice about the case (ABC News, February 13, 2015).

Counting

In Schmidt and de Graaf's typology (in Schmidt & Jongman, 2005, p. 48), terrorism is divided by targets, agents, and motives into political, criminal, and idiosyncratic types, where political includes insurgent, vigilante, and state terrorism, and insurgency includes social revolutionary, separatist (including ethnical, national, secessationist, irredentist), and single-issue terrorism. The University of Maryland's Global Terrorism Database (START) sorts the world's terrorism incidents from 1970 and may be, as self-described, "the most comprehensive unclassified data base on terrorist events in the world." It uses a variety of devices to filter and sort terrorism incidents, including, crucially the criterion that the act is aimed at a target with the motive to attain a political, economic, religious or social goal and that there is evidence of coercion, intimidation, "or some other message to a larger audience." Using this tool to discover Australian terrorism counts, and filtering down from what appears to be a gross number of over 70 events, one may derive a list exclusive of ambiguous cases of some 39 events between 1970 and 2010, with peak activity recorded between 1991 and 1998 and the most frequent targets being governments and businesses. In 30 of the 39 events, the perpetrator is unknown.

Thirty-nine incidents are far too many to analyze here, but a couple of summary points are instructive. First, the Bali bombings (2002, 2005) in which 88 and 4 Australians were killed respectively and which are considered by Australian authorities and much of the Australian public as evidence that Australia is at serious risk of terrorism, are not included in the listing because they did not occur on Australian land. Second, many of the incidents are still far too inclusive, given the little that is known about them. By way of example, ID number 200109230005 (START, 2013) provides an incident summary as follows: "A Brisbane Australia mosque was ruined in a suspected arson attack. No group claimed responsibility." In ID 20080421001 (START, 2013), a live pipe bomb was found and detonated by the police bomb squad and a person was arrested with evidence of homemade explosives. No motive or target was noted. Note that this follows choosing the restricted search to filter events to match the requirement of the ideological purpose. Third, looked at with respect to completed events, incidents of terrorism include, in the majority, the actions of ethnic, secessionist, nationalist or vigilante groups or actors that would appear to be attacking targets that are not looking to persuade Australia or Australians but rather the ethnic or factional target that happens to be located in Australia. Fourth, terrorism incidents do not include the inchoate plots that have resulted in the country's most significant terrorism prosecutions, including the 2005 Melbourne and Sydney prosecutions of *Benbrika and Ors*, and *Baldjam and Ors*, despite that the filter chosen allows inclusion of incomplete event-acts.

Before we move on, two points about the empirical underpinning need to be made. First, a note about state actor causation. Because the perpetrator is unknown, not only is the motive difficult or impossible to determine, but so too is the classification of the incident as non-state. As we shall see below, significant inchoate terrorist acts are perpetrated by non-state-state actor networks, or through terrorist/counter-terrorism plots that are commandeered by law enforcement and national security actors. The GTD, permits state actor terrorism where those states are "rogue states," such as Iran, Syria, Lebanon, etc. (START, 2013). However, as historical accounts of the Mossad and CIA amply demonstrate, established state intelligence organizations commit terrorist acts through intermediaries (see, e.g., Thomas, 2000). And, although an assassination in Dubai by Mossad agents (some of whom identified themselves by carrying false Australian passports) of Mahmud al-Mabhuh, was reported in media worldwide, it does not appear in the GTD.

Similarly, we do not find but passing reference in official documents to the interplay between foreign policy decision-making and terrorism (Cockburn, 2015; see below). In official reporting, Australian government accounting on terrorism is inclusive only of non-state terrorism, and is further reduced to criminal, idiosyncratic and/or religious, or ethnical and/or secessationist. According to the peak national security body, the Australian Security Intelligence Organisation (ASIO), it is necessary to report on terrorism incidence and dimensions in Australia to the extent that it encompasses violent jihadists, including al-Qa'ida and the Islamic State of Iraq and the Levant (ISIL). These are the groups that pose the principal threat of terrorism to Australia and Australians. ASIO's 2013–2014 Annual Report (Australian Security Intelligence Organisation [ASIO], 2014) listed 60 Australians who were "training or fighting in Syria or Iraq." The Report lists as direct involvement of Australians in acts of terrorism associated with this two suicide bombings carried out (one in Syria, one in Iraq) by Australians and the involvement of some of these 60 Australians in murders of civilians or prisoners caught up in that conflict. ASIO also reports that the reader may infer that Australians returning from participation in this conflict will participate in homegrown terrorism at a rate between 30% and 60%. This is based on 30 Australians identified to have traveled to Pakistan and Afghanistan in the late 1990s and early 2000s out of which 19 continued to engage in security concerning behaviors out of which nine were later prosecuted for terrorism-related activities.

Since the Whitlam government's dismissal by Governor General John Kerr on November 11, 1975, and perhaps the valiant efforts by Malcolm Fraser's liberal government that took office following that collapse, Australia's national security priorities have not deviated significantly from the geostrategic interests of the United States. As Phillips (2008) puts it, "nothing in Australian politics basks in a warmer, bipartisan glow that the Australian-American alliance." As Phillips notes, the ANZUS alliance has restricted and muted critical debate on Australian foreign policy alternatives, including questions of resource depletion and regional failed states. In the counter-terrorism space, there is little or no daylight between the U.S. posture, program, and implementation and that of Australia. Australia was among the first countries to pass counter-terrorism legislation following 9/11, it offered intelligence and diplomatic support not to captured Australians David Hicks and Jack Thomas, but to American authorities holding them (ultimately on illegal charges) as "enemy noncombatants" in Afghanistan and/or Guantanimo, it follows and supports official U.S. listing and delisting of terrorist organizations, and its current military support is quick to match shifting U.S. targets in the Mideast.

Disciplining or meta-framing of knowledge of terrorism generally and of Australian terrorists and terrorism specifically is predicated on a definition of terrorism and its designation by authorities that references dynamic geostrategic and domestic political interests. Note here that the ASIO and AFP are not very much interested in classifying the same number of events as listed in the GTD as terrorism. Practically, this is because despite the GTD's filtering that more or less matches Australia's legal definition of terrorism, that legal definition does not extend back to 1970, the actors involved require rather more that the GTD to include the incidents as terrorism, and the incentive to do so is sensitive to Australia's current terrorism listing and national security posture within the international unipolar order.

Here, a self-described impartial authority on terrorism would appear to augment Australia's government authority and pulls understanding of terrorism toward the realism of the security state. Accordingly, once a meta-framing of security policy has taken place that "talks up" terrorism as an existential threat or ordering principle, measuring instruments are developed, and the empirical dimensions are "fixed," at least roughly, through the orthodox view of an enemies list. The GTD has contributed, by its own account enormously, to the empirical basis of terrorism. State actors and others may now point to a reality somewhat autonomous from the framing and ordering that is already being stipulated geopolitically. A closer look at these incidents, however, draws one back to the definition issue, particularly the problem that terrorism is very much a question of review, reclassification, or simply the prerogative of the beholder – not a good launching pad for objective science.

Context

The objective counts are made sensible when we provide a context, which in the national security domain is to say something about the presumptive framing of terrorism in what we will call the first order. In first order terrorism, the terrorist event-act appears as a spectacular irruption or original sin on a tabula rasa of innocence, and there is a clean division between us and them, non-state and state, victim and offender. In first order frames, terrorism is cordoned off in its definition and incidence by an establishment narrative. That first order frame and supporting narrative rests on empirical facts or real truths that also borrow from other intersecting first order frames and their narratives, such as that, as per the U.S. state department spokeswoman Jen Psaki, that "[a]s a matter of long-standing policy, the United States does not support political transitions by non-constitutional means" (CNN February 13, 2015). Post-9/11, a first order terrorism narrative has been widely asserted. The "shock and awe" announcement provides an instantaneous clarification and reset of the ordering principle, by which "we" are distinguished from "them" (Buzan, 2000).

In many aspects, the profile of first order terrorism is consistent with the breaking news story, the medium for which it is the message. Studies consistent with the first order terrorism narrative mimic the episteme of longstanding positive science, in the development of counts of incidence, as if the ontology question of terrorism (what is it?) has been long settled (see Ranstorp, 2009). Secondly, what passes as terrorism is parsed or mediated by filters and factors. Two filters of news information in the mediation of terrorism are key. First, corporate mass media filters current events and news facts to imbricate the interests of elites in the opinion of the masses (Herman & Chomsky, 2002). Second, terrorism is mediated through the prism of the national security state, as represented by government ministers and agency directors and in legislation that structures press disclosures in their interests (for instance, as per restrictions on publicly disclosing information about whistleblowing in the *National Security Legislation Amendment Bill (No. 1) 2014*). What comes to be "widely known" or recognized as terrorism will be phenomena that take their form through both the corporate mass media and national security state filters. Accordingly,

1. Terrorism is what *they* do. The corporate mass filter and the national security filter both work to produce or reproduce an *us* versus *them* distinction. Terrorism is mostly understood as the work of non-state actors, or if state actors they are working for a pariah state.
2. Terrorism is a doubly asymmetrical political crime. It is a crime against the (conventional mode of) politics and against *our* political institutions explicitly, as narrowly defined through the prisms.

As we shall argue, the narrative and assumptions of first order terrorism do not hold up or have been superseded by a second order in which terrorism is a complex of action that includes state and non-state actors and thus makes it a crime against our political institutions that we commit against ourselves. If in first order terrorism, there is an attempt to quickly move on from the count to suggest the policy, the definition and conceptual problem is not so easily overcome where there is an interest in a more thorough analysis.

SECOND ORDER TERRORISM

> So, as this sting was progressing, the FBI squad supervisor, Richard Worms, was talking to his agents about discussions he was having with federal prosecutors, and he described how federal prosecutors wanted a "Hollywood ending" to their sting operation. What's particularly troublesome about that terminology, I think, is that it clearly shows that the FBI was not only controlling every aspect of the sting operation, but they were controlling it in such a way that they wanted a splashy ending, a Hollywood ending, as he says. They essentially got a Hollywood ending. They were able to get Sami Osmakac to record a so-called martyrdom video, in which he's wearing a suicide vest and has an AK-47 leaned up against a closet door behind him – all of which were provided by the FBI. And at the very end, they get him to attempt to deliver a car bomb, which was of course provided by the FBI. And as he backs out of a hotel parking lot, the car bomb in his trunk, FBI agents rush in and arrest him. (Trevor Aaronson, *Democracy Now*, March 19, 2015)

> Whatever the government is playing in the media and that everything that's gone on has been orchestrated by the government. They want you to see this. Behind the scenes, there's 128 agents working on this, informants and everything. All the YouTube videos and everything have been orchestrated by the government. The same day my brother was arrested, the next day, the guy that's holding the camera and everything behind, they all disappeared. There's been multiple informants. The next day, they disappeared, and nobody knew what was going on. (Avni Osmakac, *Democracy Now*, March 19, 2015)

In the post-9/11 context there is a strong belief among legislators and the executive and security actors in an "asymmetrical moral economy" in which powerful states, weakened by the very institutions by which they pronounce themselves to have gained supremacy – notably strict adherence to legality – , reassert hegemony by reference to the presumptive superiority of state actors. Although this largely subterranean belief – outside of direct conscious noting (Giddens, 1986) – is also not supported by direct testing (cf Pape, 2003), it is widespread even among the purveyors of the just world. According to Winter:

> The idea of asymmetry functions as a source of legitimacy because it frames the confrontation between states and their "asymmetric" enemies in moral terms and transposes that confrontation onto a neo-colonial template of civilized vs. uncivilized forms of warfare. The principle of distinction between combatants and civilians is being undermined in less formal and more complicated ways: through imaginative redefinitions of legal terms and creative legal interpretation. These strategies allow officials to publicly defend the integrity of domestic and international legal conventions while pursuing policies that directly contravene their very principles. (2011)

In the context of global asymmetric warfare, the reference to a presumptively just world (its innocence) permits what Requa (2011) refers to as derogations from political liberalism in the assertion of hegemony.[4] Former US Attorney General John Ashcroft dubbed the precautionary approach to counter-terrorism a "new paradigm in prevention" (Cole, 2006). Amoore and de Goede (2008, p. 8) note that the "politics of pre-emption draw on but go beyond the established language and techniques of risk."

As Aaronson reported in 2011, Sami Osmakac is one of more than 175 people since 9/11 who have been caught in counter-terrorism stings; in federal terrorism-related cases in the decade after 9/11, 243 of 508 defendants were being handled with the aid of an FBI informant. In an analysis of 50 terrorism cases since 9/11 in which the United States itself has been, or apparently has been, targeted, Muller (2012, p. 26) concludes that it seems likely that the accused in most of the cases "would never have become operationally engaged in terrorism plotting without the creative, elaborate, and costly sting efforts of the police. And, given their natural incapacities, even those who did attempt to inflict violence on their own were likely either to fail in their efforts or to commit destruction of quite limited scope." Recorded FBI agent comments suggested that as well as depending comprehensively on the FBI for the resources of the plotted attack, and believing Osmakac incapable of "committing significant violence," they were keen to provide the operational commanders with the best "Hollywood" production that limitless counter-terrorism aid to law enforcement could purchase. Osmakac was sentenced to 40 years in federal prison (Aaronson, 2015).[5]

In Australia, of the 38 terrorism prosecutions between 2001 and 2012, the extent of the role of informants is unknown, but most involved electronic intercepts and phone surveillance. In New South Wales and Victoria, the convictions of some twenty people from prosecutions stemming from the 2005 arrests relied on the precautionary crime standard that did not require evidence that an identifiable act was being planned. The Victoria prosecutions depended on the involvement of an informant "SIO 39," a Victorian police officer who infiltrated the group under the guise of a Turkish Muslim by the name of Ahmet Sonmez with explosives experience. In October 2004 SIO 39 took Benbrika to a remote location at Mt Disappointment and demonstrated detonation of a small quantity of explosives – this was recorded (video and audio) and shown to the jury. In the case against Zeky Mallah ([2005] NSWSC 317; [2005] NSWSC 317), an undercover police operative posed as journalist, paid the accused $3000 for a suicide video and engaged in conversations concerning the taking of hostages and killing of ASIO officers.

In so-called homegrown or homeland terror interdiction, precaution is now quite widely identified with the extremely proactive constructive crime or the manufacture of synthetic terrorist acts (Aaronson, 2013; Muller, 2012; Ruppert, 2012). Accordingly, involved agencies engage in "parallel construction" (Shifman & Ingram, 2013) to effect what is referred to as "create and capture" (Ruppert, 2012), summed up by Madison Ruppert (2012) as "creating terrorists" who actually have "no contact with militants of any kind." They are provided with materials to carry out attacks after which "police promptly arrest them" and "point to the case as proof that the domestic police state is working." The *conventional* prosecution of counter terrorism in Australia as in the United States now involves the precautionary or pre-crime protocol that permits security and law enforcement actors to stop terrorists before they cause damage (McCulloch & Pickering, 2009, p. 632). It should come as no surprise that this is exactly what they do. Terrorism and counter-terrorism combine as state actors assisting non-state actors prepare a crime that "we" commit against our political institutions.

There is an argument that following the drug war's modus operandi, countering terrorism may be achieved by manufacturing synthetic terrorism plots. This is refuted by the available literature (Muller, 2012; Pape, 2003, etc.). The journalist Andrew Cockburn (2015) has followed terrorist interdiction efforts by the United States and notes two studies that find that treating terrorism by applying counter-insurgency or low intensity warfare through special operations and/or drone strikes targeting cell leaders is associated with an increase in the incidence of the phenomenon which is being interdicted. The Pentagon's Institute for Defense Analysis found that the cocaine supply to the United States increased following the elimination of the leadership of drug cartels such as that adopted by the Drug Enforcement Agency in its "Kingpin Strategy." The reason given is that supply is less tight when a cartel is dismantled and the reduction of executive control allows successor kingpins to enter the market. Similarly, "a secret study of 200 cases" conducted by which "an intelligence cell attached to military HQ in Baghdad" in which high value targets (HVTs) were "killed or captured in the previous ten months" found that attacks rose sharply in nearly every case five days after the hit because, the analysts concluded, the replacement leaders were more vengeful and "aggressive" (Cockburn, 2015).

One of these alternative answers is that the eradication of certain kinds of radicalization and terror is not the first order objective, but rather the means to serve that objective, which is shifting scarce public resources to the most powerful interests, including the largest military, industrial, and security intelligence consortia that profit from ongoing or perpetual war. The global war on terror and the security intelligence infrastructure attaching domestic safety and foreign security produces the means to discipline states and governments on a common measure and assures that counter-terrorism demands and receives a vast amount of public resources.

The radicalization of persons and groups has now been much studied (e.g., Pape, 2003; 2010) and it is clear that there is a strong relationship between a country like Australia's foreign interventionism and homegrown radicalization. Given that popular support for that intervention is at best lukewarm and the stated strategic objectives of those interventions are also difficult to specify and accomplish, it is a fair question to ask how and whether the cost of counter-terrorism measures are being objectively or judiciously evaluated against those questionable interventions. Given that there does not seem to be a clear end-game for those interventions and that the strategy of using harsh military sanctions against radical groups is understood to exacerbate rather than eliminate the root problem, it would seem that answering the question as to why Australia and other middle power states are devoting so much of their treasure in this way ought to be a pressing question that entertains the possibility of alternative answers.

Demonstrating Government through Terrorism/Counter-Terrorism

A better alternative answer is that the eradication of certain kinds of radicalization and terror is not the first order objective, but rather the means to serve a second order objective, which is to structure ordering around a narrative while shifting scarce public resources to the most powerful interests, including the largest military, industrial, and security intelligence interests that profit from ongoing or perpetual war. The global war on terror and the security intelligence infrastructure attaching domestic safety and foreign security produces the means to discipline states and governments on a common measure and assures that counter-terrorism demands and receives a vast amount of public resources.

Although the effect appears as if to be a conspiracy between state and federal police, national security actors, Attorneys General or public prosecutors the ministers, and cabinet members, what we refer to as the irruptive, spectacular and increasingly regular emergency of the counter-terror cell take-down may be otherwise explained as a confluence of independent actions animated by the emergent power of the security regime and its operational standards and delivery modes. The roll-out of arrests in long-standing operations would appear at a minimum to be well-timed to effect or achieve maximum impact. Indeed, in the public imaginary, the terrorism event is broadcast as a problem at the very same time that authorities are ready to pounce on targets. In this regard the trigger must be an explicitly manufactured fear, because the object is to draw on public sentiment that has already been primed with a specific governmental direction or remedy. Governments never wish to be surprised. This, then, is consistent with *crime management* agendas as outlined by David Garland and others.

As noted by Jackson, Smyth, and Gunning (2009, p. 2), a "widely accepted wisdom" of "orthodox terrorism studies" has gradually been losing its luster in the years after 9/11. A contrasting claim is that 9/11 is blowback, in kind, for U.S.-led interventions which, in the second order terrorism narrative, does not offer a clean division between how we and they behave, blurs non-state and state culpability in big crimes, and sees victims and offenders trading places over time. Although this counter-claim may be well-known to authorities, particularly intelligence and security analysts (such as Veteran Intelligence Officers for Sanity), and is increasingly a part of public consciousness as demonstrated in public opinion surveys (Nakhaie & de Lint, 2013) the connection between the foreign policy and domestic counter-terrorism in terror criminogenesis is uncoupled as a matter of official discourse, and particularly after each "hot" new event-act. Instead, the terror file is managed (Garland, 2001) as the regular irruption of a controlled spectacle.

Here we move from first to second order terrorism frames. In second order frames, counter-terrorism is reviewed in terms of its success in delivering on objectives *other than* the stated objective (mitigating terrorism). Counter-terrorism is understood, again mostly tacitly, as a means by which to effect geostrategic ordering. As implied in Wolfowitz's statement on the "bureaucratic" decision to cite weapons of mass destruction, the ordering that requires waging war on Iraq is not at the level of first order justifications, because deciding on counter-terrorism as a means to order the world is not ripe for public approval (not to mention the International Criminal Court, the Nuremburg Principles or Geneva Conventions), particularly if that implies, as above, requiring that that world is delivering up enough terrorists to justify the intrusion (for further discussion, see de Lint & Kassa, 2015).

As evident in the gesture to more considered thinking about the nature of terrorism above, our understanding shifts as we move from an objectivist to a more discursive and constructivist understanding of the work and mediations of actors. As noted in de Lint and Kassa (2015) and de Lint (2008), measure of CT policy is adapted to suit the mode of "politics" as an extension of the war (on terrorism) footing. As policymakers "wag the dog" of public relations, there is less of a gulf between the fact and fiction of terrorism. As per an interpretation of Wolfowitz's remarks, and consistent with the political philosophy of Leo Strauss, effective rule does not simply permit but absolutely requires that messaging for the masses (there is an existential and empirical threat of terrorism) is distinguished in a nod and wink from the message to elites (terrorism consolidates 'our' order) (Crenshaw, 2001).

In this aspect, government is a demonstration, and security as perhaps the strongest claim of government is judged in terms of its alignment with the geostrategic claim. Terrorism coming to light as a spectacular irruption, is matched up with counterterrorism as an ordering spectacle, and they occur co-terminously. Both are made visible at precisely the same time, often by way of an alarmist announcement that another terrorist plot has been thwarted. Such exercises blur the distinction between the first order event as something discovered out there and the remedy or interdiction in the final act of a massive police and security operation.

As noted in de Lint and Kassa (2015, pp. 359–360), this is to adapt Garland's (2001) argument on crime and other arguments on the simulation of security to terrorism: that is to say it is increasingly a second order operation that finesses the problem of governing through, rather than in spite of, the element of surprise. By being on top of the spectacular security irruption, security is a routinization of regular "shock and awe" dosages. Terrorism/counter terrorism operations are managed as if they are costly film productions, in which each actor reads a script and the audience already anticipates the ending. This periodic second order security spectacle resonates as effective even if "the ordering that appears to be being done is not as it may appear" (de Lint & Kassa, 2015, pp. 359–360).

CONCLUSION

Baudrillard (2001) wrote in "L'esprit du terrorisme" in *Le Monde* that the assaults on the World Trade Center and Pentagon constituted a "strong event," an "event strike." He argued that the attacks were "the ultimate event, the mother of all events, the pure event uniting within itself all the events that have never taken place." Derrida has said similarly that the function of repetition of the imagery of 9/11 is one of a deadening and neutralizing. He refers to the global system ordered largely by the United States as undergoing an "autoimmunitary process ... where a living being, in quasi-suicidal fashion, 'itself' works to destroy its own protection, to immunize itself against its 'own' immunity" (Derrida, 2003, p. 94).

In first order terrorism, crime appears as a spectacular irruption or original sin on a tabula rasa of innocence, and there is a clean division between us and them, non-state and state, victim and offender. As we have been arguing, the event is perceived in this way because the context (from which it emerges) is also what is being erased. Derrida's first comment refers to 9/11 imagery as "deadening" or "neutralizing," but then appends this, suggesting reflexivity and co-authorship, consistent with second order narrative in which 9/11, while providing the appearance of the completely unexpected, is on the contrary part of a continuous operation involving many actors and blurred distinctions. The second order terrorism narrative does not offer a clean division between us and them, blurs non-state and state culpability in big crimes, and sees victims and offenders trading places over time.

While the first order has been widely effective in the short term, the second order is gaining ground. The relative purchase of each may be examined against the precautionary crime standard and the extremism concept of anti-radicalization programs. Support for radical deviations from the rule of law and legality are viewed in the first order narrative as a necessary shift to asymmetrical justice to achieve "our" victory over "them." But in asserting the neologism "precaution" as a means of neutralizing terrorism as political crime, liberal democratic institutions give way and the second order narrative gains purchase. Similarly, anti-radicalization campaigns assert intolerance for "extremism" in a first order counter-terrorism narrative that banishes reference to the "political" both as antecedent grievance and remedy. However, the false binary that is already undermined and the extremist foreign policy that is being pursued, cannot in its hypocrisy be meant to persuade in the long term. Anti-radicalization campaigns cannot assert and reach their target with a compelling message of inclusivity. On the contrary, they can only be justified on the second order narrative that both cultivates and anticipates blowback. Today, terrorism and counter-terrorism are government demonstrations blurred in event-acts carried out by non-state and state actors. First order terrorism, the narrative that has shown us the bolt out of the blue, has been eclipsed as experience has overtaken innocence.

NOTES

1. Reporting Diversity (2015) "Terrorism Raids November 2005" in *Reporting Diversity Journalism in Multicultural Australia-Case Studies*, p. 49. http://www.reportingdiversity.org.au/cs_three.pdf

2. Australia terror bill introduced, November 3, 2005. Retrieved from http://news.bbc.co.uk/2/hi/asia-pacific/4402576.stm

3. Sydney terror accused deny guilt, BBC News, http://news.bbc.co.uk/2/hi/asia-pacific/6706701.stm

4. Ex-CIA directors Porter Goss, George Tenet, and Michael Hayden publicly defended the interrogation program after the release of the Senate Intelligence Committee report. That report had concluded that the interrogation program was ineffective in producing intelligence to disrupt, capture or kill terrorists, but was responsible for serious injury, death, and permanent harm (Tenet et al., 2014).

5. We happen to know more about the Osmakac operation because Aaronson was able to obtain sealed transcripts that also inadvertently recorded confidential conversations among FBI agents.

REFERENCES

Aaronson, T. (2011). Terror trials by the numbers. *Mother Jones*. September/October.

Aaronson, T. (2013). *The Terror Factory: Inside the FBI's manufactured war on terror*. Brooklyn, NY: Ig Publishing.

Aaronson, T. (2015). How the FBI Created a Terrorist. *Democracy Now*. Retrieved from www.democracynow.org/2015/3/19/how_the_fbi_created_a_terrorist. Accessed on March 19.

Abbott, T. (2014). *The Age*, September 12, p. A1.

Amoore, L., & de Goede, M. (2008). Introduction: Governing by risk in the war on terror. In L. Amoore & M. de Goede (Eds.), *Risk and the war on terror* (pp. 5–19). Oxon: Routledge.

Australian Security Intelligence Organisation. (2014). ASIOrReport to parliament 2013–2014. Commonwealth of Australia.

Barns, G. (2014). Terrorist scaremongering threatens our democracy. *Sydney Morning Herald*. Retrieved from http://www.smh.com.au/comment/terror-scaremongering-threatens-our-democracy-20140919-10jcxq.html#ixzz3Eemg1HUC

Bateson, G. (1952). The position of humour in human communications (pp. 1–47). Paper presented at the 9th Macy Conference 1952, New York, NY.

Baudrillard, J. (2001, November 11). "L'esprit du terrorisme" *Le Monde*. In G. Borradori (Ed.), *Philosophy in a time of terror*. Chicago, IL: University of Chicago Press.

BBC News. (2005a). Australia warned of terror threat, November 2. Retrieved from http://news.bbc.co.uk/2/hi/asia-pacific/4398364.stm

BBC News. (2005b). Australia terror bill introduced, November 3. Retrieved from http://news.bbc.co.uk/2/hi/asia-pacific/4402576.stm

Berki, R. N. (1986). Security and society: Reflections on law, order and politics. Dent.

Burke, A. (2007). Beyond security, ethics and violence: War against the Other.

Buzan, B. (2000). Change and Insecurity reconsidered. In S. Croft & T. Terriff (Eds.), *Critical reflections on security and change* (pp. 1–17). London: Cass.

Cockburn, A. (2015). Why Obama's hopes of decapitating the Islamic state won't work. *Counterpunch*. 11/3. Retrieved from www.counterpunch.org/.../why-obamas-hopes-of-decapitating-the-islami...

Cole, D. (2006). Are we safer? In *The New York Review of Books*. March 9. Retrieved from www.nybooks.com/articles/archives/2006/mar/09/are-we-safer/

Corera, G. (2005). Australia arrests stir terror debate. *BBC News*, November 8. Retrieved from http://news.bbc.co.uk/2/hi/asia-pacific/4417940.stm

Crenshaw, M. (2001). Counterterrorism policy and the political process. *Studies in Conflict and Terrorism*, *24*, 329–337.

de Lint, W. (2008). The security double take: The political, simulation and the border. *Surveillance and Society: Special Issue: Smart Borders and Mobilities: Spaces, Zones and Exclusions*, *5*(2), 166–187.

de Lint, W., & Kassa, W. (2015). US counterterrorism security: Fraud, failure or fruitful spectacle. *Critical Criminology*, *23*, 349–369.

Derrida, J. (2003). Autoimmunity: Real and symbolic suicides: A dialogue with Jacques Derrida. In G. Borradori (Ed.) *Philosophy in a time of terror*. Chicago, IL: University of Chicago Press.

Foucault, M. (1972). Discourse on language. In M. Foucault (Ed.), *The archeology of knowledge*. New York, NY: Pantheon.

Fuchs, S., & Ward, S. (1994). What is deconstruction and where and when does it take place? *American Sociological Review*, *59*, 481.

Garland, D. (2001). *The culture of control. Crime and social order in contemporary society*. Chicago, IL: University of Chicago Press.

Giddens, A. (1986). Action, subjectivity, and the constitution of meaning. *Social Research*, *53*(3), 529–545.

Herman, E., & Chomsky, N. (2002). *Manufacturing consent: The political economy of the mass media*. New York, NY: Pantheon Books.

Irvine, D. (2014). ASIO Director General, *The Age*, September 12, p. A1.

Jackson, R., Smyth, M. B., & Gunning, J. (2009). The case for critical terrorism studies. In R. Jackson, M. B. Smyth, & J. Gunning (Eds.), *Critical terrorism studies: A new research agenda* (pp. 1–10). New York, NY: Routledge.

McCulloch, J., & Pickering, S. (2009). Pre crime counterterrorism: imagining future crime in the "war on terror". *British Journal of Criminology*, *49*, 628–645.

Muller, J. (2012). *Terrorism since 9/11: The American cases*. Columbus, OH: Mershon Center. Retrieved from https://edupublisher.com/EPBookstore/index.php?main_page=product_info&cPath=11&%20products_id=660&zenid=9k7a1p48uk9h917nva1hk1fqj7

Nakhaie, R. M., & de Lint, W. (2013). Security and surveillance in United States and Canadian public opinion. *International Criminal Justice Review*, *23*(2), 149–169.

National Consortium for the Study of Terrorism and Responses to Terrorism (START). (2013). *Global terrorism database* [Data file]. Retrieved from http://www.start.umd.edu/gtd

Pape, R. (2003). *Dying to win: The strategic logic of suicide terrorism*. New York, NY: Random House.

Pape, R. (2010). It's the occupation, stupid. *Foreign Policy*. Retrieved from foreignpolicy.com/2010/10/18/its-the-occupation-stupid/. Accessed on October 18.

Phillips, D. (2008). Why the American alliance should *not* be the holy grail of Australian foreign policy. *Australian Review of Public Affairs*, (July). Retrieved from http://www.australianreview.net/digest/2008/07/phillips.html

Ranstorp, M. (2009). Mapping terrorism studies after 9/11: An academic field of old problems and new prospects. In R. Jackson, M. B. Smyth, & J. Gunning (Eds.), *Critical Terrorism Studies: A new research agenda* (pp. 13–33). New York, NY: Routledge.

Requa, M. (2011). Punishing bodies, securing the nation: How rule of law can legitimate the Urbane authoritarian state. *Law & Social Inquiry*, *36*(4), 945–970.

Ruppert, M. (2012). More manufactured terrorism courtesy of the FBI. *End the Lie*. Retrieved from http://endthelie.com/2012/02/17/more-manufactured-terrorism-courtesy-of-the-fbi/#axzz2FSGO63p5

Schmidt, A., & Jongman, A. (2005). *Political terrorism: A new guide to actors, authors, concepts, data bases, theories and literature*. New Brunswick, NJ: Transaction.

Shifman, J., & Ingram, D. (2013). Exclusive: IRS manual detailed DEA's use of hidden intel evidence. *Reuters*. Retrieved from http://www.reuters.com/article/2013/08/07/us-dea-irsidUSBRE9761AZ20130807. Accessed on August 8.

Tenet, G. P., Goss, M., Hayden, J., McLaughlin, A., Calland, & Kappas, S. (2014). Ex-CIA directors: Interrogations saved lives. Wall Street Journal, December 10.

Thomas, G. (2000). *Gideon's spies: The secret history of the Mossad*. New York, NY: Dunne.

Winter, Y. (2011). The asymmetric war discourse and its moral economies: A critique. *International Theory*, *3*, 488–514.

TERROK: A HYBRID PERPETRATOR IN INDIVIDUALIZED TERRORISM WARFARE

Thomas Kron, Andreas Braun and Eva-Maria Heinke

ABSTRACT

Purpose – *This chapter looks at a new form of a hybrid perpetrator within the field of individualized political violence. We reveal, that the new thing about (transnational) terrorism overcomes current oppositions and contradictions regarding terrorists and persons running amok, which (strategically) leads to an individualization of terrorism and thereby to a hybridization of a terroristic warfare.*

Methodology/approach – *By outlining organizational and structural changes in terroristic strategy within the framework of using both modern and antimodern elements, economic thinking, acting global as well as local, and by using network structures, the individualization of terror to the point of hybrid perpetrators is presented.*

Terrorism and Counterterrorism Today
Sociology of Crime, Law and Deviance, Volume 20, 131–149

ISSN: 1521-6136/doi:10.1108/S1521-613620150000020007

Findings – *The new thing about (transnational) terrorism is the evolution of individualized perpetrators, radicalizing themselves without a clear connection to terroristic organizations. This leads to a hybridization of terroristic warfare, and within individualized single perpetrators it can be described as terrok. A terrorist running amok or a gunman on rampage with a radicalized mindset, equipped with his very individual ideology, who carries out his attacks logistically and operatively on his own while accepting his own death constitutes a new strategic way of irritating western society.*

Originality/value – *Currently, terrorists and persons running amok are separated into sharply distinguished categories. But regarding new tendencies in terroristic attacks committed by single perpetrators, this separation seems to be no longer able to capture the individualization of terrorism and thereby the linked hybridization of a terroristic warfare adequately. But in combining findings from both approaches, the new concept of terrok is able to do so.*

Keywords: Transnational terrorism; individualization; terror; amok; hybridization

INTRODUCTION

By terrorists, one usually understands actors who commit planned attacks that are part of a certain strategy aiming to provoke the government through means of repeated, credible, and systematically planned threats and/or use of violence in order to excite reactions which serve to fulfill their own political ambitions (Neumann & Smith, 2008; Steinhoff, 2005). Furthermore, terrorist attacks are often traced back to a collective responsibility, even though they were committed by a single actor. These lone perpetrators, even if they are defined as individual terrorists, are in this sense identical to a terrorist group and its ideology. This classical understanding of a group membership or an organizational affiliation of a terrorist is both part of the history and the defining criteria in politics and science[1] and is still up to date in defining terrorism, drawing a sharp distinction in categorizing elements of warfare at the same time: that is, conventional war or guerilla fights as opposed to terrorism (Hoffman, 2006; Schmid, 2011; Waldmann, 2005): Here the main differences for the creation of the distinction are based on the size of combat units (ranging from very large in a conventional war, to medium numbered units in a guerilla-fight, to small groupings of less than 10 fighters in a terroristic group), the goals (in a conventional war and in a guerilla-fight are mainly military objectives, whilst in the case of terrorism it is mostly state symbols and the public), the aspired purposes (in a conventional war: physical destruction, in a guerilla-fight: attrition of the enemy and in the case of terrorism: a political aim), as well as the final/important question of territorial control (which is the main aim of a conventional war and a guerilla-fight, whereas in the case of terrorism, this objective is secondary).

Recently, however, such classifications have been increasingly criticized, summarized by the term "fourth-generation-warfare" (Schmid, 2011). Like Beck (2004, 2007) pointed out, such clear-cut definitions and classifications are becoming less important due to the societal development in times of globalization and transnationalization. This has become recognizable in the guerilla-fighters who control a certain occupied territory with strategies that are genuinely classified terroristic; or by the terrorists who use criminal structures or guerilla tactics in order to maintain their organization, such as the Tamil Tigers (LTTE) in Sri Lanka, who controlled large swathes of territory and committed terrorist acts in the territory controlled by the Sri Lankan Government.

According to Beck, we want to broaden the following thesis: The new thing about (transnational) terrorism, taking place in a globalized world, is the overcoming of oppositions and contradictions, which, strategically leads to an *individualization of terrorism* and thereby to a hybridization of terroristic warfare. The *new terrorism* increasingly operates as a kind of *hybrid*, which we will describe in terms of *terrok*. A *terrok*, the fusion of a classical *terr*orist and am*ok* runner, is a single perpetrator – like a lone wolf – but creates his own ideological interpretations based on already existing radical ideologies or by deviating from and sometimes even overstating these. This evolutionary tendency and the rise of *terrok* as a hybrid can empirically be stated on singular cases like the Frankfurt airport perpetrator Arid Uka, the Toulouse perpetrator Mohammed Merah, or – the probably most prominent case – the Oslo/Utøya perpetrator Anders B. Breivik. And probably the latest attack on Charlie Hebdo in Paris features hints referring to this.

To establish our thesis, we outline organizational and structural changes in terroristic strategy on the example of al-Qaida as a prototype of transnational terrorism. Based on this we further point to aspects of individualization of terrorism, before we identify *terrok* as the new form of a hybrid terroristic warfare resulting from these developments.

THE EVOLUTION OF TERRORISTIC STRATEGY

Since 9/11 it has often been asserted that there is a *new form of terrorism* (Schneckener, 2006). Following the current state of research this new form can be described based on the following features: an upward trend of religious motivation, hybrid forms of organization, an increasing potential of destruction (staged by the media), a concept of enemy which is centered on Western Europe and the United States of America (USA), and the possible extension of the international toward a transnational orientation. Framed by this, scientific and political approaches to explain terrorism are often using dichotomizations that try to reduce the complexity of this phenomenon in order to deal with it more easily, as is reflected, for example, in the strategy of US counterterrorism. Therefore, the US government has resorted to the clear-cut definition of war, which is characterized by the dichotomous distinction between friend and enemy, after the attacks of 11 September: "war on terrorism" is the slogan. Those who are not in favor of America are, according to the former President *George W. Bush*, in favor of the terrorists. Either-or, *tertium non datur*. In order to simulate political power, old categories were applied to the new phenomenon, thus producing a political subject (an enemy) and hence producing political order – not indeed a nice order but at least a manageable order (of war; Nassehi, 2002, p. 179). Furthermore, science supports this political reaction, likewise resorting to bivalent distinctions to analyze the phenomenon. These features are certainly not wrong, but they miss a central point: an evolutionary process attended by an overcoming of oppositions and contradictions, like Beck (2007) pointed out with regard to the development of modern society. And in this context, the thesis of individualization of terrorism as the new thing in the evolution of terrorism is due to the contradiction blurring process of gradual vagueness, when terrorists use strategic elements and conduct operations which are, to a certain degree, opposed to their own ideology in a globalized, transnational world:

> The borderline between the duals: war and peace, civil society and military, enemy and friend, war and crime, military and police, which seem to be clear from an anthropological point of view, are becoming blurred. [...] The either-or is replaced by a 'both-and' – both war and peace, both police and military, both crime and war, both civilian and soldier. (Beck, 2004, pp. 199–206)

This exactly characterizes the "post-national war": "The vanishing of basic distinctions which constitutes interstate wars" (Beck, 2004, p. 206). In this perspective, terrorists increasingly operate as a kind of "hybrid," which does not match the established societal and scientific categorizations (see Kron, 2007, 2009, 2015). This, thus, first and foremost, contradicts the idea that terrorists generally tend to dichotomize.[2]

So, what is disregarded in the *redefinition of terrorism* (Hoffman, 2006) is the fact that transnational terrorism, like the terrorism of al-Qaida, has overcome categorical dichotomies. The following exemplary pairs of opposites, applied in the new terrorism debate, illustrate the mentioned overcoming of oppositions and contradictions above.

Terrorism as Modern Antimodernism

The new terrorism is often seen in opposition to western modernity and contrasted with the jihad of the "McWorld" (Barber, 1996). Here we find the first overcoming. From our point of view, transnational terrorism should rather be understood as a *modern antimodernism* (Beck, 2004), in which both modern *and* antimodern elements constitute a realm of ideas. Terror as a foil for comparison generates the continuous dynamism of modernity, or in other words: the evolutionary logic of modernity is related to the horror, the "fear" of disorder (Jain, 2003, p. 34). One could even refer to modernity as being born from the spirit of terror, considering the fact that the term terrorism appeared for the first time during the French Revolution and had positive connotations back then. The *régime de la terreur* was an instrument of power against nongovernmental and substate organizations, understood as a means of establishing democracy in revolutionary phases and hence at the same time an expression of virtue as the main source of a popular government and justice. Back then as well as today, terror is an instrument, which is organized, purposeful, and strategically deployed, legitimized by the creation of a better society. This is precisely what constitutes the activist momentum of modern society: the compulsion to actively engage and to directly influence the real world in order to realize the potential of what is morally required and justifiable (Münch, 1995, pp. 15). Similar to western modernity, for example, bin-Laden's world view also included the intention to fulfill moral guidelines – in this case given by divine revelation instead of reason – in terrestrial life, such as the replacement of "corrupt" political leaders by "well managed" princes (Kepel, 2004, p. 101). If terrorism is regarded as a specific form of instrumental activism, it is not surprising that terrorism is compatible with the use of modern communication technology and weaponry. Modern terrorism began with the discovery of dynamite (Laqueur, 2001, p. 74; Townshend, 2005, p. 37; Waldmann, 2005, p. 55), a technical device that impacts upon the social order. By using modern technologies, terrorism demonstrates the violability of modernity and is at the same time a highly modern phenomenon due to the increasing exploitation of the human environment (Sloterdijk, 2002, p. 26). Terror – including "negative air-conditioning" (Sloterdijk, 2004, p. 126) in high-rise buildings produced by fueled airplanes – is used as a means to point to modern values such as human rights, provided that the dead from the World-Trade-Center should (e.g.) directly allude to the Palestinian women and children that have been killed!

Economic Jihad

The *modern anti-modernity*, which al-Qaida represents, is among other things specified by the strategic use of western capitalist economy, also after the attack on the WTC as an attempt to weaken the United States and the global economy. For instance, Osama bin-Laden had stressed the significance of economic superiority within terrorist strategies in a video message from 2002, by explaining, that he would attack the interests of the American economy if the oppression in the Muslim countries was not stopped. Such an economic utility calculation is only recently being highlighted, even if there had not actually been any attacks. That is, threatening or anticipating attacks should provoke countermeasures, which have to be financed. Thus, parcel bombs, which should be sent to the USA from Yemen via Cologne/Bonn in 2010, were highly effective considering the increased safety measures for the control of cargo.

In a special edition of al-Qaida's own magazine *Inspire*, the headline read "$4,200" (Ibrahim, 2010). This was the cost of the attempted attacks, the so-called "Operation Hemorrhage," which, as its name suggests, aimed at achieving the bleeding of the enemy. It was a deliberate attack directed against the US American and European economies. It has been made clear that there is no longer a need for great attacks like those of 9/11 in order to weaken America's economy but smaller and more frequent attacks are found to be much more effective, which is known as the *strategy of thousands cuts*. This strategy adjustment, says Ibrahim (2010), leads to a high degree of efficiency in order to incapacitate the enemy. "This is what we call leverage. A $4,200 operation will cost our enemy billions of dollars." When speaking of a *judo-strategy* (Fromkin, 1977), which involves utilizing an opponent's own force against him through efficient and effective movements in order to bring him down, this fundamental idea has been translated into operational and strategic terms here. Al-Qaida has adjusted its strategy to the war on terrorism by developing it into an economic war. What is a defensive warfare (jihad) from the terrorist viewpoint is now economically implemented – the *economic jihad.*

So, recently, there are certain indications that terrorist outfits are using the capitalist economy systematically in order to weaken the west financially and to realize their own political goal. This detour of terror should hit the western economic and financial system, since this complex is globally networked and very sensible. Furthermore, it is easily influenced even by relatively slight commotions. However, all western states involved are concerned with the consequences due to economic globalization and the corresponding interdependence. To sum up, planned attacks on the western economy are an essential part of the terrorist strategy (Schäfer, 2011).

The Overcoming of Globality and Locality

Besides the use of the western capitalist economy as one part of the overcoming of modernity and premodernity, the overcoming of western bivalent ways of thinking in al-Qaida's strategy is also reflected in the question, whether the enemy of modern terrorism is internal or external. Overcoming the opposition of interior and exterior is in line with overcoming the opposition of near and far. The everyday notion in Germany not long ago was that Islamic terrorists are to be found in distant places, and that attacks were the only reason for them to approach. People thus hoped they could be able to prevent the attacks by strengthening the borders between near and far, establishing rigid asylum policy, or tight control at airports, train stations, or frontiers for example. What was overlooked was the new profile of the *homegrown terrorist* (Theveßen, 2005). In Germany, this became obvious only in 2006 when bomb attacks on regional trains failed only for technical reasons, or when the so-called *Sauerland group* was arrested in 2007 and convicted by court in 2010. In 2011, another homegrown terror cell was found in Düsseldorf, where alleged al-Qaida members who were blamed for having planned terror acts on major German cities were arrested.

Prevented as well as realized terror attacks such as 9/11 or London 2005 show that terrorism is *near and far at the same time*: Terrorists are near because they were socialized in western society and cannot be habitually distinguished from other citizens. At the same time, they are far because they do not consider themselves as a part of this society. Though they are not indoctrinated from an early age to be a suicide bomber like in Palestine, they have come to their personal conclusion that other forms of social systems are better than the western democratic society. *Terrorist sleepers* (Theveßen, 2002) seem to be adapted to society but are living in a kind of a parallel society, which does not respect values or rights of the western society.

The most important medium for the overcoming of contrasts of local and global and near and far is the internet. An advantage of this medium is the nearly anonymous and quite safe high-speed information brokerage via chat-rooms or by saving massages in draft folders of e-mail accounts. The decisive step was al-Qaida's major use of the previously mentioned medium. The control over who gets to read its material – ideological programs, technical instructions, rules of behavior, etc. – was purposely open to public and along with that the decentralization of authority was supported. Finally, a process was triggered that neither Bin Laden himself nor any other al-Qaida leader could stop. Attacks can be prepared via internet in the sense of a virtual planning, places can be spied out without physical presence, and tactics can be arranged and uploaded videos serve as propaganda. So: "the World Wide Web has become a part of al-Qaida's mutated DNA" (Musharbash, 2006).

Individualization by Network Structuring

The overcoming of globality and locality is highly relevant for the assumption of the individualization of terrorism, since terror organizations like al-Qaida have changed from being a strictly hierarchical organization to being a scale-free small world network by means of the internet.[3] It is this change in particular which paved the way for an individualization of terrorism.

For instance, after the US's interventions in Afghanistan and the hereby linked destruction of training camps during the military interventions, al-Qaida was not able to maintain its organizational structure. Al-Qaida's *adaptive response* (in terms of mutual adjustment) was the opening of its organizational structures, the characteristic feature of which is the overcoming of the opposition between globality and locality. This is achieved by generating autonomous terrorist cells which, to a certain degree, are subject to a line of command (high clustering of networks), combined with communicative links between internationally distributed cells, presuming thereby small distances within the terrorist network. Al-Qaida can thus be described as an organization that crosses boundaries, that cannot be localized (Hirschmann, 2001). It is established in transnational social spaces, which do not have a clear point of reference, because this kind of organization is "fluid, processual and aterritorial. It is neither presupposed nor given, but constructed-in-going-along" (Knorr Cetina, 2005).

Taking this into consideration, the dispute about the question, whether al-Qaida relies on a *leaderless jihad* (Sageman, 2007) or still possesses a superordinate command structure, could be defused. Our answer is: *as well as*, because the scale-free small-word network contains both. Some terror candidates are still chosen by al-Qaida leaders, and are consequently subject to their command. On the other hand, this may become less frequent, especially since the strategy deployed by Barack Obama involving U.S. tactical realignment of the targeted persecution and killing of suspected terrorists and supporters by increasing drone missions ensures that the al-Qaida leadership is under permanent pressure. In this spirit, homegrown terrorists, who radicalize themselves and organize attacks within western society, have recently become the focus of attention and therefore this development of organizational network structures is a key point referring to the individualization of terrorism.

THE INDIVIDUALIZATION OF TERROR

By overcoming the dichotomy of collective versus individual, due to the implementation of jihad in the individual process of socialization, the foundation of jihad still remains collectivist in the sense of an ideological instruction. But jihad is now increasingly practiced individualistically: young Muslims "are inspired by international sensations creating thus their own jihad" (Theveßen, 2005, p. 80). So al-Qaida's ideology develops toward a "Do-it-yourself-Dschihad" (Theveßen, 2005, p. 127), carried out by the "Mudschaheddin" (Musharbash, 2006, p. 89).

In this jihad practice, individualism and collectivism merge into one another, since the individual exercise and interpretation of the jihad is only of significance if it is exercised for the benefit of the collective. Thus, by means of this construction and by declaring the jihad first as an individual and then, when the critical number of actors is reached, which is a collective duty, the problem of the jihadists' critical mass is also solved (Saghi, 2006).

Going along with the use of the internet, terrorists are taking on a classical terror career to a lesser extent, which means that they are less embedded in Islamic groups and do not receive a specified terrorist education. Rather, they are raised in western society and develop as activists by sympathizing with the terrorist ideology. The abolishment of the distinction between the individual and collective comes along with the blurring of the distinction between the sympathizer and activist. The reason for this is the liberalization of concrete rules for membership. By means of the internet, actors are able to transform into a one-man terror cell, developing from an interested person to an activist in a short time span, and thereby crossing the borderline between interest and self-organized active terrorism by means of web-based advanced educational programs. This shows a certain deprofessionalization of terrorism. One might call this an upcoming amateur terrorism, which, in turn, increases the status of those activists with leadership capacities. They can call themselves elite, which in the jihad ideology supports the idea that an elite has to found a religious community (like al-Qaida), then emigrate from the unholy environment, picking up the fight with the enemy to finally reintroduce Islam. This results in having to be aware of the fact that, since each elimination makes room for other actors to gain an elite status, there might be successors of bin-Laden and al-Awlaki. A further consequence is that there will be more potential terrorists, who are difficult to be distinguished from nonactive terrorists, complicating the prevention of terrorist attacks. The "golden rule of terrorism" to provoke as much attention and reactions as possible the with least effort seems to have worked out perfectly fine in those cases, in which single actors claim to be terror cells, closely related to al-Qaida. They generate fear in a part of the population by only announcing terrorist attacks (Musharbash, 2006, p. 139).

TERROK: A HYBRID PERPETRATOR IN INDIVIDUALIZED TERRORISM WARFARE

Regarding the so far presented evolutionary elements of the terroristic strategy, the hereby caused structural individualization can be seen as a fundamental part, meaning that al-Qaida recommends potential activists to act as individual terrorists as Chief strategy officer Abu Mus'Ab al-Suri (2010, p. 31, 2011, p. 29) pointed out by speaking of "Individual Terrorism Jihad":

> The conclusion which we have arrived at now, is: That the basic axis of the Resistance's military activity against America and her allies now, must lie within the framework of 'light guerilla warfare', 'civilian terror' and secret methods, especially on the level of

> individual operations and small Resistance Units completely and totally separated from each other.

And this conclusion can be strengthened with Al-Awlaki's own-developed 1% doctrine – a term which was actually coined by the former US Vice President Dick Cheney and with which he expresses that even a danger of only 1% for the USA should be treated as a potential threat. If there was, for instance, a 1% probability of weapons of mass destruction in the possession of al-Qaida, one would have to act as if it was already a fact. The following imperative – "Act as soon as the probability amounts to just 1%" – has been used by al-Awlaki, being a good example for the mutual adaption. Since there is always a 1% possibility that western secret services discover single members of a cell, and thereby are able to remove the entire group, it is necessary to act as an individual terrorist:

> Group operations have a greater tendency of failing than lone operations due to the idea of the operation escaping the mind and tongue to other individuals. Even if those individuals are trustworthy in your eyes, there is still that 1% chance that someone from the intelligence agencies are listening in and paying attention to your groups' actions or that the person you are talking to might be working for the enemy or that he might be pressured at a later period to give information to them. With lone operations, however, as long as you keep it to yourself, nobody in the world would know what you're thinking and planning. That's why individuals [...] have been successful, even if they were ultimately arrested. The fact that they were able to pull off their operations without being halted by authorities is a great success. (al-Awlaki, 2011, p. 11)

Al-Qaida, one might say, now calls for realization of attacks by individualists.

Putting this development into account, recent research differentiates between four versions of individual terrorists (Pantucci, 2011): First, there is the "*lone wolf pack*": individual actors who, using al-Qaida's ideology, radicalize themselves within a group and plan attacks autonomously, without being in contact with operationally active al-Qaida members. These include, for instance, Jihad Hamad and Youssef el Hajdib, who deposited bombs in regional trains at Cologne's central train station in 2006. The missing contact to al-Qaida was probably the reason for the flawed design of the bombs, which, in fact, did not explode. Secondly, there are the *lone attackers* who operate alone but are in direct contact with al-Qaida activists, being thereby provided with instructions concerning the attack. An example of this is Richard Reid, who was radicalized in prison, returned to Afghanistan in September 2011, and he tried to blow up a commercial flight with the support of al-Qaida. Third, there are the so-called "*lone wolfs*" who organize attacks autonomously like the lone attackers but with less contact with al-Qaida activists. Here, internet contacts do exist as well but do not exert operational influence on the actual attack – like in the case of Nidal Malik Hassan who, as a US army officer, killed 12 soldiers as well as one civilian and injured several people in 2009, being in contact with al-Qaida. And finally, there is the "*loner*" who organizes single attacks, following the Islamic ideology in the absence of collectively organized operation, like Mohammed Ali Hedayat who opened fire on travelers at a ticket counter of El Al Airlines in Los Angeles in 2002, killing two people and injuring several others.

At this point, we would like to introduce a new, even more radical type of a single terrorist actor, which we call *terrok* – corresponding to the concept of a lone terrorist and a person running amok. This type is a loner, too, with the exception that he also creates his own ideological interpretations. Not only does he walk alone, like the loner/lone wolf, he also thinks alone, like the prototypical amok perpetrator. He can do this by referring to already existing ideologies or by deviating from and sometimes even overstating these, which possibly becomes relevant for the nature of the attack. We would like to emphasize that the individual terrorist is, one might say, the consistent continuation of the terrorist strategy of the economic jihad. The conjunctive alone can cause a race to the bottom. This is precisely what individual terrorists can make use of. Due to the anticipated expectations that go along with an attack it is possible that a single attack on a high-level company in the stock exchange can lead to a great loss of money in the financial market, and due to the near-zero potential of prevention, the general uncertainty of the collective consciousness and the lacking compensation, *the sole-terroristic suicide attack is the symbol of the uncertainty of expectation.*

Research is so far hardly prepared for dealing with the individual terrorist. One reason is that (in order to be able to deal with the individual terrorist) two so far separated scientific discourses would have to be combined, because the sole terrorist, who results from the strategic development of terrorism, is a hybrid of a terrorist and a person running amok. Thus, it will be necessary to investigate running amok and terrorism at the same time and in combination. While killing sprees have hardly been taken into account in previous terrorism research, scientific research characterizes killing sprees as acts of individual violence committed by individual/lone actors within public places, for the most part in urban regions and within institutions of administration or other big institutions, and, recently, often at schools or universities. The act results in the killing or injury of several people, who are selected for symbolic reasons as well (Adler, 2002; de

Becker, 1998; Hoffmann, 2003; Robertz, 2004). The typical person running amok is motivated mainly by hurtful experiences, predominantly revenge motives within the private or professional sector, whereas political or ideological motivations are quite rare (Adler, 2000; Schmidtke, Imke Müller, Lester, & Sack, 2002). Victims are accordingly those persons who are held responsible for the preceding motif. In contrast to the classical terrorist, who belongs to a certain group, the person running amok is mainly an individual actor. For a long time, persons running amok have been regarded as a "social irreality" (Vogl, 2010), as an individual manifestation of civilly dysfunctional barbarism in modern societies, which are surprised by these demotivated spontaneous acts (Adler, 2000, 2002, p. 72; Christians, 2008; Spores, 1988). Now, persons running amok will have to be considered in terrorism research, assuming that the diagnosis of the sole terrorist is correct. The structural basis for the individualization of terrorism is the described development toward a network structure, going along with broadly abdicating the control of a membership in al-Qaida. Becoming a terrorist can thus be realized in the sense of a *self-starter*. Here, like in the case of a person running amok, an individually suffered mortification,[4] which also can be an expression of a Robin Hood perspective within global relative deprivation (Reddig, 2007) in place of mortification within the family, is enough for this.[5]

Terrok illustrated a new step in terrorisms strategic evolution. Nobody imagined that there would be empirical implementations beyond radical Islamic motivations of the new social figure so quickly. Although the acts of Anders B. Breivik can of course not be linked with al-Qaida or the new Islamic terrorism, he still can be considered as an ideal type of the individual terrorist in the sense of *terrok*. On 22nd July 2011, Breivik carried out a bomb attack in Oslo and then ran amok in a summer camp on the island Utøya, where 77 people were killed and further 30 people were injured. On the one hand, this was clearly a terrorist attack. Striking is the tactic of the simultaneous attacks: first of all, Breivik could cause a 500 kg explosive device to explode in the Oslo government. After the detonation, he went to the summer camp of the Norwegian Labour Party with approximately 600–700 teenagers on Utøya and used the bomb explosion as a pretext to be ferried to the island and to shoot at the teenagers. This, in turn, shows all the characteristics of a killing spree: armed with an automatic rifle and a gun, he systematically kills 69 young people. Breivik commits these acts as an individual terrorist – up to now, there is no evidence showing that there have been links to accomplices or any other terrorist cells. His motivation can be attributed to a radical nationalistic attitude. Within this framework, he feared a European collusion in the sense of an alliance between European states and Islamic states (or rather the Islam itself), and due to the internationally widespread multicultural attitude he feared a "eurabic union." A political goal of his attacks was to take a stand against this development, pointing out this "problem" to the world. For this reason, his victims were members of the Norwegian Labor Party who, in his view, represented the multicultural replacement of national (Norwegian) values due to their immigration policy. Here, terrorist attitude and characteristics of a killing spree are being mixed. The preparation, however, rather reminds of a terrorist attack. In total, a planning period of 9 years can be reconstructed.[6] Also the ideological indoctrination is technically rather reminiscent of radical Islamists than of persons running amok; almost impressive is the manuscript "2083: A European Declaration of Independence," which was written by him and formed the basis of his actions. In the document of 1,500 pages, he lays down his political and moral attitude toward the introduction of a "cultural conservative revolution."

Again: although Breivik's acts cannot be linked with al-Qaida or Islamic terrorism – due to the fact that Breiviks fight is directed against Muslims – he can be still seen as the prototype of terrok; at least indirectly influencing other individuals in committing such new terroristic attacks in the sense of the strategic evolution. At least parallels can be drawn if one regards the Islamic-motivated terror attacks of Arid Uka in Germany and Mohammed Merah in France.

On the 2nd March 2011 the 21-year-old Arid Uka killed two and also injured two US soldiers in front of terminal 2 of the airport Frankfurt am Main. The evening before, he had seen a video sequence out of a movie on you tube, which shows the rape of a Moslem woman as well as her murder and the murder of her family – Uka claimed this sequence to be real. This video was the trigger for the crime, as Uka stated in later interrogations. Shocked by the content of this sequence, he decided to retaliate on American soldiers with the aim of killing as many of them as possible, punishing them for the crimes in Afghanistan and Iraq, which he had seen. The analysis of his computer and his Facebook profile reveals that two weeks before committing the crime, Uka, who was registered on Facebook under his battle name "Abu Reyyan," had 140 new Facebook contacts, which included militant radical Islamists, such as the Moroccan Salafist Sheikh Abdellatif, who is known by German authorities.[7]

The 23-year-old Mohammed Merah killed in sum seven people and injured three more during his several target-oriented attacks. On 11th March 2012 he killed a soldier of the French Army in Toulouse (1 Dead) and two more soldiers in Montauban on 15th March 2012, while another one was heavily injured. Also on 19th March he shot a teacher and two of his children as well as another pupil of a Jewish school in Toulouse, before he was shot by French Police Special Forces on 20th March 2012 while he tried to leave his surrounded apartment; during this police deployment he also injured two police officers. Although Merah has visited Afghanistan and Pakistan there are no signs that he has passed training camps, studied at a religious university, or has taken part in terroristic actions before, like Nicolas Sarkozy summed up the result of determination in a public speech. Following Sarkozy's speech, Mohammed Merah was not a member of a terroristic cell, but has radicalized himself via the internet and wanted to attack the French Republic.[8] Eventually, an additional influence regarding his radicalization can be linked with Merahs time in a French jail; this is also assumed to be the case with Chérif Kouachi – one of the Charlie Hebdo perpetrators.

Beside this speculation, it can be stated that both, Uka and Merah, had an ideological fundamental Islamic background on the basis of self-radicalization via the internet and without direct group contacts and memberships and both acted as individualized terrorists.

And also with respect to the latest events in Paris, the attack on Charlie Hebdo seems to show similarities with the single and self-radicalized perpetrators named above – at least following the thitherto news reports.

Although the attacks on Charlie Hebdo cannot be seen as a *pure* form of *terrok*, we would say that the attacks show at least a certain *gradual membership* to our established concept. This refers primarily to the course of action: First of all, Said and Cheri Kouachi as well as Amedy Coulibaly targeted specific buildings (publishing houses, supermarkets) and did not randomly target symbolic western institutions. Secondly they use firearms instead of bombs or other explosive devices to kill specific people (satirist, Jews, policewomen) – the target-oriented assault especially on the graphic artists, whose names and presence were asked before committing the shooting at Charlie Hebdo, can rather be seen as an act of rampage killing instead of terrorism. And at last, they try to escape and do not kill themselves as a part of the attacks; so they were not acting like suicide bombers. Of course one could counter referring to our definition above that they have been indoctrinated by Islamist views and did not create their own ideological opinion as, for example, Anders Breivik, Uka, and Merah. On the one hand this may be right, but on the other hand we would argue that the ideological frame of these attacks shows features of a new one insofar as well as al-Qaida and the Islamic State *together* build the ideological background of the three terrorists. Two terrorist groups, haven't been cooperating in the last years, but on the contrary have been hostile toward each other beginning with the imbroglio of Osama bin Laden and Abu Mus'ab az-Zarqawi.

CONCLUSION

A terrorist running amok or a gunman with a radicalized mindset, equipped with his very individual ideology, who carries out his attacks logistically and operatively on his own while accepting his own death, is a new form of terrorism, which originally seems to be used by al-Qaida as a strategic element. Up to now, this phenomenon is difficult to grasp, because (in everyday life, politics and science) terrorists and persons running amok are separated into sharply distinguished categories. For example, taking a look at the BILD's headline, you could come across the idea that there have been two different events in Norway on this day: a "massacre by a person running amok" and a "terrorist attack." Attacks carried out by such *clean face perpetrators* (Musharbash, 2006), that is to say a civilian who appears to be integrated well in society, are difficult to prevent by secret services without the support of civil society, since *terroks* do not communicate in advance. Of course, a *terrok* is not able to carry out an attack like 9/11 all by himself – at least not with planes.[9] But does this mean that attacks with extensive damage are impossible to be realized by such individual terrorists? This question has to be answered in the negative: On the one hand, *terroks*, too, are able to carry out simultaneous attacks and ignite several bombs within the same period of time, as was the case in Madrid. On the other hand, *terroks* can cause great damage if they kill themselves with a dirty bomb at a central location or if they infect themselves with a virus of high infection and high mortality rate, combined with an incubation period that is not too short.[10] Above all, however, such lone terrorists, as well as loners and lone wolves, can organize small attacks – pinpricks – which, too, like great attacks, irritate western society.

NOTES

1. This is already applied for the Jewish fanatics (ultra nationalists) in Palestine who constituted the sociohistorical background of terrorism and violently rebelled

against Roman rule, poisoned fountains and granaries of the Romans, attacked the water supply of Jerusalem (Hoffman, 2006, p. 140), and ambushed their victims – Romans as well as moderate Jews in public (Waldmann, 2005, p. 126).

2. See, for example, Waldmann (2005, p. 214): "The tendency towards black-and-white attitudes [...] is typical of most organizations."

3. The small-world network model (Watts, 2003) describes a specific organizational form that allows a signal dispersion and synchronization of high speed work in dynamic systems – a characteristic which becomes particularly relevant concerning the phenomenon of swarming, which means that several attacks are committed simultaneously – a typical characteristic of al-Qaida's attacks.

4. For more details, see Todenhöfer's striking report from 2008.

5. Occasionally, also suicide attackers are diagnosed with a "collective narcissistic slight [...], which is, on the way towards a suicidal narcissistic extreme reaction, compensated by an act of violence." (Kahre, 2002)

6. Already in 2002 (until ca. 2006), Breivik began to establish a capital basis (in total approx. 400,000–500,000€) for the realization of his plan. His intensive research and writing of a manuscript (2006–2010), on the one hand, and the operative preparation for both attacks (2009–2011), on the other hand, took place over different periods of time. The operative phase began in August 2009 when he set up his own company "Geofarm," which enabled him to provide himself with six tons of artificial fertilizer and other chemicals for the construction of the explosive device (since October 2010). For the "production" of the explosive device he bought a farmland. Also in August, he dealt with the investigation and purchase of guns that he used. The successful completion of a one-week hunting class enabled him to purchase a small caliber rapid fire gun in September 2010. In order to be able to carry the second gun, he had to be a member of a gun club, since the Norwegian national weapons legislation includes stricter regulations for the purchase of pistols than for hunting weapons. On the one hand, this preparation reminds of the killing sprees, such as in Emstetten in 2006 and Erfurt in 2002. On the other hand, however, it reminds of terrorist training camps, in which weapon skills are acquired as well. Breivik, who already has been a member of a gun club from 2005 until 2007, joined the club in June 2010 again and completed 13 to 15 training sessions with the pistol from November 2010 until January 2011, thus obtaining permission to purchase the Glock 17 in January 2011. From December 2010 to January 2011, he completed three further training sessions with his rapid fire gun. In this period, he acquired further equipment for his guns, such as a sighting telescope, a laser marker, a magazine of 30 bullets, and ammunition.

7. The informations of Uka used here are based on the released print of the press conference of the "Generalbundesanwalt" in Germany and an international media research referring to the attack.

8. The informations of Merah used here are based on an international news and media research referring to the attack.

9. Unless this is about model airplanes loaded with explosives. Such planned attacks were prevented in the USA in 2011.

10. To cite an example the so-called Marburg virus has a mortality rate of up to 90% and an incubation period of five to ten days, being enough to visit almost all airports in Europe within only a few hours.

REFERENCES

Adler, L. (2000). *Amok*. München: Belleville.

Adler, L. (2002). Amok im spektrum Homizidal-suizidale Handlungen. In M. Wolfersdorf & H. Wedler (Eds.), *Terroristen-Suizide und Amok* (pp. 71–85). Regensburg: Roderer.

al-Awlaki, A. (2011). Inspire responses. *Inspire*, *5*, 9–12.

al-Suri, A. M. (2010). The Jihad experiences. *Inspire*, *1431*, 31–35.

al-Suri, A. M. (2011). The Jihadi experiences. *Inspire*, *5*, 29–32.

Barber, B. (1996). *Jihad vs. Mc world*. New York, NY: Ballantine Books.

Beck, U. (2004). *Der kosmopolitische Blick oder: Krieg ist Frieden*. Frankfurt/Main: Suhrkamp.

Beck, U. (2007). *Weltrisikogesellschaft*. Frankfurt/Main: Suhrkamp.

Christians, H. (2008). *Amok. Geschichte einer Ausbreitung*. Bielefeld: Aisthesis.

de Becker, G. (1998). *The gift of fear. Survival signals that protect Us from violence*. New York, NY: Dell Publishing Company.

Fromkin, D. (1977). Die Strategie der Terrorismus. In M. Funke (Ed.), *Terrorismus* (pp. 83–99). Bonn: Landeszentrale für politische Bildung.

Hirschmann, K. (2001). Terrorismus in neuen Dimensionen. Hintergründe und Schlussfolgerungen. *Aus Politik und Zeitgeschichte*, *B 51*, 7–15.

Hoffman, B. (2006). *Terrorismus – der unerklärte Krieg. Neue Gefahren politischer Gewalt*. Bonn: Fischer Taschenbuch Verlag.

Hoffmann, J. (2003). Amok – ein neuer Blick auf ein altes Phänomen. In C. Lorei (Ed.), *Polizei & Psychologie* (pp. 397–414). Frankfurt/Main: Verlag für Polizeiwissenschaft.

Ibrahim, Y. (2010). $4,200. *Inspire*, 1431, 15.

Jain, A. (2003). "Terror" oder die Normalität des Schreckens. In R. Hitzler & J. Reichertz (Eds.), *Irritierte Ordnung* (pp. 31–49). Konstanz: UVK.

Kepel, G. (2004). *Die neuen Kreuzzüge*. München: Piper.

Knorr Cetina, K. (2005). Complex global microstructures. *Theory, Culture & Society*, *22*(5), 213–234.

Kron, T. (2007). Fuzzy-terrorism. In T. Kron & M. Reddig (Eds.), *Analysen des transnationalen Terrorismus* (pp. 84–121). Wiesbaden: VS.

Kron, T. (2009). Reflexive Modernisierung und die Überwindung kategorialer Dichotomien des Terrorismus. *Schweizerische Zeitschrift für Soziologie*, *1*, 117–136.

Kron, T. (2015). *Reflexiver Terrorismus*. Weilerswist: Velbrück Wissenschaft.

Laqueur, W. (2001). Left, right, and beyond. The changing face of terror. In J. Hodge & G. Rose (Eds.), *How did this happen? Terrorism and the New War* (pp. 70–82). New York, NY: Public Affairs.

Münch, R. (1995). *Dynamik der Kommunikationsgesellschaft*. Frankfurt/Main: Suhrkamp.

Musharbash, Y. (2006). Die neue al-Qaida. Innenansichten eines lernenden Terrornetzwerks. Bonn: Kiepenheuer & Witsch.

Nassehi, A. (2002). Der Erste Welt-Krieg. In D. Baecker, P. Krieg, & F. Simon (Eds.), *Terror im system* (pp. 175–200). Heidelberg: Carl-Auer-Systeme Verlag.

Neumann, P. R., & Smith, M. L. R. (2008). *The strategy of terrorism. How it works. and why it fails*. New York, NY: Routledge.

Pantucci, R. (2011). *A typology of Lone Wolves*. London: ICSR.

Reddig, M. (2007). Deprivation, Globalisierung und globaler Dschihad. In T. Kron & M. Reddig (Eds.), *Analysen des transnationalen Terrorismus* (pp. 280–309). Wiesbaden: VS.

Robertz, F. J. (2004). *School shootings. Über die Relevanz der Phantasie für die Begehung von Mehrfachtötungen durch Jugendliche*. Frankfurt/Main: Verlag für Polizeiwissenschaft.

Sageman, M. (2007). *Leaderless Jihad: Terror networks in the twenty-first century*. Philadelphia, PA: University of Pennsylvania Press.

Saghi, O. (2006). Osama Bin Laden Volkstribun im Medienzeitalter. In G. Keppel & J.-P. Milelli (Eds.), *Texte des Terrors* (pp. 25–54). München, Zürich: Piper.

Schäfer, U. (2011). *Der Angriff*. Frankfurt/Main: Campus Verlag.

Schmid, A. P. (Ed.). (2011). *The Routledge Handbook of terrorism research*. London: Taylor & Francis Ltd.

Schmidtke, A., Imke Müller, S., Lester, D., & Sack, S. (2002). Imitation von Amok und Suizid. In M. Wolfersdorf & H. Wedler (Eds.), *Terroristen-Suizide und Amok* (pp. 86–109). Regensburg: Roderer.

Schneckener, U. (2006). *Transnationaler Terrorismus. Charakter und Hintergründe des „neuen" Terrorismus*. Frankfurt/Main: Suhrkamp.

Sloterdijk, P. (2002). *Luftbeben. An den Quellen des Terrors*. Frankfurt/Main: Suhrkamp.

Sloterdijk, P. (2004). *Sphären. Plurale Sphärologie Band III: Schäume*. Frankfurt/Main: Suhrkamp.

Spores, J. C. (1988). *Running Amok. A historical inquiry*. Athens, OH: Ohio University Press.

Steinhoff, U. (2005). *Moralisch korrektes Töten. Zur Ethik des Krieges und des Terrorismus*. Neu Isenburg: Wunderkammer-Verlag.

Theveßen, E. (2002). *Schläfer mitten unter uns. Das Netzwerk des Terrors in Deutschland*. München: Knaur Taschenbuch.

Theveßen, E. (2005). *Terroralarm. Deutschland und die islamistische Bedrohung*. Berlin: Rowohlt.

Townshend, C. (2005). *Terrorismus*. Stuttgart: Reclam

Vogl, J. (2010). Der Amokläufer. In S. Moebius & M. Schroer (Eds.), *Diven, Hacker, Spekulanten. Sozialfiguren der Gegenwart* (pp. 12–25). Frankfurt/Main: Suhrkamp.

Waldmann, P. (2005). *Terrorismus. Provokation der Macht*. Hamburg: Murmann Verlag GmbH.

Watts, D. (2003). *Six degrees. The science of a connected age*. New York, NY: W. W. Norton.

SUICIDE ATTACKS AND THE SOCIAL STRUCTURE OF SACRIFICE

Jason Manning

ABSTRACT

Purpose – *In this chapter, I apply theories of conflict and social control derived from the work of Donald Black to explain when suicide attacks will occur and who will carry them out.*

Methodology/approach – *Drawing on the published literature on suicide, suicide terrorism, and social control, I present a structural analysis of suicide attacks that specifies which configurations of social space and social time are most likely to produce them.*

Findings – *I propose that suicide attacks can be explained by structural patterns such as social distance, status inferiority, organization, and large movements of social time. Furthermore, sacrifice is greater among those who are socially marginal individuals whose locations are otherwise conducive to both partisanship and self-destruction.*

Originality/value – *I highlight structural similarities between suicide attacks and other forms of violence, social control, and suicide, thus*

Terrorism and Counterterrorism Today
Sociology of Crime, Law and Deviance, Volume 20, 151–171

ISSN: 1521-6136/doi:10.1108/S1521-613620150000020009

contributing to the systemization of structural theories of human behavior and suggesting avenues for further study.

Keywords: Social control; social structure; suicide; altruism; conflict

INTRODUCTION

Suicide attacks are one of the most distinctive features of modern insurgency and terrorism. Militants give their own lives to drive explosive-laden automobiles into military checkpoints, detonate concealed explosive belts in crowded civilian marketplaces, or pilot airplanes into buildings. Others infiltrate the enemy population and launch shooting or stabbing sprees that end only when they are gunned down by others. The commonality in all these cases is that the attacker sacrifices his or her own life for the sake of killing enemies. Suicide attacks combine a high degree of self-destruction with a high level of violent aggression toward others, with modern suicide bombing being both the purest and most extreme example, as well as the form that has increased most dramatically in recent decades (Atran, 2006; Collard-Wexler, Pischedda, & Smith, 2013; Rosner, Yogev, & Schweitzer, 2014).

Because of their proliferation, suicide attacks in general and suicide bombing in particular have attracted much scholarly interest from investigators using a variety of different theoretical strategies. Some, for example, explain suicide attacks with psychological characteristics such as the personality, motives, and mental states of the attackers (e.g., Araj, 2012; Lankford, 2010, 2011; Merari, Diamant, Bibi, Broshi, & Zakin, 2010; Silke, 2008). Others focus on the external influence of ideology, socialization, and social bonds (e.g., Moghadam, 2008; Pedahzur, 2005; chapter 7; Sageman, 2004). Still others examine suicide attacks as a rational strategy for pursuing personal and political goals, such as achieving local political dominance or winning territorial concessions from foreign powers (e.g., Bloom, 2005; Ferrero, 2006; Pape, 2006). Here I draw on insights gleaned from these previous scholars, but employ a distinctive approach: the sociological paradigm known as *pure* or *Blackian* sociology. Using Blackian theories of conflict, social control, and suicide, as well as the published literature on suicide attacks, I describe key features of the social structure in which suicide attacks are most likely to arise and the social location of those most likely to sacrifice themselves in such attacks. In doing so, I highlight the structural similarities and differences between suicide attacks and other forms of suicide, and suggest relationships that can help explain other patterns of lethal self-sacrifice. First however, I outline my strategy in more detail.

SOCIAL SPACE AND ITS FLUCTUATIONS

Pure sociology, developed by sociologist Donald Black, explains human behavior with the structure and motion of social space (Black, 1995, 2011). Social space is a theoretical construct comprising various kinds of social distance. Every interaction or relationship has a social structure defined by the distances between all parties involved. Relational distance (lack of intimacy) refers to the frequency and scope of interaction, cultural distance (diversity) to differences in cultural characteristics like religion, language, or dress, and vertical distance (inequality) to differences in social status, such as varying levels of wealth, power, and prestige. Every instance of human behavior thus crosses greater or lesser distances, which in turn explains how behavior will vary. For example, Black argues that the greater the social distance between the parties in a conflict, the more likely they are to use lethal weapons to settle their dispute (Black, 2004c). Thus culturally homogeneous intimates, such as kinsmen from the same tribe, are likely to use only their fists against one another, reserving spears for fights against strangers from other ethnic groups (Black, 2004c). Behavior can also go in different directions in vertical space – upward toward a status superior or downward toward a status inferior – and this too explains variation. For example, Baumgartner (1984) observed that upward social control is more likely than downward social control to take on such covert and secretive forms as theft and sabotage. Finally, since the social world is not static but always changing, social structure fluctuates: relationships grow closer or more distant, populations grow more or less culturally diverse, and people gain or lose social stature. These fluctuations of social space – which Black (2011) calls *social time* – are what provide the cause or trigger for various behaviors. For example, a major increase in relational distance – as occurs in separation or divorce – is a movement of social time that commonly causes suicide (Manning, 2014).

Using the Blackian paradigm, one explains behavior by specifying which structural configurations of social space and social time make a behavior more or less likely. There are currently several theories of this kind that address various forms of conflict, violence, and social control (e.g., Black, 1998; Campbell, 2009, 2013; Cooney, 2014a, 2014b; Manning, 2012, 2014; Senechal de la Roche, 1996, 2001). And here I employ the same strategy to explain suicide attacks. Note that my analysis is purely structural, and as such neither confirms nor denies any assertions about the mental states of suicide attackers or the strategic rationality of the groups that dispatch them. It assumes only that the structure and motion of social space affect the likelihood and nature of suicide attacks and that knowledge of these relationships will improve our ability to explain them.

SUICIDE ATTACKS AS SOCIAL CONTROL

The purest examples of suicide attack usually occur as part of larger campaigns of terrorism and guerilla warfare, which are in turn part of larger political struggles. These struggles involve aggrieved populations that use both violent and nonviolent tactics to fight what they argue are unjust actions or circumstances. Suicide attacks, like terrorism and warfare more broadly, are thus a kind conflict management or social control (Black, 2004a, 2004b; Senechal de la Roche, 1996). That is, they are acts of moralistic violence that express grievances and punish enemies for their alleged wrongdoing (Black, 2004c). As such, they can be explained by applying Blackian theories of conflict and social control to specify why these conflicts occur and why they are handled with suicide attacks rather than something else. First, consider the origins of the conflict itself.

Social Time

Extreme violence is an unusual way of handling conflict; after all, a great number of conflicts constantly occur in every human relationship and most conflicts are handled without resort to violence of any kind. But not all conflicts are equal. We intuitively grasp that some grievances are much more serious than others – that a forcible rape is worse than unwanted flirtation, that a murder is worse than an assault, and so forth. It is likewise intuitive to propose that the most severe forms of social control – such as the mass killings carried out by suicide bombers – are more likely to arise from the most serious grievances. But what objective factors make one grievance more serious than another? Indeed, what even causes grievances in the first place?

According to Black (2011), all conflicts are sparked by the fluctuation of social space – that is, social time. Every grievance is provoked by some change in the quantity of social distance in a relationship or social setting.

Furthermore, the severity of the grievance is a direct function of the size and speed of these changes (Black, 2011, p. 6). Thus we can predict that suicide attacks are also a direct function of the size and speed of changes in social space. But what sort of changes? There are three types of structural movement that seem to cause most of the grievances associated with suicide bombing: increasing cultural diversity, increasing inequality, and increasing intimacy.

The greatest increases in cultural distance occur when a drastically foreign culture intrudes into a formerly homogenous social setting (Black, 2011, pp. 101–102). And people in more homogeneous settings are especially likely to treat these intrusions as severe offenses (Black, 2011, p. 144). Thus the technology-assisted spread of Western culture produces severe grievances in culturally distant and formerly homogenous places such as Saudi Arabia. One Western observer notes the degree of offense caused by such cultural pollution:

> I saw a Western woman, unveiled, sit down on a bench in the Najran airport ... There was an old man on that bench ... He was at one end and she sat down at the other – there was nothing like physical contact, as we would define it. But he was so outraged that he got up, leaning on his cane, and stood a few meters away, clearly in pain but preferring to stand on his one good leg rather than share a bench with an unveiled female ... Multiply shocks like that by the hundred, day after day ... and you get a sense of where jihad comes from .... (Brecher, 2014)

Another source of severe grievances is increasing inequality, as occurs when one person or group rises above others by gaining more wealth, prestige, or military power. Black (2011, pp. 70–71) argues that the United States' rapid rise to political, military, and economic dominance during the 20th century is largely responsible for the growth of anti-American grievances, including those of al Qaeda and its supporters (see also Moghadam, 2008, pp. 120–125). Nor is al Qaeda the only militant group with grievances caused by changing inequality. An especially large vertical movement occurs when a superior is usurped and dominated by a former inferior, completely reversing the initial hierarchy (Black, 2011, p. 89, citing Organski & Kugler, 1980). Such a status reversal helped spark the campaign of suicide attacks by Sri Lankan Tamils against the country's Sinhalese majority. Prior to independence from Britain, the colonial administration favored the Tamil minority, who were disproportionately represented in education and government positions. Following independence, the situation reversed as the Sinhalese systematically excluded Tamils from these same positions (Hopgood, 2005; Lewis, 2012, p. 85). A similar reversal occurred in Iraq, where first British colonial authorities and later the

Saddam Hussein regime advantaged the Sunni Arab minority at the expense of Shiite Arabs. After the US-led invasion, however Sunnis lost their former status and were dominated by a postinvasion government that increasingly sided with Iraq's Shiites (Lewis, 2012, p. 212).

Foreign invasion and occupation involves one nation subjugating and dominating another, and so is a massive increase in inequality that often causes suicide attacks. Political scientist Robert Pape (2006) may overstate the case when he says every campaign of suicide bombing is the result of foreign occupation, but subsequent research confirms that it drastically increases the odds of such attacks (see, e.g., Collard-Wexler et al., 2013). A large part of the "humiliation" and "dishonor" that occur during military occupations stems from unwanted contact and invasions of privacy, such as having one's home searched for weapons or being frisked at a security checkpoint (Hafez, 2007, pp. 142–145). Invasion causes such severe conflict because it not only increases inequality, but also intimacy, producing a sudden reduction in relational distance (Black, 2011, pp. 22–23). Thus any foreign presence may spark grievances, even if it does not occur by force. For example, Osama bin Laden and his fellow Salafi jihadists were outraged when, in 1990, King Fahd of Saudi Arabia invited US troops onto Saudi soil to defend the country against possible Iraqi attack (Moghadam, 2008, p. 124).

Military occupation is such a potent cause of suicide attacks because it combines subjugation, increased interaction with strangers, and further invasions of alien culture, combining several major structural changes that are apt to cause serious grievances. Furthermore, a prolonged occupation – such as the Israeli occupation of the West Bank and Gaza – produces many daily instances of domination and intrusion, leading to a steady accumulation of grievances that exacerbate the overall severity of the conflict (Hafez, 2006, p. 49). On the other hand, policies of restraint that reduce acts of violence and intrusion against the occupied people can reduce the severity of the conflict. For instance, historian Jeffrey Lewis argues that increasing British restraint helps explain the lack of suicide bombing by Irish Republicans during the Northern Irish Troubles (Lewis, 2012, pp. 133–135).

Social Distance

The way a given grievance is handled depends in part on the social distance between the aggrieved and the alleged offender. Building on the work of Roberta Senechal de la Roche (1996), Black (2004a, 2004b) proposes that pure terrorism – the covert mass killing of civilians by organized civilians – is more likely across extremely long social distances separating different collectivities. Terrorists, including suicide terrorists, thus attack strangers who belong to a culturally distant nation or ethnic group. The same is true of suicide attacks more generally, including those against military targets or the suicidal assassination of prominent officials. All major campaigns of suicide attack involve conflicts between groups with a slew of cultural differences, including language, ethnicity, and religion. Examples include the Japanese kamikaze attacks against US Naval forces in World War II, the suicidal attacks of Hindu Tamils against Buddhist Sinhalese in Sri Lanka, the bombing campaigns and rampage shootings carried out by Arab Muslim Palestinians against Jewish Israelis, Muslim Chechen attacks against Orthodox Russians, and attacks by Sunni Arab insurgents against US coalition forces and Shiite Arab civilians in Iraq.

Religious differences in particular are something often emphasize by scholars of suicide terrorism. For instance, Pape (2006, pp. 87–92) argues that religious differences are crucial factors and have a stronger impact than other cultural differences, partly because conflicting beliefs have a zero-sum quality that language and other cultural characteristics do not: one may be fluent in two languages, but one cannot simultaneously accept competing religions (Pape, 2006, pp. 87–88; compare Black, 2011, p. 101). Subsequent empirical research confirms that, in cases of military occupation, religious differences between the occupier and the occupied drastically increase the odds of suicide attacks (Collard-Wexler et al., 2013). Likewise, secessionist movements and civil wars are more likely to produce suicide attacks when religious differences are involved (Gambetta, 2005, p. 288). In Iraq, for instance, the Sunni militant group ISIS frequently uses suicide bombings against Shiite civilians as well as Shiite dominated government forces (Harel, 2015). And while militant Palestinian factions have had many violent conflicts with one another, they generally reserve suicide bombing for attacks against the Israelis (Kalyvas & Sanchez-Cuenca, 2005, p. 224).[1]

When different religious or ethnic groups already live in close proximity, their members might engage in peaceful interaction and so establish ties between the two groups, reducing the overall level of relational distance. Such relational closeness lowers the probability of intergroup grievances giving rise to either terrorism or suicide attacks. Conversely, the absence of such ties makes attacks more likely. Thus, during the US occupation of Iraq, most suicide attacks against Iraqi Shiites were carried out by jihadi groups staffed and led by foreigners rather than by Iraqi nationalist groups, which mostly stocked and were led by native Iraqi Sunnis (Moghadam, 2008, pp. 222–250). And because violent conflict itself often has a polarizing effect, causing members of different groups to retreat into separate areas and avoid contact with their potential enemies in the other group, it can increase relational distance and thus the frequency of suicide attacks. Increasing relational distance between Palestinians and Israelis following the first Intifada – including the reduced ability of Palestinians to work for employers in Israel, where they were largely supplanted by foreign laborers – could thus have contributed to greater violence of the second Intifada (Bartram, 1998; cf. Hafez, 2006, pp. 53–61). For instance, several would-be Palestinian bombers captured during the second uprising emphasize that they have never interacted with Israeli civilians at all (Berko & Erez, 2005, p. 610).

Vertical Direction

Social distance generally makes social control more violent and aggressive. But social inferiority encourages it to be more self-destructive (Baumgartner, 1984; Manning, 2012). In the Antebellum US South, slaves would punish their masters by hurting themselves – injuring and mutilating themselves so as to be unfit for work or to fetch a lower price for their master when sold at auction (Bauer & Bauer, 1942; Baumgartner, 1984). In highly patriarchal settings – such as rural Iran or Highland New Guinea – women sometimes turn to suicide and self-injury to protest, shame, and mobilize vengeance against abusive husbands (Aliverdinia & Pridemore, 2009; Counts, 1980). And throughout history people have used self-destruction to express grievances against their political rulers. In hunger strikes activists starve themselves – possibly even to death – to win concessions or gain support. For example, in 1981, 10 Irish republican prisoners starved themselves to death while protesting the British government's decision to treat Northern Irish militants as criminals rather than combatants (Lewis, 2012, pp. 127–131). More immediately self-destructive are those who set themselves on fire in acts of political protest – a tactic that diffused around the world after Buddhist monk Thich Quang Duc burned himself to death in 1963 to protest the Vietnamese government's suppression of Buddhism (Biggs, 2005). In sum, upward social control – toward social superiors – is more suicidal than downward social control (Manning, 2012). And this applies to violent aggression as well: upward violence is more likely than downward violence to take the form of suicide attacks.

Throughout history, suicidal tactics have been used to assassinate high-ranking targets. In the 12th century, for example, the Ismaili – a radical Shiite sect based in what is now Iran – carried out a campaign against the ruling Seljuk Turks by dispatching suicide attackers to assassinate prominent officials at the cost of the attacker's life (Lewis, 2012, p. 43; Pape, 2006). These assassins used daggers even when other weapons were feasible, preferring to get close to their targets despite the certainty they would be arrested and executed, if not killed on the spot by armed guards (Lewis, 2012, p. 43). In the early 20th century, Russian anarchists became the first militant group to use suicide bombing as a means of killing high-ranking state officials, such as in 1905 when three revolutionaries detonated the bombs they were carrying in an effort to kill the Russian prime minister (Lewis, 2012, p. 55). And during World War II, German officer Rudolph von Gersdorff planned a suicide bombing to assassinate Adolph Hitler, but was unable to execute the attack due to his target's unexpected departure from the scene (Moorehouse, 2006, pp. 249–250). In more recent times, widespread campaigns of suicide terrorism are carried out against collectivities with greater resources, such as when Palestinians attack the more educated and wealthy population of Israel or when Sri Lankan Tamils attack the more educated and politically powerful Sinhalese (Hopgood, 2005; Ricol, 2005). Black (2004a, 2004b) proposes that pure terrorism arises in upward directions and across long vertical distances – a pattern that explains why terrorism is more likely than other forms of collective violence to involve suicide attacks. Guerilla campaigns likewise have an upward direction, and so are more likely to involve suicide attacks than are counter-insurgencies or conventional warfare.

Those who study modern suicide bombing often emphasize the particular importance of military inferiority – the fact that terrorists and insurgents, due to their inferior numbers, training, and weaponry, have lesser ability to project and repel force. Pape (2006), for example, argues that militant groups turn to suicide bombing because it is the most cost-effective way to battle a militarily superior opponent. Diego Gambetta likewise notes that "all [suicide missions] are carried out by the weaker side in conflicts characterized by a marked asymmetry in the balance of military force" and refers to such attacks as "the high-precision artillery of the militarily challenged" (Gambetta, 2005, pp. 260–262, citations omitted). Members of militant organizations make similar observations, arguing that suicide bombers are a weapon analogous to the advanced military hardware used by their enemies (Hafez, 2006, pp. 25–30). Evidence from Iraq and Afghanistan suggests that, relative to other forms of violence, suicide-bombing is more likely against "hard" targets that are armed, armored, and capable of fighting back, such as military and police forces (Collard-Wexler et al., 2013).[2] Furthermore, we can observe that the probability of suicide attacks varies over the course of a given conflict as the military inferiority of one side waxes or wanes. Thus the PKK – a Kurdish separatist group in Turkey – increased its use of suicide attacks after assaults by Turkish forces destroyed PKK strongholds and left the group militarily weakened (Pedahzur, 2005, pp. 89–90). Even conflicts that begin as conventional warfare between states can generate suicidal attacks when one side gains a sufficient degree of superiority over the other (Bloom, 2005, p. 89). The destruction of Japan's navy in World War II, for instance, gave its enemies overwhelming military superiority, and led the Japanese military to launch a sustained and large-scale campaign of suicide attacks, including pilots who flew fly explosive-laden craft into US ships as well as suicide attack boats and submersibles (Hill, 2005; Lewis, 2012, pp. 59–60).

Organization

According to scholar Michael Biggs (2005, p. 191), the protest suicide of Thich Quang Duc in Vietnam was unusual in that it was planned and orchestrated with the assistance of the monk's activist colleagues, who gave their blessing to his plan, helped schedule and promote the event, and even provided assistance when his lighter failed to ignite. Most suicide protestors, however, appear to act on their own without the encouragement, support, or assistance of others. They may belong to activist groups and die on behalf of a collective cause, but the self-immolation itself is relatively spontaneous and individualized. Suicide attackers, on the other hand, are more likely to carry out their act with the planning, assistance, or encouragement of an organization. Indeed, the organized nature of suicide attacks is a factor often emphasized by previous scholars, particularly those who examine their strategic logic (e.g., Hafez, 2006; Lewis, 2012; Pape, 2006; Pedahzur, 2005). Gambetta (2005, p. 26) goes so far as to propose that "all [suicide missions] have been decided and executed with the support of an organization." And it is certainly true that the vast majority of modern suicide bombings are planned and executed by longstanding militant organizations such as Hezbollah in Lebanon, Hamas in Palestine, the Kurdistan Worker's Party (PKK) in Turkey, the Liberation Tigers of Tamil Elam (LTTE or Tamil Tigers) in Sri Lanka, the Islamic State (ISIS or ISIL) in Iraq, and Boko Haram in Nigeria.

The organizations that dispatch suicide attackers range from loose networks and small local cells to national states (Gambetta, 2005, p. 261; Pedahzur & Perliger, 2006). But even the smaller groups appear to have a relatively high degree of organization. For instance, Pedahzur (2005, p. 39) describes the division of labor in Palestinian suicide bombings, which involve the effort of leaders who plan the strikes, observers who gather intelligence on potential targets, recruiters who identify and approach potential bombers, handlers who deliver the bombers to their targets, and the bomb-makers who construct the explosive devices (Pedahzur, 2005, p. 39; see also Hafez, 2006; Lewis, 2012). When carrying out their attacks, suicide bombers may operate in teams or in coordination with conventional attacks by insurgent forces (Pape, 2006, p. 185). The LTTE, for instance, often used suicide attackers to breach military targets prior to ground assaults by its regular forces (Pedahzur, 2005, p. 86). Indeed, suicide attacks are generally part of larger campaigns that include nonsuicidal violence such as assassinations, nonsuicidal terrorism, and guerilla warfare. And since terrorism and warfare are by definition more organized and recurrent than the fleeting mob violence like riots, organization is yet another characteristic that makes terrorism likely to involve suicide attack (Black, 2004a, 2004b; Senechal de la Roche, 1996)

SUICIDE ATTACKS AS PARTISANSHIP

Why would anyone volunteer to carry out a suicide attack? The structural factors outlined above provide one answer: suicide attackers are those who have severe grievances against an enemy who is relationally and culturally distant and has superior wealth and power. For instance, Palestinian suicide bombers often have severe personal grievances against the Israelis, such as those stemming from the death of a family member (Hafez, 2006, p. 49; Kimi & Even, 2004). But not all volunteers experience personal losses. Some Palestinian bombers, for instance, are reacting not to their own losses but to the suffering of others in their community (Hafez, 2006, p. 49–50; Kimi & Even, 2004). Or consider transnational jihadists, such as the thousands of Sunni Muslims who have left their home countries to become martyrs in Syria and Iraq (Hafez, 2007, pp. 165–212; Hegghammer, 2010/11; Liddy & Gourlay, 2015). Such cases demonstrate that suicide attacks are not solely a matter of unilateral social control – one side acting against another. Suicidal attackers can also be understood as partisans – third parties who take sides in a conflict (Black, 1998; chapter 7). As such, we can further explain the behavior of those who die in suicide attacks with the conditions that promote strong partisanship.

Partisanship and Closeness

Black (1998, chapter 7) explains the likelihood and degree of partisanship with the social location of the third party relative to both sides of the conflict. More precisely, partisanship increases with social closeness to one side and social distance from the other, such that "maximal partisanship arises from a severe polarization of all the parties with knowledge of a conflict: two clusters of close people, each distant from the other" (Black, 1998, p. 126). Since dying to attack the group's enemies is extreme partisanship, we would expect it to arise only with extreme closeness to one side and extreme distance from the other. We have already considered the role of relational and cultural distance between suicide attackers and their targets. But their closeness to the militant organizations, or to the communities for which they fight, matters as well. This is most obvious with those, such as the LTTE's "Black Tigers" or the first wave of Palestinian suicide bombers, who are both members of the aggrieved community as well as longtime members of the militant organization that dispatches them (Pedahzur, 2005, p. 125). Others are members of the aggrieved community but not the militant group, as was increasingly the case during the Lebanese and Palestinian conflicts, where individuals were recruited specifically for the purpose of carrying out suicide bombings (Hafez, 2006, p. 20, 2007, pp. 165–213; Pedahzur, 2005, p. 125). Such recruits, however, typically have pre-existing relational ties to the groups that will eventually dispatch them. For instance, Pedahzur and Perliger's (2006) study of militant networks during the second Intifada showed the importance of such ties:

> Some of the suicide bombers were recruited by heads of the Kawasmeh clan from the local mosque's soccer team, which included many clan members ... In the northern Samaria network, Keis Advan exploited his position as former head of the al-Najah Student Union to recruit students to his network. Nursi Tawalbeh, hub of the Jenin network, worked with other hubs to select candidates from within their extended families and circle of friends. (Pedahzur & Perliger, 2006, p. 1995, citations omitted)

Given the extreme levels of cultural and relational distance from the enemy, as well as the longstanding and violent nature of the conflicts, many campaigns of suicide attack manage to attract even more distant partisans. The US invasion of Iraq, for example, provoked a wave of strong partisanship by those whose cultural closeness to Iraqi's Sunni Arab population and distance from the US led them to leave their homelands and join the insurgency (Hafez, 2007; Liddy & Gourlay, 2015). For example, one Lebanese teacher who decided to become a martyr in Iraq experienced an anger "that was fed by almost daily scenes on television of Iraqi women and children dying" (Moghadam, 2008, p. 231). Even these distant partisans tend to be recruited through pre-existing social ties to the local or transnational militant groups (Felter & Fishman, 2007; Hafez, 2007, pp. 165–212; see also Sageman, 2004). Indeed, a large proportion of volunteers who commit suicide bombings in Iraq, Syria, and elsewhere hail from the same foreign cities and towns and many joined together in pairs or small clusters (Felter & Fishman, 2007; Hafez, 2007, pp. 165–212; Liddy & Gourlay, 2015; Ricol, 2005, p. 133; Sageman, 2004, pp. 99–135). This pattern likely reflects not only the role of established networks in providing opportunities for partisans to join the struggle, but also the effects of social solidarity in encouraging "chains of partisanship" in which initial supporters attract their owns supporters in turn (Senechal de la Roche, 2001, pp. 38–39).

Partisanship and Inferiority

Black (1998, p. 127) also proposes that partisanship varies with the social status of the third party relative to both sides: third parties are more likely to side on behalf of social superiors against social inferiors and their degree of partisanship increases with the superiority of one side and the inferiority of the other. The upward direction of most suicide attacks shows that sufficient degrees of social distance and conflict severity can produce strong partisanship even against vastly superior enemies. But the theory would still imply that, all else equal, the ability of a militant group to attract strong partisanship would increase with its social superiority to potential volunteers. And because superiority and closeness operate jointly, organizations with greater stature should also be able to attract relatively more distant partisans. Thus in Palestine, Hamas initially relied on longstanding members to carry out suicide attacks, but as the organization grew in size and political power during the course of the conflict against Israel it was increasingly able to rely on a large supply of external volunteers (Pedahzur, 2005, p. 152). Likewise, increasing military success and resulting notoriety no doubt contributed to the ability of Iraq's Islamic State group to attract foreigners it could deploy as suicide attackers (Liddy & Gourlay, 2015). In cases of extreme superiority, such as the superiority of a dictatorial state over its citizens, the line between volunteering and being conscripted can blur, as when the Japanese military selected volunteers from among young students who had already been drafted into the military (Hill, 2005).

Leaders also show a preference for dispatching members with a relatively lower rank or with poorer records of performance. Japanese officials thus spared their best pilots from Kamikaze missions, sometimes by ordering them to be transferred from their units just prior to the unit being assigned a suicide mission (Hill, 2005, p. 22). Modern terrorist and insurgent groups likewise prefer to dispatch those who lack combat experience, technical skills, or authority within the group (Byman & Shapiro, 2014; Pedahzur, 2005, p. 126). But more inferior individuals were also more likely to volunteer in the first place: when the Japanese navy asked for volunteers to fly the first wave of suicide missions, the volunteers consisted entirely of reserve officers from within the ranks rather than the elite graduates of the prestigious naval academy (Hill, 2005, p. 4). Furthermore, the greater the stature of an organization, the greater the status of the volunteers it attracts. Due to its rapid growth in size and political influence, Hamas was able to deploy suicide bombers who had relatively high levels of wealth and education, while less prominent rivals, like Fata's al-Aqsa' Martyrs Brigades, were more likely to dispatch low-status individuals such as criminals, small children, socially disgraced women (Atran, 2014; Pedahzur & Perliger, 2006, p. 1996).

The tendency of close inferiors to commit acts of sacrificial partisanship also extends beyond suicide attacks to cases where suicide is a purely defensive action. For example, all members of Sri Lanka's Tamil Tigers wore cyanide capsules to be used for suicide when threatened with capture. More than 600 members committed suicide in this way to prevent enemy forces from coercing them into providing intelligence that could harm the group and it's charismatic leader (Hopgood, 2005, pp. 62–66; Pape, 2006, p. 143). And a similar pattern can be found far away from the battlefield: during the 1980s, Japanese businessmen sometimes killed themselves on behalf of a corporation facing public scandal, and "in such cases it is usually subordinates regarded as key witnesses who commit suicide in order to cover up the wrongdoing of their superiors" (Iga, 1986, p. 18). Likewise, high levels of social closeness and social solidarity also promote acts of defensive sacrifice, as when soldiers throw themselves on grenades to save their squad-mates (Blake, 1978). Such acts are clearly displays of strong partisanship. But to what extent are they also acts of suicide?

SUICIDE ATTACKS AS SUICIDE

There is considerable debate about the extent to which suicide attacks are similar to suicide. Much of the debate hinges on the psychological state of the attacker – whether their personality types, emotional states, and motivations resemble those typically found among suicides (see Byrm & Araj, 2012; Lankford, 2011; Merari et al., 2010). From a structural perspective, however, what matters are similarities in social structure and social time. And it appears that lethal self-sacrifice shares structural commonalities with other forms of self-destruction. Consider the role of social integration.

Suicide and Social Integration

In his classic theory of egoistic suicide, Durkheim ([1897]1951) proposed that suicide varies inversely with social integration, such that socially marginal or isolated individuals were more likely to kill themselves. Empirical research (e.g., Danigelis & Pope, 1979) generally supports the theory, finding that social marginality increases the chances of suicide in a variety of settings. Thus we might expect that, all else equal, suicide attackers tend to occupy the margins of social networks. On the other hand, suicide attacks are often a kind of self-sacrifice in which the individual gives up his or her life for others. Thus some scholars (e.g., Pape, 2006; Pedahzur, Perliger, & Weinberg, 2003) argue they are better explained by Durkheim's ([1897]1951) theory of altruistic suicide, which proposes that lethal self-sacrifice is more likely at very high levels of social integration, and should thus be most common among those who are most enmeshed in networks of strong ties.

As explanations of suicide attacks, both theories are partly true. On the one hand, lethal self-sacrifice thrives in settings of high social solidarity, such as among military units, the kin-based societies of Nigeria, Iraq, and Palestine, or the tight-knit cells of transnational terrorists. As discussed above, such solidarity is important because close ties breed strong partisanship, including sacrificial partisanship. On the other hand, the most highly integrated individuals are not necessarily the ones most likely to make a lethal sacrifice. During the second Palestinian Intifada, for example, the central hubs of the militant networks were unlikely to give their lives for the group: instead, suicide bombers were more likely to occupy a "peripheral position" and have a "relatively low number of ties" (Pedahzur & Perliger, 2006, p. 1996). Similarly, when embarrassed by the lack of elite volunteers for its first wave of Kamikaze missions, the commanders of

Japan's 201st Air Corps chose to send an academy graduate who had only recently been transferred into the fighter group from his former post as a bomber pilot in Taiwan – "he was chosen not because he was the best man for the job, but because he was an outsider" (Hill, 2005, p. 5). And marginality within a wider community matters as well. While Palestinian suicide bombers often come from relatively successful and respectable families, they themselves are usually unmarried, childless, and jobless (Hafez, 2006, p. 21; Kimi & Even, 2004; Ricol, 2005, p. 105). Hamas and Palestinian Islamic Jihad have rules against recruiting those who are "the main breadwinners in their families" (Hafez, 2006, p. 21). Many female suicide bombers are widows or divorcees. Chechen militant groups, for instance, appear to prefer to sacrifice women who have been severed from marriage and child-rearing – female bombers reportedly told Moscow hostages that "they had nothing to lose but their lives" (quoted in Elster, 2005, p. 242). And foreigners who volunteer to fight for ISIS in Syria and Iraq are especially likely to be sent on suicide missions, in part because of their lack of integration into local communities and kin groups (Byman & Shapiro, 2014). It thus appears that, given sufficient closeness and solidarity to induce partisanship, suicide attacks tend to attract the socially marginal.

Suicide and Social Time

Another similarity between suicide attacks and other forms of suicide is in the movements of social time likely to trigger both. Individual suicide typically results from losses of stature and losses of intimacy (Manning, 2014). While some suicide bombers have lost both at the hands of their enemies – and are thus volunteering partly for personal vengeance – others are responding to losses that have no connection to the conflict at all. For instance, while Palestinian nurse Wafa Idris had long "exhibited a strong sympathy" for fellow Palestinians injured at the hands of Israelis, she did not become a suicide bomber until after her husband divorced her for her inability to bear children, an increase of relational distance that also lowered her standing in the community and left her humiliated (Pedahzur, 2005, pp. 138–139). Or consider the case of a Palestinian police officer named Abdalfatah Rashid:

> He accidentally killed a Palestinian prisoner during an interrogation regarding the theft of a car. Rashid was jailed but then escaped. Now wanted by the Palestinian Authority and fearful that the family of his victim might pursue him, it was relatively easy for a

> militant from [Palestinian Islamic Jihad] whom he had met in prison to convince him to carry out a suicide attack. (Araj, 2012, p. 221)

Not all suicide bombers experience such suicidal movements of social time. Nor are all socially marginal in their communities or in the groups that dispatch them. But in settings otherwise conducive to strong partisanship, factors that encourage self-destruction will increase the probability of committing a suicide attack. Likewise, the presence of factors that increase strong partisanship makes it more likely that those in social locations conducive to suicide will choose to die by means of a suicide attack rather than pure suicide. And the degree to which suicide attackers share characteristics with ordinary suicides should vary with factors such as the distance and superiority of the enemy, the stature of the group that dispatches them, and the severity of the conflict. For instance, Ewing (1955) argues that suicide attacks by Filipino Muslims during times of relative peace appear more like ordinary suicide – stemming from factors such as an "unhappy marital life" or personal humiliation – than suicide attacks that occurred during times of open warfare against European colonists. The more partisan the structure, the less suicidal it must be to produce lethal self-sacrifice.

CONCLUSION

Modern campaigns of suicidal terrorism and insurgency are the result of a convergence between aspects of social space that encourage violent aggression, those that encourage self-destruction, and those that encourage sacrifice on behalf of others. This confluence occurs when wealthy and powerful foreigners export their culture and expand their power into settings with high degrees of social solidarity and cultural homogeneity. Add to such a volatile structure modern technology that allows the aggrieved to manufacture cheap and effective explosives, suitable for the mass killing of enemies, and suicide bombings proliferate – particularly in parts of the world where tribal levels of solidarity breed strong partisanship against outsiders. Different combinations of closeness, inferiority, marginality, and suicidal time can provoke individuals to commit such attacks, and the profile of suicide bombers is variable: some who volunteer for the duty are highly integrated veterans of the struggle expressing solidarity with their comrades, some are marginal newcomers displaying their bravery and loyalty to the honored veterans, and some are social isolates impelled by broken relationships and personal humiliations. Whatever the details, their acts are praised by other partisans, and so the status of the martyrs and the groups that dispatch them increases, as does the pool of volunteers. The conflicts are self-reinforcing in other ways as well, escalating over time as populations polarize, militant groups gain size and support, and heavy-handed counter-insurgency begets new grievances. Thus suicide attacks spread like fire. Conflicts cannot escalate indefinitely, and today's campaigns of suicide bombing will eventually subside. For the near future, however, suicide attacks are here to stay.

NOTES

1. The Liberation Tigers of Tamil Elam (LTTE) in Sri Lanka have used suicide bombing against their rivals within the Tamil community, though most of their suicide bombings are directed at the Sinhalese (Lewis, 2012, p. 100).
2. Sufficient hardening however, can cause insurgents to shift their focus to attacks against enemy civilians, transforming guerilla warfare into pure terrorism (Bloom, 2005, p. 93).

REFERENCES

Aliverdinia, A., & Pridemore, W. A. (2009). Women's fatalistic suicide in Iran: A partial test of Durkheim in an Islamic republic. *Violence Against Women*, *15*(3), 307–320.

Araj, B. (2012). The motivations of Palestinian suicide bombers in the second Intifada (2000 to 2005). *Canadian Review of Sociology/Revue canadienne de sociologie*, *49*(3), 211–232.

Atran, S. (2006). The moral logic and growth of suicide terrorism. *The Washington Quarterly*, *29*(2), 127–147.

Atran, S. (2014). Martyrdom's would-be myth buster. Open Peer Commentary on Lankford, A., Precis of The Myth of Martyrdom: What really drives suicide bombers, rampage shooters, and other self-destructive killers. *Behavioral and Brain Sciences*, *37*(4), 362–363.

Bartram, D. V. (1998). Foreign workers in Israel: History and theory. *International Migration Review*, *32*(2), 303–325.

Bauer, R. A., & Bauer, A. H. (1942). Day to day resistance to slavery. *Journal of Negro History*, *27*, 388–419.

Baumgartner, M. P. (1984). Social control from below. In D. Black (Ed.), *Toward a general theory of social control: Fundamentals* (Vol. 1, pp. 303–345). Orlando, FL: Academic Press.

Berko, A., & Erez, E. (2005). 'Ordinary people' and 'death work': Palestinian suicide bombers as victimizers and victims. *Violence and Victims*, *20*(6), 603–621.

Biggs, M. (2005). Dying without killing: Self-immolations, 1963–2002. In D. Gambetta (Ed.), *Making sense of suicide missions* (pp. 77–130). Oxford: Oxford University Press.

Black, D. (1995). The epistemology of pure sociology. *Law and Social Inquiry*, *20*(3), 829–870.

Black, D. (1998). *The social structure of right and wrong*. San Diego, CA: Academic Press.

Black, D. (2004a). Terrorism as social control. In M. Deflem (Ed.), *Terrorism and counter-terrorism: Criminological perspectives* (pp. 9–18). Bingley, UK: Emerald Publishing Group Limited.

Black, D. (2004b). The geometry of terrorism. *Sociological Theory*, *22*(1), 14–25.

Black, D. (2004c). Violent structures. In M. A. Zahn, H. H. Brownstein, & S. L. Jackson (Eds.), *Violence: From theory to research* (pp. 145–158). Newark, NJ: LexisNexis.

Black, D. (2011). *Moral time*. New York, NY: Oxford University Press.

Blake, J. A. (1978). Death by hand grenade: Altruistic suicide in combat. *Suicide and Life Threatening Behavior*, *8*(1), 46–59.

Bloom, M. (2005). *Dying to kill: The allure of suicide terrorism* New York, NY: Columbia University Press.

Brecher, G. (2014). Ward Nerd: Who exactly are the jihadis (and why aren't there more of them)? *Pando Daily*. Retrieved from http://pando.com/2014/03/28/the-war-nerd-who-exactly-are-the-jihadis-and-why-arent-there-more-of-them/

Byman, D., & Shapiro, J. (2014). *Be afraid. Be a little afraid: The threat of terrorism from Western foreign fighters in Syria and Iraq* Policy Paper 34. Washington, DC: Brookings.

Byrm, R. J., & Araj, B. (2012). Are suicide bombers suicidal? *Studies in Conflict & Terrorism*, *35*(6), 432–433.

Campbell, B. (2009). Genocide as social control. *Sociological Theory*, *27*(2), 150–172.

Campbell, B. (2013). Genocide and social time. *Dilemas: Revista de Estudos de Conflito e Controle Social*, *6*(3), 465–488.

Collard-Wexler, S., Pischedda, C., & Smith, M. G. (2013). Do foreign occupations cause suicide attacks? *Journal of Conflict Resolution*, *58*, 1–33.

Cooney, M. (2014a). Family honor and social time. *The Sociological Review*, *62*, 87–106.

Cooney, M. (2014b). Death by family: Honor violence as punishment. *Punishment and Society*, *16*(4), 406–427.

Counts, D. A. (1980). Fighting back is not the way: Suicide and the women of Kaliai. *American Ethnologist*, *7*(2), 332–351.

Danigelis, N., & Pope, W. (1979). Durkheim's theory of suicide as applied to the family an empirical test. *Social Forces*, *57*(4), 1081–1106.

Durkheim, E. ([1897]1951). *Suicide: A study in sociology*. New York, NY: The Free Press.

Elster, J. (2005). Motivations and beliefs in suicide missions. In D. Gambetta (Ed.), *Making sense of suicide missions* (pp. 233–258). Oxford: Oxford University Press.

Ewing, J. F. (1955). Juramentado: Institutionalized suicide among the Moros of the Philippines. *Anthropological Quarterly*, *28*(4), 148–155.

Felter, J., & Fishman, B. (2007). *Al-Qa'ida's foreign fighters in Iraq: A first look at the sinjar records*. West Point, NY: Combating Terrorism Center.

Ferrero, M. (2006). Martyrdom contracts. *The Journal of Conflict Resolution*, *50*(6), 855–877.

Gambetta, D. (2005). Can we make sense of suicide missions? In D. Gambetta (Ed.), *Making sense of suicide missions* (pp. 259–300). Oxford: Oxford University Press.

Hafez, M. M. (2006). *Manufacturing human bombs: The making of Palestinian suicide bombers*. Washington, DC: United States Institute of Peace Press.

Hafez, M. M. (2007). *Suicide bombers in Iraq: The strategy and ideology of martyrdom*. Washington, DC: United States Institute of Peace Press.

Harel, A. (2015). Number of suicide bombings around world surged 94% in 2014 amid rise of ISIS. *Haaretz*. Retrieved from http://www.haaretz.com/news/diplomacy-defense/.premium-1.635193

Hegghammer, T. (2010/11). The rise of Muslim foreign fighters: Islam and the globalization of jihad. *International Security*, *35*(3), 53–94.

Hill, P. (2005). Kamikaze, 1943-5. In D. Gambetta (Ed.), *Making sense of suicide missions* (pp. 1–42). Oxford: Oxford University Press.

Hopgood, S. (2005). Tamil tigers, 1987–2002. In D. Gambetta (Ed.), *Making sense of suicide missions* (pp. 43–76). Oxford: Oxford University Press.

Iga, M. (1986). *The thorn in the chrysanthemum: Suicide and economic success in modern Japan*. Berkeley, CA: University of California Press.

Kalvyas, S. N., & Sanchez-Cuenca, I. (2005). Killing without dying: The absence of suicide missions. In D. Gambetta (Ed.), *Making sense of suicide missions* (pp. 209–232). Oxford: Oxford University Press.

Kimi, S., & Even, S. (2004). Who are the Palestinian suicide bombers? *Terrorism and Political Violence*, *16*(4), 815–840.

Lankford, A. (2010). Do suicide terrorists exhibit clinically suicidal risk factors? A review of initial evidence and call for future research. *Aggression and Violent Behavior*, *15*(5), 334–340.

Lankford, A. (2011). Could suicide terrorists actually be suicidal? *Studies in Conflict & Terrorism*, *34*(4), 337–366.

Lewis, J. W. (2012). *The business of martyrdom: A history of suicide bombing*. Annapolis, MD: Naval Institute Press.

Liddy, M., & Gourlay, C. (2015). Explained: Where do foreign fighters in Iraq and Syria come from? *ABC News*. Retrieved from http://www.abc.net.au/news/2015-02-%2006/map-foreign-fighters-iraq-syria/6052544

Manning, J. (2012). Suicide as social control. *Sociological Forum*, *27*(1), 207–227.

Manning, J. (2014). Suicide and social time. *Dilemas: Revistas de Estudos de Conflicto e Controle Social*, *8*(1), 97–126.

Merari, A., Diamant, I., Bibi, A., Broshi, Y., & Zakin, G. (2010). Personality characteristics of 'self martyrs'/'suicide bombers' and organizers of suicide attacks. *Terrorism and Political Violence*, *22*(1), 87–101.

Moghadam, A. (2008). *The globalization of martyrdom: Al Qaeda, Salafi jihad, and the diffusion of suicide attacks*. Baltimore, MD: The Johns Hopkins University Press.

Moorehouse, R. (2006). *Killing Hitler: The plots, the assassins, and the dictator who cheated death*. New York, NY: Bantam Books.

Organski, A. F. K., & Kugler, J. (1980). *The war ledger*. Chicago, IL: University of Chicago Press.

Pape, R. A. (2006). *Dying to win: The strategic logic of suicide terrorism*. New York, NY: Random House Trade Paperbacks.

Pedahzur, A. (2005). *Suicide terrorism*. Malden, MA: Polity Press.

Pedahzur, A., & Perliger, A. (2006). The changing nature of suicide attacks: A social network perspective. *Social Forces*, *84*(4), 1987–2008.

Pedahzur, A., Perliger, A., & Weinberg, L. (2003). Altruism and fatalism: The characteristics of Palestinian suicide terrorists. *Deviant Behavior: An Interdisciplinary Journal*, *24*(4), 405–523.

Ricol, L. (2005). Palestinians, 1981–2003. In D. Gambetta (Ed.), *Making sense of suicide missions* (pp. 77–130). Oxford: Oxford University Press.

Rosner, Y., Yogev, E., & Schweitzer, Y. (2014). A report on suicide bombings in 2013. The Institute for National Security Studies Insight No.507. Retrieved from http://www.inss.org.il/index.aspx?id=4538&articleid=6408

Sageman, M. (2004). *Understanding terror networks*. Philadelphia, PA: University of Pennsylvania Press.

Senechal de la Roche, R. (1996). Collective violence as social control. *Sociological Forum, 11*(1), 97–128.

Senechal de la Roche, R. (2001). Why is collective violence collective? *Sociological Theory, 19*(2), 126–144.

Silke, A. (2008). Holy warriors: Exploring the psychological processes of jihadi radicalization. *European Journal of Criminology, 5*(1), 99–123.

PART III
COUNTERTERRORISM LAW, POLICY AND POLICING

PROSECUTING TERRORISM: CHALLENGES IN THE POST-9/11 WORLD

Christopher A. Shields, Brent L. Smith and Kelly R. Damphousse

ABSTRACT

Purpose – *In this chapter, we provide a brief historical framework of the events and policy changes that impacted the prosecution of terrorism over the past 50 years with emphasis placed on the changes that resulted from the 9/11 attacks.*

Methodology/approach – *We provide a review of relevant literature and complete the chapter by providing new data (2015) on case outcomes derived from the American Terrorism Study, a database housed in the Terrorism Research Center in Fulbright College, at the University of Arkansas.*

Findings – *Investigative and prosecutorial authority in U.S. terrorism cases has experienced ebbs and flows that correspond with terrorism attacks as well as missteps by the FBI, and each has impacted the success of prosecution efforts. Despite dramatic changes, the number of*

Terrorism and Counterterrorism Today
Sociology of Crime, Law and Deviance, Volume 20, 175–195

ISSN: 1521-6136/doi:10.1108/S1521-613620150000020013

cases prosecuted after 9/11 is unprecedented, and conviction rates continue to climb.

Originality/value – *This chapter provides the reader with a synopsis of the policy changes that have occurred in federal terrorism investigations and trials from the late 1960s upto the present. Based on that context, we provide an explanation of how those policy changes have impacted terrorism prosecutions.*

Keywords: Terrorism; prosecution; counterterrorism policy; counterterrorism investigation

INTRODUCTION

Over the last 15 years, America's response to terrorism has undergone a substantial overhaul, transitioning investigations and prosecutions to more proactive strategies aimed at fighting the ever-evolving threat of terrorism. As federal authorities pursued new strategies, they were confronted by new challenges and mounting public pressure. Criticism directed toward investigation techniques, such as authorities targeting mosques with undercover sting operations (Ackerman, 2014), and skepticism directed toward the FBI and the Executive Office of U.S. Attorneys concerning over- and under-reported terrorism statistics (U.S. Department of Justice, Office of the Inspector General, 2007), are just a few of the challenges raised as the government has responded to terrorism. Some of the biggest challenges have emerged from policy changes implemented by the Attorney General, by the emerging threat of homegrown Islamic extremist groups.

Often overlooked in terrorism research, Federal terrorism trials are intriguing for a number of reasons. First, terrorism is a politically motivated crime (Smith, 1994), and the prosecution strategies used to pursue those cases are often different from those used in nonterrorism criminal cases (Shields, 2012; Smith & Damphousse, 1996; Smith, Shields, & Damphousse, 2011). Changes to government intervention strategies have affected the manner in which terrorists plan terrorist activities, the structure of terrorist groups, and the manner in which they defend themselves in court (Shields, 2008). Although it is not possible to address every change in a single chapter, we will provide a historical overview of some significant events and policy changes that set the stage for the post-9/11 policy shift. Our focus then turns to some key policy changes that occurred in the wake of those attacks, a discussion of new challenges, followed by a current synopsis of federal terrorism trial outcomes.

HISTORICAL DEVELOPMENT OF ANTITERRORISM POLICY IN THE UNITED STATES

Federal authority to investigate and prosecute terrorism has both contracted and expanded over the past five decades. The ebb and flow of antiterrorism policy in the United States has come largely in reaction to both terrorism events and government action. The Executive Branch and Congress expanded the investigative power of federal agents in response to attacks perpetrated by terrorist groups, but in response to investigative abuses perpetrated by the FBI, the Executive Branch has also curtailed investigative power.

1970s and Before: Terrorism as a Conventional Crime

Before the 1980s, American jurisprudence largely avoided the concept of "political crime" and "political criminality." Some experts maintained that this was due to ideological projection, whereby the United States attempted to paint itself as a nation of consensus, immune to violent political conflict (Ingraham & Tokoro, 1969; Turk, 1982). When they were acknowledged, terrorism and political crime were associated almost exclusively with the far left and Marxist revolutionaries (Smith, 1994). Many factors, including the Cold War, communism, and the Cuban revolution, shaped America's views on those who sought political change through violence and terrorism. Federal authorities described terrorists as young, Marxist, urban, educated revolutionaries who were bent on destroying capitalism (Russell & Miller, 1977; Smith & Morgan, 1994). According to Poveda (1990), the FBI was well aware of the threat posed by these revolutionaries. The FBI engaged in efforts to suppress the activities through the counterintelligence program, COINTELPRO, from the late 1950s through the early 1970s.

Abuses in the COINTELPRO program, and the impact of Watergate in the early-1970s, tarnished the public's image of the FBI (Smith, 1994). As public lost confidence in the agency, Congress demanded change. In the wake of the post-Watergate investigation, according to Smith, two significant events occurred that helped shape the definition of American terrorism and how the federal government responded to it. First, in April 1976, Attorney General Edward Levi implemented new FBI investigative guidelines. The guidelines identified the standards by which internal security investigations could be initiated and the length of time they could last (Hearings Before the Subcommittee on Administrative Practice and Procedure of the Committee of the Judiciary on FBI Statutory Charter, 1978). The guidelines had a chilling effect on the number of domestic security investigations, which dropped from more than 20,000 in 1973 to less than 200 in 1976 (Elliff, 1979). Second, in August 1976, the FBI dismantled its domestic intelligence units and moved investigations of domestic terrorism from the Intelligence Division to the General Investigative Division (Kelley & Davis, 1987; Poveda, 1990). This move limited the types of investigative techniques that could be used in terrorism cases to the standards used for traditional crimes.

The shift resulted in the government treating terrorist acts as though they were conventional crimes, and prosecuting terrorists no differently than other federal defendants. In addition, the change altered the FBI from an agency focused on domestic intelligence gathering, to one that spent the next quarter of a century primarily concerned with law enforcement. Under the Levi Guidelines, the FBI generally avoided data collection on American citizens, and it adopted a much more reactive stance, investigating terrorist groups only when agents could establish a criminal predicate. According to Smith (1994), the domestic terrorist groups that survived COINTELPRO operated with near impunity during the late 1970s and early 1980s. Indeed, according to the FBI's annual reports on terrorism, the number of terrorism incidents in the United States reached its zenith. Far-left terrorism continued, Puerto Rican separatists targeted both the island and the U.S. mainland, and far-right terrorism emerged as a response to gains made by African Americans in the civil rights movement. But like Watergate and COINTELPRO, which triggered the changes described above, new events would swing the pendulum in the other direction (Smith, 1994).

1980s: A Terrorism Threat Impossible to Ignore

Despite the increased violence leading up to the dawn of the 1980s, the FBI was reluctant to reengage in domestic intelligence. A series of events would trigger renewed FBI vigilance. In 1981, the robbery of Brink's armored car, and the murders of two officers, served as an ignition point. The robbery involved members of the long-forgotten Weather Underground and Black

Liberation Army, which had also been providing assistance to the Puerto Rican separatist group, the Armed Forces of National Liberation (FALN). Later that year, members of another holdover leftist group from the mid-1970s, the United Freedom Front, killed a New Jersey state trooper. Congressional criticism of the FBI subsequently mounted. In 1983, Attorney General William F. Smith, reacting to congressional pressure, implemented new rules that directed the FBI to investigate domestic acts of terrorism. The new rules, which replaced the restrictive Levi guidelines, permitted the FBI to investigate terror groups for longer periods of time than possible under a general crimes investigation. In addition, a separate set of classified guidelines gave the FBI expanded authority to investigate international terrorists.

The Smith Guidelines established the standard for FBI investigations of domestic terrorism groups for the next 20 years. Although subsequent attorney generals made minor modifications over the years, the Smith Guidelines remained functionally intact until the 9/11 attacks in 2001. After the Smith guidelines were implemented, the FBI started a series of counterterrorism initiatives, including the creation of counterterrorism task forces around the country to target specific, regional threats. The success of these efforts was remarkable. Leftist groups like the Weather Underground, the May 19th Communist Organization, the United Freedom Front, and the Puerto Rican groups, the Macheteros and the FALN, were decimated by arrest, indictment, and convictions in federal courts (Smith et al., 2011). The extreme right met a similar fate. Authorities indicted and convicted members of the Order, the Sheriff's Posse Comitatus, the White Patriot Party, and the Aryan Nations in a series of publicized trials in the mid- to late 1980s.

The Smith Guidelines required FBI field offices to refer potential terrorism investigations, involving two or more persons, to the Director or Assistant Director of the FBI; only they could authorize a "terrorism enterprise" investigation (Smith, 1994). Once the Director authorized a terrorism investigation, he had to report that fact to the Office of Intelligence Policy and Review. The Smith Guidelines also required the Director or another top official to monitor the progress of the investigation at 180-day intervals (Shields, 2012). Furthermore, terrorism investigations could not be opened unless "circumstances indicate that *two or more persons* [emphasis added] are engaged in an enterprise for the purpose of furthering political or social goals … that involve force or violence and a violation of the criminal laws of the United States" (Office of the Attorney General, 1983). While the Smith Guidelines provided an opportunity for the FBI to collect domestic intelligence, the new policy was clearly intended to prevent a return to the abuses of the past. Furthermore, the FBI continued to self-impose restrictions on when terrorism investigations could be opened (Smith & Morgan, 1994). Although the new guidelines did not mandate the necessity of a "criminal predicate," the term came to be the standard descriptor used by agents when discussing the threshold for opening a terrorism enterprise investigation (Smith, 1994).

Terrorist organizations reacted to the FBI's focus on groups by implementing "leaderless resistance" or lone wolf strategies in an effort to avoid terrorism investigations (Shields, 2012; Smith, 1994). According to some scholars, the guidelines established the primary goal of decimating groups by convicting leaders, even if that meant lighter sentences for the members who carried out the attacks (Smith & Damphousse, 1996). This approach had a significant impact on negotiated pleas, and the number of defendants who turned state's evidence (Shields, 2008; Shields, Smith, & Damphousse, 2006). In addition, the FBI and the Department of Justice continued to maintain the position that terrorists should be perceived, portrayed, tried, and punished as "conventional" criminals (Smith & Damphousse, 1996). By contrast, federal officials placed renewed emphasis on international terrorism, but without a policy to recast those crimes as nonpolitical. Essentially, a dual system emerged in which domestic terrorists were portrayed as common criminals, while international terrorists were much more likely to be portrayed and described as "terrorists" (Smith, 1994).

1990s: Oklahoma City and the First World Trade Center Attack

Despite America's history with domestic terrorism, through the late 1980s Americans viewed terrorism as something that happened in Europe or the Middle East, and most probably gave no thought to the possibility that the scourge of terrorism might blight American soil. The first World Trade Center bombing in 1993 and the Murrah Federal Building bombing in 1995 changed that, awakening the American public to a terrible new reality. While Islamic extremists had targeted Americans and American interests overseas before the first WTC attack, the U.S. mainland had remained relatively secure. After the first WTC bombing, authorities uncovered subsequent plots to bomb New York City landmarks further, which emphasized that the threat of international terrorism on American soil was no longer merely a threat.

In 1996, Congress passed the *Antiterrorism and Effective Death Penalty Act* (AEDPA), which, among other things, modified habeas corpus proceedings by limiting the procedural and substantive scope of writs, established mandatory victim restitution, and under Title III, provided the government with the ability to designate Foreign Terrorist Organizations (FTOs) and punish efforts to financially support them (104th Congress, 1996). Additionally, Congress placed several terrorism-related offenses within the scope of federal jurisdiction (Giraldo & Trinkunas, 2007), and provided harsher sentences, while exposing perpetrators to the full brunt of federal law enforcement capability.

The AEDPA was a necessary policy change brought about by the collapse of the Soviet Union and globalization. Before the end of the cold war, major international terrorist groups were dependent on state sponsorship (Giraldo & Trinkunas, 2007). By the early 1990s, these groups were forced to become more self-sufficient and turned to charities, criminal behavior, and other schemes to finance their operations. Globalization permitted terrorists to utilize the increasingly integrated world financial system, provided increased opportunities for moving personnel around the globe, and enhanced communications.

For scholars studying individuals indicted for terrorism-related activities, the AEDPA created fairly large groups of persons who were indicted in federal courts. Over the next decade (1996–2006) authorities indicted more than 325 persons for providing material support to foreign terrorist groups. Emphasis on identifying these perpetrators blurred the previously rather simple distinctions between "domestic" and "international" terrorism. In the past, almost all domestic terrorists had been American citizens, while the overwhelming majority of international terrorists had been noncitizens. By the turn of the century, identifying who was being investigated under which set of Attorney General (AG) guidelines became "muddied," and that would only grow worse after the attacks of 9/11.

2000s: Policy Changes after 9/11

After 9/11, the strategies used to combat terrorism in the United States underwent a dramatic change. In broad terms, the American antiterrorism policy was refocused on terrorist organizations, affiliated networks, and state sponsors in an effort to identify potential terrorist threats and *proactively prevent* future attacks. In a seminal statement released after 9/11, Attorney General John Ashcroft explained that the policy of the United

States Government changed from prosecuting terror-related crimes that had already occurred to thwarting attacks before they could happen (Ashcroft, 2001).

Prior to this time, the FBI had remained primarily a "reactive" agency – in which preventive intelligence gathering played second fiddle to the more conservative standard associated with a criminal predicate. After September 11, 2001, Congressional and public complaints regarding the FBI's lack of an intelligence apparatus in place to prevent such an attack were commonplace.

With these new proactive goals in mind, the U.S. Congress and Executive Branch agencies changed a number of policies to provide new tools for combating terrorism. The creation of fusion centers, the National Counterterrorism Center, and passage of new, less restrictive investigative guidelines by Attorney General Ashcroft reflected this paradigm shift. Some policies expanded legal authority to engage international terrorism that occurs away from American soil (Perl, 2003). Other policies expanded legal authority to intercept, investigate, and prosecute domestic terrorists.

Terrorism Financing

Among the new areas of focus was terrorism financing. Prior to 9/11, investigating terrorism financing was neither a priority for the FBI, nor was it addressed with any sense of urgency (Eckhert, 2008). Yager (2008) noted that before 9/11, the FBI did not systematically collect or analyze data on terrorism financing, which hindered the bureau's ability to counter financing mechanisms. To address this shortcoming, the government devoted more attention to terrorism financing. What it found in the years following 9/11, was that terrorist groups were becoming even more self-sufficient – exploiting sources of funding that "require neither ideological sympathy nor consent of [donors]," such as charities (Giraldo & Trinkunas, 2007). The depth and diversity of financing schemes concerned policy makers, so considerably more focus was placed on this issue. In 2008, the DOJ said that its use of material support statutes (18 USC 2339A, et seq.) had "formed a critical component of the Department's overall terrorist prosecutorial efforts, allowing prosecutors to target … terrorists and intervene during early stages of terrorist planning" (Department of Justice, 2008). Literature on the subject verifies that assertion.

Parrott (2009) studied 328 material support cases and determined that the FBI became adept at intercepting wire transfers and placed the greatest effort on seizing assets. Accordingly, groups tried to adapt to the increased scrutiny by relying more heavily on conventional criminality for fund raising (Passas, 2007; Williams, 2007). While terrorist financing schemes continued to rely heavily on charities and wire transfers in the post 9/11 era, offenders who did engage in conventional criminality chose crimes that required skill and expertise, such as smuggling and arms trading, rather than kidnapping, robbery, or extortion (Parrott, 2009, p. 55). The FBI's emphasis on material support is telling. Since 2007, charges of Material Support for Terrorists (18 USC 2339A) and Material Support for Terrorist Groups (18 USC 2339B) are the two most frequently indicted charges in jihadist-linked terrorism cases. In 2011, 87.5% of those cases included a material support count (Terrorism Trial Report Card, 2012, p. 18).

USA PATRIOT Act and Immigration Reform

Of course, 9/11 ushered in new legislation that would impact the investigation and prosecution of terrorism. For example, Congress revisited the Anti-Terrorism and Effective Death Penalty Act, and created the USA PATRIOT Act of 2001 (PATRIOT Act) to extend and strengthen U.S. antiterrorism policy. In addition, the Executive Branch changed the Department of Justice policy on how the FBI and U.S. Attorneys would handle the investigation and prosecution of terror suspects, namely through the newly minted Ashcroft Attorney General Guidelines (Shields, 2012). The new AG Guideline changed investigation and prosecution in a number of key areas

Before 9/11, the Smith Guidelines had required FBI field offices to refer potential terrorism investigations involving two or more persons to the director or assistant director of the FBI; they could authorize a "terrorism enterprise" investigation. Once the director authorized such an investigation, he had to report that fact to the Office of Intelligence Policy and Review. The Smith Guidelines also required the director or another top official to monitor the progress of the investigation at 180-day intervals. Section (B)(4)(a) of the Ashcroft Guidelines loosened those standards by allowing agents in the field to authorize a terrorism investigation for a period of up to one year. Shields (2012) maintains that unlike the Smith Guidelines, the Ashcroft Guidelines allowed the Special Agent in Charge to renew the investigation without additional authorization from the FBI HQ. While a field office was required, within one year, to report to the FBI HQ any terrorism investigations it initiated and provide reports, permission to open an investigation was no longer necessary.

The 9/11 attack spawned reform to immigration policies as well. Change was inevitable, as investigations into the attack revealed that each of the hijackers had entered the United States with student or visitor visas. Indeed, 59% of foreign-born terrorists who operated in the United States between 1990 and 2004 had committed immigration fraud (Kephart, 2005). Congress passed several measures to enhance border security, increase data collection and information sharing, and broaden the government's power to detain and deport immigrants. Just eight days after 9/11, Congress considered the *Anti-Terrorism Act of 2001*, which provided for increased authority of domestic intelligence gathering in money laundering schemes used in terrorist financing, and a streamlined set of rules for judicial procedures for deporting suspected terrorists (Rosenblum, 2011). That act was amended to include sunset provisions placing two-year limits on the due process and indefinite detention provisions, and passed as the PATRIOT Act in October 2001 (Rosenblum, 2011).

The PATRIOT Act mandated that the FBI provide criminal records to INS and State Department officials during visa screening. Congress passed the *Enhanced Border Security and Visa Entry Reform Act* in May 2002, which mandated even more data sharing and accelerated implementation of foreign student and entry–exit tracking systems (107th Congress, 2002).

The impact of immigration policy changes on terrorism prosecutions has been significant. An examination of federal terrorism cases following 9/11 revealed that the FBI and the Executive Office of United States Attorneys (EOUSA) had begun to focus on the types of crimes (immigration violations and financial fraud) that jihadist-linked terrorists were known to engage in prior to carrying out attacks (Chesney, 2007). Further research examining pre- and post-9/11 terrorism cases from 1980 to 2004, focused on "diffusion cases," which were labeled as terrorism-related by the FBI but contained no link to a group, ideology, or planned act of terrorism (Shields, 2012). The study found that 85% of all diffusion cases involved charges of identity fraud, immigration violations, or some form of financial fraud, and the FBI had not pursued similar cases prior to 9/11 (Shields, 2012, p. 85).

The federal government reacted to 9/11 by enacting new laws and strengthening existing ones. Policymakers sought to better secure America's borders by plugging holes in immigration policy. Congress provided immigration officials with more streamlined procedures for investigating and deporting foreign nationals, and legislators made the job of assessment easier by mandating information sharing between agencies. Indeed, intelligence gathering and sharing became a cornerstone of the post-9/11 strategy. With a focus on how terror groups operate, efforts to curtail and prosecute terror financing emerged as well. By the end of the decade following 9/11, federal prosecutors were filing more material support charges than ever before.

TERRORISM ON TRIAL

Defendants investigated as suspected terrorists under the Attorney Generals' Guidelines and later charged with crimes in federal court have been the focus of empirical research for more than 25 years, in part, because they behave differently than similarly situated federal defendants and they have been processed differently by the federal criminal justice system. Each phase, from investigation strategies and charging decisions, to prosecution and defense strategies and their relationship to negotiated pleas and trial outcomes, to conviction rates and sentencing outcomes, deserves separate treatments.

Investigating and Indicting Suspected Terrorists

As mentioned above, prior to 1980, most domestic terrorists were portrayed in court as common criminals. In most cases, every effort was made to avoid raising the specter of a "political trial." Common practices used by both defense and prosecutors included filing motions "in limine" to avoid mention of the word "terrorist," the name of the terrorist group, or the ideology to which the group adhered; avoiding seditious conspiracy charges; and using "presumed" or "strict liability" counts that did not require mention of the terrorists' intent in order to obtain a conviction (Smith, 1994). That began to change in the 1980s, as prosecutors experimented with politicized prosecution strategies. Some prosecutors learned, however, that the discussion of "motive" in terrorism trials could be extremely hazardous to conviction rates.

In contrast, international terrorists were often prosecuted differently. In many cases their trials were explicitly politicized and prosecutors frequently call the defendants "terrorists" and "revolutionaries." Prosecutors used those terms, ostensibly, to evoke to the jury the threat these offenders posed to national security. The successful conviction of the first WTC bombers and their associates in 1995 represented the first successful prosecution of terrorists on seditious conspiracy charges in over a decade (Shields, 2012).

In the early 1980s, the government's response focused on infiltrating terrorist cells, either by undercover government agents or by turning rank and file members of suspected terrorist organizations into confidential informants, and gathering evidence of planned operations and attacks for the purpose of charging group leaders with conspiracy crimes centered on those plans. The impetus on indicting leaders and putting them behind bars was driven by the policy goal of tearing the organizations apart from the top down. By targeting group leaders the government hoped to disrupt the groups and help assuage the threat of their radical agendas.

This policy was time consuming, requiring time to infiltrate and build relationships with group members, but prior to 9/11, the FBI and other federal agencies had successfully infiltrated groups to the extent that 29% of all cases filed in federal court involved an undercover agent (Shields, 2012). Federal agencies were even more successful in convincing group members to turn states evidence. Prior to 9/11, prosecutors were using evidence provided by confidential informants in 59% of all federal terrorism cases.

In an effort to disrupt potential threats, the post-9/11 policy shift ushered in new strategies directing federal investigators and prosecutors to arrest and prosecute suspected terrorists as soon as sufficient evidence of criminal wrongdoing was obtained. This shift had a profound and predictable impact on the type of investigations the government conducted, as well as the proportion of cases involving successful infiltration. After 9/11, the government made use of confidential informants in just 14% of cases filed against suspected terrorists, and undercover agents in only 3% of those cases. It should be noted that Shields (2008) found no significant drop in the amount or quality of evidence provided by confidential informants after 9/11, though the average number of confidential informants per case did decrease.

With fewer informants and undercover agents to provide evidence, prosecutors sought indictments with a smaller proportion of cases involving complex conspiracies in between 2002 and 2004 than before. Consequently, prosecutors relied on a greater variety of statutes to convict suspected terrorists (Chesney, 2007; Shields, 2008, 2012; Smith et al., 2011). Indeed, the number of cases involving planned acts of terrorism dropped substantially in the first three years following 9/11 (Jackson, 2011). The proportion of cases linked to planned or completed terrorism events declined from 84.2% to 29.9% after the policy change (Jackson, 2011; Shields, 2008). However, the decreased use of CIs did not last. By the middle of the decade, the FBI was again developing CIs in terrorism investigations.

After the initial downturn following 9/11, the FBI increased the number of confidential informants in its counterterrorism network. In 2004, the FBI began recruiting confidential informants under the *Intelligence Reform and Terrorism Prevention Act of 2004*. In 2007, the FBI requested increased funding to better manage the vast network of Confidential Informants (Federal Bureau of Investigation, 2007). The proportion of cases involving confidential informants rose to nearly 50% by the time the Mukasey Guidelines were adopted in 2008 (Terrorism Trial Report Card, 2012), almost reaching pre-9/11 levels (Shields, 2012). Moreover, it is estimated that the number of confidential informants has grown from 2,800 in 1980 (Ostrow & Jackson, 1986) to more than 15,000 presently (Department of Justice, 2008).

A new challenge, centered on how informants are used, has emerged. Beginning after 9/11, the FBI no longer focused solely on individuals and groups actively engaged in terrorist activity, but according to some researchers, has begun seeking out those who would agree to participate in terrorism if the incentives are strong enough (*see* Terrorism Trial Report Card, 2011, p. 4). Aaronson (2011) maintains that a third of post-9/11 jihadist-linked terrorism arrests are the result of sting operations, and that 10% of arrests involved operations *led by* FBI informants. Between 2001 and 2011, 10 defendants unsuccessfully raised the entrapment defense (Terrorism Trial Report Card, 2011). During that same time frame, all but four of the high-profile domestic terrorism plots reported by the Department of Justice were the result of sting operations (Ismail, Shah, & Prasow, 2014, p. 21). Sting operations have met with criticism from the Muslim community and civil rights groups alike (Glionna, 2014; Markon, 2010), but a change in policy doesn't appear to be on the horizon (Holder, 2010). Not only have investigatory strategies changed, but the volume of terrorism cases has more than quadrupled (Shields, 2012).

From 1980 to 2001, the FBI referred approximately 500 individuals for prosecution following a domestic security/terrorism investigation. According to Smith et al. (2011), over 500 individuals were similarly referred and prosecuted in the first four years following September 11, 2001, and that number increased to over 1,000 by the end of 2010 (*see also*, Shields, 2012; *Terrorism Trial Report Card*, 2012). At the same time, the average number of defendants per case decreased after 9/11, dropping from

10 defendants to 4 defendants, and the average number of counts per indictment decreased from 13.8 to 7.9 (Shields, 2008; Smith et al., 2011). The average severity of charges filed against terrorist defendants also decreased (*see*, Jackson, 2011; Shields, 2008; Smith et al., 2011). Post-9/11 policy changes also impacted the prosecutorial and defense strategies used once suspected terrorists were indicted.

Prosecuting and Defending Suspected Terrorists

Unique to terrorism cases are politicized prosecution strategies employed by federal prosecutors. Similarly intriguing are the strategies used by defense attorneys to counter federal prosecutors. Smith and Damphousse (1996) first noted that federal prosecutors used explicitly politicized (explicit politicality) strategies to reveal to jurors the ideological beliefs and political motives of suspected terrorist defendants. Prosecutors using this strategy frequently sought conspiracy charges that directly tied the predicate criminal offense to the defendant's group affiliation or ideological beliefs. This, in turn, was typically done in concert with labeling the defendant as a member of an extremist group or the follower of an extremist ideology in charging documents, motions, and in open court (Shields, 2012).

Federal prosecutors used explicit politicality in 63% of the cases they pursued before 9/11 (Shields, 2008; Smith et al., 2011). Prosecutors also employed a second strategy that implied a link between the defendant and terrorism. Prosecutors using this strategy typically sought counts charging defendants with any number of crimes, but unlike the previous strategy, prosecutors make no attempt to link the defendant's alleged crimes to terrorism via indictments. Rather, prosecutors dropped "hints" during open court implying the defendant belonged to an extremist group or held extremist views. Shields (2008) reported the use of these hints at all phases of the criminal prosecution, from bail determinations to sentencing hearings. Prior to 9/11, prosecutors used this strategy about 25% of the time.

The final strategy, the conventional approach, involved treating suspected terrorist defendants as traditional offenders. Prosecutors avoid referring to the defendant's group affiliation or belief system, in essence, treating them as common criminals. Smith (1994) observed cases where federal prosecutors filed motions *in limine* to prevent defendants from using their trials as a soapbox to draw attention to their cause. While the conventional strategy was only used in one out of ten cases before 9/11, prosecutors relied on it in half of all cases later on (see Table 1). There has been a

Table 1. Prosecution Strategy before and after 9/11.

	Conventional Criminality	Implicit Politicality	Explicit Politicality	Total
Pre-9/11	67	135	348	550
	12.2%	24.5%	63.3%	100.0%
Post-9/11	200	82	129	411
	48.7%	20.0%	31.4%	100.0%
Total	174	169	419	961
	27.8%	22.6%	49.6%	100.0%

Note: $\chi^2 = 163.049$, df = 2, $p < .01$. 33 system missing (fugitive, awaiting trial, etc.).

marked and corresponding decrease in the use of both politicized strategies (explicit 31.4%; implicit 20.0%) after 9/11. When the data are disaggregated, the trend seems to be returning to a higher reliance on politicized strategies, as the use of both explicit politicality and implicit politicality has increased since 2005 (results not shown).

Shields (2008) and Smith et al. (2011) have suggested that the increased use of conventional prosecution strategies in the four years following 9/11 may be a result of the proactive policy to prosecute suspected terrorists earlier, as the practice may have resulted in a decrease in the number of confidential informants as well as the evidence they would provide. Whether that is the case, defense attorneys have responded by using more traditional defense strategies and, as will be discussed below, defendants have pleaded guilty at a higher rate since 9/11.

Responding to politicized prosecution methods, defense attorneys developed a number of strategies calculated to counter prosecutors. Defense attorneys who presented evidence that their clients were the focus of political persecution because of their beliefs dropped from 21.4% before 9/11, to 7.7% afterwards (see Table 2). Similarly, defense attorneys who tried to disassociate their clients from a terrorist group or ideology decreased from 33.5% to 10.1% after 9/11. Probably due to prosecutors increased reliance on conventional prosecution strategies, defense attorneys turned to conventional defense methods in greater numbers, from 45.1% to 82.3%, after 9/11 (Table 2).

Case Outcomes in Terrorism Trials

Investigation strategies affect prosecution strategies, which in turn, affect case outcomes (Shields, 2008, 2012; Smith et al., 2011). Smith and

Table 2. Defense Strategy before and after 9/11.

Defense Strategy				
Case type	Political persecution	Disassociate	Conventional	Total
Pre-9/11	103	161	217	481
	21.4%	33.5%	45.1%	100.0%
Post-9/11	29	38	311	378
	7.7%	10.1%	82.3%	100.0%
Total	132	199	528	859
	15.4%	23.2%	61.5%	100.0%

Note: $\chi^2 = 123.673$, df = 2, $p < .01$. 135 system missing.

Damphousse (1998) determined that terrorists behave differently at trial than similarly situated federal criminal defendants, noting that terrorists were much more likely to go to trial than their nonterrorist counterparts (see also, Shields et al., 2006). Studying cases from 1980 to 2004, Shields (2008) noted a radical shift in how the FBI and EOUSA processed cases, and a corresponding change in case outcomes, after 9/11. Interestingly, through 2015 case outcomes remain dramatically different than before 9/11. Below are results derived from an analysis of case outcomes in terrorism trials (1980–2015). The data analyzed are from the American Terrorism Study, a database housed in the Terrorism Research Center in Fulbright College at the University of Arkansas (Terrorism Research Center in Fulbright College, 2015).

As Table 3 reveals, the conviction rates for indicted defendants increased slightly from 81% in the pre-9/11 era to 87.1% in the post-9/11 era, and the means by which those defendants were convicted differ dramatically. The biggest change occurred in the proportion of defendants who entered guilty pleas versus those who went to trial between the eras. While less than one half (46.5%) of defendants indicted prior to 9/11 pleaded guilty, more than three-quarters (75.2%) did so after 9/11. Mistrials and dismissals increased after 9/11 from 10.9% to 11.4%, but jury convictions decreased from 34.5% to 11.9%.

In the first four years following 9/11, it is possible that the "early prosecution" mandate demanded by Attorney General Ashcroft impeded the government's ability to infiltrate extremist groups with agents, and likewise, it may have limited the amount of time government agents had to develop relationships with potential informants who were associated with group members. In preliminary studies, Shields (2008), Jackson (2011), and Smith

Table 3. Disposition of Defendants before and after 9/11.

Era	Dismiss/Mistrial	Acquittal at Trial	Jury Conviction	Plead Guilty	Total
Pre-9/11	55	41	174	235	505
	10.9%	8.1%	34.5%	46.5%	100.0%
Post-9/11	46	6	48	303	403
	11.4%	1.5%	11.9%	75.2%	100.0%
Total	101	47	222	538	908
	11.1%	5.2%	24.4%	59.3%	100.0%

Note: $\chi^2 = 96.737$, df = 3, $p < .01$. 86 system missing (fugitive, transferred, etc.).

et al. (2011), do suggest a significant shift in the way the government pursued and prosecuted terrorists after 9/11.

The policy shift may have been responsible for limiting the amount of evidence available to prosecutors. Shields (2008) suggested that less evidence probably caused a shift in the type of cases prosecutors pursued and the type of prosecution strategies they employed resulting in an increase in negotiated pleas. It is also possible that these lower levels of evidence might be the cause of the noted increase in the number of case dismissals. What is more intriguing, since 2005 the FBI has increased the use of confidential informants, and while the use of human intelligence has not yet returned to pre-9/11 levels, the conviction rate remains higher than observed before the September 11, 2001 attacks. More analysis is clearly needed.

Sentence Outcomes for Convicted Terrorists

While conviction rates increased after September 11, and defendants were charged with slightly less severe lead offenses, Shields (2008) noted an average drop of 138 months in average prison sentences after 9/11, from 203 months to 65 months (see also Smith et al., 2011). Although the sentence gap narrowed to 120 months when immigration and financial fraud cases (the aforementioned "diffusion" cases) were excluded from the post-9/11 sample, there remained a rather dramatic and statistically significant difference between the eras. These findings are not unique (*see also*, Terrorism Trial Report Card, 2012).

We realize that is not desirable, and perhaps misleading, to use "sentence in months" as an indicator of changes in sentence length because of alterations to federal sentencing procedures. Indeed, changes in federal sentencing policies render direct comparisons tenuous at best. One goal of the federal sentencing guidelines was to reduce disparity among "similarly situated" defendants. Smith (1994) and Smith and Damphousse (1996) addressed this issue, and found that individuals involved in terrorism cases received harsher sentences than others convicted of the same lead offenses. A later examination of postsentencing guidelines in terrorism cases found that this disparity had dropped considerably, but that it remained significant (Smith & Damphousse, 1998).

The drop in sentencing disparity in the post-9/11 era suggests that a number of other factors may be at work. We noted a small but significant decrease in count severity in lead offenses in post-9/11 cases, which may have had a small but significant impact on the average sentence length. Moreover, we should expect shorter prison sentences among defendants who pleaded guilty as compared to those who are convicted at trial. Recall, prosecutors and defendants agreed to plead guilty in three-quarters of all cases filed after 9/11, an increase of 28% from before 9/11. Third, Jackson (2011) determined that prosecutors were more likely to accept guilty pleas on fewer counts within an indictment in the post-9/11 era, reducing the opportunity for consecutive sentences and lowering overall offense severity. Jackson also found the percentage of unconvicted counts per indictment before 9/11 was roughly 37% while the percentage of unconvicted counts per indictment after 9/11 was about 82%. Therefore, several things are probably impacting the decline in sentence length. As the FBI has moved to a "proactive" rather than "reactive" stance regarding terrorism after 9/11, they have begun to intervene earlier in investigations. This frequently means evidentiary strength is not as great in these cases (Jackson, 2011), which results in greater willingness among prosecutors to negotiate a plea agreement.

CONCLUSION

While the armored car robberies of the 1980s led to a flush of terrorism cases in the federal system, 9/11 has had the most significant impact on the federal courts. Changes to government intervention strategies affected the manner in which terrorists planned terrorist activities and how they structured their groups. Each successive terrorist event impacted policy-driven strategies, changing the nature of how terrorism cases were investigated and prosecuted.

America's response to terrorism has shifted from treating politically motivated offenders as common criminals in the 1960s and 1970s, to explicitly politicizing "terrorists" group membership and ideological beliefs in the 1980s and 1990s. After 9/11, prosecution strategies shifted back again, reserving explicit politicality for only the most egregious cases. The shift in strategies may be due, in part, to the type of investigations performed by the FBI, which are in turn driven by policy considerations and the legal authority to act. Highly politicized prosecution strategies are unique to terrorism cases, and they spawned the development of defense strategies. Despite the changing legal and investigatory environment, federal prosecutors pursued several times as many "terrorism" cases after 9/11 than before. Even with the higher volume cases, conviction rates have steadily improved.

REFERENCES

104th Congress: Antiterrorism and Effective Death Penalty Act (1996). Retrieved from https://www.govtrack.us/congress/bills/104/s735

107th Congress: Enhanced Border Security and Visa Entry Reform Act (2002). Retrieved from https://www.govtrack.us/congress/bills/107/hr3525

Aaronson, T. (2011). The Informants. *Mother Jones*. September/October 2011 Issue.

Ackerman, S. (2014). *Government agents 'directly involved' in most high-profile US terror plots*. Retrieved from http://www.theguardian.com/world/2014/jul/21/government-agents-directly-involved-us-terror-plots-report

Ashcroft, J. (2001). *Remarks of attorney general John Ashcroft*. Retrieved from http://www.justice.gov/archive/ag/speeches/2002/53002agpreparedremarks.htm

Chesney, R. (2007). *Federal prosecution of terrorism-related cases: Conviction and sentencing data in light of the "Data Reliability" and "Soft Sentence" critiques*. Retrieved from http://ssrn.com/abstract_id=1005478

Department of Justice. (2008). *FY 2008 authorization and budget request of congress*. Retrieved from http://www.fas.org/irp/agency/doj/fbi/2008just.pdf

Eckhert, S. (2008). US regulatory approach. *Countering the financing of terrorism*. London: Routledge.

Elliff, J. (1979). *The reform of FBI intelligence operations*. Princeton, NJ: Princeton University Press.

Enhanced Border Security and Visa Entry Reform Act of 2002, Pub. L. No. 107-173, 107th Cong., 2nd sess. (2002, March 12). The Antiterrorism and Effective Death Penalty Act of 1996, Pub. L. No. 104-132, 104th Cong., 2nd sess. (April 15, 1996).

Federal Bureau of Investigation. (2007). *FY 2008 authorization and budget request to congress*. Retrieved from https://www.documentcloud.org/documents/238034-33-fbi-se-2.html

Giraldo, J., & Trinkunas, H. (2007). Terrorist financing: Explaining government responses. *Terrorism financing and state responses: A comparative perspective*. Stanford, CA: Stanford UP.

Glionna, J. (2014). U.S. Muslim Leader say FBI pressuring people to become informants. *Los Angeles Times*, November 3, 2014.

Hearings before the Subcommittee on Administrative Practice and Procedure of the Committee of the Judiciary on FBI Statutory Charter. (1978). 95th Cong., 2d sess., June–September (pp. 98–99). Washington, DC: U.S. Government Printing Office.

Holder, E. (2010). *Attorney general Eric Holder speaks at the Muslim advocates' annual dinner.* Retrieved from http://www.justice.gov/opa/speech/attorney-general-eric-holder-speaks-muslim-advocates-annual-dinner

Ingraham, B., & Tokoro, K. (1969). Political crime in the United States and Japan: A comparative study. *Issues in Criminology*, *4*, 145–171.

Ismail, T., Shah, N., & Prasow, A. (2014). *Illusion of justice, human rights abuses in US terrorism prosecutions.* Retrieved from http://www.hrw.org/sites/default/files/reports/usterrorism0714_ForUpload_1_0.pdf

Jackson, S. (2011). *Measuring intervention success in countering terrorism.* Thesis (defended May 2011, University of Arkansas). Unpublished manuscript.

Kelley, C., & Davis, J. (1987). *Kelley: The story of an FBI director.* Kansas City, MO: Andrews, McMeel, and Parker Publishing.

Kephart, J. (2005). *Moving beyond the 9/11 Staff report on terririst travel.* Center for Immigration Studies. Retrieved from http://cis.org/articles/2005/kephart.html

Markon, J. (2010). Tension grows between Calif. Muslims, FBI after informant infiltrates mosque. *Washington Post*, December 5, 2010.

Office of the Attorney General. (1983). *Attorney general's guidelines on domestic security/terrorism investigations.* Washington, DC: Office of the Attorney General.

Ostrow, R., & Jackson, R. (1986). U.S. Agents Make Increasing Use of Informants: But 'Handlers' Face Complex Legal Hazards When Condoning Criminal Acts. *Los Angeles Times*, June 15, 1986.

Parrott, N. (2009). *An analysis of terrorism financing court cases.* University of Arkansas. Retrieved from http://gradworks.umi.com/14/59/1459010.html

Passas, N. (2007). Terrorism financing mechanisms and policy dilemmas. *Terrorism financing and state responses: A comparative perspective.* Stanford, CA: Stanford UP.

Perl, R. (2003). Terrorism, the Future, and American Foreign Policy. *Issue Brief for Congress*, Order Code IB95112, Foreign Affairs, Trade and Research Division.

Poveda, J. (1990). *Lawlessness and Reform: The FBI in transition.* Pacific Grove, CA: Brooks/Cole.

Rosenblum, M. (2011). *US immigration policy since 9/11: Understanding the stalemate over comprehensive immigration reform.* Washington, DC: Migration Policy Institute.

Russell, C., & Miller, B. (1977). Profile of a terrorist. *Terrorism: An International Journal*, *1*, 17–27.

Shields, C. (2008). *An analysis of prosecutorial and defense strategies in federal terrorism trials from 1980 to 2004.* Dissertation (defended December 2008), UMI Number: 3341235.

Shields, C. (2012). *American terrorism trials: Prosecutorial and defense strategies.* El Paso, TX: LFB Scholarly Publishing, LLC (print release September 2012).

Shields, C., Smith, B., & Damphousse, K. (2006). Their day in court: Assessing plea bargain rates among terrorists. *Journal of Contemporary Criminal Justice, 22*(3), 261–276.

Smith, B. (1994). *Terrorism in America: Pipe bombs and pipe dreams.* Albany, NY: State University of New York Press.

Smith, B. L., & Damphousse, K. R. (1996). Punishing political offenders: The effect of political motive on federal sentencing decisions. *Criminology*, *34*(3), 289–321.

Smith, B., & Damphousse, K. (1998). Terrorism, politics, and punishment: A test of structural-contextual theory and the 'liberation hypothesis'. *Criminology, 36*(1), 67–92.

Smith, B., & Morgan, K. (1994). Terrorists right and left: Empirical issues in profiling American terrorists. *Studies in Conflict and Terrorism, 17*, 39–57.

Smith, B., Shields, C., & Damphousse, K. (2011). Patterns of Intervention in Federal Terrorism Cases. Year 2 Progress Report, June 2011, for DHS project via the START Center of Excellence, University of Maryland. Creation and Analysis of an Integrated U.S. Security Database (IUSSD), BAA number 08-01.

Terrorism Research Center in Fulbright College. (2015). *The American terrorism study (database)*. Retrieved from http://trc.uark.edu/

Terrorism Trial Report Card, Greenberg, K. J. (Eds.). (2011). *The center of law and security*. New York, NY: University School of Law.

Terrorism Trial Report Card, Greenberg, K. J. (Eds.). (2012). *The center of law and security*. New York, NY: University School of Law.

Turk, A. (1982). *Political criminality*. Beverley Hills, CA: Sage.

Uniting and Strengthening America by Providing Appropriate Tools Required to Intercept and Obstruct Terrorism Act, (P L. 107-56) enacted October 2001.

U.S. Department of Justice, Office of the Inspector General. (2007). The Department of Justice's Internal Controls over Terrorism Reporting (Audit Report 02–07). Retrieved from http://www.justice.gov/oig/reports/plus/a0720/final.pdf

Williams, P. (2007). Warning indicators. *Terrorism financing and state responses: A comparative perspective*. Stanford, CA: Stanford University Press.

Yager, L. (2008). *Terrorist financing: On deterring operations in the U.S.* New York, NY: General Accounting Office.

POSTMODERN TORTURE AND THE CONCEITS OF THE WAR ON TERROR

Michael Welch

ABSTRACT

Purpose – *This chapter delves into the controversy over detention and interrogation in the war on terror carried out by American operatives. While attending to political, legal, and ethical concerns, critical attention is directed at the manner by which certain interrogation techniques have been framed as being "scientific" and therefore effective in extracting truthful disclosures from terror suspects.*

Methodology/approach – *Drawing on extensive legal and medical literature, the critique offers a postmodern analysis by raising serious questions over the effectiveness and legitimacy of enhanced interrogation espoused by the Bush administration. By doing so, the conceits of the war on terror are exposed and confronted.*

Findings – *In 2014, the report of the Senate Select Committee on Intelligence (Study of the CIA's Detention and Interrogation Program) was unclassified and released to the public. Among other revelations, the document clearly shows that interrogators and their psychological*

Terrorism and Counterterrorism Today
Sociology of Crime, Law and Deviance, Volume 20, 197–218

ISSN: 1521-6136/doi:10.1108/S1521-613620150000020010

consultants committed torture. In doing so, they often relied on medical knowledge for harming, rather than healing. Ethical and legal remedies aimed at correcting those problems are recommended.

Originality/value – *The chapter delivers a sophisticated critique that blends recently revealed evidence of torture with postmodern interpretation. While casting doubt on the effectiveness and legitimacy of enhanced interrogation, discussion throws critical light on incidents of human rights abuses committed by health professionals. Paradoxically, those physicians and psychologists opted to use their medical skills and expertise to inflict suffering rather than alleviating it. Those acts constitute egregious ethical and legal violations that warrant prosecution.*

Keywords: Torture; human rights; war on terror; postmodernism

INTRODUCTION

The resurgence of torture as a tool for generating intelligence in the war on terror has brought about a contentious dialogue covering political, legal, and ethical issues (Cohen, 2006; Dershowitz, 2002; Gearty, 2005; Greenberg & Dratel, 2005). While not losing sight of those areas of the concern, it is also important to consider how certain interrogation methods have become framed by advocates as being "scientific" and therefore effective in extracting truthful disclosures from terror suspects. In this critique of the war on terror, in-depth analysis takes aim at the emergence of science as a model for interrogation. By doing so, serious doubts are raised, prompting reflection on torture as it passed through its premodern, modern, and postmodern phases. For instance, in medieval – premodern – times the church and monarchy resorted to brutal public spectacles to produce confessions of heresy and treason (Foucault, 1977; Garland, 1990; Langbein, 1977). The target of pain was, of course, the body even though it accompanied enormous psychological trauma. Indeed, waterboarding – a technique that injects an acute sense of drowning – was a common form of torture during the Spanish Inquisition (Cantini, 2010; Welch, 2014).

Centuries later, torture became a modern practice during the Cold War as scientists tapped into the field of psychology as a means of unlocking the unconscious mind while not "leaving marks" on the body. Toward that end, the CIA invested vast resources for mind control studies, often

involving hallucinogenic drug
Marks, 1979; McCoy, 2006).
to pass into its current postm
in the wake of 9/11. Recent
psychological consultants rel
healing but rather for harm
fessionals were not mere b
ried out techniques such
hydration (Institute on M
Human Rights [PHR], 201
[SSCI], 2014). While postr
create the illusion of humane trea
sist in the form of beatings, sexual humiliation, and s
2007).

In the pages to follow, critical attention is turned to a series of key developments. Discussion begins with a genealogy of how torture came to be understood as "scientific" amid the Cold War. In the aftermath of the attacks on September 11, 2001, torture became medicalized, albeit dubiously. Compounding matters, health care professionals engaged in activities that deliberately harmed – rather than healed – detainees. The chapter then turns to three illusions surrounding postmodern torture: the respectability of "scientific" discourse, the "reversibility" of injuries, and warping the rule of law. Overall, the objective of this critique is to call into question recent practices of torture and harsh interrogation. Along the way, postmodern reflection allows us to recognize the conceits of the war on terror as government operatives incorporate scientists, psychologists, and medical personnel into state power. Rather than advancing enlightened technological progress, however, those partnerships have paved the way for serious violations of human rights.

INVENTING "SCIENTIFIC" TORTURE

During the Cold War, the US government supported the CIA's pursuit of research on mind-control as a means to combat Communism and espionage. Billions of tax dollars were funneled into experiments aimed at studying the effects of hallucinogenic drugs, electric shock, and sensory deprivation, becoming a massive scientific campaign that McCoy calls "a veritable Manhattan Project of the mind" (2006, p. 7; Simpson, 1994).

…s are especially relevant to a genealogy of modern tor- …eflect a strong dependence on behavioral and psychological …veloping its theoretical foundation (Welch, 2009a, 2009b). …ditional forms of torture implemented physical tactics targeting …, modern torture relies increasingly on psychological techniques to … pain and suffering. Among its innovations, the emerging "science" …nterrogation produced a method known as no-touch torture. …ychologists had concluded that physical pain regardless of its intensity generated resistance, and therefore undermined efforts to extract truthful information from the subject (Biderman, 1957, 1960). To overcome that obstacle, a new psychological paradigm of torture was designed that integrated self-inflicted pain with sensory deprivation (CIA, 1963). Researchers theorized that subjects capitulate more readily to interrogation when they feel responsible for their own suffering because the synergy of physical and psychological trauma unfastens personal identity (Biderman & Zimmer, 1961; Watson, 1978). The iconic image of a hooded Iraqi detainee at Abu Ghraib standing on a box with arms extended to electrical wires suggests a CIA interrogation method geared toward both sensory deprivation (i.e., the hood) and self-inflicted pain (i.e., extended arms; McCoy, 2006).

The origins of modern torture are commonly traced to a CIA training manual titled KUBARK Counterintelligence Interrogation (1963; declassified in 1997). It is in that instructional booklet that no-touch torture was codified for purposes of teaching interrogators "scientifically-informed" techniques assumed to be effective in extracting details from persons suspected of clandestine plans or insurgent activities. The objective of KUBARK is clear:

> Unlike the police interrogation, the CI [counterterintelligence] interrogation is not aimed at causing the interrogatee to incriminate himself as a means of bringing him to trial. Admissions of complicity are not, to a CI service, ends in themselves but merely preludes to the acquisition of more information. (CIA, 1963, p. 5)

KUBARK's techniques aimed at "breaking' prisoners" (or "pulling information from a recalcitrant subject" p. 30) are different from earlier forms of interrogation, most notably due to its focus on psychological pain. Furthermore, the infliction of injuries would be difficult to detect since the scars remain deep inside the psyche (Doerr-Zegers, Hartman, Lira, & Weinstein 1992).

Written in a clinical – even cool – tone, KUBARK claims to follow some basic theoretical principles. As a central tenet, the manual theorizes that interrogation is improved significantly when the subject undergoes disorientation, leading to a regression of personality. With a weaker personal identity, according to that hypothesis, the subject becomes needy and dependent on a stronger even authoritative figure. Because the new paradigm of interrogation also strives toward efficiency, the process is accelerated by the use of isolation and sensory deprivation techniques (e.g., hooding and "sleep adjustment"). Confusion is achieved further by delivering nonviolent blows on the psyche (e.g., personal insults and sexual humiliation). The overarching objective of those psychological methods is to maximize the destructive force of self-inflicted pain. According to KUBARK: "It has been plausibly suggested that, whereas pain inflicted on a person from outside himself may actually focus or intensify his will to resist, his resistance is likelier to be sapped by the pain in which he seems to inflict upon himself" (CIA, 1963, p. 59). State power – notably the US government – has been instrumental in globalizing modern torture. Techniques devised by the CIA (contained in KUBARK) with the support of key research psychologists were propagated initially through the USAID's Office of Public Safety to police departments in Asia in the 1960s then later to Latin America after 1975. Soon the US Army Mobile Training Teams circulated the CIA's interrogation paradigm in the 1980s throughout much of Central America (Harbury, 2005; McCoy, 2006). Whereas the activities within those programs were covert, the political rationale was not: "scientific" torture would serve national security by battling the growing threat of Communism (Feitlowitz, 1998; Hinton, 2006; Huggins, Haritos-Fatouros, & Zimbardo, 2002). For the most part, torture was put back in the CIA's toolbox at the end of the Cold War while the US government resumed its public stance supporting human rights principles (e.g., participating in the World Conference on Human Rights in Vienna [1993], and ratifying the UN Convention Against Torture). After the attacks on September 11th, however, relatively dormant political ideologies surrounding the protection of national security would once again lead to the resurgence of torture as a prominent technology in the war on terror.

POSTMODERN TORTURE IN A POST-9/11 WORLD

The events of 9/11 prompted the White House to depict terrorism as an imminent and long-term threat to national security; consequently, its official response would feature a unique form of warfare directed at nonstate actors. Among the tactics used were harsh interrogation methods and torture: their purpose was to correct the information deficit since US intelligence has had but scant knowledge of Al Qaeda and its operations (Clarke, 2004). Whereas postmodern torture is not completely detached from its medieval ancestry with respect to brutality and scapegoating, the prevailing objective of enhanced interrogation was to collect intelligence in the war on terror rather than extracting a confession. That mission did not stray from the allure of "scientific" discourse in shaping its tactics. As Major General Geoffrey Miller, former administrator at Guantanamo Bay (and later Abu Ghraib) notes: "Harvesting intelligence through prisoner interrogations has become Guantanamo's principle raison d'etre" (Rose, 2004, p. 80).

As postmodern torture expanded its "scientific" thrust, it also took on a veneer of a clinical project. Toward that end, its strategies were based on truth claims involving the social need to intervene, expert knowledge, and effective results, all of which stem from state power. *Leave No Marks: Enhanced Interrogation Techniques and the Risk of Criminality*, Physicians for Human Rights and Human Rights First (Physicians for Human Rights [PHR] & Human Rights First [HRF], 2007) provides an exhaustive assessment of "enhanced" interrogation tactics employed by American operatives. It is a unique report because it combines medical literature based on survivors of torture with compelling legal narratives demonstrating the criminal nature of physical and psychological abuse. The review targets 10 methods of interrogations used in response to the events of September 11th: (1) stress positions, (2) beating, (3) temperature manipulation, (4) waterboarding, (5) threats of harm to person, family, or friends, (6) sleep deprivation, (7) sensory bombardment: noise and light, (8) violent shaking, (9) sexual humiliation, (10) prolonged isolation and sensory deprivation. In briefly describing those techniques, attention is turned to the degree of "scientific" influence contained in their development and application.

As the term suggests, stress positions refer to coercing a prisoner into painful physical posture for long periods of time (Central Intelligence Agency [CIA], 1956). CIA interrogators in Guantanamo Bay (and in Iraq and Afghanistan) were reportedly authorized to use a technique called "short shackling" whereby the subject was handcuffed and with their feet shackled to an eyebolt in the floor for more than 40 hours (Ross & Esposito, 2005). Stress positions (along with forced standing to induce fatigue) have been used to facilitate beatings, kicking, and "attention slaps" so as to promote a sense of debility, dependency, and helplessness. Such tactics also aim to humiliate detainees who are not given access to toilets, thereby leaving them to soil themselves. Another method involves subjecting detainees to "temperature manipulation" in rooms featuring extreme heat or cold and sometimes doused with cold water while being shackled. The technique called waterboarding (or mock drowning) entails strapping a prisoner down while water is poured over the face to create the sensation of asphyxiation. The practice is traced back to the Middle Ages when it was used in the Spanish and Italian inquisitions during the 1500s; in the 1970s, waterboarding was used by the Khmer Rouge regime in Cambodia as well as in Latin America where it was known as submarino (Ross, 2005; Schmitt & Marshall, 2006). Failure to cooperate with CIA interrogators was at times met with the threat to harm to the detainee or his family or friends. In a 2004 report, the International Committee of the Red Cross states that detainees in Iraq often alleged that interrogators used threats of ill-treatment, reprisals against family members, imminent execution, or transfer to Guantanamo Bay. Another common tactic used to "break down" interrogation subjects is sleep deprivation for extended periods through the use of stress positions, sensory overload, continual interruption normal sleep (CIA, 1963; Marks, 1979). In a 2002 memo that has since been rescinded, the Pentagon authorized the use of sleep deprivation for use on detainees at Guantanamo Bay in the form of 20-hour interrogations (Haynes, 2003). An investigation revealed a so-called "frequent-flyer" program in which detainees were regularly moved from one cell to another at intervals of two to four hours to interrupt their sleep (Schmidt & Furlow, 2005). Another technique, known as sensory bombardment, also disrupts sleep and disorients the detainee by barraging the subject with glaring lights and loud "aggressive" music for prolonged periods of time (Lewis, 2004). Lt. Col. V. Stuart Couch, a military prosecutor, described an incident of sensory bombardment he witnessed at Guantanamo Bay. The detainee was shackled to the floor of a cell with heavy metal music blaring. The detainee was "rocking back and forth, mumbling as strobe lights flashed." Couch said the treatment resembled the abuse he had been trained to resist if captured; "he never expected Americans would be the ones employing it" (Bravin, 2007, p. A1). The training that Couch referred to is the Survival, Evasion, Resistance, and Escape (SERE) training whereby US personnel are trained to resist torture techniques. As evidence of "reverse engineering," key aspects of SERE training became the basis for military and CIA interrogation techniques (PHR & HRF, 2007; Shane & Mazzetti, 2007). Also included in the roster of current interrogation aids is the use of violent shaking, causing pain and injury to the subject's upper torso and neck. The "attention grab" as it is known in the CIA is reminiscent of the tactic employed by the Israel security services until 1999 when the Israeli Supreme Court banned it (*Public Committee Against Torture in Israel v. The Government of Israel*, 1999). As the widely publicized photographs of Abu Ghraib illustrate, detainees in US military custody have been sexually humiliated. Forcing them naked into degrading sexual postures (e.g., simulated oral sex) is aimed to exploit cultural and religious sensitivities regarding sexual behavior in ways that induce shame, guilt, and worthlessness. The CIA, during the 1960s, began employing that interrogation tactic so as to strip its victims of their individual identities, rendering them powerless (McCoy, 2012). In 2005, U.S. Army investigation revealed the practice of sexual humiliation against detainees in Guantanamo Bay by having female interrogators attempt to physically seduce a Muslim detainee; forcing the detainee to wear a bra and placing women's underwear on his head; leading him around on a leash; forcing him to perform dog tricks; stripping him naked; and calling him a homosexual (Schmidt & Furlow, 2005).

Finally, prolonged isolation together with sensory deprivation is used to induce mental disorientation or artificial psychosis so as to "break down" the prisoner. The Pentagon authorized the use of sensory deprivation for use by the military whereby detainees were deprived of light and auditory stimuli and kept in isolation beyond 30 days (Haynes, 2003). An FBI investigation reported that a detainee at Guantanamo Bay "had been subjected to intense isolation for over three months. During that time period [the detainee] was totally isolated (with the exception of occasional interrogations) in a cell that was always flooded with light. The detainee was evidencing behavior consistent with extreme psychological trauma (talking to non-existent people, reporting hearing voices, crouching in a corner of the cell covered with a sheet for hours on end)" (Harrington, 2004, p. 1).

HEALTH PROFESSIONALS AND POSTMODERN TORTURE

In December 2014, the Senate Select Committee on Intelligence (SSCI) published their report on the CIA's detention and interrogation program. The 500-page summary is an unclassified portion of the full report that spans more than 6,700 pages (still classified). The Committee's study initially dates back to 2007 when the CIA destroyed its videotapes of interrogation of detainees, many of who were waterboarded. Given the wealth of previously uncovered human rights abuses, the Committee expanded its investigation from 2001 to 2009. In the Foreword to the Report, Senator Diane Feinstein, the Committee's Chairman, sets the record straight: detainees were, indeed, "tortured" and that the conditions of confinement were "cruel, inhuman, and degrading" (SSCI, 2014: Foreword, p. 4; see Findings and Conclusions, pp. 3–4). Furthermore, the report counters the (false) claims of torture effectiveness:

> It is my sincere and deep hope that through the release of these Findings and Conclusions and Executive Summary that U.S. policy will never again allow for secret indefinite detention and the use of coercive interrogations. As the Study describes, prior to the attacks of September 2001 the CIA itself determined from its own experience with coercive interrogations, that such techniques "do not produce intelligence," "will probably result in false answers," and had historically proven to be ineffective. Yet these conclusions were ignored. We cannot again allow history to be forgotten and grievous past mistakes to be repeated. (SSCI, 2014: Foreword p. 3; see Findings and Conclusions, pp. 2–3)

Among their Findings and Conclusions, the Committee revealed that: "Two contract psychologists devised the CIA's enhanced interrogation techniques and played a central role in the operation, assessments, and management of the CIA's Detention and Interrogation Program. By 2005, the CIA had overwhelmingly outsourced operations related to the program" (SSCI, 2014, Findings and Conclusions, p. 11). The reliance on health professionals – to a degree previously unknown – has enormous implications to postmodern reflection as well as the conceits of the war on terror. The Committee revealed that the two CIA psychologists, James Mitchell (code name "Grayson Swigert") and Bruce Jesson (code name "Hammond Dunbar") served as the torture program's chief architects. Mitchell and Jesson were granted exclusive authority to develop, operate, and assess their interrogation operations. The psychologists' prior experience was at the US Air Force Survival, Evasion, Resistance and Escape (SERE) School. However, "neither psychologist had any experience as an interrogator, nor did either have specialized knowledge of al-Qa'ida, a background in counterterrorism, or any relevant cultural or linguistic expertise" (SSCI, 2014, Findings and Conclusions, p. 11). In an eerie twist to the psychological theory, Mitchell and Jesson (mis)applied the research on "learned helplessness" (developed by esteemed scholar Martin Seligman, 1975). In a memo, Mitchell ("Grayson Swigert") proposed that "learned helplessness" would render detainees "passive and depressed in response to adverse and uncontrollable events, and would thus cooperate and provide information" (SSCI, 2014, Findings and Conclusions, p. 19).

Whereas the infliction of "learned helplessness" through an array of techniques (e.g., sensory deprivation, sensory bombardment, waterboarding) speaks of the postmodern nature of torture, recent revelations of profiteering throw critical light on the conceits of the program. Even though the Committee found that the use of "enhanced techniques was not an effective means of acquiring intelligence or gaining cooperation from detainees" (SSCI, Findings and Conclusions, p. 2), Mitchell, Jessen & Associates (the company they formed) were financially rewarded with an $81 million contract (and a budget in excess of $180 million dollars). Additionally, Mitchell and Jessen each received over $1 million from the CIA. Mitchell and Jessen were much more than architects and consultants; they become "operational psychologists" directly involved in interrogation and waterboarding. Moreover, they paid themselves handsomely. Their daily compensation reached $1,800 per day which was four times that of other interrogators (SSCI, 2014, Report, p. 66). Mitchell and Jessen were also legally immunized from potential prosecutions with a multiyear indemnification; since 2007, the CIA has paid out more than $1 million pursuant to the agreement. Overall, extensive outsourcing became a key strategy in this segment of the war on terror. In 2008, 85% of the workforce in the CIA's Rendition, Detention, and Interrogation Group comprised contractors (SSCI, 2014, Findings and Conclusions, p. 12; see Welch, 2015a).

Evidence of postmodern torture in the war on terror has attracted critical attention from human rights groups. In their report, *Doing Harm: Health Professionals' Central Role in the CIA Torture Program* (2014), Physicians for Human Rights delved into a host of ethical and legal matters. PHR highlights the crucial role of health professionals and finds that without their participation, "this illegal program might have been prevented" (2014, p. 3). PHR also concludes that "the violations committed by health professionals represent not only a gross breach of medical and professional ethics, but also violations of domestic and international law" (2014, p. 3). PHR outlines their report according to eight categories of abuse by health professionals, each of which points to the postmodern character of torture in the war on terror:

1) Designing, directing, and profiting from the torture program
2) Intentionally inflicting harm on detainees
3) Enabling DoJ lawyers to create a fiction of "safe, legal, and effective" interrogation practices
4) Engaging in potential human subjects research to provide legal cover for torture
5) Monitoring detainee torture and calibrating levels of pain
6) Evaluating and treating detainees for purposes of torture

7) Conditioning medical care on cooperation with interrogators
8) Failing to document physical and/or psychological evidence of torture. (PHR, 2014, p. 3)

PHR cites numerous incidents of CIA health professionals intentionally inflicting harm on detainees, such as administering clinical procedures for nonmedical reasons.

One of the most egregious examples of direct medical participation in torture is the use of rectal rehydration or rectal feeding. According to SSCI, a medical officer described the rectal rehydration procedure in a February 27, 2004 email: "[r]egarding the rectal tube, if you place it and open up the IV tubing, the flow will self regulate, sloshing up the large intestines .... [w]hat I infer is that you get a tube up as far as you can, then open the IV wide. No need to squeeze the bag – let gravity do the work" (2014, p. 100). While the CIA has defended its use of rectal rehydration as a "well acknowledged medical technique" (SSCI, 2014, p. 115), PHR insists that health professionals failed to establish or document medical necessity (2014, p. 6). "Moreover, the summary indicates that rectal hydration was used to control and/or punish the detainees .... Insertion of any object into the rectum of an individual without his consent constitutes a form of sexual assault" (PHR, 2014, p. 6).

In another disclosure, the SSCI (2014) revealed that health professionals collected data on interrogation practices in a manner that may constitute human subjects experimentation. PHR puts that finding into its proper historical context, noting that one of the key restrictions regarding medical ethics that came out of World War II was the prohibition against unethical human subjects experimentation. That ban was established upon discovering the atrocities committed by the Nazis and medical staff (see Lifton, 2000). To safeguard against such abuses, any research subject of a study must provide informed consent. The following entry demonstrates the type of data collection from detainees being tortured:

> NOTE: In order to best inform future medical judgments and recommendations, it is important that every application of the waterboard be thoroughly documented: how long each application (and the entire procedure) lasted, how much water was used in the process (realizing that much splashes off), how exactly the water was applied, if a seal was achieved, if the naso- or oropharynx was filled, what sort of volume was expelled, how long was the break between applications, and how the subject looked between each treatment. (PHR, 2014, p. 8)

In light of that finding, PHR (2010, 2014) contends that human subjects research without consent violates the Nuremberg Code, and could constitute a crime against humanity. SSCI (2014) clearly illustrates that health professionals were deeply involved in the CIA torture program. In violation of professional ethics, medical personnel also monitored detainee torture and calibrated levels of pain; evaluated and treated detainees for purposes of torture; conditioned medical care on cooperation with interrogators; and failed to document physical and/or psychological evidence of torture (PHR, 2014, p. 3). In response to the well-established pattern of postmodern torture that relies on medical knowledge to inflict harm, PHR advises: "Those in the healing professions, the psychologists and physicians who became part of the CIA's torture machine, must face the detainees they hurt and recognize that it is never acceptable to use the skills for healing to destroy bodies and minds" (PHR, 2014, p. 13; see Institute on Medicine as a Profession, 2013).

THE CONCEITS OF POSTMODERN TORTURE

At this stage of the critique, it is useful to elaborate on how postmodern torture contributes to the illusions, false claims, and conceits in the war on terror. Three areas of concern are especially significant: the respectability of "scientific" discourse, the "reversibility" of injuries, and warping the rule of law. As we shall see, these developments allow us to raise serious doubts about the merits of the torture program carried out by the Bush administration (see Risen, 2014; Sands, 2008; Welch, 2011, 2015b).

The Respectability of "Scientific" Discourse

Given the influence of discourse, "scientific" claims surrounding enhanced interrogation are significant because they have the potential to assuage moral objection, particularly on the part of government officials and contractors who design, order, and carry out physical and psychological abuse. Such neutralization also dampens criticism of the state, making its use of violence appear at once justified and restrained. The very term "enhanced" interrogation follows similar "scientific" rhetoric used to perpetuate the illusions of contemporary warfare, including "smart bombs" delivering "surgical strikes" that are widely – albeit falsely – believed to reduce substantially the amount of "collateral damage," a callus euphemism for the military's killing of innocent civilians. "Scientific" discourse in the war on terror eases cognitive dissonance in a few important ways. With a veneer of science, advocates of enhanced interrogation claim that those who administer such techniques are experts and professionals committed to national security. Therefore, the entire interrogation program may also be viewed by some observers – and participants – as humane since it is supervised by licensed psychologists (American Psychological Association, 2006).

Interestingly, even amid reports that mental health specialists were involved in prisoner abuse scandals at Guantanamo Bay and Abu Ghraib, the American Psychological Association in 2007 scrapped a measure that would have banned its members from assisting interrogators. The association's policy-making council voted against a proposal to prohibit its psychologists from taking part in any interrogations at US military prisons "in which detainees are deprived of adequate protection of their human rights" (Associated Press, 2007, p. EV1). Nonetheless, the APA approved a resolution that reaffirmed the group's opposition to torture and restricted members from taking part in interrogations that involved such tactics as sleep deprivation and forced nakedness. Psychologists who participate in those practices could be expelled and lose their state license. Some members of the APA went on to claim that the presence of psychologists would help ensure that interrogators did not abuse prisoners. "If we remove psychologists from these facilities, people are going to die," said Army Col. Larry James, who works as a psychologist at Guantanamo Bay (Associated Press, 2007, p. EV2). To which a colleague countered: "If psychologists have to be there so detainees don't get killed, those conditions are so horrendous that the only moral and ethical thing is to leave" (Associated Press, 2007, p. EV2; Carey, 2008).

Foucault (1980) long argued that scientific criminology and its deeply psychological orientation have always been closely aligned to the state power that shaped it (see Garland, 1990; Rodriguez, 2006). With that postmodern critique in mind, the moral objections over enhanced interrogations are muted further by the injection of American patriotism and community joined efforts to safeguard national security nationalism. Especially after September 11th, many psychologists as members of the scientific community lent their expertise to the interrogation of terror suspects (American Psychological Association, 2006). The respectability of "scientific" discourse, indeed, serves to privilege the research and clinical community while neutralizing allegations that state actors and their contractors have engaged in war crimes (see Cohen, 2001; Welch, 2009a, 2009b).

"Reversibility" of Injuries

Enhanced interrogation techniques are often (falsely) portrayed as not only effective but also relatively harmless, creating the illusion that injuries incurred – both psychological and physical – are benign and reversible. Consider, for instance, the cavalier attitude of Secretary of Defense Donald Rumsfeld who recommended the approval of several interrogation techniques for use at Guantanamo Bay, including "the use of stress positions (like standing), for a maximum of four hours." When he signed the order, he mocked the restrictions for stress positions: in a handwritten postscript to the memo: "I stand for 8–10 hours a day. Why is standing limited to 4 hours?" (Jehl, 2005, p. EV1; Sands, 2008). As physicians point out, Rumsfeld did not distinguish the difference in his working style and the experience of prisoners who are forced to maintain a painful standing position for prolonged periods of time. Prolonged standing can increase the risk of blood clots forming in the leg veins with the consequent possibility of pulmonary emboli, which can be fatal. However, in Rumsfeld's case he is able to walk around, creating a "muscle pump" in the legs which moves the blood around actively, thus preventing clots (PHR & HRF, 2007, p. 5).

In an apparent publicity stunt aimed at discrediting human rights concerns over waterboarding, Steve Harrigan, a Fox News correspondent, underwent what he described as three "phase[s]" of "waterboarding," on camera. He concluded that the technique is: "a pretty efficient mechanism to get someone to talk and then still have them alive and healthy within minutes" (Fox News, 2006). On the contrary, the medical literature indicates that brief oxygen deprivation due to waterboarding can generate neurological damage; moreover, breathing fluid into the lungs can lead to aspiration pneumonia which can be fatal. Near-suffocation can also create severe psychological effects, including panic attacks, depression, and prolonged post-traumatic stress disorder (PTSD; Bouwer & Stein, 1997; PHR & HRF, 2007; Olsen, Montgomery, Carlsson, & Foldspang, 2006).

So as to refute further the insinuation that injuries stemming from waterboarding and other enhanced interrogation are relatively minor, medical and mental health researchers have compiled lengthy reports confirming severe and prolonged problems caused by such techniques (PHR, 2005; PHR & HRF, 2007). As just noted, forced standing causes symptoms such as swollen ankles, severe blisters and may also lead to a delirious mental state, delusions, and visual hallucinations; similarly, stress positions can produce long lasting and even permanent nerve, joint, and circulatory damage (Leth & Banner, 2005). Beatings, even those delivered with an open palm, can lead to blunt trauma, and especially when applied to sensitive areas of the body may produce long-term musculoskeletal pain (Thomsen et al., 2000). When subjected to temperature manipulation, detainees risk hypothermia and heat stroke which in some cases can be fatal; additionally, those conditions can cause cognitive problems such as amnesia (Bouchama & Knochel, 2002; Jurkovich, 2007).

Detainees who have been threatened with harm (as well as threats to their family) can experience a long-lasting psychological harm; extreme fear and anxiety and loss of control and flashbacks which are strongly associated with PTSD (Ferrada-Noli, Asberg, & Ormstad, 1998). Sleep deprivation causes significant cognitive impairments including deficits in memory, learning, logical reasoning, complex verbal processing, and decision-making (Kim et al., 2001). Sensory (audio and visual) bombardment throws the body into extreme disorientation and withdrawal from reality as a defense; those danger signals induce the release of stress hormones that increase the risk of heart disease or heart attack (Ising & Kruppa, 2004; Metternich & Brusis, 1999).

Not surprisingly, violent shaking – whiplash – can produce serious neck and back injuries as well as trauma to the brain (Carrigan, Walker, & Barnes, 2000). Sexual humiliation not only debases the prisoner but such intense indignity can result in lasting psychological harm in the form of PTSD and deep depression (PHR, 2005). Moreover, sexual victimization – including sexual threats and humiliation – may be particularly debilitating for detainees due to the nature of confinement that prevents flight; consequently, it brings on trauma and feelings of helplessness. Constant worrying and anxiety can result in an array of psycho-physiological conditions: ulcers, colitis, and hypertension (McCorkle, 1993). Finally, detainees subjected to prolonged isolation together with sensory deprivation develop extreme disorientation, anxiety, and even hallucinations (Andersen, Sestoft, Lillebæk, Gabrielsen, & Hemmingsen, 2003; Haney, 2003; Shalev, 2008; Wexler, Mendelson, Leiderman & Solomon 1958). Dispelling the illusion that enhanced interrogation is relatively harmless is important as we consider the rule of law aimed at enforcing international and US federal laws against torture and the mistreatment of detainees.

Warping the Rule of Law

Key figures in the Bush administration have gone to great lengths to perpetuate the illusion that enhanced interrogations did not constitute torture and so therefore are not unlawful (Sands, 2008; Yoo, 2006). Following the events of 9/11, the White House developed its own definition of torture in an attempt to render inapplicable the Convention Against Torture, an international treaty that the US ratified in 1994. In a memorandum to the President, Alberto R. Gonzales, then White House Counsel and later Attorney General, altered the meaning of the longstanding Convention Against Torture by arguing: "Physical pain amounting to torture must be equivalent in intensity to the pain accompanying serious injury, such as organ failure, impairment of bodily function, or even death" (Gonzales, 2002; see Greenberg & Dratel, 2005, 172; Danner, 2004). Efforts by the Bush administration to evade its obligations under the Convention Against Torture, in addition to the International Covenant on Civil and Political Rights ICCPR ratified in 1992 and key federal statutes that prohibit torture, continue to worry the human rights community.

Compounding matters, several government officials have publicly revealed that they endorse interrogation tactics that squarely fit into the ambit of torture. While being questioned by the Senate, Porter J. Goss, director of the CIA, was confronted by Senator John McCain (AZ, R) who spent five years as a prisoner of war in Vietnam. When McCain asked Goss about the CIA's reported use of waterboarding (mock drowning), Goss replied that the approach fell into "an area of what I will call professional interrogation techniques" (Jehl, 2005, p. A11).

Despite claims by the Bush White House that the 2007 executive order authorizing the most recent version of interrogation program is lawful, human rights lawyers insist that those who participate in enhanced techniques could face criminal sanctions (Brody, 2005; Malinowski, 2005; Mazzetti, 2007; Roth, 2005).

> U.S. policy makers and interrogation personnel should understand that if such ["enhanced"] techniques are practiced, it would be reasonable for courts to conclude that the resulting harm was inflicted intentionally. The interrogation techniques analyzed above – and other techniques that have comparable medical consequences – implicate legal prohibitions and could result in felony criminal prosecutions. It is therefore inappropriate that any such techniques be available for use by U.S. personnel in interrogations, and it is the responsibility of U.S. policy makers to ensure that the use of such techniques is effectively precluded. (PHR & HRF, 2007, p. 35)

Among the U.S. statutes available to prosecutors and victims of torture are: the Torture Act (1994), the Torture Victims Protection Act (1991), the Foreign Sovereign Immunities Act (1976), the War Crimes Act (1996), the Detainee Treatment Act (2005) (see PHR & HRF, 2007). In response to emerging prospects for litigation, CIA counterterrorism officers in growing numbers have signed up for a government-reimbursed, private insurance plan that would pay their civil judgments and legal expenses should they be sued or charged with criminal wrongdoing, particularly in cases involving abuse and harsh interrogation tactics. Whereas the Bush administration argued that the methods are legal some CIA officers are concerned that they may have violated international law or domestic criminal statutes; furthermore, they fear that they will not have Justice Department representation in court or during congressional inquiries. Incriminating details of enhanced interrogations also could come to light if tribunals taking place for detainees at Guantanamo Bay somehow reach civilian courts. As evidence of human rights abuses become more frequently aired, government agents are "worried about a pendulum swing" that could lead to accusations of wrongdoing, said a former CIA officer (Smith, 2006, p. A1).

In sum, the illusions contained in postmodern torture speak of the power and consequences of "scientific" discourse (see Foucault, 1980). Such rhetoric in the war on terror reproduces the misleading impression that enhanced interrogation is not only a legitimate offspring of science but also is a legally justified tactic. Consequently, the political and ideological status of science is maintained which in turn lends (erroneous) rightfulness to the state and its unlawful policies.

CONCLUSION

This postmodern critique situates torture within a framework of "scientific" claims making that (falsely) purports an effectiveness and appropriateness of enhanced interrogations in the war on terror. Overall, the analysis demonstrates the extent to which the development of enhanced interrogation was influenced by specialists who claim to have expert knowledge regarding a methodical use of pain. However, the government's rationale for enhanced methods does not live up to its billing. Whereas the Bush administration insists that enhanced interrogations were lawful, effective, and necessary to safeguard national security, human rights lawyers insist that those who participate in the use of such techniques could face criminal sanctions (Brody, 2005; Roth, 2005). Of course, it is with that worry in mind that key enhanced procedures were further refined so as to "leave no marks." Indeed, "no touch" torture and waterboarding were designed to conceal injuries from forensic investigators in search of evidence of detainee mistreatment and torture (see PHR & HRF, 2007; Welch, 2011, 2009b).

As a remedy to those problems, Physicians for Human Rights strongly recommends that all government employees – and contractors – who have "engaged in and/or authorized torture and ill-treatment of detainees should be held legally responsible for their roles" (PHR, 2014, p. 14). So as to impose greater transparency and comprehensive accounting on the CIA torture program, the full report of the SSCI should be released to the public. Moreover, President Barack Obama and the U.S. Congress should create a federal commission to investigate and document the role that health professionals played in all interrogation and detention programs related to the war on terror. Members of that nonpartisan panel would have appropriate security clearance to conduct a thorough investigation as well as possess the authority to exercise subpoena powers. Based on its findings, the commission would have the power to refer cases to the U.S. Department of Justice for prosecutions. Other recommendations apply to national associations of health professionals. For instance, the American Psychological Association and other health professional organizations should join the American Medical Association and American Psychiatric Association in strictly prohibiting members from directly or indirectly participating in the interrogation of individuals. To further regain the public confidence, those health professionals should reaffirm the ethical obligation to do no harm and declare that their skills and expertise will not be used to participate in torture, ill-treatment, or unethical human subjects research.

REFERENCES

American Psychological Association. (2006). Role of psychologists in interrogations. *The Military Psychologist: The Official Newsletter of Division 19 of the APA*, *22*(2), 13–15.

Andersen, H. S., Sestoft, D., Lillebæk, T., Gabrielsen, G. & Hemmingsen, R. (2003). A longitudinal study of prisoners on remand: Repeated measures of psychopathology in the initial phase of solitary versus nonsolitary confinement. *International Journal of Law & Psychiatry*, *26*, 165–177.

Associated Press. (2007). U.S. psychologists scrap interrogation ban. August 20, EV1-2.

Biderman, A. D. (1957). Communist attempts to elicit false confession from Air Force prisoners of war. *Bulletin of the New York Academy of Medicine*, *33*, 31–44.

Biderman, A. D. (1960). Social psychological needs and 'involuntary' behavior as illustrated by compliance in interrogation. *Sociometry*, *23*, 61–76.

Biderman, A. D., & Zimmer, H. (1961). *The manipulation of human behavior*. New York, NY: Wiley.

Bouchama, A., & Knochel, J. (2002). Heat stroke. *New England Journal of Medicine*, 346, 1978–1991.

Bouwer, C., & Stein, D. J. (1997). Association of panic disorder with a history of traumatic suffocation. *American Journal of Psychiatry*, *154*, 1566–1579.

Bravin, J. (2007). The conscience of the colonel. *Wall Street Journal*, March 31, A1.

Brody, R. (2005). The road to Abu Ghraib: Torture and impunity in U.S. detention. In K. Roth & M. Worden (Eds.), *Torture: Does it make us safe? Is it ever OK?* New York, NY: The New Press.

Cantini, L. (2010). *Torture instruments: From the middle ages to the industrial era*. Mexico City: Mexican Academy of Human Rights.

Carey, B. (2008). Psychologists clash on aiding interrogations. *New York Times*, August 15, EV1-4.

Carrigan, T. D., Walker, E., & Barnes, S. (2000). Domestic violence: The shaken adult syndrome. *Journal of Accident & Emergency Medicine*, *17*, 138–139.

Central Intelligence Agency. (1956). *Communist control techniques: An analysis of the methods used by communist state police in the arrest, interrogation, and indoctrination of persons regarded as 'enemies of the state*. Retrieved from http://www.americantorture.com/documents/cold_war/01.pdf

Central Intelligence Agency. (1963). *KUBARK counterintelligence interrogation*. Retrieved from http://www.kimsoft.com/2000/kubark.Html

Clarke, R. (2004). *Against all enemies: Inside America's war on terror*. New York, NY: Simon and Schuster.

Cohen, S. (2001). *States of denial: Knowing about atrocities and suffering*. Cambridge: Polity.

Cohen, S. (2006). Neither honesty nor hypocrisy: The legal reconstruction of torture. In T. Newburn & P. Rock (Eds.). *Politics of crime control: Essays in honour of David Downes*. Oxford: Oxford University Press.

Danner, M. (2004). *Torture and truth: America, Abu Ghraib, and the war on terror*. London: Granta Books.

Dershowitz, A. (2002). *Why terrorism works*. New Haven, CT: Yale University Press.

Doerr-Zegers, O., Hartman, O., Lira, E., & Weinstein, E. (1992). Torture: Psychiatric sequelae and phenomenology, *Psychiatry* 55(2), 177–184.

Feitlowitz, M. (1998). *A lexicon of terror: Argentina and the legacies of torture*. New York, NY: Oxford University Press.

Ferrada-Noli, M., Asberg, M., & Ormstad, K. (1998). Suicidal behavior after severe trauma. Part 2: The association between methods of torture and of suicidal ideation in post-traumatic stress disorder. *Journal of Traumatic Stress*, *11*, 113–124.

Foucault, M. (1977). *Discipline and punish: The birth of the prison*. New York, NY: Vintage.

Foucault, M. (1980). The eye of power. In C. Gordon (Ed.), *Power/knowledge: Selected interviews and other writings*. New York, NY: Pantheon.

Fox News. (2006). On the record with Greta Van Susteren: (FOX News television broadcast November 3, 2006). See also mediamatters.org, Fox News correspondent on his on-air "waterboarding". Retrieved from http://mediamatters.org/items/200611060004. Accessed on November 6, 2006.

Garland, D. (1990). *Punishment and modern society*. Chicago, IL: University of Chicago Press.

Gearty, C. (2005). With a little help from our friends. *Index on Censorship*, *34*(1), 46–51.

Gonzales, A. R. (2002). Memorandum to the president. Re: Standards for conduct for interrogation under 18 U.S.C. Sections 2340-2340A. August 1.

Greenberg, K., & Dratel, J. (2005). *The torture papers: The road to Abu Ghraib*. Cambridge: Cambridge University Press.

Haney, C. (2003). Mental health Issues in long-term solitary and 'supermax' confinement. *Crime & Delinquency*, *49*, 124–137.

Harbury, J. (2005). *Truth, torture, and the American way: The history and consequences of U.S. involvement in torture*. Boston, MA: Beacon Press.

Harrington, T. J. (2004). *Letter from T. J. Harrington, Deputy Assistant Director FBI Counterterrorism Division, to Major General Donald J. Ryder, DOA Criminal Investigation Command, Re: Suspected Mistreatment of detainees, Document #: DOJFBI001914-DOJFBI001916; Date of Record: 2004-07-14*. Retrieved from http://www.aclu.org/projects/foiasearch/pdf/DOJFBI001914.pdf

Haynes, W. (2003). *Memorandum from William Haynes, Gen. counsel of the Dept. of Def. to Donald Rumsfeld, Sec'y of Def. (January 15)*. Retrieved From http://www.humanrightsfirst%20http://www.humanrightsfirst.org/us_law/etn/pdf/dod%20memos-120202.pdf

Hinton, M. (2006). *The state on the streets: Police and politics in Argentina and Brazil*. Boulder, CO: Lynne Rienner.

Huggins, M., Haritos-Fatouros, M., & Zimbardo, P. (2002). *Violence workers: Police torturers and murderers reconstruct Brazilian atrocities*. Berkeley, CA: University of California Press.

Institute on Medicine as a Profession. (2013). *Ethics abandoned: Medical professionalism and detainee abuse in the war on terror*. New York, NY: Institute on Medicine as a Profession.

Ising, H., & Kruppa, B. (2004). Health effects caused by noise: Evidence in the literature from the past 25 years. *Noise and Health*, *6*(5), 21–33.

Jehl, D. (2005). Questions left by C.I.A. chief on torture use: Goss vouches only for current practices. *New York Times*, March 18, A1, A11.

Jurkovich, G. J. (2007). Environmental cold-induced injury. *Surgical Clinics North America*, *87*, 247–259.

Kim, D. J., Lee, H. P., Kim, M. S., Park, Y. J., Go, H. J., Kim, K. S., … Lee, C. T. (2001). The effect of total sleep deprivation on cognitive functions in normal adult male subjects. *International Journal of Neuroscience*, *109*, 127–137.

Langbein, J. (1977). *Torture and the law of proof: Europe and England in the Ancien Regime*. Chicago, IL: University of Chicago Press.

Leth, P. M., & Banner, J. (2005). Forensic medical examination of refugees who claim to have been tortured. *American Journal of Forensic Medicine & Pathology*, *26*, 125–138.

Lewis, N. (2004). Broad use of harsh tactics is described at Cuba base. *New York Times*, October 17, EV1-3.

Lifton, R. J. (2000). *The Nazi doctors: Medical killing and the psychology of genocide*. New York, NY: Basic Books.

Malinowski, T. (2005). Banned State Department practices. In K. Roth & M. Worden (Eds.), *Torture: Does it make us safe? Is it ever OK?* New York, NY: The New Press.

Marks, J. (1979). *The search for the Manchurian Candidate: The CIA and mind control*. New York, NY: Times Books.

Mazzetti, M. (2007). C.I.A. destroyed tapes of interrogations. *New York Times*, December 6, EV1-5.

McCorkle, R. C. (1993). Fear of victimization and symptoms of psychopathology among prison inmates. *Journal of Offender Rehabilitation*, *19*, 27–44.

McCoy, A. (2006). *A question of torture: CIA interrogation, from the Cold War to the war on terror*. New York, NY: Metropolitan Books.

McCoy, A. (2012). *Torture and impunity: The U.S. doctrine of coercive interrogation*. Madison, WI: University of Wisconsin Press.

Metternich, F. U., & Brusis, T. (1999). Acute hearing loss and tinnitus caused by amplified recreational music. *Laryngorhinootologie*, *78*, 614–623.

Olsen, D. R., Montgomery, E., Carlsson, J., & Foldspang, A. (2006). Prevalent pain and pain level among torture survivors. *Danish Medical Bulletin*, *53*, 210–214.

Physicians for Human Rights. (2005). *Break them down: The systematic use of psychological torture by U.S. forces*. Washington, DC: Physicians for Human Rights.

Physicians for Human Rights. (2014). *Doing harm: Health professionals' central role in the CIA torture program*. New York, NY: Physicians for Human Rights.

Physicians for Human Rights and Human Rights First. (2007). *Leave no marks: Enhanced interrogation techniques and the risk of criminality*. Washington, DC: Physicians for Human Rights and Human Rights First.

Public Committee Against Torture in Israel v. The Government of Israel. (1999). 53(4) PD 817. Retrieved from http://wwwstoptorture.org.il/eng/images/%20uploaded/publications/18.pdf. Accessed on September 6.

Risen, J. (2014). *Pay any price: Greed, power, and endless war*. New York, NY: Houghton Mifflin Harcourt.

Rodriguez, J. (2006). *Civilizing Argentina: Science, medicine, and the modern state*. Chapel Hill, NC: University of North Carolina Press.

Rose, D. (2004). *Guantanamo: America's war on human rights*. London: Faber and Faber.

Ross, B. (2005). A partial history on waterboarding. *ABC News.com*, November 29. Retrieved from http://abcnews.go.com/WNT/Investigation/story?id=1356870

Ross, B., & Esposito, R. (2005). CIA's harsh interrogation techniques described. *ABC News Online*, November 18 Retrieved from http://abcnews.go.com/WNT/Investigation/story?id=1322866

Roth, K. (2005). Justifying torture. In K. Roth & M. Worden (Eds.), *Torture: Does it make us safe? Is it ever OK?* New York, NY: The New Press.

Sands, P. (2008). *Torture team: Rumsfeld's memo and the betrayal of American values*. New York, NY: St. Martin's Press.

Schmidt, R., Gen., & Furlow, J., Brig. Gen. (2005). U.S. Army, Investigation into FBI allegations of detainee abuse at Guantanamo Bay, Cuba Detention Facility. Army Regulation 15-6: Final Report. Retrieved from http://www.defenselink.mil/news/Jul2005/d20050714report.pdf

Schmitt, E., & Marshall, C. (2006). In secret unit's 'black room,' A grim portrait of U.S. abuse. *New York Times*, June 17 EV1-3.

Seligman, M. (1975). *Helplessness: On depression, development, and death*. San Francisco, CA: W.H. Freeman.

Senate Select Committee on Intelligence. (2014). *Study of the Central Intelligence Agency's detention and interrogation program*. Unclassified. Washington, DC: U.S. Government Printing.

Shalev, S. (2008). *A sourcebook on solitary confinement*. London: Mannheim Centre for Criminology, London School of Economics.

Shane, S., & Mazzetti, M. (2007). Interrogation methods are criticized. *New York Times*, May 30, EV1-6.

Simpson, C. (1994). *Science of coercion: Communication research and psychological warfare, 1945-1960*. Oxford: Oxford University Press.

Smith, R. J. (2006). Worried C.I.A. officers buy legal insurance: Plans fund defense in anti-terror cases. *Washington Post*, September, 11, A1.

Thomsen, A. B., Eriksen, J., & Smidt-Nielsen, K. (2000). Chronic pain in torture survivors. *Forensic Science International*, *108*, 155–163.

Watson, P. (1978). *War on the mind: The military uses and abuses of psychology*. New York, NY: Basic Books.

Welch, M. (2006). *Scapegoats of September 11th: Hate crimes & state crimes in the war on terror*. New Brunswick, NJ: Rutgers University Press.

Welch, M. (2007). Fare l'impensabile. Genealogia della tortura moderna (Doing the unthinkable: A genealogy of modern torture). *Studi Sulla Questione Criminale*, *3*, 41–64.

Welch, M. (2009a). *Crimes of power & states of impunity: The U.S. response to terror*. New Brunswick, NJ: Rutgers University Press.

Welch, M. (2009b). American painology in the war on terror: A critique of 'scientific' torture. *Theoretical Criminology*, *13*(4), 451–474.

Welch, M. (2011). Illusions in truth seeking: The perils of interrogation and torture in the war on terror. *Social Justice A Journal of Crime, Conflict & World Order*, *37*(2–3), 123–148.

Welch, M. (2014). La reaparicion de la tortura en la cultura politica: Siguiendo su discurso y genealogia. [The re-emergence of torture in political culture: Tracking its discourse and genealogy]. In G. I. Anitua & D. Z. Quiros (Eds.), *La tortura: Una práctica estructural del sistema penal, el delito más grave*. CABA: Ediciones Didot.

Welch, M. (2015a). Torture and its division of labor. A paper presented at the workshop: The politics and jurisprudence of group offending, coordinated by Anthony Amatrudo (Middlesex University, London) at Institut Internationale de Sociologie Juridique (International Institute for the Sociology of Law), Onati, Spain, July 23–25.

Welch, M. (2015b). On the ethics of torture by Uwe Steinhoff, 2013. *Punishment & Society*, *17*(2), 261–262.

Wexler, D., Mendelson, J., Leiderman, H., & Solomon, P. (1958). Sensory deprivation. *A.M. A. Archives of Neurology and Psychiatry*, *79*, 225–233.

Yoo, J. (2006). *The powers of war and peace: The constitution and foreign affairs after 9/11*. Chicago, IL: University of Chicago Press.

CHANGES IN LOCAL LAW ENFORCEMENT BROUGHT ABOUT BY 9/11

Gregg W. Etter, Sr.

ABSTRACT

Purpose – *The terrorist attacks on the United States on September 11, 2001 were a very traumatic event for the entire nation. This was especially true for law enforcement. Many law enforcement officers and other first responders lost their lives in the initial response to the attack while attempting to save the lives of the citizens they were sworn to protect. As a result of the 9/11 attacks, many changes have occurred in the missions, operations and tactics of local law enforcement agencies in the United States.*

Methodology/approach – *This chapter attempts to examine the changes that were forced upon law enforcement by the events of 9/11 and to look at what the future might hold for law enforcement in an enhanced homeland security environment.*

Terrorism and Counterterrorism Today
Sociology of Crime, Law and Deviance, Volume 20, 219–240

ISSN: 1521-6136/doi:10.1108/S1521-613620150000020011

Findings – *Terrorism presents additional duties for law enforcement. Traditional police missions have not been lessened, but new threats to the public have arisen.*

Keywords: policing; militarization; terrorist threats; homeland security

INTRODUCTION

The only constant is change. After the terrorist attacks against the United States on September 11, 2001 the paradigm of American law enforcement was forced to expand in ways that were unplanned. Suddenly local cops were thrust into a role that was more familiar to either federal law enforcement agents or the military. The local cops were charged with not only taking care of local law enforcement, but guarding the homeland as well. Not since World War II, has local law enforcement been this involved in national security threats.

White (2004) has observed that:

> On the morning of September 11, 2001, law enforcement officers carried out their duties in normal fashion. All across the country local and state police officers pieced together drug raids, murder investigations, barking dogs, lost children, family fights, and a variety of serious and non-serious crimes into a patchwork cops call "routine." Morning shifts went home and day shifts reported for briefings. Many rookies enjoyed Tuesday as the first day of their 'weekend' while chiefs and sheriffs prepared for staff meetings and budget reports. Some officers arrived for court testimony. September 11 was just another Tuesday. It was routine. All that changed shortly after 8:30 A.M. (p. 4)

Prior to September 11, 2001, law enforcement as a whole had been primarily focused on internal domestic terrorist threats and those racist or radical groups from the left wing and right wing that posed a danger. Groups like the Animal Liberation Front, Black Liberation Army, Black Panthers, Earth Liberation Front, Symbionese Liberation Army, and the Weathermen on the left were viewed as revolutionary groups and possible terrorist threats. The right had the Army of God, Aryan Nations, American Nazi Party, CSA (Covenant, the Sword, and the Arm of the Lord), the Ku Klux Klan, Militias, The Order, Phineas Priesthood, Posse Comitatus, and Sovereign Citizen groups that were considered to be threats of domestic terrorism or civil unrest (Gurr, 1988, pp. 549–578). These threats were all domestic. While their activities have been well documented, they were sporadic. They did not occur every day and most law enforcement officers at the local and state level did not deal with them directly.

However, this was the threat that the local and state law enforcement officers were familiar with and trained for. Criminal activities of these groups usually involved anti-government actions, bank robberies, bombings, church arsons, or violence against minorities. These were individual crimes that were committed by individual "lone wolves" or by small organized conspiracies (Levitas, 2002).

THE CHALLENGE OF TERRORISM

Lone Wolf v. Conspiracy

There are two basic types of terrorist acts: those committed by a single individual which are called "Lone Wolf" attacks and those attacks that involved a group. Mouras (2015) found that: "The term 'lone wolf' is often used to describe individuals who act alone to commit terrorist acts. Lone wolf attacks are often motivated by political, religious, and/or ideological reasoning." For example, the Unabomber (Ted Kaczynski) who conducted a series of bombing attacks from 1978 to 1995 is an example of a "Lone Wolf" terrorist. Kacrynski acted alone in the planning and execution of his criminal acts. As a terrorist, he would be considered as being a domestic terrorist from the left wing of the political spectrum (Martinez, 2012, pp. 239–274; McCann, 2006, pp. 221–230).

While the motivations may be the same when more people are involved, the planning need for a group criminal activity makes the existence of a conspiracy necessary. The Oklahoma City bombing on April 19, 1995, for example, was a conspiracy between Timothy McVeigh, Terry Nichols, and Michael Fortier. These domestic terrorists were considered to be from the right wing of the political spectrum (Martinez, 2012, pp. 275–318; McCann, 2006, pp. 211–220; Michel & Herbeck, 2001).

9/11

On September 11, 2001 four aircrafts that had been hijacked by foreign terrorists deliberately set out to crash into buildings in an al-Qaeda plot involving 19 hijackers. Two of the aircraft flew into the twin towers of the World Trade Center in New York City. One aircraft flew into the Pentagon in Washington, DC. The last aircraft crashed into a field in Pennsylvania killing all aboard. In the overall attack, 2,977 people were killed plus the 19 hijackers. Thousands were injured. There was hundreds of millions of dollars in property damage. In the initial attacks 72 law enforcement officers and 343 firefighters/paramedics lost their lives. Others have died since of related illnesses. In the attack on the Twin Towers in New York City, 23 NYPD officers died when the towers collapsed. Another 70 NYPD officers have died from 9/11 related illnesses since (McCann, 2006, pp. 276–281; ODMP, 2015).

IN THE AFTERMATH OF 9/11

While the attacks of September 11 were an outright act of war against the American people, the loss of so many police officials and firefighters in one day sent shock waves through the first responder communities. As White (2004) observed, "Never in history had America lost firefighters and police officers on such a scale. The families of the New York fire and police departments and eventually the nation went numb. The United States of America was in a shadow war" (p. 5).

As the federal government reorganized their emergency response apparatus in the Department of Homeland Security, the question became "What is the new role of local and state law enforcement?" Bodrero (2002) made the argument that law enforcement had acquired a new mission to investigate, interdict, and prevent terrorism. However, in his analysis of the changing mission of law enforcement Bodrero (2002) also realized that:

> During this period of change, one thing is likely to remain the same. State and local law enforcement's role in tomorrow's world will be the same as it has always been to protect the lives and property of their citizens. While some states have mobilized National Guard troops, the primary source of protection of America's communities remains the thin blue line provided by America's law enforcement community. Unless there are additional catastrophic attacks, it is doubtful that federal military troops will be patrolling the cities and counties of America. State and local law enforcement agencies will be performing the job they have traditionally performed, only in a drastically altered environment. (p. 43)

Bodrero (2002) went on to observe that local law enforcement had been investigating domestic terrorist groups for years especially in the wake of the Oklahoma City Bombing in 1995. The author advocated that local law enforcement expand its intelligence gathering capabilities to meet this new threat.

In observing the changes in law enforcement that began to occur after 9/11, Bridges (2002) has argued that: "On September 11, 2001, our world changed. Our security weaknesses were not just exposed – they had been exposed and known for years – but exploited, and to an unprecedented degree. Because of the viciousness and success of the attacks, Americans have a sense of vulnerability that permeates their everyday lives. Future U.S. military action will likely participate in further terrorist acts in our country, which will affect local law enforcement more than any of the previous wars in the last century." Bridges cited several areas that he felt would be of critical concern to local law enforcement as a result of 9/11, among these areas of concern were: security at major events; tactical actions; nuclear, biological, and chemical threats; investigations of suspected terrorist activity; intelligence; bomb threats; suspicious people; suspicious packages; hate crimes; civil unrest; critical facility security; dignitary protection; regional coordination of intelligence gathering and anti-terrorism efforts; and balancing civil liberties with security needs (pp. 35–36).

In a nationwide survey of local and state law enforcement agencies conducted by the International Association of Chiefs of Police in 2005 on post 9-11 policing, Lynn et al. (2005) found that mission changes had occurred in local and state law enforcement with the additional duties of a possible anti-terrorism response mission mandated by Homeland Security. The study recommended the incorporation of intelligence-led policing in order to accomplish these additional duties. Chief among the concerns expressed to the researchers about the new Homeland Security mission were funding issues, training issues, equipment issues, intelligence sharing issues, and creating multijurisdictional partnerships to accomplish the new tasks at hand while maintaining the capabilities to accomplish currently mandated law enforcement missions such as patrol, investigations, etc. The primary issue expressed by the law enforcement leaders was the issue of funding. Most were scared of another unfunded mandate from Washington that required more services, equipment, or personnel without providing adequate long-term funding to pay for it.

THE STRUCTURAL CHANGE FROM CIVIL DEFENSE TO FEMA BROUGHT ON BY 9/11

Local and state law enforcement was familiar with the various civil defense and later FEMA organizations that responded to attacks and natural disasters. The Office of Civil Defense was established in 1941 to assist United States citizens in the event of an attack on the United States. Later versions expanded their role to include natural disasters. The OCD and successor agencies were replaced in 1979 by the Federal Emergency Management Agency or FEMA (Bullock et al., 2006, p. 5). FEMA continued the OCD mission of providing civil defense and disaster relief. Many of the offices were on the state or county levels. Extensive training to EMS, Fire and law enforcement was provided by FEMA along with equipment for disaster relief provided to state and local governments. Training exercises such as mass casualty exercises, prepared local emergency managers, hospitals, and first responders for disasters such as airplane crashes, earthquakes, hurricanes, and tornadoes. As a direct result of the attacks on 9/11, FEMA was one of 23 federal agencies incorporated into the new Department of Homeland Security on March 1, 2003 (FEMA, 2015).

The National Incident Management System

In order to coordinate the emergency efforts of multiple emergency responding agencies to emergencies, disasters, and threats FEMA developed the National Incident Management System or N.I.M.S. According to FEMA (2015): "The National Incident Management System (NIMS) is a systematic, proactive approach to guide departments and agencies at all levels of government, nongovernmental organizations, and the private sector to work together seamlessly and manage incidents involving all threats and hazards – regardless of cause, size, location, or complexity – in order to reduce loss of life, property and harm to the environment." FEMA provides training to Law Enforcement and other emergency managers at no cost on how to implement the N.I.M.S. system. As designed, N.I.M.S. is a unified system of command to be used in the case of emergencies that allows various emergency agencies to operate together more efficiently.

After 9/11, the need for law enforcement to successfully be able to operate under N.I.M.S. was reemphasized when the order to evacuate the Twin Towers of the World Trade Center did not come over the FDNY radio channel in a timely manner and many firefighters were killed when the building collapsed. Atkins (2011) observed that in the 9/11 response at the World Trade Center in New York City: "Two factors hindered the efforts of firefighters to be more effective. One was the failure of the communication systems. Radios did not work, and other communication systems were overwhelmed by the traffic. Almost as serious was the lack of coordination between the firefighters and the police." Interagency coordination, unified command, and interoperable communications capability are central tenants of N.I.M.S.

N.I.M.S. Failure: Hurricane Katrina, New Orleans, Louisiana

In New Orleans, when Hurricane Katrina hit, the N.I.M.S. system did not function as designed. Due to inadequacies in the local government and the police, instead of an orderly response to the disaster and evacuation chaos reigned. In effect the local government collapsed and was unable to respond effectively to the threat posed by the disaster. While individual police officers attempted to perform their duty (some very heroically), many abandoned their posts and fled. Rather than rescuing people or helping to maintain order, some NOPD officers were even caught on camera joining in the looting of flooded stores. As a result of this failure the number of dead and injured was far larger than what it might have been if an effective N.I.M.S. response had been implemented. In addition to the hundreds of millions of dollars in property damage that occurred as a result of the hurricane and the flooding that followed, there were a reported 1,464 dead and many thousands more injured. There were widespread civil disturbances, increased crime, and looting that the New Orleans Police Department was unable to effectively control. All of this tragedy was played out on national television as the nation watched in horror (Greene, 2008, p. 208).

In assessing the outright collapse of the local government and police in New Orleans during Hurricane Katrina, Waugh (2006) observed that: "Poor implementation of emergency plans, poor communications, and poor decision processes were evident in the lack of congruence between conditions 'on the ground' in the disaster areas and local, state and national decision making. Local, state and federal leaders appeared disconnected at best and insensitive and incompetent at worse" (p. 11).

In the aftermath of the failure of N.I.M S. and the overall government collapse of police and local government response to Hurricane Katrina in New Orleans The Chief of the New Orleans Police Department, Superintendent Eddie Compass resigned (AP, 2005). Congress passed the Post-Katrina Emergency Reform Act in October 2006 which significantly reorganized FEMA (FEMA, 2015). Former New Orleans Mayor Ray Nagin was indicted on January 18, 2013 on charges of corruption (Lewis, 2013). Nagin was found guilty on February 12, 2014 (AP, 2014).

N.I.M.S. Success: Hurricane Katrina, Biloxi, Mississippi

Hurricane Katrina did not spare Mississippi. The Gulf Coast cities of Gulfport and Biloxi were devastated and billions of dollars of property damage occurred. However, the loss of life was not nearly as severe as it was in New Orleans. This was due in part to the successful usage of N.I.M.S. and the timely evacuation of most citizens by the local and Mississippi state governments directing their first responders to act quickly. In the aftermath of the storm, the local law enforcement agencies used N.I.M.S. to coordinate command and control of the many law enforcement agencies from several states that sent officers to assist (the author's own agency sent officers from Kansas to assist in the recovery). Looting, chaos, and loss of life were limited by the swift and well-coordinated actions of local law enforcement and other first responders. Although Smith (2012) noted that there were some problems with the initial FEMA response, the N.I.M.S. systems worked as designed and the efforts of volunteers and first responders were able to assist in the recovery successfully (pp. 55, 86).

SOCIAL MEDIA

Social media has long played a part in terrorist or revolutionary activities. In the 1960s and 1970s, left wing radicals were inspired by political posters, pamphlets, and books. Bomb making techniques were acquired by reading books such as *The Anarchist Cookbook* (Powell, 1971). In the 1990s, right wing radicals were inspired by reading books such as *The Turner Diaries* (Macdonald, 1980). The type of bomb used in the Oklahoma City Bombing in 1995 was similar to the bomb described in the text of that book and the target in the novel was a government building also.

Although the telephone has been around for over one hundred years, extremists and revolutionaries have used the telephone and telephone trees to maintain communications for years. The telephone tree is a type of calling list where if one person is called with a message, they call three others and each of those calls three more. Thus the telephone tree allows a large amount of people to be contacted in a short period of time. The advent of the cell phone allowed everyone to be in constant communication with their friends and comrades. Texting provided a secure form of communication. Texting trees and twitter replaced the telephone tree and hundreds could now be contacted at once. This tool proved useful to those that would cause social disruption. Disorderly groups called flash mobs were summoned to cause chaos at a particular location via this method (Du Comb & Benmen, 2014, pp. 34–40; Smith & Rush, 2012, pp. 33–50). Cell phones even began to be used as triggering mechanisms for improvised explosive devices (IEDs) used in terrorist bombings (McKenna, 2004, pp. 43–49).

Mouras (2015) observed that the internet can play a primary part in the radicalization of lone wolf terrorists by providing them an informational outlet to contact others of a like mind or to study political/religious ideas or terrorist techniques. Internet magazines such as Al Qaeda's *Inspire* encourage would be radicals to join the jihad and is printed in English. The first issue in 2010 even had an article on how to make a pressure cooker bomb titled: "Make a Bomb in the Kitchen of Your Mom" (CNN, 2010). The technology that was covered in the article outlined tried and true Al Qaeda bomb making methods that had been used previously in Afghanistan, India, and Pakistan using a pressure cooker as the casing for the bomb. The terrorist article bore fruit and soon pressure cooker bombs were used in the United States in the attempted bombing of Times Square in May, 2010 and again in the Boston Marathon Bombing that occurred in April 2013. In yet another incident, Ryan and Ferran (2012), in investigating a bombing plot near Ft. Hood, Texas involving AWOL Army PFC Jason Naser Abdo, found that at least some of his radical Islamist views had been inspired by the internet. They reported that: He was arrested on July 21, 2011 at a Killeen hotel after arousing the suspicions of the staff of a local gun store when he tried to purchase smokeless gunpowder and shotgun and pistol ammunition. A handgun, bomb-making materials, and an article from the Al Qaeda magazine "Inspire" called "How to Make a Bomb in the Kitchen of Your Mom" were found in his room. Jason Naser Abdo received a life sentence for his plot (FBI, 2012). Abdo was arrested by officers of the Killeen Police Department.

Other internet social media sites such as Facebook and My Space have been used to communicate, radicalize, and post propaganda videos in support of radical groups. Local law enforcement officers have had to begin to scan the websites and Facebook pages of gangs and radical groups to gather intelligence about the groups and information about suspects. Some criminals have even confessed crimes or boasted about criminal plots on social media.

For American local and state law enforcement, the other 800 pound elephant in the room is language. Frankly most American cops only speak English. If they have any foreign language abilities they usually involve some dialect of Spanish. The main languages of those that are currently involved in terrorist type activities are Arabic, Aramaic, Chechen, Dari, Farsi, Kurdish, Pashto, Punjabi, and Urdu. The average American beat cop can't speak any of these languages, much less read them. Many of these languages use the Arabic or Cyrillic alphabets rather than the Latin one. This adds a whole new level of difficulty to reading a website or means of communication for the law enforcement investigator. The federal law enforcement agencies have many more resources available to them. Silber (2015) observed that the arrest of three Brooklyn residents of Central Asian descent that were arrested on February 25, 2015 for trying to join the Islamic State were recruited on the internet and discovered by agents of the FBI on an "obscure Uzbek-language website, Hilofatnews, provided the initial thread that would lead to the unraveling of the terrorist plot" (p. A11). Local law enforcement does not have a large number of Uzbeck-language speaking officers at its disposal or the manpower to monitor such terrorist websites.

INTELLIGENCE-LED POLICING

In 1994, Reibling (1994) advocated that cops should become more like spies, gathering data on criminals and using it to develop police strategies based on risk-assessment and risk management. Riebling's writings became the basis for the police strategies known as intelligence-based policing. Intelligence-based policing gained popularity after 9/11 with many law enforcement leaders especially with the New York City Police Department. Intelligence-led policing conducts a crime analysis of data gathered using overt/covert means including: physical surveillance (in person or by videotape), electronic surveillance (trap and trace or wiretap), confidential informants, undercover operators, newspaper reports (including internet), and searches of public records (data mining: deeds, property tax records, etc.).

In a Bureau of Justice Assistance study, Peterson (2005) advocated that:

> Because effective intelligence operations can be applied equally well to terrorist threats and crimes in the community, homeland security and local crime prevention are not mutually exclusive. Officers "on the beat" are an excellent resource for gathering information on all kinds of potential threats and vulnerabilities. However, the intelligence operations of state and local law enforcement agencies often are plagued by a lack of policies, procedures, and training for gathering and assessing essential information. To correct this problem, fundamental changes are needed in the way information is gathered, assessed, and redistributed. Traditional, hierarchical intelligence functions need to be reexamined and replaced with cooperative, fluid structures that can collect information and move intelligence to end users more quickly. Intelligence in today's policing

environment must adapt to the new realities presented by terrorism and conventional crimes.

One of the main grievances that local law enforcement official had was that before 9/11 local and state law enforcement agencies would send information to federal law enforcement agencies but would very seldom get any information back in return. Reibling (1994) and others criticized federal agencies for not even talking with each other, much less the locals. After 9/11 this began to change and local law enforcement leaders were given security clearances and access to more information on a need-to-know basis. White (2004) observed that local and state law enforcement agencies already had a framework to conduct intelligence type operations because of their involvement in the "War on Drugs" (p. 8). A recent example of the federal government sharing intelligence with local law enforcement was the February, 2015 internet threat made by the Somali-based terrorist group al-Shabaab to attack the Mall of the Americas in Minnesota. This threat was taken very seriously by both local and federal law enforcement because of the 2013 attack by the same terrorist group on the Westgate Shopping Mall in Nairobi, Kenya that killed 67 people. A shopping mall in the United Kingdom was also threatened at the same time (Radnofsky & Madigan, 2015, p. A3). In this new threat environment, the terrorists can cause a law enforcement reaction by merely posting a threat on the internet, it would be simply too dangerous to ignore.

However, there was some controversy about NYPD's use of intelligence-led policing tactics. Calderone (2013) reported that: "The NYPD, under commissioner Ray Kelly, interpreted the revised (Handschu) guidelines to permit intelligence-gathering on Muslim restaurants, mosques and neighborhoods, including Zazi's. And yet the NYPD's extensive, years-long surveillance operation didn't play a role in stopping the Zazi plot." (In 2009, Zazi had plotted to attack the New York Subway system, but was arrested before he could do so.) The NYPD's surveillance program was criticized in the press, by the Muslim community and by the ACLU. In 2014, under Police Commissioner Bill Bratton the NYPD surveillance program was discontinued and the unit's personnel reassigned.

Training for New Threats and the Alleged Militarization of the Police

The police constantly have to train just to maintain their skills. The amount of required annual in-service training varies by state (Etter & Griffin, 2011,

p. 235). Laws change in every state, every year. There is new equipment and there are new tactics to be learned. In post 9/11 policing, law enforcement had to learn how to cope with new threats such as terrorism and the possibility of chemical, biological, radiological, nuclear, and explosive weapons (CRBNE). Just learning about the personal protective equipment that is needed to survive in a CBRNE environment was a training issue. Training costs money. Even if the federal government provides the instructors for free, the wages of the law enforcement officers being trained must be paid. Every officer in training is not on the street that day and has to have their job covered by another officer. Therefore, in some agencies law enforcement training in antiterrorism subjects was limited to a few officers rather than the whole department. But when you consider that the New York City Police Department has over 49,000 employees alone, the salary cost on even one 8-hours training day is staggering. Similar situations exist across the United States as police budgets were froze or cut in the economic downturn that followed 9/11. Squad tactics and anti-riot tactics were a part of the training. This along with equipment upgrades to meet the new threat level has resulted in some groups decrying the militarization of the police (Grossman, 2014, p. A3). According to Stalcup and Craze (2011), another issue is the quality of the instructors that are teaching some of the anti-terrorist curriculum. They allege that some instructors view all Moslems as potential terrorist and pass that view to their trainees. Keeping a realistic view of the threat and of who might be potentially involved is crucial, but racial or religious profiling is not only illegal but counterproductive.

Equipping Local Law Enforcement to Meet the New Threats of the 21st Century

Body cameras are devices that are designed to see what the law enforcement officer is seeing at the time. Kaste (2014) observed that police body cameras have limitations and some unintended effects. The traditional problems of cameras of lighting, angle, and focus also apply to body cameras worn by the police. Body cameras are expensive. The question as to who is to pay for these body cameras becomes central to the discussion. Is this another unfunded federal mandate that will stretch slender police budgets even further? There is some confusion as to when they are to be turned on (Mims, 2014). Although, some crimes have already been recorded on police body cameras including the murder of a police officer. Kaste (2014) also observed that in one study that was conducted in a small California police department after the agency adopted body cameras there was a significant reduction in the number of use of force incidents.

Closed Circuit Television Cameras (CCTV) are not new. However law enforcement is making much more use of them in the fight against street crime and terrorism. In a crime prevention sense, CCTV cameras were first used in the United States to prevent robberies in banks and convenience stores. Many home security systems have them. Some cites use CCTV cameras for traffic enforcement. This application has proved controversial and there are mixed court rulings on the legality of this practice. In some larger cities like Boston, Chicago, or New York, CCTV cameras have been installed by the police to monitor public traffic ways as a crime prevention measure. This has raised privacy concerns among some Americans although it is a common practice in Europe and elsewhere (Welsh & Farrington, 2009, p. 717). The usage of CCTV cameras is a reactive type of police work. Usually the crime has already occurred and the CCTV footage is a part of the resulting law enforcement investigation.

Many law enforcement agencies have patrol cars equipped with dashboard cameras. Cameras are expensive and many law enforcement agencies do not have them in every patrol car due to expense. However, according to Stateline (2014), in New Jersey, new city police cars must have dashboard video cameras starting March 1, 2015. Dashboard cameras can provide valuable evidence in police stops and investigations. Police dashboard cameras are a DOJ recommended solution to racial profiling.

Laptop computers in patrol cars are a relatively recent phenomena. They can be used as a secure communications device, a way to check on warrants or driver's licenses, or to type reports. Although this technology has been around for more than 20 years, due to the expense (usually over $1,000.00 per unit) many agencies have not yet installed them in their patrol cars or if they have, they have not installed them in all departmental cars (Siuru, 1994, p. 59). Many departments have spent federal grant money on this technology.

Another promising technology is Automatic License Plate Readers in patrol cars. The ALPR reads and records the license plate from the automobile and records it to a data base The license plate is checked to see the registered owner, the vehicle it is registered on, if the car or plate is stolen. If you are looking for a fugitive, their license plate information can be fed into the data base as well. The unit cost is about $15,000.00 each and many police agencies use them. They are very effective in detecting stolen autos (Weise & Toppo, 2013, p. 3a). They also have antiterrorism uses to identify suspects. However, ACLU attorneys advocate that they are being used to spy on innocent civilians and have filed lawsuits against the police in several states. None of the lawsuits have been successful so far (Insinna & Magason, 2012, p. 11; Li, 2014).

The possibility of having to operate in a CRBNE environment led to the need for Personal Protective Equipment (PPE). PPE consists of things such as gas masks and HAZMAT suits. Upgraded hard shell body armor and ballistic helmets were also on the list of equipment that was acquired.

CIVIL UNREST AND THE POLICE

Civil Unrest Threat: Occupy Wall Street

Occupy Wall Street (2015) is described on the group's own website as follows:

> Occupy Wall Street is a people-powered movement that began on September 17, 2011 in Liberty Square in Manhattan's Financial District, and has spread to over 100 cities in the United States and actions in over 1,500 cities globally. #OWS [Occupy Wall Street] is fighting back against the corrosive power of major banks and multinational corporations over the democratic process, and the role of Wall Street in creating an economic collapse that has caused the greatest recession in generations. The movement is inspired by popular uprisings in Egypt and Tunisia, and aims to fight back against the richest 1% of people that are writing the rules of an unfair global economy that is foreclosing on our future.

The Occupy Wall Street movement is often said to be inspired by the earlier Spanish 15-M movement. Occupy Wall Street and other Occupy movements express anarchist political philosophies about income inequality, capitalist control of production, and call for redistribution of wealth. OWS displays anarchist symbols on their website and states "World Revolution is the Only Solution." The police in the United States are no strangers to the anarchist movement. In 1881, President James Garfield was assassinated by an anarchist named Charles Guiteau in Elberon, New Jersey (Parissen, 2008, pp. 73–76). In 1901, President William McKinley was assassinated in Buffalo, New York by an anarchist named Leo Czolgosz (Parissen, 2008, pp. 85–88). In 1920, on Wall Street in New York City, an anarchist bomb contained in a horse drawn cart exploded killing more than 30 people and caused panic on the New York Stock Exchange. The case was never solved (Martinez, 2012, pp. 123–147). In 1933, anarchist Giuseppe Zangara attempted to assassinate President-Elect Franklin

D. Roosevelt in Miami, Florida. Zangara's pistol was deflected by a bystander in the crowd and the bullets struck and killed Chicago Mayor Anton Cermak instead (McCann, 2006, pp. 69–85).

In 2011–2012 thousands of Occupy Wall Street protesters filled the streets and parks of downtown New York. While being loud, there was not much violence and only a minor amount of street crime was reported. However some sexual assaults were alleged by Occupy Wall Street members that allegedly were committed by other Occupy Wall Street members. Overall, arrests were few. A large NYPD presence was needed for crowd control. However, the same cannot be said of Occupy Oakland. The demonstrations that began in October of 2011 were marred by sometimes violent clashes with police (Wood, 2011). Wolf (2012) alleged that the FBI and DHS saw the OWS movement as a possible terrorist threat and that this had caused some of the alleged police overreaction in Oakland. In one of the demonstrations the Occupy Oakland protesters managed to actually shut down the Port of Oakland for a time. Other Occupy movements have been largely peaceful in their demonstrations in other cities.

Civil Unrest Threat: Ferguson, Missouri

On August 9, 2014 after committing a strong arm robbery of cigars at a convenience store, 18-year-old Michael Brown was stopped by a Ferguson Police officer for an unrelated matter. A struggle ensued and Brown, who was an African American and unarmed, was shot and killed by the white police officer while attacking the police officer. There were conflicting stories from the witnesses about the shooting. Demonstrations and riots occurred. The St. Louis County Prosecutor took the case in front of a grand jury in an effort to indict the police officer for a wrongful shooting. The state grand jury failed to indict Officer Darren Wilson (Von Drehle & Altman, 2014). This touched off another wave of protests. Two area police officers were shot. The federal government also declined to indict Wilson but found that the Furguson Police Department and Municipal Court system had showed racial bias (Grossman, 2015). Wilson resigned. The Furguson Police Chief resigned. Several officers, a municipal judge and the city manager were dismissed (Kesling, 2015b).

The St. Louis County Police Department used CCTV footage of the looters and arsonists to attempt to identify and prosecute those responsible for the destruction. They posted the CCTV pictures on the public crime stoppers website and asked the public's assistance to help identify those responsible (Kesling, 2015a).

TERRORIST THREATS AND THE POLICE

Terrorist Threat: The Little Rock, Arkansas Army Recruiter Murder

On June 1, 2009, two uniformed U.S. Army personnel, Pvt. William Long and Pvt. Quinton Ezeagwula were taking a short break outside the U.S. Army recruiting station that was located in a local strip mall. A black SUV drove by and the driver later identified as Abdulhakim Mujahid Muhammad (AKA Carlos Bledsoe) fired at the soldiers. Long was hit several times and later died of his injuries. Ezeagwula was wounded, but survived. The Little Rock Police caught Abdulhakim Muhammad in his vehicle shortly after the shooting and recovered several weapons including a SKS rifle and two hand guns. Muhammad's original name was Bledsoe, but he changed it when he converted to Islam. He was a U.S. Citizen. Shortly before this incident Muhammad had traveled to Yemen using a Somali passport and was being looked at by the FBI's Joint Terrorism Task Force (Eaton, 2009; Esposito, Thomas, & Date, 2009).

Terrorist Threat: The New York City Times Square Attempted Bombing

On May 1, 2010, Faisal Shahzad, parked his blue Nissan Pathfinder in Times Square in New York City. He activated the fuse of the homemade car bomb that he had constructed and walked away. Some citizens observed smoke coming from the car and informed a New York City Police horse mounted patrolman. The patrolman examined the vehicle and observed what he believed to be explosives. The patrolman called for backup and the bomb squad. He also notified the FDNY who responded to the smoking car. The bomb was disarmed and did not explode (Moynihan & Cohen, 2010). Shahzad was arrested by federal authorities at John F. Kennedy Airport as he attempted to flee the country. Shahzad was charged and pled guilty in federal court to a 10 count indictment. He was sentenced to life imprisonment. According to Weiser (2010), Shahzad was a Pakistani immigrant who was a United States citizen. Weiser citing the indictment observed that: "In December 2009, Mr. Shahzad received explosives training in Waziristan, Pakistan, from trainers affiliated with Tehrik-i-Taliban."

Terrorist Threat: The Boston Marathon Bombing

The Boston Marathon is a very public athletic event that has been celebrated in Boston, Massachusetts for many years. On April 15, 2013, two brothers, Dzhokhar Tsarnev (age 19) and Tamerlan Tsarnev (age 26) were observed on CCTV camera walking through the crowd of spectators carrying backpacks. The backpacks contained homemade bombs that had been constructed from pressure cookers. The bombs had been constructed in a similar fashion as had been described in the Al Qaeda's magazine *Inspire* article that was posted on the internet (Kamp, 2015). When the bombs detonated in the crowds, three spectators were killed and another 284 were injured. The Boston Police Department responded and activated the emergency plans that they had made for any problem that might arise during the Marathon. The bombers had escaped unnoticed.

The Tsarnev brothers had come to the United States from Russia in 2002. Tamerlan and Dzhokhar both thought of themselves as Chechen by ancestry although neither of them had ever lived in Chechnya. Both brothers were Muslim. Tamerlan had been a boxer at one time and had attend Bunker Hill Community College for a short while He later enrolled at Mass Bay Community College but dropped out of that school as well. Prior to the Boston Marathon Bombing, Tamerlan had begun to argue with the Iman at the Mosque that he attended. Dzhokhar was a student at the University of Massachusetts at Dartmouth. He was described as easy going and liked to use marijuana (Jammet, 2013).

While they were on the run from law enforcement, the Tsarnaev brothers stayed in the Boston area hiding in the suburbs. The FBI had released CCTV photographs of the suspects on April 19, 2013. Later that day in an attempt to get another firearm, the Tsarnaev brothers killed Massachusetts Institute of Technology police officer Sean A. Collier shooting him several times. They were then unable to get the officer's pistol because of the weapons retention system of the slain officer's holster (Haven, 2013; Miller, 2013). The Tsarnev brothers later carjacked a Mercedes Benz SUV and took the owner hostage. They forced the owner to withdraw $800 from an ATM machine. The SUV owner was able to escape. The Tsarnaev brothers vehicles were spotted by an officer of the Watertown police and a pursuit ensured. Tamerlan began to exchange gunfire with the police, while Dzhokhar attempt to escape in the stolen car. Tamerlan was hit several times by police gunfire and then was struck by the car driven by his brother. He died as a result of his wounds (Levitz, 2015). Dzhokhar was captured shortly thereafter while hiding in a boat in the neighborhood. Several other suspects were looked at by federal authorities.

Terrorist Threat: The Overland Park, Kansas Jewish Center Shooting

Sometimes the threat comes as an act of domestic terrorism. In a lone wolf attack, Frazier Glenn Cross attacked two Jewish facilities in Overland Park, Kansas (a suburb of Kansas City) on April 13, 2014. Using a shotgun and a handgun, Frazier opened fire at the Jewish Community Center of Greater Kansas City and at the nearby Village Shalom Retirement Community in Leawood, Kansas. According to Stucker and Shoichet (2014), Frazier shot at a total of five people and killed three in the shooting spree. The shooting occurred the day before the Jewish holiday of Passover began. Frazier had an anti-Semitic motive in his attacks, but ironically the people he shot were not Jewish, but participants in the various social activities that were being offered at the facilities. Frazier was captured shortly after the shootings by local police officers.

CONCLUSION

In the aftermath of the attacks of 9/11, many saw a terrorist hiding under every bush. In truth, as the United States went to war, only some were found. Some of the terrorists that were discovered were foreign born and some were natural born American citizens who had become radicalized. However, the actual numbers of terrorists discovered were quite small. Some incidents were not classified as terrorism, such the 2014 beheading of a women by a recently fired native born Muslim fellow worker in Oklahoma City. That incident was classified as workplace violence and was stopped when a reserve deputy sheriff shot the perpetrator as he was attacking a second victim (Bustillo & Campoy, 2014).

As White (2004) has argued, "Law enforcement management frequently favors local issues over national ones" (p.18). Nonetheless, as Shallwani, Elinson, and Fileds (2014) have observed, many police departments are being forced to change their tactics and their operational procedures based on the changing tactical and political landscapes that exist in the United States today (pp. A1, A6).

REFERENCES

AP. (2005). New Orleans police chief resigns. *NBC News.com*. 09/29/05. Retrieved from http://www.nbcnews.com/id/9503273/ns/us_news-katrina_the_long_road_back/t/new-orleans-police-chief-resigns/#.VMKgY6Pnbmg. Accessed on January 13, 2015.

AP. (2014). Ray Nagin, Ex-New Orleans Mayor, found guilty on corruption charges. *Huffington Post*. 02/12/14. Retrieved from http://www.huffingtonpost.com/2014/02/12/ray-nagin-guilty_n_4775601.html. Accessed on January 23, 2015.

Atkins, S. (2011). Firefighters at ground zero. *The 9/11 encyclopedia*. Santa Barbara, CA: ABC-CLIO.

Bodrero, D. (2002). Law enforcement s new challenge to investigate, interdict, and prevent terrorism. *The Police Chief*, *69*(2), 41–48.

Bridges, D. (2002). It's a police problem: The terrorist threat's impact on state and local law enforcement. *The Police Chief*, *69*(2), 35–36.

Bullock, J., Haddow, G., Cappola, D., Ergin, E., Westerman, L., & Yeletaysi, S. (2006). *Introduction to homeland security* (2nd ed.). Burlington, MA: Elsevier.

Bustillo, M., & Campoy, A. (2014). FBI probes beheading in Oklahoma. *The Wall Street Journal*, September 27–28, p. A3.

Calderone, M. (2013). AP's Matt Apuzzo And Adam Goldman crack open secretive institutions, From NYPD to CIA. *Huffington Post*, September 3. Retrieved from http://www.huffingtonpost.com/2013/09/03/ap-nypd-matt-apuzzo-adam-goldman_n_3861444.html. Accessed on February 26, 25.

CNN. (2010). Al Qaeda launches English language magazine. *CNN*, July 1. Retrieved from http://www.cnn.com/2010/WORLD/meast/07/01/al.qaeda.magazine/. Accessed on February 10, 2015.

Du Comb, C., & Benmen, J. (2014). Flash mobs, violence and the turbulent crowd. *Performance Research*, *19*(5), 34–40.

Eaton, S. (2009). Army recruiter killed in shooting. *WLTX*, June 2. Retrieved from http://archive.wltx.com/news/article/74497/0/Army-Recruiter-Killed-in-Shooting. Accessed on March 16, 2015.

Esposito, R., Thomas, P., & Date, J. (2009). Recruiter shooting suspect under FBI investigation. *ABC News*, June 1. Retrieved from http://abcnews.go.com/Politics/story?id=7730637&page=1. Accessed on March 16, 2015.

Etter, G., & Griffin, R. (2011). In-service training of older law enforcement officers: An andragogical argument. *Policing: An International Journal of Police Strategies & Management*, *34*(2), 233–245.

FBI. (2012). *Naser Jason Abdo sentenced to life in federal prison in connection with Killeen bomb plot*. Retrieved from http://abcnews.go com/Blotter/naser-jaon-abdo-ft-hood-plotter-life-prison/story?id=16978363. Accessed on February 10, 2015.

FEMA. (2015). *FEMA: 35 years of commitment*. Retrieved from http://www.fema.gov/fema-35-years-commitment. Accessed on January 23, 2015.

Greene, L. (2008). Governmental liability for the Katrina failure. In J. Levitt & M. Whitaker (Eds.), *Hurricane Katrina: America's unnatural disaster*. Lincoln, NE: University of Nebraska Press.

Grossman, A. (2014). Congress probes police militarization. *The Wall Street Journal*, September 10, p. A3.

Grossman, A. (2015). Federal Probe finds Ferguson police bias. *The Wall Street Journal*, March 4, p. A3.

Gurr, T. (1988). Political terrorism in the United States: Historical antecedents and contemporary trends. In M. Stohl (Ed.), In *The politics of terrorism* (3rd ed.). New York, NY: Marcel Dekker, Inc.

Haven, S. (2013). Officer killed in MIT standoff ID'd as Sean Collier, 26. *USA Today*, April 19. Retrieved from http://www.usatoday.com/story/news/nation/2013/04/19/boston-mit-officer-collier/2096329/. Accessed on March 20, 2015.

Insinna, V., & Magason, S. (2012). License plate reader technology sparks lawsuit. *National Defense*, *97*(708), 11.

Jammet, J. (2013). The fall of the hose of Tsarnaev. *The Boston Globe*. Retrieved from http://www.bostonglobe.com/Page/Boston/2011-020/WebGraphics/Metro/BostonGlobe.com/2013/12/15tsarnaev/tsarnaev.html. Accessed on March 20, 2015.

Kamp, J. (2015). Bomb suspect admits role. *The Wall Street Journal*, March 5, p. A3.

Kaste, M. (2014). Even police body cameras can lose sight of the truth. *NPR*. Retrieved from http://www.npr.org/2014/08/23/342623830/even-police-body-cameras-can-lose-sight-of-the-truth. Accessed on January 27, 2015.

Kesling, B. (2015a). Arson and looting in Ferguson investigated. *The Wall Street Journal*, February 6, p. A3.

Kesling, B. (2015b). State judge to take over Ferguson cases. *The Wall Street Journal*, March 10, p. A3.

Levitas, D. (2002). *The terrorist next door: The Militia movement and the radical right*. New York, NY: St. Martin's Press.

Levitz, J. (2015). Police describe gun fight in bombing trial. *The Wall Street Journal*. March 17, p. A5.

Lewis, R. (2013). Former New Orleans Mayor Ray Nagin indicted. *USA Today*. January 18. Retrieved from http://www.usatoday.com/story/news/nation/2013/01/18/new-orleans-mayor-ray%20nagin/1845617/. Accessed on January 23, 2015.

Li, V. (2014). Law enforcement's latest highway tech speeds up info-gathering, but critics say it violates privacy. *ABA Journal*, October 100(10).

Lynn, P., Scrivner, E., Wilson, F., Lee, J., Hamilton, E., McDonald, P., & Greenburg, S. (2005). *Post 9-11 policing: The crime control-homeland security paradigm, taking command of new realities*. Alexandria, VA: IACP.

Macdonald, A. (pseudonym for William L. Pierce) (1980). *The turner diaries* (2nd ed.). Arlington, VA: National Vanguard Books.

Martinez, J. M. (2012). *Terrorist attacks on American soil from the civil war era to the present*. Lanham, MD: Rowman & Littlefield Publishers, Inc.

McCann, J. (2006). *Terrorism on American soil: A concise history of plots and perpetrators from the famous to the forgotten*. Boulder, CO: Sentient Publications.

McKenna, T. (2004). Blast from the past. *The Journal of Electronic Defense*, *27*(6), 43–49.

Michel, L., & Herbeck, D. (2001). *American terrorist: Timothy McVeigh & the Oklahoma city bombing*. New York, NY: Harper Collins.

Miller, J. (2013). Police believe Tsarnev brothers killed officers for his gun. *CBS News*, April 23. Retrieved from http://www.cbsnews.com/news/police-believe-tsarnaev-brothers-killed-officer-for-his-gun/. Accessed on March 20, 2015.

Mims, C. (2014). What happens when police officers wear body cameras. *The Wall Street Journal*, August 18, p. B1.

Mouras, T. (2015). Lone wolves: Are they really alone in the radicalization process? *In Public Safety*. Retrieved from http://inpublicsafety.com/2015/02/lone-wolves-are-they-really-alone-in-the-radicalization-process/. Accessed on February 06, 2015.

Moynihan, C., & Cohen, M. (2010). Bomb scare reveals another side of Times Square. May 2. Retrieved from http://www.nytimes.com/2010/05/03/nyregion/03scene.html. Accessed on March 16, 2015.

Occupy Wall Street. (2015). *Occupy Wall Street*. Retrieved from http://occupywallst.org/about/. Accessed on February 18, 2015.

ODMP. (2015). *Officer down memorial page, New York, New York*. Retrieved from http://www.odmp.org/agency/2758-new-york-city-police-department-new-york. Accessed on January 29, 2015.

Parissen, S. (2008). *Assassins: Assassinations that shock the world. From Julius Ceasar to JFK*. London: Quercus.

Peterson, M. (2005). Intelligence-led policing: The new intelligence architecture. In *New Realities: Law Enforcement in the Post9/11 Era*. Washington, DC: Office of Justice Programs. BJA Product 2003-DD-BX-K002.

Powell, W. (1971). *The anarchist cookbook*. New York, NY: Barricade Book, Inc.

Radnofsky, L., & Madigan, K. (2015). Mall security tightens after threat. *The Wall Street Journal*, February 23, p. A3.

Reibling, M. (1994). *Wedge: The secret war between the FBI and CIA*. New York, NY: Knopf Publishers.

Ryan, J., & Ferran, L. (2012). Naser Jason Abdo, Ft. Hood Plotter, gets life in prison. *ABC News*. Retrieved from http://abcnews.go.com/Blotter/naser-jaon-abdo-ft-hood-plotter-life-prison/story?id=16978363. Accessed on February 10, 2015.

Shallwani, P., Elinson, Z., & Fields, G. (2014). Police move to revamp tactics. *The Wall Street Journal*, December 5, pp. A1 and A6.

Silber, M. (2015). Fighting Islamic state in Brooklyn. *The Wall Street Journal*, February 27, p. A11.

Siuru, B. (1994). Police cars go high-tech. *Poplar Electronics*, *11*(8), 59.

Smith, C., & Rush, J. (2012). Flashgangs and flashbanging: How can local police prepare? *Journal of Gang Research*, *20*(2), 33–50.

Smith, J. (2012). *Hurricane Katrina: The Mississippi Story*. Jackson, MS: University of Mississippi.

Stalcup, M., & Craze, J. (2011). How we train our cops to fear Islam. *Current*, *535*, 16–21.

Stateline. (2014). Cop Cams. *State Legislatures*. October/November, p. 14.

Stucker, M., & Shoichet, C. (2014). 3 Killed in shootings at Kansas city-area Jewish centers. *CNN*, April 14. Retrieved from http://www.cnn.com/2014/04/13/us/kansas-jewish-center-shooting/index.html. Accessed on January 20, 2015.

Von Drehle, D., & Altman, A. (2014). The tragedy of Ferguson. *Time*, September 1, pp. 22–27.

Waugh, W. (2006). The political costs of failure in the Katrina and Rita disasters. *The Annals of the American Academy of Political and Social Science*, *604*(1), 10–25.

Weise, E., & Toppo, G. (2013). License plate scanners: Love 'em or loathe'em: Calif. town's police say the devices have nearly eliminated car thefts. *USA Today*, July 19, p. 3a.

Weiser, B. (2010). Suspect in times Sq. Bomb attempt is indicted. *The New York Times*, June 17. Retrieved from http://www.nytimes.com/2010/06/18/nyregion/18terror.html?ref=topics. Accessed on March 16, 2015.

Welsh, B., & Farrington, D. (2009). Public area CCTV and crime prevention: An updated systematic review and meta-analysis. *Justice Quarterly*, *26*(4), 716–745.

White, J. (2004). *Defending the homeland: Domestic intelligence, law enforcement, and security*. Belmont, CA: Thompson-Wadsworth.

Wolf, N. (2012). Revealed: How the FBI coordinated the crackdown on occupy. *The Guardian*, December 29. Retrieved from http://www.theguardian.com/commentisfree/2012/dec/29/fbi-coordinated-crackdown-occupy. Accessed on February 18, 2015.

Wood, D. (2011). Occupy Wall Street clash in Oakland: How should police handle protests? *Christian Science Monitor*. November 4. Retrieved from http://www.csmonitor.com/USA/2011/1104/Occupy-Wall-Street-clash-in-Oakland-How-should-police-handle-pro tests-video. Accessed on February 18, 2015.

STATE LEGITIMACY AND TERRORISM: IMPLICATIONS FOR COUNTERTERRORISM POLICY

Jennifer C. Gibbs

ABSTRACT

Purpose – *Scholars often suggest that violent extremism or terrorism – "the threatened or actual use of illegal force and violence to attain a political, economic, religious or social goal through fear, coercion or intimidation" (LaFree, G., & Dugan, L. (2007). Introducing the Global Terrorism Database.* Terrorism and Political Violence, 19, *181–204, 184) – is a battle for legitimacy. However, the ambiguous definition of legitimacy often makes its application to counterterrorism measures difficult at best. The purpose of this chapter is to define legitimacy to connect policies designed to counter violent extremism.*

Methodology/approach – *The main impediment in the study of the influence of legitimacy on terrorism is the debate over the meaning and measurement of legitimacy. This debate is reviewed, and a recent resolution is presented, grouping the many conceptualizations of legitimacy into three broad categories and identifying empirical indicators for each. These categories are then used to distinguish counterterrorism policies that can be used to boost legitimacy.*

Terrorism and Counterterrorism Today
Sociology of Crime, Law and Deviance, Volume 20, 241–259

ISSN: 1521-6136/doi:10.1108/S1521-613620150000020012

Originality/value – *This chapter organizes counterterrorism policies into a recently developed framework as a tool for researchers, practitioners, and policymakers.*

Keywords: Terrorism; state legitimacy; political violence; counterterrorism; common vulnerabilities and exposures

INTRODUCTION

Several scholars have noted the significance of legitimacy for inhibiting violence – especially political violence (e.g., Gurr, 1970). Terrorism and other political violence, in fact, may be reduced to a battle over legitimacy between a government and its opponents, especially considering one of the defining characteristics of terrorism is a grievance (see LaFree & Ackerman, 2009). Cronin (2009) explains that "terrorist campaigns succeed when groups can convince more powerful actors of the legitimacy of their cause ..." (p. 92).

History is ripe with examples of illegitimacy leading to increased terrorist attacks. Police illegitimately using excessive force – or allowing such force – can create a violent backlash, which was the case during the second intifada of the Israeli–Palestinian conflict (Cronin, 2009). Cronin reports:

> The uprising began [in late September of 2000] with widespread rioting among Israeli Arabs, blocking streets, looting stores, and assaulting Jewish Israeli citizens. The police opened fire, killing 12 Israeli Arabs and one Palestinian. When two Israeli reservists entered the Palestinian city of Ramallah, they were arrested by the Palestinian Authority police. A mob rushed the police station, then brutally beat the two soldiers to death, throwing their mutilated corpses onto the street .... The Israelis responded with air strikes by helicopter gunships, pummeling the police station into rubble .... A major campaign of suicide attacks and targeted killings was well under way by the next summer. (pp. 54–55)

The Liberation Tigers of Tamil Eelam was formed in Sri Lanka in response to police illegitimacy – police killed civilians at the World Tamil Conference – and have specifically targeted police, like in 1990, when they murdered more than 600 officers (Cronin, 2009).

Legitimacy is important for voluntary citizen obedience to government authority and citizen support of the government's rule. Legitimacy leads to many desirable outcomes, including citizens' voluntary obedience to the law (i.e., reduced crime), citizen support for and cooperation with authorities, citizen willingness to follow government directives, and support for empowering authorities. Conversely, illegitimacy leads to many negative consequences, including retaliation, possibly serving to delegitimize a government by attacking its representatives.

While scholars have suggested the influence of legitimacy on terrorism (e.g., Chalk, 1998; Gurr, 1970), both empirical studies testing this relationship and connecting policy with legitimacy are challenging, perhaps due to the difficulty in operationalizing this concept. However, the myriad definitions of legitimacy found in the literature can be organized into three broad categories: (1) the government has the legal right to rule; (2) the government has the moral right to rule; and (3) citizens actively consent to the government's rule (Beetham, 1991). Following this classification, Gilley (2006, 2009) recently suggested empirical indicators for each category. The purpose of this chapter is to link policies designed to reduce violent extremism with legitimacy. First, legitimacy is defined, explaining the meaning behind the three categories and identifying ways to operationalize each. Next, the desirable outcomes of high legitimacy are reviewed, followed by a summary of the few studies empirically linking legitimacy with terrorism. The chapter concludes with implications for counterterrorism policy.

WHAT IS LEGITIMACY?

As "legitimacy" has evolved throughout history, its definition, too, has had several incarnations. Sternberger (1968) describes the etymology of state legitimacy, showing three main advancements. The earliest was the Roman *legitimus*, meaning "lawful, according to law" (Sternberger, 1968, p. 245). In medieval times, *legitimus* referred to conforming to custom or customary procedure. Finally, in 1338, popular consent became part of the definition of legitimacy. While contemporary scholars debate about the meaning and measure of legitimacy, these three topical areas dominate the literature. Summarizing this literature, Beetham (1991, 1993) redefined these categories as *views of legality* (lawful or according to law), *views of justification* (conforming to customary procedure), and *acts of consent* (citizens actively accepting the authority of the government).

Views of legality is Weber's classical view of legitimacy: the predictable rules and laws that the government follows (Gilley, 2009). Here, people know what to expect; laws are not arbitrary (Gilley, 2009). Citizens "trust that institutions responsible for the implementation of public policies are run and guided by the principles of impartiality and fairness" (Rothstein & Stolle, 2001, p. 7, as cited in Ivkovic, 2008). Levi,

Sacks, and Tyler (2009) "find that citizens everywhere are capable of determining whether government is meeting its obligations to them, and they are likely to withdraw their deference and compliance if it is not" (pp. 370–371). Adopting this element, some scholars have operationalized legitimacy as confidence in the government, its representatives, or civil servants (Gilley, 2006, 2009). The absence of government corruption may also be an indicator of this element of legitimacy, showing that government officials tend to follow the rules (see Fig. 1).

However, this traditional element of legitimacy has been criticized for ignoring morality (Beetham, 1991, 1993; Breitmeier, 2008). Breitmeier (2008) argues "A conception of legitimacy which ignores the weight of morality takes the risk to justify authoritarian political power as legitimate then if the people are convinced of the adequacy of immoral power" (p. 19). This leads to the next component of state legitimacy.

Under the *views of justification* element, citizens believe that the state reflects a shared moral consensus. This component is also referred to as "congruence" in Norway or "vertical social contract" by political philosophers (Gilley, 2009). Kennedy (1998) reminds us that the difference between terrorism and the legitimate actions of a sovereign state is the moral authority of the government in pursuit of its national interests. When citizens perceive that moral authority can be weakened, terrorist groups justify their violent behavior as taking the moral high ground – as was the case of the 1995 bombing of the Alfred P. Murrah Federal Building in Oklahoma City, Oklahoma in the United States (Kennedy, 1998). The state failing to adopt the values of citizen groups can be evidenced by mass emigration of particular groups, the number of political prisoners (Gilley, 2006, 2009), genocide, or political discrimination of minority groups. When these are low, views of justification are high (see Fig. 1).

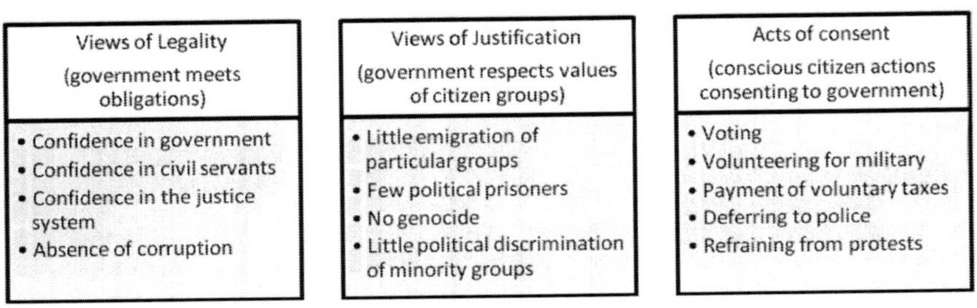

Fig.1. Possible Ways to Operationalize State Legitimacy.

The third component of state legitimacy is *acts of consent* – conscious citizen actions, obeying the government. Here, citizens actively recognize the government's authority through activities like voting, voluntarily joining the military, paying taxes, deferring to police, or reporting crimes to police (Gilley, 2009; see Fig. 1). Rothstein and Stolle (2001) argue:

> it makes no sense to pay your taxes if you think that the tax authorities are discriminating against you or are heavily corrupt. You would not take your dispute to a court if you did not trust the judge to be impartial and to follow the universal rules guaranteeing equality before the law. (p. 10, as cited in Ivkovic, 2008)

In other words, when the state is "legitimate," people are more likely to voluntarily consent to its rules. Consent may be based on whether the government is following clearly established rules or is respecting the shared belief system of the public, demonstrating that each of these three elements may depend on one of the other elements (Beetham, 1993). Accordingly, any complete measure of state legitimacy should recognize all three elements dominating the literature.

While scholars generally focus on one or more of these elements when discussing legitimacy, few have empirically tested whether the full model holds water. One exception is Gilley (2006, 2009), who created a composite measure of legitimacy using a cross-sectional sample of 72 countries, representing 83% of the world's population. He computed a legitimacy score (ranging from 0 to 10) for each country and ranked countries according to their legitimacy scores. The legitimacy score incorporated both attitudinal and behavioral measures representing the three subtypes of legitimacy described above (views of legality, views of justification, and acts of consent). Gilley finds that Denmark, Norway, the Netherlands, and Canada rank highest (with the United States ranking 8th – just behind Sweden) and the Dominican Republic, Armenia, Pakistan, and Russia ranked last of the 72 countries included in his study. On average, countries in the West and Asia enjoy higher legitimacy scores than states in Latin America and Eastern Europe, which one might expect given that countries in Latin America and Eastern Europe are commonly viewed as less stable (e.g., the dissolutions of the USSR, Czechoslovakia, and Yugoslavia) than those in the Western or Asian regions. So, Gilley's legitimacy measure is valid on its face. Additionally, his convergent and discriminant validity tests confirm his conceptualization of legitimacy. For example, good governance (measured by the World Bank Governance Indicators) and civil liberties (drawn from Freedom House) were highly correlated with the legitimacy measure, while population size was not (Gilley, 2006). Further, the legitimacy score had a high positive correlation with political stability (drawn from the World Bank), considered an outcome of legitimate states (Gilley, 2006). Recent research using Gilley's legitimacy index across 65 countries found that illegitimate states have higher homicide rates than legitimate states (Nivette & Eisner, 2013).

While incorporating these three elements is only one – and perhaps the most comprehensive – measure of legitimacy, its impact on other important outcomes like terrorism has yet to be tested. Assessing the impact of legitimacy on terrorism is important because the literature suggests that there may be a link between legitimacy and terrorism. Gurr (1970) hypothesized that "people who regard their regimes as legitimate will regard political violence as unjustified ..." (p. 186). This may be the case, given the many positive results of legitimacy.

DESIRABLE OUTCOMES OF LEGITIMACY

Collaboration, Cooperation, and Support

The impact of perceptions of legitimacy on public support cannot be understated because terrorist groups, as organizations (Crenshaw, 2001; Dugan & Gibbs, 2008), are potentially competing with the state for support from the same public constituency. McCauley (2006) summarizes:

> ... terrorists depend upon their civilian base of sympathizers and supporters. The terrorist apex cannot survive long without cover, information, money, supplies, expertise, and, especially, recruits from lower in the pyramid. ... terrorists cannot be beaten so long as they can disappear into and recruit from the pyramid that supports them. (p. 250)

When the public believes the government is legitimate, citizens support the state and its representatives – not terrorists. Terrorist attacks are viewed by the public as unjust, and the public will abhor the terrorist group; in cases of higher state legitimacy, the lack of public support for terrorist attacks against government representatives provides little incentive (unless, of course, such terrorist groups are disinterested in an earthly constituency). For example, this lack of support may have led to the downfall of the Armenian Secret Army for the Liberation of Armenia (ASALA), as they lost the legitimacy awarded to them by their constituents after a botched bombing at the Orly Airport in 1983 that killed many innocent civilians, followed by targeting fellow Armenians and extorting constituents (Dugan, Huang, LaFree, & McCauley, 2008).

Alternatively, when the public believes the government is illegitimate, citizens are less supportive of the state and its representatives. At the very least, "When members of a society begin to doubt the fairness of their political institutions, even if they do not themselves violate laws, they become less enthusiastic agents for the social control of others" (LaFree, 1998, p. 80). Terrorist attacks in this instance are viewed as just, terrorist groups are viewed as heroes for attacking the "villains," and terrorist groups have a larger pool of supporters from which to recruit.

There is some empirical evidence of the relationship between perceptions of legitimacy and support for authorities. For example, using the 2005 Afrobarometer survey data, Levi et al. (2009) found that the administrative competence of the government (measured as the belief that the government will enforce criminal law, even among top officials, and the belief that the police are not corrupt) and procedural justice (beliefs that the government fairly treats citizens, as well as members of their own ethnic group) increased the likelihood that citizens would report accepting governmental authority (i.e., authority of the police, the court, and the tax department).

Compliance with the Law and Consent to Decisions

Following a Weberian tradition, most writers agree that legitimacy encourages a voluntary willingness of the public to obey government directives because citizens believe this authority *ought* to be obeyed (LaFree, 1998; Sherman, 1998; Sunshine & Tyler, 2003, p. 514; Weber, 1984; see also Tyler & Huo, 2002, p. xiv). Legitimacy induces a sense of obligation to defer to government rules and regulations, bolstering obedience to the law (Levi et al., 2009; Tyler, 1990, 2006) and to authorities. Alternatively, when confidence in the system is low, the stigma associated with formal social control is reduced (Hirschfield & Piquero, 2010). Voluntary citizen compliance with the law is crucial to an orderly society, as the alternative means that such behavior must be coerced – usually at great cost. In short, political legitimacy decreases citizen motivation to engage in deviance and increases the effectiveness of social control (LaFree, 1998).

Motivation to voluntarily comply with the law is different from deterrence (obeying the law due to fear of punishment; Sunshine & Tyler, 2003). Indeed, Freeman, Liossis, and David (2006) found in a survey of Australian driving-while-intoxicated recidivists that those participants who reported lower government legitimacy related to drinking and driving interventions were more likely to report intentions to drive intoxicated in the future. This finding was more robust than participants' perceptions of swift, severe, and certain penalties, which were used to test the deterrence doctrine. In other words, legitimacy may have a greater impact on compliance than does deterrence (see also Murphy, 2004).

Empirical evidence supports the influence of legitimacy in decreasing crime (LaFree, 1998). Studying a sample of 586 New Yorkers in the spring and summer of 2001 (before the terrorist attacks on 9/11), Sunshine and Tyler (2003) found that respondents' perceptions of police legitimacy (19 Likert-response items asking about perceived obligation to obey police, trust in police and emotions about police) directly influenced their reported compliance with the law (e.g., legally parking and disposing of trash, not purchasing stolen goods, refraining from shoplifting, not using drugs).[1] Similarly, results from a United States nationwide telephone survey of 432 adults indicated that legitimacy (as measured by reported trust in the police) was more important to citizen compliance than perceptions of distributive fairness (Reisig, Bratton, & Gertz, 2007). LaFree (1998), too, found that legitimacy of institutions in the United States and US crime rates were inversely related.

Summary

While legitimacy produces many desired outcomes, public perceptions of illegitimacy have negative outcomes – perceptions of illegitimacy have the power to restructure government institutions and practices. For example, the community policing movement – which arguably changed the structure and practices of police agencies in the United States and created new government agencies – stemmed from a "legitimacy crisis" in policing, arising in the tumultuous 1960s and 1970s (Hawdon, Ryan, & Griffin, 2003; Sunshine & Tyler, 2003). Illegitimacy also has the potential to generate grievances strong enough to propel extremists into terrorist violence.

CONNECTION BETWEEN LEGITIMACY AND TERRORISM

Many scholars suggest legitimacy plays a central role in terrorism (e.g., Crenshaw, 1981; Cronin, 2009; Gurr, 1970). "When individuals do not believe that a state's laws are binding or legitimate, they will be less likely to orient their actions in accordance with these laws, and conflict may ensue" (Cook, 2003, p. 112). So, legitimacy is a motivation for violence against the state. Terrorists simultaneously attempt to increase their own legitimacy while decreasing the legitimacy of the state (Cook, 2003). Terrorist organizations with high legitimacy can use it to recruit and to generate sympathy for their cause. According to Cronin (2009), because they are in the weaker position, "terrorist violence seeks to challenge the state on two levels: among its citizens, by creating doubt about the state's ability to protect them from harm; and internationally, by undermining traditional notions of national sovereignty" (p. 116).

However, few have empirically tested this assumption, perhaps due to the vague definition of legitimacy and its ambiguous measurement. Cook (2003) summarizes the empirical issues between legitimacy and terrorism:

> Since it is a normative concept, legitimacy … confronts analysts with moral and political issues that defy social scientific measurement. (pp. 109–110) … [A]ttempts have been made to define legitimacy in some of the philosophical literature. Yet, where definitions have been advanced, philosophers seldom address the problem of terrorism. Conversely, when terrorism is examined by philosophers, they seldom deal with the issue of legitimacy. (p. 111)

Despite this challenge, there is some empirical evidence linking terrorism with legitimacy. For example, in a content analysis of the speeches and writings of 22 twentieth-century revolutionary leaders, Martin, Scully, and Levitt (1990) found that legitimacy played an important role in justifying violence. Additionally, Hussain (2010) found support for Sherman's defiance theory, indicating that legitimacy plays a role in terrorism – at least in Pakistan.

My previous research found a link between legitimacy measures and terrorist attacks targeting the police in 82 countries between 1999 and 2008 (Gibbs, 2011). Considering the earlier discussion about the three categories of legitimacy, views of legality (the legal right to rule) might be operationalized as low corruption (measured by Transparency International's Corruption Perceptions Index); views of justification (the moral right to rule) could be operationalized as minority groups at risk who have greater differences from the dominant group in terms of language, customs, religion, and appearance (drawn from the Minorities at Risk dataset); and acts of consent may be indicated by the willingness to engage in nonviolent protest.[2] Tobit and negative binomial regression models found that these three indicators were significantly related to the proportion and the count of terrorist attacks targeting the police in the expected direction (Gibbs, 2011).

Gurr (1970) defined illegitimacy "in terms of the extent people regard their regimes as improper and deserving of opposition"; in other words, "the polar opposite of legitimacy" (p. 186). When the state or its representatives are viewed as illegitimate and deserving of opposition, terrorist violence against these targets may result. This offers an important lesson for reducing terrorist violence.

IMPLICATIONS FOR COUNTERTERRORISM POLICY

Combating terrorism is expensive in terms of both monetary expenditures and human capital. Unintended consequences of counterterrorism measures may actually aid in terrorist recruitment, furthering the problem – especially considering that a goal of terrorist attacks is to coerce governments into using excessive force, thereby reducing state legitimacy (Abrahms, 2007; Fromkin, 1975; LaFree, Yang, & Crenshaw, 2009; Mueller, 2005). Given its importance, counterterrorism policies may be well-served in deliberately including efforts to boost legitimacy. Several approaches can be used to address each of the three conceptualizations of legitimacy.

Maintaining Legitimacy through Following the Law

Recall that one group of definitions of legitimacy focus on the legal right to rule. Following this, states should consider adhering to the rule of law. One way to do this is to reduce corruption across all levels of the government. Corruption decreases confidence in government agencies (Jang, Lee, and Gibbs, Forthcoming), thereby reducing legitimacy, and increases terrorist attacks – especially attacks targeting government agents like the police (Gibbs, 2011). However, anticorruption programs are noticeably absent from many policies designed to counter violent extremism. Shelley (2014) confirms: "Corruption is central to the dirty entanglement with crime and terrorism, yet it commands too little attention in efforts to address terrorism" (p. 18).

One organization that has become a leader in combating state-level corruption worldwide is Transparency International. In addition to its thorough research on corruption in most countries, Transparency International compiles evidence-based best practices to reduce corruption, like sample policies for businesses to counter bribery (Transparency International, 2013) and a summary of a national integrity assessment system implemented in France and Norway (Transparence International France, 2011; Transparency International Norge, 2012). These measures, though, focus solely on anticorruption and might not necessarily touch on counterterrorism. Shelley recommends incorporating anticorruption programs into measures designed to counter violent extremism in a *whole-of-society approach*. That is, the government must work with private sector industries, the media, educational institutions, nonprofit groups, and others in civil society as well as the international community to reduce corruption and strengthen resilient communities (Shelley, 2014).

The government also can demonstrate a commitment to respecting the law by treating terrorism as a crime, processing violent extremists through the criminal justice system. Involving civilian police dispels the notion of war and reduces the sensationalism surrounding terrorism (Cronin, 2009). Trying terrorists in open criminal court – instead of secretive military tribunals – shows due process and demonstrates proper application of justice, identifies the perpetrators as criminals, and shifts the focus from the group's cause to the illegal act that was committed (Cronin, 2009). Incarcerating violent extremists decreases their martyrability, showing their mortality to the public (Cronin, 2009). Of course, the criminal justice system is not a panacea – especially where there is rampant corruption and terrorists can network and otherwise continue working toward their goals in criminal justice institutions. That said, the criminal justice system can be a promising alternative to military interventions, which can increase terrorism in the short-term and are unsustainable over the long term for an overall null effect or worse (Lum, Kennedy, & Sherley, 2006).

At the international level, countries can work with their neighbors and allies to foster human rights and civil liberties. Abrahms (2007) recommends that the international community consistently encourage states to protect civil liberties and avoid policies involving torture and violation of due process. Abrahms (2007) highlights the importance of respecting civil liberties in counterterrorist measures: "Civil liberties are invaluable not just because of their moral benefits to society, but also because of their practical counterterrorism advantages" (p. 250). In this way, the government maintains constituency support, avoiding losing legitimacy to violent extremists, as well as preserves respect from the international community (Abrahms, 2007).

Increasing Legitimacy through Respecting Customs

Operationalizing legitimacy as the moral right to rule ("views of justification" definitions), states should consider giving all group representatives "voice" – that is, a seat at the political table. Dugan and Young (2009) argue that extremist groups target the disenfranchised, who may be more vulnerable during certain political and economic climates, so the policy should target the same group "to engage in the policy process, making them active stakeholders and reducing their vulnerability to radical rhetoric" (p. 160).

Offering extremist groups a seat at the political table does not necessarily mean negotiating with terrorists. On the contrary, offering concessions can increase terrorist attacks, as only moderates agree to them leaving extremists in charge of the group (Bueno de Mesquita, 2005). Giving voice also does not necessarily imply liberating states to allow free elections, as more often than not such policies have had the unintended consequence of allowing extremists to take power and foreign military intervention can increase extremist violence (Abrahms, 2007; Pape, 2003, 2005, 2008). Further, this approach is likely effective for extremist groups who have political goals and likely ineffective for groups with religious or apocalyptic goals (Nussbaum, 2009).

Instead, providing opportunities for members of all constituencies to participate meaningfully to have their concerns heard can be as simple as representatives having a social media presence or answering citizens' questions through a website (see Dugan & Young, 2009). At the community level, ensuring government representatives take time to listen to people's concerns can be beneficial. Local governments may wish to hold more community forums. If they haven't done so already, police agencies should make a point to adopt provisions of community policing where they invite the public to partner with them to reduce crime and, by extension, terrorism (Donner, Maskaly, Fridell, & Jennings, 2015; see also Lee & Gibbs, 2015). Police have the daily opportunity to build trusting relationships with citizens and, as public servants, ensure that the state is providing basic services so that no void exists for extremist groups to fill. According to the Law Enforcement Management and Administrative Statistics (LEMAS) survey, many police agencies throughout the United States are focusing counterterrorism efforts by increasing police presence in critical areas rather than partnering with the community (Lum, Haberfeld, Fachner, & Lieberman, 2009).

Securing Citizen Consent

The last group of legitimacy definitions operationalizes the concept in terms of citizens' actively consenting to state rule. Policies drawing from this view of legitimacy should encourage citizens' participation in countering violent extremism. A promising new approach is CVE (Common Vulnerabilities and Exposures)-enhanced community oriented policing (COP). This strategy moves beyond traditional community policing in that it involves police working together with *specific* communities without necessarily "targeting" them. The International Association of Chiefs of Police (2014) outlines five key principles for CVE-COP programs: (1) build police–community partnerships based on trust; (2) involve all community residents; (3) involve both public and private stakeholders to expand the breadth of resources available to police; (4) adopt a supporting role, serving as an educator and government representative, to empower these partners to strengthen community resilience against violent extremism; and (5) educate all members of the police agency with up-to-date, unbiased training

Several cities in the United States are piloting CVE-enhanced COP programs in various forms, including Montgomery County, Maryland; Dearborn, Michigan; and Minneapolis-St. Paul, Minnesota. The Los Angeles Police Department (LAPD), for example, centers on Muslim-American communities. Directing efforts at one community reframes the community in the eyes of the police from being part of the problem to becoming part of the solution (Weine, 2014). The program involves a unit of 25 officers who partner with willing and cooperative leaders from the Los Angeles Muslim-American community; they also hold quarterly forums with the larger community in an effort to build trust so that people will notify police when they notice friends or family members pursuing violent, radicalized teachings (Bennett, Rubin, & Kim, 2014; Weine, 2014). In addition to working with the community, the government also partners with schools and health-care providers to identify individuals who may be radicalizing and are vulnerable to terrorist group recruitment (Bennett et al., 2014). Other countries, like Australia, Canada, and Germany, also are adopting programs to counter violent extremism programs (Weine, 2014).

Programs such as this new effort, but involving federal policing agencies, were promoted in the United States during the 1990s, following the Oklahoma City bombing. In particular, the FBI launched a program encouraging agents at field offices to meet their local militia members

(Hull, 1999). This strategy humanized FBI agents in the eyes of the militia and helped them differentiate violent extremists from members loyal to the militia cause of protecting constitutional rights – a goal shared by federal agents (Hull, 1999). Only time will tell whether these programs are helpful. At the time of this writing, evaluations of CVE-enhanced COP are underway in some cities, but building police–community partnerships is a promising approach.

Local community buy-in is especially important for immigrant communities to thwart *international* terrorist threats. As LaFree and colleagues suggest, "Foreign attackers typically face an environment in which they have an imperfect understanding of local language, culture, and daily life .... [thus] foreign terrorist groups need locals" (p. 125). As mentioned earlier, any CVE measure, though, must take care to respect civil liberties (Abrahms, 2007; see also Robison, 2010), and this message must be heard by the targeted communities. In the LAPD CVE-COP pilot program, one difficulty was focusing on the Muslim-American community without stigmatizing them (Weine, 2014), and there was some backlash against the program. This backlash against preventing violent extremism programs in the United Kingdom was noted by Kahn (2009), who wrote that such approaches discriminate against Muslims and seem to be a way for the government to collect intelligence. Program evaluations can serve as a way to identify these community concerns early on to redirect efforts.

Importance of Evaluation

Any discussion of policies countering violent extremism would be incomplete without a mention of the importance of evaluation. Unfortunately, we know very little about the effectiveness of counterterrorism strategies or unintended consequences of such measures because of the lack of assessment: "there is more uncertainty than certainty about the effectiveness of counter-terrorism programs, mostly because only a small subset of strategies have actually been evaluated, and some evaluations are of modest quality" (Lum et al., 2006, p. 508). To put this into perspective, of the 6,041 peer-reviewed studies evaluating counter-terrorism strategies identified by Lum et al. (2006), only seven assessed counterterrorist strategies with moderate methodological rigor. Overall, instead of the intended deterrent effects, Lum et al. (2006) found backlash effects and other unintended consequences (e.g., metal detectors in airports led to a displacement effect, with terrorists seeking other attack modalities like kidnapping). These findings highlight the importance of evaluation in policy considerations (see also Lum et al., 2009).

Despite the dearth of evaluation, any policy should incorporate both process and outcome assessments to ensure its success. Evaluations of counterterrorism policies should include assessing perceptions of legitimacy. Given Gilley's (2006, 2009) suggested indicators of legitimacy, the concept can now be relatively easily operationalized in policy assessment and academic research. When doing so, legitimacy must be considered from all levels – how the public perceives the government is only one piece. Any strategy to reduce violent extremism must take into account how legitimacy is perceived by the international community (see Maller, 2009), the government itself, and the government agents implementing policy (e.g., police and military). This is especially important in today's climate, as countering violent extremism is a collaborative international duty.

CONCLUDING THOUGHTS

Legitimacy has long been used as an explanation for terrorism, yet research establishing this relationship and counterterrorism policies targeting legitimacy were prohibited by ongoing debate over the meaning and measure of legitimacy. Recently developed operationalization of this concept recommended indicators to tap into three main groups of definitions of legitimacy, paving the way for both research and policy development.

As expected, empirical evidence confirmed political and academic speculation of the link between legitimacy and terrorism. Policies designed to counter violent extremism also can be tied into the various definitions of legitimacy to foster its growth and development. Through evaluation, policymakers can confirm that measures to counter violent extremism are effectively reducing harm to society.

NOTES

1. There may be some overlap with the legitimacy measure and outcomes in this study, as the legitimacy measure includes the respondents' perceived obligation to obey authorities and the outcome measure is compliance with the law.
2. The legitimacy indicators from this earlier work were slightly different. Corruption originally was included as a control variable and minorities at risk data were incorporated as a measure of societal schism, an alternative explanation for

terrorist attacks targeting the police. Gilley's (2006) composite measure could not be used, as it included terrorism as an indicator of legitimacy (rather, illegitimacy); thus, incorporating it as an independent variable into any statistical model would put terrorism on both sides of the equation.

REFERENCES

Abrahms, M. (2007). Why democracies make superior counterterrorists. *Security Studies, 16*(2), 223–253.

Beetham, D. (1991). *The legitimation of power*. London: Macmillan.

Beetham, D. (1993). In defence of legitimacy. *Political Studies, 41*, 488–491.

Bennett, B., Rubin, J., & Kim, V. (2014). L.A. chosen for pilot program on dissuading militant recruits. *LA Times*, Retrieved from http://www.latimes.com/local/la-me-terror-jihad-program-20140923-story.html. Accessed on September 23, 2014

Breitmeier, H. (2008). *The legitimacy of international regimes*. Burlington, VT: Ashgate Publishing Company.

Bueno de Mesquita, E. (2005). Conciliation, counterterrorism, and patterns of terrorist violence. *International Organization, 59*(Winter), 145–176.

Chalk, P. (1998). The response to terrorism as a threat to liberal democracy. *Australian Journal of Politics and History, 44*(3), 373–388.

Cook, D. (2003). Legitimacy and political violence: A Habermasian perspective. *Social Justice, 30*(3), 108–126.

Crenshaw, M. (1981). The causes of terrorism. *Comparative Politics, 13*(4), 379–399.

Crenshaw, M. (2001). Theories of terrorism: instrumental and organizational approaches. In D. C. Rapoport (Ed.), *Inside terrorist organizations* (pp. 13–31). London: Frank Cass.

Cronin, A. K. (2009). *How terrorism ends: Understanding the decline and demise of terrorist campaigns*. Princeton, NJ: Princeton University Press.

Donner, C., Maskaly, J., Fridell, L., & Jennings, W. G. (2015). Policing and procedural justice: A state-of-the-art review. *Policing: An International Journal of Police Strategies & Management, 28*(1), 153–172.

Dugan, L., & Gibbs, C. (2008). The role of organizational structure in the control of corporate crime and terrorism. In S. Simpson & D. Weisburd (Eds.), *The criminology of white-collar crime* (pp. 111–128). New York, NY: Springer.

Dugan, L., Huang, J. Y., LaFree, G., & McCauley, C. (2008). Sudden desistance from terrorism: The Armenian Secret Army for the Liberation of Armenia and the justice commandos of the Armenian genocide. *Dynamics of Asymmetric Conflict, 1*(3), 231–249.

Dugan, L., & Young, J. K. (2009). Allow extremist participation in the policy making process. In N. A. Frost, J. D. Freilich, & T. R. Clear (Eds.), *Contemporary issues in criminal justice policy: Policy proposals from the American Society of criminology conference* (pp. 159–168). Belmont, CA: Cengage/Wadsworth.

Freeman, J., Liossis, P., & David, N. (2006). Deterrence, defiance and deviance: An investigation into a group of recidivist drink drivers' self-reported offending behaviours. *The Australian and New Zealand Journal of Criminology, 39*(1), 1–19.

Fromkin, D. (1975). The strategy of terrorism. *Foreign Affairs, 53*(4), 683–698.

Gibbs, J. C. (2011). *The relationship between legitimacy, terrorist attacks and police*. Doctoral dissertation, University of Maryland, College Park.

Gilley, B. (2006). The meaning and measure of state legitimacy: Results for 72 countries. *European Journal of Political Research*, *45*, 499–525.

Gilley, B. (2009). *The right to rule: How states win and lose legitimacy*. New York, NY: Columbia University Press.

Gurr, T. R. (1970). *Why men rebel*. Princeton, NJ: Princeton University Press.

Hawdon, J. E., Ryan, J., & Griffin, S. P. (2003). Policing tactics and perceptions of police legitimacy. *Police Quarterly*, *6*(4), 469–491.

Hirschfield, P. J., & Piquero, A. P. (2010). Normalization and legitimation: Modeling stigmatizing attitudes toward ex-offenders. *Criminology*, *48*(1), 27–56.

Hull, C. B. (1999, July 12). *FBI meets with militia groups; program is legacy of Oklahoma City Bombing*. New York, NY: Associated Press.

Hussain, S. E. (2010). *Terrorism in Pakistan: Incident patterns, terrorists' characteristics and the impact of terrorist arrests on terrorism*. Doctoral dissertation, University of Pennsylvania.

International Association of Chiefs of Police. (2014). *Using community policing to counter violent extremism: 5 key principles for law enforcement*. Washington, DC: Office of Community Oriented Policing Services. Retrieved from http://www.theiacp.org/Portals/0/documents/pdfs/Final%20Key%20Principles%20Guide.pdf

Ivkovic, S. K. (2008). A comparative study of public support for the police. *International Criminal Justice Review*, *18*(4), 406–434.

Jang, H., Lee, J., & Gibbs, J. C. (Forthcoming). The role of the national government on confidence in the police: A focus on corruption. *International Journal of Law, Crime and Justice*. doi:10.1016/j.ijlcj.2015.01.003

Kahn, K. (2009). *Preventing violent extremism (PVE) and PREVENT: A response from the Muslim community*. London: An-Nisa Society Retrieved from https://muslimyouthskills.files.wordpress.com/2010/05/pve__prevent_-__a_muslim_response.pdf

Kennedy, M. (1998). The 21st-Century conditions likely to inspire terrorism. In H. W. Kushner (Ed.), *The future of terrorism: Violence in the new millennium* (pp. 185–194). Thousand Oaks, CA: Sage.

LaFree, G. (1998). *Losing legitimacy: Street crime and the decline of social institutions in America*. Boulder, CO: Westview Press.

LaFree, G., & Ackerman, G. (2009). The empirical study of terrorism: Social and legal research. *Annual Review of Law and Social Sciences*, *5*, 347–374.

LaFree, G., Yang, S.-M., & Crenshaw M. (2009). International cooperation, not unilateral policies may be the best counterterrorist strategy. In N. A. Frost, J. D. Freilich, & T. R. Clear (Eds.), *Contemporary issues in criminal justice policy: Policy proposals from the American society of criminology conference* (pp. 121–128). Belmont, CA: Cengage/Wadsworth.

Lee, J., & Gibbs, J. C. (2015). Race and attitudes toward police: The mediating effect of social distance. *Policing: An International Journal of Police Strategies and Management*, *38*(2), 314–332.

Levi, M., Sacks, A., & Tyler, T. (2009). Conceptualizing legitimacy, measuring legitimating beliefs. *American Behavioral Scientist*, *53*(3), 354–375.

Lum, C., Haberfeld, M., Fachner, G., & Lieberman, C. (2009). Police activities to counter terrorism: What we know and what we need to know. In D. Weisburg, T. E. Feucht, I. Hakimi, L. F. Mock, & S. Perry (Eds.), *To protect and to serve: Policing in an age of terrorism* (pp. 101–141). New York, NY: Springer.

Lum, C., Kennedy, L. W., & Sherley, A. (2006). Are counter-terrorism strategies effective? The results of the Campbell systematic review on counter-terrorism evaluation research. *Journal of Experimental Criminology*, *2*, 489–516.

Maller, T. (2009). The dangers of diplomatic disengagement in counterterrorism. *Studies in Conflict & Terrorism*, *32*, 511–536.

Martin, J., Scully, M., & Levitt, B. (1990). Injustice and the legitimation of revolution: Damning the past, excusing the present, and neglecting the future. *Journal of Personality and Social Psychology*, *59*(2), 281–290.

McCauley, C. R. (2006). Terrorism and the state: the logic of killing civilians. In J. J. F. Forest (Ed.), *The making of a terrorist: Recruitment, training and root causes* (Vol. 3, pp. 238–253). Root causes. Westport, CT: Praeger Security International.

Mueller, J. (2005). Six rather unusual propositions about terrorism. *Terrorism and Political Violence*, *17*(4), 491.

Murphy, K. (2004). The role of trust in nurturing compliance: A study of accused tax avoiders. *Law and Human Behavior*, *28*(2), 187–209.

Nivette, A. E., & Eisner, M. (2013). Do legitimate polities have fewer homicides? A cross-national analysis. *Homicide Studies*, *17*(1), 3–26.

Nussbaum, B. (2009). Including extremists in the political process: "Irreconcilables," constraints on violence, and the social scientific analysis of terrorism. In N. A. Frost, J. D. Freilich, & T. R. Clear (Eds.), *Contemporary issues in criminal justice policy: Policy proposals from the American society of criminology conference* (pp. 169–174). Belmont, CA: Cengage/Wadsworth.

Pape, R. A. (2003). The strategic logic of suicide terrorism. *The American Political Science Review*, *97*(3), 343–361.

Pape, R. A. (2005). *Dying to win: The strategic logic of suicide terrorism*. New York, NY: Random House Trade Paperbacks.

Pape, R. A. (2008). Methods and findings in the study of suicide terrorism. *American Political Science Review*, *102*(2), 275–277.

Reisig, M. D., Bratton, J., & Gertz, M. G. (2007). The construct validity and refinement of process-based policing measures. *Criminal Justice and Behavior*, *34*, 1005–1028.

Robison, K. K. (2010). Terror's true nightmare? Reevaluating the consequences of terrorism on democratic governance. *Terrorism and Political Violence*, *22*, 62–82.

Shelley, L. I. (2014). *Dirty entanglements: Corruption, crime, and terrorism*. New York, NY: Cambridge University Press.

Sherman, L. W. (1998). American policing. In M. Tonry (Ed.), *The handbook of crime and punishment* (pp. 429–456). New York, NY: Oxford University Press.

Sternberger, D. (1968). Legitimacy. In David L. Sills (Ed.), *International encyclopedia of the social sciences* (Vol. 9, pp. 244–248). New York, NY: The Macmillan Company.

Sunshine, J., & Tyler, T. (2003). The role of procedural justice and legitimacy in shaping public support for policing. *Law and Society Review*, *37*(3), 513–548.

Transparence International France. (2011). *National integrity system assessment: France*. Retrieved from http://www.transparency.org/whatwedo/publication/national_integrity_system_assessment_france_executive_summary

Transparency International. (2013). *Business principles for countering bribery: A multi-stakeholder initiative led by Transparency International* (3rd ed.). Berlin: Author. Retrieved from http://issuu.com/transparencyinternational/docs/business_principles_web_final/16?e=2496456/6040471

Transparency International Norge. (2012). *National integrity system assessment: Norway*. Retrieved from http://www.transparency.org/whatwedo/publication/national_integrity_system_assessment_norway_executive_summary_english

Tyler, T. (1990). Why do people obey the law? New Haven, CT: Yale University Press.

Tyler, T. (2006). Why do people obey the law? Princeton, NJ: Princeton University Press.

Tyler, T. R., & Huo, Y. J. (2002). *Trust in the law: Encouraging public cooperation with the police and courts*. New York, NY: Russell Sage.

Weber, M. (1984). Legitimacy, politics and the state. In W. Connolly (Ed.), *Legitimacy and the state* (pp. 32–62). New York, NY: New York University Press. (Reprinted from Max Weber: Essays in Sociology, pp. 77–83, 95–105, 196–201, 230–235, 253–255, 261–264, by H. Gerth & C. W. Mills (Eds.), 1958. New York, NY: Oxford University Press).

Weine, S. (2014). CVE enhanced community policing & accelerating CVE. Paper presented at the annual meeting of the National Consortium for the Study of Terrorism and Responses to Terrorism, College Park, MD. Retrieved from http://www.start.umd.edu/pubs/START_Weine_CVEEnhancedCommunityPolicingAcceleratingCVE.pdf

To Amelia

For making me want to be more

The Boys of Summer

By Ciarán West

One

It'd been boiling for weeks. Mam said last time we'd a summer like this was in 1977, when she was pregnant with me. I used to wonder what she'd looked like; twelve years younger, with a big belly on her. I'd seen pictures of her from before that, when she was young; people always said she was beautiful. She just looked like Mam to me.

'Scatter!' The big wall behind us was the only way to get out. I didn't have to look back to know Colm and Willum were coming. Paddy too; with the blood gushing out of him. I wasn't a good runner anyway, and being scared made my legs into lead. Sometimes it was better to just stop running; curl up in a ball. Let them kick you, until they felt sorry for you and went away. I was sprinting now though. Dead fast, for me. Shane was already up and over; he'd a massive grin on him going past me. Dara was on top of the wall, reaching down to Seán.

'Give him a legger!' I didn't want to give Seán a legger; I didn't even know if I could get up there myself. I turned away from them and took a jump at the wall. My hands caught onto the top, but my feet just scraped the front of it, and I fell on my backside. I was bricking it; they'd be over in a second. I looked round for another way. Dara had pulled Seán up on his own; I couldn't see Dermot at all.

There was a gate there. It was the same height as the wall but it looked easier to climb; there was places to put your feet. I didn't check for splinters or spiders; I just threw myself over. I knew they were right behind me; I didn't have to look. The other side of the wall was all trees and thorny bushes. I'd get slowed down, but it'd slow them down too. There was two or three ways to get through there, it was like a maze; they might get lost in there looking for me. Paddy had no idea who'd hit him, neither did Willum or Colm. They'd still beat the face off the first one of us they caught though. I tore through, ninety miles an hour; my arms got scraped by the thorns, but I didn't feel it hurting.

'Willuuuuum!' That was Colm. I stopped moving and went all still, like the mouse when he hears the owl's wings.

'Willuuuuuum! Come-here-I-want-ya!' He was over the gate into where I was. Willum would be over too in a second. I couldn't stay still; I had to keep moving, even if it made noise. I sprinted off through the bushes. I heard them again, but not loud. There was another wall in front of me; that one got you out of the place altogether. Someone had put an auld palette against it, so's you could hop over. I ran up it like a stairs and dived over the wall. I landed the tarmac, and it took the skin off my hands and my wrists.

I was in a back alley behind some houses; I'd never been there before, but it was definitely in Kileely. Dolan's field backed onto Kileely, cos you could see down into it from Jonathan Musgrave's bedroom. There was noise behind me on the other side of the wall. Someone was screaming; they must've caught one of the

boys. Dermot would be all right, cos Colm was his brother. None of them would touch Shane either. It'd be Dara they'd caught, or Seán. Whoever it was, they screamed again. It was awful screaming altogether. Sounded like they were murdering him.

There was four gates in the alley and they all looked the same, but I'd no idea what was behind them. I hopped over the near one, on to some soft grass. It was someone's house. No dog or anything, but the garden smelt like something dead. They'd a side gate going out the front. A cat jumped down off the windowsill and meowed. He'd sharp teeth on him. Mam didn't like cats, she didn't trust them; we'd a dog instead. I could hear shouting and laughing behind me; they must've been catching up. I'd no idea how long I could keep running. I didn't look back. I tore down the side, through the gate. I just had to get across the front garden now.

'Hoy you! What you think you're doing? Hoy! I'm talking to you!' It was a man, upstairs in the house. He'd opened the window; he must've been in the bathroom, because he'd soap or cream all over his face. Dad never shaved like that; he'd a Philishave. The man picked something up off the sink and I thought he was going to throw it; but he put it down again. I gulped like someone off a cartoon, and hopped over the front wall.

'Hoy! Come back, you! Come… you little… you fecking blaggard you!' He'd run down the stairs in about two seconds, and come out onto the porch. I tore down the road; no idea where I was getting the energy. My teacher read out a line

from a poem, once: 'fear lent him wings,' and asked us what it meant. I think this was what it meant. Yer man from the window was still shouting, but he'd stayed on the porch, cos he was still in his jocks. Purple y-fronts. Pure old-fashioned.

At the end of the street, I ran out of breath and collapsed. I was amazed I'd lasted that long. I was useless at running; I never won nothing in the Sports Day or in P.E. I closed my eyes and waited; if you made yourself small it didn't hurt you as much, and they'd less of you to kick.

Nothing happened. I opened my eyes. No Paddy; no Willum; no Colm. They'd been there though! I'd heard them behind me. There was a few mams on their front porches; talking, or having a fag. I got up off the ground; mortified. I was in Hogan Avenue.

The street was next to St Lelia's School, near the Quarry. You could see our house from there; I could run home in two minutes, if I ever got my breath back. I was dying for a glass of water. Where'd they gone? Who was screaming? I didn't want Paddy Hooley turning up at my door with his mother, giving out about him having to get stitches. Mam would go spare. She wasn't one of those mams who thought her kids were angels and didn't believe nothing no one said about them. She'd kill me stone dead.

I was on the green now; it felt safer with people around. Alan Devlin and Dave Mahon were playing Headers and Volleys at the other end. I didn't have a key; Chris didn't even have a key. You didn't get a key til you were about fifteen. I got the jitters after I knocked: what if they'd called in and told on me? Dad

wouldn't do anything, but Mam was different. The door opened; it was him, not her.

'Well?' It wasn't a question; that was just how he said hello. I went into the kitchen and opened our fridge. No fizzy; just milk and water. Mam filled old lemonade bottles with tap water during the summer; the cold made it taste less horrible. I took a long swig out of the bottle; I never drank milk; it made my spits all stringy. Chris was in the front room, watching The Crystal Maze. I went upstairs to the computer.

Mam's room was open when I passed; she'd probably been at work the night before. She worked waitressing in lots of places, but she'd started in a new place now. Bella Italia, in O'Connell Street. It was a posh place, but Mam said she didn't get posh wages. I got to my room without her hearing me, which was good because I didn't want to have to make her a cuppa. Mam would forget that I didn't drink tea or coffee; she'd put on the kettle on Saturday morning and take a cup out for me with the rest of them. I hated tea; I'd never even tasted it. Sometimes on days like this when she was tired, she'd call out to me to make her some. I didn't like doing it, because I didn't know what tea was supposed to look like when it was done properly; I'd be afraid that I hadn't left the bag in long enough, because you couldn't put it back in later. I'd be afraid that I'd put too much milk in, because you couldn't take it out later. There were too many things to get wrong, and Mam would get cross if you took too long. 'It's just common sense', she'd say. She said that about a lot of things I was no good at. She hadn't heard me this time; I was safe. Chris could make it for her, later; he'd be better at it. I wasn't

being lazy; I just didn't want her to be disappointed.

Me and Chris had never been best buds or anything, but now that he was fourteen, he hardly talked to me at all. He just grunted at me or sneered, or told me to get out when I came into our bedroom. People changed when they turned into teenagers. He was always slamming doors or locking them; he'd a suitcase in the wardrobe, with a padlock on it, but I couldn't find the key.

We'd been in a camp earlier. We'd built it ourselves, by putting galvanised metal over the top of an old shed that had no roof. When we were younger, we'd make camps every day, and play Army or have mock wars with each other. We were too old for that now. I was going to Secondary in September; so were the rest of them, except Seán. Nowadays we'd just make camps for a bit of shelter; or so you could have a sneaky fag without your mam catching you. We'd just been sitting around talking. Shane had been saying about going to St Nessan's in September. I'd really wanted to go there too; you got to have girls in your class, and you could wear jeans jackets if you liked, and earrings. I was going to Ardscoil Rís, cos you had to go to the same school as your brother. Dara was going to Sexton's, in the middle of town. That was all boys, just like Ardscoil. Dara was mad into girls; he'd shifted loads of them. I couldn't believe he was going to a school with only fellas. I'd never gone away with a girl yet. All the lads had gone to St. Munchin's down the road, but Mam had sent me and Chris to JFK on the Ennis Road. It was posh and full of rich kids; the boys gave me an awful

slagging over it, especially Shane.

We'd been sitting there in the camp, talking away, happy as Larry. Then Colm, Willum and Paddy had come along on their bikes; we'd heard them outside, then the stones started hitting our galvanise roof. We hadn't started it. We didn't ever start it.

Teenage Mutant Hero Turtles was in the tape deck; I hadn't been playing it, so it must've been Chris. It wasn't fair; Mam had got me the computer, not him. He'd got a bike for Christmas and I wasn't allowed on that. I wouldn't want to go on it anyway; it was a racer, like Seán Kelly or Stephen Roche rode in the Tour De France. I couldn't stay up on a racer. He'd wanted a Raleigh Banana, but Mam said a Peugeot was all we could afford, because of getting the Commodore. They didn't even get me a colour monitor; it was a green one. They couldn't afford a colour one, cos of getting Chris' bike. I switched on the monitor and heard the Turtles music; Chris had left the computer plugged in and just turned off the button on the screen. I nearly shouted for Mam to tell on him. Then I remembered that I didn't want to make her tea. The game was paused on level seven; it was a water level. The bedroom window was open, because it was summer.

They'd started firing little stones at us, with their slings. We'd thrown the galvanise up as a shield though, so then they started throwing bricks. Shane had a

Black Widow; much better than a normal forksling. He'd got it in a fishing shop, he said. I picked up a rock. It was heavy; it'd split someone's head open if it hit them. I wasn't going to hit anyone with it though; I'd just throw it over at the bush and hope it missed everyone. That's how you played war with the big lads: let them win and wait until they got bored and went away. The last time one of us actually got one of them had been a good few months ago: Dermot had hit Danny O'Neill in the eye with a bit of red brick. Danny beat him so hard that Dermot's brother Dennis had to take him to the Regional on the bus, to get stitches. No one called the Gards or anything; you didn't do that where we lived. A fight was a fight.

I wasn't as strong as I'd thought; the rock didn't even get half way to the bush. Their gang let out a 'Waaaaaah', and I even heard Shane and Dara laughing. I hated doing anything in front of people. Whenever I walked past lads playing soccer, I'd pray the ball never came off the pitch, towards me. I always made a hames of kicking it back. My legs went like jelly any time I did something and thought about it at the same time.

I was getting nowhere; the water level was deadly to do, and there was no cheat. I looked in the big shoebox for another game. I had loads, but most of them were crap. You could get games for £2.99 in Eason's, but they were usually awful yokes. You were better off saving up for a good one, but I hated saving up. I loved soccer games, but the ones for the Commodore were pathetic. I'd got a lend of

Microprose Soccer off Joe a few weeks ago; that was good, if you were playing someone who agreed not to do the cheat goal, so you'd have a fair match. Or if you played someone who didn't even know you could do the cheat goal; then you could hockey them ten-nil.

I hadn't meant to hit Paddy at all. I'd been firing my stones way off target, and just staying down when they were firing theirs. I wasn't too good at soccer, and I wasn't too good at fishing, and I definitely wasn't a good shot with a forksling. Any time I ever got a goal or a bite off a fish, I couldn't enjoy it. I'd be too busy waiting for someone to cop on that I'd only fluked it. I'd put a bit of slate in the tongue of my sling, and fired it off over. I was more surprised than any of them. It hit him smack in the mouth and his lip just bursted open. It was the worst thing that could have happened. I was dead. If he didn't catch me straight away, he'd catch me the next day, or the next week, or some time. I was already running when Dermot shouted for us to scatter.

There was a knock on the front door; we'd no doorbell. Mam had bought one, but there had been a fight with Dad about putting it in, and then I'd just never seen it again; Mam was from County Clare, not Limerick; so she'd grown up without a doorbell, or a phone, or a middle name. I heard her feet outside on the landing, then down the stairs to the hall.

'Richard?' She called my name up the stairs, but not very loud; she must've thought I was out.

'Coming!' I switched the monitor off and left the computer on. It was Joe at the door; he had an Italy 90 soccer ball.

'I'm going out, Mam.' She said something back at me, but I was gone. It was boiling hot out. I'd already got sunburned twice this year.

Joe was two months older than me; he lived across the green. I didn't have a best friend, but he'd a been the nearest one to it. I was getting to be better friends with Dermot too these days. Joe was rapid at soccer; he was nearly on the first team for Balla last year. I was useless; I'd just play Full Back and stay out of the way. Sometimes, I'd go in for slide tackles and clatter people. One time Colm O' Halloran was running in to shoot and I slid around him and hooked the ball away, like Paul McGrath. It was honestly a fair tackle, but he hopped his forehead off the tarmac and everyone around us made that 'Ooh' noise that you make when you know someone is going to get a beating. My nose bled all the way home and half way through Coronation Street.

'The Shades were all over the Quarry a while ago,' he said, dribbling the ball. He meant the Gards; I didn't know why people called them Shades.

'Yeah?' I hadn't seen anything when I'd come down from Hogan Avenue, but I hadn't been looking either, really.

'Yeah! Loads of them: three squad cars and a paddy wagon.' It wasn't

really big news or anything. There was loads of criminals living ‘round this place. That was a lot of police though.

‘Jaysus. What was going on?’

‘I dunno, shur… Probably found a big stash of coke or something,’ he said. I didn’t think there was any cocaine in Thomondgate. Nothing exciting ever happened here at all, let alone stashes of cocaine. Hash, maybe. Hash was a new thing; Mam hadn’t heard of it yet. She was still warning me and Chris about sniffing glue.

He passed me the ball and I trapped it, like Liam Brady; I didn’t feel that nervous around him with a soccer ball, but I still wasn’t able to do anything fancy. I hadn’t the skill.

‘We’ll ask Dara when we see him.’ Dara’s dad was a sergeant in the Gards. My dad didn’t have a job these days; he used to be a train driver, but there was a big accident, and he got blind in one eye, cos some glass went in it. He got a pension every fortnight now, even though he didn’t look old. Mam worked instead; in restaurants. She was always going on about her poor feet. I wasn’t sure what I wanted to do when I grew up, but I was going to make sure it was a job where you could sit down. I said that to Dad, and he said:

'I was sitting down when I crashed that train.' I didn’t know whether I was supposed to laugh, so I didn’t.

We passed Seán’s, but we didn’t call in for him. Their house looked

awful from the outside, and when you got inside, it looked worse. The mother was big and fat, same as the kids; Seán said instead of cooking dinner, she'd bring a takeaway home from Gino's in William Street. Mam would never do that; she cooked a dinner every day. Sometimes I'd rather have a Gino's for dinner, but I didn't want to be fat.

'Dare you,' said Joe, pointing at the knocker. A dare was serious; you couldn't just not do it. That was chicken.

'My leg's killing me, shur.' I was lying; I hated playing Knockadally, and Seán's father was lanky; he could probably tear after you and catch you easy. I'd end up getting leathered, and Joe would get away.

'Bawk! Bawk!' He was only messing. He was sound, Joe. He was a laugh, and he'd back up for you in a fight, no problem. That's what made someone sound.

We passed the ball a bit on the way. I didn't like doing it while we were walking; the ball could go under a car. We went past Pa's shop, and saw Punch Drunk coming out, with a litre of skimmed milk. We didn't salute him, cos we didn't really know him. Punch Drunk was Shane's brother Alan; they said he had been hit too many times in the boxing ring and he'd gone soft in the head. One time me and Shane snuck into his bedroom, and there was posters of English fellas on the wall; black and white pictures of miserable looking yokes. They looked like steamers, Shane said. They were in bands called 'The Smiths' and 'Joy Division'; we tried to listen to one of the tapes once, but we couldn't get the stereo to work.

There was loads of magazines too: Hot Press and NME and Melody Maker. They were full of steamers as well, according to Shane. I was thinking of joining boxing in September, but I changed my mind after we were in that room. I didn't like hitting people or getting hit anyway, so it was lucky really.

There was nobody on the green when we got there, but Danny O'Neill and them were on the proper pitch. They played serious games, in boots and shorts; if you wanted to use the goalposts to play Headers & Volleys or a mess game, you'd have to come along early in the morning when they weren't there. Joe put his tracksuit top down for a left post; the big rock was the other one. Being in goals here was dangerous; you'd never want to dive when they shot low on the side with the rock; Dermot got two stitches last summer. Me and Joe took turns in goal while I told him what had happened earlier with Colm and all them.

'Colm's only an aul' waster, shur,' I nodded, but that was easy for Joe to say; he was massive. Everyone probably seemed like a waster when you were big. When you were the size of me, you'd to be more careful. Joe probably wasn't afraid of no one, except maybe Shane.

You needed at least three for Headers & Volleys, but no one else was around. Dermot, Shane and Dara must've been inside home. It was that, or Colm's boys had caught them and were holding them prisoner somewhere. He did that a few times before to us; put on a Nazi voice, and walked around with a twig under his arm, and whipped us with it, like it was a jockey's stick. He was a bit mad in the head, Colm. He'd always let you off to have your supper though; or your Mam

would go round his house and give out stink to his Mam. Mothers were the ones who did the real giving out; Dads stayed well out of it.

'D'you think we're going to get to Italy?' Joe asked; he did that: starting a conversation when he was in goals, so you'd forget about taking shots.

'I think so. We beat Spain, like.'

'Own goal though.' He was doing keepy-uppies, even though he was supposed to be in goals. I wouldn't have a hope of doing those. I could manage about three in a row.

'Yeah, but Malta and Hungary too, so it wasn't a fluke,' I didn't know much about soccer. I couldn't name one Irish soccer player until they got into Euro '88. I'd read about it all in the back pages of the Star though, or the Herald.

'Shur they're only wasters, will you go way. We'll have to beat the Prods in October though, like.' He meant Northern Ireland. 'Cos Spain are going to kick the bollix off a Hungary, both times. If we beat Northern Ireland, we'll be away, says you.' He kneed the ball up over his head, and then caught it on the back of his neck. He was rapid at it. I nodded at him to agree. Soccer was one of those things that you had to do around this place; you couldn't just tell them that you were no good at it, because they didn't care. They needed to make up teams for games, and if you got picked, they picked you last and just shoved you in goal, or Full Back. I didn't mind being Full Back; you could just hoof it away when anyone came near. There was no hiding when you were in goals though. Sometimes they'd play

hurling on the green, or tennis when it was Wimbledon, but it was mostly soccer.

Some lads walked past on the other side of the green; Joe knew them from St Munchin's.

'Come here an' I tell you, sham. Did ye see the Gards did ye?' said the tall one; his name was Sully.

'I did, yeah; what's the scala, like?' asked Joe, stopping my shot with one hand. Sully shrugged,

'No idea, boss. Just seen 'em down there. Good few of 'em, mind. Loada squad cars and a paddywagon. Gerry Mac said he seen a load of blood, but you know him, like.'

'Blood? Ah, shur he's only an aul' gowl, though.' Joe laughed. I didn't say nothing, cos I didn't know any of these lads. I didn't know if it was right to laugh if you didn't know the person who was saying something funny.

'You up Balla tomorrow?' yer man asked him.

'Nah,' said Joe. I wondered why not; maybe he was injured. He'd a few scrapes on his knee, but so did I. You'd get that from climbing over walls and all that. Mam was always giving out to me for it.

'Ah, right. Anyway, we've to g'way. Listen, you going to Kilkee this year, boss?' said Sully.

'Yeah. For two weeks, shur.'

‘Yeah? I’ll be down myself, sham. Going on Wednesday, like.’ Kilkee was always full of Limerick people. We didn’t go, cos we’d no caravan and Mam couldn’t afford a Bed And Breakfast for us, cos of Dad not being in work.

‘I’ll see you then, shur,’ said Joe.

‘Sound, boss.’

Sully went back to his lads. He sort of saluted me, and I sort of saluted him back. I still didn’t know him, though. I wouldn’t have saluted him if I was on my own.

Gerry Mac was full of it, definitely. He told us his uncle owned King John’s Castle, and that he’d let Gerry go in when no one was around, and fire the canons at swans. Another time, he convinced us his Da was in Vietnam. Shane figured out he was lying after he watched Platoon on Sky Movies, and recognised all of Gerry’s stories happening in the film. He was only a chancer.

Seán and his brother Golly showed up then. Seán had changed his top since the morning. He’d a yellow Arsenal jersey on; the away one.

‘What happened ye? Did ye get caught?’ I said.

‘Yeah… Willum got me…’ He didn’t look hurt; maybe his other top was covered in blood.

‘What did he do to you?’ I wiped some sweat off my forehead. It was boiling still.

‘He didn’t do nothing really; he gemme a dead leg and he spitted at me, but he missed me with it.’

‘Paddy’s after you though,’ said Golly, scratching his scalp, like he always did. We called him Golly, cos he’d hair like a black. His real name was Eamonn, but even his Mam called him Golly half the time. ‘He says he’s gonna bate you. He’s probably gonna have to get stitches.’ He wasn’t even there; I didn’t know why he was the one telling me. I asked Seán:

‘What about Dermot and Shane and them? Did they get away?’

‘Colm ran after Dermot, like. Follied him for ages, but Dermot stood his ground when Colm caught him, and Colm didn’t do nothing to him though.' That was what usually happened, yeah; Colm wouldn’t hit Dermot, their Da would batter him.

'What about Dara?'

'Dara went over the wall, same as you. None of them did nothing to Shane.’ That must’ve been who I’d heard screaming; poor Dara, cos he hadn’t caught up with me at all. I’d been sure it was Seán though. The scream was all high pitched and squeaky, like a girl or a little kid. Seán was the youngest, not including Golly. I knew Shane would’ve been safe anyway. Wouldn’t have been him screaming. He wasn’t even that big for his age, but everyone knew he was good in a fight. Both his brothers won medals for boxing, and he was doing boxing too now. I never saw him look scared. We wouldn't go up to Kileely or Ballynanty

without him; even people who didn't know him would get scared of him. He had a look on him. No one ever said nothing about our gang having a leader, but we all knew it was Shane.

Dermot showed up next; I didn't see him until Joe kicked him over the ball. Dermot was good at soccer as well, but he never played in a real team. Colm played in goals for Balla a few times, but Dermot had never signed up, and he wasn't on his school team either. He could be strange.

'Well, bud?' he said, lobbing the ball at me. I managed to kick it on the volley, but too high. It still looked good though.

'Howrya?' I said. Joe ran behind, to pick up the ball. I wasn't in the mood for a game, and if someone else came along, they'd probably want to play three on three.

'Where'd you run away to anyway?' asked Dermot. I didn't like the way he'd said it; he'd run away too, and so had Dara. He was making it sound like I was a chicken.

'I got away over a gate. Then I went through the bushes at the back of …' I stopped talking when I saw that he wasn't really listening. I did that sometimes, because a lot of the time it seemed like no one really listened to you.

'Paddy says he's gonna kill you. That was some shot, bud.' It had been way too good a shot for me; I didn't even aim the forksling properly; it was a pure fluke that I'd hit him.

‘He’ll have to catch me first.’ It was a stupid thing for me to say; they all knew I was a slow runner. Well, I had been before today anyway. Dermot laughed; he was all right, Dermot.

'Shane'll back you up, anyway; so will I,' said Joe. I wasn't sure if that was true, about Shane. Joe definitely would though. He’d always stick up for you in a fight. I was afraid, but you’d never admit it front of the lads. You had to pretend you didn’t really care. I did though; Paddy was a beast. People with that slow look in their eyes, they were always hard. He was Chris’ age, but he was still in St.Munchin’s. He’d failed the entrance exam for The Tech, and that was the stupidest school in Ireland.

‘How does he know I was the one that hit him anyway?’ I looked at Seán.

‘What? Am, I dunno. He just… must’ve seen you do it.’

‘He couldn’t have! I ducked straight down after, shur!’ I had. Straight away. Dermot agreed with me:

‘He’s right, bud. I seen him, cos I looked over when I seen Paddy get split, and Rich was already ducked down, then I said ‘Scatter’ and we all legged it. They didn’t see nothing.’ I was glad Dermot was backing me.

‘Ah well, yeah. But he must’ve seen… someone must’ve told…’ He stopped talking, cos we’d all turned around to look at something else now. A squad car had pulled up outside Kelly’s. More Gards. I pulled my T-Shirt down over my back jeans pocket to hide the fork-sling; sometimes the Gards were

sound, but sometimes they'd take it off you.

A Gard got out of the front of the car, then another one from the back; the second one was a Ban-Garda. There was someone else with her; it was Mrs Kelly. Her face was all red and her eyes were bloodshot. The woman from next door was in her porch, and she said something to Mrs Kelly, but Mrs Kelly didn't even look at her. The Ban-Garda shook her head at the neighbour, and walked Mrs Kelly to the porch. Someone inside opened the door and the three of them went in.

'Bridie Kelly's after getting arrested, sham,' said Seán. Golly sniggered beside him. That wasn't how it looked to me, but I didn't say anything. 'Probably got caught down the docks. .' he said. People would say that sometimes, as a slagging; that your mother worked down the docks.

'Shut up, you gowl. What if she's got raped?' Dermot threw a dirty look at Seán and Golly. I nodded, cos Dermot had backed me a minute ago.

'Dara will know, we'll ask him,' I said, and everyone nodded. Dara was the man, definitely; his da would let it slip later, after he'd had a few sups.

'Ask him what?' It was Shane; he'd pulled up on his mountain bike. He'd got it last Christmas; it used to be his brother Alan's. We told him about Mrs Kelly, but he didn't think it was anything.

'G'way will you. Probably Fin, getting caught robbing again.' Fintan Kelly was their oldest, about Chris' age or a little bit younger. I'd never heard of him being in trouble with the Gards before, but Shane knew more about stuff like

that than me. His brothers had all sorts of connections like that. Shane told me once that Damien and Alan went over to the posh areas and rob money or tackies off the kids that lived there. I was shocked by that. Robbing from a shop was one thing, but mugging someone… that was lousy.

No one disagreed with Shane about the Mrs Kelly thing, cos you didn't really disagree with him about anything. There was enough of us for soccer now anyway. We'd a game of two on two, with Seán in goals. Golly didn't play; he never played soccer. Joe was on my team. They won it four-three. I only scored one, but it was a beaut. Even Shane said so, and slapped me on the back to congratulate me. Joe wanted to play first to five, but no one else really did. The heat was making us all exhausted. I couldn't even remember the last time we'd had rain.

The front door was open when I got home, and I could hear Mam and Dad talking quiet in the sitting room. We used our front room all the time; we weren't like them families that kept it for special occasions. Dara was never allowed in his front room. They had a massive twenty four inch telly in there, but their Mam made them all sit in the kitchen and watch a black and white portable. We were halfway through one of Ireland's games in Euro 88 before his Mam and his sister realised they were cheering for Russia.

'…not around here, anyway. You wouldn't see that sort of thing in a film, God bless us and save us.' I caught the last of what Mam was saying, but she

stopped when she saw me in the doorway. Dad looked very serious, like a teacher or a priest. I suddenly got guilty, in case they'd been talking about Paddy or something.

'Well?' He was smiling now, but it looked all false. Mam sniffled a bit, and looked around for her fags. I just nodded at them, and went into the kitchen. Sometimes they'd get funny with me, usually after they'd been at the pub. This was different though; they both seemed kind of sad. I shouted back in to Mam,

'What's for dinner?' She said nothing for ages, then:

'I'll throw on some chips in a while. What do you want; burgers, is it?'

'Is there fish fingers?' I asked. The burgers she got from Pa's were rotten altogether. They tasted like cardboard.

'I don't know shur. Can ye check the freezer for me?' I opened the top door; there was fuzzy snow stuff on everything. Eventually I found the box of Bird's Eye, with the Captain looking out at me.

'Yeah. There's a whole box, like.'

'Grand. I'll have my fag and then I'll put it on for ye.' Mam made lovely dinners. You'd have sausages and mash on a Monday; bacon and cabbage on Tuesday; maybe a stew for Wednesday; breast bones or spare ribs on a Thursday, and fish and chips on a Friday. Saturday was anything you wanted. She could make other things too. Fancy stuff that she learned in work, in the restaurant. I

wouldn't eat anything like that though. I didn't like sauce or curry or gravy. She'd make stuff like that when we'd visitors round. I shut the freezer door, but it popped open again. I scraped a little bit of the snow off the rubber bit, and it shut properly the second time. I could hear voices out the back, probably next door.

I lied down on my bed, reading a comic. There'd been a sale in Todd's; they'd big boxes of these American comics for 25p each. They were smaller than the ones you'd buy in the shops over here, but thicker, so you got lots more story. I was reading a Captain America one. My favourite part of the Marvel comics was the adverts bit in the back pages. You could buy X-Ray glasses that made you be able to see through your hand, and something called Sea Monkeys; creatures that you grew out of dried eggs, and they'd live in a tank in your room and do all sorts of stuff. You couldn't send away for them in Ireland though; that was always lousy.

I could hear Mam downstairs, cutting the potatoes into chips. I always preferred her ones; Dad cut the chips okay, but he didn't know exactly how yellow I like them, and if you were having sausages, he'd throw the sausages in the chip pan at the same time as the chips, so you'd end up with horrible chips, and sausages that had the skin hanging off them. The cutting stopped, and I heard the sound of the first chip go into the oil. That's how you made chips: you put one chip into the oil on its own, and when that chip came up to the top and started sizzling, it was time to do the rest. Mam would definitely wait until the chips were done before she put the fish fingers in; she wasn't an eejit.

Christopher came in the front door, and Mam shouted at him to leave his bike outside:

'Not on my good floor!'

'Ah Mam, I can't leave it out!'

'Why not?'

'It'll get robbed,' It was his new one, from Christmas; the Peugeot that wasn't a Raleigh Banana.

'Will you go way oura that; shur who'd be robbing it?'

'Leonard Power's one got robbed last week' Chris wasn't going to give in.

'Did it? His new one and everything?'

'Yep. With the mag wheels an' all.'

'Jesus, all right so. You'd better leave it in, so. I don't have money to burn like Deirdre Power. This place is going to the dogs, so it is…'

'Sound!'

Chris got away with murder; he was only a Mammy's Boy. He'd better not go near my chips. I wanted to be an only child, like Jonathan Musgrave. Mam said it was awful to be an only child, cos even though you got spoilt rotten, you didn't have any brothers and sisters to play with, so you were lonely. When you

thought about it, that was bull; because I never played with my brother, and being lonely wouldn't be that bad if you had all the He-Mans, and Castle Greyskull. Jon Musgrave probably got as much chips as he wanted, too. I put the comic book away; I'd finished it, but it was a To Be Continued, and I didn't have the next one.

'Heard about the Quarry?' Chris was in the doorway. He meant the old quarry at the end of the big field; we sometimes had forksling wars there. It was overgrown now, so it didn't look like a quarry any more.

'Yeah. The Gards, like? What happened?' This was good, cos I might be the first of the lads to find out; even before Dara.

'Someone got *murdered.*' He'd whispered the last word, like he didn't want Mam or anyone to hear him.

'G'way, will you.' I didn't believe him; he was always messing. He'd probably seen the Gards down at the Quarry earlier, and thought up a story to take the mick out of me.

'Christopher!' It was Mam. I looked at Chris again; his face looked like he was holding back a smile. He was only having a mess, obviously.

'Richie; your fish fingers are ready!' she said. Rapid, I was starving.

'Eat it at the table …' Mam's voice was nice tonight, but it sounded like there was a warning in it too, so I put my plate back and chomped down a few

chips; they were gorgeous. Dad was watching telly in the front room; the news was on again about Poland. President Bush was doing something over there. There was lots of mad stuff going on in other countries, like Poland and Hungary and China. Dad would try to explain it to me when we were watching the news, but I didn't really understand. I didn't like the news; I still liked cartoons, like Transformers, or Centurions.

'Had you a nice day?' Mam asked, moving the chip pan to the back of the cooker, so's nobody would knock it over themselves. That's what happened our cousin Agnes from Shannon.

'Hmmmff' I said; mouth full of chips. Mam was sound; she'd always ask you if you were all right, or if you were tired. When you were sick, she'd get you some Seven-Up from Pa's Shop, and do a cup of Disprin for you. I hated the taste of Disprin. The fish fingers were good. Mams always said that the ones you got that were Dunne's Stores own brand were just as nice, but Findus or Bird's Eye were way better. I loved fish, except kippers. I'd never had one, but they looked rank. And sardines; sardines looked like they'd taste rotten. I liked the tin though, with the key. Sometimes Mam did haddock in sort of white looking sauce, and that was okay if you didn't look at it. My favourite was whiting, or cod maybe. Whiting tasted good if you covered it with salt and vinegar.

I thought about what Chris had said. Normally I'd think he was messing straight away, but the Gards had been around; everyone was talking about it. It could be true as well. And what about Bridie Kelly? That was very strange. Chris

was gone out again now, so I couldn't ask him.

Mam was doing the crossword; usually it was Dad you saw doing that. He'd have the hard one from the Irish Times; the cryptic one. Much harder than a normal one. Mam would save the Big One from the Sun Day magazine that came with The News of the World. I wasn't allowed to read The News of the World, because it was full of things about sex and other things that weren't suitable. They let me read the magazine though.

'Rich, love; will ye do me a favour and stay in tonight?'

'What? I'm going out with the boys!' Janey Mack! I hadn't done nothing; she couldn't ground me.

'Yeah, well. Can't they come over here? Ye can go out the back; the shed is nice and big too since your Dad got rid of the lawnmower.' That lawnmower had been as big as a tank.

'Ah, Mam...'

'Please, Rich…' She looked sad instead of cross.

I suppose… Okay.' This was stupid; I wasn't a baby. I still gave in though. I couldn't argue her round like Chris could. The boys might like coming over to the shed; 'specially if it was cold later.

'Good man yourself,' she was cheered up now; was better to see her smiling. I liked pleasing Mam; it didn't make me a swot or anything. It was better

than telling her to eff off, like some kids did round here.

'You know I love the bones of you, don't you?' She turned off the gas under the kettle, cos it had started whistling.

'Yeh-huh,' I could feel a blush coming all over me, and I didn't want her to see it. I loved her too, but you couldn't really say it.

Two

I finished the end of my chips. They'd gone all cold; it made the ketchup taste rotten. I headed out.

'Plate!' said Mam. I always forgot to put my plate in the basin. Mam never made us wash up, except on some Saturdays, or if she had visitors. When she had visitors we'd have to behave ourselves, like we were on The Waltons or something. She'd hide all the dirty washing in the hot press, and she'd be up all morning polishing.

'Where are ye going now?'

'Out.'

'Out where, shur?'

'Dermot's.' Short answers were better to give when you wanted to get away. I didn't even know if I was going to call for him; I was just going out.

'Ah now, Rich...'

'What?'

'Aren't ye after saying to me that ye were going to stay in?'

'Yeah… But you said the lads could come over!'

'So?' She scrunched up her face at me.

'Well I have to go and call over for them, don't I? To tell them I can't come out!'

‘Ah right, so. Go on. Be quick, though; before it's dark.’ She was being stupid now; it didn't even get dark till half nine in the summer.

‘Why can't I go out, anyway?’

‘Because I asked you to, Rich.’ That’s the sort of answer mams and dads gave you, when they didn’t have an answer.

‘Okay, so. I'll be back in a bit.’ She looked at me strange, then:

‘Good boy. Be careful now, won't you? Be careful.’

‘Ah, yeah. I will Mam.’

I went out the front. There was no murderers in Thomondgate. Half the things Chris said were only rubbish. Naughton's door was open, which was strange, cos they'd moved out in February. They'd got a new Corporation house in Castletroy View. I couldn't see in the door, but I heard a man talking. He sounded pure Limerick, like he was from Southill, or Moyross. I walked down the path to Dermot's, then I remembered about Colm and Paddy, so I legged it past, ducking down under the windows in case they were in the front room. Dermot and Colm's dad was called Colm as well; he was sound, sometimes he called Colm 'Colmkille', for the sneer.

I crossed over to Cannon Breen Park, where Shane and Dara's houses were.

Danny O’Neill, Shane’s brother Damien and the rest of them were in the alley where everyone played handball. They were rolling ten pence pieces against the wall, and cheering. It was a game they played for money. I kept my head down; older lads would salute you sometimes, but if you saluted them first, they

thought you were cheeky. Shane's house had an aluminium porch and windows. I didn't know what the difference was between aluminium windows and normal ones; they looked like normal glass to me. Same with PVC.

Sheriff ran over and jumped up on me, trying to lick me on my face. He used to be Damien's dog, but he'd let Shane have him for keeps when he got bored of looking after him. His mother answered the door; she looked like him, but her voice was really slow.

'Shaaaaaney!' she shouted up the stairs to him; she hadn't even said hello to us. She called him 'Shaney' all the time; so did his brothers. We wouldn't have dared to.

'Comin'!' His voice came out a window over our heads. I heard it, but his mother didn't.

'Shaaaaaaane! You're wanted!'

I suddenly wanted to laugh, so I bit my tongue. She looked at me, then back up the stairs. Shane was behind her now.

'I heard you the first time, you fucking handicap!' He was one of those kids that cursed in front of his parents; I'd have been clattered. Some children round here got away with murder compared to me, and some others got away with nothing. Seán and Golly cursed in front of their mam, but they wouldn't have done it in front of their Dad. I didn't even swear in front of Chris; he'd tell Mam on me.

Shane had a Michael Jackson 'Bad' T-shirt on; it was all faded away at the front. He probably wouldn't have cursed in front of his Dad either, but you never saw his Dad much. He was a docker, and he worked nights. That's why you

couldn’t go up to Shane's room in the daytime. He looked like Eddie from Coronation Street: like a binman. Shane didn’t look nothing like him. We walked over to Joe's.

I knocked on the door, but no one came out. That's what happened at Joe's: you'd knock, and one of the parents would shout out for one of the kids to get the door. It was usually his Mam. His Da was an alcoholic, so he'd either be down the pub or asleep. Joe came running down the stairs like Indiana Jones; I thought he was going to smack into the door.

‘Don't stay out too late, Joe!’ That was his mam’s voice, from the sitting room.

'Shur go way, will you! It's holidays!'

'All right, all right. Don't go too far though.'

'God's sake!'

'And don't go near the Quarry, will you?' My heart did a little jump when she said that.

'Why not?'

'Cos I said, Joe. All right?’ she said.

That was that. Joe slammed the door, and we heard his Mam shout something else, he didn’t turn around.

'What are ye up to, shur?' He was chewing some gum; I could smell it off his breath.

'Nothing.' I said. Then:

‘Oh, d’you know you were saying about the Quarry and the Gards?’

‘Yeah…’ he raised his eyebrows at me.

‘Chris says someone’s after getting murdered down there.’

‘Hah?’ said Joe. Shane looked at me like I had two heads. Before Joe could answer, he butted in:

'Murdered? What are you on? You spa.'

‘That’s what Chris said, yeah; mad, isn’t it?'

'Will you g'way, will you! Your brother’s full of shit,' said Shane, sneering at me.

'I know, but imagine it, like: a *serial killer*, in Thomondgate…' I said. Shane snorted now.

‘What would you know about serial killers, sham? There’s no serial killers in Ireland, you gowl.’ He always made you feel small. Joe changed the subject:

‘What are we doing tonight anyway, shur?’ I remembered Mam and the shed.

'I’ve to stay in tonight, like.'

'Why’s that?' Shane again, still cross-sounding.

'Dunno… My mother asked me to. She said we could go in the shed, though. Out the back, like.'

‘The shed? What are we supposed to do in there, sham?'

‘I dunno, we could…’

'Anyone got fags?' he asked. I shook my head.

'Dermot will,' said Joe. Dermot usually had fags. I couldn't care less about cigarettes. The way my Mam went on, you'd swear they were the best thing in the world. They tasted rank, you coughed like mad, and you wanted to puke your ring up. You got a head rush and felt a bit dizzy. You could do that rolling down a hill. You couldn't say any of that to anyone though. You didn't want to be called a *steamer*.

'Dara might be able to get some gear, shur.' Dara's auld fella smoked hash, even though he was a Gard; he'd rob it off the druggies they stopped and searched in Moyross or Southill. Dara would wait until he fell asleep, then he'd rob a nodge off the block. Hash was a different story to fags. Hash was actually *drugs*.

'You can't smoke gear in my shed! They'll smell it a mile away.' I said.

'Your Mam wouldn't know what hash smells like, you gowl.' Shane was right, but I didn't want to give in to him.

'Yeah, she'll know we're smoking something, though.'

'Shur, we smoked fags there before; we'll do it out the window,' said Joe; I was getting outnumbered here, it was no use. I could still smell his gum; it was Juicy Fruit. Shane picked up a bit of slate, and threw it at a crow; it flew away; crows weren't as brave as pigeons.

'Why don't we get a few cans, shur; from Quiltys,' said Joe. If I'd said it, Shane would have wet himself laughing. Joe was big, though. He could probably get served. Shane nodded at him.

'Yeah, rapid. I'm broke though, sham. What have ye?' Shane was the first person I'd ever heard say 'sham'. After I started hanging round with him, Mam

gave out to me for saying it too much.

'I've a tenner,' said Joe.

'Janey Mack!' I said.

'Where'd you rob that, you latchie?' Shane punched him on the arm. Joe went like he was gonna hit him back, but we all knew they were only joking. Shane would have killed him; didn't matter how big he was.

'Got it off my Auntie in England. For my birthday,' He was twelve a few weeks ago; he looked about fifteen, at least. The *size* of him.

'Nice one,' said Shane. I had a couple of pounds; Dermot might have money too, but if he didn't, he'd have fags.

'I've two quid. We can get flagons, and we'll pay you back the rest, like.' I said.

'Rapid,' Joe said. Shane wasn't ever gonna pay him nothing back, that was obvious to me. Shane never paid you back. Two flagons would be plenty; I'd be dizzy after a few swigs; especially if we got Linden Village.

We waited around the corner at Dermot's house. I wasn't going to take the chance of running into Paddy. Shane didn't care; he walked straight up and banged the knocker. We could hear him talking to Dermot's Mam, all charming. The mothers and fathers around our place all thought he was a proper little gentleman; he'd cut the grass on Saturdays to earn a few bob; they all loved him. Dermot hopped over his side wall and nearly landed on top of me.

'Jesus Christ, Dermot!' I shouted, but I was already laughing. Shane came

back from around the front with a bag of Taytos.

'Where'd ye get those?' asked Joe.

'Mrs. McCarthy' said Shane, like it was the most normal thing in the world for someone's Mam to give you a pack of crisps out of the blue. Dermot rolled his eyes, and said:

'How're ye anyway? Calling for Seán and Golly, are we?' He was messing.

'Fuck off; they're only a pair of gowls; I'm not sharing my flagons with them, sham. There's enough of us already.' They were *his* flagons now. We hadn't even got them yet.

'Have you fags, sham?'

'Yeah, bud. Only Silk Cut Blue, though. Who's got flagons, what?'

'Blue? They're like smoking air, sham.' Shane smoked John Players himself. I didn't smoke anything; I'd smoke whatever someone else had, or whatever was the cheapest when you were chipping in for some.

'Ah well, beggars can't be choosers, bud. Am I right?' said Dermot. Shane shrugged his shoulders and nodded.

'My Da's gone over to Frazer's to watch Liverpool, so I'd to take some of Mam's Duty Free.' He'd a whole twenty box. My Mam went to Frazer's too. It was only down the road, but she'd usually come home in a taxi. Dad hardly ever went over these days, cos we'd the Discovery Channel now, and he loved watching things about sharks.

I pushed the doorbell at Dara's house, nice and hard; it was one of the

ones that you could only hear from inside. The door opened; it was one of his sisters. I didn't know all their names, but everyone knew this one: Natalie, the ride. She was about fourteen, but she looked way older. She barely looked at me.

'Dara! You're wanted!'

I didn't know where to look. I tried not to stare, but Janey Mack! She'd some chest on her. And lovely lips, like Kylie Minogue. She was wearing a T-Shirt and jeans shorts. Pure tanned all over her legs, and her chest looked all swelled up; in a good way, not in a sore way. I was trying not to look at the nipples. Dara said that when a woman was on the horn, her left one got hard. Both of hers looked hard, now. I could feel myself going red. She tsss'd, and went back upstairs.

'Fuckin' arse on her, bud…' whispered Dermot. We all murmured, agreeing with him. Dara came out the door all red-faced and out of breath.

'What were you doing; riding the dog?' said Shane. We all burst out laughing. He was funny sometimes. Dara looked like he'd forgotten how to talk.

'What? I was... I was asleep.' He'd probably been pulling himself. Dara had his own skin mags; he'd bought them when he was on holiday in Spain with his Mam and Dad, and hid them in his suitcase, going home. In Spain and France and places like that, you could walk into any shop and buy skin mags.

'Oh! Come here and I tell ye. Did ye hear about yer one getting raped?' Dermot said, taking a fag out of the box for himself. Shane shook his head, and screwed his face up.

'What? Raped? A minute ago it was serial killers, sham. Are ye all on

tablets or what?'

'I don't know anything about serial killers now, bud. I heard Dennis talking to my Da about the Shades being around by the Quarry, and Dad said something to him about rape, or rapists. Then they saw me, and they shut up; I'll ask Dennis again, later; when my Da's not around.'

I said:

'Chris told me someone's after being murdered... In the Quarry as well, like.'

'Janey Mack… I dunno, bud; something's going on, anyway,' Dermot looked like an old man sometimes; he'd creases on his forehead that were like wrinkles. 'Stab City, wha?'

That was the thing, though: you'd hear people say 'Stab City' about Limerick, but it wasn't really true. Thomondgate was safe enough. Balla was a bit more dangerous, and Moyross was worse. But you never thought someone was gonna murder you, like. Or rape you, even.

'One of us has to go get the drink, sham.' Shane was looking at Joe. He'd have loved to be able to stroll in and buy the cider, but Joe was the only one of us who'd look old enough.

'All right; will I get fags as well, sham?' asked Joe, holding his hand out to me for my money. Dara had a few quid too. There was about sixteen pounds together.

'Have ye gear?' Shane asked. Dara looked annoyed, but he nodded.

'Right, we'll use Silk Cuts for the joints, but get ten Johnny Blue too, for

smoking.' Joints were better if you made them with the low-tar fags, people said. Shane wanted the Johnny Blue for himself to smoke; he was a real smoker; I'd seen him stubbing out butts before going into school. He didn't even care that the teachers would smell it off him.

Joe headed off to Quilty's to get the stuff. He didn't complain, even though most of the money was his, and he didn't even smoke. He'd have a few drags, though; everyone had a few drags when they had booze in them.

'Get Rizlas too! Green ones!' said Shane. We went down the alley where all the back doors were for my block. The gates all looked the same, just different colours. I hopped over first, to shut the dog up. I held him back with my leg, and let the lads in, quickly. Shane bent down and started playing with him; I never played with Rex, really. I didn't like animals that much, not even dogs.

The shed was right down at the end of the garden; miles away from our kitchen. I went to get the key from under a flowerpot, but the door was already open. There was someone in there. I shhhh'd the lads, and got ready to scatter, in case it was Paddy. I opened the door slow, and saw who it was.

'Who let you in?' I asked him, knowing it'd been Mam. Seán smiled up at me and said nothing. He picked snot out of his nose, and then he ate it. I dunno why we let him hang round with us at all. The others followed me in, after.

'Aboy the head, Golly!' said Dara. People did that; called you by your brother's nickname; even if his nickname was 'Lanky', and you were short. People didn't call me anything, cos Chris had no nicknames.

The walls of the shed had my posters on them: they were of planes, now;

that was what I was into. I was collecting a magazine about them every two weeks, and the posters from it were rapid. There was an F-14 Tomcat, the F-16 Interceptor, the Blackbird SR-71- that one looked like a space ship. It was only for taking pictures, though; it didn't have no weapons. The lads wouldn't have been interested in planes. If I wanted to talk about planes, I'd hang around with Jonathan Musgrave. He was into war, and guns and stuff. Dermot was having a look through the drawers.

'Have ye any cups, Rich; even plastic or paper ones?' I'd no idea if we did. 'An ashtray? Have ye ashtrays?'

'Don't need any, shur; we'll be tipping it out the window.' I wasn't letting them smoke in here; Mam would go spare.

'Fair enough, bud. Cups, though?'

'I'll try and sneak a few out from the house in a bit,' I probably wouldn't. We could drink out of the bottle; we weren't in Adare Manor, as Mam would say. Shane put a chair under the window at the back; he'd got a Silk Cut off Dermot. The smoke blew back in straight away, but most of it would go out. The Silk Cuts were supposed to be for the joint, but there were loads of them. Duty Free meant they were from Spain, or France.

'After you on that!' said Dara. You never got a full fag; someone always called After on it. Shane huffed, but he nodded; they weren't his fags anyway. Dermot was still looking in the drawers. I remembered I'd given him a lend of my Ghostbusters game. I'd have to get that back off him later.

'Richie love?' Jesus It was Mam Everyone panicked, and we started

shouting at each other to hide things, but whispering the shouts, so she wouldn't hear. Dara threw the butt out the window, and waved the smoke out with his hands. I grabbed the matches off the table and shoved them in my pocket. She banged on the door. It wasn't locked; she was being polite. I said:

'Am, come in!' She opened it a bit, and put her head in. She clocked the boys.

'Oh, hiya lads...' They saluted her and mumbled stuff, like you do when one of yeer parents is there.

'Rich, one of your other friends is at the front door; will I let him through?' Joe must've come round the front, the eejit. How was he hiding the flagons from her? He must've not got served.

'Yeah, go on, shur; let him through.' I said. Then Shane says:

'Hang on a sec. Mrs. South? What's he look like, yer man? Is it a tall blond fella?' What was he on about? Joe had black hair.

'Uh, yeah. That's it, Shane. Blondey hair on him. Older fella really. I was a bit surprised. I've never seen him with ye before.' Jaysus! It was Paddy!

'Tell him I'm not here, Mam,'

'Ah Rich; I'm not telling lies for ye...'

'Mam! Please?' She looked at me, then she rolled her eyes:

'Oh, go on then, shur. Just the once...'

'Thanks, Mam.'

'Ah, shur. Are ye all right otherwise so?'

'Have ye any cups, Mrs. South? Like, Party Cups…?' Shane, again.

'Ah, I don't know, Shane. Paper ones do ye mean? Would they do ye?'

'Oh they'd be perfect, yeah. Thank you very much, Mrs. South. I'll come in with ye so.' He was something else. Watching her walking off into the house with him, I realised just then how small Mam was. He was already taller than her, and he had years left to grow.

After they went, Seán took one of the fags and hopped on the chair; brazen as anything. I'd the matches, though; he'd have to ask me for a light. I turned around to talk to Dermot, but I smelt smoke straight away. He must've had a lighter. Dermot was looking through an old Sun Day magazine. Kylie Minogue was on the front of it, in a green top. She was a ride, she was.

'Cheeky cunt isn't he, like?' said Dermot; he was talking about Paddy, not Seán.

'I know; calling up to the door, like!' I said. The thing with Paddy wasn't going to go away; I was going to get a beating eventually. I wondered if I should go out and take it now. Maybe the longer he had to wait, the worse it would be for me. Revenge was colder the longer you waited to do it.

'Colm was probably hiding; he'd know your Mam knows him, and she'd've told you,' said Dermot.

'I seen them on the wall earlier,' Seán said. He hadn't given anyone a smoke on the fag. He'd horsed it down. Silk Cut Blue had their own smell; different to Mam's fags. She smoked Rothman's now; before that, it was Major like Dad. She was always telling me never to start.

'Would you say they'll get Joe?' asked Seán.

'Joe wasn’t there today, bud.' said Dermot. That was true, cos I’d been the one who’d told him all about what’d happened.

'D'you think they'll come round the back of here? They wouldn’t, would they? Cos of the dog? Rex will savage them, shur,’ Seán said.

'Rex wouldn't savage a plate of chips', I said. The lads laughed and so did I, but it was true. Rex was only an 'aul coss. He wasn’t no guard dog. Shane came back through the door with a big stack of paper party cups.

'What did ye tell her they were for?' I felt a weird feeling in my stomach about Shane being all pally with Mam. I didn't know what it was. Jealousy was the wrong word for it.

'Coke. I said Joe's gone down to Pa's for a bottle of Coke, and some Taytos for us.'

‘Nice one,’ said Dermot.

'Rapid, I’m starving.' said Seán.

‘He’s not actually gone to Pa’s, you gowlawalla.’ We sniggered.

‘Oh, yeah; right.’

‘Any sign of Paddy or Colm?’ I asked.

‘Would you say they’d come round the back?’ asked Seán. ‘I said Rex would savage them, but Rich says Rex wouldn’t savage a bag of chips!’

I looked over at him, the cheek of him, stealing my joke. Shane didn’t laugh anyway.

‘They won't come round the back,’ he said. ‘And if they do: I'll fucking lace into them, sham.' He’d one of Dad's hammers in his hand.

Suddenly, someone started banging the door down; I gulped. It wasn't Mam, and there was no other way out of the shed. We were trapped. I got ready, maybe to fight or to run. Shane ran over with the hammer above his head, like a psycho. My brain made it all slow down again, and in my head I saw us in court; little suits like we were making our First Holy Communion, listening to the judge hand down our sentences; Paddy Hooley's mother bawling her head off in the seats for the victim's family.

'Jesus fucking Christ, will you cop on, will you, shur?' It was only Joe, thank God. Shane put down the hammer and burst out laughing. Joe was shaking like Rex did when he came out of the river. He didn't have no liquor with him either.

Turned out Joe had actually got on well for a bit in Quilty's. He'd found one flagon of Linden in the fridge, and yer man had said 'One ninety nine, boss' to him. He needed two flagons though, and there was only Dry Blackthorn in the fridge, so he asks yer man if there's more Linden in the back. Obviously Joe's voice don't sound as old as how tall he was, 'cause yer man takes one listen, looks him up and down and tells him to eff off out of it. He didn't even get the Linden. We were all raging.

'What else will we do?' said Seán. His nails were filthy and black.

'Have ye booze over home?' Shane asked Joe. The rest of us went quiet, cos we all knew Joe's father was an alko. There'd be no drink left in that house. He'd neck the Listerine if you left him on his own in the bathroom, Dad said. Joe

shook his head, mortified looking. He took one of Dermot's fags and went over to the chair by the window. I looked somewhere else, instead of at him. It wasn't his fault his da was a wino.

'After you on that,' said Dermot. Joe mumbled something back.

'Mulcahy's?' asked Seán.

'Go way, will you. None of ye would get served in there, and I'm not going all the way into town.' said Shane.

'Can any of ye get Donkey's?' asked Shane. Donkey's Bollocks was the easiest way to get drunk. You'd get an empty Shannon lemonade bottle, or a big Lucozade one, then you'd put a little bit out of all the drink bottles in your house into it. I said I could probably rob one of Mam's baby bottles of Power's for it. Seán said his Mam and Dad didn't drink, which sounded like a lie. Dara's Dad had a big liquor cabinet, and he never noticed any of it going. He'd already brought the hash though.

'Go on, shur,' said Shane, to him. It was risky for Dara to go out there, with Paddy and Colm around. They were after me, but they might settle for him.

'Right, but I'm having some of that.' He pointed at the money on the table.

'What for?' It wasn't even Shane's money, but he still didn't want to give any of it to Dara.

'Danger money,' said Dara.

'What you mean, sham?'

'Paddy and Colm and Willum, like. They haven't catched any of us yet,

I'll get a battering…'

'They caught you though, shur.' I said. He'd been the one screaming.

'No they fucking didn't.'

'They did! I was running away and I heard someone screaming. Seán said it wasn't…'

'Well it wasn't me, shur. Why would I be screaming? I got away through the bushes, Rich.'

'Oh.'

'Yeah, anyway so. They'll bate the shit out of me if they see me. Danger Money please.' He was half laughing, but he meant it. Me and Joe nodded. Shane didn't look happy, but it was me and Joe's money.

'You can have a fiver between us; cos you got the gear, too,' Joe said. He'd have to have coins; there was only a tenner and a load of coins. Hopefully he'd be all right. I'd no idea who'd been screaming now though. I got a chill down me then, but I'd no idea why.

It was mad the way we were: playing Forty-Five or Bulldog some days; drinking booze and smoking gear other days. We weren't teenagers yet, but we weren't kids any more either. We were too big for the schools we'd left, but we'd be the babies in our new schools in September. Me especially, cos I'd skipped a year. I'd probably be the smallest. Chris was never drinking or smoking gear when he was our age. Kids were more… advanced, now. I would've preferred to be eleven back in them days, instead of now. I was no good at smoking or drinking. The rest of them were from rougher families though, and the scobier the family,

the earlier the kids got up to messing. Mam thought I was an angel. She'd drop dead if she knew half the stuff we did.

I liked messing around with the boys, even though they went a bit too far sometimes. It was a mad laugh.Mam had all these visions of me going to Trinity College or something. I wasn't *that* clever. I read lots of books and stuff, but I'd get bored easy. None of this lot would end up in college though. Some of them would probably end up in jail. Or worse.

Dara went off to his place; Shane followed him out. He came back in with a nodge and some skins, and Dermot threw him two fags from the box. Me and Dermot were talking about Mrs. Kelly:

'D'you think she was robbing, like? In Quinnsworth or something?' he said, rooting around in his ear with a finger.

'Nah, they're loaded,' I answered. The Kelly kids always had mad loads of toys and bikes at Christmas.

'Maybe that's why they're loaded?' Dermot said, smiling.

'True,' I said. Mam said most rich people were only rich because they were misers, like Scrooge. She'd say 'Fur coat and no knickers.' I didn't know what it meant, but I'd still laugh cos it was funny.

'What if she's the murderer, though?' he said. 'This is serious, bud. We need to get Jessica Fletcher on the case, like.' We laughed; Mrs. Kelly was small, like a bird. She wouldn't be able to hurt no one, even if she wanted to. I took a stick of Wrigley's out of my pocket; it was old, so it didn't taste very minty.

'There is something going on, though.' I said.

'Yep, definitely something, bud.' His face looked older again, especially in his eyes. I'd a rotten feeling in the bottom of my gut; I got it when I knew bad news was coming. I wasn't scared. This whole thing didn't feel scary to me.I didn't have to walk home from here tonight though.

Shane was rolling. I'd no idea how to do it; I'd never even tried it. He held up the nodge of hash in his fingers and burnt it with the lighter. It catched fire, he blew it out, then he crushed the dust into the tobacco. It looked like the coolest thing you could ever see someone do. I felt like we were in a movie, but we were the bad guys. Shane ripped a bit of cardboard off the packet to make a roach. I was glad that he was rolling, cos that meant he'd go first. There'd be other people calling second and third, so there was a good chance that they might skip me altogether. I didn't want to be getting wrecked in here, with Mam up in the house.

'First!' said Seán. Shane looked at him like he'd two heads.

'Second, I mean...'

'*Never*, you mean.' Shane sparked it up, and the first blast of smoke was so strong, I nearly got stoned just smelling it.

'The window!' I said, doing my best Friendly Face at Shane. He tutted at me and rolled his eyes, but he got up on the chair.

'Who's the murderer then, would ye say?' he asked. Up there, looking down at us, he was kind of like our King. He was messing; he didn't think anyone'd got murdered.

'Golly's Dad,' said Dermot.

'Fuck off!' said Seán, pretending to go to punch him.

'Ah lads, don't be lousy. His Da's sound,' I said. Seán looked at me, surprised. 'It's obviously his Ma.' The lads laughed. Seán went back to sulking.

Shane was well used to smoking; he didn't cough once. The smell was going right out the window as well. Joe was next, but he didn't need the chair to reach the window. Dermot was talking now:

'It's mad, like. Someone going around murdering people, in Thomondgate. No wonder Richie's Mam doesn't want him out tonight. One of us might be next, bud.'

'It's all only bollocks, sham. I'm telling you, the Gards probably found a stash of robbed videos, or a burnt out car.' said Shane. *Doubting Thomas*, Mam would call someone like him.

'Rich? Smoke here for you,' said Joe. I couldn't say no now. I climbed up on the chair, and it wobbled. I took a pull. It tasted horrible; worse than fags. I felt sick off it. I looked outside across the back gardens. The Cronins were the first ones to build a wall; the rest of us had bollards and plastic chains that the Corporation had put there. I didn't want to smoke this; I was a lightweight compared to any of them. My heart was beating fast from worry; Mam always knocked, but she might walk around the back of the shed too, and see me with a big joint in my mouth. I could feel it hitting me already; it was supposed to take a while, but I was already dizzy, and my thinking was getting mixed up. Even simple things. I was glad the others weren't really paying attention to me, cos it meant I didn't have to breathe in too much smoke. I saw Dara coming through the

green, with something under his arm. I hopped down and passed the joint over to Dermot; the paper was all see-through, from the grease on our fingers. I felt sick still. Seán was gone.

'Where's he?' I asked.

'Went over to tell his Mam he's over here; he has to check in, like. Fucking steamer,' said Shane. Seemed like a babyish thing to do, but Seán was younger than us. He was going on holiday the next day anyway, he'd said. He might have said; I hadn't been listening, and he hadn't been saying it to me anyway. Portugal. Or the port of something else. Couldn't remember now.

'Fair enough,' I said. My eyes were slitty, like a Chinaman. Music came out of nowhere: 'She Drives Me Crazy' was the song. The drum sounded like slaps. Loud slaps. Joe had found the radio. A white one, with a digital clock on it. The clock didn't say the time, it just flashed 00:00. I thought music might be a bad idea, cos we wouldn't be able to hear Mam or any of them coming in, but the way I was feeling made me want to hear it. I'd heard this one lots of times before, but it sounded different now. The beats felt like they were inside of me- like the sea is inside a shell or your heartbeat is inside your ear when you're lying on your pillow. I wanted to dance to it, and I would have if none of them had been there.

Dara was back, and he'd filled the whole bottle up with Donkeys'. Shane took a swig, and his face crinkled like he was after drinking vinegar.

'That's the good stuff, sham,' he said; wheezing like an auld man. Dara giggled. He'd come in time to rob the end of the joint. Shane was rolling another

one. The music was still going through me, like it was inside my blood. I was tapping my fingers to the drums, on the side of my leg. It felt rapid. 'Beat It' was on now. I had to stop my legs from dancing to it, in case they'd all look at me and laugh. I was wrecked; I didn't want the booze that was in my hand. The lads were in full swing, talking about girls off the TV and girls around here and riding. I had a gulp of Donkey's; it tasted like whiskey, or the smell of whiskey.

Dara thought Paula Abdul was a ride; Shane didn't know who she was. Dermot said Kylie was his one, and we all knew her. Shane said if you wanted to ride Kylie Minogue, you were a steamer. I was staying out of it, cos I didn't want to say 'Dara's sister', by accident. I was off my tree. I closed my eyes for a bit, and thought about Natalie, Dara's sister. The bones in my face felt warm, and there was a nice feeling in my langer. Words were wriggling around in my brain behind my eyeballs, like baby worms. Words were like worms, worms were like words. I tried to say things, but my voice barely came out, and the lads turned and laughed at me. I didn't know why they'd all suddenly turned on me, but they probably hadn't at all. I was thinking backwards. I saw Seán rush in the door, and call the lads over to him. There was wind going across the holes of my ears, like I was a tinwhistle or a flute.

'Here!' Dermot was on the chair, calling me over for some more joint. I must've staggered, cos everyone was laughing. When I looked at them, their mouths didn't move; but I heard the laughing in my head. I got up by the window, and took a pull. I could hear them talking behind me.

'... yeah, swear on my mother's life. Alan Devlin was over on the green a

minute ago, he told me,' said Seán.

'Jaysus, bud. Are ye sure?'

'Yep. Definitely one of the Kellys, anyway.'

'*Raped*'

'Raped and murdered.' –Seán again. My head started spinning. All of the voices sounded wrong, like my ears were underwater in the bath.

'Jaysus Christ, lads. Who'd do something like that?'

'Was it Aoife? Or the other one, what's her name, again?'

'Caoimhe…'

'Who did it? Who was it?' Shane punched the door of the press, with his bare knuckles. One was still raw since the morning, when one of their lot had got him with a stone. I looked at his face and looked away again quickly. His face had been different. Like a demon's face.

'Would you think it's someone from 'round here, like?'

'G'way, will you? There's no child molesters around here, bud.' Dermot's voice was the only one that sounded normal to me. I didn't look at him though, in case he looked like a demon too.

'I dunno, though… You never know with some people; it's always the quiet ones,' said Dara, walking over to me to swap places. I joined them now, but I didn't say anything. I'd a weird feeling, like terror. I wasn't afraid of them, I was just *afraid*. Of everything.

'Who's going around raping little girls, like?' Dermot was passing a Silk Cut through his fingers and turning it over and over; it wasn't lit, though.

‘And killing them…’ Dara said, from the window.

'Perverts, steamers, child molesters,' said Shane. He said it like 'chime-lesters'. I used to think that that was how you actually spelled it. Joe wasn't saying anything; he'd gone over to wait for the joint off Dara. My tongue felt weird, and my hands were all sweaty. I needed some water, but the tap was in the kitchen and I didn't want Mam to see me. Would she know what *stoned* looked like though? She only really knew about glue-sniffers. She did grow up in the sixties, mind. The Irish sixties, though. In Clare.

I loved Mam. I probably loved Dad, too; he didn't do any real Dad things, like kick a ball around with me, or go fishing. He didn't shout at us or hit us either though. I had a better Mam and Dad than most of my friends. I felt happy, but I felt like crying too. My mouth was still dry. I wiped my hands on my jeans. I was getting a whitener. Closing my eyes didn't help. I was less dizzy with them open.

Sometimes, before I went to sleep, I'd be able to have mad little dreams about stuff, but dreams that I'd be in control of. You could fly through the air or drive a car, or shift a nice looking girl. Other times I couldn't control the dreams, and I got more and more frightened. Running through glue, or punching nothing with hands that never made fists. This was kind of like that. I was thinking about Paula Abdul and the cat. *Opposites attract.* Is a cat the opposite of a human? What about dogs, then? Why do opposites attract? Do you have to hate someone for them to go out with you? Is that why Mams and Dads were always fighting? Magnets. Mouth really dry; hands really sweaty. Maybe I should lick my tongue with my hands. I felt like vomiting. Twopences would stick to a magnet, but a can

of Coke wouldn't.

'You all right?' It was Dara. I opened my eyes; it felt like the morning. My mouth tasted like morning. It was still night time though. The street light in the alley outside was giving me a headache, and I was still in the shed. I'd been thinking about Portugal. It must've been a dream. I must've been asleep. You can't sleep sitting down on the ground though. My eyes went closed again for a second or a minute. I was in Portugal again; Seán and Golly were there, and Paula Abdul.

'Are you all right, man!? You were out cold.' Dara gave me a little shake, and my eyes were open again. I felt sick come up my throat, but I swallowed it. My eyes went watery.

'Yeah... Yeah, I'm grand,' I said. I tried to straighten myself out, in case he saw that I was having a whitener. He knew, though. Everyone knew. Mam knew. The teachers at school knew. Father Sheehan knew. I closed my eyes and imagined I was in the Garda station. Mam was crying; Dad looked angry. The music from the radio took me back to the real world. *I Think We're Alone Now*. She was sort of a ride, even though she'd ginger hair.

I looked around. Seán and Dermot were looking through a skin mag. Shane and Joe were gone. I could hear voices whispering outside the window. Dara gave me the Donkey's and went over to look at the skin mag. It was probably his. There was plenty in the bottle. I didn't want any, but my mouth wanted something to wet it, and I'd no water still. I took a slug of it, and said over:

'Where's the other two?'

'Outside...' Dara said. 'I think Joe might a had a whitener...'

I said nothing; I knew that everyone knew I'd had one. I could feel it. Shane's voice was really soft outside, like whispering, or singing. Joe sounded like he was crying. Dara was still talking to me, but I couldn't listen; he sounded like bees inside a balloon. Aoife Kelly's face kept coming into my head; it was covered in blood, and her eyes were Xs, like when you're dead in a cartoon. I didn't really know what Caoimhe looked like.

'Want some?' Seán had a glass of water. I blinked at him. I thought he was going to disappear, like those things where the soldier in the desert thinks he sees a pool, and then he ends up drinking sand. I grabbed the pint glass off him. My tongue went into the water and soaked it all up like a sponge; I didn't even need to tilt my head back, it went up into my throat, like magic. I felt like a lizard, and then I stopped thinking that, because the pictures in my head of me being a lizard were too real. I shaked my face from side to side to get rid of the thoughts. I imagined my face was an Etch-A-Sketch, and when I'd shaked it, all my eyes and nose and mouth fell down and crumbled into dust. I wanted to see a mirror to check that it hadn't happened. My hands felt horrible against the outside of the glass, and I kept wiping them on my T-shirt.

'What's in it, anyway?' I asked Dara, pointing at the Donkey's. Talking out loud was hard, but it kept me from going mental.

'Vodka, Jameson, Rum, Bacardi, Malibu, Power's and Huzzar', he said.

'Huzzar is vodka, shur.' said Dermot.

'And Bacardi is rum, like.' I said. Dara nodded.

'So, is there other vodka and other rum in it, or just Huzzar and Bacardi?' asked Dermot. Dara looked blank.

'Uh, yeah. Vodka, Bacardi, Rum, Huzzar, Jameson's, Power's and whiskey.'

'Power's and Jameson *are* whiskey, shur.' said Dermot.

'Yeah'

'And Malibu!' said Seán.

'Malibu isn't whiskey, you gombeen!' Dara said. They were making my head spin. My eyes wanted to close. I wandered out. Shane was still whispering to Joe:

'Naw, man. We'll get him all right. We'll get him...'

'Get who?' I said. Both of them jumped.

'Nothing.' said Shane. Joe nodded, and sniffed a big load of snot up his nose. I didn't care what they were on about; I wanted my head to stop spinning and my brain to be quiet. I took the pint glass down the garden into the kitchen. I needed some more water; Mam was probably gone to Frazer's.

The kitchen was quiet, but I could hear Dad's TV in the front room. He wasn't going to come out now; not until bedtime. I ran the tap to get the colder water, but I didn't put the glass under yet. Mam killed me for doing that; it left rings on the table. I took a big gulp that disappeared into my tongue without even going down my throat, and then filled the glass up again. You couldn't hear the radio from up here, and you couldn't smell our smoke. That was good. I sort of

didn’t recognise my own kitchen, or I did, but I was scared of it. It’s stupid to think that you could be scared of a tap or a jug kettle, but I was, and I wanted to get out of there fast.

Back in the shed, they were all inside again. Seán was acting the clown for them: he did this thing where he stuck his elbows out the arms of his T-shirt, and pretended he was a chicken. It was funny. No one was talking about murder or rape or me.

'Give us a swig off that, sham.' said Shane. I gave him the last of my water. He handed me the end of the third joint, or maybe the fifth. I was wondering how to get rid of it, when I heard Chris's voice behind me, and lobbed it out the window. What was he doing here?

'Fuck off, really?' Shane couldn't believe what Chris was telling us. I couldn't either, but I was keeping quiet; he'd know I was wrecked if I tried to talk; he’d tell Mam, straight away. The whitener was wearing off, but still.

'Really, yeah. Fin was down in Frazer’s this morning with his da. Tony served him a Carling and everything; didn't say nothing.' Fintan Kelly was older than us, but he was still only fourteen. Tony Frazer wouldn't sell you a pack of fags without a note from your mother.

'Tom, though? Small little Tom. How? He’s only a toddler, shur.' Dermot looked like he was angry; he was nearly crying. I wanted to be in bed. I was too young to be drinking or smoking gear, and I wanted Mam. I kept looking at Chris, then looking away before he looked back.

'Some dirty old steamer, d'you know what I mean, lads? A queer, like. They're all the same. Should be fucking hanged, all of them. Awful carry on, altogether, shur. Give us a slug off that, will yuh? What is it? Whiskey?' he grabbed the bottle off Dara. I didn't understand: It was Tom Kelly who'd been murdered, now; not Aoife, or Caoimhe. That was the story now. That was the scala.

'Fucking… Jesus Christ, sham; we'll kill him,' said Shane. Seán looked white as a sheet. Joe looked like he was going to throw up, but he stopped himself. I watched him do it again, then he covered his mouth with his hand, and ran outside. Chris saw me, finally.

'What's the matter with you?' he laughed. I looked at him, saying nothing. I couldn't speak. My throat was dry again, and I'd nothing to say back to him anyway.

'Is he drunk, lads?' They did that Not Really Answering thing that your friends did so's not to get you into trouble. I didn't mind him thinking I was drunk; he couldn't tell Mam, cos I seen him drinking loads of times, with his friends from Garryowen.

'G'way you steamer, you.' I said. I'd never given him cheek before in my life. It didn't feel like I'd said it. It was like I'd been watching someone else say it. I had said it though. He looked gobsmacked, then he burst out laughing. They did as well.

He punched me in my ribs, messing, but I didn't feel it. I twisted away and went out the door. He called something after me, and they all laughed again,

but he didn’t follow me out. The hash was so strong, my thoughts were everywhere. I loved Mam; I loved Chris, even if he was acting the steamer; I felt sad for the Kellys. I wanted to be in my bed, away from all the drink and hash and murderers. My mouth was dry again. Chris was going to find out that I was high on drugs, and he was going to tell Mam, and she'd have to tell the Gards, and they'd take me down the Quarry, and some old queer fella would pull his mickey out in front of me, and then he'd murder me, and Dad and Chris would be in Frazer’s in the morning drinking Carling and crying, and Tony Frazer wouldn't even say nothing to Chris, even though he’s only fourteen.

I squinted over at someone in the garden; I couldn’t see who it was. If it was Paddy Hooley, he was welcome to me. I couldn’t move a muscle. He could kill me all he liked. It was just Joe, though. He was puking his ring up. He must’ve been wrecked as well. It was too much, the drinking and the gear. We were only kids. His puking sounded all wrong; like he’d run out of stuff to vomit, and was just making the noise, still. The dry heaves, Mam called them. It sounded a bit like he was crying too, but he probably wasn’t at all. I was too wrecked. The knees of my jeans were wet, but I couldn’t remember what’d happened to them.

Three

The sunshine and Mam's voice came into my head at the same time, and both of them hurt. My skin felt like I'd the Flu, and my mouth tasted like I'd been licking sand.

'Shane's here for ye, love; what's wrong, Rich? Are ye sick is it?' She was only talking soft, but her voice was going through me like a drill. I made some sort of noise, and she stopped and went away. How was I in bed? I was only wearing my jocks, but I didn't remember taking off my clothes. Then I felt a lump inside my chest: guilty feelings, what'd I done? Chris! He was there last night. Oh God.

Shane was standing inside the door when I got downstairs. On his own, which was strange.

'How's the head, sham?' I just groaned. He sniggered. 'Have ye fags?'

'Shhhh, will you?' Mam was only in the kitchen.

'I've nothing; I didn't have the fags last night.' I remembered that; Dermot had had them.

'Rob one for us.' said Shane. He was looking past me into the kitchen; Mam's were open on the table. I really didn't want to, but it was Shane saying to.

Outside, he waited until we were at the end of the path, then he lit it up.

'I'll leave you a smoke.'

'I'm all right,' I shook my head at him. I'd have puked my ring up; even the smell of it was enough.

'Don't tell no-one this, right?' he said.

'Tell them what?' I raised my eyebrow. Mam said I looked the spit of Dad when I did it.

'Swear first.'

'Right, I swear.' I said. There was an orange ball on the grass belonging to someone. It didn't look punctured or anything.

'On your mother's life?'

'Cross my heart and hope to die.'

'Good. Right, you know little Tommy Kelly?'

'Yeah…' Last night came back to me. I felt sick.

'You know the way some dirty old steamer strangled him?' I hadn't known that he'd been strangled, or if I had, I'd forgotten it. I nodded anyway though.

'And you know they interfered with him, sham?' I nodded at him again. The whole of yesterday was a blur still though; not just the night time part.

'We know the fucker who did it, sham.' I stopped walking; I was wide awake now.

'How? Who? How did...' I couldn't get the questions out.

'Joe, sham. Joe knows who did it; he's the one told me.' He passed me the very end of the butt, and I took it, cos I needed it now.

We walked the long way, while Shane told me it all. It had been a long time since I'd hung around with him on his own.

Joe'd got really drunk and started spilling his guts to Shane last night.

He'd started crying, and when Shane pushed him to say what was wrong, he'd told him that when he was small, some auld fella had *interfered* with him. Molested him. Touched him on his privates or whatever. He'd never told no one about it before.

He was all right when we'd all thought it was a woman that had been raped. When we started saying it was a kid though, he'd lost it; he was stoned as well, like me. Probably paranoid too. All these bad memories had come back. He'd gone outside, and Shane came looking for him, to see was he puking or something. He'd just been sitting against the wall, staring into space, shaking like anything. It wasn't even cold out. Shane gave him a fag, then they just talked and talked. Shane waited until he'd made Joe pull himself together before they went back inside. Then when they'd got in, Chris was there, telling everyone about little Tommy. Joe'd gone back outside and puked his ring up. He was bawling crying too, Shane said.

'I don't remember him being that bad,' I said.

'He was, sham. You were asleep for half the night.' I couldn't argue with that, cos I couldn't remember still. Then a little bit of last night came back to me, and I remembered someone in the garden; the dry heaving, and the rest of it.

'Who's it, then?'

'Who's what?'

'Who's after doing that, to that little boy?'

'Paudie,' said Shane, flicking away the butt.

'Paudie Collins?'

‘Yep.’

'Jaysus...'

Paudie Collins was a bit of a weirdo. You couldn't really tell what age he was, cos he didn't dress nice, and his hair was a state. I'd’ve guessed he was at least thirty. Maybe forty even. He was harmless. One of those fellas you'd salute in the street, for a sneer.

'Aboy the head, Paudie!' we’d shout. He'd salute you back sometimes; other times he'd look at you like to say 'Eff off, will ye?’ He had a fat porter-belly that hung over his tracksuit bottoms and he wore a Man Utd shellsuit top as a jacket. We'd thrown eggs at his windows on Halloween, and he hadn't even come out to shout at us. I'd felt lousy then: it was scary when someone chased you after ye’d egged their house; it was kind of sad when they didn't, cos they were afraid or cos they were handicapped, or a bit slow. I wasn’t able to be really horrible. I’d a guilty conscience. I always thought of what Mam would say to me if she knew; that stopped me being too bad.

'Ah no. He’s a bit weird, but… I mean, he wouldn’t… something like that, I mean… No,' I said. Paudie was just a bit pathetic; he didn’t look dangerous.

‘Yes he would, sham.’

‘Nah, he’s not like that, though…I, ’

'He fucking is, okay?’ He shouted it. His spits went onto my cheek.

'Okay. Okay, I believe you. How… how do you know, though?’

He didn't answer me properly, he just raised his eyebrows; like I was being thick. It took me a few seconds.

' Jaysus.'

'Yeah.'

'But, why didn't he say nothing? To the Gards, like?'

'I dunno, sham. He was pure ashamed, like. Picture it: a steamer, touching your langer and stuff. Making you give him blow jobs... you couldn't just go tell someone.'

'Because they'd think he was, a you know, a *queer* too?' We were outside Brian and Orlaith's house. Their mam was in the garden watering the bushes.

'Yep. And they would, like. How could you tell your Da something like that? Mine would fuckin' kick the shit out of me, sham. He'd put me in the grave.' I nodded, because he was telling the truth there.

'Yeah, I suppose.' I agreed with him, but I didn't think his dad would be right to do that. You can't be like that. Something like this... it was called *abuse*; I'd seen a thing about it on That's Life, about the Childline in England. We had it here too. If an adult was doing things to you, it wasn't your fault. It wasn't you. Joe wasn't a gay, really. I thought of the times when we d got changed in front of him for swimming, and I felt like getting sick. It wasn't his fault... he wasn't really queer. It was still disgusting, though. Poor Joe.

'Why did he tell it all to you, though? Last night, like. After all this time?'

'He was para, sham, just came out. You know what it's like, on the gear...' I did. Shane didn't seem like he'd know though. He was one of those fellas who could smoke a rake of the stuff. Same with the drink. Some people were just born cool.

I couldn't imagine anyone being able to do anything to Joe. Big Joe, like. Paudie was only a little fella; he was fat, but he wasn't tall, and he'd no muscles on him. Joe wouldn't have been big back then though. He'd have only been a little boy, like Tommy Kelly. It was shocking, all of it. It was a bit exciting too though, like a film. I felt lousy for thinking that though.

We were outside Dara's. He must've seen us out the window; he came out the gate, pulling on his jeans jacket. His cheeks were all red. Shane looked at me, to say that the conversation was over. It was kind of mad that he'd called up for me 'specially, and told me all that. That was the soundest he'd been to me in a while. Since before last Christmas. I liked it. I'd missed it.

We were going to go into town, so we had to go get the rest of them. Dermot and Joe were kicking a ball around in the green. I couldn't look Joe in the face, but he wasn't being that friendly anyway.

'Where's Seán and Golly?' I asked Dermot.

'Gone to Portugal, 'member? Two weeks, bud.' I didn't remember at all.

'He is in his bollocks. How would they afford to go to Portugal, sham?' said Shane.

'I dunno, sham. That's where he said he was going… Don't shoot the messenger, bud.' Dermot looked annoyed at Shane. He was the only one of us who was well able for him. I sort of remembered something about Portugal from the night before. Felt like I'd dreamed it though. Joe would be going soon, too. There'd be hardly any of us left. Another One Bites The Dust came into my head.

We walked down Pa's first, and I got a Fat Frog ice pop. Pa made some joke about it, but I didn't get it. He was always making jokes; he was sound enough. He didn’t say anything about little Tommy, but he told us to be careful. Every time we passed someone old on the street, they saluted us. Mrs. O’Neill asked us were we all right; Tom Horan gave us a wave from the Calor Gas truck, and Dermot Sheehan’s mam stopped us to tell us not to be hanging around in the Quarry or behind the White Wall when it got dark. None of them actually said anything about it to us, but it was the thing with little Tommy. Everyone knew about it.

The lads kept asking me how my head was. I didn’t like being the joke, I wasn’t used to it. I still couldn't remember getting into bed. I'd already met Mam though, and she hadn't said nothing. That meant I hadn't got sick in the toilet or anything. We walked in by The Maternity, instead of along the strand. Dara needed a slash, so he went behind the bushes in Jury's car park; this woman nearly saw him, but he zipped up in time.

'She wanted my mickey, she did,' he said, when he caught up with us.

'She did in her ring' said Dermot.

'Exactly!' We all laughed.

‘Did Chris tuck ye in?' Dermot asked me when we were walking next to each other.

'Er, I... what?'

'Chris, like. You vanished, bud. We thought you'd gone up to bed. When we were going away home, Chris found ye in the garden, panned out.'

'Ah, yeah. Yeah, I was knackered. Over-did it on the gear.' I tried to sound like someone cool; like off the telly or in a film.

'Fair enough, like. Chris had an auld smoke with us. He's all right.' That bit was news as well.

'He's not. He's a langer to me, most of the time...'

'He's your brother, shur,' Dermot said, and shrugged his shoulders.

'I suppose.' Dermot had one fool of a brother and one sound one. He'd Bermudas on today; I hated wearing shorts, cos I'd milk bottle legs. The other three were up ahead, they walked faster than us.

'Listen and I'll tell you. Swear to God you'll keep this to yourself?' he said. I nodded at him; everyone was telling me things today.

'Swear on your mother's life?'

'I swear...' I crossed my heart as well. I wasn't afraid of lying on a swear. That stuff was all bull.

'You know the *murder*?'

'Yeah…' I nodded. He told me the exact same story, about Joe and Paudie, and the thing that had happened years ago. Shane had told him, last night. Dermot went into more detail about it though. I didn't know that gay fellas put their mickeys up each other. It sounded *sore*. I didn't let on that I already knew the story. I felt a bit crap now that I wasn't the first one that Shane had told, but I felt a bit better that someone else knew about it, too.

'D'you definitely think he did it?' I asked.

'To Joe or to Tommy?'

'Both of them, I suppose.'

'Definitely, like. What's the chances a there been *two* fucking childmolesters living round here?'

'What we gonna do?' I asked. Shane hadn't actually said a plan.

'Dunno, shur. Tell the Shades?' He was biting the skin off his finger, cos he'd no nails left.

'Would they believe us, though?'

'They'd believe *him*,' he said, looking at the back of Joe's head. Then, quieter, 'I dunno if he'd say anything, though, without the drink.'

We were over Sarsfield's Bridge already. We just bummed round town in the summer; there wasn't nothing to do except for sit by the river, or go to the Pound Shop, or go to Harry's. Harry's was a café next to Dunnes Stores that I went into with Mam sometimes, when she'd take me with her to get the messages from town. It was old fashioned looking, with red checkered tablecloths made of lino. There was always red sauce on them, and fag burns. We'd never buy anything; we'd just go in when it was quiet, and sit at a table where other people left their plates. Me and Dermot would look round at all the people, and make up funny voices for them. Shane would throw chips at people's heads, and then look all innocent when they turned around to see who'd done it. It was a mad laugh.

Shane wanted to go to Wisebuy, to get some Action Force. He said Marc Reagan had told him they'd Cobra Commander, Destro and The Baroness; all mad hard to get. Shane was the best at robbing; I was useless at it, cos I'd get nervous, and go scarlet, and end up just leaving the stuff there. It was all right for him; my

family was actually decent. His mother would probably just clip him round the ear if a Garda car brought him home. She'd be more angry at him for getting caught than for robbing. Mam would drop dead.

Wisebuy was kind of like a Pound Shop. We didn't walk in in one big gang; Dara said that would make them suspicious. Shane went straight over to where the Action Force were, on hooks in the wall near the back of the shop. He was bauld as brass. Me and Joe were looking at the comics; He'd a Roy of the Rovers, and I could see his lips moving when he read the words. I was probably the best reader out of us; none of the rest of them would read a book, unless a teacher said to. Shane read his mam's True Crime magazines.

I looked around to see if I could see the detective. They usually had a leather jacket on, and a gold watch. They were always fat; Dara said they were people who were too short or too fat to get into the Gards. It was so hot this summer, you'd boil in a leather jacket; especially if you were fat.

Dermot had an Indiana Jones key ring. He passed it from hand to hand, like a magician, while talking to Dara about something. I didn't even see him put it in his pocket; it was just there one second, gone the next. Like a magician. Shane was looking really closely at the front of the Action Force packets, and ripping through the cardboard on the back with his fingernails. I'd seen him do it before. That's how he had so many Cobra Troopers. You'd think his Mam would've asked him where they all came from. I still couldn't see a detective.

'*Get out of here, ye robbers!*' Dara had put on an auld fella's voice; he'd scared the crap out of me. He had a sticker album of The Bangles in his hand:

'Yer one there's a ride, isn't she? The singer, like?'

'Yeah. Gorgeous.' I didn't actually agree; I didn't like the way she done her hair. You couldn't say something like that though; people would think you were bent.

'Listen, I've to tell you something later. Not now though...' He looked over near where Joe and Dermot were, then back at me. I nodded. Shane or Dermot must've told him the story too. You couldn't keep a secret for long.

I'd been holding a can of Seven Up in my hand, from the fridge. Shane had shown us this trick: you picked up a can of fizzy, and maybe a book or something else. Then you joined the queue to the till. While you were queuing, you'd act annoyed, like you were in a hurry. Eventually you'd do a big huff, leave the queue, and put the book back on the shelf. Then you'd just walk out the shop with the can. No one ever noticed. Shane said no one is ever paying as much attention to you as you think they are. They're too busy worrying about themselves.

I looked around for something to pretend to buy. There was a Beetlejuice pencil parer there, and a U2 cap. I didn't really get that film; yer man from Batman was supposed to be in it, but I couldn't see him at all when we watched it. Chris liked it. Chris liked U2 and all. I was half way along the queue when I saw the detective. He'd a leather jacket on all right, and a gold watch. He was looking straight at the back of Shane, with a big rotten smile on his face.

Dara and Joe were outside by now, waiting for us. Dermot was over in the corner, looking through a book about Crocodile Dundee. I was stuck in the

queue; I hadn't the balls to do the Seven Up thing, now I'd seen yer man. I wasn't going to pay for it either though. Shane had no idea. He was shoving The Baroness down his jeans, while yer man stood behind him, watching everything. He was going to be caught red-handed. I'd to get his attention quick. I came out of the queue without doing the huffing thing. I didn't bother going back to the fridge; I just put the can on the shelf in front of me. That made the detective look over at me. I was crapping myself, even though he couldn't get me for nothing now.

Shane finished and started walking out. I hadn't counted, but he'd probably at least five Action Force down the legs of his jeans. Derm was already outside. I was going to have to catch up with Shane and stall him. They couldn't get him unless he walked out carrying it. How was I supposed to tell him though, without yer man hearing me?

I speeded up a little bit; the detective was near enough to Shane to be able to touch him. Some posh eejit wearing a Guns N Roses T-Shirt got in my way, and slowed me down. I wasn't quick enough; Shane was at the door. I had a little vision of what was going to happen to us. Shane was going to get arrested, and we'd all be brought down the station as well. They couldn't get us for anything, obviously. But they'd call Mam, and she'd have to come down, and all the neighbours would know about it, and she'd be a disgrace, and tell me that I'd made a holy show of her. I closed my eyes, then I had to open them again, cos I had to see it.

Shane stopped about a foot from the door. He stopped so quickly that the detective bashed into the back of him; like a pile-up in traffic. He put his hand

down the legs of his jeans, and pulled all the Action Force men out, one by one. And the weapons. He started whistling.

Looking straight at yer man, he puts them all on top of a pile of colouring books. Still whistling; the tune of Pop Goes The Weasel. Then he pats himself down like a policeman in the movies would; front and back. The detective couldn't believe what was goin' on. Then Shane just turns around and walks out, with me following him; my jaw on the floor.

Once we turned the next corner, we scattered for it. The law is the law, and they can't do you for shoplifting if you don't have the stuff on you; there was no law against him running after us and beating the crap out of us though.

We kept on running, down William Street, around by Todd's, down Cecil Street, and past Henry Street, where the Garda Station was. We didn't stop until we were on the grass under the New Bridge. I was laughing so much, it was like I was having one of Chris's asthma attacks.

'Aw, man! How did you know he was following ye?' asked Dara; he was still out of breath and his face was even more redder than usual.

'G'way will you, sham. I seen him ages ago, like. That's why I was being pure obvious.'

'I thought you were a goner,' I said. He rolled his eyes at me. I blushed, and felt like I shouldn't have said nothing. The rest of the lads carried on asking him questions and licking up to him, like you do whenever anyone's done anything rapid. Dara came over to me, fag in his mouth.

'Light? I'll leave you a smoke.' He nodded over towards the rock for us to

go sit down, where the rest of them couldn't hear us.

'Guess what, anyway.' I knew what was coming, but I still acted like I didn't:

'What?'

'I seen who's moving into Naughton's.'

'What? When was this?'

'In the Square, earlier. They had a big van full of furniture; yer man was asking how to get in the back of number 46,' said Dara.

'Oh, right.' I said. I'd thought he was going to tell me about the other thing. This wasn't important. I didn't care who was moving in next door.

'There's more, though, right…' He'd a big smile- he looked like one of the blacks on a jam jar, only he was white.

'They've a daughter, like. And she's a ride,' he said.

'Oh, right.' I said. I wasn't sure what to say. I wasn't any good at talking to girls. Especially not good looking ones.

'Mad, isn't it? You lucky bastard! You can watch her getting changed, with binoculars,' said Dara. I think he thought we lived in a Hollywood movie. I didn't even have binoculars.

'Yeah, I suppose. What's she look like?'

'Blonde hair, brown tan, lovely knockers, sham. She's about thirteen or fourteen, like; from the size of 'um.' I didn't fancy blonde girls at all. In the films or in real life. I liked brown haired ones, like yer one from Labyrinth.

'Yeah,' I said. It was all right for him; he was rapid with girls. He'd come

back from Kilkee and tell us all about the ones he'd shifted over the holidays, and what he'd got off them. I couldn't remember him going away with anyone from round Thomondgate, but he probably did.

'Why aren't you telling the boys?'

'Ah... I just didn't want to say anything, cos… I mean, Dermot's all right, but the other two've never gone away with a girl in their lives. I swear they're a pair-a-queers.' I looked at him and felt my face blushing. He didn't know that I'd never gone away with anyone; I wasn't going to tell him either though.

'Yeah. Good idea. Keep her for ourselves, like.' I said, trying to sound like a big man. He smirked.

'Would you say she's riding?'

'I haven't even seen her yet, Dara.'

'Oh right, yeah. Rest of that?' There was about a third of the fag left.

'Go on, shur.'

We walked back over the New Bridge; the one that whistled when the wind blew. My other friends, from school, lived around here; I was hoping we didn't run into any of them. My school was kind of a rich people school, even though it was free to go there. It was like I was two different people sometimes: all nice and polite and posh at school; one of the boys at home. My friends from Caherdavin and the North Circular road wouldn't get on with my Thomondgate friends; they'd think they were knackers. My Thomondgate friends wouldn't like my posh friends, either; Shane would say they were steamers.

There were some lads down on the wooden bit, where they push the boats

out, at St Michael's Rowing Club; Shane was slagging off their cycling shorts, saying they must be gay. I liked the yellow and blue colours, but he was kind of right: why would you wear cycling shorts if you weren't on a bike? Seemed a bit dodgy all right. Dermot threw some stones at the swans on the quay, but they didn't even turn around. He'd actually robbed loads of stuff, while the detective had been spying on Shane: that key ring; some Superman chewing gums; a necklace made of sweets. He gave me one of the Supermans; they had a tattoo in them, but they were only for kids. I'd stopped putting mock tattoos on me ages ago; before last Christmas.

It was sunny now; I could feel myself getting burnt on the back of my neck, and the end of my nose. There was nothing I could do, though; you had to put the cream on before you went out. We walked down the strand, towards Jury's. Dara had wanted to go up by Arscoil, but Shane said no. I was glad, because even though it was a laugh in the bushes behind the rugby pitch there, I didn't want to end up getting caught by the caretaker, cos it was going to be *my* school in September. I didn't want to think about that, now; I wanted to enjoy the holidays.

We split up after Shane's house- Dara only lived a few doors down, and I couldn't walk to Dermot's. It was mad how when you were on your own, things felt different. All the stuff about murder and rape and whatever felt exciting and fun and not really real when I was with the lads. Now it gave me the chills. It was mad sunny out, but it *felt* dark. I was still looking out for Paddy, too. That was another thing that didn't feel so scary when the boys were around. I didn't want a beating; the worst part would be having to explain to Mam why it happened. Or

lying to her about it instead.

There was a van in front of Naughton's, although it wasn't really Naughton's any more. The new people, the ones Dara saw; they didn't have a name yet. There was no road outside our block of houses, so the van had to park up on the grass. Our door was open, so I went straight in. I heard something then; like a child's voice. I stopped and listened harder, but it was gone. Probably came from over in the Square.

Mam was in the kitchen; smoking a fag. When you really smoked, not just messing about, you could just go have a fag, and do nothing else. I couldn't do that. Shane did it; so did Mam. Sometimes she said she had to have one, or she couldn't do anything else. I never got that with them.

'How'rya, Richie love?' she'd a great smile, Mam. I didn't. People said I had a puss on me most of the time. I think I got it from Dad's side. My teeth were no good either.

'I'm grand. Is there corned beef?' I was hungry, after everything.

'There's ham, actually.'

'Picnic ham or real?' Picnic was rank.

'Picnic ham *is* real ham, Richard, shur.' She gave me a bit of a look. It was definitely picnic then.

'Did ye want me to make it for ye?' said Mam; she was sound out.

'Nah, it's all right, shur; have we cheese?'

'Only the Easi Singles…'

'Rapid,' I loved Easi Singles; real cheese was rotten. The picnic ham

didn't look too bad, cos it was fresh from Pa's, not out of a packet. I spread the Dairygold carefully, cos it was hard from the fridge; I hated having holes in the bread.

'Where were ye, town was it?'

'Yep,' I said; my mouth full of sandwich.

'Where did ye go?'

'Ah, just around, like.' I could hardly tell her I'd been out robbing Action Force. There probably were kids round here who would though. I probably knew a few of them.

'Ah, right. Lovely day to be out in the fresh air, says you' she said; the smoke coming out of her nostrils. I touched the back of my neck, and did a 'ffffssss': I'd got burnt, definitely.

'Yeah. We were down by the New Bridge earlier, sitting on the grass.'

'Yeah? Who was there with ye?'

I told her, and she asked me some more stuff, and I answered all her questions, cos I didn't mind talking to her at all. These conversations we had were never about important stuff, but they were my thing with her; I didn't talk to Dad like that, and her and Chris weren't close like this. I wondered sometimes if we'd always be like this together, for our whole lives. Or did it all stop when you grew up and had your own kids? I finished up my food; I ate the crusts to make her happy, even though crusts were rank.

The front room smelt of dog, but Rex wasn't in there. Dad was reading the Limerick Leader; there'd be nothing in it about Tommy Kelly, because they

printed it on a Friday or a Thursday. Mam or Dad hadn't said nothing to me about the whole thing, but they must've known. We knew, and we were only kids. Dad took his eyes off the paper and looked over.

'Well?'

'Well.'

That was a conversation with us. Dad was like a cat: he could be great company, when he wanted to be. He'd come over to you and be nice, when he was bored, or wanted a laugh and a joke. He could be funny sometimes. If you wanted him, though, he was usually never there. Just like a cat.

There were no covers on my bed upstairs. The continental quilt and the pillows were stacked up on the bare mattress; Mam must've taken everything off to wash them. The mattress was full of knobbly bits, and they scratched the sunburn on my arms when I tried to get comfortable. I was reading a book that Chris had for school, called Catcher in the Rye. I didn't really understand it; it was too American. There was noise out the back; I got up on Chris's bed, and looked out through the net curtains.

A man in blue was bringing a couch in along the back garden, with another fella who was fat, and looked a bit slow. They were definitely moving in; that van from outside had come round to the back gate. The man shouted out something at someone inside the house.

Then I saw her: yer one Dara had been talking about- the ride. She was older than me, I'd say. And taller. Girls always got taller first than boys. She'd

some tan on her. And her body was like she was off Baywatch. My langer was twitching just from looking at her. I could only see the back of her, but her face was obviously going to be gorgeous when the rest of her looked like that. I felt a bit drunk, looking at her. I put my hand down the front of my pants; not to do anything; just to move it, cos it was getting sore. While I was doing that, she looked straight up at the window, into my face. I dropped down under the windowsill like I was dodging snipers.

'Who are ye spying on, sham?' It was Chris. He'd took the heart out of me. He had cycling gloves on.

'What? No one. Just looking out the back.' I didn't want him seeing yer one.

'Sleep all right last night?' He had a big grin on him. I wished I could remember more.

'Yeah, grand.'

'What did Mam say?'

'About what?'

'About you, you spa.'

'She didn't say nothing. Don't call me a spa, Chris.'

'What are you gonna do about it?' He always said that.

'Nothing.'

'Exactly. Have you something else to do in here?'

'What d'you mean, like?'

'I'm gonna listen to some music.'

'Yeah?'

'Yeah. Fuck off out of it.'

Downstairs, I went out into the back garden, looking for a tennis ball. I wasn't actually looking for one; I was just nosing. There was no one in their garden now, but they'd the kitchen window open, and I could hear talking. One of the men was probably yer one's father; dunno about the other fella.

'Will ye be right so, Mick?'

'Ah yeah, shur. Ye're after doin' enough today, Sheamie. Cheers for that, boy.'

'Shur t'was nothing, says you.'

'Did ye want another coffee, while I've the kettle boiled? Or a glass of porter is it?'

'Ah, no… arra go on then, shur. Just coffee though. I've to drive up to Mama's after,'

The girl wasn't saying anything. Maybe she wasn't there anymore.

'Hey!' It was her; standing right in front of me, in their garden. My mouth hung open for a bit, then I tried to answer her,

'Hi you'. Hi you? That sounded wrong; I was already making a hames of it.

'I'm Marian.' She was gorgeous from the front too. Much better than any of Dara's sisters.

'Hi,' I said, again; even that was a struggle. She was an absolute ride. I'd no idea what you'd say to someone who looked like that. I couldn't look away

though.

'Have you a name too, or is "Hi" your name?' Her teeth were gorgeous and white; like someone from the Colgate ads. I was awful at remembering to brush mine.

'Richie…*Richard.* Richard… Rich, Rich- Richie.'

'Hello, Richie Richard.' She was smiling again. Smiling at me, like.

'Are you moving in, are ye?'

'Yes…' Well, of course she was moving in.

'Where've ye come from?'

'Erm, we used to live in Kennedy Park.' She spoke way too posh for someone from Kennedy- that was up near Southill; full of knackers, Dad would say. I nodded. I couldn't ask her if she knew so-and-so from Kennedy, like people usually would. I didn't know any knackers. I went to Ardscoil, nearly.

'What age are you then, Richie?'

Was I supposed to tell the truth?

'Eleven. And, and three quarters.' Her face dropped.

'Oh right; I thought you were older.' I could see through her T-shirt, but she was wearing a bra, so I couldn't see anything.

'Nice, aren't they?' She said.

'What? Yeah. I mean, what?' Jesus, she didn't even mind me gawking at them? She was like an English one or something. God bless us and save us, as Mam would say.

'My uncle bought them for me, in America.' What? Janey Mack, I never

what… Ah, right! She meant her tackies; Converse All Star. That made more sense. Jesus.

'Yeah, rapid. What was he in America for?'

'He looks after kids for a charity; they were taking them to Disneyland.'

'Ah, right, so. That's nice. America, though? Rapid.'

'Have you been over, yourself?' she said. I'd never been anywhere; Mam said we couldn't afford holidays. I'd lie about it in school, otherwise you'd get a slagging for being poor.

'Nah. My Mam hates aeroplanes.' That was true, actually. She'd never been on one or anything, but she did hate them. Marian nodded, then:

'You've a brother?'

'What? Yeah. Yeah'

'Yes, I saw him.' Of course. She'd be more into lads Chris's age; I was only being an eejit. I was only a child.

'You're more handsome; you've lovely eyes.'

I said nothing. I just looked at her, like it was a trick.

'See ya later anyway, Richie Richard.' She skipped off into her kitchen. My jaw was still hanging open when Chris appeared beside me.

'Jaysus, who's that, like?'

'Yer one from next door.' I wasn't going to tell him her name; I wanted her all to myself.

'What's she talking to you for?'

'Dunno. She has American tackies; her uncle bought them for her.

'She has American diddies, is what she has. Go on!' I didn't like that; he shouldn't be allowed to say things like that about her; she was sound out, as well as being a ride.

Four

'Right! Cop on, a minute, will ye? Shhhh!'

Shane, me and Dermot were in the alley behind Paudie's. I was supposed to be at Mass; we all were. Dara had gone with his family; we could ask him later what the sermon had been about, and who the priest was. That was all Mam'd ask me when I went home. Sometimes I just made it up; she didn't know the difference.

'Is he there?' Dermot asked me. I was up on top of a big yellow Calor Gas bottle, peeking over the wall into the garden. There was no one in there, but I could hear whistling.

'Nothing yet,' I said. My accent changed when I was home from school for a few weeks. With the lads, 'nothing' was 'nottin'', 'beat' was 'bate'; little things like that. The boys from Castletroy or the North Circular Road had no idea where Thomondgate was; they probably thought it was a lovely place, from the way I talked at school. They'd drop dead if they knew there was horses on the green outside my house. Or if they saw the carts from Balla, that sold coal, blocks and briquettes.

'Give us a gawk, sham.' Shane swapped places with me, but he couldn't see anyone either. Paudie had a dog, called Molly; she was half a boxer, half something else. He'd probably let her in the house today, cos I hadn't seen her and you couldn't hear any barking.

‘He’s in there all right,’ said Shane; he’d heard the whistling too.

‘We can get over the gate easy, but I dunno if she bites,’ said Dermot. He was the one who told us the dog’s name. Paudie had got her as a pup off Colm Senior, when their own boxer bitch had got pregnant by some mongrel. That was her last lot of pups anyway; she’d died a few months later.

‘Yeah, sham. We could get in the shed now no problem, cos there’s no dog. But it’s broad daylight, like. If we go in in the night, we can have a good look ‘round; see if there’s *clues*.’

Shane had set this all up earlier. He made sure it was only him and me and Dermot, cos we were the ones that knew about the Paudie thing. We’d gone over to the big stones in the green to sit down. He’d said:

‘C’mere an' I tell ye. We’re going to catch Paudie, for Joe, sham.’

‘Whatcha mean, *catch* him?’ said Dermot.

‘For the murder, you spa. What you think I meant? We need to *investigate*, like. Folly him. See what we can find out.’ Shane said this like it was the most normal thing in the world. Like we did this every week; following suspects and collecting fingerprints.

‘Who are we now, the Scooby Doos? Why don’t we just tell the Gards, like?’ asked Dermot. I’d nodded too.

‘No, you fucking steamer!’ Shane’d stamped his foot on the grass. ‘The Gards won’t believe nothing coming from us, sham. How many times we been gived out to by the Shades, Dermot? Paudie’s probably reported us before; for the

eggs on Halloween, or putting them fireworks in his letterbox.' I'd forgotten that we did that; I'd looked at my feet with the shame when he'd reminded us.

'No Gard is going to believe someone from my family; or yours.' He meant Dermot.

'True, like. But what if Joe tells them? They'd have to take him serious, bud; it was him that...'

'Joe hasn't said a word to me since, sham. And he won't either. I don't blame him; no one wants to be a steamer. We've to catch this prick ourselves.'

'How?' It sounded stupid. Shane wasn't Poirot, or Columbo, it didn't matter how many magazines he'd read. I was cleverer than any of the boys, but what were we going to be looking for? We were only eleven or twelve, for God's sake.

'*Trophies*,' said Shane. We looked at him.

'What…' I said, 'like medals, for running?'

'Not sports trophies, no; trophies like hunters have. Like the heads on the wall.'

'Jaysus!' said Dermot. 'Did they not find his head, so? Tommy? That's… that's fucking rank, bud.'

'Will you get a grip, sham.' Shane had rolled his eyes at Dermot, and took a Silk Cut Blue off him. They must've been a new box, it was nearly full. 'I was watching this yoke the other night, see; on the cable. It was about serial killers, and the things they do. Fucking mad altogether, like.' We'd nodded at him to carry on. I liked this sort of stuff too, but Shane knew loads about it. 'Anyways,

that's one of the things they said,'

'Keeping the heads!' said Dermot.

'No, you gowlawalla. Keeping trophies. So he might take something, like her tights, or a necklace; to remind him of when he killed them, sham.'

'Ah, right…' I'd said. 'D'you think he's done it before, though?' Shane had been sniggering at us for saying 'serial killer' two days ago in the shed. Now he was mad into the whole idea.

'Of course he has, like. What about poor Joe?' Dermot had answered instead of Shane.

'Naw, I mean has he killed someone as well before?'

'We don't know, do we? I never heard nothing like that round here. He's not from Thomondgate though. Maybe he done it somewhere else. Or maybe he done it before, but no one found the body. Kids go missing all the time; some of them never get found.' We'd both nodded at him, even though we didn't know if it was true, cos it sounded true.

That's how we'd ended up here. Shane was going to let Dara in too, he said. Seán and Golly were gone, and even if they weren't, they'd have been too young and none of us trusted them; they'd only squeal. Joe was going to Kilkee on Monday, for two weeks. That would give us time. Shane thought that we'd have found the truth out by then. We'd be in the paper, and on telly. It *did* feel like we were in Scooby Doo, except we weren't looking for ghosts.

I hadn't told either of them about meeting yer one the day before. I

wasn't even sure if I was going to tell Dara about it now. She'd said she thought I was handsome. I didn't even think she was only taking the mick. I wasn't the handsomest one out of our lot. Girls liked Dara, and Shane was tough. Girls liked tough guys; well they did in the movies. Joe was tall; girls liked tall fellas as well. If I could just keep her to myself for a while, you never know what might happen. We went away from Paudie's; Shane said we'd come back later with Dara, after we'd told him the story.

Dad was out the front, cutting the grass with a pair of clippers. We'd no lawnmower any more; we normally borrowed Ger next door's one, but they were gone down to Lahinch, since yesterday. Everyone was on holiday except my family. It was lousy.

'Well?'

'How'rya.' I said. That wasn't a question either. I went to go past him into the house.

'Rich, wait a second…' He put the clippers down, and took off the gardening glove he had on one hand. The dog had ate the other one.

'Listen, come here. What have ye heard about the Kellys over the road, Rich?' His face didn't look sad or happy.

'We… we heard that the little boy's after . . he's after being killed; down the Quarry. Murdered.' I wasn't going to say 'raped' to Dad. You couldn't talk about sex things with your mam or dad.

'Ah, yeah. Yeah, tis awful all right. Well, your Mam wanted me to talk to you about it, but…' He stopped; he didn't know what else to say.

'Yeah? Ah, I know the score, Dad. She wants me to be careful, is it?'

'Ah, no. Well, yeah; there's that, of course. No, she wanted… well, if you'd any questions, you know?' I wasn't sure if he wanted me to say yes, or if he just wanted me to say no, and save him having to be awkward. He looked lost. I felt like I wanted to save him

'No, I've no questions, Dad. It's all right, shur.' He looked at me then. His eyes went wet, like he was going to start bawling. If we were in a film, he might have hugged me. But we were in Limerick, so he just said:

'Well, so,' and put his one glove back on.

It was a Sunday, so Mam was off doing a wedding. She'd bring back cake later, wrapped in a bit of tissue. It was nice, except for the marzipan. Chris wasn't upstairs, so I'd the room to myself. I didn't feel like doing anything, though. All my computer games were either rubbish or boring now. I'd got a big 90 minute cassette off Anthony up the road, with loads of pirated games taped on to it, but only about three of them worked. I lay down on my bed and thought about yer one yesterday. Marian. She was some ride altogether. I'd seen this film on video, called Can't Buy Me Love. Yer man in it was an awful nerd, but he had money. So he pays this gorgeous one a thousand dollars to pretend to be his girlfriend. Good film, like; until it got all mushy. But yer one in it; the girlfriend- she was something else altogether. That's who she reminded me of, that one in the film. I'd my hand inside my jocks now, thinking of her. I wasn't doing nothing. I wouldn't have known what to do: I'd heard people saying 'pull yourself' and 'go way and

pull your wire', nothing happened for me when I tried pulling it. It was hard as anything now, though. If anyone came into the room I'd be mortified.

She'd actually said she liked me. Well, she'd said something. I closed my eyes and thought about touching them tanned legs, or seeing her with her bra off, or kissing them gorgeous lips. I'd never kissed a girl properly, though. I didn't know how to. I shouldn't have thought about that, because it was putting me off now. My langer went back to normal, and I took my hand away from it. I took down a Fantastic Four from Chris' shelf; it was about the Silver Surfer. Yer one Sue Storm was a ride too. When she wasn't being invisible.

I'd dozed off for a while, then Joe called over. Dad sent him upstairs to my room; I was only half awake when he came in. I did up the buttons on my jeans fast when I heard him on the stairs. I could feel my face going scarlet. The last button wouldn't close. I just left it.

'All right, shur?' He was wearing his Celtic top; the home gear, green and white stripes.

'Yeah' I said, and I yawned at the same time. He yawned as well, cos yawns are catching.

'When you off to Kilkee?' I knew when he was off there; it was tomorrow. Small talk, though.

'In the morning, shur.'

'Rapid. Ye've a caravan down there, so?'

'A mobile home,' Joe said. A mobile home was a caravan with no wheels. Same thing.

'All right, so. Peter going down with ye?'

'Nah. He's working,' Peter was Joe's big brother; he used to live in England before. He'd an Englishman's haircut now; a side parting and a quiff. People changed when they went over there.

We went out the front. We were nearly out the gate, when I heard a girl's voice:

'Hiya, Richard.' It was yer one. She'd a strange voice; nothing Limerick about her. But I liked it. She sounded like the women off RTE.

'Uh, hi. You right, yourself?' I said. I could feel Joe's eyes burning into me.

'I'm good, yeah. Had to go confession.' She had black cycling shorts on, with luminous green stripes on. I was trying to not look at the bit between her legs.

'You did? Oh right.' I wasn't sure if she was serious; I didn't know her enough yet to know if she was joking. The skin on her arms looked as soft as butter; I wanted to touch her.

'Yeah. I got forty Our Fathers; thirty Hail Marys and ten Glory Bes.' She was only messing; I could tell now.

'What did you do?' I was still too awkward to say anything smart to her, but talking was getting easier.

'That's for me to know and you to find out.' She was gorgeous. I tried to think of something funny to say back to her, but Joe says:

'Are we going or what?' I looked at him, but he was looking at the floor; scarlet cheeks on him.

‘Ah, yeah. We are.’ I looked at her. She winked at me, and I almost had to turn around to stop her seeing my langer jump. She wouldn’t have seen it anyway, but still.

‘See ya round, Rich…’ She went back in the door.

‘Who’s she, like?’ said Joe, after a few minutes. He still sounded cross.

‘That’s yer one from next door,’ I said, but he already knew that.

There was no one out around, so we went to his place to have a go on the computer; he’d the same one as me, but his parents had got him a colour monitor, and it was a bigger one than mine, too. He had his a few years now, that was where I first played one. We were playing International Karate Plus, which was a mad laugh. Joe was saying he was looking forward to going away, even if it was only to Kilkee. I wasn’t even going to Kilkee this year, or Ballybunion, but I didn’t say nothing. I’d been hoping I wouldn’t see him before he went, cos I felt awkward about everything. It was all fine now, though. He seemed normal. He hadn’t said anything about Marian, and that kind of got me thinking about whether he actually might be one of them. But if he was, it wasn’t his fault. He couldn’t help what that man had made him into. It was lousy, though. I was no good at talking to girls, but at least I… anyway, he seemed all right today.

‘D’you want a drink?’ he said.

‘Yeah, go on.’ I was thirsty, definitely. He went into the kitchen, and came back with two cans of Harp.

‘Jaysus, what? Will they not notice?’ I said ‘they’; I meant his dad. His

mam didn't drink at all really.

'Nah. They'd a party last night, shur. Here, have some of them too:' He handed me a bowl of cocktail sausages. They were cold, but they were still good. I opened the can, and it bubbled up a bit too much. I took a swig; it was actually nice. Harp was what Mam used to drink before she started on Carling. She'd give me a little sip of it if I was in Frazer's to watch the match, or if she had to have me over with her cos there was no one to watch me at home for her. Mam was sound. It was scorching hot outside and inside too. Cold beer was lovely on those sorts of days. Cold anything was lovely. I was beating him in IK+, but he was a good loser, so we kept on playing.

After a bit, we heard the door opening, and Joe hid the empty cans under his chair It was his Da. I got very awkward, because I knew Jack would be drunk, and I knew Joe would be mortified, cos I was there. I sat silent for a bit, then we heard him go straight up to his bed. There was silence between us then, for ages.

'Probably polluted,' Joe said, finally. I'd never heard him say anything like that about his Da. I said nothing back.

'I'll go up later and rob a few pound out of his pockets. Fucking alcoholic cunt,' he said. I just looked straight forwards at the screen, and made sure my karate fella lost this one. Poor Joe; he'd had some life.

His mam came home later, and hunted me out so he could have his Sunday dinner. We weren't having one at ours, cos Mam was working. I went down to Pa's for a Calypso bar, or some Taytos.

I was still looking out for Paddy, but he didn't live in Thomondgate, so I

was safe enough. I thought about Paudie. When Dermot was telling me about what Paudie'd done to Joe, it was like my ears weren't listing to the disgusting bits. There was no need to know things that gays got up to; or the things that'd happen to you if a child molester got you. Child molester was a new word; before we used to call them 'kidnappers'; if you'd see a weird car pull up when you were out playing, one of you'd whisper 'Kidnappers!', then ye'd all scatter, for the laugh. There really was kidnappers in the world, though; Mam had warned us about them a few years ago. She hadn't explained it properly or anything, cos we were only small. She'd just said that there were bad people out there, who wanted to hurt kids. She said they wanted to hurt them in a really bad way, that she couldn't really tell us about. Mam was no good with that sort of thing; sex, I mean. I think it was because she was from Clare. Pa had no Calypsos, so I got a packet of So Longs, and some Banshee Bones.

'Well?' said Pa. He was chewing a match, or a toothpick. He hadn't shaved, so it made him look like Clint Eastwood.

'All right, Pa? Just these, please.' Pa'd only had the shop a few years; when we first moved here, it was owned by a woman called Suzie Wong. She wasn't a Chinee or anything; that was just her name.

'Twenty pence, pal. Ye know about the boy of the Kellys, yeah?' Pa said. I nodded at him, but I didn't say nothing.

'The Leader'll be full of it tomorrow, shur.' He was right. The Limerick Leader was a boring paper, but they'd go mad over this whole thing. Pa took the money out of my hand; there was no change off it. The So Longs were sticky; I ate

one, but the paper had got stuck to it.

'Hey!' Some blonde girl was standing in my way on the path. Took me a few seconds to realise who.

'Hi!' I wanted to say something clever, like 'We have to stop bumping into each other like this.' I didn't, though. No one said stuff like that in real life, and if they did, they didn't say it in Limerick.

'You going to the shop?' I asked. Of course she was going to the shop. Well done, Rich.

'Yeah. I've never been in there before though. Is it scary? Is the man a pervert?'

'What? Nah, it's fine.'

'Will you mind me?' Was she messing ? What if I took her seriously, when she was taking the mick? Mortified, I'd be.

'I, ah; I'll go in with you so.'

'My hero,' She smiled a little smile, and pretended to faint towards me, so I had to catch her. Her arms felt warm, and her hair smelt lovely; like shampoo and something else.

'Back again?' said Pa. He was only about five foot tall; not that scary at all.

'He couldn't keep away,' said Marian.

'Who's this, then?' said Pa; the dirty old man.

'She's Marian,' said Marian, before I could speak.

'The new girlfriend, is it?' Ah no, Pa. Mortify me anyway.

She smiled again, at him and then me. Gorgeous smile. I didn't know where to look.

'Anyway, milk!' she said. She was standing very close to me, and when she'd talk to me, she'd keep touching me; on the arm or the chest. Just for a second each time, but it felt like she was giving me electric shocks. She whispered to me:

'Do you think he has six other friends?'

'How d'you mean, like?'

'You know; so they can help with the housework?'

'Huh?' She was making no sense.

'In Snow White's house.'

'Hah!' Her head was close enough for her hair to tickle my face. Her skin didn't smell like anything I knew from before, but there was something in me that wanted to get her really near to me and breathe it all in. I felt dizzy just being close to her. I'd never be able to say something like that to the lads; it sounded handicapped.

She handed Pa the money for the milk, and we went outside. She was asking me things about Thomondgate; I didn't know all the answers. She was still close to me when we were walking, and she still touched me when we were talking. A few lads that I half-knew gave us the odd gawk. I felt a bit embarrassed, but kind of proud as well. She was the biggest ride in Thomondgate; Sandra Carey or Samantha Horan weren't half as gorgeous as her.

We turned the corner by Dara's house, and I seen the blondey hair poking

out from behind the skip outside Seán's house.

'Jakers!' I didn't think, I just pushed her into one of the doorways along the street. Paddy was right across the road. My face was in her neck; her head was on my shoulder. Her skin smelt gorgeous. My leg was sort of in between hers. She started talking, but I Shhhh'd her; she spoke again, but whispering:

'Hey! You could have just asked, Rich.'

'Huh? Oh, no. Naw. I'm hiding. I've to hide,' I said. My lips were so near the skin between her shoulder and her neck; I wanted to kiss it.

'Is that what they're calling it these days? What is it you're trying to hide, Rich? Where are you hiding it?' I couldn't see her, but I heard her giggling and I felt her face smile.

'I, ah. There's a lad called Paddy; he's after me.'

'Shur who'd blame him? Aren't you gorgeous altogether?' Janey Mack, she was going to give me the horn in a minute, and she'd feel it as well; our legs were that close. I was still breathing in the smell of her.

'Will I look out and see if he's gone? What's he look like?' she whispered. Her voice was so nice. I was going to be on the bone in a minute if she didn't shush.

'NO! Erm, naw. Thanks. Just… just stay here a minute; honestly.' I didn't give a fiddler's if Paddy was still out there; this was lovely. She didn't say nothing, but she did a little giggle again.

Paddy was gone, so we walked up to her house to give the milk in. I waited outside; I didn't want to meet no one's Mam or Dad. I was no good at that

sort of thing, and when your daughter's that much of a ride, you're probably horrible to any boys hanging around her. Especially if you're the dad. She came out in no time.

'Come on,' she said. She grabbed the sleeve of my T-shirt, and dragged me after her.

'Where we goin'?'

'What's in that field over there, behind the houses?' She meant Dolan's.

'Ah, nothing really. A few sheds, and some old banjaxed cars.' I nearly told her that me and the lads made camps there, but that'd make me sound about ten.

'Cool out. Let's go there.'

She kept walking through, until we were in a part of the field that you couldn't see from the outside. Jesus, was she going to get me to shift her? I couldn't shift her; I didn't know how to do it. I got scared and excited and mortified all at the same time. I looked at her legs and her backside, and the bra showing through the back of the T-Shirt. Janey Mack…

'D'you want to do something naughty, Richard?' She put her hand down the front of her shorts. Jesus Christ, she was going to take her fanny out and show me it and everything!

'Sorry about the squashing, I had to find somewhere to put them.' She'd pulled two fags out of her knickers. Thank God!

'Have you a light?' I did. I stayed standing up; she was sitting on the

grass. The fag tasted gorgeous, cos I was smoking it with her.

'It was funny when yer man in the shop asked was I your girlfriend, wasn't it?' she said, dragging on her fag.

'Yeah.' I said. No it wasn't funny; I'd nearly gone purple.

'Have you a girlfriend, no?' she said, in a little quiet voice. I liked all of her voices.

'Ah, not at the moment, no.' Not ever.

'Awww. Why not?'

'Dunno,' I said. I didn't like how she'd said 'Awww'. Like she was feeling sorry for me.

'You never know, eh?' she said, winking at me.

'What you mean?'

'Someone might come along…' She was beautiful. Her fingernails were shiny, and she hadn't been biting them; her hair was long and blonde and curly; her skin was perfect, like a painting. What was she doing here, smoking in a field, with me?

'I like you, Richie. You're cute. You don't say much, but you're handsome.' I couldn't take much more of this. If she was taking the mick after all that, I'd probably end up crying.

'Thanks,' I said. What else was I going to say?

We talked for a while. She asked me what school I was going to go to; she was in Salesian's secondary, across the road from Ardscoil. We'd be neighbours in September, kind of. We talked about our Mams and Dads: her Da

worked for the Corporation, her Mam worked in a clothes shop. She was an only child, but she wasn't spoiled. She didn't have a boyfriend. She accidentally put her hand in my hand for a second, and I wanted to keep it there, but I didn't. It was tea time way too soon, and I walked her over to her house, which was the same as walking over to my own house. I was already mad about her, but it didn't feel good. It felt like I sort of wanted to get sick, or it felt like someone was sticking their knuckles into my chest. It didn't feel good to be this mad about someone who had no idea you were mad about them, cos you didn't get any of the good stuff like the shifting, or the boys being jealous. You just got the horrible pains when you thought of someone else taking her off you.

It was dull out, later on; it wasn't dark though. Summer days were long, especially this summer. When I was small, I used to hate going to bed while it was still bright. We were up on the roof of Dara's shed; he knew about the Joe and Paudie thing now. Shane must've told him, cos I hadn't.

'Is that the telly, sham?' asked Shane. We were looking across at Paudie's; you could see it easily from up on this roof.

'I think so, yeah. Would he have a telly in his bedroom?' Dara asked.

'He could. He mightn't have one downstairs. Or it might be a computer, or something,' I said. You could get computer games for adults, like Leisure Suit Larry, for the IBM. That had a load of cursing in it, and sex. It was only cartoons though. You couldn't really see nothing.

'He has one downstairs, bud. I seen it. Maybe he has two?' Dermot had

been in there before, when they'd sold the dog to Paudie, probably.

'Smoke on that, sham,' said Shane to Dermot. Dara'd brought his binoculars; Shane was hogging them.

'Throw us over them, a sec,' said Dara.

'Naw, g'way. I'm not finished.'

'You can't smoke a fag and look through binoculars, like.'

'Watch me, sham.' He was something else.

We'd been there for a half an hour, keeping tabs on Paudie. We were going to wait and see if he went out. Or if he went to bed. Then we could go have a root around out the back; and the shed, if it was open. You'd have to be careful doing stuff like that, cos you couldn't just break a window to get in; he'd be onto you. The police were allowed to do anything they like; we were more like Magnum P.I. He was a private detective, so even though he'd a gun, he wasn't a policeman. He could get arrested by the real police. So could we.

'There he is! Shhhh, will ye?' Dunno what Shane was shushing us for; we were miles away from the house. I ducked down anyway, like an eejit. Paudie was in one of the upstairs rooms; the one on the right. There was no net curtains, so you could see straight in. The light in there looked funny; like it wasn't coming from the ceiling.

'What ye think he's doing, lads?' said Dara. I looked at Paudie, in the room with the funny light. He wasn't doing anything. The room was kind of green looking; the parts that weren't dark, anyway.

'That's probably the room where he keeps the trophies…' said Shane.

'And clippings from the newspapers…' That youngfella watched too many videos, I swear to God. His mind was *warped*, as Mam would say.

'Shur there's been nothing in the papers, yet,' I said, then straight away wished I hadn't. It was never worth arguing with Shane; you wouldn't win.

'I meant from all the other murders, you handicap. Anyway, there'll be loads in the Leader tomorrow…'

'Would you say he pulls himself in there, like? Thinking of little boys?' said Dara.

'You're some steamer altogether,' Shane stubbed the fag out. Dara just sniggered. I'd come along, but my mind was somewhere else. I was wondering if she'd wanted me to shift her, earlier. And was she disappointed in me now? When you'd hear anyone talking about shifting a girl, they'd usually do it somewhere like that, away from anyone else. That was cos if she let you get anything, no one would be walking past and say something to ye. You'd always hear stories about people getting caught shifting by someone's mam or dad. Or by a priest.

I only knew what I'd heard from other people; I'd never done nothing with no one. Shifting was the proper kissing they did in films, French kissing. If she was easy, she'd let you raise the hand. If ye'd been going away with each other for a few weeks, she'd let you drop the hand. Girls would do things to you as well, but that didn't happen as much. Dara said that he'd had a few girls pull his mickey for him. He'd got half a blow job once, too. Off a tinker girl, at the Two Mile Inn disco. Yer one Marian was gorgeous, and she was older than us. She'd probably had loads of fellas; she'd laugh her head off at me if I tried to shift her.

'Wait a minute, bud; what's that?' Dermot had the binoculars now. I squinted over at the room again. There must've been a lamp on the floor, or on a bedside locker. That's why the light looked so weird in there, with the shadows on the ceiling. Paudie had gone out, and come back with only a towel on. He was white looking. Milk bottle skin on him.

'Jaysus, will you look at the state of him.' Shane said. Paudie had one towel around his waist, and another one now in his hands. His belly shook when he dried his hair with the second one.

'He *looks* like a child molester, though,' said Dara. He looked disgusting. He was rubbing the hair faster now; he shook so much that the towel around his middle came open and dropped off. He caught it before we saw his langer, though. We all went 'Ewwww' at the same time. Then he turned around and looked straight at us.

'Jaysus fuck!' said Dara.

'Get down!' said Dermot. We did, crapping ourselves. Then the scared feeling turned into a funny feeling, and we all started giggling, and I burst out laughing. He hadn't seen us. We were miles away. What was he doing being half naked in front of a window with no curtains, anyway? That was a bit sick. Kids could be watching. I wished we could just go to the Gards now; he was getting away with everything. Poor Tommy. Poor Joe.

'Fucking hell, bud. That was close,' Dermot sparked up another fag; Dara shouted 'After' on it. It smelt nice. Sometimes they smelt nice.

'It was in its bollix, close. Shur he has no idea we're over here. He just

looked to see did anyone see his mickey,' said Shane. It was true; I nodded. I was glad I hadn't the binoculars when that towel fell.

'Sup on that?' I said; Dermot had a supercan of Lilt.

'Yeah, no probs, bud.' Paudie was finished drying himself. There must've been a mirror in front of him, because he kept leaning in and checking his hair, or what was left of it, as Mam would say. The window was big and low; you could see into the room, and the bed in there was high enough so it came up over the top of the sill. Paudie sat down, and started rooting around underneath it. I had the binoculars.

'Here, bud.' Dermot was passing me the Lilt, but I pushed it away, cos I couldn't do two things at the one time. Paudie'd a magazine now. He'd got it out from under the mattress.

'What's that in his hand, sham? Gissa look, will ye? Here!' Shane tried to grab the binoculars off me, but I wriggled away.

'Skin mag, I think,' I said. My heart was speeding. I couldn't see a name on it or anything; he'd already it open and folded over. It was a skin, though. Lots of nudey pictures in it. I was holding my breath. The lads were all trying to see what was going on, without binoculars.

'Jaysus, he's going to pull himself. With the curtains open,' said Dara. I was rooted to the spot. I didn't want to see that. Couldn't look away either though.

He put the magazine on his lap. Then he put his hand down the front of the towel, having a feel of himself.

'Jaysus, bud. The dirty fucker.' Dermot was whispering, even though we

were miles away.

'Fucking hell, sham. What's in the magazine? Steamers is it? Is it steamers? Lemme have a see.'

'Nah. Girls, I think,' I said. I ignored what he said about seeing. I was holding on to the binoculars. Paudie was having a go at himself under the towel with one hand, and turning the pages of the magazine with the other one. His belly was jiggling, and he had sort of got diddies, like a woman. I couldn't see his langer, but I didn't want to either. This was bad enough.

'Aw, lads. God help us, like,' said Dara, laughing. I was holding onto the binoculars like they were the bars on a rollercoaster. Paudie's hand was moving up and down faster, and he was flicking through it pure quickly. This was wanking; this was pulling your wire; this was tossing off. He moved around a little, and pushed the towel off himself.

'Jesus, Mary and Joseph,' said Dermot. Dara's eyes were bulging. Shane had his hands half over his eyes, like it was a horror movie.

'Ah, lads. Jaysus. I'm going to vomit, sham. You can keep them binoculars, Richie; you steamer.'

Paudie's langer was all swelled up, and red like a dog's one. It was bigger than his hand, and he was pulling the skin on it up and down. He'd his eyes closed now, the magazine had fell on the floor.

'He's going to spunk off,' said Dara. I didn't know; maybe he was. I didn't want to see that, but I did as well. Janey Mack…

'Ye're all steamers, lads. Watching a steamer pulling his wire.' Shane

wasn't even looking any more. He was having a fag. Dermot called smoke on it. Paudie slowed down and stopped pulling himself. His langer was gone smaller. I froze for a second, in case he stopped altogether and looked over at us. I'd actually been thinking that he might be doing this on purpose in this room, and hoping someone would see him. Like when flashers show their mickeys to old ladies. Or he might just not care. He went under the bed again.

'Has he spunked?' said Dara. I shook my head. Paudie came out from under the bed with a shoebox. He took something out of it; small and white and square. He spitted into his hand, and rubbed the spit on his langer, and it started to get big again. My stomach did a little cat's tumble, and I took the binoculars away from my eyes for a second. He looked at the white thing, and started pulling himself again. The towel was long gone; you could see the lot. His balls were hairy, and bright red as well.

'What is it?' said Dermot.

'It's a photo!' Dara answered.

'That's not a photo: it's not big enough.' Shane was looking again. He had to squint.

'It's a Polaroid, you eejit.' Dara was being brave, all of a sudden. He was right though; it was a Polaroid. Paudie was wanking like mad now: eyes open, staring at the Polaroid.

'Ah, Jaysus,' went Shane. 'It's a photo of Tommy…'

Oh God, he could have been right. You didn't need to bring Polaroids into the chemist to get them developed. They were automatic. If you wanted no

one to look at what you were talking pictures of, Polaroids would be how you did it. Mam said they were too expensive, and they faded after a while. All photos faded, though.

'The fucking dirty cunt.' Shane was really angry. I looked in the binoculars again; Paudie's hand had stopped. We must've missed him spunking off while we were talking. He was panned out on the bed, his belly was going up and down with the breath. He was disgusting. After a while, he sat up.

'Is he finished or what?' said Dermot. I shhhh'd him. Paudie took the hand he'd been pulling himself with, and licked the back of it, and then the front. He was after eating his own spunk.

I gave the binoculars back to Dara, and took out a fag that I'd robbed off Mam. Shane looked over to claim a smoke. I'd never seen him look so angry before. A feeling came into my head then, very hard to describe. It was like one of us there was after dying, even though I was looking at them all, and they were fine. I smoked nearly half of the fag with one pull, but it didn't do me no good. Mam said they only calmed you down if you were a real smoker. Shane's smoke didn't calm him down either. Me and Dermot and Dara had to actually convince him not to go straight over to the house and knock on the door. I was glad we did, cos he was so raging, I'd've doubted even the three of us together could have holded him back.

We waited there a while more, even when it got cold, but Paudie wasn't going anywhere that night. He got dressed after a while, then went downstairs. We could only see him when he went into the kitchen, cos the other back room had

blinds. He made some food in a massive frying pan, like you'd see in a Chinese restaurants in the karate movies; there was a load of smoke, so he opened the window. We got bored very quickly, even Shane did. He was saying we should go over there and have a look in his shed, but the dog was out the back. I'd said why didn't we wait until we saw him out walking the dog in the morning, and couldn't we go in then? Everyone agreed, they must've been as tired as me.

They were all sitting in front of the telly like zombies, when I got in.

'How're ya, Rich?' Mam said, when I went past. She was still in her work clothes from doing the wedding.

'Grand.' I went out the back, to see if yer one was around. No one except Rex was there. I wanted to go upstairs anyway, for a while.

'What are ye watching?'

'A film' said Mam

'What is it?'

'Shhhhh, will you?' said Chris.

'Will ye leave him alone now, Christopher. Big Gun it's cal-'

'Top Gun!'

'It's only started, shur. Sit down there for yourself, now.' Mam said.

'Nah, I seen it already.'

'You have in your ring!' said Chris

'Christopher! Language!'

'Sorry, Mam.' He got away with murder. I went on up the stairs, and

closed our room door behind me.

The curtains were still open, and the room was lovely and warm from all the sun that had got trapped in there during the day. I lifted up my mattress, and felt around under it. I found what I was looking for, and put it under the pillow, in case anyone came in. I was going to have to get under the quilt; that was the safest. I took off my top and my jeans, and got in under. That way, it looked like I'd just gone to bed early, if anyone asked. Under the covers, I sat up a little bit, so it was like a tent. I had my torch with me, the one I got in the pound shop. It really did feel like I was camping, only it was warm and dry. I took the thing out from under the pillow, and switched on the torch. I wasn't going to be able to hold on to it, so I propped it up with the pillow, and let it shine down.

The magazine was an English one; I'd robbed it from Dara's house a few weeks ago. My heart was racing. I flicked through the letters page, and all the jokes. There were ads to phone up girls and stuff, with dirty words under them. They were all naked, the girls. The words were all filthy, I didn't understand half of them. My langer was already stiff. I looked at the first girl; her name was Jasmine. She'd black hair, and normal sized diddies. As you went through, she'd take more clothes off. I was flicking the pages with my right hand first, but then I swapped hands, cos I wanted my good hand for the other thing. I tried to remember what Paudie had been doing, even though I didn't want to think about him, or the things he'd done to little boys. Jasmine was smiling out at me, with her bra off, and her legs open. She'd a hairy fanny; I didn't know if that was cos she was English or what. I wondered if there was any Irish girls who were in skin

mags or blue movies; and what did their mothers think of them?

The next girl was called Harriet. She was a blonde one, with golden legs, like Marian. My mickey got fierce hard looking at her, but I still wasn't sure if I was doing it right. I got to the end of Harriet's photos very quickly; that was disappointing. The girl after that was rotten; I even stopped pulling myself until I got past her. Ginger hair and freckles- disgusting. The next bit made me nearly explode; two gorgeous yokes, shifting each other, like. Tongues and everything. Lesbians. There was a blonde one, with massive diddies, and a black one. I'd never seen a black girl with no clothes on. The blonde one was giving her a lickout, and you could see right up her fanny. It was pink inside, same as a white girl's one would be. I liked the black one; she was called Shaz, or she might a been Denise. They didn't say.

What I was doing was the same as what he'd been doing. I was holding it in my fist, and stroking it up and down. Nothing was happening, though. There was a feeling like an itch or a tickle in the head of it, but I didn't know what it was supposed to feel like when you were doing it right. I went through another few girls, but after a while I was just getting sore. I stopped, and put the magazine back under. I flipped my pillow over onto the cold side, and lay there thinking about Marian, and what she'd look like with no clothes on. I'd my hand inside my jocks, just touching it, but not pulling it any more. That was nice. She was more gorgeous than any of them nudey English girls. I felt lovely, nice, love feelings for her. Like in a Disney cartoon, or a romantic film. I felt dirty, disgusting feelings about her too, though; those were the ones in my head when I fell asleep.

I had to sneak past Mam in the morning, and put my sheets and my quilt cover and my jocks in the washing machine. She came in while I was trying to turn it on, and she showed me how. She'd a big proud look on her face, cos I'd brought my washing down by myself. I'd nearly had a heart attack when I woke up; then I realised what had happened. Dara had told us before about Wet Dreams. It was all normal; he'd had them himself, shur. I was a man now, whether I wanted to be or not.

Five

Paudie took the dog out for a walk at about eleven the next morning. The plan was: two of us would follow him, and the other two would go inside and see what we could find. I wanted to be one of the ones following, but Shane picked me to go inside, along with him. It felt good that he wanted me to do it, so I said yes. We were sitting on the grass across from the house, pretending that we weren't watching.

'He's not coming out, lads,' said Dara. 'I don't think that dog gets any walks.'

'She does, bud. I seen him over in Shelbourne with her the other day. My da wouldn't've given it to him if he wasn't gonna walk her.'

'He'll be out, sham,' said Shane. I was trying to get some bits of Stinger bar out of the cavities in my teeth, with my tongue. I needed fillings the last time I was at the dentist, but I'd missed the appointment to come back. Dara leaned over to me, keeping his voice down:

'Have you seen yer one, yet?'

'Who's that?' I knew who he meant.

'The little ride; next door to ye. I seen her again this morning.' Had he?

'Did you?'

'Yeah. She was wearing a little pair of jeans shorts. And a bra.'

'A bra?' He was just making things up, now.

'Yeah, well a bikini top. Have ye seen her yet? Rich… Fu-ckin tits on it…' I wanted to hit him in the face.

'I spoke to her a few times, yeah…' He was going to find out anyway.

'Jaysus, have you? What's she like? Is she a knacker?'

'No!' I said it way too loud, and Shane looked over for a sec. Then he just went back to talking to Dermot. Dara goes:

'All right, Rich; I was only asking. Is she sound, then? Or is she an aul' bitch? Rides are usually bitches.' He'd know, I supposed; with his sisters.

'Naw, she's sound. 'I didn't want to say any more. I didn't want him to meet her; I didn't want any of them to. She liked me, maybe. If she thought I was handsome, she was bound to think Dara or Dermot were even handsomer. I'd to keep her for myself a bit more.

'I don't give a fiddler's anyway; I only want her for her body, like.' I still wanted to hit him, but he was only being Dara.

'Right, whisht!' Shane said, in a quiet voice. We sneaked a look over, and saw Paudie coming out the gate, with Molly in front of him. She wasn't on the leash, but he had it in his hand. He looked at us for a second, and we all looked away at the same time. Pure obvious.

Dermot and Dara waited until Paudie'd got to the bollards at the end of the path, then they got up to follow him. Dermot had a ball with him, cos they were probably going to Shelbourne Park. Shane and me had a Frisbee. We walked around the back of Paudie's. We didn't need anyone to be a look-out; when the walk was over, Dermot and Dara were going to run back before Paudie, and give

us the shout to get out. It was a good plan.

'Right. I'll go over here, and you throw it to me,' said Shane. We'd have a few goes of throwing it to each other first, before we threw it over the wall.

'Okay. Who's climbing over anyway?' I said. I didn't want to go in there; anyone from the other houses could see us. One of them might phone the Gards.

'You climb over; then, you open the gate for me.' Hang on… How did that work? If one of us went over, we could say that it was to get the Frisbee, yeah. But why would I be letting him in through the gate?

'We'll say that you couldn't find it by yourself. We'll say it went in the big bushes.' Shane was way ahead of me as usual.

'Sound. Go on then.' I threw the Frisbee nice and soft. It curved over his head, and went straight over the wall. Jakers!

'Jesus fucking Christ…What the fuck do we do now? You handicap.' He was angry with me, but it was an accident. I couldn't help it if I was bad at sports.

'I'll go over now.' It was the only thing I could think of saying. He gave me a legger, and I missed the wall first, but I went straight over the second time. I landed on hard grass and a thistle. I pulled the thorns of it out of my tracksuit bottoms, and looked around the garden. He didn't have any flowers, but the grass was cut short. Molly'd gone to the jacks everywhere though; I had to tiptoe around all the dog do. I wasn't sure if I was supposed to walk up and down, pretending to look for the Frisbee. It was right in front of me. I walked all over the garden, saying things like 'Damn it!' and 'Where's it gone?' just in case any of the neighbours were looking at me from their windows. We were lucky that the

Frisbee was green, so it didn't stick out straight away when you looked at the garden.

'Pssst' It was Shane, outside the gate. I turned around, and dodged more lumps of kacka, on the way to the gate. The lock was stiff, but I opened it with a push.

'Right, sham. Is his shed locked?' said Shane.

'I didn't… I haven't been over-

- watch out!' I stopped him walking in the dog mess.

'Fuck! You'd think he'd clean that up.'

'Yeah, it's rank all right.' I looked on the bottom of my shoes, but they were fine. The shed was a wooden one; like one you buy and build yourself. Much smaller than ours. There was a bolt going across, with a padlock on it.

'Fuck's sake!' Shane hit the door with the palm of his hand. Paudie would have that key; either on him, or inside the house.

'Hang on,' I said. I'd seen a window round the back of it. We went to look.

'Ah, shur; I'll never get in through that,' said Shane. He was right; it was very small altogether. I tried putting my arm through, then my head. The window was one of those wide ones, but it was only a few inches high.

'Go on, sham,' said Shane, excited. I got my other shoulder in, and then my back.

'Gimme a hand!' I said. I'd be able to get in, but I might end up hopping my forehead off the floor. Shane got his hand round my waist; then, he held me

steady while I went through, bit by bit. I felt like I was the thread that he was putting through the needle.

'Go on, sham; you're nearly in!' I was upside down now; my fingers were touching the floor. It smelt like old newspapers in there, and mouldy orange skins. It was dark, too.

Shane had to let go of me eventually; there was too much weight on my side of the window, like on a see-saw. I didn't fall that hard, my hands saved me.

'Right. Have a look around, sham. I'll keep a look out.' I heard him striking a match, and the smell of fags came through the window. It wasn't easy to see things in here, but the sunlight was pretty strong down this end. I was crapping myself, though. It'd take a good while to get back out that window, so even if he was keeping a look-out, I was screwed if Paudie came back. I mightn't get caught straight away, but I'd have to hide in here until tonight. I wished I was back home now, maybe talking to Marian.

'Anything good?' said Shane, between pulls.

'Nothing yet; I'll give you a shout,' I said.

'Right… look for trophies, sham.' He was going to attract attention if he didn't keep quiet. I couldn't say that to him, obviously. There were piles of magazines on the table; some of them were just the sort you'd get with the Sunday papers. There was ones called 'Observer', ones from the Sunday Times and a few News of the World ones. Those ones had some women in bikinis in them, but they weren't skin mags. Even if he had some dirty magazines, it didn't prove nothing about him. Lots of men liked looking at naked women. The one he'd been looking

at the night before had been of naked women, not little boys. There probably wasn't skin mags with little boys in them, though. These magazines here weren't evidence; there was nothing.

Up on one of the shelves, there was a bottle of liquid. Kidnappers always put some sort of liquid on a cloth, and when they put the cloth under your nose, you'd faint. Clora foam is was called. There was a label on the bottle, but it had got faded away. The only thing I could still see on it was an orange box, with a black X in it. I couldn't remember if that meant 'poisonous' or 'don't get it near your skin', but I'd seen it on bottles under the sink in our house, so it probably wasn't any sort of special kidnapper stuff. There was nothing here; I wanted to go back out now, before Paudie got back and I ended up being caught over nothing.

'Richie? Rich?'

'What?'

'What's in there?'

'Nothing. Just a few magazines. Some turps, or something. Few tins of paint.'

'No drawers or presses?'

'Naw. Oh, wait. Maybe.' I hadn't looked in the chest of drawers.

'No sign of the other two; carry on, sham,' he said. Easy for him to say; when Paudie came back, he'd just be able to hop over the gate and get away.

The top drawer had nothing in it, only an empty naggin of Power's. The second one looked like it had jumpers in it. The last one was full of empty Tayto packets, and mouldy crusts off of bread. I'd to close my nose. I was about to tell

Shane to help me get out the window, when something told me to have another look in the middle one. I lifted up a few jumpers, and my heart leapt when I saw what was under them.

They were magazines, in another language; it looked like German. They'd men on the front of them, but they looked like very strange men. They'd all got 'taches, and no tops on. Like builders in the summer, only none of them had porter bellies. I flicked through one, and nearly screamed. They were full of men, having sex with men. They were looking straight out of the page at me, while some other fella was riding them from behind. You could see everything: the langer going inside their backside; fellas licking each other's balls; one fella was even pulling another guy's behind open, and licking his hole. Janey Mack, I couldn't look at it any more. I did, though. I looked at them all. There were orgies, with loads of men riding each other at the same time. There were auld fellas riding little skinny fellas. And there was spunk; so much spunk. Spunk on fella's faces; spunk all over their backsides; spunk dribbling out of lad's mouths. This was worse than any skin mag I'd ever seen. I'd one last one to look at, when Shane whistled outside the door. Jaysus! They were back, that must be it. I was trapped in here, with Paudie's dirty gay mags, and the liquid for making you unconscious. Then, something dropped out of the magazine that was in my hand. It was a Polaroid picture. Shane banged the door down.

'Get out, sham! Get fucking out, now! SOS! Mayday!' My eyes went to the door, then to window, then to the photo on the ground, then to the window. I picked it up, and shoved it back into the magazine. Shane was banging again.

'Richie! Can ye hear me?! The lads are here! Paudie's gone in the front!' I put the magazine back underneath the rest. I didn't know what page the photo had fell out from. In two seconds, I was hanging out the window. Shane nearly pulled my arms out of my sockets, dragging me out. I was halfway through now…

'C'mon to fuck, will ye?' Shane's face was red, and his eyes looked crazy.

'I'm trying; I'm trying!' I wanted to cry, a proper cry like you'd do and them your Mam would hug it better. I was almost out, but the more I panicked, the bigger I got, and the harder it was to get me through the gap.

'Richie! He'll be putting the fucking dog out in a minute; come out the fucking window, will ye?'

'I'm trying!' I said again, but my voice had got tiny. Jesus Christ; they'd been licking each other's holes. Licking the spunk out of each other's holes. He hadn't seen it; He hadn't had to look at it. I heard Molly barking. I felt like my life was going to flash in front of my eyes now. Shane looked at me, all helpless; then his face got angrier than I'd ever seen it, and he put one foot against the shed, and dragged the whole of my body through the window frame. I felt the skin on my hips tear on the side of the window frame; it stung like mad. I was through though. We both belted for the gate; he got there first. He stopped.

'What are you doing?' I screamed at him. He was going to get us killed!

'We cant leave it open, sham. He'll know we were in here.' He was right, but I didn't feel like agreeing with him now. Why couldn't one of us go through first, then the other one stay and lock it? There wasn't time to ask. I heard Paudie

somewhere behind, talking to the dog.

'Go on, so. Go on and have your water; good girl, shur.'

Shane pushed the stiff lock down, and got over the gate in two seconds. I was next; I'd never moved so fast in my life.

We hit the ground on the other side, and didn't stop. We were in the green around the corner before either of us even took a breath. I lay back on the grass and rubbed my sore hip. Dara and Dermot had been outside the gate, but they'd scattered before me and Shane had got out; I'd have been annoyed with them if I'd had the energy. Shane was gasping like someone who'd just done a marathon; the fags were going to kill him some day and he wasn't even a teenager yet. My head was spinning with dirty pictures of gay fellas doing things to each other's holes. I wanted to get sick, but I'd nothing in my belly except the Stinger. I wasn't going to tell them about the Polaroid.

Mam was home when I got in. She was in the kitchen, rolling some dough; she made a lovely soda bread sometimes.

'How're ya, love?' she said. She was wearing her jeans, so she probably didn't have work today.

'Grand. What you making?'

'Ah, just an auld soda, love.' Her smile was back to normal. She'd still said nothing to me about Tommy Kelly. She'd asked Dad to have a word, and he probably told her that he'd taken care of it. I couldn't picture Mam talking to me about something like that. I wondered what was for lunch, or maybe it was time

for dinner, even.

The lads had all wanted to know about the shed. They couldn't believe their ears when I told them about the mags. Shane thought I was making it up:

'You're only shitting us, sham. There's no skin mags with faggets in them, is there, Dara?'

'Ah, I dunno, shur. I did see some magazines in Spain with fellas on the front, but I just thought they'd have the girls on the inside. I don't think you'd be able to buy steamer magazines in the corner shop over there, no.'

'See?' Shane says, at me.

'You might have to get them in the sex shop, like,' said Dara. I'd never heard of a sex shop.

'What's that?'

'The sex shops are where you get the blue movies; if you want to buy them.' I didn't know you could buy them. The ones we'd watched were always terrible looking, and Dermot said that was because people would rent them from the shop, then record them with their video camera and keep them to pass round.

I carried on telling them what the gays were doing in the magazines. Dermot was skitting; Dara looked like he'd heard it all before. Shane was raging.

'I knew he was a fucking child molester,'

'Well, a steamer anyway,' said Dara.

'Same fucking thing,' said Shane.

‘Would chips and something do you, Rich? I’ve hardly anything in the house til I go get the messages.’ said Mam.

‘Yeah; have ye sausages?’ I rubbed my cut, and made a face cos of the stinging.

‘What have ye done to yerself, Rich. Show me and I see.’ She lifted my T-Shirt up, and she done a ‘Fssssss’.

‘Jesus, let me get the lotion.’ She meant iodine; I didn’t want that, it would sting worser.

‘Nah, I’m all right, shur,’ I said, but she took no notice.

I bit my lip when the iodine got in the cut and stung it. When you were getting something like this done, it was half like you were in the war and the nurse was treating you, and half like you were only a baby, and your mam was rubbing Sudocreme on your sore backside. She put the lotion away, and kissed me on the forehead. That definitely wasn’t what the nurse in the war would’ve done, but it felt nice, so it was grand.

The lads had asked lots more questions about the skin mags. I’d answered everything I could, and made up answers if I couldn’t. Talking about it was making me feel sick in one way, but it was actually making me on the horn a bit too, just because I was talking about riding. I wasn’t a gay, though. Marian was what I wanted; she was the one I had dirty dreams about that I couldn’t remember. I wanted to go home now and see her. Seeing her would clean the gay feelings out of me. It was around lunch time; the lads would be going home in a bit.

'That be enough chips for you, Rich?' said Mam, showing me three potatoes. One was big, and the other two were small, but I had no idea how many chips you get from a potato.

'Was it fell over you did, yeah?' she asked.

'Yeah. I was up on Joe's skateboard, and I came off of it.' That was a stupid lie; what if she knew that Joe was in Kilkee?

'Ah, well; I told you to be careful on those things, didn't I, Rich?'

'Yep.' Mam hated anything dangerous; she'd seen a fella's head come off once, in a bike crash in front of Jury's. We weren't even allowed to mention motorbike in our house, let alone talk about wanting one. Dad was gone out. Mam said he'd gone to a funeral. She didn't say whose funeral. I wondered would it have been little Tommy's. Dad went to a lot of funerals. I'd never been to one; I was too young to know anyone that would be dying. The chips were on, and Mam had taken out the big frying pan to do the sausages

'Ye know I worry about ye, don't ye, Rich?' Mam was in one of her moods.

'Yeah, Mam.' I was getting an appetite, smelling the fat in the pan.

'I wouldn't want nothing to happen to ye, shur; and Christopher.'

'Yeah, I know.'

'Ye haven't met anyone acting… weird, around here, have ye?'

'No. No one weird, Mam. Why?'

'Ah, oh. Nothing, Rich. I'm just checking. Ye're all right, shur. There's

no fear of ye.'

'Yeah, shur. I'm fine, Mam. Just a little scratched,'

The food was ready; she put the chips on a plate with a clean tea towel on it; to soak up the grease.

'Wash yeer hands before ye eat, Rich,' she said. I took a smell of my fingers, then I turned the hot tap on. Mam hung round me while I ate my chips and sausages; she looked like she was going to say something a few times, but then she looked like she'd changed her mind. I looked at her with my eyebrows up, like to say: -Is there something you want to tell me?- but she just looked away.

I heard Dad coming in from the funeral. Chris didn't seem to be around, but he could've been upstairs again. Dad came into the kitchen, but he didn't say nothing to me or to Mam; not even a 'Well?', like we'd normally get. Mam was washing the cups and saucers, and Dad tried to get past her for an ashtray. She stood where she was, and didn't get out of the way. Dad tried to get to the press where the clean ones were, but he couldn't get to them. He made a huffing sound, and then turned to go away into the hall. Mam said:

'Here, shur,' and got him one down. He didn't look at her when he took it, but he said:

'Thanks' in a small voice. I don't like any of what was happening, or the way it made me feel. I brought my plate over to the sink, and said:

'Thanks' in an even smaller voice than Dad's. I smelled my fingers again, walking up the stairs. Hopefully, Chris wouldn't be in the bedroom.

I'd walked up the road with Dermot, cos he lived the nearest to me. He wanted to know about the skin mags again; I was tired of telling it by now.

'Was there no girls at all, like? Just men?' His face was blushing.

'Nope. No women. Just fellas with their clothes off. Touching each other's mickeys,' I'd told them all of this already. It still felt cool, though; being the one who had the scala.

'And they were sucking each other's langers, like?'

'Yeah,'

'Sixty nines?'

'A few, yeah.' I'd no idea, I was just saying yes.

'Jaysus, bud. How is that even legal?'

'It was German, or something.' I had no idea what that language had been, but he wasn't going to be able to check.

'Ah right, bud; I suppose they might allow it over there. They're all evil, aren't they; the Nazis, shur.'

'Yeah. Probably different laws, like.'

'D'you think yer man Paudie did it, then?' he asked me. It was a good question.

'Well, if Joe says that he… you know, with him… you'd say Yeah, wouldn't you?' I wished I'd heard Joe saying it, myself. He was in Kilkee now, but even if he wasn't, I wouldn't have asked him.

'I dunno, bud. It's a bit mad. He's definitely a steamer, but…'

'Yeah.' I remembered the fellas in the magazine. I remembered the

Polaroid, too.

'It's disgusting, like. I'm glad it wasn't me that seen them skin mags, bud. No offence, like.' Dermot was sound.

'Yep, rotten.' I couldn't get the pictures out of my head, now. The worst thing about seeing gays, was how hairy everyone was. At least in a normal skin mag or a blue, the women would only have hair on their fannies. Men were hairy all over, so when you had two men, or three men…

'Well, if he's looking at that sort of thing, there's something not right about him anyway,' Dermot said. I was gasping with the thirst.

'I don't know, Derm.'

'I dunno either, bud. Shane thinks we should just hang them all. The steamers, like.'

Shane wasn't here now, so I could disagree with him:

'Ah now, they can't help it if they're gay, can they?'

'What you mean?' Dermot raised his eyebrows.

'I mean like, if you wanted to be normal, but you just don't fancy women,'

'How could you not fancy women? I mean, like… I don't fancy Paula O'Keefe… but how could you not fancy a ride? How could you not fancy Kylie?'

'Shane doesn't fancy Kylie,' I sniggered, but so did Dermot.

'I'll tell him you said he was a steamer!' He was messing. We stopped outside his house.

'Right, bud. See you later.' He hopped over the small gate, without

opening it.

'All right, sound.'

Marian was in sitting on the pillar outside their front garden. I suddenly felt like my face was too hot; my tongue was too big, and my feet were on the wrong legs.

'How're ya, handsome?' she said; that smile again. Janey Mack. She was wearing a yellow T-Shirt that said 'Malibu'. I tried looking at her face and not at her chest.

'Ah, hi. What are you?'

'I'm a human being, Richie. What are you?' Ah Jesus anyway.

'I meant *how* are you…'

'I know what you meant; have you to go in now, for your lunch?' She'd a skirt on today; short, so you could see all of her legs.

'No. No, I had it already.' I hadn't, but I was suddenly not hungry any more.

'Jeez, you must eat early, so. It's only twelve o'clock.' She had sandals on; her toes had pink nail varnish on them.

We went for a walk out past Kileely, cos she wanted a walk, and that was the only one I knew. We talked about the films we liked: she knew way more films than me; girls normally didn't know stuff like that. She was older though. I asked her about her school: she had lots of friends there, but there were a lot of cows there too. The nuns were horrors, as well. I told her that there was no nuns in

Ardscoil where I was going in September, but they'd have the Christian Brothers, who were the same thing, really. Up past the Barrack Lane, we went over to the pond with the swans. There was some auld one there, throwing bread in.

'This is nice, Rich.' She sat on the ground and put her hands around her knees, even though it wasn't cold.

'Yeah, we used to come down here loads, last Summer.' I picked up a slate, and skimmed it over the water. A good one: four bumps.

'Nice! Do it again.' She made me nervous talking, but she made me comfortable as well. I threw another one, but I made of a hames of it cos she was watching. She giggled and said it was all right.

'Light?' She had two fags in her mouth at the same time. I tried to light them, but the wind kept blowing the flame out. I put my hand over it and tried again. Then she put both her hands over it, and they touched my hands. The lighter worked, and she took them away again. I squatted down with my fag.

Her skirt was going up, and she kept pulling it back down. I could see the front of her knickers; they were pink, like her nails. It said something on them, but I couldn't read it. I didn't want to get caught looking. They looked very soft; I thought about what it would be like to touch her there; not inside them, just on the material. I was sweating, and it wasn't cos of the sun.

'You enjoying that?' she said. I went scarlet, and tried to look everywhere except her knickers.

'Nice, aren't they?' Jesus Christ.

'Eh, yeah. Lovely.' I nearly choked, then pretending I was coughing from

the smoke.

'All right, maybe not that nice!' she laughed.

'Huh?'

'Well, if they're giving you a cough, like. Yeah, Silk Cut Purple; I smoke them when I'm at school,' she said. I was a gombeen sometimes.

She done a big yawn, closed her eyes and stretched out all the way. Her legs went high, and her skirt fell out of the way, and I could see the back of her knickers.

'They're nice too, hah?' she had her eyes open again, laughing. I wasn't able to speak.

'So, what do you like in a girl, Rich?' She sitted back up properly.

'What d'you mean?'

'Like, do you like a girl with a nice boobs, or nice legs, or a nice bum?' she said; she looked grown up when she smoked. Like someone in a French film.

'Ah, I dunno really…' What was the best answer to say? Were these questions like a test? What answer would get her all offended? She had a nice all of them things; she wouldn't mind anything I said…

'Ah, the face?' I said. That was the smart answer.

'Hah!' She laughed, and smoke came out of her nose.

'Naw, no. I just mean like, I like girls who are pretty. And ones that aren't, I suppose.'

'You like ugly girls?'

'No! I mean, I don't mind. A nice personality?' What did she want me to

say?'

'Tits or arse, Richie?' she was smiling. She had a filthy mouth for someone who sounded so posh.

'Ah, am. The second one.' I was scarlet.

'Do you like mine, then?'

'Well, I..' Jesus Christ. I wasn't able for her at all sometimes.

'C'mere and I show you.' She pulled me by my T-Shirt, over to behind the toilets at the edge of the pond. She looked around for a minute, then she pulled the skirt up.

'Go on, then. Look!' she said. I looked down at her, in those pink knickers. They weren't tiny like a bikini but they weren't big like little girl's knickers either. You could see a little bit of the cheeks; near the tops of the back of her legs. They were round, and soft looking, but none of her was fat. My langer was gone so hard that it was hurting me.

'Ta-da!' she said, then she turned around to face me. She looked me in the eye, then nodded down to her knickers. It said 'Hang Loose' on the front, in furry white letters.

'Touch them,' she said, in a funny, wobbly voice. I was pretty sure now that this was a dream, and I was going to wake up, riding my pillow.

'What? Touch what?'

'The letters! Touch them; They're *furry*.' I put my two fingers out in front of me, and it seemed to take about twenty minutes before they got to the letters. I rubbed them slowly.They were like felt, or velvet. She giggled like it was tickling.

I took my fingers away, but she stopped me, and put them back. She whispered:

'Softly. Gently.' Her breath was hot like fire inside my ear, and the hot went all the way down my body and between my legs and I nearly groaned at how good it felt down there. She'd put my fingers back on the letters. She was all quiet first. Then, when I got to the first 'O', she made a little sound, like a cat when he's purring. I did the other O, then I went back and did the first O again. She made more purring sounds, only louder. I went back to the second O, but her hand was there stopping me, and she put me back where I'd been. I didn't know what I was doing, but I couldn't speak, or ask her anything.

We stood there for ages. I didn't look her in the eye; she didn't say anything. I kept going; even when my hand got tired. She pushed herself nearer and nearer to me. I was thinking a million things. She wasn't doing nothing to me, but my breathing got fast when hers did, and my langer was still hard, rubbing against my trousers. I got tired, and my hand needed to slow down, but she grabbed it again, and wouldn't let me take it away.

'No! Keep… just keep doing it.'

I didn't know what to do with my other hand: I tried putting it around her waist, but it felt wrong. I put it on her arm, but it got too clammy, and I had to take it off. I looked at her face a few times, but her eyes were always closed. Her lips were gorgeous, but I couldn't kiss her, because I didn't know how. And anyway, we weren't even shifting. This wasn't even fingering; I didn't know what it was. Her breath got really fast, and she put her face onto my shoulder, like she had in the doorway before. She was moving now, rubbing herself onto my fingers. I felt

like I was going to spunk off, even though I didn't know what that felt like. My legs were wobbling, and so were hers. She stopped me for a minute, and made us lie down on the grass. There was no one around, only the ducks.

Her hand was down near my hand now; she took my fingers away from the letter O, and put them down inside the front of her knickers. Jesus Christ... It was slippery, but nice, not slimy. A smell came up at my nose, but it wasn't fishy, like you'd hear the lads saying in jokes. It was another smell, not like anything. I put my middle finger up into her, and she froze:

'Fssssssssssssss! No!' She put her own hand down there again, and moved my fingers to another bit. She whispered:

'Same way! Same way as before...' I rubbed her the same way, only it wasn't as easy, cos of the slipperiness, and cos there was no O any more. She kept making noises, I hoped they were the good ones. I kept on going and going, even though my hand was nearly broke. She was a ride, and I'd my fingers in her knickers. I wanted to tell everyone.

And then she was finished. I didn't know the name for what we'd done. She hadn't shifted me or anything, but she'd run her fingers through my hair near the end, when she'd been breathing really fast, and swearing under her breath. She pulled her knickers up, cos they'd slipped down by her knees. She threw me over a cigarette, but I didn't really look at her. I could smell my fingers when I took a pull on the fag. I wished she wasn't there for a minute, because I wanted to just breathe it into me; the smell of her. After a while, she stood up and said:

'Will you walk me home?' So I did. When we got to our houses, she gave

me a hug.

'You're very good, you know.' she whispered in my ear.

'Good at what?'

'At lots of things, probably.' Then she skipped away up the driveway and in home. I was starving.

Six

'Come on, will ye!' Shane was already up, and leaning down to give me a hand.

'I can't,' I said. I really didn't think I could. I wasn't afraid of heights like Dermot; I just wasn't strong. Shane grabbed both of my wrists, and made a noise like the fellas on World's Strongest Man. I concentrated hard, but it was no good.

'For fuck's sake, go round, then!' He gave up. It'd take me a good bit of time to get round the side, while he just went straight over. We were going into the old butcher's, to see could we get some lead. We used to collect it to make soldiers before, but now we were doing it for a bit of cash. I went down the path around the side. There was wood over the windows now, and people had put up posters on them. Fosset's Circus were coming to the Crescent shopping centre, it said. Ah, no; it was old. 'January 1989'. Shane'd called in for me by himself again.

'Where are you now, sham?'

'Outside…'

'Come in then, shur.'

'Open the gate for us, will you?' No point in me having walked all the way round, just so I have to climb something else.

'For fuck's sake, anyway. You're only a…' He stopped the sentence when he opened the door. He'd a Liverpool top on; the yellow one, with Crown Paints as the sponsor, even though the new one had Candy, the ones who made our fridge.

'C'mon in, you gowl.'

'Anything good in here?' I said. I did that; tried to come up with something to say, to get rid of the silence when someone was angry with me. It never sounded like real words to me when I said it; they were words, but they were empty, really. They were see through.

'What? Naw, I haven't looked yet, sham. Here, get that.' He pointed at a big roll of black cable. Cable always had metal wires inside. You got copper out of there. It was seven quid if you gave them a tonne of copper, Dermot said. That didn't sound much, for a tonne. I'd never been to the scrapyard; Mam said I wasn't allowed go, it was for tinkers.

'You talking to that girl who's moved into Naughton's, sham?' He took me by surprise with this.

'Who? No...' I didn't want him to know about her. He was my friend, and he was all right sometimes; but I didn't want him near her.

'Yeah you fuckin' have, sham.' He punched me on the arm; friendly for him, but it still hurt more than I'd have liked. 'Dara told me you were talkin' away to her, like. You steamer, you.' He was smiling. He scared me; I couldn't be relaxed with him.

'Ah, yeah. Yeah, sorry; I spoke to her, all right. I forgot that.' Empty, see through words again.

'She's only an aul' slut anyway, I hear.' He was kneeling down, cutting one of the cables open with a penknife. I was raging at him, but I pretended not to be.

'Oh right…Who says that, then?'

'Damien. He says she went away with Danny at Poldark's disco last year, sham.'

'Yeah?' Pain digged into my chest, and filled me up to my throat. I wanted to strangle him with that cable; I wanted to tear out his eyes.

'Yep. Dirty little bitch, Dame says.' The knife was making a scraping noise, and I could really notice it, and I wanted it to stop.

'Gave him a hand job and everything; says he would have got the blow too, only one of her friends came over and collected her. The fucking sluts, the lot of 'em, sham.' I wanted him to stop talking. I was raging. I went into the next room, so he didn't see me getting a red face.

I wanted to kill Danny O'Neill, but I wanted to kill Shane more, cos he'd told me about it, and because he was there in front of me, and what you don't know can't hurt you, but he was after making me know, and he was after hurting me. I felt like telling him straight out what me and her had done. I didn't though, cos you're not supposed to tell. I wasn't a gentleman, but I knew that. Girls didn't like it if you were boasting about what they let you get off them. He wouldn't have believed me anyway.

'What's in there, sham?' he shouted from out the front.

'Nothing. An old fridge; broken glass…'

'Fuck it anyway, sham.'

'Yeah.'

‘You not going on holiday this year?’ Me and Dermot were down by Quarry Road.

‘Nah,’ I said.

‘Why not?’

‘Don’t want to.’ I did want to. We couldn’t afford it. I didn’t want to say that though.

‘Yeah.’

‘How ‘bout you?’ I hoped he wasn’t; there was hardly any of us left.

‘Nah. Can’t be bothered either, bud. Fucking holidays are stupid.’

‘Yep.’

We were outside where the front wall used to be. The Quarry was all covered in green now, and trees. There was still rocks there, but most of them were under bushes and grass. Mam said a *quarry* meant that in the old days they’d have dug up rocks there, to build things. The houses ‘round here were made of red bricks though. No rocks or stones. The front wall here had been made of old rocks itself, so they were probably from inside. It was half gone; a car crash, a few years ago.

Today was the first day we were able to go down, cos the Gards had had tape all round it and signs up that told everyone stay out. Dermot had seen them take it all away earlier, so he’d called for me, and we’d walked down.

He went over the low bit of the wall. The last of the Gards had only drove away a few minutes ago, so we were the first people in there since the thing happened.

'Is that it?' Dermot asked me, pointing over at a pile of rocks. The paper said Tommy's body was found near rocks; you couldn't really see any other bare rocks around.

'Maybe. I think so.' I didn't know, though. We were whispering, like in the library; but we were outside, and there was no one else around. You did that sometimes, though. Out of respect. Whenever we went messing in the graveyard of St Mary's Cathedral, I'd keep my voice down too. And they were only Protestants in them graves. Tommy wasn't buried here, obviously. But it still felt like a place you had to show respect in.

'Creepy, bud.' He nodded at the place where we thought it had happened. I got a chill down me. I squatted down for a second, because I needed to. I breathed out slow, through my lips. I'd tried to have a read of the Leader in the morning, but Mam had took it off me. She'd said it was to look at her Stars, but she was probably trying to stop me from the reading the gory bits.

'Want one?' Dermot had fags; Silk Cut Blue again.

'Yeah, sound.' He threw me one over; it was bent, cos he'd squashed the box in his pocket. I looked around; we'd had some mad auld laughs in here, running from Colm and his boys, or having forksling wars with lads from Balla or Kileely. I loved the smell of the trees and the rocks here. Smells were always good when they'd good memories attached to them. This place was ruined now, though. This was the place where a bad thing had happened; that's what it would be from now on. When we got older and had our own kids, they'd probably tell ghost stories about this place, and about poor Tommy.

‘How did he get down here in the first place, bud?’ asked Dermot. The thing had happened in the morning. The Kellys were always leaving their kids run around in the green though. It was no wonder someone had taken one of them. *Neglect*, Mam would say.

‘Paudie probably brought him down. Gave him sweets.’ It was weird to say that. We all knew Joe’s story, and we’d all gone along with Shane’s plan; but we hadn’t really said it out loud like that. Not like it was a fact.

‘D’you believe it was him did it?’ Dermot squinted at me from the sun.

‘I suppose. I mean, Joe said, didn’t he?’

‘I didn’t hear him say nothing; did you?’ Dermot wasn’t looking at me; he was turning a bit of slate over and over in his fingers. It was like he was deliberately not looking at me.

‘Well, no. But Shane said… And we seen him in the bedroom, pulling himself. And the magazines in the shed.’ I still hadn’t told them about the Polaroid; I’d forgotten it myself until then.

‘Shane says loadsa things. Anyway, what if Joe was just stoned, like? Hallucinating A *bad trip*, bud?’

‘Yeah, but. I mean, how would your brain come up with something like that?’

‘Drugs are mad, Rich. Drugs’ll make you do anything. People take drugs and they hop off the top of skyscrapers, cos they think they can fly…’ I’d heard that as well, loads of times.

‘And the magazines, like?’ I’d seen them myself. They weren’t

hallucinations.

'Yeah. Well, I mean it's disgusting, like. But I dunno… Just cos he's a fagget, it don't make him someone who kills children… does it?'

There was gay people on telly sometimes; famous ones. They were just harmless, really. They weren't a danger. I didn't understand their jokes, but they were just men who were a bit like girls. I felt sorry for most of them, cos sometimes I'd feel a bit like I wasn't a real man, around people like Shane, or Dara. Sometimes when boys were acting too much like men around you, you'd feel like a sissy. I wasn't a gay though. I thought about Marian then, and the wet stuff. I was definitely not one of them.

'We're not doing no harm, though; just following him, or looking.' I shrugged when I said it.

'Yeah, until *Shaney* tells us it's not enough.' We never called him Shaney. I felt a little excited, like we were plotting against him, behind his back. It felt good.

'No shoes on my good floor, Rich!' said Mam. She'd been singing 'California Dreaming' before I'd come in.

'I haven't been in no mud, though!' It was dry out, my shoes were fine.

'Doesn't matter, still. I just washed it.'

'Ah, Mam…'

'Off!' she said; snappy this time. I took my tackies off and dropped them on the ground outside. The kitchen smelled like rashers.

'Did ye want something now, or is it early?' Mam was always trying to feed you.

'Nah, I'm all right. Not hungry.' I went over to the press where we kept the Taytos.

'What are ye looking for?'

'Have we any Cheese and Onion, shur?' I hated Salt and Vinegar.

'I thought ye weren't hungry?'

'Ah, I'm peckish.'

'Peckish, says you. You're only an aul' blaggard, so you are. What will we do with you at all, at all?'

She was smiling. I liked that; there'd been a few times in the last few days when I'd seen her looking sad. It might have been all that business with Tommy Kelly. It wouldn't be Dad; I'd never seen them have a fight. Although there was that thing with the ashtray the day before...

'Listen, are ye keeping out of trouble, now?' she said. She wasn't serious; she'd no idea the sort of bloody trouble I'd been getting into. She'd've dropped dead.

'Yeah. I've just been hanging around, you know. With the boys.'

'Are ye still friends with that youngfella of the McCarthys, Rich?' She meant Dermot.

'Yeah'

'Rich now, be careful of him. I don't want ye getting into any bother with the Gards. I don't like the look of them kids.' Dermot always got a bad name cos

of Colm; I think it was cos they looked like each other. Dermot was actually an angel compared to him. Dennis used to be wild, but he'd calmed down.

'Dermot's grand, Mam. It's Colm that's always in trouble, sham.'

'Don't say that word, please Richard. Is Colm the tall one?'

Yeah. With the darker hair, sh- shur.' I couldn't help it if I talked normal.

'Ah, right; yeah, he's not the full shilling, that fella. Touch of the tar brush about him, too,' said Mam. I didn't know what she meant.

'Have ye seen your father today?' she asked

'Not today, no. Why?' Your father; she never called him that. It was like she was on Upstairs Downstairs.

'Ah, no reason, shur. Are ye sure ye're all right now for food?'

'Yeah, I'm grand, sham…'

'Rich!'

'Sorry!'

'Go on, shur. G'way out of it with you,' she smiled. I watched her walk out of the kitchen, looking small again.

I finished the Taytos, then I heard our door going. Mam shouted in:

'Rich? Shane's here for you, love,' then in a quieter voice, 'Stand in there out of it, Shane shur. Is your Mother all right?'

'She's grand, Mrs South. Tipping away, says you.'

I was getting better at fingering her. We were in the small space between Naughton's shed, and their back wall. It was Marian's shed now, of course. I was

up really close; I could feel the heat coming off her face onto mine. I tried to tell what she liked and what she didn't, but I'd no clue. I just kept on doing the same thing and she didn't tell me to stop, so she must've liked it. My langer was crushed between my jeans and my leg, really sore cos it was so hard. She was making little squeaky noises in my ear, and her breathing was all fast and loud. She was wearing jeans shorts; ones you made yourself with a scissors from real jeans. I hadn't opened the top button on them, but I wished I had now, cos my wrist was all sore.

Her eyes were closed, and it made her face look even more gorgeous. She was pushed up right against me; her bra was rubbing off my T-Shirt. Everything was making my thing harder and stiffer, and I was in agony, but it was great. I went to feel her through the T-Shirt, and she didn't stop me. I tried to put it up under there then, and she wriggled away a bit. I got mortified then and I nearly stopped. Any time I ever thought about what I was doing, I felt like I wanted to stop. It felt weird when you thought about it, but it felt good when you just did it. My other hand was mad tired, but the slipperiness of her felt brilliant, and the smell…

I wasn't really even moving my hand any more; she was rubbing herself on my fingers. I sort of wanted to kiss her, or to tell her 'I love you' but I couldn't, cos I didn't really know how to kiss someone properly and no one says 'I love you' in real life. I kept sneaking a look at different bits of her, she was such a ride.

She rubbed on me faster and faster now, and the squeaks got louder. It would've been pure embarrassing, but it wasn't at all. We were both breathing like

mad, like we'd been in a race. Then, right at the end, she opens her eyes- the most beautiful eyes I'd ever seen- and she kisses me. On the lips. I froze solid, my whole body did. She was shaking all over. She didn't put the tongue in, or do anything like French kissing on the telly. She just pushed her lips onto my lips, hard and for long, until she stopped rubbing herself on my fingers, and she stopped shaking. In a small voice that didn't really sound like her at all, she said

'Heh,' and then she sparked up a fag. I didn't say anything, and I didn't look at her either.

'Can you get over by yourself?' asked Shane. We could have just gone out the gate, but you couldn't shut it behind you from the outside. Someone would know we'd been inside there. We didn't care about getting caught, really. We just liked being able to go there, for some shelter, or for a smoke. It had still been a Butcher's last year, so there was electricity and everything in there; you could still switch on some of the lights. We never went in there at night, though; yer man who owned it only lived across the road, so he'd see the place lit up. I got over the gate fine; there was grips.

'Will we go in to Styx?' he said, once we were out behind the bins.

'Nah; I've no money. Have you?' I didn't want to go there anyway; I was no good at pool, or snooker.

'Nope, I'm broke, sham. D'you want to go rob something from Feehan's?' Nearly everything Shane wanted to do was illegal.

'Nah. Last time he nearly caught me. Can't go in again for a while.' That

was completely made up; every word of it. I didn't care, though.

'When was that, sham?' He looked suspicious.

'Am, last week?'

'Who were ye with?'

'Ah… Joe.' That would do. He wouldn't be able to check.

'Ah, right. Actually, why don't we go spy on Paudie?' He had a little bit of hair growing under his arms already. When he put his hands up, there was a smell like cheese and onion Taytos.

'Will he be there?' I didn't want to go spy on Paudie. I wanted Joe to be here, so I could ask him what he'd said that night. I didn't really want that, though; I'd be too mortified to say anything to him.

'Hopefully not, sham. We'll have a see anyway, shur.' He had a stick in his hand, and he was rattling it off the bars of someone's fence while we walked along.

'Will we call in for Derm?' he asked.

'Not there.'

'Where is he, so?' He threw the stick over someone's back wall; we heard it clattering off the ground inside.

'The Forty Foot. Went out for a cycle; with his Dad and Dennis…'

'Ah, right. We should go out again soon, sham. Get some trout.' Shane was rapid at fishing. I didn't like it, but only cos I wasn't no good at it. We got to Paudie's, and walked past all casual, like we weren't trying to see who was inside. We couldn't, anyway. There was no way to know.

'C'mon. We'll find out if he's there.'

'How?' I asked.

'Watch me.' He opened the gate and walked up the path.

'Shane! What're you doing?!' I hissed it, under my breath. He was going to get us killed.

'Calm down, sham.' He pushed the doorbell, and the dog inside started barking. We waited ages, but no Paudie. I was bricking it. What would Shane say if he actually did come out to answer the door? That boy was tapped. He pushed the bell again.

'Janey Mack! What are you doing?!'

'Shush, will you?' Molly was still barking inside. He was definitely not there, but we'd no idea when he went out, or when he was coming home again. It still wasn't safe or anything.

'Right, sham; round the back,' said Shane. I didn't know what he expected to find, going in there again. We'd no Frisbee either.

The shed window wasn't open at all this time. That made me scared; he must've gone in there, and seen that someone had been in there. I wanted to get out when I saw that. I hadn't moved lots of stuff or anything, but I'd been rushing when we had to get out of there. And the Polaroid; that might have been slipped into a special page in the magazine. I'd just shoved it back in anywhere. I felt like I felt when I broke something at home, but Mam hadn't found out yet. He must've known someone had been in there. He'd shut the window.

'Ah, well. Will we go, so?' I said.

'Nah, sham. Hang on a few minutes.' He was looking around the garden. He picked up a rock from the grass, and for a minute I thought he was going to break the window with it. He dropped it. He was over by the kitchen. The sun was bright, so he'd to put his hands up round his eyes like binoculars to see in the window. I looked around for anyone watching us, but I wouldn't have been able to see them. People spying on you usually hid when they were doing it. Like Mam, behind the net curtains in the sitting room.

'What's in there?'

'Nothing really, sham.'

I walked over to him at the window of the back door; it was one of them ones with all the black wire in it, that made it safe when you broke it. I couldn't see nothing in there

'Hang on, sham! There's something on the ironing board there.'

'What is it?'

'Shorts. Little boy's shorts!' He was excited. He done a hock with his nose, and spat a big greener on the ground.

'Really? D'you think they're Tommy's?' He'd said to us before, about trophies. My face went hot, especially on my forehead.

'Yeah! Maybe,' he said. 'They might just be his own jocks though, sham. They're grey.' Of course they were going to be his jocks. You didn't murder a child and then leave his shorts in your house for anyone to find. Or if you did, you didn't iron them. It was just a dead herring.

She hadn't said much to me before we'd gone behind the shed. She wasn't saying much now, either. This was the second time she'd done that stuff with me. I felt mad, and excited, and I wanted to tell someone about it, but I didn't want anyone to find out.

'Do anything special today?' she asked. I wanted to get out of her back garden now, in case her parents were here. I didn't want to go away from her though.

'Went down the quarry, with Dermot.'

'Oh Jesus. Did you see where it happened?' Her face went sad.

'Nah, well yeah. We seen… the quarry. And it happened there, definitely. But we dunno exactly where they found him…' This was sort of a lie, but I didn't want to talk about it with her, cos her face was too sad.

'On the rocks, they said...'

'There's loads of rocks, shur.'

'Ah, yeah. I suppose. I haven't been down there ever. I suppose it's all rocks, if it's a quarry.'

'Kind of, yeah.' I didn't want to argue with her; she was too pretty, and I wanted her to smile again.

'D'you think they'll find who did it?' she asked, looking in her fag box. Why couldn't I just tell her what we knew? There'd be no harm in it. No, though.

'I dunno. It's not like the films, is it? Sometimes they just never find out, in real life.'

'Do you know them; The Kellys?'

'Yeah. A bit.' Not at all, really. Chris hung round with Fintan sometimes; that was about it.

'Must be awful,' Her legs were perfect. Her skin felt lovely, like when you pressed into a balloon. Not rubbery, just springy. I loved how golden she was; if you looked close at her skin, there was little glittery bits.

'Here, a second.' She got up, and came over. I was sitting on the concrete, and she sat down too, her back to me, in between my knees.

'I feel funny thinking about all that stuff, Richie. Make me safe.' She put my arms around her. I could smell her neck, and her hair, and the perfumey smell that wasn't even perfume; it was just the smell of her. I felt like I could sink into her, but I knew that wasn't what she wanted. She wanted me to be strong. So I was strong.

'Tell me about you,' she said, without looking back at me.

'How do you mean?'

'Just tell me a story. Something that tells me the kind of person you are.' She slipped her hand under my hand, and opened her fingers so that mine opened too, and we were kind of holding hands. I told her about the time when we were in Cubs, and Joe fell into a deep pond out in Castleconnell. I'd lied down on the ground and held onto his wrist with my two hands, to stop him going under the water. I'd held him until one of the Venture Scouts came and helped us get him out. She laughed, and said 'My hero!' and I didn't let go of her hand.

I asked her to tell me a story about her, and she told me about when she went to a disco in Kennedy Park Boxing Club when she was eleven, and her and

her friends sneaked in a naggin of vodka. They'd got langers drunk, and her friends found her in the toilets, in nothing except her knickers and vest, singing songs from Oliver Twist. One of the adults called the Gards, and she'd to escape out the window in her underwear, and sneak in the back door while her parents were watching The Late Late Show. I'd forgotten that she was older than me, for a bit. She was wild, even though she looked kind of quiet. I think that was the voice too; posh accents made you think girls were all innocent. I pictured her in her knickers. I wasn't sure if it was wrong to be thinking of her like that when she was eleven, but cos I was only eleven now myself, it was probably all right.

We walked up the other end of the quarry too. Dermot said that the newspaper hadn't said where in here they'd found Tommy's body, so it might have been over past the trees, just as much as it might have been where we first looked. It was so quiet, like a graveyard. We'd been in the place a million times, but it was never going to feel normal again. We'd even been in here when it was dark; I shivered thinking about what that would be like now. I didn't believe in ghosts anymore, but there were worse things to get scared of than ghosts.

'Come up here and see…' We walked up a sort of hill, into the top corner of the quarry. It wasn't steep or high; Dermot hated heights. Once you were up there though, there was a wall you could sit on and you could see most of the quarry, and a fair bit of Thomondgate. The drop on the other side was only about three feet, onto the school road in Kileely. You'd be grand as long as you fell off that side.

Neither of us stood up, we just sat on it, holding on tight. Shane would have cracked up laughing at the two of us. I didn't say nothing to Dermot about being afraid of heights, cos it was hardly like I was Geronimo or something. I was afraid of some heights, and plenty of other things. I looked out at Crossroads, it looked golden. I didn't like the sun on my skin, but sometimes it made normal things look rapid when you were looking at them; like real life was a painting. There wasn't a cloud up in the sky, so you'd probably have been able to see the Clare Hills easily. We weren't facing the right way though.

'Smoke?' He'd the box out again.

'Nah, just leave me a few pulls…'

'A drag so, bud?'

'Sound'. I was smoking loads lately; I hardly never did normally. Marian smoked; that was another reason to keep it up, and get better at it.

'Well, I can see two bits with rocks, now, yeah? The place where we came in, and that bit over there, by St.Lelia's.' He pointed to the corner; over a little wall was the graveyard of the church. I remembered the other day, running from Paddy.

'Is he still after me, or what?' I hadn't really forgotten about it, it was just that you didn't see him around that much, so you didn't think about him.

'I don't know really, bud. Colm ha'nt said nothing. Still, I'd be careful if I was you.' The fag smelt rotten around all these plants and flowers.

'Yeah. They can come out of anywhere, you know? Can't relax…' I took a smoke off him, or a drag even. It was rotten, cos he'd squeezed the butt too hard,

and made it all wet.

'Yep. Well, if I hear he's coming down to see Colm, I'll give you a shout.' Paddy didn't live in Thomondgate. I wasn't sure where he was actually from. Balla or Kileely, probably.

We crawled along along the top of the old walls on our hands and knees, then we jumped down behind the trees that backed into the gardens in Kileely. It must've been mad to live there, and be able to just hop over the back fence, and be down the quarry. It must've been horrible as well, though; reading in the paper, about a murder happening a few feet outside your house. Especially if you'd kids yourself. Unless the murderer lived in one of these houses. That was something we hadn't thought of.

'So, d'you think Joe just made it all up?' I asked. I didn't think that at all; I knew Joe nearly all my life. He wouldn't do something like that.

'I dunno, bud.' He was trying to get one of the smaller knives out of his Swiss Army.

'So, you just think he was langered, and stoned, and he thought it was true, like?' I didn't think that was true either.

'Naw, bud.... I think maybe, someone put words into his mouth, like.' I knew who he meant, but he didn't say the name.

'Like, deliberately?' I wasn't sure, but I wondered if Dermot knew more than me. He looked up from messing with the penknife.

'I dunno. See, right...' He took a deep breath. 'One time our school was doing a flag day, yeah? And we were collecting money in town; giving people

stickers, when they gave us ten or twenty pence, like.' I nodded at him to go on. I didn't know this story.

'So, like; I'd collected a bomb of fucking money, right. I'd a pure good spot, outside the Augustinians, up O' Connell Street. Shane was down outside Supermacs. I mean, that's a good spot too, but he must've been messing, cos his tin had hardly nothing in it.' He jammed the blade of the Swiss Army into the muck between the bricks of the wall, and left it sticking out there. 'So, he comes over to me, and tells me that we should rob some of the money. I'm all right with that, like; I don't give a shit, bud. Charity begins at home, what? But the tins was sealed pure tight, and you couldn't get nothing out of them by turning them upside down. So he says that we'll just bust one of them, and we'll say that it got robbed off us.'

'By who, like?' Dudu Mac had mugged a few of the lads from my school last year when they were collecting for St John's Ambulance. Pulled a Stanley knife on them and everything.

'I dunno, bud. By tinkers or something. Anyway, he says to me- yours is the heaviest, we'll bust that one, and we'll give them mine.' I raised my eyebrows.

'I says hang on, like; I collected that money fair and square. But, of course, he says yeah, so don't I want some of it for myself? And I says I suppose so, but I still didn't feel right, you know yourself. I'm fuckin' awful at lying, 'specially to teachers, like.' He was lighting up another fag.

'So he says to me, shur: you don't have to lie. You take my tin and pretend it's yours, and I'll say the tinkers robbed my one off me. I thinks fair

enough, like.'

'So what happened then?' I was watching the fag in his mouth, hoping he wasn't going to crush this one too, and fill the butt with spit.

'Well, just before we gets to Mrs Garvey's, he turns around to me pure serious, sort of with a scared look on his face, and starts going on about how they'll never believe that he let tinkers take his tin, cos he's known around the school as pure hard like, and they think his brothers are all only thieves and his family is only scum. I mean, I'm not known around the school as Walter The Softy, you know? I was pure… insulted, bud.' He passed the smoke over; it was soaking, but I took it anyway.

'What happened then though; did he go in and tell her?'

'He just… it was the qeerest thing, bud. He just starts talking to me- for ages, in this quiet voice. I can't even remember what he said, like. Swear on my mother's life. He was just saying all this stuff about me, and how they'd believe me more, and how his family had a bad reputation, and so on, and whatever. Just like he'd said already, but... different? And I don't know really how or anything, but I ends up walking in there with no tin, and telling Mrs Garvey that tinkers robbed me on the way out Clancy Strand, and that they took everything, and they hit me, and whatever else, bud.'

'Janey Mack. Did she believe ye?'

'Like fuck, did she, bud. Suspended me for two weeks, like. Brought my da in, he gave me a leathering, like. He'd to pay back the money, but they didn't know what it was. So they checked what the other boys collected on the day, and

said twenty quid.'

'Jesus! And did he pay all that?'

'Oh yeah. I mean, there was forty four quid in my tin; they'd no idea how good I'd done. I'd have been able to give him the money myself straight away, but I'd told him that I didn't steal it. So I couldn't just *happen* to have twenty quid on me, bud. D'you know what I mean?' He smiled, but his eyes didn't smile with his mouth.

'Jaysus. How'd you pay him back?'

'Odd jobs, or whatever. Cutting the grass or washing windows. He didn't give me no pocket money for five months, neither.'

'Bloody hell! What about Shane?'

'What about him, like? He fucked off with his twenty two quid. Never even said sorry, Rich. That's what I'm saying though. I've still no idea to this day, bud… how he convinced me to go in there and take the blame for that. He's a snakey cunt. I don't trust him.'

'Yeah… still, though. I don't see why he'd make Joe say all that.'

'I don't either, bud. He mightn't a done it at all; it might be all true. I'm just saying, that Shane? You'd wanna watch him, bud.' We'd been walking and talking, we were at the second rocky place now. It felt worse, here. The other rocks were just rocks, but this place felt wrong. Dermot must've read my mind.

'Here, sham. Here... It happened here, bud. You can… you can feel it, like. And that smell…' He was right; it felt chilly here, even in the sun. There was rubbish on the ground; not like rubbish from someone's bin at the end of the week,

but like someone was moving house, and they were throwing out stuff they didn't want any more. There were table mats, with pictures of trains on them. A candlestick that was broken. A plastic Holy Water thing, with The Virgin Mary on it. The smell wasn't coming from the rubbish, though. It was just hanging in the air. A graveyard smell; like stones, and old water.

'There's some of the tape, there,' I said, pointing at some yellow plastic in the rocks. I couldn't tell if it was really Police tape, or just part of a Quinnsworth bag. This was where he'd died, though. Just being here made me want to cry. Dermot was squatting down, moving the rocks around.

'What are you looking for?'

'Blood…'

'I thought he was strangled?'

'He was. There'd still be blood, though. From… what yer man did to him… He was only a baby, bud. He'd've bled all right. Poor misfortune.'

'Janey Mack…' I wanted to get sick as well as cry now.

'What'll we do now?' I asked. I'd climbed up on the small wall back at the front of the quarry. I hadn't wanted to stay in that spot any longer; it felt like death and ghosts, even though I didn't believe in ghosts anymore. Or I didn't think I did anyway.

'Dunno. What time's it?'

'Half ten.' I'd got a Pop Swatch with my Confirmation money. I didn't really like the strap, but you could get new straps for them.

'I've to g'way, bud…' He hopped over in one jump.

'Where you off to?'

'Forty Foot.'

'Oh right. With who?'

'Have you ever had a girlfriend, Rich? A proper one, I mean.' We were still sitting with me behind her; I was glad of that now, cos my face must've been scarlet.

'Yeah, of course.'

'Really? When was that?'

'Ah, last year.' I was thinking fast; I hated lying. Mam said liars always got caught, cos they tangled themselves up in a spiders web.

'Really? What was her name?'

'Am, Sarah Jane.' That was Seán's sister's name, but she was only four.

'Are you sure?' She giggled as she said it. I didn't like this conversation.

'What? Ah, yeah. I mean, no. I mean…'

'It's okay if you haven't, you know…' She squeezed my hand.

'What d'you mean?'

'It's okay if you've never had a girlfriend. I think it's nice, actually.'

'Yeah. Yeah, I suppose.' I was mortified. I wanted to tell her everything now; that I'd never had a girlfriend, or that I'd never even kissed no one. Nothing came out of my mouth though.

'Here…' She turned all the way round, so she was facing me. She was so gorgeous, I'd stopped being mortified about getting the horn around her. I was just

on the bone all the time around her. I couldn't stop it.

'Close your eyes.'

'Why?'

'Shhhh, and just because.' She touched her fingers on my eyelids, one by one, like a magician. I couldn't say anything, I just closed them. I felt her fingers on my neck; they were cold, or my neck was hot. Then they were on my mouth, but they were soft. They weren't her fingers at all, she was kissing me again. I opened my mouth, and tried to shift her like I'd seen other people do it on telly. Her teeth were closed first, then they came apart. My tongue was touching her tongue; I didn't know what to do, so I wiggled it about. I was shifting a ride. I felt like I was going to burst.

'Hey.' She pulled away from me for a second. Her eyes looked massive.

'Hi,' I said. I was so on the horn that my brain had stopped working. My body wanted to make all the decisions. I wanted to lie down on top of her, and rub myself against her.

'Hey… you haven't shifted a lot of girls, have you?'

'Uh, am…' I felt like I was slipping down somewhere, like someone in a cartoon falling down a well.

'It's okay, Rich. It's fine. It's sweet. But here…' she leaned in, and kissed me, soft. No tongues.

'Let me show you the best way…' She kissed me again; little small baby kisses, on the lips. No open mouths. Then she kept going, and I started kissing her back. This was better. It felt better. I kissed her bottom lip, a little bit hard, with

both my lips. She liked that. I put my bottom lip between the two of hers, and pressed it against her teeth. She liked that, too. She showed me how to kiss her with my tongue; no wiggling around, just in and out, together. One tongue rubbing over the other, touching as you took it back out, or touching as you put it in. I learned fast off her. It was easy, when you got to learn off someone who looked like her. I felt like the King of the World. I could shift now, and my first shift had been her. I couldn't tell anyone that part though. You had to lie about your first shift, so people thought you'd actually done it ages ago.

We couldn't believe our luck. Shane had been peering in through Paudie's window, when his foot had knocked over the flower pot. The key to the shed padlock shone up at the both of us, like a gold coin in a pirate film.

'Is that…' I started to say.

'Has to be, sham. Too small to go in the back door.' He picked up the key, and ran over to the shed. He put in, and turned it. Nothing happened.

'Fuck anyway.'

'Here, let me…' There might just have been a knack to it. There was a knack to the key on our back door, and to the padlock on Chris's Peugeot.

'G'way, no. I have it…' he pushed me off.

'All right. It's just…'

'Shush. I have it now.' He screwed up his face, he wasn't getting anywhere with it. We were running out of time here. I grabbed it out of his hand. This Marian thing was making me feel like a much stronger person. I didn't know

that shifting someone could make you more brave or more tough. Talking to Dermot in the morning had done something to me too.

‘What the fuck? You cheeky…’ I stopped listening to him. I let my hand go relaxed, then just turned the key softly. It clicked open straight away. Shane’s face changed.

‘Aboy the head, kid!’ Then, straight away: ‘Beginner’s luck, sham.’ He took the padlock off the bolt, and opened the shed door. My heart was beating quick; half cos we’d got into the shed, half cos I’d kind of stood up to him.

‘Here, is that the drawers with the skin mags?’

‘Yep. Inside that one, under the jumpers.’ I pointed at the drawer, then I remembered the Polaroid. Part of me whished I’d looked at it, the other day; in case it was a clue. The other part of me was glad that I hadn’t, because it was probably something much worse than what was in them magazines. I pulled the drawer open, and lifted up the jumpers.

‘I’m not looking at them fucking things, sham. You’ll turn into a steamer if you go looking at that.’ He still lifted up a few pages of the top magazine, called ‘Rustlers’. He looked more disgusted, the longer he looked.

‘Fucking pervert, sham. We should just wait here for him, and kick the fucking shit out of him for being a steamer.’

‘Yeah… d’you definitely think it was him?’ I asked. He got a wild look on him, and grabbed me by the arm.

‘Are you fucking calling Joe a liar, sham?’ His nails were digging into me.

'Wha- no, I…'

'You're calling me a liar, so?'

'No, no! I was just saying… I know he… he was *at* Joe, like. I was just sayin' how do we know that he done the *murder*?' The skin on my arm felt like it was bleeding.

'We just do. Fucking steamers are all the same, sham. Kids aren't safe around them. Ask your dad if you don't believe me; ask anyone actually.' He stared me down. 'What's this? Did you look in here before?' It was a green shoebox, a Clark's one. There was dust all over the lid. Was it the one Paudie had? My heart was going ninety.

'Nope. I don't think that was there before.' It could've been; I just didn't want him giving out to me. He took the top off.

'Jesus fucking Christ…' He was looking inside it now. I went over by his side.

'Janey Mack.'

She and me stayed there for ages, kissing. My lips felt like they had pins and needles in them after a while. Every time I kissed her, I got better at it; I could tell from the way she way moving, and from the noises. I'd my hands everywhere, but not really. I didn't go near the bra; I just felt the skin on her back. I didn't touch her backside, and I didn't put my hand down the front of her knickers. That stuff didn't feel like it was part of the same thing as the kissing.

'I told you you were good at lots of things…' she whispered. I'd my

fingers in her hair; it felt like Mam's silky green top that she wore for people's weddings. She smelled sweet and perfumey again. She put her head back a second and I kissed her neck. She liked that too. She kissed my neck, but I didn't feel nothing. I just kind of sat there, and waited until it was time to kiss her again.

'My lips are tingly!' she said. Her face was all pink, but she wasn't blushing.

'Yeah,' I said. I didn't want to talk during any of this; it was like I thought it would break the spell. It felt like that, a spell. There was so many thoughts in my head when I kissed her. None of them were like real thoughts. It was like I was thinking in feelings, instead of words.

She took my hand and put it up under her T-Shirt. I'd the bottom half of it on the bra, and the fingers on the skin above. It was soft and warm. She put her own hand up under there, and lifted the bra up for me, without opening it. Janey Mack.

'Rough…' she said.

'Hah?'

'Don't be gentle with them- be rough.' She wasn't looking in my eyes. I touched the nipple gently, first. Then I sort of rubbed it.

'Rough!' I squeezed it, but she squirmed away like I was hurting her.

'Sorry!' I was no good at this.

'No, it's all right. You're just… stronger than you look.'

'Sorry…'

'No, I like it. It's good. Pull them.'

'What?'

'Pull them, Richie. Pull them; hurt me a little.' She was mad. I didn't want to hurt her. I did what I was told though. She made the good noises. I carried on like that, being rough with this ride of a girl, in her own back garden. I pulled her nipples, I dug my nails into her. I bit her lips, and her neck. I wanted to do this forever, and at the same time, I wanted to go home, and write her name on my pencil case, and all my copies. I wanted everyone to know, but I wanted to keep her to myself too. She was lovely and strange and she was mad into me. I didn't want no one to steal her away from me. Cos someone would; cos she was a ride, and I was no good at this.

Her Mam called out from the kitchen for her to come in. She stood up and fixed herself. I couldn't stand up yet. She smiled at me; she was gorgeous.

'Right. Catch you later?'

'Ah, yeah.' I was mortified now, for some reason. All the strong in me sort of leaked out the second she went away. I tried a smile myself.

'You're so handsome; do you know that?' She said these things to me; things that no one else did. I didn't know how to feel and I didn't know what to say.

'Thank you…'

'You're funny.' Then she walked off, and I watched her go, wondering did I have a girlfriend now. I could hear Mam in the kitchen, singing or whistling or something.

It was more Polaroids; loads of them. They were all of kids, some of them just in swimming trunks. Kids on the beach; in the park. Little boys and little girls. Shane got more and more angry while we were going through them. There was nothing actually dirty about them, but finding them out here in his shed, near the filthy skin mags with men in them… it made them seem horrible and wrong.

'Janey Mack…'

'Jesus fucking Christ, sham' It was just a picture of a little boy with no top on, in the park. Now though, it looked disgusting. I was still trying to remember the night of the bedroom and the binoculars; the colour of that box Paudie had. It had to have been this one though. There was Polaroids in it. It was a shoebox. Case closed, as Matlock would say.

'D'you think these are kids he's… *interfered* with, like?'

'Of course they are, sham. Or ones he wants to. He prolly hangs around in the park and takes pictures. There's always little kiddies running round in the summer with hardly no clothes on. Jaysus Christ, Richie. How could anyone be like that?'

He threw the photos back into the shoebox and spitted onto the ground. I thought about Paudie maybe seeing the spit later, but I didn't say nothing. I didn't want to be in here any more. I wanted to go. I wanted to be at home. I should have had something to eat when Mam had offered it earlier.

'C'mon. We'll go,' he said. We locked it up again, and put the key back where we'd got it from. There was no sign of Paudie, and Molly hadn't barked in ages. When we were out in the alley, Shane turned and pointed back at the house.

‘We need to get inside there. That’s where we’ll find all the real clues. That’s where we’ll get the evidence. That’s where he’ll have the trophies.’ I didn’t like the idea of that. If Paudie really was the killer, inside his house was the last place we should be.

Seven

Last year, in the few months before Christmas, I knew Mam and Dad were getting me a computer. I'd been going on and on about the Commodore 64 ever since I'd played it over at Joe's, and Mam knew that the Atari we had was ancient now, and the games were only for babies. We'd agreed that she'd get it if I only got the green screen monitor; that was the only way they could afford it. Shane actually started being sound out to me around then, bringing me over to his house all the time, so we could look at Commodore magazines and talk about games. He was getting one for Christmas too, he said. Target Renegade was my favourite game that I'd played; I liked how you had to jump-kick the fellas off the bike. We used to both mitch school and go into Smyth's toy shop in Henry Street to look at the boxes. They'd a picture of the keyboard on them, the joystick and screenshots whatever games came with them that year. The graphics looked rapid. I couldn't wait. Shane even robbed some games from this little computer shop on Parnell Street, and game some of them to me. There was a Strip Poker game, with real naked women in it and everything. I'd have to hide that one from Mam.

It was a rapid time; I'd never seen Shane be that sound before. We'd spend hours in town, looking at games and playing demos in shops, and cos it was winter, it'd always be dark when we walked home. Cold too, I think it snowed one day and everything. When our Mams and Dads were out of the house, we'd try and find our Commodores hidden away around the houses, but we never could,

cos I suppose people put stuff like that in the attic.

Then Christmas day came, and I got my Commodore and my green screen and a whole rake of games and I played all of them, all morning. Even let Chris have a few goes, cos Mam made me. I still had the Strip Poker one hidden away for later. I really wanted to go down to Shane's house though. Mam said I had to wait until after lunch. I tore down the road, past all the lads riding new bikes and all the remote controlled cars in the street. I got to Shane's house and banged down the door, but it was only his Mam who answered. She said he didn't want to come out. I didn't know what to say to that, so I turned around and walked back home, feeling like crying, but not knowing why. It was really cold out and I didn't have no jacket on.

I didn't see Shane at all that day. Or on Stephen's Day. When I finally ran into him in the Square a few days later he was on his new bike; Alan's old one. He looked different. He didn't look happy to see me. I asked him about his Commodore and he said he'd changed his mind. He said computers were only for steamers and nerds, and he'd got that bike instead, and a rapid bomber jacket with a jaguar on the back, and some blank tapes for his stereo. And I didn't even argue with him, I just nodded and changed the subject and shut up about my Christmas presents. Cos I was angry that his Mam and Dad could do that to him and I was sad cos I couldn't do nothing to make it better.

****

'Why do you put them in the water, Mam?' I was eating a raw carrot out of a bowl in the fridge. I liked them, and the stalks from cabbage.

'I don't know really, Rich. I suppose it keeps them fresh. My own Mam used to do it.' It was early now, about eleven in the morning; she'd cut those ones the day before, though.

'What are ye making?'

'Bolognese.'

'Ugh.'

'What d'you mean, ugh? You've never had it.' She took an onion out of the plastic crate on the ground, near the cooker.

'I don't like spaghetti, though.'

'We're not having spaghetti. And anyway, you've never had spaghetti either, Rich.' She was smiling. She'd a little white thing in her hand that looked like an onion as well, and she was pulling bits off it.

'Hah?'

'Bolognese is the name of the sauce; the sauce and the mince. I usually make it with sauce from a jar. Same as when I make Chilli Con Carne with the Knorr powder, remember?'

'Ugh.' Chilli Con Carne was rank.

'I'm going to try making the sauce myself today, with a recipe I got from… a friend. You'd like it, Rich.'

'You sure?' I wouldn't. I hated sauce and gravy.

'I promise.' She was a great cook, Mam. I just didn't like a lot of foods. I'd been in someone's house once when they'd had spaghetti; it looked like worms, and it dropped out of your mouth and back into the dinner.

'Can we've chips with it?'

'We'll see…'

That meant 'no'. She took out a few of her good sharp knives.

'D'you want to help me make it, so?' She nodded at the onion and the carrots, and the white thing that was in bits now.

'I'm going out.'

'Ah Rich; shur wouldn't you stay here with me for a bit, and keep me company?' I couldn't really say no to her; she was sound.

Dara was the one I wanted to talk to; *needed* to talk to. He knew everything. I pushed the doorbell, but I didn't care if Natalie came out, or any of his sisters. Marian was a bigger ride than any of them; I wasn't going to be nervous around no girls now. And even if I was, who cared? I waited and I thought about how to start the conversation. You couldn't just ask someone how to get a girl to pull your langer. You couldn't act like you knew nothing, if you wanted some information. You had to act like you already knew everything.

'Jesus, you up already?' said Dara, when he came out to the door. He looked like he was still asleep.

'It's twelve o' clock, shur.' I'd been up since ten.

'Is it? Oh right, so. Where you off?'

'Dunno, out. Will we get Dermot?' I didn't say to call for Shane, even though we'd have to do it. You couldn't leave him out of anything, or he'd call you a sneak-off. We walked and we talked. You talked to Dara about TV usually.

He loved telly. McGyver was one of his favourites. Or The A Team. Or Knight Rider. Or Airwolf. Any of them ones; they were the sort of programmes he liked. I liked most of them too. I'd watch them if they were on. I liked Quantum Leap the best. Every Tuesday night at 8.00, on BBC2. I never missed it.

After a bit I just said:

'You know when you're fingering a girl?' I said it all calm, like I said that sort of thing all the time. He looked at me, wide-eyed.

'Yeah, er. Yeah. Course I do, like. Obviously. What about it?'

'D'you ever be fingering her for ages like, and shifting her, but she doesn't do nothing?'

'What you mean she doesn't do nothing? Like, she doesn't make no noises, like?' He made a sort of girly moaning sound that was a bit creepy.

'Nah. I mean, she's not like, doing nothing. Yeah?' I pointed down at my....

'Oh. Oh right, yeah. She don't do nothing to you like? No hand jobs; no feeling the balls; no blow jobs? Yeah, she's just *frigid*.'

'What does that mean?' I'd heard that word before. Shane had said it about Joy Hogan. And that she had a caved-in fanny.

'Means she doesn't like doing anything with boys; she might be a lesbian, shur.'

'But why is she letting me finger her then, or shift her?'

'Dunno, sham. Wait, is this real?'

'What?'

'You're talking about something that you're really doing, like; with a girl? Is this with yer one from Naughton's? The big ride? Aboy the Richie, sham. You're a dark horse, boy! Wehey!' His face was red; he smacked me on the back with his hand.

'I'm, err… Don't tell no one, like.' I hadn't ever talked to Marian about telling anyone what we did; I didn't know if it was a secret. I didn't know why it would be a secret, but still. We weren't *going together* or anything. She hadn't said we were.

'You dirty bollicks, you. What's she like? Has she nice diddies? Has she big brown nipples? D'you think you'll ride her?' There were too many questions. I looked, and we were at the bollards by Dermot's. I'd to stay there, in case of Paddy. He walked on, up to the door.

'Say nothing to Dermot, will you?'

'Course not.' I didn't even mind Dermot knowing; he wouldn't even care. The more of them that knew though, the sooner I'd have to tell Shane. I didn't want him to know yet. I didn't want him to ruin it for me.

'Do you want a go at doing this?' She had a half an onion in her hand, the other half was on the chopping board. I looked at the long knife; it was old. She'd had a whole set of them once.

'How d'you do it?'

'C'mere and I show you. You put it face down, first. Right? Then you hold your three fingers like this…' I watched her, and made the same shape with

my fingers.

'Then you make a few slits in the onion, like that. You don't cut it all the way, just a few slits. You get that?' I nodded. Cutting onions was supposed to make you cry; I didn't know why. She must've read my mind though.

'Now, this bit is the root. If you don't want to end up crying, you don't cut that bit, Rich. It bleeds, see; then the fumes make your eyes water.' She held the onion together, then she turned it around and sliced it again, three times, in the other direction. She was very good; like a chef in a movie.

'Then, now watch me, Rich; this is the hard bit. You hold the whole thing together, and make one last lot of slits…' She sliced through the onion again, and turned it into a load of little tiny square onions, like in the sauce at Burgerland.

'Ta-da! And then you can keep chopping them if you like, but that size is grand, says you. Now, you want to try?' I didn't want to; cos I knew I'd make a hames of it. I took the knife anyway, though. She stood over me.

'Right, that's it. Not too deep, Rich!' The first cut I made went straight through the onion, nearly straight through the table. I tutted, and carried on.

'That's it, that's better!' The second and third cuts weren't too bad. I turned it round like she had, and cut into the other side, and over the cuts I'd just made.

'Right Rich, you can be a little rougher with this now. Not so gentle…'

'I don't want to break it…'

'You can't break an onion, love.'

'You know what I mean…' I'd done the second cuts. I turned it back

around, but it looked nothing like hers. I tried to do the last cuts, but the whole thing just fell apart. She laughed a big loud laugh, but it was a nice one.

'Ah well, nearly had it.' She took the knife, and chopped up the rest of mine, really quickly. She pushed it all to one side, and picked up one of the bits of the weird onion thing. It looked like the bulbs you planted to make flowers.

'What's that thing?'

'That's fresh garlic, Rich.'

'Bluh!' I made a face.

'What? What's wrong with garlic, love? Shur there's garlic in most things. You've just never seen one up close.' She squeezed the little white thing between her thumb and her finger.

'I dunno. Sounds disgusting. And vampires.' She pulled the wrinkly skin off it, like when you have to take the red stuff off the peanuts inside monkey nuts at Halloween. It was creamy white and smooth underneath the skin.

'Vampires aren't real, Rich.' She took the knife, and cut the garlic into very thin slices. They looked greasy. The smell wasn't nice and it wasn't horrible, it just smelt like flavour.

'Do want to chop that for me?' She handed me some celery. Celery was rank.

'What size?' I had the knife again; I felt cool.

'Little bits will be fine, love.' She showed me the size with her hand. I put my three fingers on the stalk, and chopped away. Not too fast, but faster than most kids could do, I'd say. I was being careful, cos you could cut yourself with a

knife like that, pure easy.

‘What’s the scala, anyway?’ Dermot had walked out of the house with a lit fag in his mouth; his mam and dad must’ve been out.

‘Nothing,’ I said.

‘Richie has news, sham,’ Dara said. I looked at him, feeling my cheeks go red.

‘Dara!’

‘What’s the news, bud?’ Dermot was looking from one of our faces to the other, like he was watching the tennis. I looked at Dara again, pleading with him. He winked at me.

‘He, ah. He…. Well, the thing is, he… He’s got his first pube.’. I could have killed him. Dermot laughed.

‘Congratulations, bud. You’ll be getting your period next, shur.’ Now Dara laughed. I laughed too. Dermot handed me a smoke off his fag; I hadn’t even asked for it. I was beginning to wonder these days why I used to think Joe was my best friend. Dermot was much sounder, and Joe hadn’t told me nothing about Paudie, but he’d told Shane.

‘Cheers,’ I said. Dermot had surprised me in the quarry, telling me all that. If I wanted to sneak off and stop palling round with Shane, I’d go to Dermot now, not Joe. I didn’t have nothing against Joe; it wasn’t his fault that someone had touched him when he was a kid. Dermot was just sounder, and he didn’t argue with you. He wasn’t into skateboards or TV, or computers really. He was more

into soccer, but not as much as Joe was.

'Where's Shane?'

'We didn't call in yet,' said Dara. We'd walked all the way down near the quarry now, but not on purpose.

'You been in there, since?' Dermot asked Dara.

'Nah. You?' We nodded. I shivered when I remembered the rocky corner, with the smell, and the plastic Holy Mary.

'D'ye see any blood or anything, sham?' He was standing on the broken wall now. I wondered if I should answer, but Dermot said:

'Nah. Pure creepy though; cos, you know…' He raised his eyebrow. Dara nodded, and blew air out over his lips. He'd an Ireland soccer jersey on; I didn't ever think of Dara as being into soccer. Lots of people were into Ireland now though, after last year in the Euros. He stepped down, and carried on walking with us. We headed down towards Distillery. I never knew why it was called that; there was no distillery there. There was a salmon weir, over the water, with the Island Field on the other side. We never went over there. Lads from the Island were more scobey than even lads from Balla or Moyross. Dudu Mac and all them.

'Into the Weir?' said Dermot. You could climb up the wall and go into the yard of the building that worked the salmon weir. I wasn't even sure if the weir still worked, or even what it did when it did work. It was a sort of bridge that caught fish, Dad had said. I wasn't sure if he'd been taking the mick.

Inside was all deserted looking, but there was lots of cool looking metal stuff, going rusty now. I was sitting on an auld tea chest. Dermot was trying to

smash a bit of machine, to get the ball bearings out of it. We'd use them as leadners, when it was marbles season again, when we went back to school. He was standing over the thing, with a brick in his hands. I knew the bang was going to come, but I still jumped when he dropped it.

'Quiet, isn't it? Without Joe,' said Dara.

'Or the Gollies,' Dermot said. He dropped the brick again. I was thirsty now.

'Jaysus, yeah. I'd forgotten about them two gowls.' Dara was breaking a stick off one of the trees in the yard. It was thorny, like a walking stick.

'Gone off to Portugal…' I said. I'd been quiet since Dara nearly said the thing about Marian.

'Yeah. Or they might've just gone to Tramore,' he laughed. It still would have been more of a holiday than I was going to get.

'Is Joe gone for two weeks as well, then?' I said. I knew he was; he'd told me he was. I was just looking for stuff to talk about. It was sort of boring today, without Shane.

'Yeah, bud. They got the weather for it anyway. Jesus, there's no need to be going to Portugal when you have this weather.' He was right; I was sitting in the shade, so's to not get burnt.

I was thinking about Shane, and about the Paudie thing. I'd got the feeling the day before off Dermot that he didn't agree with Shane, and he didn't think we should be doing it at all. I wanted to know what Dara thought about it. If he was against Shane too, then that was all of us against one. Joe didn't know

nothing about what we were doing, and Seán didn't matter, cos he wasn't really my friend, and he wasn't in our gang. If I got Dermot to start saying something about it…

'D'you know like in Back To The Future, right?' Dara said. 'You know how he goes back in time, and he meets his mam when she was young?'

'Yeah. And she's trynta ride him, like.' Dermot smiled. He'd one tooth yellower than the others.

'Yeah, sham.' Dara nodded. 'Well, like. If that was you, would you do it?'

'Do what?' I said.

'Would you ride her, if you were him?'

'Who, bud; yer one in the film? She was nice all right…' said Dermot. I didn't think that was the question Dara was asking us.

'Naw, not her. If you were yer man, I mean…'

'Marty,' I said.

'Yeah. Marty McFly. If he was you, and you went back in time, would you…'

'Would I ride my mother?'

'Yeah, would you ride her like, if she was all young like. I mean, if she was a ride?'

'Dara, you're one sick puppy, bud,' said Dermot, shaking his head. He was holding in a smirk though, cos it was funny as well.

'I was just saying, like…' Dara said. 'I mean, if she was nice lookin', and

you were back in time, and no one would find out, like…'

'Would you, like?' I said, to Dara.

'What, ride your mother? She's a bit old for me, Rich. Thanks for offering, though.' We all burst out laughing at that, even me. It wasn't really him slagging my mother, so it was all right. We were only having a mess. I liked it. There was no fear here, when you didn't have Shane. It was like we were *real* friends, the three of us. I was going to say something to them now, I had to.

'Whisht!' said Dermot, with his fingers to his lips. Someone was outside. We got ready to scatter. We were trespassing, and the sign said No Trespassing. I looked over at the gate, to see was it going to open, and was the man going to come in. There was no other way to get out of there, unless you went over the weir itself, to the Island Field. None of us were going to do that. I couldn't even stand up to walk over the Metal Bridge out by the dump; I'd to do it on my hands and knees. The weir would be way worse, probably. Someone thumped loudly on the gate from outside, then a voice shouted:

'Get out of there, ye cunts ye!' It was loud enough, but none of us moved. It was someone our age, trying to do a man's voice. We saw a hand on top of the gate, then another. Then Shane's face looked over.

'That's where ye are, ye bollixes.'

'Right. How are them carrots, Rich?' she nodded at the small black pot.

'I dunno?' I said. My fingers smelt like onions and celery; rotten.

'Ah, Rich.' She came over to look herself, and they must've been okay,

cos she turned the gas off.

'Here and I show you now.' She had the board we'd been chopping on in her hand; there was her garlic and onion, and my celery, and my banjaxed half of the onion.

'Get me that cooking oil there, love.' I picked the bottle up; it was heavier than it looked.

'Pour a bit in there; just a little, mind!' she pointed at the big pot. She lit the gas under it. I watched the oil get hot; it moved around and got bigger and smaller. She took the knife and scraped all the onions into the pot. The tiny garlic bits too, and the celery. She gave me the wooden spoon.

'Here, Rich; keep stirring them; make sure they're covered with oil, don't let them stay still too long. They'll burn if they do.' She took a carrot out of the pot, and bit a piece off it. Then she drained them off, and put them in my saucepan too. My eyes were stinging a bit; it must've been from the onions. It was all actually starting to smell nice together in the pot. Not quite sure what it smelt of yet, it just smelt like someone cooking.

'Girls like a fella who can cook, you know,' said Mam. I looked at her like I'd been daydreaming, and she'd woken me up.

'Who?'

'Girls. Like yer one next door you've been hanging around with… Marian, is it?' What? How did she know all this? I was mortified.

'Eh, yeah. Yeah, Marian.' I didn't know her second name yet.

'She's a bit old for you, isn't she?' She wasn't smiling at me, but she

wasn't frowning. I couldn't tell what she was thinking.

'Ah, it's not like that,' I lied. It was like that.

'Oh, is it not? It looked a lot like that to me…' She smiled this time, but there was still something up.

'What you mean?' What was she doing, spying on me? Where had she seen us? God, if she'd seen some of the stuff we'd been doing, she definitely wouldn't be smiling.

'I was young once too, you know Rich.'

'Yeah. Back in the dark ages.'

'Cheeky get!' That was a real smile.

'Keep stirring, mind.' I'd forgotten the onions. They were making a crackling sound in the oil now; smelled like burgers from a van at the seaside. The little bits of garlic looked all oily and wet, but I couldn't smell them.

'Yeah. We like a man who's good in the kitchen.' I didn't like how she said 'we', there. She wasn't that old, but she wasn't a girl. Her and Marian weren't going to be sitting over in Dolan's Field, smoking fags and talking about boys' langers. Talking about my langer. Jesus. I kept on stirring.

'Your Dad couldn't cook when I met him,' she went on. He still couldn't cook now; I'd had a few of his dinners.

'He could dance, though. Jesus he was some mover. We like that too. D'you like dancing, Rich?' She had a look in her eye that I couldn't tell if it was sad, or just the look you get when you're remembering nice things.

'Ah, nah. I dunno. Never tried.'

'Oh, it's easy. C'mere a minute, shur…' she took my wrists, and started trying to dance with me; the spoon fell into the onions.

'Mam! My stirring!' I was beetroot now. She was drunk or something; drunk or mad.

'All right, all right, Chef.' She giggled and gave me back my hands.

'Are they nearly done?' she asked, lighting up a fag. Her fags never made me want a fag too; they smelt rotten.

'How do I know if they're done?'

'C'mere and we see.' She came over again, and looked in the pot. She turned the onions over a few times with the spoon, then she smelled the steam that was coming off it.

'That's grand, shur. Let me finish my fag, and then we'll put the mince in.'

I didn't know how he'd found us. He'd walked straight over and scobed a fag off Dermot; a whole one, not a smoke.

'Never guess what who I just seen, sham.' He'd a horrible smile, and I hated his freckly face.

'What you mean, bud?'

'Over your house it was.' He was halfway down the fag already. None of us called afters on it.

'My house? Who was it, Paddy?' said Dermot. I looked up now; not this crap again.

'Nah, what? Paddy? Fuck Paddy, sham. I don't give a shit about him. It was Paudie Collins!'

'Paudie came to my house?'

'Yeah! I honestly nearly shitted myself, sham. I was ready to do a legger, when your da says hello to me.'

'My da's not at home though.' He was right, cos he'd been smoking in the house when we called in for him.

'Well he was there. So was Paudie.' He got three quarters of the way down the fag, then he just stubbed it out. What a waste.

'What was he doing there? Did he say something to you?' asked Dara.

'Well, he wasn't there to say nothing about us. He doesn't know nothing about that, said Shane.

'Jaysus, thank fuck!'

'Yeah, I know. Anyway, c'mere though, wait and you hear this!'

'G'wan…' Dara sparked up a fag now; he must've had his own. They were Carroll's.

'Well, he was there so he could ask Colm, I mean ask *your da,* to look after Molly.'

'Why?' I asked, cos no one else did.

'Cos he's going away! He gave Molly into Colm, into your da, and then he got in the car, and drove away. He'd a suitcase and everything. He's gone.'

'So you think he's running away?'

'No! Well, yeah he might be. He told your Dad he'd be gone two nights.'

'Ah right, so.'

'What I mean is, we can get in there now!' He was excited. I knew what was coming, and I didn't like it, but I wasn't going to be the first one to say something.

Dermot was.

'Yeah, well. You can go in the back again. Or the shed. But the house, d'you mean? How'd we do that? I'm not a cat burglar, bud.'

Shane looked at him with a sneer. '*You're* not, no. You couldn't climb up *me*. Don't worry about that, sham. I'll figure that out.'

'I dunno, shur. My da…' said Dara.

'Your da thinks you're an angel, sham. Picture it though, lads. All the trophies. Me and Rich found some clues already yesterday, didn't we?' The others looked at me funny, cos I hadn't said nothing about it. I'd just wanted a break from it all; the whole thing gave me the creeps. I wasn't going to talk about Shane when he wasn't there. Not in that way anyway.

'What kind of clues? What ye find, bud?'

'We found the shoebox, with the photos. Why didn't you tell them, Rich?' I didn't have any answer.

'The shoebox! Jaysus, what was in it, bud?'

Shane filled them in on everything. His version made everything sound way more like real evidence. I wanted to say to them that the shoebox was green, and I thought that the shoebox the other night might have been brown. I was the one with the binoculars; I'd seen it up close. But I couldn't say that, cos I wasn't

sure, and cos the box me and him had found was full of photos too. And cos it was Shane.

'Right, just take about three quarters of that, Rich…' The mince was raw and pink, and it didn't smell of anything. I was a little bit afraid to touch it, but it wasn't too bad.

'Did you wash your hands today?

'Yeah, of course,' I was lying.

'Right, well just plop it in there, says you. Yeah, straight in. Mind the paper underneath, love.'

I dropped the mince in on top of the onions and celery and garlic and carrots. It didn't hiss or sizzle cos Mam had turned the gas down while she finished her fag.

'Right now, take that…' she pointed at a flat wooden thing, with long holes in it.

'…and turn the mince over. Not yet, Rich love. Leave the first lot in there a minute.' I'd no idea what was going on now, but it felt like I was cooking.

'Now, love; flip some of it over. Is it brown underneath?' I gave her a nod; the pink had gone from underneath it It smelled like burgers, only different. More oniony.

'Right, turn it over now, and get the rest of the pink bits brown. There's a good boy.'

'Rapid.' I smiled.

'D'ye like that, so? Easy, isn't it?' Mam smiled too.

'It is, yeah.' It was simple. You didn't even need to wear gloves or nothing.

'Ah, it's not all easy. The hard part is the flavour. Well, getting it right, anyway. Takes years of practice, says you.'

Mam poured herself a cup of tea from the pot. She'd only offered me one once so far; she was learning. I kept turning the meat, probably more than I should have been turning it. I didn't care though, I felt like a chef.

'Where does she go to school, then?' She was back on this, for God's sake.

'Ah, Salesian's. The secondary, though.'

'I'd guessed it was the secondary, yeah. The figure on her, God bless us and save us.' Again, I couldn't tell if she was happy or cross.

'And what does she want with my baby?' she said, sipping her tea now that it was cool enough.

'I dunno…' I was embarrassed now, I wanted her to stop. I knew she wasn't giving out to me, but it felt like she was cross with someone.

'Ah, I'll leave you alone about it, Rich. Tis not your fault you're so handsome, is it shur?' I blushed again, like I did when Marian said things like that. Mam had never said anything like that about me before.

'Where's Dad?' Time to change the subject.

'Ah, he's… he's gone to see your grandmother.' She said that last word like it was lemons in her mouth. Mam hated Nana South. I didn't really know

why, I just knew that Mam would call her every name under the sun if you listened at the right time. Nana South probably didn't like her either, but I didn't know, cos I only saw her on Christmas, and Easter.

'Will he be back later?'

'I, I'm not sure. Probably, love…' she didn't look at me when she said it. I had that bad feeling again; the one where it feels like someone's died.

'How's it now, Rich? The mince?' There was a wobble in her voice, like she was going to cry. She came over; I wanted to hug her, but you didn't do that. Mams hugged you, it didn't go the other way.

'Ah, that's grand. We can put the flavours in now.' She had a big rack on the wall, with all her spices and leaves. I hated the smell of it. It was like sneezing powder from the trick shop.

'Get me the rosemary, the thyme, and the oregano, Rich…' I rooted through all the little pots, 'til I found those three. I opened them all up and smelled them; the oregano was the nice one, the other two I didn't like.

'Right, then. Give us those over.' She took them off me, and shook them one by one, into the brown mince, giving it a stir as well.

'How do you know how much is the right amount?'

'Well, there's recipes of course. The books. But I think it's just experience, Rich. I think you just learn by making it over and over. You learn by making mistakes. That's how you know.'

'But you haven't made this before?' What was she on about? We'd never had Bolognese.

'Ah, shur we make food in work all the time, Rich. Me and… me and the *chefs*.' It was weird, thinking of Mam with this other life, where she made Bolognese, and ate spaghetti. I felt the same way that I did when I saw her being pally with Shane. I watched her add salt and pepper to it, and stir it a bit more. It smelt better now.

'When is it going to be a sauce, Mam?' It just looked like mince.

'That's the next part, Rich. Patience. We've already the hardest bit done.'

It was after Tea when we all met up again, in the alley behind Paudie's. He was definitely gone; Dermot had asked Colm Sr. about it when he saw Molly in their garden at home.

'Right, sham. Anyone looking?' said Shane. I didn't know which of us he was asking. He didn't wait for an answer anyway. He hopped straight over the gate. We heard the catch pop, and he let us in.

'Shhhh now.' We walked in pure careful, keeping up next to the sides, like we were ninjas. There was no real point in doing it; it was still bright out, so anyone looking would still see us. Paudie's windows weren't very clean; you could see that now in the sunshine.

'Look!' Shane was pointing up. The sun was in my eyes.

'What is it?' Dara asked. He had a Fiori polo neck, with long sleeves on; it was too hot to be wearing that.

'The window, sham.'

I squinted, with my hands over my eyes. The small top window of the

bathroom was a little bit open. It was all the way up there though.

'Oh right, yeah.'

'D'you think you'd get in there, sham?' He was talking to me.

'Me?'

'Yeah. You got in the other one, no problem.' There'd been plenty of problems. Especially when I was trying to get out.

'No. Well, I… How would I get up there, like?' I wasn't going up there. At all.

'Like that, sham.' He stood closer to me, and then he pointed his finger, so I could follow it with my eyes. Up the small side wall; along the top of it; step over onto next door's porch roof, then up a metal drainpipe to the windowsill. I laughed, a bit too loud.

'What's funny?' He looked angry.

'You're joking, shur; aren't you? Climb up the drainpipe? What is this, a cartoon?' I was smiling at him, but I was already regretting saying anything at all. He wasn't smiling back.

'Will you g'way, sham. I climb up drainpipes all the time, you gowl.' I wanted to ask him when was this, or something else smart, but I was pushing it already. I didn't want a burst lip.

'Oh right, yeah. So, can you not climb this one then?' I did my best to not look cheeky.

'What? Yeah, course I could. You calling me a liar, sham?'

'No, I…' Bloody hell.

‘I’d climb that easy, sham. I’d do it with my eyes closed; one hand tied behind my back. Tis no use me climbing it, though.’ He hocked a spit. It was at the ground, not at me; still felt a bit like it was at me.

‘Why?’

‘Cos I can’t fit in the fuckin’ window, you gowlawalla. I’m not a skinny little weed like you.’ He spitted on the ground again; a normal spit, nearly hit me on the tackie. Dermot interrupted us:

‘I’m probably skinnier than him, bud.’ They were all like rakes in that family; the Mam and Dad as well.

‘Yeah, sham. You’re no good, though.’ Shane sparked up a John Player Blue. I couldn’t see Dara, but he’d definitely come in with us.

‘Why’s that, bud?’ Dermot was kind of standing up to him too. Something felt different. Things were changing.

‘Fraid of heights, aren’t you?’ He was right; Dermot never went up anywhere high, which was weird, cos he wasn’t a chicken about nothing else.

‘I’m not,’ said Dermot. This was mad; he was arguing just so that he could argue. He was afraid of heights, but he wasn’t afraid of Shane today.

‘Do it, so. You steamer. You’d last about five seconds up on that.’

‘I will, then.’

‘You will in your arse, sham.’ Shane looked around for one of us to join in with him laughing at Dermot, but me and Dara just looked at the ground.

‘Fucking watch me, bud.’ Dermot looked all serious. I liked it, until I realised that Shane was after getting his way. Dermot thought he was standing up

for himself, but really Shane was winning. It was exactly like Dermot had said about the Flag Day and the tins; Shane had a way of making you do things.

'Here, lads; look at this!' Dara'd a magazine in his hand; all torn pages.

'What's it? A skin?' said Dermot.

'I dunno. Might be. It's Chinese or something.' All the girls in it looked Chinese or Japanese; so did the writing. They had all their clothes on, though. It wasn't a skin mag.

I didn't care. I was wondering what was going to happen. I looked over at Shane, and I realised that I hated him. I just didn't know how to be not friends with him yet.

Mam got a tin out of the press where all the tins were; it had tomatoes on the front of it. I made a face, cos I didn't like things coming out of tins.

'It's just tomatoes, Rich; chopped up.' She put the tin opener on the edge, and started turning it. Her arms were mad freckly, even though she was a grown-up.

'What else is in it?' I was going to hate this Bolognese. I didn't like onions, and I probably didn't like garlic. *Rosemary, thyme, oregano*; I'd never heard of them.

'Tomato juice.' She poured the whole can in.

'D'ye want to give it a stir for me now?' She was getting another fag out; I nearly asked her for a smoke. I took the big wooden spoon. Chris would get hit with the wooden spoon when he was my age. He said I was lucky; he said she'd

gone mellow in her old age. Even though she wasn't old at all.

The whole thing actually started to smell quite nice. Not like soup and not like stew, but in between them. Then the smell of fags went into my nose instead.

'What age is yer one anyway?' she said, after a long pull. She squeezed the butt too much as well, and she took so much off the fag in one go, that the orange hot bit went really long, like a spear.

'I dunno. Thirteen?' I didn't actually know. I just knew she was in Second Year, in Salesian's, so thirteen was about right. Although, she was going into Third Year, so…

'Jaysus that's old, Rich.'

'What you mean?'

'Give that another stir, Rich. I just… I just mean she's a bit old for you. You're only eleven, shur.'

'Nearly twelve!' She talked to me like I was ten sometimes.

'Ah, I know, love. I'm just saying is all. She's a bit…' She stopped, like she couldn't think of the right word.

'… she's a bit more Chris' age, you know?' I could feel my face going red. I wanted to scream at her, or start crying. She was *mine*. Bloody Chris, I was more handsomer, she said. Mam should be on my side:

'I… I… I'm nearly twelve…' was all I could say though. Mam nodded at me, and stubbed out the fag.

'That's stirred enough now, Rich. You can leave that.' She came over, and put a big lid over the top of it.

'What do we do now, then?'

'Nothing now, love. We just wait.' She picked up the Limerick Leader off the table. The front of it had Tommy Kelly on it.

'Wait until what?'

'Until it's ready.' She twisted the knob for the gas, and turned down the heat.

It was boiling. I was standing over in the shade with Dara, looking at Dermot climb up Paudie's side wall. He'd gone through with it. Shane still wasn't happy; he was over near him sneering.

'Pffft, you'll be down again in two seconds!' He hocked another spit on the ground. I was sharing a Carroll's with Dara.

'Fucking wanker, like. He's gonna put him off,' Dara whispered to me.

'Yeah,'

My hands smelt weird. It was the onions, or the garlic. Dinner had been nice, I'd had chips with it in the end.

'I mean, like, that's not on.' Dara was trying to get a big drag off the fag before he had to hand it over.

'Yeah.'

I watched Dermot get up on the wall, then get down on his hands and knees, like we'd done in the quarry. That was the way I used to climb walls, when I was younger. I still did it that way if it was a really high wall, or the Metal Bridge, or a small wall when no one else was looking. Shane was sniggering.

Dermot just ignored him, and went along, slowly. Dara gave the fag, it was less than a smoke, but I didn't care.

'Smoke on that!' Shane was over with us, now.

'I only just gived it to him,' said Dara. I handed Shane the butt anyway. He grabbed it, and took a big pull.

'I'm only messing with him, sham,' he said, to me or to Dara; I wasn't sure.

'Ah, yeah. We know that, shur,' said Dara. I threw a look at him. They were all such cowards around Shane. So was I though.

'He's not gonna get up that pipe though, sham.'

I looked over at Dermot, he was nearly at the end of the wall.

'Ah, he might…'

'G'way will you, sham. He'll be back down in two minutes.'

Dermot was trying to stand up now, but he was wobbling. These weren't corporation houses like ours; they were much taller. The bathroom window was very far up altogether. He was going to have to climb up high. I shivered. It was too hot out for a breeze though.

I'd met Dermot the first day I'd moved to Thomondgate. There'd been a bunch of kids playing round on the green, and me and Chris came out of our new house. Dermot had a hurley in his hand, but he'd no ball for it. I'd walked around for a few hours with him, talking. We'd ended up down the Barrack Lane, near the river. I thought he was kind of weird looking. He was skinny, and his skin was

dark. Not dark like a black, but darker than you should be if you were just Irish. He told me lots of things that day; like how the fish that swum around near the sewerage pipe were called 'bream', and how if you caught one of them, the Chinese next to Munchin's church would give you four quid for it. He showed me how to tie the knots in the elastic to make a good forksling. Mam didn't let me have a forksling; I had to hide mine from her.

He was sound out. His brother Dennis was sound too, and the dad. Colm was the only one who was a bit of a fool. Their da fixed old motorbikes and scooters. He let us ride on a Honda 50 once, just on the grass though. It was only going a few miles an hour, but it felt very fast altogether.

I had my tea at his house that first day. His mam was quiet, but she made gorgeous sausages and rashers. She'd stood next to us while were eating, and the second we were finished, she took the plates and the knives and forks off us, and washed them up in the sink. I liked going over there It was rapid.

He was standing up fully now. I wanted to say 'go on!' or 'Aboy the Dermot!', but I didn't want to jinx him. Shane was quiet. He'd said that if Dermot got in, he could come downstairs and let us in the back door. Even if you didn't break a window or anything, going into someone's house was still burglary. It was still breaking and entering, even if you didn't break nothing. I'd seen it on telly, on The Bill.

Dermot took a big breath, then he stretched his leg out, off the wall, and onto the roof of the porch next door. I was holding my breath too, just looking at

him. He hadn't looked over at us once since he'd got up there. That made it feel weirder. Made it feel silent. There was noises all around, from the kids in other gardens, or out on the green. But it still felt silent, looking at him. No one was saying anything. His foot touched the roof of the porch, and he stood there for ages, with one leg there, and the other leg still on the small wall.

'G'wan Dermo, will you…' said Dara, but he whispered it. Dermot stood up a bit, to get his balance.

'Pffft. He's not gonna do it,' said Shane. Dara shhhh'd him; Shane didn't even tell him to eff off. He leaned back a little. We all gasped. He got steady again, and then like one, two three, he just hopped over, and landed on his knees.

'Woo!' said Shane.

'Aboy the head!' Dara said. We were all smiling and patting each other on the backs. Even Shane. It felt rapid.

Dermot turned around for the first time, and gave us a smirk. He stayed on his knees, probably so next door wouldn't see him up there. It was their drainpipe he'd to climb up. It was a metal one, greenish blue. It looked strong, but for all I knew it might collapse the second he got up on it. There was grips on it though. And it wasn't too far from the porch to the window.

'He's half way there…' said Shane. Dara sparked up another fag. Dermot was up on the first bit of the pipe already, but he wasn't moving. Shane shook his head.

'Nah, he's not goin' up that.'.

'Give him a minute, shur,' said Dara. Still noise from outside in the

street, but inside where we were no one was even breathing He lifted one leg, and started to climb the pipe like it was a ladder. I swallowed, but I'd no spit in my throat.

I'd stayed in the kitchen for a good while with Mam, after we'd made the Bolognese. She'd kept asking sly questions about Marian; I kept dodging having to answer them. The mince just cooked away on the hob, she said she'd be cooking it all day, until dinner time. I'd looked in a few times; let the steam out and had a good smell of it. It was nice.

She'd the gas on very low, but it was on all the same. Dinnertime wasn't for ages yet.

'Will you not burn it?' I asked. She shook her head and smiled,

'Oh no, Rich. Shur the Italians cook theirs for a whole day, then they put it in the fridge, and warm it up the next day. The longer you cook it, the better; brings out the flavour.'

'Janey Mack, a whole day?' I looked in the pot again. The sauce was bright red, thick and gloopy. It looked like the fake blood they used in horror films. Real blood was that colour too, but it went brown after a minute or two.

Dermot was at the top of the drainpipe now. He must've been crapping himself; I would've been, and I wasn't even that scared of heights.

'Aboy the Dermot!'

Dermot didn't look down. He put his right foot on the windowsill of next

door's bedroom window, to steady himself. Paudie's bathroom window was on the other side, so he was going to have to bring that leg back over, then swing his left leg over. He was really close; he wouldn't have to stretch much at all. I was wondering if the back door was locked. Even if it was, he'd be able to open the windows when he came downstairs. I wasn't going in there, though. I tapped Shane on the shoulder,

'Listen, I'll keep a lookout, yeah?' He looked at me, blinking from the sun. Then,

'All right, sham. You don't wanna come in, though? Have a look 'round, like?'

'Nah. I'm all right,' I said. He looked into my eyes without blinking, and I stared back into his. I wasn't changing my mind.

'Okay, sham. Give us a good loud shout if anyone comes though.' He slapped me on the arm. It was always a little bit too hard.

'Of course.' Part of me hoped Paudie would come back and catch him in there. I'd be long gone.

'Whisht! He's going over!' said Dara. I looked up, and Dermot's two legs were back on the pipe now. He still hadn't looked down to where we were standing, but that was more to do with not looking down than it was to do with us. He poked the toes of his left foot out, and you could hear nothing on the ground, cos none of us were even breathing.

He missed, first time. The rest of him jerked and shook from the surprise, and the three of us gasped at the same time, when we ran out of breath to hold.

'Fucking hell, sham…'

'Jesus…'

Up above, he gave it another go. This time his foot actually got onto the sill. Shane did a quiet whistle. I couldn't see Dermot's face, cos of the sun and cos he was too far up.

'Good man yourself,' said Dara. The inside of my mouth felt as dry as tissues. Shane was biting his nails and looking up, with his other hand shading the sun. Dermot put his left hand all the way out now, and grabbed onto the brick at the side of Paudie's bathroom window. He stayed there like that for a few seconds, and I wanted to look away, but I couldn't.

'Go on…' Shane said, whispering. He put the fingers of this hand up, and crossed them for good luck. I did the same; Dara had his hands in his pockets.

Dermot made the jump. His right foot came off the pipe and landed on the windowsill. His hands grabbed onto the bricks on the side, first. Then he stood himself up tall, and held onto the inside of the open window. I nearly cheered. Shane and Dara were beaming. He still had to get in that really small window, but all the hard work was done now. And he'd be able to come out the back door when he was finished as well; he wouldn't have to do no more climbing. He turned around to look at us. He gave me and Dara a big grin, but I think the smile he gave Shane was a different one. It was like 'I told you so'. I started to change my mind about going in, now. I didn't trust Shane. I should go up there and have a look for myself, and see was it a different shoebox. It'd be fine; Paudie wasn't going to come back for a few days; we were safe.

Dermot's tackies must've had no grips in them at all, and the paint on Paudie's windowsills must've been pure shiny, cos his foot just seemed to slide off, then the rest of him did. It was so quick that none of us down below knew what was happening until it was over. In a movie, there's music that tells you something bad is going to happen, and when the bad thing does happen, the music gets the loudest, and then the camera shows you everyone's faces. Our faces did nothing, until he was on the concrete in front of us, with his face in two pieces, and his eyes still looking. The sound of him hitting the ground had been pure normal, like a bag of sugar, or a litre of milk.

Eight

Dermot was fine. I dunno how I'd been so stupid. It was all so simple now, after he'd explained it to me. We were down by the New Bridge, with Dara and Shane, laughing about it all. It had been a joke, like April Fool's. Shane had known about it, Dara too. I felt stupid, but I felt glad that Dermot was okay. It'd seemed so real, though. I tried to remember what Dermot had said; when he'd told me how they'd done it. My head kept drifting off to other things, though. It hadn't been blood at all; it'd been Bolognese sauce. Thick and gloopy and bright red.

We were in Wisebuy, but I had no idea how we'd got here so quickly. Shane was talking with the store detective from the other day; they were laughing. I wanted to ask Dermot more questions, but I kept losing him in the crowd. How did he fall that far and not hurt himself? I found him eventually. Well, the back of him. He'd his bomber jacket on, the one with the jaguar on the back. I tried to reach out to him, but I couldn't touch him. My hand was moving slow through the air, like it was going through glue.

I called his name, but no noise came out of me. I stretched out some more, nearly touching his shoulder now. My legs felt like they were in glue too, or honey. The noise of everything had stopped, and the crowd was gone. We were on our own, floating through space, and now I didn't mind that my arms were stuck in glue, cos I didn't actually want to touch him on the shoulder; cos none of this was real, and Dermot was dead, and that thing I was trying to touch wasn't him, and I

didn't want it to turn around, because I didn't want to see the face, or what was left of it.

I woke up in my bed, and vomited inside my mouth. It was only a small bit of sick, so I swallowed it back down. Then I remembered everything, and I sicked it up again, onto the quilt. I got up and looked around the room for something to wipe it with. Chris had the box of tissues on his locker; I took a handful of them. The sick was red and tomatoey, from yesterday's dinner. I felt more of it coming up in my throat, and tried to swallow it back. I didn't want to go back to sleep, but I did want to go back to the first part of that dream, where Dermot was okay.

'S'wrong with you?' It was Chris, in the doorway. He took the heart out of me.

'Huh? Nothing, why?' I hadn't seen him the day before; he had dinner over in Ivan Hayes' house, so it had just been me and Mam and Dad.

'You been drinking again?' he said, looking at the tissues in my hands, with a big smirk on his face.

'What? Naw. I think I've food poisoning.' That's what you'd hear people say, when they'd been puking their ring up. Mam said you got it from not cooking your fried eggs right, or from putting hot water in Ribena.

'Food poisoning… anyway listen, have you seen Dermot Mac?' Silence from me; eyes wide open. Heart going ninety.

'Yes or no, Rich...'

‘Ah, yes. I mean no. Not since; not since yesterday. Yesterday morning. After that I didn’t…’

‘All right, all right. I didn’t ask you for your life story, Rich. I just seen Colm Sr down the shop, and he says Dermot didn’t come home last night; thought he might have been with ye lot…’

‘No, I came home last night. Early.’ We hadn’t even come up with a story. We’d just gone home. For all I knew, Dara had already told his Da everything. Shane wouldn’t have told no one nothing though.

‘All right, so. Well if you do see him, tell him get the fuck home, sham. His ma’s pure worried.’ There was a knock on the door downstairs.

‘I’ll get it, Mam!’ He ran down to the door. I just sat there for a while, not thinking. I looked at my Pop Swatch; it was quarter to eleven. I had been in bed for ages, but I hadn’t really slept. Dreams and nightmares all night, and I kept waking up thirsty. It was hot all through the night; I couldn’t have the quilt on me properly. I closed my eyes, but I saw Dermot on the concrete, with his head in pieces, and all the blood. I opened them again, and tried not to be sick.

We’d panicked. What else would we have done? We were only children. No one spoke; we just stared at him there on the ground. I knew he was dead. In the films, they check the pulse on their neck, then they shake their head and say, ‘He’s gone…’ I already knew he was gone. His body wasn’t moving; it looked like a scarecrow’s body, with no life inside, only straw. He’d been upside down when he fell; straight onto his head.

'J-j-j-Jesus fucking Christ!' said Dara. I'd been in a trance until that second, where everything sounded like when you had your head under the water in the bath. Hearing his voice snapped me out of it.

'Janey Mack, lads. What'll we do?' I asked both of them, but it was really a question to Shane. He'd gone white as a ghost. He was staring at Dermot, and all the blood. He wasn't blinking.

'Shane!' said Dara now, almost shouting. Shane turned around, without blinking.

'Eh, yeah. Yeah, we have to get out of here, sham…'

'You're right,' I said; 'Let's get him out of here.' We'd have to lift him between us. It was going to be messy, no matter which way we did it. I wasn't sure I had the stomach for it.

'No,' Shane said, putting his hand on my arm. His eyes had gone back to normal. 'No, we've got to get out of here. Now.' I didn't get it; Dara didn't look like he did either.

'What about him?' I was very close to crying now, but I wasn't going to do it in front of him.

'We have to leave him. He's dead, Rich…' He said it so… matter of fact. Like he was talking about a fish, or a pigeon.

'But we should call the ambulance…' I was losing.

'An ambulance is no good when you're dead, sham. We need to get out of here fast, or we're all gonna get nabbed.'

'I'm not leaving him!' The tears were nearly there; I was fighting them

back as hard as I could. He looked at me like I was an eejit.

'Fine. Fucking do what you want, sham. You stay here, and let the Shades find you with him.' His eyes were nearly black with the anger. I couldn't remember what colour they were supposed to be.

'C'mon, Rich. We should go, like' said Dara. I threw a look at him, to say he should stay out of it. He had his hand on my back, but he took it off.

'I will, then,' I said to Shane. 'You leave him here, if you like. I'm staying.'

'And what are you going to tell them, sham? What are you going to say you were doing here, hah? You going to tell them you were breaking into the house? You fucking gowlawalla,' said Shane. He was up really close to me now, in my face. I was shaking, but I kept arguing. I hated him.

'I'll tell them what happened. I'll tell them he fell.'

'Fell doing what?'

'Am, climbing. I dunno, like, but…' He had me. There wasn't any way I could explain it, without getting myself into trouble. But that didn't matter. Dermot was dead; me getting into trouble was nothing.

The first day I'd met Shane, I had Bigfoot truck. It wasn't as good as a remote controlled car; you could only go forward and back, with no turning. It was good for driving through mud, though; or you could pretend it was crushing your other toys, same way the real Bigfoot truck smashed smaller cars. I'd been driving it up and down the path outside Dermot and Colm's house. I wasn't allowed across

the road, but that's where Shane was; in his garden. He called me over, and there was something about him that made me not want to tell him that I wasn't allowed, so I just went over. Mam wasn't going to find out anyway.

He'd asked me a big load of questions, like who did I follow in soccer, and where did I go to school, or when was my birthday. The grass in their garden was really short, like on a golf course. He took a load of goes on the Bigfoot; every time it was my go, he'd say hang on a second, then he'd have another go himself. He said 'sham' a lot, and he cursed more than anyone I'd ever heard; even more than adults. I was afraid of him, a bit. I wanted him to be my friend though. I hadn't many friends yet in Thomondgate, and he seemed like a good one to have, cos he was tough and he had brothers.

We'd stayed there for ages in the garden; me watching him play with my toy. He was making it drive over some Cobra troopers, and we made the noises for them screaming. He made it drive over his James Bond car; the silver one with the ejector seat. He made it drive over a ramp he'd made out of cardboard, but it was too heavy to jump, so the whole thing just collapsed.

He'd had to go in for his tea later, and when he did, he asked me could he have a loan of the Bigfoot, and he'd give it back tomorrow. Mam would have killed me if I came home without that truck, so I tried to say no, even though I didn't want to seem like I wasn't sound. I tried to say it, but he kept convincing me and convincing me and making me feel bad, and in the end I said yes, and when I went over home, I sneaked in the back way, so Mam wouldn't see me not having it.

‘Rich!’ Mam was calling me from downstairs. My heart went ninety straight it way. It must be the Gards; they must’ve found Dermot’s body in Paudie’s; they must’ve looked for footprints in the garden, and traced them back to here.

‘Rich, you’re wanted.’ Maybe it wasn’t the Gards. She wouldn’t have sounded like that, if it was the Gards. All calm. Mam wasn’t calm over things like that. I got up off the bed, but it was hard. My legs didn’t want to come with me. I put on my Adidas tracksuit pants, with the loops at the bottom.

Mam was in the hallway with Marian when I got to the landing. She hadn’t said it was her; she should’ve said. I squinted through the sun at them.

‘Morning, Sailor,’ said Marian. This was mortifying. Still, I was glad it was Marian and not any of the boys. I didn’t feel like I could face Dara today; and Shane, well…

‘Well, so,’ said Mam. I could feel that she was going to say something stupid or embarrassing; I said a prayer in my head to make her stop.

‘Are you off for a walk, is it?’

‘Probably, yeah.’ Marian said it with a giggle; I could feel myself going red. I didn’t say nothing.

‘Right, so. Listen, Rich… here.’ She held out her hand; there was a tenner in it. She’d want me to go to Pa’s, for fags.

‘Ah, Mam. I’m busy, like. Can’t you send Chris?’

‘What? No, love; this is for you. Get yourself some sw- Get yourself

something nice. Or save it up, you know.' I blinked at her, not believing. Ten quid was a fortune!

'Nice for some, eh?' Marian giggled again, and winked at Mam. Mam looked at her a bit funny, but not in a cross way. Then she hugged me; in front of Marian. Like I was six. Janey Mack.

'Mam!'

'Ah, go on with ye. Off on yeer walk, so.' I looked back at her as we were going out the gate, and I thought I saw a tear. It was probably just the sun though.

'Do you know what *manslaughter* is, sham?' Shane was so near me now that I could smell his breath. It was like stale fags and Coke.

'Yeah, of course I do.' I didn't know what it meant exactly; I'd heard of it, though. I hated admitting that I didn't know something.

'Well, then.' He smirked into my face.

'Well then what?' This was the nearest thing to an argument as I'd ever had with him. It wasn't cos I wasn't scared, either; I was terrified.

'Well then, if the Shades find you here with him, they'll arrest you for manslaughter, you fucking eejit.' He hocked a spit in his throat, but he spat it away from me, on the ground. Dara nodded. I'd no idea, but I'd already pretended that I knew what it meant. I had to think fast.

'Yeah. But ye were all here too, like.'

'Oh! So you're going to squeal? Grass us up to the Gards, yeah? Your

best friends?' He had me now. I had nowhere to go in this. That was his trick all right. I could see now.

'I, ah, I, I dunno.' I looked at the ground.

'Exactly. Now come will ye? Let's go. And watch yeer feet; don't get blood on yeer tackies.' He was already on his way to the gate.

I stayed for as long as I could next to Dermot, before I followed them over. I only looked down at him once. The bone of his skull was sticking up through the blood, which wasn't bright red any more. A horsefly landed on the darkest part of it, and dipped his sucker in.. I wanted to be in my bed.

'*Will* we go for a walk then?' said Marian when were outside. I didn't want to go for a walk; I didn't want to go anywhere. I didn't want to run into anyone.

'Nah. Is there anybody in yours?'

'My mother; we could go out the back, though.'

'Go on then, shur.' I touched her on the arm; the back of her elbow. It wasn't really on purpose.

We sat behind the shed again, but she didn't look like she wanted me to make a move on her or anything. She'd fags with her.

'What did you do last night?' She said it normal, but I heard it like she was one of the Gards, interrogating me.

'Nothing.' I pronounced it right; she spoke so posh it made me bring out my JFK voice when I was around her. She'd say things like 'Mum' instead of

'Mam'.

'Oh, right. I went to the pictures.' She blew smoke out slowly, doing a kiss shape with her lips.

'Who'd you go with?' I felt the jealousy stabbing in my chest.

'Dierdre. You don't know her…' Thank God for that. Unless she was lying.

'What you see?'

'Back To The Future? Back To The Future Two, I mean…'

'Oh, rapid. Any good?' I wanted to see that.

'Ah, it's was all right. Bit of a boy's film.'

'Yeah…'

I was glad she'd called in. I'd have to go out there and face them eventually. But I could put it off for a bit, and this was a good way of putting it off. If they called in for me, Mam would tell them I was out. Dara would probably call in; Shane probably wouldn't. We talked about lots of things; nothing important or anything. She was always going on about Pat, her uncle. She was mad about him; he used to look after her a few years ago, when he lived in Kennedy as well. I didn't know any Pats, unless you counted Pa who owned Pa's shop. Then she said something weird:

'Do you know any gay people, Rich?'

'What?'

'Gay people. You know… boys who fancy boys. Or girls who fancy girls.'

'Steamers, you mean?' I said it, and I straight away knew it was the wrong thing. Her face went all cross. I started panicking.

'Richie! That's a *horrible* word. You shouldn't say that. Ever!' She almost got up to walk away.

'What? Ah Janey Mack, I'm sorry, like.' I was panicking. Don't do this to me, God. 'I just, I well I just, it's just a word, sorry. Sorry!' I looked at her. She wasn't happy.

'It's a fucking horrible bad word, Rich. It's the sort of word that people shouldn't use about people like that. They're human beings. I bloody hate people who use word like that, and worse ones…' Jesus, I'd no idea where this had come from.

'I'm sorry, Mar. I'm really sorry. I am. I didn't… I didn't mean anything. I just… I'm sorry.' She started to look a little bit less cross. My heart was going a hundred miles an hour now. I couldn't have this happen. I couldn't fall out with her now.

'It's… it's okay. I'm just a bit sensitive about it. I've… Don't tell anyone this, right?' She looked at me to make sure.

'No, swear to God I won't, Mar.' She was back on my side, thank the Lord.

'I've this cousin, right? And he's only seventeen. And well, he's *gay*…' She said the last bit quiet. I nodded at her and tried to make sure I was doing the right face.

'Right, well anyway… he decided when he was sixteen that he was going

to tell my Uncle and Auntie about it.'

'About him being a… about him being *like that*?' I asked her. I wasn't quite able to say the right word, but at least I hadn't said the other word.

'Yeah. Coming out of the closet, they call it.' She was nearly smiling.

'The closet? A press, like?'

'Not literally, Rich. I think it's cos you've hidden away what you are. I dunno really.'

'Ah, I see.'

'Anyway, it turned out it was the wrong thing to do. My uncle went mental. Wanted to kill him.'

'Jaysus. Your uncle Pat?'

'Oh no, not Pat. It was my uncle Sammy. He was ragin'. He used worse words than *steamer*, Richie. I'll tell you that for nothing.'

'Janey Mack. And what happened so?'

'He had to run away from home.'

'What about his mam?'

'Susie? Oh, she couldn't do anything. My uncle Sammy rules the roost there. Auntie Susan is only a mouse.'

'Jaysus. So he was on the streets so?' I'd never seen a young tramp before; they were always ancient, with beards. Like Willy Joyce.

'Well, yeah. For a couple of nights anyway.' She passed me the smoke without me even asking.

'Then what happened?'

‘My other uncle came to the rescue. Pat, I mean.’ She smiled when she said his name.

‘Oh, right. What did he do?’

‘Well, he let my cousin stay with him.’

‘Nice. For how long?’

‘About six months, until he found his own place I think. He didn’t have a spare room for him, so he let him have the shed.’

‘Still sound of him though.’

‘Oh, that’s Pat really. He’s the nicest fella you’d ever meet.’

‘Yep. Sounds like it, sham.’

We were good again. I’d had a panic, but it was over. She scooched closer to me. She did this thing that I noticed, and maybe all girls did it, but I wouldn’t know: She’d start off with her arms folded, far away from you. Then, the more and more you talked to her or made her laugh, the arms would come down and she’d move closer to you. After a while, she’d be touching you on your arm or your leg every few minutes. Then, one time, she’d leave her hand there. Then you’d end up shifting. Next time you saw her though, the arms would be folded and you’d have to go through the whole thing again. It was probably something all girls did, but I wouldn’t know.

My favourite memory with Dermot was from a few years back;. We’d gone out to the Blackwater, on our bikes. You could walk there, along the train tracks; cycling was faster though. It wasn’t too hot, but Dermot and Joe had their

T-Shirts off anyway. I never took mine off, cos I'd milk bottle skin. I never tanned at all, it was lousy.

We'd taken our rods with us, to see if we could get some trout. There were supposed to be loads down by the bridge. Christy and them lads had told us. I wasn't that good at fishing, but I liked it. Putting the bait on, casting off; all that stuff. We didn't have worms with us; we'd gone to the sport shop and bought maggots. They were the red ones, which was better, cos they were dry. The white ones were all slimy and I didn't want to touch them.

Dermot had an old rod of Dennis's and I had my yellow fibreglass one. Joe was the only one with proper gear: a Shakespeare rod, and an expensive reel on it. His Mam got him it for his birthday. Must have cost a bomb.

'Watch out for the maggots when you've them in your hands,' Joe had said;

'They lay eggs under your fingernails.'

'Janey Mack, do they?' I was terrified by the sound of that.

'Yep.' Joe knew loads about fishing.

'Real fishermen put the maggots in their mouths, bud. To keep 'em warm…' Dermot had a ream of them wriggling in his hand. They smelt like something; fish, maybe.

'Jaysus, g'way!'

'I'm telling you, bud. Makes the fish like 'em more as well, cos your spit is delicious to fish.'

'I've never heard of anyone putting them in their mouth. Shur wouldn't

they lay eggs in your mouth too?' Joe was putting a bit of gut through the hole in a hook, carefully.

'Nah. They don't lay eggs. They are the eggs, if you think about it. Flies hatch out of them, bud.' I hadn't thought about it like that; Dermot was right. Joe looked morta.

'G'way will you; you don't know nothing. Maggots aren't eggs; they're insects.'

'They're maggots, bud. They're lavas, or something. We did it in school, in Nature Studies.' You'd forget Dermot was clever sometimes, cos he never acted like he was good at school like a swot or anything, and he wanted to leave when he was sixteen and get an apprenticeship. Joe looked embarrassed now, but Dermot was sound out, not like Shane. He just changed the subject, so Joe wouldn't feel like an eejit.

'D'you think we'll get the trout today, anyway?' He had red wellies on that looked too small for his feet.

'Ah, yeah. I think. There's lots around, Alan Devlin said yesterday.' Joe was wearing real rushers, like a professional fisherman would. They were up to his waist, nearly.

'Rapid. I'll bring a few home for tea, so.' We went down by the bridge with our rods and our bikes and our maggots, and we started catching trout nearly straight away. My line tugged only a few minutes after I cast off, and I managed to pull him nearly all the way in, but the hook ripped out of his lip. I imagined him swimming away, and having to live the rest of his life with only half a lip. I felt

sorry for him, cos he didn't do nothing to deserve getting half his mouth ripped off like that by me. Fishes were innocent.

'Nearly, bud! Next time!' said Dermot, slapping me on the back. He'd four little trout already, and Joe had one big one and one small. We stayed there for ages, reeling in more and more of them, and having a laugh. You could eat trout, so that meant you had to kill them, not just throw them back. They'd jump and wiggle around on the ground; all frightened looking. You'd have to take a stick and bash the head until they stopped wiggling. I let Joe do all mine; I couldn't kill something as easily as he could.

When we'd got enough trout, we went into the woods, and lit a fire. The three of us played Lives and Black Jack, with the pack of cards Dermot had brought. I won four games. We were going to cook one of the fish and everything, but then none of us really knew how to take the guts and the bones out. We stuck a stick through one of them anyway, and we held it over the fire, like they did in the films. None of us knew what we were doing. Dermot dared Joe to eat it, but Joe chickened out, and he had to let Dermot do slaps on his knuckles with the cards. That's what happened if you didn't do a dare. Such a rapid day, it was.

She was sitting on my lap, with her legs over mine and her knees around the back of me. We were shifting properly now; I'd my hand up the back of her top, and I could feel her bra strap. She'd one of her hands in the hair at the back of my neck; there was no tickling feeling, just her nails on my skin. The whole thing felt different today; there was more feelings. I think it was cos we'd nearly had a

fight, about the steamer thing. Nearly our first fight.

Her mouth was wetter than before; not sloppy or horrible- wetter in a good way. She was sitting right on my langer, and I was sort of pushing it into her. We'd still all our clothes on, obviously. I didn't know could she feel it, but it felt like she was pushing down onto me too. I was sweating everywhere, but I didn't think I'd a smell off me yet. I kept opening my eyes during the shifting, to look at her. She always had hers closed.

She had on a t-shirt with a V neck, and I could see down the top of it. Her bra was yellow, and it had pink flowers on it. She was more gorgeous than all the women I'd ever seen on telly or in films; anyone who'd ever given me the horn. She was more of a ride than any of them. She'd pink shorts on, that went right up to the top of her legs. There was little drops of sweat all the way up her thighs; from the sun, or from what we were doing. She took my hand, and put it on the clip bit of her bra. I fiddled with it for a bit, but I didn't know what to do with it. She laughed and tutted and went back there with her own hand. I stayed very still now. She looked at me with her big, pretty eyes, then she closed them, and went to kiss me again. I put my hand up under the front of her bra now, cos it was loose and hanging off. The palm of my hand rubbed over her nipple; it was stiff and hot as well. I pulled on it, then on the other one. She made a sighing noise, and grinded herself a little bit harder into my lap. I felt like I was going to explode.

Outside Paudie's, in the alley, we were all still shell-shocked. We knew we'd to get away, but we couldn't just scatter. People would remember that later,

if the Gards came round asking. Shane was looking at the bottom of his shoes, like he'd stood in dog do.

'Check for blood, sham; that's how they catch you.'

'Who's gonna catch us? For what?'

'The shades. It's called *forensics*; they get your DNA off you, and they trace it back to the crime, like. You can't leave any clues. They look everywhere.'

I didn't know what he was on about, but the programmes he watched about serial killers and investigations and all that were about America. The Gards probably didn't have DNA. He was just getting us terrified for nothing.

'I've nothing on me, shur,' said Dara. His face was redder than usual. He looked so young. We were all young, only children. Except Dermot. He wasn't anything no more now.

'It's invisible, sham. Even if you can't see blood, the DNA might still be there.'

'What's DNA, though?' I wondered if he actually knew, or was he just talking through his backside.

'It's like… it's like a fingerprint, but it's in blood, or hair, or spit.'

'Well, you were spitting load in there…' Dara said. It was the wrong thing to say.

'What? Nah, that won't prove nothing; you don't know nothing about it, you fucking steamer. They can't prove fucking nothing with a bit of spit. That'd just prove that I spitted in there. I could have spitted over the fucking wall, sham.' He didn't look like he believed himself. His voice went a little bit high, like a

girl's voice. I hated him.

'When a serial killer does a killing, he usually burns all his clothes, and his shoes,' he said.

'Ah, Jaysus! I can't burn these tackies; I got 'em with my Confirmation money. My Mam would kill me!' Dara had one of his off and in his hand, looking into the grips.

None of this was helping. If there was such thing as DNA, we'd all left loads of ours in Paudie's today. We were leaving even more now, outside his back gate.

'C'mon,' I said, walking out of the alley. The other two followed; Dara hopping on one foot, trying to put his tackie back on. I felt in charge for a second. I wasn't though.

'Where we goin' sham?' Shane whispered.

'I'm going home.' That was the only thing I wanted to do now.

'You can't just go home, you gowl. What if someone finds out? What if they ask us questions? We need a story, sham. And we all need to know it off by heart.' I didn't know if he knew this stuff cos he watched too many films or TV programmes about murderers, or cos his family were all criminals. He was right, but I didn't care.

'I want to go home!' I didn't shout it, but he backed away a little.

'All right, all right, sham. Say nothing to no one, though. Right?'

'Who'd I be saying something to?' I was still angry. He'd done this; he'd made Dermot die. He'd wanted to break into Paudie's. It was his fault.

'Chris, or your Mam, or…'

'I'm not an eejit.'

We were around by the green now. There was no one around.

'All right, sham. You too, Dara.'

'What?' Dara still looked all red and sweaty. We were nearly outside his house now.

'Say nothing to no one; especially your Da.' That was a stupid thing to say. Of course he wouldn't. A lot of things Shane said were stupid; he just said them in a way that made you think he was *wise*. Dara just nodded. He hadn't realised Shane's game the way me and Dermot had. It hit me again that he was dead. Like someone kicking me full force in the chest. I needed to be out of there. Dara went in home, and we carried on walking.

'D'you think he'll say something?' Shane always talked about people behind their backs. When that sort of thing happened, you never really thought he did the same to you when you weren't around. He did, though. He must've.

'Nah, he'll be fine.' I didn't know if that was true, I just wanted to be on someone else's side, other than Shane's. Dermot hated him, same as I did. Dermot would have come away from Shane with me, definitely.

She was on top of me now, my back was on the ground. Her Mam was at home, for God's sake; up in the kitchen. It was mad the way they hadn't come down to check on us, when they knew I was with her. Maybe they thought she wouldn't have been getting up to anything with me, cos I was younger. They

might have thought we were *just friends*. We'd been shifting for nearly an hour I'd say; she hadn't put my hand down her knickers though. I was really hard down there now, and it was getting sore. She was pressing herself into me, and rubbing off me like we were riding. It felt better than anything we'd ever done. I started moving the same way as her, and that was even better. She moaned. It wasn't real riding, but it felt good. We were breathing heavy, and I felt hot. We might as well have been riding.

I was always thinking too much about everything, and when we did the things we did, I'd be thinking things all the way through them too, and sometimes that would ruin it. It wasn't like that today, though. I had been thinking a million things about Dermot and Shane and the Gards and prison and everything like that before I saw her today. The minute we started kissing though, it went away. I wasn't thinking now, I was feeling. The rest of the world was gone: the only thing I could see was her, when I sneaked a look while we were shifting. The only thing I could smell was her. The skin on her neck, the perfume on her. The only thing I could feel was her skin against my skin, and little puffs of her breath, and the heat between her legs. The only thing I could taste was her mouth, and her skin, and her spit mixed up with mine. The hardness, rubbing against her like that; it made nothing important any more, just what we were doing. It was like being drunk, or stoned; but without the bad bits.

I put my hand down towards her shorts, but she pushed it away. I could feel myself going scarlet, and she seemed to feel it too, cos she said,

'It's okay; I'm fine,' and then she kissed me again, and rubbed herself off

me some more. I was a bit jittery, but it was all so good. After more of it, I put my hand down the back instead, and she didn't stop me this time. The skin on her backside was soft, like the rest of her. I grabbed onto it, and pushed her down onto me more; she made a noise that told me she liked that; she liked it when I was rough to her. I wanted it to be rough today. I would have thought that after everything the day before, I'd have wanted someone to talk to, or to hug, or something like that. But I didn't at all. I wanted this, what was happening here. I grinded her into me some more, and she made the small whimpering noises that I knew meant that she was liking it. I was moving back and forward really fast now. I wanted to put my hand down into her knickers though; I wanted that wetness, and that smell. I dropped the hand on her again, rougher, thinking she'd like it. She took it away again, kissed me, and said,

'I can't today, hun. You know…' I didn't know. I was going to explode in a minute. I put my hand up her t-shirt again, and squeezed hard. Her skin was warm and sweaty, and it smelt amazing now.

I took her hand, but not to hold it. I stretched my back out a bit, so that there was more of a gap between us. She stopped kissing me, and looked at my eyes, then at our hands. I didn't really know what I was doing or what she was going to say, but I just carried on anyway. I put her hands down the front of my tracksuit, into my jocks. She froze. I'd done the wrong thing. Jesus Christ… I'd already nearly screwed up today, now I was-

Then she started moving her fingers. My breath stopped in my throat; this was the best feeling I'd ever had. She was so soft, the way she touched me. No

pulling or *jerking*, or any of the words the boys used. Just soft fingers, almost tickly. Now I was the one making the moaning sounds. She carried on, and I lay back, in Heaven. I'd my eyes closed, but I peeked at her one time, and she'd a strange look on her face; like she was concentrating. My langer was still inside the tracksuit pants, but it was standing up, like a tent. She was just running her fingers up and down it, barely touching. I was going to spunk off. I wondered if I should tell her. She was such a ride, and I was so lucky. I squinted out at her again, looking at how gorgeous her skin was, how lovely everything on her body was. She moved her hand faster now, but not harder. It was still tiny touches. I looked at how long her neck was, and how small her ears were. I'd never noticed that before. She used the back of the wrist on her other hand to hold the elastic waist of the pants up. I felt a breeze come in, and it was nice, in a weird way. Her fingers went faster and faster. I felt my leg start twitching. I wondered do you tell the girl, if you're going to spunk off, cos otherwise they might get it on their hand. I'd a pack of tissues in my back pocket. She peeked under the waistband herself, and I suddenly got all weird, and I thought she might see my langer, and think it was too small or something, and just stop. She didn't though; she kept on with her soft fingers. Up and down. Fast. I was going to explode; I couldn't say something; my leg was going mad; I was going to spunk off now; she was so gorgeous. I looked at her one more time, and she caught me. Beautiful eyes. My leg shook like mad, my balls went really tight, and then it happened. Hot, sticky pee, it was like. She pulled her hand off straight away, but some of it got on her.

'Sorry! Sorry! Sorry, sorry, sorry!' It was the only thing I could think of

to say. My whole body felt like it was jelly.

'Shhhh, shhhh. You're all right, shur,' she giggled. 'Did you like it?'

'Huh?' I looked at her like she was speaking Chinese. My body was like jelly and my brain was too.

'I'll take that as a yes, Rich. Here…' she handed me a clean tissue she'd got from somewhere. I wiped up all the stuff I could see, but there was probably more. I suddenly felt very small and very weak, and very younger than her. The happiness all seemed to have come out of me when I finished, there. Something hit me on the cheek; it was a cigarette that she'd thrown over.

'Cheers, thanks… for the fag, I mean. Not ther- So, did you not want to…' I wanted to ask her if she wanted me to finger her, but there really wasn't a nice way of saying it, and now that I'd spunked off, I felt kind of guilty and dirty about things like that. But I felt lousy, so…

'Course I did, but you know…' She pointed down there.

'What?'

'Period!' She whispered it, but loudly. I was such an eejit; obviously that was what she had meant earlier, when I was trying to…

'Otherwise, yeah. Of course.' She didn't want to talk about it either, maybe. We never talked about it really. We talked about normal stuff, and we shifted; we never talked about shifting.

Doing these things with her made me feel like I'd known her for much longer than I had. All I wanted to do was tell her about Paudie, and what we'd been doing, and how it went too far, and about Dermot, lying there in that garden;

dead, and foxes eating him. How could I tell her, though? What would she think of me? Would it mean that she'd never do this with me again? I didn't care that much about the shifting. I just liked her, I liked being with her. The shifting was still great, though. I wouldn't want that to stop, no matter how much I liked her as a friend. I didn't want her to be just my friend; I wanted this. She got up, and put herself sitting into me; her back to me, but my arm around her, cuddling her.

'So, have you told your friends ?' She didn't turn around to me. I could smell her neck; it was lovely altogether.

'Ah, well, no. No, I don't think so.'

'Why not? Are you ashamed of me?' She turned to me now, and put on a face; pretending she was hurt.

'Janey Mack, no. I just, I didn't- I wouldn't know what to tell them, if you get me.' I'd said that stuff to Dara, and I wasn't sure if I'd been really asking his advice, or if I'd been boasting. But I hadn't really said nothing to no one, cos I'd no idea myself what we were doing.

'Shur wouldn't you just tell them that you'd met a girl? A nice girl, from Kennedy Park?' She winked at me. No one would ever believe she was from Kennedy Park.

'Ah well, yeah. I mean I told Dara…'

'Which one is he?'

'The blond one…'

'No, I haven't seen him. I've seen the tall fella, with the brown hair…'

'That's Joe.'

'Right'

'Anyway, I told Dara that I'd met you, and I'd talked to you… but that's all.'

'You mean to tell me haven't told any of your friends that you've been going with the new girl that moved in next door? Jaysus, Rich; aren't you the perfect gentleman.' She was smiling now, her teeth were as white as someone from Hollywood. It reminded me to keep my mouth shut when I smiled around her; mine were awful; I was always forgetting to brush them.

'Er, yeah. I didn't want to be saying nothing, you know.' I felt guilty now, cos I'd told Dara I'd been fingering her. I'd forgot that.

'Well, I don't mind, really. So long as you aren't making fun of me, you know? I've had some boys tell tales about me… not nice.' I thought about Danny O'Neill and felt angry. Mostly at him, some at Shane, and a little bit at her. I swallowed it down.

'Yeah. Lads like that are terrible.'

'Anyway, if you wanted to tell people about us; that we're going with each other, I mean. You can.' She winked again.

We're going with each other? That was mad. I should've felt as happy as Larry. I wasn't though, cos I was thinking about Dermot. There was a chance we might get away with it. He could just have been in there by himself for all anyone knew. And we didn't have Seán with us, so out of me, Shane and Dara, there wasn't anyone known for squealing. It didn't matter though, getting away with it. He was still dead. He was still dead, and his Mam and Dad just thought he was

missing; that he'd stayed over in one of our houses, and forgot to tell them.

'What're you thinking?' Her voice took me out of the daydream.

'Ah, nothing. Just something.' I blinked; the sun was in my eyes now.

'You were miles away there… you looked sad.' She'd scooched around again now, so she was looking into my face. Her skin was even more golden today. There was a sort of shimmer off it.

'Ah no. Tis nothing,' I said. I'd said it really Thomondgate as well, and it made me want to shut my mouth to hide my words in front of her, same as I did to hide my yellow teeth. I was still thinking about the day before.

I'd run from Shane's house to mine, but it had taken me ages to go through the front door once I got there. Nothing felt real at all, and I was paranoid as anything. The more I thought about it all, the less real it was. Dermot was back there, all alone and dead. They were going to find him, and they were going to come and get us. We'd been in there for ages; there was no way one of the neighbours hadn't heard us or seen us. They wouldn't have done nothing at the time, but if the Gards came round asking questions about a dead boy, they'd remember us.

'Is that you, Rich?' Mam was in the kitchen; I could smell her smoking. The light was off in the sitting room, but the light of a TV was flickering out the door.

'Yeah. I'm goin' up to bed.'

'Jaysus, Rich. Bed? At this time?' It was still bright outside.

‘I feel a bit sick…’ I was halfway up the stairs now.

‘Aw, God help us. What’s wrong, Rich; your tummy is it? Did ye want some milk of magnesia?’

‘Naw, no. I’ve a headache is all, Mam.’ I wasn’t drinking no milk of magnesia; that stuff was rotten.

Upstairs I left the light off, and closed the curtains. They were only kids’ ones; Return Of The Jedi, so they didn’t block out the light properly. I took my clothes off and got under the quilt. Chris was staying over at the Hayes’, Mam had said at dinner. I wrapped the covers round me tight, like I was a baby. My heart was thumping now; I could hear it in my ear. We’d just left him there. He’d be so cold after it got dark. And alone. I knew he was dead, but I still felt like he shouldn’t be out in the cold like that all night. Rats would come, too. Rats and cats and dogs and foxes. They’d eat the face off him before anyone found him, and his Mam and Dad would have to go down the Garda station to see him, but there’d be no face there any more. I closed my eyes to stop myself thinking about it, but with my eyes closed, I saw worse stuff. At least with them open, I could only see what was actually there. The sun was nearly down now; the curtains were kind of glowing with the light coming through. I stared at C3PO and Chewbacca, and wondered if I was ever going to get to sleep.

After a while, I could hear them downstairs. First I thought someone had come to the door and told on me, cos Mam’s voice sounded cross. I went through all the things I was going to say; wondered who I could blame that wasn’t me; I even thought about climbing out the window. Then I noticed that the other cross

voice was Dad's. Dad never got angry, or shouted a lot. He was just himself, most of the time. I couldn't hear what they were saying, but it was a fight, definitely. Or an argument. I didn't like it.

When we'd had our dinner, neither of them had said nothing to each other. I hadn't noticed it that much, cos I was thinking about Marian and her cousin and what we'd done and all of that stuff. But there was definitely something wrong. Mam had been talking to me about random things, like she always did. I'd answered her, but Dad didn't join in at all. And usually you'd get a sarcastic comment from him, or a joke that you didn't really understand. He just sat there, eating his Bolognese. He didn't even complain that Mam had done chips for me instead of spaghetti, and he'd usually have made a smart comment about that.

Mam's voice got louder downstairs now, and Dad's did too. She was shrieking, kind of. His voice was pure low, but you could hear that he was angry. I could hear a chair being scraped on the kitchen floor, then something bigger- the table, probably. Then Dad's voice, really loud. Then Mam screamed, like a banshee. Then there was a sound like a plate, or a cup breaking. A door opened, and there were footsteps on the stairs. I turned towards the wall, and wrapped myself up tighter. I stayed as still as possible. If one of them opened my door, I was gonna pretend I was asleep. Otherwise they might try and talk to me, and I couldn't handle that tonight. They just went past, though. The door to Mam and Dad's room slammed shut. Downstairs, there was more noise of moving furniture, but it was quieter now; like they were putting it back. I wrapped the quilt over my

ears, cos I didn't want to hear the noise of Mam crying next door.

Marian had been gone for a fair bit now. She only went in for a glass of water. I wondered if I should just go. I hated things like that; the bits in life where you'd no one to ask what to do, only yourself. There was a beetle on the ground in front of me; a big one. I didn't like creepy crawlies, but I didn't like killing things either. I always got Joe or someone to kill a spider for me. I watched it walk along over the concrete, in and out of the pebbles. I kept looking at, until it was gone. Once you knew it was gone, you didn't be wondering if it was crawling on you later. I scratched my neck from thinking about it.

I stuck my head around the corner, to see where she was. Their kitchen window had the blinds open. Her da was home. My heart leapt a bit, cos what if he was giving out to her for being down here with me? He didn't look cross, though.

She was sitting up on their counter; not on a stool, on the counter itself. Her da was a big fella; you wouldn't want to get on the wrong side of him. You couldn't hear what they were saying, but it must've been serious, cos his face was sad or cross, and she was fiddling with the sleeve of her T-shirt, like she did when she was nervous. I didn't know that I knew that about her, until just then. But I must've done. They kept on talking for a while, then he turned and looked at me. I swung back around the corner of the shed. Janey Mack! Did he see me? I thought about leaving again, but he was probably just looking down there for some other reason.

She'd left her fags on the ground. She wouldn't have minded me having

one, but it wasn't a good idea, just in case he had been looking at me, and he was going to come down to give out to me. Or just to meet me. That's what you did; you met their dads, and the dad gave you the once over, and growled at you a bit, and told you to make sure she was back by whatever time. That's how it was in the films. I took a fag out, but I didn't light it yet. Paudie had gone yesterday morning; he was going to be back tomorrow; maybe in the evening. There was some time to make up a story, or an excuse. There was time to tell someone too; to come clean, but Shane was probably right. We'd all get into so much trouble for it. Mam would be mortified, and she wanted me to go to college; you couldn't go to college if you'd a criminal record, probably. I lit the fag; hanged for a sheep, hanged for a lamb, as Mam herself would say. There were footsteps coming down the path; I dropped it on the ground and stamped on it. It was only Marian by herself, though.

'Hey,' I said. Waste of a whole fag.

'Uh, hey.' She wasn't smiling.

'What's up?'

'Oh. It's Dad. Oh, Richie… He's seen, he's found…' She picked her fags up, and looked in the box. Damn, I was going to get nabbed.

'Did you take… never mind. Dad's just come back from Pat's house…'

'Oh right, yeah?' Maybe something had happened to the Uncle. She'd need comforting, like the girls in the films. I could do that.

'Yeah. There's been… an accident.'

'Janey Mack, is he all right shur?'

'Who, Pat? Oh he's fine. He's not even there. He's away for a few days.

He asked Dad to call in this morning and make sure the place was all right. He left the dog with someone to mind, but Dad said he'd call in anyway and check that everything was okay… So he went in the garden this morning, and…' Her hands had a cigarette in them, but she'd forgot to light it.

'And what?' I said. But I knew the answer already.

Nine

'C'mere I wantcha' Chris was at the bedroom door. I was in no mood for him. I just wanted to be on my own. Actually, I didn't want to be on my own, cos my thoughts were driving me mental. I didn't want to be with other people either though.

'I'm here, what you want?' I wasn't getting off the bed.

'Fine. Listen…' He came over. 'You know Mam and Dad have been fighting a lot, right?' What was he on about now? I'd heard the thing last night. And they'd been funny at dinner. And the other day in kitchen… but they weren't *fighting*. They were fine. They were happy.

'Well, Mam's decided… Mam's gone to Auntie Maggie's for a few days, okay?' He didn't look like the Chris I was used to. He looked like he was trying to be… *nice*.

'What? What d'you mean? Why?

'I mean, she just, look… she needs a bit of *space*, all right?'

I just stared at him; I didn't even nod.

'Will you be all right here with Dad? For a week or two, like?'

'A week or two? What you mean *with Dad*? Where will you be, like?'

'I'm… going to Maggie's too.'

'What? Why?' What I meant was, why wasn't she taking me? What was going on here? Me and Mam were the close ones. She didn't like Chris like she

liked me.

'She needs someone there with her, okay? And I'm the oldest. I've a few friends over that way, anyway. Eric and Matthew.' Maggie and Joe lived in Pineview; they'd no kids.

'Rich, I've me bike, so I can come see you during the week…' He was doing the kind face again; it made me hate him.

'I don't need you to come back! Where's Mam? I want to talk to her.'

'You can't…'

'WHY NOT?' I wanted to hit him, but he'd have killed me. I didn't care though. I needed Mam.

'She's already gone, in the taxi. I'm sorry, Rich.' He put his arm around me, like he was pretending he loved me; like we were on TV. He was pure awkward, though. It didn't help at all. I was trying not to cry. Everything was falling apart.

'Listen, I've to go myself, okay?' I didn't look at him; I was slumped on the bed.

'If you need me, you know where I am.'

'I don't know where Maggie lives,' I mumbled at him. They'd moved last year, and I hadn't been to the new house. There was no point. Like I said, they'd no children.

'Don't worry about that; I'll see you soon, bud.' He went, then. I waited until he was out the front door, then I put my face right into the pillow, and tried to cry. Nothing came out though. I'd no feelings left.

Chris hadn't said anything about Dermot. That meant that the word hadn't got round. It wouldn't have, in fairness. Marian's Dad wasn't from round here, so he wouldn't have recognised Dermot, or what was left of him. He wouldn't know that there was a boy gone missing, either. The Gards would put two and two together though. It was only a matter of time. I kneeled up and looked out the window at Dermot and Colm's house. If I stayed there long enough, I'd see a squad car pull up outside. The Gards would go in, and Mrs McCarthy would see them on the doorstep, and she'd collapse in tears. Colm Sr would be strong, and hold onto her while they listened to the Gard telling them that they'd found Dermot's body. Then the word would start to leak out. People would know that he was dead; that he was found in Paudie's. The bits they didn't know, like why he was there, or how he died, they'd start to fill in themselves. That's how it happened; Chinese whispers. None of them would guess what had actually gone on, of course. But we could still be caught for it. We'd no story, and we were just stupid little kids. The chances were, if any Gard thought we had something to do with it, he'd be able to get it out of us no problem. Even Shane; he was hard, but he was still a kid. We were all just kids, like Dermot. Now he was a dead kid, and that made two dead kids in a week.

I was losing my mind now, and I didn't even have Mam. I wouldn't have told her anything anyway, but sometimes you need your mother. I never said two words to Dad, and all he ever did was make smart comments, or burn the dinner. Chris was a sneaky get; jumping in there first. He must've asked her could he come with her, and she wasn't able to say no, cos he's her son. If I'd known first;

if I'd been able to ask first, she'd have said yes to me instead. That was the truth. She didn't love him more than me. Why was she even going, though? Was she leaving for good? You couldn't get divorced in Ireland. You could be separated, though.

It was sunny out again; I wasn't leaving the house though. It felt like as long as I stayed in, the bad stuff couldn't get to me. As long as I didn't talk to no one, or see no one, everything would be fine. It wouldn't be fine forever, but it would be fine for a while. I needed time.

Dad wasn't downstairs, so I'd robbed a few packs of salt and vinegar Taytos and a 54321 bar, and brought them back upstairs with me for my lunch. I turned the Commodore on. I loaded up Silkworm. It was impossible with just one player, but I'd the cheat. You were the helicopter in one player; you couldn't be the jeep on its own.

Mam and Dad had never been lovey-dovey, but no one's parents were around here. In real life, most people didn't hold hands or kiss after they were married. Most of the lads' parents argued with each other, or said sly comments. If you were ever round someone's house when their mam had her friends around, they'd always be laughing and slagging off their husbands, behind their back. Mam never said nothing about Dad, though. Nothing nasty anyway. And they did do lovey-dovey stuff, sometimes. If there was a party, or it was Christmas, and they'd had a few drinks. Dad didn't drink a lot of the time, though. He was kind of too serious. He wasn't serious at all in other ways, though; he was always making jokes. Chris was saying about them arguing like it was obvious to everyone or

something. Like it had been going on for ages. Maybe I was too busy with everything else. I'd had so much stuff in my head, and with Marian as well. I was blasting the enemies off the screen with my guns and missiles, but I was cheating and I couldn't die, so it didn't even feel good.

The Gards would already be over there. Marian's dad would have called them straight away; maybe from the phone inside Paudie's, if he had the keys. I wondered if they'd search the house… if they'd find the box of photos. If they did, they might think that Paudie had something to do with Dermot dying, and we might get away with it. They wouldn't though. Even if they searched his house, and they found a box of normal photos of kids, they wouldn't think nothing. If they went in the shed and found those skin mags, they wouldn't do nothing about it. That wasn't illegal, being like that; neither was pulling yourself. They'd have nothing on him, and neither did we. Even if Dermot had got in, we'd probably have found nothing.

I wanted to talk to Joe, to ask him what he'd said to Shane that night. He'd tell us now, cos of what happened to Dermot. If I got him on my own, and told him everything, he'd tell me everything. He wouldn't want Dermot being dead to be his fault. He'd tell the truth. But he was in Kilkee, and he didn't know nothing yet. He was probably in the arcade now, playing Double Dragon.

I pictured the whole thing, and in my head, Joe had been stoned, and drunk and didn't know what he'd been saying. Shane had put words into his mouth, and Joe had been confused, and just agreed, and then Shane had told us all the next day. That still didn't make any sense, though. Why would Shane do any

of it?

I hadn't known Marian's last name. It was probably Collins, like Paudie. Paudie, Padraig, Patrick, Pat. Maybe nobody who really knew him called him 'Paudie'. I couldn't remember when I saw him first, or how I'd found out his name; he was just always around. Her Da looked very like Paudie, now that I thought about it. They'd be brothers. Why hadn't I noticed it before? Why would you notice it, though? Why would I ever look at her, with her gorgeous skin, and her lovely face, and the way she made me feel- why would I look at that, and think she was related to Paudie Collins? No one would. I cared more about messing things up with her than I did about the Gards finding out, or getting into trouble with Mam.

And what about Paudie? What if he really had touched Joe, and what if he really had killed little Tommy? That meant her uncle was a child molester; and he was a murderer. She'd said he used to babysit her. What if he'd done things to her too? What if that's why she was so mad into shifting and stuff? I was two years younger than her at least. What if she was childmolesting me?

'Are ye winning?' Dad was standing in the doorway, with a glass of something in his hand. I'd no idea how long he'd been there.

'What, huh… uh, yeah. I've it on cheat, though.'

'So you can't die?' He took a sip; it looked like whiskey. I could smell it off him.

'Yeah. Infinite lives.'

'Ah shur that's no fun. Is there two player on that one?'

'No,' I lied. Was he drunk?

'Ah well.'

He'd normally have left by now, but he was still here. He walked in behind me, and sat down on Chris' bed.

'Chris talked to you?' His voice was quiet.

'Er, yeah.' I wasn't ready for this, I wanted him to get out and leave me alone.

'Well… what do you think?'

'I… I dunno, Dad.'

The Gards would still be over there. Dermot's body would be covered with a blanket. Some of them would stay with him, and they'd send other ones over in the squad car, to tell his Mam and Dad. Jesus.

'D'you think she'll be coming back?' He was flicking through Chris's tapes now with his fingers. It made a clack-clack-clack noise.

'What will you do if she doesn't, Rich?' He said my name in a strange way, there. He sounded like a Dad from TV. Was he trying to tell me that he loved me? It was a bit late. But then I thought Mam loved me, and she'd run away and left me here.

'I dunno. I dunno nothing, Dad.' The helicopter on the screen flew into a power-up that made you invincible, but I didn't need it. I got it anyway. If you got another one at the same time, it made all the enemies on the screen blow up. I didn't need that either, but I'd still go for it.

'Anything…' He stopped.

'What?'

'Nothing… look I know, Rich. Sorry, I know you must be confused. Sorry.' Now he just sounded sad, and I didn't want that either. He wasn't a bad person; he didn't hit us, or Mam. He just was no good at being a Dad. I didn't say anything back to him.

'It's tough, is all. It's tough on all of us. Your mother, too; and Chris.' He was still talking; still here. I was hungry, even after the crisps and chocolate. There might be bread below in the fridge, and corned beef.

The kitchen smelt of burnt something. Dad had been using the big frying pan. He was still up in my room; he hadn't come down after me. I took a swig of cold water out of the bottle in the fridge. There was too many things going on in my head. Everything was okay now, but it was all going to go very bad. Quickly. There was bread, but it was brown. I'd have to have it anyway. The fridge had loads of stuff in it. Mam must've filled it up for us. She'd be back. She wouldn't just go away. Dad wasn't that bad. They'd make it up. There was Denny corned beef there, and Denny cooked ham. I actually wanted the corned beef. I thought about having lettuce, but I was too lazy to wash it.

They'd have told them by now, Dermot's parents. No one else around the block would know, for a bit anyway. Then they might phone some of the family. They'd stay in the house all day, and people would come over to visit. They'd tell Colm; he was old enough to know. That would be how it got out; Colm would tell Paddy, or Willum, and they'd go telling everyone then. It'd be all round the

Square by tonight, or maybe tomorrow. Shane wouldn't know yet. Dara would find out from his Dad. It was probably Dara's Dad they'd send to tell them; cos he knew Colm Sr.

There was no Dairygold spread that I could see, only butter. You were supposed to leave the butter out, so it wouldn't get hard. We didn't in our house, though. I tried doing it like Mam; scraping little bits off onto the knife, but I still ended up tearing holes in the bread. Nothing was going right for me today.

The lads must've been thinking things as well. Dermot being found a day early was going to take them by surprise too. Shane was brazen. He'd just sit there with a straight face through everything, and never even go red, or get scared. Dara wasn't as tough as him; if his da started questioning him, he might say something. I wasn't saying nothing to no one. If Marian ever found out anything about what we'd been doing in Paudie's, that would be it. She'd never speak to me again, and I'd have no girl, and I'd be back to where I was before; no clue about girls, and no idea what to say to any of them. Mam had gone off and left me here with *him*, and I'd no one to talk to, and she was the only good thing left.

I felt sad about Dermot, but I wasn't gonna tell no one. It was like they said on TV or in films: he was dead now, and no amount of anything was going to bring him back. I put salt on the corned beef, then on the cheese. Four slices of bread, two sandwiches; each sandwich cut into two. I didn't like eating things if they weren't in twos or fours.

I'd been expecting Dermot being missing to be a big thing. Thought Mam and Dad would be asking me stuff, and I'd get nervous, and act all obvious and

stuff. Thought everyone in the estate would be out looking for him; his Mam crying on the porch, and all that sort of thing. Nothing like that had happened though, it was all too quick. It made it less easy to believe that he was dead. There'd be a funeral, though. Tomorrow, maybe; or the next day. I'd never been at a funeral before; I didn't want to see a dead body, I told Mam. Nanna on her side died two years ago, and Dad's da got cancer last year. He was gone before Christmas. I'd already seen this dead body, but I still didn't want to see it again. Shane and Dara would be there. That'd be the first time I'd seen either of them, since. I didn't want that either.

'Hungry, is it?' Dad was back, with an empty glass. He went over to the freezer, and got the ice thing out. He held it over the sink, and pushed the ice out with his thumbs pressing the back of it. The cold made his fingers go red.

'Ah, yeah. Corn beef.'

'Oh right. Yeah, I picked up the Denny stuff in Quinnsworth. That's the one ye like, yeah?' *He'd* done the shopping? Janey Mack.

'Yeah. Yeah, I like that one.' Dad wouldn't know about them finding Dermot yet. He probably didn't even know he'd been missing. The McCarthys wouldn't have thought anything was wrong until well late in the night. In the summer holidays, no one went in home until about ten. Sometimes you'd stay out til eleven, if you were watching a video in someone's house.

'Well, if there's anything you need. Food and drink… let me know, and I'll get it for you.' He was being nice, but it was just like Mam giving me the tenner. It didn't feel like they were doing something for me, really. It felt like they

were feeling guilty.

'I'm all right.'

'Okay. As long as you're all right.' He took the cap off the bottle of Jameson, and poured it over the ice in his glass. There was some left in a bottle of Shannon lemonade in the fridge, and he poured that in on top of it. It was dead flat, so it didn't make a fizzy noise.

'Yeah, sound.' I wasn't all right, there was nothing I could say to him now, though. He was probably feeling bad enough with Mam gone. He took a sip, and he did that face that adults do when they have some liquor- the face that looks like they hate the taste, but they love it as well. Dermot did it too; well, he used to.

'You know, I…' He started saying something, and I looked over; he must've changed his mind, though.

'I'm going to go sit out in the garden…' Dunno why he was telling me for. I scoffed the end of my sandwich and went back upstairs.

I looked out the window again, at Dermot's. There was a black car outside, with dark windows. Could've been detectives. I jumped back from the window when I saw it, but that was stupid, cos no one could see me through the nets. I looked over at Kelly's. They'd had the funeral the other day; that was the one Dad had gone to, Mam had told me. I'd forgotten about Tommy, in all the drama. Stupid, really; cos he was the reason for all of this. Or Joe was. I wanted to talk to Joe. Before Shane got a chance to talk to him though. Dermot was on my side, but Dara had just done what Shane said, yesterday. I'd have no chance getting him now. If Joe knew what Shane had made us do though. If he knew that

Shane had told us his secret…

Maybe there was no secret though. There was no one going in or out of Dermot's yet. The record player came on loud downstairs; the Beatles. Dad was singing along, he was tapped in the head. I'd no idea what we were going to have for dinner tonight. He couldn't cook nothing. I was still hungry, like there was a hole in me. I needed a fag. I'd two saved, under the bed. I'd have to go out, cos he'd smell it if I had one out the bathroom window now. He was out the back though, he'd said. I didn't want to go out the front. I looked out the window again; he was out the back all right. He'd the deckchair put out, and he was listening to the stereo coming out the kitchen window.

I lit up the fag on the front porch. I'd never risk it normally, but he was out the back, and Mam and Chris were in Pineview. The worst that was gonna happen was one of the neighbours would see me, and tell on me. I wasn't going anywhere though, so it'd have to do.

There was no one out on the green at all. It was scorching out, but you couldn't hear a single kid. It was like a ghost town in the westerns. That sun would have rotted Dermot away pure quickly, so it was good that they'd found him soon. Ah, Jesus, poor Dermot. Imagine his mam trying to identify him down the Garda station, and all maggots crawling out of his eyes. I gulped. I hated doing that; thinking things like that, and scaring myself. Mam said I was worse than any horror film, with my imagination.

The fag tasted good. Sometimes they did; most times they were rank.

People always wanted one when they were trying to concentrate, or if they'd had a big mad shock. Dermot had been in a car accident once, and he said that afterwards the Gard had given him a fag to calm him down. When he was nine, this was. He might have made it up, but it was a rapid story. Dermot was really sound; I kept thinking that. I dunno was it just because he was dead; did you like people more because they died? You probably did, because on telly when there was a funeral, people only said nice things about the dead person. And you couldn't speak badly of the dead, neither; Mam always said that. I wished Mam wasn't gone away. When Dad found out about Dermot, he probably wouldn't even say anything to me. He was too awkward at talking about anything. Mam would have said something; or she'd have told us at least. She'd say: 'God bless us and save us' or 'the poor misfortune', and she'd look for a lesson that I should learn from it, and tell me to be careful. Dad never talked to me like that; he was just a messer. That's what he was like; a messer in class at school, only he was an adult.

I was half trying to keep the fag away from the front door, so Dad wouldn't see it, and half trying to keep myself inside the porch, so no one would see me. Marian's mam was in their front garden, doing the weeds. I didn't salute her, cos I didn't know her, yet. I hadn't met either of them. It wasn't like on TV, where you got a new neighbour, and they called in to say hello. People weren't as nice in real life. Of course, when they built this estate, everyone that moved into it was new, all at the same time. That was different, and for a while all the people here were friends with each other. But after a while there'd be fights and arguments, or someone's child would break someone else's window with a ball,

and their da wouldn't pay for it, and then they'd stop talking to each other. The first year we were here, there was a Sports Day and everything. That was the first time I met Joe.

I had different friends for different things; every kid probably had that. Like, there were things me and Jonathan Musgrave would talk about that I'd never talk about in front of the others. We both liked ghosts and vampires. When we were small, we used to rob big sheets of paper out of his father's shed, and draw mad pictures of ghosts and ghouls on them. The sheets were orange instead of white, but we didn't care. Joe was my friend for video games, though. We both had the Commodore 64 now, and we swapped games all the time, and played Microprose all the time. He always had good games magazines in his house. He bought lots of them, even the ones that weren't just for the Commodore.

Joe's older brother Peter liked Iron Maiden; he had mad posters of them in his room. We'd loved to have been able to draw like that, but neither of us was very good. My skeletons looked like onions half the time. Me and Joe had always been the closest. He used to come over every day before, and hang around. I wasn't ever allowed to go to his house, but I didn't know back then that it was because of his dad. We had sleepovers sometimes. There was a space under our stairs that we didn't really use for nothing. Other people put the linen basket in there, in their houses, or hung up their coats. Mam didn't put nothing under there, though. I used to think it looked like the cockpit of one of the ships from Battlestar Galactica; me and Joe would sit under there, and pretend we were fighting the Cylons. There was a pipe that came up for the gas meter that we pretended was the

joystick thing for flying and firing lasers.

We were so close back then that people even said we looked like each other. Strangers would ask us if we were brothers. This was before he got so big, though. We never had fights, we just suited each other. We told each other everything as well.

So why wouldn't he have told me about Paudie? When did it happen? That was another thing I couldn't work out. Joe and me had moved to Thomondgate at the same time; when we were seven. Was it before that? Little Tommy Kelly was younger than seven. Joe lived in Balla before he moved here, and from what Marian said, Paudie used to live in Kennedy Park. They were nowhere near each other. A memory came into my head, but I couldn't figure out what it was. It was like an old photograph, but I couldn't remember if I was remembering something, or actually remembering seeing a photograph.

I stubbed out the fag on the ground, and picked the butt up, to throw in the bin. A photograph… or a memory of a photograph. It was on the tip of my tongue, whatever it was. There was a breeze out here, now. There hadn't been a good cool breeze in weeks. It didn't feel like it was ever going to rain again.

'D'you like music, Rich?' He was looking through a stack of his LPs, when I went into the kitchen. He'd another drink in his hand. He must've got more lemonade somewhere. Do I like music… that was a stupid question; everyone likes music.

'Uh, yeah.' I wished I'd gone straight upstairs, now.

‘Pop music, yeah? Stuff off the radio?’ He didn’t look at me when he spoke; he was taking a record out of its sleeve. It was red. There was a blonde girl on the front; she’d a white dress on, and long boots.

‘Yeah. I suppose.’ She looked a bit like Marian, only her hair was all old fashioned. He put the record on.

‘Yeah. See, with music you go through three stages. Three periods in your life…’ His voice was different, like someone on the telly. I knew this song; it was the one about These Boots Are Made For Walking. Mam liked it.

‘When you’re your age, you like the pop music. That’s when you start buying records; they’re the records that get in the charts. Singles, I mean. Who do you like?’ It was definitely new lemonade, cos when he put it on the counter, it fizzed up.

‘Uh, I dunno really. A-ha?’ They were the only ones I could think of where I knew more than one song. I didn’t follow bands.

‘What ones do they do, again? Remind your Dad, Rich. He’s an old fogey.’ He was smiling, but he didn’t look happy or anything. It was a drunk smile. Dad used to play the drums when he was younger. In a Showband, with my uncle Terry. They still did a show every Christmas, up in the hall at Thomond Rugby Club. They weren’t even too bad, except it was all old music, for the mams and dads.

‘Ah, Take Me On? The Sun Always Shines On TV?’ I liked The Bangles as well, but you couldn’t say that; they were for girls.

‘Hmmm, yeah. I think I know. Well, anyway- when you’re young, you

like pop. When you get to be a teenager, you start liking the old music. You know, like The Beatles, or the Rolling Stones?' I didn't like either of them; they were boring. I wasn't going to suddenly start liking boring old sixties music when I was a teenager. He was definitely drunk.

'Yeah? Listen, Dad, I've to…'

'And then, when you get into your thirties and forties, you end up liking classical music.' He just ignored what I said, and carried on talking. It was a good song, this one. Even if it was ancient. It was catchy. I wondered could Marian sing. She probably could. Some people just got to be everything: gorgeous, clever, funny, good at stuff. Some other people didn't get to be nothing.

'Did you have an argument?' He looked at me more serious now, but he was still sort of smiling.

'What? With who?'

'With your… your friends. The lads. The boys… You've been in here all day; it's not like you. The weather's nice outside.' The song stopped, and another one came on, but he picked the needle off the record, and put it at the start of another one. I didn't know this one.

'Am, no. No, nothing happened.' How did he know? Was someone after telling him something?

'It was Shane, yeah?' The song was about when she was five, and yer man was six. It was very different to the last one. I didn't answer, but he could see in my face that he'd got it nearly right, anyway.

'Listen and I tell you about people like Shane, Rich. I knew his father

when I was growing up, and he's the very same as him. They're bullies, Rich.' I didn't know he'd known Shane's dad. He hadn't grown up around here.

'Bullies with a bit of charm; that's the worst. I see him, coming in here. I see how he fools your Mam into thinking butter wouldn't melt, Rich. But there's nothing sweet about that fella, is there?' He finished his drink, and got straight up to go for the bottle again. I'd never seen Dad drink properly. He'd never talked to me like this, either.

'Well, yeah. He's…' I started, but he didn't really need me to talk. He carried on anyway:

'People like Shane, Rich… people like that, your Mam will tell you that people like that never win in the end. That everyone gets their just desserts… all that fucking shite, pardon my language.' I'd never heard him swear like that before.

'People like that usually end up getting everything they want in life, because life isn't fair. That's the most important thing I could ever teach you, right now, before your life even starts. Life isn't fucking fair.'

'But, what about…' I stopped. Couldn't put it into words, what I wanted to say. It was something about good deeds, and rewards, but I didn't want to sound stupid.

'Nothing about nothing, Richie. Life isn't fair, and being nice won't get you anywhere. People like them will get the jobs, the women, the money. The only thing you can try and do, is use that' -he pointed at his head-

'Use that, to try and get ahead of them. Do good in school, get into

college… get yourself out of this shithole.' He put way too much whiskey in the glass; he noticed it too, and he picked the glass up, and took a swig out of it, to make room for the lemonade. He hadn't thought that through. I nearly giggled.

'Fuck people like them, Rich. I'd love to tell you that they all end up in prison, or homeless, or stabbed to death, but most of them don't. They just meet some woman, and pop out some kids, and those kids grow up to be the same as them, and it goes on and on.' He took another drink, and wiped his mouth with the back of his hand. I'd stopped trying to join in the conversation; I was letting him get on with it. The woman on the record was saying Bang Bang, My Baby Shot Me Down.

'What you don't do, Rich, is let cunts like them drag you down and hold you back. Do you like him; Shane I mean?'

'Yeah, I mean no. I mean, I don't know.'

'I'll take that as No. So what's stopping you just telling him to…to eff off, eh? Why can't you just be friends with the others?' He'd stopped himself saying the F word there. Probably cos he'd said the C word. His face was red.

'Well, because… because you can't just…' He didn't understand; he was too old.

'Ah yeah, I know. I suppose you can't, can you… I'm sorry Rich, I'm rambling. I'm a little tipsy. It's your Mam, you know… and everything. I just want you to be happy. Life isn't fair, though…'

'Yeah, I know, Dad.' He looked sad, now. I wanted to make him better.

'What, I'm… I suppose what I was trying to say, is that it's your life.

Don't let someone else ruin it for you. Make your own choices. You think I know nothing, and I'm an old fart, or whatever. But I see you, with those guys. I see how he bullies you, and the other lads. It doesn't have to be like that. Ye're only kids, still. If ye all got together and talked, without him there, ye'd realise that it was easy to just walk away… from someone like him. He only seems strong when you're thinking about doing it on your own. When it's the lot of ye together… well, it's a whole different story.' He put his hand on my arm. It felt like a scene from the movies, only in those movies, your dad wouldn't have been drunk.

I never thought Dad paid any attention to what I got up to, but he knew a lot. He was right, as well. I needed to do something about Shane. We needed to. I just knew that when it came down to it, I wouldn't be able to. I was like the Lion from the Yellow Brick Road; I'd no courage.

Sometimes, when it was after Lights Out, and I was nearly asleep, I'd think about everything in my life, and it would be like all the answers became clear, and I'd make all these plans about what I was going to do, and who I was going to say what to, the next day. Then I'd wake up in the morning, and all the courage would be gone again, and even thinking about the things I'd been thinking the night before would make me scared. A sort of crushing on my chest scared, like in a film, when they play the music that sounds like the part of a piano that has all the low down notes. Some of the lads in JFK got piano lessons. I just liked messing around with it. Plink plink plink on one end; dumm dumm dumm on the other.

I went out into the back garden and sat down. The Gards would have been and gone from Dermot's now. They'd have taken him out of Paudie's house too, to the hospital, or the morgue; wherever it was you took dead bodies. I was hungry again. Someone knocked on the front door. No one got it. I wasn't going to get it either. Knocking again, now; a little harder. It could be the Gards. I thought about running.

I heard Dad open the door and talk to someone in a mumbled voice. He was so drunk, it would have been funny another time. He shut the door again, must've been some Jehovahs or something. He was coming out here now, I could hear footsteps.

'Oh, Richie, love. I'm so sorry.' Marian came through our back door and put her arms around me. She smelt clean, like shampoo and soap. My bones felt like they'd turned to water. I'd lost everyone; I needed to keep her. I opened my eyes and saw Dad in the kitchen. He gave me a smile, and a wink. Not meaning something dirty or anything. He just looked happy; for me. He'd no idea what was really going on, though.

I felt like a liar, of course. Sitting there with a straight face, while she told me that the boy they'd found in her uncle Pat's garden was one of the McCarthys. The youngest fella; the one who I was friends with. I acted shocked, like people did in films. I did the whole shebang; choked a little bit, stuttered, looked like I was going to faint. She believed me all right, but she'd no reason not to. I couldn't tell her anything. Most of the story of how Dermot got there was stuff I never wanted her to find out.

We talked for a while, about Dermot and how long I knew him for; were we close; had I known he was missing? She'd listened in while her dad was talking to the Gards in their house. That's how she'd found out Dermot's name, and it clicked that he was someone I knew.

She was good at this; making me feel better. Even though she hadn't known Dermot, she knew how to say the right things. It was good to be able to talk, even if I was mostly telling lies.

She talked about Paudie, and how they were trying to phone him all morning. Whenever she said 'Pat', I had a blank space in my brain, then I'd fill it in with Paudie, and get a little sick feeling in my stomach. They'd got hold of him eventually, and he was on the way home now, from wherever he'd been. Her Dad had gone over to McCarthys and picked up the dog, to get her out of their way. He'd said the mother was sitting on the couch, bawling crying. Colm Sr was chain-smoking, and shaking his head. I could picture it all, and I felt as guilty as sin. I shouldn't have, though. Shane was the one who brought us in there; Joe was the one we were doing everything for; Dermot himself had gone up there. He'd insisted. I'd nothing to feel guilty about, but I did all the same, cos I was keeping a secret.

We'd gone down behind the shed, for some privacy. Dad wouldn't come out here, anyway. Not when I'd a girl with me. Dads were different to mams like that. Mams wanted to keep you out of trouble like that; Dads didn't mind you having a bit of fun with a girl. Well, in the movies anyway. Marian had fags, and

we were having one each, instead of smokes. She was so beautiful, and I was enjoying this attention. That made me feel even more guilty, with poor Dermot rotting away, wherever he was. I had to forget about it though. The guilt would eat me up, like it did in the films, then I'd have to tell someone. The rest of them wouldn't join in either. They'd just let me take the blame. Then I'd definitely lose her, for good.

I looked down at her chest, and her bra showing through the top. I wanted to shift her now, but that felt wrong. Like we were doing it on Dermot's grave, or something. He wasn't in a grave yet though.

We talked about Tommy Kelly, and what had happened to him. She understood the whole thing much better than me, probably cos she was older. She said that when she'd lived in Kennedy Park, a little boy near her house got touched by someone, but they never found out who it was. I tried to hide my reaction to that; Paudie lived in Kennedy back then. He must've done it before. He'd been doing it for years. Shane had been right. We'd been right. We had to be right. We could be wrong, though. People got molested all the time, probably. It didn't mean that Paudie was the one doing it. Jesus Christ. I couldn't make up my mind about nothing until I talked to Joe again. That mightn't be for ages though.

We talked about when the funeral would be, and would they have to put it off, cos they'd be doing an autopsy. You always had to do an autopsy if someone died suspiciously. I didn't know if it was called an autopsy in Ireland though. She asked me what I thought he had been doing in Paudie's; why he'd been up so high, to have fallen that far down. I gave her no answers, in case I told her the truth, by

accident. She said that they'd probably have a mass for Dermot tomorrow. The funeral would be on another day. I wondered who'd be at that Mass. I'd have to go. I told her I'd never been to a funeral, and she said they were okay, and that you didn't have to look into the coffin or anything. I thought of Dermot in the coffin, with his busted face, and I remembered the horsefly, and I wanted to vomit.

We went over into her house after a bit. She was dead cool with her Mam; she just told her she was going upstairs to watch a video with me. The Mam said nothing. I looked at her, wondering should I say hello or something, but she just carried on filling up the washing machine.

'She's such a gowl,' Marian said, once we were upstairs.

'Ah, she seems sound…' Mam would never have let me bring a girl up to my room.

'Trust me, she's a twat. What do you want to watch?' We were actually going to watch a video then. It wasn't just an excuse. I was disappointed again. I'd still got the horn, even though it was wrong.

'Ah, what have ye?' She'd probably only mushy romances.

'Have a look yourself, there.' She sparked up a fag. In her own bedroom, with her mam downstairs. She looked at me like she was expecting me to say something about it, so I didn't. I had a root through the tapes on the side. Some were copies or pirates, but most of them were real ones. She'd The Breakfast Club, and Pretty In Pink, and Dirty Dancing… all those girly ones. But she'd good ones as well, like Top Gun, and Terminator. I picked out a tape.

'How about this one; you watched it yet?'

‘I’ve watched them all, hon. That’s a good one though. We’ll watch that.’ She looked gorgeous. The TV and video were on a stand facing the side of the bed. I didn’t know if she was going to come sit with me or not.

‘Want this?’ She had half the fag left.

‘Nah I’m all right.’ I did want it, but I didn’t want her mam or dad to burst in and catch me smoking, on top of everything else.

‘Okey doke.’ She just threw it out the window. Cool as a cucumber. She pushed all the teddy bears over to the side so we could sit. I put the pillows up behind us as well. The windowsill was sticking into my back a bit, but I didn’t mind it. I put my arm around her, still awkward doing it. She snuggled into me, and I forgot every bad thing in my head for a while.

The film was rapid. There was a fella into it that was mad into computers. Hawky-looking old fashioned looking ones, compared to mine. But he could plug his into the telephone, and it talked to other computers on the other side of the country. Mad, like. There was a girl in it too; a ride, she was. She liked him, even though he was a computer geek. That happened in films. He nearly started the Nuclear War by accident, from playing a game against a computer. Marian was dead quiet all the way through, but not in a bad way. She was just enjoying the film; she laughed at all the funny bits, same as me.

We didn’t shift each other or anything, probably cos of her period. She didn’t start anything anyway, and I definitely wasn’t going to. I didn’t want to get up to anything in here anyway, in case her dad kicked down the door or something. We ended up falling asleep on the bed. I must’ve been exhausted. A

knock on the bedroom door woke me up, but I didn't remember hearing it.

'Marian, love?'

'WHAT?' She was a bit of a brat, Marian ; she gave her mam an awful time.

'Oh, hi Mar. Listen, it's nearly half ten…'

'So?' She winked at me when she said it, and I smiled. Her mam hadn't even opened the door or anything.

'So maybe your, um… *friend* should go home now, all right?' I thought she was going to start an argument with the mother for a second, then she just shrugged and said,

'Pfffft. Okay. Five minutes, right?'

'Five minutes so.' I got up to leave, but she put her hand on my arm, and sat me down again. Then she took one of my hands, and put it straight up her top, and pulled me into her to kiss me. The first thing that came into my head was my breath must be rank from the sleep, but I forgot about it straight away; she was all wet and hot inside her mouth, and her nipple was hard and soft at the same time. I got a bit lost inside her for a while, like she was a dream I was having, and when stopped so we could breathe, she said

'I love you' and I said

'I love you too,' because that's what you did, and because I meant it as well.

My good mood lasted all the five minutes it took me to get into my kitchen, until Dad told me to sit down, while he told me about poor Dermot

McCarthy, and I had to act like I was surprised.

Ten

I still had one Nana and one Granddad left, so I'd thought that the first funeral I went to would be one of theirs. I'd no hope of getting out of this one though. Dad didn't say much on the way. It felt weird being outside. I didn't feel safe. Shane and Dara were going to be there; Colm as well, and maybe Paddy. Mam and Chris weren't coming. The sun was too nice for this. In a film, it would be raining. In the films, you saw the coffin going into the ground, as well. The thing we were going to was the mass. Tomorrow, they'd take the coffin to the graveyard, but I wasn't going to go to that, I didn't think.

We came in at the back. I'd my head down. I'd no idea how long funeral masses went on for. Most mass was short, but when you had your communion or your confirmation they'd drag on for ages. I couldn't see any of the lads yet. If we stayed back here, I might be able to get through the whole thing without seeing Shane or Colm or Dermot's mam and dad. I definitely didn't want to see *them*. All the back rows were full. It was the opposite of a wedding; no one wanted to be at the front. Dad had told me that you have to shake the hand of Colm, or Dermot's mam, and say 'Sorry for your loss.' He said that I was all right though; kids didn't have to do it. Sometimes you hated your parents calling you a child, but sometimes it was handy to be one.

The next few rows were full again. There was lots of people there I didn't recognise; kids, so probably from Munchin's. There was people from

Thomondgate that weren't even friends with Dermot; their mothers or fathers must've known Colm Sr and Mrs McCarthy. Dad and me kept walking up, but there was no spaces for us; no one was moving to let us in either. I started to crap myself, because I knew that we were going to have to sit right up the front, and there'd be no hiding there.

'Here! Here, there's space here, boss…' someone said. Dad grabbed me by the wrist and pushed me into where they'd said to go. I sat down and tried to make myself small. I could see the coffin now; it wasn't as big as a real coffin, and that made me want to cry. Dad leaned across me, to whoever had let us in the seat:

'Thanks, Paudie. How are you yourself?' I froze.

'Ah, shur… still a bit, you know, Mick. Thanks.'

'Ah, of course. Nothing you could have done, Paud. These things just happen.' Dad patted him on the leg. I couldn't move, now. I didn't look at either of them while they were talking. Paudie smelled like something I couldn't put my finger on. It wasn't sweat, and it wasn't food. It was something, though. The coffin was white, with brass handles. It looked tiny, even from here. It looked like a baby's coffin.

The priest was by the altar, with the altar boys, but mass wasn't starting yet. People were being quiet, but there was so many of them whispering, that the sound of it all together was actually loud. Every few minutes, the priest would get annoyed at it, and look over, or say 'Shhhh!' Then everyone would stop, but only for a few minutes, then the whispers would start again. Mass was weird cos it had been ages since any of these grown-ups had been in school, but when the priest

was around, they still acted a bit like kids. The altar boys had a big gold yoke with chains on it. That was for burning the smelly stuff. I'd been avoiding looking at the row beyond the coffin, cos I knew who'd be there. I looked now and saw Colm Senior and Mrs McCarthy, looking very sad. People all over the church were trying to catch their eye for a second, so they could give them a sad nod, or mouth Sorry For Your Loss at them. Colm Junior had a suit on, a black one. He looked like he was going to a Debs. I looked away when my eyes got to him, and I shrank back into where I was sitting. Paudie was whispering to whoever was on his other side. I looked over again, and saw Dennis, with some girl; must've been his girlfriend. She was crying, and he looked awful. Him and Dermot were the close ones; neither of them got on with Colm. The whisper around the room got loud, and the priest had to Shhhh them all again.

I could see the door from my seat. Every time it creaked, people would look to see who was coming in. The Mass had to be starting soon; it was boiling in here. I looked over across again at Dermot's family. People in the rows behind were leaning in to talk to them, and the whispering all over the church was getting fierce loud. Then I saw Shane.

He was dressed in black, but not in a shirt and trousers or anything. He'd black jeans on, and a Raiders t-shirt. He was sitting with Dara. That was the worst bit. They weren't looking over this way, thank God. The priest started the Mass, and everyone stood up. I never knew which bits you stood up for or sat down again for. There was the bit where you hit your chest and said 'Lamb of God', and the bit where you shook hands with the guy next to you… Janey Mack, I'd have to

shake his hand.

There was a bang down at the doors, cos someone was coming in late. A few of us looked around to see who it was; the auld biddies would tsk and tut at you for having no respect for Our Lord. My mouth nearly hit the floor though, cos the people coming in late now were Mrs McNamara, and Joe. They must've come back from Kilkee. It was only in County Clare; you could drive there in two hours.

Joe was dressed in black trousers and a black tie, but he'd a white shirt on. It made him look like he was a waiter. He was kind of shy, Joe, so he never really looked straight at you. He always had his eyes on the floor when he was just walking around, so I'd no chance of him saluting me. I watched them walk up to look for seats. The priest stopped what he was saying for a few second, and did one of those coughs that you know aren't really coughs; it's just someone trying to drop a hint. I held my breath when they got to the seats where Shane and Dara were, but there was no room there, and they went over to the other side.

The Mass was long and boring, and nothing like a funeral was like on the telly. On the telly or in a film, you'd be watching it, and there'd be sad music, and you'd get all caught up in it, and you'd feel like crying too. Even though it was just made up, and you didn't even know them. This was a real funeral though, and one of my friends was dead in a coffin there, and I was bored stiff, and I wanted to go home. The whole thing just felt like normal Mass, and there was a reason why none of us ever wanted to go to that.

I stood up for the hymns, but I didn't sing them. Dad didn't sing them either. There would be Holy Communion near the end. I was dreading that, cos I

might run into Shane at the altar, or Dara, or Colm. I hadn't seen Paddy at all; I'd nearly forgot him. I wanted to talk to Joe. I wanted to talk to him before Shane did. This wasn't the place though. You couldn't talk in Mass, you'd get killed for it.

'I might head over to Frazer's, so. To pay my respects,' Dad said; when we were outside.

'Weren't we just paying our respects there?' I suddenly felt scared. We were a good bit away from our house. Being outside somewhere was always less safe than being inside, near people.

'Ah yeah, but you know…' He didn't look in my eyes when he said it. He wanted to go for a drink. Frazer's was on the way; it was half way between Munchin's church and our place. I walked up with him. Other people from the mass were all over the place; I couldn't see Shane or any of them, though. If I could catch Joe on his own, I could maybe say something. Dad was right; there was no reason why we had to hang around with Shane. We were our own bosses. If I could get Joe on his own, and he agreed with me, we'd only have to get Dara. I didn't care if he was sitting next to Shane at Mass; I knew him, he wasn't that close to him. He wasn't close to any of us really, but I'd prefer him with us instead of Shane. It wasn't about who you got with you in a gang, it was about how many. If Shane was left on his own, it didn't matter how hard he was. He'd never start nothing with one of us if he knew we were all against him. I had to get Joe, though. I hadn't seen him at the end at all. When I'd come down from Communion, the seat next to his mam had been empty. Shane and Dara were gone

too. We did that all the time; left after Communion, or left while everyone was going up. Mam said it was okay to do it, cos the bit after Communion wasn't that holy. Paudie hadn't looked at me, when he shaked my hand and said 'Peace be with you'. That probably didn't mean nothing though. He couldn't've known anything yet. He couldn't.

Dad had gone into the pub, now. I walked along the side of the road with Dolan's Field on it, cos there was shade there. If you kept your head down, and kept in the shade, no one would ever see you. Not unless they were really looking for you. I kept my head low and my eyes down. That was probably why I didn't see Colm and Paddy. They were waiting for me, on top of a wall.

'Get his arms, sham,' said Paddy. Colm was behind me, holding me in a lock, like a wrestler would do. I didn't even struggle. I couldn't have got out of it anyway. He pulled my arms up higher, and squeezed harder; I was in agony. My brain just said to me, sort of calmly:

'This is it. You're going to die.' And it felt all right. Felt like someone had taken a big brick off my chest. Paddy squared up to me, face to face. I looked in his eyes, and my brain said the same thing to me, even calmer:

'This is it. You're going to die,' and then: 'You're not afraid.' I felt all relaxed, and this big smile came over my face. Paddy looked confused. Colm was still holding me.

'Hit him, will you, sham. Hit him!' Paddy was blank.

If I'd've laughed at him, he'd probably have broke my nose. Smiling was

different than laughing though. Laughing at someone was cheeky; it made them angry. He pulled his fist back, like he was going to punch me in the face. I closed my eyes and waited for it. I was already imagining it in my head; the skin of his knuckles, smashing into my nose. All the bones in my face being smashed. It didn't feel scary. I looked straight into his eyes, and smiled. He swung for me, and my eyes closed without me closing them. There was no hit, just the wind on my face when his hand went past.

'Leave him off, sham. G'wan.'

'Huh? What you mean leave him off, bud?' said Colm. My eyes were still closed, and he still had a hold of me. He sounded a little bit like Dermot when you'd your eyes closed.

'Leave him off, I said.' He sounded angry now, but at Colm not me. The hands around my arms were gone and I fell onto my knees. I stood up and rubbed myself down, even though there was no mud anywhere. It was just what you saw people do in films after there was a fight.

'He burst your lip, sham! What are you doing, like? Hit him!' Colm couldn't believe it.

'Ah, t'was only messing, boy. If I'd a hit him, it'd be the same. T'was forkslings, sham. If you're afraid a getting hurt, you shun't play. Am I right, boss?' He meant me. I nodded; I must've been dreaming again. Paddy had his hand out.

'Shake on it, pal.' I went to shake his hand, for a second I thought there might be a looger in it or something, but it was dry.

'I'll tell you what, sham; you've a pair of bollix on you all right. Ha'nt he, Colm?' Colm didn't say anything, but he grunted like he was agreeing. I'd been calm a minute ago, but my heart was going ninety now.

'No way a getting' away, like, an' he just stands there; smiling at me. Big grin on his chops. I'll tell you what, pal; any your little buds woulda shit themselves there. You're a fucking headcase, boss. You're not all there, like. D'you smoke?' His eyes were wild.

'No. Yeah, I mean, yeah. I smoke, yeah. I've none, though, sorry.' He laughed, and took out a box of Rothman's. He gave me one, and one to Colm as well. Colm still looked like he didn't know what was going on. He looked pee'd off, probably at me.

'What you giving him fags for?'

'Whisht, you; they're my fags,'

We were standing in one of the gate bits that came off the side of Dolan's. No one knew who Dolan was; it was just some name. But the field used to belong to people, and there used to be houses here too. All that was left was a few front walls, and the gates. Paddy pushed open the gate and walked in. I stopped.

'C'mon. You're all right, sham. We're not gonna touch you, are we, Colm?' Colm didn't answer him. 'You'll be all right.'

I didn't believe him. All of this was too weird. I wondered for a second if I'd actually died, and this was all just a dream that my brain was playing to make me feel better. The fag was really strong, and it reminded me of Mam. We went

through the field. Paddy had a big blackthorn branch; like you'd make a walking stick out of, and he was using it to thrash the nettles. Colm looked like he was in a world of his own. We weren't going near where the thing had happened with the forksling; thank God for that. Paddy hadn't forgotten it or anything, but remembering it like that wasn't going to help me.

We hopped over a little wall, into a place where they must've been using as a camp, or whatever older fellas had instead of camps. They'd a little shelter built, in case it rained, but the rest of it was all out under the sun. They'd a plastic chair, like the ones in school. And a big bean bag, and a table as well. There was an ashtray that someone had robbed from home or the pub; it had Guinness on it. There was a crate with skin mags in it; some of them were a bit torn up. Dermot told us before about the camps his brothers made. They'd always make one around Halloween, to keep trays of eggs in, cos you couldn't keep them at home, or your mam and dad would find them. Paddy lifted up a piece of plywood. There was a hole dug under it. He took out a can of Carling.

'Here!' He threw it over to me. This was mad. Much more better than any camp we'd ever made. They'd shelves and everything, with spray cans on them. They'd do mad graffiti around the place, Dermot had said. I opened the can. Paddy had one too, and Colm. I said

'Cheers', cos that's what you say, and they said it too. I looked over at Colm; he was still in his smart suit, with red rings around his eyes that gave it away that he'd been crying. I wanted to tell him I was sorry for his loss, or to say anything to him at all, but I didn't know him properly. I didn't know where to start

with a thing like that.

'Was he robbing houses long?' he said, out of the blue.

'What? Who?'

'Who, says you. My brother is who. Dermot…' He drank a long swig of Carling, and done a burp that made echoes around us. He was obnoxious, as Mam would say. I was frightened of him.

'Janey Mack, no. He wasn't robbing no houses, Colm.' I knew his name, but saying it to him felt funny. It always did, when you didn't really know someone.

'What was he doing in there, so? Ye musta known he was doing it; ye're always together; you, him, Shane Collopy, that Dara steamer. Ye musta known. Or were ye all doin' it?'

'I didn't ever hear nothing like that, Colm. Honest to God; swear on my Mother's life.' I was finished my can already, but I kept it in my hand like it still had something in it. I did that a lot. It gave you something to do with yourself, pretending to drink out of it.

'If he says he dun't know, he dun't know, Colm. Lee'm alone,' said Paddy. He put another can of Carling in front of me. His eyes were all bloodshot.

'Finished already, boss? You're a fucking animal, hah? Hahahah. G'wan.' He was kind of sound, but in that way people you were afraid of were kind of sound. Like Shane.

'Why're you wasting the drink, bud?' Colm crushed his own can in his hand, and got another one out of the hole.

'Ah, leave him alone will you, sham. They're my beers. Half of 'em, anyway.' He looked at Colm without blinking, the way hard fellas do to you. Colm was hard too, but Paddy was a beast.

We sat there for a few hours, or it must've been a few hours anyway; I'd left my watch at home, cos the strap had got red sauce on it. Colm got more friendlier after a few more cans, and Paddy took a shine to me, as Dad would have said. We talked about who we knew around Thomondgate and Kileely and Balla. People did that all the time. Do you know so-and-so? Do you know my cousin from there? They asked me about going to JFK, and I told them about the poshies I went to school with; slagging them off and doing impressions of them, cos that's what you do, if you want to get in with lads like them two. Paddy was in stitches. There was loads of cans in the hole, and they kept giving me fags, too. We didn't talk about Dermot again, until much later on, when Colm said:

'Here, d'you think he was in trouble, Rich?'

'How d'you mean?' I asked. I was langered now. All the fags hadn't helped either; you always felt way more drunk if you'd fags. My eyes were trying to close.

'D'you think he owed someone money, and he'd to go robbing for it?' Colm's eyes were all sad now.

'Nah, he never said nothing, Colm man. Nothing like that at all. I'd a known.' I felt so guilty, but I wasn't going to start confessing stuff. I wasn't the bad guy anyway. Think of Marian, I kept telling myself. She was the only thing I cared about now. I missed her. I wanted to go call in for her. Not even to shift her;

just to see her. I was mad about her.

'And there was no one around ye that might have been making him do stuff? No older fellas, asking you do a little favour, for money?'

'What you mean, like?' It probably wasn't complicated; I was just drunk. Paddy answered for Colm:

'Well, like… when me and Colm war your age, we hanged round 'side Extra Vision in Caherdavin… d'you know're I mean, sham?' He threw me over a fag, and it landed in the foldy bits of my t-shirt.

'I do, yeah. Next to the garage?' I'd friends from school lived there. Dermot Sheehan and all them. It wasn't actually in Caherdavin, it was near it though.

'That's it, boss. Anyway, we'd go up outside there every night, having a schneer with the lads from Woodview. One night these fellas from Balla comes round, in a van. We thinks they war gonna bate us, right, the first time they pulled up. They war sound though, warn't they, man?'

'Yep. Flipper and them lads.'

'Yeah. Flipper Carney. Hahaha, sham. Flipper… Anyways, they invites us into the van, like. They'd gear in there and everything; pure generous too, like. Giving us smokes off a joint an' all, they war. Even gave us a few nodges to take away, sham. One time Flipper gives me £10, a fuckin' note, like; as a loan. And when I says t'im when d'you want it back, he says 'don't worry about it.' Right?' I nodded. I got him, so far.

'Ten quid was a lot in them days, bud. This is was when a bag of Taytos

was only twelve pence. Hahaha.' He was scary when he laughed. He didn't make you feel like joining in.

'Jaysus, yeah.' I'd found the fag, but I'd no light now.

'So then Mark, that's Flipper's real name, starts asking us little favours. Like could you keep this video in your shed for me, I've no room f'rit over home. Or can you bring these fags across town to my brother; I'll get you a taxi.' He looked at me to see did I get it. I did, kind of.

'Rich, we weren't eejits. I'm pure thick, like. But I'm not stupid. In't that right, Colm?'

'Yep,' said Colm. For some reason, I joined in and nodded too. Paddy stopped and looked at me.

'What? You calling me thick, boss?' He looked like he was going to murder me. What had I done?

'I, no, I, well, you said that… I'm sorry. I'm sorry, please don't…' I closed my eyes and waited for it.

'Hahaha, I'm only pulling your leg, sham.' He whacked me on the arm, but friendly. He was right, though; there was nothing stupid about him really. I hadn't known nothing about him before; except what people said, and all they said was he was pure hard, and pure thick. There was more to him though. I tried to think about it some more, but my head was spinning, and I had to listen to the story.

'We knew them videos were robbed, sham. I knew there was an ounce of gear in that fag box. They were using us, sham; cos we were kids. If the shades

caught us, they couldn't do nothing. We knew what they were doing, but we were getting booze and gear and money off them, so we din't give a shit, sham.'

'Janey Mack!' It was mad. I'd heard of Flipper before. The lads talked about him, cos he sold hash up in Balla. This was like being part of a gang, listening to this stuff.

'So you don't know if anyone was doing anything like that, bud? If there was, you should tell us, sham. The youngfella's dead, like. Someone's gon'ta pay for it. Aren't they, Colm?' Colm nodded, but he'd gone very quiet now. I didn't want to look at him, cos I had the feeling he'd cry. The drink made you giddy to begin with. After a while though, the mood you were in would catch up with you. That's what Mam said. I didn't really understand it when she'd said it.

'No. Naw, I don't think anything like that was going on. He never said nothing about nothing like that. Swear to God. Swear on my mother's life, like.'

I could have told them the truth. Shane would have wanted to kill me, but they'd probably have protected me from him. I'd have been safe. But it would have all come out. Joe being messed around with; us breaking into that shed; Paudie's magazines. There'd be no secrets then. Marian would find out everything. I couldn't do it. Couldn't lose her. Mam had walked out on Dad because he hadn't done enough to make her stay. I wasn't going to be like that. She was too old for me, yeah, and when she went back to school in September, she might think different about going out with me. But I was in Ardscoil now, and I was nearly twelve, and I was getting taller. Mam said. She said I could tell people we were going with each other. That meant something. I wasn't telling no one

about what had happened. I was going to keep her.

The sun was going down; I'd no idea what time it was. I was drunk, and I needed to get out of there. Colm almost looked like he was asleep now, but Paddy was still raring to go; telling me stories about people I'd never heard of.

'Listen, I've to go way home,' I said. It was easy to say stuff when you were drunk. It just came out of your mouth. You were never shy when you were drunk.

'Ah no! Tis early, boss.' Paddy had a very childish face, on a big man's body.

'Stay and have another beer, sham. Shun't he, Colm?' Colm didn't even look over. He was langered. There was spit coming out of the side of his mouth.

'Ah, me Ma will go spare.' Any lie would do to get me out of here. Mam was in Pineview. Dad was probably still in Frazer's.

'Ah, the Mammy's boy, hah?' He was smiling, but God he was frightening. I stared at him, without blinking.

'I'm only codding you, boss. Here, have one more, yeah?' He bent down to get another beer from the whole. Colm made a snoring noise. He actually was asleep. I wanted to go now, before Paddy got too drunk. I'd just say no to another beer. He'd respect that, like he'd respected me a few hours back. Or he might kill me.

'Here, hang on,' said Paddy. He was on his hands and knees now, looking in the hole.

'Nah, I'm grand, Paddy.' He froze. I'd said the wrong thing. He stood up

and walked over, as big as the Hulk. The relaxed feeling I had earlier was gone now, and the drunk braveness suddenly wasn't working either. He put his face right up to mine, and the smell of fags and beer went right up my nostrils.

'What the FUCK did you call me, boss?' His eyes were mental. I couldn't answer; my mouth had stopped working. I knew it was all too good to be true. I closed my eyes to stop myself from crying.

'Hahahaha! He thought I was serious, Colm. What? G'way, will you. Hahahaha!' Jesus Christ. I wasn't able for this. Let me go.

'Ah, you got me, yep. Listen… I do have to go…' I was still shaking.

'Ah, you'll stay for another can, like.'

'I can't, I've to…' He just wasn't listening to me.

'Oh wait, hang on, actually; there's none left.' He took another fag out, and gave me one. I'd had too much fags, but he'd scared the crap out of me, so I wanted one. Mam always had a fag when she'd had a shock.

'What?'

'Lager, sham. There's none left. In the hole.'

'Oh right, so.' Thank God for that. I was sort of thirsty now though.

'So you going then?' He'd already gone through about a third of the fag. He must've had a throat like steel.

'I have to, yeah…' I hadn't lit the fag, cos I'd no light again.

'Your Mam, yeah?'

'Yeah.' I was never going to get to leave. I was wobbling a bit, from the drink.

‘All right so, sham. Listen…’ There was a big pause. I looked in his eyes and for a minute I thought he was going to turn on me again, but for real this time. Then he smiled,

‘Look after yourself, right?’ He slapped me on the back.

‘You’ll be all right going up the road, sham?’ He looked over at Colm; still snoozing in the plastic chair. He looked back at me and sniggered.

‘Dead to the world, what? Go on. Listen…’ Jesus Christ, come on. Let me go!

‘Listen, if anyone gives you any trouble, right? You let us know, sham.’ I hoped he meant it, cos I might need him on my side, if Shane came after me. It had been a mad day altogether.

Eleven

I felt able for anything, walking down the road. Strong from the drink. I was walking straight enough, but my body kept trying to go faster than I could, so I tripped a few times. Everything was going to be fine, now. Shane could go and shag himself. I was finished with him. He had nothing to hold over me, neither. If he told anyone anything, he'd be getting himself into trouble. I realised that now, it was clear as crystal. My mouth was watering, but the spit was kind of salty, or bitter. They could all go and shag themselves. I didn't really mean that; Dara was okay, and Joe used to nearly be my best friend. I didn't care about the Gollies, and I still had Jonathan Musgrave, or even the lads from school. I'd be in Ardscoil too, in September. I'd have loads of new friends there; good fellas, not scobes and scumbags. Paddy thought I was sound now, too. He was sound. Colm was sound. And Marian! She loved me. She'd said it. I was going to marry her, and have babies. We'd be riding every night. Mam would come back as well. I thought about Mam smiling, and I knew she'd come back. Dad was all right, she loved him. I knew she did. Chris would come back too, but who cares about Chris anyway, he's only an auld-

God I was langered. Mam was gone, and she wasn't coming back at all. She'd tricked us. She, she… Oh, Dermot. I wanted to cry, but I wasn't crying, I was laughing. Some auld one from the bungalows looked over; giving me the evil eye, as Mam woul say.

‘Feck off you, will you?’ I screamed at her so loud that she jumped with the shock. She nearly fell over. I didn’t like this feeling. You couldn’t get this langered from just Carling. But I’d had loads. Twelve cans, maybe. Or eight. Or six. They must’ve spiked my drink, like they did in the films. That was it; they’d put a tablet or something in my Carling, and any minute now I was going to collapse, and I’d wake up, and all my money’d be gone, and my credit cards. I’d no money though; I hadn’t even fags. No wait, I’d one fag. I’d kept it, when Paddy wasn’t looking. He was sound, though. He’d mad stories altogether. I’d the fag out now, bent. No light. I asked some businessman looking fella outside the chip shop near Ladbroke’s. He ignored me, though. He was stuck up, Dermot would have said.

‘You prick, you!’ I screamed at him as well. My head was like I was after being on a merry go round, or the teacups at Funderland. Yer man looks back at me, almost scared, like. A fully grown man, scared of me. He kept moving. He’d want to keep moving, and all. I’d a battered him.

‘I know Paddy Hooley, ye’re all… ye’re… yeah.’ I was just mumbling now; gibberish, as Mam would say.

‘G’me a light!’ There was no one around. I was asking the air. I started looking on the ground for matches or a lighter; I was always finding lighters on the ground, and matches, when I didn’t need them. One time I found half a pack of Silk Cut outside Frazer’s. Shane made me give him half of them, though. Even though it was me who’d found them. I was gasping now. Matches were only ten pence, but I’d nothing. I could go in the shop and ask yer one could I borrow a

lighter for a second. She'd tell me to g'way, though. Too young. I didn't even like smoking.

'He's DEAD! He's dead. My best f…. my best feckin' friend and he's dead and it's all my fault, sham.' I was just scuttering words out of my mouth, now. I'd said that quiet, though, not shouted it. A few people stopped and gawked at me, and I could tell from their faces that they were saying to each other that I was drunk and wasn't it a disgrace, and wasn't that Mick South's youngfella, and isn't he one of the ones that broke into that poor Paudie's house, and aren't the Gards going to catch them soon, and won't it be an awful thing altogether for their mothers and fathers, god-bless-us-and-save-us.

I watched the vomit fall down onto my shoes like as if it was someone else puking, on their shoes, and I was watching it on the telly. I tried to think what I'd had to eat, but I couldn't think and it had been a long auld day and it was probably only cornflakes this morning and that was what the white stuff must be. I smelt the sick in my nostrils, and another blurk of it came up my neck and over my tongue; it was fizzy from the beer, and sour from how long the milk had been inside me. I felt like I'd run a marathon, I was sweating so much now, from the sick and the heat. Except it was late, now and it wasn't hot. As soon as I even thought that thought, a shiver came over me. I needed a jumper, or a blanket, and I needed to be at home.

'Here. Come on. You're all right, shur.' Someone big was around me, holding me up. Dad. I'd got him all wrong, all my life. He was sound out. I'd no

idea where I was when he found me. I'd been heading off towards home; round the long way now. I couldn't even see properly. Drunk and sick, eyes not working properly, I was only a disgrace so I was. My lids keeped trying to close, but I had to go on walking, cos Dad was tall, but he wouldn't have been able to carry me. I kept my mouth shut, so he wouldn't smell the booze. He wasn't saying nothing anyway. My eyes went closed for a while, and I thought about everything. The funeral, Marian, Paudie, Tommy, Mam. I opened my eyes a few times, couldn't open them full, just slits. I could see the cement of the path, and all the chewing gum stuck to it that got melty in the summer. I could see my own shoes, covered in puke, and Dad's tackies beside them; they were Nike Air, his ones. Rapid. It got dark really quickly all of a sudden after a while, and there were loads of voices, but I couldn't hear nothing properly. Someone put me on a chair. People were whispering. I couldn't hear. I squinted, cos it felt like squinting my eyes would make me hear better. Dad had no idea how drunk I was. He must've just thought I was sick. Was Mam here now? And Chris? Loads of voices. Laughing. I had to try to keep it together. I needed the toilet bad, but I wasn't able to get out of the chair. Someone was asking Dad; I couldn't catch all the words.

'But how, like? How'd you get him to ___ all the ___ over here?'

'I've no ___, shur. I _____ in for him and ___ ___ said he wasn't ___ so I goes away, and then who does I meet only ___. Honest to God, ___ just ___ the road with me. He's ____ altogether…'

'Fucking hell. It's your ____ day, sham.' They laughed. Dad sounded weird. I was nodding off again, then I felt someone put their hands on me, on my

shoulders.

'Here, c'mere. Are you awake? Richie?' It wasn't Dad, it must've been Chris. Must've come home from Pineview. I'd ask him if Mam was here too. Only I didn't really want to speak, cos…

'Wake him up,' someone else said. Wasn't Chris' voice though, or Mam's.

'What you mean?' said yer man who was holding me, and didn't sound like Dad. It was Dad, though. Cos he'd brought me home. Don't be an eejit, Richie. The room looked weird. It was green instead of orange, like my kitchen was supposed to be. I saw Dara in the corner, and saluted him.

'Wake him up, sham!' said the other voice, then someone slapped me full force across the face. It stinged like mad, even with all the drink in me.

'Oi! What you do that for?' My head was spinning twice as fast now. I tried to focus my eyes onto Dad, but they wouldn't work. Why was Dara in my house? Why were people slapping me? All the doors of the presses were green. Joe's hands on my neck held me down when I tried to get up. He wasn't Dad at all. Dad wasn't here, and I wasn't at home. It looked familiar, though. I was langered still, but this was sobering me up. Someone else's face was really near mine now again, not Joe though. I could smell old fags, and cider. I could smell him too, though. I knew who that smell was of.

'Aboy, Rich. What's happening, sham?' It was Shane. He was smiling.

'What, why, what am I here… what?' I was just babbling. Dara sniggered over in the corner. I thought Dara was all right. Why was he being a gowl to me?

Why were they all being gowls to me? What was going on?

'Where am I?' They all laughed when I said that.

'D'you not recognise it, sham?' Shane had a flagon of Linden in his hand; nearly half gone. I looked around at the kitchen. No, I did and I didn't know it. There was an ironing board that made me look at it twice, but no. Still too langered.

'How about now?' He stepped out of the way, and I could see that there was someone else there, on a chair like me. It took me a while to see who it was; the face was covered with a bag, a cloth one, like you'd bring a packed lunch to school in. They'd tied him to the chair, with blue plastic rope; the sort that cut you when you tried to get out of it. I only recognised him because he was wearing the same top he'd been wearing at the funeral, only now it was covered in blood. Paudie Collins looked like he was dead. I closed my eyes again, in case I was dreaming. My stomach did a somersault, and filled my mouth up with warm sick. What had they done to him?

'You missed most of the party, sham.' We sent Joe over to call in for you, like. Your Da said you were with your woman, though. You riding that yet? Course you fucking aren't, you steamer. Fucking slut like that, wasted on you. Danny O'Neill knows all about that one, sham.' They all laughed again. Shane's knuckles were covered in dried blood, and there were splashes of red all on the white bits of his Raiders t-shirt. I said nothing to him. I was filling up with rage though, not filling up with sadness. You don't talk about her like that. No one does.

‘So, yeah. Anyway. We thought we’d come pay Paud a visit, like. After Dermot’s funeral, like. That’s another little boy’s got killed cos of you, Paud. Eh? EH?’ He punched Paudie in the guts as he said it, and Paudie let out a shriek; he was still alive. Jesus Christ. Thank God. I’d been sure he was a goner.

‘You like killing little boys, don’t you Paud?’ He leaned his ear towards the bag, but there was no answer. Then he punched Paudie full force in the side of the head, and there was another shriek from under the bag. Shane must’ve hurted himself, though; cos he shook his hand after, like you do when you burn yourself under the hot tap. I caught Dara’s eye, but he looked away soon as he saw me. I was still drunk. They didn’t need to tie me to a chair, I couldn’t go nowhere. This was mental though, even if he was still alive. How’d they gotten in here? Why were they doing this? Paudie didn’t kill Dermot. I didn’t even think he killed Tommy. But then, Joe… I just didn’t know nothing no more.

‘Why… why am I here, like? Why are ye at me? What did I do?’ I didn’t know which of them I was even asking. Joe hadn’t been here all week; he hadn’t known nothing about what we’d been doing, or what Shane had said to us. Now he was here, and we all knew about him being touched by Paudie, and he was fine with that, was he? I wasn’t able to follow any of it. I hadn’t said nothing to Shane or Dara since Dermot died. Had they been planning this behind my back? What were they planning; to kill him? Joe was the one that answered me

‘You’re here cos he killed your friend too. And you’re gonna get him back too, like we are.’

‘He didn’t kill Dermot, though, he…’

'HE FUCKIN' DID, ALL RIGHT?' Shane shouted it so close to my face that his spit went all over me. I tried to remember what I'd done earlier with Paddy, but my head was spinning now. I'd the dizzy too, that you got when you'd been puking but you'd no food in you.

'Yeah,' said Joe. 'He might as well, right? Cos it's his fault Dermot was in there, sham. Use your fucking head, like.' I didn't recognise this Joe at all. He was polluted drunk, obviously. But I'd seen him drunk before. This was like a whole different youngfella. I looked down at his Nike Air tackies, and said nothing. I needed a plan. In the movies, they always had a plan.

'So, you were there; you're in this with us.' Shane was crouching down now, to get in my face.

'What you mean, in with ye?'

'We all were there. We all know what this cunt did…' he turned to point at Paudie, and I saw that he'd a knife in his hand. A hunting one; a Rambo knife. Aw Jesus…

'Ah, now lads… What you gonna do with that?'

'He's not gonna do nothing with it,' said Joe, standing next to Paudie's chair.

'You are.' Shane nodded at me, and leaned in close.

'See, we're all buddies here, Rich. And Dermot was too. He was my best fucking friend, yeah? We're all buddies, and you used to be a buddy, but I han't heard a peep from you in the last few days. Dara's been round my house every day, and I been talking to Joe in Kilkee on the phone, telling him all about it. But

when we look for you, you're not around.' He was doing that thing again, the friendly voice, saying scary things. I wasn't scared of him now, though. He was a coward. That's why he'd needed Dara and Joe. I'd been surviving on my own the past few days. Without Mam, either. Shane had to surround himself with his buddies. He was a chicken.

'For all I knew, you'd gone and squealed on us, Richie.' He looked in my eyes and I knew he was looking to see would I flinch or twitch, or whatever it is people did that gave them away when they were lying or guilty. I was looking at the knife in his hand though I was having some terrible thoughts.

'For all we knew, you were down the Garda station, telling them all the things we'd been doing, sham.' He put the sharp part of the blade against the pocket of my jeans. My heart was going mental, like at the start of a race. I didn't know what I was going to do with it when I got it, but if I had it, I'd be better off than now.

'And now, you'll tell us that you were with your little girlfriend all that time. That little whore that Danny O'Neill got a blowjob off?' Dara and Joe laughed loud, drunk laughs at that. I got my hand ready to make a move.

'Well, I dunno if I believe you. I dunno if I'd believe a ride like her would go 'way with a little faggot like you who's never got his hole in his life. And I'll tell you something else…' My fingers were almost on the blade now. If I grabbed it that way though, I'd get cut, and he still might keep hold of it by the handle. Had to wait…

'Cos see, Dermot told me something about you, Rich.' I stopped.

'What?'

'Oh yeah, sham. He told me you and him been talking, in the Quarry, like.' Oh, God.

'We… yeah, we were talking, what about it, like?'

Dermot wouldn't have said nothing to him about me. Not Dermot… He wouldn't. He wouldn't. This was called *calling your bluff*. I'd seen it in a film. Shane was trying to call my bluff. I'd to try and call his first.

'He told me you thought Joe ha'nt said nothing to me that night, sham.'

'That's not true!' I was sobering up quickly. I couldn't tell if he was bluffing me or not; my head was too spinny.

'Well… that's what he said. Said you'd said I musta made it up, like. Made up that Paudie Collins fucking *raped* poor Joe. What kind of a buddy says that, sham?'

I didn't look over at Joe, but I could almost feel him raging. He was shy enough as it was, normally. Jesus Christ, why were we doing this? Why couldn't we all just be friends? Shane was why. He was the one that was doing this.

'Is that what you think, like? Is that what you think of me, Rich?' It dawned on me then that the bag over Paudie's head meant nothing, cos we were all saying our names in front of him. Shane wasn't going to let him out of here alive.

'Well I amn't no liar. And I fucking stick up for my pals, even if you don't think you fucking have to. You fucking JFK prick, always thinking he's better than us, in't he, lads?'

Joe and Dara mumbled at us, agreeing with him. They were ganging up on me. I always kind of knew they hated me for going to that school.

'What do you want me to do?' I needed to stall him. The knife was too far away for me to grab straight out, now If they wanted me to do something though; to stab him, then they'd give me the knife. All I had to do was go along with it. My body still felt drunk, but my brain was wide awake.

'Aboy the kid. C'mere and I'll show you.' He was smiling again, but I wasn't falling for that.

I stood up and walked with him, still wobbly. I was slipping in and out of drunk. Shane took me to Paudie's chair, and just whipped the bag off his head. He looked terrified, like a fox when it stops in front of your car in the night. There was blood all over his face; it made me think of Dermot. One of his eyes was completely closed over and swelled, like yer man in Raging Bull. He started whimpering, but no words were coming out.

'Now, sham. This dirty fucker rapes little boys. Takes them off their Mammies and Daddies, and he brings them somewhere quiet, and he takes their little jocks off, and he puts his mickey in their mouths and up their holes, Richie.' Paudie sort of weakly shook his head, and mumbled something. I thought I heard the word 'please'. I wanted to cry.

'Shut the fuck up, you fucking pervert steamer cunt, you.' Shane put the blade up to Paudie's throat, and I held my breath like I was underwater. He kept it there, and then carried on talking:

'We're going to give him what he deserves, Rich. But you have to do it

too, sham. All for one, and one for all. Like the Muskahounds, wha?' The others laughed again. I just looked at the knife against Paudie's throat. I couldn't let him do it. I didn't know if Paudie was actually guilty of anything. Marian had said that thing about Kennedy Park, and there'd been the photos of little kids… but none of that was actual proof. I'd wanted to talk to Joe about it, but... I needed that knife. I put my hand out to Shane for it. He shook his head

'All right, take your time, sham. Have a few digs first.' He nodded at Paudie, who groaned and said something I couldn't hear.

'What, with my hands?' They all laughed at me.

'Yeah with your hands, you steamer. Go on, sham. Go Rocky!'

I had to do it. I was awful at fighting, so the punches probably weren't even going to hurt Paudie. I closed my eyes and said a bit of the Our Father, then I punched at his swelled up face.

'Wehay!' Shane was cheering me; it was like being in school. The first punch was useless though; I'd left my thumb inside my fist. Felt like I'd broke it nearly. I tried with my other hand this time.

'Oh, the South Paw now!' Shane's whole family were boxers. The next punch landed on Paudie's sore eye. It wasn't properly scabbed over. When my knuckles hit him, it burst open like a gone-off peach. Blood and orange stuff dribbled out of the slit, and down his cheek. I felt dizzy.

'One more for good luck, Rich; get the dirty cunt. For Dermot!' I was still saying the Our Father in my head; the Hail Mary and the Glory Be. The last punch hit him on his mouth, and I mostly hit teeth, so it hurt me more than him again.

'All right, all right.' Shane was looking at me a bit funny; like he was suspicious. I was probably putting the act on too strong, now. I was going to ask for the knife, but I needed to wait a bit.

'Dara, come over here and have a go, sham.' Dara wobbled over, he was hammered altogether. I wondered how long they'd been drinking for, cos they all looked wrecked. Maybe they'd just thought of doing this whole thing at the last minute. It didn't matter, anyway. I was gonna get the knife and get out of there. I didn't know what I was gonna do after that; I didn't care. I didn't know what they were going to do to Paudie when I was gone, but I couldn't do nothing about that. I couldn't be thinking about it. I knew he was Marian's uncle, but I wasn't able to save him.

Dara was even worse at punching than me. After two feeble little digs, Joe pushed him out of the way.

'Here, shur.' He started karate kicking him. In the shins first; then the ribs. Then in the head. I didn't know how much more of this Paudie was going to be able to take. I had to do something soon. The chair kept nearly falling over; Joe caught it before it went.

'I'm going for a piss, lads.' Dara's eyes were bloodshot, and he could barely stand up.

'It's upstairs,' said Shane. He had the knife by his side now, not even gripping the handle. It was time to do it.

'I know where toilets are, you don't have to tell me about where toilets are, Shane… I know where a toilet is…' He went into the hall. Joe was still

kicking and punching Paudie. The sounds were sickening. Not like when someone got hit on TV. Real sounds of were much worse. Bones hitting bones, skin bursting. Joe was like a machine. His eyes were terrifying, there was so much rage in them. I believed it then. Paudie must've interfered with him. No one could be that angry over nothing.

Finally, Paudie said something.

'Stop! Stop it! Please! Why? Why are ye… why? Stop it, please…'

Joe did stop, but it wasn't a good sort of stop. It made me feel worse, not better. He stepped back, and wiped the sweat off his forehead with the sleeve of his shirt that used to be white.

'Please? Stop?' Then he started sniggering.

'Did you stop what you were doing to Tommy when he said stop, Paud?'

'What? Listen I don't…'

'You FUCKING DIDN'T! Did he say stop, Paudie? Did he say please? Please stop?' Shane and me stood there with our mouths open.

'I don't, I don't know what ye're talking about, lads. Ye've me mixed up with someone. Heheh. That's all it is. Shur can't ye just untie me now, and I won't tell yeer Mams and Dads? How about it? Anyone can make a mistake, hahahaha. We, we all make…'

'D'you remember *me* saying stop, Paudie?' Joe had tears in his eyes. I did too. Shane looked like he was fighting back his.

'What, I… who?' Paudie looked blank. He was bleeding from his ear now; I couldn't stop looking at it.

'D'you remember me saying please? Please stop… please stop, Mister. I wanna go home…' The tears were just rolling down his cheeks; he wasn't actually crying. He wasn't even blinking.

'I don't know what ye're talking about, boss. I don't even know who ye are. Just let me go, yeah? I'll say nothing to no one. It'll be our little secret. Please. Please just stop…' He looked straight into Joe's eyes, then he smiled. His teeth were pink from the blood.

I made a grab for Shane's knife. It didn't come out of his hand at all, he just turned around and smiled at me.

'Hah! You cheeky fucking cunt, you.' The smile went away. He went to grab me, and I stepped back. He lost his balance, but he held onto me while he was falling. We both went down on the floor, and he was on top of me. I tried to get my knee into his balls, but he was squirming away. I couldn't get a real grip on him at all, he was like a snake, or an eelfry. My heart was going nintety; I'd no plan without the knife. I'd no plan with the knife either. Just to get it and to get away. I was never going to stab them; just use it as a threat. Now though, if I got it off him I'd have to use it, cos he was gonna use it on me. Would he, though? Was it just drink? He wasn't gonna stab me, his friend. He wasn't gonna stab Paudie either. I rolled over so I was on top now. He was so bloody strong. I needed both my hands just to keep him pinned down; I'd no chance of getting the knife. He was just drunk; they all were. It was just a drunk idea that had gone too far. We could fix it. We'd make a deal with Paudie. We'd get money or something. I

caught Shane's eyes, and I tried to see something in them. There it was; just for a second, he looked sort of… kind. I remembered that time he'd brought me over to his place and we'd had Viennetta ice cream in the back garden.

I heard the insides of my nose go snap when he headbutted me, and then the blood started gushing out. I didn't let go of him. I just kept holding him down, pinning him to the floor so he couldn't move. The snotty blood was streaming out of me, down on top of his face. He closed his mouth to stop it getting in, then his eyes.

My head was throbbing, and I was probably going to have two shiners, cos that's what happened when you broke your nose; you got two black eyes. I moved in closer and grabbed his bottom lip with my teeth, and started pulling and biting and pulling and biting. He screeched like a banshee. I didn't care; I kept biting, and pulling. I was going to bite his whole lip off. I hated him now. I was going to kill him. The blood from my nose was all in the back of my throat and my mouth, and I could taste it, all salty on my tongue. My teeth were clamped closed around his lip, and there was more blood coming out of that too, into my mouth and mixing with my own. I felt like a dog, tearing apart a rat. I shook my head from side to side, ripping the lip away from his mouth. He shouldn't have said them things about her; he shouldn't have made us break in there, in here. He shouldn't have pushed us; he shouldn't have pushed me. He shouldn't have…

'Lads! Lads! LADS! Stop! Stop, will ye…' It was Dara, bending down to us. We let go of each other, and I straight away grabbed for the knife. There was

no knife, though. I looked at Shane; his face was covered in blood now. Mine and his. His lip was nearly torn off; it was hanging down onto his chin. I felt sick, but still angry. My heart was beating in my ears. I kept an eye on him. He didn't move much. He wouldn't fight me any more.

Something wasn't right. Dara looked like he'd seen a ghost. What was the noise? The squelching? And the smell? Like sewerage or something. Like a blocked toilet.

We all looked over at the same time. The chair was on the ground with Paudie still in it. Joe was kneeling over him with the knife, bawling his eyes out and muttering something I couldn't hear. There was this whistling, gargling sound. Paudie's neck was in tatters. No skin on it any more, just blood and holes. He looked at me with his one good eye for a second; I'd never seen anyone look as terrified. Then I swear to this day I saw him smile; not like something was funny, or not like he was crazy. It was a smile that just said 'This is it. I'm going to die. I'm not afraid.'

Then the whistling and the gurgling didn't happen any more. Joe didn't stop stabbing him after he was dead. It took the three of us to pull him away. Dara said he was going upstairs to the toilet again. I sat there in silence with the other two. Joe didn't let go of the knife, and neither of us tried taking it off him. Shane looked weak now. Like a kid. He'd been crying, and trying to hold onto the bits of his mouth, probably so the doctors could stitch it for him. I didn't care. I wasn't drunk any more, but I was still high on something. I didn't feel scared. I looked over at him, but I didn't feel sorry. Fuck him.

Ten minutes later, Dara's father was at the door, with three other Gards. Dara must've used the phone upstairs. One of them took something off him. It was the shoebox from upstairs. I remember thinking that it was a different colour to the one we'd found in the shed. It was a different box. I knew that meant something important, but I didn't say nothing to no one. The Gards were nice to us down the station; pure friendly. Real life is hardly ever like the films.

Epilogue

Nothing happened. No one was arrested; no court case; no one went to jail. The local Garda sergeant (who also happened to be Dara's father) decided that big Joe McNamara who played centre forward for Balla had had enough suffering in his life, and that the death of a paedophile was no loss to any community. The case was recorded as a burglary that had gone wrong. They had no suspects. It was over. We all kept our mouths shut too, for our own reasons. Mine was the same reason as ever. I would have done anything to keep her.

We stayed together for a few years after that, but she was never going to be The One. I suppose a part of me was glad when it was over, because every day since Paudie had felt like a lie, no matter how much I enjoyed it. I loved her, though. That much had been true, and I'll always believe it. All the years that passed never changed my mind about how real those feelings had been.

Mam came back to look after me of course, but she wasn't home for good. After that Christmas she moved out properly. She had a new fella, a chef from the Italian restaurant. The one who'd taught her to cook more exciting meals, and want more exciting things from life. Dad hadn't stood a chance. Parents breaking up was still a big thing back then in Ireland. I think I cried, but I don't remember now. Dad never found anyone else, and I don't think he looked either. We get on better now, whenever I come home to see him.

I ended up working in films, on the writing side; married a Canadian girl

who loved Christy Moore and good cognac. Her name was Trudy. It still is, I guess. Shane managed to stay out of Jail for another six years, before he got sent down for GBH. No one was really surprised. Dara joined the Gards, like his Dad wanted him to. Quite a few people were surprised.

Joe moved to England when he was seventeen, and none of us ever heard from him again. One day in 2003, I watched a report on Sky News about a man who'd been arrested on suspicion of the rape and murder of eleven children, over the last five years, in Coventry. They'd all been around five years old and they'd all been boys. The policemen both looked very short next to him when they brought him into the court. He'd got even taller since I'd seen him last. The shy face was still the same, although he had an Englishman's haircut now; a side parting and a quiff. They showed a picture of him that must have been off his passport. I looked at the quiet face with the sad eyes, and thought: he's the only one of us who'll ever know the truth about that night in Paudie's kitchen.

I was still crying when Trudy came in after midnight. I wasn't sure if they were tears for Paudie, or those little boys, or for my friend Joe, who someone must have hurt so very badly. We stayed up together until the next morning; drinking warm Hennessy, and remembering how great it was and how terrible it was to be eleven.

The End

19581213R00171

Printed in Poland
by Amazon Fulfillment
Poland Sp. z o.o., Wrocław

CONTRIBUTORS

J. R. Alexander Jr.
Towson State University,
Towson, MD 21032, USA.
Email: e7c1ale@toe.towson.edu

D. Allen
Centre for Neural Networks,
Department of Mathematics,
King's College London,
London WC2R 1LS UK.

N. M. Allinson
Department of Electrical
Engineering and Electronics,
UMIST, Manchester M60 1QD, UK.
Email: allinson@umist.ac.uk

Shun-ichi Amari
University of Tokyo, Tokyo, Japan,
RIKEN Frontier Research Program,
Wako-City, Saitama, Japan.
Email: amari@sat.t.u-tokyo.ac.jp

P. Edgar An
Department of Ocean Engineering,
Florida Atlantic University,
Boca Raton, FL 33431, USA.
Email: ean@oe.fau.edu

I. J. Anderson
School of Computing and Mathematics,
University of Huddersfield, Queensgate,
Huddersfield HD1 3DH, UK.
Email: scomija@zeus.hud.ac.uk

G.S. Androulakis
Department of Mathematics,
University of Patras,
GR-261.10 Patras, Greece.
Email: gsa@math.upatras.gr

James Austin
Advanced Computer Architecture Group,
Department of Computer Science,
University of York,
Heslington, YO1 5DD, UK.

E.D. Aved'yan
Russian Academy of Sciences,
Institute of Control Sciences,
65 Profsoyuznaya str.,
Moscow 117342, Russia.
Email: avedyan@dep07.ics.msk.su

David Barber
Dept. Comp, Sci. and Appl. Maths.,
Aston University, Birmingham B4 7ET, UK.
Web: http://www.ncrg.aston.ac.uk/

V. Beiu
Los Alamos National Laboratory,
Division NIS-1,
Los Alamos, New Mexico 87545, USA.
Email: beiu@lanl.gov

Jan van den Berg
Department of Computer Science,
Erasmus University Rotterdam,
The Netherlands.
Email: jvandenberg@few.eur.nl

N Benjathapanun
Department of Electrical, Electronic and
Information Engineering
City University, Northampton Square,
London EC1V OHB, UK.

Monica Bianchini
Dipartimento di Sistemi e Informatica,
Università degli Studi di Firenze,
Via di Santa Marta, 3,
50139 Firenze, Italy.
Email: monica,marco@mcculloch.ing.unifi.it

Jan C. Bioch
Department of Computer Science,
Erasmus University Rotterdam,
The Netherlands.
Email: bioch@cs.few.eur.nl

Christopher M. Bishop
Neural Computing Research Group,
Dept. of Computer Science and
Applied Mathematics,
Aston University, Birmingham B4 7ET, UK.
Email: c.m.bishop@aston.ac.uk

D. Bockus
Dept. Computing and Information Science,
University of Guelph,
Ontario NIG 2W1, Canada.

Hamid Bolouri
Engineering Research and
Development Centre,
University of Hertfordshire,
College Lane, Hatfield,
Herts, AL10 9AB, UK.

W J O Boyle
Department of Electrical, Electronic and
Information Engineering
City University, Northampton Square,
London EC1V OHB, UK.

J. Bradford
Brock University,
St. Catharines, Ontario, Canada.

Paul C. Bressloff
Department of Mathematical Sciences,
Loughborough University,
Leics. LE11 3TU, UK.
Email : P.C.Bressloff@lut.ac.uk

Susan Brittain
University of Natal,
Pietermaritzburg, South Africa.

M. Brown
ISIS research group,
Dept of Electronics and Computer Science,
Southampton University, Highfield,
Southampton, SO17 1BJ, UK.
Email: mqb@ecs.soton.ac.uk

Marco Budinich
Dipartimento di Fisica & INFN,
Via Valerio 2, 34127, Trieste, Italy.
Email: mbh@trieste.infn.it

William Burckel
Phillips Laboratory,
Kirtland Air Force Base
Albuquerque, New Mexico, USA.

Terry M. Caelli
School of Computing,
Curtin University of Technology,
Perth, Western Australia.
Email: tmc@cs.curtin.edu.au

Enrico Capobianco
Stanford University,
Stanford, CA 94305, USA.
Email: enrico@psych.stanford.edu

Robert Carsouw
Department of Computer Science,
Erasmus University Rotterdam,
The Netherlands.

B. Cessac
University of New-Mexico,
Department of Electrical and
Computer Engineering,
Albuquerque, NM 87131, USA.

S. Chen
Dept. of E.E.E.,
The University of Portsmouth, UK.

Xavier Clastres
Centre d'Etudes et de
Recherches de Toulouse,
2 avenue Edouard Belin, BP 4025,
31055 Toulouse Cedex, France.

D.K.Y. Chiu
Dept. Computing and Information Science,
University of Guelph,
Ontario NIG 2W1, Canada.
Email: dchiu@snowhite.cis.uoguelph.ca

E.S Chng
National University of Singapore,
Institute of System Science,
Heng Mui Keng Terrace,
Kent Ridge, 119597 Singapore.
Email : eschng@iss.nus.sg.

J. P. Coughlin
Towson State University,
Towson, MD 21032, USA.

Jack D. Cowan
Departments of Mathematics and
Neurology, The University of Chicago,
Chicago, IL 60637, USA.
Email: cowan@synapse.uchicago.edu

Carol G. Crawford
U.S. Naval Academy,
Department of Mathematics,
Annapolis MD 21402, USA.
Email: cgc@sma.usna.navy.mil

George Cybenko
Thayer School of Engineering,
8000 Cummings Hall, Dartmouth College,
Hanover, NH 03755 USA.
Email: gvc@dartmouth.edu

Laurence C Dixon
Engineering Research and
Development Centre,
University of Hertfordshire,
College Lane, Hatfield,
Herts, AL10 9AB, UK.

Christopher Dehainaut
Phillips Laboratory,
Kirtland Air Force Base
Albuquerque, New Mexico, USA.

A. Delgado
National University of Columbia,
Elec. Eng. Dept., AA No. 25268, Bogota,
D C, Columbia SA.
Email: adelgado@col1.telecom.com.co

B. Doyon
Unité INSERM 230, Service de Neurologie,
CHU Purpan,
31059 Toulouse Cédex, France.

Andrzej Dzielinski
Department of Mechanical Engineering,
James Watt Building,
University of Glasgow,
Glasgow G12 8QQ, Scotland, UK.
Email: andrzej@mech.gla.ac.uk

A. Easdown
School of Computing and
Mathematical Sciences,
University of Brighton,
Brighton BN1 4GJ, UK.
Email: A.Easdown@brighton.ac.uk

Michael Eisele
The Salk Institute,
Computational Neurobiology Laboratory,
PO Box 85800, San Diego,
CA 92186 - 5800, USA.
Email: eisele@salk.edu

S.W. Ellacott
School of Computing and
Mathematical Sciences,
University of Brighton,
Brighton BN1 4GJ, UK.
Email: S.W.Ellacott@brighton.ac.uk

Stefano Fanelli
Dipartimento di Matematica,
Università di Roma,
"Tor Vergata" Via della Ricerca Scientifica,
00133 Roma, Italy.
Email: fanelli@mat.utovrm.it

Alistair Ferguson
Engineering Research and
Development Centre,
University of Hertfordshire,
College Lane, Hatfield,
Herts, AL10 9AB, UK.
Email: A.Ferguson@herts.ac.uk

Richard Filer
Advanced Computer Architecture Group,
Department of Computer Science,
University of York,
Heslington, YO1 5DD, UK.
Email: rjhf@minster.york.ac.uk

Jason A.S. Freeman
Centre for Neural Systems,
University of Edinburgh,
Edinburgh EH8 9LW, UK.
Email: jason@cns.ed.ac.uk

Laurent Freyss
Centre d'Etudes et de
Recherches de Toulouse,
2 avenue Edouard Belin,BP 4025,
31055 Toulouse Cedex, France.

Jock H. Geselschap
Department of Computer Science,
Erasmus University Rotterdam,
The Netherlands.

G. Gibson
Biomathematics and Statistics,
The University of Edinburgh, UK.

Marco Gori
Dipartimento di Sistemi e Informatica,
Università degli Studi di Firenze,
Via di Santa Marta, 3, 50139 Firenze, Italy.
Email: marco@mcculloch.ing.unifi.it

T.N. Grapsa
Department of Mathematics,
University of Patras,
GR-261.10 Patras, Greece.
Email:grapsa@math.upatras.gr

K T V Grattan
Department of Electrical, Electronic and
Information Engineering
City University, Northampton Square,
London EC1V OHB, UK.

Robert Gray
Thayer School of Engineering,
8000 Cummings Hall, Dartmouth College,
Hanover, NH 03755 USA.

G.G.R. Green
Dept. of Physiological Sciences,
University of Newcastle upon Tyne,
Newcastle upon Tyne, NE1 7RU, UK.
Email: gary.green@ncl.ac.uk

Stephen Grossberg
Boston University, Department of Cognitive
and Neural Systems, and
Center for Adaptive Systems,
677 Beacon Street, Boston, Massachusetts
02215 USA

Linda M. Haines
University of Natal,
Pietermaritzburg, South Africa.
Email: haines@stat.unp.ac.za

C.J. Harris
ISIS research group,
Dept of Electronics and Computer Science,
Southampton University, Highfield,
Southampton, SO17 1BJ, UK.

Morris W. Hirsch
Department of Mathematics,
University of California at Berkeley,
CA 94720-3840 USA.
Email: hirsch@math.berkeley.edu

D. Husmeier
Centre for Neural Networks,
Department of Mathematics,
King's College London,
London WC2R 1LS, UK.
Email: D.Husmeier@bay.cc.kcl.ac.uk

Koji Ito
Interdisciplinary Graduate School of
Science and Engineering, Tokyo Institute of
Technology, 4259, Nagatsuda,
Midori-ku, Yokohama 226, Japan.
Email: ito@ssie.titech.ac.jp

Mark P. Joy
Centre for Research in Information
Engineering, School of Electrical,
Electronic and Information Enineering,
South Bank University, 103, Borough Rd.,
London SE1 OAA, UK.
Email: joympa@vax.sbu.ac.uk

C. Kambhampati
Cybernetics Department,
University of Reading, Whiteknights,
Reading RG6 6AY, UK.

S. Kasderidis
Department of Mathematics,
King's College London,
London WC2R 1LS, UK.

Jim Kay
Dept. of Statistics, University of Glasgow,
Mathematics Building,
Glasgow G12 8QW, UK.
Email: jim@stats.glasgow.ac.uk

Petri Koistinen
Rolf Nevanlinna Institute,
P.O. Box 4, FIN-00014
University of Helsinki, Finland.
Email: petri.koistinen@rni.helsinki.fi

A. R. Kolcz
Department of Electrical
Engineering and Electronics,
UMIST, Manchester M60 1QD, UK.

Bart Krekelberg
Centre for Neural Networks,
King's College London
London WC2R 2LS, UK
Email: bart@mth.kcl.ac.uk

Sabine Kroener
Technische Informatik I,
TU Hamburg-Harburg,
Harburger Schloßstr. 20,
D-21071 Hamburg, Germany.
Email: Kroener@tu-harburg.d400.de

Abderrahim Labbi
Dept. of Computer Science,
University of Geneva,
24 Rue General Dufour, 1121 Geneva 4,
Switzerland.
Email: labbi@cui.unige.ch

Bao-Liang Lu
The Institute of Physical and
Chemical Research (RIKEN),
3-8-31 Rokuban,Atsuta-ku,
Nagoya 456, Japan.
Email: lbl@nagoya.bmc.riken.go.jp

S P Luttrell
Defence Research Agency,
Malvern, Worcs, WR14 3PS, UK.
Email: luttrell@signal.dra.hmg.gb

G.D. Magoulas
Department of Electrical and
Computer Engineering,
University of Patras,
GR-261.10, Patras, Greece.
Email: magoulas@ee-gw.ee.upatras.gr

S. Manchanda
Dept. of Chemical and Process Engineering,
University of Newcastle upon Tyne,
Newcastle upon Tyne, NE1 7RU, UK.
Email: Sunil.Manchanda@ncl.ac.uk

Glenn Marion
Department of Statistics and
Modelling Science, Livingstone Tower,
26 Richmond Street, Glasgow G1 1XH, UK.
Email: glenn@stams.strath.ac.uk

J. C. Mason
School of Computing and Mathematics,
University of Huddersfield, Queensgate,
Huddersfield HD1 3DH, UK.
Email: J.C.Mason@hud.ac.uk

Ronny Meir
Electrical Engineering Department,
Technion, Haifa 32000, Israel.
Email: rmeir@ee.technion.ac.il

H. N. Mhaskar
Department of Mathematics,
California State University,
Los Angeles, California 90032, USA.
Email: hmhaska@calstatela.edu

Katsuhiro Moizumi
Thayer School of Engineering,
8000 Cummings Hall, Dartmouth College,
Hanover, NH 03755 USA.

Christophe Molina
Cambridge University
Engineering Department,
Trumpington Street, Cambridge CB2 1PZ, UK.
Email: cm3@eng.cam.ac.uk

Reinhard Moratz
AG Angewandte Informatik,
Universität Bielefeld, Postfach 100131,
D-33501 Bielefeld, Germany.

Yves Moreau
Katholieke Universiteit Leuven,
Dept. of Electrical Engineering,
ESAT-SISTA Kardinaal Mercierlaan 94,
B-3001 Leuven (Heverlee), Belgium.
Email: moreau@esat.kuleuven.ac.be

B. Mulgrew
Dept. of Electrical Eng.,
The University of Edinburgh, UK.

Ian T Nabney
Neural Computing Research Group,
Aston University, Birmingham, B4 7ET, UK.
Email: nabneyit@aston.ac.uk

Mahesan Niranjan
Cambridge University
Engineering Department,
Trumpington Street, Cambridge CB2 1PZ, UK.
Email: niranjan@eng.cam.ac.uk

Toru Ohira
Sony Computer Science Laboratory
3-14-13 Higashi-gotanda, Shinagawa,
Tokyo 141, Japan.
Email: ohira@csl.sony.co.jp

Rob Potharst
Department of Computer Science,
Erasmus University Rotterdam,
The Netherlands.
Email: robp@cs.few.eur.nl

Marco Protasi
Dipartimento di Matematica,
Università di Roma,"Tor Vergata"
Via della Ricerca Scientifica,
00133 Roma, Italy.
Email: protasi@mat.utovrm.it

Adam Pruegel-Bennett
NORDITA Blegdamsvej 17,
DK-2100 Copenhagen Ø, Denmark.

Cazhaow S. Qazaz
Neural Computing Research Group,
Dept. of Computer Science and
Applied Mathematics,
Aston University, Birmingham B4 7ET, UK.

M. Quoy
Universität Bielefeld,
BiBos, Postfach 100131,
33501 Bielefeld, Germany.

Magnus Rattray
Department of Computer Science,
University of Manchester,
Manchester, M13 9PL, UK.

Peter Rieper
FB Mathematik, Universitaet Hamburg,
Bundesstr. 55, D-20146 Hamburg, Germany.

G. Rodriguez
Department of Mathematics,
University of Cagliari,
viale Merello 92,09123 Cagliari, Italy.

Richard Rohwer
Prediction Co.,
320 Aztec Street, SuiteB,
Santa Fe, NM87501, USA.

Barbara Rosario
Dipartimento di Fisica & INFN,
Via Valerio 2, 34127, Trieste, Italy.
Email: mbh@trieste.infn.it

David Saad
Dept. of Computer Science and
Applied Mathematics, University of Aston,
Birmingham B4 7ET, UK.
Email: D.Saad@aston.ac.uk

M. Samuelides
Centre d'Etudes et de
Recherches de Toulouse,
2 avenue Edouard Belin, BP 4025,
31055 Toulouse Cedex, France.
Email: samuelid@cert.fr.

S. Seatzu
Department of Mathematics,
University of Cagliari,
viale Merello 92, 09123 Cagliari, Italy.

Jonathan L. Shapiro
Department of Computer Science,
University of Manchester,
Manchester, M13 9PL, UK.

Sergey A. Shumsky
P.N.Lebedev Physics Institute,
Leninsky pr.53, Moscow, Russia.
Email: serge@mart7.demos.su

A. Shustorovich
Business Imaging Systems,
Eastman Kodak Company, Rochester, USA.
Email: Sasha@kodak.com

J. Smid
Department of Mathematics,
Morgan State University,
Baltimore, MD 21239 USA.
Email: smid@ltpsun.gsfc.nasa.gov

Sara A. Solla
CONNECT, The Niels Bohr Institute,
Blegdamsvej 17,Copenhagen 2100, Denmark.

Peter Sollich
Department of Physics,
University of Edinburgh,
Edinburgh EH9 3JZ, UK.
Email: P.Sollich@ed.ac.uk

David McG. Squire
School of Computing,
Curtin University of Technology,
Perth, Western Australia.
Email: squizz@cs.curtin.edu.au

Shin Suzuki
Information Science Research Laboratory,
NTT Basic Research Laboratories,
3-1 Morinosato-Wakamiya,
Atsugi-Shi, Kanagawa Pref., 243-01 Japan.
Email: shin@idea.brl.ntt.jp

G.Tambouratzis
Dept. of Mathematics,
Agricultural Univ.of Athens,
Iera Odos 75,
Athens 118 55, Greece.
Email: giorg_t@ilsp.gr

D.Tambouratzis
Dept. of Mathematics,
Agricultural Univ.of Athens,
Iera Odos 75,
Athens 118 55, Greece.

T.Tambouratzis
Institute of Nuclear Technology - Radiation
Protection, NRCPS "Demokritos",
Aghia Paraskevi 153 10, Greece.

Gregory L. Tarr
Phillips Laboratory,
Kirtland Air Force Base
Albuquerque, New Mexico, USA.
Email: Gtarr@euler.plt.af.mil

J. G. Taylor
Department of Mathematics and
Centre for Neural Networks,
King's College, London WC2R 1LS, UK.

Rua-Huan R. Tsaih
Department of Management
Information Systems,
National Chengchi University,
Taipei, Taiwan, ROC.
Email: tsaih@mis.nccu.edu.tw

Joos Vandewalle
Katholieke Universiteit Leuven,
Dept. of Electrical Engineering,
ESAT-SISTA Kardinaal Mercierlaan 94,
B-3001 Leuven (Heverlee), Belgium.

P. Volf
UTIA The Czech Academy of Sciences,
Prague 8, CZ 180 00 Czech Republic.
Email: volf@utia.cas.cz

M.N. Vrahatis
Department of Mathematics,
University of Patras,
GR-261.10 Patras, Greece.
Email: vrahatis@math.upatras.gr

K. Warwick
Cybernetics Department,
University of Reading, Whiteknights,
Reading RG6 6AY, UK.
Email: kw@cyber.reading.ac.uk

Ansgar H. L. West
Neural Computing Research Group,
Aston University,
Aston Triangle, Birmingham B4 7ET, UK.
Email: A.H.L.West@aston.ac.uk

Christopher K. I. Williams
Neural Computing Research Group
Department of Computer Science and
Applied Mathematics,
Aston University, Birmingham B4 7ET, UK.
Email: c.k.i.williams@aston.ac.uk

Li-Qun Xu
Intelligent Systems Research Group,
BT Research Laboratories
Martlesham Heath,
Ipswich, IP5 7RE, UK.
Email: xulq@info.bt.co.uk

Howard Hua Yang
Lab for Information Representation
FRP, RIKEN, 2-1 Hirosawa,
Wako-Shi, Saitama 351-01, Japan.
Email: hhy@murasaki.riken.go.jp

Rafal Zbikowski
Department of Mechanical Engineering,
James Watt Building,
University of Glasgow,
Glasgow G12 8QQ, Scotland, UK.

Assaf J. Zeevi
Electrical Engineering Department,
Technion, Haifa 32000, Israel.

Huaiyu Zhu
Santa Fe Institute,
1399 Hyde Park Road,
Santa Fe, NM87501, USA.
Email: zhuh@santafe.edu

R. Zimmer
Computer Science Department,
Brunel University,
Uxbridge, Middx. UB8 3PH, UK.
Email: Robert.Zimmer@brunel.ac.uk

Dedication

This volume is dedicated to Professor Patrick Parks who died in 1995. Patrick was famous both for his work in nonlinear stability and automatic control and for his more recent contributions to neural networks—especially on learning procedures for CMAC systems. Patrick was known to many as a good friend and colleague, and as a gentleman, and he is greatly missed.

PREFACE

This volume of research papers comprises the proceedings of the first International Conference on Mathematics of Neural Networks and Applications (MANNA), which was held at Lady Margaret Hall, Oxford from July 3rd to 7th, 1995 and attended by 116 people. The meeting was strongly supported and, in addition to a stimulating academic programme, it featured a delightful venue, excellent food and accommodation, a full social programme and fine weather - all of which made for a very enjoyable week.

This was the first meeting with this title and it was run under the auspices of the Universities of Huddersfield and Brighton, with sponsorship from the US Air Force (European Office of Aerospace Research and Development) and the London Mathematical Society. This enabled a very interesting and wide-ranging conference programme to be offered. We sincerely thank all these organisations, USAF-EOARD, LMS, and Universities of Huddersfield and Brighton for their invaluable support.

The conference organisers were John Mason (Huddersfield) and Steve Ellacott (Brighton), supported by a programme committee consisting of Nigel Allinson (UMIST), Norman Biggs (London School of Economics), Chris Bishop (Aston), David Lowe (Aston), Patrick Parks (Oxford), John Taylor (King's College, London) and Kevin Warwick (Reading). The local organiser from Huddersfield was Ros Hawkins, who took responsibility for much of the administration with great efficiency and energy. The Lady Margaret Hall organisation was led by their bursar, Jeanette Griffiths, who ensured that the week was very smoothly run.

It was very sad that Professor Patrick Parks died shortly before the conference. He made important contributions to the field and was to have given an invited talk at the meeting.

Leading the academic programme at the meeting were nine invited speakers. Nigel Allinson (UMIST), Shun-ichi Amari (Tokyo), Norman Biggs (LSE), George Cybenko (Dartmouth), Frederico Girosi (MIT), Stephen Grossberg (Boston), Morris Hirsch (Berkeley), Helge Ritter (Bielefeld) and John Taylor (King's College, London). The supporting programme was substantial; out of about 110 who submitted abstracts, 78 delegates were offered and accepted opportunities to contribute papers. An abundance of relevant topics and areas were therefore covered, which was indeed one of the primary objectives.

The main aim of the conference and of this volume was to bring together researchers and their work in the many areas in which mathematics impinges on and contributes to neural networks, including a number of key applications areas, in order to expose current research and stimulate new ideas. We believe that this aim was achieved. In particular the meeting attracted significant contributions in such mathematical aspects as statistics and probability, statistical mechanics, dynamics, mathematical biology and neural sciences, approximation theory and numerical analysis: algebra, geometry and combinatorics, and control theory. It also covered a considerable range of neural network topics in such areas as learning and training, neural network classifiers, memory based networks, self organising maps and unsupervised learning, Hopfield networks, radial basis function networks, and the general area of neural network modelling and theory. Finally, applications of neural networks were considered in such topics as chemistry, speech recognition, automatic control, nonlinear programming, medicine, image processing, finance, time series, and dynamics. The final collection of papers in this volume consists of 6 invited papers and over 60 contributed papers, selected from the papers presented at the conference following a refereeing procedure of both the talks and the final papers. We seriously considered dividing the material into subject areas, but in the end decided that this would be arbitrary and difficult - since so many papers addressed more than one key area or issue.

We cannot conclude without mentioning some social aspects of the conference. The reception in the atmospheric Old Library at LMH was accompanied by music from a fine woodwind duo, Margaret and Richard Thorne, who had first met one of the organisers during a sabbatical visit to Canberra, Australia! The conference dinner was memorable for preliminary drinks in the lovely setting of the Fellows Garden, excellent food, and an inspirational after-dinner speech by Professor John Taylor. Finally the participants found some time to investigate the local area, including a group excursion to Blenheim Palace.

We must finish by giving further broad expressions of thanks to the many staff at Universities of Huddersfield and Brighton, US Air Force (EOARD), London Mathematical Society, and Lady Margaret Hall who helped make the conference possible. We also thank the publishers for their co-operation and support in the publication of the proceedings. Finally we must thank all the authors who contributed papers without whom this volume could not have existed.

PART I

INVITED PAPERS

N-TUPLE NEURAL NETWORKS

N. M. Allinson and A. R. Kolcz

Department of Electrical Engineering and Electronics, UMIST, Manchester, UK.

The N-Tuple Neural Network (NTNN) is a fast, efficient memory-based neural network capable of performing non-linear function approximation and pattern classification. The random nature of the N-tuple sampling of the input vectors makes precise analysis difficult. Here, the NTNN is considered within a unifying framework of the General Memory Neural Network (GMNN) — a family of networks which include such important types as radial basis function networks. By discussing the NTNN within such a framework, a clearer understanding of its operation and efficient application can be gained. The nature of the intrinsic tuple distances, and the resultant kernel, is also discussed, together with techniques for handling non-binary input patterns. An example of a tuple-based network, which is a simple extension of the conventional NTNN, is shown to yield the best estimate of the underlying regression function, $E(Y|\mathbf{X})$, for a finite training set. Finally, the pattern classification capabilities of the NTNN are considered.

1 Introduction

The origins of the N-tuple neural network date from 1959 when Bledsoe and Browning [1] proposed a pattern classification system that employed random sampling of a binary retina by taking N-bit long ordered samples (i.e., N-tuples) from the retina. These samples form the addresses to a number of memory nodes — with each bit in the sample corresponds to an individual address line. The N-tuple sampling is sensitive to correlations occurring between different regions for a given class of input patterns. Certain patterns will yield regions of the retina where the probability of a particular state of a selected N-tuple will be very high for a pattern class (e.g., predominately 'white' or 'black' if we are considering binary images of textual characters). If a set of exemplar patterns is presented to the retina, each of the N-tuple samples can be thought of as estimating the probability of occurrence of its individual states for each class. A cellular neural network interpretation of N-tuple sampling was provided by Aleksander [2]; and as we attempt to demonstrate in this paper its architecture conforms to what we term as the *General Memory Neural Network* (GMNN). Though the N-tuple neural network is more commonly thought of as a supervised pattern classifier, we will consider first the general problem of approximating a function, f, which exists in a D–dimensional real space, IR^D. This function is assumed to be smooth and continuous and that we possess a finite number of sample pairs $\{(\mathbf{x}_i, y_i) : i = 1, 2 \ldots, T\}$. We will further assume that this training data is subject to a noise component, that is $y_i = f(\mathbf{x}_i) + \varepsilon$, where ε is a random error term with zero mean. A variant of the NTNN for function approximation was first proposed by Tattersall *et al* [3] and termed the *Single-Layer-Lookup-Perceptron* (SLLUP). The essential elements of the SLLUP are the same as the basic NTNN except that the nodal memories contain numeric weights. A further extension of the basic NTNN, originally developed by Bledsoe and Bisson [4], records the relative frequencies at which the various nodal memories are addressed during training. The network introduced in Section 4 combines aspects of these two networks and follows directly from the consolidated approach presented in Section 2.

We discuss, in Section 3, some details of the NTNN with particular reference to its mapping between sampled patterns on the retina and the N-tuple distance metric, and the transformation of non-binary element vectors onto the binary retina. The form of the first mapping, which is an approximately exponential function, is the kernel function of the NTNN — though due to the random nature of the sampling, this must be considered in a statistical sense. Finally, a brief note is given on a Bayesian approximation that indicate how these networks can be employed as pattern classifiers.

2 The General Memory Neural Network

Examples of GMNN include *Radial Basis Function* (RBF) [5] networks and the *General Regression Neural Network* (GRNN) [6]. These networks can provide powerful approximation capabilities and have been subject to rigorous analysis. A further class of networks, of which the NTNN is one, have not been treated to such detailed examination. However, these networks (together with others such as the CMAC [7] and the Multi-Resolution Network [8]) are computationally very efficient and better suited to hardware implementation. The essential architectural components of GMNNs are a layer of memory nodes, arranged into a number of blocks, and an addressing element that selects the set of locations participating in the computation of the output response. An extended version of this section is given in [9].

2.1 Canonical Form of the General Memory Neural Network

The GMNN can be defined in terms of the following elements:

- A set of K memory nodes, each possessing a finite number of $|A_k|$ addressable locations.

- An address generator which assigns an address vector
$$A(\mathbf{x}) = [A_1(\mathbf{x}), A_2(\mathbf{x}), \ldots, A_K(\mathbf{x})]$$
to each input point $\mathbf{x}$. The address generated for the kth memory node is denoted by $A_k(\mathbf{x})$.

- The network's output, g, is obtained by combining the contents of selected memory locations, that is
$$[m_1(A_1(\mathbf{x})), m_2(A_2(\mathbf{x})), \ldots, m_k(A_k(\mathbf{x}))] \rightarrow \mathrm{I\!R}, \tag{1}$$
where $m_k(A_k(\mathbf{x}))$ is the content of the memory location selected by the kth memory node by the address generated by $\mathbf{x}$ for that node (this will be identified as simply $m_k(\mathbf{x})$). No specific format is imposed on the nature of the memories other than that the format is uniform for all K nodes.

- A learning procedure exists which permits the network to adjust the nodal memory contents, in response to the training set, so that some error criterion, $\pi(f, g)$, is minimised.

Each node of the network performs a simple vector quantization of the input space into $|A_k|$ cells. For each node, the address generating element can be split into an *index generator* and an *address decoder*. The index generator, I_k, selects a cell for every $\mathbf{x} \in \Omega$ and assigns it a unique index value, $I_k(\mathbf{x}) \in \{1, 2, \ldots, |A_k|\}$; hence the index generator identifies the quantization cell to which the input points belongs. The address decoder uses this generated index value to specify the physical memory address which then selects the relevant node k. Hence, $A_k(\mathbf{x}) = A_k(I_k(\mathbf{x}))$. Therefore, a cell, R_i^k, can be defined as the set of all input points which result in the selection of an address corresponding to the ith index of the kth node.

$$R_i^k = \{\mathbf{x} \in \Omega : I_k(\mathbf{x}) = i\} \tag{2}$$

Each of the cells is closed and bounded as the input space is compact in $\mathbb{R}^D$. The selection of a cell is given by the following operator or *activation function*

$$S_i^k(\mathbf{x}) = (I_k(\mathbf{x}) = i) = \begin{cases} 1 & \text{if } \mathbf{x} \in R_i^k : i = 1, \ldots, |A_k| \\ 0 & \text{otherwise} \end{cases} \tag{3}$$

The quantization of Ω performed by the individual nodes is combined, through the intersection of the K cells being superimposed, to yield a global quantizer. The number of cells $|A|$ is given by the number of all such distinct intersections.

$$|A| = \sum_{i_1=1}^{|A_1|} \sum_{i_2=1}^{|A_2|} \cdots \sum_{i_k=1}^{|A_k|} \prod_{k=1}^{K} (\{\mathbf{x} \in \Omega : I_k(\mathbf{x}) = i_k\} \neq \emptyset) \tag{4}$$

The upper bound being given by $|A|_{\max} = \prod_{k=1}^{K} |A_k|$. The address generation element of the network is distributed across the nodes, so that the general structure of Figure 1a emerges. Alternatively, the address generation can be considered at the global level (Figure 1b). These two variants are equivalent.

The quantization of the input space by the network produces values that are constant over each cell (We are ignoring, for the present, external kernel functions). The value of f assigned to the ith cell is normally expressed as the average value of f over the cell.

$$f : R_i \rightarrow \frac{\int_{R_i} d_f(\mathbf{u}) f_x(\mathbf{u})\, d\mathbf{u}}{\int_{R_i} f_x(\mathbf{u})\, d\mathbf{u}}, \tag{5}$$

where d_f is given by the squared error function. In most supervised learning schemes, this representation of $f(R_i)$ is estimated inherently through the minimisation of an error function.

For $K = 1$, the GMNN could be simply replaced to a VQ followed by a look-up table. There would need to be at least one input point per quantization cell. The granularity of the quantization needs to be sufficient to meet the degree of approximation performance appropriate for the required task. When there are multiple nodes ($K > 1$), the quantization at the node level can be much coarser which, in turn, increases the probability of input points lying inside a cell. The fine granularity being achieved through the superposition of nodal quantizers. Learning and generalisation are only possible through the use of multiple nodes. Points that are close to each other in the Ω space should share many addresses, and *vice versa*.

2.2 GMNN Distance Metrics

The *address proximity function*, which quantifies the proximity of points in Ω and so the number of generated identical nodal addresses, is given by

$$\kappa : \Omega^2 \rightarrow \{0, 1, \ldots, K\} \quad \kappa(\mathbf{x}, \mathbf{y}) = \sum_{k=1}^{K} (A_k(\mathbf{x}) = A_k(\mathbf{y})) = \sum_{k=1}^{K} (I_k(\mathbf{x}) = I_k(\mathbf{y})) \tag{6}$$

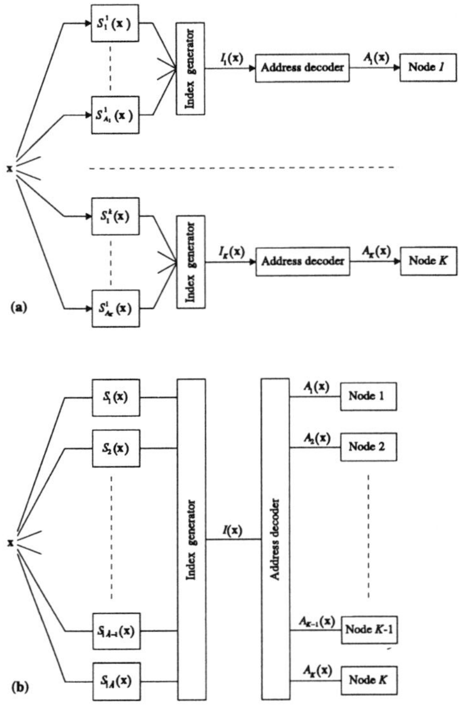

Figure 1 (a) GMNN — address generation considered at the nodal level. (b) GMNN — address generation considered at the global level. These two variants are identical in terms of overall functionality.

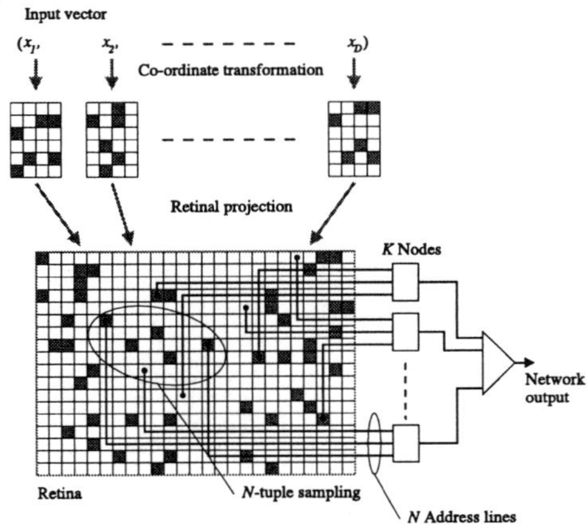

Figure 2 General structure of an NTNN.

The *address distance function*, defined as the number of different generated nodal addresses, is given by

$$\rho : \Omega^2 \to \{0, 1, \ldots, K\} \quad \rho(\mathbf{x}, \mathbf{y}) = \sum_{k=1}^{K} (A_k(\mathbf{x}) \neq A_k(\mathbf{y})) = \sum_{k=1}^{K} (I_k(\mathbf{x}) \neq I_k(\mathbf{y})) \quad (7)$$

The *binary nodal incidence function*, which returns '1' if two inputs share a common address at a given network node and '0' otherwise, is defined as

$$M_k(\mathbf{x}, \mathbf{y}) = (I_k(\mathbf{x}) = I_k(\mathbf{y})) = \begin{cases} 1 & \Leftrightarrow \quad I_k(\mathbf{x}) = I_k(\mathbf{y}) \\ 0 & \Leftrightarrow \quad I_k(\mathbf{x}) \neq I_k(\mathbf{y}) \end{cases} \quad (8)$$

From these definitions, several properties directly follow.

$$\begin{array}{lll} \forall(\mathbf{x}, \mathbf{y} \in \Omega) & \rho(\mathbf{x}, \mathbf{x}) = 0 & \rho(\mathbf{x}, \mathbf{y}) = \rho(\mathbf{y}, \mathbf{x}) \\ & \kappa(\mathbf{x}, \mathbf{x}) = K & \kappa(\mathbf{x}, \mathbf{y}) = \kappa(\mathbf{y}, \mathbf{x}) \\ & \kappa(\mathbf{x}, \mathbf{y}) = K - \rho(\mathbf{x}, \mathbf{y}) & \end{array} \quad (9)$$

$$\sum_{k=1}^{K} M_k(\mathbf{x}, \mathbf{y}) = \kappa(\mathbf{x}, \mathbf{y}) \quad (10)$$

2.3 GMNN Error-Based Training

If the address generation elements of the GMNN have been established (based on some *a priori* knowledge about the function to be approximated), then the only element which is modifiable through training is the contents of the nodal memory locations (e.g., the weights). If these locations contain real-valued numbers and the output of the network is formed by summing these numbers, then the response of the GMNN is linear in terms of this weight space. Learning methods based on the minimisation of the square error function are guaranteed to converge under these general circumstances. In the following analysis, we will therefore assume an iterative LMS learning schedule. For a finite training set of T paired samples, the error produced by the network for the jth presentation of the ith training sample is given by

$$y^i - \sum_{k=1}^{K} w_k(\mathbf{x}^i) \tag{11}$$

where $w_k(\mathbf{x}^i)$ is the value of the weight selected by $\mathbf{x}^i$ at the kth node. The participating weights are modified by a value, Δ_j^i, proportional to this error so as to reduce the error.

$$w_k(\mathbf{x}^i) \leftarrow w_k(\mathbf{x}^i) + \Delta_j^i \, : k = 1, 2, \ldots, K \tag{12}$$

Initially, all weight values are set to zero. As $w_k(\mathbf{x}^i)$ is shared by all points within the neighbourhood $N_k(\mathbf{x}^i)$, this weight updating can affect the network response for points from outside the training set. That is within an input space region given by

$$w_k(\mathbf{x}) \leftarrow w_k(\mathbf{x}) + \Delta_j^i \cdot M_k(\mathbf{x}, \mathbf{x}^i) \tag{13}$$

The output of the network after the training is complete, for an arbitrary $\mathbf{x} \in \Omega$, will depend on all training samples lying within the neighbourhood of $\mathbf{x}$.

$$g(\mathbf{x}) = \sum_{k=1}^{K} w_k(\mathbf{x}) = \sum_{k=1}^{K} \sum_{i=1}^{T} \left(M_k(\mathbf{x}, \mathbf{x}^i) \sum_{j=1}^{T_i} \Delta_j^i \right) \tag{14}$$

Rearranging this expression and using the identity (10), yields

$$g(\mathbf{x}) = \sum_{i=1}^{T} \sum_{j=1}^{T_i} \Delta_j^i \sum_{k=1}^{K} M_k(\mathbf{x}, \mathbf{x}^i) = \sum_{i=1}^{T} \Delta^i \cdot \kappa(\mathbf{x}, \mathbf{x}^i), \text{ where } \sum_{j=1}^{T_i} \Delta_j^i = \Delta^i. \tag{15}$$

We can compare this result with the response of a trained RBF network.

$$g(\mathbf{x}) = \sum_{i=1}^{T} w^i \cdot \kappa(\mathbf{x}, \mathbf{x}^i) \tag{16}$$

For the normalised RBF network, the response is given by

$$g(\mathbf{x}) = \frac{\sum_{i=1}^{T} w^i \cdot \kappa(\mathbf{x}, \mathbf{x}^i)}{\sum_{i=1}^{T} \kappa(\mathbf{x}, \mathbf{x}^i)} \tag{17}$$

and for the GRNN (where the training set response values replace the weight values).

$$g(\mathbf{x}) = \frac{\sum_{i=1}^{T} y^i \cdot \kappa(\mathbf{x}, \mathbf{x}^i)}{\sum_{i=1}^{T} \kappa(\mathbf{x}, \mathbf{x}^i)} \tag{18}$$

Though there are obvious similarities, we can further extend the functionality of the GMNN by incorporating into each nodal memory an integer counter. This nodal counter is incremented whenever the node is addressed, that is $c_k(\mathbf{x}^i) \leftarrow c_k(\mathbf{x}^i) + 1$ (Initially, all counter values are set to zero). Now the response of the GMNN is given by

$$g(\mathbf{x}) = \frac{\sum_{i=1}^{T} \Delta^i \cdot \kappa(\mathbf{x}, \mathbf{x}^i)}{\sum_{i=1}^{T} \kappa(\mathbf{x}, \mathbf{x}^i)} \tag{19}$$

The trained GMNN is equivalent to a set of T units, each centred at one of the training samples, $\mathbf{x}^t$, and possessing height Δ^t and kernel weighting function $\kappa(\cdot, \mathbf{x}^t)$. To complete the equivalence of the GMNN and the GRNN, κ must satisfy the general conditions imposed on kernel functions [10].

2.4 Introduction of External Kernels

The network output is given by the sum of weights corresponding to the selected locations, but the output remains constant over each quantization cell — regardless of the relative position of the input point inside a cell. The network mapping thus becomes discontinuous at the cell boundaries. A solution would be to emphasise weights that correspond to quantization cells that are closer to the current excitation, $\mathbf{x}$, than others. This distance can be defined in terms of the distance between $\mathbf{x}$ and the centroid of R_i^k (where $i = I_k(\mathbf{x})$).

$$d(\mathbf{x}, R_i^k) = d(\mathbf{x}, c_i^k) \tag{20}$$

A smooth, continuous and monotonically decreasing kernel function is then introduced to weight the contributions of the respective nodes to the values of $d(\mathbf{x}, R_i^k(\mathbf{x}))$, where $R_i^k(\mathbf{x})$ is the cell selected by $\mathbf{x}$ for the kth node. The network output now becomes

$$g(\mathbf{x}) = \sum_{k=1}^{K} \sum_{i=1}^{|A_k|} w_i^k \cdot \varphi_i^k(d(\mathbf{x}, R_i^k(\mathbf{x}))) \cdot M_k(c_i^k, \mathbf{x}) \tag{21}$$

A set of $K \cdot |A_k|$ kernel or basis functions can be defined, with centres given by the centroid set $\{c_i^k\}$ and where each kernel has its support truncated to its corresponding quantization region. The network mapping can be expressed as

$$g(\mathbf{x}) = \sum_{k=1}^{K} \sum_{i=1}^{|A_k|} w_i^k \cdot \varphi_i^k(\mathbf{x}) \tag{22}$$

or in its normalised form as

$$g(\mathbf{x}) = \frac{\sum_{k=1}^{K} \sum_{i=1}^{|A_k|} w_i^k \cdot \varphi_i^k(\mathbf{x})}{\sum_{k=1}^{K} \sum_{i=1}^{|A_k|} \varphi_i^k(\mathbf{x})} \tag{23}$$

$\varphi_i^k(\mathbf{x})$ is the kernel function associated with the ith quantization cell of the kth node and truncated to zero at its cell boundaries. Gaussian kernels provide an approximation to this last condition, though B-spline kernels [11] can lead to the total absence of cell discontinuities. The introduction of external weighting kernels is the final step in the GMNN architecture.

3 The N-Tuple Neural Network

The general form of the NTNN was described in the introduction and is shown in Figure 2. The following two sections consider the mapping functions inherent to this network. Namely:

- Conversion of the input vector into the binary format needed for the retina
- Sampling the retina by taking N bit values at a time to the address of one of the K memory nodes.

There is some choice in what form the first of these mappings may take depending on the application, but the retinal N-tuple sampling is common to all NTNNs. Figure 3a indicates how the threshold decision planes of the individual elements of a tuple delineate the input space into discrete regions and why the Hamming distance between tuple values is the obvious choice for a distance metric. Further details of the N-tuple distance metric and input encoding are given in [12, 13].

3.1 Retinal Sampling

The relationship between the number of different addresses generated for two arbitrary inputs, $\mathbf{x}$ and $\mathbf{y}$, and the Hamming distance $H(\mathbf{x}, \mathbf{y})$ (i.e., the number of bits for which $\mathbf{x}$ and $\mathbf{y}$ differ) is important as it reveals the nature of the distance metric necessary when a NTNN is used for pattern classification and the form of the kernel for the approximation-NTNN. This relationship can only be expressed in terms of an expectation due the random nature of the sampling. For sampling without repetitions, the expected value of $\rho_{\text{NTNN}}(\mathbf{x}, \mathbf{y}) = \rho_{\text{NTNN}}(H)$ is given by

$$E(\rho_{\text{NTNN}}(H)) = K\left(1 - \left(1 - \frac{1}{K}\right)^H\right) \tag{24}$$

For small values of H, this can be simplified to

$$E(\rho_{\text{NTNN}}(H)) \approx K\left(1 - \exp\left(-\frac{H}{K}\right)\right) \tag{25}$$

For sampling with repetitions, the expected value is

$$E(\rho_{\text{NTNN}}(H)) = K\left(1 - \exp\left(N \cdot \left(h - \frac{h^2}{2} + \frac{h^3}{3} - \cdots\right)\right)\right) \tag{26}$$

where h is the normalised Hamming distance ($= H/R$). Again, this can be simplified for small values of h, to yield

$$E(\rho_{\text{NTNN}}(H)) \approx K(1 - \exp(-N \cdot h)) \tag{27}$$

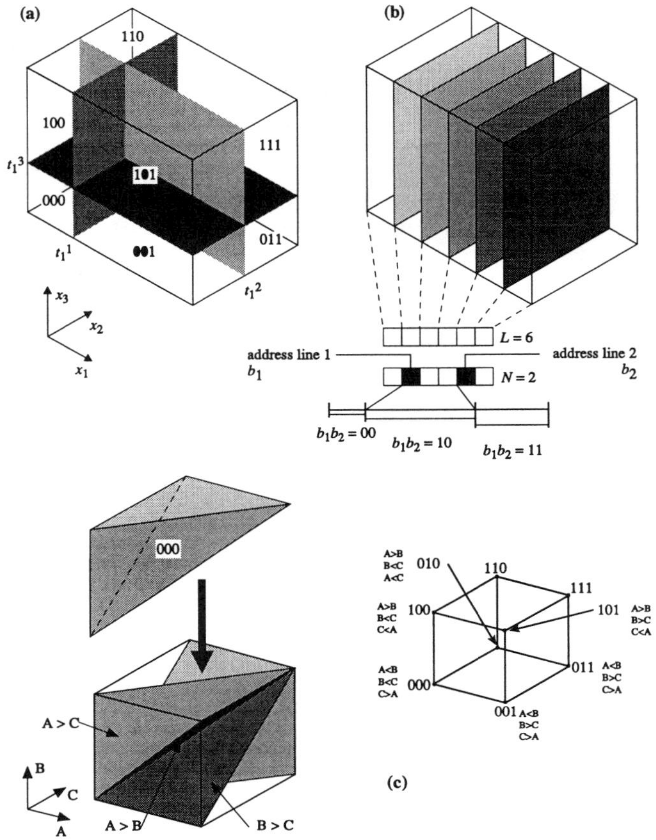

Figure 3 (a) The delineation of input space by the hard decision planes of each tuple element's threshold. Each region is marked by its specific binary state of the 3-tuple, t_1. (b) The thermometer coding inherent in N-tuple sampling. The variable, x_1, is uniformly quantized into six discrete regions ($L = 6$). The indicated 2-tuple partitions this interval into three unequal quantization regions, with the binary state of the 2-tuple indicated. (c) The delineation of the 3-dimensional input space into tetrahedral regions through the use of a ranking code. The binary space representation of the input space is also shown.

There is little difference in the general form of these two sampling methods, though there may be crucial differences in performance for specific tasks. The distance function depends exponentially on the ratio of the Hamming distance, H, between patterns to the retinal size, R. The rate of decrease is proportional to the tuple size.

3.2 Input Encoding

There is a direct and monotonic dependence of ρ_{NTNN} on the Hamming distance in the binary space of the network's retina. For binary patterns, the N-tuple sampling provides the desired mapping between the input and output addresses. For non-binary input patterns, the situation is not so clear. One obvious solution is to use a thermometer or bar-chart code, where one bit is associated to every level of an input integer. This creates a linear array of 2^n bits for an n-bit long integer. This can produce very large retinas if the input dimensionality and quantization level are large. The use of the natural binary code or Gray code is not feasible. Though these are compact codes, there is no monotonic relationship between input and pattern distances. The concatenation of several Gray codes [3] offers an improvement over a limited region and enhances the dynamic range over the binary and straight Gray code. The exponential dependence of the ρ_{NTNN} on the Hamming distance means that strict proportionality is not required but monotonicity is required within an *active* region of Hamming distances.

The potential of CMAC encoding, and further aspects of input coding methods, are discussed in Kolcz and Allinson [14]. Improvements in the input mapping, which in turn produce a more isotropic kernel, are given in Kolcz and Allinson [15], where rotation and hyper-sphere codings are described. Two further techniques will be briefly introduced here in order to indicate the wide range of possible sampling and coding schemes. Figure 3b shows one input variable, x_1, which is uniformly quantized to six levels and this is sampled by the indicated 2-tuple. The corresponding states of the resultant tuple for the three resulting sub-intervals indicate that thermometer encoding can be inherent in tuple sampling. This concept can be extended to the multivariate case. If the input space, Ω, is a D-dimensional hypercube and each memory node distributes its N address lines among these dimensions, then the space is effectively quantized into $\prod_{d=1}^{D}(N_d+1)$ hyper-rectangular cells. This assumes random sampling, such that there are N_d address lines per input dimensions (where $N_d = N/D$). The placement of tuples can be very flexible (i.e., uniform quantization is not essential) and the sampling process can take into account the density of training points within the input space.

In rank-order coding, the non-binary N-tuple is transformed to a tuple of ranked values (e.g., $\langle 20, 63, 40, 84, 122, 38\rangle$ becomes, in ascending order, the ranked tuple $\langle 0, 3, 2, 4, 5, 1\rangle$). Each possible ordering is assigned a unique consecutive ranking number, which is converted to binary format and then used as the retinal input. Rank-order coding produces an equal significance code The use of these relationships is equivalent to delineating the input space into hyper-tetrahedrons rather than the usual hyper-rectangles (Figure 3c).

4 N-tuple Regression Network

The framework for GMNN proposed earlier together with the derivation the tuple distance metric are employed here in the development of a modified NTNN which operates as a non-parametric regression estimator. The formal derivation of this network and that the N-tuple kernel is a valid one for estimating the underlying probability function is given in Kolcz and Allinson [16]. The purpose of this section is to show the relative simplicity of this network compared with other implementations.

During the training phase, the network is presented with T data pairs, $(\mathbf{x}^i, y^i)$, where $\mathbf{x}^i$ is the D-dimensional input vector and y^i is the corresponding scalar output of the system under consideration. The input vector is represented by a unique selection of the K tuple addresses with their associated weight and counter values.

$$\mathbf{x} \rightarrow \left\{ \begin{array}{c} \{t_1(\mathbf{x}), t_2(\mathbf{x}), \ldots, t_K(\mathbf{x})\} \\ \{w_1(\mathbf{x}), w_2(\mathbf{x}), \ldots, w_K(\mathbf{x})\} \\ \{a_1(\mathbf{x}), a_2(\mathbf{x}), \ldots, a_K(\mathbf{x})\} \end{array} \right. \tag{28}$$

During training, each addressed tuple location is updated according to

$$w_k(\mathbf{x}^i) \leftarrow w_k(\mathbf{x}^i) + y^i \text{ and } a_k(\mathbf{x}^i) \leftarrow a_k(\mathbf{x}^i) + 1 \tag{29}$$
$$\text{for } i = 1, 2, \ldots, T \text{ and } k = 1, 2, \ldots, K$$

Initially all weight and counter values are set to zero. After training, the network output, $\hat{y}(\mathbf{x})$, is obtained from

$$\hat{y}(\mathbf{x}) = \frac{\sum_{k=1}^{K} w_k(\mathbf{x})}{\sum_{k=1}^{K} a_k(\mathbf{x})} \tag{30}$$

An additional condition is where all addressed locations are zero. In this case, the output is set to zero.

$$\sum_{k=1}^{K} a_k(\mathbf{x}) = 0 \rightarrow \hat{y}(\mathbf{x}) = 0 \tag{31}$$

Figure 4 shows the modifications needed to a conventional NTNN to form the N-

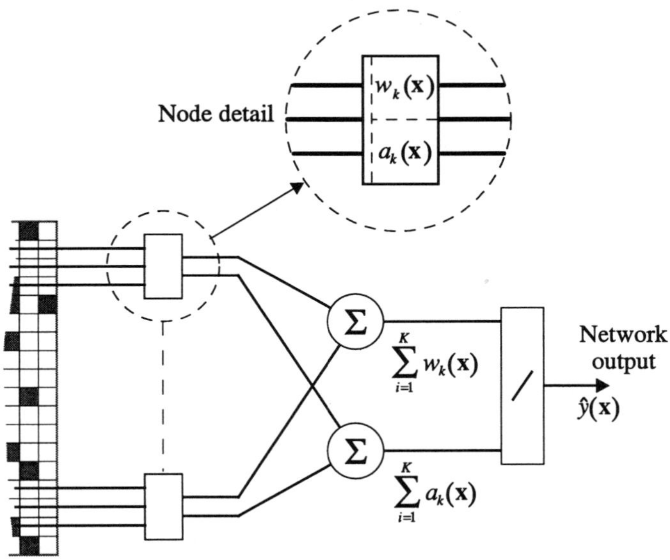

Figure 4 Modifications to the nodes and output elements of the NTNN to yield the N-tuple regression network.

tuple regression network. By considering the tuple distances between inputs, as defined in terms of the number of different tuple addresses generated, then (30) can be extended to

$$\hat{y}(\mathbf{x}) = \frac{\sum_{k=1}^{K} w_k(\mathbf{x})}{\sum_{k=1}^{K} a_k(\mathbf{x})} = \frac{\sum_{i=1}^{T} y^i \cdot \left(1 - \frac{\rho(\mathbf{x},\mathbf{x}^i)}{K}\right)}{\sum_{i=1}^{T} \left(1 - \frac{\rho(\mathbf{x},\mathbf{x}^i)}{K}\right)} \tag{32}$$

This suggests that the network output is an approximate solution of the generalised regression function, $E(Y|\mathbf{x})$, provided that the bracketed term in (32) is a valid kernel function. This function is continuous, symmetrical, non-negative and possesses finite support. These are all necessary conditions. A close approximation (based on the exponential approximation of tuple distances) is also representable as a product of univariate kernel functions. Taken together these provide sufficient conditions for a valid kernel function [17]. A wide ranging set of experiments on chaotic time-series prediction and non-linear system modelling has been conducted [16], which confirm the successful operation of this network. A major advantage of the NTNN implementation over other approaches is its fast, and fixed, speed of operation. Each recall operation involves addressing a fixed number of locations. There is no need for preprocessing large data sets, through data clustering, as is often the case for RBF networks [18].

5 Pattern Classification

So far we have restricted our considerations to the approximation properties of the NTNN, but the other major application — namely, pattern classification — can be discussed within this common framework. The training phase of a supervised network provides estimates of the conditional probabilities of individual pattern classes. The class membership probabilities can be formulated through the Bayes relationship, i.e.,

$$P(\mathbf{x} \in c) = \frac{P(\mathbf{x}\ c)P(c)}{P(\mathbf{x})} \tag{33}$$

where c is the class label for a particular class $\{c = 1, 2, \ldots, C\}$. The modified NTNN discussed in Section 4 can be reformulated in terms of this classification. The network through training approximates C indicator functions, which denote membership to an individual class.

$$I_c(\mathbf{x}) = \begin{cases} 1 & \text{if } x \subset c \\ 0 & \text{otherwise} \end{cases} \tag{34}$$

Modifying (32), the indicator functions can be approximated, after training, by

$$I_c(\mathbf{x}) = \frac{\sum_{i=1}^{T} (\mathbf{x}^i \subset c)(1 - \rho(\mathbf{x},\mathbf{x}^i)/K)}{\sum_{i=1}^{T} (1 - \rho(\mathbf{x},\mathbf{x}^i)/K)} = \frac{\sum_{k=1}^{K} w_k^c}{\sum_{k=1}^{K} a_k} \equiv P(c)\frac{\sum_{k=1}^{K} P(t_k|c)}{\sum_{k=1}^{K} P(t_k)} \tag{35}$$

This relationship gives the ratio of the cumulative summation of all training points belonging to a class c, which have an N-tuple distance at $0, 1, \ldots, (K-1)$ from $\mathbf{x}$ to a similar cumulative summation for all training points. The decision surfaces present in the K-dimensional weight space are described by $\sum_{k=1}^{K} w_k = \text{const}$, and the winning class is given by $c_{\text{winner}} = \max_{c=1,2,\ldots,C} \sum_{k=1}^{K} w_k^c$.

6 Conclusions

The unifying approach proposed for a wide class of memory-based neural networks means that practical, but poorly understood, networks (such as the NTNN) can be considered in direct comparison with networks (such as RBF networks) that possess a much firmer theoretical foundation. The random sampling inherent in the N-tuple approach makes detailed analysis difficult so this link is all the more important. The pragmatic advantages of NTNNs has been demonstrated in the regression network described above, where large data-sets can be accommodated with fixed computational overheads. The possible range of input sampling and encoding strategies has been illustrated, but by no means exhaustively. There is still a need to seek other strategies that will provide optimum kernel functions for specified recognition or approximation tasks. The power and flexibility of Bledsoe and Browning's original concept has not, as yet, been fully exploited.

REFERENCES

[1] Bledsoe W W and Browning I, *Pattern recognition and reading by machine*, IRE Joint Computer Conference, 1959, 225–232.

[2] Aleksander I, *Fused adative circuit which learns by example*, Electronics Letters, 1965, 1, 173–174.

[3] Tattersall G D, Foster S and Johnston R D, *Single-layer lookup perceptrons*, IEE Proceedings — F: Radar and Signal Processing, 1991, 138, 46–54.

[4] Bledsoe W W and Bisson C L, *Improved memory matrices for the N-tuple pattern recognition method*, IRE Transactions on Electronic Computers, 1962, 11, 414–415.

[5] Broomhead D S and Lowe D, *Multivariable functional interpolation and adaptive networks*, Complex Systems, 1988, 2, 321–355.

[6] Specht D F, *A general regression neural network*, IEEE Transactions on Neural Networks, 1991, 2, 568–576.

[7] Albus J S, *A new approach to manipulator control: the cerebellar model articulation controller (CMAC)*, Journal of Dynamic Systems, Measurement and Control, 1975, 97, 220–227.

[8] Moody J, *Fast learning in multi-resolution hierarchies*, in Advances in Neural Information Processing 1 (Touretzky D S, ed.), 1989, Morgan Kaufmann: San Mateo, CA, 29–39.

[9] Kolcz A and Allinson N M, *General Memory Neural Network — extending the properties of basis networks to RAM-based architectures*, 1995 IEEE International Conference on Neural Networks, Perth, Western Australia.

[10] Park J and Sandberg, I W, *Universal approximation using radial basis function networks*, Neural Computation, 1991, 3, 246–257.

[11] Kavli T, *ASMOD - an algorithm for adaptive modelling of observational data*, International Journal of Control, 1993, 58, 947–967.

[12] Kolcz A and Allinson N M, *Application of the CMAC-input encoding scheme in the N-tuple approximation network*, IEE Proceedings - E Computers and Digital Techniques, 1994, 141, 177–183.

[13] Kolcz A and Allinson N M, *Enhanced N-tuple approximators*, Proceedings of Weightless Neural Network Workshop 93, 1993, 38–45.

[14] Allinson N M and Kolcz A, *The theory and practice of N-tuple neural networks*, in Neural Networks (Taylor J G, ed.), 1995, Alfred Waller, 53–70.

[15] Kolcz A and Allinson N M, *Euclidean mapping in an N-tuple approximation network*, Sixth IEEE Digital Signal Processing Workshop, 1994, 285–289.

[16] Kolcz A and Allinson N M, *N-tuple regression network*, Neural Networks vol 9 No.5 pp855-870.

[17] Parzen E, *On estimation of a probability density function and mode*, Annals of Mathematical Statistics, 1962, 33, 1065–1076.

[18] Moody J and Darken C J, *Fast learning in networks of locally-tuned processing units*, Neural Computation, 1989, 1, 281–294.

INFORMATION GEOMETRY OF NEURAL NETWORKS —AN OVERVIEW—

Shun-ichi Amari

University of Tokyo, Tokyo, Japan, RIKEN Frontier Research Program, Wako-City, Saitama, Japan. Email: amari@sat.t.u-tokyo.ac.jp

The set of all the neural networks of a fixed architecture forms a geometrical manifold where the modifable connection weights play the role of coordinates. It is important to study all such networks as a whole rather than the behavior of each network in order to understand the capability of information processing of neural networks. What is the natural geometry to be introduced in the manifold of neural networks? Information geometry gives an answer, giving the Riemannian metric and a dual pair of affine connections. An overview is given to information geometry of neural networks.

1 Introduction to Neural Manifolds

Let us consider a neural network of fixed architecture specified by parameters $\boldsymbol{w} = (w_1, \cdots, w_p)$ which represent the connection weights and thresholds of the network. The parameters are usually modifiable by learning. The set N of all such networks is considered a p-dimensional neural manifold, where $\boldsymbol{w}$ is a coordinate system in N. Because it includes all the possible networks belonging to that architecture, the total capabilities of the networks are made clear by studying the manifold N itself. To be specific, let N be the set of multilayer feedforward networks each of which receives an input $\boldsymbol{x}$ and emits an output $\boldsymbol{z}$. The input-output relation is described as

$$\boldsymbol{z} = \boldsymbol{f}(\boldsymbol{x}; \boldsymbol{w})$$

where the total output $\boldsymbol{z}$ depends on $\boldsymbol{w}$ which describes all the connection weights and thresholds of the hidden and output neurons. Let us consider the space S of all the square integrable functions of $\boldsymbol{x}$

$$S = \{\boldsymbol{k}(\boldsymbol{x})\}$$

and assume for the moment that $\boldsymbol{f}(\boldsymbol{x}; \boldsymbol{w})$ is square integrable. The set S is infinite-dimensional L_2 space, and the neural manifold N is a part of it, that is, a p-dimensional subspace embedded in S. This shows that not all the functions are realizable by neural networks.

Given a function $\boldsymbol{k}(\boldsymbol{x})$, we would like to find a neural network whose behavior $\boldsymbol{f}(\boldsymbol{x}; \boldsymbol{w})$ approximates $\boldsymbol{k}(\boldsymbol{x})$ as well as possible. The best approximation is given by projecting $\boldsymbol{k}(\boldsymbol{x})$ to N in the entire space S. The approximation power depends on the shape of N in S. This shows that geometrical considerations are important.

When the behavior of a network is stochastic, it is given by the conditional probability $p(\boldsymbol{z}|\boldsymbol{x}; \boldsymbol{w})$ of $\boldsymbol{z}$ conditioned on input $\boldsymbol{x}$, where $\boldsymbol{w}$ is the network parameters. A typical example is a network composed of binary stochatic neurons: The probability $z = 1$ of such a stochastic neuron is given by

$$\text{Prob}\{z = 1; \boldsymbol{w}\} = \frac{\exp\{\boldsymbol{w} \cdot \boldsymbol{x}\}}{1 + \exp\{\boldsymbol{w} \cdot \boldsymbol{x}\}}, \tag{1}$$

where $z = 0$ or 1. Another typical case is a noise-contaminated network whose output $\boldsymbol{z}$ is written as

$$\boldsymbol{z} = \boldsymbol{f}(\boldsymbol{x}; \boldsymbol{w}) + \boldsymbol{n}, \tag{2}$$

where $\boldsymbol{n}$ is a random noise independent of $\boldsymbol{w}$. If $\boldsymbol{n}$ is subject to the normal distribution with mean 0 and covariance $\sigma^2 I$, I being the identity matrix,

$$\boldsymbol{n} \sim N(0, \sigma^2 I),$$

the conditional probability is given by

$$p(\boldsymbol{z}|\boldsymbol{x};\boldsymbol{w}) = \text{const } \exp\left\{-\frac{[\boldsymbol{z} - \boldsymbol{f}(\boldsymbol{x},\boldsymbol{w})]^2}{2\sigma^2}\right\}. \tag{3}$$

When input signals $\boldsymbol{x}$ are produced independently from a distribution $q(\boldsymbol{x})$, the joint distribution of $(\boldsymbol{x}, \boldsymbol{z})$ is given by

$$p(\boldsymbol{x}, \boldsymbol{z}; \boldsymbol{w}) = q(\boldsymbol{x}) p(\boldsymbol{z}|\boldsymbol{x}; \boldsymbol{w}). \tag{4}$$

Let S be the set of all the conditional probability distributions (or joint distributions). Let $q(\boldsymbol{z}|\boldsymbol{x})$ be an arbitrary probability distribution in S which is to be approximated by a stochastic neural network of the behavior $p(\boldsymbol{z}|\boldsymbol{x};\boldsymbol{w})$. The neural manifold N consists of all the conditional probability distributions $p(\boldsymbol{z}|\boldsymbol{x};\boldsymbol{w})$ (or the joint probability distributions $p(\boldsymbol{x},\boldsymbol{z};\boldsymbol{w})$) and is a p-dimensional submanifold of S. A fundamental question arises : What is the natural geometry of S and N? How should the distance between two distributions be measured? What is the geodesic connecting two distributions? It is important to have a definite answer to these problems not only for studying stochastic networks but also for deterministic networks which are not free of random noises and whose stochastic interpretation is sometimes very useful. Information geometry ([3], [17]) answers all of these problems.

2 A Short Review of Information Geometry

Let us consider probability distributions $p(\boldsymbol{y}, \boldsymbol{\xi})$ of random variable $\boldsymbol{y}$, where $\boldsymbol{\xi} = (\xi_1, \cdots, \xi_n)$ is the parameters to specify a distribution. When $\boldsymbol{y}$ is a scalar and normally distributed, we have

$$p(y, \boldsymbol{\xi}) = \frac{1}{\sqrt{2\pi}\sigma} \exp\left\{-\frac{(y-\mu)^2}{2\sigma^2}\right\},$$

where $\boldsymbol{\xi} = (\mu, \sigma)$ is the parameters to specify it. When y is discrete, taking values on $\{0, 1, \cdots, n\}$, we have

$$\text{Prob}\{y, \boldsymbol{\xi}\} = \sum_{i=1}^{n} \xi_i \delta_i(y) + \left(1 - \sum_{i=1}^{n} \xi_i\right) \delta_0(y)$$

where $\delta_i(y) = 1$ when $y = i$ and is equal to 0 otherwise and $\xi_i = \text{Prob}\{y = i\}$. Let S be the set of such distributions

$$S = \{p(\boldsymbol{y}, \boldsymbol{\xi})\}$$

specified by $\boldsymbol{\xi}$. Then, S can be regarded as an n-dimensional manifold, where $\boldsymbol{\xi}$ is a coordinate system. If we can introduce a distance measure between two nearby points specified by $\boldsymbol{\xi}$ and $\boldsymbol{\xi} + d\boldsymbol{\xi}$ by the quadratic form

$$|d\boldsymbol{\xi}|^2 = \sum_{i,j} g_{ij}(\boldsymbol{\xi}) d\xi_i d\xi_j, \tag{5}$$

the manifold S is said to be Riemannian. The quantity $\{g_{ij}(\boldsymbol{\xi})\}$ is the Riemannian metric tensor. Another important concept is the affine connection by which a geodesic line (an extention of the concept of the straight line in the Euclidean geometry) is defined. The affine connection is defined by the covariant derivative, and is represented by the three-index parameters $\Gamma_{ijk}(\boldsymbol{\xi})$ formally defined by

$$\Gamma_{ijk} = \langle \nabla_{\boldsymbol{e}_i} \boldsymbol{e}_j, \boldsymbol{e}_k \rangle \tag{6}$$

where $\boldsymbol{e}_i = \partial/\partial\xi_i$ is the natural basis vector field, $\langle \cdot, \cdot \rangle$ is the inner product and ∇ is the covariant derivative. The metric tensor is written as

$$\langle \boldsymbol{e}_i, \boldsymbol{e}_j \rangle = g_{ij}. \tag{7}$$

In the Riemannian geometry, the Levi-Civita connection

$$\Gamma^{(0)}_{ijk} = \frac{1}{2}\left(\frac{\partial}{\partial\xi_i} g_{jk} + \frac{\partial}{\partial\xi_j} g_{ik} - \frac{\partial}{\partial\xi_k} g_{ij} \right) \tag{8}$$

is used usually. This is the only torsion-free metric connection satisfying

$$X\langle Y, Z\rangle = \langle \nabla_X Y, Z\rangle + \langle Y, \nabla_X Z\rangle, \tag{9}$$

for vector fieds, X, Y and Z. More intuitively, a geodesic is the minimum distance curve connecting two points under the Levi-Civita connection.

Information geometry ([3], [17]) defines a new pair of affine connections given, respectively, by

$$\Gamma^{(e)}_{ijk}(\boldsymbol{\xi}) = \Gamma^{(0)}_{ijk} - \frac{1}{2} T_{ijk}, \tag{10}$$

$$\Gamma^{(m)}_{ijk}(\boldsymbol{\xi}) = \Gamma^{(0)}_{ijk} + \frac{1}{2} T_{ijk}, \tag{11}$$

where $T_{ijk}(\boldsymbol{\xi})$ is the tensor defined by

$$T_{ijk} = E\left[\frac{\partial}{\partial\xi_i} \log p \frac{\partial}{\partial\xi_j} \log p \frac{\partial}{\partial\xi_k} \log p \right]. \tag{12}$$

They are called the e- and m-connection, respectively, and are dual in the sense of

$$X\langle Y, Z\rangle = \langle \nabla^{(e)}_X Y, Z\rangle + \langle Y, \nabla^{(m)}_X Z\rangle. \tag{13}$$

The duality of connections is a new concept given rise to by information geometry. When a manifold has a dually flat structure in the sense that the e- and m-Riemann-Christoffel curvature vanish (but the Levi-Civita connection has non-vanishing curvature in general), it has remarkable properties that are dual extensions of Euclidean properties. Exponential families of probability distributions are proved to be dually flat. Intuitively speaking, the set of all the probability distributions $\{p(\boldsymbol{y})\}$ are dually flat, and any parameterized model $S = \{p(\boldsymbol{y}, \boldsymbol{\xi})\}$ is a flat or curved submanifold embedded in it. Hence, it is important to study properties of the dually flat manifold.

When S is dually flat, the divergence function

$$D(\boldsymbol{\xi} : \boldsymbol{\xi}') = \int p(\boldsymbol{y}, \boldsymbol{\xi}) \log \frac{p(\boldsymbol{y}, \boldsymbol{\xi})}{p(\boldsymbol{y}, \boldsymbol{\xi}')} d\boldsymbol{y} \tag{14}$$

is naturally and automatically introduced to S. This is an extension of the square of the Riemannian distance, because it satisfies

$$D(\boldsymbol{\xi} : \boldsymbol{\xi} + d\boldsymbol{\xi}) = \frac{1}{2} \sum g_{ij}(\boldsymbol{\xi}) d\xi_i \xi_j. \tag{15}$$

The divergence satisfies $D(\boldsymbol{\xi}, \boldsymbol{\xi}') \geq 0$ with equality when and only when $\boldsymbol{\xi} = \boldsymbol{\xi}'$. But it is not symmetric in general.

We have the generalized Pythagorus theorem.

Theorem 1 *Let ξ_1, ξ_2 and ξ_3 be three distributions in a dually flat manifold. Then, when the m-geodesic connecting ξ_1 and ξ_2 is orthogonal at ξ_2 to the e-geodesic connecting ξ_2 and ξ_3,*

$$D(\xi_1 : \xi_2) + D(\xi_2 : \xi_3) = D(\xi_1 : \xi_3). \tag{16}$$

The projection theorem is a consequence of this theorem.

Theorem 2 *Let M be a submanifold embedded in a dually flat manifold S. Let P be a point in S, and let $\hat{Q}_P$ is the point in M that minimizes $D(P : Q)$, $Q \in M$, that is, the point in M that gives the best approximation to P. Then, the $\hat{Q}_P$ is the m-geodesic projection of Q to M.*

These properties are applied to various fields of information sciences such as statistics ([3], [11], [16], information theory ([5],[9], control systems theory ([4],[19]), dynamical systems ([14],[18]) etc. It is also useful for neural networks ([6], [10], [7]). We will show how it is applied to neural networks.

3 Manifold of Feedforward Networks and EM Algorithm

In the begining, we show a very simple case of the manifold M of simple stochastic perceptrons or single stochastic neurons. It receives input $\boldsymbol{x}$ and emits a binary output z stochastically, based on the weighted sum $\boldsymbol{w} \cdot \boldsymbol{x}$ of input $\boldsymbol{x}$. The conditional probability of z is written as

$$p(z|\boldsymbol{x}; \boldsymbol{w}) = \frac{e^{z\boldsymbol{w}\cdot\boldsymbol{x}}}{1 + e^{\boldsymbol{w}\cdot\boldsymbol{x}}}. \tag{17}$$

The joint distribution is given by

$$p(\boldsymbol{x}, z; \boldsymbol{w}) = q(\boldsymbol{x})p(z|\boldsymbol{x}; \boldsymbol{w}). \tag{18}$$

Here, we assume that $q(\boldsymbol{x})$ is the normal distribution $N(0, I)$ with mean 0 and covariance metrix I, the identity matrix.

Let M be the set of all the stochastic perceptrons. Since a perceptron is specified by a vector $\boldsymbol{w}$, M is regarded as a manifold homeomorphic to $\boldsymbol{R}^n$ where n is the dimensions of $\boldsymbol{x}$ and $\boldsymbol{w}$. Here, $\boldsymbol{w}$ is a coordinate system of M. We introduce a natural Riemannian geometric structure to M. Then, it is possible to define the distance between two perceptrons, the volume of M itself, and so on. This is done through the Fisher information, since each point (perceptron) in M is regarded as a probability distribution (18). Let $G(\boldsymbol{w}) = \{g_{ij}(\boldsymbol{w})\}$ be a matrix representing the Riemannian metric tensor at point $\boldsymbol{w}$. We define the Riemannian metric by the Fisher information matrix,

$$g_{ij}(\boldsymbol{w}) = E\left[\frac{\partial}{\partial w_i}\log p(z, \boldsymbol{x}; \boldsymbol{w})\frac{\partial}{\partial w_j}\log p(z, \boldsymbol{x}; \boldsymbol{w})\right], \tag{19}$$

where E denotes the expectation over $(z, \boldsymbol{x})$ with respect to the distribution $p(z, \boldsymbol{x}; \boldsymbol{w})$. In order to calculate the metric G explicitly, let $\boldsymbol{e_w}$ be the unit column vector in the direction of $\boldsymbol{w}$ in the Euclidean space $\boldsymbol{R}^n$,

$$\boldsymbol{e_w} = \frac{\boldsymbol{w}}{|\boldsymbol{w}|},$$

where $|\boldsymbol{w}|$ is the Euclidean norm, and $\boldsymbol{e}_{\boldsymbol{w}}^T$ its transpose. We then have the following theorem.

Theorem 3 *The Fisher information metric is given by*

$$g(\boldsymbol{w}) = c_1(w)I + \{c_2(w) - c_1(w)\}\boldsymbol{e_w e_w^T}, \tag{20}$$

where $w = |\boldsymbol{w}|$ *(Euclidean norm) and* $c_1(w)$ *and* $c_2(w)$ *are given by*

$$c_1(w) = \frac{1}{\sqrt{2\pi}} \int f(w\varepsilon)\{1 - f(w\varepsilon)\} \exp\left\{-\frac{1}{2}\varepsilon^2\right\} d\varepsilon, \tag{21}$$

$$c_2(w) = \frac{1}{\sqrt{2\pi}} \int f(w\varepsilon)\{1 - f(w\varepsilon)\}\varepsilon^2 \exp\left\{-\frac{1}{2}\varepsilon^2\right\} d\varepsilon. \tag{22}$$

The theorem shows that M is a Riemannaian manifold with Riemannian metric $G(\boldsymbol{w})$ which has spherical symmetry. It is remarked that the skewness tensor $T = (t_{ijk})$,

$$t_{ijk} = E\left[\frac{\partial}{\partial w_i} \log p \frac{\partial}{\partial w_j} \log p \frac{\partial}{\partial w_k} \log p\right]$$

vanishes under the distribution $q(\boldsymbol{x}) \sim N(0, I)$. Hence, M is a self-dual Riemannian manifold and no dual affine connections appear in this special case.
We now show some applications of the Riemannian structure.
The volume V_n of the perceptron manifold M is measured by

$$V_n = \int \sqrt{|G(\boldsymbol{w})|} d\boldsymbol{w} \tag{23}$$

where $|G(\boldsymbol{w})|$ is the determinant of $G = (g_{ij})$ which represents the volume density by the Riemanian metric. Let us consider the problem of estimating $\boldsymbol{w}$ from examples. ¿From the Bayesian viewpoint, we consider that $\boldsymbol{w}$ is chosen randomly subject to a prior distribution $p_{\rm pr}(\boldsymbol{w})$. A natural choice of $p_{\rm pr}(\boldsymbol{w})$ is the Jeffrey prior or non-informative prior given by

$$p_{\rm pr}(\boldsymbol{w}) = \frac{1}{V_n} \sqrt{|G(\boldsymbol{w})|}. \tag{24}$$

When one studies learning curve and overtraining ([8]), it is important to take the effect of $p_{\rm pr}(\boldsymbol{w})$ into account. The Jeffrey prior is calculated as follows.

Theorem 4 *The Jeffrey prior and the volume of the manifold are given by*

$$\sqrt{|G(\boldsymbol{w})|} = \frac{1}{V_n} \sqrt{c_2(w)\{c_1(w)\}^{n-1}}, \tag{25}$$

$$V_n = \int \sqrt{c_2(w)\{c_1(w)\}^{n-1}} a_n w^{n-1} dw, \tag{26}$$

respectively, where a_n *is the volume of the unit n-sphere.*

The gradient descent is a well known learning method, which was proposed by Widrow for the analog linear perceptron and extended to non-linear multilayer networks with hidden units ([2],[20] and others). Let $l(\boldsymbol{x}, z; \boldsymbol{w})$ be the loss function when the perceptron with weight $\boldsymbol{w}$ processes an input-output pair $(\boldsymbol{x}, z)$. In many cases, the squared error

$$l(\boldsymbol{x}, z; \boldsymbol{w}) = \frac{1}{2}|z - f(\boldsymbol{w} \cdot \boldsymbol{x})|^2$$

is used. When input-output examples $(\boldsymbol{x}_t, z_t)$, $t = 1, 2, \cdots$, are given, we train the perceptron by the gradient-descent method:

$$\boldsymbol{w}_{t+1} = \boldsymbol{w}_t - c\frac{\partial l(\boldsymbol{x}_t, z_t; \boldsymbol{w}_t)}{\partial \boldsymbol{w}} \tag{27}$$

where $\boldsymbol{w}_t$ is the current value of the weight and it is modified to give $\boldsymbol{w}_{t+1}$ by using the current input-output $(\boldsymbol{x}_t, z_t)$. It was shown that the learning constant c can be replaced by any positive-definite matrix cK ([2]). The natural choice of this matrix is the inverse of the Fisher information metric,

$$\boldsymbol{w}_{t+1} = \boldsymbol{w}_t - cG^{-1}(\boldsymbol{w}_t)\frac{\partial l}{\partial \boldsymbol{w}} \tag{28}$$

from the geometrical point of view, since this is the invariant gradient under general coordinate transformations. However, it is in general not easy to calculate G^{-1} so that this excellent schema is not usually used (see [10]). We can calculate $G^{-1}(\boldsymbol{w})$ explicitly in the perceptron case.

Theorem 5 *The inverse of the Fisher information metric is*

$$G^{-1}(\boldsymbol{w}) = \frac{1}{c_1(w)}I + \left(\frac{1}{c_2(w)} - \frac{1}{c_1(w)}\right)\boldsymbol{e}_{\boldsymbol{w}}\boldsymbol{e}_w^T. \tag{29}$$

This leads to a very simple form of learning

$$\begin{aligned}\boldsymbol{w}_{t+1} &= \boldsymbol{w}_t - c\{z_t - f(\boldsymbol{w}_t.\boldsymbol{x}_t)\}f'(\boldsymbol{w}_t\cdot\boldsymbol{x}_t)\\ &\quad\left[\frac{1}{c_1(w_t)}\boldsymbol{x}_t - \frac{1}{w_t^2}\left(\frac{1}{c_2(w_t)} - \frac{1}{c_1(w_t)}\right)(\boldsymbol{w}_t\cdot\boldsymbol{x}_t)\boldsymbol{w}_t.\right].\end{aligned} \tag{30}$$

This is much more efficient compared to the prevailing simple gradient method. Any acceleration methods can be incorporated with this.

The geometry of the manifold N of multilayer feedforward neural networks can be constructed in principle in the same way. However, it is not so easy to calculate the explicit forms of the metric $g_{ij}(\boldsymbol{w})$ and the connections $\Gamma_{ijk}^{(e)}$ and $\Gamma_{ijk}^{(m)}$. The geometrical structure becomes very complicated because of hidden units.

Neural network researchers sometimes use statistical methods such as the EM algorithm [15]. Information geometry is useful for elucidating such a method [7]. Let $(\boldsymbol{x}, \boldsymbol{y}, \boldsymbol{z})$ be the random variables representing the input, outputs of hidden units and the final output. Let S be the manifold of all the joint probability distributions $q(\boldsymbol{x}, \boldsymbol{y}, \boldsymbol{z})$. The manifold N of the probability distributions $p(\boldsymbol{x}, \boldsymbol{y}, \boldsymbol{z}; \boldsymbol{w})$ realized by the network specified by $\boldsymbol{w}$ forms a submanifold in S.

We want to realize a stochastic input-output relation $q(\boldsymbol{z}|\boldsymbol{x})$ or $q(\boldsymbol{x}, \boldsymbol{z})$ and we do not care about the values $\boldsymbol{y}$ of hidden units so far as the input-output relation is well approximated. All the probability distributions whose marginal distributions are the same, that is, those satisfying

$$\sum_{\boldsymbol{y}} q(\boldsymbol{x}, \boldsymbol{y}, \boldsymbol{z}) = q^*(\boldsymbol{x}, \boldsymbol{z}) \tag{31}$$

form an m-flat submanifold D in S,

$$D_{q^*} = \{q(\boldsymbol{x}, \boldsymbol{y}, \boldsymbol{z}) | \sum_{\boldsymbol{y}} q(\boldsymbol{x}, \boldsymbol{y}, \boldsymbol{z}) = q^*(\boldsymbol{x}, \boldsymbol{z})\}.$$

This is called the data submanifold. The problem of approximation is formulated as follows : Given $q^*(\boldsymbol{x}, \boldsymbol{z})$ obtain the neural network $\boldsymbol{w}^*$ that minimizes $D[q(\boldsymbol{x}, \boldsymbol{y}, \boldsymbol{z}) : p(\boldsymbol{x}, \boldsymbol{y}, \boldsymbol{z}; \boldsymbol{w})]$, that is

$$\min_{q\in D_{q^*},\ p\in N} D[q : p]. \tag{32}$$

Hence, the problem is minimization of the divergence between two submanifolds N and D_{q^*}.

This is iteratively solved as follows:

Step 1 : Given $p_i \in N$, obtain $q_i \in D_{q^*}$ that minimizes $D[q, p_i]$.

Step 2 : Given $q_i \in D_{q^*}$. obtain $p_{i+1} \in N$ that minimizes $D[q_i, p]$.

The step 1 is solved by e-projecting p_i to D_{q^*}. This is equivalent to taking the conditional expectation of hidden variables with respect to p_i. The step 2 is the maximization of the likelihood and is given by m-projecting q_i to N. Hence, the procedure is called the *em*-algorithm in geometry ([12], [13], [7], [10]) and the *EM*-algorithm in statistics. The algorithm was shown very effective in the model of mixture of expert nets ([15], and many others). Its geometry was studied by Amari [7]. Xu [21] extended the idea to be applicable to more general neural network learning problems.

4 Manifold of Boltzmann Machines

A Boltzmann machine is a recurrently connected neural network composed of binary stochastic neurons. We show in the beginning a simple Boltzmann machine without hidden units and then study that with hidden units. The behavior of a Boltzmann machine is shown by the following stochastic dynamics : Let $\boldsymbol{x}(t) = (x_1(t), \cdots, x_n(t))$ be the state of the network at time t, where x_i takes on 0 and 1 representing the quiescent and excited states of the ith neuron. At time $t+1$, choose one neuron at random. Let the ith neuron be chosen. Then, the state of the ith neuron changes stochastically by

$$\text{Prob}\{x_i(t+1) = 1\} = \frac{\exp\{u_i\}}{1 + \exp\{u_i\}}, \tag{33}$$

where

$$u_i = \sum_j w_{ij} x_j(t) - w_{i0}, \tag{34}$$

w_{ij} being the connection weights of the ith and jth neurons and w_{i0} being the biasing term of the ith neuron. All the other neurons are unchanged, $x_j(t+1) = x_j(t)$.

The $\boldsymbol{x}(t)$, $t = 1, 2, \cdots$, is a Markov process, and its stationary distribution is explicitly given by

$$p(\boldsymbol{x}, W) = \exp\left\{\frac{1}{2}\sum w_{ij} x_i x_j - \psi(W)\right\} \tag{35}$$

when $w_{ij} = w_{ji}$, $w_{ii} = 0$ hold, where $x_0 = 1$. The set of all the Boltzmann machines forms an $n(n+1)/2$-dimensional manifold B, and $W = \{w_{0i}, w_{ij}, i < j\}$ is a coordinate system of the Boltzmann neural manifold. To each Boltzmann machine W corresponds a probability distribution (35) and vice versa. Therefore, B is identified with the set of all the probability distributions of form (35).

Let S be the set of all the distributions over 2^n states $\boldsymbol{x}$,

$$S = \{q(\boldsymbol{x}) \mid q(\boldsymbol{x}) > 0, \sum_{\boldsymbol{x}} q(\boldsymbol{x}) = 1\}. \tag{36}$$

Then, B is an $n(n+1)/2$-dimensional submanifold embedded in the $(2^n - 1)$-dimensional manifold S. We can show that B is a flat submanifold of S, and that both S and B are dually flat, although they are curved from the Riemannian metric point of view [10].

Given a distribution $q(\boldsymbol{x})$, we train the Boltzmann machine by modifying w_{ij} based on independent examples $\boldsymbol{x}_1, \boldsymbol{x}_2 \cdots$ from the distribution q, for the purpose of obtaining $\hat{W}$ such that $p(\boldsymbol{x}, \hat{W})$ approximates $q(\boldsymbol{x})$ as well as possible. The degree of approximation is measured by the divergence $D[q(\boldsymbol{x}) : p(\boldsymbol{x}, W)]$. The best approximation is given by m-projecting q to B. We have an explicit solution since the manifolds are flat. The stochastic gradient learning was proposed by Ackley, Hinton and Sejnowski [1],

$$W_{t+1} = W_t - \eta \frac{\partial}{\partial W} D[q; p] \tag{37}$$

where the gradient term is not the expectatio form but is evaluated by random example $\boldsymbol{x}_t$. However, from the geometrical poit of view, it is more natural to use

$$W_{t+1} = W_t - \eta G^{-1} \frac{\partial}{\partial W} D[q; p], \tag{38}$$

where G^{-1} is the Fisher information matrix. In this case, the expectation of the trajectory $\hat{W}_t$ of learning is the e-geodesic of B (when the continuous time version is used), see [10]. It is shown that the convergence is much faster in this case, although calculations of G^{-1} are sometimes not easy.

When hidden units exist, we divide $\boldsymbol{x}$ into

$$\boldsymbol{x} = (\boldsymbol{x}^V, \boldsymbol{x}^H), \tag{39}$$

where $\boldsymbol{x}^V$ represents the state of the visible part and $\boldsymbol{x}^H$ represents that of the hidden part. The connection weights are also divided naturally into the three parts $W = (W^V, W^H, W^{VH})$. The probability distribution of the visible part is given by

$$p(\boldsymbol{x}^V; W) = \sum_{\boldsymbol{x}^H} p(\boldsymbol{x}^V, \boldsymbol{x}^H; W). \tag{40}$$

Let S^V and B^V be the manifolds of all the distributions over $\boldsymbol{x}^V$ and those realizable by Boltzmann machines in the form of (40). Then, S^V is flat but B^V is not.

It is easier to treat the extended manifolds of $S^{V,H}$ and $B^{V,H}$ including hidden units. However, only a distribution $q(\boldsymbol{x}^V)$ is specified from the outside in the learning process and its hidden part is not. Let us consider a submanifold

$$D = \{q(\boldsymbol{x}^V, \boldsymbol{x}^H) | \sum_{\boldsymbol{x}^H} q(\boldsymbol{x}^V, \boldsymbol{x}^H) = q(\boldsymbol{x}^V)\}. \tag{41}$$

The submanifold D is m-flat. Because we want to approximate $q(\boldsymbol{x}^V)$ but we do not care about $q(\boldsymbol{x}^H)$ nor the interaction of $\boldsymbol{x}^V$ and $\boldsymbol{x}^H$, the problem reduces to minimizing

$$D[q(\boldsymbol{x}^V, \boldsymbol{x}^H) \ : \ p(\boldsymbol{x}^V, \boldsymbol{x}^H; W)]$$

over all W and $q \in D$, or

$$D[q : p]$$

over all $p \in B^{S,V}$ and $q \in D$. This is the minimization of the divergence between two submanifold D and $B^{S,V}$.

We can use the geometric *em* algorithm which is equivalent to the statistical *EM* algorithm in this case, too. Since D is m-flat and $B^{S,V}$ is e-flat, the problem is relatively easy to solve (see [7]).

5 Conclusion

We have shown the framework of the information-geometrical method of neural networks. Information geometry has originated from the research on statistical manifolds or families of probability distributions. It proposes a new geometrical notion of the duality of affine connections. It has successfully been applied to statistics, information theory, control systems theory and many others. Neural networks research is one of the promissing fields of applications of information geometry. Its research has just started with expectation that it opens new perspectives to neural networks

REFERENCES

[1] Ackley, D., Hinton, G., and Sejnowski, T., *A learning algorithm for Boltzmann machines*, Cognitive Science, Vol. 9 (1985), pp147–169.

[2] Amari, S., *Theory of adaptive pattern classifiers*, IEEE Trans., Vol. EC-16 (1967), pp299–307.

[3] Amari, S., *Differential-Geometircal Methods in Statistics*, Springer-Verlag, New York (1985).

[4] Amari, S., *Differential geometry of a parametric family of invertible linear systems — Riemannian metric, dual affine connections and divergence*, Mathematical Systems Theory, Vol. 20 (1987), pp53–82.

[5] Amari, S., *Fisher information under restriction of Shannon information in multiterminal situations*, Annals of Institute of Statistical Mathematics, Vol. 41 (1989), pp623–648.

[6] Amari, S., *Dualistic geometry of the manifold of higher-order neurons*, Neural Networks, Vol. 4 (1991), pp443-451.

[7] Amari, S., *Information geometry of EM and em algorithms for neural networks*, Neural Networks, Vol. 8 (1995), No.5.

[8] Amari, S., Murata, N., Müller, K.-R., Finke, M. and Yang, H., *Asymptotic statistical theory of overtraining and cross-validation*, IEEE Trans. NN, submitted (1995).

[9] Amari, S. and Han, T.S., *Statistical inference under multi-terminal rate restrictions — a differential geometrical approach*, IEEE Trans. on Information Theory, Vol. IT-35 (1989), pp217–227.

[10] Amari, S., Kurata, K. and Nagaoka, H., *Information geometry of Boltzmann machines*, IEEE Trans. Neural Networks, Vol. 3 (1992), pp260-277.

[11] Barndorff-Nielsen, O.E., Cox, R.D., and Reid, N., *The role of differential geometry in statistical theory*, International Statistical Review, Vol. 54 (1986), pp83–96.

[12] Csiszár, I., *I-divergence geometry of probability distributions and minimization problems*, Annals of Probability, Vol. 3 (1975), pp146–158.

[13] Csiszár, I. and Tusnády, G., *Information geometry and alternating minimization procedures*, in E.F. Dedewicz, et al. (eds), Statistics and Decisions (Supplementary Issue, No.1 (1984), pp205–237), Munich: Oldenburg Verlag.

[14] Fujiwara, A. and Amari, S., *Dualistic dynamical systems in the framework of information geometry*, Physica D, Vol. 80 (1995), pp317–327.

[15] Jordan, M.I. and Jacobs, R.A., *Higherarchical mixtures of experts and the EM-algorithm*, Neural Computation, Vol. 6 (1994), pp181–214.

[16] Kass, R. E., *The geometry of asymptotic inference (with discussions)*, Statistical Science, Vol. 4 (1989), pp188–234.

[17] Murray, M.K. and Rice, J.W., *Differential Geometry and Statistics*, Chapman & Hall (1993).

[18] Nakamura, Y., *A tau-function for the finite Toda molecule, and information spaces*, Contemporary Mathematics, Vol. 179 (1994), pp205–211.

[19] Ohara, A. and Amari, S., *Differential geometric structures of stable state feedback systems with dual connections*, Kybernetika, Vol. 30 (1994), pp369–386.

[20] Rumelhart, D., Hinton, G.E. and Williams, R.J., *Learning internal representations by error propagation*, in: Parallel Distributed Processing: Explorations in the Microstructure of Cognition, Vol.Vol. 1, Foundations, MIT Press (1986), Cambridge, MA.

[21] Xu, L., *YING-YANG machine: A Bayesian-Kullback scheme for unified learnings and new results on vector quantization*, Proc. ICONIP'95-Beijing (1995).

Q-LEARNING: A TUTORIAL AND EXTENSIONS

George Cybenko, Robert Gray and Katsuhiro Moizumi
Thayer School of Engineering, 8000 Cummings Hall, Dartmouth College, Hanover, NH 03755 USA. Email: gvc@dartmouth.edu

In the past decade, research in neurocomputing has been divided into two relatively well-defined tracks: one track dealing with cognition and the other with behavior. Cognition deals with organizing, classifying and recognizing sensory stimuli. Behavior is more dynamic, involving sequences of actions and changing interactions with an external environment. The mathematical techniques that apply to these areas, at least from the point of neurocomputing, appear to have been quite separate as well. The purpose of this paper is to give an overview of some recent powerful mathematical results in behavioral neurocomputing, specifically the concept of Q-learning due to C. Watkins, and some new extensions. Finally, we propose ways in which the mathematics of cognition and the mathematics of behavior can move closer to build more unified systems of information processing and action.

1 Introduction

The study of artificial neural networks has burgeoned in the past decade. Two distinct lines of research have emerged: the cognitive and the behavioral. Cognitive research deals with the biological phenomenon of recognition, the mathematics of pattern analysis and statistics, and applications in automatic pattern recognition. Behavioral research deals with the biological phenomena of planning and action, the mathematics of time dependent processes, and applications in control and decision-making.

To be mathematically precise, let us discuss simple formulations of each problem type. A cognitive problem typically involves so-called *feature* vectors, $x \in \mathbb{R}^n$. These feature vectors are sensory stimuli or measurements and are presented to us in some random way – that is, we cannot predict with certainty which stimuli will occur next. These observations must be classified and the classification is accomplished by a function $f : \mathbb{R}^n \rightarrow \mathbb{R}^m$. The problem is to build an estimate of the true function, f, based on a sample set of the form $S = \{(x_i, y_i), i = 1, ..., N\}$ which are drawn according to a joint probability distribution on $(x, y) \in \mathbb{R}^{n+m}$, say $\mu(x, y)$. Call the estimate $g(x)$. Typically, $f(x)$ is the conditional expected value of y: $f(x) = \int_y y d\mu(x, y) / \int_y d\mu(x, y)$. A number of distinct situations in cognitive neurocomputing arise depending on the type of information available for estimating f. (See one of the numerous excellent textbooks on neural computing and machine learning for more details.)

- Supervised Learning – The sample data, S, is as above so that correct classifications, apart from noise, are part of the data. Moreover, an error criterion is typically provided or constructed on the classifications: $|g(x) - f(x)|$ is some error metric. This situation is closest to traditional statistical regression and uses many classical statistical methods.

- Unsupervised Learning – No corrrect or approximate classification values, y, are given. The problem is to organize the data into equivalence classes or clusters and then to label the classes. These labels serve to define f from above and the performance criterion is related to how accurately the equivalence classes are formed. Unsupervised learning is closely related to clustering and uses techniques from that area.

- REINFORCEMENT LEARNING – As in unsupervised learning, no "correct" response is given but a *reinforcement* is available. A reinforcement can be thought of as an error when $g(x)$ is the estimated response for feature vector x but the correct response f is not available. Reinforcement learning is thus between supervised and unsupervised learning: some performance feedback is provided but not in the form of the correct answer and the deviation of the response from it. The difference between supervised and reinforcement learning has been characterized as the difference between learning from a teacher and learning from a critic. The teacher provides the correct response but the critic only states how bad the system's response was. Reinforcements are often referred to as "rewards" and "punishments" depending on their sizes and the context.

Behavioral neurocomputing derives its problems from planning, decision-making and other applications in which actions over time are of fundamental interest. The mathematical framework, which will be formalized below, involves a system with *states*. Actions are available to move the system into another state, perhaps stochastically. There is an immediate cost associated with taking an action. An action at any given time may be optimal in the short run but may not be the best over the long run when future costs and actions are taken into account. Behavioral applications are therefore most naturally cast as reinforcement learning problems. The goal of behavioral learning is to have a system infer, from empirical data, the state-action pairs which give the smallest average cost.

There are a number of ways that such a behavioral system could be reduced to a cognitive problem. One involves building the following type of training set. Given some initial state, generate a sequence of actions randomly, stopping at some future time. Record the initial state, the action sequence and the ultimate cost of taking that action sequence from that initial state. From this data, build a classifier whose input feature vector is a state and whose output is the action sequence which has minimal cost over all sequences tried. This estimate of the minimal cost to solve the problem from an initial state is an estimate of the *cost-to-go* function.

A related way to solve the problem involves estimating these *cost-to-go* values for each state-action pair. Notice that in a stochastic setting, the action which empirically resulted in the least cost solution may not be the action which leads to the least cost expected value. So averaging is more appropriate than merely keeping track of the minimum cost solution for a given action sequence. The artificial intelligence community has had considerable difficulties with behavioral learning because of difficulties with temporal delays and combinatorial explosions resulting from brute force approaches. Only recently has the mathematics of controlled Markov chains been explored along with solution techniques such as dynamic programming. A major breakthrough in learning optimal actions for such processes has been Watkins' Q-learning [3, 2, 4, 1].

In this paper, we give a quick overview of controlled Markov processes in Section 2. Section 3 presents Watkins' basic results and Section 4 extends those results to describe a system that learns and simultaneously converges to the optimal policy

	Cognitive Learning	Behavioral Learning
Goal	Classifying inputs	Optimizing actions
Related Areas	Statistics Pattern recognition	Control theory Operations research
Relevant Mathematics	Approximation theory Probability	Dynamic programming Stochastic Systems
Status	Sound Theoretical Foundations	Emerging Analytic Theory

Table 1 Cognitive vs. Behavioral Learning.

solution. Section 5 discusses possible areas of intersection between the cognitive and behavioral problems.

2 Markov Decision Processes

The paradigm for *behavioral* neurocomputing can typically be cast as a controlled Markov process which is described below. An environment has a number of states, $X = \{x_i\}$. For each state, there is a set of actions, $A_i = \{a_{ij}\}$, each of which transforms the current state to another state stochastically. This is quantified as a collection of transition probabilities: $p(x_i, a_{ij}, x_k)$ being the probability that applying action a_{ij} in state x_i we land in state x_k at the next time step. These probabilities are independent of time and previous states, hence the stationary Markov character.

Each action engenders a *cost*, $k(x_i, a_{ij})$, which depends only on the state and the action. The goal of a behavioral problem is to minimize this cost over time. Such a temporal cost depends on a *policy* which specifies the actions to be taken at various times in various states. Thus for each time, t, in a policy, we have a vector of actions a_t which tells us which action to apply for any of the possible states the system could be in at time t. Specifically, $a_t(x_i)$ is one of the allowable actions a_{ij} for state x_i. There are a number of ways in which to quantify this temporal cost minimization:

- FREE-TIME MINIMIZATION – A designated state, x_0, terminates the process. We are concerned with the cost of the behavior up to the time this state is reached. Starting in some state x_i and following a policy, $\pi = (a_0, a_1, a_2, ...)$, suppose we follow the trajectory $x_i, x_{i_1}, x_{i_2}, ..., x_{i_{\tau-1}}, x_{0_j}$ the cost will then be

$$\sum_{j=0}^{\tau-1} k(x_{i_j}, a_j(x_{i_j})).$$

However, since the transitions are stochastic, we must take an expectation over all possible trajectories, starting with x_i and terminating in x_0 with probabilities determined by the policy, π, and the corresponding transitions.

$$V(\pi, i) = E\{\sum_{j=0}^{\tau-1} k(x_{i_j}, a_j(x_{i_j}))\}.$$

- FIXED-TIME MINIMIZATION – As above but the cost is computed up to a fixed time as opposed to when a terminal state is reached.
- AVERAGE-COST MINIMIZATION – The average future cost is minimized (here $0 < \gamma \leq 1$ is the discount factor):
$$V(\pi, i) = \lim_{L\to\infty} \frac{1}{L+1} E\{\sum_{j=0}^{L} \gamma^j k(x_{i_j}, a_j(x_{i_j}))\}.$$
- DISCOUNTED COST MINIMIZATION – Here the cost of future actions are discounted by a constant rate $0 < \gamma < 1$, so that
$$V(\pi, i) = E[\sum_{j=0}^{\infty} \gamma^j k(x_{i_j}, a_j(x_{i_j}))].$$

We consider only discounted cost minimization problems here. A large body of literature in optimal control theory has been devoted to solving such problems and we review the key elements, leaving out the occasional technical requirements for the results to hold. We focus instead on the general flow of ideas.

First of all, we need only consider policies which are independent of time if we are interested in the optimal policy. The reason is that the process is Markovian and once we reach a state at a point in time, only the future costs can be affected. Since the costs are additive (in a discounted way), an optimal choice of action depends only on the current state. This simplification allows us to consider only policies that are of the form $\pi = (a, a, a, ...)$ where a is a mapping from states to actions.

Secondly, the cost-to-go functions, which we now write as $V(a, i)$ because we are restricting ourselves to stationary policies, satisfy a recurrence relation of the form:
$$V(a, i) = k(x_i, a(x_i)) + \gamma \sum_j p(x_i, a(x_i), x_j)V(a, j).$$

This identity has the following interpretation: using action $a(x_i)$ we go to state x_j with probability $p(x_i, a(x_i), x_j)$; once in state x_j we have the cost-to-go value $V(a, j)$. Weighing these cost-to-go values with the corresponding transition probabilities and adding gives the identity. Stacking these values to form a vector $V(a)$, the above equation becomes a vector-matrix equation of the form:
$$V(a) = k(a) + \gamma P(a)V(a).$$

Thus, every stationary policy satisfies an equation of the above form which can be solved by rewriting it as:
$$(I - \gamma P(a))V(a) = k(a)$$
where it is assumed that $P(a)$ and $k(a)$ are known for a given policy a. Thus this is a simple linear system of equations which can be solved using standard matrix iterative techniques.

What this shows is that for any policy, there is a computational procedure for computing the cost-to-go function for a fixed action policy. What remains is to find an action policy which will lead to the overall optimal strategy – one that minimizes the cost-to-go function for each state.

Specifically, the optimal policy a^* has the property that
$$V(a^*) = V^* = min_a\{k(a) + \gamma P(a)V^*\}.$$

This policy can be computed using the iteration, starting with V_0 arbitrary,

$$V_{n+1} = min_a\{k(a) + \gamma P(a)V_n\}.$$

Then $V_n \longrightarrow V^*$ and the optimal policy is the policy which realizes the minimization above.

3 Watkins' Q-Learning

The behavioral learning problem is to learn the optimal (minimal cost) policy using samples of the following form:

$$s_i = (\eta_i, \zeta_i, \alpha_i, k_i), i = 1, 2, 3, ...$$

These samples are four-tuples with the interpretation that s_i involves a trial use of action α_i on state η_i which resulted in a transition to state ζ_i at a cost of k_i. Given many samples with the same initial state and action, we can estimate the transition probabilities as well as the expected cost of taking that action from that state. With such estimates, a standard solution procedure for computing optimal policies for a Markov decision process can be carried out. This is an off-line, batch approach.

Is there an on-line approach which will learn the optimal strategy adaptively, with guaranteed convergence? The on-line strategy does not compute transition probabilities or costs explicitly. Watkins has given an elegant solution to this problem which he named *Q-learning.* Q-learning uses samples of the above form to update a simple table whose entries converge and whose limit values can easily be used to infer an optimal policy.

Q-learning is motivated by so-called Q-values which are defined as follows:

$$Q^a(x_i, a_{ij}) = K(x_i, a_{ij}) + \gamma P(a)V(a).$$

$Q^a(x_i, a_{ij})$ is the expected cost when starting in state x_i, performing action a_{ij}, and then following policy a thereafter. Let Q^* be the Q-values for the optimal policy a^*, meaning we take some initial action and then follow it with optimal actions thereafter. For these Q-values, we have

$$V(a^*)_i = \min_{a_{ij}}\{Q^*(x_i, a_{ij})\}$$

and the optimal action from state x_i is precisely the action a_{ij} which achieves the minimum.

The beauty of Watkins' Q-learning is that we can adaptively estimate the Q-values for the optimal policy using samples of the above type. The Q-learning algorithm begins with a tableau, $Q_0(x_i, a_{ij})$, initialized arbitrarily. Using samples of the form

$$s_i = (\eta_i, \zeta_i, \alpha_i, k_i), i = 1, 2, 3, ...$$

we perform the following update on the Q-value tableau:

$$Q_i(\eta_i, \alpha_i) = (1 - \beta_i)Q_{i-1}(\eta_i, \alpha_i) + \beta_i(k_i + \gamma V(\zeta_i))$$

where $V(\zeta_i) = \min_\alpha\{Q_{i-1}(\zeta_i, \alpha)\}$. All other elements of Q_i are merely copied from Q_{i-1} without change. The parameters $\beta_i \rightarrow 0$ as $i \rightarrow \infty$.

Theorem 1 *(Watkins [6, 7, 5]) – Let $\{i(x, \alpha)\}$ be the set of indices for which the (x, α) entry of the Q-tableau is updated. If*

$$\sum_{i(x,\alpha)} \beta_{i(x,\alpha)} = \infty \quad \text{and} \quad \sum_{i(x,\alpha)} \beta^2_{i(x,\alpha)} < \infty$$

then $Q_i(x, \alpha) \rightarrow Q^*(x, \alpha)$ as $i \rightarrow \infty$. Accordingly, $\alpha_i(x) = \text{argmax}_\alpha Q_i(x, \alpha)$ converges to the optimal action for state x.

Proof See [7, 5]. □

This result is remarkable in that it demonstrates that a simple update rule on the Q-tableau results in a learning system which computes the optimal policy. In the next section we show how this method can be embedded into an online system which simultaneously uses the current Q-values to generate policies *and* uses the results to update Q-values in such a way as to satisfy Watkin's theorem. Consequently, the online system learns the optimal policy to which it ultimately converges.

4 Universal On-line Q-Learning

Online optimal learning and asymptotic optimal performance must be a compromise between performing what the learning system estimates to be the optimal actions and persistently exciting all possible state-action possibilities often enough to satisfy the frequencies stipulated in Watkins' Q-learning theorem.

To begin, let us introduce a notion of asymptotically optimal performance. Suppose we have an infinite sequence of state-action pairs that result from an actual realization of the Markov decision process, say $\{(y_i, \alpha_i), i = 0, 1, ...\}$ with (y_i, α_i) meaning that at time i we are in state y_i and execute action α_i resulting in a transition to state y_{i+1} at the next time. For such a sequence, we have a corresponding sequence of costs v_i which represent the actual costs computed from the realized sequence, v_i being the cost of following the sequence from time i onwards.

We now define *asyptotic average optimality.* Suppose that V_i is the optimal expected cost-to-go for state i. Let $v_i(n_{ij})$ be the observed cost-to-go values for state i when the system is in state i at time n_{ij}. Let $N_M(i)$ be the number of times the process has visited state i up to time M. Then we say that the policy is *asyptotically optimal on average for state* i if

$$\frac{1}{N_M(i)} \sum_{n_{ij}<M} v_i(n_{ij}) \rightarrow V_i$$

as $M \rightarrow \infty$.

In order to establish this result, we need to construct an auxiliary Markov process with states (x_i, a_{ij}) and transition probabilities,

$$p((x_i, a_{ij}), (x_m, a_{mn})) = p(x_i, a_{ij}, x_m)/J_m$$

where J_m is the number of allowable actions in state x_m. This auxiliary process has the following interpretation: the transition probabilities between states are determined by the transition probabilities of the original controlled process with the added ingredient that the actions corresponding to the resulting state are uniformly randomized.

Theorem 2 – *Suppose that there is at least one stationary policy under which the states of the resulting Markov process constitute a single recurrent class (that is, the process is ergodic). Then, with probability 1, there is a mixed nonstationary strategy for controlling the Markov decision process with the following two properties:*
1. The optimal policy is estimated by Q-learning asymptotically;
2. The control is asymptotically optimal on average for all states that have a nonzero stationary occupancy probability under the process' optimal policy.

Proof – The proof consists of three parts. We begin by showing that under the hypothesis that the original process has a stationary policy under which the Markov

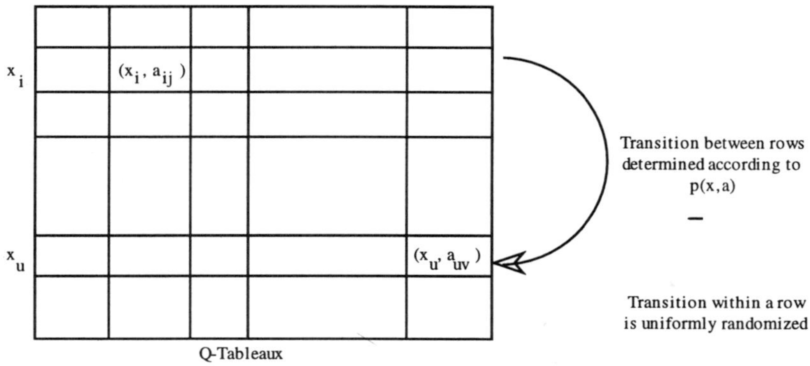

Figure 1 Auxiliary Process Schematic.

process consists of a single recurrent class, the corresponding auxiliary process also has a single recurrent class. Let $a(x)$ be the action for a state x which makes the original process have a single recurrent set. Denote the corresponding transition probabilities by $p_*(x, x') = p(x, a(x), x')$. Let D be the maximal number of actions per state: $D \geq |\{a_{ij}\}|$ for all i. Consider the auxiliary process' canonical partitioning into subclasses of states in which each set of the partition consists of states which are either a) transient or b) recurrent and communicate with each other. Now the $(x, a(x))$ form a subset of the states of the auxiliary process.

Step 1. The auxiliary Process is Recurrent – We will show that any given state of the auxiliary process communicates with every other state. Let (x, a) and (x', a') be any two states of the auxiliary process. We must show that

$$p^{(n)}((x, a), (x', a')) > 0$$

for some n. Pick any state y for which $p(x, a, y) > 0$. By assumption, there is an m for which

$$p_*^{(m)}(y, x') > 0$$

under the special choice of actions, $a(x)$. This means that there is a sequence of states $y_1 = y, y_2, ..., y_m = x'$ for which

$$p(y_i, a(y_i), y_{i+1}) > 0$$

and so

$$p^{(m+1)}((x, a), (x', a')) \geq \frac{p(x, a, y)}{D} \Pi_{i=1}^{m-1} [p(y_i, a(y_i), y_{i+1})/D] > 0.$$

Since all states of the auxiliary process communicate with each other, all states must be recurrent. Thus the auxiliary process consists of a single recurrent set of states. Because the auxiliary process consists of recurrent states, the expected time to visit all states of the auxiliary process is finite and all states will be visited in a finite time with probability 1.

Step 2. A Mixed Policy – We next define a mixed time-dependent strategy for switching between the auxiliary process and a stationary policy based on an estimate of the optimal policy. The mixed strategy begins by choosing actions according to the auxiliary process. At time n_k we switch from the auxiliary process to the process controlled by the policy determined by the Q-table according to

$$a_j(n_k) = \text{argmin}_\alpha Q_{n_k}(x_j, \alpha).$$

At time m_k we switch back to the auxiliary process. For $k = 1, 2, 3, \ldots$ we have $1 = m_0 < n_k < m_k < n_{k+1} < m_{k+1} \ldots < \infty$. Let N' the largest expected time to visit all states of the auxiliary process starting from any state and let $N = 2 * N'$. Consider the following experiment which is relevant to the discussion below. Start in any state of the auxiliary process and follow it for N steps at which time we jump to an arbitrary state and run for another N steps, repeating this process indefinitely. Call each such run of N steps a *frame*, numbering them F_i for $i = 1, 2, 3, \ldots$. We want to concatenate the frames to produce a realization of the auxiliary process. To do this, consider the final state of frame F_i. Since N was chosen to be twice as large as the expected time to visit all states starting from any state, with probability 1 some future frame, say F_{i+j}, includes a visit to the final state of F_i in the first $N/2 = N'$ states of that frame. Concatenate to the end of F_i the history in F_{i+j} following the visit to the final state of F_i. Each step of this concatenation adds at least N' consecutive steps of the auxiliary process so there are an infinite number of visits to all states in the concatenation with probability 1. In the following construction, we implicitly use this property of a concatenation of frames. The definition of n_k is as

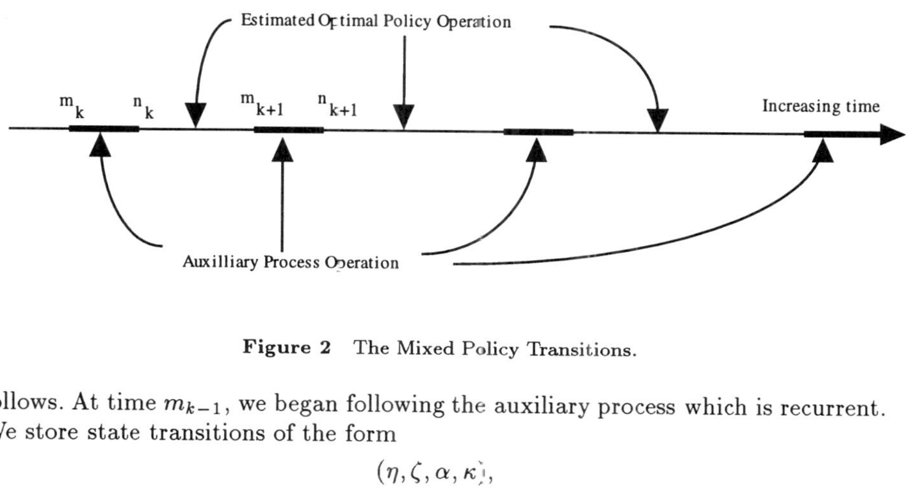

Figure 2 The Mixed Policy Transitions.

follows. At time m_{k-1}, we began following the auxiliary process which is recurrent. We store state transitions of the form

$$(\eta, \zeta, \alpha, \kappa),$$

where η is a state x_i, α is an action taken by the auxiliiary process, ζ is the state of the original process to which the process transitioned and κ is the observed cost of that transition, in a list. Proceed in this manner until either N steps have been taken in this way or until the list contains a sample for each element in the Q-table. If the list to update the Q-table is completed first, we update the Q-table and compute the current optimal actions. In this case, n_k is defined as the time after which the Q-table was updated. Otherwise, define $n_k = m_{k-1} + N$ and continue using the previous estimated optimal actions as a policy. In either case, $m_k = n_k + k * N$ so

we operate the process using the estimated optimal policy for increasingly longer periods of time $k * N$. We then use this list to update the Q-table with the samples in the list.
Assume that the Q-table has M entries. Then for updating the ith element for the jth time in the Q-table from the sample list, use

$$\beta_{j*M+i} = \frac{1}{j * M + i}.$$

According to this scheme, element i is updated for $j = 1, 2, 3, \ldots$ and the corresponding subset of β's forms an arithmetic subsequence of the harmonic sequence; hence it satifies Watkins' criteria for divergence and squared-convergence.
By the discussion above about frames, this list is filled in a finite amount of time infinitely often with probability 1, but we impose a deterministic limit on the time spent in this mode generating a frame. By construction and Watkins' Theorem, the Q-table values converge to the optimal Q-values and hence the optimal action policy is eventually found.
Step 3. Asymptotic Optimal Convergence – To prove the asymptotic optimal convergence, note that the Q-table updates are performed according to Watkins' criteria so that in the limit the Q-table values determine an optimal stationary policy. Moreover, the time spent operating in the auxiliary mode becomes an asymptotically small fraction of the time spent operating in the estimated optimal policy. Hence, the asymptotic convergence to optimality.
To make this formal, note that asymptotic average optimality depends only on what happens in the limit. Specifically, if we can show that the average of the observed cost-to-go values after some fixed time converges to the optimal value then we are done.
To see this, run the process long enough so that the estimated optimal policy determined by the Q-table is as close as desired to the optimal cost-to-go for the process. This will happen at some finite time with probability 1 although the time is not known a priori. Since we can also wait until k is arbitrarily large, the fraction of time spent in the appoximately optimal mode can be made as close to 1 as we like. Now for a state that has nonzero stationary occupancy probability under the optimal policy, the fraction of time spent operating under the estimated optimal policy approaches 1 and so the empirical cost-to-go also approaches the optimal. For states that have zero occupancy probability under the optimal policy, the empirical cost-to-go will be dominated by the empirical values determined during the auxiliary process operation which will not be optimal in general. Thus the average within the mixed mode of operation is guaranteed to converge to the estimated cost-to-go for the optimal policy but only for states that have nonzero stationary occupancy probabilities under the optimal policy. □

5 Discussion

We have shown that there exists a strategy for operating a Markov Decision Process (under simple conditions) in such a way that the optimal strategy is both learned and the asymptotic operation of the system approaches optimality for states that have nonzero occupancy probabilities under the computed optimal policy. This is only one of many possible strategies for performing both of these simultaneously. The question of which operating procedures are best for fastest convergence to the

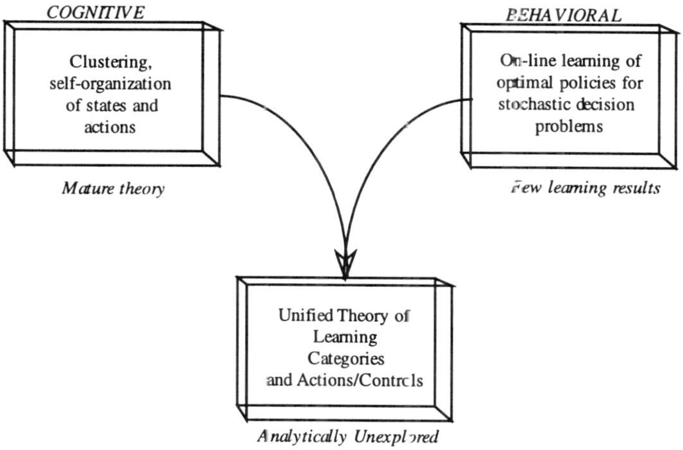

Figure 3 A Unified Learning Theory.

optimal cost-to-go values is beyond the scope of the techniques that we use. It is an important question to pursue in the future.

One of the weaknesses of the Q-Learning framework is that states and actions for the Q-Tableaux must be known a priori. This is restrictive in most dynamic learning situations – it may not be appropriate or possible to select the actual states or actions of a system without significant experimentation first. In general, we would like to simultaneously learn the states, actions and corresponding optimal policies at one time. This subject has been looked into by various researchers but with few analytic results yet. There has been growing interest in dealing with systems that have an infinite (contiuum) of possible states and actions, requiring discretization for Q-Learning. How these states can be clustered or otherwise organized to achieve optimal operation is a challenging question that requires serious future research.

REFERENCES

[1] D. Bertsekas, *Dynamic Programming and Optimal Control.* Athena Scientific, Belmont, MA (1995).

[2] R. Howard, *Dynamic Programming and Markov Processes.* MIT Press, Cambridge, MA (1960).

[3] W.T. Miller III, R.S. Sutton, and P.J. Werbos, *Neural Networks for Control.* MIT Press, Cambridge, MA (1990).

[4] R.S. Sutton, A.G. Barto, and R.J. Williams, *Reinforcement learning is direct adaptive control,* IEEE Control Systems Magazine (April 1992), pp19–22.

[5] J. Tsitsiklis, *Asynchronous stochastic approximation and Q-Learning,* Machine Learning, Vol. 16 (1994), pp185–202.

[6] C.I.C.H. Watkins, *Learning from delayed rewards* Ph.D. Dissertation, University of Cambridge (1989).

[7] C.I.C.H. Watkins and P. Dayan, *Q-Learning,* Machine Learning, Vol.8 (1989), pp279–292.

Acknowledgements

Supported in part by the Air Force Office of Scientific Research research grant F49620-93-1-0266.

ARE THERE UNIVERSAL PRINCIPLES OF BRAIN COMPUTATION?

Stephen Grossberg

Boston University, Department of Cognitive and Neural Systems and Center for Adaptive Systems, 677 Beacon Street, Boston, Massachusetts 02215 USA

1 Introduction

Are there universal computational principles that the brain uses to self-organize its intelligent properties? This lecture suggests that common principles are used in brain systems for early vision, visual object recognition, auditory source identification, variable-rate speech perception, and adaptive sensory-motor control, among others. These are principles of matching and resonance that form part of Adaptive Resonance Theory, or ART. In particular, bottom-up signals in an ART system can automatically activate target cells to levels capable of generating suprathreshold output signals. Top-down expectation signals can only excite, or prime, target cells to subthreshold levels. When both bottom-up and top-down signals are simultaneously active, only the bottom-up signals that receive top-down support can remain active. All other cells, even those receiving large bottom-up inputs, are inhibited. Top-down matching hereby generates a focus of attention that can resonate across processing levels, including those that generate the top-down signals. Such a resonance acts as a trigger that activates learning processes within the system.
In the examples described herein, these effects are due to a top-down nonspecific inhibitory gain control signal that is released in parallel with specific excitatory signals.

2 Neural Dynamics of Multi-Source Audition

How does the brain's auditory system construct coherent representations of acoustic objects from the jumble of noise and harmonics that relentlessly bombards our ears throughout life? Bregman [1] has distinguished at least two levels of auditory organization, called primitive streaming and schema-based segregation, at which such representations are formed in order to accomplish auditory scene analysis. The present work models data about both levels of organization, and shows that ART mechanisms of matching and resonance play a key role in achieving the selectivity and coherence that are characteristic of our auditory experience.

In environments with multiple sound sources, the auditory system is capable of teasing apart the impinging jumbled signal into different mental objects, or streams, as in its ability to solve the cocktail party problem. With my colleagues Krishna Govindarajan, Lonce Wyse, and Michael Cohen [5], a neural network model of this primitive streaming process, called the ARTSTREAM model (Figure 1), has been developed that groups different frequency components based on pitch and spatial location cues, and selectively allocates the components to different streams. The grouping is accomplished through a resonance that develops between a given object's pitch, its harmonic spectral components, and (to a lesser extent) its spatial location. Those spectral components that are not reinforced by being matched with the top-down prototype read-out by the selected object's pitch representation are suppressed, thereby allowing another stream to capture these components, as in the "old-plus-new heuristic" of Bregman [1]. These resonance and matching mechanisms are specialized versions of ART mechanisms

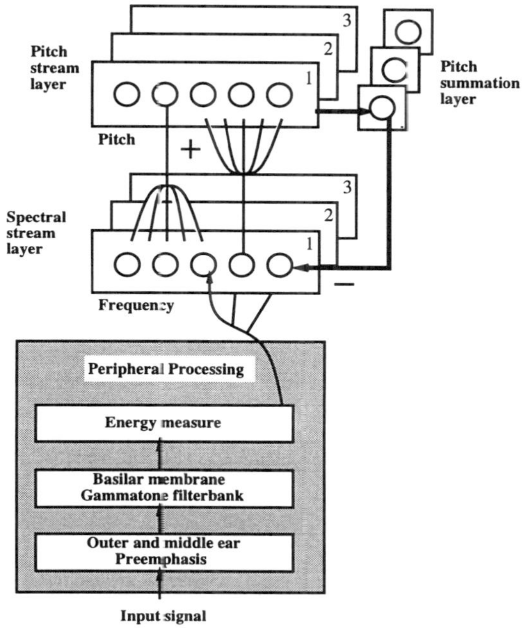

Figure 1 Block diagram of the ARTSTREAM auditory streaming model. Note the nonspecific inhibitory feedback from pitch representations to spectral representations.

The model is used to simulate data from psychophysical grouping experiments, such as how a tone sweeping upwards in frequency creates a bounce percept by grouping with a downward sweeping tone due to proximity in frequency, even if noise replaces the tones at their intersection point. The model also simulates illusory auditory percepts such as the auditory continuity illusion of a tone continuing through a noise burst even if the tone is not present during the noise, and the scale illusion of Deutsch whereby downward and upward scales presented alternately to the two ears are regrouped based on frequency proximity, leading to a bounce percept. The stream resonances provide the coherence that allows one voice or instrument to be tracked through a multiple source environment.

3 Neural Dynamics of Variable-Rate Speech Categorization

What is the neural representation of a speech code as it evolves in real time? With my colleagues Ian Boardman and Michael Cohen [6], a neural model of this schema-based segregation process, called the ARTPHONE model (Figure 2), has been developed to quantitatively simulate data concerning segregation and integration of phonetic percepts, as exemplified by the problem of distinguishing "topic" from "top pick" in natural discourse. Psychoacoustic data concerning categorization of stop consonant pairs indicate that the closure time between syllable final (VC)

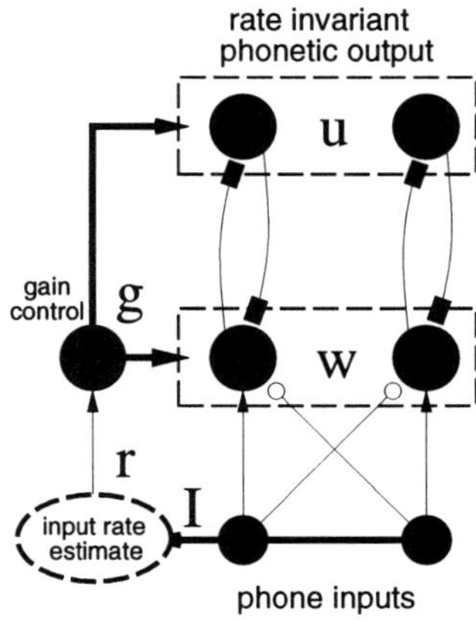

Figure 2 The ARTPHONE model. Working memory nodes (**w**) excite chunks (**u**) through previously learned pathways. List chunks send excitatory feedback down to their item source nodes. Bottom-up and top-down pathways are modulated by habituative transmitter gates (filled squares). Item nodes receive input in an on-center off-surround anatomy. Total input (I) is averaged to control an item rate signal (r) that adjusts the working memory gain (g). Excitatory paths are marked with arrowheads, inhibitory paths with small open circles.

and syllable initial (CV) transitions determines whether consonants are segregated, i.e., perceived as distinct, or integrated, i.e. fused into a single percept. Hearing two stops in a VC–CV pair that are phonetically the same, as in "top pick," requires about 150 msec more closure time than hearing two stops in a VC_1–C_2V pair that are phonetically different, as in "odd ball." As shown by Repp [10], when the distribution of closure intervals over trials is experimentally varied, subjects' decision boundaries between one-stop and two-stop percepts always occurred near the mean closure interval.

The ARTPHONE model traces these properties to dynamical interactions between a working memory for short-term storage of phonetic items and a list categorization network that groups, or chunks, sequences of the phonetic items in working memory. These interactions automatically adjust their processing rate to the speech rate via automatic gain control. The speech code in the model is a resonant wave that emerges after bottom-up signals from the working memory select list chunks which, in turn, read out top-down expectations that amplify consistent working memory items. This resonance may be rapidly reset by inputs, such as C_2, that are inconsistent with a top-down expectation, say of C_1; or by a collapse of resonant activation due to a habituative process that can take a much longer time to occur, as illustrated by the categorical boundary between VCV and VC–CV. The categorization data may thus be understood as emergent properties of a resonant process that adjusts its dynamics to track the speech rate.

4 Neural Dynamics of Boundary and Surface Representation

With my colleagues Alan Gove and Ennio Mingolla [4], a neural network model, called a FACADE theory model (Figure 3), has been developed to explain how

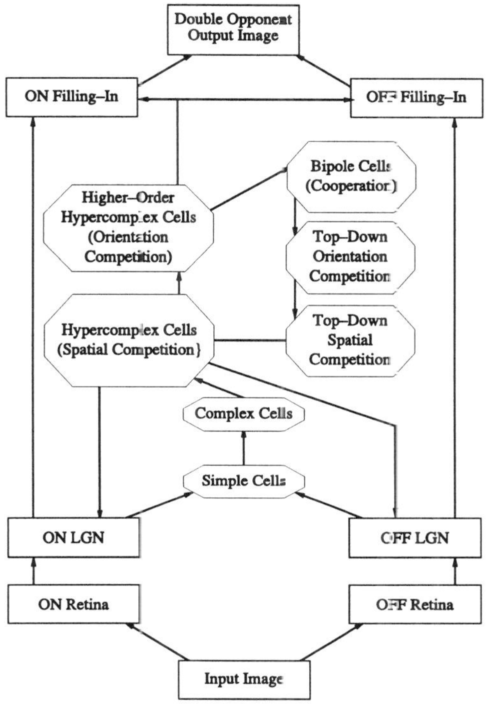

Figure 3 FACADE model macrocircuit. Boundary representation, or BCS, stages are designated by octagonal boxes, surface representation, or FCS, stages by rectangular boxes.

visual thalamocortical interactions give rise to boundary percepts such as illusory contours and surface percepts such as filled-in brightnesses. Top-down feedback interactions are needed in addition to bottom-up feedforward interactions to simulate these data. One feedback loop is modeled between lateral geniculate nucleus (LGN) and cortical area V1, and another within cortical areas V1 and V2. The first feedback loop realizes a resonant matching process, as in ART, which enhances LGN cell activities that are consistent with those of active cortical cells, and suppresses LGN activities that are not. This corticogeniculate feedback, being endstopped and oriented, also enhances LGN ON cell activations at the ends of thin dark lines, thereby leading to enhanced cortical brightness percepts when the lines group into closed illusory contours. The second feedback loop generates boundary representations, including illusory contours, that coherently bind distributed cortical features together. Brightness percepts form within the surface representations through a diffusive filling-in process that is contained by resistive gating signals from the boundary representations. The model is used to simulate illusory contours and surface brightnesses induced by Ehrenstein disks, Kanizsa squares, Glass patterns, and café wall patterns in single contrast, reverse contrast, and mixed contrast configurations. These examples illustrate how boundary and surface mechanisms can generate percepts that are highly context-sensitive, including how illusory contours can be amodally recognized without being seen, how model simple cells in V1 respond preferentially to luminance discontinuities using inputs from both LGN ON and OFF cells, how model bipole cells in V2 with two colinear receptive fields can help to complete curved illusory contours, how short-range simple cell groupings and long-range bipole cell groupings can sometimes generate different outcomes, and how model double-opponent, filling-in and boundary segmentation mechanisms in V4 interact to generate surface brightness percepts in which filling-in of enhanced brightness and darkness can occur before the net brightness distribution is computed by double-opponent interactions. Taken together, these results emphasize the importance of resonant feedback processes in generating conscious percepts in the visual brain.

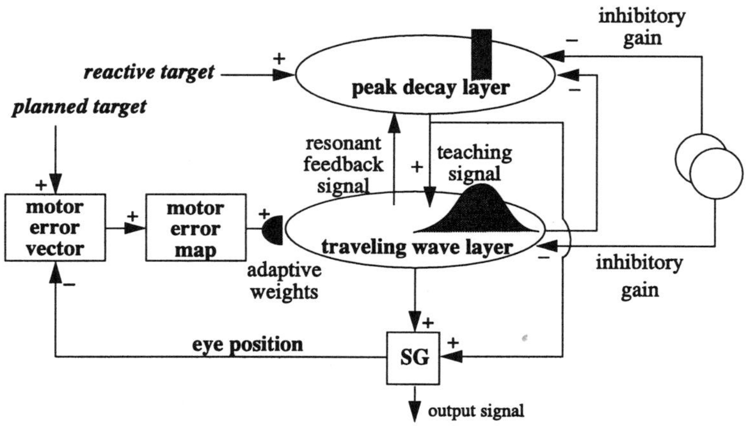

Figure 4 SACCART model for multimodal control of saccadic eye movements by the superior colliculus.

5 Neural Dynamics for Multimodal Control of Saccadic Eye Movements

Saccades are eye movements by which an animal can scan a rapidly changing environment. While the saccadic system plans where to move the eyes, it also retains reflexive responsiveness to fluctuating light sources. These two types of saccades ultimately result in control of the same set of eye muscles. Visually reactive cells encode gaze error in a *retinotopically* activated motor map. Planned targets are coded in *head–centered* coordinates. When two conflicting commands attempt to share control of the saccadic eye movement system, the system must resolve the conflict and coordinate command of one set of eye muscles.

The superior colliculus is a brainstem region that plays a prominent role in both planned and reactive saccades. This region coordinates information to adjust movements of the head and eyes to a stimulus. In order to combine these visual, somatic, and auditory saccade targets in the superior colliculus, the targets in head–centered coordinates are mapped to a gaze motor error in retinotopic coordinates.

How does the saccadic movement system select a target when visual and planned movement commands differ? How do retinal, head–centered, and motor error coordinates interact during the selection process? How are these coordinate systems rendered consistent through learning? Recent data on superior colliculus (SC) reveal a travelling wave of activation whose peak codes the current gaze error [9]. In contrast, Waitzman [12] found that the locus of peak activity in SC remains constant while the activity level at this locus decays as a function of residual gaze error. Why do these distinct cell types exist?

With my colleagues Mario Aguilar, Dan Bullock, and Karen Roberts [8], a neural network model has been developed that answers these questions while providing a functional rationale for both signal patterns (Figure 4). The model assumes that calibration between visual inputs and eye movement commands is learned early in development within a visually reactive saccade system [7]. Visual error signals coded in retinotopic coordinates calibrate adaptive gains to achieve accurate foveation. The accuracy of planned saccades derives from using the gains learned by the reactive system. For this, a transformation between a planned head–centered and a retinotopic target representation needs to be learned. ART matching and resonance control the stability of this learning and the attentive selection of saccadic target locations. Targets in retinotopic and head–centered coordinates are rendered dimensionally consistent so that they can compete for attention to generate a movement command in motor error coordinates. Simulations show how a decaying, stationary activity profile is obtained in the pre–motor layer due to feedback modulation. In addition, a travelling wave activity profile is produced in the motor layer due to modulation from the pre–motor layer and the nature of the local connectivity. The simulations show how this model reproduces physiological data of these two classes of collicular neurons simultaneously during a variety of behavioral tasks (e.g., visual, memory, gap, and overlap conditions), an achievement previously unattained by eye movement models. In addition, the model also clarifies how the SC integrates signals from multiple modalities, and simulates collicular response enhancement and depression produced by multimodal stimuli [11].

6 Concluding Remarks

In addition to these systems are the more familiar ART systems for explaining visual object recognition and its breakdown due to hippocampal lesions that lead to medial temporal amnesia [2]. Taken together, these results provide accumulating evidence that the brain parsimoniously specifies a small set of computational principles to ensure its stability and adaptability in responding to many different types of environmental challenges.

REFERENCES

[1] Bregman, A.S., *Auditory scene analysis.* Cambridge, MA: MIT Press (1990).

[2] Carpenter, G.A. and Grossberg, S., *Normal and amnesic learning, recognition, and memory by a neural model of cortico-hippocampal interactions.* Trends in Neurosciences, Vol. 16 (1993), pp131–137.

[3] Cohen, M.A., Grossberg, S., and Wyse, L.L., *A spectral network model of pitch perception.* Journal of the Acoustical Society of America, Vol. 98 (1995), pp862–879.

[4] Gove, A., Grossberg, S., and Mingolla, E. *Brightness perception, illusory contours, and corticogeniculate feedback.* Visual Neuroscience, Vol. 12 (1995), pp1027–1052.

[5] Govindarajan, K.K., Grossberg, S., Wyse, L.L., and Cohen, M.A., *A neural network model of auditory scene analysis and source segregation.* Technical Report CAS/CNS-TR-94-039,

Boston University (1994).

[6] Grossberg, S., Boardman, I., and Cohen, M.A., *Neural dynamics of variable-rate speech categorization.* Journal of Experimental Psychology: Human Perception and Performance, in press (1994).

[7] Grossberg, S. and Kuperstein, M., *Neural dynamics of adaptive sensory motor control: Expanded edition.* Elmsford, NY: Pergamon Press (1989).

[8] Grossberg, S., Roberts K., Aguilar M. and Bullock, D., *A neural model of multimodal adaptive saccadic eye movement control by superior colliculus.* Tech. Rept. CAS/CNS TR-96-029 (1996).

[9] Munoz, D., Guitton, D., and Pélisson, D., *Control of orienting gaze shifts by the tectoreticulospinal system in the head-free cat, III: Spatiotemporal characteristics of phasic motor discharges.* Journal of Neurophysiology, Vol. 66(5) (1991), pp1642–1666.

[10] Repp, B.H., *A range-frequency effect on perception of silence in speech.* Haskins Laboratories Status Report on Speech Research, SR-61 (1980), pp151–165.

[11] Stein, B.E. and Meredith, M.A., *The merging of the senses.* Cambridge, MA: MIT Press (1993).

[12] Waitzman, D., Ma, T., Optican, L., and Wurtz, R., *Superior colliculus neurons mediate the dynamic characteristics of saccades.* Journal of Neurophysiology, Vol. 66(5) (1991), pp1716–1737.

Acknowledgements

Supported in part by the Air Force Office of Scientific Research (AFOSR F49620-92-J-0225), the Advanced Research Projects Agency (ONR N00014-92-J-4015), and the Office of Naval Research (ONR N00014-91-J-4100 and ONR N00014-92-J-1309). The author wishes to thank Diana Meyers and Cynthia Bradford for their valuable assistance in the preparation of the manuscript.

ON-LINE TRAINING OF MEMORY-DRIVEN ATTRACTOR NETWORKS

Morris W. Hirsch

Department of Mathematics, University of California at Berkeley, USA.

A rigorous mathematical analysis is presented of a class of continuous networks having rather arbitrary activation dynamics, with input patterns classified by attractors by a special training scheme. Memory adapts continually, whether or not a training signal is present. It is shown that consistent input-output pairs can be learned perfectly provided every pattern is repeated sufficiently often, and input patterns are nearly orthogonal.

1 Introduction

Most neural networks used for pattern classification have the following features:

- The training dynamics is separate from the activation dynamics.
- Patterns are classified by fixed points or limit cycles of the activation dynamics.

But biological neural networks— nervous systems— do not conform to these rules. We learn while doing— we learn *by* doing, and if we don't do, we may forget. And chaotic dynamics is the rule in many parts of the cerebral cortex (see the papers by Freeman *et al.*).

Here we look at supervised learning in continuous time nets in which:

- The memory matrix is *always* adapting: the only difference between training and testing is the presence of a training signal. Testing reinforces learning, lack of testing can lead to forgetting, and retraining at any time is possible.
- Patterns are classified by possibly chaotic attractors.
- Training is completed on any single pass through the training set.

The fundamental problem faced by such a system is that presentation of new input patterns affects the memory of old patterns, whether or not a training signal is present; consequently there is a tendency for previously trained memories to degrade. To prevent this from occurring, we constrain the system in two ways:

- Each input pattern is repeated sufficiently frequently, with or without a training signal.
- Input patterns are nearly orthogonal.

When the input patterns are sufficiently orthogonal, depending on the number of patterns, then system parameters can be chosen robustly so that the system learns to give the correct output for each input pattern on which it has consistently trained. The net comprises an input layer of d units which feeds into a recurrently connected activation layer of n units. Inputs and activations can take any real number values. Inputs are drawn from a fixed list of patterns, taken for convenience to be unit vectors. With any input a training signal may be presented for minimum time and then shut off. These training signals need not be consistent, but those patterns that are trained consistently and tested sufficiently frequently, will respond with the correct output.

Rather than taking outputs to be the usual stable equilibria or limit cycles, we consider outputs to be the attractors (more precisely, their basins) to which the activation dynamics tends. (Compare [2], [4]). Each training signal directs the activation dynamics into the basin of an attractor.

In some biological models it is the attractor as a geometric object, rather than the dynamics in the attractor, that classifies the input. If the components of the activation vector x represent firing rates of cells, then the attractor may corresond to a particular cell assembly, and the useful information is which cell assembly is active, with dynamical details being irrelevant. In this connection compare [8]; [1].

Before giving details of the dynamics, we first describe how the network looks from the outside. From this black box point of view the activation dynamics *appears* to be governed by a differential equation in Euclidean n-space $\mathbb{R}^n$,

$$\frac{dx}{dt} = F(x) + I \tag{1}$$

$$\equiv -x + f(x) + I \tag{2}$$

where $f : \mathbb{R}^n \to \mathbb{R}^n$ is bounded and $I \in \mathbb{R}^n$ is a constant training signal which may be 0. Input patterns are chosen from a finite set of distinct vectors $\xi^a \in \mathbb{R}^d$, $a = 1, \ldots, m$. Training signals are selected from a compact set $S \subset \mathbb{R}^n$ which contains the origin.

At stage k of running the net, an input and a possibly null training signal are presented simultaneously to the net for a certain time interval $[t_{k-1}, t'_k]$ called the k'th *instruction period*, followed by the *computation period* $[t'_k, t_k]$ during which training signal is removed (set to 0) while the same input is present. The activation vector x then settles down to an attractor for the dynamics of the vector field F, that is, for the differential equation

$$\frac{dx}{dt} = -x + f(x), \tag{3}$$

When this process is repeated with a different input and training signal, the activation variable x jumps instantaneously to a new initial position.

To each pattern ξ^a there is associated a special attractor $A^a \subset \mathbb{R}^n$ for (3), and a *target* U^a, which is a positively invariant neighborhood of A^a in $B(A^a)$. It is desired that when ξ^a is input, $x(t)$ goes into U^a and stays there (thus approaching A^a), until the input is changed.

Training consists in using training signals from a special subset $S^a \subset S$ of *proper* training signals asociated with ξ^a. Other nonzero training signals are *improper*.

It turns out that with sufficiently orthogonal input patterns and suitable parameters, any pattern that is trained on a proper training signal at stage k will go to its correct target at a later stage provided that at intervening stages the pattern was presented sufficiently often and no improper training signals were used.

Now we explain how the memory evolves. The time varying *memory matrix* $M \in \mathbb{R}^{n\times d}$ maps static input patterns (column vectors) ξ to dynamic activation vectors x by $x(t) = M(t)\xi$. An auxiliary fast variable $y \in \mathbb{R}^n$ provides a delay between $x(t)$ and $M(t)$: The true dynamics is given by the following *Main System*, where

ξ^T denotes the transpose of ξ:

$$\frac{dM}{dt} = [-x + y + I]\xi^T, \tag{4}$$

$$\lambda \frac{dy}{dt} = f(x) - y, \tag{5}$$

$$x = M\xi. \tag{6}$$

The system's dynamics is thus driven by $M(t)$; there is no independent activation dynamics.

Computing dx/dt and using the fact that $\xi^T\xi = ||\xi||^2 = 1$, we obtain the following system:

$$\frac{dx}{dt} = -x - y + I, \tag{7}$$

$$\lambda \frac{dy}{dt} = f(x) - y. \tag{8}$$

This system is independent of the input ξ; but the interpretation of x depends on ξ, and x (but not y) jumps discontinuously when ξ is changed.

It is interesting to observe that System (7), (8) is equivalent to a single second order equation in x, namely:

$$\lambda \frac{d^2x}{dt^2} + (\lambda + 1)\frac{dx}{dt} + x = f(x) - I, \tag{9}$$

similar to the second order activation dynamics used by W. Freeman *et al.* (see References). The following fact is used:

Proposition 1 *If $x(t)$ obeys Equation (9) and $||f(x)|| \leq \rho$, then $x(t) \to N_\rho(I)$.*

Standard dynamical system techniques (singular perturbations, invariant manifolds) show that the dynamics of System (7), (8) is closely approximated by the that of the simpler system

$$\frac{dx}{dt} = -x + f(x) + I \tag{10}$$

provided λ is small enough.

Example 1 A simple but interesting system of this type has 1-dimensional activation dynamics. For f we take any smooth (Lipschitz also works) sigmoid with high gain $\kappa \gg 1$, having limiting values ± 1. The dynamics of (10) with $I = 0$ has stable equilibria at (approximately) $x = \pm 1$ and an unstable equilibrium at $x = 0$. The 2-dimensional dynamics of System (7), (8) with $I = 0$ has two attracting equilibria near $(1, 1)$ and $(-1, -1)$, and an unstable equilibrium near $(0, 0)$. Every trajectory tends to one of these three equilibria. As training signals we take $I_- = -1$, $I_+ = +1$. When I takes either of these values I^a, (x, y) settles to the global attractor near $(2I^a, 2I^a)$. When I is then set to 0, keeping the same input pattern, then (x, y) relaxes toward (I^a, I^a). This system learns to sort any number of sufficiently orthogonal input patterns into two arbitrary classes after a single pass through the pattern set. A similar system is treated in detail in [9].

Higher dimensional examples can be obtained from this one by taking Cartesian products of n such vector fields, yielding 2^n attracting equilibria. More interesting dynamics can be constructed by changing the vector field in small neighborhoods of the attracting equilibria. In this way attractors with arbitrary dynamics can be constructed.

2 Statement of Results

Notation. $||u|| = \sqrt{u \cdot u}$ denotes the Euclidean norm of vector u. The closed ball of radius ρ about a point z is denoted by $N_\rho(z)$. The closed ρ-neighborhood of a set A is $\bigcup_{z\in A} N_\rho(z)$.

We start with the *data*: f, $\{A^a\}$, $\{U^a\}$, $\{S^a\}$.

We assume given an increasing sequence of times $t_{k-1} < t'_k < t_k$, $k \in \mathbb{N}$. The Main System is run during stage k as described above, taking as initial values at t_{k-1} whatever the terminal values were in the previous stage (if $k > 1$).

We make the following asumptions, in terms of parameters $\epsilon > 0, T > 0, N \geq 1, R > 0, \rho > 0$:

Hypothesis 2

Unit pattern vectors: $||\xi^a|| = 1$.
Separation of patterns: $|\xi^a \cdot \xi^b| < \epsilon$ *for distinct* a, b
Duration of presentation: $t'_k - t_{k-1} > T$ *and* $t_k - t'_k > T$ *for all* k.
Frequency of presentation: *Each pattern* ξ^a *is used as input at least once in every* N *successive stages.*
Initial values: $|y(0)| < 1$, $||M(0)\xi^a|| < R$.
Bound on f**:** $||f(x)|| < \rho$.
Proper training signals: $S^a = \{I \in \S : N_\rho(I) \subset B(A^a)\}$.

The following theorems refer to the main system. They mean that robust parameters can be chosen so that that whenever the pattern from a consistent pair is input after being properly trained once, the output is always correct, whether or not a training signal is input, and regardless of the training signals when other patterns are input; and moreover, all the variables stay within given bounds.

Define time-varying vectors $x^a(t) = M(t)\xi^a \in \mathbb{R}$— the net's *current recall of input* ξ^a.

A pattern ξ^a is *consistently trained* from stages k to l provided that at stage k the input is ξ^a and the training signal is proper, while at each stage r, $k < r \leq l$ at which ξ^a is input,the training signal is either proper or 0 (both may occur at different stages).

ξ^a *tests successfully* during stages k to l provided $x^a(t_j) \in U^a$ whenever $k \leq j \leq l$ and the input for stage j is ξ^a.

Recall that λ is the time constant in Equation (5).

Theorem 3 *There exist positive constants* T_*, τ_*, λ_* *independent of* $N, \epsilon, \{\xi^a\}$ *and computable from the data, with the following property. Assume* $0 < \lambda < \lambda_*$ *and Hypothesis 2 holds with* $T \geq T_*, R \geq R_*$*, and in addition* $\epsilon N \leq \tau_*$*. Then every pattern which is consistently trained from stages* k *to* l*, tests successfully during those stages.*

The quantity

$$\theta = \epsilon N(1+\epsilon)^N$$

plays a key role. Notice that $\theta \to 0$ as $\epsilon N \to 0$.

Theorem 4 *There exist positive constants T_*, R_*, λ_*, independent of $\epsilon, N, \{\xi^a\}$ and computable from the data, with the following property. If $0 < \lambda < \lambda_*$ and Hypothesis 2 holds with $T \geq T_*, R \geq R_*$, then:*

$$||M(t)\xi^a|| < \theta R \tag{11}$$

for all $t \geq 0,\ a = 1, \ldots, m$.

It is clear from (4) that if a vector $\eta \in \mathbb{R}^d$ is orthogonal to all the input patterns, then $M(t)\eta$ is constant. Therefore the Theorem 4 implies that the entries in $M(t)$ are uniformly bounded.
The key to the proofs is the following lemma. Suppose the input is $\xi = \xi^a$ in System (4), (5),(6). Computing dx^b/dt shows $dx^b/dt = (\xi^b \cdot \xi^a)dx^a/dt$, yielding the crucial estimate:

Lemma 5 *If the input is ξ^a and $b \neq a$, then for $t_1 > t_0 \geq 0$ we have:*

$$|x^b(s_1) - x^b(s_0)| \leq \epsilon|x^a(s_1) - x^a(s_0)|. \tag{12}$$

This means that after presentation of ξ^b, subsequent presentation of ξ^a does not alter the net's recall of ξ^b by very much provided ϵ is sufficiently small.

3 Discussion

Theorem 3 means that each consistently trained input pattern yields the correct output attractor regardless of the training of the other patterns, which may be untrained or even inconsistently trained. Moreover the system can be trained or retrained on any patterns without impairing the previous training of the other patterns.
Example 2 An example which illustrates the difficulty in verifying the assumption on proper training signals in Hypothesis 2 is obtained by replacing f in Example 1 by $f_1(x) = f(x) + f(x-1)$. (If f approximates a step function, then f_1 approximates a staircase function.) For high gain the vector field $-x + f_1(x)$ has attracting equilibria very near $-2, 0$ and 2, and unstable equilibria near -1 and 1. The basin of the attraction for the equibrium near 0 is contained in the interval $(-1, 1)$. As we must take $\rho \approx 2$, Hypothesis 2 is violated because $N_2(0) \not\subset (-1, 1)$.
The requirement that input patterns be unit vectors is made only for simplicity. If they are not unit vectors then the assumption on separation of distinct patterns in Hypothesis 2 is changed to

$$\frac{|\xi^a \cdot \xi^b|\ ||\xi^b||}{||\xi^a||} < \epsilon,$$

with similar results. The dimension d of the input space is irrelevant to our results. In fact the input patterns could be members of an arbitrary inner product space.
It is not hard to see that some restrictions on the geometry of the patterns is necessary. For example, a set of linearly dependent patterns severely constrains the associated outputs that can be learned.
The training-testing schedule is also crucial. Simple examples show that, as with natural learning systems, if a pattern is not repeated sufficiently often it may be forgotten.
Interesting stochastic questions arise. Suppose, for example, that instead of considering consistently trained patterns, we allow the wrong teaching signal to be given

with small positive probability. Is it true, as seems likely, that under some similar training scheme there is a high probability of correct output?

Some other issues: Is incremental learning possible? Can such nets be usefully coupled? Can more than one layer of memory be trained this way? Is there a good way to approximately orthogonalize inputs by preprocessing?

REFERENCES

[1] Amit, D. J., *The Hebbian paradigm reintegrated: local reverberations as internal representations*, Behavioral and Brain Sciences in press (1995).

[2] Baird, B. & Eeckmann, F. H., *A hierarchical sensory-motor architecture of oscillating cortical area subnetworks*, in: Analysis and Modeling of Neural Systems II, F. H. Eeckman (ed.) Boston: Kluwer (1992), pp96–104.

[3] Baird, B. & Eeckman, F. & Hirsch, M. W., *A neural network associative memory fdor handwritten character recognition using multiple Chua attractors*, IEEE Trans. Circuits & Systems Vol. 40 (1993), pp667–674.

[4] Baird, B. & Hirsch, M. W., *Computing with dynamic attractors*, Biosystems Vol. 34 (1995), pp173–195.

[5] Freeman, W. J., *Simulation of chaotic EEG patterns with a dynamic model of the olfactory system* , Biological Cybernetics Vol. 56 (1987), pp139–143

[6] Freeman, W. J. & Baird, B., *Relation of olfactory EEG to behavior: spatial analysis*, Behavioral Neuroscience Vol. 101 (1987), pp393–408

[7] Freeman, W. J. & Viana di Prisco, G., *EEG spatial pattern differences with discriminated odors manifest chaotic and limit cycle attractors in olfactory bulb of rabbits*, in: Proceedings First Trieste Meeting on Brain Theory, G. Palm & A. Aertsen (eds.) New York: Springer-Verlag (1986).

[8] Hebb, D. O., *The Organization of Behavior*, New York: Wiley (1949).

[9] Hirsch, M. W., *On-line Training of a Continually Adapting Perceptron-Like Network*, Neurocomputing, in press 1996.

Acknowledgements

Partially supported by a grant from the National Science Foundation.

MATHEMATICAL PROBLEMS ARISING FROM CONSTRUCTING AN ARTIFICIAL BRAIN

J. G. Taylor

Department of Mathematics and Centre for Neural Networks, King's College, London, UK.

A beginning is being made on the hard problem of constructing an artificial brain, to try to bridge the gap between neurophysiology and psychology. The approach uses especially the increasing number of results obtained by means of non-invasive instruments (EEG,MEG,PET,fMRI), and the related psychological tasks. The paper describes the program and some of the mathematical problems that it is producing. In particular the class of problems associated with the activities of various coupled modules used in higher order control and attention will be discussed. These include posterior attentional coupled systems, and the anterior motor/action/attention "ACTION" networks, based on biological circuits. The relevance of these modules, and the associated problems, for higher order cognition, are emphasised.

1 Introduction

The Harvard neurologist Gerald Fishbach stated recently "The human brain is the most complicated object on earth". That does indeed seem to be the case, and for a considerable period of time since the beginning of the scientific revolution this fact seems to have led to despair in ever being able to have a reasonable comprehension of it. However there is now a strong sense of optimism in the field of brain sciences that serious progress is being made in the search for comprehension of the mechanisms used by the brain to achieve its amazing powers, even up to the level of consciousness. Part of this optimism stems from the discovery and development of new windows with which to look at the brain, with large groups now being established to exploit the power of the available instruments. There are also new theories of how neurons might combine their activities to produce mind-like behaviour, based on recent developments in the field of artificial neural networks. At the same time there is an ever increasing understanding of the subtleties of the mechanisms used by living neurons. It would thus appear that the mind and brain are being attacked at many levels. The paper attempts to contribute towards this program by starting with a brief survey of the results of non-invasive instruments. Then it turns to consider the inverse problem before discussing the nature of past global brain models. An overview is then given of the manner in which neural modelling may attempt to begin to achieve perception. Problems of neuropsychological modelling are then considered, with the breakdown of tasks into component sub-processes. Mathematical problems associated with constructing neural modules to achieve the required functionality of sub-process are then discussed. Modules to produce possible conscious processing are then considered, and the paper concludes with a summary and discussion of further questions.

2 Non-Invasive Results

There are amazing new windows on the mind. These measure either the magnetic or electric fields caused by neural activity, or the change in blood flow in active regions of the brain to allow oxygen to be brought to support the neural activity. The former techniques are termed magnetoencephalography (MEG) and electroencephalography (EEG), the latter positron emission tomography (PET) and functional magnetic resonance imaging (fMRI) respectively. The techniques of MEG, EEG and fMRI are truly non-invasive since there is no substance penetrating the body, whilst that is not so with PET, in which a subject imbibes a radioactive material which will decay rapidly with emission of positrons (with their ensuing decay to two photons).

The methods have different advantages and disadvantages. Thus EEG is a very accurate measure of the time course of the average electrical current from an aggregate of neurons firing in unison, but is contaminated with conduction currents flowing through the conducting material of the head. Thus although temporal accuracy of a few milliseconds can be obtained spatial accuracy is mainly limited to surface effects, and deep currents are difficult to detect with certainty. MEG does not have the defect of being broadened out spatially by the conduction currents, but has the problem of spatial accuracy, which is slowly becoming resolved (but also has a more difficult one of expense due to the need for special screening and low temperature apparatus for the SQUID devices). fMRI also has considerable expense and low temporal accuracy. Even though the activity from each slice of brain may be assessed in an fMRI machine within about 100 or so milliseconds the blood flow related to the underlying brain activity still requires about 7 seconds to reach its peak. There has been a recent suggestion that hypo-activity from the deoxygenated blood will 'peak' after only about 1 or 2 seconds of input [1], but that is still to be confirmed. Finally PET also has the same problems of slow blood flow possessed by fMRI, but good spatial accuracy. Combining two or more of the above techniques together makes it possible to follow the temporal development of spatially well defined activity [2]. The results stemming from such a combination are already showing clear trends.

The most important result being discovered by these techniques is that

1. activity of the brain for solving a given task is localised mainly in a distinct network of modules,
2. the temporal flow of activity between the modules is itself very specific,
3. the network used for a given task is different, in general, from that used for another task.

It is not proposed to give here a more detailed description of the enormous number of results now being obtained by these techniques, but refer the reader, for example, to the recent book of [2], or the excellent discussion in [3]. However it is important finally to note that the fact there are distinctive signatures that can be picked up by these instruments indicate that aggregates of nerve cells are involved in solving the relevant tasks by the subjects. Thus population activity is involved, and "grandmother" cells are not in evidence. Of course if they were important they would slip through the net. However that there are such characteristic signatures seems to show that the net is sharp enough to detect relevant aggregated activity.

3 Inverse Problems

There has been much work done to decipher the detailed form of the underlying neural activity that gives rise to a particular MEG or EEG pattern, the so-called "inverse problem". Various approaches have been used to read off the relevant neural processing, mainly in terms of the distribution of the underlying sources of current flow. This latter might be chosen to be extremely discrete, as in the case of the single dipole fits to some of the data. However more complete current flow analyses have been performed recently, as in the case of MFT [4]. This leads to a continuous distribution of current over the brain, in terms of the lead fields describing the effectiveness of a given sensor to detect current at the position of the field in question.

It has been possible to extend this approach to use cross entropy minimisation so as to determine the statistics of the current density distribution in terms of the covariance matrix of the measurements and the sensor mean results [5]. This approach is presently being extended to attempt to incorporate the iteration procedure in the MFT method of [4] so as to make the approach more effective [6].

There are further deep difficulties with the inverse problem. Thus one has to face up to the question of single trials versus averaged values. Averaging has especially been performed on the EEG data so as to remove the noise present. However in the case of successful task performance the subject must have used activity of a set of modules, in a single trial, in a way which avoided the noise. This is an important question that will be taken up in the next section: how is successful performance achieved in an apparently noisy or chaotic dynamical system such as the brain [7]? Averaging only removes the crucial data indicating as to how the solution to this task might be achieved. But single trials appear to be very, very noisy. How do modules share in the processing so as to overcome the variability of neural activity in each of them?

One way to begin to answer this, and the earlier problem about the inverse problem, is to model the neural activity in a direct manner. In other words the actual flow of nerve impulses, and their resultant stimulation of other neural modules, must be attempted. The resulting electric and magnetic fields of this neural activity must then be calculated. This approach will allow more knowledge to be inserted in the model being built than by use of methods like MFT, and so help constrain the solution space better.

4 Neural Modules for Perception

It is possible to develop a program of modelling for the whole brain, so that the spatial and temporal flow patterns that arise from given inputs can be simulated. That also requires the simulation of reasonably accurate input sensors, such as the retina, the nose or the cochlea. There are already simple neural models of such input processors (such as in [8]), so that with care the effects of early processing could already be included.

The order of work then to be performed is that of the development of simple neural modules, say each with about a thousand neurons, and connected up to others in a manner already being determined from known connectivities, such as that of the macaque [9]. An important question of homology has to be solved here, but there is increasing understanding of how to relate the monkey brain to that of the human, so that problem may not be impossible. There is also the difficulty of relating the resulting set of, say, a hundred simplified modules to their correct places on the cortical surface (and to appropriate sub-cortical places) for a particular human subject. Even assuming the cortical surface is known from an MRI scan, the actual placing of the modules corresponding to different areas might be difficult. However this may be tackled by considering it as a task of minimization of the mismatch between the predictions of the model and the actual values of EEG and MEG signals during a range of input processing, and including sub-cortical structures, such as discussed in [10].

5 Neuropsychological Modelling

There is a big gap between neurons in the brain and the concepts which they support. The job of explaining how the latter arise from the former is formidable. Indeed it is even harder to consider the ultimate of experiences supported, that of consciousness itself. One approach has been to consider the brain as carrying out simple computations. However there has recently been an attack on the notion of the brain as a 'computational' organ, in the sense that "nervous systems represent and they respond on the basis of the representations" [11]. It has been suggested, instead, that brains do not perform such simple computations. Thus "It is shown that simplified silicon nets can be thought of as computing, but biologically realistic nets are non-computational. Rather than structure sensitive rules governed operations on symbolic representations, there is an evolution of self-organising non-linear dynamic systems in a process of 'differing and deferring' " [7].

This claim of non-computationality of the brain is supported by appeals to the discovery of chaos in EEG traces, and also that low-dimensional motion may be involved in the production of percepts in ambiguity removal. However it is well known that neural systems are non-linear, and that such systems can easily have chaotic motions if forced into certain parameter regimes. Thus the dynamics of the whole brain, written as the dynamical system

$$dX/dt = F(X, a)$$

in terms of the high dimensional state vector X, is expected to have chaotic motion for some of the parameter range a, on which the vector field F depends. Thus X could denote the set of compartmental membrane potentials, and F denotes the non-linear Hodgkin-Huxley equations for the production of the nerve impulses. However there are still expected to be "representations" brought about by the changes of the function F by, for example, synaptic modifications caused by learning. If there is no change in the transform function F there seems to be no chance for learning. Hence the claim of [7] seems to be incorrect when the notion of representation is extended to the more general transform function F. This uses the notion of coupled modules in the whole brain, as are observed to be needed by the non-invasive techniques mentioned earlier. Thus the possibility of chaos will not be regarded as problematic to the program being proposed.

It is possible to build neural modules to model some of the important processes observed in psychology. Thus the various sorts of memory and other processes may be modelled as:

- working memory (as a set of neuron buffers)
- semantic memory (as an associative memory)
- episodic memory (as a recurrent net)

- attention (as a lateral inhibitory net)
- action (by means of a population vector encoding)

This is an incomplete list, but can be begun to be made complete. However in order to do that it would appear necessary to consider the manner in which psychological tasks may themselves be broken down. That is done in the next section.

6 Component Sub-Processes

The method to be developed here is to try to decompose complex psychological functions into a set of lower order component sub-processes (CSPs). These latter will attempted to be chosen so as to be independent of each other. That would then make the identification of neural substrates for their performance easier, in the sense that separate neural modules would be expected to support the different CSPs. Lesion deficits would then be expected to show loss of different components of the complex tasks, and hopefully even allow better identification of the CSPs involved. Such a program has already been started for the frontal lobes in [12], where the supposed executive function action of that region has been attempted to be decomposed into a set of CSPs in the case of attention.
The conjecture, then, is that

> Any complex psychological task is decomposable into a set of independent component sub-processes, each of which is distributed across only a few separate brain areas.

Such a conjecture would make the analysis of brain function a problem of mapping the corresponding CSPs onto the appropriate brain areas. There may well be a limit as to how far it is possible to break down a complex psychological task in a manner which still has psychological observability. Thus it might be supposed that some small brain areas may give a contribution to a task which does not have any clearly observable effect on task performance. However the principle of parsimony would lead one to expect that such areas would be rather unlikely, since they do not appear to possess much survival value to the system and so could be dispensed with.
It is possible to group complex tasks under the four main headings:

- Perception
- Movement
- Memory
- Thought

It is further seen that perception itself has at least the two component sub-tasks of construction of codes (in the five separate modalities) and that of representations (such as at feature, object, category, position, body matrix, lexical, phonological and word level). There are numerous sub-divisions of memory (episodic, semantic, implicit, priming, working, active) with considerable overlap with representations (which are the objects of memory). There are functions which are strongly associated with limbic regions, such as goals, values, drives and self representations.

There are also frontally-sited functions, as in attention, social behaviour, planning and actions [13].
The above set of functions is performed by complex brain networks, as demonstrated clearly in [2]. It is a very important but difficult task to attempt to reduce this broad range to a smaller set of underlying elements, the CSPs alluded to above. The following set is proposed as a preliminary version of the required list:

- Analyser (into features, objects or categories)
- Predictor/Actor (as a generator of schema)
- Monitor (for assessing goodness of fit)
- Activator (to promote or inhibit on-going schema or other forms of processing)
- Buffer (for holding activity over a fixed or variable time)
- Clock (for estimating temporal duration)
- Long-term memory stores (both implicit and declarative)
- Goal formation (involving value-memory)
- Drive (arising from internal bodily sources, and being independent of the activator)

There may be other CSPs which must be added to the above list. Moreover the CSPs of a given sort specified above may have different properties amongst each other. Thus there are buffers which hold activity for a fixed time (such as the phonological store [14]) and those which can preserve it over a variable time of up to 30 or so seconds (associated specifically with frontal lobe). Similarly activators can either excite or inhibit, and there may thus be two quite separate sub-classes of modules performing these two disparate functions. However the suggested list of CSPs given above seems to be of enough interest to explore its use in attempting to reduce the complexity of psychological tasks to more manageable proportions. It includes those suggested in [12] for the frontal lobe, where the 'logic CSP' introduced there is assumed to be the schema generator above, and compression of separate inhibitor and excitor modules has been introduced in our list to give a common activator sub-set.
The next step is to develop a neural underpinning for the mental processes at the level of the CSPs listed above. Thus single modules or small coupled nets of them must be constructed which (a) have a close relation to neural modules in the brain from an anatomical and functional point of view (b) appear to cause deficits in processing when there is loss of the relevant module (c) are seen to be active in the performance of a task as determined by some non-invasive measurement.

7 Neural Modules for Component Sub-Processes

There are already a number of modules which may be suggested to solve the above problems (a), (b) and (c). Thus

(i) an *analyser* may be designed from a convolution filter, such as by the use of a Gabor function kernel. Such a filter has similarity to the action of striate visual cortex, and may be directly mapped onto the action of simple cells in area V1, say. There is also a considerable level of understanding of the manner in which such a filter may arise from adaptation to visual input.

(ii) a *predictor* may be constructed as a recurrent net of the form

$$x(t+1) = F(I(t), x(t), x(t-1), ...)$$

where such recurrence leads to the generation of a sequence stored in the nature of the response function F, which may also be modulated by the external input I. Identification of such a system is in terms of well defined recurrence of neural output, as is well known as occurring in hippocampus, for example [15].

(iii) an *activator* may be constructed as a set-point detector, say in the form

$$x(t+1) = Y(-I(t) + s)$$

where Y is the Heaviside step function. Then neuron x is active (to initiate search, say) if the input I (which may be some internal energy level, say) drops below the threshold or set-point s. This can be mapped onto various brain-stem systems.

(iv) *active memory , comparator action, etc*: there are several tasks associated with actions which are not so simple to relate to actual neuranatomical structures, although there is now increasing work on this area of investigation. Some of these are specifically associated with frontal functions. The approach to be adopted here now is to take a specific architecture, that of the ACTION network [16], and determine in which manner it may be able to support the CSPs associated with monitoring, prediction/action (schema generation) and active memory.

The ACTION network comprises the frontal cortex, basal ganglia and associated thalamic nuclei. It is decomposable at least into the four main loops of motor action, frontal eye fields, limbic activity, and cognitive activity [17]. These loops are supposed to have a certain degree of autonomy, so might be expected to play an important role in the support of CSPs.

The architecture of the ACTION net is one of a feedback loop between cortex and thalamus which has threshold modulation by a non-reciprocal disinhibitory feed from cortex down through the basal ganglia to the same area of thalamus as was in contact with the cortex in the first place. The ACTION network is built to capitalise on this structure so as to allow for the development of a flip-flop action between cortex and thalamus. Thus activity arriving at a cortical region from posterior cortex (parietal or temporal areas have important cortico-cortical connections with frontal cortex) may cause the cortico-thalamic loop to be activated, and stay on. Such persistence may crucially require support from the basal ganglia disinhibition, which may be achievable by means of cingulate activation (as 'drive') from some set point detector, or from some goal memory set up there or on another portion of the ACTION network.

Such functionality may thus be seen to support active memory. By the addition of lateral inhibition in the two levels of the basal ganglia it may also be shown to function as a comparator. Again the successful performance by ACTION to achieve this can be argued for, since if there is an active memory being preserved on cortex and thalamus then a new, but different, one arriving on cortex will produce lateral inhibitory activity in basal ganglia. A competitive action is then fought on the basal ganglia between the earlier activity and that newly arriving. Assuming that there is support for the earlier activity from cingulate, say, as part of drive, then the former activity will win this competition on the basal ganglia. That means that the new activity will not be able to persist on cortex, since its threshold disihibiting mechanism has been lost. Only new activity in agreement with the past activity will be able to continue its activity unchecked, and contribute positively to the previously stored activity on cortex. This latter may then exceed some detection threshold to indicate that a search has been completed successfully, say.

Besides the obvious mathematical questions associated with the development and storage capacity of the proposed cortico-thalamic flip-flop and of the lateral competitive system on the basal ganglia, there is a more fundamental question that needs answering. It is well established experimentally that coding of action in motor or premotor cortex is in terms of a population code. Many cells in motor cortex contribute to the determination of the direction an action will take. Each has its own preferred direction, say α_i, and resulting activity proportional to $[1 + \cos(\theta - \alpha_i)]$, if θ is the direction of the upcoming movement. However it does not seem easy to preserve this activity level by means of a flip-flop memory, since in that case activity is either on or off, and is not graded. Therefore there seems to be a contradiction between the proposed functioning of ACTION as a flip-flop and the presence of a range of preserved activities by population coding.

One way to understand the mode of persistence of the motor cortex population vector is to suppose that the motor cortex has an attractor behaviour arising from its structure as a recurrent net due to the lateral connections it possesses. These connections have been observed as having weights anticorrelated with the preferred direction of movement vector for each cell; the value $w_{ij} = \cos(\alpha_i - \alpha_j)$ would roughly fit the data of [18. In that case the value of the quantity $\sum w_{ij}[1 + \cos(\theta - \alpha_j)]$ may be seen to be proportional to $\cos(\theta - \alpha_i)$ (with constant of proportionality 1/3). In order to obtain the additional term 1 in the cortical neuron activity it seems necessary to use disinhibition from the basal ganglia side line. This can be achieved by the use of summation of activity from a set of N cortical neurons onto a single basal ganglia neurons (experimentally there is at least a ratio of a hundred cortical neurons to one basal ganglia neuron) and thence to the thalamic cell; the weight of the basal ganglia neurons need only be of order $1/N$ for preservation of the activity.

There now seems to be two possible sources of active memory in frontal cortex. One is that developed in the previous paragraph, which uses a relaxation net of recurrent connections which seems to fit the observed pattern of persistence in motor cortex. The other is that of the previous paragraph, with a set of attractors developed by thalamo-cortical feedback connections (functioning somewhat as a bidirectional associative memory or BAM might). However the former model also needs the activity of appropriately connected, and active, thalamic neurons to feed the threshold disinhibition from thalamus up to the relevant cortical cells. Thus there appears to be some sort of a reconciliation of these two proposed modes of action of the cortico-thalamic- basal ganglia system. It is clear that further analysis, and much simulation, needs to be performed in order to determine the effectiveness of the ACTION network in this case.

8 Modules for the Mind

There are clearly many modules involved in the creation of consciousness. An important question is if there is a distributed action of the brain to achieve conscious awareness or if there are discrete centres which are to be regarded as the true sites of such experience which is then shared around or broadcast to other such sites so as to give a unified system of response. There is some support for the latter form of neural system for consciousness, since inputs are known to be processed up to a semantic level without reaching awareness. This is associated with the phenomenon of subliminal processing. It is now reasonably well established that awareness and response to a later word or other input may be modified by earlier inputs which have not gained access to the awareness system but which have been processed up to a reasonably high level. The highest level, as noted above, was up to semantic memory, but only for words and not for sentences. It is therefore clear that there are quite high level modules in the brain whose activation does not directly produce consciousness but which are important in the influence their activity may exert on later conscious experiences.

Such a modulating influence has been modelled [19] by means of a coupled set of semantic/ working memory modules. The first of these acts in a feedforward excitatory manner with dedicated nodes (which might arise from some form of topographic map) which feed to similar nodes on a working memory module with longer time constants. This latter net acts as a buffer so as to hold activity for a second or so, in order that earlier context can be properly incorporated in any decision that is taken on the working memory module. This latter has inhibitory connections between incompatible nodes, so that their activity may effect the time to reach a certain threshold of nodes activated by later inputs from the semantic net. It is possible in this manner to model with some accuracy the changes in reaction time in lexical decision tasks brought about by subliminally processed letter strings at an earlier time.

Consciousness seems to reside, therefore, on the working memory modules of the posterior cortex. These are present for a variety of codes, and allow a detailed implementation of the Relational Mind model developed by the author over 20 years ago, and published more recently in a more developed form [20]. However there are various features of consciousness that are missing from this model, in particular the emergence of its uniqueness. Such a feature might be expected to arise from some form of competitive action between the different working memory modules. Such an action might be able to occur in cortex by suitable connection of excitatory outputs from a given working memory module to others. However there is no clear picture of such inhibition, especially between the working memory modules which appear to be at about the same level in the hierarchy of brain modules following cytoarchitectonic and myeloarchitectonic reasoning; these working memory sites may be classified as heteromodal cortex.

In order to resolve this issue of the putative source of long range inhibition in cortex (which is also seen to be absent in the modelling of global EEG patterns) it may be that there are sub-cortical sites of such inhibition which are of importance. It has been suggested that there are indeed such sites, in particular in the nucleus reticularis thalami (NRT for short) which is a sheet of totally inhibitory neurons which surround the upper and lateral parts of the thalamic nuclei. NRT cells are activated by thalamo-cortical axon collaterals piercing the NRT, as also by cortico-thalamic axon collaterals. A model of this system has been constructed [21] which has been shown to lead to global competition, and even to allow explanation of the relatively long time to reach consciousness determined by the beautiful experiments of Libet and his colleagues [22].

The picture that emerges from these analyses is of a set of coupled semantic (SM)/ working (WM) memories, each for a given code A. There is a competition between the activities of the WMs, the winner being that whose content emerges into consciousness. However this account only deals with posterior sites, so is more correctly denoted C_p, the subscript denoting both posterior and passive. The other important component of consciousness will be denoted as C_a, the subscript now denoting anterior and active. It is that aspect of awareness which the ACTION network, introduced above, can also begin to tackle in terms of the various control operations it can perform. Various aspects of this have been discussed earlier, as part of the consideration of active memory and the comparator action it may support.

9 Conclusions

From what has been outlined briefly above the time seems opportune to mount a program attempting to simulate the brain on a large scale by modelling it as a set of connected modules, each composed of simple neurons connected together by a set of well defined rules. The program can be broken down into separate tasks:

- construct a software simulation with about 100 modules, each with ever more complex neurons,
- include increasingly detailed neuroanatomical analyses so as to include increasing realism,
- develop the simulation so as to allow for a modular analysis of psychological functions and their component sub-processes,
- test the simulation results against non-invasive instrument measurements,
- perform mathematical analyses of the resulting equations using techniques from dynamical systems and statistical mechanics.

The resulting set of models will be able to provide an increasingly detailed basis to explore the manner in which the brain can support the mind.

REFERENCES

[1] Prof H Muller-Gartner, private communication.

[2] MI Posner and ME Raichle *Images of the Mind* Scientific American Library, Freeman (1994).

[3] J Grafman, A Partiot and C Hollnagel, *Fables of the prefrontal cortex* , Behaviour and Brain Sciences, Vol. 18 (1995), pp349–358.

[4] A Ioannides, JPR Bolton and CJS Clarke, *Continuous Probabilistic Solutions to the Biomagnetic Inverse Problem* , Inverse Problems Vol. 6 (1990), pp523–542.

[5] F Alavi, A Ioannides and JG Taylor, *The Biomagnetic Inverse Problem* , in Artificial Neural Networks 2, I Aleksander and JG Taylor (eds), Elsevier Science Publishers (1992).

[6] Ibid, work in progress.

[7] GG Globus, *Towards a Noncomputational Cognitive Neuroscience* J Cognitive Neuroscience Vol. 4, pp299–310.

[8] JG Taylor, *A Silicon Model of Vertbetrate Retinal Processing* , Neural Networks Vol.3 (1990), pp171–178.

[9] DJ Felleman and DC Van Essen, *Distributed Hierarchical Processing in the Primate Cerebral Cortex* , Cerebral Cortex, Vol. 1 (1991), pp1–47.

[10] F Alavi and JG Taylor, *A global competitive network* , Biol Cyb. Vol. 72 (1995), pp233–248.

[11] M Steriade, DA McCormick and TJ Sejnowski, *Thlamocortical Oscillations in the Sleeping and Aroused Brain* , Science Vol. 262 (1993), pp679–685.

[12] DT Stuss, T Shallice, MP Alexander and TW Picton, *A Multidisciplinary Approach to Anterior Attentional Functions* Univ of Toronto preprint, unpublished, (April 1995).

[13] R Bappi, G Bugmann, D Levine and JG Taylor, *Neural Models of Executive Function* , in preparation (1996).

[14] A Baddeley, *Working Memory*, Oxford Univ Press (1986).

[15] M Reiss and JG Taylor, *Does the Hippocampus Store Temporal Patterns?* , Neural Network World Vol. 3 (1992), pp365–384.

[16] JG Taylor, *Modules for the Mind of PSYCHE* , Proc WCNN95, II-967-972 (1995), Lawrence Erlbaum Associates.

[17] GE Alexander, MD Crutcher and MR DeLong, *Basal ganglia thalamocortical circuits: parallel substrates for motor, oculomotor, 'prefrontal' and 'limbic' functions* Prog Brain Res. Vol. 85 (1990), pp119–146.

[18] AP Georgopoulos, M Taira and A Lukashin, *Cognitive Neurophysiology of the Motor Cortex*, Science Vol. 260 (1993), pp47–52.

[19] JG Taylor *Breakthrough to Awareness*, Neural Computation, in press.

[20] JG Taylor *The Relational Mind*, Seminars at Tubingen and London Universities (1973); ibid *Can a Neural Network ever be made to think?*, Neural Network World Vol.1 (1991), pp4–12.

[21] JG Taylor, *Towards a neural network model of the mind* , Neural Network World Vol.2 (1992), pp797–812.

[22] B Libet, WW Alberts, EW Wright Jr, DL Delattre, G Levin and B Feinstein, *Production of Threshold Levels of Conscious Sensation by Electrical Stimulation of Human Somato-Sensory Cortex* , J Neurophysiol Vol.27 (1964), pp546–578.

PART II

SUBMITTED PAPERS

THE SUCCESSFUL USE OF PROBABILITY DATA IN CONNECTIONIST MODELS

J. R. Alexander Jr. and J. P. Coughlin

Towson State University, Towson, USA.

Reggia [10] explored connectionist models which employed "virtual" lateral inhibition, and included the activation of the receiving node in the equations for the flow of activation. Ahuja [1] extended these concepts to include summing the total excitatory and inhibitory flow into a node. He thus introduced the concept that the change of activation of a node depended on the integral of the flow into that node and not just the present activation levels of the nodes to which it is connected. Both Reggia's and Ahuja's models used probability data for the weights. Ahuja's model was further extended by Alexander [2], [3], [4] in the RX model to allow both the weights and the activations of Ahuja's model to be negative, and further, Alexander's model included the prior probabilities of all nodes. Section 1 of this paper contains a complete listing of the RX equations and describes their development. The main result of this paper, the demonstration of the convergence of the system is presented in Section 2. Section 3 briefly describes the experiments testing the RX system and summarizes this article.

1 The RX Equations

The net is two-layered, with the lower level being the J input nodes and upper level the N output nodes. The values of the upper level nodes, $a_i(t)$, are on $[0,1]$. The prior probability of the existence of the feature associated with the ith node is called $\overline{a}_i$. Values of $a_i(t)$ greater than $\overline{a}_i$ indicate a higher than average chance of occurrence of the feature represented by node i, and those lower, indicate a less than average chance. The activation on the lower level nodes is computed from the range of possible input values to a node. If the smallest observed value is Min_j, the largest Max_j and the average Ave_j. Let $Observ_j$ be the observed value. Then define:

$$m_j = \frac{[Observ_j - Ave_j]}{[Max_j - Ave_j]} \text{ if } Observ_j > Ave_j \quad \text{and}$$

$$m_j = \frac{[Observ_j - Ave_j]}{[Ave_j - Min_j]} \text{ otherwise} \tag{1}$$

Clearly m_j lies on $[-1,1]$. When m_j assumes the value 1, then the feature represented by m_j is present, with probability one. When m_j is -1 the feature is absent with probability one. A value of zero indicates that no information exists concerning the absence or presence of this feature. Two sets of weights exist. The first is called w_{ij}, and in absolute value indicates the probability of occurrence (if positive, and non-occurrence if negative) of the feature associated with the upper level node (ith), given the existence of activation on the lower level node (jth). The second weight is called v_{ij}, and in absolute value indicates the probability of occurrence (if positive, and non-occurrence if negative) of the feature associated with the lower level node, given the existence of activation on the upper level node.

Two auxiliary functions are to be associated with each $a_i(t)$. The function which conveys the excitatory activation is called $Exc_i(t)$, and the one which conveys the inhibitory is called $Inh_i(t)$. Each is the sum of all the excitatory and inhibitory flow of activation into node i. These functions are defined by their derivatives and, since the latter are sums of everywhere positive terms, the former are monotone-increasing. Each of the terms used in defining the derivative is a function of all the $a_i(t)$ and is the variable forcing term. There will be one such function for each lower level (j) node, hence a sum need be taken over all the j nodes connected to any given i node. The bounded characteristic is achieved by including in the equation a factor of the form $[N - Exc_i(t)]$. The choice of N as the bound to which $Exc_i(t)$ approaches is somewhat arbitrary.

2 Convergence of the RX Equations

2.1 The RX Equations

$$\dot{a}_i(t) = K_3 * c_u * [1 - a_i(t)] * [Exc_i(t) - Inh_i(t)] \tag{2}$$

$$\dot{a}_i(t) = K_3 * c_l * [a_i(t)] * [Exc_i - Inh_i] \tag{3}$$

According as $a_i(t) \geq \overline{a}_i$ or $a_i(t) \leq \overline{a}_i$ respectively. K_3 is a constant of proportionality, and the values of c_l and c_u are chosen to keep the derivative continuous at $\overline{a}_i$:

$$c_u = 1/(1 - \overline{a}_i), \qquad c_l = 1/\overline{a}_i.$$

$$\begin{aligned} \dot{Exc_i}(t) = {} & K_1 * \overline{a}_i * [N - Exc_i(t)] * \\ & \sum_j [k_{11} * OUTPP_{ij}(t) + k_{12} * outpm_{ij}(t) \\ & + k_{13} * outmp_{ij}(t) + k_{14} * OUTMM_{ij}(t)] \end{aligned} \tag{4}$$

$$\begin{aligned} \dot{Inh_i}(t) = {} & K_2 * \overline{a}_i * [N - Inh_i(t)] * \\ & \sum_j [k_{21} * outpp_{ij}(t) + k_{22} * OUTPM_{ij}(t) \\ & + k_{23} * OUTMP_{ij}(t) + k_{24} * outmm_{ij}(t)] \end{aligned} \tag{5}$$

Here $k_{11}, \ldots, k_{24}$ are included for generality.

$$OUTPP_{ij}(t) = \frac{W_{ij} * |a_i(t) - \overline{a}_i|}{\sum_l W_{lj} * |a_l(t) - \overline{a}_l| + \epsilon_d} * m_j \tag{6}$$

with similar expressions for the other $OUTP$ terms and

$$outpp_{ij}(t) = \frac{\sum_{k \neq i} V_{kj} * |a_k(t) - \overline{a}_k|}{\sum V_{lj} * |a_l(t) - \overline{a}_l| + \epsilon_d} * m_j * |a_i(t) - \overline{a}_i| \tag{7}$$

with similar expressions for the other $outp$ terms. The ϵ_d is included so that the denominator never vanishes.

2.2 The Dynamics of the RX Net

The principal result of this section, that the dynamics of the RX system converges, is given in Section 2.3 below. Hirsch [8] defines convergent dynamics by stating that "the trajectory of every initial condition tends to some equilibrium". Prior to stating the theorem, we make some observations about the critical points.
They are labeled as follows:

$$CP_0 = (r_1, r_2, ..r_i, ..r_N, N_1, ..N_N, N_1, ..N_N) \tag{8}$$

and

$$CP_L = (r_1, r_2, ..r_{N-L}, \overline{a}_{N-L+1..N}, N_1, ..N_{N-L}, d_{N-L+1}..d_N, N_1, ..N_{N-L}, d_N..d_N) \tag{9}$$

where r_i (the value of a_i) $\in (0, 1)$, and the d_i (the value of Exc_i or Inh_i) $\in [0, N)$. By letting L (the number of the $a_i(t)$ that approach $\overline{a}_i$) range from 0 through N, all critical points may be described simply by stating the value of L, and that of each d_i. Note that the critical points need <u>NOT</u> be isolated. One of the lemmas in [2] has demonstrated that $Exc_i(t)$ and $Inh_i(t)$ are monotone increasing functions. As a result, points of type CP_L may be thought of as "on the way" to CP_0. If $Exc_i(t)$ and $Inh_i(t)$ approach N, then the critical point becomes of type $CP_{(L-1)}$.

The norm adopted in the sequel is the ℓ_1 norm [6] where: $\|X\| = \sum_i |x_i|$. We proved [2] that both $Exc_i(t)$ and $Inh_i(t)$ are bounded monotone increasing functions and that the RX functions are Lipschitzian throughout their domain of definition.

We now discuss the details of the interface of the upper and the lower branches of the equations. Recall, the upper branch is defined for $a_i \in [\overline{a}_i, 1]$, and the lower branch for $a_i \in [0, \overline{a}_i]$, Since each branch is analytic on its domain of definition, and the composite (upper and lower branches considered as one) function is Lipschitzian where the branches meet (at $a_i = \overline{a}_i$), the solutions through any point exist and are unique. To examine stability it is necessary to look at the derivatives of the RX function and we are confronted with the problem that the derivative, per se, does not exist on the hyper-plane $a_i = \overline{a}_i$. However, the left-hand and right-hand derivatives do exist and for the purpose of calculating stability (in our case convergence) of the solution, we contend that the above conditions are sufficient since convergence is concerned with the behavior of the solutions passing near the critical points.

2.3 Demonstration of the Convergence of the $a_i(t)$:

Theorem 1 *Consider the equations (2) through (9). Given:*

$$0 \leq Exc_i(t_0), Inh_i(t_0) \leq N \text{ and } 0 \leq a_i(t_0) \leq 1, \text{ all } i; -1 \leq m_j \leq 1, \text{ some } m_j \neq 0. \tag{10}$$

Then, under the above initial conditions, all trajectories of the RX system tend to some equilibrium point.

Proof From the definition, $Exc_i(t)$ and $Inh_i(t)$ can be shown to be bounded monotone functions [2], and therefore approach limits, LE_i and LI_i, respectively (see Buck [7], pg 26). The cases that may occur are:

$$\begin{array}{llcl} (1) & LE_i & \neq & LI_i; \\ (2a) & LE_i & = & LI_i = d_i, (d_i < N) \text{ and;} \\ (2b) & LE_i & = & LI_i = N. \end{array}$$

Case (1) By examining separately the cases where $LE_i > LI_i$ and $LI_i > LE_i$, it is easily shown that $a_i(t)$ approaches a limit in either case. (See [2].)

The remaining two cases are, (2a) in which $LE_i = LI_i = d_i < N$, and (2b) in which $LE_i = LI_i = N$. For the space of any triple, a_i, Exc_i, and Inh_i, a plane is formed by $Exc_i = Inh_i$. This is pictured in Figure 1. The line formed by the intersection of the plane with the plane $a_i = \overline{a}_i$ constitutes the ith component of a CP_L type critical point. Thus, this line forms a continuum of critical points.

The flow, in both Cases (2a) and (2b), is considered (1) outside a 2η band (η positive and small) about the plane $a_i = \overline{a}_i$ and (2) inside this band. It is not difficult to analyze what happens outside the band, but pure analysis proofs could not be obtained inside the band. Hence, within the 2η band of the $\overline{a}_i$ plane, the associated linear system was used to analyze the flow of activation.

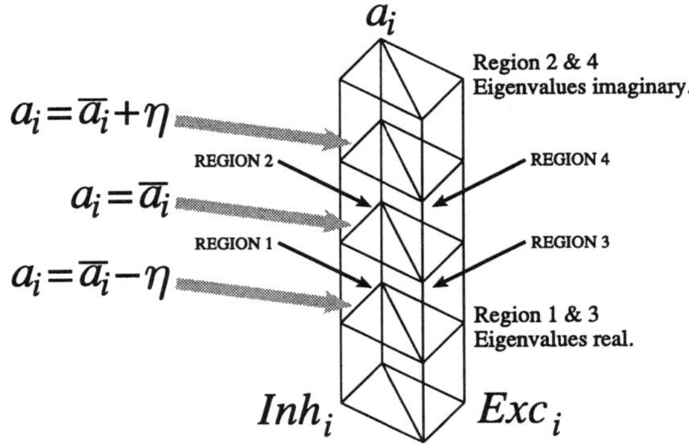

Figure 1 Details of the volume V.

Case (2a) $LE_i = LI_i = d_i$, where $0 < d_i < N$.
(1) Flow outside the 2η band. Equations (8) furnished the result of formally integrating equation (4) and equation (5). The results were:

$$Exc_i(t) = N - [N - Exc_i(t_0)] * e^{-K_1 \overline{a}_i * \int_{t_0}^{t} OUT_i(s)\,ds} \tag{11}$$

$$Inh_i(t) = N - [N - Inh_i(t_0)] * e^{-K_2 \overline{a}_i * \int_{t_0}^{t} out_i(s)\,ds} \tag{12}$$

Assume that after some time T, $a_i(t)$ remains bounded away from the $\overline{a}_i$ plane, by some arbitrarily small amount η. Therefore:

$$I_1 = \int_0^\infty OUT_i(t)\,dt = \int_0^\infty g_1|a_i - \overline{a}_i|\,dt > \int_0^\infty |g_1|_{\min}\eta\,dt \tag{13}$$

$$I_2 = \int_0^\infty out(t)\,dt = \int_0^\infty g_2|a_i - \overline{a}_i|\,dt > \int_0^\infty |g_2|_{\min}\eta\,dt. \tag{14}$$

In equation (9), g_1 is $W_{ij}/(\sum_l W_{lj}|a_l - \overline{a}_l| + \epsilon_d)$, and g_2 is

$$(\sum_{k\neq i} V_{kj}|a_l - \overline{a}_l|)/(\sum_l V_{lj}|a_l - \overline{a}_l| + \epsilon_d)$$

Not all the $a_k(t)$ may approach their $\overline{a}_k$. Were this to occur, then I_2 would approach a limit different from I_1. Therefore, LE_i would be greater than LI_i and contrary to the assumption ($LE_i = LI_i = d_i$) would not converge to d_i, contrary to hypothesis.

Under the assumption that $\sum_{k\neq i} V_{kj}|a_k(t) - \overline{a}_k| \neq 0$ we assert that, $g_2 = \mathcal{O}(g_1)$ and $g_1 = \mathcal{O}(g_2)$ ($\mathcal{O}$ stands for "order of"). That is, g_1 and g_2 are of the same order of magnitude (Olmstead [9], p141.) since they are both ratios of fractions whose denominators are not zero. The integrals I_1, and I_2 will therefore diverge and, $Exc_i(t)$ and $Inh_i(t)$ will approach N and not d_i contrary to assumption.

(2) The flow inside the 2η band. Elsewhere [2], the eigenvalues and eigenvectors of the Jacobians on each side of the $a_i(t) = \overline{a}_i$ hyperplane are calculated, and solutions of the associated linear system discussed in detail. It suffices to say that on one side of the hyperplane $a_i(t) = \overline{a}_i$, the eigenvalues are imaginary, and cause elliptical motion about the line, $Exc_i(t) = Inh_i(t)$ (at d_i), which is in the hyperplane

$a_i(t) = \overline{a}_i$. In Figure 1 the imaginary eigenvalues from the linear system characterize the motion above the $\overline{a}_i$ plane, and the real eigenvalues that below this plane. From below the $\overline{a}_i$ plane trajectories in the region where $Exc_i > Inh_i$ (called Region 1 in Figure 1) approach the $\overline{a}_i$ plane from below, and penetrate it. Above the $\overline{a}_i$ plane (Region 2 where $Exc_i > Inh_i$) trajectories travel an elliptic path about the line $Exc_i = Inh_i$ and enter Region 4, (where $Inh_i > Exc_i$). Two situations may occur. First, they may leave the η band and go far enough above it that they may not return. It is known that the integrals diverge in this region and hence $Exc_i(t)$ and $Inh_i(t)$ do not converge to d_i. Second, the trajectories may move back towards the hyperplane $a_i(t) = \overline{a}_i$. They penetrate this plane and pass through to the other side. Once beneath the $\overline{a}_i$ plane they are in Region 3, where $a_i < \overline{a}_i$, and $Inh_i > Exc_i$. The trajectory then moves away from the critical point. Since both Exc_i and Inh_i are monotone non-decreasing, once past d_i, they cannot approach this point again. Therefore, unless trajectories actually encounter a CP_L type critical point, they are driven away from it and into the region where $|a_i - \overline{a}_i| \geq \eta$. The integrals I_1 and I_2 therefore increase, and hence Exc_i and Inh_i, being monotone increasing, will exceed d_i and not approach it as a limit.

Below the $\overline{a}_i$ plane, the eigenvalues are real, but one of them is positive. Bellman, [6] (Theorem 3, p88) has shown that, under conditions which the RX equations obey, (i.e. differentiability Rudin [11], pg 189) critical points possessing positive eigenvalues are unstable. As such, CP_L type critical points are unstable equilibrium points. Instability is not a strong property, and therefore, the possibility of points approaching a CP_L type critical point cannot be dismissed. Elsewhere [2] it is demonstrated that a solution of the linear system does indeed approach $\overline{a}_i$.

We now move on to the last remaining possibility for $Exc_i(t)$ and $Inh_i(t)$: $LE_i = LI_i = N$. {Case (2b)}

(1) Flow outside the 2η band. In this case as in the preceding case it is fairly simple to show that $a_i(t)$ approaches a limit.

(2) Flow inside the 2η band. Flow inside the band is approximated by the linear system, but all trajectories are now those for which $Exc_i(t)$ and $Inh_i(t)$ are within ϵ of N. The approximating linear equations are presented in [2]. As before, the trajectories will eventually reach Region 3, where, although the constants multiplying it are small, the motion is still governed by a positive exponential and $a_i(t)$ will be directed away from $\overline{a}_i$. Thus, it would appear that when $a_i(t)$ leaves the cube of figure 1, it will approach a limit. □

We conclude by proving a lemma.

Lemma 2 *If* $\lim_{t\to\infty} Exc_i(t) = Inh_i(t) = N$, *then* $a_i(t)$ *will not attain* $\overline{a}_i$ *in finite time.*

Proof The proof is by contradiction. Assume for $t > t^*$ that $a_i(t) = \overline{a}_i$. Then, for $t > t^*$, $OUT_i(t) = out_i(t) = 0$. Therefore:

$$\int_0^\infty OUT_i(t)\,dt = \int_0^{t^*} OUT_i(t)\,dt = \alpha \qquad \int_0^\infty out_i(t)\,dt = \int_0^{t^*} out_i(t)\,dt = \beta \tag{15}$$

where α and β are finite numbers. Integrating (4) we have for a solution to $Exc_i(t)$:

$$\lim_{t\to\infty} Exc_i(t) \quad = \quad N - [N - Exc_i(t_0)]e^{-K_1\overline{a}_i \int_0^\infty OUT_i(t)\,dt}$$

$$= \quad N - [N - Exc_i(t_0)]e^{-K_1\overline{a}_i\alpha} \neq N.$$

The same can be shown for $Inh_i(t)$. □

It would appear from this lemma, and from the fact that $a_i(t)$ is very near the $\overline{a}_i$ plane, that the trajectories within the volume being considered are moving very slowly. This is to be expected since all terms are small.

We have thus shown in all three cases (1), (2a) and (2b) that all trajectories of the RX system approach limits and hence the demonstration of the convergence of $a_i(t)$ is complete.

3 Summary

The RX equations have been tested both in associative memory and control applications. In associative memory abilities, a back-propagating net's performance only slightly exceeded that of the RX net in a test involving classifying RADAR signals. In control applications a two input, one output node RX net (three neuron controller) performed as well or better than a fuzzy controller in the task of backing a truck to a loading dock. Because of the apparent biological plausibility of the three neuron controller, and the existence of elementary life forms with control circuitry yet no memory circuitry, we offer the speculation that neural memory circuitry has evolved from neural control circuitry [5]. Recall, that the RX net uses probability data as weights and that it involves no learning. In the future, we intend to study more biologically plausible versions of the RX net both in memory and control applications.

REFERENCES

[1] Ahuja S., Soh W., Schwartz A. *A Connectionist Processing Metaphor for Diagnostic Reasoning.* International Journal of Intelligent Systems, (1988).

[2] Alexander, J.R. . *An Analysis of the General Properties and Convergence of a Connectionist Model Employing Probability Data as Weights and Parameters.* PhD Dissertation (1991), University of Maryland Baltimore County, Baltimore MD.

[3] Alexander, J.R. *A Connectionist Model Employing Probability Data as Weights and Parameters.* Intelligent Engineering Systems Through Artificial Neural Networks, Vol 2. (1992), ASME Press, New York NY.

[4] Alexander, J.R. *Calculating the Centroid of a Fuzzy Logic Controller Using an Artificial Neural Net.* Intelligent Engineering Systems Through Artificial Neural Networks, Vol 3. (1993), ASME Press, New York NY.

[5] Alexander, J.R. and Bradley, J. B. *The Three Neuron Controller — History, Theoretical Foundations, and Possible Employment in Adaptive Control.* Intelligent Engineering Systems Through Artificial Neural Networks, Vol 5. (1995), ASME Press, New York NY.

[6] Bellman R. *Stability Theory of Differential Equations,* (1953), New York: McGraw-Hill.

[7] Buck R.C. *Advanced Calculus,* (1956), New York: McGraw-Hill.

[8] Hirsch M. *Convergent Activation Dynamics in Continuous Time Networks.* Neural Networks 2 (1989), pp331–349.

[9] Olmstead J.M.H. *Advanced Calculus.* (1961), New York: Appleton-Century-Crafts, Inc.

[10] Reggia J. *Virtual Lateral Inhibition in Parallel Activation Models of Associative Memory.* Proceedings Ninth International Conference on Artificial Intelligence (1985), pp 244–248.

[11] Rudin W. *Principles of Mathematical Analysis.* (1976), New York: McGraw Hill.

WEIGHTED MIXTURE OF MODELS FOR ON-LINE LEARNING

P. Edgar An

Department of Ocean Engineering,
Florida Atlantic University, Boca Raton, FL 33431, USA.

This paper proposes a weighted mixture of locally generalizing models in an attempt to resolve the trade-off between model mismatch and measurement noise given a sparse set of training samples so that the conditional mean estimation performance of the desired response can be made adequate over the input region of interest. In this architecture, each expert model has its corresponding variance model for estimating the expert's modeling performance. Parameters associated with individual expert models are adapted in the usual least-mean-square sense, weighted by its variance model output. Whereas the variance models are adapted in such a way that expert models of higher-resolution (or greater modeling capability) are discouraged to contribute, except when the local modeling performance becomes inadequate.

1 Background

Artificial neural networks have been widely used in modeling and classification applications because of their flexible nonlinear modeling capabilities over the input region of interest [3]. The merit of individual networks is generally evaluated in terms of cost criterion and learning algorithm by which the free parameters are adapted, and the characteristics of the parametric model. These networks often employ minimum sum-squared error criteria for parameter estimation such that the desired solution is a conditional mean estimator for the given data set, provided that the model is sufficiently flexible [2]. The use of such criterion not only provides a simple iterative procedure for parameter estimation but also the adaptation follows the Maximum Likelihood (ML) principle when the model uncertainty is a realization of independent Gaussian process. Nevertheless in many applications, the generalization performance which utilizes the least-square criterion breaks down when the conditional mean response is estimated using a small set of data samples with an unknown degree of noise uncertainty. This is because the LS criterion maximizes *only* the overall fitting performance defined by the data set, rather than evaluating the model mismatch in any local input region. Thus, a sufficiently flexible model often overfits undesirable noisy components in the data samples whereas a model with restricted degrees of freedom is less likely to converge to the conditional mean of the data response [4]. This paper focuses on an alternative approach in dealing with the bias/variance dilemma, which is based on a variation of the "Mixture-of-Experts" (or ME) [5].

2 Weighted Mixture of Experts (WME)

One alternative solution to the bias/variance dilemma is to incorporate a weighted mixture of expert (or WME) models so that only few experts contribute in any particular input region [5]. The internal structure in each of these experts is fixed, and a separate variance model is used, one for each expert, to evaluate its corresponding expert's performance. If the expert and variance models are chosen to be linear with respect to their adaptable parameters, the resulting learning process can be formulated as a linear optimization problem which enables rapid learning convergence.

The learning process for the WME algorithm is based on the competitive nature among experts in modeling an unknown mapping, and the overall WME output, $\hat{y}(x)$, is simply a linear combination of individual expert model outputs weighted by their variance model outputs, $\alpha_j(x)$, at x

$$\hat{y}(x) = \sum_{j=1}^{m} \frac{\exp(-\alpha_j(x))}{\sum_{k=1}^{m} \exp(-\alpha_k(x))} \hat{y}_j(x) = \sum_{j=1}^{m} p_j(x)\hat{y}_j(x) \tag{1}$$

where $\hat{y}_j(x)$ is the jth expert model output, and α_j is the corresponding variance model output (associated with the jth expert output). $p_j(x)$ can be interpreted as a local fitness measure of the jth expert modeling performance at x, and is bounded $\in [0, 1]$. The error criterion for individual expert models is defined as

$$E_y = \frac{1}{2n} \sum_{i=1}^{n} \left[\sum_{j=1}^{m} p_j(x_i)(y(x_i) - \hat{y}_j(x_i))^2 \right] \tag{2}$$

whereas the cost criterion for adapting the variance models is

$$E_\alpha = \frac{1}{n} \sum_{i=1}^{n} \left[\sum_{j=1}^{m} \lambda_j p_j(x_i) (y(x_i) - \hat{y}_j(x_i))^2 \right] \tag{3}$$

where n is the number of data samples, and $y(x_i)$ is the data output for x_i. E_y ensures that each of the experts is allowed to best approximate $y(x_i)$, weighted by $p_j(x_i)$, whereas E_α ensures that all experts are specialized in unique input regions by assigning a smaller $p_j(i)$ for a larger error variance, and vice versa. The term λ_j in (3) regulates the variance estimation among models of varying resolution so that λ_j is larger for higher-resolution experts, and vice versa. If this term was not included, the resulting adaptation would lead to a WME model consisting mainly of high-resolution experts. λ_j can thus be interpreted as a form of regularization which takes in prior knowledge about the set of experts for modeling, and can be set inversely proportional to their degrees of freedom (e.g. total number of free parameters). This criterion is thus different from that proposed in [5] as a result of this regularizing factor λ. In the case where the model structure of any expert is non-uniform across the input region of interest (such as clustering-based radial-basis-functions network), λ_j can be modified in such a way that it varies from one input segment to another.

Like in many artificial neural networks, the iterative procedure can be modified so that the adaptation is carried out sample by sample, and the corresponding cost criterion can be reduced by dropping the first summation term in (2,3). It is generally desirable to maintain equal variance model outputs prior to *on-line* learning to avoid bias toward any particular model structure, unless prior knowledge of the unknown mapping is available (e.g. $\alpha_j(\cdot) = 0$). As training proceeds, the variance models are adapted to form appropriate prior knowledge for combining the experts. These parameterized models can be chosen from a variety of existing locally-generalizing models, such as radial-basis-functions, B-Splines or Cerebellar Model Articulation Controller (or CMAC) networks. These networks are particularly well suited to the WME model implementation because their internal structures are fixed and their parameters are defined over a local region of support, thus enabling rapid learning convergence. Also, the influence of the variance model is restricted to within the local extent of the training input, and equal contribution will be assigned to regions of unseen data samples. If both variance and expert models generalize globally, the conditional mean estimation performance is likely to deteriorate considerably as a result of temporal instability.

3 Example

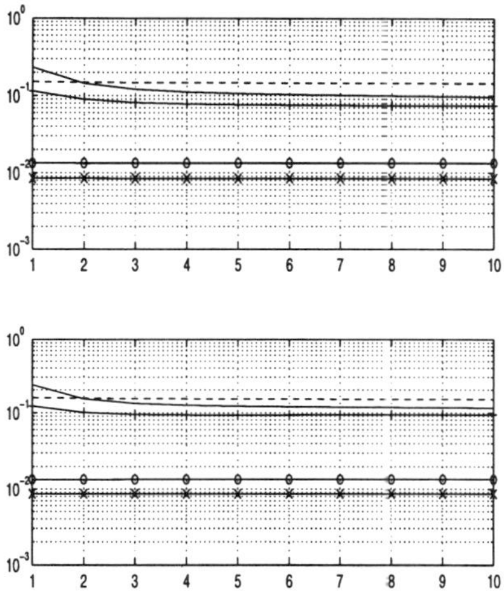

Figure 1 (a) Top: The RMS curves as a function of training cycle number for five different models averaging over 10 independent sets of 500 noiseless (randomly drawn) training samples. '–': single CMAC (C = 2); '- -': single CMAC (C = 7); '+': additive CMACs (C = 2, 7); 'o': WME CMACs (1:1 λ ratio, C = 2, 7); 'x': WME CMACs (1:3 λ ratio, C = 2, 7). (b) bottom: same RMS curves as described in (a) except that the samples are contaminated with zero-mean Gaussian noise of variance 0.1.

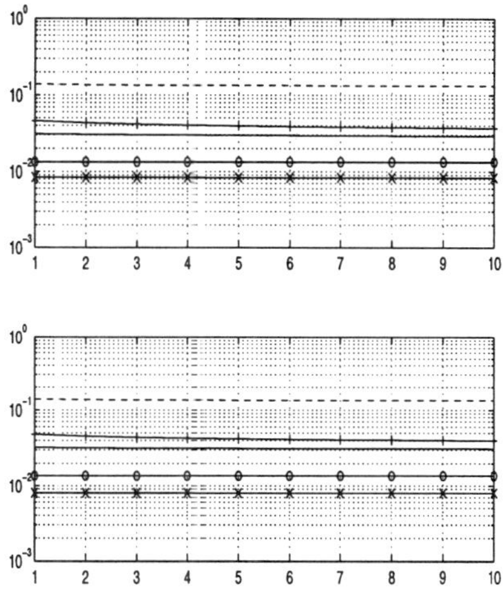

Figure 2 (a) Similar configuration to those described in Figure 1 except that each independent training set contains 5000 samples. (b) bottom: same RMS curves as described in (a) except that the samples are contaminated with zero-mean Gaussian noise of variance 0.1.

In this section, the generalization performance and implementation of the WME model are illustrated with an example using a sigmoidal function as desired surface

$$y(x_1, x_2) = 1 + 1/(1 + \exp[-100(x_1 + x_2)]) \tag{4}$$

This surface has a significant gradient along the ridge on the anti-diagonal but zero elsewhere, and thus the WME model is particularly well suited to the surface by fitting high-resolution experts near the anti-diagonal and low-resolution experts to regions with zero gradient. In this example, the WME model is based on two independent expert models, each parameterized as a form of CMAC. As a form of a generalized look-up-table, the CMAC output is a linear combination of a set of submodel's output weighted by a set of adaptable parameters. Each of the submodels is defined as a union of non-overlapping basis functions of hypercubic support on the input lattice (with the support spanning C number of cells along each input axis), and these submodels are offset relatively along the input diagonal in the standard CMAC where the generalization power is dominant. As the number of submodels is also constrained to be C, which is generally greater than 1, the entire set of basis functions associated with all submodels are thus sparsely distributed on the input lattice. The individual basis function for any input can be either binary or continuous (tapered basis function) so that its response is proportional to some chosen metric norm between the input and the support center. In addition, the layout of the submodels ensures that exactly C parameters are updated at every iteration for a given training sample. One important property of the CMAC network is that a larger C leads to a larger degree of generalization but with fewer adaptable parameters, and vice versa. Thus, the trade-off between the computational cost and modeling capability must be balanced with great care. The CMAC parameters are commonly adapted using the normalized LMS algorithm in order to facilitate fast convergence. Further detail of the CMAC modeling capability and learning convergence can be found in [3].

In the sigmoidal example, the input domains were restricted to $[-1.5, 1.5]^2$ and their submodel offsets were uniform along univariate axes (see [1] for the improved offset scheme). The nonlinear input transformation function associated with each of the parameters was chosen to be linearly tapered along each input axis, and the function output was formed using the standard product operator. The individual expert model output was self-normalized in order to produce a smoother response by minimizing bias toward any particular input region. In both expert models, each input axis was partitioned into 20 intervals, and the learning rate was initially set to 1 (decreased slowly to zero). The generalization parameters, C_1 and C_2, for both expert models (identified as y_1 and y_2) were chosen to be 7 and 2. Thus, the basis support of each cell was seven intervals wide in y_1, but only two in y_2, and there were 186 and 481 adaptable parameters in y_1 and y_2 respectively. λ_1 and λ_2 were chosen to be 1 and 3 respectively because of the approximate ratio of free parameters. The variance models, α_1 and α_2, were parameterized using the same internal structure and learning rule as those of the y_1 and y_2 respectively, but with independent parameter vectors, and the model parameters were adapted using least-mean-squares method. In addition to the WME model ($M1$), four independent models were considered as control comparisons; $M2$: single CMAC (C = 2); $M3$: single CMAC (C = 7); $M4$: additive CMACs (C = 2, 7) where p_1 and p_2 were each set to 0.5, and finally $M5$: WME but with $\lambda_1 = \lambda_2 = 1$. That is, $M2 - M4$ shared identical learning rules and input partitioning with $M1$, except the generalization width, whereas $M1$ and $M5$ were only different in λ_1 and λ_2.

Case 1: RMS Study for Sparse Training Samples

In this case study, 10 independent sets of 500 data samples $\{S1, S2, \cdots, S10\}$ were generated by uniformly randomly interrogating the sigmoidal function within the hypercubic input region $\in [-1, 1]^2$. Each of the five models was independently adapted using individual sample sequentially drawn from $S1$, and the training was carried out over ten sweeps of $S1$. Parameters of these models were then nullified, and the same run was repeated for the rest of the data sets. An expected root-mean-square (RMS) generalization error curve as a function of training cycle was then generated using 3000 independent testing samples for the five models by averaging the individual RMS performance over the ten data sets. Figure 1a shows the corresponding RMS curves for these models, and Figure 1b shows the similar curves except that the same set of training samples were contaminated with additive Gaussian noise of variance 0.1. It is interesting to observe that $M1$ and $M5$ performed significantly better than the single and additive CMACs (of fixed-$p_{1,2}$), indicating the importance of estimating the variance from the data samples. Also, $M1$ provides a better RMS fit as compared to $M5$, suggesting that the use of λ can be tuned to provide optimal resource sharing. Similar RMS curves for the first 500 training samples averaged over the ten runs also indicated similar profiles as compared to those in Figure 1, suggesting that the WME model consistently performed better than the other four models for on-line learning [1]. More work needs to be investigated on the choice of λ.

Case 2: RMS Study for Abundant Training Samples

In this case study, 10 independent sets of 5000 data samples were instead generated using the identical method described above, and the same procedure was carried out to form the expected RMS curves for the five models. Figure 2a shows the corresponding curves using noiseless samples whereas Figure 2b shows the similar curves using noisy samples. It can be observed that except $M3$ which had almost the same RMS characteristics as those shown in case 1, the modeling performances among the four models were relatively closer, suggesting that for more abundant training samples and sufficient modeling capability, the process for estimating the variance becomes less critical, as expected. Note that for all the RMS curves, noise overfitting problem was not observed because of the diminishing learning rate for adaptation, which can be interpreted as a form of regularization, and is conceptually similar to early-stop training approach [6].

Case 3: Surface Evaluation

To visualize the modeling performance, Figure 3 shows the individual model outputs evaluated at every point of a 50 X 50 grid after 10 training cycles (1 run) using a single set of 500 noisy training samples. The rough surface of $M2$ was due to the smaller local support (less noise averaging) and sparse training samples (insufficient generalization), as opposed to that of $M3$. By estimating the variance over the input region of interest, the surface reconstruction was comparatively better, as compared to that of $M4$. Also, the relative weighting surfaces of p_1 and p_2 of $M1$ were found to follow closely the relative gradient of the sigmoidal surface, as desired.

4 Conclusion

The validity of the WME model is based on the assumption that the conditional mean estimation is the desired learning objective, and the proposed architecture makes use of variance models which estimate the error variance for their expert models, and assign less weighting to those expert models with larger variance. The estimation performance is adapted using a given set of training data, and the set of variance models evolves to form the desired prior in choosing an appropriate set of expert models. It is intuitive that in order for each and every expert to excel in different input regions, their model structures must be unique otherwise the

[1] Results were omitted for space reason.

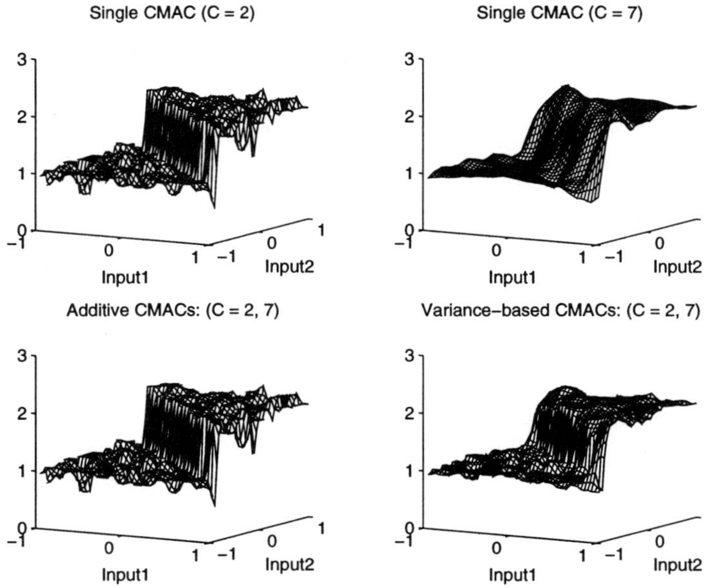

Figure 3 Surface reconstruction after 10 training cycles of iterations using four different models and a single set of 500 noisy training samples. (a) top left: single CMAC (C = 2); (b) top right: single CMAC (C = 7); (c) bottom left: additive CMACs (C = 2, 7); (d) bottom right: WME CMACs (1:3 λ ratio, C = 2, 7).

bias/variance dilemma issue will remain unresolved. Having unique internal expert structures also facilitates implicit model selection problems such that one does not need to search for an *optimal* structure for a single model. It would appear that having a mixture of experts increases the total number of free parameters for optimization, and the resulting network will not be parsimonous. Quite differently, the objective is not to reduce the number of physical parameters, as advocated in many proposed architectures, but rather to reduce the number of effective parameters, governed by the variance models, in such a way that the WME model can be more robust with respect to noise and model mismatch.

REFERENCES

[1] An P.E., Miller W.T., Parks P.C. *Design Improvements in Associative Memories for Cerebellar Model Articulation Controllers (CMAC)*, Proc. Intl. Conf. on Artificial Neural Networks, Helsinki, North Holland, Vol.2 (1991), pp.1207-1210.

[2] Bishop C. *Mixture Density Networks*, Neural Computing Research Group Report NCRG/4288 (1994), Department of Computer Science, Aston University, UK.

[3] Brown M., Harris C.J. NeuroFuzzy Adaptive Modelling and Control (1994), Prentice-Hall.

[4] Geman S., Bienenstock E. *Neural Networks and the Bias/Variance Dilemma*, Neural Computation, Vol. 4 (1992), pp.1-58.

[5] Jacobs R., Jordan M., Nowlan S., Hinton G. *Adaptive Mixtures of Local Experts*, Neural Computation, Vol. 3 (1991), pp.79-87.

[6] Sjoberg J., Ljung L. *Overtraining, Regularization, and Searching for Minimum in Neural Networks*, the 4th IFAC Symposium on Adaptive Systems in Control and Signal Processing, France, (1992) pp.669-674.

LOCAL MODIFICATIONS TO RADIAL BASIS NETWORKS

I. J. Anderson

School of Computing and Mathematics, University of Huddersfield, Queensgate, Huddersfield HD1 3DH, UK.

The form of a radial basis network is a linear combination of translates of a given radial basis function, $\phi(r)$. The radial basis method involves determining the values of the unknown parameters within the network given a set of inputs, $\{\mathbf{x}_k\}$, and their corresponding outputs, $\{f_k\}$. It is usual for some of the parameters of the network to be fixed. If the positions of the centres of the basis functions are known and constant, the radial basis problem reduces to a standard linear system of equations and many techniques are available for calculating the values of the unknown coefficients efficiently. However, if both the positions of the centres and the values of the coefficients are allowed to vary, the problem becomes considerably more difficult. A highly non-linear problem is produced and solved in an iterative manner. An initial guess for the best positions of the centres is made and the coefficients for this particular choice of centres are calculated as before. For each iteration, a small change to the position of the centres is made in order to improve the quality of the network and the values of the coefficients for these new centre positions are determined. The overall algorithm is computationally expensive and here we consider ways of improving the efficiency of the method by exploiting the local stability of the thin plate spline basis function. At each step of the iteration, only a small change is made to the positions of the centres and so we can reasonably expect that there is only a small change to the values of the corresponding coefficients. These small changes are estimated using *local modifications*.

1 Introduction

We consider the thin plate spline basis function

$$\phi(r) = r^2 \log r.$$

This basis function has not been as popular as the Gaussian, $\phi(r) = \exp(-r^2/2\sigma)$, mainly due to its unbounded nature. The thinking behind this is that it is desirable to use a basis function that has near compact support so that the approximating function behaves in a local manner.

A suitable definition of local behaviour for an approximating function of the form given in equation (1) is as follows. The ith coefficient, c_i, of the approximant should be related to the values $\{f_k\}$ for values of k where $\|\mathbf{x}_k - \boldsymbol{\lambda}_i\|$ is small. Thus, the value of the coefficient should be influenced only by the data ordinates whose abscissae values are close to the centre of the corresponding basis function. From this definition one deduces that it is advisable to use basis functions that decay, hence the desire for basis functions with near compact support. However many authors have shown that this deduction is unfounded and it is in fact easier to produce the properties of local behaviour by using unbounded functions [4, 2, 3, 1].

1.1 The Approximation Problem

Given a set of m data points, $(\mathbf{x}_k, f_k)$, for $k = 1, 2, \ldots, m$, it is possible to produce an approximation of the form

$$f(\mathbf{x}) = \sum_{i=1}^{n} c_i \phi(\|\mathbf{x} - \boldsymbol{\lambda}_i\|), \tag{1}$$

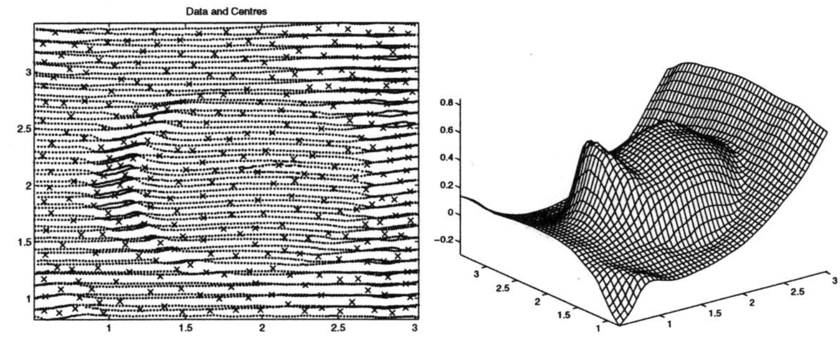

Figure 1 The positions of the data abscissae and the centres of the basis functions, and the surface approximant to the data.

such that

$$f(\mathbf{x}_k) \approx f_k.$$

It is usual for this approximation problem to be solved in the least-squares sense. There are two important categories for such an approximation. The easiest approach is to consider the positions of the centres to be fixed, in which case the approximation problem is linear and is therefore reasonably efficient to solve. The alternative is to allow the positions of the centres to vary or indeed for the number of centres to change. For example, once a preliminary approximation has been completed it is worth examining the results to determine the quality of the approximation. It may be decided that one (or more) regions are unsatisfactory and so extra basis functions or an adjustment of the centres of the current basis functions would be suitable.

Under such circumstances it is usual to recalculate the new coefficients for the approximation problem with respect to the new positions of the centres. Repeating this process too often can be computationally expensive and it is more appropriate to modify the current approximation to take into account the small changes that have been made to the centres.

2 Local Stability of the Thin Plate Spline

This local behaviour of the thin plate spline is demonstrated by the use of an example that consists of approximating $m = 6{,}864$ data points using $n = 320$ basis functions. The centres for these basis functions are produced using a clustering algorithm and the data are fitted in the least-squares sense. Formally, let I be the set of indices for the basis functions, $\{1, 2, \ldots, n\}$. We wish to calculate the values of the coefficients $\{c_i\}$ that minimize the ℓ_2-norm of the residual vector $\mathbf{e}$ which has the components

$$e_k = f_k - \sum_{i \in I} c_i \phi(\|\mathbf{x} - \boldsymbol{\lambda}_i\|),$$

for $k = 1, 2, \ldots, m$. The data, centres and the resulting approximant are shown in Figure 1.

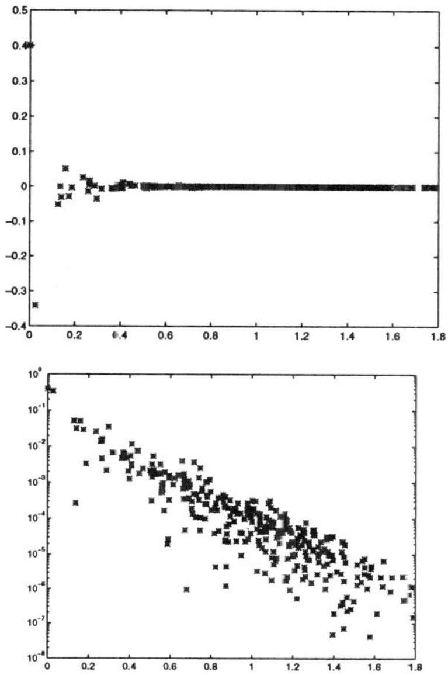

Figure 2 The differences in the coefficients between the two approximants as a function of distance. Standard and logarithmic axes are shown.

Let $j \in I$ be the index for one of the centres. We now perturb this centre by a small amount, $\boldsymbol{\delta}$, such that we produce a new centre;

$$\boldsymbol{\lambda}_j^* = \boldsymbol{\lambda}_j + \boldsymbol{\delta}.$$

All of the other centres are left undisturbed. That is $\boldsymbol{\lambda}_i^* = \boldsymbol{\lambda}_i$ for $i \in I, i \neq j$. Again the data are fitted in the least-squares sense but this time we use the new set of centres, $\{\boldsymbol{\lambda}_i^*\}$. Thus we calculate the values of the coefficients c_i^*, for each $i \in I$, that minimize the ℓ_2-norm of the residual vector $\mathbf{e}^*$ which has the components

$$e_k^* = f_k - \sum_{i \in I} c_i^* \phi(\|\mathbf{x} - \boldsymbol{\lambda}_i^*\|),$$

for $k = 1, 2, \ldots, m$. The two approximants are visually indistinguishable and so we compare the coefficients of the respective fits.

Let d_i be the distance between the centre of the ith basis function and the position of the perturbed centre, $d_i = \|\boldsymbol{\lambda}_i^* - \boldsymbol{\lambda}_j^*\|$. Figure 2 shows the differences between the respective coefficients, $\{(c_i - c_i^*)\}$ of the two fits against the distances $\{d_i\}$. Also shown is the logarithm of the absolute values of the differences between the respective coefficients against the same set of distances.

It can be seen that the differences between the coefficients decay exponentially as the distance between the corresponding centre and the perturbation increases. It is in this sense that we say that the thin plate spline behaves locally.

3 Exploiting the Local Behaviour

Since the effects of perturbing the position of a given centre are only noticeable for the coefficients which correspond to basis functions that are centred in the neighbourhood of the perturbed centre, it seems reasonable that we should be able to retrain the network with these new centre positions by using only the basis functions from this neighbourhood. The coefficients for the other basis functions can be left unchanged on the assumption that they will not be affected by a significant amount. By using only a small number of centres we can expect this local approximation to be significantly faster than the global approach which uses all of the centres.

We adopt an iterative refinement type approach. First we choose to use a given number, q, of basis functions whose centres are nearest to the position of the new perturbed centre. Let $I^* \subset I$ be the set of indices for these q basis functions. Then we calculate the residuals between the original function values and the current estimate for the approximating function. This current estimate is based on the best approximant using the original positions of the centres, but with the basis functions for the new positions of the centres,

$$e_k^* = f_k - \sum_{i \in I} c_i \phi(\|\mathbf{x} - \boldsymbol{\lambda}_i^*\|).$$

We wish to approximate these residuals using the approximating form

$$\sum_{i \in I^*} \delta c_i^* \phi(\|\mathbf{x} - \boldsymbol{\lambda}_i^*\|).$$

This approximation is again done in the least-squares sense. This produces a "correction surface" that we combine with the current estimate for the approximant in order to produce an updated estimate (or combined surface) for the required approximant. The new approximant has the coefficients

$$c_i^{(\text{new})} = \begin{cases} c_i + \delta c_i^* & i \in I^*, \\ c_i & i \notin I^*. \end{cases}$$

The experiment is repeated for various values of q and the results are discussed below.

3.1 Choice of the Data Subset

If we use all of the data and therefore all of the residuals, we find that the resulting correction surface is flat in nature and the local variation around the position of the perturbation has been largely ignored. The reason for this phenomenon is that we are treating each of the data points with equal importance and since there are many more data outside the neighbourhood of interest than the number inside, the former group of data tend to dominate the approximation.

Since we are only using the basis functions that are local to the position of the perturbation, it seems reasonable to use only the data that lie in the neighbourhood of interest. Unfortunately this too has a problem in that we are effectively assigning no importance to the "far-away" data points and so the approximation has a tendency to behave in an uncontrolled manner away from the neighbourhood, in much the same way that the basis functions are uncontrolled.

As a compromise we use a subset of data that consists of all of the data points that are close to the perturbation and a few data points that are sampled randomly from the remainder of the data domain. In the example that we are considering 512 data points were used for the local subset and 512 data points were used to represent the remainder of the domain. By doing this we wish to give more importance to the local data while still considering the global effect of the correction approximant. An advantage that accrues from this approach is that the local approximation uses fewer data points than the global method and so we can expect the speed of calculating the approximation to be significantly faster.

4 Concluding Remarks

Various values for q were chosen and the local modifications were calculated. The value of the square root of the mean of the squares of the errors (R.M.S.) between all of the original ordinates and the values of the combined surface at the data points produced using the global approach was 7.50×10^{-3} which took about 2,870 seconds to calculate, and the R.M.S. value for the current approximation with the new centres was 15.73×10^{-3}. By applying the local modification, using $q = 7$ an R.M.S. value of 7.52×10^{-3} was obtained in less than three tenths of a second.
Clearly it can be seen that an excellent improvement in the R.M.S. value can be achieved using only a very small number of basis functions. The required fit has been achieved to within an accuracy of one per cent in approximately one ten thousandth of the time needed by the global approach. Visually, there is no difference between the approximations produced by a) the global approach and b) the local modification method.
Future work in this area would concentrate on the following areas.

- Convergence. Since each iteration is so much faster than the global approach we can afford to use the technique many times, using different sets of basis functions. However it would be necessary to confirm that such an approach would continually refine and improve the quality of the approximation.

- No attempt has been made to optimize the size or the positions of the subset of data used for the local modification. It is envisaged that a small but significant improvement in the quality of the approach could be made using such a technique.

- Similarly the size and position of the subset of centres could be optimized. Particular attention could be directed towards the effects of larger perturbations and/or several small perturbations.

REFERENCES

[1] I. J. Anderson. *Local modifications to radial basis networks.* Technical Report RR9505, School of Computing and Mathematics, University of Huddersfield, Huddersfield, UK, (1995).

[2] M. D. Buhmann and C. K. Chui. *A note on the local stability of translates of radial basis functions.* Journal of Approximation Theory, Vol. 74 (1993), pp36–40.

[3] J. Levesley. *Local stability of translates of polyharmonic splines in even space dimension.* Numer. Funct. Anal. and Optimiz., Vol.15 (1994) pp327–333.

[4] M. J. D. Powell. *Radial basis function approximations to polynomials.* In D. F. Griffiths and G. A. Watson, editors, Numerical Analysis, (1987), pp 223–241. Longman Scientific and Technical, 1988.

Acknowledgements

The author wishes to thank C. K. Pink for his comments on earlier drafts of this paper, and also the Department of Conservative Dentistry in the Dental School at the London Hospital Medical College for supplying the data.

A STATISTICAL ANALYSIS OF THE MODIFIED NLMS RULES

E.D. Aved'yan, M. Brown* and C.J. Harris*

Russian Academy of Sciences, Institute of Control Sciences, 65 Profsoyuznaya str., Moscow 117342, Russia. Email: avedyan@dep07.ics.msk.su

**ISIS research group, Dept of Electronics and Computer Science, Southampton University, Highfield, Southampton, SO17 1BJ, UK. Email: mqb@ecs.soton.ac.uk*

This paper analyses the statistical convergence properties of the modified NLMS rules which were formulated in an attempt to produce more robust and faster converging training algorithms. However, the statistical analysis described in this paper leads us to the conjecture that the standard NLMS rule is the only *unconditionally stable* modified NLMS training algorithm, and that the optimal value of the learning rate and region of convergence for the modified NLMS rules is generally less than for the standard NLMS rule.

1 Adaptive Systems and the NLMS Algorithm

Nonlinear networks, such as the Cerebellar Model Articulation Controller (CMAC), Radial Basis Functions (RBF) and B-splines have an "output layer" of linear parameters that can be directly trained using any of the linear learning algorithms that have been developed over the past 40 years. So consider a linear in its parameter vector network of the form:

$$\begin{aligned} y(t) &= \sum_{i=1}^{n} x_i(t)\, w_i(t-1) \\ &= \mathbf{x}^T(t)\, \mathbf{w}(t-1) \end{aligned} \tag{1}$$

where $y(t)$ is the system's output, $\mathbf{w}(t-1) = (w_1(t-1), \ldots, w_n(t-1))$ is the n-dimensional weight vector and $\mathbf{x}(t) = (x_1(t), \ldots, x_n(t))$ is the n-dimensional transformed input vector at time t. This "input" vector $\mathbf{x}$ could possibly be a nonlinear transformation of the network's original input measurements. For a linear system described by equation 1, the Normalised Least Mean Squares (NLMS) learning algorithm for a single training sample $\{\mathbf{x}(t), \widehat{y}(t)\}$ is given by:

$$\Delta\mathbf{w}(t) = \mu \frac{\epsilon_y(t)}{\|\mathbf{x}(t)\|_2^2}\, \mathbf{x}(t) \tag{2}$$

where $\Delta\mathbf{w}(t) = \mathbf{w}(t) - \mathbf{w}(t-1)$ is the weight vector update, $\epsilon_y(t) = (\widehat{y}(t) - y(t))$ is the output error, $\widehat{y}(t)$ is the desired network output at time t and $\mu \in [0, 2]$ is the learning rate. This simple learning rule has a long history, as it was originally derived by Kaczmarz in 1937 [6] and was re-derived numerous times in the adaptive control [7] and neural network literature. When the training data are generated by an equivalent model with an unknown "optimal" parameter vector $\widehat{\mathbf{w}}$ (i.e. there is no modelling error or measurement noise), the NLMS algorithm possesses the property that:

$$\|\epsilon_{\mathrm{w}}(t)\|_2 \leq \|\epsilon_{\mathrm{w}}(t-1)\|_2 \tag{3}$$

where $\epsilon_{\mathrm{w}}(t) = \widehat{\mathbf{w}} - \mathbf{w}(t)$ is the weight error at time t. Hence the estimates of the weight vector approach (monotonically) the true values and this learning rule has many other desirable properties [3].

2 Modified NLMS algorithms

In 1971, a set of Modified NLMS (MNLMS) algorithms was proposed by Aved'yan [1, 2] and they were again rediscovered over 20 years later by Douglas [5]. The MNLMS learning algorithms are derived from the two conditions:

$$\text{Find } \mathbf{w}(t) \text{ such that: } \quad \widehat{y}(t) = \mathbf{x}^T(t)\mathbf{w}(t) \quad \text{and} \quad \|\Delta \mathbf{w}(t)\|_p \text{ is minimised.} \tag{4}$$

for different values of p where $1 \leq p < \infty$.

These instantaneous learning rules are based on generating a new search direction by minimising an alternative norm in weight space, and three special cases which are worthy of attention are the 1, 2 and ∞-norms. The 2-norm corresponds to the standard NLMS rule which is denoted by **std NLMS**, but the L_1 learning algorithm is:

$$\Delta w_i(t) = \mu \frac{\epsilon_y(t)}{x_k(t)} \delta_{i,k} \tag{5}$$

where $k = \arg\max_i |x_i(t)|$, and this will be referred to as the **max NLMS** rule. The L_∞ training rule is given by:

$$\Delta \mathbf{w}(t) = \mu \frac{\epsilon_y(t)\text{sgn}(\mathbf{x}(t))}{\|\mathbf{x}(t)\|_1} \tag{6}$$

and this will be referred to as the **sgn NLMS** rule [7]. It is fairly simple to show that the *a posteriori* output error is always zero for these learning rules (with $\mu = 1$), so the only difference between them is how they search the weight space. The max NLMS algorithm always updates the weight vector parallel to an axis, and the sgn NLMS rule causes the weight vector update to be at 45° to an axis. This is in contrast to the std NLMS training procedure which always projects the weight vector perpendicularly onto the solution hyperplane generated by the training data [6].

3 A Statistical Analysis

A deterministic analysis of the MNLMS rules has already been completed and it is shown in [4] that certain finite training sets can cause unstable learning in the linear network for the sgn and max NLMS rules, irrespective of the size of the (non-zero) learning rate. The statistical analysis of the MNLMS rules in this paper is based on a model of the input vector where all components are mutually independent random processes with zero mean values, each of which is a sequence of independent identically symmetric distributed random variables. This proivdes the conditions of convergence for the modified algorithms, the optimal value of the learning rate, and the influence of a noise and the mean value of the input process on the convergence conditions.

3.1 Convergence

The process $\mathbf{w}(t)$ converges (in the statistical mean-square sense) to the optimal weight vector, $\widehat{\mathbf{w}}$, if it satisfies the condition $\lim_{t\to\infty} E\left(\epsilon_{\mathbf{w}}^T(t)\epsilon_{\mathbf{w}}(t)\right) = 0$, where $E\,()$ denotes the statistical expectation operator. The convergence depends greatly on the properties of the input process $\mathbf{x}(t)$, for instance the standard NLMS algorithm does not converge to its optimal values, when the process $\mathbf{x}(t)$ quickly settles to a constant value or when it is varies very slowly: the input signal is not *persistently exciting.* This situation is even worse for both the max and sgn NLMS algorithms as they search a restricted section of the parameter space and an optimal solution for the training date does not always lie in this region [3].

It is possible to write the Euclidean squared norm of the error in the weight vector $\epsilon_{\mathrm{w}}^T(t)\epsilon_{\mathrm{w}}(t)$ as:

$$\epsilon_{\mathrm{w}}^T(t)\epsilon_{\mathrm{w}}(t) = \epsilon_{\mathrm{w}}^T(t-1)\left(\mathbf{I} - \mu\frac{\mathbf{x}(t)\mathbf{s}^T(t)}{\mathbf{x}^T(t)\mathbf{s}(t)} - \mu\frac{\mathbf{s}(t)\mathbf{x}^T(t)}{\mathbf{x}^T(t)\mathbf{s}(t)} + \mu^2\frac{\mathbf{x}(t)\mathbf{s}^T(t)\mathbf{s}(t)\mathbf{x}^T(t)}{(\mathbf{x}^T(t)\mathbf{s}(t))^2}\right)\epsilon_{\mathrm{w}}(t-1)x \quad (7)$$

where $\mathbf{s}(t)$ is the current search direction for the different learning rules, when the training data contain no measurment or modelling errors.

Let us denote by $V^2(t) = E\left(\epsilon_{\mathrm{w}}^T(t)\epsilon_{\mathrm{w}}(t)\right)$ the statistical expectation of the Euclidean squared norm of the error in the weight vectors in equation 7. Taking into account the statistical properties of the input vector $\mathbf{x}(t)$ and the fact that the trace of each matrix in these equations is equal to one, it is possible to generate first-order relations:

$$V_*^2(t) = \left(1 - 2n^{-1}\mu + \beta_*\mu^2\right)V_*^2(t-1) \quad (8)$$

where a $*$ is used instead of std, sgn and max, and:

$$\beta_{\mathrm{std}} = n^{-1} \quad (9)$$

$$\beta_{\mathrm{sgn}} = E\left(\frac{\mathbf{x}^T(t)\mathbf{x}(t)}{(\mathbf{x}^T(t)\mathrm{sgn}(\mathbf{x}(t)))^2}\right) \quad (10)$$

$$\beta_{\max} = n^{-1}E\left(\frac{\mathbf{x}^T(t)\mathbf{x}(t)}{x_k^2(t)}\right) \quad (11)$$

For these parameters we have the following inequalities:

$$n^{-1} \le \beta_{\mathrm{sgn}} \le 1 \quad (12)$$

$$n^{-1} \le \beta_{\max} \le 1 \quad (13)$$

The value of the parameters β_{sgn} and $\beta_{\max}$ depends on the probability distribution function of the vector $\mathbf{x}(t)$ and can be calculated analytically in the special cases shown below.

From equation 8, it follows that not only are the convergence conditions for the std, sgn and max NLMS algorithms, respectively:

$$0 < q_* = \left(1 - 2n^{-1}\mu + \beta_*\mu^2\right) < 1 \quad (14)$$

but also the optimal value of the learning rate $\widehat{\mu}$ by which values of $q_{\mathrm{std}}, q_{\mathrm{sgn}}$ and $q_{\max}$ are minimal:

$$\widehat{\mu}_* = (n\beta_*)^{-1} \quad (15)$$

and consequently:

$$\widehat{q}_* = \left(1 - \beta_* n^{-1}\right) \quad (16)$$

These values determine the convergence time of the respective algorithms, and:

$$\mu_{\mathrm{sgn}}^* \le \mu_{\mathrm{std}}^* = 1 \quad (17)$$

$$\mu_{\max}^* \le \mu_{\mathrm{std}}^* = 1 \quad (18)$$

$$q_{\mathrm{sgn}}^* \ge q_{\mathrm{std}}^* = \left(1 - n^{-1}\right) \quad (19)$$

$$q_{\max}^* \ge q_{\mathrm{std}}^* = \left(1 - n^{-1}\right) \quad (20)$$

Hence it follows that optimal value of the learning rate and the region of convergence for the sgn and max NLMS rules are less than for the std NLMS rule, and that the convergence time for the std NLMS rule is less than for the other sgn and max NLMS rules. However, it is possible to get the analytical expression for β in equations 10 and 11 in certain special cases.

When $x_i(t)$ has a *Laplace* distribution: $p(x_i) = \alpha^{-1}\exp\left(-|x_i|/\alpha\right)$, then $\beta_{\text{sgn}} = 2/(n+1)$ and $\widehat{\mu}_{\text{sgn}} = (n+1)/2n$ for the sgn NLMS rule. The corresponding region of convergence is equal to $0 < \mu_{\max} < (n+1)$ in contrast with the std NLMS rule where $0 < \mu_{\text{std}} < 2$. Hence, for large n, the convergence rate of the sgn NLMS rule is approximately twice as large as the std NLMS rule.

When $x_i(t)$ has a *uniform* distribution $p(x_i) = 1/2\alpha$, $|x_i| < \alpha$, then $\beta_{\max} = (n+2)/3n$, and $\widehat{\mu}_{\max} = 3/(n+2)$. The corresponding region of convergence is $0 < \mu_{\max} < 6/(n+2)$ and it follows that for large n, the time of convergence of the std NLMS rule is equal to cn where c is a constant whereas for the max NLMS rule this time is equal to $cn(n+2)/3$.

These examples shows that the std NLMS rule has a larger convergence rate when compared with the sgn and the max NLMS algorithm for these *specific* input distributions. The MNLMS rules therefore represent a tradeoff between computational simplicity and stability/convergence rate.

3.2 The Influence of Noise

Assuming that the output data are corrupted with an additive, statistically independent, white noise sequence $\xi(k)$, with variance σ_ξ^2, and that the input vector has the same statistical properties as were mentioned above, then:

$$V_*^2(t) = (1 - 2n\mu + \beta_*\mu^2)V_*^2(t-1) + \mu^2\sigma_\xi^2 d_* \tag{21}$$

where the disturbance terms d_* are given by:

$$d_{\text{std}} = E\left(\left(\mathbf{x}^T(t)\mathbf{x}(t)\right)^{-1}\right) \tag{22}$$

$$d_{\text{sgn}} = nE\left(\left(\mathbf{x}^T(t)\text{sgn}(\mathbf{x}(t))\right)^{-1}\right) \tag{23}$$

$$d_{\max} = E\left(\left|x_k^{-1}(t)\right|\right) \tag{24}$$

Comparing equations 8 and 21, it follows that if the convergence conditions for the std, sgn and max NLMS algorithms (see inequality 14) remain constant, then after a transient period, the variance equals:

$$V_{\text{std}}^2 = n\sigma_\xi^2\frac{\mu}{2-\mu} \tag{25}$$

$$V_{\text{sgn}}^2 = n\sigma_\xi^2 d_{\text{sgn}}\frac{\mu}{2-\beta_{\text{sgn}}\mu n} \tag{26}$$

$$V_{\max}^2 = n\sigma_\xi^2 d_{\max}\frac{\mu}{2-\beta_{\max}\mu n} \tag{27}$$

After the initial "transient" convergence, the mean value of the process $\mathbf{w}(t)$ will be equal to $\widehat{\mathbf{w}}$ and the weight vector will "jitter" around the mean value with a variance given in equations 25-27. This region of convergence was termed a *minimal capture zone* by Parks and Militzer [8]. For a specific input distribution, the size of the minimal capture zone can be made arbitrary small by choosing a small learning rate, μ, but this would also decrease the rate of convergence.

3.3 The Influence of Mean Value of the Input Process

The presence of the mean value in the input vector decreases the rate of convergence for all these algorithms. For the std NLMS algorithm, the presence of non zero mean value, m_x, in the input vector increases the time of convergence approximately $(1 + m_x^2/\sigma_x)$ times in comparison with the case when the mean value is zero. Hence, it is desirable to both centralise the input vector and also transform it such that all components of the vector have the same variances.

3.4 Simulation and Discussion

The simulation, shown in Figure 1, illustrates the dynamical evolution of the Euclidean norm of the error in the weight vector for these algorithms. In this figure, the learning rates are set to their near-optimal values derived above. The adaptive system has 5 inputs, the optimal weight vector is $\widehat{\mathbf{w}} = (0.22, 0.32, 0.42, 0.53, 0.63)$ and the random, Gaussian input vector has the statistical properties described above and these results support the theoretical conclusions.

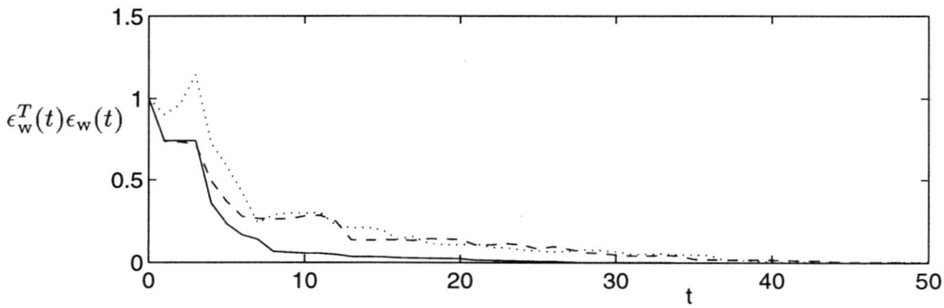

Figure 1 The evolution of the magnitude of the error in the weight vector when it is trained using the std NLMS rule (solid line), sgn NLMS rule (dashed line) and the max NLMS rule (dotted line), with $\mu_{\mathrm{std}} = 1$ and $\mu_{\mathrm{sgn}} = \mu_{\mathrm{max}} = 0.5$.

The MNLMS rules were originally proposed as a computationally efficient method for increasing the rate of convergence of the NLMS algorithm as they search weight space in orthogonal directions. However, this has serious implications for the stability and rate of convergence of these instantaneous algorithms as has been pointed out in this paper. For any network with 3 or more coefficients, the MNLMS procedures could potentially be unstable and their persistently exciting conditions are more severe than the standard NLMS rule.

REFERENCES

[1] E.D. Aved'yan, *Bestimmung der Parameter linearer Modelle stationärer und instationärer Strecken*, Messen, Steuern, Regeln, Vol.14:9 (1971) 348–350.

[2] E.D. Aved'yan, *Learning Systems*, Springer Verlag, London, UK, (1995).

[3] M. Brown and C. Harris, *Neurofuzzy Adaptive Modelling and Control*, Prentice Hall, Hemel-Hempstead, UK, (1994).

[4] M. Brown and P.E. An and C.J. Harris, *A Stability Analysis of the Modified NLMS Rules*, submitted to IEEE Trans. Signal Processing, (1995).

[5] S.C. Douglas, *A Family of Normalised LMS Algorithms*, IEEE Signal Processing Letters, Vol.1:3 (1994) pp49–51.

[6] S. Kaczmarz, *Angenäherte Auflösung von Systemen Linearer Gleichungen*, Bull. Int. Acad. Pol. Sci. Lett and Cl. Sci. Math. Nat. Ser. A., (1937) pp355–357.
[7] J.I. Nagumo and A. Noda, *A Learning Method for System Identification*, IEEE Trans. Automatic Control, Vol.12:3 (1967) pp282–287.
[8] P.C. Parks and J. Militzer, *Convergence Properties of Associative Memory Storage for Learning Control Systems*, Automation and Remote Control, Vol. 50:2 (1989) 254–286.

Acknowledgements

The authors gratefully acknowledge the financial support of Lucas aerospace during the preparation of this manuscript and Dr Aved'yan also acknowledges the financial support of the Fundamental Research Foundation of Russia, grant 93-012-448. He also wishes to thank the Royal Society of London for their support through a joint project on "Overall Behaviour of Adaptive Control Systems Using Neural Networks for Identification or Learning", (1993-1996), Ref. No. 638072.P622.
This paper is dedicated to the memory of Patrick Parks.

FINITE SIZE EFFECTS IN ON-LINE LEARNING OF MULTI-LAYER NEURAL NETWORKS.

David Barber, Peter Sollich* and David Saad

Dept. Comp, Sci. and Appl. Maths., Aston University, Birmingham B4 7ET, UK. Web: http://www.ncrg.aston.ac.uk/

** Department of Physics, University of Edinburgh, Mayfield Road, Edinburgh EH9 3JZ, UK.*

We extend the recent progress in thermodynamic limit analyses of mean on-line gradient descent learning dynamics in multi-layer networks by calculating the fluctuations possessed by finite dimensional systems. Fluctuations from the mean dynamics are largest at the onset of specialisation as student hidden unit weight vectors begin to imitate specific teacher vectors, and increase with the degree of symmetry of the initial conditions. Including a term to stimulate asymmetry in the learning process typically significantly decreases finite size effects and training time.

Recent advances in the theory of on-line learning have yielded insights into the training dynamics of multi-layer neural networks. In *on-line learning*, the *weights* parametrizing the *student* network are updated according to the error on a single example from a stream of examples, $\{\boldsymbol{\xi}^\mu, \tau(\boldsymbol{\xi}^\mu)\}$, generated by a *teacher* network $\tau(\cdot)$[1]. The analysis of the resulting weight dynamics has previously been treated by assuming an infinite input dimension (*thermodynamic limit*) such that a mean dynamics analysis is exact[2]. We present a more realistic treatment by calculating corrections to the mean dynamics induced by finite dimensional inputs[3].
We assume that the *teacher* network the student attempts to learn is a *soft committee machine*[1] of N inputs, and M hidden units, this being a one hidden layer network with weights connecting each hidden to output unit set to $+1$, and with each hidden unit n connected to all input units by $\mathbf{B}_n (n = 1..M)$. Explicitly, for the N dimensional training input vector $\boldsymbol{\xi}^\mu$, the output of the teacher is given by,

$$\zeta^\mu = \sum_{n=1}^{M} g(\mathbf{B}_n \cdot \boldsymbol{\xi}^\mu), \tag{1}$$

where $g(x)$ is the activation function of the hidden units, and we take $g(x) = \mathrm{erf}(x/\sqrt{2})$. The teacher generates a stream of training examples $(\boldsymbol{\xi}^\mu, \zeta^\mu)$, with input components drawn from a normal distribution of zero mean, unit variance. The *student* network that attempts to learn the teacher, by fitting the training examples, is also a soft committee machine, but with K hidden units. For input $\boldsymbol{\xi}^\mu$, the student output is,

$$\sigma(\mathbf{J}, \boldsymbol{\xi}^\mu) = \sum_{i=1}^{K} g(\mathbf{J}_i \cdot \boldsymbol{\xi}^\mu), \tag{2}$$

where the student weights $\mathbf{J} = \{\mathbf{J}_i\} (i = 1..K)$ are sequentially modified to reduce the *error* that the student makes on an input $\boldsymbol{\xi}^\mu$,

$$\epsilon(\mathbf{J}, \boldsymbol{\xi}^\mu) = \frac{1}{2}\left(\sigma(\mathbf{J}, \boldsymbol{\xi}^\mu) - \zeta^\mu\right)^2 = \frac{1}{2}\left(\sum_{i=1}^{K} g(x_i^\mu) - \sum_{n=1}^{M} g(y_n^\mu)\right)^2, \tag{3}$$

with the *activations* defined $x_i^\mu = \mathbf{J}_i \cdot \boldsymbol{\xi}^\mu$, and $y_n^\mu = \mathbf{B}_n \cdot \boldsymbol{\xi}^\mu$. Gradient descent on the error (3) results in an update of the student weight vectors,

$$\mathbf{J}^{\mu+1} = \mathbf{J}^\mu - \frac{\eta}{N}\delta_i^\mu \boldsymbol{\xi}^\mu, \tag{4}$$

where,

$$\delta_i^\mu = g'(x_i^\mu)\left[\sum_{n=1}^{M} g(y_n^\mu) - \sum_{j=1}^{K} g(x_j^\mu)\right], \tag{5}$$

and g' is the derivative of the activation function g. The typical performance of the student on a randomly selected input example is given by the generalisation error,

$$\epsilon_g = \langle \epsilon(\mathbf{J}, \boldsymbol{\xi}) \rangle, \tag{6}$$

where $\langle .. \rangle$ represents an average over the gaussian input distribution. One finds that ϵ_g depends only on the *overlap parameters*, $R_{in} = \mathbf{J}_i \cdot \mathbf{B}_n$, $Q_{ij} = \mathbf{J}_i \cdot \mathbf{J}_j$, and $T_{nm} = \mathbf{B}_n \cdot \mathbf{B}_m (i, j = 1..K; n, m = 1..M)$[2], for which, using (4), we derive (stochastic) *update equations*,

$$R_{in}^{\mu+1} - R_{in}^\mu = \frac{\eta}{N}\delta_i^\mu y_n^\mu, \tag{7}$$

$$Q_{ik}^{\mu+1} - Q_{ik}^\mu = \frac{\eta}{N}\left(\delta_i^\mu x_j^\mu + \delta_k^\mu x_i^\mu\right) + \frac{\eta^2}{N^2}\delta_i \delta_k \boldsymbol{\xi}^\mu \cdot \boldsymbol{\xi}^\mu. \tag{8}$$

We average over the input distribution to obtain deterministic equations for the mean values of the overlap parameters, which are self-averaging in the thermodynamic limit. In this limit we treat $\mu/N = \alpha$ as a continuous variable and form differential equations for the *thermodynamic overlaps*, R_{in}^0, Q_{ik}^0,

$$\frac{dR_{in}^0}{d\alpha} = \eta \langle \delta_i y_n \rangle, \tag{9}$$

$$\frac{dQ_{ik}^0}{d\alpha} = \eta \langle \delta_i x_k + \delta_k x_i \rangle + \eta^2 \langle \delta_i \delta_k \rangle. \tag{10}$$

For given initial overlap conditions, (9,10) are integrated to find the mean dynamical behaviour of a student learning a teacher with an arbitrary numbers of hidden units[2] (see fig.(1a)). Typically, ϵ_g decays rapidly to a *symmetric phase* in which there is near perfect symmetry between the hidden units. Such phases exist in learnable scenarios until sufficient examples have been presented to determine which student hidden unit will mimic which teacher hidden unit. For perfectly symmetric initial conditions, such *specialisation* is impossible in a mean dynamics analysis. The more symmetric the initial conditions are, the longer the trapping in the symmetric phase (see fig.(2a)). Large deviations from the mean dynamics can exist in this symmetric phase, as a small perturbation from symmetry can determine which student hidden unit will specialise on which teacher hidden unit[1].
We rewrite (7,8) in the general form

$$a^{\mu+1} - a^\mu = \frac{\eta}{N}(F_a + \eta G_a), \tag{11}$$

where $F_a + \eta G_a$ is the *update rule* for a general overlap parameter a. In order to investigate finite size effects, we make the following ansaetze for the deviations of the update rules F_a (the same form is made for G_a) and overlap parameters a from their thermodynamic values,[1]

$$F_a = F_a^0 + \triangle F_a + \frac{1}{N} F_a^1, \qquad a = a^0 + \sqrt{\frac{\eta}{N}} \triangle a + \frac{\eta}{N} a^1, \tag{12}$$

where $\langle \triangle F_a \rangle = \langle \triangle a \rangle = 0$. The update rule *ansatz* is motivated by observing that the activations have variance $\mathcal{O}(1)$ which, iterated through (11) yield overlap variances of $\mathcal{O}(N^{-1})$. Terms of the form, $\triangle a$ represent *dynamic* corrections that arise due to the random examples, and a^1 represent *static* corrections such that the mean of the overlap parameter a is given by $a^0 + \eta a^1/N$ - the thermodynamic average plus a correction. In order to simplify the analysis, we assume a small learning rate, η, so that the thermodynamic overlaps are governed by,

$$\frac{da^0}{d\tilde{\alpha}} = F_a^0, \tag{13}$$

where F_a^0 is the update rule F_a averaged over the input distribution, and the rescaled learning rate is given by

$$\tilde{\alpha} = \eta \alpha. \tag{14}$$

Substituting (12) in (11) and averaging over the input distribution, we derive a set of coupled differential equations [2] for the (scaled) covariances $\langle \triangle a \triangle b \rangle$, and static corrections a^1,

$$\frac{d\langle \triangle a \triangle b \rangle}{d\tilde{\alpha}} = \sum_c \langle \triangle a \triangle c \rangle \frac{\partial F_b^0}{\partial c^0} + \sum_c \langle \triangle b \triangle c \rangle \frac{\partial F_a^0}{\partial c^0} + \langle \triangle F_a \triangle F_b \rangle \tag{15}$$

$$\frac{1}{2}\frac{d^2 a^0}{d\tilde{\alpha}^2} + \frac{da^1}{d\tilde{\alpha}} = \sum_b b^1 \frac{\partial F_a^0}{\partial b^0} + \frac{1}{2} \sum_{bc} \langle \triangle b \triangle c \rangle \frac{\partial^2 F_a^0}{\partial b^0 \partial c^0} + G_a^1. \tag{16}$$

Summations are over all overlap parameters, $\{Q_{ij}, R_{in} | i,j = 1..K, n = 1..M\}$. The elements $\langle \triangle F_a \triangle F_b \rangle$ are found explicitly by calculating the covariance of the update rules F_a, and F_b. Initially, the fluctuations $\langle \triangle F_a \triangle F_b \rangle$ are set to zero, and equations (13,15) are then integrated to find the evolution of the covariances, $\text{cov}(a,b) = (\eta/N) \langle \triangle a \triangle b \rangle$, and the corrections to the thermodynamic average values, $(\eta/N) a^1$. The average finite size correction to the generalisation error is given by

$$\epsilon_g = \epsilon_g^0 + \frac{\eta}{N} \epsilon_g^1, \tag{17}$$

where,

$$\epsilon_g^1 = \sum_a a^1 \frac{\partial e_g^0}{\partial a} + \frac{1}{2} \sum_{ab} \langle \triangle a \triangle b \rangle \frac{\partial^2 \epsilon_g^0}{\partial a^0 \partial b^0}. \tag{18}$$

These results enable the calculation of finite size effects for an arbitrary learning scenario. For demonstration, we calculate the finite size effects for a student with two hidden units learning a teacher with one hidden unit. In this over-realisable case, one of the student hidden units eventually specialises on the single teacher hidden unit, while the other student hidden unit decays to zero. In fig.(1), we plot the thermodynamic limit generalisation error alongside the $\mathcal{O}(N^{-1})$ correction. In fig.(1a) there is no significant symmetric phase, and the finite size corrections (fig.(1b))

[1] If the order parameter represented by c is Q_{11}, then $c^0 = Q_{11}^0$, and $\triangle c = \triangle Q_{11}$.

[2] The small-fluctuations *ansatz* necessarily yields equations of the same form as presented in [4] for the weight component dynamics. Here they are for the order parameter of the system.

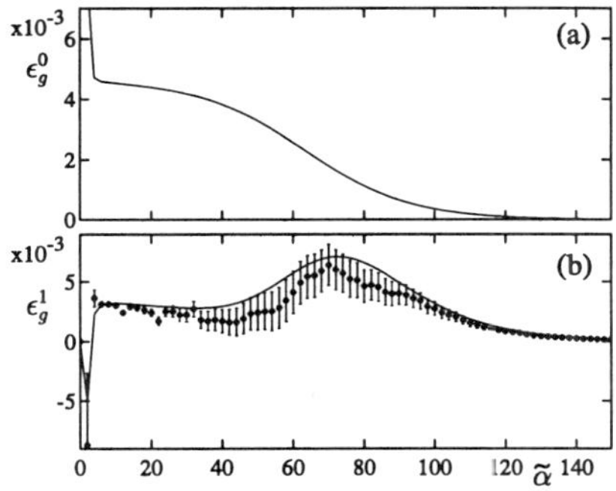

Figure 1 Two student hidden units, one teacher hidden unit. Non zero initial parameters: $Q_{11} = 0.2, Q_{22} = R_{11} = 0.1$. (a) Thermodynamic generalisation error, ϵ_g^0. (b) $\mathcal{O}\left(N^{-1}\right)$ correction to the generalisation error , ϵ_g^1. Simulation results for $N = 10, \eta = 0.1$ and (half standard deviation) error bars are drawn.

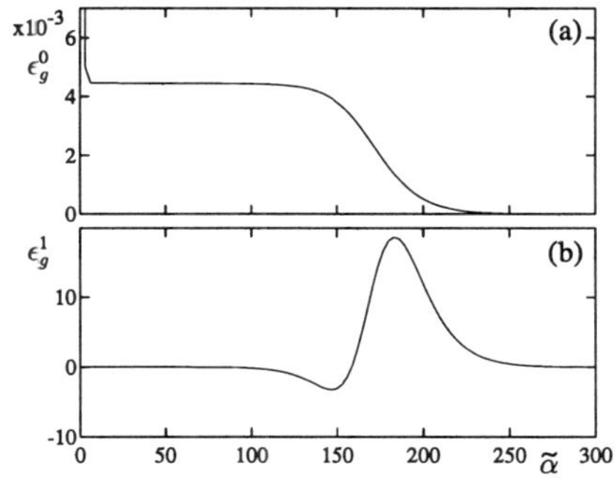

Figure 2 Two student hidden units, one teacher hidden unit. Initially, $Q_{11} = 0.1$, with all other parameters set to zero. (a) Thermodynamic generalisation error ϵ_g^0. (b) $\mathcal{O}\left(N^{-1}\right)$ correction to the generalisation error, ϵ_g^1.

are small. For a finite size correction of less than 10%, we would require an input dimension of around $N > 25\eta$. For the more symmetric initial conditions (fig.(2a)) there is a very definite symmetric phase, for which a finite size correction of less than 10% (fig.(2b)) would require an input dimension of around $N > 50,000\eta$. As the initial conditions approach perfect symmetry, the finite size effects diverge, and the mean dynamical theory becomes inexact. Using the covariances, we can analyse

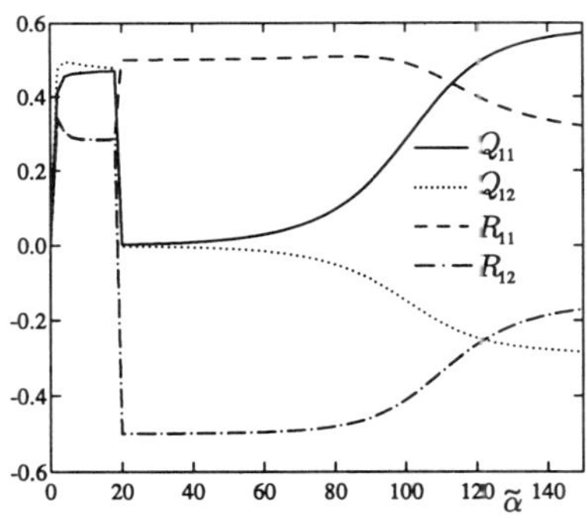

Figure 3 (a) The normalised components of the principal eigenvector for the isotropic teacher. $M = K = 2$, ($Q_{22} = Q_{11}, R_{22} = R_{11}$). Non zero initial parameters $Q_{11} = 0.2$, $Q_{22} = 0.1$, $R_{11} = 0.001$,$R_{22} = 0.001$.

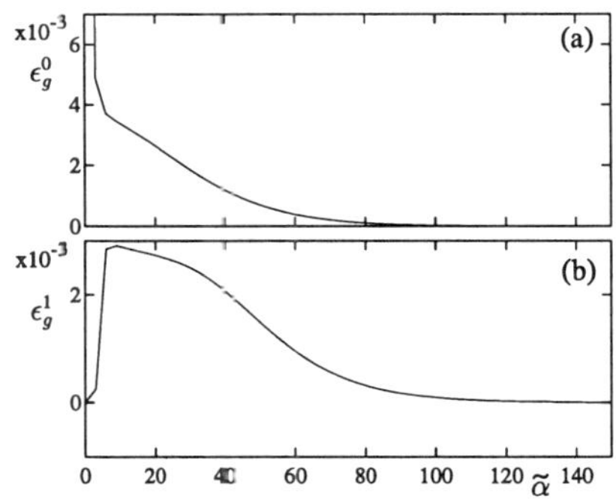

Figure 4 Two student hidden units, one teacher hidden unit. The initial conditions are as in fig.(2).(a) Thermodynamic generalisation error, ϵ_g^0. (b) $\mathcal{O}\left(N^{-1}\right)$ correction to the generalisation error, ϵ_g^1.

the way in which the student breaks out of the symmetric phase by specialising its hidden units. For the isotropic teacher scenario $T_{nm} = \delta_{nm}$, and $M = K = 2$, learning proceeds such that one can approximate, $Q_{22} = Q_{11}, R_{22} = R_{11}$. By analysing the eigenvalues of the covariance matrix $\langle \Delta a \Delta b \rangle$, we found that there is a sharply defined principal direction, the components of which we show in fig.(3). Initially, all components of the principal direction are similarly correlated, which corresponds to the symmetric region. Then, around $\tilde{\alpha} = 20$, as the symmetry breaks, R_{11} and R_{21} become maximally anti-correlated, whilst there is minimal correlation between the Q_{11} and Q_{12} components. This corresponds well with predictions from perturbation analysis[2]. The symmetry breaking is characterised by a specialisation process in which each student vector increases its overlap with one particular teacher weight, whilst decreasing its overlap with other teacher weights. After the specialisation has occured, there is a growth in the anti-correlation between the student length and its overlap with other students. The asymptotic values of these correlations are in agreement with the convergence fixed point, $R^2 = Q = 1$.

In light of possible prolonged symmetric phases, we break the symmetry of the student hidden units by imposing an ordering on the student lengths, $Q_{11} \geq Q_{22} \geq \ldots \geq Q_{KK}$, which is enforced in a 'soft' manner by including an extra term to (3),

$$\epsilon^{\dagger} = \frac{1}{2} \sum_{j=1}^{K-1} h\left(Q_{j+1j+1} - Q_{jj}\right), \tag{19}$$

where $h(x)$ approximates the step function,

$$h(x) = \frac{1}{2}\left(1 + \operatorname{erf}\left(\frac{\beta}{\sqrt{2}}x\right)\right). \tag{20}$$

This straightforward modification involves the addition of a gaussian term in the student weight lengths to the weight update rule (4). In fig.(4), we show the overlap parameters and their fluctuations for β=10, $K = 2, M = 1$. This graph is to be compared to fig.(2) for which the initial conditions are the same. There is now no collapse to an initial symmetric phase from which the student will eventually specialize. Also, the initial convergence to the optimal values is much faster. As there is no symmetric phase, the finite size corrections are much reduced and are largest around the initial value of $\tilde{\alpha}$ where the overlap parameters are most symmetric, decreasing rapidly due to the driving force away from this near-symmetric region. For the case in which the teacher weights are equal, the constraint (19) prevents the student from converging optimally. A naive scheme to prevent this is to adapt the steepness, β, such that it is inversely proportional to the average of the gradients Q_{ii}, which decreases as the dynamics converge asymptotically.

We conjecture that such symmetry breaking is potentially of great benefit in the practical field of neural network training.

REFERENCES

[1] M. Biehl and H. Schwarze, *Learning by online gradient descent*, Journal of Physics A Vol.28 (1995), pp643–656.

[2] D. Saad and S .Solla, *Exact solution for online learning in multilayer neural networks.* Physical Review Letters, Vol. 74(21) (1995). pp4337-4340.

[3] P. Sollich, *Finite size effects in learning and generalization in linear perceptrons*, Journal of Physics A Vol.27 (1994), pp7771–7784.

[4] T. Heskes, Journal of Physics A Vol.27 (1994), pp5145–5160.

Acknowledgements

This work was partially supported by the EU grant ERB CHRX-CT92-0063.

CONSTANT FAN-IN DIGITAL NEURAL NETWORKS ARE VLSI-OPTIMAL

V. Beiu

Los Alamos National Laboratory, Division NIS-1, Los Alamos, New Mexico 87545, USA. Email: beiu@lanl.gov

The paper presents a theoretical proof revealing an intrinsic limitation of digital VLSI technology: its inability to cope with highly connected structures (e.g. neural networks). We are in fact able to prove that efficient digital VLSI implementations (known as *VLSI-optimal* when minimising the AT^2 complexity measure — A being the *area* of the chip, and T the *delay* for propagating the inputs to the outputs) of neural networks are achieved for small-constant *fan-in* gates. This result builds on quite recent ones dealing with a very close estimate of the *area* of neural networks when implemented by threshold gates, but it is also valid for classical Boolean gates. Limitations and open questions are presented in the conclusions.

Keywords: neural networks, VLSI, fan-in, Boolean circuits, threshold circuits, $\mathbf{F}_{n,m}$ functions.

1 Introduction

In this paper a *network* will be considered an acyclic graph having several input nodes (*inputs*) and some (at least one) output nodes (*outputs*). The nodes are characterised by *fan-in* (the number of incoming edges — denoted by Δ) and *fan-out* (the number of outgoing edges), while the network has a certain *size* (the number of nodes) and *depth* (the number of edges on the longest input to output path). If with each edge a synaptic *weight* is associated and each node computes the weighted sum of its inputs to which a non-linear activation function is then applied (*artificial neuron*), the network is a *neural network* (NN):

$$\mathbb{Z}_k = (z_0, ..., z_{n-1}) \in \mathbb{R}^n, k = 1, ..., m, \text{ and } f(\mathbb{Z}_k) = \sigma\left(\sum_{i=0}^{n-1} w_i z_i + \theta\right), \quad (1)$$

with $w_i \in \mathbb{R}$ the synaptic *weights*, $\theta \in \mathbb{R}$ known as the *threshold*, and *sigma* a non-linear activation function. If the non-linear activation function is the threshold (logistic) function, the neurons are *threshold gates* (TGs) and the network is just a *threshold gate circuit* (TGC) computing a *Boolean function* (BF). The cost functions associated to a NN are *depth* and *size*. These are linked to $T \approx$ *depth* and $A \approx$ *size* of a VLSI chip. Unfortunately, NNs do not closely follow these proportionalities as:

- the *area* of the connections counts [2, 3, 9];
- the *area* of one neuron is related to its associated *weights*.

That is why the *size* and *depth* complexity measures are not the best criteria for ranking different solutions when going to silicon [11]. Several authors have taken into account the *fan-in* [1, 9, 10, 12], the total number of connections, the *total number of bits needed to represent the weights* [8, 15] or even more precise approximations like the *sum of all the weights and thresholds* [2–7]:

$$area \propto \sum_{all\ neurons}\left(\sum_{i=0}^{n-1} |w_i| + |\theta|\right). \quad (2)$$

An equivalent definition of 'complexity' for a NN is $\sum_{i=0}^{n-1} w_i^2$ [16]. It is worth mentioning that there are also several sharp limitations for VLSI implementations like: (i) the maximal value of the *fan-in* cannot grow over a certain limit; (ii) the maximal ratio between the largest and the smallest *weight*. For simplification, in the following we shall consider only NNs having n binary inputs and k binary outputs. If real inputs and outputs are needed, it is always possible to quantize them up to a certain number of bits such as to achieve a desired precision. The *fan-in* of a gate will be denoted by Δ and all the logarithms are taken to base 2 except mentioned otherwise. Section 2 will present previous results for which proofs have already been given [2–7]. In section 3 we shall prove our main claim while also showing several simulation results.

2 Background

A novel synthesis algorithm evolving from the decomposition of *COMPARISON* has recently been proposed. We have been able to prove that [2, 3]:

Proposition 1 The computation of *COMPARISON* of two n-bit numbers can be realised by a Δ-ary tree of *size* $\mathcal{O}(n/\Delta)$ and *depth* $\mathcal{O}(\log n/\log\Delta)$ for any integer *fan-in* $2 \le \Delta \le n$.

A class of Boolean functions $\mathbb{F}_\Delta$ having the property that $\forall f_\Delta \in \mathbb{F}_\Delta$ is linearly separable has afterwards been introduced as: *"the class of functions f_Δ of Δ input variables, with Δ even, $f_\Delta = f_\Delta(g_{\Delta/2-1}, e_{\Delta/2-1}, \ldots, g_0, e_0)$, and computing $f_\Delta \stackrel{def}{=} \bigvee_{j=0}^{\Delta/2-1}\left[g_j \wedge \left(\bigwedge_{k=j+1}^{\Delta/2-1} e_k\right)\right]$"*. By convention, we consider $\bigwedge_{i=\alpha}^{\alpha-1} e_i \stackrel{def}{=} 1$. One restriction is that the input variables are pair-dependent, meaning that we can group the Δ input variables in $\Delta/2$ pairs of two input variables each: $(g_{\Delta/2-1}, e_{\Delta/2-1}), \ldots, (g_0, e_0)$, and that in each such group one variable is 'dominant' (i.e. when a dominant variable is 1, the other variable forming the pair will also be 1):

$$\mathbb{F}_\Delta \stackrel{def}{=} \Big\{f_\Delta | f_\Delta : \{(0,0),(0,1),(1,1)\}^{\Delta/2} \to \{0,1\}, \Delta/2 \in \mathbb{N}^*,$$
$$f_\Delta = \bigvee_{j=0}^{\Delta/2-1}\left[g_j \wedge \left(\bigwedge_{k=j+1}^{\Delta/2-1} e_k\right)\right], g_i \Rightarrow e_i, i = 0, 1, \ldots, \Delta/2-1\Big\}.$$

Each f_Δ can be built starting from the previous one $f_{\Delta-2}$ (having a lower *fan-in*) by copying its synaptic *weights*; the constructive proof has led to [5]:

Proposition 2 The *COMPARISON* of two n-bit numbers can be computed by a Δ-ary tree neural network with polynomially bounded integer *weights* and *thresholds* ($\le n^k$) having *size* $\mathcal{O}(n/\Delta)$ and *depth* $\mathcal{O}(\log n/\log\Delta)$ for any integer *fan-in* $3 \le \Delta \le \log^k n$.

For a closer estimate of the *area* we have used equation (2) and proved [5]:

Proposition 3 The neural network with polynomially bounded integer *weights* (and *thresholds*) computing the *COMPARISON* of two n-bit numbers occupies an *area* of $\mathcal{O}(n \cdot 2^{\Delta/2}/\Delta)$ for all the values of the *fan-in* (Δ) in the range 3 to $\mathcal{O}(\log n)$.

The result presented there is:

$$AT^2(n,\Delta) \cong \frac{2^{\Delta/2}}{\Delta} \cdot \frac{8n\Delta - 6n - 5\Delta}{\Delta - 2} \cdot \frac{\log^2 n}{\log^2 \Delta} = \mathcal{O}\left(\frac{n\log^2 n \cdot 2^{\Delta/2}}{\Delta \log^2 \Delta}\right) \quad (3)$$

and for $\Delta = \log n$ this is the best (i.e. smallest) one reported in the literature. Further, the synthesis of a class of Boolean functions $\mathbf{F}_{n,m}$ — functions of n input variables having m groups of ones in their truth table [13] — has been detailed [4]:

Proposition 4 Any function $f \in \mathbf{F}_{n,m}$ can be computed by a neural network with polynomially bounded integer *weights* (and *thresholds*) of *size* $\mathcal{O}(mn/\Delta)$ and

depth $\mathcal{O}(\log(mn)/\log\Delta)$ and occupying an *area* of $\mathcal{O}(mn \cdot 2^\Delta/\Delta)$ if $2m \leq 2^\Delta$ for all the values of the *fan-in* (Δ) in the range 3 to $\mathcal{O}(\log n)$.
More precisely we have:

$$T(n,m,\Delta) = \left\lceil \frac{\log n - 1}{\log\Delta - 1} \right\rceil + \left\lceil \frac{\log m + 1}{\log\Delta} \right\rceil = \mathcal{O}\left(\frac{\log(mn)}{\log\Delta}\right) \quad \text{and}$$

$$A(n,m,\Delta) < 2m \cdot \left(\frac{4n \cdot 2^\Delta}{\Delta} + \frac{5(n-\Delta)\cdot 2^{\Delta/2}}{\Delta(\Delta-2)}\right) + \Delta \cdot \left\lceil \frac{2m-1}{\Delta-1} \right\rceil = \mathcal{O}\left(\frac{mn \cdot 2^\Delta}{\Delta}\right)$$

which leads to:

$$AT^2(n,m,\Delta) = \mathcal{O}\left(\frac{mn \cdot \log^2(mn) \cdot 2^\Delta}{\Delta \cdot \log^2\Delta}\right). \tag{4}$$

For $2m > 2^\Delta$ the equations are much more intricate, while the complexity values for *area* and for AT^2 are only reduced by a factor (equal to the *fan-in* [6, 7]). If we now suppose that a feed-forward NN of n inputs and k outputs is described by m examples, it can be directly constructed as simultaneously implementing k different functions from $\mathbf{F}_{n,m}$ [4, 6, 7]:

Proposition 5 Any set of k functions $f \in \mathbf{F}_{n,i}$, $i = 1, 2, ..., m$, $i \leq m \leq 2^{\Delta-1}$ can be computed by a neural network with polynomially bounded integer *weights* (and *thresholds*) having *size* $\mathcal{O}(m(2n+k)/\Delta)$, *depth* $\mathcal{O}(\log(mn)/\log\Delta)$ and occupying an *area* of $\mathcal{O}(mn \cdot 2^\Delta/\Delta + mk)$ if $2m \leq 2^\Delta$, for all the values of the *fan-in* (Δ) in the range 3 to $\mathcal{O}(\log n)$.

The architecture has a first layer of COMPARISONs which can either be implemented using classical Boolean gates (BGs) or — as it has been shown previously — by TGs. The desired function can be synthesised either by one more layer of TGs, or by a classical two layers AND-OR structure (a second hidden layer of AND gates — one for each hypercube), and a third layer of k OR gates represents the outputs. For minimising the *area* some COMPARISONs could be replaced by AND gates (like in a classical disjunctive normal form implementation).

3 Which is the VLSI-Optimal Fan-In?

Not wanting to complicate the proofs, we shall determine the VLSI-optimal *fan-in* when implementing *COMPARISON* (in fact: $\mathbf{F}_{n,1}$ functions) for which the solution was detailed in *Propositions 1* to *3*. The same result is valid for $\mathbf{F}_{n,m}$ functions as can be intuitively expected either by comparing equations (3) and (4), or because:

- the *delay* is determined by the first layer of COMPARISONs; while
- the *area* is determined by the same first layer of COMPARISONs (the additional *area* for implementing the symmetric 'alternate addition' [4] can be neglected).

For a better understanding we have plotted equation (3) in Figure 1.

Proposition 6 The VLSI-*optimal* (which minimises the AT^2) neural network which computes the *COMPARISON* of two n-bit numbers has small-constant *fan-in* 'neurons' with small-constant bounded *weights* and *thresholds*.

Proof: Starting from the first part of equation (3) we can compute its derivative:

$$\frac{d(AT^2)}{d\Delta} = \frac{2^{\Delta/2}\log^2 n}{\Delta^2(\Delta-2)^2\log^3\Delta} \times \left(8n\Delta^3\log\Delta - 22n\Delta^2\log\Delta + 12n\Delta\log\Delta\right.$$

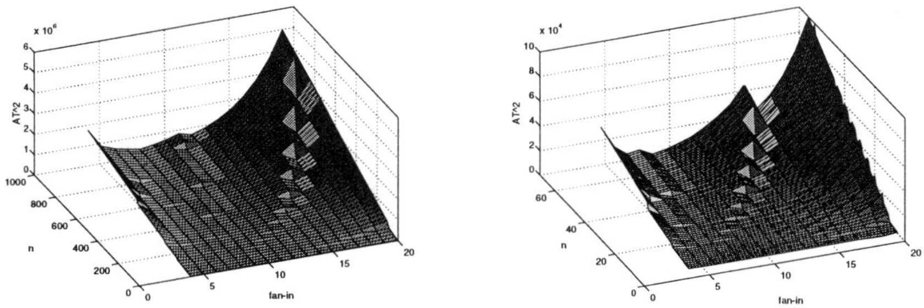

Figure 1 The AT^2 values of COMPARISON — plotted as a 3D surface — versus the number of inputs n and the *fan-in* Δ for: (a) many inputs $n \leq 1024$ $(4 \leq \Delta \leq 20)$; and (b) few inputs $n \leq 64$ $(4 \leq \Delta \leq 20)$. It can be very clearly seen that a 'valley' is formed and that the 'deepest' points constantly lie somewhere between $\Delta_{minim} = 5$ and $\Delta_{maxim} = 10$.

$$- 5\Delta^3 \log \Delta + 10\Delta^2 \log \Delta - \frac{16}{\ln 2} n\Delta^2 \log \Delta + \frac{24}{\ln 2} n\Delta \log \Delta$$
$$- \frac{24}{\ln 2} n \log \Delta + \frac{10}{\ln 2}\Delta^2 \log \Delta - \frac{32}{\ln 2} n\Delta^2 + \frac{88}{\ln 2} n\Delta - \frac{48}{\ln 2} n$$
$$+ \frac{20}{\ln 2}\Delta^2 - \frac{40}{\ln 2}\Delta \Bigg)$$

which — unfortunately — involves transcendental functions of the variables in an essentially non-algebraic way. If we consider the simplified 'complexity' version of equation (3) we have:

$$\frac{d(AT^2)}{d\Delta} \cong \frac{d}{d\Delta}\left(\frac{n \log^2 n \cdot 2^{\Delta/2}}{\Delta \log^2 \Delta}\right) = \frac{2^{\Delta/2}}{\Delta \log^2 \Delta} \cdot \left(\frac{\ln 2}{2} - \frac{1}{\Delta} - \frac{2}{\Delta \ln \Delta}\right)$$

which when equated to zero leads to $\ln \Delta(\Delta \ln 2 - 2) = 4$ (also a transcendental equation). This has $\Delta = 6$ as 'solution' and as the *weights* and the *thresholds* are bounded by $2^{\Delta/2}$ (*Proposition 4*) the proof is concluded. □

The proof has been obtained using several successive approximations: neglecting the ceilings and using a 'simplified' complexity estimate. That is why we present in Figure 2 exact plots of the AT^2 measure which support our previous claim. It can be seen that the optimal *fan-in* 'constantly' lies between 6 and 9 (as $\Delta_{optim} = 6...9$, one can minimise the *area* by using COMPARISONs only if the group of ones has a length of $\alpha \geq 64$ — see [4–7]). Some plots in Figure 2 are also including a TG-optimal solution denoted by SRK [14] and the logarithmic *fan-in* solution ($\Delta = \log n$) denoted B_lg [5].

4 Conclusions

This paper has presented a theoretical proof for one of the intrinsic limitations of digital VLSI technology: *there are no 'optimal' solutions able to cope with highly connected structures.* For doing that we have proven the contrary, namely that constant *fan-in* NNs are VLSI-*optimal* for digital architectures (either Boolean or using TGs). Open questions remain concerning *'if'* and *'how'* such a result could be extended to purely analog or mixed analog/digital VLSI circuits.

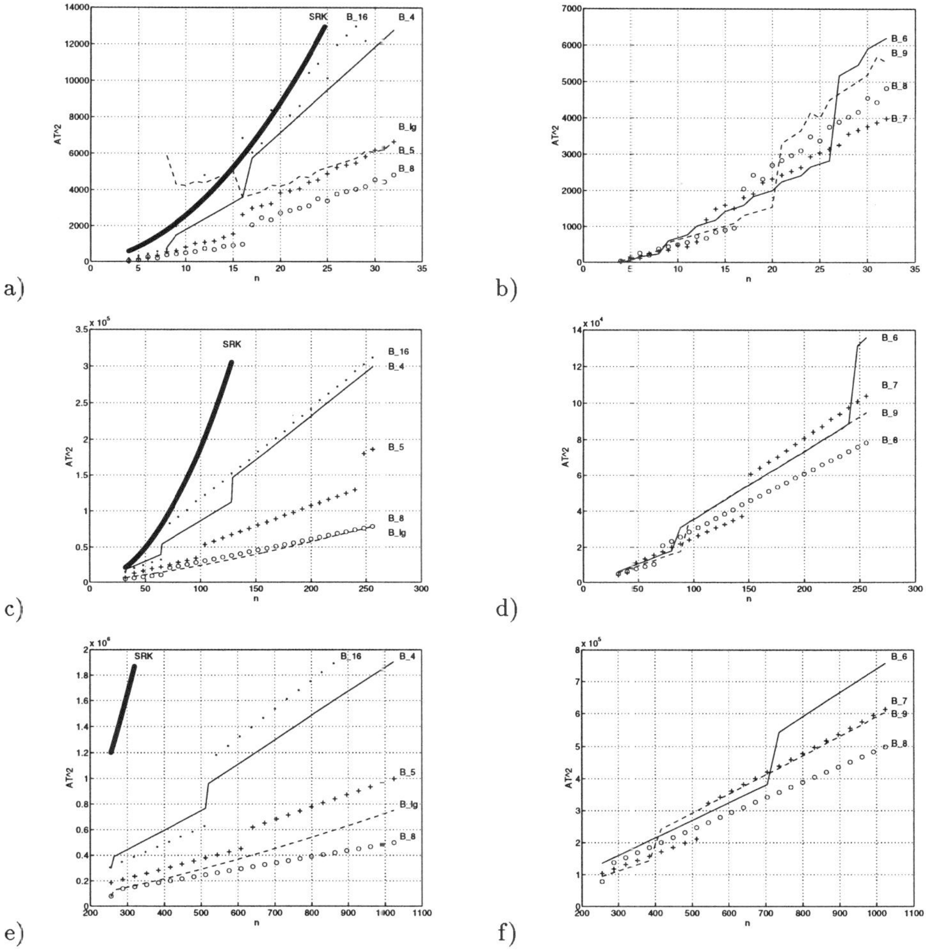

Figure 2 The AT^2 values of COMPARISON for different number of inputs n and *fan-in* Δ (B_Δ): (a) for $4 \leq n \leq 32$ including the SRK [14] solution; (b) detail showing the optimum *fan-in* for the same interval ($4 \leq n \leq 32$); (c) for $32 \leq n \leq 256$ including the SRK [14] solution; (d) detail showing the optimum *fan-in* for the same interval ($32 \leq n \leq 256$); (e) for $256 \leq n \leq 1024$ including the SRK [14] solution; (f) detail showing the optimum *fan-in* for the same interval ($256 \leq n \leq 1024$).

REFERENCES

[1] Y.S. Abu-Mostafa, *Connectivity Versus Entropy*, in: Neural Information Processing Systems (Proc. NIPS*87, Denver, Colorado), ed. D.Z. Anderson, American Institute of Physics, New York, (1988) pp1–8.

[2] V. Beiu, J.A. Peperstraete, J. Vandewalle and R. Lauwereins, *Efficient Decomposition of COMPARISON and Its Applications*, in: ESANN'93 (Proc. European Symposium on Artificial Neural Networks '93, Brussels, Belgium), ed. M. Verleysen, Dfacto, Brussels, (1993) pp45–50.

[3] V. Beiu, J.A. Peperstraete, J. Vandewalle and R. Lauwereins, *COMPARISON and Threshold Gate Decomposition*, in: MicroNeuro '93 (Proc. International Conference on Microelectronics for Neural Networks '93, Edinburgh, UK), eds. D.J. Myers and A.F. Murray, UnivEd Tech. Ltd., Edinburgh, (1993) pp83–90.

[4] V. Beiu, J.A. Peperstraete, J. Vandewalle and R. Lauwereins, *Learning from Examples and VLSI Implementation of Neural Networks*, in: Cybernetics and System Research '94 (Proc. European Meeting on Cybernetics and System Research '94, Vienna, Austria), ed. R. Trappl, World Scientific Publishing, Singapore, (1994) pp1767–1774.

[5] V. Beiu, J.A. Peperstraete, J. Vandewalle and R. Lauwereins, *Area-Time Performances of Some Neural Computations*, in: SPRANN '94 (Proc. International Symposium on Signal Processing, Robotics and Neural Networks '94, Lille, France), eds. P. Borne, T. Fukuda and S.G. Tzafestas, GERF EC, Lille, (1994) pp664–668.

[6] V. Beiu and J.G. Taylor, *VLSI Optimal Neural Network Learning Algorithm*, in: Artificial Neural Nets and Genetic Algorithms (Proc. Int. Conf., Ales, France), eds. D.W. Pearson, N.C. Steele and R.F. Albrecht, Springer-Verlag, Vienna, (1995) pp61–64.

[7] V. Beiu and J.G. Taylor, *Area-Efficient Constructive Learning Algorithms*, in Proc. CSCS-10 (10th International Conference on Control System and Computer Science, Bucharest, România), ed. I. Dumitrache, PUBucharest, Bucharest, (1995), pp293–310.

[8] J. Bruck and J. Goodman, *On the Power of Neural Networks for Solving Hard Problems*, in: Neural Information Processing Systems (Proc. NIPS*87, Denver, Colorado), ed. D.Z. Anderson, American Institute of Physics, New York, (1988) pp137–143.

[9] D. Hammerstrom, *The Connectivity Analysis of Simple Associations -or- How Many Connections Do You Need*, in: Neural Information Processing Systems (Proc. NIPS*87, November, Denver, Colorado), ed. D.Z. Anderson, American Institute of Physics, New York, (1988) pp338–347.

[10] H. Klaggers and M. Soegtrop, *Limited Fan-In Random Wired Cascade-Correlation*, in: MicroNeuro'93 (Proc. International Conference on Microelectronics for Neural Networks, Edinburgh '93, UK), eds. D.J. Myers and A.F. Murray, UnivEd Tech. Ltd., Edinburgh, (1993) pp79–82.

[11] A.V. Krishnamoorthy, R. Paturi, M. Blume, G.D. Linden, L.H. Linden and S.C. Esener, *Hardware Tradeoffs for Boolean Concept Learning*, in WCNN'94 (Proc. World Conference on Neural Networks '94, San Diego, USA), Lawrence Erlbaum and INNS Press, Hillsdale, (1994) Vol. 1, pp551–559.

[12] D.S. Phatak and I. Koren, *Connectivity and Performance Tredeoffs in the Cascade-Correlation Learning Architecture*, IEEE Trans. on Neural Networks Vol. 5(6) (1994), pp930–935.

[13] N.P. Red'kin, *Synthesis of Threshold Circuits for certain Classes of Boolean Functions*, Kibernetica Vol. 5 (1970), pp6–9. Translated in Cybernetics Vol. 6(5) (1973), pp540–544.

[14] K.-Y. Siu, V. Roychowdhury and T. Kailath, *Depth-Size Tradeoffs for Neural Computations*, IEEE Trans. on Computers Vol. 40(12) (1991), pp1402–1412.

[15] R.C. Williamson, *ϵ-Entropy and the Complexity of Feedforward Neural Networks*, in: Neural Information Processing Systems (Proc. NIPS*90, Denver, Colorado), eds. R.P. Lippmann, J.E. Moody and D.S. Touretzky, Morgan Kaufmann, San Mateo, (1991), pp946–952.

[16] B.-T. Zhang and H. Mühlenbein, *Genetic Programming of Minimal Neural Networks Using Occam's Razor*, Technical Report: Arbeitspapiere der GMD 734, Schloß Birlinghoven, Sankt Augustin, Germany (1993).

Acknowledgements

This research work has been started while Dr. Beiu was with the Katholieke Universiteit Leuven, Belgium, and has been supported by a grant from the Concerted Research Action of the Flemish Community entitled: "Applicable Neural Networks". The research has been continued under the Human Capital and Mobility programme of the European Community as an Individual Research Training Fellowship ERB4001GT941815: "Programmable Neural Arrays", under contract ERBCHBICT941741. The scientific responsibility is assumed by the author, who is on leave of absence from the "Politechnica" University of Bucharest, Romania.

THE APPLICATION OF BINARY ENCODED 2ND DIFFERENTIAL SPECTROMETRY IN PREPROCESSING OF UV-VIS ABSORPTION SPECTRAL DATA

N Benjathapanun, W J O Boyle and K T V Grattan

Department of Electrical, Electronic and Information Engineering City University, Northampton Square, London EC1V OHB, UK.

This paper describes classification of UV-Vis optical absorption spectra by binary encoding segments of the second derivative of the absorption spectra according to their shape. This allows successful classification of spectra using the Back Propagation Neural Network analysis (BPNN) algorithm where other preprocessing schemes have failed. It is also shown that once classified, estimation of chemical species concentration using a further stage of BPNN is possible. Data for the study are derived from laboratory-based measurements of UV-Vis optical absorption spectra from mixtures of common chemical pollutants.

1 Introduction

This study has the goal of developing artificial intelligence methods, to analyse UV-Vis spectra and hence determine actual chemical species and their concentrations in real-time in-line monitor systems. Prior to the study, a wide range of NN methods (BP, Radial Base, Kohonen, etc.), topologies and iteration conditions were evaluated for their ability to classify and/or estimate components in the data. All these methods were unsuccessful and pointed to the need for a more knowledge-based approach. In the present work two approaches to preprocessing the data before classification by BPNN are evaluated. The first method, 2nd derivative spectrometry, relies only on the spectral data and if successful would give self-classifying, self learning solutions. The second method, a modification of 2nd derivative spectrometry [1], depends on knowledge of the absorption spectra of expected constituent species.

2 Experimental

Data for the study were obtained from laboratory-based UV-Vis optical absorption spectra measurements taken from mixtures of three common chemical pollutants in water prepared at three different concentrations. Stock solutions were prepared from addition of *Sodium Nitrate*, *Ammonia* solution and *Sodium Hypochlorite* to distilled water and these were mixed in all possible combinations to provide a set of training data with 64 members. 64 samples were also mixed for a test set at concentrations approximately 30% greater than those for the training set. Species and concentrations are summarised in Table 1. The apparatus used in the experiments consisted of a Hewlett-Packard 8452A diode array spectrometer equipped with a 1 cm quartz cell operated remotely using proprietary software. All spectroscopic data were transferred to computer via a serial interface for analysis using Microsoft Windows based software including the Neural Desk v2.1 Neural Network software package[2]. UV intensity spectra of the solution were recorded from 190 to 820 nm with 2 nm interval. Absorption spectra were calculated from the intensity spectra using equation (1) with spectra from distilled water as a reference. For data

TRAINING SET								
NH_3-A	=	105.83 mg/l	Cl_2-A	=	49.23 mg/l	NO_3-A	=	7.75 mg/l
NH_3-B	=	32.55 mg/l	Cl_2-B	=	24.62 mg/l	NO_3-B	=	3.88 mg/l
NH_3-C	=	11.18 mg/l	Cl_2-C	=	6.15 mg/l	NO_3-C	=	1.94 mg/l
TESTING SET								
NH_3-D	=	137.7 mg/l	Cl_2-D	=	60.48 mg/l	NO_3-D	=	9.75 mg/l
NH_3-E	=	45.9 mg/l	Cl_2-E	=	30.24 mg/l	NO_3-E	=	4.88 mg/l
NH_3-F	=	15.3 mg/l	Cl_2-F	=	5.04 mg/l	NO_3-F	=	1.95 mg/l

Table 1 Chemical species and concentrations used to obtain the data sets.

analysis, data points 4nm apart were used, giving data arrays of 43 points.

$$A = \log_{10}\left(\frac{I_{blank} - \text{darkcurrent}}{I_{sample} - \text{darkcurrent}}\right) \quad (1)$$

Figure 1 shows absorption spectra obtained for the three individual species and the spectra when these are mixed together. These spectra are typical of those obtained for this study and they exemplify two important features of UV-Vis spectrometry. Firstly, UV-Vis spectral peaks from water are in general broad and overlapping, typically 30nm wide - this makes them difficult to discern. Secondly, the dynamic range in absorption for the contaminant species is high. Consequently when two or more species are mixed at high concentrations very little light is left for measurement, and the signal to noise level is reduced. The experimental data set is also subject to some systematic error due to base line shifts representative of drift in the experimental apparatus over long time periods (days) and also because of undetermined chemistry due to reactions between components in the mixture. However these factors should not limit the ability to classify the spectra, only the ability to quantify, as each constituent in a sample should result in its own distinctive adsorption peak, even if the relationship between peak height and concentration contains some error and/or is non-linear.

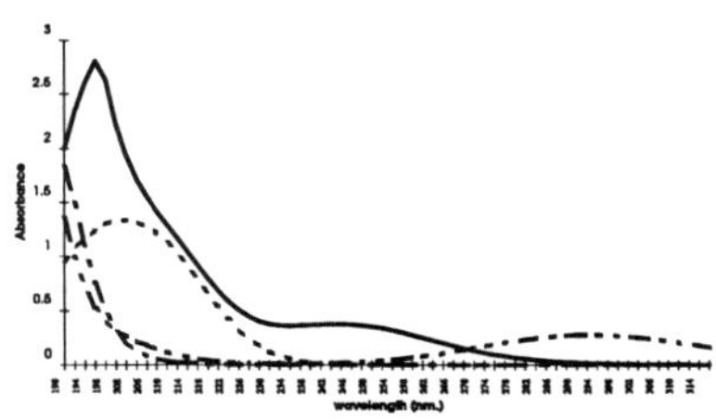

Figure 1 The absorbance spectra of NO_3 7.75 mg/l, NH_3 105.83 mg/l and Cl_2 49.23mg/l and a mixture of these (solid line).

3 Simulating Data Patterns by Adding Systematic Noise

To obtain sufficient training and testing sample sets [3], a systematic noise characteristic of stray light in the optical system was added to the raw data in the range

0-5% in intervals of 0.5%, using formula (2), in a similar manner to the work of Gemperline et al [4]. This generated 704 training patterns and 704 test patterns

$$A_{i\lambda}(generate) = A_{i\lambda} + \log\left(1 + \frac{E}{10^{A_{i\lambda}}}\right) \tag{2}$$

where $A_{i\lambda}$ is the absorption of the ith component at the wavelength λ, and E is the fraction of stray light added.

4 Results

A summary of conditions for the BPNN classifiers used after the preprocessing steps is given in Table 2. Figure 2 shows a diagram of the root mean square training error against iteration epoch and Figure 3 is a diagram of the percentage error in the testing set after intervals of 200 epochs. A minimum in the error in Figure 3 indicates the best compromise between under training and over training.

Stochastic back-propagation: learning rate = 0.1, alpha = 0.9	Network Topology		
Pre-processing	inputs	hidden	outputs
2nd derivative values	21	5	3
Encode the shape of 2nd derivative spectra	22	5	3

Table 2 Summary of conditions for the BPNN classifiers used after the preprocessing steps.

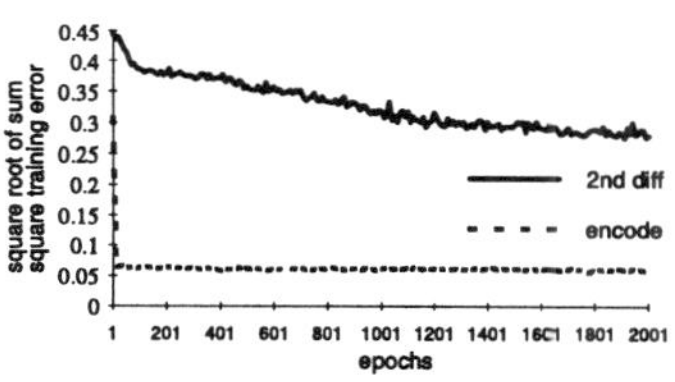

Figure 2 Training error as a function of epoch for preprocessing with PCA, 2nd Derivative spectra, and Binary Encoded 2nd Derivative Spectra.

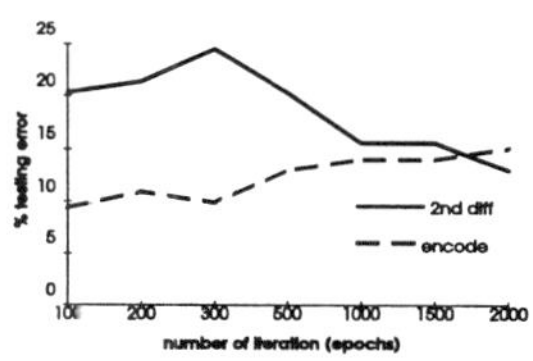

Figure 3 Testing error after every 200 training epochs as a function of epoch for preprocessing with PCA, 2nd Derivative spectra, and Binary Encoded 2nd Derivative Spectra.

5 2nd Derivative Preprocessing with BPNN classification

Following the procedure of Antonov and Stoyanov [5] whereby the spectra are transformed into differential absorption spectra which increase the likelihood of discerning spectral features related to the presence of a species, in this trial, a data set of 704 spectra of 21 values of the second derivative with respect to wavelength ($d^2A/d\lambda^2$) were prepared. As shown in Figure 2 and Figure 3 this scheme is not successful at classifying the data.

6 Binary Encoded 2nd Derivative Preprocessing

The idea behind binary encoding the 2nd derivative spectra is to obtain a code that represents the shape of the spectral data that is as independent as possible of the intensity of the data. The procedure consists of binary encoding segments of the second derivative of the absorption spectra according to the state of the slope, i.e. of the third derivative. Only relevant data are used, that is data from around the absorption speaks of expected species. In detail the binary encoding scheme consists of: firstly, segmenting the 2nd derivative spectra between 190 - 350 nm into 10 segments as shown in Figure 3, with the segment between 206 and 224 divided into two segments to ensure that the minimum in this region is included; secondly, encoding the slope in each segment with a 2 bit binary code of 01 for decreasing, 10 for increasing, 11 for convex, and 00 for unchanged; and thirdly, using the resulting 22 bit code as input to a classifying BPNN network. The topology of this network is 22 input nodes, 5 hidden nodes, and 3 output nodes. The three outputs determine whether Nitrate, Chlorine, or Ammonia are present. As can be seen in Figures 2 and 3, the classification was much more accurate than in the previous attempt and the training error converged to a small value very quickly. This results in a 93.75% prediction confidence overall for classification. However an error of 6.25% is obtained for the case of a mixture of Ammonia and Nitrate which is mis-predicted as a mixture of Ammonia, Nitrate and Chlorine. However as will be shown in the next section when this classification was followed up by the third stage of estimation the mis-identified chlorine is predicted as occurring at a low, insignificant level. Thus overall the two stages tend to cancel out the error.

7 Estimation of Concentration

Following on from the binary encoded second derivative preprocessing, the scheme for estimation of concentration also uses a knowledge of components expected in the spectra. Here one of seven possible networks which predict concentration is chosen depending on the output of the classification network. The seven networks cover all the possibilities of the 1. Chlorine, 2. Nitrate, 3. Chlorine and Nitrate, 4. Ammonia, 5. Chlorine and Ammonia, 6. Nitrate and Ammonia and 7. Chlorine, Nitrate and Ammonia. These are described in the next section. In this scheme absorption peak shape data for the various components; Nitrate at 210 nm, Hypochlorite at 290 nm and Monochloramine at 245 nm are used to determine the input variables for the seven BPNNs used for estimating concentration. The inputs used are the 7 values of absorbance centred around the peak region of each species as depicted in Table 4. Training and Testing data for these BPNN was generated, using extinction coefficient data for each of the expected components and varying the concentration of each species over the ranges shown in Table 3. The extinction coefficients data sets required for this were obtained by partial least squares fitting the absorption spectra using the combined original raw training and testing data sets. Data from this new training set was used with one of the following network topologies, depending on the output of the classification network. The various networks were: 3 hidden nodes for 7 inputs for the cases with 1 outputs node, 4 hidden nodes for 14 inputs for the cases with 2 outputs, and 5 hidden nodes for 21 inputs for the cases with 3 outputs. The algorithm used was Stochastic BP with 0.1 learning rate and 0.9 momentum. It is worth noting that these estimation networks are linear since they were trained using data from a linear model of absorbance. Testing data for the estimating networks were generated by selecting the values of absorption half way between the values of absorption used for the training set and adding 5% stray light; i.e. $E = 0.05$ in (2).

The training and testing error for the Ammonia and Chlorine network was typical of the result obtained for all the estimation networks. For this the network error converged very quickly from an error of 0.1889 at 1st epoch to less than 0.0025 after only 100 epochs. The testing error also reduced to a minimum of 0.015 after 500 training epochs. The overall accuracy of the estimating networks is shown in Table 4. This figure tabulates the number of training patterns and the resulting error for the networks described in the text.

Concentration Varying (mg/l)				
Net	Chlorine	Nitrate	Ammonia	INPUTS Absorption units at
1.	4.5 – 40.0	—	—	279–303 nm
2.	—	1.2 – 8.0	—	203–227 nm
3.	4.0 – 40.0	1.2 – 8.0	—	279–303 & 203–227 nm
4.	—	—	4.5 – 40.0	191–219 nm
5.	4.0 – 40.0	—	4.0 – 38.0	191–219 & 231–255 & 279–303 nm
6.	—	1.2 – 8.0	4.0 – 40.0	191–227 nm
7.	5.0 – 40.0	1.0 – 8.0	5.0 – 40.0	191–227 & 231–255 & 279–303 nm

Table 3 Concentration range of each species used in generating training patterns. 1.Chlorine (7 inputs) 2. Nitrate (7 inputs) 3. Chlorine and Nitrate (14 inputs) 4. Ammonia (7 inputs) 5.Chlorine and Ammonia (21 inputs) 6. Nitrate and Ammonia (9 inputs) 7. Chlorine, Nitrate and Ammonia (23 inputs).

ALGORITHM	Stochastic BP with 0.1 learning rate and 0.9 momentum	
Network	patterns	Result Error
1. Chlorine	356	0.03%
2. Nitrate	137	0.05%
3. Chlorine and Nitrate	350	0.18% & 0.20%
4. Ammonia	356	0.04%
5. Chlorine and Ammonia	350	0.72% & 0.17%
6. Nitrate and Ammonia	350	0.68% & 0.56%
7. Chlorine, Nitrate and Ammonia	512	0.13% & 1.72% & 1.03%

Table 4 Network's Topology and Performance.

8 Conclusions

In laboratory-based trials, 2nd-derivative analysis is found to be an ineffective preprocessing method in BPNN classification of UV-Vis absorption from water samples. This follows on from earlier work in which various NN algorithms including BPNN were evaluated for classification and estimation and also found ineffective. Subsequently a more knowledge-based approach has been formulated which restricts itself to determining the presence and concentration of a range of expected species. The scheme involves a three stage process. In the first stage shape information is derived by binary encoding segments of the second derivative of the absorp-

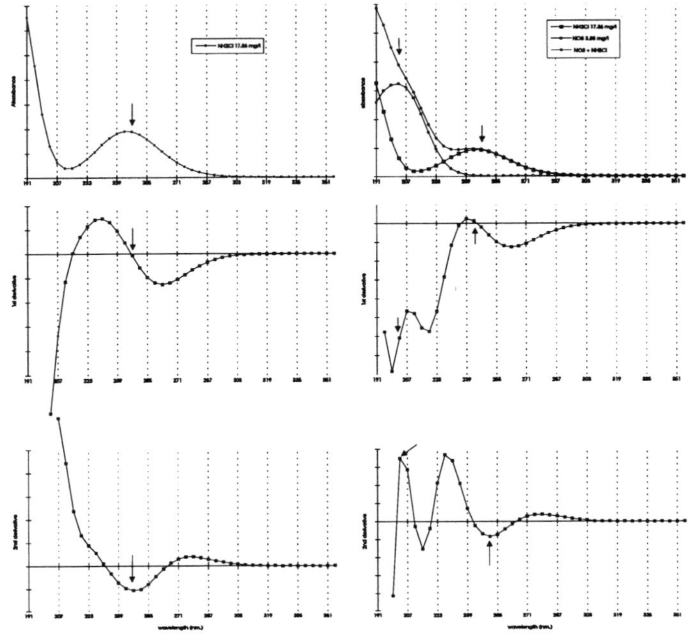

Figure 4 Absorption spectra and 1st and 2nd derivative spectra for monochloroamine and monochloroamine plus nitrate.

tion spectra according to their shape. The rationale of this stage is to reduce the spectral information to shape sensitive factors. This is found significantly to ease classification of the spectra by a second stage of BPNN analysis. For estimation of concentration of species absorption data for the expected species is used to train a second stage of BPNN, segmentation of the spectra and selection of relevant inputs for the second stage BPNN is determined from the absorption data for the expected species, to give the best segmentation pattern and minimum number of network inputs. The two-step approach taken to classification and then estimation is better than a one step approach. The first-step network specifies which species are likely to occur and the second-step network can then focus on a few inputs that strongly correlate with the presence of the expected species. Also the second-step provides a filter that compensates for classification of species at low concentration levels or incorrect identification of species due to low level signals with noise.

REFERENCES

[1] Sommer, L., *Analytical absorption spectrophotometry in the visible and ultraviolet: the principles*, (1989) Elsevir.

[2] *Neural Desk: User's Guide*, Neural Computer Sciences, (1992).

[3] Hammerstrom, D. M., *Working with neural networks*, IEEE Spectrum, July (1993), pp46–53.

[4] Gemperline, P. J., Long, J. R. and Gregoriou, V. J., *Nonlinear Multivarate Calibration Using Principal Components Regression and Artificial Neural Networks*, Anal. Chem., Vol. 63 (1991), pp2313–2323.

[5] Antonov, L. and Stoyanov, S., *Analysis of the Overlapping Bands in UV-Vis Absorption spectroscopy*, Applied Spectroscopy, Vol. 47 (1993), no. 7, pp1030–1035.

A NON-EQUIDISTANT ELASTIC NET ALGORITHM

Jan van den Berg and Jock H. Geselschap
Department of Computer Science,
Erasmus University Rotterdam, The Netherlands.
Email: jvandenberg@few.eur.nl

The statistical mechanical derivation by Simic of the Elastic Net Algorithm (ENA) from a stochastic Hopfield neural network is criticized. In our view, the ENA should be considered a *dynamic penalty method*. Using a linear distance measure, a *Non-equidistant* Elastic Net Algorithm (NENA) is presented. Finally, a *Hybrid* Elastic Net Algorithm (HENA) is discussed.

1 Stochastic Hopfield and Elastic Neural Networks

Hopfield introduced the idea of an energy function into neural network theory [5]. Like Simic [8], we use Hopfield's energy expression multiplied by -1, i.e.

$$E(\mathbf{S}) = \tfrac{1}{2}\sum_{ij} w_{ij} S_i S_j + \sum_i I_i S_i, \tag{1}$$

where $\mathbf{S} \in \{0,1\}^n$ and all $w_{ij} \geq 0$. Making the units stochastic, the network can be analyzed applying statistical mechanics. We concentrate on the free energy [6, 6]

$$F = \langle E(\mathbf{S})\rangle - T\mathcal{S}, \tag{2}$$

where $T = 1/\beta$ is the temperature, where $\langle E(\mathbf{S})\rangle$ represents the average energy, and where $\mathcal{S}$ equals the so-called entropy. A minimum of F corresponds to a thermal equilibrium state [6]. We shall apply the next theorem [10, 11]:

Theorem 1 *In mean field approximation, the free energy F_c of constrained stochastic binary Hopfield networks, submitted to the constraint $\sum_i S_i = 1$ equals*

$$F_c(\mathbf{V}) = -\tfrac{1}{2}\sum_{ij} w_{ij} V_i V_j - \tfrac{1}{\beta}\ln[\sum_i \exp(-\beta(\sum_j w_{ij} V_j + I_i))]. \tag{3}$$

The stationary points of F_c are found at state space points where

$$V_i = \mathrm{P}(S_i = 1 \ \wedge\ \forall j \neq i : S_j = 0) = \frac{\exp(-\beta(\sum_j w_{ij} V_j + I_i))}{\sum_l \exp(-\beta(\sum_j w_{lj} V_j + I_l))}. \tag{4}$$

Let S_p^i denote whether the salesman at time i occupies space-point p or not ($S_p^i = 1$ or 0). Then the corresponding Hamiltonian may be stated as [8]

$$E(\mathbf{S}) = \tfrac{1}{4}\sum_i \sum_{pq} d_{pq}^2 S_p^i (S_q^{i+1} + S_q^{i-1}) + \tfrac{\alpha}{4}\sum_i \sum_{pq} d_{pq}^2 S_p^i S_q^i. \tag{5}$$

The first term represents the sum of distance-squares, the second term penalizes the simultaneous presence of the salesman at more than one position. The other constraints, which should guarantee that every city is visited once, can be built-in 'strongly' using $\forall i : \sum_j S_{ij} = 1$. Eventually, one finds [8, 12] the free energy

$$\begin{aligned} F_{\text{tsp}}(\mathbf{V}) \ = \ & -\tfrac{1}{4}\sum_i \sum_{pq} d_{pq}^2 V_p^i (V_q^{i+1} + V_q^{i-1}) - \tfrac{\alpha}{4}\sum_i \sum_{pq} d_{pq}^2 V_p^i V_q^i - \\ & \tfrac{1}{\beta}\sum_p \ln\big[\sum_i \exp(-\tfrac{\beta}{2}\sum_q d_{pq}^2(\alpha V_q^i + V_q^{i+1} + V_q^{i-1}))\big]. \end{aligned} \tag{6}$$

On the other hand, the 'elastic net' algorithm [2] has the energy function

$$E_{\text{en}}(\mathbf{x}) = \tfrac{\alpha_2}{2} \sum_i \mid \mathbf{x}^{i+1} - \mathbf{x}^i \mid^2 - \tfrac{\alpha_1}{\beta} \sum_p \ln \sum_j \exp(\tfrac{-\beta^2}{2} \mid \mathbf{x}_p - \mathbf{x}^j \mid^2). \quad (7)$$

Here, $\mathbf{x}^i$ represents the i-th elastic net point and $\mathbf{x}_p$ represents the location of city p. Application of gradient descent on (7) yields the updating rule:

$$\Delta \mathbf{x}^i = \tfrac{\alpha_2}{\beta}(\mathbf{x}^{i+1} - 2\mathbf{x}^i + \mathbf{x}^{i-1}) + \alpha_1 \sum_p \Lambda^p(i)(\mathbf{x}_p - \mathbf{x}^i), \quad (8)$$

where $\Lambda^p(i) = \exp(-\frac{\beta^2}{2} \mid \mathbf{x}_p - \mathbf{x}^i \mid^2)/\sum_l \exp(-\frac{\beta^2}{2} \mid \mathbf{x}_p - \mathbf{x}^l \mid^2)$ and where the time-step $\Delta t = 1/\beta$ equals the current temperature T.

2 Why the ENA is a Dynamic Penalty Method

Three objections against Simic's derivation of (7) (with $\alpha_1 = \alpha_2 = 1$) from (6) are given. To derive a free energy expression in the standard form (2), Simic applies a Taylor series expansion on the last term of (6). We try to do the same. Taking

$$f(\mathbf{x}) = \sum_p \ln \big[\sum_i \exp(x_p^i) \big], \quad (9)$$

$$a_p^i = -\beta \tfrac{\alpha}{2} \sum_q d_{pq}^2 V_q^i, \quad \text{and} \quad h_p^i = -\beta \tfrac{1}{2} \sum_q d_{pq}^2 (V_q^{i+1} + V_q^{i-1}), \quad (10)$$

and using (4) (adapted to the TSP, with $\alpha \gg 1$), we obtain [12]

$$\begin{aligned} f(\mathbf{a}+\mathbf{h}) &= \sum_p \ln \big[\sum_i \exp(a_p^i) \big] + \sum_{ip} h_p^i \frac{\partial f}{\partial x_p^i}(a_p^i) + \mathcal{O}(\mathbf{h}^2) \quad (11) \\ &\approx \sum_p \ln \sum_i \exp\big(-\beta \tfrac{\alpha}{2} \sum_q d_{pq}^2 V_q^i \big) - \tfrac{\beta}{2} \sum_i \sum_{pq} d_{pq}^2 V_p^i (V_q^{i+1} + V_q^{i-1}). \end{aligned}$$

Substitution of this result in (6) yields:

$$\begin{aligned} F_{\text{app}}(\mathbf{V}) &= \tfrac{1}{4} \sum_i \sum_{pq} d_{pq}^2 V_p^i (V_q^{i+1} + V_q^{i-1}) - \tfrac{\alpha}{4} \sum_i \sum_{pq} d_{pq}^2 V_p^i V_q^i - \\ &\qquad \tfrac{1}{\beta} \sum_p \ln \sum_i \exp\big(-\beta \tfrac{\alpha}{2} \sum_q d_{pq}^2 V_q^i \big). \quad (12) \end{aligned}$$

Objection 1. Since h_p^i is proportional to β, the Taylor-approximation (11) does not hold for high values of β. This is a fundamental objection because during the execution of the ENA, β is increased step by step. □

Next, Simic performs a 'decomposition of the particle (salesman) trajectory':

$$\mathbf{x}^i = \langle \mathbf{x}(i) \rangle = \sum_p \mathbf{x}_p \langle S_p^i \rangle = \sum_p \mathbf{x}_p V_p^i. \quad (13)$$

$\mathbf{x}(i)$ is the stochastic and $\mathbf{x}^i$ the average position of the salesman at time i. Using the decomposition, Simic writes $\sum_q d_{pq}^2 V_q^i = \mid \mathbf{x}_p - \mathbf{x}^i \mid^2$. By this, he makes a crucial transformation from a linear function in V_p^i into a quadratic one in $\mathbf{x}^i$. Substitution of the result in (12) (with $\alpha = \beta$), neglect of the second term, and application of the decomposition (13) on the first term of (12) finally yield (7).

Objection 2. Careful analysis [12] shows that in general

$$\sum_q d_{pq}^2 V_q^i = \sum_q (\mathbf{x}_p - \mathbf{x}_q)^2 V_q^i \neq \mid \mathbf{x}_p - \mathbf{x}^i \mid^2 .$$ □

Energy (6) is a special case of a generalized free energy of type (3), whose stationary points are solutions of $V_p^i = \exp(-\beta \sum_{jq} w_{pq}^{ij} V_q^j) / \sum_l \exp(-\beta \sum_{jq} w_{pq}^{lj} V_q^j)$. Whatever is the temperature, these stationary points are found at states where on average, *all* strongly submitted *constraints are fulfilled*. Moreover, stationary points of a free energy of type (3) are often maxima [11, 12].

Objection 3. An analysis of the free energy of the ENA (section 3) yields a very different view: both terms of (7) create a set of minima. A *competition* takes place between feasibility and optimality, where the current temperature determines the overall effect. This corresponds to the classical penalty method. A difference from that approach is that here – like in the Hopfield-Lagrange model [9] – the penalty weights change dynamically. Consequently, we consider the ENA a *dynamic penalty method*. □

The last observation corresponds to the theory of so-called deformable templates [7, 13], where the corresponding Hamiltonian equals

$$E_{\rm dt}(\mathbf{S}, \mathbf{x}) = \tfrac{\alpha_2}{2} \sum_i \mid \mathbf{x}^{i+1} - \mathbf{x}^i \mid^2 + \sum_{pj} S_p^j \mid \mathbf{x}_p - \mathbf{x}^j \mid^2 . \tag{14}$$

A statistical analysis [7, 13] of $E_{\rm dt}$ yields the free energy (7). A comparison between (7) and (14) clarifies that the first energy expression is derived from the second one by adding noise exclusively to the penalty terms.

3 An Analysis of the ENA

We can analyze the ENA by inspection of the energy landscape [3, 12]. The general behavior of the algorithm leads to large-scale, global adjustments early on. Later on, smaller, more local refinements occur. *Equidistance* is enforced by the first, 'elastic ring term' of (7), which corresponds to parabolic pits in the energy landscape. *Feasibility* is enforced by the second, 'mapping term' corresponding to pits whose width and depth depend on T. Initially, the energy landscape appears to shelve slightly and is lowest in regions with high city density. On lowering the temperature a little, the mapping term becomes more important: it creates steeper pits around cities. By this, the elastic net starts to stretch out. We next consider two potential, nearly final states of a problem instance with 5 *permanently* fixed cities and 5 variable elastic net points, of which 4 are *temporarily* fixed. The energy landscape of the remaining elastic net point is displayed. Figure 1 shows the case where 4 of the 5 cities have already caught an elastic net point.

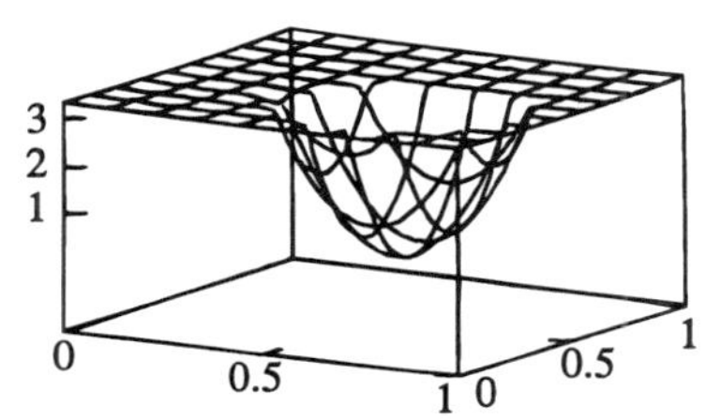

Figure 1 The energy landscape, a non-feasible state.

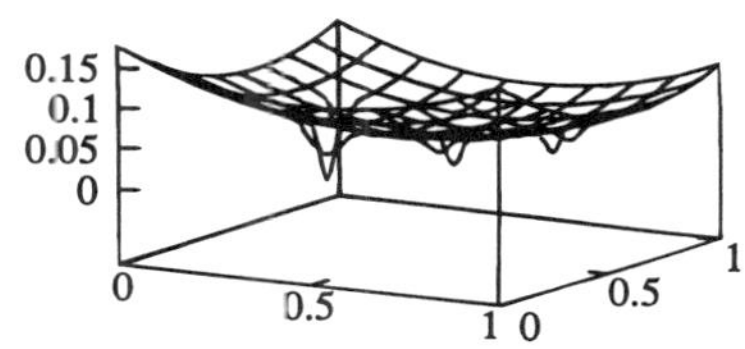

Figure 2 The energy landscape, an almost feasible state.

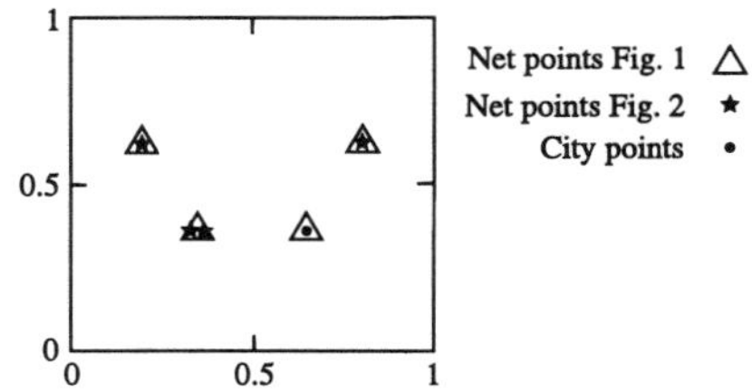

Figure 3 Net points and city point positions.

The landscape of the 5-th ring point exhibits a large pit situated above the only non-visited city. If the point is not too far away from the non-visited city, it can still be caught by it. It demonstrates, that a too rapid lowering of the temperature may lead to a non-valid solution. In figure 2, an almost feasible final solution is shown, where 3 net points coincide with 3 cities. A 4-th elastic net point is precisely in the middle between the two close cities. Now, the mapping term only produces some small pits. The elastic net term has become perceptible too. Hence, the remaining elastic net point is most probably forced to the middle of its neighbors making the final state more or less equidistant, but not feasible! Thus, it is possible to end up in a non-feasible solution if (a) the parameter T is lowered too rapidly[1] or if (b) two close cities have caught the same net point.

4 Alternative Elastic Net Algorithms

In order to use a correct distance measure and at the same time, to get rid of the equidistance property, we adopt a *linear* distance measure in (7):

$$F_{\text{lin}}(\mathbf{x}) = \alpha_2 \sum_i \mid \mathbf{x}^{i+1} - \mathbf{x}^i \mid - \frac{\alpha_1}{\beta} \sum_p \ln \sum_j \exp\left(\frac{-\beta^2}{2} \mid \mathbf{x}_p - \mathbf{x}^j \mid^2\right). \qquad (15)$$

Applying gradient descent, the corresponding motion equations are found [3]. A self-evident analysis shows that, like in the original ENA, the elastic net forces try to push elastic net points onto a straight line. There is, however, an important difference: once a net point is situated in *any* point on the straight line between its neighboring net points, it no longer feels an elastic net force. Equidistance is not pursued anymore and the net points have more freedom to move towards cities. We therefore conjecture that the NENA will find feasible solutions more easily. Since the elastic net forces are normalized by the new algorithm, a tuning problem arises. To solve this problem, all elastic net forces are multiplied by a same factor. The final updating rule becomes:

$$\Delta\mathbf{x}^i = \frac{\alpha_2}{\beta}\frac{1}{m} \sum_1^m \mid \mathbf{x}^{i+1} - \mathbf{x}^i \mid \left(\frac{\mathbf{x}^{i+1} - \mathbf{x}^i}{\mid \mathbf{x}^{i+1} - \mathbf{x}^i \mid} + \frac{\mathbf{x}^{i-1} - \mathbf{x}^i}{\mid \mathbf{x}^{i-1} - \mathbf{x}^i \mid} \right) + \alpha_1 \sum_p \Lambda^p(i)(\mathbf{x}_p - \mathbf{x}^i).$$

Finally, we merged the ENA and the NENA into a hybrid one (HENA): the algorithm starts using ENA (to get a balanced stretching out) and, after a certain number of steps, switches to NENA (to try to guarantee feasibility).

[1] In optimal annealing[1], the temperature is decreased carefully to *escape* from local minima. Instead, here this is done to *end up* in a local (i.e., a constrained) minimum.

5 Experiments

We started using the 5-city configuration of section 3. Using 5 up to 12 elastic net points, the ENA produced only non-feasible solutions. Using 15 elastic net points, the optimal feasible solution is always found. Using 5 elastic net points, the NENA occasionally produced the optimal solution. A gradual increase of the number of elastic net points results into a rise of the percentage of optimal solutions found. Using only 10 elastic net points, we obtained a 100% score. Testing a 15-city-problem, we had the similar experiences. However, the picture started to change having 30-city problem instances. As a rule, both algorithms are equally disposed to find a valid solution, but the quality of the solutions of the original ENA is generally better. Trying even larger problem instances, the NENA more frequently found a non-valid solution: inspection shows a strong *lumping* effect of net points around cities and sometimes a certain city is completely left out. At this point, the hybrid approach of HENA comes to mind. Up to 100 cities, we were unable to find parameters which yield better solutions than the original ENA.

6 Conclusions and Outlook

Elastic neural networks are *dynamic penalty methods*, therefore always having a *tuning* problem. Contrary to simulated annealing, the network should *end up* in a local, constrained minimum. Trying the ENA, it may come up with a non-valid solution if two cities are close to each other. To guarantee feasibility more easily, we implemented a new algorithm, having a *linear* distance measure. The success of it is limited to small problem instances, showing that the *quadratic distance measure* is an *essential* ingredient of the original ENA. Trying a hybrid algorithm, we did not find parameters which yield a better performance. In future research, an alternative for HENA can be considered by realizing a *gradual* switch from the ENA to the NENA. Likewise, other formulations of penalty terms can be tested.

REFERENCES

[1] E. Aarts and J. Korst, *Simulated Annealing and Boltzmann Machines, A Stochastic Approach to Combinatorial Optimization and Neural Computing*, John Wiley & Sons (1989).

[2] R. Durbin and D. Willshaw, *An Analogue Approach of the Travelling Salesman Problem Using an Elastic Net Method*, Nature, Vol. 326 (1987), pp689–691.

[3] J.H. Geselschap, *Een Verbeterd 'Elastic Net' Algoritme (An Improved Elastic Net Algorithm)*, Master's thesis, Erasmus University Rotterdam, Comp. Sc. Dept., (1994).

[4] J. Hertz, A. Krogh, and R.G. Palmer, *Introduction to the Theory of Neural Computation*, Addison-Wesley (1991).

[5] J.J. Hopfield, *Neural Networks and Physical Systems with Emergent Collective Computational Abilities*, Proceedings of the National Academy of Sciences, USA Vol. 79 (1982), pp2554–2558.

[6] G. Parisi, *Statistical Field Theory*, Addison-Wesley (1988).

[7] C. Peterson and B. Söderberg, *Artificial Neural Networks and Combinatorial Optimization Problems*, to appear in: Local Search in Combinatorial Optimization, E.H.L. Aarts and J.K. Lenstra eds., John Wiley & Sons.

[8] P.D. Simic, *Statistical Mechanics as the Underlying Theory of 'Elastic' and 'Neural' Optimisations*, Network, Vol. 1 (1990), pp88–103.

[9] J. van den Berg and J.C. Bioch, *Constrained Optimization with the Hopfield-Lagrange Model*, in: Proceedings of the 14th IMACS World Congress (1994), pp470–473.

[10] J. van den Berg and J. C. Bioch, *On the (Free) Energy of Stochastic and Continuous Hopfield Neural Networks*, in: Neural Networks: The Statistical Mechanics Perspective, J.-H. Oh, C. Kwon, S. Cho eds., World Scientific (1995), pp233–244.

[11] J. van den Berg and J.C. Bioch, *Some Theorems Concerning the Free Energy of (Un)Constrained Stochastic Hopfield Neural Networks*, in: Lecture Notes in Artificial Intelligence 904,

EuroCOLT'95 (1995), pp298–312.

[12] J. van den Berg and J.H. Geselschap, *An analysis of various elastic net algorithms*, Technical Report EUR-CS-95-06, Erasmus University Rotterdam, Comp. Sc. Dept. (1995).

[13] A.L. Yuille, *Generalized Deformable Models, Statistical Physics, and Matching Problems*, Neural Computation, Vol. 2 (1990), pp1–24.

UNIMODAL LOADING PROBLEMS

Monica Bianchini, Stefano Fanelli*, Marco Gori and Marco Protasi*

Dipartimento di Sistemi e Informatica, Università degli Studi di Firenze, Via di Santa Marta, 3, 50139 Firenze, Italy.

Email: monica,marco@mcculloch.ing.unifi.it

** Dipartimento di Matematica, Università di Roma, "Tor Vergata" Via della Ricerca Scientifica, 00133 Roma, Italy.*

Email: fanelli,protasi@mat.utovrm.it

This paper deals with optimal learning and provides a unified viewpoint of most significant results in the field. The focus is on the problem of local minima in the cost function that is likely to affect more or less any learning algorithm. We give some intriguing links between optimal learning and the computational complexity of loading problems. We exhibit a computational model such that the solution of all loading problems giving rise to unimodal error functions require the same time, thus suggesting that they belong to the same computational class.

Keywords: Backpropagation, computational complexity, optimal learning, premature saturation, spurious and structural local minima, terminal attractor.

1 Learning as Optimisation

Supervised learning in multilayered networks (MLNs) can be accomplished thanks to Backpropagation (BP), which is used to minimise pattern misclassifications by means of gradient descent for a particular nonlinear least squares fitting problem. Unfortunately, BP is likely to be trapped in local minima and indeed many examples of local extremes have been reported in the literature.

The presence of local minima derives essentially from two different reasons. First, they may arise because of an *unsuitable* joint choice of the functions which defines the network dynamics and the error function. Second, local minima may be inherently related to the structure of the problem at hand. In [5], these two cases have been referred to as *spurious* and *structural* local minima, respectively. Problems of sub-optimal solutions may also arise when learning with *high* initial weights, as a sort of *premature neuron saturation* arises, which is strictly related to the neuron fan-in. An interesting way of facing this problem is to use the "*relative cross-entropy metric*" [10], for which the erroneous saturation of the output neurons does not lead to plateaux, but to very high values of the cost. When using the cross-entropy metric, the repulsion from such configurations is much more effective, and underflow errors are likely to be avoided.

There have also been attempts to provide theoretical conditions aimed at guaranteeing local minima free error surfaces. So far, however, only some sufficient conditions have been identified that give rise to unimodal error surfaces. Examples are the the case of *pyramidal networks* [8], commonly used in pattern recognition, *radial basis function networks* [2], and *non-linear autoassociators* [3]. The identification of similar conditions ensures global optimisation just by using simple gradient descent.

Instead of looking for local algorithms like gradient descent, techniques that guarantee global optimisation may be explored. Of course, one of the main problems to face is that most interesting tasks give rise to the optimisation of functions with even several thousand variables. This makes it very unlikely that most classic approaches [11] can be directly and successfully applied. Instead, the proposal of successful algorithms has to face effectively the *curse of dimensionality* typical of most interesting practical problems.

Statistical training methods have been previously proposed in order to alleviate the local convergence problem. These methods introduce noise to connection weights during training, but suffer from extremely slow convergence due to their probabilistic nature.

Several numerical algorithms for global optimisation have also been presented, in which BP is revisited from the viewpoint of dynamical system theory. Barhen *et al.* [1] have proposed the *TRUST* algorithm (for *Terminal Repeller Unconstrained Subenergy Tunneling*) that formulates global optimisation as the solution of a system of deterministic differential equations, where $E(W)$ is the function to be optimised, while the connection weights are the states of the system. The dynamics used is achieved upon application of the gradient descent to a modified cost which transforms each encountered local minimum into a maximum, so that the gradient descent can escape from it to a lower valley. A related algorithm, called *Magic Hair-Brushing*, has been proposed in [6]. The system dynamics is now modified through a deformation of the gradient field for eliminating the local minima, while preserving the global structure of the function. All these algorithms exhibit a good performance in many practical cases but, unfortunately, their optimal convergence is not formally guaranteed, unless starting from a "*good*" initial point.

2 The Class of Unimodal Loading Problems

Most experiments with multilayer perceptrons and BP are performed in a sort of *magic* atmosphere where data are properly supplied to the network which begins learning without knowing whether or not the experiment will be successful either in terms of optimal convergence and generalisation. A *trial and error* scheme is usually employed, aimed at adjusting the architecture in subsequent experiments so as to meet the desired requirements. To some extent, this way of performing experiments is inherently plagued by the suspect that the used numerical optimisation algorithm might fail. Moreover, though optimal learning may be attained with networks having a growing number of hidden neurons [14], the generalisation to new examples is not guaranteed. The intuitive feeling that, in order to obtain a good convergence behaviour, generalisation must be sacrificed, may be effectively formalised in a sort of "*uncertainty principle of learning*" in which the variable representing optimal convergence and generalisation are like conjugate variable in Quantum Mechanics [7]. These potential sources of failure of learning algorithms give rise to a sort of *suspiciousness* that turns out to be the unpleasant companion of every experiment. This seems to be interwound with the ambitious task of learning too general functions.

Let us focus on the complexity issues related to the loading of the weights independently of the consequent generalisation to new examples. This makes sense once a consistent formulation of the learning problem in terms of both the chosen examples and the neural architecture was provided. We address the problem of establishing the computational requirements of special cases in which the loading of the weights can be expressed in terms of optimisation of unimodal error functions.

2.1 Canonical Form of Gradient Descent Learning

Let us consider the following learning equation:

$$\frac{dW}{dt} = -\gamma \nabla_W E = f(t, W), \tag{1}$$

where $E(W)$ is the cost function and $W \in \mathbb{R}^m$ is the weight vector. Let us choose $\gamma \doteq \frac{\Psi(E)}{\|\nabla_W E\|^2}$, being Ψ a non-negative continuous function of E. Based on this choice of the learning rate, the dynamics of the error function becomes

$$\frac{dE}{dt} = (\nabla_W E)^T \frac{dW}{dt} = (\nabla_W E)^T \left(-\frac{\Psi(E)}{\| \nabla_W E \|^2} \nabla_W E \right) = -\Psi(E), \tag{2}$$

which makes the cost function continuously decreasing to zero. Those configurations for which $\nabla_W E = 0$ are singular points that attract the learning trajectory [4]. Special cases of this reduction to a canonical structure, where the learning is forced by function Ψ and is independent of the problem at hand, have been explored in the literature. White [13] has suggested to introduce a varying learning rate so that the error dynamics evolves following the equation $\frac{dE}{dt} = -\Psi(E) \doteq -aE$, $a > 0$, whose solution is a decaying exponential such that reaching the $E = 0$ *attractor* will theoretically take infinite time. In practice, this may not necessarily be a problem, as the attractor may be approached sufficiently close in a reasonable amount of time, even if, for ill-conditioned systems, it can still be prohibitive to reach a satisfactory solution. Unfortunately, feedforward neural networks do often result in dynamical systems that are ill-conditioned or mathematically *stiff* and thus the convergence is generally very slow.

In [12] the canonical reduction of equation (2) is based on choosing $\Psi(E) \doteq E^k$, $0 < k < 1$, which leads to an error dynamics based on the differential equation $\frac{dE}{dt} = -E^k$, having a singularity at $E = 0$ violating the Lipschitz condition. If $E_0 \geq 0$ is the initial value of the cost, then the closed form solution is $E(t) = (E_0^{1-k} - (1-k)t)^{\frac{1}{1-k}}$, $t \leq t_e$, where $t_e = \frac{E_0^{1-k}}{1-k}$ (Fig. 1a). In the finite time t_e the transient beginning from $E(0) = E_0$ reaches the equilibrium point $E = 0$, which is a "*terminal attractor.*"

In this paper, we are interested in finding terminal attractors and, particularly, in minimising the time t_e required to approach the optimal solution. The choice $\Psi(E) \doteq \eta$ fulfills our needs. Consequently $t_e = E_0/\eta$ and, in particular, when selecting $\eta = E_0/\sigma$, the terminal attractor is approached for $t_e = \sigma$ (Fig. 1b), independently of the problem at hand, while the corresponding weight updating equation becomes

$$\frac{dW}{dt} = -\frac{E_0}{\sigma} \frac{\nabla E}{\|\nabla E\|^2}. \tag{3}$$

This way of forcing the dynamics leads to establish intriguing links between the concept of unimodal problems and their computational complexity. In fact, learning attractors in finite time is not only useful from a numerical point of view but, in the light of the considerations on the canonical equations (2), is interesting for the relationships that can be established between different problems giving rise to local minima free cost functions.

2.2 Computational analyses

Let us introduce the following classes of loading problems [9].

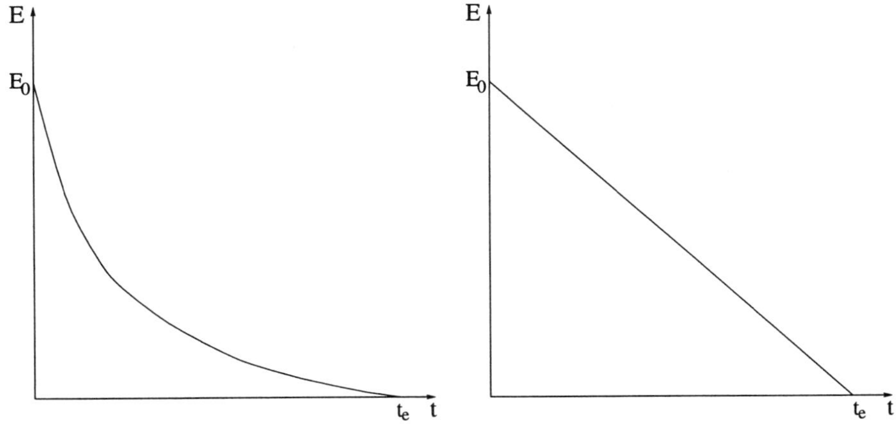

(a) (b)

Figure 1 Terminal attraction using (a) $\Psi(E) \doteq E^k, 0 < k < 1$, and (b) $\Psi(E) \doteq \eta$.

Definition 1 *A loading problem P is unimodal, $P \in \mathcal{UP}$, provided that there exists an associated unimodal error function $E(P, W)$ whose optimisation represents the solution of P.*

Note that a given loading problem can be approached in the framework of optimisation using different error functions. For example, the loading of the weights in a multilayer perceptron using linearly-separable patterns may led to sub-optimal solution when choosing error functions where the targets are different from the asymptotical values of the squashing functions. Nevertheless, it is always possible to get rid of these spurious local minima and provide a formulation based on a local minima free error function.
In order to evaluate the computational cost for learning problems belonging to $\mathcal{UP}$ it is convenient to refer to the parallel computational model offered by differential equation (1). We assume that there exists a continuous system implementing this differential equation and then consider the following computational class.

Definition 2 *Let us consider the class of loading problems P for which there exists a formulation according to the differential equation (1) such that $\forall \tau > 0$ the loading of the weights ends in a finite time $t_e : t_e \leq \tau$. This class is referred to as the class of finite time loading problems and is denoted by $\mathcal{FT}$.*

Because of the previous analysis on gradient descent the following result holds.

Theorem 3 $\mathcal{UP} \subset \mathcal{FT}$.

Proof If $P \in \mathcal{UP}$ then one can always formulate the loading according to differential equation (3) and the gradient descent is guaranteed not to get stuck in local minima. Because of equation (2) the learning process ends for $t_e = \sigma$. Hence, $\forall \tau > 0$, if we choose $\sigma \leq \tau$ we conclude that $P \in \mathcal{FT}$. □
This theoretical result should not be overvalued since it is based on a computational

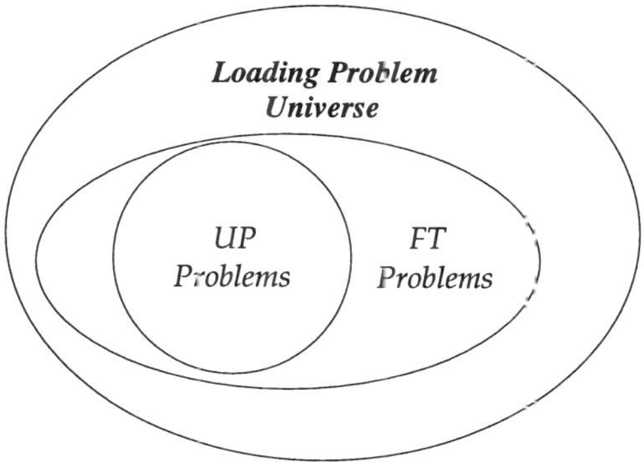

Figure 2 The class of unimodal learning problem can be learned in constant time.

model that does not care of problems due to limited energy. When choosing τ arbitrarily small, the slope of the energy in Fig. 1b goes in fact to infinite.
One may wonder whether problems can be found in $\mathcal{FT}$ that are not in $\mathcal{UP}$ (see Fig. 2). This does not seem easy to establish and is an open problem that we think deserves further attention.

3 Conclusions

The presence of local minima does not necessarily imply that a learning algorithm will fail to discover an optimal solution, but we can think of their presence as a boundary beyond which troubles for any learning technique are likely to begin.
In this paper we have proposed a brief review of results dealing with optimal learning, and we have discussed of problems of sub-optimal learning. Most importantly, when referring to a continuous computational model, we have shown that there are some intriguing links between computational complexity and the absence of local minima. Basically all loading problems that can be formulated as the optimisation of unimodal functions are proven to belong to a unique computational class. Note that this class is defined on the basis of computational requirements and, therefore, seems to be of interest independently of the neural network context in which it has been formulated.
We are confident that these theoretical results open the doors for more thoroughly analyses involving discrete computations, that could shed light on the computational complexity based on ordinary models of Computer Science.

REFERENCES

[1] J. Barhen, J. W. Burdick, and B. C. Cetin, *Terminal Repeller Unconstrained Subenergy Tunneling (TRUST) for fast global optimization*, Journal of Optimization Theory and Applications, Vol.77 (1993), pp97–126.

[2] M. Bianchini, P. Frasconi, and M. Gori, *Learning without local minima in radial basis function networks*, IEEE Transactions on Neural Networks, Vol. 6, (1995), pp749–756.

[3] M. Bianchini, P. Frasconi, and M. Gori, *Learning in multilayered networks used as autoassociators*, IEEE Transactions on Neural Networks, Vol. 6, (1995), pp512–515.

[4] M. Bianchini, M. Gori, and M. Maggini, *Does terminal attractor backpropagation guarantee global optimization?*, in International Conference on Artificial Neural Networks, Springer-Verlag, (1994), pp377–380.

[5] M. Bianchini and M. Gori, *Optimal learning in artificial neural networks: A review of theoretical results*, Neurocomputing, Vol.13 (October 1996), No.5, pp313–346.

[6] J. Chao, W. Ratanasuwan, and S. Tsujii, *How to find global minima in finite times of search for multilayer perceptrons training*, in International Joint Conference on Neural Networks, IEEE Press, Singapore, (1991), pp1079–1083.

[7] P. Frasconi and M. Gori, *Multilayered networks and the C-G uncertainty principle*, in SPIE International Conference, Science of Artificial Neural Networks, Orlando, Florida, 1993, pp396–401.

[8] M. Gori and A. Tesi, *On the problem of local minima in backpropagation*, Transactions on Pattern Analysis and Machine Intelligence, Vol. 14 (1992), pp76–86.

[9] J. S. Judd, *Neural Network Design and the Complexity of Learning.* Cambridge (1990), London: The MIT Press.

[10] T. Samad, *Backpropagation improvements based on heuristic arguments*, in International Joint Conference on Neural Networks, IEEE Press, Washington DC, (1990), pp565–568.

[11] Torn and Zilinkas, *Global Optimization*, Lecture Notes in Computer Sciences, (1987).

[12] S. Wang and C. H. Hsu, *Terminal attractor learning algorithms for backpropagation neural networks*, in International Joint Conference on Neural Networks, IEEE Press, Singapore, 1991, pp183–189.

[13] H. White, *The learning rate in backpropagation systems: an application of Newton's method*, in International Joint Conference on Neural Networks, IEEE Press, Singapore, 1991, pp679–684.

[14] X. Yu, *Can backpropagation error surface not have local minima?*, IEEE Transactions on Neural Networks, Vol. 3 (1992), pp1019–1020.

Acknowledgements

We thank P. Frasconi, M. Maggini, F. Scarselli, and F. Schoen for fruitful discussions and suggestions.

ON THE USE OF SIMPLE CLASSIFIERS FOR THE INITIALISATION OF ONE-HIDDEN-LAYER NEURAL NETS

Jan C. Bioch, Robert Carsouw and Rob Potharst
Department of Computer Science, Erasmus University Rotterdam, The Netherlands. Email: bioch,robp@cs.few.eur.nl

Linear decision tree classifiers and LVQ-networks divide the input space into convex regions that can be represented by membership functions. These functions are then used to determine the weights of the first layer of a feedforward network.

Subject classification: AMS(MOS) 68T05, 92B20

Keywords: decision tree, feedforward neural network, LVQ-network, classification, initialisation

1 Introduction

In this paper we mainly discuss the mapping of a linear tree classifier (LTC) onto a feedforward neural net classifier (NNC) with one hidden layer. According to Park [9] such a mapping results in a faster convergence of the neural net and in avoiding local minima in network training. In general these mappings are also interesting because they determine an appropriate architecture of the neural net. The LTC used here is a hierarchical classifier that employs linear functions at each node in the tree. For the construction of decision trees we refer to [10, 5, 12]. Several authors [11, 4, 9] discuss the mapping of an LTC onto a feedforward net with one or two hidden layers, see also [3, 2]. A discussion of a mapping onto a net with two hidden layers can be found in Sethi [11] and Ivanova&Kubat [4]. A mapping onto a net with *one* hidden layer is discussed in Park [9]. In his approach the mapping is based on representing the convex regions induced by an LTC by linear membership functions. However, in Park [9] no explicit expression for the coefficients of the membership functions is given. These coefficients depend on a parameter ρ that in his paper has to be supplied by the user. In section 2 we show that in general it is not possible to find linear membership functions that represent the convex regions induced by an LTC. It is however possible to find subregions that can be represented by linear membership functions. We derive explicit expressions for the aforementioned parameter ρ, in section 3. This makes it possible to control the approximation of the convex regions by membership functions and therefore of the initialisation of the neural net. In section 4 we also briefly discuss the use of LVQ-networks [6, 7] for such an initialisation.

2 Non-existence of Linear Membership Functions

Suppose we are given a multivariate decision tree $(\mathcal{N}, \mathcal{L}, \mathcal{D})$. In this notation, $\mathcal{N}$ is the set of nodes of the tree, $\mathcal{L}$ is the set of leaves of the tree and $\mathcal{D}$ is the set of linear functions $d_k : \mathbb{R}^n \to \mathbb{R}, k \in \mathcal{N}$. In any node k of the tree, the linear function d_k is used to decide which branch to take. Specifically, we go left if $d_k(x) > 0$, right if $d_k(x) \leq 0$, see figure 1. A decision tree induces a partitioning of $\mathbb{R}^n$: each leaf ℓ corresponds with a convex region R_ℓ, which consists of all points $x \in \mathbb{R}^n$, that get assigned to leaf ℓ by the decision tree. For example, region R_5 consists of all $x \in \mathbb{R}^n$ with $d_1(x) \leq 0$ and $d_3(x) \leq 0$.

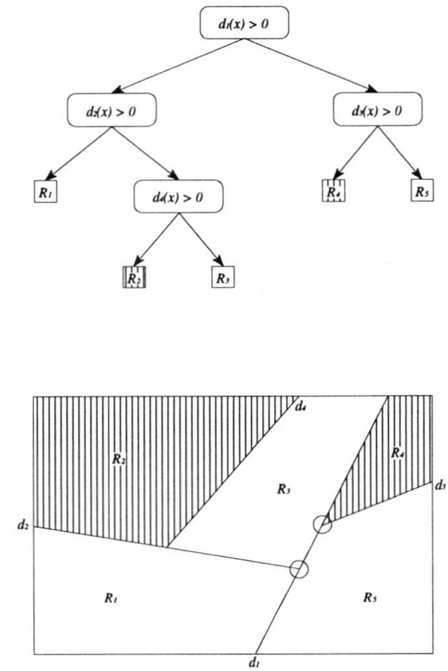

Figure 1 The convex regions induced by a classification tree.

We will now discuss the idea of linear membership functions to represent the convex regions induced by an LTC, and we show that these functions are in general not possible.
In [9] the following 'theorem' is given without proof, though supplied with heuristic reasoning for its plausibility, see also equation 2 in the next section:

Conjecture (Park[9]) *For every decision tree* $(\mathcal{N}, \mathcal{L}, \mathcal{D})$ *there exists a set of linear membership functions* $M = \{m_\ell, \ell \in \mathcal{L}\}$, *such that for any* $\ell, \ell' \in \mathcal{L}$, *with* $\ell \neq \ell'$:

$$m_\ell(x) > m_{\ell'}(x), \forall x \in R_\ell. \quad (1)$$

According to [9] the coefficients of a linear membership function can be used to initialise the weights of the connections of a hidden unit with the input layer. For example, the decision tree in figure 1 can be mapped onto a one-hidden-layer network with 3 inputs, 5 hidden units and 2 outputs. The weights in the input-to-hidden layer are chosen according to the membership functions.
In [2] we have presented a minimal counterexample to Park's conjecture, and we also argued that a mapping is only possible if the decision boundaries are parallel. In

the next theorem we show that neither linear nor quadratic membership functions that represent the convex regions induced by an LTC can exist.

Theorem 1 *Let $(\mathcal{N}, \mathcal{L}, \mathcal{D})$ be a decision tree, with at least two non-parallel decision boundaries. Then the convex regions induced by this tree cannot be represented by a set of quadratic polynomials.*

Proof Let R_1, R_2 and R_3 be regions induced by a decision tree such that the regions R_1 and $R_2 \cup R_3$ are separated by the hyperplane $d_1(x) = 0, x \in \mathrm{IR}^n$. We assume that $d_1(x) > 0$ on R_1 and $d_1(x) < 0$ on $R_2 \cup R_3$. Similarly, R_2 and R_3 are separated by $d_2(x) = 0$, such that $d_2(x) > 0$ on R_2 and $d_2(x) < 0$ on R_3. Note that such regions will always be induced by a subtree of a decision tree, unless all decision boundaries are parallel. Let m_1, m_2 and m_3 respectively denote the membership functions of R_1, R_2 and R_3. By definition $m_1 = 0$ on the hyperplane $d_1(x) = 0$. Similarly, $m_2 = 0$ on $d_2(x) = 0$. (Note, that we actually know only that m_2 is zero on half of the hyperplane $d_2(x) = 0$. However, using a simple result from algebraic geometry it follows that m_2 must be zero on the whole hyperplane $d_2(x) = 0$.)
Now, let $D_{12} = m_1 - m_2$. Then D_{12} is zero on $d_1(x) = 0$, because $D_{12} > 0$ on R_1 and $D_{12} < 0$ on $R_2 \cup R_3$. As a consequence of Hilbert's Nullstellensatz d_1 is a factor of D_{12}. Therefore, there exists a polynomial function e such that $D_{12} = d_1 e$. Since D_{12} is at most quadratic by assumption, we conclude that e is a constant or a linear function. However, since both $d_1 e$ and d_1 are positive on R_1 and negative on R_2, the function e is positive on $R_1 \cup R_2$. Since the degree of e is ≤ 1, e must be a positive constant. Similarly, we have $D_{13} = d_1 f$, where f is a positive constant. Therefore $D_{23} = d_1(f - e)$. This contradicts the fact that D_{23} is zero on $d_2(x) = 0$.
□

Remark In [2] it is shown that under the conditions of Theorem 1, the membership functions m_i can be represented by multivariate polynomials, albeit of degree ≥ 5.

3 An Approximated Mapping of a Decision Tree onto a One-hidden-layer Neural Network

We will show in this section that the difficulties encountered in the preceding section may be circumvented by requiring that the points we consider are not too close to the hyperplanes associated with the decision tree.
Let $(\mathcal{N}, \mathcal{L}, \mathcal{D})$ be a decision tree. We will restrict the regions R_ℓ by assuming that $\forall k \in \mathcal{N} : 0 < e \leq |d_k(x)| \leq E$, where e and E are positive constants. The set of points in R_ℓ satisfying this condition will be denoted by S_ℓ. Hence, S_ℓ is a convex subregion of R_ℓ. Note also that R_ℓ can be approximated by S_ℓ with arbitrary precision, by varying the constants e and E.
In [9] Park considers the following set of linear membership functions:

$$m_\ell(x) = \sum_{k \in P_\ell} s_{\ell k} c_k d_k(x), \tag{2}$$

where P_ℓ is the set of nodes on the path from the root to the leaf ℓ. The constants $s_{\ell k}$ are defined such that:

$$s_{\ell k} d_k(x) > 0. \tag{3}$$

The constants $c_k > 0$ are determined experimentally in [9]. Here we will derive an explicit expression for these constants. Since as we have shown above that in general these constants cannot exist if $x \in R_\ell, \ell \in \mathcal{L}$, we will now assume that $x \in S_\ell$.

Theorem 2 *Let $(\mathcal{N}, \mathcal{L}, \mathcal{D})$ be a decision tree. Then there exists a set of linear functions $M = \{m_\ell, \ell \in \mathcal{L}\}$, such that for any $\ell, \ell' \in \mathcal{L}$, with $\ell \neq \ell'$:*

$$\forall x \in S_\ell : m_\ell(x) > m_{\ell'}(x). \tag{4}$$

Proof Let $\mathcal{T}$ be the set of terminal nodes of the tree. An internal node t is called terminal if both children of t are leaves. Further, if n_1 and n_2 are two nodes, then we write $n_1 < n_2$ if n_1 is an ancestor of n_2. Suppose that $n_a \notin \mathcal{T}$, and ℓ, ℓ' are two leaves such that n_a is the *last common ancestor* of ℓ and ℓ'.
We decompose the function $m_{\ell'}$ as follows: $m_{\ell'}(x) = \sum_{n_i<n_a} s_{\ell i} c_i d_i(x) + \sum_{n_j \geq n_a} s_{\ell' j} c_i d_j(x)$, where $n_i \in P_\ell$ and $n_j \in P_{\ell'}$. By applying (3) to the node n_a, it can be seen that $s_{\ell a} = -s_{\ell' a}$. From this we conclude $m_\ell(x) - m_{\ell'}(x) = 2 s_{\ell a} c_a d_a(x) + \Sigma_1 - \Sigma_2$, where $\Sigma_1 = \sum_{n_i>n_a} s_{\ell i} c_i d_i(x)$, with $n_i \in P_\ell$ and $\Sigma_2 = \sum_{n_j>n_a} s_{\ell' j} c_j d_j(x)$, with $n_j \in P_{\ell'}$. To assure that (4) holds, we require that $(\Sigma_2 - \Sigma_1)/(2 s_{\ell a} d_a(x)) < c_a$. Since Σ_1 is positive we can satisfy the last condition by taking $\Sigma_2/(2 s_{\ell a} d_a(x)) < c_a$, or $\frac{E}{2e} \sum_{n_j>n_a} c_j \leq c_a$. This yields the following sufficient condition for the constants c_j:

$$\frac{E}{2e} \max_{\ell \in \mathcal{L}_a} \left\{ \sum_{n_j > n_a} c_j \right\} \leq c_a, \tag{5}$$

where $n_j \in P_\ell$ and $\mathcal{L}_a$ is the set of leaves of the subtree with root n_a. Condition (5) implies: $c_a \geq \frac{E}{2e} \sum_{n_j>n_a} c_j$, where $n_j \in \mathcal{P}$ and $\mathcal{P}$ is the *longest* possible path from node n_a to some leaf. From condition (5) it also follows that the constants c_a are determined up to a constant factor. It is easy to see that the constants can be determined recursively by choosing positive values c_t for the set of terminal nodes $t \in \mathcal{T}$. □

Theorem 3 *Let $\rho = 1/(1 + \frac{E}{2e})$. Then $m_\ell(x) = \sum_k s_{k\ell} \rho^{\delta(r)-\delta(k)} d_k(x)$ are linear functions for which (4) holds. Here $\delta(k)$ denotes the length of the longest possible path from node n_k to a terminal node.*

Proof Using the formula for the partial sum of a geometric series this result can be obtained straightforwardly, see [2]. □
Another expression for the constants c_a can be obtained by using the fact that a decision tree $(\mathcal{N}, \mathcal{L}, \mathcal{D})$ in practical situations is derived from a finite set of examples $V \subset \mathbb{R}^n$. See [2].

4 Another Initialisation Method

In this section we consider another well-known classifier: Learning Vector Quantisation (LVQ) networks [6, 7]. This method can be used to solve a classification problem with m classes and data-vectors $x \in \mathbb{R}^n$. It is known that the LVQ-network induces a so-called Voronoi tesselation of the input space, see [6] chapter 9. Training of an LVQ-network yields prototype vectors $w_j \in \mathbb{R}^n, j = 1, \ldots, m$ such that an input vector x belongs to class j iff the distance to w_j is smallest:

$$\forall i \neq j : ||w_j - x|| \leq ||w_i - x|| \Rightarrow x \in R_j.$$

It is easy to see that this is equivalent with

$$w_j^T x - \frac{1}{2} w_j^T w_j \geq w_i^T x - \frac{1}{2} w_i^T w_i.$$

Now define the linear membership function m_i as:

$$m_i(x) = w_i^T x - \frac{1}{2} w_i^T w_i.$$

Then

$$x \in R_i \iff m_i(x) > m_j(x), \forall j \neq i.$$

Since an LVQ-network is good classifier and can be trained relatively fast, it is a good alternative for the initialisation of a neural net using linear membership functions. In [2] we show that an LVQ-network cannot induce the convex regions induced by an LTC.

Discussion: We have proven that linear (or quadratic) membership functions representing the convex regions of a linear decision tree in general do not exist. However, we give explicit formulae for the approximation of such functions. This allows us to control the degree of approximation. Currently, we are investigating how to determine an appropriate approximation in a given application. Furthermore, we discussed the use of another simple classifier, namely an LVQ-network for initialising neural nets, see also [2].

REFERENCES

[1] J.C. Bioch, M. van Dijk and W. Verbeke, *Neural Networks. New Tools for Data Analysis?*, in: M. Taylor and P. Lisboa (eds.) Proceedings of Neural Networks Applications and Tools, IEEE Computer Society Press, pp28–38 (1994).

[2] J.C. Bioch, R. Carsouw and R. Potharst, *On the Use of Simple Classifiers for the Initialisation of One-Hidden-Layer Neural Nets*, Technical Report eur-cs-95-08, Dept. of Computer Science, Erasmus University Rotterdam (1995).

[3] R. Carsouw, *Learning to Classify: Classification by neural nets based on decision trees*, Masterthesis (in Dutch), Dept. of Computer Science, Erasmus University Rotterdam, February (1995).

[4] I. Ivanova, M. Kubat and G. Pfurtscheller, *The System TBNN for Learning of 'Difficult' Concepts*, in: J.C. Bioch and S.H. Nienhuys-Cheng (eds), Proceedings of Benelearn94, Tech. Rep. eur-09-94, Dept. of Computer Science, Erasmus University Rotterdam, pp230–241 (1994).

[5] U.M. Fayad and K.B. Irani, *On the Handling of Continuous-Valued Attributes in Decision Tree Generation*, Machine Learning, Vol. 8 (1992), pp88–102.

[6] J. Hertz, A. Krogh, R.G. Palmer, *Introduction to the theory of neural computation*, Addison-Wesley (1991).

[7] T. Kohonen, *Self-Organization and Associative Memory*, Berlin: Springer Verlag, 3rd edition (1989).

[8] M.L. Minsky, S.A. Papert, *Perceptrons*, 2nd edition, MIT Press (1988).

[9] Y. Park, *A Mapping From Linear Tree Classifiers to Neural Net Classifiers*, Proceedings of IEEE ICNN, Vol. I (1994), pp94–100, Orlando, Florida,.

[10] Y. Park and J. Sklansky, *Automated Design of Linear Tree Classifiers*, Pattern Recognition, Vol. 23, No. 12 (1990), pp1393-1412.

[11] A.K. Sethi, *Entropy Nets: From Decision Trees to Neural Networks*, Proceedings of the IEEE, Vol. 78, No. 10 (1990), pp1606–1613.

[12] J.R. Quinlan; *C4.5 Programs for Machine Learning*, Morgan Kaufmann (1993).

MODELLING CONDITIONAL PROBABILITY DISTRIBUTIONS FOR PERIODIC VARIABLES

Christopher M Bishop and Ian T Nabney

Neural Computing Research Group, Aston University, Birmingham, B4 7ET, UK. Email: c.m.bishop@aston.ac.uk

Most conventional techniques for estimating conditional probability densities are inappropriate for applications involving periodic variables. In this paper we introduce three related techniques for tackling such problems, and test them using synthetic data. We then apply them to the problem of extracting the distribution of wind vector directions from radar scatterometer data.

1 Introduction

Many applications of neural networks can be formulated in terms of a multi-variate non-linear mapping from an input vector x to a target vector t: a conventional network approximates the regression (i.e. average) of t given x. But for mappings which are multi-valued, the average of two solutions is not necessarily a valid solution. This problem can be resolved by estimating the conditional probability $p(t|x)$. In this paper, we consider techniques for modelling the conditional distribution of a periodic variable.

2 Density Estimation for Periodic Variables

A commonly used technique for *unconditional* density estimation is based on mixture models of the form

$$p(t) = \sum_{i=1}^{m} \alpha_i \phi_i(t) \tag{1}$$

where α_i are called mixing coefficients, and the component functions, or kernels, $\phi_i(t)$ are typically chosen to be Gaussians [7, 9]. In order to turn this into a model for conditional density estimation, we simply make the coefficients and adaptive parameters into functions of the input vector x using a neural network which takes x as input [4, 1, 5]. We propose three methods for modelling the conditional density.

2.1 Mixtures of Wrapped Normal Densities

The first technique transforms $\chi \in \mathbb{R}$ to the periodic variable $\theta \in [0, 2\pi)$ by $\theta = \chi \bmod 2\pi$. The transformation maps density functions p with domain $\mathbb{R}$ into density functions $\widetilde{p}$ with domain $[0, 2\pi)$ as follows:

$$\widetilde{p}(\theta|x) = \sum_{N=-\infty}^{\infty} p(\theta + N2\pi|x) \tag{2}$$

This periodic function is normalized on the interval $[0, 2\pi)$, since

$$\int_0^{2\pi} \widetilde{p}(\theta|x)d\theta = \int_{-\infty}^{\infty} p(\chi|x)d\chi = 1 \tag{3}$$

Here we shall restrict attention to Gaussian ϕ:

$$\phi(t|x) = \frac{1}{(2\pi)^{c/2}\sigma_i(x)^c} \exp\left\{-\frac{\|t - \mu_i(x)\|^2}{2\sigma_i(x)^2}\right\} \tag{4}$$

where $t \in \mathbb{R}^c$.

A mixture model with kernels as in equation (4) can approximate any density function to arbitrary accuracy with suitable choice of parameters [7, 9]. We use a standard multi-layer perceptron with a single hidden layer of sigmoidal units and an output layer of linear units. It is necessary that the mixing coefficients $\alpha_i(x)$ satisfy the constraints

$$\sum_{i=1}^{m} \alpha_i(x) = 1, \qquad 0 \leq \alpha_i(x) \leq 1. \tag{5}$$

This can be achieved by choosing the $\alpha_i(x)$ to be related to the corresponding network outputs by a normalized exponential, or *softmax* function [4]. The centres μ_i of the kernel functions are represented directly by the network outputs; this was motivated by the corresponding choice of an uninformative Bayesian prior [4]. The standard deviations $\sigma_i(x)$ of the kernel functions represent *scale* parameters and so it is convenient to represent them in terms of the exponentials of the corresponding network outputs. This ensures that $\sigma_i(x) > 0$ and discourages $\sigma_i(x)$ from tending to 0. Again, it corresponds to an uninformative prior. To obtain the parameters of the model we minimize an error function E given by the negative logarithm of the likelihood function, using conjugate gradients. (The maximum likelihood approach underestimates the variance of a distribution in regions of low data density [1]. For our application, this effect will be small since the number of data points is large.) In practice, we must restrict the value of N. We have taken the summation over 7 complete periods of 2π. Since the component Gaussians have exponentially decaying tails, this introduces negligible error provided the network is intialized so that the kernels have their centres close to 0.

2.2 Mixtures of Circular Normal Densities

The second approach is to make the kernels themselves periodic. Consider a velocity vector v in two-dimensional Euclidean space for which the probability distribution $p(v)$ is a symmetric Gaussian. By using the transformation $v_x = \|v\| \cos\theta$, $v_y = \|v\| \sin\theta$, we can show that the conditional distribution of the direction θ, given the vector magnitude $\|v\|$, is given by

$$\phi(\theta) = \frac{1}{2\pi I_0(m)} \exp\{m\cos(\theta - \psi)\} \tag{6}$$

which is known as a *circular normal* or *von Mises* distribution [6]. The normalization coefficient is expressed in terms of the modified Bessel function, $I_0(m)$, and the parameter m (which depends on $\|v\|$) is analogous to the inverse variance parameter in a conventional normal distribution. The parameter ψ gives the peak of the density function. Because of the $I_0(m)$ term, care must be taken in the implementation of the error function to avoid overflow.

2.3 Expansion in Fixed Kernels

The third technique uses a model consisting of a fixed set of periodic kernels, again given by circular normal functions as in equation (6). In this case the mixing proportions alone are determined by the outputs of a neural network (through a softmax activation function) and the centres ψ_i and width parameters m_i are fixed. We selected a uniform distribution of centres, and $m_i = m$ for each kernel, where the value for m was chosen to give moderate overlap between the component functions.

3 Application to Synthetic Data

We first consider some synthetic test data. It is generated from a mixture of two triangular distributions where the centres and widths are taken to be linear functions

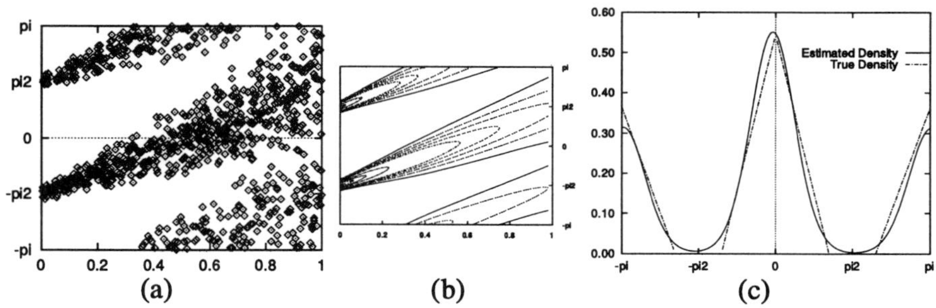

Figure 1 (a) Scatter plot of the synthetic training data. (b) Contours of the conditional density $p(\theta|x)$ obtained from a mixture of adaptive circular normal functions as described in Section 2.2. (c) The distribution $p(\theta|x)$ for $x = 0.5$ (solid curve) from the adaptive circular normal model, compared with the true distribution (dashed curve) from which the data was generated.

of a single input variable x. The mixing coefficients are fixed at 0.6 and 0.4. Any values of θ which fall outside $(-\pi, \pi)$ are mapped back into this range by shifting in multiples of 2π. An example data set generated in this way is shown in Figure 1. Three independent datasets (for training, validation and testing) were generated, each containing 1000 data points. Training runs were carried out in which the number of hidden units and the number of kernels were varied to determine good values on the validation set. Table 1 gives a summary of the best results obtained, as determined from the test set. The mixture of adaptive circular normal functions performed best. Plots of the distribution from the adaptive circular normal model are shown in Figure 1.

Method	Centres	Hidden Units	Validation Error	Test Error
Wrapped normal	6	7	1177.1	1184.4
Adaptive circular normal	6	8	1109.5	1133.9
Fixed kernel	36	7	1184.6	1223.5

Table 1 Results obtained using synthetic data.

4 Application to Radar Scatterometer Data

The European Remote Sensing satellite ERS-1 [8, 3] has three C-band radar antennae which measure the total backscattered power σ_0 along three directions. When the satellite passes over the ocean, the strengths of the backscattered signals are related to the surface ripples of the water which in turn are determined by the low-level winds. Extraction of the wind vector from the radar signals represents an inverse problem which is typically multi-valued. Although determining the wind speed is relatively straightforward, the data gives rise to *aliases* for the direction. For example, a wind direction of θ will sometimes give rise to similar radar signals to a wind direction of $\theta + \pi$, and there may be further aliases at other angles. Modelling the conditional distribution of wind direction provides the most complete information for further processing to 'de-alias' the wind directions.

A large set of ERS-1 measurements has been assembled by the European Space Agency in collaboration with the UK Meteorological Office. Labelling of the dataset was performed using wind vectors from the Meteorological Office Numerical Weather Prediction model. These values were interpolated from the inherently coarse-grained model to regions coincident with the scatterometer cells. To provide a challenging task, the data was selected from low pressure (cyclonic) and high pressure (anti-cyclonic) circulations. Ten wind fields from each of the two categories were used: each wind field contains $19 \times 19 = 361$ cells each of which represents an area of approximately 26km × 26km. Training, validation and test sets each contained 1963 patterns.

The inputs used were the three values of σ_0 for the aft-beam, mid-beam and fore-beam, and the sine of the incidence angle of the mid-beam (which strongly influences the signal received). The σ_0 inputs were scaled to have zero mean and unit variance. The target value was expressed as an angle (in radians) clockwise from the satellite's forward path. Table 2 gives a summary of the preliminary results obtained. This is a more complex domain than the synthetic problem so there were more difficulties with local optima. This problem was considerably reduced (to about 25% of the runs) by starting training with the centres of the kernel functions approximately uniformly spaced in $[0, 2\pi)$. Of the adaptive-centre models, the one with six centres

Method	Centres	Hidden Units	Validation Error	Test Error
Wrapped normal	4	20	2474.6	2446.2
Adaptive circular normal	6	20	2308.0	2337.9
Fixed kernel	36	24	2028.9	1908.9

Table 2 Results on satellite data.

has the lowest error on the validation data: however fewer centres are actually required to model the conditional density function reasonably well.

5 Discussion

All three methods give reasonable results, with the adaptive-kernel approaches beating the fixed-kernel technique on synthetic data, and the reverse on the scatterometer data. The two fully adaptive methods give similar results.

Note that there are two structural parameters to select: the number of hidden units in the network and the number of components in the mixture model. The use of a larger, fixed network structure, together with regularization to control the effective model complexity, would probably simplify the process of model order selection.

REFERENCES

[1] C M Bishop, *Mixture density networks.* Technical Report NCRG/4288, Neural Computing Research Group, Aston University, U.K. (1994).

[2] C. M. Bishop, *Neural Networks for Pattern Recognition.* Oxford University Press (1995).

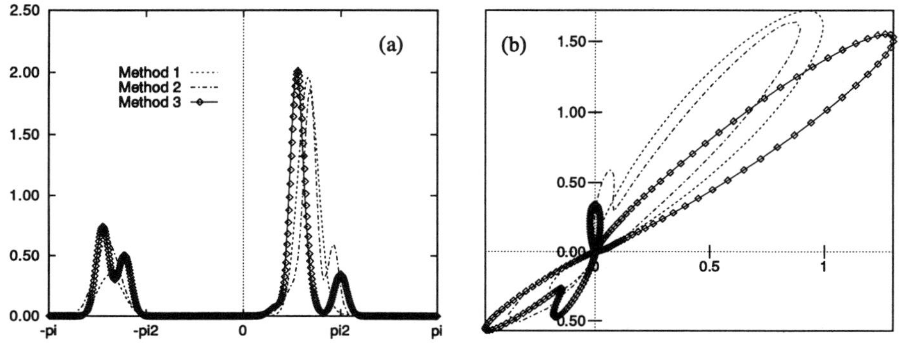

Figure 2 Plots of the conditional distribution $p(\theta|\mathbf{x})$ obtained using all three methods. (a) and (b) show linear and polar plots of the distributions for a given input vector from the test set. The dominant alias at π is evident. In both plots, the solid curve represents method 1, the dashed curve represents method 2, and the curve with circles represents method 3.

[3] C. M. Bishop and C. Legleye, *Estimating conditional probability distributions for periodic variables*, in: D. S. Touretzky, G. Tesauro, and T. K. Leen, editors, Advances in Neural Information Processing Systems, Vol. 7 (1995), pp641–648, Cambridge MA, MIT Press.

[4] R A Jacobs, M I Jordan, S J Nowlan, and G E Hinton, *Adaptive mixtures of local experts*, Neural Computation, Vol. 3 (1991), pp79–87.

[5] Y Liu, *Robust neural network parameter estimation and model selection for regression*, in: Advances in Neural Information Processing Systems, Vol.6 (1994), pp192–199, Morgan Kaufmann.

[6] K V Mardia, *Statistics of Directional Data.* Academic Press, London (1972).

[7] G J McLachlan and K E Basford, *Mixture models: Inference and Applications to Clustering.* Marcel Dekker, New York (1988).

[8] S Thiria, C Mejia, F Badran, and M Crepon, *A neural network approach for modeling non-linear transfer functions: Application for wind retrieval from spaceborne scatterometer data*, Journal of Geophysical Research, Vol. 98(C12) (1993), pp22827–22841.

[9] D M Titterington, A F M Smith, and U E Makov, *Statistical Analysis of Finite Mixture Distributions*, John Wiley, Chichester (1985).

Acknowledgements

We are grateful to the European Space Agency and the UK Meteorological Office for making available the ERS-1 data. The contributions of Claire Legleye in the early stages of this project are also gratefully acknowledged. We would also like to thank Iain Strachan and Ian Kirk of AEA Technology for a number of useful discussions relating to the interpretation of this data.

INTEGRO-DIFFERENTIAL EQUATIONS IN COMPARTMENTAL MODEL NEURODYNAMICS

Paul C. Bressloff

Department of Mathematical Sciences, Loughborough University, Leics. LE11 3TU, UK.

Most neural network models take a neuron to be a point processor by neglecting the extensive spatial structure of the dendritic tree system. When such structure is included, the dynamics of a neural network can be formulated in terms of a set of coupled nonlinear integro-differential equations. The kernel of these equations contains all information concerning the effects of the dendritic tree, and can be calculated explicitly. We describe recent results on the analysis of these integro-differential equations.

The local diffusive spread of electrical activity along a cylindrical region of a neuron's dendrites can be described by the *cable equation*

$$\frac{\partial V}{\partial t} = -\epsilon V + D\frac{\partial^2 V}{\partial \xi^2} + I(x,t) \tag{1}$$

where x is the spatial location along the cable, $V(x,t)$ is the local membrane potential at time t, ϵ is the decay rate, D is the diffusion coefficient and $I(x,t)$ is any external input. Note that equation (1) is valid provided that conductance changes induced by synaptic inputs are small; in the dendritic spines the full Nernst-Planck equations must be considered [1]. A *compartmental model* replaces the cable equation by a system of coupled ordinary differential equations according to a space-discretization scheme [2]. The complex topology of the dendrites is represented by a simply-connected graph or tree Γ. Each node of the tree $\alpha \in \Gamma$ corresponds to a small region of dendrite (compartment) over which the spatial variation of physical properties is negligible. Each compartment α can be represented by an equivalent circuit consisting of a resistor R_α and capacitor C_α in parallel, which is joined to its nearest neighbours $<\beta,\alpha>$ by junctional resistors $R_{\alpha\beta}$. We shall assume for simplicity that the tree Γ is coupled to a single somatic compartment via a junctional resistor $\hat{R}$ from node $\alpha_0 \in \Gamma$. (Figure 1). The boundary conditions at the terminal nodes of the tree can either be open (membrane potential is clamped at zero) or closed (no current can flow beyond the terminal node).
An application of Kirchoff's law yields the result

$$C_\alpha \frac{dV_\alpha}{dt} = -\frac{V_\alpha}{R_\alpha} + \sum_{<\beta,\alpha>} \frac{V_\beta - V_\alpha}{R_{\alpha\beta}} + \frac{U - V_{\alpha_0}}{\hat{R}}\delta_{\alpha,\alpha_0} + I_\alpha(t), \quad \alpha \in \Gamma \tag{2}$$

$$C\frac{dU}{dt} = -\frac{U}{R} + \frac{V_{\alpha_0} - U}{\hat{R}} \tag{3}$$

where $V_\alpha(t)$ is the membrane potential of compartment $\alpha \in \Gamma$ and $U(t)$ is the membrane potential of the soma. It can be shown that there exists a choice of parameterisation (where all branches are uniform) for which equation (2) reduces to the matrix form [3]

$$\frac{d\mathbf{V}}{dt} = 2\sigma\mathbf{Q}\mathbf{V}(t) - (\epsilon + 2\sigma)\mathbf{V}(t) + U(t)\mathbf{a} + \mathbf{I}(t) \tag{4}$$

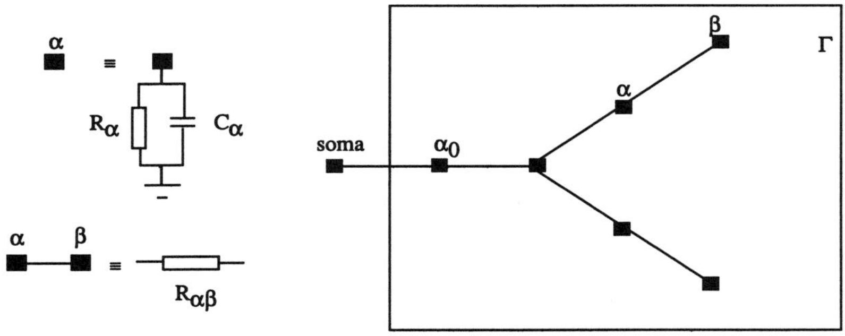

Figure 1 Compartmental model of a neuron.

where $a_\alpha = \delta_{\alpha,\alpha_0}$ and σ, ϵ are global longitudinal and transverse decay rates respectively. The matrix $\mathbf{Q}$ generates an unbiased random walk on the tree Γ. That is, $\mathbf{Q} = \mathbf{D}^{-1}\mathbf{A}$ where $\mathbf{A}$ is the adjacency matrix of Γ, $A_{\alpha\beta} = 1$ if the nodes α and β are adjacent and $A_{\alpha\beta} = 0$ otherwise, and $\mathbf{D} = \text{diag}(d_\alpha)$ where d_α is the coordination number of node α. Our choice of parameterisation is particularly useful since it allows one to study the effects of dendritic structure using algebraic graph theory (see below). More general choices of parameterisation where each branch is nonuniform, say, can be handled using perturbation theory.

Since the output of the neuron is determined by the somatic potential $U(t)$, we can view the dendritic potentials as auxiliary variables. In particular, using an integrating factor we can solve equation (4) for $\mathbf{V}(t)$ in terms of $U(t)$ and $\mathbf{I}(t)$. Substitution into equation (3) then yields the integro-differential equation (assuming without loss of generality that $\mathbf{V}(0) = 0$ and $\hat{R}C = 1$)

$$\frac{dU}{dt} = -\rho U(t) + \int_0^t \sum_{\alpha\in\Gamma} G_{\alpha_0\alpha}(t-t')\left[U(t')\delta_{\alpha,\alpha_0} + I_\alpha(t')\right] dt' \tag{5}$$

where $\rho = 1/RC + 1/\hat{R}C$ and

$$G_{\alpha\beta}(t) = \mathrm{e}^{-(\epsilon+2\sigma)t}\left[\mathrm{e}^{2\sigma t\mathbf{Q}}\right]_{\alpha\beta} \tag{6}$$

is the dendritic membrane potential response of compartment α at time t due to a unit impulse stimulation of node β at time $t = 0$ in the absence of the term $U(t)\mathbf{a}$ on the right-hand side of equation (4). All details concerning the passive effects of dendritic structure are contained within $\mathbf{G}(t)$. Note that in deriving equation (5) we have assumed that the inputs $I_\alpha(t)$ are voltage-independent. Thus we are ignoring the effects of shunting and voltage-dependent ionic gates.

One way to calculate $G_{\alpha\beta}(t)$, equation (6), would be to diagonalize the matrix $\mathbf{Q}$ to obtain (for a finite tree)

$$G_{\alpha\beta}(t) = \mathrm{e}^{-(\epsilon+2\sigma)t}\sum_r u_{r\alpha}u_{r\beta}\mathrm{e}^{2\sigma\lambda_r t} \tag{7}$$

where $\{\lambda_r\}$ forms the discrete spectrum of $\mathbf{Q}$ and $\mathbf{u}_r$ are the associated eigenvectors. It can be shown that the spectral radius $\rho(\mathbf{Q}) = 1$ and an application of the *Perron-Frobenius Theorem* establishes that (a) $\lambda = 1$ is a nondegenerate eigenvalue and (b) eigenvalues appear in real pairs $\pm\lambda_r$. However, such a diagonalization procedure is rather cumbersome for large trees and does not explicitly yield the dependence on tree topology. An alternative approach is to exploit the fact that $\mathbf{Q}$ generates a random walk on Γ. That is, expand equation (6) to obtain

$$G_{\alpha\beta}(t) = \mathrm{e}^{-(\epsilon+2\sigma)t} \sum_{r=0}^{\infty} \frac{(2\sigma t)^r}{r!} [\mathbf{Q}^r]_{\alpha\beta} \tag{8}$$

where $[\mathbf{Q}^r]_{\alpha\beta}$ is equal to the probability of an unbiased random walk on Γ reaching α from β in r steps. Using various reflection arguments, which is equivalent to a *generalized method of images*, one can express $G_{\alpha\beta}(t)$ as a series involving the response function of an infinite, uniform chain of dendritic compartments [3,4],

$$G_{\alpha\beta}(t) = \mathrm{e}^{-(\epsilon+2\sigma)t} \sum_{\mu}^{(\alpha\beta)} b_\mu I_{M_\mu}(2\sigma t) \tag{9}$$

where I_n is the modified Bessel function of integer order n. In equation (9), the summation is over trips μ starting at node β and ending at node α, and a trip is a restricted kind of walk in which changes of direction can only take place at branching nodes or terminal nodes of the tree. The length of a trip (number of steps) is given by M_μ. The constant coefficients b_μ are determined by various factors picked up along a trip according to the following "Feynman Rules". (i) A factor of $+1$ on reflection from a closed terminal node and a factor of -1 on reflection from an open terminal node. (ii) A factor of $2/d_\alpha$ when a trip passes through a branching node with coordination number $d_\alpha > 2$. (iii) A factor of $2/d_\alpha - 1$ when a trip reflects at a branching node of coordination number d_α. (iv) A factor of $2/d_\alpha$ when a trip terminates at a branching node ($d_\alpha > 2$) or a closed terminal node ($d_\alpha = 1$).

The series (9) will typically involve an infinite number of terms. However, for any fixed t, trips with length $M_\mu >> \sqrt{\sigma t}$ can be neglected so that the sum over μ can be truncated to include only a finite number of terms. Thus, using an efficient algorithm for generating trips should provide an efficient method for calculating $\mathbf{G}(t)$ at small and intermediate times. Moreover, one can also extract information concerning the long-time behaviour by Laplace-transforming (9)

$$\begin{aligned} \tilde{G}_{\alpha\beta}(z) &= \frac{1}{2\sigma[\lambda_+(z) - \lambda_-(z)]} \sum_{\mu}^{(\alpha\beta)} b_\mu \lambda_-(z)^{M_\mu}, \\ \lambda_\pm(z) &= \frac{z+\hat{\epsilon}}{2\sigma} \pm \sqrt{\left(\frac{z+\hat{\epsilon}}{2\sigma}\right)^2 - 1} \end{aligned} \tag{10}$$

where $\hat{\epsilon} = \epsilon + 2\sigma$. The resulting summation over trips can be performed explicitly to yield a closed expression for $\tilde{\mathbf{G}}(z)$ [5]. In the remainder of this paper we consider some examples illustrating the effects of dendritic structure on neurodynamics. We shall find that the Laplace transform $\tilde{\mathbf{G}}(z)$ plays a crucial role in determining the stability of these systems.

A major issue at the single neuron level is the effect of the coupling between soma and dendrites on the input-output response of a neuron satisfying equation (5), which may be rewritten in the form

$$\frac{dU}{dt} = -\rho U(t) + \int_0^t H(t-t')U(t')dt' + \hat{I}(t),$$

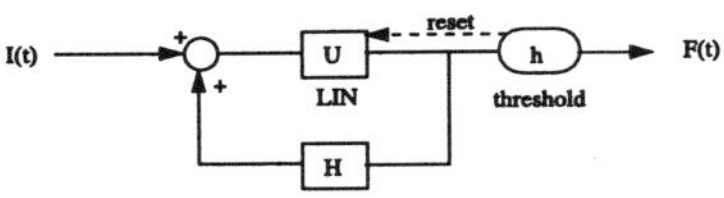

Figure 2 Schematic diagram of a compartmental model leaky integrator neuron (LIN) indicating the feedback arising from the electrical coupling between the soma and dendrites.

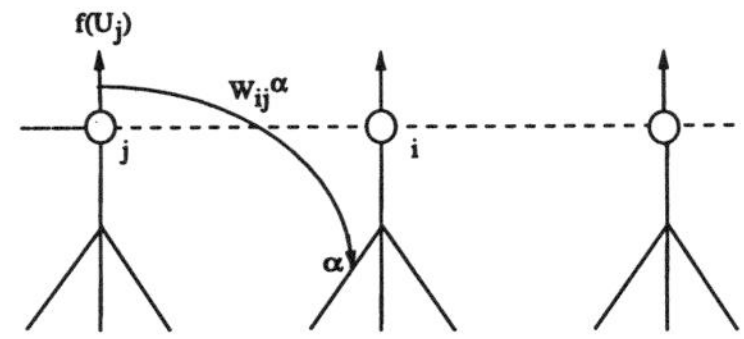

Figure 3 A network of compartmental model neurons indicating the axo-dendritic connection from neuron j to compartment α of neuron i.

$$\hat{I}(t) = \int_0^t \sum_{\alpha\in\Gamma} G_{\alpha_0\alpha}(t-t')I_\alpha(t')dt' \tag{11}$$

This describes a leaky-integrator neuron with external input $\hat{I}(t)$ and an additional feedback term mediated by the kernel $H(t) = G_{\alpha_0\alpha_0}(t)$, which takes into account the underlying coupling between $U(t)$ and the dendritic potentials. The model is represented schematically in figure 2. Since both $H(t)$ and $\hat{I}(t)$ are continuous on $[0,\infty)$ we can apply a variation of parameters formula to obtain

$$U(t) = Z(t)U(0) + \int_0^t Z(t-t')\hat{I}(t')dt', \quad Z(t) = \mathcal{L}^{-1}\left[\frac{1}{z+\rho-\tilde{H}(z)}\right](t) \tag{12}$$

where $\mathcal{L}^{-1}$ indicates the inverse Laplace transform. An interesting application of the model is to the case of *reset* where the neuron's somatic potential is reset to a zero resting level whenever it reaches a threshold h and fires. Let T_n denote the nth firing-time of the neuron. Then $U(t)$ evolves according to equation (11) for $T_n < t < T_{n+1}$ and $U(T_N) = h$ so that $U(T_n^+) = 0$. It can be shown that the firing-times evolve according to a *second-order* difference equation rather than a first-order one typical of standard *integrate-and-fire* models. (For more details see Ref. [6]). Thus the coupling between soma and dendrites can have non-trivial consequences for dynamical behaviour.

Now consider a network of N neurons labelled $i = 1, ..., N$ each with identical dendritic structure. Let W_{ij}^α denote the synaptic weight of the connection from neuron j impinging on compartment $\alpha \in \Gamma$ of neuron i. The associated output is taken to be of the form $W_{ij}^\alpha f(U_j)$ where f is a sigmoidal output function, (see figure 3). Equation (5) then leads to a set of coupled integro-differential equations

$$\frac{dU_i}{dt} = -\rho U_i(t) + \int_0^t \left[\sum_{j\neq i}\sum_{\beta\in\Gamma} W_{ij}^\beta G_{\alpha_0\beta}(t-t')f(U_j(t'))\right] dt' \tag{13}$$

Note that for simplicity we are neglecting the feedback arising from the coupling between the soma and dendrites of the same neuron. Further, let the output function f satisfy $f(x) = \tanh(\kappa x)$. Then $f(0) = 0$ so that $\mathbf{U} = 0$ is a fixed point solution of (13). Linearization about the zero solution with $f'(0) = \kappa$ gives

$$\frac{dU_i}{dt} = -\rho U_i(t) + \int_0^t \sum_{j\neq i} H_{ij}(t-t')U_j(t')dt' \tag{14}$$

$$H_{ij}(t) = \kappa \sum_{\beta} W_{ij}^{\beta} G_{\alpha_0\beta}(t) \tag{15}$$

Assume that the weights satisfy the condition $\sum_{\beta\in\Gamma} |W_{ij}^{\beta}| < \infty$ for all $i, j = 1, ..., N$ so that the convolution kernel $\mathbf{H}(t)$ is a continuous $N \times N$ matrix whose elements lie in $L^1[0, \infty)$. That is, $\int_0^{\infty} |H_{ij}(t)| dt < \infty$ for all $i, j = 1, ..., N$ It can then be proven [7] that the zero solution of equation (14) is asymptotically stable if and only if

$$\Delta(z) \equiv \det \left[(\rho + z)\mathbf{I} - \tilde{\mathbf{H}}(z) \right] \neq 0 \quad \text{when} \quad \text{Re} z \geq 0 \tag{16}$$

where $\tilde{\mathbf{H}}(z)$ is the Laplace transform of the kernel $\mathbf{H}$ and $\mathbf{I}$ is the $N \times N$ unit matrix, which can be calculated explicitly from equations (15) and (10). Condition (16) requires that no roots of the so called *characteristic function* should lie in the right-half complex plane.

It can also be established that if the stability condition (16) is met for the linear system (14), then the zero solution of the full nonlinear system (13) is locally asymptotically stable [7]. On the other hand, if $\Delta(z)$ has at least one root in the right-half complex plane then the linear system (14) is unstable. The corresponding instability of the full nonlinear system is harder to analyse; in such cases one has to bring in techniques such as bifurcation theory to investigate the effects of the nonlinearities on the behaviour of the system at the point of marginal stability where one or more eigenvalues cross the imaginary axis [8].

It is clear from equation (15) that the stability of a recurrent network depends on the particular distribution of axo-dendritic connections across the network. We end this paper by presenting some recent results concerning such stability. Detailed proofs are presented elsewhere [8,9]. First, suppose that the weights decompose into the product form $W_{ij}^{\alpha} = J_{ij} P_{\alpha}$, $P_{\alpha} \geq 0$, and $\sum_{\alpha} P_{\alpha} = 1$. Thus the distribution of axon collaterals across the dendritic tree of a neuron is *uncorrelated* with the location of the presynaptic and postsynaptic neurons in the network. Assuming that the weight matrix $\mathbf{J}$ can be diagonalized with eigenvalues w_r, $r = 1, ..., N$ then equation (16) reduces to

$$(z + \rho) - \kappa w_r \sum_{\beta\in\Gamma} P_{\beta} \tilde{G}_{\alpha_0\beta}(z) = 0 \tag{17}$$

Two particular results follow from equation (17).

I. The zero solution is (locally) asymptotically stable if

$$\kappa |w_r| < \rho \left[\sum_{\beta\in\Gamma} P_{\beta} \tilde{G}_{\alpha_0\beta}(0) \right]^{-1}$$

for all $r = 1, ..., N$. Taking $P_{\beta} = \delta_{\beta,\bar{\beta}}$, for example, shows that the passive membrane properties of the dendritic tree can stabilize an equilibrium. This follows from the property that for compartments sufficiently far from the soma, $\tilde{G}_{\alpha_0\bar{\beta}}(0) < \tilde{G}_{\alpha_0\alpha_0}(0)$.

II. The passive membrane properties of the dendrites can induce oscillations via a supercritical Hopf bifurcation [8]. At the point of marginal stability there exists a pair of pure imaginary roots $z = \pm i\omega$ satisfying equation (17) for a nondegenerate eigenvalues $w^* = \min_r \{w_r\}$ such that $w^* < 0$ and all roots of equation (17) for $w_r > w^*$ have negative definite real part.

When one considers the synaptic organisation of the brain, it becomes apparent that the decoupling of network and dendritic coordinates is an oversimplification. One example of this concerns the recurrent collaterals of pyramidal cells in the olfactory cortex [10]. These collateralls feed back excitation onto the basal dendrites of nearby pyramidal cells and onto the apical dendrites of distant pyramidal cells. This suggests that in our model the distance of a synapse from the soma should increase with the separation $|i-j|$; this leads to a reduction in the effectiveness of the connection (ignoring active processes). On the other hand, there is growing experimental evidence that the reduction in the effectiveness of distal synapses may be compensated by a number of mechanisms including increases in the density of synapses at distal locations and voltage-dependent gates on dendritic spines [10]. We can incorporate the former possibility by taking W_{ij}^{α} to be an increasing function of the degree of separation of compartment α from the soma at α_0. If this is combined with the previous feature then we have a third result.

III. The passive membrane properties of the dendritic tree can induce spatial pattern formation (arising from a Turing-like instability) in a purely excitatory or inhibitory network when the dependence of the weight distribution on dendritic and network coordinates is correlated. Thus one does not require a competition between excitatory and inhibitory connections (Mexican hat function) to induce the formation of coherent spatial structures.

Finally, note that all the results presented in this paper have a well-defined continuum limit. In particular, introduce a length-scale l corresponding to the length of an individual compartment. One then finds that in the limit $l \to 0$ such that $\sigma/l^2 \to D$, equation (4) reduces to the cable equation (1) on each branch of the tree such that current $\partial V/\partial x$ is conserved at each branching node and V is continuous at a branching node. Equation (10) with $\alpha l = \xi, \beta l = \xi', L_\mu = M_\mu l$ becomes

$$\lim_{l\to 0} \frac{\tilde{G}_{\alpha\beta}(z)}{l} = \tilde{G}(\xi,\xi';z) = \frac{1}{2}\sqrt{\frac{1}{D(z+\epsilon)}} \sum_{\mu}^{(\xi,\xi')} b_\mu \exp\left(-\sqrt{\frac{z+\epsilon}{D}} L_\mu\right)$$

REFERENCES

[1] Sejnowski TJ and Qian N. In *Single neuron computation* (ed. T. Mckenna, J. Davis and S. F. Zornetzer), San Diego: Academic Press (1992) pp117–139.

[2] Rall W. In: *Neural Theory and Modeling* (R. F. Reiss ed.), Stanford University Press, Stanford (1964), pp73–97.

[3] Bressloff PC and Taylor JG, *Biol. Cybern.* Vol.70, pp199–207.

[4] Abbott LF, Farhi E and Gutmann S, *Biol. Cybern.* Vol.66 (1991), pp49–60.

[5] Bressloff PC, Dwyer VM and Kearney MJ, *J. Phys. A*, Vol.29 (1996), pp1881–1896.

[6] Bressloff PC, *Physica D* Vol.80 (1995), p399.

[7] Burton TA , *Volterra Integral and Differential Equations* Academic Press, London (1983).

[8] Bressloff PC , *Phys. Rev. E* Vol.50 (1994), pp2308-2319.

[9] Bressloff PC, *Biol. Cybern.*, Vol.73 (1995), pp281–290.

[10] Shepherd GM ed., *The Synaptic Organization of the Brain* Oxford University Press, Oxford (1990).

NONLINEAR MODELS FOR NEURAL NETWORKS

Susan Brittain and Linda M. Haines

University of Natal, Pietermaritzburg, South Africa. Email: haines@stat.unp.ac.za

The statistical principles underpinning hidden-layer feed-forward neural networks for fitting smooth curves to regression data are explained and used as a basis for developing likelihood- and bootstrap-based methods for obtaining confidence intervals for predicted outputs.

Keywords: Hidden–layer feed–forward neural networks; nonlinear regression; nonparametric regression; confidence limits; predicted values.

1 Introduction

Hidden-layer feed–forward neural networks are used extensively to fit curves to regression data and to provide surfaces from which classification rules can be deduced. The focus of this article is on curve-fitting applications and two crucial statistical insights into the workings of neural networks in this context are presented in Section 2. Approaches to developing confidence limits for predicted outputs are explored in Section 3 and some conclusions given in Section 4.

2 Statistical Insights

Consider the following single hidden-layer feed–forward neural network used to model regression data of the form, $(x_i, y_i), i = 1, \ldots, n$. The input layer comprises a neuron which inputs the x-variable and a second neuron which inputs a constant or bias term into the network. The hidden–layer comprises two neurons with logistic activation functions and an additional neuron which inputs a bias term and the output layer provides the predicted y-value through a neuron with a linear activation function. The connection weights, $\theta = (\theta_1, \ldots, \theta_7)$, are defined in such a way that the output, o, from the network corresponding to an input, x, can be written explicitly as

$$o = \theta_5 + \frac{\theta_6}{1 + e^{-(\theta_1+\theta_2 x)}} + \frac{\theta_7}{1 + e^{-(\theta_3+\theta_4 x)}}. \quad (1)$$

If in addition the network is trained to minimize the error sum-of-squares, $\sum_{i=1}^{n}(y_i - o_i)^2$, then it is clear that implementing this neural network is *equivalent* to using the method of least squares to fit the nonlinear regression model, $y_i = o_i + \epsilon_i, i = 1, \ldots, n$, where the error terms, ϵ_i, are independently and identically distributed with zero mean and constant variance, to the data. The weights of the network correspond to parameters in the regression model, training corresponds to iteration in an appropriate optimization algorithm, and generalization to prediction. In fact the nonlinear regression model just described is not in any way *meaningful* in relation to the data and the broad modelling procedure should rather be viewed as one of smoothing. In the present example, two logistic functions are scaled and located so that their sum, together with a constant term, approximates an appropriate smooth curve. Overall therefore it is clear that the underlying mechanism of a hidden-layer feed–forward neural network is that of nonlinear regression and that the broad principle underpinning such a network is that of nonparametric regression.

3 Confidence Limits for the True Predicted Values

Consider a hidden-layer feed–forward neural network represented formally as the nonlinear regression model,

$$y_i = \eta(x_i, \theta) + \epsilon_i, \quad i = 1, \ldots, n, \quad (2)$$

where y_i is the observed value at x_i, $\theta = (\theta_1, \ldots, \theta_p)$ is a $p \times 1$ vector of unknown parameters, $\eta(\cdot)$ is a nonlinear function describing the network, and the error terms, ϵ_i, are uncorrelated with mean, 0, and constant variance, σ^2. Then the least squares estimator of θ, denoted $\hat{\theta}$, is that value of θ which minimizes the error sum-of-squares, $S(\theta) = \sum_{i=1}^{n}[y_i - \eta(x_i, \theta)]^2$, and the estimator of σ^2, denoted s^2, is given by $S(\hat{\theta})/(n-p)$. The mean predicted value at x_g for model (2), and hence for the underlying neural network, is given by $\eta(x_g, \hat{\theta})$ and confidence intervals for the corresponding true value, $\eta(x_g, \theta)$, can be derived from likelihood theory or by resampling methods.

3.1 Likelihood Theory

Linearization method : Suppose that the errors in model (2) are normally distributed and suppose further that this model can be satisfactorily approximated by a linear one, and that $V(\hat{\theta})$, the estimated asymptotic variance of the least squares estimator, $\hat{\theta}$, is taken to be $s^2 \left[\sum_{i=1}^{n} g(x_i, \theta) g(x_i, \theta)^T\right]_{\hat{\theta}}^{-1}$, where $g(x_i, \theta) = \partial\eta(x_i, \theta)/\partial\theta, i = 1, \ldots, n$, and the subscript $\hat{\theta}$ denotes evaluation at that point. Then the standard error of the mean predicted value at x_g is given by $SE[\eta(x_g, \hat{\theta})] = s\sqrt{g(x_g, \theta)_{\hat{\theta}}^T \; V(\hat{\theta}) \; g(x_g, \theta)_{\hat{\theta}}}$, where $g(x_g, \theta) = \partial\eta(x_g, \theta)/\partial\theta$, and an approximate $100(1-\alpha)\%$ confidence interval for $\eta(x_g, \theta)$ can be expressed quite simply as

$$\eta(x_g, \hat{\theta}) \pm t^{\star} SE[\eta(x_g, \hat{\theta})], \tag{3}$$

where $t^{\star}$ denotes the appropriate critical t-value with $n-p$ degrees of freedom.

Example 1 : Data were generated from model (2) with deterministic component (1) corresponding to the neural network described in Section 2 and with normally distributed error terms. The parameter values were taken to be

$$\theta = (0.5, 0.5, 1, -1, 0.1, 1, 1.5)$$

and $\sigma = 0.01$, 25 x-values, equally spaced between -12 and 12, were selected, and simulated y-values, corresponding to these x-values, were obtained. The approximate 95% confidence limits to $\eta(x_g, \theta)$ for $x_g \in [-12, 12]$, were calculated using formula (3) and are summarized in the plots of $\pm t^{\star} SE[\eta(x_g, \hat{\theta})]$ against x_g shown in Figure 1. The interesting, systematic pattern exhibited by these limits depends on the design points, $x_i, i = 1, \ldots, n$.

Profile likelihood method : Suppose again that the errors in model (2) are normally distributed and let $S(\hat{\theta}|\eta_g^c)$ denote the minimum error sum-of-squares for a fixed value, η_g^c, of the true predicted value, $\eta(x_g, \theta)$. Then the profile log-likelihood for $\eta(x_g, \theta)$ is described, up to an additive constant, by the curve with generic point, $(\eta_g^c, S(\hat{\theta}|\eta_g^c))$, and a likelihood-based $100(1-\alpha)\%$ confidence interval for $\eta(x_g, \theta)$ comprises those values of η_g^c for which

$$S(\hat{\theta}|\eta_g^c) - S(\hat{\theta}) \leq t^{\star 2} s^2. \tag{4}$$

For Example 1 the requisite values of the conditional sum-of-squares, $S(\hat{\theta}|\eta_g^c)$, for a particular x-value, x_g, were obtained by reformulating the deterministic component of the model as $\eta(x, \theta) = \eta_g + \eta_1(x, \theta) - \eta_1(x_g, \theta)$ with $\eta_1(x, \theta) = \frac{\theta_6}{1+e^{-(\theta_1+\theta_2 x)}} + \frac{\theta_7}{1+e^{-(\theta_3+\theta_4 x)}}$, and by minimizing the resultant error sum-of-squares for appropriate fixed values of the parameter, $\eta_g = \eta(x_g, \theta)$. For each value of $x_g \in [-12, 12]$

so considered, the profile log-likelihood for the true predicted value, $\eta(x_g, \theta)$, was approximately quadratic and the attendant 95% confidence limits were calculated as the two values of η_g^c satisfying the equality condition in expression (4) by using the bisection method. A plot of these 95% confidence limits, centered at the maximum likelihood estimator, $\eta(x_g, \hat{\theta})$, against x_g, are shown, together with those found by the linearization method, in Figure 1. It is clear from this figure that the confidence

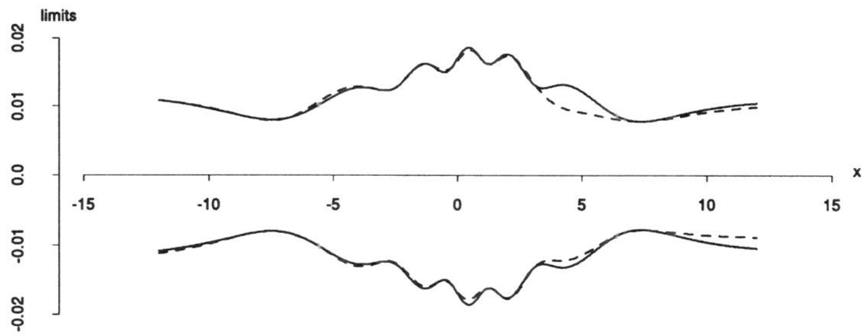

Figure 1 Linearization (solid line) and profile likelihood (dashed line) methods.

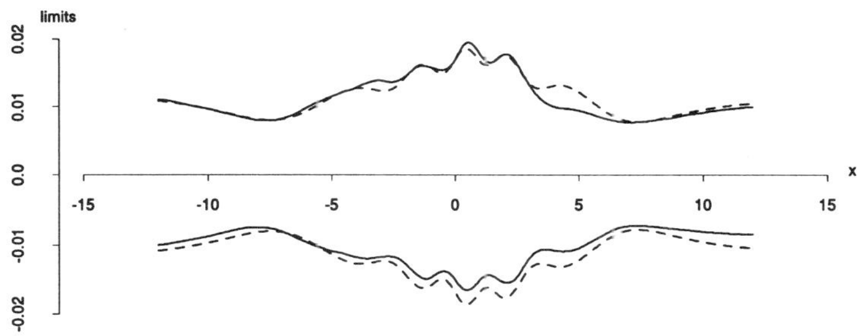

Figure 2 Bootstrap residuals (solid line) and linearization (dashed line) methods.

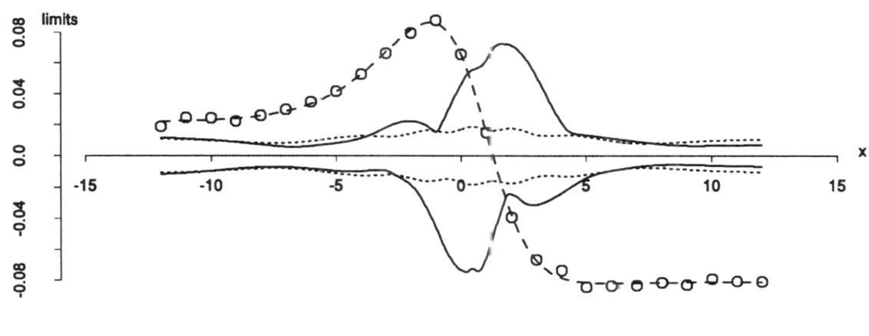

Figure 3 Bootstrap pairs (solid line) and linearization (dotted line) methods; fitted curve (dashed line) and data points (circles).

limits for $\eta(x_g, \theta)$ obtained from these two methods are very similar.

3.2 Bootstrap Methods

Bootstrapping residuals : Suppose that the least squares estimate, $\hat{\theta}$, of the parameters in model (2) is available. Then confidence intervals for true predicted values, $\eta(x_g, \theta)$, can be obtained by bootstrapping the standardized residuals, $e_i = [y_i - \eta(x_i, \hat{\theta})]\sqrt{\frac{n}{n-p}}$ for $i = 1, \ldots, n$, following the procedure for regression models outlined in [1]. For example 1, the resultant 95% bootstrap confidence limits for predicted values, $\eta(x_g, \theta)$, with $x \in [-12, 12]$ were centered at the corresponding bootstrap means, and a plot of these limits against x is shown in Figure 2, together with the the corresponding limits obtained from the linearization method. It is clear from this figure that the broad pattern exhibited by the two sets of confidence limits is the same but that the limits are systematically displaced. An attempt to correct the bootstrap percentiles for bias by implementing the BC_a method of [1] produced limits which were very different from the uncorrected ones.

Bootstrapping pairs : An alternative to bootstrapping the residuals is to bootstrap the data pairs, $(x_i, y_i), i = 1, \ldots, n$, directly, following the procedure given in [1]. Approximate 95% confidence intervals for the true predicted values of Example 1 were obtained in this way and the results, in the form of plots of the confidence limits centered about the bootstrap mean against x, are shown in Figure 3, together with a plot of the corresponding centered limits obtained from the linearization method. Clearly the confidence limits obtained by bootstrapping the data pairs are *wildly* different from those found by the other methods investigated in this study. The reason for this is clear from the suitably scaled plots of the data points and the fitted curve which are superimposed on the plots of the confidence limits in Figure 3 so that the x-values coincide. In particular, only 4 of the 25 observations are taken at x-values corresponding to the steep slope of the fitted curve between $x = -1$ and $x = 2.5$ and the probability that at least one of these points is *excluded* from the bootstrap sample is high, *viz.* 0.8463. As a consequence the bootstrap least squares fitted curve is expected to be, and indeed is, extremely unstable in the region of this slope.

3.3 Comparison of Methods

It is clearly important to generalize the results found thus far. To this end, 400 data sets were simulated from the model setting of Example 1 and, from these, coverage probabilities with a nominal level of 95% for a representative set of true predicted values were evaluated using the likelihood-based and the bootstrap methods of the previous two subsections. The results are summarized in Table 1 and clearly reinforce those obtained for Example 1. In particular, the coverage probabilities provided by the linearization and the profile likelihood-based methods are close to nominal, while those obtained by bootstrapping the residuals are consistently low over the range of x-values considered and those obtained by bootstrapping the data pairs are very erratic.

4 Conclusions

The aim of this present study has been to critically compare selected methods for setting confidence limits to the predicted outputs from a neural network. Both of the likelihood-based methods investigated produced surprisingly good results. In particular, the linearization method proved quick and easy to use, while the profile

Method	x-values for true predicted outputs						
	-10	-5	-2.5	0	2.5	5	10
Linearization	95	95.75	95.75	94.75	92.25	92.5	94.75
Profile likelihood	95.5	94.5	93.5	96	95.25	95	93.25
Bootstrap residuals	91.75	93.5	94	91.5	90	91.75	94.5
Bootstrap pairs	89.75	90.75	96.5	97.25	98.5	92.5	91

Table 1 Coverage probabilities for a nominal level of 95% and 400 simulations.

likelihood approach, which is more rigorous, was a little more difficult to implement. In contrast, the bootstrap methods for finding the required confidence limits were, necessarily, highly computer-intensive, and the results disappointing. On balance, it would seem that, to quote Wu [2], "The linearization method is a winner".

REFERENCES

[1] Efron, B. and Tibshirani, R.J., *An Introduction to the Bootstrap*. Chapman & Hall (1994), New York.

[2] Wu, C.F.J., *Jackknife, bootstrap and other resampling methods in regression analysis*, Annals of Statistics, Vol. 14 (1986), pp1261–1295.

Acknowledgements

The authors wish to thank the University of Natal and the Foundation for Research Development, South Africa, for funding this work.

A NEURAL NETWORK FOR THE TRAVELLING SALESMAN PROBLEM WITH A WELL BEHAVED ENERGY FUNCTION

Marco Budinich and Barbara Rosario

Dipartimento di Fisica & INFN, Via Valerio 2, 34127, Trieste, Italy.
Email: mbh@trieste.infn.it

We present and analyze a Self Organizing Feature Map (SOFM) for the NP-complete problem of the travelling salesman (TSP): finding the shortest closed path joining N cities. Since the SOFM has discrete input patterns (the cities of the TSP) one can examine its dynamics analytically. We show that, with a particular choice of the distance function for the net, the energy associated to the SOFM has its absolute minimum at the shortest TSP path. Numerical simulations confirm that this distance augments performances. It is curious that the distance function having this property combines the distances of the neuron and of the weight spaces.

1 Introduction

Solving difficult problems is a natural arena for a would-be new calculus paradigm like that of neural networks. One can delineate a sharper image of their potential with respect to the blurred image obtained in simpler problems.

Here we tackle the Travelling Salesman Problem (TSP, see [Lawler 1985], [Johnson 1990]) with a Self Organizing Feature Map (SOFM). This approach, proposed by [Angéniol 1988] and [Favata 1991], started to produce respectable performances with the elimination of the non- injective outputs produced by the SOFM [Budinich 1995]. In this paper we further improve its performances by choosing a suitable distance function for the SOFM.

An interesting feature is that this net is open to analytical inspection down to a level that is not usually reachable [Ritter 1992]. This happens because the input patterns of the SOFM, namely the cities of the TSP, are discrete. As a consequence we can show that the energy function, associated with SOFM learning, has its absolute minimum in correspondence to the shortest TSP path.

In what follows we start with a brief presentation of the working principles of this net and of its basic theoretical analysis (section 2). In section 3 we propose a new distance function for the network and show its theoretical advantages while section 4 contains numerical results. The appendix contains the detailed description of parameters needed to reproduce these results.

2 Solving the TSP with self-organizing maps

The basic idea comes from the observation that in one dimension the exact solution to the TSP is trivial: always travel to the nearest unvisited city. Consequently, let us suppose we have a smart map of the TSP cities onto a set of cities distributed on a circle, we will easily find the shortest tour for these "image cities" that will give also a path for the original cities. It is reasonable to conjecture that the better the distance relations are preserved, the better will be the approximate solution found. In this way, the original TSP is reduced to a search of a good neighborhood-preserving map: here we build it via unsupervised learning of a SOFM.

The TSP we consider is constituted of N cities randomly distributed in the plane (actually in the (0,1) square). The net is formed by N neurons logically organized

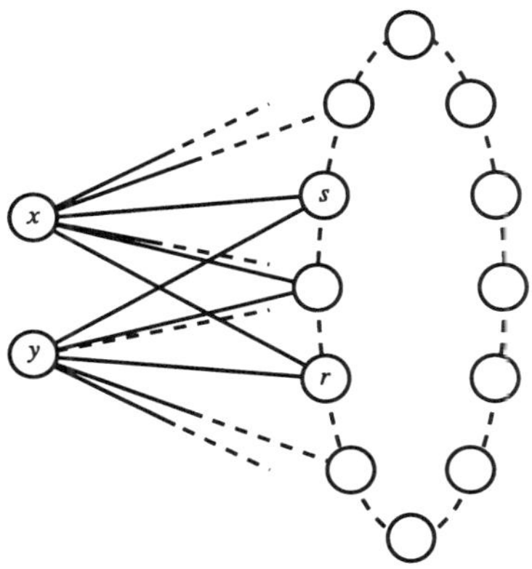

Figure 1 Schematic net: not all connections from input neurons are drawn.

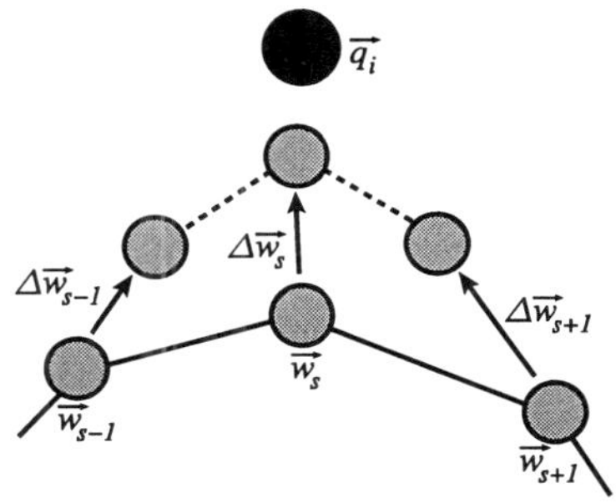

Figure 2 Weights modification in a learning step: neurons (small gray circles) are moved towards the pattern $\vec{q}$ (black circle) by an amount given by (1). The solid line represents the neuron ring. The shape of the deformation of the ring is given by the relative magnitude of the $\Delta\vec{w}$ that is in turn given by the distance function h_{rs}.

in a ring. The cities are the input patterns of the network and the (0,1) square its input space.

Each neuron receives the $(x, y) = \vec{q}$ coordinates of the cities and has thus two weights: $(w_x, w_y) = \vec{w}$. In this view both patterns and neurons can be thought as points in two dimensional space. In response to input $\vec{q}$, the r-th neuron produces output $o_r = \vec{q}\cdot\vec{w}_r$. Figure 1 gives a schematic view of the net while figure 2 represents both patterns and neurons as points in the plane.

Learning follows the standard algorithm [Kohonen 1984]: a city $\vec{q_i}$ is selected at random and proposed to the net; let S be the most responding neuron (ie the neuron nearest to $\vec{q_i}$) then all neuron weights are updated with the rule:

$$\Delta\vec{w}_r = \epsilon h_{rs} (\vec{q_i} - \vec{w}_r) \tag{1}$$

where $0 < \epsilon < 1$ is the learning constant and h_{rs} is the distance function.

This function determines the local deformations along the chain and controls the number of neurons affected by the adaptation step (1); thus it is crucial for the evolution of the network and for the whole learning process (see figure 2).

Step (1) is repeated several times while ϵ and the width of the distance function are being reduced at the same time. A common choice for h_{rs} is a Gaussian-like function like $h_{rs} = e^{-\left(\frac{d_{rs}}{\sigma}\right)^2}$ where d_{rs} is the distance between neurons r and s (the number of steps r and s) and σ is a parameter which determines the number of neurons r such that $\Delta\vec{w}_r \neq 0$; during learning $\epsilon, \sigma \to 0$ so that $\Delta\vec{w}_r \to 0$ and $h_{rs} \to \delta_{rs}$.

After learning, the network maps the two dimensional input space onto the one dimensional space given by the ring of neurons and neighboring cities are mapped onto neighboring neurons. For each city its image is given by the nearest neuron. From the tour on the neuron ring one obtains the path for the original TSP[1]

The standard theoretical approach to these nets considers the expectation value $E[\Delta\vec{w}_r|\vec{w}_r]$ [Ritter 1992]. In general $E[\Delta\vec{w}_r|\vec{w}_r]$ cannot be treated analytically except when the input patterns have a discrete probability distribution as it happens for the TSP. In this case, $E[\Delta\vec{w}_r|\vec{w}_r]$ can be expressed as the gradient of an energy function, i.e. $E[\Delta\vec{w}_r|\vec{w}_r] = -\epsilon\Delta_{\vec{w}_r}V(W)$, with

$$V(W) = \frac{1}{2N}\sum_{rs} h_{rs} \sum_{q_i \in F_s} (\vec{q}_i - \vec{w}_r)^2 \tag{2}$$

where $W = \{\vec{w}_r\}$ and the second sum is over the set of all the cities $\vec{q}_i$ having $\vec{w}_s$ as nearest neuron, i.e. the cities contained in F_s , the Voronoi cell of neuron having $\vec{w}_s$. On average, $V(W)$ decreases during learning since . $E[\Delta V|W] = -\epsilon\sum_r \|\nabla_{\vec{w}_r}V\|^2$. Substantially, in this case, there exists an energy function which describes the dynamics of the SOFM and which is minimized during learning; formally, the learning process is the descent along the gradient of $V(W)$. Unfortunately $V(W)$ escapes analytical treatment until the end of the learning process when some simplifications are applicable. Since at the end of learning $h_{rs} \to \delta_{rs}$, we can suppose h_{rs} is significantly different from zero only for $r = s, s \pm 1$; in this case (2) becomes

$$V(W) \cong \frac{1}{2N}\sum_{s}\sum_{q_i \in F_s} \left[h_{s-1,s}(\vec{q}_i - \vec{w}_{s-1})^2 + h_{ss}(\vec{q}_i - \vec{w}_s)^2 + h_{s+1,s}(\vec{q}_i - \vec{w}_{s+1})^2\right] \tag{3}$$

In addition, simulations support that, at the end of learning, most neurons are selected by just one city to which they get nearer and nearer. This means that F_s, contains just one city, let's call it $\vec{q}_{i(s)}$, and that $\vec{w}_s \to \vec{q}_{i(s)}$, consequently

$$V(W) \cong \frac{1}{2N}\sum_{s} \left[h_{s-1,s}(\vec{q}_{i(s)} - \vec{q}_{i(s-1)})^2 + h_{s+1,s}(\vec{q}_{i(s)} - \vec{q}_{i(s+1)})^2\right] \tag{4}$$

and assuming h_{rs} symmetric i.e. $h_{s-1,s} = h_{s+1,s} = h$, we get

$$\begin{aligned} V(W) &= \frac{h}{2N}\sum_{s} \left[(\vec{q}_{i(s)} - \vec{q}_{i(s-1)})^2 + (\vec{q}_{i(s)} - \vec{q}_{i(s+1)})^2\right] \\ &= \frac{h}{N}L_{TSP^2} \end{aligned}$$

where L_{TSP^2} is the length of the tour of TSP considering the squares of the distances between cities. Thus the Kohonen algorithm for TSP minimizes an energy function which, at the end of the leaning process, is proportional to the sum of the squares of the distances. Numerical simulations confirm this result.

3 A New Distance Function

Our hypothesis is that we can obtain better results for the TSP using a distance function h_{rs} such that, at the end of the process, $V(W)$ is proportional to the simple length of the tour L_{TSP}, namely $V(W) \propto \sum_s(\vec{q}_{i(s)} - \vec{q}_{i(s-1)}) = L_{TSP}$ since, in general, minimizing L_{TSP^2} is not equivalent to minimizing L_{TSP}. We thus consider

[1] The main weakness of this algorithm is that, in about half of the cases, the map produced is not injective. The definition of a continuous coordinate along the neuron ring solves this problem yielding a competitive algorithm [Budinich 1995].

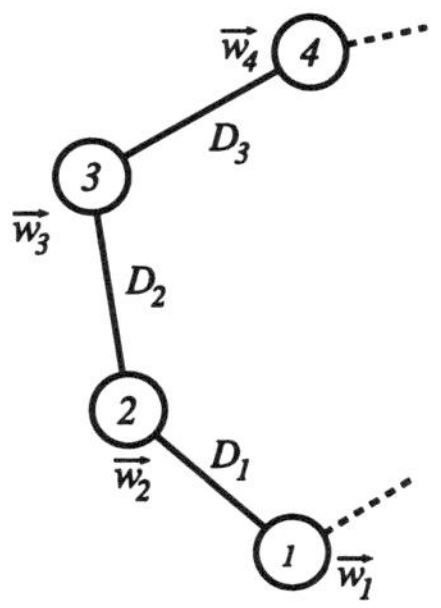

Figure 3 Distances between neurons $s = 4$ and $r = 1$: $D_{1,4} = D_1 + D_2 + D_3$ and $d_{1,4} = 3$.

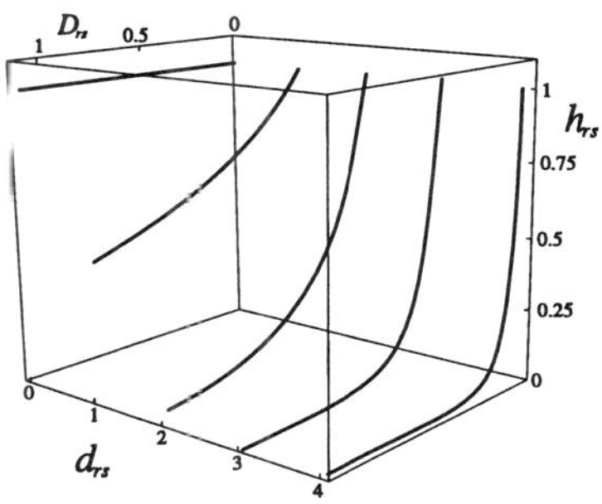

Figure 4 Set of h_{is} given by (5) for $0 < D_{is} < 1$ and $d_{is} = 0, 1, \ldots, 4$.

a function h_{rs} depending both on the distance d_{rs} and on another distance D_{rs} defined in weight space:

$$D_{rs} = \sum_{j=r+1}^{3} |\vec{w}_j - \vec{w}_{j-1}|$$

If we define

$$h_{rs} = \left(1 + \frac{D_{rs}}{\sigma}\right)^{-d_{rs}^2} \tag{5}$$

when $\sigma \to 0$, we get for $h_{s\pm1,s}$

$$h_{s\pm1,s} = \left(1 + \frac{D_{s\pm1,s}}{\sigma}\right)^{-1} \cong \frac{\sigma}{D_{s\pm1,s}} = \frac{\sigma}{|\vec{w}_s - \vec{w}_{s\pm1}|} \cong \frac{\sigma}{|\vec{q}_{i(s)} - \vec{q}_{i(s\pm1)}|}$$

and substituting this expression in (4) we obtain $V(W)$

$$\begin{aligned} &\cong \frac{1}{2N}\sum_s \left[\frac{\sigma}{|\vec{q}_{i(s)} - \vec{q}_{i(s-1)}|}(\vec{q}_{i(s)} - \vec{q}_{i(s-1)})^2 + \frac{\sigma}{|\vec{q}_{i(s)} - \vec{q}_{i(s+1)}|}(\vec{q}_{i(s)} - \vec{q}_{i(s+1)})^2\right] \\ &= \frac{\sigma}{N}\sum_s |\vec{q}_{i(s)} - \vec{q}_{i(s+1)}| \\ &= \frac{\sigma}{N} L_{TSP} \end{aligned}$$

With this choice of h_{rs} the minimization of the energy $V(W)$ is equivalent to the minimization of the TSP path. We remark that the introduction of the distance D_{rs} between weights is a slightly unusual hypothesis for this kind of nets that usually keep well separated neuron and weight spaces in the sense that the distance function h_{rs} depends only on the distance d_{rs}.

4 Numerical Results

Since the performances of this kind of TSP algorithms are good for problems with more than 500 cities and more critical in smaller problems [Budinich 1995], we began testing the performances produced by the new distance function (5) in problems with 50 cities.

City set	Min. length	[Durbin 1987]	[Budinich 1995]	This algorithm
1	5.8358	2.47%	1.65%	0.96%
2	5.9945	0.59%	1.66%	0.31%
3	5.5749	2.24%	1.06%	1.05%
4	5.6978	2.85%	1.37%	0.70%
5	6.1673	5.23%	5.25%	0.43%
Average		2.68%	2.20%	0.69%

Table 1 Comparison of the best TSP solution obtained in 10 runs of the various algorithms. Rows refer to the 5 different problems each of 50 cities randomly distributed in the (0,1) square. Column 2 reports the length of the best known solution for the given problem. Columns 3 to 5 contain the best lengths obtained by the three algorithms under study expressed as percentual increments from the minimal length; the number of runs of the algorithms is respectively: unknown, 5 and 10. Last row gives the increment averaged over the 5 city sets.

We compared the quality of TSP solutions obtained with this net to those of two other algorithms both deriving from the idea of a topology preserving map and that both actually minimizes L_{TSP^2} : the elastic net of Durbin and Willshaw [Durbin 1987] and this same algorithm with a standard distance choice.
As a test set, we considered the very same 5 sets of 50 randomly distributed cities used for the elastic net.
Table 1 contains a comparison of the best TSP path obtained in several runs of the different algorithms expressed as percentual increments over the best known solution for the given problem. Another measure of the quality of the solution is the mean length obtained in the 10 runs. The percentual increment of these mean lengths, averaged over the 5 sets, was for this algorithm 2.49%, showing that even the averages found with the new distance function are better than the minima found with the elastic net.
These results clearly show that distance choice (5) gives better solutions in this SOFM application, thus supporting the guess that an energy $V(W)$ directly proportional to the length of the tour L_{TSP}, is better tuned to this problem.
One could wonder if adding weight space information to the distance function could give interesting results also in other SOFM applications.

Appendix

Here we describe the network setting that produces the quoted numerical results. Apart from the distance definition (5) we apply a standard Kohonen algorithm and exponentially decrease parameters ϵ and σ with learning epoch n_e (a learning epoch corresponds to N weights update with rule (1))

$$\epsilon = \epsilon_0 \alpha^{n_e} \qquad \sigma = \sigma_0 \beta^{n_e}$$

and learning stops when ϵ reaches $5 \cdot 10^{-3}$. Numerical simulations clearly indicate that best results are obtained when the final value of σ is very small ($\approx 5 \cdot 10^{-3}$) and when ϵ and σ decrease together reaching their final value at the same time. Consequently given values for α and σ_0 one easily finds β. In other words there are just three free parameters to play with to optimize results, namely ϵ_0 and σ_0 and α.

After some investigation we obtained the following values that produce the quoted results: $\epsilon_0 = 0.8$, $\sigma_0 = 14$ and $\alpha = 0.9996$.

REFERENCES

[1] B Angeniol, de G. La Croix Vaubois and J.-Y. Le Texier, *Self Organising Feature Maps and the Travelling Salesman Problem*, Neural Networks Vol.1 (1988), pp289–293.

[2] M Budinich, *A Self-Organising Neural Network for the Travelling Salesman Problem that is Competitive with Simulated Annealing*, to appear in: Neural Computation.

[3] R. Durbin and D. Willshaw, *An Analogue Approach to the Travelling Salesman Problem using an Elastic Net Method*, Nature Vol.336 (1987), pp689–691.

[4] F Favata amd R Walker. *A Study of the Application of Kohonen-type Neural Networks to the Travelling Salesman Problem*, Biological Cybernetics Vol. 64 (1991), pp463–468.

[5] D. S. Johnson, *Local Optimization and the Traveling Salesman Problem*, in: Proceedings of the 17th Colloquium on Automata Languages and Programming, Springer-Verlag (1990) New York, pp446–461.

[6] T. Kohonen, *Self-Organisation and Associative Memory*, Springer-Verlag (1984, 3rd Ed. 1989), Berlin Heidelberg.

[7] E. L. Lawler, J. K. Lenstra , A. G. Rinnoy Kan and D. B. Shmoys (editors), *The Traveling Salesman Problem — A Guided Tour of Combinatorial Optimization*, John Wiley & Sons, New York (1990), IV Reprint, p474.

[8] H. Ritter, T. Martinez and K. Schultern, *Neural Computation and Self Organising Maps*, Addison-Wesley Publishing Company (1992), Reading Massachusetts , p306.

SEMIPARAMETRIC ARTIFICIAL NEURAL NETWORKS

Enrico Capobianco

Stanford University, Stanford, CA 94305, USA.

Email: enrico@psych.stanford.edu

In this paper Artificial Neural Networks are considered as an example of the semiparametric class of models which has become very popular among statisticians and econometricians in recent years. Modelling and learning aspects are discussed. Some statistical procedures are described in order to learn with infinite-dimensional nuisance parameters, and adaptive estimators are presented.

Keywords: Semiparametric Artificial Neural Networks; Profile Likelihood; Efficiency Bounds; Asymptotic Adaptive Estimators

1 Introduction

We look at the interface between statistics and artificial neural networks (ANN) and study stochastic multilayer neural networks with unspecified functional components. We call them **Semiparametric Neural Networks** (SNN). The fact that no absolute requirements come from biological considerations represents an important motivation for SNN. Many technical issues arise from the statistical inference perspective; we (**A**) stress the importance of computing likelihood-based criterion functions in order to exploit the large sample statistical properties pertaining to the related estimators and (**B**) measure the asymptotic efficiency of the estimators from given network architectures.

2 ANN and Likelihood Theory

A stochastic machine with a vector of synaptic weights w, the input(output) vectors $x(y)$ (given a conditional density function $f(y/x)$) and the data set dimension T, is used to compute w through a learning algorithm based on the minimization of some fitting criterion function of estimated residuals or prediction errors. Consider a likelihood function $L(Y,\theta)$, where $Y = (y_1, \dots, y_T)'$ is the sample observation vector and $\theta = (\theta_1, \dots, \theta_p)'$ is a vector of parameters. These three elements can fully characterize a taxonomy of models, differentiated by the sample size and the dimension of the parameter space where the optimization of the chosen criterion function must be done. For instance, in a network where all the activation functions are specified and the dimension of θ is $p < \infty$, i.e., in a fully parametric situation, the solution to the optimization problem is to maximize $l = \sum_{i=1}^{T} lnL(y_i,\theta)$ over the weight space Θ. On the other hand, the activation functions can be reasonably left unspecified, apart from some smoothness conditions. This choice permits a shift from a parametric to a more nonparametric setting, where the likelihood function now admits a modified form $L(Y,\lambda)$, with $\lambda = (w,g,h)$ and w,g,h that indicate respectively the weight vector, the unknown output and hidden layer activation functions. A more restricted context, but still semiparametric in nature, occurs when g or h are in fact specified; networks here closely resemble the semiparametric and nonparametric extensions of the Generalized Linear Models [7] described in [6]. As a result, the likelihood function is now more constrained, with $L(Y,\delta)$ and $\delta = (w,g,\bar{h})$ or $\delta = (w,\bar{g},h)$. If a stochastic one-hidden layer feedforward neural network is represented by:

$$y = G(x, w) = F[\gamma_0 + \sum_{j=1}^{q} \alpha_j f(\gamma_j + \sum_{i=1}^{s} v_{ij} x_i)] \tag{1}$$

where $w = (\alpha', v', \gamma')'$ is the vector of weights and F/f are the specified output/hidden layer activation functions, then a likelihood-based criterion function, under a gaussian distribution of p(y/x,w), is directly related to the sum-of-squared errors scaled by the output variance. For $F(z) = z$, we have that:

$$max \sum_t lnp(y_t/x_t, w) \equiv min \ \frac{1}{2} \sum_t \frac{1}{\sigma_t^2}(y_t - G(x_t, w))^2 \tag{2}$$

Whenever Gaussianity is assumed but not verified, a **quasi-maximum likelihood** criterion is given. Conditionally gaussian time series models are specified in terms of a gaussian distribution for y_t, conditioned on the information available at time t-1; here too a likelihood function can be computed and thus (2) holds[1]. When the likelihood function relies on unknown components we deal with an ill-posed optimization problem and some form of regularization is required. If the entire parameter vector can be decomposed in "interest" w and "nuisance" η components, such that $\hat{\theta} = (\hat{w}, \hat{\eta})$ represents the ML estimator of θ, $\tilde{\theta}(w) = (w, \tilde{\eta}_{\bar{w}})$ is a constrained initial estimator for θ, i.e., an estimator computed from an initially fixed value of the parameters of interest, not necessarily a ML value. Inference for w can be based on the so-called **profile** or **concentrated** log-likelihood function $PL(w) = L(\tilde{\theta}(w))$. We seek the value w^* which maximizes PL(w); it is $w^* = \hat{w}$, at least for the case of a finite dimensional nuisance parameter space. In other words, a ML estimate is computed in two sequential stages: (1) an estimate is obtained for η, given an initial consistent value of w; (2) the MLE for w conditional to $\tilde{\eta}_{\bar{w}}$ is calculated by maximizing a likelihood-based criterion function where the previous estimate of η has been plugged-in. Hence the name profile log-likelihood.

3 The Semiparametric Approach to ANN

The bias/variance dilemma [4] is crucial in ANN as it is in nonparametric statistical inference. If the relation between the input and the output variables is unknown, as for the function $E(y_t/\mathcal{F}_t)$ in nonlinear regression or $E(y_t/\mathcal{Y}_{t-1})$ in time series prediction problems [2] ANN will try to exploit their "universal approximation" properties. But whereas parametric and potentially incorrect models lead to high bias, nonparametric models lead to high variance, given the presence of parameters of infinite dimension; therefore, the loss of efficiency is a likely price to pay. We usually observe noisy input data, according to some underlying probability distribution; thus, for some aspects, the advantage is that data could be replicated under certain conditions that offer a solution for the data-size constraint and thus soften

[1] The normalized mean squared error [12] cost function $E = \frac{1}{T\hat{\sigma}_T^2}\sum_t(y_t - \hat{y}_t)^2$ can also be used. Otherwise, the likelihood can be formed in terms of the prediction errors $v_t = y_t - E(y_t/y_{t-1}, \ldots, y_1)$, given that $var(v_t) = var(y_t/y_{t-1}, \ldots, y_1)$. Moreover, the $\hat{w}$ value that minimizes $\frac{1}{T}\sum_t(y_t - G(x_t, w))^2$ is equivalent to the NLS estimator [13] and this converges to the network optimal weights w^* as $n \to \infty$.

[2] $\mathcal{F}_t$ or $\mathcal{Y}_{t-1}$ represent information up to the time t or t-1 (lags only included for $\mathcal{Y}_{t-1}$).

the "curse of dimensionality"[3].

An important aspect in SNN is related to the functional form of the I/O relation. The approximation ability of the network depends on the characteristics of the underlying functional relation; usually sigmoidal-type or RBF-type ANN work well, but when the activation functions are left unspecified, projection pursuit regression [3] and other highly parameterized techniques represent possible solutions. We consider pure minimization and iterative estimation strategies; the former are based on the decomposition of the parameter vector, $\theta = (w, \eta)$, where w represents the weights and the bias terms considered together and η represents the infinite-dimensional nuisance parameter[4], and the latter are **Newton-Raphson** (NR)-type procedures. We address the optimization problem in the Profile ML setting introduced before. But another challenging issue is the weight estimation accuracy, at least asymptotically. By working with an initially unrestricted likelihood-based performance measure we would like to obtain, in statistical terms, a lower bound [8, 9, 10] for the asymptotic variance (AV) of the parametric component of the semiparametric model such that we are able to generalize the usual parametric bound given by the inverse of the **Fisher Information Matrix** (FIM). We equivalently calculate the **Semiparametric Efficiency Bounds** (SEB) for the parameters of interest, which quantify the efficiency loss resulting from a semiparametric model compared to a parametric one[5].

4 Parametric and Nonparametric Estimation Theory

The discussion here draws mainly on [8], [10] and [11], where the concept of marginal Fisher's bound for asymptotic variances in parametric models is generalized. If it is true that *a nonparametric problem is at least as difficult as any of the parametric problems obtained by assuming we have enough knowledge of the unknown state of nature to restrict it to a finite dimensional set*, it is important to look for a method that obtains a lower bound for the AV of the parametric component of the initially unrestricted model[6]. Since a one-dimensional sub-problem asymptotically as difficult as the original multidimensional problem often exists, *we could express the parameter space as a union* of these one-dimensional sub-problems (paths or directions along w, like $F_w : F_w \in \mathcal{F}$) and estimate the parameter of interest *to select one of the sub-problems proceeding as if the true parameter would lay on this curve.* The question is: which sub-problem should be selected? First, we should verify the existence of an estimator for a " curve " defined in the infinite-dimensional nuisance parameter space, corresponding to one of the possible one-dimensional

[3]These distributional assumptions make a substantial difference in terms of the **global or local statistical efficiency** that an estimator can achieve. While for global efficiency we mean that an estimator is accurate regardless of the true underlying distributions, for local efficiency the same holds only for some specific distributions related to the nonparametric component of the model.

[4]η can stand for the unknown hidden layer activation functions, the noise density which randomly perturbs the input/output pattern data, the weights or even the same activation functions.

[5]In the ANN context we could make comparisons between SNN and sigmoidal-type or other networks on the grounds of the statistical efficiency of the related learning algorithms.

[6]If a sequence of estimators (θ_n) satisfies $\sqrt{n}(\theta_n - \theta) \rightarrow_d N(0, V)$, then V is the asymptotic variance of (θ_n) and for the ML estimator, under regular conditions, equals I_θ^{-1}, where I_θ is the FIM.

sub-problems. Given $\theta = (w, \eta)$, consider the smooth curve $\theta(t) : \; a < t < b$ designed in the space $W \times \Upsilon$ by the map $t \rightarrow \theta(t) = (w(t), \eta(t))$. According to a possible parameterization inducted by $w(t) = t$, the map becomes $w \rightarrow (w, \eta_w)$ with $\eta_{w_0} = \eta_0$ and for each curve η_w we can compute the associated score functions U_w ,U_η such that, $\frac{d}{dw} l(w, \eta_w) \mid_{w=w_0} = \frac{\partial l}{\partial w}(w_0, \eta_0) + \frac{\partial l}{\partial \eta}(w_0, \eta_0)(\frac{d}{dw}\eta_w \mid_{w=w_0})$ (or simply $U_w + U_\eta$) and the information matrix $E_0(\frac{d}{dw} l(w, \eta_w) \mid_{w=w_0})^2 = E(U_w + U)^2$, where $U \in span(U_\eta)$. Repeating the procedure for all the possible η_w we can find the minimum FIM, which is given by $inf(E_0(U_w + U)^2 = E_0(U_w + U^*) = i_w$, where U^* is the projection of U_w onto $span(U_\eta)$. In particular, we define the curve η^*_w for which this minimum is achieved as the **Least Favorable Curve** (LFC). With a semiparametric model, in order for η^*_w to be LFC, the following relation must be satisfied:

$$E([\frac{\partial l(w, \eta^*_w)}{\partial w}] \mid_{w=w_0})^2 \leq E([\frac{\partial l(w, \eta_w)}{\partial w}] \mid_{w=w_0})^2 \tag{3}$$

for each curve $w \rightarrow \eta_w$ in the nuisance functional space Υ[7]. Following the parametric case, the marginal FIM for w in a semiparametric model is given by:

$$i_w = inf_\eta E([\frac{\partial l(w, \eta_w)}{\partial w}] \mid_{w=w_0})^2 \tag{4}$$

or alternatively $i_w = E_0(U_w + U^*_\eta)$, with $U^*_\eta = \frac{\partial}{\partial \eta} \dot{l}(w_0, \eta_0)(t^*))^2$, where $t^* \in \Upsilon$ represents the tangent vector to the curve η_w at w_0 and $\frac{\partial \dot{l}}{\partial \eta}$ is a Frechet derivative[8]. Now, $i_w^{-1} = V$ is the lower bound for the AV of a regular[9] estimator of w in the semiparametric model. In summary, every semiparametric estimator has an AV comparable to the Cramer-Rao bound of a semiparametric model; therefore, the bound is not less than the bound of every parametric sub-model, i.e. the *sup V* of all these bounds. This is the semiparametric AV bound or SEB, whose attainment reflects the ability to estimate adaptively.

5 Adaptive Estimation

In practice, accurate estimation and unrestricted model specification can be contrasting aspects of a problem. Adaptive estimation is a solution since it suggests that full efficiency can still be attained even under an initially unrestricted model[10]. A pure minimization method for adaptively estimating semiparametric models is the one described in Section 2 and adopted in [10], the **Generalized Profile Likelihood** (GPL)[11]. For a regular estimator the **convolution theorem** [2] applies,

[7] In practice [10] for a nonparametric regression or density estimation problem $\hat{\eta}_w$ often converges to the LFC; otherwise, we could verify that its limit is such that a least favorable direction is found.

[8] We say that T is *Frechet differentiable* at x if there exists a function $\dot{T}_x : X \rightarrow Y$ which is linear and continuous such that $lim_{|h| \rightarrow 0} \frac{||T(x+h) - T(x) - \dot{T}_x(h)||}{||h||} = 0$ (see [2]).

[9] Given a local DGP, i.e. a stochastic process where for every sample size n the data are distributed according to θ_n, with $\sqrt{n}(\theta_n - \theta_0)$ bounded, an estimator $W \subset \Theta$ is called **regular in a parametric sub-model** if, for each true value θ_0 of the parameter vector, $\sqrt{n}(\hat{w} - w(\theta_n))$ has a limit distribution not dependent on the local DGP and **regular** if the property holds for every parametric sub-model.

[10] An adaptive estimator can be found to exist or not. In any case, the model is required to satisfy conditions related more to the underlying structure or functional relations than to the possible adaptive estimation procedures [9].

[11] Generalized because the first step estimator for the nuisance parameter vector is not required to be an ML estimator.

thus giving an asymptotic distribution for $\sqrt{n}(\hat{w} - w_0)$ equal to that of Z+U, where $Z \sim N(0, V)$ and U an independent noise; V is the SEB, as shown when U is gaussian and thus $Var(\hat{w}) = V + E(UU') >> V$. If η_w is a curve in Υ, we require that the estimator $\hat{w}$ obtained by maximizing $l(w, \tilde{\eta}_{\bar{w}})$ has an asymptotic distribution as the one of the estimator obtained by $l(w, \eta_w)$, or equivalently we require that the two functions have the same local behavior; then, the SEB should be attained. If $\hat{w}$ is the maximizer of $l(w, \tilde{\eta}_{\bar{w}})$, then $\sqrt{n}(\hat{w} - w_0) \rightarrow_D N(0, i_{\bar{w}}^{-1})$ is expected, because when η_w is LFC the bias disappears asymptotically, due to the orthogonality of the score functions. Thus, under some regularity conditions, an estimator for w can be obtained by maximizing the GPL criterion function and the estimator is asymptotically efficient. The value of the SEB is given by the inverse of:

$$\hat{i}_w = -\frac{1}{n}\left[\frac{\partial^2 l(w, \tilde{\eta}_{\bar{w}})}{\partial w' \partial w}\right] |_{w=\hat{w}} \tag{5}$$

5.1 The Algorithm Applied to ANN; an Example

Consider the example in [1]: suppose we have a stochastic machine with an input vector $x \subset R^s$, a p-dimensional weight vector w and the binary output is $y = \pm 1$ according to p(y/x,w), where $p(y = 1/x, w) = k[f(x, w)]$ and $p(y = -1/x, w) = 1 - k[f(x, w)]$, $k(f) = \frac{1}{1+e^{-\beta f}}$, β is the inverse of the so-called temperature parameter and f represents a smooth hidden layer activation function (therefore our nuisance parameters). The general form of the conditional log-likelihood function $l(y/x, w) = lnp(y/x, w)$ is $\mathcal{L} = \sum_i [y_i \ln D(w)] + (1 - y_i)\ln[(1 - D(w))]$, where $D(w) = k[f(x_i, w)]$. According to the GPL procedure, we *(**1**) estimate initially w via BP with a network of fixed structure (i.e. f represented with one of the usually specified forms) (**2**) obtain a nonparametric estimate $\hat{f}$ conditionally on the estimated w, thus finding $\hat{D}$ (**3**) plug in $\hat{f}_{\bar{w}}$ and maximize the GPL criterion function w.r.t. w (where $\hat{D}$ in fact replaces D^* which represents an estimable and locally approximating version of the unknown function D) (4) calculate $\hat{w}$ and repeat steps 2-3-4 till we go as close as possible to the SEB*[12]. Thus the stochastic machine specifies the probabilities $p(y = \pm 1/x, w)$.

5.2 Relationships between GPL and Learning Consolidation

When fully iterative algorithms are considered, **consolidation of network learning** proposed in [13] becomes important, since BP is only one of the possible **recursive m-estimators** that locally solve optimization problems and is asymptotically inefficient relative to a NR-type estimator, regardless of the local minimizer. Thus, BP can be improved with regard to the accuracy of the estimate through just one NR step. In [8] one-step *semiparametric m-estimators* are considered[13]; they are based on the zero mean and finite variance *influence function* (IF) $\psi(z)$ of a single observation on the estimator, such that $\sqrt{n}(\hat{\phi} - \phi) = \sum_i \frac{\psi_i}{\sqrt{n}} + o_p(1)$, and they

[12]Note that (**A**) $\hat{w}(\hat{D})$ that maximizes $L(\hat{D}(w))$ should behave like $\hat{w}(D)$, where $\hat{w}(D) = argsup_w L(D(w))$ (a consistent estimator is required, given that $L(\hat{D}(w) \rightarrow_{pr} L(D(w))$ uniformly in w) (**B**) given $AV = \frac{1}{G}$, where according to [1] $G = (g_{ij})$ is the FIM and $g_{ij} = \beta^2 \int \sum_y k(1-k)\frac{\partial f}{\partial w_i}\frac{\partial f}{\partial w_j} p(x)dx$ is the generic component of G, we must compare AV with the inverse of (5).

[13]These estimators are asymptotically efficient after one iteration from a consistent initial estimate of the parameter of interest and with the functions of the likelihood consistently estimated.

solve moment equations of the form $\frac{\sum_i m(z_i,\phi,\tilde{\eta})}{n} = 0$, given a general interest parameter ϕ. The m(.) function, similar to the *estimating functions* adopted in [5], can represent the *First Order Conditions* for the *maximum* of a criterion function Q, and η maximizes the expected value of the same function. This method is equivalent to GPL when f is the density from a given distribution function F, Q is the log-likelihood function, m(.) the score function and $\eta(\phi, F)$ is the limit, for the nonparametric component, that maximizes the expected value of $lnf(z/\phi, \eta)$. With $\hat{\phi} = argmax_\phi \sum_i lnf(z_i/\phi, \tilde{\eta}_{\bar{\phi}})$ as the GP(Max)L estimator, where the estimation of η does not affect the AV, and given $M = \frac{\partial E(m(z,\phi,\eta_0))}{\partial \phi} |_{\phi=\phi_0}$ nonsingular, we have $\psi(z) = M^{-1}m(z,\phi,\eta_0)$ and $\dot{\phi} = \hat{\phi} + \frac{\sum_i \hat{\psi}(z_i,\hat{\phi})}{n}$, which is the one-step version of GP(Max)L estimator.

6 Conclusions

We analyzed semiparametric neural networks, described a general model set-up and discussed the related asymptotic estimation issues. The degree of success in solving the bias/variance dilemma is often a case-dependent problem requiring a reparameterization of the model in the hope of finding adaptive estimators. SEB tell us about the asymptotic statistical efficiency of the chosen estimator.

REFERENCES

[1] S.Amari and N.Murata, Statistical *Theory of Learning Curves under Entropic Loss Criterion*, Neural Comput., Vol.5 (1993), pp140–153.

[2] P.Bickel, C.A.J.Klaassen, Y.Ritov and J.A.Wellner, *Efficient and Adaptive Estimation of Semiparametric Models.* The John Hopkins University Press (1993).

[3] J.H.Friedman and W.Stuetzle, *Projection Pursuit Regression*, JASA, Vol. 76 (1981), pp817–823.

[4] S.Geman, E.Bienenstock and R.Doursat, *Neural Networks and the bias/variance dilemma*, Neural Comput., Vol. 4 (1992), pp1–58.

[5] M.Kawanabe and S.Amari, *Estimation of networks parameters in semiparametric stochastic perceptron*, Neural Comput., Vol. 6 (1994), pp1244–1261.

[6] P.A.Jokinen, *A nonlinear network model for continuous learning*, Neurocomp., Vol. 3 (1991), pp157–176.

[7] R.McCullagh and J.A.Nelder, *Generalized Linear Models*, Chapman and Hall (1989).

[8] W.K.Newey, *Semiparametric efficiency bounds*, J. Appl. Ec.trics, Vol. 5 (1990), pp99–135.

[9] W.K.Newey, *The asymptotic variance of semiparametric estimators*, Econometrica, Vol.62 (1994), pp1349–1382.

[10] T. Severini and W.H. Wong, *Profile likelihood and conditionally parametric models*, An. Stat., Vol. 20 (1992), pp1768–1802.

[11] C. Stein, *Efficient nonparametric testing and estimation*, in: Proceedings Third Berkeley Symposium in Mathematics, Statistics and Probability, University of California Press, Berkeley, (1956) Vol. 1, pp187–196.

[12] A.S.Weigend and N.A.Gershenfeld, *Time series prediction: forecasting the future and understanding the past*, Santa Fe, Proc. Vol. XV (1994), Addison-Wesley.

[13] H. White, *Artificial Neural Networks. Approximation and learning theory*, Blackwell, (1992).

Acknowledgements

The author thanks two anonymous referees for their suggestions.

AN EVENT-SPACE FEEDFORWARD NETWORK USING MAXIMUM ENTROPY PARTITIONING WITH APPLICATION TO LOW LEVEL SPEECH DATA

D.K.Y. Chiu, D. Bockus and J. Bradford*

University of Guelph, Ontario, Canada.

** Brock University, St. Catharines, Ontario, Canada.*

This paper describes an event-space feedforward network based on partitioning of the input space using maximum entropy criterion. It shows how primitives defined as partitioned hypercells (event space) can be selected for the purpose of class discrimination. Class discrimination of a hypercell is evaluated statistically. Observed primitives corresponding to observed characteristics in selected hypercells are used as inputs to a feedforward network in classification. Preliminary experimental results using simulated data and as it pertains to speaker discrimination using low-level speech data have shown very good classification rates.

1 Introduction

This paper proposes a feedforward network whose input layer is reconfigured during the training phase depending on the generation and selection of newly defined primitives. As the primitives are identified through partitioning of the input outcome space, so would the construction of the input nodes which corresponds to defining the primitive set. The primitives are defined through the selection of partitioned hypercells corresponding to certain feature values of the data selected for classification. Thus, an observed primitive in a datum would correspond to an observed selected characteristic (or range of values) which eventually determine the datum's classification. Since the input layer in the network is reconfigured depending on the selected hypercells identified, we call it a self-configurable neural network [2]. The two processes of primitive generation and classification are integrated and "closely coupled".

2 Maximum Entropy Partitioning

When discretizing the outcome space based on partitioning of the data, the discretization process becomes a partitioning process. The Maximum Entropy Partitioning (MEP) process generates a set of hypercells through partitioning of the outcome space of n continuous valued variables (or features) [1,3,4,7]. This method bypasses the problem of non-uniform scaling for different variables in multivariate datum compared to the commonly used equal-width partitioning algorithm, and minimizes the information loss after partitioning [3].

Given n variables in n-dimensional space, the MEP process partitions a data set into k^n hypercells based on the estimated probabilities of the data. The value k represents the number of intervals that a dimension is divided into. Let P be the probability distribution where the process produces a quantization of P into:

$$P(R_i), i = 1, 2, \ldots, k^n, \tag{1}$$

where R_i denotes a hypercell. To maximize the information represented by R_i, the partitioning scheme which maximizes Shannon's entropy function defined below is used:

$$H(R) = -\sum_{i=1}^{k^n} P(R_i) \log P(R_i). \tag{2}$$

The function $H(R)$ now becomes the objective function where information can be maximized according to the maximization of $H(R)$. With one variable, maximization occurs when the expected probability $P(R_i)$ is approximately $1/k$ of the training data with repeated observations. This creates a narrower interval where the probability density is higher [3] In the proposed method, the partitioning process is done based on the marginal probability distribution on each variable to avoid combinatorial complexity.

In our data representation (such as low-level speech data), the jth datum is represented by a set of $I(j)$ points which are denoted by $Z_j = \{x_i = (x_{1i}, x_{2i}, ..., x_{ni}) | i = 1, ..., I(j)\}$. That is, Z_j composes of sets of n-vectors. A set of partition boundaries are determined by combining all the data into a single set that we call the "data universe" denoted by U. Hence, U is defined as the union of all the training data:

$$U = \{Z_j \,|\, j = 1, \ldots, J\} = Z_1 \cup Z_2 \cup \cdots \cup Z_J \tag{3}$$

Each data is assumed to have an assigned class label C_m in L_c classes, $1 \leq m \leq L_c$. In n-dimensional space, the set of hypercells generated after partitioning is then defined as $R = \{R_i | i = 1, 2, ..., k^n\}$, where each R_i is bounded by intervals that partition the data universe. The intervals that bound R_i are composed of the boundary points which will be determined by an algorithm [3].

3 Selection of the Partitioned Hypercells

Representation of individual datum Z_j is based on the same partitioning scheme generated from partitioning the data universe. Each generated hypercells from the partitioning cordons off a set of points in Z_j. Since our partitioning is based on the marginal probability distributions, a hypercell R_i on datum Z_j that has significantly more points than expected can be evaluated using the following statistic also known as the standard residual [5]:

$$D(R_i, Z_j) = \frac{\text{obs}(R_i, Z_j) - \exp(R_i, Z_j)}{\sqrt{\exp(R_i, Z_j)}} \tag{4}$$

where $\exp(R_i, Z_j)$ is defined as the average number of points observed in a hypercell R_i, calculated as $M(Z_j)/k^n$, and $\text{obs}(R_i, Z_j)$ is the number of points in Z_j observed in the same hypercell given that $M(Z_j)$ is the total number of points in Z_j. Since the statistic follows a normal distribution, it is therefore possible to evaluate a hypercell which has significant characteristic in the data, based on the normal distribution according to a confidence level. If the expected value calculated using the null hypothesis so that each hypercell has equal probability of occurrence, then this equation has the properties of an approximate normal distribution with a mean of 0 and a variance of 1. In cases where the asymptotic variance differs from 1, then an adjustment to the standard residual is required in order to yield better approximations [5]. The significance of a hypercell is determined by comparing $D(R_i, Z_j)$ to the tabulated z-values of a predefined confidence level using the standard normal distribution. That is, the hypercell R_i is selected as significant based on:

$$\delta(R_i, Z_j) = \begin{cases} 1 & D(R_i, Z_j) \geq z \\ 0 & \text{otherwise} \end{cases} \tag{5}$$

where z is the tabulated z-value of a certain degree of confidence level.
As each datum is partitioned using the same scheme generated from partitioning the data universe, the number of data Z_j with significant $D(R_i, Z_j)$ (or $\delta(R_i, Z_j) = 1$) and class label C_m is denoted as $\eta(R_i, C_m)$, (or $\eta(R_i, C_m) = \sum_{Z_j} \delta(R_i, Z_j)$ for $Z_j \in C_m$). Let $e(R_i)$ be the average number of data per class whose hypercell R_i is significant, or:

$$e(R_i) = \frac{\sum_{m=1}^{L_c} \eta(R_i, C_m)}{L_c}, \quad \forall Z_j \in U \tag{6}$$

and let

$$\theta(R_i) = \sum_{m=1}^{L_c} \frac{[\eta(R_i, C_m) - e(R_i)]^2}{e(R_i)}, \quad \forall Z_j \in U \tag{7}$$

reflects the extent of class discrimination for a hypercell R_i in the data universe. Since $\theta(R_i)$ has an asymptotic Chi-square distribution, the relevance of a hypercell can be evaluated by applying the Chi-square test. After $\theta(R_i)$ is calculated, it is compared to a tabulated χ^2 value with $L_c - 1$ degrees of freedom based on a presumed confidence level. The function described in equation (3.5) indicates the hypercell's statistical relevance for class discrimination:

$$\beta(R_i) = \begin{cases} 1 & \text{if } \theta(R_i) \geq \chi^2_{L_c-1} \\ 0 & \text{otherwise} \end{cases} \tag{8}$$

Hypercells that are not identified as statistically relevant are partitioned further, using the same criterion of maximum entropy, until there exists an insufficient number of points, or a predefined depth has been reached. We call this method hierarchical maximum entropy partitioning [1,3]. The rationale of using partitioning iteratively is to identify useful characteristics at a more restricted interval when relevant characteristic is not found at a larger interval. The hypercells that surpass the threshold value are marked as having an acceptable degree of class discrimination with $\beta(R_i) = 1$, and these selected hypercells can be relabeled as $\{R_s^*\}$ indicated by the superscript. The set $\{R_S^*\}$ corresponds to the set of input nodes in the feedforward network. When labeled, as $(R_1^*, R_2^*, \ldots, R_S^*)$, they correspond to a set of data value characteristics that are selected to have acceptable class discrimination information.

4 Self Configurable Event-Space Feedforward Network

The number of inputs to the feedforward network depends on the number of iterations and selected hypercells. As more iterations of the partitioning process are performed, then more hypercells are generated and identified as statistically relevant. This is analogous to the use of more refined characteristics of the data for class discrimination if sampling reliability is not a concern.
Given a datum Z_j and the generated hypercell R_S^*. Let $\text{obs}(R_S^*, Z_j)$ be the number of points Z_j has in R_S^*, $\exp(R_S^*, Z_j) = M(Z_j)/k^n$ be the expected average number of points, where $M(Z_j)$ is the total number of points in Z_j. Substituting $\text{obs}(R_S^*, Z_j)$ and $\exp(R_S^*, Z_j)$ into equation (4), we calculate the statistic for Z_j, denoted as $D(R_S^*, Z_j)$. Define a binary decision function for all the selected hypercells $\{R_S^*\}$ for Z_j as:

$$\alpha(R_s^*, Z_j) = \begin{cases} 1 & \text{if } D(R_s^*, Z_j) \geq z \\ 0 & \text{otherwise} \end{cases} \tag{9}$$

where z is a tabulated z-value for a given confidence level. Then Z_j is represented by a vector as:

$$W_j = (\alpha(R_1^*, Z_j)\theta(R_1^*), \alpha(R_2^*, Z_j)\theta(R_2^*), \ldots \alpha(R_s^*, Z_j)\theta(R_s^*),) \quad (10)$$

where $\alpha(R_s^*, Z_j)$ indicates whether a selected characteristic is observed in Z_j , that is, a selected primitive is observed, and $\theta(R_s^*)$ is the estimated relevance of R_s^* based on the analysis from the data universe.

A binary vector V_j can be used as an approximation to W_j, for each data where simplicity of inputs is desired. It is defined as:

$$V_j = (\alpha(R_1^*, Z_j)\beta(R_1^*), \alpha(R_2^*, Z_j)\beta(R_2^*), \ldots \alpha(R_s^*, Z_j)\beta(R_s^*),) \quad (11)$$

Each component $\alpha(R_i^*, Z_j)\beta(R_s^*)$ is the product of $\alpha(R_i^*, Z_j)$ which identifies significant characteristics in the data Z_j, and $\beta(R_s^*)$, which identifies the hypercells (or primitives) based on the data universe. In other words, a component is 1 only if the primitive is statistically significant in Z_j, and statistically discriminating in U.

This approximation does not provide the detailed information contribution to the class discrimination as does the W_j vector. However, V_j usually provides faster training times with additional analysis information. $\beta(R_i^*)$ is defined as a binary element in the vector V_j and is always equal to 1 for the selected hypercells. The $\beta(R_i^*)$ value replaces $\theta(R_i^*)$ in equation (10) so that it is now represented by a 1, thus V_j is rewritten as:

$$V_j = (\alpha(R_1^*, Z_j), \alpha(R_2^*, Z_j), \ldots \alpha(R_s^*, Z_j),) \quad (12)$$

5 Training and Classification of the Network

A network can be trained using the standard back-propagation algorithm with the supervised class label for each datum where the vector W_j or V_j is the input. In the testing phase, a new datum Z_j with an unknown class label is assumed to belong to one of the given classes, hence it is expected that the partitioning scheme generated from the training session can be applied as well. Z_j is partitioned to the predefined levels according to the same scheme identified in training on the data universe. Then Z_j is converted to the corresponding vectors W_j or V_j using equation (10) or (12).

These vectors are applied to the feedforward network. The output node with the highest activation which surpasses a threshold value, identifies the class of the unknown input datum. If there is no output node with an activation surpassing the threshold, then the datum remains as unclassified (or rejected).

6 Experimentation with Speech Data

To show how the algorithm performs on low level speech data, we performed an experiment on its ability to identify relevant speech characteristics as well as its ability to distinguish the speaker identity. The data used for these experiments involved 3 speakers, on 3 words pronounced as "quit", "printer" and "end". Three classes of data were defined, one corresponding to each speaker. Each of the three words was spoken 10 times by each speaker, resulting in 30 speech sample data per speaker, and a total of 90 samples. Each speech sample is represented by a set of points composed of three variables as a 3-vector (time, frequency, amplitude). A single utterance generated slightly over 12,000 data points.

The experiment used the "hold-out test" to evaluate the algorithm for speaker identification. Each run consisted of selecting 5 samples on a word randomly from each speaker class for training. The remaining 5 samples were used for testing. With 3 speakers, each run consists of 15 test data and 15 training data. With 3 words, and performing 10 runs on each word, a total of 30 runs was done for a total of 450 test samples. The results from the experiments showed that the system performed reasonably well. A total of 369 out of 450 were classified correctly. Of those that were not classified, about half were rejected. Total success rate was about 82%.

7 Experimentation with Classifying Data Forming Interlocking Spirals

These experiments illustrate the algorithm on classifying overlapping interlocking spirals of points [6]. In this set of experiments, the data are generated using different parameters to define two classes of data so that each data consists of a number of points forming spirals. Here, the points in a spiral were artificially generated so that the points in a spiral could overlap with points in another data even though they may belong to different class. Thus classification of each data has to depend on a large number of points jointly. Each data sample was composed of 96 points. To create a problem with probabilistic uncertainty, but more difficult, a degree of randomness was introduced so that each spiral as well as each point in it had the radius shifted by a random quantity.

In total, 60 data samples were generated for use in all the experiments. The experiment consisted of 10 runs where each run was composed of 30 training data, 15 per class. The test set then used the remaining 30 unchosen samples, once again 15 per class. In 89 runs, using different confidence levels and number of intervals. The results based on a total of 2670 test samples were: correctly recognized 92.9%, rejected 5.0% and incorrectly classified 2.1%.

REFERENCES

[1] Bie C., Shen H. and Chiu D.K.Y., *Hierarchical maximum entropy partitioning in texture image analysis*, Pattern Recognition Letter, Vol. 14 (1993), pp421–429.

[2] Chiu, D.K.Y. *Towards an event-space self-configurable neural network*, Proc. 1993 IEEE Intern. Conference on Neural Networks (1993), pp956–961.

[3] Chiu D.K.Y. *Information discovery through hierarchical maximum entropy discretization and synthesis*, Knowledge Discovery in Databases, G. Piatetsky, Shapiro and W.J. Frwley, MIT/AAAI press (1991), pp125–140.

[4] Shen, H.C., Bie C. and Chiu D.K.Y., *A texture-based distance measure for classification*, Pattern Recognition, Vol. 26 (1993), No. 9, pp1429–1437.

[5] Haberman, S.J. *The analysis of residuals in cross- classified tables*, Biometrics 29 (1973), pp205–209.

[6] Lang, K.J. and Witbrock, M.J *Learning to tell two spirals apart*, Proc 1988 Connectionist Models Summer School, Carnegie Mellon University, Morgan Kaufman Publishers (1988), pp52–59.

[7] Wong, A.K.C. and Chiu, D.K.Y., *Synthesizing statistical knowledge from incomplete mixed-mode data*, IEEE Trans. PAMI, Vol. PAMI-9 (1987), No.6, pp796–805.

APPROXIMATING THE BAYESIAN DECISION BOUNDARY FOR CHANNEL EQUALISATION USING SUBSET RADIAL BASIS FUNCTION NETWORK

E.S. Chng, B. Mulgrew* , S. Chen and G. Gibson*****

National University of Singapore, Institute of System Science, Heng Mui Keng Terrace, Kent Ridge, 119597 Singapore. Email : eschng@iss.nus.sg.

** Dept. of Electrical Eng., The University of Edinburgh, UK.*

*** Dept. of E.E.E., The University of Portsmouth, UK.*

**** Biomathematics and Statistics, The University of Edinburgh, UK.*

The aim of this paper is to examine the application of radial basis function (RBF) network to realise the decision function of a symbol-decision equaliser for digital communication system. The paper first study the Bayesian equaliser's decision function to show that the decision function is nonlinear and has a structure identical to the RBF model. To implement the full Bayesian equaliser using RBF network however requires very large complexity which is not feasible for practical applications. To reduce the implementation complexity, we propose a model selection technique to choose the important centres of the RBF equaliser. Our results indicate that reduced-sized RBF equaliser can be found with no significant degradation in performance if the subset models are selected appropriately.

Keywords: RBF network, Bayesian equaliser, neural networks.

1 Introduction

The transmission of digital signals across a communication channel is subjected to noise and intersymbol interference (ISI). At the receiver, these effects must be compensated to achieve reliable data communications[1, 2]. The channel, consisting of the transmission filter, transmission medium and receiver filter, is modelled as a finite impulse response (FIR) filter with a transfer function $H(z) = \sum_{i=0}^{n_a-1} a(i)z^{-i}$. The effects on the randomly transmitted signal $s(k) = s = \{\pm 1\}$ through the channel is described by

$$r(k) = \hat{r}(k) + n(k) = \sum_{i=0}^{n_a-1} s(k-i)a(i) + n(k) \tag{1}$$

where $r(k)$ is the corrupted signal of $s(k)$ received by the equaliser at sampled instant time k, $\hat{r}(k)$ is the noise-free observed signal, $n(k)$ is the additive Gaussian white noise, $a(i)$ are the channel impulse response coefficients, and n_a is the channel's memory length[1, 2]. Using a vector of the noisy received signal $\mathbf{r}(k) = [r(k), \cdots, r(k-m+1)]^T$, the equaliser's task is to reconstruct the transmitted symbol $s(k-d)$ with the minimum probability of mis-classification, P_E. The integers m and d are known as the feedforward and delay order respectively. The measure of an equaliser's performance P_E, or more commonly expressed as the bit error rate (BER), BER $= \log_{10} P_E$, in communication literature [1], is expressed with respect to the signal to noise ratio (SNR) where the SNR is defined by

$$\text{SNR} = \frac{E[\hat{\mathbf{r}}(k)]}{E[n^2(k)]} = \frac{\sigma_s^2(\sum_{i=0}^{i=n_a-1} a(i)^2)}{\sigma_e^2} = \frac{\sum_{i=0}^{i=n_a-1} a(i)^2}{\sigma_e^2} \tag{2}$$

where $\sigma_s^2 = 1$ is the transmit symbol variance and σ_e^2 is the noise variance.
The transmitted symbols that affect the input vector $\mathbf{r}(k)$ is the transmit sequence $\mathbf{s}(k) = [s(k), \cdots, s(k-m-n_a+2)]^T$. There are $N_s = 2^{m+n_a-1}$ possible combinations

of these input sequences, i.e. $\{\mathbf{s}_j\}, 1 \leq j \leq N_s$[2]. In the absence of noise, there are N_s corresponding received sequences $\hat{\mathbf{r}}_j(k), 1 \leq j \leq N_s$, which are referred to as channel states. The values of the channel states are defined by,

$$\mathbf{c}_j = \hat{\mathbf{r}}_j(k) = F[\mathbf{s}_j], \qquad 1 \leq j \leq N_s, \tag{3}$$

where the matrix $F \in R^{m\times(m+n_a-1)}$ is

$$\begin{bmatrix} a(0) & a(1) & \dots & a(n_a-1) & 0 & \dots & \dots & \dots & \dots & 0 \\ 0 & a(0) & a(1) & \dots & a(n_a-1) & 0 & \dots & \dots & \dots & 0 \\ \vdots & \vdots & \vdots & & & & & & & \\ & & & \dots & \dots & \dots & \dots & \dots & \dots & 0 \\ 0 & \dots & \dots & \dots & \dots & \dots & a(0) & a(1) & \dots & a(n_a-1) \end{bmatrix} \tag{4}$$

Due to the additive noise, the observed sequence $\mathbf{r}(k)$ conditioned on the channel state $\hat{\mathbf{r}}(k) = \mathbf{c}_j$ is a multi-variable Gaussian distribution with mean at $\mathbf{c}_j$,

$$p(\mathbf{r}(k)|\mathbf{c}_j) = (2\pi\sigma_e^2)^{-m/2}\exp(-\|\mathbf{r}(k) - \mathbf{c}_j\|^2/(2\sigma_e^2)). \tag{5}$$

The set of channel states $C_d = \{\mathbf{c}_j\}_{j=1}^{N_s}$ can be divided into two subsets according to the value of $s(k-d)$, i.e.

$$C_d^{(+)} = \{\hat{\mathbf{r}}(k)|s(k-d) = +1)\}, \tag{6}$$

$$C_d^{(-)} = \{\hat{\mathbf{r}}(k)|s(k-d) = -1)\}, \tag{7}$$

where the subscript d in C_d denotes the equaliser's delay order applied.
To minimise the probability of wrong decision, the optimum decision function is based on determining the maximum *a posteriori* probability $P(s(k-d) = s|\mathbf{r}(k))$ [2] given observed vector $\mathbf{r}(k)$, i.e.,

$$\hat{s}(k-d) = \text{sgn}(\ P(s(k-d) = +1|\mathbf{r}(k)) - P(s(k-d) = -1|\mathbf{r}(k))\ ) \tag{8}$$

where $\hat{s}(k-d)$ is the estimated value of $s(k-d)$. It has been shown in [2] that the Bayesian decision function can be reduced to the following form,
$f_b(\mathbf{r}(k)) =$

$$\sum_{\mathbf{c}_j \in C_d^{(+)}} \exp(-\|\mathbf{r}(k) - \mathbf{c}_j\|^2/(2\sigma_e^2)) - \sum_{\mathbf{c}_k \in C_d^{(-)}} \exp(-\|\mathbf{r}(k) - \mathbf{c}_k\|^2/(2\sigma_e^2)) \tag{9}$$

It is therefore obvious that $f_b(.)$ has the same functional form as the RBF model [2, 3] $f_{\text{rbf}}(\mathbf{r})$,

$$f_{\text{rbf}}(\mathbf{r}) = \sum_{i=1}^{N} w_i\phi(\|\mathbf{r} - \mathbf{c}_i\|^2/\alpha) \tag{10}$$

where N is the number of centres, w_i are the feedforward weights, $\phi(.)$ are the nonlinearity, $\mathbf{c}_i$ are the centres of the RBF model, and α is a constant. The RBF network is therefore ideal to model the optimal Bayesian equaliser [2].

Example of decision boundary: As an example, the Bayesian decision boundaries realised by a RBF equaliser with feedforward order $m = 2$ for channel $H(z) = 0.5 + 1.0z^{-1}$ is considered. Fig 1a lists all the 8 possible combinations of the transmitted signal sequence $\mathbf{s}(k)$ and the corresponding channel states $\mathbf{c}_i$. Fig. 1b depicts the corresponding decision boundaries for the different delay orders. Note that the decision boundary is dependent on the channel state positions and delay order parameter.

S/No i	Transmitted symbols $\mathbf{s}(k)$ [$s(k)$	$s(k-1)$	$s(k-2)$]	Channel State $\mathbf{c}_i$ [$\hat{r}(k)$	$\hat{r}(k-1)$]
1	1	1	1	1.5	1.5
2	1	1	-1	1.5	-0.5
3	1	-1	1	-0.5	0.5
4	1	-1	-1	-0.5	-1.5
5	-1	1	1	0.5	1.5
6	-1	1	-1	0.5	-0.5
7	-1	-1	1	-1.5	0.5
8	-1	-1	-1	-1.5	-1.5

Fig (a) : State Table

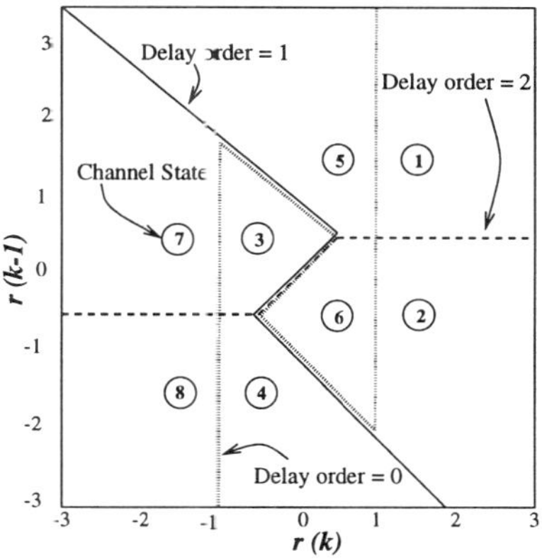

Fig (b) : Decision boundaries

Figure 1 (a) Transmit sequences and channel states for channel $H(z)$, (b) Corresponding Bayesian decision boundaries for various delay orders.

2 Selecting Subset RBF Model

The implementation of the full RBF Bayesian equaliser requires the use of all N_s channel states. Such implementation however may be impractical if N_s is large. In some cases, the complexity may be reduced by using a subset of the N_s channel states to generate the RBF decision function. For example, it is obvious that the decision boundary using delay $d = 1$ for $H(z)$ (Fig. 1b) can be realised approximately by a RBF network using $\{\mathbf{c}_3, \mathbf{c}_4, \mathbf{c}_5, \mathbf{c}_6\}$ as centres. If the realised decision boundary using the subset RBF equaliser is very similar to the full Bayesian equaliser, the classification performance of the two equalisers would also be very similar. That is, the implementation complexity of the RBF equaliser is reduced by using only the important channel states that define the decision boundary.

To understand how centres affect decision boundary, we analyse the effects of centre positions on boundary position when $\sigma_e \to 0$. Let $\mathbf{r}_0$ be the set of all boundary points. I.e., $f_b(\mathbf{r}_0)$ equals to 0. Therefore, if $\mathbf{r}(k) \in \mathbf{r}_0$, Eq. 9 becomes

$$\sum_{\mathbf{c}_j \in C_d^{(+)}} \exp(-\|\mathbf{r}_0 - \mathbf{c}_j\|^2/(2\sigma_e^2)) = \sum_{\mathbf{c}_k \in C_d^{(-)}} \exp(-\|\mathbf{r}_0 - \mathbf{c}_k\|^2/(2\sigma_e^2)). \quad (11)$$

When $\sigma_e \to 0$, the sum on the l.h.s. of Eq. 11 becomes dominated by the closest centres to $\mathbf{r}_0$, i.e.

$$\{U_d^+\} = \min_{\mathbf{c}_j \in C_d^{(+)}} \{\|\mathbf{r}_0 - \mathbf{c}_j\|\}. \quad (12)$$

This is because the contribution from the terms $\exp(-\|\mathbf{r}_0 - \mathbf{c}_j\|^2/(2\sigma_e^2))$ for centres $\mathbf{c}_j \notin U_d^+$ converges much more quickly to zero when $\sigma_e \to 0$ than terms for centres belonging to U_d^+. Similarly, the sum on the r.h.s of Eq. 11 becomes dominated by the closest terms for centres belonging to U_d^-, where $U_d^- = \min_{\mathbf{c}_k \in C_d^{(-)}} \{\|\mathbf{r}_0 - \mathbf{c}_k\|\}$.

At very high SNR, the asymptotic decision boundaries are hyper-planes between pairs of channel states belonging to $\{U_d^+\}$ and $\{U_d^-\}$ [4].
However, not all channel states of $\{U_d^+, U_d^-\}$ are required to define the decision boundary. This can be observed from the example illustrated in Fig. 1b for decision boundary realised using delay order $d = 2$. By visual insepection (Fig. 1b), it is obvious that $\{\mathbf{c}_3, \mathbf{c}_7\} \in U_d^+$ and $\{\mathbf{c}_4, \mathbf{c}_8\} \in U_d^-$. The decision boundary formed using centres $\{\mathbf{c}_3, \mathbf{c}_4\}$ and $\{\mathbf{c}_7, \mathbf{c}_8\}$ are however the same. Therefore, in this case, only 1 pair of channel states, either $\{\mathbf{c}_3, \mathbf{c}_4\}$ or $\{\mathbf{c}_7, \mathbf{c}_8\}$, is sufficient to approximate that region of decision boundary.
To find the set of important centres $\{U_{ds}^+, U_{ds}^-\}$ for the subset RBF equaliser, we propose the following algorithm,

Algorithm 1 : Finding U_{ds}^+, U_{ds}^-

For $\mathbf{c}_j \in C_d^{(+)}$
For $\mathbf{c}_k \in C_d^{(-)}$

$$\mathbf{r}_{j,k}^* = \mathbf{c}_j + \left(\frac{\mathbf{c}_k - \mathbf{c}_j}{2}\right)$$

$$\text{if} \left[\begin{array}{l} f_b(\mathbf{r}_{j,k}^*) = 0 \text{ and} \\ \mathbf{c}_j = \min_{\mathbf{c}_i \in C_d^{(+)}} \{\|\mathbf{r}_0 - \mathbf{c}_i\|\} \text{ and} \\ f_s(\mathbf{r}_{j,k}^*) \neq 0 \end{array} \right]$$

$$\mathbf{c}_j \to U_{ds}^+, \ \mathbf{c}_k \to U_{ds}^-$$

next $\mathbf{c}_k$,
next $\mathbf{c}_j$.

where $f_s(.)$ = RBF model formed using the current selected channel states from $\{U_{ds}^+, U_{ds}^-\}$ as centres and $f_b(.)$ is the full RBF Bayesian equaliser's decision function.

2.1 Subset Model Selection : Some Simulation Results

Simulations were conducted to select subset RBF equalisers from the full model. The following channels which have the same magnitude but different phase response were used,

$$H1(z) = 0.8745 + 0.4372z^{-1} - 0.2098z^{-2} \quad (13)$$

$$H2(z) = 0.2620 - 0.6647z^{-1} - 0.6995z^{-2} \quad (14)$$

The feedforward order used was $m = 4$, resulting in a full model with $N_s = 2^{m+n_a-1} = 64$ centres. Using SNR condition at 16dB, simulations were conducted to compare the performance of the subset RBF and full RBF equalisers for the two channels. The results are tabulated in Table 1a and 1b respectively; The first column of each table indicates the delay order parameter, the second column indicates the number of channel states selected to form the subset model while the third and fourth columns list the BER performance of the two equalisers and the last column indicates if the channel states belonging to the different transmit symbol, i.e. $C_d^{(+)}$ and $C_d^{(-)}$, are linearly or not-linearly separable. Our results show that reduced size RBF equaliser with performance very similar to the full model's performance can usually be found for equalisation problem that is linearly separable.

Delay	Subset Size	Subset log(Pe)	Full-model log(Pe)	Decision Boundary
0	56	-4.09	-4.09	Linear Sep.
1	57	-4.14	-4.14	Linear Sep.
2	32	-4.11	-4.12	Linear Sep.
3	32	-4.11	-4.12	Linear Sep.
4	48	-1.91	-1.91	Not-Linear Sep.
5	64	-0.97	-0.97	Not-Linear Sep.

Table a : Channel H1(z)

Delay	Subset Size	Subset log(Pe)	Full-model log(Pe)	Decision Boundary
0	56	-0.80	-1.30	Not-Linear Sep.
1	46	-2.99	-2.99	Linear Sep.
2	38	-3.38	-3.38	Linear Sep.
3	56	-3.43	-3.43	Linear Sep.
4	55	-3.32	-3.32	Not-Linear Sep.
5	64	-3.41	-3.41	Not-Linear Sep.

Table b : Channel H2(z)

Table 1 Comparing the performance of the full-size (64 centres) RBF equaliser, subset RBF equaliser for Channel $H1(z)$ (Table 1a) and Channel $H2(z)$ (Table 1b) at SNR=16db.

3 Conclusions

This paper examined the application of RBF network for channel equalisation. It was shown that the optimum symbol-decision equaliser can be realised by a RBF model if channel statistic is known. The computational complexity required to implement the full Bayesian function using the RBF network is however considerable. To reduce implementation complexity, a method of model selection to reduce the number of centres in the RBF model is proposed. Our results indicate that the model size, and hence implementation complexity, can be reduced without significantly compromising classification performance in some cases.

REFERENCES

[1] S.U.H.Qureshi, *Adaptive equalization*, Proc. IEEE, Vol. 73 (1985), No. 9, pp1349–1387.

[2] S.Chen, B.Mulgrew and P.M.Grant, *A clustering technique for digital communications channel equalization using radial basis function networks*, IEEE Trans. Neural Networks, Vol. 4 (1993), No. 4, pp570–579.

[3] M.J.D.Powell, *Radial basis functions for multivariable interpolation: a review*, Algorithms for Approximation, J.C.Mason and M.G.Cox (Eds), Oxford (1987) pp143–167.

[4] R.A.Iltis, *A randomized bias technique for the importance sampling simulation of Bayesian equalisers*, IEEE Trans. Communications, Vol. 43 (1995), pp1107–1115.

APPLICATIONS OF GRAPH THEORY TO THE DESIGN OF NEURAL NETWORKS FOR AUTOMATED FINGERPRINT IDENTIFICATION

Carol G. Crawford

U.S. Naval Academy, Department of Mathematics, Annapolis, USA.

This paper presents applications of graph theory to the design of graph matching neural networks for automated fingerprint identification. Given a sparse set of minutiae from a fingerprint image, complete with locations in the plane and (optionally) other labels such as ridge angles, ridge counts to nearby minutiae and so on, this approach to matching begins by constructing a graph-like representation of the minutiae map, utilizing proximity graphs, such as the sphere-of-influence graphs. These graph representations are more robust to noise such as translations, rotations and deformations. This paper presents the role of these graph representations in the design of graph matching neural networks for the matching and classification of fingerprint images.

1 Introduction

Matching the representations of two images has been the focus of extensive research in computer vision and artificial intelligence. In particular, the problem of matching fingerprint, images has received wide attention and varying approaches to its solution. In this paper we present results of an ongoing collaborative research program which combines techniques and methods from graph theory and neural science to design algorithms for graph matching neural networks.

This collaborative approach with Eric Mjolsness, University of Southern California, San Diego, and Anand Rangarajan, Center for Theoretical and Applied Neural Science at Yale, is an outgrowth of an initial investigation for the Federal Bureau of Investigation to their existing Integrated Automated Fingerprint Identification System, IAFIS.

In this research program, algorithms and techniques from discrete mathematics, graph theory and computer science are combined to develop methods and algorithms for representing and matching fingerprints in a very large database, such as the one at the FBI. The Federal Bureau of Investigation and National Institute of Standards and Technology provided a small database of fingerprints. This database, together with the software environment at the Center for Theoretical and Applied Neural Science at Yale University have provided a test bed for these algorithms. The following presents the background of the fingerprint problem and this research together with a special emphasis on the role of proximity graphs in the design of the graph matching neural networks.

2 Fingerprint Images, Minutiae and Graph Representations

2.1 Minutiae Maps

Fingerprint matching and identification dates back to 1901 when it was introduced by Sir Edward Henry for Scotland Yard. After sorting the fingerprints into classes such as whorls, loops and arches, matches are made according to comparisons of minutiae. Minutiae include such indications as ridge endings, islands and bifurcations, with fingerprints averaging 100 or more per print. Today fingerprints are initially stored on computer as a raw minutiae map in the form of a list of minutiae positions and ridge angles in a raster-scan order. In American courts a positive matching of a dozen minutiae usually suffices for identification. However, for an average computer to make these dozen matches the process would entail locating every minutiae in both prints and then comparing all ten-thousand-plus possible pairings of these minutiae. In addition, the minutiae map itself is very non-robust to likely noise such as translations, rotations, and deformations, which can change every minutiae positions. A subtler form of noise is the gradual increase in ridge width or image scale typically encountered in moving from the top of the image to the bottom. Thus, it is desirable to determine graph- like representations which are more robust to noise and less susceptible to problems with missing minutiae.

2.2 Graph Representations of Minutiae Maps

Given a sparse set of minutiae from one fingerprint image, complete with their locations in the plane and (optionally) other labels such as ridge angles, ridge counts to nearby minutiae and so on, we construct a graph- like representation of the minutiae map. By considering relationships between pairs of minutiae such as their geometric distance in the plane, or the number of intervening ridges between them, we can begin to construct features which are robust against translations and rotations at least. However, there still exists the very serious problem of reorderings of the minutiae forced by rotation and missing or extra minutiae. This "problem" must be addresses by defining a reordering- independent match metric between two such graphs.

Complete Graphs and Planar Distances

The simplest example of a labelled graph representation would be the complete graph where every pair of minutiae are linked by an "edge" in the graph. Edges would be labelled by the 2-d Euclidean distance between the minutiae. Note that this graph would require a special definition of the match metric to handle missing, extra and reordered minutiae. Furthermore, most of the edges would connect distant minutiae whose relationships, such as planar distance or ridge count, are subject to noise and provide less real information than nearby edges. So for reasons of robustness and computational cost, it makes sense to consider instead various kinds of "proximity graphs", which keep only the edges between minutiae that are "neighbors" according to some criterion.

Sphere-of-influence Graphs and Other Proximity Graph Representations

Sphere-of-Influence graphs comprise the first set of proximity graphs which we considered in our goal of determining a better class of minutiae map representations. First introduced by Toussaint [9], sphere- of-influence graphs provide a potentially robust representation for minutiae maps. These graphs are capable of capturing low-level perceptual structures of visual scenes consisting of dot patterns. . A very active group of researchers have developed a series of significant results dealing with this class of graphs. We refer the reader to the work of M. Lipman, [4,5,6]; F. Harary, [5,6]; M. Jacobson, [5,6] T. S. Michael,[7,8]; and T. Quint, [7,8].

The following definition is referred to by Toussaint, [9]. Let $V = (P_1, \ldots, P_n)$ be a finite set of points in the plane. For each point p in V, let r_p be the closest distance to any other set of points in the set, and let C_p be the circle of radius r_p centered at p. The *sphere- of-influence graph, or SIG*, is a graph on V with an edge between points p, q if and only if the circles C_p, C_q intersect in at least two places. For various illustrations of sphere-of-influence graphs we refer the reader to the excellent presentation by Toussaint in [9].

One can note from the prior example that perceptually salient groups of dots become even more distinct in the corresponding sphere-of-influence graph. However, SIGs represent only one group of an even richer class of graphs we refer to as proximity graphs. These graphs also offer various benefits in their potential for providing robust representations of minutiae maps. Proximity graphs all share the property that they only contain edges corresponding between minutiae that are "neighbors" according to some given criterion. The graphs which have turned out to be most promising representations include *relative neighborhood graphs, delauney triangulations, voronoi diagrams, minutiae distance graphs and generalized sphere-of-influence graphs.* We refer the reader to an excellent survey article by Toussaint for more details on proximity graphs. [9]

Generalized Sphere-of-Influence Graph Representations

K-sphere-of-influence graphs (k-SIGs) are generalizations of SIGs, in which a vertex is connected to k nearby. vertices depending only on their relative distances, not absolute distances.(Guibas, Pach, and Sharir [10]). Given a set V of n points in R^d, the *kth sphere-of- influence* of a point x in V is the smallest closed ball centered at x and containing more than k points of V (including x). The case for $k = 1$ yields the standard sphere-of-influence graph. The it kth sphere-of-influence graph, $G_k(V)$ *of* V is a graph whose vertices are the points of V, and two points are connected by an edge if their k-th spheres -of - influence intersect.

K-SIGs are especially suitable for minutiae map representations because of the fact that connections depend on relative distances. This property provides a form of scale invariance. Each edge can be labelled with the integer k, recording whether it connects nearby ($k = 1$) or farther minutiae pairs. Unfortunately, this scale robustness is bought at the price of increased susceptibility to missing minutiae. When a minutiae goes missing, not only is there an unavoidable effect on the graph by the deletion of the node, but there is a gratuitous "splash" effect of the edges between nearby pairs of the remaining minutiae: their k-numbers change despite the fact that their planar distance do not. This effect is mitigated by the match metric, which changes only gradually with k, but it is still undesirable.

Finally, we define yet another graph which is a hybrid between planar distance graphs and k-SIGs. We begin by creating a k-SIG with an overly large value of k. However, we label the edges with the planar distance d. Next we find the local image scale factor by finding the best constant of proportionality between d and k in each image region. Divide all d's by this coefficient to turn them into less noisy, noninteger versions of k, and then let this scaled version of d be the importance rating for an edge. Then proceed to a graph and a match metric as in the planar distance example. For this hybrid representation minutiae deletion only affects d via the local scaling factor, which is determined by many different value of k and is therefore fairly robust, preserving scale invariance.

3 Graph-Matching Neural Network Implementation

Graph representations of minutiae maps provide only the first step in developing a matching scheme for fingerprints. This second part of this research effort is devoted to the design of graph matching algorithms and their implementation as neural networks. As outlined in prior sections these algorithms are based on proximity graphs which only contain edges for nearby minutiae. These edges are then labelled with features and with and "edge importance rating" that directly affects the weight given to that edge in the match metric. In this scenario one can construct a nested series of graphs including more and more edges of less and less importance or greater and greater distance, until either some cut off limit is reached or all possible edges between minutiae in the map are included in the largest graph. In this class of algorithms the match metric between two such graphs is insensitive to arbitrary reorderings of the minutiae in either graph, and is implementable as an analog neural network. Finally, the match metric will contain adjustable weighting parameters which determine the relative weights of matching edges as a function of their importance rating, and the relative weights of any other labelling information attached to the vertices or edges of the graphs These parameters are then determined statistically by a steepest-descent training algorithm applied to a data base of minutiae maps, followed by testing-set validations, exactly as is done in the conventional neural network paradigm.

3.1 Relaxation Networks for Graph Matching — Deterministic Annealing and Lagrangian Decomposition

The neural network implementation of this research effort has been conducted at Yale University's Center for Theoretical and Applied Neural Science in cooperative efforts with E. Mjolsness and A. Rangarajan. This implementation has concentrated on the use of relaxation neural networks for matching the labelled graphs corresponding to minutiae maps. It should be noted that neural network approaches to graph matching share the feature of other recent approaches to graph matching in that they are not restricted to looking for isomorphisms, but seek to minimize the distance between two graphs. Graph isomorphism occurs when the distance is zero. The approach at Yale utilizes deterministic annealing to generalize to inexact, weighted graph matching.

In [11] Mjolsness and Rangarajan formulate the problems as follows: given graphs G and g, find a permutation matrix m that brings the two sets of vertices into correspondence. A permutation matrix is a zero one matrix whose rows and columns sum to one. Within the framework of *deterministic annealing* one can easily formulate the permutation matrix constraints. In this setting the row or column constraints are *winner-take-alls* and either set (but not both sets) of constraints separately can be exactly imposed used deterministic annealing methods.

This deterministic annealing approach is similar to a *Lagrangian decomposition* approach in that the row and column constraints are satisfied separately. Lagrange multipliers are then used to equate the two solutions. Other methods do exist to satisfy both the row and column constraints and this method (for obtaining a permutation matrix) is equivalent w.r.t. fixpoints to the one presented in [12]. A fixpoint preserving transformation [13] is applied to the graph matching distance resulting in the ability to express the combination of the graph matching distance constraint and the permutation matrix constraint using terms that are linear in the permutation matrix M.

Due to the existence of unavoidable symmetries in graph matching and the resulting global minima, a symmetry- breaking term is added in order to always obtain a permutation matrix. The symmetry-breaking term is similar to the hysteretic annealing performed in [14,15] and is suitable for the deterministic approach being used. The symmetry-breaking term is reversed via another fixpoint preserving transformation. The network then performs minimization with respect to the Lagrange parameters and maximization with respect to the permutation matrix. In 11] simulation results are shown for the isomorphism problem with 100 node random, undirected graphs and for the weighted graph matching problem with 100 node random graphs with uniform noise added to the connections.

REFERENCES

[1] Chen Gould, M S Jacobson Schelp and D West, *A characterization of influence graphs of prescribed graph*, Vishwa Internat. J. Graph Theory, Vol.1 (1992), pp77–81.

[2] C. Crawford and E Mjolsness, *Graph Matching and Image Processing Neural Networks for Fingerprint Identification*, Technical Report for The Federal Bureau of Investigation, (September 1992), pp1–14.

[3] C. Crawford and E Mjolsness, *Automated Fingerprint Identification: An Independent Study, Research Report* YALE/DCS/RR-920, (October 1991), pp1–30, also published as Technical Report for The Federal Bureau of Investigation.

[4] M J.Lipman, *Integer realizations of sphere-of-influence graphs*, Congress Numerantium, Vol. 91 (1991), pp63–70.

[5] Harary, M S Jacobson, M J Lipman, and F R McMorris, *Abstract sphere-of-influence graphs*, Math. Comput. Modelling, Vol. 17 (1993), pp77–83.

[6] T. S. Michael and T Quint, *Sphere-of-influence graphs defined on a prescribed graph.* (submitted).

[7] T S. Michael and T Quint, *On Sphere-of-influence graphs in the plane*, (submitted)

[8] T S Michael and T Quint, *Sphere-of-influence graphs: small clique and star factors*, (submitted)

[9] G T Toussaint, *A graph-theoretic primal sketch*, Computational Morphology, Elsevier North Holland, Arnsterdarn (1988), pp229–260.

[10] Guibas, Pach and Sharir, *Generalized sphere-of-influence graphs in higher dimensions*, manuscript, Tel-Aviv University, (1992).

[11] A Rangarajan and E Mjolsness, *A Lagrangian Relaxation Network for Graph Matching*, (submitted).

[12] A L Yuille and J J Kosowsky, *Statistical physics algorithms that converge*, Technical Report 92–7 (1992), Harvard Robotics Laboratory.

[13] A H Gee and R W Prager, *Polyhedral combinatorics and neural networks*, Neural Computation, Vol.6 (1994), pp161–180.

[14] S. V. B Aiyer, M Niranjan, and F Fallside, *A Theoretical investigation into the performance of the Hopfield model*, IEEE, Trans. Neural Networks. Vol.1 (1990), pp204–215.

Acknowledgements

Research supported by The Office of Naval Research contract N0001494WR23025. This work is an outgrowth of a cooperative program with Eric Mjolsness of The University of Southern California and Anand Rangarajan of The Center for Theoretical and Applied Neural Science at Yale University This program was originally funded by The Federal Bureau of Investigation.

ZERO DYNAMICS AND RELATIVE DEGREE OF DYNAMIC RECURRENT NEURAL NETWORKS

A. Delgado, C. Kambhampati* and K. Warwick*

National University of Columbia, Elec. Eng. Dept., AA No. 25268, Bogota, D C, Columbia SA. Email: adelgado@col1.telecom.com.co

**Cybernetics Department, University of Reading, UK.*

In this paper the differential geometric control theory is used to define the key concepts of relative degree and zero dynamics for a Dynamic Recurrent Neural Network (DRNN). It is shown that the relative degree is the lower bound for the number of neurons and the zero dynamics are responsible for the approximating capabilities of the network.

1 Introduction

Most of the current applications of neural networks to control nonlinear systems rely on the classical NARMA approach [1,2]. This procedure, powerful in itself, has some drawbacks [3]. On the other hand, a DRNN is described by a set of nonlinear differential equations and can be analysed using differential geometric techniques [4].

In this work, the important concepts of zero dynamics and relative degree from the differential geometric control theory are formulated for a control affine DRNN.

2 Mathematical Preliminaries

Consider the nonlinear control affine system

$$\begin{aligned}
\dot{x}_1 &= x_2\\
\dot{x}_2 &= x_3\\
&\vdots\\
\dot{x}_{r-1} &= x_r\\
\dot{x}_r &= f_r(x_1 \ldots, x_r, x_{r+1}, \ldots, x_n) + g_r \cdot u\\
\dot{x}_{r+1} &= f_{r+1}(x_1, \ldots, x_r, x_{r+1}, \ldots, x_n) + g_{r+1} \cdot u\\
&\vdots\\
\dot{x}_n &= f_n(x_1, \ldots, x_r, x_{r+1}, \ldots, x_n) + g_n \cdot u\\
y &= x_1
\end{aligned} \tag{1}$$

these equations can be written in compact form

$$\begin{aligned}
\dot{x} &= f(x) + g \cdot u\\
y &= h(x)
\end{aligned} \tag{2}$$

where $x \in \mathrm{IR}^n$, $u \in \mathrm{IR}$, $y \in \mathrm{IR}$, $f(x)$ and g are vector fields, $h(x)$ is a scalar field. For the system (1) there are two key concepts in the differential geometric framework, that is the zero dynamics and the relative degree.

2.1 Zero Dynamics

The zero dynamics of the system (1) describe its behaviour when the output $y(t)$ is forced to be zero [4]. With the output zero, the initial state of the system must be set to a value such that $(x_1(0), \ldots, x_r(0))$ are zero, whereas $(x_{r+1}(0), \ldots, x_n(0))$ can be chosen arbitrarily. In addition, the input $u(t)$ must be the solution of the equation

$$0 = f_r(0,\ldots,0,x_{r+1}(t),\ldots,x_n(t)) + g_r \cdot u \tag{3}$$

Solving for $u(t)$ in (3) and replacing in the remaining equations, the zero dynamics are given by the set of differential equations

$$\begin{aligned}\dot{x}_{r+1} &= f_{r+1}(0,\ldots,0,x_{r+1},\ldots,x_n) - \frac{g_{r+1}}{g_r} f_r(0,\ldots,0,x_{r+1},\ldots,x_n) \\ &\vdots \\ \dot{x}_n &= f_n(0,\ldots,0,x_{r+1},\ldots,x_n) - \frac{g_n}{g_r} f_r(0,\ldots,0,x_{r+1},\ldots,x_n)\end{aligned} \tag{4}$$

The zero dynamics play a role similar to that of the zeros of the transfer function in a linear system. If the zero dynamics are stable then the system (1) is said to be minimum phase.

2.2 Relative Degree

The relative degree of a dynamical system is defined as the number of times that the output $y(t)$ must be differentiated with respect to time in order to have the input $u(t)$ appearing explicitly or is the number of state equations that the input $u(t)$ must go through in order to reach the output $y(t)$.

The nonlinear system (2) is said to have relative degree r [3,4] if

$$\begin{aligned} L_g L^i{}_f h(x) &= 0, \qquad i = 0,\ldots,r-2 \\ L_g L_f^{r-1} h(x) &\neq 0 \end{aligned}$$

3 DRNN

A DRNN is described by the set of nonlinear differential equations

$$\begin{aligned}\dot{\chi}_i &= -\chi_i + \sum_{j=1}^{N} w_{ij}\cdot\sigma(\chi_j) + \gamma_i \cdot u \\ y &= \chi_1, \qquad i = 1,\ldots,N\end{aligned} \tag{5}$$

or in matrix form

$$\begin{aligned}\dot{\chi} &= -\chi + W\cdot\Sigma(\chi) + \Gamma\cdot u \\ y &= \chi_1\end{aligned} \tag{6}$$

where $\chi \in \mathbb{R}^N$, $W \in \mathbb{R}^{N\times N}$, $\Gamma \in \mathbb{R}^{N\times 1}$, and $\Sigma(\chi) = (\sigma(\chi_1),\ldots,\sigma(\chi_N))^{\mathrm{T}}$.

For control purposes it was demonstrated [3] that the network (6) can approximate nonlinear systems of the class (2), the resulting model can be analysed using the differential geometric framework. The aim of this paper is to propose a canonical structure for the network (6) in order to get any desired relative degree with a zero dynamics similar to (4).

Theorem 1 *The DRNN (6) with the following matrices W and Γ can have any relative degree $r \in [2, N]$*

$$W = \begin{bmatrix} \omega_{11} & \omega_{12} & 0 & \cdot & \cdot & \cdot & \cdot & \cdot & \cdot & 0 \\ \omega_{21} & \omega_{22} & \omega_{23} & 0 & \cdot & \cdot & \cdot & \cdot & \cdot & 0 \\ \cdot & \cdot & \cdot & \cdot & \cdot & \cdot & \cdot & \cdot & \cdot & \cdot \\ \cdot & \cdot & \cdot & \cdot & \cdot & \cdot & \cdot & \cdot & \cdot & \cdot \\ \omega_{r-11} & \omega_{r-12} & \cdot & \cdot & \cdot & \omega_{r-1r} & 0 & \cdot & \cdot & 0 \\ \omega_{r1} & \omega_{r2} & \cdot & \cdot & \cdot & \omega_{rr} & \cdot & \cdot & \cdot & \omega_{rN} \\ \omega_{r+11} & \omega_{r+12} & \cdot & \cdot & \cdot & \omega_{r+1r} & \cdot & \cdot & \cdot & \omega_{r+1N} \\ \cdot & \cdot & \cdot & \cdot & \cdot & \cdot & \cdot & \cdot & \cdot & \cdot \\ \cdot & \cdot & \cdot & \cdot & \cdot & \cdot & \cdot & \cdot & \cdot & \cdot \\ \omega_{N1} & \omega_{N2} & \cdot & \cdot & \cdot & \omega_{Nr} & \cdot & \cdot & \cdot & \omega_{NN} \end{bmatrix}$$

$$\Gamma = \begin{bmatrix} 0 & 0 & \cdot & \cdot & 0 & \gamma_r & \gamma_r & \cdot & \cdot & \gamma_N \end{bmatrix}^{\mathrm{T}}$$

in other terms

$$\omega_{ij} = 0; \gamma_i = 0, \quad i = 1, \ldots, r-1, \quad j = i+2, \ldots, N$$

This particular structure is called the **staircase** structure. Note that the minimum number of neurons is the relative degree r. For a desired relative degree $r = 1$, the coefficient γ_1 must be nonzero.

Proof Applying the definition of relative degree

$$\begin{aligned} y &= \chi_1 \\ \dot{y} &= \dot{\chi}_1 = \omega_{11} \cdot \sigma(\chi_1) + \omega_{12} \cdot \sigma(\chi_2) \end{aligned}$$

after the first derivative, every new derivative of $y(t)$ introduces a new state equation (staircase structure). Then after r derivatives of the output $y(t)$, the input $u(t)$ appears explicitly. □

Theorem 2 *The network of the* **Theorem 1** *with a sigmoid function $\sigma(0) = 0$ has a zero dynamics described by the set of differential equations*

$$\dot{\chi}_i = -\chi_i + \sum_{j=r+i}^{N} (\omega_{ij} - \frac{\gamma_i}{\gamma_r}\omega_{rj}) \cdot \sigma(\chi_j), \qquad i = r+1, \ldots, N$$

Proof The zero dynamics are defined as the resulting dynamics when the output $y(t)$ is constrained to be zero. In the structure proposed $y(t) = 0$ means that the first r state variables are zero $\chi_1(t) = \cdots = \chi_r(t) = 0$ and $\sigma(\chi_1(t)) = \sigma(\cdots) = \sigma(\chi_r(t)) = 0$ The equation for $\dot{\chi}_r(t)$ becomes

$$0 = \sum_{j=r+i}^{N} \omega_{rj} \cdot \sigma(\chi_j) + \gamma_r \cdot u$$

solving for u

$$u = -\frac{1}{\gamma_r} \sum_{j=r+i}^{N} \omega_{rj} \cdot \sigma(\chi_j)$$

replacing the control u in the last $N - r$ equations

$$\dot{\chi}_i = -\chi_i + \sum_{j=r+1}^{N} \omega_{ij} \cdot \sigma(\chi_j) - \frac{\gamma_i}{\gamma_r} \sum_{j=r+1}^{N} \omega_{rj} \cdot \sigma(\chi_j) \qquad i = r+1, \ldots, N$$

Finally

$$\dot{\chi}_i = -\chi_i + \sum_{j=r+1}^{N} (\omega_{ij} - \frac{\gamma_i}{\gamma_r}\omega_{rj}) \cdot \sigma(\chi_j) \qquad i = r+1, \ldots, N$$

□

Example: Consider the following staircase DRNN

$$\begin{aligned}
\dot{\chi}_1 &= -\chi_1 + \omega_{11} \cdot \sigma(\chi_1) + \omega_{12} \cdot \sigma(\chi_2) \\
\dot{\chi}_2 &= -\chi_2 + \omega_{21} \cdot \sigma(\chi_1) + \omega_{22} \cdot \sigma(\chi_2) + \omega_{23} \cdot \sigma(\chi_3) + \gamma_2 \cdot u \\
\dot{\chi}_3 &= -\chi_3 + \omega_{31} \cdot \sigma(\chi_1) + \omega_{32} \cdot \sigma(\chi_2) + \omega_{33} \cdot \sigma(\chi_3) + \gamma_3 \cdot u \\
y &= \chi_1 \\
\sigma(0) &= 0
\end{aligned}$$

Relative Degree: The first derivative of the output is

$$\dot{y} = \dot{\chi}_1 = -\chi_1 + \omega_{11} \cdot \sigma(\chi_1) + \omega_{12} \cdot \sigma(\chi_2)$$

the input u does not appear so the relative degree is greater than one. The second derivative of the output is

$$\ddot{y} = -\dot{\chi}_1 + \omega_{11} \cdot \sigma'(\chi_1) \cdot \dot{\chi}_1 + \omega_{12} \cdot \sigma'(\chi_2) \cdot \dot{\chi}_2$$

where

$$\sigma'(\chi_i) = \frac{d\sigma(\chi_i)}{d\chi_i}.$$

Replacing $\dot{\chi}_1$ and $\dot{\chi}_2$

$$\begin{aligned}
\ddot{y} &= (-1 + \omega_{11} \cdot \sigma'(\chi_1))(-\chi_1 + \omega_{11} \cdot \sigma(\chi_1) + \omega_{12} \cdot \sigma(\chi_2)) \\
&\quad + \omega_{12} \cdot \sigma'(\chi_2) \cdot (-\chi_2 + \omega_{21} \cdot \sigma(\chi_1) + \omega_{22} \cdot \sigma(\chi_2) + \omega_{23} \cdot \sigma(\chi_3) + \gamma_2 \cdot u)
\end{aligned}$$

notice that the input appears explicitly so the relative degree is $r = 2$.
Zero Dynamics: The proposed network has three states and relative degree two, so the zero dynamics has one state.
Following the definition of zero dynamics [4], $y = \chi_1 = 0$. The first state equation is reduced to

$$0 = -0 + \omega_{11} \cdot \sigma(0) + \omega_{12} \cdot \sigma(\chi_2)$$

this yields $\chi_2 = 00$. The second state equation is

$$0 = -0 + \omega_{21} \cdot \sigma(0) + \omega_{22} \cdot \sigma(0) + \omega_{23} \cdot \sigma(\chi_3) + \gamma_2 \cdot u$$

solving for the input

$$u = -\frac{\omega_{23}}{\gamma_2} \cdot \sigma(\chi_3)$$

replacing u in the remaining state equation, the zero dynamics is

$$\dot{\chi}_3 = -\chi_3 + (\omega_{33} - \frac{\gamma_3}{\gamma_2}\omega_{23}) \cdot \sigma(\chi_3)$$

In the simulations [5, 6] a single link manipulator of relative degree 2 and without zero dynamics was identified with a DRNN, the resulting model has the same relative degree but **it needs** the zero dynamics in order to improve the plant approximation.

4 Conclusions

A DRNN, is described naturally by a set of nonlinear differential equations and can be analysed within the framework of the differential geometric control theory. There are two key concepts in this framework : the zero dynamics and the relative degree.

Two theorems were formulated and proved, as a result a particular structure is proposed for a DRNN in order to get any desired relative degree $r \in [1, N]$ and the canonical zero dynamics (4). The **relative degree** is a **lower bound** for the **number of neurons** and the **zero dynamics** are responsible for the **approximating capabilities** of the neural network. That is, for multilayer networks the approximating capabilities reside in the hidden layers and for recurrent networks the approximating capabilities reside in the zero dynamics.

REFERENCES

[1] Chen, S. and Billings, S. A., *Neural networks for nonlinear dynamic system modelling and identification*, Int. J. Control, Vol. 56 (1992). pp319–346.

[2] Narendra, K.S. and Parthasarathy, K., *Identification and control of dynamical systems using neural networks*, IEEE Transactions on Neural Networks, Vol.1 (1990), pp4–26.

[3] Delgado, A., Kambhampati, C. and Warwick, K., *Dynamic recurrent neural network for system identification and control*, IEE Proceedings, Part D, Vol. 142 (1995), pp307–314.

[4] Isidori, A., *Nonlinear Control Systems*, Springer-Verlag (1989).

[5] Delgado, A., Kambhampati, C. and Warwick, K., *Identification of nonlinear systems with a dynamic recurrent neural network*, Proceedings of the IEE — IV international conference on ANNs. Cambridge (1995), pp318–322.

[6] Delgado, *Input/output linearization of control affine systems using neural networks* PhD Thesis, Dept. Cybernetics, Reading University (1996).

Acknowledgements

The author A. Delgado would like to thank to the Colombian Institute for the Development of Science and Technology (COLCIENCIAS) and to the National University of Colombia for supporting his PhD studies at the Cybernetics Department of the University of Reading.

IRREGULAR SAMPLING APPROACH TO NEUROCONTROL: THE BAND-AND SPACE-LIMITED FUNCTIONS QUESTIONS

Andrzej Dzieliński and Rafał Żbikowski

Department of Mechanical Engineering, James Watt Building, University of Glasgow, Glasgow G12 8QQ, Scotland, UK. Email: andrzej@mech.gla.ac.uk

The use of feedforward neural networks (FNNs) for non-linear control based on the input-output discrete-time description of systems is presented. The discussion focusses on coupling of reconstruction techniques for n-D irregularly sampled space- and/or band-limited functions with feedforward neural networks. The essence of the approach is to use the multi-dimensional irregular sampling theory to obtain the neural network representation of interpolating filter as well as bounds for accuracy of the interpolation from the finite set. Key questions from the relations between band- and space-limited functions are addressed and their consequence on neurocontrol are underlined.

Subject classification: AMS(MOS) 62D05, 93C10, 92B20, 93C35

Keywords: sampling theory, nonlinear control systems, neural networks, multi-dimensional systems

1 Introduction

This paper focusses on the discrete-time input-output model of a deterministic non-linear single-input single-output (SISO) system

$$y(k+1) = f(y(k), \dots, y(k-n+1), u(k), \dots, u(k-m+1)) \tag{1}$$

with output $y \in [a,b] \subset \mathbb{R}$, and input $u \in [c,d] \subset \mathbb{R}$ and $f\colon D \to [a,b]$ with the domain of definition $D = [a,b]^n \times [c,d]^m \subset \mathbb{R}^{n+m}$. This model is referred to as NARMA (Non-linear Auto-Regressive Moving Average) model (see [1]) and is usually obtained by discretisation of a deterministic non-linear (Lipschitz) continuous-time SISO system described by controlled ordinary differential equations. NARMA models are valid only locally and with this caveat it may be a starting point for the considerations of non-linear dynamic systems modelling in the context of neurocontrol (see [6])

2 Generation of Irregular Samples by a Dynamic System

In practice f in (1) is often unknown, and modelling has to be based on the given pairs of multi-dimensional samples $((y_k, \dots, y_{k-n+1}, u_k, \dots, u_{k-m+1}), y_{k+1})$, where we put $y_k = y(k)$ etc. for brevity. Given the samples

$$\xi_k = (y_k, \dots, y_{k-n+1}, u_k, \dots, u_{k-m+1})$$

and $f(\xi_k)$, the issue is to reconstruct the multi-variable function f, a problem from multi-dimensional signal processing (note that it is completely separate from the question of band-limiting of y). The approach was introduced by Sanner & Slotine [3], but they assumed that the multi-dimensional samples are uniform, i.e., regularly distributed in the domain D of f. This seems to be a simplification, as the dynamics of (1) manifest themselves through irregular samples. For example, if f is linear, i.e., $y_{k+1} = a_0 y_k + \dots + a_{n-1} y_{k-n+1} + b_0 u_k + \dots + b_{m-1} u_{k-m+1}$, then even for constant input the output will not take values in constant increments, but according to the slope of the hyperplane determined by f. Thus even uniformity of u cannot, in general, ensure regular distribution of values of y, because the irregularity of the distribution represents f.

We now examine in detail the nature of this process in low dimensions (as this can be illustrated graphically). We look at the way nonuniform samples, i.e., ξ_k in the

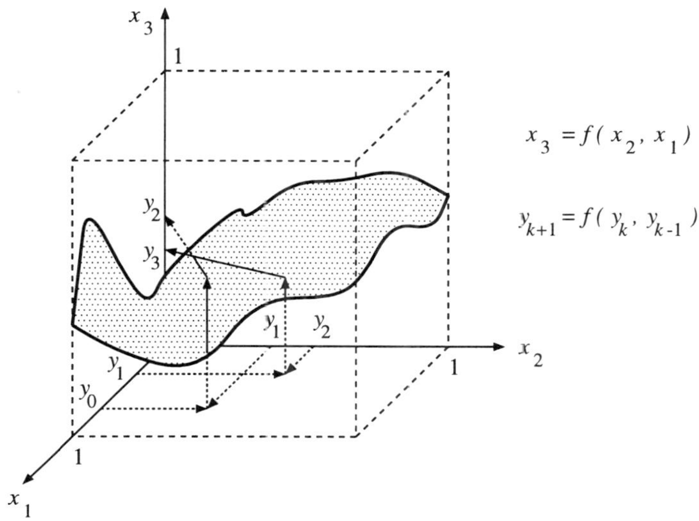

Figure 1 Iterative map $f: [0, 1] \times [0, 1] \to [0, 1]$ defined by $y_{k+1} = f(y_k, y_{k-1})$.

pairs $(\xi_k, f(\xi_k))$, are generated when f is the right-hand side (RHS) of a dynamic system. For simplicity, instead of dealing with a controlled system of type (1), we concentrate on the low-order autonomous case

$$y_{k+1} = f(y_k, y_{k-1}), \tag{2}$$

with $y \in [0, 1]$. Thus $\xi_k = (y_k, y_{k-1})$. We also assume that f is continuous; its domain, $D = [0, 1]^2$ for (2), is compact (and connected).

The essential observation is that y_k, i.e., ξ_k of the pairs $(\xi_k, f(\xi_k))$ occur in the x_1x_2 plane in a nonuniform (irregular) way. They will be, in general, unevenly spaced and their pattern of appearance will depend on the dynamics of (2), or the shape of $f: [0, 1] \times [0, 1] \to [0, 1]$.

The sample points $\xi_k = (y_k, y_{k-1})$ appear in the x_1x_2 plane, according to the iterative process (2); see Fig. 1. If we start with $\xi_1 = (y_1, y_0)$, where $y_1 \in Ox_2$ and $y_0 \in Ox_1$, then we can read out y_2 from the surface representing f. Then y_2 is reflected through $x_3 = x_2$ on the x_2x_3 plane, becoming a point on the Ox_2 axis. In the same time y_1 is reflected through $x_2 = x_1$ on the x_1x_2 plane, becoming a point on the Ox_1 axis. This results in the point (y_1, y_2) in the x_1x_2 plane, corresponding to the sample $\xi_2 = (y_2, y_1)$. We can now read out y_3 from the surface representing f and repeat the process for $k = 3$. Now y_3 'migrates' from Ox_3 to Ox_2 and y_2 from Ox_2 to Ox_1 generating the point (y_2, y_3) on the x_1x_2 plane corresponding to the sample $\xi_3 = (y_3, y_2)$ etc.

Thus, we have to address the issue of nonuniform sampling and to provide at least the existence conditions for function recovery with any degree of accuracy from a sufficiently large *finite* number of irregular samples making this way the application of neural networks plausible.

3 Band-limited and Space-limited Functions

The crucial question we are dealing with is whether the non-linear functions describing dynamical systems as NARMA models (1) are strictly band-limited or space-limited in the sense usually used in Signal Processing. Also important are the consequences of these properties for the reconstruction of such functions. The related question is how their extensions to the whole domain $\mathbb{R}^{n+m}$ functions are constructed. This is important, because we are going to use the harmonic analysis tools and especially Fourier Transform or Fourier Series. Thus we extend f to be equal to 0 outside its natural domain $D = [a, b]^n \times [c, d]^m$. For simplicity, the subsequent considerations concern mainly the 1-D case.

We shall say that a function $f(x)$ is *band-limited* if its Fourier transform (multi-dimensional) is zero outside a finite region, and its energy is finite, i.e.,

$$F(\omega) = 0 \qquad \text{for} \qquad |\omega| > \Omega \qquad \text{and} \qquad \mathrm{E} = \frac{1}{2\pi}\int_{-\Omega}^{\Omega} |\mathrm{F}(\omega)|^2 \mathrm{d}\omega < \infty.$$

ω and Ω being vectors, in general. Analogously we shall say that a function is *space-limited* in multi-dimensional case if

$$f(x) = 0 \qquad \text{for} \qquad |\mathrm{x}| > \mathrm{X} \qquad \text{and} \qquad \mathrm{E} < \infty.$$

The problem is: are the 'usual' functions encountered in dynamic systems description really band-limited or space-limited? From the theory of complex functions we know that any function that is band-limited is analytic in its domain, i.e., is an entire function. On the other hand, an entire function cannot vanish on an interval, except for the case $f(x) \equiv 0$; thus it is not space-limited. So f cannot be band-limited and space-limited at the same time. This is a manifestation of the *uncertainty principle* of harmonic analysis. For if we want to localise a function $f(x)$ in its (spatial) domain, it must be composed of very many $\sin \omega x$ and thus $\Delta\omega$ must be large and vice-versa. Generally, the uncertainty principle of harmonic analysis says: *It is impossible for a non-zero function and its Fourier transform to be simultaneously very small.*

4 Concentration Problem and Prolate Spheroidal Wave Functions

Knowing that a non-trivial band-limited function cannot be space-limited we naturally come to the question: what kind of *approximately* space-limited function corresponds to a given band-limited function. In practical terms we are looking for a function whose 'energy' outside the given spatial region is small enough to be indistinguishable from the energy of (strictly) space-limited function. Therefore, we may define a meaningful measure of concentration of a function as

$$\alpha^2(X) = \frac{\int_{-X/2}^{X/2} |f(x)|^2 dx}{\int_{-\infty}^{\infty} |f(x)|^2 dx}.$$

We want to determine how large $\alpha^2(X)$ can be for a given band-limited f; dually one may define an appropriate measure of concentration of the amplitude spectrum of $f(x)$, say $\beta^2(\Omega)$. Note that if $f(x)$ were indeed space-limited to $(-X/2, X/2)$, then $\alpha^2(X)$ would have its largest value, namely unity. To solve the problem of maximising $\alpha^2(X)$ we have to express $f(x)$ in terms of its amplitude spectrum $F(\omega)$ and find the $F(\omega)$ for which $\alpha^2(X)$ achieves maximal value. This is a classical problem of mathematical physics (see [2]) and we know that the maximising $F(\omega)$ must satisfy the integral homogeneous Fredholm equation of the second kind

$$\int_{-\Omega}^{\Omega} \frac{\sin \pi T(\omega' - \omega'')}{\pi(\omega' - \omega'')} F(\omega'') d\omega'' = \alpha^2(X) F(\omega'), \qquad |\omega'| \leq \Omega. \tag{3}$$

The solutions to equation (3) are known as *prolate spheroidal wave functions (pswf)* and they provide a useful set of band-limited functions (see [5] for more details).

5 The $2X\Omega$ Theorem

Our principal question was how well the band-limited and space-limited functions (with above mentioned restrictions) are suited to model real-world dynamic automatic control systems. To shed more light on it let us recall the so-called $2X\Omega$ Theorem [4]. Its practical engineering formulation says that if $X\Omega$ is large enough, then the space of functions of space range X and 'bandwidth' Ω has dimension $\lceil 2X\Omega \rceil$. To formulate it in a more rigorous manner we have to introduce the notion of space-limited and band-limited functions in a way avoiding their dependence on the detailed behaviour of functions or their Fourier transforms at infinity.

So, we say that a function $f(x)$ is space-limited in multi-dimensional case to the interval $(X/2, X/2)$ at level ε if

$$\int_{|x|>X/2} |f(x)|^2 dx < \varepsilon,$$

i.e., if the energy outside this space region is less than it is, in some sense, essential for us. The same way we say that a function is band-limited with bandwidth Ω at level ε if

$$\int_{|\omega|>\Omega/2} |F(\omega)|^2 d\omega < \varepsilon,$$

i.e., the energy outside the frequency range is less than the value we are interested in. Using these newly defined functions we may state that every function is both space-limited and band-limited at level ε (for some X and Ω) as opposed to only one function ($f(x) \equiv 0$) which is both space-limited and band-limited in the strict sense.

To complete the reformulation of the $2X\Omega$ Theorem we need one more definition. We say that a set of functions $\mathcal{F}$ has an approximate dimension N at level ε on the interval $(-X/2, X/2)$ if there exists a set of $N = N(X, \varepsilon)$ functions $\phi_1, \phi_2, \ldots, \phi_N$ such that for each $f(x) \in \mathcal{F}$ there exist $a_1, a_2, \ldots, a_N$ such that

$$\int_{-X/2}^{X/2} \left[f(x) - \sum_{j=1}^{N} a_j \phi_j(x) \right]^2 dx < \varepsilon \tag{4}$$

and there is no set of $N-1$ functions that will approximate every $f(x) \in \mathcal{F}$ this way. This definition says, in other words, that every function in $\mathcal{F}$ can be approximated in $-X/2 < x < X/2$ by a function in the linear span of $\phi_1, \phi_2, \ldots, \phi_N$, so that the difference between the function and its approximation is less than ε.

Restated version of the theorem has now the following form:

Theorem 1 *Let $\mathcal{F}_\varepsilon$ be the set of functions space-limited to $(-X/2, X/2)$ at level ε and band-limited to $(-\Omega, \Omega)$ at level ε. Let $N(\Omega, X, \varepsilon, \varepsilon')$ be the approximate dimension of $\mathcal{F}_\varepsilon$ at level ε'. Then for every $\varepsilon' > \varepsilon$*

$$\lim_{X\to\infty} \frac{N(\Omega, X, \varepsilon, \varepsilon')}{X} = 2\Omega, \qquad \lim_{\Omega\to\infty} \frac{N(\Omega, X, \varepsilon, \varepsilon')}{\Omega} = 2X.$$

In fact these limits do not depend on ε and the set of functions which in real world we must consider to be limited both in space and frequency will be always asymptotically $2X\Omega$-dimensional.

6 Conclusions

In this paper we have shown how the irregular samples are generated by a dynamic system. We argue that in general this is an intrinsic feature of the NARMA model and our attempts to reconstruct the function f should be set in the irregular sampling context. The most important question in this setting is the one of space- and band-limitedness of the function under consideration. The result of paramount importance from the point of view of function approximation by *finite, linear* combinations of functions is given in the form of the $2X\Omega$ theorem. Equation (4) stipulates the existence of a *finite* approximation of a given nonlinear function by a *linear* combination of functions. It also gives the lower bound for the number of these functions. This allows the application of neural network with known (finite) number of neurons.

On the other hand, the $2X\Omega$ theorem is also interesting from the point of view of function reconstruction from its irregularly spaced samples. In this case we have to assume that our function to be reconstructed is band-limited. From practical considerations it has to be space-limited as well. This problem is normally solved in the context of the theory of complex functions analytic in the entire domain (entire functions and their special types). Let us notice that applying the $2X\Omega$ Theorem, instead of using entire functions of exponential type (as is usually the case in irregular sampling), which is quite restrictive, we deal with functions which are square-integrable—a condition that is easily fulfilled in most practical cases.

REFERENCES

[1] S. Chen and S. A. Billings. *Representation of non-linear systems: the NARMAX model.* International Journal of Control, Vol. 49 (1989), pp1013–1032.

[2] R. Courant and D. Hilbert. *Methods of Mathematical Physics*, Vol. 1. Interscience Publishers (1955), New York.

[3] R. M. Sanner and J.-J. E. Slotine. *Gaussian networks for direct adaptive control.* IEEE Transactions on Neural Networks, Vol. 3 (1992), pp837–863.

[4] D. Slepian. *Some comments on Fourier analysis, uncertainty and modelling.* SIAM Review, Vol. 25(3) (July 1983), pp379–393.

[5] D. Slepian and H. O. Pollak. *Prolate spheroidal wave functions, Fourier analysis and uncertainty, I.* The Bell System Technical Journal, Vol. 40(1) (January 1961), pp43–64.

[6] R. Żbikowski, K. J. Hunt, A. Dzieliński, R. Murray-Smith, and P. J. Gawthrop. *A review of advances in neural adaptive control systems.* Technical Report of the ESPRIT NACT Project TP-1, Glasgow University and Daimler-Benz Research, (1994). (Available from FTP server ftp.mech.gla.ac.uk as PostScript file /nact/nact_tp1.ps).

Acknowledgements

Work supported by ESPRIT III Basic Research Project No. 8039 *Neural Adaptive Control Technology*

UNSUPERVISED LEARNING OF TEMPORAL CONSTANCIES BY PYRAMIDAL-TYPE NEURONS.

Michael Eisele

The Salk Institute, Computational Neurobiology Laboratory, PO Box 85800, San Diego, CA 92186 - 5800, USA. Email: eisele@salk.edu

An unsupervised learning principle is proposed for individual neurons with complex synaptic structure and dynamical input. The learning goal is a neuronal response to temporal constancies: If some input patterns often occur in close temporal succession, then the neuron should respond either to all of them or to none. It is shown that linear threshold neurons can achieve this learning goal, if each synapse stores not only a weight, but also a short-term memory trace. The online learning process requires no biologically implausible interactions. The sequence of temporal associations can be interpreted as a random walk on the state transition graph of the input dynamics. In numerical simulations the learning process turned out to be robust against parameter changes.

1 Introduction

Many neocortical neurons show responses that are invariant to changes in position, size, illumination, or other properties of their preferred stimuli (see review [5]). These temporal "constancies" or "invariants" do not have to be inborn: In numerical simulations [2, 3, 6] neurons could learn such responses by associating stimuli that occur in close temporal succession. Similar temporal associations have also been observed experimentally [4].

In most numerical simulations [2, 6] temporal associations were formed with the help of "memory traces" which are running averages of the neuron's recent activity: If the stimulus S_i is often followed by the stimulus S_j, a strong response of the neuron to S_i causes a large memory trace at the time of stimulus S_j, which teaches the neuron to respont to S_j, too. By presenting the stimuli in reverse temporal order $S_j \rightarrow S_i$, the response to stimuli S_i is likewise strengthened by the response to stimulus S_i.

This simple learning scheme does no longer work, if the input dynamics is irreversible, that is if only the transition $S_i \rightarrow S_j$ occurs. In the following a more complex learning scheme will be presented, which can form associations in both temporal directions of an irreversible input dynamics. For this purpose an additional memory trace will have to be stored in each synapse. Numerical results are presented for neuronal input generated by a Markov process which is simpler than naturally occuring input, but irreversible and highly stochastic. A temporal constancy in such a dynamics consists of a set of states which are closely connected to each other by temporal transitions. The learned synaptic excitation can be derived from the neuronal firing pattern by interpreting the sequence of temporal associations as a random walk between Markov states.

2 Neuron Model

The model neuron was chosen to have the simple activation dynamics of a linear threshold unit, but a complicated learning dynamics. The input signal is generated by a temporally discrete, autonomous, stochastic dynamics with a finite number N of states S_i. Each state is connected with a sensory afferent. At any time t the afferent of the present state $R(t) \in \{S_0, \ldots S_N\}$ is set active ($x_j(t) = 1$ for

$R(t) = S_j$), while all the other afferents are set passive ($x_i(t) = 0$ for $R(t) \neq S_i$). Each afferent forms one synapse with the model neuron. The sum of weighted inputs is called the neuron's activity $a(R(t)) = \sum_i w_i x_i(t)$. If the activity exceeds a threshold θ, the neurons output $y(R(t))$ is 1, otherwise it is 0.

The memory trace $<p>_r$ of any quantity p is defined as its exponentially weighted past average at time t. The subscript r indicates over which time scale $1/\eta_r$ the average is done (with $0 < \eta_r < 1$).

$$<p>_r(t) \quad := \quad \eta_r \sum_{\tau=1}^{\infty} p(t-\tau) \cdot (1-\eta_r)^{(\tau-1)} \tag{1}$$

$$\Rightarrow \quad <p>_r(t+1) - <p>_r(t) \quad = \quad \eta_r \cdot (p(t) - <p>_r(t)) \tag{2}$$

The neuron model includes a variable threshold $\theta(t)$ and a variable synaptic decay term $\rho(t)$, which serve to keep the neuron's average output y and activity a near the preset values $\overline{y}, \overline{a} > 0$.

$$\theta(t) \quad := \quad <\theta>_\theta(t) \cdot (1 + \eta_y \cdot (<y>_\theta(t) - \overline{y})) \tag{3}$$

$$\rho(t) \quad := \quad <\rho>_\rho(t) + \frac{1}{\eta_w <a>_\rho(t)} \cdot \left(<\sum_i \Delta w_i>_\rho(t) + \eta_\rho \cdot (<a>_\rho(t) - \overline{a}) \right) \tag{4}$$

(Remember that the memory traces $<\theta>_\theta(t)$ and $<\rho>_\rho(t)$ at time t do not depend on $\theta(t)$ or $\rho(t)$.) If the total synaptic change $\sum_i \Delta w_i$ is positive and if the activity a exceeds its target $\overline{a}$, ρ will decrease on a time scale $1/\eta_\rho$, causing a subsequent decrease of synaptic weights in eq. (6). The time scales $1/\eta_\theta$ and $1/\eta_\rho$ of the averages are set large compared to the recurrence time of sensory input patterns. The rate $\eta_y \approx 1/3$ determines how much the threshold θ is increased, if the average output $<y>_\theta$ exceeds its target $\overline{y}$.

Synaptic learning processes determine the synaptic weights w_i and the synaptic short-term memory traces q_i, which measure the contribution that a synapse has recently made to the neuronal activity a.

$$q_i(t) \quad := \quad \left\langle \frac{w_i \cdot x_i}{a} \right\rangle_f (t) \tag{5}$$

$$\Delta w_i(t) \quad := \quad \eta_w w_i(t) x_i(t) \left(\alpha_p \frac{<z>_p(t)}{a(t)} - \rho(t) \right) + \eta_w \alpha_f z(t) q_i(t) \tag{6}$$

The decay term $\rho(t)$ was defined above. The past and future prefactors α_f and α_p will be discussed below. The quantity $z(t)$ models the postsynaptic depolarization that effects the learning process. It is defined as a sum $z(t) := a(t) + \gamma y(t)$ of the depolarization a caused by other synaptic inputs and the depolarization caused by the firing y of the postsynaptic neuron, weighted by a factor $\gamma > 0$.

This synaptic learning rule can be rewritten into a more comprehensible form by defining modified synaptic changes $\widetilde{\Delta w_i}$:

$$\widetilde{\Delta w_i}(t) \quad := \quad \eta_w w_i(t) x_i(t) \left(\frac{\alpha_p}{a(t)} \eta_p \sum_{\tau=1}^{\infty} z(t-\tau) \cdot (1-\eta_p)^{(\tau-1)} + \frac{\alpha_f}{a(t)} \eta_f \sum_{\tau=1}^{\infty} z(t+\tau) \cdot (1-\eta_f)^{(\tau-1)} - \rho(t) \right) \tag{7}$$

By inserting definitions (1) and (5) into eq. (6) one can easily show that the modified synaptic changes cause approximately the same total changes in the long run:

$\sum_{t=1}^{T} \Delta w_i(t) \approx \sum_{t=1}^{T} \widetilde{\Delta w_i}(t)$ for large T. The approximation is good, if the learning period T is much larger than the duration $1/\eta_f$ of the synaptic memory trace q_i. It is exact, if the depolarization $z(t)$ is zero for $t < 1$ and $t > T$.

The definition (7) of $\widetilde{\Delta w_i}$ resembles resembles an unsupervised Widrow-Hoff-rule, in which the desired activity of the neuron depends on an exponentially weighted average of past and future postsynaptic depolarizations $z(t \pm \tau)$. Because the future depolarizations $z(t + \tau)$ are not yet known at time t, the memory traces q_i had to be introduced in order to construct the online learning rule (6) of $\Delta w_i(t)$.

3 Interpretation of Temporal Associations as a Random Walk

After a sufficiently long time t_0, any successful learning process should reach a quasistationary state, in which synaptic changes cancel each other in the long run. In the following we will derive the neural activities $a(S_i)$ in the quasistationary state from the neural outputs $y(S_j)$ and the transition rules of the input dynamics. Even in the quasistationarity state, the quantities w_i, θ, and ρ will fluctuate irregularily, if the input is generated by a stochastic dynamics. We assume that the learning rates η_w, η_θ and η_ρ are so small that these fluctuations can be neglected. Then the activity a, the output y, and the depolarization $z = a + \gamma y$ depend on time t only through the state $R(t)$ of the input dynamics. Under the assumption that the input dynamics is ergodic, the temporal average $\sum_{t=1}^{T} \widetilde{\Delta w_i}(t+t_0)/T$ can be replaced by an average over all possible trajectories $\ldots \to R(-1) \to R(0) \to R(1) \to \ldots$ of the input dynamics. By definition, quasistationarity has been reached, if these average weight changes vanish for all synapses. Using definition (7) of $\widetilde{\Delta w_i}$, the condition of quasistationarity now reads:

$$\begin{aligned} a(R(0)) \;&\stackrel{!}{=}\; \frac{\alpha_f}{\rho} \cdot \sum_{R(1),R(2),\ldots} \left(P_f(R(0) \to R(1) \to R(2) \ldots) \eta_f \sum_{\tau=1}^{\infty} z(R(\tau))(1-\eta_f)^{(\tau-1)} \right) \\ &+ \frac{\alpha_p}{\rho} \cdot \sum_{\ldots,R(-2),R(-1)} \left(P_p(\ldots R(-2) \to R(-1) \to R(0)) \eta_p \sum_{\tau=1}^{\infty} z(R(-\tau))(1-\eta_p)^{(\tau-1)} \right) \quad (8) \end{aligned}$$

for any state $R(0)$. Here $P_f(R(0) \to R(1) \to \ldots)$ denotes the probability measure that a trajectory starting at $R(0)$ will subsequently pass through $R(1)$, $R(2)$, ... Analogously, $P_p(\ldots \to R(-1) \to R(0))$ denotes the relative probabilities of trajectories ending at $R(0)$.

The right hand side of eq. (8) can be interpreted as an average over random jumps between states of the input dynamics. Every jump starts at state $R(0)$. It jumps with probability α_f/ρ into the future and with probability α_p/ρ into the past. The jump length τ is exponentially distributed, with a mean of $1/\eta_f$ (or $1/\eta_p$) time steps being transversed. If the dynamics is stochastic, several end states may be reached after $\pm\tau$ time steps. The end state $R(\pm\tau)$ is then chosen according to the transition probabilities P_f or P_p, which were defined above. The effective depolarization $z = a + \gamma y$ of the end state is averaged over all possible jumps. According to eq. (8), this average should equal the activity $a(R(0))$ at the start state $R(0)$.

The activity $a(R(0))$ at the start state still depends on the unknown activity $a(R(\pm\tau))$ at the end state. The latter can again be interpreted as an average over random jumps, which start from state $R(\pm\tau)$. By repeating this concatenation of

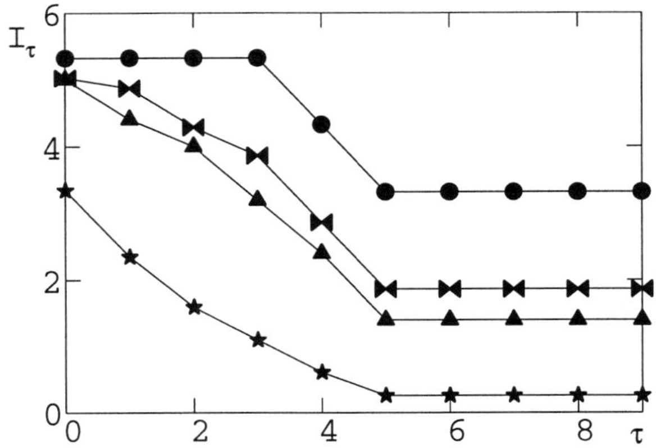

Figure 1 I_τ is the information which a first spike at time t transmits about the state of the input dynamics at time $t+\tau$. A neuron responding to a randomly chosen set of 32 states would convey very little information (stars). A neuron with suitable learning parameters (see text) can improve its response: Circle: response to an optimal set of 32 states at $t \approx 10^6$. Triangle: response to 33 states at $t \approx 2 \cdot 10^6$, if the "drift" is slightly positive ($\alpha_f = 0.55$; $\alpha_p = 0.45$; $\eta_f = \eta_p = 0.8$). Bowtie: response to 31 states at $t \approx 2.5 \cdot 10^6$, if a maximal drift ($\alpha_f^a = \alpha_p^b = 0$) is compensated by interactions of two different dendrites.

jumps, one forms a random walk (which should not be confused with a trajectory of the input dynamics). By averaging eq. (8) over all start states $R(0)$ one can easily show that the total jump probability $\alpha_f/\rho + \alpha_p/\rho \approx 1/(1+\gamma\overline{y}/\overline{a}) < 1$, so that the random walk is of finite mean length $\overline{a}/(\gamma\overline{y})$. Thus one can sum γy over the end states of all jumps in a random walk and average this sum over all the random walks starting at S_j. According to construction, this average shold equal the activity $a(S_j)$, once that the learning process has reached quasistationarity.

4 Numerical Results

The learning algorithm was tested with input generated by a special Markov process, whose high internal symmetry permits an accurate assessment of the learning process. Each of its $10 \cdot 2^5 = 320$ equally probable states is denoted by a digit sequence $C\ B_1B_2B_3B_4B_5$, with $C \in \{0,1,\ldots 9\}$ and $B_i \in \{0,1\}$. Each state $C\ B_1B_2B_3B_4B_5$ forms two equally probable transitions to the states $C'\ B_2B_3B_4B_50$ and $C'\ B_2B_3B_4B_51$, with $C' \equiv C+1 \bmod 10$.

With suitable learning parameters ($\overline{y} = 0.1$, $\gamma = 0.1$, $\alpha_f = \alpha_p = 0.5$, and $1/\eta_f = 1/\eta_p = 1.25$, $\eta_w \approx 0.04$) and random initial synaptic weights the neuron needed 1 million time steps of online learning to develop a quasistationary response. It responded to 32 states of the Markov process, namely the 8 states $0\ B_1B_2B_301$ (with $B_1B_2B_3 \in \{000, 001, \ldots 111\}$), the 8 states $1\ B_1B_201B_5$, the 8 states $2\ B_101B_4B_5$, and the 8 states $3\ 01B_3B_4B_5$. According to the rules of the input dynamics, these four groups of states are always passed in the given order. Thus the neuron always responds for 4 consequetive time steps. By its first spike ($y(t) = 1$ after $y(t-1) = 0$) it transmits an information $I_\tau = \log_2(320/8) \approx 5.3$ about the state $R(t=\tau)$ of the input dynamics at the present moment $\tau = 0$ and the next three time steps

$\tau = 1, 2$ or 3 (see fig. 1). One can prove that this is one of the "most constant" responses to the input dynamics, in the sense that no neuron with mean firing rate $\overline{y} = 0.1$ can transmit more information I_τ by its first spike or show more than 4 consequetive responses at some times without showing less than 4 consequetive responses at other times.

A deeper analysis of the properties of the random walk showed that the learning process is robust against almost all parameter changes (as long as $\eta_f, \eta_p, \eta_w, \eta_\theta, \eta_\rho$, and γ remain small enough). The one critical learning parameter is $\alpha_f/\eta_f - \alpha_p/\eta_p$, the mean drift of the random walk into the future direction per jump. In the extreme case $\alpha_p = 0$ the learning goal (8) would require the neuron's strongest activity to preceed its output $y = 1$ in time, which is inconsistent with the output being caused by the neuron's strongest activity. Only if the drift was rather small, did the learning process converge to quasistationarity (triangles in fig. 1).

There is a way to turn the learning process robust against changes in α_f and α_p. One constructs a neuron with two different dendrites, differing in the values ρ, $<\rho>_\rho$, $<\sum_i \Delta w_i>_\rho$, and $<a>_\rho$ and the synaptic learning parameters $\alpha_f, \alpha_p, \eta_f, \eta_p$: In dendrite a the drift $\alpha_f^a/\eta_f^a - \alpha_p^a/\eta_p^a$ is chosen negative, in dendrite b the drift $\alpha_f^b/\eta_f^b - \alpha_p^b/\eta_p^b$ is chosen positive. This learning process always reached quasistationarity in numerical simulation. The early part of neuronal responses was caused by dendrite b, the late part by dendrite a. The worst choice of learning parameters (maximal drift $\alpha_f^a = \alpha_p^b = 0$) still produced a rather good neuronal response (bowties in fig. 1). The known anatomical connections in the neocortex suggest that dendritic type a might correspond to apical dendrites and dendritic type b to basal dendrites[1]. This speculative hypothesis might be tested by simulating networks of such neurons.

REFERENCES

[1] Eisele, M., *Vereinfachung generierender Partitionen von chaotischen Attraktoren,* (German) PhD-thesis, Appendix D, ISSN 0944-2952 Jül-report 3021, KFA-Jülich, Jülich (1995).

[2] Földiak, P., *Learning invariance from transformation sequences,* Neural Computation, Vol.3 (1991), pp194–200.

[3] Mitchison, G. J., *Removing time variation with the anti-hebbian differential synapse,* Neural Computation, Vol.3 (1991), pp312–320.

[4] Miyashita, Y. & Chang, H.-S., *Neuronal correlate of pictorial short-term memory in the primate temporal cortex,* Nature, Vol. 331 (1988), pp68–70.

[5] Oram, M. W. & Perret, D. I., *Modeling visual recognition from neurobiological constraints,* Neural Networks, Vol.7 (1994), pp945–972.

[6] Wallis, G., Rolls, E. T., & Foldiak, P., *Learning invariant responses to the natural transformations of objects,* Int. Joint Conf. on Neural Net., Vol.2 (1993), pp1087–1090.

Acknowledgements

The author thanks F. Pasemann for many useful discussions and E. Pöppel and G. Eilenberger for general support. This work was done at the KFA Jülich, Germany.

NUMERICAL ASPECTS OF MACHINE LEARNING IN ARTIFICIAL NEURAL NETWORKS

S.W. Ellacott and A. Easdown

School of Computing and Mathematical Sciences, University of Brighton, Brighton BN1 4GJ, UK. Email: S.W.Ellacott@brighton.ac.uk

In previous papers e.g. [5] the effect on the learning properties of filtering or other preprocessing of input data to networks was considered. A strategy for adaptive filtering based directly on this analysis will be presented. We focus in Section 2 on linear networks and the delta rule since this simple case permits the approach to be easily tested. Numerical experiments on some simple problems show that the method does indeed enhance the performance of the epoch or off line method considerably. In Section 3, we discuss briefly the extension to non-linear networks and in particuar to backpropagation. The algorithm in its simple form is, however, less successful and current research focuses on a practicable extension to non-linear networks.

1 Introduction

In previous papers e.g. [5] the effect on the learning properties of filtering or other preprocessing of input data to networks was considered. Such filters are usually constructed either on the basis of knowledge of the problem domain or on statistical or other properties of the input space. However in the paper cited it was briefly pointed out that it would be possible to construct filters designed to optimise the learning properties directly by inferring spectral properties of the iteration matrix during the learning process, permitting the process to be conditioned dynamically. The resulting technique is naturally parallel and easily carried out alongside the learning rule itself, incurring only a small computational overhead. Here we explore this idea.

2 Linear Theory

Although not the original perceptron algorithm, the following method known as the *delta rule* is generally accepted as the best way to train a simple perceptron. Since there is no coupling between the rows we may consider the single output perceptron. Denote the required output for an input pattern $\mathbf{x}$ by y, and the weights by the vector $\mathbf{w}^T$. Then,

$$\delta\mathbf{w} = \eta(y - \mathbf{w}^T\mathbf{x})\mathbf{x}$$

where η is a parameter to be chosen called the *learning rate* [7],p.322 . Thus given a current iterate weight vector $\mathbf{w_k}$,

$$\mathbf{w_{k+1}} = \mathbf{w_k} + \eta(y - \mathbf{w_k}^T\mathbf{x})\mathbf{x} = (I - \eta\mathbf{x}\mathbf{x}^T)\mathbf{w_k} + \eta y\mathbf{x} \quad (1)$$

since the quantity in the brackets is scalar. The bold subscript $\mathbf{k}$ here, denotes the *kth* iterate, not the *kth* element. We will consider a fixed and finite set of input patterns $\mathbf{x_p}$, $p = 1 \dots t$, with corresponding output y_p. If we assume that the patterns are presented in repeated cyclic order, the presented $\mathbf{x}$ and corresponding y of (1) repeat every t iterations, and given a sufficiently small η, the corresponding weights go into a limit t-cycle: see [3] or [5]. Of course this is not the only or necessarily best possible presentation scheme [2], but other methods require *a priori* analysis of the data or dynamic reordering. Since we are assuming that we have a fixed and finite set of patterns $\mathbf{x_p}$, $p = 1 \dots t$, an alternative strategy is not to update the weight vector until the whole epoch of t patterns has been presented.

This idea is attractive since it actually generates the steepest descent direction for the least sum of squares error over all the patterns. We will call this the *epoch method* to distinguish it from the usual delta rule. (Other authors use the term *off line learning.*) This leads to the iteration

$$\mathbf{w_{k+1}} = \Omega\mathbf{w_{k+1}} + \eta\sum_{p=1}^{t}(y_p\mathbf{x_p}) \tag{2}$$

where $\Omega = (I - \eta XX^T) = (I - \eta L)$. Here X is the $n \times t$ matrix whose columns are the $\mathbf{x_p}$'s. The k in (2) is, of course, not equivalent to that in (1), since it corresponds to a complete epoch of patterns. There is no question of limit cycling, and, indeed a fixed point will be a true least squares minimum $\mathbf{w}^*$. To see this, put $\mathbf{w_{k+1}} = \mathbf{w_k} = \mathbf{w}^*$ and observe that (2) reduces to the normal equations for the least squares problem. Moreover the iteration (2) is simply steepest descent for the least squares problem, applied with a fixed step length. Clearly $L = XX^T$ is symmetric and positive semi definite. In fact, provided the $\mathbf{x_p}$ span, it is (as is well known) strictly positive definite. The eigenvalues of Ω are $1 - \eta(\textit{the corresponding eigenvalues of } L)$, and hence for η sufficiently small $\varrho(\Omega) = \|\Omega\|_2 < 1$. Unfortunately, however, (2) generally requires a smaller value of η than (1) to retain numerical stability [3], [5]. How can we improve stability of (2) or indeed (1)? Since these are linear iterations it is only necessary to remove the leading eigenvalue of the iteration matrix. Specifically we seek a matrix T such that if each input vector $\mathbf{x_p}$ is replaced by $T\mathbf{x_p}$, more rapid convergence will result. We see from (2) that the crucial issue is the relationship between the unfiltered update matrix $\Omega = (I - \eta XX^T)$ and its filtered equivalent $(I - \eta TXX^TT^T) = \Omega'$ say. In general these operations may be defined on spaces of different dimension: see e.g. [5], but here we assume T is $n \times n$. To choose T we compute the largest eigenvalue and corresponding eigenvevtor of XX^T. This may be carried out by the power method [6], p.147 at the same time as the ordinary delta rule or epoch iteration: the computation can be performed by running through patterns one at a time, just as for the learning rule itself. We get a normalised eigenvector $\mathbf{p_1}$ of XX^T corresponding to the largest eigenvalue λ_1 of XX^T. Set

$$T = I + (\lambda_1^{-1/2} - 1)\mathbf{p_1}\mathbf{p_1}^T. \tag{3}$$

A routine calculation shows that TXX^TT^T has the same eigenvectors as XX^T, and the same eigenvalues but with λ_1 replaced by 1. Each pattern $\mathbf{x_p}$ should then be multiplied by T, and, since we are now iterating with different data, the current weight estimate $\mathbf{w}$ should be multiplied by

$$T^{-1} = I + (\lambda_1^{1/2} - 1)\mathbf{p_1}\mathbf{p_1}^T. \tag{4}$$

We may then repeat the process to remove further eigenvalues. Basically the same idea can be used for the iteration with the weights updated after each pattern as in (1), but it is less convenient: for simplicity, our numerical experiments refer only to the application to (2). Two small examples are discussed: in each case four eigenvalues are removed though in fact for the first example, only the first eigenvalue is significant.

The first example is a 'toy' problem taken from [5],p113. There are four patterns and $n = 3$: $\mathbf{x_1} = (1,0,0)^T, \mathbf{x_2} = (1,1,0)^T, \mathbf{x_3} = (1,1,1)^T$ and $\mathbf{x_4} = (1,0,1)^T$. The corresponding outputs are $y_1 = 0, y_2 = y_3 = y_4 = 1$. Figure 1 shows the number of

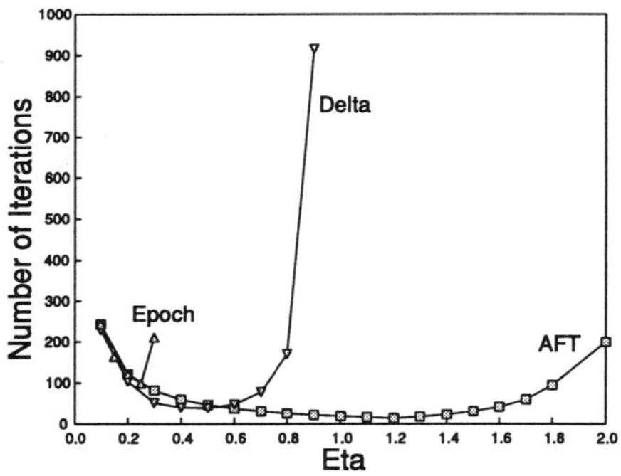

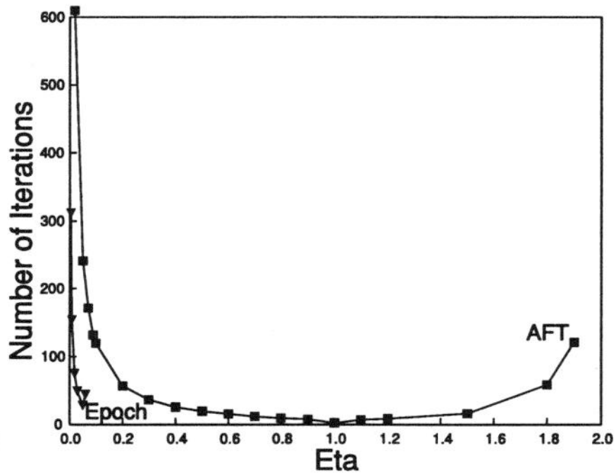

Figure 1 **Figure 2**

epochs required to obtain agreement in the weights (at the end of the epoch for the delta rule) to an error or 1E-8, for various values of η and for the three methods: the delta rule (1), the epoch or off line method (2) and the Adaptive Filtering Method (AFT) using (3).

As a slightly more realistic example we also considered the Balloon Database B from the UCI Repository of Machine learning and domain theories [1]. This is a set of sixteen 4-vectors which are linearly separable. Figure 2 compares the perfomance of the epoch and AFT methods: on this very well behaved database the epoch method actually performs better in terms of iterations than the delta rule even though it requires a larger value of η. With $\eta = 1$, AFT requires only three epochs and good performance is obtained over a wide range, whereas the best obtainable with the epoch method is 28 with $\eta = 0.05$ and this is a very sharp minimum: $\eta = 0.03$ requires 49 iterations, and $\eta = 0.06$ requires 45.

3 Non-linear Networks

The usefulness of linear neural systems is limited, since many pattern recognition problems are not linearly separable. We will define a general nonlinear delta rule. The *backpropagation rule* [7], pp.322-328 used in many neural net applications is a special case of this. For the linear network the dimension of the input space and the number of weights are the same: n in our previous notation. Now we will let M denote the *total number* of weights and n the input dimension. So the input patterns $\mathbf{x}$ to our network are in $\mathbb{R}^n$, and we have a vector $\mathbf{w}$ of parameters in $\mathbb{R}^M$ describing the particular instance of our network: i.e. the vector of synaptic weights. For a single layer perceptron with m outputs, the vector $\mathbf{w}$ is the the $m \times n$ weight matrix, and thus $M = mn$. For a multilayer perceptron, $\mathbf{w}$ is the cartesian product of the weight matrices in each layer. For brevity we consider just a single output. The network computes a function $g : \mathbb{R}^M \times \mathbb{R}^n \rightarrow \mathbb{R}$. In [4] or [5] it is shown that the generalised delta rule becomes

$$\delta \mathbf{w} = \eta(y - g(\mathbf{w}, \mathbf{x}) \nabla g(\mathbf{w}, \mathbf{x}) \qquad (5)$$

∇g takes the place of $\mathbf{x}$ in (1). Observe that a change of weights in any given layer will cause a (linear) change in the *input* vector to the succesive hidden layer. Thus the required gradient is obtained by i) differentiating the current layer with respect

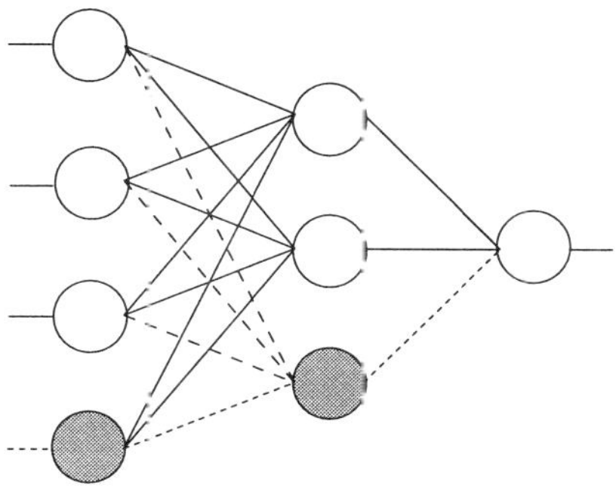

Figure 3

to the weights in the layer and ii) multiplying this by the matrix representation of the Fréchet derivative *with respect to the inputs* in the succeeding layers. Thus, let the kth weight layer, $k = 1, 2, \ldots K$, say, have weight matrix W_k : each row of these matrices forms part of the parameter vector $\mathbf{w}$. On top of each weight layer is a (possibly) non-linear layer. At each of the m (say) hidden units we have an activation function: h_j for the jth unit. The function $\mathbf{h}$ whose jth co-ordinate function is h_j is a mapping $\mathbb{R}^n \to \mathbb{R}^m$. However for a multilayer perceptron it is rather special in that h_j only depends on the jth element of its argument: in terms of derivatives this means that the Jacobian H of $\mathbf{h}$ is diagonal. Let the H and $\mathbf{h}$ for the units layer *after* the kth weight layer also be subscripted k. (Input units to the bottom layer just have identity activation, as is conventional.) Finally suppose that the input to the kth weight layer (i.e. the output from the units of the previous layer) are denoted $\mathbf{v_k}$, with $\mathbf{v_1} = \mathbf{x}$. A small change δW_k in the kth weight matrix causes the input to the corresponding unit layer to change by $\delta W_k \mathbf{v_k}$. The Fréchet derivative of a weight layer $W_r \mathbf{v_r}$ with respect to its input $\mathbf{v_r}$ is of course just W_r. Thus the output is changed by $H_K W_K H_{K-1} W_{K-1} \ldots H_k \delta W_k \mathbf{v_k}$. Since this expression is linear in δW_k it yields for each individual element that component of the gradient of g corresponding to the weights in the kth layer. To see this, recall that the gradient is actually just a Fréchet derivative, i.e. a linear map approximating the change in output. In fact we might as well split up W_k by rows and consider a change $(\delta \mathbf{w_{i,k}})^T$ in the ith row (only). This corresponds to $\delta W_k = \mathbf{e_i}(\delta \mathbf{w_{i,k}})$, so $\delta W_k \mathbf{v_k} = \mathbf{e_i}(\delta \mathbf{w_{i,k}})\mathbf{v_k} = \mathbf{e_i}\mathbf{v_k}^T(\delta \mathbf{w_{i,k}})^T = V_{i,k}(\delta \mathbf{w_{i,k}})^T$, say, where $V_{i,k}$ is the matrix with ith row $\mathbf{v_k}$, and zeros elsewhere. Thus, that section of ∇g in (5) which corresponds to changes in the ith row of the kth weight matrix is $H_K W_K H_{K-1} W_{K-1} \ldots H_k V_{i,k}$. The calculation is illustrated in the following example. Figure 3 shows the architecture. The shaded neurons represent bias neurons with activation functions the identity, and the input to the bias neuron in the input layer is fixed at 1. The smaller dashed connections have weights fixed at 1, and the larger dashed ones have weights fixed at 0. (This approach to bias has been adopted to keep the matrix dimensions consistent.) All other neurons have the standard activation function $a = 1/(1 + e^x)$. Other than the bias input, the data is the same as the first example in Section 2. Let the initial weights be

0.01	0.03	0.05	0
0.02	0.04	0.06	0
0	0	0	1

between the inputs and hidden layers numbering from the top in 3. Thus no bias is applied (but weights in rows 1 and 2 in the last column are trainable), and the bottom row of weights is fixed. Weights are

0.01	0.02	0.02

between hidden and output layer, so a bias of 0.03 is applied to the output neuron and this is trainable. With input $\mathbf{x_1} = (1,0,0,0)^T$ and $y_1 = 1$, we find that (working to 4dp) the output from the non-bias hidden units are 0.5025 and 0.5050. The bias output is of course 1. The output from the output unit is 0.5113. Using the fact that the derivative of the standard activation function is $a(1-a)$, the diagonal elements of the 3×3 matrix H_1 are 0.2500, 0.2500 and 1 from the bias unit. The off diagonal elements are, of course, 0. H_2 is a 1×1 matrix (i.e. a scalar) with value 0.2499. Ignoring terms corresponding to fixed weights we have 11 trainable weights: 8 below the hidden layer and 3 above. ∇g is a thus an 11-vector with the first three elements (say) corresponding to the hidden-to-output weights. (This is the convenient ordering for backpropagation, as the output gradient terms must be computed first.) So the first three elements of ∇g are given by $H_2 V_{1,2} = 0.2499 V_{1,2} = 0.2499 \mathbf{v}_2^T$ (since $\mathbf{e_1}$ is here a 1-vector with element 1) = (0.1256, 0.1262, 0.2499). Proceeding to the sub-hidden layer weights, the first four elements are given by $H_2 W_2 H_1 V_{1,1}$. The product $H_2 W_2 H_1$ evaluates to (0.0006, 0.0012, 0.0075). $V_{1,1} = \mathbf{e_1}\mathbf{v_1^T}$, which has (1,0,0,1) as first row and zeros elsewhere. Hence elements 4 to 7 of ∇g are (0.0006, 0, 0, 0.0006). Similarly elements 8 to 11 of ∇g are (0.0012, 0, 0, 0.0012).
Experiments with the adaptive filtering algorithm have as yet been less successful than in the linear case, due to problems of underdetermination and non-stationarity. These difficulties, which do not appear to be insurmountable, are the focus of current research.

REFERENCES

[1] *The uci repository of machine learning and domain theories*, ftp from ics.uci.edu: /pub/machine-learning-database.

[2] C. Cachin, *Pedagogical pattern selection strategies*, Neural Networks Vol.7 No.1 (1994), pp175–181.

[3] S.W. Ellacott, *An analyis of the delta rule*, in Proceedings of the International Neural Net Conference, Kluwer Academic Publishers (1990), pp956–959.

[4] S.W. Ellacott, *Techniques for the mathematical analysis of neural networks*, J. Computational and Applied Mathematics, Vol.50 (1993), pp283–297.

[5] S.W. Ellacott, *Aspects of the numerical analysis of neural networks* Acta Numerica, Cambridge University Press (1994).

[6] E Isaacson and H.B. Keller, *Analysis of numerical methods*, Wiley (1966).

[7] D.E. Rumelhart and J.L. McClelland. *Parallel and distributed processing: explorations in the microstructure of cognition*, Vols.1 and 2, MIT (1986).

LEARNING ALGORITHMS FOR RAM-BASED NEURAL NETWORKS

Alistair Ferguson, Laurence C Dixon and Hamid Bolouri

Engineering Research and Development Centre, University of Hertfordshire College Lane, Hatfield, Herts, AL10 9AB, UK.

RAM-based neural networks are designed to be hardware amenable, which affects the choice of learning algorithms. Reverse differentiation enables derivatives to be obtained efficiently on any architecture. The performance of four learning methods on three progressively more difficult problems are compared using a simulated RAM network. The learning algorithms are: reward-penalty, batched gradient descent, steepest descent and conjugate gradient. The applications are: the 838 encoder, character recognition, and particle classification. The results indicate that reward-penalty can solve only the simplest problem. All the gradient-based methods solve the particle task, but the simpler ones require more CPU time.

1 Introduction

The driving force behind RAM-based neural networks is their ease of hardware realisation. The desire to retain this property influences the design of learning algorithms. Traditionally, this has led to the use of the reward-penalty algorithm, since only a single scalar value needs to be communicated to every node [7]. The mathematical tool of *reverse differentiation* enables derivatives of an arbitrary function to be obtained efficiently at an operational cost of less than three times the original function. Using three progressively more complex problems, the performance of three gradient-based algorithms and reward-penalty are compared.

2 HyperNet Architecture

HyperNet is the term used to denote the hardware model of a RAM-based neural architecture proposed by Gurney [5], which is similar to the pRAM of Gorse and Taylor [4]. A neuron is termed a multi-cube unit (MCU), and consists of a number of subunits, each with an arbitrary number of inputs. j and k reference nodes in the hidden and output layers respectively, with $i = 1, \dots I$ indexing the subunits. μ denotes the site addresses, and is the set of bit strings $\mu_1, \dots, \mu_n$ where n denotes the number of inputs to the subunit. z_c refers to the cth real-valued input, with $z_c \in [0, 1]$ and $\hat{z}_c \equiv (1 - z_c)$. For each of the 2^n site store locations, two sets are defined: $c \in M^{ij}_{\mu 0}$ if $\mu_c = 0$; $c \in M^{ij}_{\mu 1}$ if $\mu_c = 1$. The access probability $P(\mu^{ij})$ for location μ in subunit i of hidden layer node j is therefore $P(\mu^{ij}) = \prod_{c \in M^{ij}_{\mu 0}} \hat{z}_c \prod_{c \in M^{ij}_{\mu 1}} z_c$. The subunit response (s) is then gained by summing the proportional site values, which are in turn accumulated to form the multi-cube activation (a). The node's output (y) is given by passing the MCU activation through a sigmoid transfer function $(y = \sigma(a) = 1/(1 + e^{-\frac{a}{\rho}}))$. The complete forward pass of a two layer network of HyperNet nodes is given in Table 1. in the form of a computational graph.

Gradient-based algorithms require the extraction of error gradient terms. Reverse differentiation [10] enables derivatives to be obtained efficiently on any architecture. Functions are usually composed of simple operations, and this is the basis on which reverse accumulation works. A computational graph with vertices 1 to N connected by arcs is constructed. The first n vertices are the independent variables, with the results of subsequent basic operations $f_u(.)$ stored in intermediate variables

Computational Graph	Reverse Accumulation

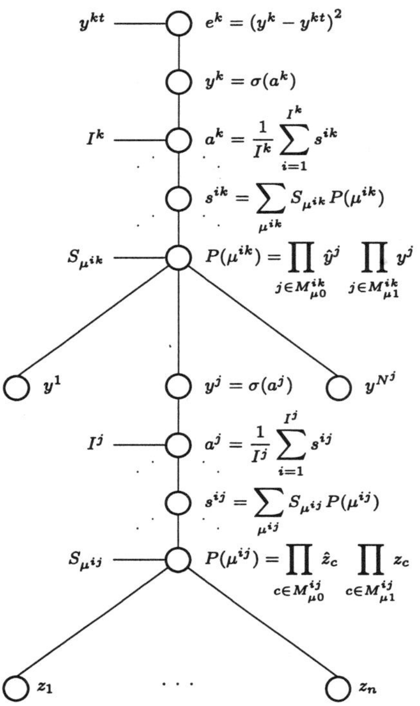

$$\bar{e}^k = 1$$

$$\bar{y}^k = 2(y^k - y^{kt})\bar{e}^k$$

$$\bar{a}^k = \sigma\prime(a^k)\bar{y}^k$$

$$\bar{s}^{ik} = \frac{1}{I^k}\bar{a}^k$$

$$\bar{S}_{\mu^{ik}} = P(\mu^{ik})\bar{s}^{ik}$$

$$\bar{P}(\mu^{ik}) = S_{\mu^{ik}}\bar{s}^{ik}$$

$$\bar{y}^j = \sum_{\substack{k \text{ where} \\ j \in M^{ik}_{\mu 1}}} \left(\prod_{\substack{c \in M^{ik}_{\mu 1} \\ c \neq j}} y^c \prod_{c \in M^{ik}_{\mu 0}} \hat{y}^c \right) \bar{P}(\mu^{ik}) - \sum_{\substack{k \text{ where} \\ j \in M^{ik}_{\mu 0}}} \left(\prod_{c \in M^{ik}_{\mu 1}} y^c \prod_{\substack{c \in M^{ik}_{\mu 0} \\ c \neq j}} \hat{y}^c \right) \bar{P}(\mu^{ik})$$

$$\bar{a}^j = \sigma\prime(a^j)\bar{y}^j$$

$$\bar{s}^{ij} = \frac{1}{I^j}\bar{a}^j$$

$$\bar{S}_{\mu^{ik}} = P(\mu^{ij})\bar{s}^{ij}$$

Table 1 Forward and reverse accumulation of a two layer network of real-valued HyperNet nodes.

$x_u = f_u(.), u = n+1, \ldots, N$ with $F(x) = x_N$. The gradient vector $g(x) = \partial F(x)/\partial x$ can then be obtained by defining $\bar{x} = \partial x_v/\partial x_u, u = 1, \ldots, v$ for vertex u, and applying the chain rule. The process thus starts at vertex N, where $\bar{x}_N = 1$, and percolates down. The reverse accumulation of a two layer HyperNet network is also given in Table 1.

3 Learning Algorithms

The reward-penalty algorithm used is an adaptation of the P-model associative algorithm devised by Barto [2] and modified for HyperNet nodes by Gurney [5]. A single scalar reinforcement signal, calculated from a performance measure, is globally broadcast. The internal parameters are updated using this signal, and local information. The performance metric used is the mean-squared error on the output layer ($e = 1/N^k \sum_{k=1}^{N^k}[\sigma(a^k) - y^{kt}]^2$ where y^{kt} is the target output for node k, and N^k is the number of output layer nodes). The binary reward signal is then probabilistically generated: $r = 1$ with the probability $(1 - e)$; $r = 0$

otherwise. Given a reward signal ($r = 1$) the node's internal parameters are modified so that the current output is more likely to occur from the same stimulus. A penalising step ($r = 0$) should have the opposite effect. The update is therefore $\Delta S_\mu = \alpha\,[r(\breve{y} - y) + \hat{r}\lambda(1 - \breve{y} - y)]$ where α is the learning rate, λ is the degree of penalising, and $\breve{y} \equiv y^{kt}$ for output layer nodes and is the closest extreme for hidden layer nodes: $\breve{y} = 1$ if $y > 0.5$; $\breve{y} = 0$ if $y < 0.5$; or $\breve{y} = 1$ with probability 0.5 if $y = 0.5$.

Gradient descent is the simplest gradient technique, with the update $\Delta S = -\alpha\bar{S}$, where α is the step size and $\bar{S}$ is the gradient term. In the trials reported here, *batched* updating was used, where the gradients are accumulated over the training set (an epoch) before being applied. Gradient descent has also been applied to RAM-based nodes by Gurney [5], and Gorse and Taylor [4].

Steepest Descent represents one of the simplest learning rate adaption techniques. A line search is employed to determine the minimum error along the search direction. The line search used was proposed by Armijo [1], and selects the largest power of two learning rate that reduces the network error.

Successive steps in steepest descent are inherently perpendicular [6], thus leading to a zig-zag path to the minimum. A better search direction can be obtained by incorporating some of the previous search direction. Momentum is a crude example. Conjugate gradient utilises the previous direction with the update rule $\Delta S = \alpha\,\delta S = \alpha(-\bar{S} + \beta\,\delta S^-)$ where δS^- refers to the change on the previous iteration. β is calculated to ensure that successive steps are conjugate, and was calculated using the Polak-Ribiere rule [9].

4 Benchmark Applications

The 838 encoder is an auto-associative problem which has been widely used to demonstrate the ability of learning algorithms [6]. Both the input and output layers contain $n = 8$ nodes, with $\log_2 n = 3$ hidden layer nodes. Presentation of n distinct patterns requires a unique encoding for each to be formulated at the hidden layer. Of the n^n possible encodings, $n!$ are unique. Thus for the 838 encoder, only 40,320 unique encodings exist in the 16,777,216 possible, or 0.24%. The network is fully connected, with every MCU containing only one subunit. The training vectors consist of a single set bit, which is progressively shifted right.

The character set database is a subset of that utilised by Williams [11], and consists of twenty-four examples of each letter of the alphabet, excluding 'I' and 'O'. Each are sixteen by twenty-four binary pixels in size, and were generated from UK postcodes. Nineteen examples of each letter form the training set. A randomly generated configuration was utilised, with each pixel mapped only once. Eight inputs per subunit, and seven subunits per MCU resulted in seven neurons in the hidden layer. The output layer contains twelve nodes, each with a single subunit fully connected to the hidden layer.

The particle scattering images were generated by a pollution monitoring instrument previously described by Kaye [8]. Data was collected on eight particle types, namely: long and short caffeine fibres; 12μm and 3μm silicon dioxide fibres; copper flakes; 3μm and 4.3μm polystyrene spheres; and salt crystals. The training set comprised fifty randomly selected images of each type, quantised to 16^2 5-bit images to reduce computational load. A fully connected network was used, with sixteen hidden, and six output layer MCUs. Every MCU consisted of two subunits, each with eight randomly generated connections. A more complete description of the airborne particle application can be found in [3].

5 Experimental Results

The site store locations were randomly initialised for all but reward-penalty, where they simply set to zero. The convergence criteria was 100% classification for the 838 encoder, and 95% for the other applications. Parameter settings were gleaned experimentally for the reward-penalty and gradient descent algorithms. The gradient descent setting of ρ was also used for steepest descent and conjugate gradient. The results are averaged over ten networks for the simpler problems, and five for the particle task. Table 2 summarises the parameter settings, and results for the four algorithms on the three applications. "Maximum", "mean", "deviation", and "coefficient" are in epochs, with the latter two being the standard deviation and coefficient of variation ($V = \frac{s}{\bar{x}} \cdot 100$) respectively. * denotes unconverged networks, and hence the maximum cycle limit. "CPU / cycle" is based on actual CPU time (secs) required on a Sun SPARCstation 10 model 40. "Total time" is given by "mean" × "CPU / cycle".

For the 838 encoder, conjugate gradient was the fastest, requiring marginally less time than reward-penalty and almost six and a half times fewer cycles. The character recognition task highlights the difference in learning ability. Reward-penalty was unable to converge, being more than three orders of magnitude away from the desired error. Batched gradient descent again demonstrated consistent learning, but was still the slowest of the gradient-based algorithms. The results for the particle task exemplify the problem of steepest descent: every network became trapped and required a relatively large number of cycles to be freed. The power of conjugate gradient also becomes clear, needing five times fewer cycles then gradient or steepest descent. Reward-penalty was not tried due to its failure on the simpler character problem.

6 Conclusions

The performance of various learning algorithms applied to a RAM-based artificial neural network have been investigated. Traditionally, reward-penalty has been applied to these nodes due to its inherent hardware amenability. The experiments reported here suggest that reinforcement learning is bested suited to simple problems. With respect to the gradient-based algorithms, gradient descent was consistently the slowest algorithm. While steepest descent was the fastest on the character recognition task, it had a tendency to become trapped. Conjugate gradient was by far the best algorithm, being fastest on two of the three applications.

REFERENCES

[1] L. Armijo, *Minimisation of functions having lipschitz continuous first partial derivatives.* Pacific Journal on Mathematics, Vol. 16 (1966), pp1–3.

[2] A. G. Barto and M. I. Jordan, *Gradient following without back-propagation in layered networks*, in: Proc. Int. Conf. Neural Networks (ICNN '87), IEEE, Vol. II (1987), pp629–636.

[3] A. Ferguson, T. Sabisch, P.H. Kaye, L.C.W. Dixon and H. Bolouri, *High-speed airborne particle monitoring using artificial neural networks*, Advances in Neural Information Processing Systems 8 (1996), MIT Press, pp980–986.

[4] D. Gorse and J.G. Taylor, *Training strategies for probabilistic RAMs*, Parallel Processing in Neural Systems and Computers, Elsevier Science Publishers (1990), pp31–42.

Task	Parameters	Reward-Penalty	Gradient Descent	Steepest Descent	Conjugate Gradient
838 Encoder	ρ	0.35	0.21	0.21	0.21
	λ	0.7	NA	NA	NA
	α	32	4	NA	NA
	Maximum	449	578	107	75
	Mean ($\bar{x}$)	239	499	55	37
	Deviation (s)	181	74	32	23
	Coefficient (V)	76	15	58	62
	CPU / cycle (secs)	0.004	0.006	0.020	0.024
	Total time (secs)	0.980	2.944	1.089	0.881
Alphabetic Character Recognition	ρ	1.75	0.21	0.21	0.21
	λ	0.8	NA	NA	NA
	α	4	2	NA	NA
	Maximum	10000*	259	60	63
	Mean ($\bar{x}$)	-	244	50	41
	Deviation (s)	-	19	8	14
	Coefficient (V)	-	8	16	34
	CPU / cycle (secs)	2.90	6.47	13.85	32.45
	Total time (secs)	-	1579	692	1331
Airborne Particle Classification	ρ	-	0.9	0.9	0.9
	α	-	1	NA	NA
	Maximum	-	1014	1190	197
	Mean ($\bar{x}$)	-	828	890	156
	Deviation (s)	-	111	250	49
	Coefficient (V)	-	13	28	31
	CPU / cycle (secs)	-	56.44	133.93	190.55
	Total time (secs)	-	46733	119199	29726

Table 2 Summary of the performance of the training algorithms applied to the benchmark tests.

[5] K. N. Gurney, *Training nets of hardware realisable sigma-pi units*, Neural Networks, Vol. 5 (1992), pp289–303.

[6] J. Hertz, A. Krogh and R.G. Palmer, *Introduction to the Theory of Neural Computation*, Addison-Wesley (1991).

[7] T. K. L. Hui, P. Morgan, K.N. Gurney and H. Bolouri, *A cascadable 2048-neuron VLSI artificial neural network with on-board learning*, in: Artificial Neural Networks 2, North-Holland (1992), pp647–651.

[8] P. H. Kaye, E. Hirst, J.M. Clark and M. Francesca, *Airborne particle shape and size classification from spatial light scattering profiles*, Journal of Aerosol Science, Vol. 23 (1992), pp597–611.

[9] E. Polak, *Computational Methods in Optimisation*, Academic Press (1971).

[10] L. B. Rall, *Automatic Differentiation*, Springer-Verlag (1981).

[11] P. M. Williams, *Some experiments using n-tuple techniques for alphanumeric pattern classification*, report 575, The Post Office Research Centre, Ipswich, (1977).

ANALYSIS OF CORRELATION MATRIX MEMORY AND PARTIAL MATCH–IMPLICATIONS FOR COGNITIVE PSYCHOLOGY

Richard Filer and James Austin

Advanced Computer Architecture Group, Department of Computer Science, University of York, Heslington, YO1 5DD, UK. Email: rjhf@minster.york.ac.uk

This paper describes new work on partial match using Correlation Matrix Memory (CMM), a type of binary associative neural network. It has been proposed that CMM can be used as an inference engine for expert systems, and we suggest that a partial match ability is essential to enable a system to deal with real world problems. Now, an emergent property of CMM is an ability to perform partial match, which may make CMM a better choice of inference engine than other methods that do not have partial match. Given this, the partial match characteristics of CMM have been investigated both analytically and experimentally, and these characteristics are shown to be very desirable. CMM partial match performance is also compared with a standard database indexing method that supports partial match (Multilevel Superimposed Coding), which shows CMM to compare well under certain cirumstances, even with this heavily optimised method. Parallels are drawn with cognitive psychology and human memory.

Keywords: Correlation Matrix Memory, Neural Network, Partial Match, Human Memory.

1 Introduction

Correlation Matrix Memory (CMM) [4] has been suggested as an inference engine, possibly for use in an expert system [1]. Touretsky and Hinton [7] were the first to implement successfully a reasoning system in a connectionist architecture, and there have been several neural network based systems suggested since. However, only the systems [1, 7] can be said to use a truly distributed knowledge representation (the issue of localist versus distributed knowledge representation will not be discussed here), for instance SHRUTI [6] is an elaborate system using temporal synchrony. The SHRUTI model was developed with a localist representation and, although a way of extending the model to incorporate a semi-distributed representation is given, this is not a natural extension of the model; moreover, it is difficult to see how learning could occur with either form of knowledge representation. Many of the properties that have become synonymous with neural networks actually rely on the use of a distributed knowledge representation. These are: (a) a graceful degradation of performance with input data corruption; (b) the ability to interpolate between input data and give a sensible output, and (c) a robustness to system damage. Partial match ability is very much connected with (a) and (b), which give neural network systems their characteristic flexibility. Here we suggest that a certain flexibility in reasoning is invaluable in an inference engine because, in real world problems, the input data is unlikely to be a perfect match for much of the time. The CMM-based inference engine suggested by Austin [1] uses a distributed knowledge representation, and therefore this system can, in principle, offer the desired flexibility. The focus of this paper is a full analysis of the partial match ability of CMM, including a comparison with a conventional database indexing method that offers partial match. This conventional database indexing method is Multilevel Superimposed Coding [3]. Section 2 contains a more detailed description of CMM and partial match, including an analysis of the theoretical partial match performance of CMM. Section 3 compares CMM partial match with Multilevel

Superimposed Coding, and Section 4 considers how these results may be relevant to cognitive psychology and the study of human memory.

2 CMM and Partial Match

CMM is a type of binary associative memory, which can be thought of as a matrix of binary weights. The fundamental process which occurs in CMM is the association by Hebbian learning of binary vectors representing items of information, which subsequently allows an item of information to be retrieved given the appropriate input. CMM allows very fast retrieval and, particularly, *retrieval in a time which is independent of the total amount of information stored in the memory for given CMM size.* In [1], a symbolic rule such as X⇒Y can be encoded by associating a binary vector code for X, the rule antecedent, with a binary vector code for Y, the rule consequent. The rule can be recalled subsequently by applying the code for X to the memory and retrieving the code for Y. Multiple antecedent items can be represented by superimposing (bitwise OR) the binary vector codes for each item prior to learning. A fixed weight, sparse encoding is used to generate codes with a coding rate that optimizes storage wrt. number of error bits set in the output, which are bits set *in error* due to interactions between the binary representations stored in the CMM [11]. CMM learning is given by:

$$\boldsymbol{M}^{i+1} = \boldsymbol{M}^{i} \oplus I\,\overline{O} \tag{1}$$

where $\boldsymbol{M}^i$ is the $m \times m$ CMM at iteration i, I and O are m-bit binary vector codes to be associated, and $\oplus$ means OR each corresponding element. Hence to obtain CMM at iteration $i+1$, I and O are multiplied and the result ORed with $\boldsymbol{M}^i$. Note that learning is accomplished in a single iteration. CMM retrieval is given by:

$$\overline{\Gamma} = \overline{I}\,\boldsymbol{M} \tag{2}$$

$$O = \text{L–max}(\Gamma, l) \tag{3}$$

where I would be one of a pair of vectors previously associated in $\boldsymbol{M}$, and the function L–max(Γ, l) [2] selects the l highest integers in the integer vector, Γ, to be the l set bits in the output, O. Storage wrt. error is maximised when [11]:

$$n = \log_2 m \tag{4}$$

where n is the number of set bits in each m-bit binary vector; usually, we choose $l = n$. In a symbolic rule matching context, partial match would allow a rule that has multiple items in the antecedent to fire when only a subset of the items are present. In terms of the binary vector code representation being considered here and if the input to the CMM contains z set bits, a full match input is characterised by the greatest possible number of set bits ($z = n$), while a partial match has less set bits than this ($\frac{n}{k} \leq z < n$, where k is the number of antecedent items). Because of the way in which multiple input data are superimposed, CMM partial match is em insensitive to the order in which items are presented as input. For example, consider the following symbolic rule:

engine_stalled ∧ ignition_ok ∧ fuelgauge_low ⟹ refuel

Normally, to check if a subset {engine_stalled , ignition_ok} is a partial match, it would be necessary at least to look at all the possible orderings of the subset, but with CMM this is not necessary. We term this emergent property **Combinatorial**

Partial Match. CMM could equally be used in frame based reasoning, where partial match would allow an entire frame to be recalled given a subset of the frame.

Partial Match Performance

If each input learned by the CMM, I, is obtained by hashing and superimposing the attributes that identify each record, then the CMM can be used subsequently to locate the record in memory, using I (or a partial match for I), by associating I with an output code, O, that represents the location of the record. Hence CMM can be used as a database indexing method. However, if multiple matches occur and multiple locations are represented in the CMM output, then output codes may be so overlapped that it is impossible to identify individual codes. Therefore, a method is needed to decode the CMM output but giving the minimum number of false positives (records that appear to be a match in the CMM but are not true matches) and no false negatives (records that appear not to be a match in the CMM but are true matches). We suggest here a novel method of identifying which output codes may be present in the CMM output, whereby output codes are subdivided and stored in buckets in memory, according to where the middle set bit (MB) appears in each code (Fig. 1). This approach allows us simply to identify all set bits in the output that could be MBs, then if all the buckets corresponding to these bits are searched, we are guaranteed no false negative matches.

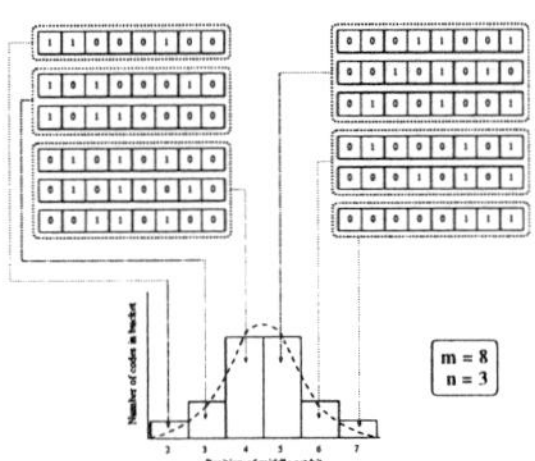

Figure 1 How output codes are divided up into buckets in secondary storage according to the position of the middle set bit (MB); in general, $m-(n-1)$ buckets are needed.

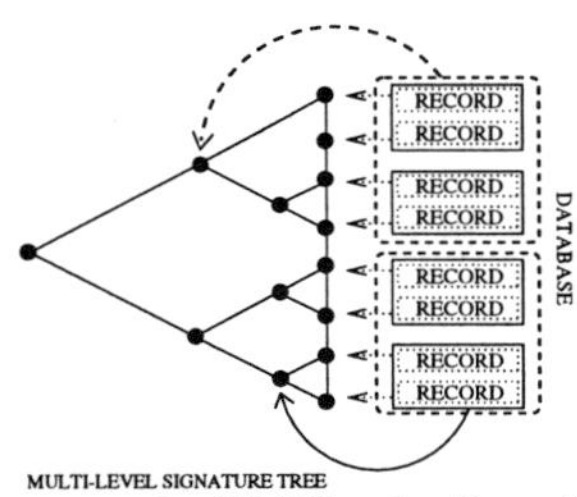

Figure 2 Multilevel Superimposed Coding (from [3]).

The partial match performance of CMM is considered in terms of the fraction, γ, of the index memory (which may be held in a slow secondary storage device) that must be searched in order to answer a given partial match query; the smaller this fraction is, the better. Other measures of performance are: computation reduction (the proportion of the total number of bits in the index that must be searched — not considered here), and the physical size of the index (in the comparison, we allow both methods the same index size). We show that this fraction, γ, depends only on: m, the dimension of the $m \times m$ CMM; z, the number of set bits in I, and t, the expected number of matches that will be found. If we first consider the absolute amount of memory that must be searched, this amount is due to two components: ω_1, the amount of memory that must be searched in order to obtain the CMM output, and ω_2, the amount of memory representing output codes that must be searched in order to decode the CMM output. For ω_1, only z rows of the $m \times m$

CMM are needed to obtain the CMM output, hence:

$$\omega_1 = zm \text{ bits} \tag{5}$$

To derive an expression for ω_2, we first look at the expected number of matches with items stored in the CMM that will be found, t, which gives us the expected number of set bits in the CMM output due only to true matches:

$$\kappa_1 = (1 - \left(\frac{m-n}{m}\right)^t)m \text{ bits} \tag{6}$$

But we must also take account of erroneously set bits, which occur due to interactions between the binary representations stored in the CMM (see [11] for an eloquent explanation of why this occurs):

$$\kappa_2 = (m-n)q^3 \text{ bits} \tag{7}$$

where q is the proportion of all m^2 bits in the CMM that are set, which at maximum storage is 50%. $\kappa_1 + \kappa_2$ is now the total expected number of set bits in O; however, for our purposes, we can ignore $n-1$ of these bits because these $n-1$ bits represent bits that cannot possibly be MBs[1], giving:

$$\kappa_3 = \kappa_1 + \kappa_2 - (n-1) \text{ bits} \tag{8}$$

κ_3 is the number of set bits in O that could be MBs, or equivalently *the number of output code buckets that must be searched.* Now, each output code bucket contains on average $\frac{p}{m-(n-1)}$ output codes, where p is the number of records in the CMM, and each output code can be encoded in n^2 bits, hence:

$$\omega_2 = \frac{pn^2}{m-(n-1)}\kappa_3 \approx \frac{pn^2}{m}\kappa_3 \text{ bits} \tag{9}$$

Note that, for a given p, if m is chosen such that $q = 50\%$, then $p \approx \frac{m^2}{3(\ln m)^2}$ [5] (i.e. p may be expressed in terms of m). We can now write:

$$\gamma = \frac{\omega_1 + \omega_2}{m^2 + pn^2} \tag{10}$$

This result has been verified experimentally (up to $m = 1000$, however a lack of space unfortunately does not permit the discussion of these experimental results here).

3 A Comparison with Multilevel Superimposed Coding

Multilevel Superimposed Coding (MSC) [3] has been chosen as the conventional database indexing method that supports partial match because of the similarities of this method with our method, also MSC is used by several companies (e.g. Daylight CIS Inc.) for indexing their large databases. In MSC (Fig. 2), records are identified by hashing and superimposing attribute values into a binary code using multiple hash functions to gain access at multiple levels to a binary tree. Note that the resultant codes are of a different length, which is why multiple hash functions are needed. As before, the idea is to search as little of the index as possible, and the ideal state of affairs when locating a single record would be if at each node only one branch were taken. However, if the index is poorly conditioned then all branches may need to be searched, which would then be equivalent to performing a linear search on the entire index.

[1] Consider O comprising just one output code: O has n set bits, only one of which can be a middle set bit (MB); therefore $n-1$ of the set bits are not MBs (this generalises to the general case of O comprising multiple output codes).

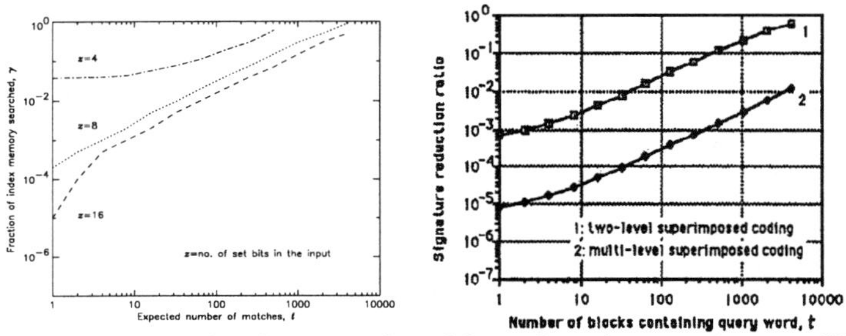

Figure 3 A comparison in terms of partial match performance between CMM (left) and MSC (right, (2); from [3]), for varying expected number of matches. Overall index size = 1.5 GB (both methods).

Kim and Lee [3] consider an example case of an index for a database of 2^{24} records, for which MSC requires a 24 level tree with *24 hash functions.* The analysis for MSC relies on specifying t, the expected number of matches, and both methods are allowed the same amount of storage (1.5 GB). The results are shown in Fig. 3, and concern the fraction of each index that must be searched versus the expected number of matches. Remembering that a full match input is characterised by the greatest possible number of set bits ($z = n$), while a partial match has less set bits than this ($\frac{n}{k} \le z < n$), we observe from Fig. 3 that CMM approaches the performance achieved by MSC provided (1) that the input is well specified, and (2) that few true matches exist in the database. Even with a less well specified input and with several matches, CMM still performs reasonably well (especially considering the relative simplicity of the CMM method in comparison with the heavily optimised and much less straightforward MSC method).

4 Implications for Cognitive Psychology

In presenting this work to colleagues from differing backgrounds — some in psychology — it has become clear that this work may have relevance to cognitive psychology and the study of human memory. The **Encoding Specificity Principle** due to Endel Tulving [10] states: *"Only that can be retrieved that has been stored, and how it can be retrieved depends on how it was stored."* And in [8] Tulving states: *"On the unassailable assumption that cue A has more information in common with the trace of the A-T [T for target word] pair of studied items than with the trace of the B-T pair, we can say that the probability of successful retrieval of the target item is a monotonically increasing function of the information overlap between the information present at retrieval and the information stored in memory."* The Encoding Specificity Principle is by no means the only theory to explain this aspect of human memory function, and a number of experiments have been performed by protagonists of this or other theories. The work presented in this paper could be taken in support of the Encoding Specificity Principle, but this is not the intention of the authors. However, CMM could provide a model of the low level workings of human memory and, as such, the results of those experiments performed in relation to the Encoding Specificity Principle are most interesting. For instance, in [9], 674 subjects learned a list of 24 target words, (1) with one of two sets of cue words, or (2) without cue words; the cue words were chosen to each have an association of 1%

with the corresponding target word. In retrieval, subjects were asked to remember the list (a) with cues; (b) without cues, or (c) with wrong cues (a cue word taken from the alternative list). The experimental results are given in terms of the mean number of words remembered and are as follows, given in descending order of the mean number of words remembered: (1a) 14.93; (2b) 10.62; (1b) 8.72; (2a) 8.52; (1c) 7.45. What is interesting for CMM as a model of memory, is the difference between the results of experiments (1a) and (1b). If one postulates that the target word and the cue word are somehow stored together, like the input to a CMM, and that the output would be the equivalent of a pointer to the target word then the results of this paper can be interpreted in the light of the results in [9]. To do so, it is necessary to envisage some indexing mechanism in the human brain for retrieving information from memory that works best when there is little index memory to be searched, which is perfectly plausible. Then (1a) would correspond to a full match input, which would be expected to give best retrieval performance, as was found to be the case in the experiments; similarly, (1b) would correspond to a partial match input, which would be expected to give a rather worse retrieval performance, again as was found to be the case.

5 Conclusions

We have analysed the partial match performance of CMM, in line with the proposed use of CMM as an inference engine for an expert system that must solve real world problems. The analysis has enabled a comparison with a conventional database indexing technique that supports partial match, the results of which suggest CMM is good at performing partial match when the input is well specified and few matches exist. Interestingly, a similar behaviour is observed in human memory experiments and, although we would not go so far as to suggest that human memory is so simple as CMM, we observe that there are similarities that would support the use of CMM, or CMM partial match, as a model of some of the low level workings of human memory in further experiments in cognitive psychology.

REFERENCES

[1] J. Austin, *Correlation Matrix Memories for Knowledge Manipulation*, in: International Conference on Neural Networks, Fuzzy Logic, and Soft Computing, Japan (1994), Iizuka.

[2] D. Casasent and B. Telfer, *High Capacity Pattern Recognition and Associative Processors*, Neural Networks, Vol. 4(5) (1994), pp687–98.

[3] Y.M. Kim and D.L. Lee, *An Optimal Multilevel Signature File for Large Databases*, In Fourth International Conference on Computing and Information, IEEE (1992).

[4] T. Kohonen and M. Ruohonen, *Representation Of Associated Data By Matrix Operators*, IEEE Transactions on Computers, (July 1973).

[5] J-P. Nadal and G. Toulouse, *Information Storage in Sparsely Coded Memory Networks*, Network, Vol. 1 (1990), pp61–74.

[6] L. Shastri and V. Ajjanagadde, *From Simple Associations to Systematic Reasoning*, Behavioural & Brain Sciences, Vol. 16(3) (1993), pp417–93.

[7] D.S. Touretsky and G.E. Hinton *A Distributed Connectionist Production System*, Cognitive Science, Vol. 12 (1988), pp423–66.

[8] E. Tulving, *Relation Between Encoding Specificity and Levels of Processing*, in: Levels of Processing in Human Memory. John Wiley & Sons (1979), London.

[9] E. Tulving and S. Osler, *Effectiveness of Retrieval Cues in Memory for Words*, Journal of Experimental Psychology, Vol. 77(4) (1968), pp593–601.

[10] E. Tulving and D.M. Thomson, *Encoding Specificity and Retrieval Processes in Episodic Memory*, Psychological Review, Vol. 80 (1973), pp352–73.

[11] D.J. Willshaw, O.P. Buneman, and H.C. Longuet-Higgins, *Non-Holographic Associative Memory*, Nature, Vol. 222 (1969), pp960–62.

REGULARIZATION AND REALIZABILITY IN RADIAL BASIS FUNCTION NETWORKS

Jason A.S. Freeman and David Saad*

Centre for Neural Systems, University of Edinburgh, Edinburgh EH8 9LW, UK. Email: jason@cns.ed.ac.uk

** Department of Computer Science & Applied Mathematics, University of Aston, Birmingham B4 7ET, UK. Email: D.Saad@aston.ac.uk*

Learning and generalization in a two-layer Radial Basis Function network (RBF) is examined within a stochastic training paradigm. Employing a Bayesian approach, expressions for generalization error are derived under the assumption that the generating mechanism (teacher) for the training data is also an RBF, but one for which the basis function centres and widths need not correspond to those of the student network. The effects of regularization, via a weight decay term, are examined. The cases in which the student has greater representational power than the teacher (over-realizable), and in which the teacher has greater power than the student (unrealizable) are studied. Finally, simulations are performed which validate the analytic results.

1 Introduction

When considering supervised learning in neural networks, a quantity of particular interest is the *generalization error*, a measure of the average deviation between desired and actual network output across the space of possible inputs. Generalization error consists of two components: approximation error and estimation error. Given a particular architecture, approximation error is the error made by the optimal student of that architecture, and is caused by the architecture having insufficient representational power to exactly emulate the teacher; it is an asymptotic quantity as it cannot be overcome even in the limit of an infinite amount of training data. If the approximation error is zero, the problem is termed realizable; if not, it is termed unrealizable. Estimation error is the error due to not having selected an optimal student of the chosen architecture; it is a dynamic quantity as it changes during training and is caused by having insufficient data, noisy data or a learning algorithm which is not guaranteed to reach an optimal solution in the limit of an infinite amount of data. There is a trade-off between representational power and the amount of data required to achieve a particular error value (the sample complexity) in that the more powerful the student, the greater the ability to eliminate the approximation error but the larger the amount of data required to find a good student.

This paper employs a Bayesian scheme in which a probability distribution is derived for the weights of the student; similar approaches can be found in [6, 1, 2] and [3]. In [7], a bound is derived for generalization error in RBFs under the assumption that the training algorithm finds a global minimum in the error surface; regularization is not considered. For the exactly realizable case, Freeman *et al.* calculate generalization error for RBFs using a similar framework to that employed here [2].

2 The RBF Network and Generalization Error

The RBF architecture consists of a two-layer fully-connected network, and is a universal approximator for continuous functions given a sufficient number of hidden units [4]. The hidden units will be considered to be Gaussian basis functions, parameterised by a vector representing the position of the basis function centre in input space and a scalar representing the width of the basis function. These parameters are assumed to be fixed by a suitable process, such as a clustering algorithm. The output layer computes a linear combination of the activations of the basis functions, parameterised by the adaptive weights $\mathbf{w}$ between hidden and output layers.

Training examples consist of input-output pairs $(\boldsymbol{\xi}, \zeta)$. The components of $\boldsymbol{\xi}$ are uncorrelated Gaussian random variables of mean 0, variance σ_ξ^2, while ζ is generated by applying $\boldsymbol{\xi}$ to a teacher RBF and corrupting the output with zero-mean additive Gaussian noise, variance σ_η^2. The number, position and widths of the teacher hidden units need not correspond to those of the student, allowing investigation of over-realizable and unrealizable cases. The mapping implemented by the teacher is denoted f_T, and that of the student f_S. Note it is impossible to examine generalization error without some *a priori* belief in the teacher mechanism [9]. The training algorithm for the adaptive weights is considered stochastic in nature; the selected noise process leads to the following form for the likelihood:

$$\mathcal{P}(D|\mathbf{w}, \beta) \propto \exp(-\beta E_D) \tag{1}$$

where E_D is the training error. This form resembles a Gibbs distribution; it also corresponds to the constraint that minimizing the training error is equivalent to maximizing the likelihood [5]. This distribution can be realised by employing the Langevin algorithm, which is simply gradient descent with an appropriate noise term added to the weights at each update [8]. To prevent over-dependence of the distribution of student weight vectors on the noise, it is necessary to introduce a regularizing factor, which can be viewed as a Bayesian *prior*:

$$\mathcal{P}(\mathbf{w}|\gamma) \propto \exp(-\gamma E_W) \tag{2}$$

where E_W is a penalty term based here on the magnitude of the student weight vector. Employing Bayes' theorem, one can derive an expression for the probability of a student weight vector given the training data and training parameters:

$$\mathcal{P}(\mathbf{w}|D, \gamma, \beta) \propto \exp\left(-\beta E_D - \gamma E_W\right) \tag{3}$$

The common definition of generalization error is the average squared difference between the target function and the estimating function:

$$E(\boldsymbol{w}) = \left\langle \left(f_S(\boldsymbol{\xi}, \boldsymbol{w}) - f_T(\boldsymbol{\xi})\right)^2 \right\rangle \tag{4}$$

where $\langle \cdots \rangle$ denotes an average w.r.t. the input distribution. In practice, one only has access to the test error, $\frac{1}{P_{TEST}} \sum_{p=1}^{P_{TEST}} (\zeta_p - f_S(\boldsymbol{\xi}_p, \mathbf{w}))^2$. This quantity is an approximation to the expected risk, defined as the expectation of $(\zeta - f_S(\boldsymbol{\xi}, \mathbf{w}))^2$ w.r.t. the joint distribution $\mathcal{P}(\boldsymbol{\xi}, \zeta)$. With an additive noise model, the expected risk decomposes to $E + \sigma_\eta^2$, where σ_η^2 is the variance of the noise.

When employing stochastic training, two possibilities for average generalization error arise. If one weight vector is selected from the ensemble, as in usually the case in practice, equation (4) becomes:

$$E_G(\gamma, \beta) = \left\langle \int d\mathbf{w}\, \mathcal{P}(\mathbf{w}|D, \gamma, \beta)\left(f_S(\boldsymbol{\xi}, \boldsymbol{w}) - f_T(\boldsymbol{\xi})\right)^2 \right\rangle \tag{5}$$

Alternatively, one can take a Bayes-optimal approach which, for squared error, requires taking the mean estimate of the network. It is computationally impractical to find this, but it is interesting as it represents the result of the best guess, in an average sense. In this case generalization error takes the form :

$$E_B(\gamma,\beta) = \left\langle \left(\int d\mathbf{w}\, \mathcal{P}(\mathbf{w}|D,\gamma,\beta)\, f_S(\boldsymbol{\xi},\mathbf{w}) - f_T(\boldsymbol{\xi}) \right)^2 \right\rangle \tag{6}$$

In order to examine generic architecture performance independently of the particular data employed, an average over datasets is performed, taking into account both the position of the data in input space and the noise.

Defining E_D as the sum of squared errors over the training set and defining the regularization term $E_W = \|\boldsymbol{w}\|^2$, E_G and E_B can be found from equations (3), (5) and (6). The calculation is straightforward until the average over the dataset; the complications and their resolution are discussed in [3]. Schematically:

$$E_G = \text{Student Output Variance} + \text{Noise Error} + \text{Student-Teacher Mismatch} \tag{7}$$

$$E_B = \text{Noise Error} + \text{Student-Teacher Mismatch} \tag{8}$$

The student output variance and noise error are estimation error only; the student-teacher mismatch is both estimation and approximation error.

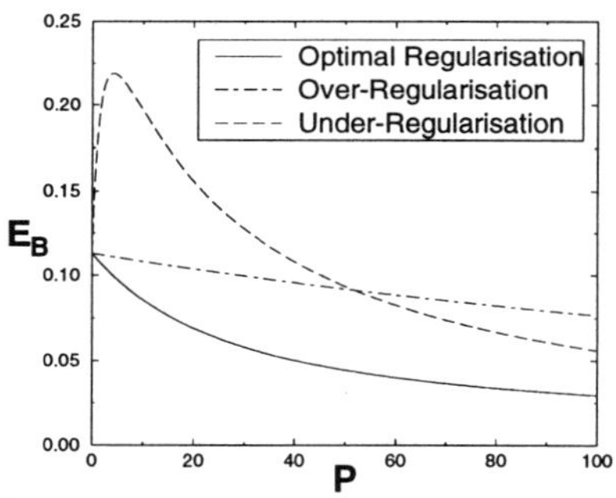

Figure 1 The effects of regularization: the solid curve represents optimal regularization($\gamma = 2.7, \beta = 1.6$), the dot-dash curve illustrates the over-regularised case ($\gamma = 2.7, \beta = 0.16$), and the dashed curve shows the highly under-regularised case ($\gamma = 2.7, \beta = 16$). The student and teacher were matched, each consisting of 3 centres at $(1,0), (-0.5, \sqrt{3}/2)$ and $(-0.5, -\sqrt{3}/2)$. Noise of variance 1 was employed.

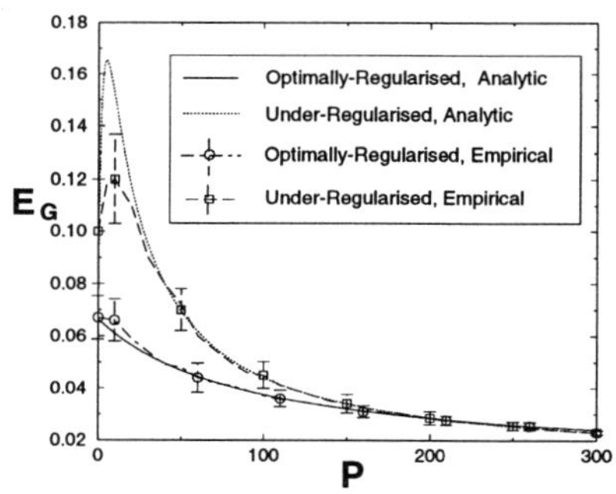

Figure 2 Simulation results. The curves are for a realizable case with three centres at $(1,0)$, $(-0.5, \sqrt{3}/2)$ and $(-0.5, -\sqrt{3}/2)$, with centre width $\sqrt{2}/2$ and noise of variance $2/\beta$. The empirical curves were generated by exhaustive training at each value of P, and represent averages over 100 trials. The error bars are at 1 standard deviation of the empirical distribution.

3 Analysis of Generalization Error

3.1 The Effects of Regularization

While the effects of regularization are similar for E_G and E_B, the optimal parameter settings, found by minimizing equations (7) and (8) w.r.t. γ and β, are quite

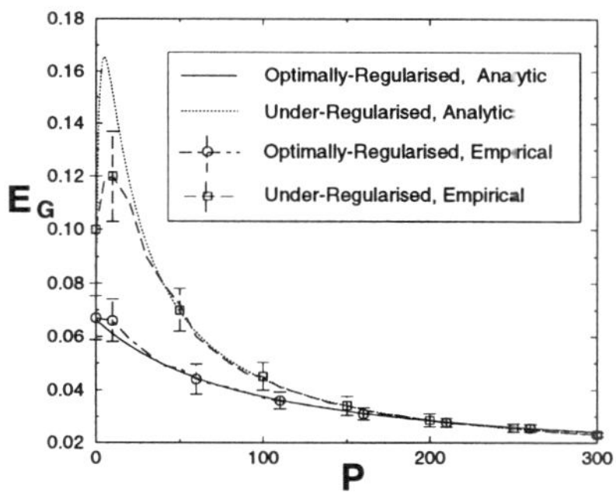

Figure 3 The Over-realizable Case: the dashed curve shows the over-realizable case with training optimised as if the student matches the teacher ($\gamma = 3.59, \beta = 2.56$), the solid curve illustrates the over-realizable case with training optimised with respect to the true teacher ($\gamma = 3.59, \beta = 1.44$), while the dot-dash curve is for the student matching the teacher ($\gamma = 6.52, \beta = 4.39$). All the curves were generated with one teacher centre at (1,0); the over-realizable curves had two student centres at (1,0) and (−1,0). Noise with variance 1 was employed.

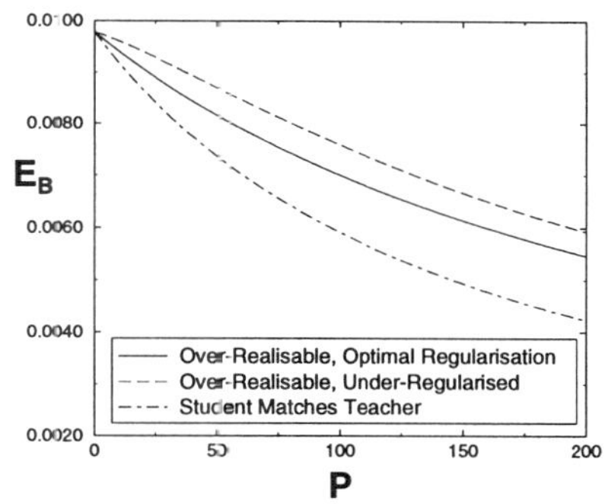

Figure 4 The unrealizable case: the solid curve denotes the case where the student is optimised as if the teacher is identical to it ($\gamma = 2.22, \beta = 1.55$); the dashed curve demonstrates the student optimised with knowledge of the true teacher ($\gamma = 2.22, \beta = 3.05$), while, for comparison, the dot-dash curve shows a student which matches the teacher ($\gamma = 2.22, \beta = 1.05$). The curves were generated with two teacher centres at (1,0) and (−1,0); the unrealizable curves employed a single student at (1,0); noise of variance 1 was utilised.

different. As discussed in [2], for E_G it is necessary to optimise γ and β jointly, while for E_B, only the *ratio* of γ to β need be considered; this optimal ratio is independent of P. This dissimilarity is due to the variance term in E_G, which is minimised by taking $\beta \to \infty$. These findings hold for both realizable and unrealizable cases. To demonstrate the effects of regularization in a realizable scenario, consider figure 1 where E_B is plotted versus P for three cases. The solid curve illustrates optimal regularization and shows the lowest value of generalization error that can be achieved on average; the dot-dash curve represents the over-regularised case, in which the prior dominates the likelihood, showing how reduction in generalization error is substantially slowed. The dashed curve is for the highly under-regularised case, which in the $\gamma/\beta \to 0$ case gives a divergence in both E_G and E_B. Although under-regularization is initially more damaging than over-regularization, its effects are recovered from more rapidly. As training proceeds, the likelihood comes to dominate the prior, making the incorrect setting of the prior irrelevant; this proceeds more rapidly when the prior is weak with respect to the likelihood.

3.2 The Over-Realizable and Unrealizable Scenarios

Operationally, selecting a form for the student implies that one is prepared to believe that the teacher has an identical form. Therefore optimization of training parameters must be performed on this basis. When the student is overly powerful this leads to under-regularization, as the magnitude of the teacher weight vector is believed to be larger than the true case. This is shown in figure 3; the dashed curve represents generalization error for the under-regularised case where the training parameters have been optimised as if the teacher matches the student, while the solid curve represents the same student, but with training optimised with respect to the true teacher. Employing an overly-powerful student rather than the optimally-matched student can drastically slow the reduction of generalization error. Even with training optimised with respect to the true teacher, the matching student greatly out-performs the overly-powerful version due to the necessity to suppress the redundant parameters. The effect is shown in figure 3; generalization error for the matching student is given by the dot-dash curve, while that of the overly-powerful but correctly optimised student is given by the solid curve. In the unrealizable scenario, where the teacher is more powerful than the student, optimization of training parameters under the belief that the teacher has the same form as the student leads to over-regularization, as the assumed magnitude of the teacher weight vector is greater than the true magnitude. This effect is shown in figure 4, in which the solid curve denotes generalization error for the over-regularised case based on the belief that the teacher matches the student, while the dashed curve shows the error for an identical student when the parameters of the true teacher are known; this knowledge permits optimal regularization. The most significant effect of the teacher being more powerful than the student is the fact that the approximation error is no longer zero, as the teacher can never be exactly emulated by the student. This is also illustrated in figure 4, where the dot-dash curve represents the learning curve when the student matches the teacher (with zero asymptote), while the two upper curves show an under-powerful student, and have non-zero asymptotes.

3.3 Simulations

To validate the analytic results, simulations were performed for optimally-regularised and under-regularised realizable cases. The simulations involved exhaustive training of RBF networks using Langevin updating. The empirical results were generated by averaging over 100 runs, approximating generalization error using a large, noiseless test set. The results are shown in figure 2; an excellent fit between analytic and simulated results is found for $P > 50$. In the region where P is small in the under-regularised case, the analytic mean is larger than the simulation result. In the small P region, this case is particularly vulnerable to the approximation employed in the dataset average (see [3]). The errorbars are also large in this region, as the distribution of student weights is relatively unconstrained.

4 Conclusion

Under-regularization initially causes very poor generalization, which can be overcome rapidly with the addition of more training data. Over-regularization is initially less damaging, but requires a large quantity of training data in order to overcome the effect. In the over-realizable case, there is a tendency to under-regularise due to over-estimating the complexity of the teacher. There is also an increase in sample complexity. In the unrealizable case, under-estimating the complexity of the teacher leads to over-regularization.

REFERENCES

[1] A. Bruce and D. Saad, *Statistical mechanics of hypothesis evaluation*, J. Phys. A: Math. Gen., Vol. 27 (1994), pp3355 – 3363.

[2] J. Freeman and D. Saad, *Learning and generalization in radial basis function networks*, Neural Computation, Vol. 7 (1995), pp1000–1020.

[3] J. Freeman and D. Saad, To appear in *Neural Networks*, (1995),

[4] E. Hartman, J. Keeler, and J. Kowalski, *Layered neural networks with gaussian hidden units as universal approximators*, Neural Computation, Vol. 2 (1990), pp210–215.

[5] E. Levin, N. Tishby, and S. Solla, *A statistical approach to learning and generalization in layered neural networks*, In Colt (1989), pp245–260.

[6] D. MacKay, *Bayesian interpolation*, Neural Computation, Vol. 4 (1992), pp415–447.

[7] P. Niyogi and F. Girosi, *On the relationship between generalization error, hypothesis complexity and sample complexity for radial basis functions*, Technical report, AI Laboratory, MIT (1994).

[8] T. Rögnvaldsson, *On langevin updating in multilayer perceptrons*, Neural Computation, Vol. 6 (1994), pp916–926.

[9] D. Wolpert, *On the connection between in-sample testing and generalization error*, Complex Systems, Vol. 6 (1992), pp47–94.

Acknowledgements

This work was supported by EU grant ERB CHRX-CT92-0063.

A UNIVERSAL APPROXIMATOR NETWORK FOR LEARNING CONDITIONAL PROBABILITY DENSITIES

D. Husmeier, D. Allen and J. G. Taylor

Centre for Neural Networks, Department of Mathematics, King's College London, UK.

A general approach is developed to learn the conditional probability density for a noisy time series. A universal architecture is proposed, which avoids difficulties with the singular low-noise limit. A suitable error function is presented enabling the probability density to be learnt. The method is compared with other recently developed approaches, and its effectiveness demonstrated on a time series generated from a non-trivial stochastic dynamical system.

1 Introduction

Neural networks are used extensively to learn time series, but most of the approaches, especially those associated with the mean square error function whose minimisation implies approximating the predictor $x(t) \rightarrow x(t+1)$, will only give information on a mean estimate of such a prediction. It is becoming increasingly important to learn more about a time series, especially when it involves a considerable amount of noise, as in the case of financial time series. This note is on more recent attempts to learn the conditional probability distribution of the time series, so the quantity

$$P(x(t+1)|\mathbf{x}(t)) \tag{1}$$

where $\mathbf{x}(t)$ denotes the time-delayed vector with components $(x(t), x(t-1), \ldots, x(t-m))$, for some suitable integer m.

An important question is as to the nature of a neural network architecture that can learn such a distribution when both very noisy and nearly deterministic time series have to be considered. A variety of approaches have independently been recently proposed (Weigend and Nix, 1994; Srivastava and Weigend, 1994; Neuneier et al, 1994), and this plethora of methods may lead to a degree of uncertainty as to their relative effectiveness. We here want to extend the discussion of an earlier paper (Allen and Taylor, 1994) and will derive the minimal structure of a universal approximator for learning conditional probability distributions. We will then point out the relation of this structure to the concepts mentioned above, and will finally apply the method to a time series generated from a stochastic dynamical system.

2 The General ANN Approach

2.1 Minimal Required Network Structure

Let us formulate the problem in terms of the cumulative probability distribution

$$F(y|\mathbf{x}(t)) = p(x(t+1) \leq y|\mathbf{x}(t)) = \int_{-\infty}^{y} p(y'|\mathbf{x}(t))\, dy' \tag{2}$$

first, as this function does not become singular in the noise-free limit of a deterministic process, but reduces to

$$F(y|\mathbf{x}(t)) = \theta(y - f(\mathbf{x}(t))) \tag{3}$$

(where $\theta(.)$ is the threshold or Heaviside function, $\theta(x) = 1$ if $x \geq 0$, 0 otherwise). We want to derive the structure of a network that, firstly, is a universal approximator for $F(.)$ and, secondly, obtains the noise-free limit of (3). It is clear that a difficulty would arise if the universal approximation theorem of neural networks were applied directly to the function $F(y, \mathbf{x}(t))$ so as to expand it in terms of the output of a single hidden layer net,

$$F(y|\mathbf{x}(t)) = \sum_i a_i S\left(\sum_{j=0}^{m} w_{ij} x_j + b_i y - \vartheta_i\right), \tag{4}$$

where $x_j := x(t-j+1)$, $S(x) = 1/(1+e^{-x})$, and a_i, w_{ij}, b_i, ϑ_i are constants with obvious interpretation in neural network terms (a_i output weights, ϑ_i thresholds, w_{ij}, b_i weights between input and hidden layer). Trying to obtain the deterministic case (3), the best one can get from (4) in the limit when $a_i \rightarrow \delta_{i,i_0}$ (Kronecker delta) and the weights of the hidden nodes become very large (so that each sigmoid function $S(.)$ entering in (4) becomes a threshold function $\theta(.)$), is the expression

$$F(y|\mathbf{x}(t)) \rightarrow \theta\left(y - \sum_j c_j x_j - s\right), \tag{5}$$

with constants c_j, s. Thus at best it is only possible to approximate the deterministic limit of a linear process, with $f(\mathbf{x})$ a linear function of its variable.
To be able to handle the split between the single predicted variable y and the input variable $\mathbf{x}$, we proceed by developing a universal one-layer representation for y first, and then do the same for the remaining variable $\mathbf{x}$ successively. Thus at the first step results

$$F(y|\mathbf{x}(t)) = \sum_i a_i S(\beta_i(y - \mu_i)), \tag{6}$$

where β_i is the steepness of the sigmoid function, and μ_i a given threshold. We then expand each μ_i by means of the universal approximation theorem in terms of a further hidden layer network, resulting in

$$\mu_i(\mathbf{x}) = \sum_j b_{ij} S\left(\sum_k c_{ijk} x_k - \vartheta_{ij}\right). \tag{7}$$

In order that the right hand side of (6) be a cumulative probabilty distribution, i.e. $F(-\infty|\mathbf{x}) = 0$, $F(\infty|\mathbf{x}) = 1$ and $F(y|\mathbf{x})$ monotone increasing in the variable y, the following conditions are imposed on the coefficients entering eq.(6):

$$\beta_i > 0, \quad a_i \geq 0, \quad \sum_i a_i = 1 \tag{8}$$

This can be realized by taking β_i and a_i as functions of new variables ξ_i and ς_i, e.g. $\beta_i = (\xi_i)^2$, and $a_i = (\varsigma_i)^2 / \sum_k (\varsigma_k)^2$ or $a_i = \exp(\varsigma_i) / \sum_k \exp(\varsigma_k)$.
It is now possible to see that the deterministic limit (3) arises smoothly from the universal two-hidden-layer architecture of equations (6) and (7) when $a_i \rightarrow \delta_{i,j}$ and $\beta_j \rightarrow \infty$, i.e., for one output weight one and all the others zero, and a large steepness parameter for the unit connected to the non-vanishing weight.

2.2 Moments

One of the attractive properties of the use of sigmoid response functions is that it is possible to give (after some algebra) a closed form for the moment generating function (Allen, Taylor, 1994),

$$M(t) := \int_{-\infty}^{\infty} \exp(ty)p(y|\mathbf{x})\,dy = \sum_i \frac{a_i(\pi t/\beta_i)\exp(\mu_i t)}{\sin(\pi t/\beta_i)}, \tag{9}$$

from which all the moments arising from the conditional probability density (1) can be calculated, e.g.

$$E(Y) = \lim_{t\to 0} \frac{dM(t)}{dt} = \sum_i a_i \mu_i \tag{10}$$

$$E(Y^2) = \lim_{t\to 0} \frac{d^2M(t)}{dt^2} = \sum_i a_i \left[\mu_i^2 + \frac{1}{3}\left(\frac{\pi}{\beta_i}\right)^2\right] \tag{11}$$

For $a_i \to \delta_{ij}$, $\beta_j \to \infty$ the deterministic limit ensues, with $E(Y^m) = [E(Y)]^m$.

2.3 The Error Function

It is now necessary to suggest a suitable error function in order to make the universal expression given by (6) and (7) the true conditional cumulative distribution function given by the available data. As the true value for $x(t+1)$ is not known, one cannot use standard mean square error. Let us assume that the process is stationary. Then the negative expectation value of the logarithm of the likelihood,

$$E = -\langle \log(p(x(t+1)|\mathbf{x}(t)))\rangle \approx -\frac{1}{N}p(x(t+1)|\mathbf{x}(t)), \tag{12}$$

is the appropriate choice, based on Kullback's Lemma (see, e.g., Papoulis, 1984), according to which (12) in terms of the true (unknown) probability density, p_{true}, is always smaller than (12) in terms of the probability density predicted by the network, p. Hence by minimising (12) one can hope to always "get closer" to p_{true}.

2.4 Regaining the Conditional Probability Density

In order to get back to the conditional probability density, we have to take the derivative of the output of (6) with respect to the target, y, yielding

$$p(y|\mathbf{x}) = \frac{\partial F(y|\mathbf{x})}{\partial y} = \frac{\partial S(\beta(y-\mu(\mathbf{x})))}{\partial y} = \beta S(\beta(y-\mu(\mathbf{x})))(1-S(\beta(y-\mu(\mathbf{x}))) \tag{13}$$

This function is Gaussian-shaped, so our resulting network structure can be summarized as follows: The output node, which predicts the conditional probability density $p(x(t+1) = y|\mathbf{x}(t))$, is connected to a layer of RBF-like nodes. The output of the ith "RBF"-unit is determined by its input, $x(t+1)$ (the same for all nodes), and its centre, μ_i, the latter being an $\mathbf{x}$-dependent function implemented in a seperate one-hidden- layer network with the usual sigmoidal hidden nodes. The parameters a_i and β_i have obvious interpretations as a priori probability and inverse kernel width, respectively. (Note that from (10) and (11) one gets $\sigma_i = \pi/(\sqrt{3}\beta_i)$ for the standard deviation of the ith kernel, i.e. its "width"). The same structure can basically be found in the other approaches mentioned above too, with the following differences and simplifications.

3 Comparison with Other Approaches

The CDEN (Conditional Density Estimation Network) of Neuneier et al. (1994) uses only one hidden layer for computing all of the $\mu_i(\mathbf{x})$, which corresponds to simplifying (7) by making c_{ijk} and ϑ_{ij} independent of the subscript i. This simplification is certainly justified when the $\mu_i(\mathbf{x})$ are of a similar functional form, with

Network	"RBF" kernel function	μ_i x-dependent	σ_i x-dependent	a_i x-dependent
As proposed here	$S'(.)$	yes, seperate hidden layers	no	no
CDEN	Gaussian	yes, 1 shared hidden layer	yes	yes
Soft histograms	triangular	no, from preprocessing	no, from preprocessing	yes
Weigend, Nix	1 Gaussian	yes	yes	unity

Table 1 Comparison between the different network architectures mentioned in the text.

similar a priori probabilities, but may cause difficulties when this assumption is strictly violated. On the other hand, the CDEN includes a further generalisation of the architecture proposed here by making the kernel widths, σ_i, and the output weights, a_i, $\mathbf{x}$-dependent, computing them as outputs of seperate one- hidden-layer networks. This is not necessary in order for the architecture to be a universal approximator, but may lead to a considerable reduction of the "RBF"-layer size, the latter, though, at the expense of additional complexity in other parts of the network. It thus depends on the specific problem under consideration if this further generalisation is an advantage.

The *soft histogram* approach proposed by Srivastava and Weigend (1994) is identical to a mixture of triangular-shaped "RBF"-nodes, $P(y|\mathbf{x}) = \sum_i a_i(\mathbf{x})R_i(y)$, with $R_i(y) = h_i(y-\mu_{i-1})/(\mu_i-\mu_{i-1})$ if $\mu_{i-1} \le y \le \mu_i$, $R_i(y) = h_i(\mu_{i+1}-y)/(\mu_{i+1}-\mu_i)$ if $\mu_i \le y \le \mu_{i+1}$, and $R_i(y) = 0$ otherwise. The "heights" h_i are related to the kernel widths $\sigma_i =: \mu_{i+1} - \mu_{i-1}$ by $h_i = 2/\sigma_i$ in order to ensure that the the normalisation condition $\int_{-\infty}^{\infty} P(y|\mathbf{x})\,dy = 1$ is satisfied. The kernel centres result from a preprocessing "binning" procedure (described in [Srivastava, Weigend 1994]). The output of the network is thus similar to the CDEN and the model proposed in this paper, with the difference that now only the output weights $a_i(\mathbf{x})$ are $\mathbf{x}$-dependent, whereas the kernel centres, μ_i, are held constant.

Finally the architecture introduced by Weigend and Nix (1994) reduces the size of the "RBF" layer to only one node, assuming a Gaussian probability distribution, which is completely specified by μ and σ, both of which are given as the ($\mathbf{x}$-dependent) output of a seperate network branch. Obviously, this parametric approximation reduces the network complexity, but leads to a biased prediction.

4 Simulation

We tested the performance of our method on an artificial time series generated from a stochastic coupling of two stochastic dynamical systems,

$$x(t+1) = \Theta(\xi - \vartheta)\alpha x(t)[1-x(t)] + (1-\Theta(\xi-\vartheta))\,[1-x^{\kappa}(t)]\,, \qquad (14)$$

where $\Theta(.)$ symbolizes the Heaviside function, as before, and the parameters α, κ and ξ are random variables drawn from a uniform distribution, $\xi \in [0,1]$, $\alpha \in [3,4]$, $\kappa \in [0.5, 1.25]$. The prior probabilities of the two processes are determined by the

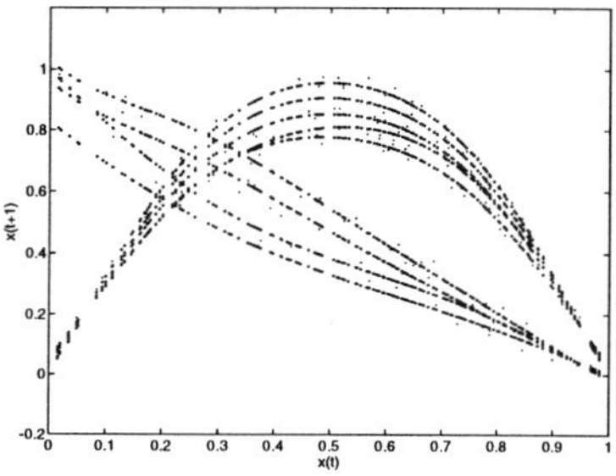

Figure 1 Centres of the "RBF"-kernels, $\mu_i(x(t))$, after training (black lines). The grey dots show a state-space plot of the time series.

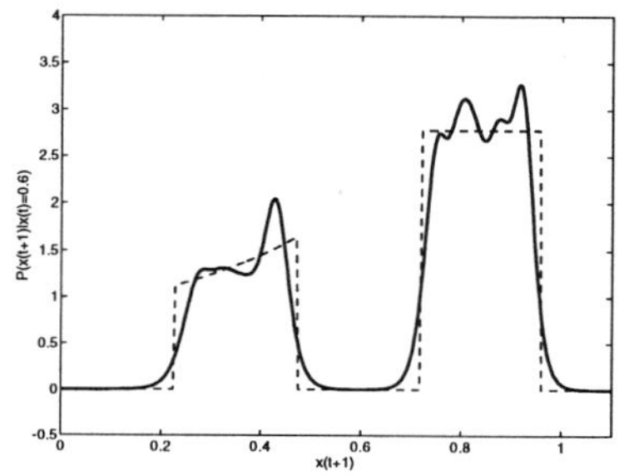

Figure 2 Cross section of the true (narrow graph) and predicted (bold graph) conditional probability density, $P(x(t+1) = y|x(t) = 0.6)$.

treshold constant ϑ, which was chosen such that we got a ratio of 2:1 in favour of the left process (i.e., $\vartheta = 1/3$). We applied a network with ten "RBF"-nodes to learn the conditional probability density of this time series. Figure 1 shows a state space plot of the time series (dots) and the centre positions of the "RBF"-kernels, $\mu_i(x(t))$ (black lines). Figure 2 shows a cross-section of the conditional probability density for $x(t) = 0.6$, $P(x(t+1) = y|x(t) = 0.6)$, and compares the correct function (narrow grey line) with the one predicted by the network (bold black line). Apparently the network has captured the relevant features of the stochastic process and correctly predicts the existence of two clusters. Note that a conventional network for time series prediction, which only predicts the conditional mean of the process, would be completely inappropriate in this case as it would predict a value between the two clusters, which actually never occurs. The same holds for the network proposed by Weigend and Nix, which would predict a value for $x(t+1)$ between the two clusters, too, and a much too large error bar resulting from the assumption of a Gaussian distribution.

5 Conclusions

A general approach to the learning of conditional probability densities for stationary stochastic time series has been presented, which overcomes the limitation of restricted reduction to the noise-free case. The minimal architecture required for the network to be a universal approximator *and* to contain the non-restricted noise-free case was found to be of a two-hidden-layer structure. We have shown that the other recently developed approaches to the same problem are of a very similar form, differing basically only with respect to the $\mathbf{x}$-dependence of the parameters and the functional form of the "RBF"-kernels. Which architecture one should finally adopt depends on the specific problem under consideration. While the structure proposed by Weigend and Nix is suitable for a computationally cheap, but biased approximation of $p(x(t+1)|\mathbf{x}(t))$ (approximation by a single Gaussian), the CDEN, the method of soft histograms and the network proposed here offer a more accurate, but also computationally more expensive determination of the whole conditional probability density. It is an important subject of further research to assess the relative merits and drawbacks of the latter three models by carrying out comparative simulations on a set of benchmark problems.

REFERENCES

[1] Allen DW and Taylor JG , *Learning Time Series by Neural Networks*, Proc ICANN (1994), ed Marinaro M and Morasso P, Springer, pp529–532.

[2] Neuneier R, Hergert F, Finnoff W and Ormoneit D, *Estimation of Conditional Densities: A Comparison of Neural Network Approaches*, Proc ICANN (1994), ed Marinaro M and Morasso P, Springer, pp689–692.

[3] Papoulis, A., *Probability, Random Variables and Stochastic Processes*, McGraw-Hill (1984).

[4] Srivastava AN and Weigend AS, *Computing the Probability Density in Connectionist Regression*, Proc ICANN (1994), ed Marinaro M and Morasso P, Springer, pp685–688.

[5] Weigend AS and Nix DA, *Predictions with Confidence Intervals (Local Error Bars)*, Proc ICONIP (1994), ed Kim M-W and Lee S-Y,Korea Advanced Institute of Technology, pp847–852.

CONVERGENCE OF A CLASS OF NEURAL NETWORKS

Mark P. Joy

Centre for Research in Information Engineering,
School of Electrical, Electronic and Information Enineering,
South Bank University, 103, Borough Rd., London SE1 OAA, UK.
Email: joympa@vax.sbu.ac.uk

The additive neural network model is a nonlinear dynamical system and it is well-known that if either the weight matrices are symmetric or the dynamical system is cooperative and irreducible (with isolated equilibria) then the net exhibits convergent activation dynamics. In this paper we present a convegence thoerem for additive neural nets with ramp sigmoid activation functions having a row-dominant weight matrix. Of course, such nets are not, in general, cooperative or possess symmetic weight matices. We also indicate the application of this theorem to a new class of neural networks – the Cellular Neural Networks – and consider its usefulness as a practical result in image processing applications.

1 Introduction

In the last few years the definition of the neural network dynamical system has expanded rapidly. This paper concerns neural networks associated with the set of ODEs:

$$\dot{x}_i = -x_i + \sum_{j=1}^{n} b_{ij} f(x_j) + I, \tag{1}$$

where $x \in \mathbb{R}^n$, describes the activity levels of n 'neurons', b_{ij} is a real constant representing the connection strength from neuron j to neuron i, f is a sigmoid function and I represents a clamped input. In order to facilitate the analysis of (1) we define f as a *ramp* sigmoid:

$$f(x) = \frac{1}{2}(\mid x+1 \mid - \mid x-1 \mid). \tag{2}$$

We wish to investigate the activation dynamics of these nets operating as CAMs. Upon presentation of an input the net should 'flow', eventually settling at a stationary point of the dynamical system which represents output in the form of n reals. With this dynamic in mind we wish to prevent, by judicious design, any of the more exotic dynamical behaviour exhibited by nonlinear systems. What we seek to prove is that the union of the basins of attraction of equilibria comprises the whole phase space. It is natural then to make the following definition:

Definition 1 *A dynamical system is said to be convergent if for every trajectory $\phi_t(x)$ we have:*

$$\lim_{t \to \infty} \phi_t(x) = \eta,$$

where η is an equilibrium point.

It is possible to relax this definition in different ways and still have workable definitions of the behaviour we require. For more details, see the excellent paper by Hirsch, [1].

It is easy enough to show that solutions, $x(t, x_0)$ to (1), have bounded forward closure if $\|x_0\| \leq K$, $K > 0$, in the sup norm. We will assume boundedness of inital conditions throughout, so that the phase space Ω is a compact subset of $\mathbb{R}^n$. By standard theory, all trajectories can be extended to have domain of definitions equal to the whole of $\mathbb{R}$.

Since f is linear in the three segments defined by: $| x | \leq 1, x > 1$ and $x < -1$, the CNN vector field is piecewise linear. The regions of Ω on which the vector field is constant will be called *partial* or *total saturation* regions depending on whether some cells are in their linear region or not. It is clear (by piecewise linearity) that if any total saturation region contains a stable equilibrium it is a trapping region; whilst the absence of an equilibrium means that all trajectories will leave such a region. Finally, Jacobians are constant on the various partial saturation regions.

The analysis of large-scale interconnected systems often proceeds by investigating the behaviour of the system thought of as a collection of subunits. When we can describe the dynamical behaviour of the subunits successfully we may make progress towards the description of the behaviour of the system as a whole by supposing that the connections between units are so weak that the dynamical behaviour of the isolated units dominate. In [2] an analysis of a type of additive neural net was presented which presumed a *strict row-diagonally dominant* condition on the feedback matrix $B = (b_{ij})$; namely:

$$b_{ii} - 1 > \sum_{i \neq j} | b_{ij} | . \tag{3}$$

Roughly speaking (3) says that in terms of the dynamics, the self-feedback of each CNN cell dominates over the summed influences from its neighbours and may therefore be viewed as an example of the above large-scale system analysis. In section III of [2], the authors conjectured that (3) is sufficient to ensure convergence of the associated net; furthermore they outlined a method of proof. In this note we show that this conjecture is true by giving a rigorous argument built on their ideas.

2 Convergence of the Dynamical System.

Of prime importance to our result is the fact that if $B - I$ satisfies (3), then each total saturation region contains a (unique) equilibrium point; this is the substance of:

Lemma 2 *If B is strictly row-diagonally dominant, then every total saturation region contains an equilibrium.*

Proof We borrow some notation from [3]; let $S \subset \{1, \dots, n\}$ be of cardinality m and define the following sets:

$$\Lambda_m = \{\varepsilon = (\varepsilon_1, \dots, \varepsilon_n) \mid \varepsilon_i = 0, i \in S \text{ and } \varepsilon \in \{-1, 1\}, \text{ for } i \notin S\},$$

where:

$$\Lambda = \{(\varepsilon_1, \dots, \varepsilon_n) \mid \varepsilon_i \in \{-1, 1\}\}.$$

Then for each $\varepsilon \in \Lambda$ define:

$C(\varepsilon) = \{(x_1, \dots x_n) \in \Omega \mid | x_i | < 1, \text{ if } \varepsilon_i = 0, x_i \geq 1, \text{ if } \varepsilon_i = 1, x_i \leq -1, \text{otherwise}\}$.

Firstly we consider the total saturation region $C(\varepsilon_s)$, for some $\varepsilon_s \in \Lambda_0$. Suppose that an equilibrium $\bar{x}$ for the linear system of equations restricted to $C(\varepsilon_s)$, satisfies $f(\bar{x}_i) = 1$; then:

$$\bar{x}_i = b_{ii} + \sum_{j \neq i} b_{ij} f(\bar{x}_j) \geq b_{ii} - \sum_{j \neq i} | b_{ij} | \geq 1,$$

provided that (3) is satisfied. Similarly, if $f(\bar{x}_i) = -1$, $\bar{x}_i \leq -1$. Thus each total saturation region contains a (unique) equilibrium. □

Much more than lemma (2) is true, in fact it is possible to show that there exists an equilibrium in each partial and total saturation region, if and only if $B - I$ satisfies (3). In this case it is possible, by a linearly invertible change of variables (Grossberg's $S\Sigma$-exchange), to consider the dynamical system operating on a closed hypercube, a so-called BSB system ("Brain-State-In-A-Box"), then the existence equilibria at each corner of the hypercube is shown in [4].

Our main theorem is:

Theorem 3 *If $B-I$ is strictly row-diagonally dominant then the dynamical system (1) with N cells defined by:*

$$\dot{x} = -x + Bf(x),$$

is convergent.

Proof By Gerschgorin's Circle theorem (see [5]), if (3) is satisfied all the Gerschgorin discs lie in the right half-plane. Thus any unsaturated variable, corresponding to a cell operating in its linear region, has an associated eigenvalue with positive real part. It follows that trajectories decay from partial saturation regions and the linear region since at least one eigenvalue of the Jacobian has positive real part there (unless, of course a trajectory lies in the stable manifold of an unstable equilibrium point, in which case it converges to an equilibrium anyway).

Once a hyperplane $x_i = \pm 1$ has been crossed by a trajectory $\phi(t)$, say at at time t_0, then at no future time $t > t_0$, will this trajectory satisfy $\mid \phi_i(t) \mid < 1$. To see this consider the vector field along the hyperplane H_i^+, defined by $x_i = 1$. We have:

$$\dot{x}_i = b_{ii} - 1 + \sum_{j \neq i} b_{ij} f(x_j), \tag{4}$$

and it follows that $\dot{x}_i > 0$ along H_i^+ since the maximum value that the summation term in (4) attains equals:

$$\sum_{j \neq i} \mid b_{ij} \mid,$$

because $\mid f(x) \mid \leq 1$ for all x. (An identical argument along $x_i = -1$ holds). Thus the vector field points 'outwards', i.e in the direction of increasing $\mid x_i \mid$, along the hyperplanes forming the boundary of the individual linear regions and therefore no trajectory can decay across any $H_i^{\pm}$ with $\mid \phi_i \mid$ decreasing.

If we define:

$$\rho(\phi(t, x)) = \# \text{ (saturated components of } \phi(t, x)),$$

then the argument in the previous paragraph shows that $\rho(t)$ is a non-decreasing function (defined on $\{x\} \times [0, \infty)$), which is bounded above by N. Thus $\lim_{t \to \infty} \rho(t)$ exists and actually must equal N (if not, given some $T > 0$, there is at least one unsaturated cell, i.e there exists i_k, say, such that $\mid \phi_{i_k}(x, t) \mid < 1$, for all $t \geq T$ and $1 \leq k \leq N$. However, since the real parts of the corresponding eigenvalues are positive, there exists a $t_0 > T$ such that $\mid \phi_{i_k}(x, t_0) \mid > 1$, which is a contradiction). Since all total saturation regions contain a stable equilibrium point by Lemma 2, and the basin of attraction of such an equilibrium contains the total saturation region, all trajectories converge. □

By an identical argument we are able to prove the more general result:

Theorem 4 *If an additive neural network described by (1) satisfies the condition:*

$$b_{ii} - 1 > \sum_{j \neq i}^{n} | b_{ij} | + | I_i | \tag{5}$$

then it is convergent.

3 Applications to CNNs and Final Remarks

Recently a new class of neural networks called *Cellular Neural Networks (CNNs)*, has been introduced, (see [6]); such nets are recurrent, continuous time networks described by (1), with a particular structure on B, called the *feedback* matrix, (that arises from the architecture of the net), together with a ramp sigmoid activation function. Therefore our results (3) and (4) from the previous section apply to such nets.

The concept of a CNN is rooted in 2D nonlinear Filter Theory, and Cellular Automata. The neurons are arrayed on a two-dimensional grid and any fixed neuron can be thought of as a centre neuron which is connected, through a neighbourhood of size $r \geq 1$, to its nearest neighbours; i. e. any cell which can be arrived at in a kings walk of length $\leq r$ on a chessboard. Neighbourhood sizes can increase in size up to a fully interconnected net, but usually we insist on $r = 1$ so that only the 'nearest' neighbours are connected. The intention of this architecture is to facilitate the fabrication of such a device onto a chip, for reducing connections increases the chances of a successful implementation.

CNNs have found a variety of interesting and useful applications and most cases share the common idea that solutions to processing tasks are represented as constant attracting trajectories of the associated dynamical system. Upon presentation of an input image, coded as an array of grey-scale pixels, the CNN should operate as a CAM, 'flowing' to an output image.

The strict row-diagonal dominance of the feedback matrix is a severe restriction on the parameters because in practical terms such a CNN would not process bipolar images. A trajectory with a 'bipolar' initial condition would of course lie in a total saturation region. If (3) holds all such regions are contained in the basin of attraction of a stable equilibrium point $\bar{x}$. The output of the CNN, $f(\bar{x})$, would then be identical to the input image and we would observe no transformation of such an image. As proved in [2], (3) is a necessary and sufficient condition for the existence of a stable equilibrium in each total saturation region. Conditions weaker than (3) would therefore allow bipolar images to undergo change because any trajectory with initial conditions in a total saturation region which contains no equilibrium must leave this region and hence undergo a nonlinear transformation. In practice therefore we seek weaker conditions which ensure complete stability.

As a final remark, let us return to the more general case considered in the first sections of this paper. We have a compact phase space, partitioned by the PWL vector field. If the matrix B has eigenvalues with positive real parts one would like to be able to say that trajectories are 'expanding' and thus reach total saturation regions. However, there are examples of CNNs with such eigenvalues possessing closed orbits – all that one can say is that no trajectory can remain in a partial saturation region if such an eigenvalue exists. The diagonal dominance condition ensures that recrossing of a partial saturation boundary cannot occur and as we have seen this has a profound effect on the global behaviour of trajectories.

REFERENCES

[1] M. W. Hirsch, *Activation dynamics in continous time nets*, Neural Networks, Vol. 2 (1989), pp331–349.

[2] F. A. Savaci and J. Vandewalle, *On the stability analysis of cellular neural networks*, IEEE Trans. Circuits Syst., Vol. 40 (1993), pp213 – 215.

[3] J. H. Li, A. N. Michel, and W. Porod, *Analysis and synthesis of a class of neural networks: Linear systems operating on a closed hypercube*, IEEE Trans. Circuits Syst., Vol. 36 (1989), pp1405–1422.

[4] S. Hui and S. H. Zak, *Dynamical analysis of the brain-state-in-a-box (BSB) neural models*, IEEE Trans. Neural Networks, Vol. 3 (1992), pp86–94.

[5] R. A. Horn and C. R. Johnson, *Matrix Analysis*, Cambridge University Press (1990), Cambridge UK.

[6] L.O. Chua and L. Yang, *Cellular neural networks: Theory*, IEEE Trans. Circuits Syst., Vol. 35, (1988), pp1257 – 1272.

APPLICATIONS OF THE COMPARTMENTAL MODEL NEURON TO TIME SERIES ANALYSIS

S. Kasderidis and J. G. Taylor

Department of Mathematics, King's College London, UK.

In this paper we discuss an extended model neuron in ANN. It is the compartmental model which has already been developed to model living neurons. This type of neuron belongs to the class of temporal processing neurons. Learning of these neurons can be achieved by extending the model of Temporal Backpropagation. The basic assumption behind the model is that the single neuron is considered as possessing finite spatial dimension and not being a point processor (integrate and fire). Simulations and numerical results are presented and discussed for three applications to time series problems.

1 Introduction

Most models of a neuron used in ANN neglect the spatial structure of a neuron's extensive dendritic tree system. However, from a computational viewpoint there are a number of reasons for taking into account such a structure. (i) The passive membrane properties of a neuron's dendritic tree leads to a spread of activity through the tree from the point of stimulation at a synapse. Hence spatial structure influences the temporal processing of synaptic inputs. (ii) The spatial relationship of synapses relative to each other and the soma is important. (iii) The geometry of the dendritic tree ensures that different branches can function almost independently of one another. Moreover, there is growing evidence that quite complex computations are being performed within the dendrites prior to subsequent processing at the soma.

The (linear) cable theory models try to explain the creation of the action potential [1]. These models belong to the class of Hodgkin-Huxley derived models. The one-dimensional cable theory describes current flow in a continuous passive dendritic tree using P.D.E.s. These equations have straightforward solutions for an idealised class of dendritic trees that are equivalent to unbranched cylinders. For cases of passive dendritic trees with a general branching structure the solutions are more complicated. When the membrane properties are voltage dependant then the analytical approach using linear cable theory is no longer valid. One way to account for the geometry of complex neurons has been explored by Abbott et al. [2]. Using path-integral techniques, they construct the membrane potential response function (Green's function) of a dendritic tree described by a linear cable equation. The response function determines the membrane potential arising from the instantaneous injection of a unit current impulse at a given point on the tree.

A complementary approach to modelling a neuron's dendritic tree is to use a compartmental model in which the dendritic system is divided into sufficiently small regions or compartments such that spatial variations of the electrical properties within a region are negligible. The P.D.E.s of cable theory then simplify to a system of first order O.D.E.s. From these equations we can then calculate the response function, i.e. the law with which the action potential is created, see [3], [4], [5]. Using the previous ideas, we construct an artificial neuron through appropriate simplifications in the structure of the neurobiological compartmental model and its response function.

2 The Compartmental Model Neuron

2.1 The Transfer Function

The artificial neuron is composed of a set of compartments, in which connections from other neurons of the network are arriving. The transfer function for neuron i in the layer l in time instance t has the form:

$$y_{li}(t) = s(V_{li}^0(t)) = s\left(\sum_{n=0}^{T}\sum_{\beta=0}^{m} f_{|\beta|}(n)u^{\beta}(n)\right) \tag{1}$$

$$u_{\beta}(n) = \sum_{j=1}^{M_{li}^{\beta}} w_{lij}^{\beta}(n)y_{(l-1)j}(t-n) \tag{2}$$

where s is any suitable nonlinear function, usually the sigmoid, $V_{li}^0(t)$ is the net potential at "soma" (compartment 0) at time t, T is the number of time steps used to keep a history of the neuron, m is the number of compartments in the neuron, M_{li}^{β} is the number of incoming weights to compartment β (note that this number is compartment related), $u^{\beta}(n)$ is the net potential at compartment β at time instance n and $f_{|\beta|}(n)$ is a kernel function corresponding to the response function of the respective neurobiological model and has the following general form:

$$f_{|\alpha-\beta|}(t) = G(\alpha, t; \beta, 0) = e^{\frac{-t}{\tau}} I_{|\alpha-\beta|}\left[\frac{2t}{\gamma}\right] \tag{3}$$

The parameters γ and τ determine effectively the delay rate in the propagation of the signal from compartment β at time 0 (a stimulus is coming there) to compartment α at time t. The function $I_n(t)$ is the modified Bessel function of integer order n.

For the purpose of the artificial neuron the parameters can either remain constant or adapt during the simulation. The connections that exist between neurons are assumed to be like the ones of the Temporal Backpropagation case, i.e. having tapped delays up to a desirable order N, see [6]. In this way the neuron produces a signal that depends also on the previous values of its input.

2.2 The Learning Law

In applying the compartmental model to problems of supervised learning we devise a learning law that is based on Temporal Backpropagation, but is modified appropriately to account for the existence of distinct compartments. Assuming an MSE error function and a sigmoid transfer function of the type:

$$f(x) = \frac{1}{1+e^{-x}} \tag{4}$$

then the learning law (stochastic case) has the following form:

$$w_{lij}^{x(new)}(s) = w_{lij}^{x(old)}(s) + \Delta w_{lij}^{x(new)}(s) \tag{5}$$

$$\Delta w_{lij}^{x(new)}(s) = (-\eta) f_{|x|}(s) y_{(l-1)j}(t-s)\delta_{li}(t) + \alpha\Delta w_{lij}^{x(old)}(s) \tag{6}$$

$$\delta_{li}(t) = s'(t)(-2)e_{li}(t) \quad \text{for} l = L \tag{7}$$

$$\delta_{li}(t) = s_{li}'(t)\sum_{p=1}^{M_{li}'}\sum_{t'=t}^{t+T_{(l+1)p}} \delta_{(l+1)p}(t') f_{|d|}(t'-t) w_{(l+1)pi}^{d}(t'-t) \tag{8}$$

In the above equations, η and α are the learning rate and momentum coefficients, $s = 0...T_{li}$ is a temporal index, T_{li} is the temporal dimension of neuron i at layer l. In equation (6) t is referring to current time and s is then the time delay from current time. L is the output layer, $e_{li}(t)$ is the error in the output layer, s' is the derivative of the transfer function, M'_{li} is the number of outgoing connections from neuron i. W_{lij} are the weights connecting neuron j at layer $(l-1)$ to neuron i at layer l. In the notation we take into account that the weights are associated with different compartments. The index x in the weights denotes that compartment in which an incoming connection is terminated and the index d is the compartment (of neuron p at layer $(l+1)$) to which an outgoing connection of i is connected. Finally the δ_{li} are defined as follows:

$$\delta_{li}(t) \equiv \frac{\partial E}{\partial V_{li}(t)} \tag{9}$$

where E is the error function and $V_{li}(t)$ is the activation of the neuron before the transfer function.

3 Simulation Results

We tested the model using three time series: the logistic map series near its chaotic region, an astronomical series which describes the interaction of a gravitational wave with a distribution of particles in the interstellar media [7], and a solid state physics series which describes the chaotic voltage oscillations in the NDR region of the I-U characteristics registered in V_2O_5 single crystals [8]. In all cases the parameters γ and τ were kept constant.

3.1 Logistic Map

In Fig. 1 we see the performance of the model in comparison with a Temporal Backpropagation network of same degrees of freedom. The network for the compartmental model employed was a 1-15-1 architecture with 3 tapped delay lines for the case of hidden neurons and 1 line for the output unit. In both networks we used 400 points for training, 200 points for validation and 250 points for testing the mapping that was achieved. In the testing set after the first 200 points we used multi-step iterative prediction for the remaining 50 points. The parameters γ and τ had values 1.0 and 2.0 respectively. The incoming connections from the hidden neurons to the output neuron were connected to compartment number zero ("soma").

The parameters for the logistic map were $\lambda = 3.8$ and the initial condition was $x_0 = 0.1$ In Fig. 1 we see the region of multi-step prediction, ranging from number 900 up to number 932 for both methods. The solid line is the logistic map series, the sparse dashed line is the Compartmental model prediction and the dense dashed line is the Temporal Backpropagation model.

We see initially that after two points with correct match the Compartmental model does not predict correctly the following twelve points. The same behaviour is observed for the Temporal Backpropagation model. But afterwards, strangely enough, the model closely follows the underlying mapping for the remaining points. This behaviour extends further in the series.

3.2 Astronomical Series

In Fig. 2 we see a series that is describing the interaction of a gravitational wave with the interstellar plasma. The interaction that is shown is chaotic.

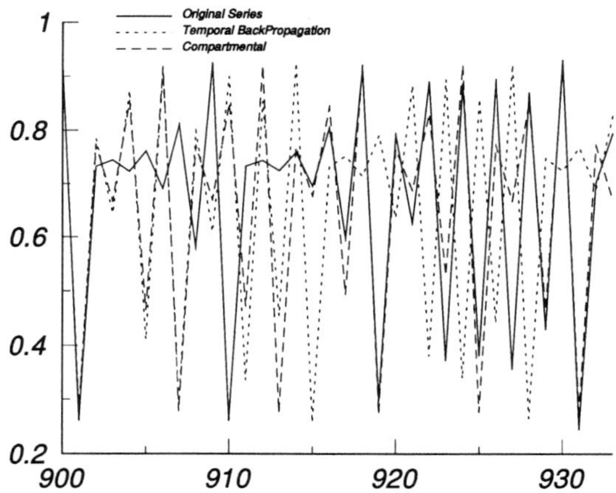

Figure 1 Logistic Time Series. Logistic map, I=3.8. T=1, G=2. Network 1-15-1. TDimH = 3, TDimO = 1. Multistep Prediction region 900-932.

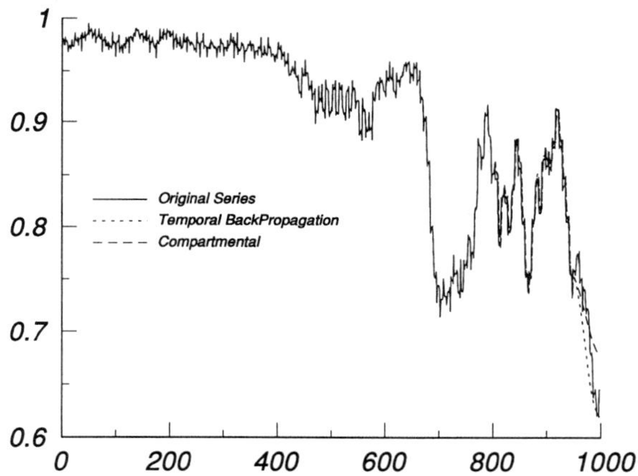

Figure 2 Astrophysical Time Series. T = 1, G = 1. Network 1-5-1. TDimH = 3, TDimO = 1. Connections to "soma".

Again the Compartmental and Temporal Backpropagation models were used for comparison. The architecture that was employed was a 1-5-1 network with 3 tapped delays for the hidden neurons and 1 delay line for the output neuron. The τ and γ parameters were 1.0 and 1.0 respectively. The incoming connections to output neuron were connected to the "soma" . Again 400 points were used, here though from the range 400–800, because we wanted to avoid the initial transient period. The prediction that was sought was in the range of 800–1000, and 150 points were used for single step prediction and the remaining 50 points were generated by a multi-step prediction scheme.

The solid line corresponds to the original series, the sparse and dense dashed lines represent the Compartmental and Temporal Backpropagation model predictions respectively.
Fig. 2 shows that a good approximation of the underlying map was achieved by both models even though a fairly simple architecture was employed and the training set was not the most representative.

3.3 Solid State Series

In Fig. 3 we see a series that is describing the chaotic voltage oscillations in the NDR region of the crystal.

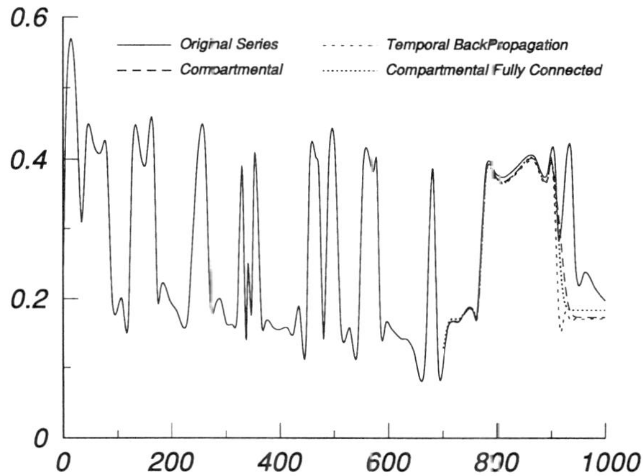

Figure 3 Solid State Physics Time Series. T=1, G=2. Network 1-5-1. TDimH = 8, TDimO = 2. Connections to "soma". Network 1-5-1. TDimH = TDimO = 1.5 comps/neuron. Fully connected.

Again the Compartmental and Temporal Backpropagation models were used for comparison. The architecture that was employed was a 1-5-1 network with 8 tapped delays for the hidden neurons and 2 delay line for the output neuron. The τ and γ parameters were 1.0 and 2.0 respectively. The incoming connections to output neuron were connected to the "soma". For training, 450 points were used, from the range 1–450, 200 points were used for validation in the range 500–700. The prediction that was sought was in the range of 700–1000, and 200 points were used for single step prediction and the remaining 100 points were generated by a multi-step prediction scheme.
Here we try to tackle also the problem of how the incoming weights to a neuron should be distributed among its compartments. Here instead of connecting just to one compartment, we tested the idea of connecting to all the compartments. For this purpose we used a 1-5-1 network structure, with 1 tapped delay line per hidden and output neuron. But instead the neurons consist of 5 compartments each, where we are connecting the incoming signal from every other neuron. The key to note here is that the value of the incoming signal is the same for all the five compartments, but different weights exist for every connection to a specific compartment.

In Fig. 3 the solid line corresponds to the original series, the flat sparse and exponentially decaying dense dashed lines represent the Compartmental and Temporal Backpropagation model predictions respectively. The dense dashed line is the Compartmental model with full connectivity to all compartments.

Fig. 3 shows that a good approximation of the underlying map was achieved by both models even though a fairly simple architecture was employed. We were surprised by the fact that the best approximation to the underlying map was achieved by the fully connected model.

Finally we have to mention here, that for comparison the parameters of the nets were chosen to produce exactly the same number of free parameters (weights) namely fifty for all three models.

4 Conclusion

From these initial simulations we see that in general the Compartmental model is at least as successful as the Temporal Backpropagation model for the time series involved. Even though fairly simple architectures were used, the underlying mapping was approximated reasonably well as the single step predictions are showing. For the multi-step predictions further simulations are needed, in order to specify a more appropriate architecture and parameter range that leads to better performance.

Further research is now being carried out to investigate the complex couplings of the parameters that control the behaviour of the model. Also a major issue of the model is the scheme with which we choose to assign the incoming connections of each neuron to its compartments [11].

REFERENCES

[1] Koch and Segev, editors, *Methods in Neural Modeling*, MIT Press (1989).

[2] Abbott, L. F., Farhi, E., Gutmann, S., *The path integral for dendritic trees*, Biological Cybernetics, Vol. 66 (1991), pp61–70.

[3] Bressloff, P. C., *Dynamics of a compartmental model integrate-and-fire neuron with somatic potential reset*, Physica D, submitted.

[4] Bressloff, P. C., Taylor, J. G., *Compartmental response function for dendritic trees*, Biological Cybernetics, Vol. 70 (1993), pp199–207.

[5] Bressloff, P. C., Taylor, J. G., *Spatio-temporal pattern processing a compartmental model neuron*, Physica Review E, Vol. 47 (1993), pp2899–2912.

[6] Wan, E., *Finite Impulse Response Neural Networks for Autoregressive Time Series Prediction*, in: Predicting the Future and Understanding the Past, eds. by A. Weigend and N. Gershenfeld, SFI Studies in the Sciences of Complexity, Proc. Vol. XVII (1993), Addison-Wesley.

[7] Kleidis, K., Varvoglis, H., Papadopoulos, D., *Interaction of charged particles with gravitational waves of various polarizations and directions of propagation*, Astronomy and Astrophysics, Vol. 275 (1993), pp309–317.

[8] Karakotsou, C., Anagnostopoulos, A., Kambas, K., Spyridelis, J., *Chaotic voltage oscillations in the negative-differential-resistance region of the I-U curves of* V_2O_5 *crystals*, Physical Review B, Vol. 46 (1992), No. 24, p16144.

[9] Kasderidis, S., Taylor, J. G., *The compartmental model neuron and its application to time series analysis*, in proceedings of IEEE Workshop on Nonlinear Signal and Image Processing, Neos Marmaras, Greece, (June 20–22 1995), p58.

[10] Kasderidis, S., Taylor, J. G., *The compartmental model neuron*, proceedings of WCNN (July 17–21 1995), Washington D.C., USA.

[11] Kasderidis, S., Taylor, J. G., King's College preprint (to appear).

Acknowledgements

During this work the first author was supported by a grant of the Greek State Scholarship Foundation.

INFORMATION THEORETIC NEURAL NETWORKS FOR CONTEXTUALLY GUIDED UNSUPERVISED LEARNING

Jim Kay

Dept. of Statistics, University of Glasgow, Mathematics Building, Glasgow G12 8QW, UK. Email: jim@stats.glasgow.ac.uk

The purpose of this article is to describe some new applications of information-theoretic concepts in unsupervised learning with particular emphasis on the implementation of contextual guidance during learning and processing.

1 Introduction

Building on earlier work by Linsker, and Becker and Hinton [8, 2] , Kay and Phillips [7] used the concept of three-way mutual information in order to define a new class of objective functions designed to maximise the transfer of the information shared between a set of inputs (the receptive field) and outputs that is predictably related to the context(the contextual field) in which the learning occurs and termed one of this new class of objective functions **Coherent Infomax**. In addition they introduced a new activation function which combines information flowing from the receptive and contextual fields in a novel way within local processors. Two illustrations of the role of contextual guidance are given in [7] and further demonstrations are provided in [9]. This work, however, considered only the case where the local processors have binary output units. In this article the methodology proposed in [7] is extended to the case of general multivariate Gibbs distributions but will be described, for simplicity, in the particular case of multivariate binary outputs. The article proceeds as follows. In section 2 notation will be described and probabilistic modelling of the multivariate outputs considered. The definition of suitable objective functions will be discussed in section 3 and various local objective functions introduced. The learning rules will be presented in section 4 and finally in section 5 computational issues will be briefly considered.

2 Probabilistic Modelling

We consider a local processor having multiple outputs. This processor receives input from two distinct sources, namely, its receptive field inputs,$\mathbf{R} = \{R_1, R_2, ..., R_m\}$ and its contextual field inputs,$\mathbf{C} = \{C_1, C_2, ..., C_n\}$ and produces its outputs,$\mathbf{X} = \{X_1, X_2, ..., X_p\}$, where $\mathbf{R}$, $\mathbf{C}$ and $\mathbf{X}$ are taken to be random vectors and we adopt the usual device of denoting a random variable by a capital letter and its observed value by the corresponding lower-case letter. In order to allow explicitly for the possibility of incomplete connectivity we define connection neighbourhoods for the ith ouput unit X_i. Let $\partial i(r)$, $\partial i(c)$ and $\partial i(x)$ denote, respectively, the set of indices of the RF input units, the set of indices of the CF inputs and the set of indices of the outputs that are connected to the ith output unit X_i. The corresponding random variables are denoted by $\mathbf{R}_{\partial i}, \mathbf{C}_{\partial i}, \mathbf{X}_{\partial i}$ respectively and the set of all components of $\mathbf{X}$ excluding the ith component is $\mathbf{X}_{-i}$. The weights on the connections into the ith output unit are given by w_{ij}, v_{ij} and u_{ij} for the jth RF input, jth CF input and the jth output unit respectively and we assume that the weights connecting

the output units to each other are symmetric. We now define the integrated fields in relation to the ith output unit.
$S_i(r) = \sum_{j\in\partial i(r)} w_{ij}R_j - w_{i0}$ is the RF integrated field.
$S_i(c) = \sum_{j\in\partial i(c)} v_{ij}C_j - v_{i0}$ is the CF integrated field.
$S_i(x) = \sum_{j\in\partial i(x)} u_{ij}X_j$ is the output integrated field.
The weights w_{i0} and v_{i0} are biases.
The activation function at the ith output unit is now a function of three integrated fields and we shall take it to have the following form

$$A_i = A(s_i(r), s_i(c)) + s_i(x) \equiv a_i + s_i(x). \qquad (1)$$

although we shall derive the learning rules in the general case. This particular way of incorporating the integrated output has been chosen so that this local activation function at the ith output unit is consistent with the definition of a multivariate model for **X**. The activation function A which binds the activity of the RF and CF integrated fields is that proposed in [7] defined by

$$A(s_1, s_2) = \frac{1}{2}s_1(1 + \exp(2s_1s_2)) \qquad (2)$$

We assume that the output vector **X** follows a binary markov random field model [3] conditional on the RF and CF inputs, with probability mass function

$$Pr(\mathbf{X} = \mathbf{x}|\mathbf{R} = \mathbf{r}, \mathbf{C} = \mathbf{c}) = \frac{\exp(\sum_{i=1}^{p} a_i x_i + \frac{1}{2}\sum_{i=1}^{p}\sum_{j\in\partial i(x)} u_{ij}x_ix_j)}{Z(\mathbf{a}, \mathbf{u})} \qquad (3)$$

where $Z(\mathbf{a}, \mathbf{u})$ is the normalisation constant (i.e. not a function of **x**) required to ensure that the probabilities sum to unity. This model is a regression model in two distinct senses. Firstly, via the terms $\{a_i\}$ which are general nonlinear functions of the RF and CF inputs, it is a nonlinear regression of the outputs with respect to all of the inputs. Secondly, when written in conditional form in equation (3), it expresses an auto-regression for each output unit in terms of the other output units in its neighbourhood. The formulation developed in the above model has the advantage of interfacing a feed-forward network between layers with a recurrent network structure within the output layer within a single coherent probabilistic framework. Not only that but it is also possible to connect the multiple output local processors themselves in a multi-layered network structure in a probabilistically coherent manner.
From this model the local conditional distributions may be derived. As we shall see using these distributions provides a local structure to the learning rules and, under the restrictions on the output connection weights, the Hammersley-Clifford theorem [3] ensures that working locally with the conditional models is equivalent to assuming a coherent global model for the outputs. However in the case were the output units are fully, mutually connected the equations presented here hold without any necessity to invoke this theorem to ensure probabilistic coherence and are derived using the basic rules of probability.
The local conditional distribution for the ith output is

$$\theta_i \equiv Pr(X_i = 1|\mathbf{R}_{\partial i} = \mathbf{r}_{\partial i}, \mathbf{C}_{\partial i} = \mathbf{c}_{\partial i}, \mathbf{X}_{\partial i} = \mathbf{x}_{\partial i}) = 1/(1 + \exp(-A_i)). \qquad (4)$$

Here $A_i = a_i + s_i(x)$, where a_i is any general differentiable function of the integrated RF and CF fields.

3 Global and Local Objective Functions

We now consider a global objective function based on the joint distribution of all outputs, RF inputs and CF inputs. In the case of multivariate outputs, we consider the general version of the objective function introduced in [7] which is

$$F = I(\mathbf{X};\mathbf{R};\mathbf{C}) + \phi_1 I(\mathbf{X};\mathbf{R}|\mathbf{C}) + \phi_2 I(\mathbf{X};\mathbf{C}|\mathbf{R}) + \phi_3 H(\mathbf{X}|\mathbf{R},\mathbf{C}). \qquad (5)$$

Here the term I(**X**;**R**;**C**) is the three-way mutual information between the random vectors **X**,**R** and **C** given by

$$I(\mathbf{X};\mathbf{R};\mathbf{C}) = I(\mathbf{X};\mathbf{R}) - I(\mathbf{X};\mathbf{R}|\mathbf{C}) \qquad (6)$$

and

$$I(\mathbf{X};\mathbf{R}) = H(\mathbf{X}) - H(\mathbf{X}|\mathbf{R}) \qquad (7)$$

is the mutual information shared between the random vectors **X** and **R** and the symbol H denotes Shannon's entropy. For further details see [4]. The objective function in equation (5) is based on the three-way mutual information and the three possible conditional measures of (two-way) mutual information.
For the purposes of modelling this is expressed as

$$F = H(\mathbf{X}) - \psi_1 H(\mathbf{X}|\mathbf{R}) - \psi_2 H(\mathbf{X}|\mathbf{C}) - \psi_3 H(\mathbf{X}|\mathbf{R},\mathbf{C}). \qquad (8)$$

In terms of the output, and indeed the input, units this is a **global** objective function and general learning rules have been derived in the general case of Gibbs distributions. However these lead to learning rules that are global and also computationally challenging in their exact form and so we now describe a particular local approximation to the global objective function F; other definitions of locality are possible [5]. In this multiple output case, it is natural to think of the processing locally in terms of each output unit using the information available to it from its RF, CF and output neighbourhoods. This suggests that one might focus in turn on the joint distribution of, say, the ith output and its RF and CF inputs **given** the neighbouring output units. From this perspective it then seems natural to introduce the concept of the **conditional** three-way mutual information shared by the ith output and its RF and CF inputs given the neighbouring outputs denoted by

$$I(X_i;\mathbf{R}_{\partial i};\mathbf{C}_{\partial i}|\mathbf{X}_{\partial i}) = I(X_i;\mathbf{R}_{\partial i}|\mathbf{X}_{\partial i}) - I(X_i;\mathbf{R}_{\partial i}|\mathbf{C}_{\partial i},\mathbf{X}_{\partial i}) \qquad (9)$$

It is possible to decompose the global three-way mutual information as follows.

$$I(\mathbf{X};\mathbf{R};\mathbf{C}) = I(X_i;\mathbf{R}_{\partial i};\mathbf{C}_{\partial i}|\mathbf{X}_{\partial i}) + I(\mathbf{X}_{-i};\mathbf{R};\mathbf{C}) \qquad (10)$$

This decomposition may be repeated recursively and is of particular relevance when the output units represent some one-dimensional structure such as a time series ; then the well-known general factorisation of joint probability into a product of a marginal and conditional distributions allows the general three-way mutual information to be written as a sum of local conditional three-way mutual information terms. However such simplicity is not possible here, although this first-step decomposition shows that the conditional three-way information is a part of the global three-way information in a well-defined sense. The same conditioning idea may be applied to the other components of information within the objective function F and this leads to the specification of a local objective function for the ith output unit defined as follows

$$\begin{aligned} F_i &= I(X_i;\mathbf{R}_{\partial i};\mathbf{C}_{\partial i}|\mathbf{X}_{\partial i}) + \phi_1 I(X_i;\mathbf{R}_{\partial i}|\mathbf{C}_{\partial i},\mathbf{X}_{\partial i}) \\ &\quad + \phi_2 I(X_i;\mathbf{C}_{\partial i}|\mathbf{R}_{\partial i},\mathbf{X}_{\partial i}) + \phi_3 H(X_i|\mathbf{R}_{\partial i},\mathbf{C}_{\partial i},\mathbf{X}_{\partial i}), \end{aligned} \qquad (11)$$

and we express $\{F_i\}$ in the more useful form

$$F_i = H(X_i|\mathbf{X}_{\partial i}) - \psi_1 H(X_i|\mathbf{R}_{\partial i}, \mathbf{X}_{\partial i}) - \psi_2 H(X_i|\mathbf{C}_{\partial i}, \mathbf{X}_{\partial i}) - \psi_3 H(X_i|\mathbf{R}_{\partial i}, \mathbf{C}_{\partial i}, \mathbf{X}_{\partial i}) \quad (12)$$

This means that we envisage each output unit working to maximise F_i and because of the the fact that mutually distinct sets of weights connect into each of the outputs this is equivalent to maximising the sum of the $F_i s$. We view this sum as a locally-based approximation to the global objective function F. In the extreme case where the outputs are conditionally independent this sum is equivalent to F. Obviously the approximation will be better the smaller are the sizes of the output neighbourhood sets relative to the number of outputs. We now provide formulae for the local entropic terms and the components of local information for the ith output unit.

$$H(X_i|\mathbf{R}_{\partial i}, \mathbf{C}_{\partial i}, \mathbf{X}_{\partial i}) = \langle \theta_i \log \theta_i + (1-\theta_i)\log(1-\theta_i)\rangle_{\mathbf{R}_{\partial i}, \mathbf{C}_{\partial i}, \mathbf{X}_{\partial i}} \quad (13)$$

$$H(X_i|\mathbf{R}_{\partial i}, \mathbf{X}_{\partial i}) = \langle E^{(i)}_{\mathbf{R}_{\partial i}, \mathbf{X}_{\partial i}} \log E^{(i)}_{\mathbf{R}_{\partial i}, \mathbf{X}_{\partial i}} + (1 - E^{(i)}_{\mathbf{R}_{\partial i}, \mathbf{X}_{\partial i}}) \log(1 - E^{(i)}_{\mathbf{R}_{\partial i}, \mathbf{X}_{\partial i}})\rangle_{\mathbf{R}_{\partial i}, \mathbf{X}_{\partial i}} \quad (14)$$

$$H(X_i|\mathbf{C}_{\partial i}, \mathbf{X}_{\partial i}) = \langle E^{(i)}_{\mathbf{C}_{\partial i}, \mathbf{X}_{\partial i}} \log E^{(i)}_{\mathbf{C}_{\partial i}, \mathbf{X}_{\partial i}} + (1 - E^{(i)}_{\mathbf{C}_{\partial i}, \mathbf{X}_{\partial i}}) \log(1 - E^{(i)}_{\mathbf{C}_{\partial i}, \mathbf{X}_{\partial i}})\rangle_{\mathbf{C}_{\partial i}, \mathbf{X}_{\partial i}} \quad (15)$$

$$H(X_i|\mathbf{X}_{\partial i}) = \langle E^{(i)}_{\mathbf{X}_{\partial i}} \log E^{(i)}_{\mathbf{X}_{\partial i}} + (1 - E^{(i)}_{\mathbf{X}_{\partial i}}) \log(1 - E^{(i)}_{\mathbf{X}_{\partial i}})\rangle_{\mathbf{X}_{\partial i}} \quad (16)$$

It follows that the components of local information at the ith output unit are as follows.

$$I(X_i; \mathbf{R}_{\partial i}; \mathbf{C}_{\partial i}|\mathbf{X}_{\partial i}) = (16) - (15) - (14) + (13),$$

$$I(X_i; \mathbf{R}_{\partial i}|\mathbf{C}_{\partial i}, \mathbf{X}_{\partial i}) = (15) - (13),$$

$$I(X_i; \mathbf{C}_{\partial i}|\mathbf{R}_{\partial i}, \mathbf{X}_{\partial i}) = (14) - (13),$$

$$H(X_i|\mathbf{R}_{\partial i}, \mathbf{C}_{\partial i}, \mathbf{X}_{\partial i}) = (13)$$

The $\{E\}$ terms are averages of the output probabilities at the ith unit and are defined at the end of section 4.

4 The Learning Rules

Using the locally-based objective functions developed in section 2 and the formulation so far, it turns out that the learning rules for all weights have the same general structure as those introduced in [7].

We describe the gradient ascent learning rules in relation to the ith output unit.

$$\frac{\partial F_i}{w_{is}} = \langle(\psi_3 A_i - \bar{O}_i)\theta_i(1-\theta_i)\frac{\partial A_i}{\partial s_i(r)} R_s\rangle_{\mathbf{R}_{\partial i}, \mathbf{C}_{\partial i}, \mathbf{X}_{\partial i}}, \quad (17)$$

for each RF input s which connects into the ith output unit.

$$\frac{\partial F_i}{v_{is}} = \langle(\psi_3 A_i - \bar{O}_i)\theta_i(1-\theta_i)\frac{\partial A_i}{\partial s_i(c)} C_s\rangle_{\mathbf{R}_{\partial i}, \mathbf{C}_{\partial i}, \mathbf{X}_{\partial i}}, \quad (18)$$

for each CF input s which connects into the ith output.

$$\frac{\partial F_i}{\partial u_{is}} = \langle(\psi_3 A_i - \bar{O}_i)\theta_i(1-\theta_i)\frac{\partial A_i}{\partial s_i(x)} X_s\rangle_{\mathbf{R}_{\partial i}, \mathbf{C}_{\partial i}, \mathbf{C}_{\partial i}}, \quad (19)$$

for each output unit s which connects into the ith output. Note that these learning rules are **local** and this results from the decision to separately maximise the local objective functions $\{F_i\}$(or equivalently to maximise the sum of the $\{F_i\}$). The dynamic average for the ith output unit is

$$\bar{O}_i = \log \frac{E^{(i)}_{\mathbf{X}_{\partial i}}}{(1 - E^{(i)}_{\mathbf{X}_{\partial i}})} - \psi_1 \log \frac{E^{(i)}_{\mathbf{R}_{\partial i},\mathbf{X}_{\partial i}}}{(1 - E^{(i)}_{\mathbf{R}_{\partial i},\mathbf{X}_{\partial i}})} - \psi_2 \log \frac{E^{(i)}_{\mathbf{C}_{\partial i},\mathbf{X}_{\partial i}}}{(1 - E^{(i)}_{\mathbf{C}_{\partial i},\mathbf{X}_{\partial i}})}. \tag{20}$$

Here the dynamic averages are more complicated than in the single output case and their calculation involves storing the average probability at the ith output unit for each pattern of the other outputs that connect into the ith output unit, for the combination of each of the neighbouring output and RF input patterns and for the combination of each of the neighbouring output and CF input patterns. However various approximations are possible [5] The various averages of the probability at the ith output unit are defined as follows. $E^{(i)}_{\mathbf{X}_{\partial i}} = \langle\theta_i\rangle_{\mathbf{R}_{\partial i},\mathbf{C}_{\partial i}|\mathbf{X}_{\partial i}}$, $E^{(i)}_{\mathbf{R}_{\partial i},\mathbf{X}_{\partial i}} = \langle\theta_i\rangle_{\mathbf{C}_{\partial i}|\mathbf{R}_{\partial i},\mathbf{X}_{\partial i}}$, $E^{(i)}_{\mathbf{C}_{\partial i},\mathbf{X}_{\partial i}} = \langle\theta_i\rangle_{\mathbf{R}_{\partial i}|\mathbf{C}_{\partial i},\mathbf{X}_{\partial i}}$, and the required partial derivatives may be easily calculated.

5 Some Computational Details

The computation may be performed using on-line learning as was the case in [7] or, alternatively, using batch learning. In the case of on-line learning the weight change rules are applied with the averaging brackets removed and the required conditional averages of output probabilities may be updated dynamically during learning after the presentation of each pattern via recursive computation. In particular recursive computation may be used to avoid the need to explicitly calculate the statistics of the input data and then employ a two-stage approach to the learning. The methodology has been applied in a number of computational experiments described in [6] which demonstrate the feasibility of the approach. It is shown there that the differences between the Infomax and Coherent Infomax computational goals described by [7] hold in this more general set up and that the multiple output unit is capable of representing its inputs by means of population codes. Further experimentation is currently in progress and this will address the computational feasibility of scaling up to large multiple output units and evaluate various approximations for the conditional dynamic averages.

REFERENCES

[1] M. W. Hirsch, *Activation dynamics in continous time nets*, Neural Networks, Vol.2 (1989), pp331–349.

[2] Becker S and Hinton G E, *Self-organizing neural network that discovers surfaces in random-dot stereograms.* Nature Vol. 355 (1992), pp161-3

[3] Besag J E, *Spatial analysis and the statistical analysis of lattice systems (with discussion)*, J. R. Statist. Soc. Ser. B Vol. 36 (1974), pp192-236.

[4] Hamming R W, *Coding and Information Theory* Englewood Cliffs, NJ: Prentice-Hall (1980).

[5] Kay J W, *Information-theoretic neural networks for the contextual guidance of learning and processing: mathematical and statistical considerations*, Technical Report, Biomathematics and Statistics Scotland (1994). (See http://www.stats.gla.ac.uk/~jim/)

[6] Kay J W, Floreano D and Phillips W A, *Contextually guided unsupervised learning using multivariate binary local processors*, submitted to Neural Networks, (1996).

[7] Kay J W and Phillips W A, *Activation functions, computational goals and learning rules for local processors with contextual guidance*, Neural Computation, in press (1997).

[8] Linsker R, *Self-organization in a perceptual network*, IEEE Computer, March (1988), pp105-17.

[9] Phillips W A Kay J W and Smyth D, *The discovery of structure by multi-stream networks of local processors with contextual guidance*, Network Vol. 6 (1995), pp225-246.

CONVERGENCE IN NOISY TRAINING

Petri Koistinen

Rolf Nevanlinna Institute, P.O. Box 4, FIN-00014 University of Helsinki, Finland. Email: petri.koistinen@rni.helsinki.fi

A minimization estimator minimizes the empirical risk associated with a given sample. Sometimes one calculates such an estimator based not on the original sample but on a pseudo sample obtained by adding noise to the original sample points. This may improve the generalization performance of the estimator. We consider the convergence properties (consistency and asymptotic distribution) of such an estimation procedure. Subject classification: AMS(MOS)62F12

1 Introduction

In backpropagation training one usually tries to minimize the empirical risk

$$r_n(t) := \frac{1}{n}\sum_{i=1}^{n} \|Y_i - g(X_i, t)\|^2 = \min!,$$

where $x \mapsto g(x,t)$ denotes the input/output mapping of a multilayer perceptron whose weights comprise the vector t. When the training sequence $\{Z_i\}$, $Z_i = (X_i, Y_i)$, consists of i.i.d. (independent and identically distributed) random vectors, it is known that under general conditions the parameter τ_n minimizing the empirical risk is strongly consistent for the minimizer set of the population risk $r(t) = E\|Y_1 - g(X_1, t)\|^2$. Further, if the sequence $\{\tau_n\}$ converges towards an isolated minimizer t^* of r, then under reasonable conditions, $\sqrt{n}(\tau_n - t^*)$ converges in distribution to a normal distribution with mean zero, see White [8].

Here we consider what happens in the above procedure when instead of the original data one uses data generated by adding noise to the original sample points. Such a practice has been suggested by several authors, see [4] for references. The relationship of this procedure to regularization has been investigated in many recent papers, see [6, 3, 1, 7]. In the present paper we outline both consistency and asymptotic distribution results for noisy training. The results are based on the doctoral thesis of the author [5], where the interested reader can find rigorous proofs and results which are more general than what can be covered here. The consistency results obtained in the thesis are much stronger than the previous results of Holmström and Koistinen [4]. Asymptotic distribution results in our setting have not been available previously.

2 The Statistical Setting

The original sample is part of a sequence $Z_1, Z_2, \ldots$ of random vectors taking values in $\mathbb{R}^k$. The noisy sample is generated by replacing each original sample point $Z_1, \ldots, Z_n$ with $s \geq 1$ pseudo sample points

$$Z^{\#}_{nij} = Z_i + h_n N_{ij}, \quad i = 1, \ldots, n, j = 1, \ldots, s. \tag{1}$$

Here the h_n's are positive random variables called the smoothing parameters. We assume that the noise vectors N_{ij}'s are i.i.d. and independent of the Z_i's and the h_n's. The smoothing parameters are allowed to depend on the $\{Z_i\}$-sequence. We need to let h_n converge to zero to ensure consistency, and therefore the pseudo sample points are not i.i.d. This prevents us from using standard convergence results for minimization estimators to analyze the convergence properties of noisy training.

We next define empirical measures associated with the original and the pseudo observations. Let δ_x denote the probability measure with mass one at $x \in \mathbb{R}^k$, and define the probability measure

$$\mu_n := n^{-1} \sum_{i=1}^{n} \delta_{Z_i},$$

i.e., μ_n places mass $1/n$ at each of the observations $Z_1, \ldots, Z_n$. We call μ_n the empirical measure of the first n observations. Similarly, we define the empirical measure $\mu^{\#}_{ns}$ of the pseudo observations $Z^{\#}_{nij}, i = 1, \ldots, n, j = 1, \ldots, s$ as the probability measure which places mass $1/(ns)$ at each of these ns points. The measures μ_n and $\mu^{\#}_{ns}$ are examples of what are called random probability measures; the randomness arises from the fact that the measures depend on the observed values of random vectors.

For the consistency results, we need to assume that the empirical measures μ_n converge weakly, almost surely, towards some probability measure μ in $\mathbb{R}^k$; in symbols, $\mu_n \overset{\text{a.s.}}{\Rightarrow} \mu$. The definition of this mode of convergence for any sequence $\{\lambda_n\}$ of random probability measures in $\mathbb{R}^k$ is as follows,

$$\lambda_n \overset{\text{a.s.}}{\Rightarrow} \mu \quad \text{if and only if} \quad \left(\forall f \in C_b : \int f \, d\lambda_n \to \int f \, d\mu\right), \quad \text{almost surely,}$$

where C_b is the set of bounded continuous functions $\mathbb{R}^k \to \mathbb{R}$. An argument due to Varadarajan [2, Th 11.4.1] then implies that for measures in $\mathbb{R}^k$,

$$\lambda_n \overset{\text{a.s.}}{\Rightarrow} \mu \quad \text{if and only if} \quad \int f \, d\lambda_n \overset{\text{a.s.}}{\rightarrow} \int f \, d\mu, \quad \forall f \in C_b. \tag{2}$$

Unlike the condition of the actual definition, condition (2) is often easy to verify. E.g., if $Z_1, Z_2, \ldots$ are i.i.d., then the strong law of large numbers implies that the empirical measures $\mu_n \overset{\text{a.s.}}{\Rightarrow} \mu$, where μ denotes the common law of the Z_i's on $\mathbb{R}^k$. The same conclusion holds by the ergodic theorem, if the sequence $\{Z_i\}$ is stationary and ergodic.

Suppose that the empirical measures $\mu_n \overset{\text{a.s.}}{\Rightarrow} \mu$, where μ is some (nonrandom) probability measure in $\mathbb{R}^k$. Let $T \subset \mathbb{R}^m$ be our parameter set and let there be defined a loss function ℓ on $\mathbb{R}^k \times \mathbb{R}^m$. The aim is to select the parameter $t \in T$ such that the risk

$$r(t) := \int \ell(z, t) \, \mu(dz), \quad t \in T \tag{3}$$

is minimal. Here the measure μ is supposed to be unknown, so we cannot solve the problem directly. Instead we may try to minimize either the empirical risk associated with the original observations

$$r_n(t) := \frac{1}{n} \sum_{i=1}^{n} \ell(Z_i, t) = \int \ell(z, t) \, \mu_n(dz) \tag{4}$$

or the empirical risk associated with the noisy observations

$$r^{\#}_{ns}(t) := \frac{1}{ns} \sum_{i=1}^{n} \sum_{j=1}^{s} \ell(Z^{\#}_{nij}, t) = \int \ell(z, t) \, \mu^{\#}_{ns}(dz). \tag{5}$$

3 Consistency

If $A \subset T$, define the distance of $t \in T$ from A by $d(t, A) := \inf\{\|t-y\| : y \in A\}$, with the convention that $d(t, \emptyset) = \infty$. We write $\operatorname{argmin}_T r$ for the (possibly empty) set of points that minimize r on T. We seek conditions guaranteeing for our estimators θ_n that

$$d(\theta_n, \operatorname*{argmin}_T r) \overset{\text{a.s.}}{\longrightarrow} 0.$$

If this holds, we say that θ_n is strongly consistent for the set $\operatorname{argmin}_T r$.
The following result is proved in [5].

Theorem 1 *Let $s \geq 1$. If $h_n \overset{\text{a.s.}}{\longrightarrow} 0$, and for some probability measure μ, $\mu_n \overset{\text{a.s.}}{\Rightarrow} \mu$, then also $\mu^{\#}_{ns} \overset{\text{a.s.}}{\Rightarrow} \mu$, as $n \to \infty$.*

This motivates the following approach. Let $\{\lambda_n\}$ be a sequence of random probability measures and μ a nonrandom probability measure such that $\lambda_n \overset{\text{a.s.}}{\Rightarrow} \mu$ and let

$$R_n(t) := \int \ell(z, t)\, \lambda_n(dz). \tag{6}$$

Suppose that θ_n is a random vector with values in T such that

$$R_n(\theta_n) = \inf_T R_n + o(1), \quad \text{(a.s.)}. \tag{7}$$

Under certain conditions, θ_n is then strongly consistent for the set $\operatorname{argmin}_T r$, as is formulated in the following theorem. Hence we obtain a consistency theorem for any estimator τ_n coming close enough to minimizing r_n. Provided $h_n \overset{\text{a.s.}}{\longrightarrow} 0$, we also obtain a consistency theorem for any estimator $\tau^{\#}_{ns}$ coming close enough to minimizing $r^{\#}_{ns}$.

Theorem 2 *Let the parameter set T be compact and let $\lambda_n \overset{\text{a.s.}}{\Rightarrow} \mu$. Suppose ℓ is continuous on $\mathbb{R}^k \times T$ and dominated by a continuous, μ-integrable function, i.e.,*

$$|\ell(z, t)| \leq L(z), \quad z \in \mathbb{R}^k, t \in T,$$

where $L \geq 0$ is continuous and $\int L\, d\mu < \infty$. If in addition, $\int L\, d\lambda_n \overset{\text{a.s.}}{\longrightarrow} \int L\, d\mu$, then any random vector satisfying (7) is strongly consistent for the set $\operatorname{argmin}_T r$.

In practice, the most useful dominating functions are the scalar multiples of the powers $|z|^p, p \geq 1$. If $\int |z|^p\, \mu_n(dz) \overset{\text{a.s.}}{\longrightarrow} \int |z|^p\, \mu(dz) < \infty$ and $E|N|^p < \infty$, then it can be shown that also $\int |z|^p\, \mu^{\#}_{ns}(dz) \overset{\text{a.s.}}{\longrightarrow} \int |z|^p\, \mu(dz)$. This facilitates checking the conditions of the previous theorem.

4 Asymptotic Distribution

A consistency result does not tell how quickly the estimator converges. One way to characterize this rate is by giving an asymptotic distribution for the estimator. Our asymptotic distribution results are of the form $\sqrt{n}(\theta_n - t^*) \overset{\text{d}}{\longrightarrow} N(0, C)$, i.e., they state that $\sqrt{n}(\theta_n - t^*)$ converges in distribution to a normal law with mean zero and a covariance matrix C. Here t^* denotes a minimizer of r. Such a result says that the law of θ_n collapses towards a point mass at t^* at a very specific rate, e.g., in the sense that for any $\epsilon > 0$, $n^{1/2-\epsilon}|\theta_n - t^*|$ converges to zero in probability and $n^{1/2+\epsilon}|\theta_n - t^*|$ converges to infinity in probability.
Henceforth we assume that the original observations $Z_1, Z_2, \ldots$ are i.i.d. and that the noise vectors have mean zero. The effect of noisy training in linear regression is

relatively straightforward to analyze. This is the case where z is the pair $(x, y), x \in \mathbb{R}^{k-1}, y \in \mathbb{R}$ and $\ell(z,t) = (x^T t - y)^2$. Denote the minimizer of r_n by τ_n and the minimizer of $r^{\#}_{ns}$ by $\tau^{\#}_{ns}$. If $h_n = o_p(n^{-1/4})$, i.e., if $n^{1/4}h_n$ converges in probability to zero, then it turns out that $\tau^{\#}_{ns}$ and τ_n have the same asymptotic distribution. If h_n converges to zero at some slower rate, then the situation is more complicated; when it can be obtained, the asymptotic distribution of $\tau^{\#}_{ns}$ then typically depends on the sequence $\{h_n\}$.

The same kind of results hold also more generally. Let now $t^* \in T$ satisfy $\nabla r(t^*) = 0$, i.e., t^* is a stationary point of the risk r. We assume that t^* is an isolated stationary point in the interior of T. Further, we assume that ℓ is a C^3-function on $\mathbb{R}^k \times \mathbb{R}^m$, and that Z_1 has a compactly supported law. Then the matrices

$$A := E[\nabla^2_{tt}\, \ell(Z_1, t^*)], \quad B := \mathrm{Cov}[\nabla_t\, \ell(Z_1, t^*)]$$

are well defined. Here ∇_t and ∇^2_{tt} denote the gradient and Hessian operators with respect to t, respectively. We assume that A is invertible and that B is nonzero. Further, we assume that the noise vectors have a compactly supported law and that the smoothing parameters satisfy $0 \le h_n \le M$ for some constant M.

Under these assumptions, let $h_n = o_p(n^{-1/4})$. Let $\{\tau_n\}$ be a sequence of T-valued random vectors such that

$$\tau_n \xrightarrow{\text{P}} t^*, \quad \text{and} \quad \int \nabla_t\, \ell(z, \tau_n)\, \mu_n(dz) = o_p(n^{-1/2}),$$

and let $\{\tau^{\#}_{ns}\}$ be a sequence of T-valued random vectors such that

$$\tau^{\#}_{ns} \xrightarrow{\text{P}} t^*, \quad \text{and} \quad \int \nabla_t\, \ell(z, \tau^{\#}_{ns})\, \mu^{\#}_{ns}(dz) = o_p(n^{-1/2}).$$

Here τ_n and $\tau^{\#}_{ns}$ renders the respective empirical risk stationary in an asymptotic sense. It is shown in [5] that then

$$\sqrt{n}(\tau_n - t^*) \xrightarrow{\text{d}} N(0, A^{-1}BA^{-1}) \quad \text{and} \quad \sqrt{n}(\tau^{\#}_{ns} - t^*) \xrightarrow{\text{d}} N(0, A^{-1}BA^{-1}). \tag{8}$$

That is, the asymptotic distributions of τ_n and $\tau^{\#}_{ns}$ coincide. The asymptotic distribution for τ_n is naturally the same as in [8, Th. 2]; the result for $\tau^{\#}_{ns}$ is new.

This asymptotic distribution can be used, e.g., to construct an asymptotic confidence interval for t^* or for $r(t^*)$, the risk at t^*. Instead of this, we now use this result to characterize the generalization performance of our estimators. Let the sequence $\{\theta_n\}$ stand either for $\{\tau_n\}$ or for $\{\tau^{\#}_{ns}\}$. The generalization performance of θ_n can be characterized by the law of $r(\theta_n)$, the risk evaluated at the estimator. It can be shown that its asymptotic distribution is now given by

$$n[r(\theta_n) - r(t^*)] \xrightarrow{\text{d}} \frac{1}{2} U^T A U, \quad \text{where} \quad U \sim N(0, A^{-1}BA^{-1}). \tag{9}$$

5 Conclusions

We have outlined new results for the convergence properties of minimization estimators in noisy training. The main conditions in the consistency result are that the empirical measures associated with the original sample converge weakly, almost surely, towards some measure μ and that the smoothing parameters $h_n \to 0$, almost surely.

The main conditions for the asymptotic distribution result are the following: the original sample points are i.i.d., the noise vectors have zero mean and $h_n = o_p(n^{-1/4})$.

Under certain additional conditions we then have that the asymptotic distributions of τ_n and $\tau_{ns}^{\#}$ are identical, where τ_n denotes the minimizer of the empirical risk associated with original sample and $\tau_{ns}^{\#}$ the minimizer of the empirical risk associated with the noisy sample. This implies that the asymptotic distributions of $r(\tau_n)$ and $r(\tau_{ns}^{\#})$ coincide and hence additive noise can have only a higher-order effect on the performance of a minimization estimator as the sample size goes to infinity. However, numerical evidence indicates that additive noise sometimes does improve the generalization performance of a minimization estimator, at least with small sample sizes. It remains to be seen whether this effect can be quantified by analyzing the distribution of $r(\tau_{ns}^{\#})$ using more refined asymptotic methods.

REFERENCES

[1] C.M. Bishop, *Training with noise is equivalent to Tikhonov regularization*, Neural Computation, Vol. 7 (1995), pp108–116.

[2] R.M. Dudley, *Real Analysis and Probability*, Wadsworth & Brooks/Cole, Pacific Grove, CA, (1989).

[3] Y. Grandvalet and S. Canu, *Comments on "noise injection into inputs in back propagation learning"*, IEEE Trans. Systems, Man, and Cybernetics, Vol. 25 (1995), pp678–681.

[4] L. Holmström and P. Koistinen, *Using additive noise in back-propagation training*, IEEE Trans. Neural Networks, Vol. 3 (1992), pp24–38.

[5] P. Koistinen, *Convergence of minimization estimators trained under additive noise*, Research reports A 12, Rolf Nevanlinna Institute, Helsinki University of Technology (1995), (Doctoral thesis).

[6] K. Matsuoka, *Noise injection into inputs in back-propagation learning*, IEEE Trans. Systems, Man, and Cybernetics, Vol. 22 (1992), pp436–440.

[7] R. Reed, R.J. Marks II, and S. Oh, *Similarities of error regularization, sigmoid gain scaling, target smoothing, and training with jitter*, IEEE Trans. Neural Networks, Vol. 6 (1995), pp529–538.

[8] H. White, *Learning in artificial neural networks: A statistical perspective*, Neural Computation, Vol. 1 (1989), pp425–464.

NON-LINEAR LEARNING DYNAMICS WITH A DIFFUSING MESSENGER

Bart Krekelberg and John G. Taylor

Centre for Neural Networks, King's College London, London WC2R 2LS, UK. Email: bart@mth.kcl.ac.uk

The diffusing messenger Nitric Oxide plays an important role in the learning processes in the brain. This diffusive learning mechanism adds a non-linear and non-local effect to the standard Hebbian learning rule. A diffusive learning rule can lead to topographic map formation but also has a strong tendency to homogenise the synaptic strengths. We derive a non-linear integral equation that describes the fixed point and show which parameter regimes lead to non-trivial solutions.

Keywords: Nitric Oxide, self-organization, topographic maps

Introduction

Most learning rules used in neurobiological modelling are based on Hebb's postulate that a synaptic connection is strengthened if and only if there is both a post-synaptic and pre-synaptic depolarization at that particular synapse. Recent physiological research, however, shows that this assumption is not always warranted. Experiments in areas varying from rat hippocampus to cats' visual cortex show that there is a non-local effect in learning.

This non-local learning is often thought to be mediated by *retrograde messengers.* Nitric Oxide (NO) is a candidate for such a messenger which is produced post-synaptically (both in the dendrites and the soma [1]), then diffuses through the intracellular space and is taken up pre-synaptically. The chemical properties of NO allow it to diffuse over relatively long distances in the cortex; with a diffusion constant of $3.3 \times 10^{-5} cm^2/s$ and a half-life in the intracellular fluid of $4 \sim 6$ seconds, it has an effective range of at least $150 \mu m$. If NO were an ordinary neurotransmitter it would be hard to understand how the specificity of neuronal connections in the brain on a scale smaller than this could be achieved. An explanation has been found in experimental setups with locally modifiable concentration of NO: physiologists have been able to demonstrate that low levels of NO lead to *depression* of synaptic strengths (LTD) and high levels lead to Long Term Potentiation (LTP) (For recent reviews see [3, 8]). This non-linearity in the dependence of the synaptic change on the NO concentration is crucial to attain specificity in a network with a diffusing messenger.

Detailed simulations of such a a non-linear and non-local learning rule have been performed in [2, 7]. In these simulations pattern formation in the weights was seen to occur but, as the input patterns and the initial (partly topographic) weight distributions were already organized, it is difficult to tell how general these results are. In [5] we analysed networks with a diffusing messenger in a linearised reaction-diffusion framework and found that homogeneous weights were the dominant solutions of the dynamics. Following up a suggestion in [4] that Nitric Oxide could underlie a mechanism similar to the neighbourhood function in the SOFM. we showed in [6] that a diffusing messenger can indeed support the development of topographic maps without the need for a Mexican Hat lateral interaction.

Here we extend our previous analysis to arrive at a fuller account of the non-linear effects. We derive a general fixed point equation for the weights and determine which parameter regimes admit non-zero homogeneous solutions.

1 The Model

We consider a neural field consisting of leaky integrator neurons with activity u, all *sampling* their input with a synaptic density function r from a field of synapses with strengths s. Note that this implies that synapses do not "belong" to a neuron, a neuron just takes its input from the synapses within its reach (determined by the function r). Inputs $a(x, x_0)$ are Gaussian shaped with the maximum at x_0 and spread σ. The inputs are presented with equal probability at each position x_0. Nitric Oxide is produced *in the dendrites* at a rate proportional to the local depolarization, decays at a rate -1 and has diffusion constant κ. Learning is non-linearly dependent on the local NO level through the function f which captures the qualitative effects described above (see also 2). Given an input centred at x_0, the dynamical equations can be written as:

$$\begin{aligned}\dot{u}(x, x_0) &= -u(x) + \int dx' r(x, x') s(x') a(x', x_0),\\ \dot{n}(x, x_0) &= -n(x) + s(x) a(x, x_0) + \kappa \nabla^2 n(x, x_0),\\ \dot{s}(x) &= -s(x) + f[n(x, x_0)] a(x, x_0).\end{aligned}$$

We assume (as in [7]) that *all* learning is dependent on the local NO level and there is no *direct* dependence on the post-synaptic depolarization (see Discussion). The local NO level that determines the change in synaptic strength depends on the details of the post-synaptic production of NO and the pre-synaptic *measurement* process. As the details of this process are as yet unknown, we use a Gaussian Green's function ($G(x, x')$) to model the spatial distribution of NO. This approximation is exact if the NO is produced in a short burst and measured some fixed period of time later. The real process of production and measurement will presumably be more complicated, but we expect that at least the qualitative features are well described by a Gaussian kernel. With these approximations and averaging over all patterns, the fixed point equation for the learning dynamics can be written in the form of the following non-linear Fredholm integral equation.

$$s(x) = \int dx_0\, a(x, x_0) f\left[\int dx'\, G(x, x') s(x') a(x', x_0)\right]. \qquad (1)$$

In section 2 we substitute the simplest non-linear function that still captures the qualitative features observed in experiments:

$$f(n) = -n(n - D)(n - P) \qquad (2)$$

with D and P two parameters that can be determined directly from experiments. The unphysical values of f for negative NO concentration merely stabilise the trivial fixed point, and the decrease of f after its positive maximum can either be interpreted as toxicity of a high concentration of NO or an easy way of modelling a saturation of the NO production. The important features of the function are the negative values for small NO concentration (LTD) and positive values (LTP) for high NO concentration.

2 Analysis

In appendix 4 we use the assumptions about the non-linearity, the spread of NO (ρ) and the width (σ) of the Gaussian inputs in equation 1 to derive the following expression in Fourier space for the fixed point of the dynamics.

$$\begin{aligned} s(k) &= -DPN_1 s(k)\mathrm{e}^{-\beta_1 k^2} \\ &+ (D+P)N_2 \int dk'\, s(k')s(k'-k)\mathrm{e}^{-(k'^2-k'k)/2(\rho+\sigma)}\mathrm{e}^{-k^2\beta_2} \\ &- N_3 \iint dk'dk''\, s(k')s(k'')s(k'+k''-k)\mathrm{e}^{-\frac{(k'^2-(k'-k'')k+k''^2)}{2(\rho+\sigma)}}\mathrm{e}^{-\beta_3 k^2} \end{aligned} \tag{3}$$

where the parameters are defined by:

$$\begin{aligned} N_n &= \left(\frac{a_0^{n+1}\pi^{(n+1)/2}}{\sqrt{(\rho+\sigma)^{(n-1)}(\sigma^2+(n+1)\rho\sigma)}}\right) \\ \beta_n &= \frac{1}{4}\left(\frac{1}{\rho+\sigma}+\frac{\sigma^2}{(\rho+\sigma)^n(\rho^2+(n+1)\rho\sigma)}\right) \end{aligned}$$

To derive the conditions under which the dynamics admit homogeneous solutions for the weights, we substitute the solution $s(k) = s_h\delta(k)$ in equation 3 and derive the following third order polynomial in s_h:

$$s_h = -DPN_1 s_h + (D+P)N_2 s_h^2 - N_3 s_h^3. \tag{4}$$

Clearly, the zero-weight solution is a fixed point, and non-trivial homogeneous solutions can be determined by finding the two remaining roots of this equation. Non-trivial homogeneous solutions exist if s_h has at least one positive real solution. This is the case if the width σ of the stimuli satisfies the following constraint:

$$\frac{\rho}{\sigma(\sigma+3\rho)^2} \leq 1 - \frac{4DP}{(D+P)^2}, \tag{5}$$

and in the limiting case, the homogeneous solution is given by

$$s_h = \frac{D+P}{\sqrt{4\pi}a_0}\sqrt{(\rho+\sigma)\left(\frac{\sigma^2+4\rho\sigma}{\sigma^2+3\rho\sigma}\right)}$$

For widths larger than this limiting case there will be *two* fixed points of which only the largest is a stable solution. This is evident from figure 1 in which we solve equation 4 pictorially.

Even though the couplings between the different Fourier components of the weights in equation 3 are limited, a general *periodic* solution is not easily found. From substituting $s(k) = \delta(k) - \delta(k-k^*)$ in the equation it can be seen that in this case there is a coupling with only one higher harmonic $s(k) = \delta(k-2k^*)$. This suggests that a (numerical) iterative procedure to solve the integal equation could be fruitful. We will attempt such a solution in future work.

3 Discussion

We have shown that the weight dynamics of a neural field with a diffusing messenger can be described by a non-linear Fredholm integral equation and that non-zero honogeneous solutions for the weights are stable for stimuli wider than a critical width. We expect that in real tissue some mechanism would be needed to prevent this tendency to homogenise the weights: either the production of NO or its diffusion through the tissue has to be controlled. We expect such a mechanism to be found when the chemical process by which NO is synthesized is more fully understood.

The current model assumes that *all* learning is NO dependent and ignores any influence of the activity of the post-synaptic neurons. In reality, the NO effects we

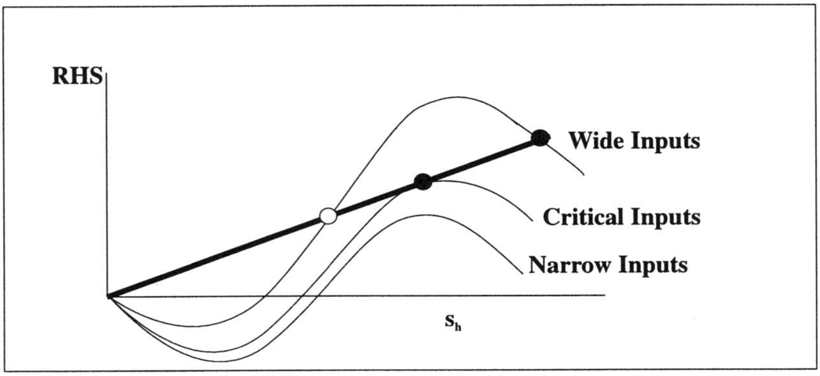

Figure 1 Solving for the homogeneous solutions of equation 3. **RHS** indicates the Right Hand Side of this equation and the solid line is the Left Hand Side. The closed bullets show stable fixed points whereas the open bullets are unstable fixed points. The critical size of the inputs is given by equation 5.

model and the more standard Hebbian learning rules could operate concurrently. In that case the interaction between the two learning rules needs to be investigated. Furthermore, we assumed that all NO is produced in the dendrites. There is evidence, however, that the production can take place in the soma and even the axons [1]. Our previous analyses [5, 6] considered production of NO in the soma, and showed different behaviour than that described here. A full model would include all the sources of NO and the interaction between them.
Lastly, we have modelled all time-dependent effects of the diffusion with the single parameter ρ. Interesting dynamics could result from including the time dependence explicitly, especially if the inputs are temporally correlated. We will address this issue in future work.

4 Appendix

Starting from equation 1 we substitute the Gaussian Green's function with spread ρ and the inputs to derive the fixed point equation. First we derive the NO concentration at position x when a stimulus is presented at x_0. The weights are written as an integral of Fourier components $s(k)$:

$$n(x, x_0) = \int dk' s(k') \int dx' \, e^{ik'x'} a_0 e^{-\sigma(x'-x_0)^2} e^{-\rho(x-x')^2}.$$

This Fourier integral over a shifted gaussian can be evaluated explicitly:

$$n(x, x_0) = a_0 \sqrt{\frac{\pi}{\rho+\sigma}} \int dk' s(k') e^{-\frac{k'^2}{4(\rho+\sigma)}} e^{-ik'(\frac{\rho}{\rho+\sigma})x} e^{-ik'(\frac{\rho}{\rho+\sigma})x_0} e^{-(\frac{\sigma\rho}{\sigma+\rho})(x-x_0)^2}.$$

For the averaged weights' fixed point equation we have to average over all the patterns:

$$s(x) = \int dx_0 \, a_0 e^{-\sigma(x-x_0)^2} f\left[n(x, x_0)\right].$$

For each of the terms in f, the integral over the distribution of patterns has to be done seperately. Here we do the linear case; the quadratic and cubic terms follow by analogy but will include interactions betweeen the different fourier components. Substituting the non-linearity f from equation 2, the integral over the pattern positions x_0 in the linear term ($s^{(1)}$) is another Fourier integral and gives:

$$\begin{aligned} s^{(1)}(x) &= -a_0^2 DP \sqrt{\frac{\pi}{\rho+\sigma}} \sqrt{\frac{\pi}{\sigma + \frac{\rho\sigma}{\rho+\sigma}}} \\ &* \int dk'\, s(k')\mathrm{e}^{-ik'x}\mathrm{e}^{-k'^2/4(\rho+\sigma)}\mathrm{e}^{-\sigma^2 x'^2/((\rho+\sigma)(\sigma^2+2\rho\sigma))}. \end{aligned}$$

In Fourier space this integral equation can be written as:

$$s^{(1)}(k) = -DPN_1 s^{(1)}(k)\mathrm{e}^{-\beta_1 k^2}.$$

The quadratic and cubic terms can be determined analogously which results in equation 3.

REFERENCES

[1] C. Aoki, S. Fenstemaker, M. Lubin, C.-G. Go, *Nitric oxide synthase in the visual cortex of monocular monkeys as revealed by light and electron microscopic immunocytochemistry*, Brain Research, Vol. 620 (1993), pp97–113.

[2] Joseph A. Gally, P. Read Montague, George N., Reeke Jr., Gerald M. Edelman, *The NO hypothesis: Possible effects of a short-lived, rapidly diffusing signal in the development and function of the nervous system*, Proceedings of the National Academy of Sciences, USA (1990), pp3547–3551.

[3] J. Garthwaite, C.L. Boulton, *Nitric oxide signalling in the central nervous system*, Annual Review of Physiology, Vol. 57 (1995), pp683–706.

[4] Teuvo Kohonen, *Physiological interpretation of the self-organizing map*, Neural Networks, Vol. 6 (1993), pp895–905.

[5] Bart Krekelberg, John G. Taylor, *Modelling a diffusing messenger*, in: Proceedings of the WCNN, Washington DC., Vol. I (July 1995), pp557–560, New Jersey, Lawrence Erlbaum Associates, Inc.

[6] Bart Krekelberg, John G. Taylor, *Nitric oxide: A diffusing messenger in a topographic map*, in: Proceedings of ICANN (October 1995), pp525–530.

[7] P. Read Montague, Joseph A. Gally, Gerald M. Edelman, *Spatial signalling in the development of neural connections*, Cerebral Cortex, Vol. 1 (1991), pp199–220.

[8] Erin M. Schuman, Daniel V. Madison, *Nitric oxide and synaptic function*, Annual Review of Neuroscience., Vol. 17 (1994), pp153–183.

Acknowledgements

B. Krekelberg was supported by a grant from the European Human Capital and Mobility Programme.

A VARIATIONAL APPROACH TO ASSOCIATIVE MEMORY

Abderrahim Labbi

Dept. of Computer Science, University of Geneva, 24 Rue General Dufour, 1121 Geneva 4, Switzerland. Email: labbi@cui.unige.ch

The purpose of this paper is to show how fundamental results from variational approximation theory can be exploited to design recurrent associative memory networks. We begin by stating the problem of learning a set of given patterns with an associative memory network as a hypersurface construction problem, then we show that the associated approximation problem is well-posed. Characterizing and determining such a solution will lead us to introduce the desired associative memory network which can be viewed as a recurrent radial basis function (RBF) network which has as many attractor states as there are fundamental patterns (no spurious memories).

Subject classification: AMS(MOS) 65F10, 65B05.
Keywords: Associative Memory, Variational Approximation, RBF Networks.

1 Introduction

Learning from a set of input-output patterns, and sometimes from additional *a priori* knowledge, in neural networks usually amounts to determining a set of parameters relative to a given network. In the case of feedforward networks, the problem may be equivalent to determining a continuous mapping. Such a problem can be stated in the framework of multivariate approximation theory which, in some cases, is closely linked to regularization [11]. Concerning learning in recurrent associative memory networks, one usually has to determine a set of parameters connected with the dynamics of a given network so that the patterns (memories) to be stored are stable states of such a network [1, 3, 7]. Complete characterization of the network dynamics may be achieved by defining a global Lyapunov function (energy) which decreases during the network evolution (the recalling process) and whose local minima are the network's stable states [3, 6, 7].

The procedure followed here for the design of an associative memory network is the reverse of the general approach: using methods from variational approximation, we determine a function (or a hypersurface) which has as many local maxima as the number of patterns to be memorized, and then define a dynamics on such a hypersurface (actually, the gradient dynamics) which has its stable states *close* to the patterns to be memorized.

We begin by proving that the problem is well posed from the approximation point of view, and that the desired function can be explicitly computed when choosing convenient constraints and parameters in the variational formulation of the problem. We finally show that the derived gradient dynamics can be implemented by an associative memory network. Such a network can be viewed as a recurrent radial basis function network which has as many stable states as there are fundamental patterns to be stored. We also discuss how basins of attraction can be shaped so that no spurious stable states can be encountered during the recalling process.

2 Statement of the Problem

Let us consider a set of patterns, $\mathcal{A} = \{S_1, S_2, ..., S_m\} \subset \Omega \subset \mathrm{IR}^n$. The first stage of the proposed approach is to construct a hypersurface defined by a bounded smooth function, $F : \mathrm{IR}^n \rightarrow \mathrm{IR}$ whose unique local maxima are *close* to the patterns $S_i, i = 1, ..., m$. Therefore, we will reduce the problem to a functionnal minimization

under constraints which aim to translate the following assumptions: i) F should interpolate the data $(S_i, y_i), i = 1, ..., m$, where $y_i = F(S_i)$ are large positive real values, and F should tend to zero outside of the data. This constraint is reduced here to the minimization of the L_2 norm of F. ii) F should not oscillate between the data. This constraint is reduced to *surface tension* minimization, which usually amounts to minimize the L_2 norm of the gradient of F. iii) F should be smooth *enough*. This constraint is usually imposed by minimizing the L_2 norm of smoothing differential operators (D^p) to be introduced in the following.
Let us define $C_Y = \{f \in \mathbb{R}^n \mapsto \mathbb{R}, f \in \mathcal{C}(\mathbb{R}^n), r > 0, \text{and } f(S_i) = y_i\}$. Determining an approximation of F regarding the given three constraints can be reduced to the minimization of a cost functional J over C_Y,

$$J(f) = \lambda_0 \|D^0 f\|^2 + \lambda_1 \|D^1 f\|^2 + ... + \lambda_p \|D^p f\|^2 \qquad f \in C_Y \qquad (1)$$

The operators D^k are defined by: $D^k f(X) = \sum_{i_1+...+i_n=k} \frac{\partial^k}{\partial x_1^{i_1} ... \partial x_n^{i_n}} f(X), k \geq 0$.
To solve the minimization problem, we can either use standard methods from the calculus of variations by means of the Euler-Lagrange equation [4, 11], or use direct methods based on functional analysis. Herein, we use the latter method which is closely related to the reproducing kernels method [5, 15].
First, let us consider the Hilbert space, $H^p(\mathbb{R}^n) = \{f \in L_2(\mathbb{R}^n); \sum_{k=0}^{p} \|D^k f\|^2 < \infty\}$endowed with the inner product, $< f, g >_{H^p} = \sum_{k=0}^{p} < f, g >_k$, where $< f, g >_k = < D^k f, D^k g >$. When p and n satisfy the condition, $p > \frac{n}{2} + r, r \geq 0$,then $H^p(\mathbb{R}^n)$ is a subset of $C^r(\mathbb{R}^n)$ [12]. We assume this condition is satisfied in the following.
To show that the problem is well-posed (i.e. it has a unique solution in C_Y), we consider the following vector space, $H^p_\Lambda(\mathbb{R}^n) = \{f \in L_2(R^n), \sum_{k=0}^{p} \lambda_k \|D^k f\|^2 < \infty, \text{and } \lambda_k > 0\}$. It can easily be shown [8, 12] that $H^p_\Lambda(\mathbb{R}^n)$ endowed with the inner product, $< f, g >_{H^p_\Lambda} = \sum_{k=0}^{p} \lambda_k < f, g >_k$, is a Hilbert space whose norm is, $\|f\|_{H^p_\Lambda} = (< f, f >_{H^p_\Lambda})^{\frac{1}{2}}$. Moreover, H^p and H^p_Λ are topologically equivalent since their norms are equivalent.
Now, observe that the norm of $H^p_\Lambda(\mathbb{R}^n)$ is identical to the functional J to be minimized, so the minimization problem can be rewritten as,

$$(\mathcal{P}) \quad Minimize \;\; J(f) = \| f \|^2_{H^p_\Lambda}, f \in \mathcal{C}_Y$$

($\mathcal{P}$) is then reduced to a special class of approximation problems in normed linear spaces [14, 9]. We will use convenient methods of such theory to prove the existence and give a characterization of a solution to the problem.

Theorem 1 *Given strictly positive real parameters, $\lambda_k, k = 1, ..., p$, the problem ($\mathcal{P}$) has a unique solution $F \in H^p_\Lambda(\mathbb{R}^n)$, which is characterized by, $< F, u >_{H^p_\Lambda} = \sum_{i=1}^{m} \beta_i . < \delta_i, u >$, $\forall u \in H^p_\Lambda$, where β_i are real parameters and $< \delta_i, . >$ are Dirac operators supported by $S_i, i = 1, ..., m$.*

Proof The proof[1] is based on the projection theorem for the existence and the charactrization of the best approximation in a linear manifold of a Hilbert space [8, 9, 14]. In order to use such results, we first show that $\mathcal{C}_Y$ is a linear manifold of H^p_Λ. This is achieved by considering the set $\mathcal{C}_0$ defined as,

[1]the details of the proof can be found in [8]

$\mathcal{C}_0 = \{v \in H^p_\Lambda, < \delta_i, v > = v(S_i) = 0, \ i = 1, ..., m\}$, which is a vector subspace of H^p_Λ, and observing that $\mathcal{C}_Y$ is a translation of $\mathcal{C}_0$. Therefore, the projection theorem asserts that there is a unique function $F \in \mathcal{C}_Y$ which solves $(\mathcal{P})$, and since $\mathcal{C}_Y$ is linear manifold associated to $\mathcal{C}_0$, F can be characterized by the relation, $< F, u >_{H^p_\Lambda} = \sum_{i=1}^m \beta_i . < \delta_i, u >, \quad \forall u \in H^p_\Lambda$ where β_i are real parameters. □
The previous theorem provides only a characterization of the solution, but we are interested in determining explicitly such a solution. Therefore, we consider the differential operator P defined as a combination of iterated Laplacians, $Pf = \lambda_0 f - \lambda_1 \Delta f + ... + (-1)^p \lambda_p \Delta^{2p} f, \quad \forall f \in H^p_\Lambda(\mathrm{I\!R}^n)$, which leads us to the following theorem.

Theorem 2 *Consider the functions (kernels)* $G(., S_1), G(., S_2), ..., G(., S_m)$ *as respective solutions of the partial differential equations (in the distributions sense),* $PG(X, S_i) = \delta(X - S_i), i = 1, ..., m, \forall X \in \mathrm{I\!R}^n$. *Then, there exist unique parameters* $\beta_1, \beta_2, ..., \beta_m$ *such that the solution* F *of the problem* $(\mathcal{P})$ *is,* $F(X) = \sum_{i=1}^m \beta_i . G(X, S_i)$, *where* $(\beta_1, ..., \beta_m)$ *is the solution of the linear system,* $F(S_j) = \sum_{i=1}^m \beta_i . G(S_j, S_i) = y_j, \ j = 1, ..., m.$

Proof First, let us show that any function $f(X) = \sum_{i=1}^m \beta_i . G(X, S_i)$, with arbitrary β_i's, satisfies the characterization of theorem (1). If we consider any pair of functions ϕ and ψ in H^p_Λ, an integration by parts in the sense of distributions gives [13], $< \phi, \psi >_k = (-1)^k < \Delta^{2k} \phi, \psi >$. This relation allows us to write, for any $u \in H^p_\Lambda$,

$$\begin{aligned} < F, u >_{H^p_\Lambda} &= \sum_{i=1}^m \beta_i < G(X, S_i), u >_{H^p_\Lambda} = \sum_{i=1}^m \beta_i < \sum_{k=0}^p (-1)^k \lambda_k \Delta^{2k} G(X, S_i), u > \\ &= \sum_{i=1}^m \beta_i < \delta_i, u > \end{aligned}$$

So the function F given in the theorem satisfies the characterization stated in theorem (1). Finally, to show that F is the solution of the problem $(\mathcal{P})$, we have to show that $F \in \mathcal{C}_Y$, which amounts to show that there is a unique solution (in β_i's) to the following linear system, $F(S_i) = \sum_{j=1}^m \beta_i G(S_j, S_i) = y_i, i = 1, ..., m$. Since P is a linear combination of iterated Laplacians, it is rotation and translation invariant [5, 13], and the kernels $G(., S_i)$ are radial, centered respectively on S_i, and can be written as, $G(X, S_i) = G(\|X - X_i\|)$.
To show that the linear system has a unique solution, it suffices to show that the function $G(t)$ is positive definite [10]. Since G verifies the equations,

$$\lambda_0 G(\|X - S_i\|) - \lambda_1 \Delta G(\|X - S_i\|) + ... + (-1)^p \lambda_p \Delta^p G(\|X - S_i\|) = \delta(\|X - S_i\|)$$

it can be shown that $G(t)$ can be written as [11], $G(t) = \int_{\mathrm{I\!R}} \frac{\exp(it\omega)}{\lambda_0 + \lambda_1 \omega^2 + ... + \lambda_p \omega^{2p}} d\omega = \int_{\mathrm{I\!R}} \exp(it\omega) dV(\omega)$, where V is a bounded nondecreasing function. G is then written in the form required by the Bochner theorem [2] which characterizes positive definite functions. Therefore, $F(X) = \sum_{i=1}^m \beta_i . G(X, S_i)$ is the solution of $(\mathcal{P})$. □
Poggio & Girosi [11] considered a similar variational problem for learning continuous mappings under *a priori* assumptions. They derived similar kernels $G(t)$ using the Euler-Lagrange equation. Setting λ_k to some particular values gives some illustrations of the solution F in figure 1. If we let p tend to infinity in the problem $(\mathcal{P})$ as in [11] (considering only functions with infinite smoothness degree), and

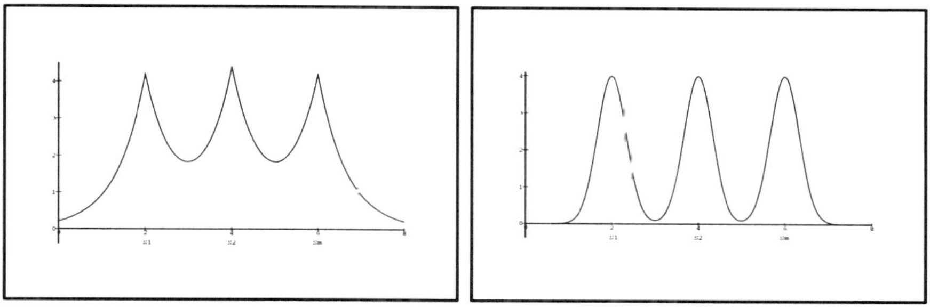

Figure 1 The solution F: (*left*) for $\lambda_0 = \sigma > 0, \lambda_1 = 1$, and $\lambda_k = 0$, $k \geq 2$, we have $G_1(t) = \frac{1}{2\sigma}.\exp(-\sigma.|t|)$ which is not differentiable at the origin; (*right*) for $\lambda_0 = \sigma^4, \lambda_1 = 2\sigma^2, \lambda_2 = 1$, and $\lambda_k = 0$, $k \geq 3$, we have $G_2(t) = G_1(t) * G_1(t)$ (the convolution product) which is differentiable.

choose $\lambda_k = \frac{1}{k!2^k\sigma^{2k}}$, then following the same reasoning as the previous sections, we obtain, $G(\omega) = \exp(-\frac{\omega^2}{2\sigma^2})$, and hence F is a linear combination of Gaussians centered on S_i's with positive coefficients β_i since, in the linear system, $Y = G.\mathcal{B}$ where $(\mathcal{B})_i = \beta_i, (G)_{ij} = \exp(-\frac{\|S_i - S_j\|^2}{2\sigma^2})$, and $(Y)_i = y_i >> 0$, if we take a small σ, and decompose the matrix G as $G = I + \mathcal{G}$, where I is the identity matrix, and $(\mathcal{G})_{ij} = \exp(-\frac{\|S_i - S_j\|^2}{2\sigma^2})$ for $i \neq j$, we can make the approximation, $G^{-1} = I - \mathcal{G}$. Therefore, we get, $\mathcal{B} = G^{-1}.Y \simeq (I - \mathcal{G}).Y$. Since the elements of $\mathcal{G}$ can be reduced as desired by choosing a small σ, we get positive $\beta_i's$, and so the computed function preserves the *a priori* constraints imposed on the desired function (see figure 1).

3 Building an Associative Memory Network

Let us consider the solution $F(X) = \sum_{j=1}^{m} \beta_j \exp(-\frac{\|X - S_j\|^2}{2\sigma^2})$ obtained by setting $\lambda_k = \frac{1}{k!2^k\sigma^{2k}}$. The last stage of our approach is to build an associative memory network whose unique attractor states are *close* to the patterns S_i. If we consider the gradient dynamics applied to F, then from any initial state X_0, we stabilize on a local maximum of F which is *close* to a pattern S_i. The closeness of the actual maxima of F to the patterns S_i depends on the size of σ. For a large σ, the deviation is more important because of the overlap between Gaussians, while it is less important for a small σ. This is a natural consequence, since large *penalty* parameters λ_k would result from a small σ, and hence the constraints would be better preserved. A discretization of the gradient dynamics applied to F gives,

$x_i(t+1) = x_i(t) + \alpha.\sum_{j=1}^{m}(x_i - S_j^i)\frac{\beta_j}{\sigma^2}\exp(-\frac{\|X - S_i\|^2}{2\sigma^2}),\ i = 1, ..., n$

This dynamics can be implemented by a two-layer recurrent RBF network (see figure 2). The first layer consists of n units encoding the input/output pattern, and the second -hidden- layer consists of m units computing radial functions centered on the patterns S_j, $G_j(X) = \frac{\beta_j}{\sigma^2}\exp(-\frac{\|X - S_j\|^2}{2\sigma^2})$. The connection weight between an input/output unit i and a hidden unit j is S_i^j (j^{th} component of S_i). The network has been used as a part of a system for handwritten character recognition and reconstruction [8].

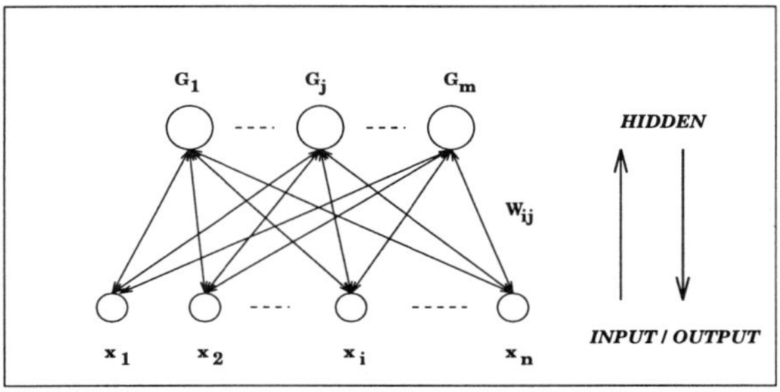

Figure 2 The associative memory network architecture.

REFERENCES

[1] Amari S., *Statistical Neurodynamics of Associative Memory* Neural Net, Vol. 1 (1988).

[2] Bochner S., *Lectures on Fourier Integrals*, Annals of Mathematical Studies, No. 42 (1959), Princeton Univ. Press.

[3] Cohen M.A., Grossberg S., *Absolute Stability of Global Pattern Formation and Parallel Memory Storage by Competitive Neural Networks*, IEEE Trans. on SMC, Vol. SMC-13 (1983).

[4] Courant R., Hilbert D., *Methods of Mathematical Physics*, Interscience, London (1962).

[5] Duchon J., *Spline Minimizing Rotation-Invariant Semi-norms in Sobolev Spaces*, Constructive Theory of Several Variables, in W. Schempp & K. Zeeller (Eds), Lecture Notes in Mathematics, No. 571 (1977), Springer-Verlag, Berlin.

[6] Goles E. *Lyapunov Functions Associated to Automata Networks*, in: Automata Networks in Computer Science, F. Fogelman et al. (eds), Manchester Univ. Press (1987).

[7] Hopfield J.J., *Neural Networks and Physical Systems with Emergent Collective Computational Abilities*, Proc. of the Nat. Acad. of Science, USA, Vol. 79 (1982).

[8] Labbi A., *On Approximation Theory and Dynamical Systems in Neural Networks*, Ph.D. Dissertation in Applied Mathematics, INPG, Grenoble (1993).

[9] Laurent P.J. *Approximation et Optimisation*, Hermann, Paris (1973).

[10] Micchelli C.A. *Interpolation of Scattered Data: Distance Matrices and Condionally Definite Functions*, Constr. Approx., Vol. 2 (1986).

[11] Poggio T., Girosi F. *Networks for Approximation and Learning*, Proc. IEEE, Vol. 78 (1990).

[12] Rudin W. *Functional Analysis.* McGraw-Hill, New York, St Louis, San Fransisco (1991).

[13] Schwartz L. *Théorie des Distributions.* Hermann, Paris (1966).

[14] Singer I. *Best Approximation in Normed Linear Spaces by Elements of Linear Subspaces.* Springer-Verlag, New York, Heidelberg, Berlin (1970).

[15] Wahba G. *Splines Models for Observational Data. Series in Applied Mathematics*, Vol. 59 (1990), SIAM, Philadelphia.

TRANSFORMATION OF NONLINEAR PROGRAMMING PROBLEMS INTO SEPARABLE ONES USING MULTILAYER NEURAL NETWORKS

Bao-Liang Lu and Koji Ito*

The Institute of Physical and Chemical Research (RIKEN), 3-8-31 Rokuban, Atsuta-ku, Nagoya 456, Japan. Email: lbl@nagoya.bmc.riken.go.jp

** Interdisciplinary Graduate School of Science and Engineering, Tokyo Institute of Technology, 4259, Nagatsuda, Midori-ku, Yokohama 226, Japan. Email: ito@ssie.titech.ac.jp*

In this paper we present a novel method for transforming nonseparable nonlinear programming (NLP) problems into separable ones using multilayer neural networks. This method is based on a useful feature of multilayer neural networks, i.e., any nonseparable function can be approximately expressed as a separable one by a multilayer neural network. By use of this method, the nonseparable objective and (or) constraint functions in NLP problems can be approximated by multilayer neural networks, and therefore, any nonseparable NLP problem can be transformed into a separable one. The importance of this method lies in the fact that it provides us with a promising approach to using modified simplex methods to solve general NLP problems.

Keywords: separable nonlinear programming, linear programming, multilayer neural network.

1 Introduction

Consider the following NLP problem:

$$\begin{array}{lll} \text{Minimize} & p(\boldsymbol{x}) & \text{for } \boldsymbol{x} \in \mathbb{R}^n \\ \text{subject to} & g_i(\boldsymbol{x}) \geq 0 & \text{for } i = 1, 2, \cdots, m, \\ & h_j(\boldsymbol{x}) = 0 & \text{for } j = 1, 2, \cdots, r. \end{array} \tag{1}$$

where $p(\boldsymbol{x})$ is called the objective function, $g_i(\boldsymbol{x})$ is called an inequality constraint and $h_j(\boldsymbol{x})$ is called an equality constraint.

NLP problems are widespread in the mathematical modeling of engineering design problems such as VLSI chip design, mechanical design, and chemical design. Unfortunately, for the general NLP problems, computer programs are not available for problems of very large size. For a class of NLP problems known as separable [4, 1], some variation of the simplex method, a well-developed and efficient method for solving linear programming (LP) problems, can be used as a solution procedure. Separable nonlinear programming (SNLP) problem refers to a NLP problem where the objective function and the constraint functions can be expressed as the sum of functions of a single variable. A SNLP problem can be expressed as follows:

$$\begin{array}{lll} \text{Minimize} & \displaystyle\sum_{k=1}^{n} p_k(x_k) & \\ \text{subject to} & \displaystyle\sum_{k=1}^{n} g_{ik}(x_k) \geq 0 & \text{for } i = 1, 2, \cdots, m, \\ & \displaystyle\sum_{k=1}^{n} h_{jk}(x_k) = 0 & \text{for } j = 1, 2, \cdots, r. \end{array} \tag{2}$$

An important problem in mathematical programming is to generalize the simplex method to solve NLP problems. In this paper we discuss how to use multilayer neural networks to transform nonseparable NLP problems into SNLP problems.

2 Transformation of Nonseparable Functions

Let $q(\boldsymbol{x})$ be a multivariable function. Given a set of training data sampled over $q(\boldsymbol{x})$, we can train a three-layer network[1] to approximate $q(\boldsymbol{x})$ [2]. After training the mapping $\hat{q}(\boldsymbol{x})$ formed by the network can be regarded as an approximation of $q(\boldsymbol{x})$ and expressed as follows:

$$\hat{q}(\boldsymbol{x}) = \alpha + \beta(f\left(\sum_{j=1}^{N_2} w_{31j} f\left(\sum_{i=1}^{N_1} w_{2ji}x_i + bias_{2j}\right) + bias_{31}\right) - \gamma), \tag{3}$$

where x_j is the input of the jth unit in the input layer, w_{kji} is the weight connecting the ith unit in the layer $(k-1)$ to the jth unit in the layer k, $bias_{kj}$ is the bias of the jth unit in the layer k, f is the sigmoidal activation function, N_k is the number of units in the layer k, α, β, and γ are three constants which are determined by the formula used for normalizing training data.

Introducing auxiliary variables b_{31}, b_{21}, b_{22}, $\cdots$, and b_{2N_2} into Eq. (3), we can obtain the following simultaneous equation

$$\begin{cases} \hat{q}(b_{31}) = \alpha + \beta(f(b_{31}) - \gamma) \\ b_{31} - \sum_{j=1}^{N_2} w_{31j} f(b_{2j}) = bias_{31} \\ b_{21} - \sum_{i=1}^{N_1} w_{21i}x_i = bias_{21} \\ \vdots \\ b_{2N_2} - \sum_{i=1}^{N_1} w_{2N_2i}x_i = bias_{2N_2}, \end{cases} \tag{4}$$

where b_{kj} for $k = 2, 3$, $j = 1, 2, \cdots, N_K$, and x_i for $i = 1, 2, \cdots, N_1$, are variables. We see that all of the functions in Eq. (4) are separable. The importance of Eq. (4) lies in the fact that it provides us with an approach to approximately expressing nonseparable functions as separable ones by multilayer neural networks.

In comparison with conventional function approximation problems the training task mentioned above is easier to be dealt with. The reasons for this are that (a) an arbitrary large number of sample data for training and test can be obtained from $q(\boldsymbol{x})$, and (b) the goal of training is to approximate a given function $q(\boldsymbol{x})$, so the performance of the trained network can be easily checked.

3 Transformation of Nonseparable NLP problems

According to the locations of nonseparable functions in NLP problems, nonseparable NLP problems can be classified into three types: (I) only the objective function is nonseparable function; (II) only the constraint functions are nonseparable

[1] For simplicity of description, we consider only three-layer networks throughout the paper. The results can be extended to M-layer ($M > 3$) networks easily.

functions; and (III) both the objective and constraint functions are nonseparable functions.

For Type I nonseparable NLP problems, we only need to transform the objective function into separable one. Replacing the objective function with its approximation in Eq. (4), we can transform a Type I nonseparable NLP problem into a SNLP problem as follows:

$$
\begin{array}{ll}
\text{Minimize} & \alpha + \beta(f(b_{31}^O) - \gamma) \\
\text{subject to} & b_{31}^C - \sum_{j=1}^{N_2^O} w_{31j}^O f(b_{2j}^O) = bias_{31}^O \\
& b_{21}^C - \sum_{i=1}^{N_1} w_{21i}^O x_i = bias_{21}^O \\
& \vdots \\
& b_{2N_2^O}^C - \sum_{i=1}^{N_1} w_{2N_2^O i} x_i = bias_{2N_2^O}^O \\
& \sum_{k=1}^{n} g_{ik}(x_k) \geq 0 \quad \text{for } i = 1, \cdots, m, \\
& \sum_{k=1}^{n} h_{jk}(x_k) = 0 \quad \text{for } j = 1, \cdots, r,
\end{array}
\tag{5}
$$

where the "O" superscript refers to quantities on the *objective function*.

Using the similar approach mentioned above, we can transform the Type II and III nonseparable NLP problems into SNLP problems, and deal with unconstrained nonlinear programming problems.

Suppose that the accuracy of approximating nonseparable functions is good enough for a given problem. The transformed SNLP problems are equivalent to their original nonseparable NLP problems, since the transformations only change the expression forms of the objective function and (or) the constraint functions. The accuracy of approximation may be effected by many factors such as the network size, the learning algorithms and the number of training data. There are several methods for dealing with this problem, for example see [3, 8, 7]. We can use these results to guide our training and get a good accuracy.

4 Analysis of Complexity

Now let us analyze complexity of the original and transformed problems. Suppose that each nonseparable function is approximated by the network with same number of hidden units (N). Also suppose that there are s ($s \leq m$) nonseparable inequality and t ($t \leq r$) nonseparable equality constraint functions in Type II and III problems. The numbers of variables and constraints in original and transforming problems are shown in Table 1.

From Table 1 we see that as the number of hidden units grows both the number of variables and the number of constraints in the transformed problems increase. Therefore, it is desirable that each nonseparable function is approximated by a network with as few number of hidden units as possible. But on the other hand

Problem	No. of variables	No. of constraints
Original	n	$m+r$
I	$n+N+1$	$m+r+N+1$
II	$n+sN+tN+(s+t)$	$(m-s)+(r-t)$ $+sN+tN+s+t$
III	$n+N+sN+tN+(1+s+t)$	$(m-s)+(r-t)+N$ $+sN+tN+(1+s+t)$

Table 1 The numbers of variables and constraints in the original and transformed problems.

it may become more difficult for a smaller network (e.g., fewer number of hidden units) to approximate a nonseparable function. There exists a trade-off between the complexity of the transformed SNLP problems and the approximating capability of neural networks.

5 Simulation Results

Consider the following simple NLP problem:

$$\begin{aligned} \text{Minimize} \quad & 2-\sin^2 x_1 \sin^2 x_2 \\ \text{subject to} \quad & 0.5 \le x_1 \le 2.5 \\ & 0.5 \le x_2 \le 2.5 \end{aligned} \tag{6}$$

Clearly, this is a Type I nonseparable NLP problem. A three-layer perceptron with two input, ten hidden, and one output units is used to approximate the objective function. The training data set consists of 524 input-output data which are gathered by sampling the input space $[0.5, 2.5] \times [0.5, 2.5]$ in a uniform grid. The network is trained by the back-propagation algorithm [6]. In this simulation, the learning is considered complete when the sum of squared error between the target and actual outputs gets less than 0.05. Replacing the objective function with its approximation formed by the network, we obtain a SNLP problem.

Approximating the sigmoidal activation function in the SNLP problem over the interval $[-16, 16]$ via 14 grid points, we obtain an approximate SNLP problem. Solving this problem with the simplex method with the *restricted basis entry rule* [4], we obtain the solution: $x_1^* = 1.531488$ and $x_2^* = 1.595567$. If the sigmoidal activation function is approximated over the interval $[-16, 16]$ via 40 grid points, we can obtain a better solution: $x_1^* = 1.564015$ and $x_2^* = 1.569683$. Solving this problem directly with the Powell method [5], we obtain a more accurate solution: $x_1^* = 1.57079$ and $x_2^* = 1.57079$. It should be noted that there exits a trade-off between the accuracy of the approximation of SNLP problems and the number of grid points for each variable.

In general, several local solutions may exist in a SNLP problem. But only one solution can be obtained by solving the approximate SNLP problem using the simplex method with the restricted basis entry rule. It has been shown that if the objective function is strictly convex and all the constraint functions are convex, the solution obtained by the modified simplex method is sufficiently close to the global optimal solution of the original problem by choosing a small grid. Unfortunately, the SNLP problems transformed by our method are non-convex since the sigmoidal activation function is non-convex. In such case, even though optimality of the solution can not be claimed with the restricted basis entry rule, good solutions can be obtained [1].

6 Conclusion and Future Work

We have demonstrated how multilayer neural networks can be used to transform nonseparable functions into separable ones. Applying this useful feature to nonlinear programming, we have proposed a novel method for transforming nonseparable NLP problems into separable ones. This result opens up a way for solving general NLP problems by some variation of the simplex method, and makes connection between multilayer neural networks and mathematical programming techniques. As future work we will perform simulations on large-scale nonseparable NLP problems.

REFERENCES

[1] M. S. Bazaraa, H. D. Sherali, and C. M. Shetty, *Nonlinear Programming: Theory and Algorithms*, 2nd Edition, John Wiley & Sons, Inc. (1993).

[2] K. Hornik, M. Stinchcombe and H. White, *Multilayer feedforward networks are universal approximators*, Neural Networks, Vol.2 (1989), pp359-366.

[3] J. Lee, *A novel design method for multilayer feedforward neural networks*, Neural Computation, Vol.6 (1994), pp885-901.

[4] C. E. Miller, *The Simplex Method for Local Separable Programming*, in: Recent Advances in Mathematical Programming, R. L. Graves and P. Wolfe eds., McGraw-Hill (1963), pp89-100.

[5] M. J. D. Powell, *A fast algorithm for nonlinearly constrained optimization calculations*, in: Lecture Notes in Mathematics No. 630 (1978), G. A. Waston ed., Springer-Verlag, Berlin.

[6] D. E. Rumelhart, G. E. Hinton and R. J. Williams, *Learning representations by backpropagating errors*, Nature, Vol. 323 (1986), pp533-536.

[7] X. H. Yu, G. A. Chen and S. X. Cheng, *Dynamic learning rate optimization of the backpropagation algorithm*, IEEE Transactions on Neural Networks, Vol.6 (1995), pp669-677.

[8] Z. Wang, C. D. Massimo, M. T. Tham, and A. J. Morris, *A procedure for determining the topology of multilayer feedforwar neural networks*, Neural Networks, Vol. 7 (1994), pp291-300.

Acknowledgements

We would like to thank Steve W. Ellacott and the reviewer for valuable comments and suggestions on the manuscript.

A THEORY OF SELF-ORGANISING NEURAL NETWORKS

S P Luttrell

Defence Research Agency, Malvern, Worcs, WR14 3PS, UK.
Email: luttrell@signal.dra.hmg.gb

The purpose of this paper is to present a probabilistic theory of self-organising networks based on the results published in [1]. This approach allows vector quantisers and topographic mappings to be treated as different limiting cases of the same theoretical framework. The full theoretical machinery allows a visual cortex-like network to be built.

1 Introduction

The purpose of this paper is to present a generalisation of the probabilistic approach to the static analysis of self-organising neural networks that appeared in [1]. In the simplest case the network has two layers: an input and an output layer. An input vector is used to clamp the pattern of activity of the nodes in the input layer, and the resulting pattern of individual "firing" events of the nodes in the output layer is described probabilistically. Finally, an attempt is made to reconstruct the pattern of activity in the input layer from knowledge of the location of the firing events in the output layer. This inversion from output to input is achieved by using Bayes' theorem to invert the probabilistic feed-forward mapping from input to output. A network objective function is then introduced in order to optimise the overall network performance. If the average Euclidean error between an input vector and its corresponding reconstruction is used as the objective function, then many standard self-organising networks emerge as special cases [1, 2].

In section 2 the network objective function is introduced, in section 3 a simpler form is derived which is an upper bound to the true objective function, and in section 4 the derivatives with respect to various parameters of this upper bound are derived. Finally, in section 5 various standard neural networks are analysed within this framework.

2 Objective Function

The basic mathematical object is the objective function D, which is defined as

$$\sum_{\mathbf{y}_1,\mathbf{y}_2,\cdots,\mathbf{y}_n=1}^{\mathbf{m}} \int d\mathbf{x}\, d\mathbf{x}'\, \Pr(\mathbf{x}) \Pr(\mathbf{y}_1,\mathbf{y}_2,\cdots,\mathbf{y}_n|\mathbf{x}) \Pr(\mathbf{x}'|\mathbf{y}_1,\mathbf{y}_2,\cdots,\mathbf{y}_n) \left\|\mathbf{x}-\mathbf{x}'\right\|^2 \tag{1}$$

where $\mathbf{x}$ is the input vector and $\mathbf{x}'$ is its reconstruction, $(\mathbf{y}_1,\mathbf{y}_2,\cdots,\mathbf{y}_n)$ are the locations in the output layer of n firing events, and $\left\|\mathbf{x}-\mathbf{x}'\right\|^2$ is the Euclidean distance between the input vector and its reconstruction. The various probabilities arise as follows: $\int d\mathbf{x} \Pr(\mathbf{x}) (\cdots)$ integrates over the training set of input vectors, $\Pr(\mathbf{y}_1,\mathbf{y}_2,\cdots,\mathbf{y}_n|\mathbf{x})$ is the joint probability of n firing events at locations $(\mathbf{y}_1,\mathbf{y}_2,\cdots,\mathbf{y}_n)$, $\Pr(\mathbf{x}'|\mathbf{y}_1,\mathbf{y}_2,\cdots,\mathbf{y}_n)$ is the Bayes' inverse probability that input vector $\mathbf{x}'$ is inferred as the cause of the n firing events, $\sum_{\mathbf{y}_1,\mathbf{y}_2,\cdots,\mathbf{y}_n=1}^{\mathbf{m}}(\cdots)$ sums over all possible locations (on an assumed rectangular lattice of size $\mathbf{m}$) of the n firing events. The order in which the n firing events occurs will be assumed not to be observed, so that $\Pr(\mathbf{y}_1,\mathbf{y}_2,\cdots,\mathbf{y}_n|\mathbf{x})$ is a symmetric function of $(\mathbf{y}_1,\mathbf{y}_2,\cdots,\mathbf{y}_n)$.

A simplifying assumption will be made where the observed firing events are assumed to be statistically independent, so that

$$\Pr(\mathbf{y}_1, \mathbf{y}_2, \cdots, \mathbf{y}_n|\mathbf{x}) = \Pr(\mathbf{y}_1|\mathbf{x}) \Pr(\mathbf{y}_2|\mathbf{x}) \cdots \Pr(\mathbf{y}_n|\mathbf{x}) \tag{2}$$

Normally, a simple form for $\Pr(\mathbf{y}|\mathbf{x})$ is used such as

$$\Pr(\mathbf{y}|\mathbf{x}) = Q(\mathbf{x}|\mathbf{y}) \Big/ \sum_{\mathbf{y}'=1}^{\mathbf{m}} Q(\mathbf{x}|\mathbf{y}')$$

where $Q(\mathbf{x}|\mathbf{y}) \geq 0$, which guarantees that the normalisation condition $\sum_{\mathbf{y}=1}^{\mathbf{m}} \Pr(\mathbf{y}|\mathbf{x}) = 1$ holds. However, a more general expression will be used here based on the definition

$$\Pr(\mathbf{y}|\mathbf{x}; \mathbf{y}') \equiv \frac{Q(\mathbf{x}|\mathbf{y})\, \delta_{\mathbf{y}\in\mathcal{N}(\mathbf{y}')}}{\sum_{\mathbf{y}''\in\mathcal{N}(\mathbf{y}')} Q(\mathbf{x}|\mathbf{y}'')} \tag{3}$$

which implies that $\sum_{\mathbf{y}\in\mathcal{N}(\mathbf{y}')} \Pr(\mathbf{y}|\mathbf{x};\mathbf{y}') = 1$, where $\mathcal{N}(\mathbf{y}')$ is the set of node locations that lie in a predefined "neighbourhood" of $\mathbf{y}'$. This neighbourhood can be used to introduce "lateral inhibition" between the firing neurons if the expression for $\Pr(\mathbf{y}|\mathbf{x})$ is written as a sum over $\Pr(\mathbf{y}|\mathbf{x};\mathbf{y}')$ as follows

$$\Pr(\mathbf{y}|\mathbf{x}) = \frac{1}{M} \sum_{\mathbf{y}'\in\mathcal{N}^{-1}(\mathbf{y})} \Pr(\mathbf{y}|\mathbf{x};\mathbf{y}') = \frac{1}{M} Q(\mathbf{x}|\mathbf{y}) \sum_{\mathbf{y}'\in\mathcal{N}^{-1}(\mathbf{y})} \frac{1}{\sum_{\mathbf{y}''\in\mathcal{N}(\mathbf{y}')} Q(\mathbf{x}|\mathbf{y}'')} \tag{4}$$

where $\mathcal{N}^{-1}(\mathbf{y})$ is the "inverse neighbourhood" of $\mathbf{y}$ defined as $\mathcal{N}^{-1}(\mathbf{y}) \equiv \{\mathbf{y}' : \mathbf{y} \in \mathcal{N}(\mathbf{y}')\}$, and M is the total number of locations in the output layer that have a non-zero neighbourhood size ($M \equiv \sum_{\mathbf{y}:\mathcal{N}(\mathbf{y})\neq\emptyset} 1$). This expression for $\Pr(\mathbf{y}|\mathbf{x})$ is identical to one that arises in the context of optimising a special class of mixture distributions [3], and it satisfies $\sum_{\mathbf{y}=1}^{\mathbf{m}} \Pr(\mathbf{y}|\mathbf{x}) = 1$. The expresson for $\Pr(\mathbf{y}|\mathbf{x})$ in (4) may readily be generalised to the case where the neighbourhood is non-uniformly weighted. The expression for D in (1) and the expression for $\Pr(\mathbf{y}|\mathbf{x})$ in (4) are the two basic ingredients in the theory of self-organising neural networks presented in this paper.

There is one further ingredient that proves to be very useful. $\Pr(\mathbf{y}|\mathbf{x})$ will be allowed to "leak" as follows [1, 3]

$$\Pr(\mathbf{y}|\mathbf{x}) \to \sum_{\mathbf{y}'\in\mathcal{L}^{-1}(\mathbf{y})} \Pr(\mathbf{y}|\mathbf{y}') \Pr(\mathbf{y}'|\mathbf{x}) \tag{5}$$

where $\Pr(\mathbf{y}|\mathbf{y}')$ is the amount of probability that leaks from location $\mathbf{y}'$ to location $\mathbf{y}$, and $\mathcal{L}^{-1}(\mathbf{y})$ is the "inverse leakage neighbourhood" of $\mathbf{y}$ defined as $\mathcal{L}^{-1}(\mathbf{y}) \equiv \{\mathbf{y}' : \mathbf{y} \in \mathcal{L}(\mathbf{y}')\}$, where $\mathcal{L}(\mathbf{y}')$ is the "leakage neighbourhood" of $\mathbf{y}'$. The purpose of leakage is to allow the network output to be "damaged" in a controlled way, so that when the network is optimised it automatically becomes robust with respect to such damage. For instance, if each node is allowed to leak probability onto its neighbours in the output layer, then when the network is optimised the node properties become topographically ordered.

3 Simplify the Objective Function

The network objective function can be simplified to yield [1]

$$D = 2\int d\mathbf{x} \Pr(\mathbf{x}) \sum_{\mathbf{y}_1,\mathbf{y}_2,\cdots,\mathbf{y}_n=1}^{\mathbf{m}} \Pr(\mathbf{y}_1, \mathbf{y}_2, \cdots, \mathbf{y}_n|\mathbf{x}) \left\|\mathbf{x} - \mathbf{x}'(\mathbf{y}_1, \mathbf{y}_2, \cdots, \mathbf{y}_n)\right\|^2 \tag{6}$$

where $\mathbf{x}'(\mathbf{y}_1, \mathbf{y}_2, \cdots, \mathbf{y}_n)$ is a "reference vector" defined as $\mathbf{x}'(\mathbf{y}_1, \mathbf{y}_2, \cdots, \mathbf{y}_n) \equiv \int d\mathbf{x} \Pr(\mathbf{x}|\mathbf{y}_1, \mathbf{y}_2, \cdots, \mathbf{y}_n)\, \mathbf{x}$. If $\mathbf{x}'(\mathbf{y}_1, \mathbf{y}_2, \cdots, \mathbf{y}_n)$ is treated as an independent variable (i.e. its definition is ignored) then minimisation of D with respect to it yields the result $\mathbf{x}'(\mathbf{y}_1, \mathbf{y}_2, \cdots, \mathbf{y}_n) = \int d\mathbf{x} \Pr(\mathbf{x}|\mathbf{y}_1, \mathbf{y}_2, \cdots, \mathbf{y}_n)\, \mathbf{x}$, which is consistent with how it should have been defined anyway. This convenient trick allows the inverse probability $\Pr(\mathbf{x}|\mathbf{y}_1, \mathbf{y}_2, \cdots, \mathbf{y}_n)$ to be eliminated henceforth, provided that D in (6) is tacitly assumed to be minimised with respect to $\mathbf{x}'(\mathbf{y}_1, \mathbf{y}_2, \cdots, \mathbf{y}_n)$.
D can be further simplified to the form $D = D_1 + D_2 - D_3$ [2], where

$$D_1 \equiv \frac{2}{n} \int d\mathbf{x} \Pr(\mathbf{x}) \sum_{\mathbf{y}=1}^{\mathbf{m}} \Pr(\mathbf{y}|\mathbf{x}) \left\|\mathbf{x} - \mathbf{x}'(\mathbf{y})\right\|^2 \tag{7}$$

$$D_2 \equiv \frac{2(n-1)}{n} \int d\mathbf{x} \Pr(\mathbf{x}) \sum_{\mathbf{y}_1, \mathbf{y}_2=1}^{\mathbf{m}} \Pr(\mathbf{y}_1, \mathbf{y}_2|\mathbf{x}) (\mathbf{x} - \mathbf{x}'(\mathbf{y}_1)) \cdot (\mathbf{x} - \mathbf{x}'(\mathbf{y}_2))$$

$$D_3 \equiv 2 \sum_{\mathbf{y}_1, \mathbf{y}_2, \cdots \mathbf{y}_n=1}^{\mathbf{m}} \Pr(\mathbf{y}_1, \mathbf{y}_2, \cdots \mathbf{y}_n) \left\| \mathbf{x}'(\mathbf{y}_1, \mathbf{y}_2, \cdots \mathbf{y}_n) - \frac{1}{n} \sum_{i=1}^{n} \mathbf{x}'(\mathbf{y}_i) \right\|^2$$

To obtain this result $\Pr(\mathbf{y}_1, \mathbf{y}_2, \cdots, \mathbf{y}_n|\mathbf{x})$ has been assumed to be symmetric under permutation of the locations $\mathbf{y}_1, \mathbf{y}_2, \cdots, \mathbf{y}_n$ (e.g. the locations, but not the order of occurrence of the n firing events is known). If the independence assumption in (2) is now invoked, then D_2 may be simplified to

$$D_2 = \frac{2(n-1)}{n} \int d\mathbf{x} \Pr(\mathbf{x}) \left\| \mathbf{x} - \sum_{\mathbf{y}=1}^{\mathbf{m}} \Pr(\mathbf{y}|\mathbf{x})\, \mathbf{x}'(\mathbf{y}) \right\|^2 \tag{8}$$

The dependence of D_3 on the n-argument reference vectors $\mathbf{x}'(\mathbf{y}_1, \mathbf{y}_2, \cdots \mathbf{y}_n)$ is inconvenient, because the total number of such reference vectors is $\mathcal{O}(|\mathbf{m}|^n)$, where $|\mathbf{m}|$ is the total number of output nodes ($|\mathbf{m}| = m_1 m_2 \cdots m_d$ for a d-dimensional rectangular lattice of size $\mathbf{m}$). However, the positivity of D_3, together with $D = D_1 + D_2 - D_3$, will be used to obtain an upper bound to D as $D \leq D_1 + D_2$, which depends only on 1-argument reference vectors $\mathbf{x}'(\mathbf{y})$. The total number of 1-argument reference vectors is equal to $|\mathbf{m}|$.

4 Differentiate the Objective Function

In order to implement an optimisation algorithm the derivatives of D_1 and D_2 with respect to the various parameters must be obtained. The expressions that are encountered when differentiating are rather cumbersome, but they have a simple structure which can be made clear by the introduction of the following notation

$$\begin{array}{ll}
L_{\mathbf{y},\mathbf{y}'} \equiv \Pr(\mathbf{y}'|\mathbf{y}) & P_{\mathbf{y},\mathbf{y}'} \equiv \Pr(\mathbf{y}'|\mathbf{x};\mathbf{y}) \\
p_{\mathbf{y}} \equiv \sum_{\mathbf{y}' \in \mathcal{N}^{-1}(\mathbf{y})} P_{\mathbf{y}',\mathbf{y}} & \left(L^T p\right)_{\mathbf{y}} \equiv \sum_{\mathbf{y}' \in \mathcal{L}^{-1}(\mathbf{y})} L_{\mathbf{y}',\mathbf{y}} p_{\mathbf{y}'} \\
\mathbf{d}_{\mathbf{y}} \equiv \mathbf{x} - \mathbf{x}'(\mathbf{y}) & (L\mathbf{d})_{\mathbf{y}} \equiv \sum_{\mathbf{y}' \in \mathcal{L}(\mathbf{y})} L_{\mathbf{y},\mathbf{y}'} \mathbf{d}_{\mathbf{y}'} \\
(PL\mathbf{d})_{\mathbf{y}} \equiv \sum_{\mathbf{y}' \in \mathcal{N}(\mathbf{y})} P_{\mathbf{y},\mathbf{y}'} (L\mathbf{d})_{\mathbf{y}'} & \left(P^T PL\mathbf{d}\right)_{\mathbf{y}} \equiv \sum_{\mathbf{y}' \in \mathcal{N}^{-1}(\mathbf{y})} P_{\mathbf{y}',\mathbf{y}} (PL\mathbf{d})_{\mathbf{y}'} \\
e_{\mathbf{y}} \equiv \left\|\mathbf{x} - \mathbf{x}'(\mathbf{y})\right\|^2 & (Le)_{\mathbf{y}} \equiv \sum_{\mathbf{y}' \in \mathcal{L}(\mathbf{y})} L_{\mathbf{y},\mathbf{y}'} e_{\mathbf{y}'} \\
(PLe)_{\mathbf{y}} \equiv \sum_{\mathbf{y}' \in \mathcal{N}(\mathbf{y})} P_{\mathbf{y},\mathbf{y}'} (Le)_{\mathbf{y}'} & \left(P^T PLe\right)_{\mathbf{y}} \equiv \sum_{\mathbf{y}' \in \mathcal{N}^{-1}(\mathbf{y})} P_{\mathbf{y}',\mathbf{y}} (PLe)_{\mathbf{y}'} \\
\bar{\mathbf{d}} \equiv \sum_{\mathbf{y}=1}^{\mathbf{m}} \left(L^T p\right)_{\mathbf{y}} \mathbf{d}_{\mathbf{y}} & \text{or } \bar{\mathbf{d}} \equiv \sum_{\mathbf{y}=1}^{\mathbf{m}} (PL\mathbf{d})_{\mathbf{y}}
\end{array} \tag{9}$$

which allows (5) to be written as $\Pr(\mathbf{y}|\mathbf{x}) \to \frac{1}{M}\left(L^T p\right)_{\mathbf{y}}$. D_1 and D_2 may be differentiated with respect to $\mathbf{x}'(\mathbf{y})$ to obtain

$$\begin{aligned}\frac{\partial D_1}{\partial \mathbf{x}'(\mathbf{y})} &= -\frac{4}{nM}\int d\mathbf{x}\Pr(\mathbf{x})\left(L^T p\right)_{\mathbf{y}} \mathbf{d}_{\mathbf{y}} \\ \frac{\partial D_2}{\partial \mathbf{x}'(\mathbf{y})} &= -\frac{4(n-1)}{nM^2}\int d\mathbf{x}\Pr(\mathbf{x})\left(L^T p\right)_{\mathbf{y}} \bar{\mathbf{d}} \end{aligned} \tag{10}$$

D_1 and D_2 may be functionally varied with respect to $\log Q(\mathbf{x}|\mathbf{y})$ to obtain

$$\begin{aligned}\delta D_1 &= \frac{2}{nM}\int d\mathbf{x}\Pr(\mathbf{x})\sum_{\mathbf{y}=1}^{\mathbf{m}} \delta\log Q(\mathbf{x}|\mathbf{y})\left(p_{\mathbf{y}}(Le)_{\mathbf{y}} - \left(P^T P L e\right)_{\mathbf{y}}\right) \\ \delta D_2 &= \frac{4(n-1)}{nM^2}\int d\mathbf{x}\Pr(\mathbf{x})\sum_{\mathbf{y}=1}^{\mathbf{m}} \delta\log Q(\mathbf{x}|\mathbf{y})\left(p_{\mathbf{y}}(L\mathbf{d})_{\mathbf{y}} - \left(P^T P L\mathbf{d}\right)_{\mathbf{y}}\right)\cdot\bar{\mathbf{d}}\end{aligned} \tag{11}$$

If $Q(\mathbf{x}|\mathbf{y})$ is assumed to be a sigmoid function

$$Q(\mathbf{x}|\mathbf{y}) = 1/\left(1+\exp\left(-\mathbf{w}(\mathbf{y})\cdot\mathbf{x} - b(\mathbf{y})\right)\right)$$

then the derivatives of D_1 and D_2 with respect to the "weight" vector $\mathbf{w}(\mathbf{y})$ and "bias" $b(\mathbf{y})$ may be written as

$$\begin{aligned}\frac{\partial D_1}{\partial\begin{pmatrix} b(\mathbf{y}) \\ \mathbf{w}(\mathbf{y})\end{pmatrix}} &= \frac{2}{nM}\int d\mathbf{x}\Pr(\mathbf{x})\begin{bmatrix}\left(p_{\mathbf{y}}(Le)_{\mathbf{y}} - \left(P^T P L e\right)_{\mathbf{y}}\right) \\ \times\left(1 - Q(\mathbf{x}|\mathbf{y})\right)\begin{pmatrix}1 \\ \mathbf{x}\end{pmatrix}\end{bmatrix} \\ \frac{\partial D_2}{\partial\begin{pmatrix} b(\mathbf{y}) \\ \mathbf{w}(\mathbf{y})\end{pmatrix}} &= \frac{4(n-1)}{nM^2}\int d\mathbf{x}\Pr(\mathbf{x})\begin{bmatrix}\left(p_{\mathbf{y}}(L\mathbf{d})_{\mathbf{y}} - \left(P^T P L\mathbf{d}\right)_{\mathbf{y}}\right)\cdot\bar{\mathbf{d}} \\ \times\left(1 - Q(\mathbf{x}|\mathbf{y})\right)\begin{pmatrix}1 \\ \mathbf{x}\end{pmatrix}\end{bmatrix}\end{aligned} \tag{12}$$

The gradients in (10) and (12) may be used to implement a gradient descent algorithm for optimising $D_1 + D_2$, which then leads to a least upper bound on the full objective function D $(= D_1 + D_2 - D_3)$.

5 Special Cases

Various standard results that are special cases of the model presented above are discussed in the following subsections.

5.1 Vector Quantiser and Topographic Mapping

Assume $n = 1$ so that only 1 firing event is observed so that $D_2 = D_3 = 0$, $\mathbf{y} \in \mathcal{N}(\mathbf{y}')\ \forall \mathbf{y}, \mathbf{y}'$ so that the neighbourhood embraces all of the output nodes, and probability leakage of the type given in (5) is allowed. Then D reduces to $D = 2\int d\mathbf{x}\Pr(\mathbf{x})\sum_{\mathbf{y}=1}^{\mathbf{m}}\Pr(\mathbf{y}|\mathbf{y}(\mathbf{x}))\left\|\mathbf{x} - \mathbf{x}'(\mathbf{y})\right\|^2$ [1], which leads to a behaviour that is very similar to the topographic mappings described in [5], where $\Pr(\mathbf{y}|\mathbf{y}')$ now corresponds to the topographic neighbourhood function. In the limit where $\Pr(\mathbf{y}|\mathbf{y}(\mathbf{x})) = \delta_{\mathbf{y},\mathbf{y}(\mathbf{x})}$ this reduces to the criterion for optimising a vector quantiser [4].

5.2 Visual Cortex Network

A "visual cortex"-like network can be built if the full theoretical machinery presented earlier is used. This network has many of the emergent properties of the mammalian visual cortex, such as orientation maps, centre-on/surround-off detectors, dominance stripes, etc (see e.g. [7] for a review of these phenomena). There is an input layer with a pattern of activity representing the input vector, an output layer with nodes firing in response to feed-forward connections (i.e. a "recognition" model), and a mechanism for reconstructing the input from the firing events via feed-back connections (i.e. a "generative" model). The output layer has lateral inhibition implemented as in (4); the neighbourhood of node $\mathbf{y}'$ has an associated inhibition factor $1/\sum_{\mathbf{y}''\in\mathcal{N}(\mathbf{y}')} Q\left(\mathbf{x}|\mathbf{y}''\right)$, and the overall inhibition factor for node $\mathbf{y}$ is $\sum_{\mathbf{y}'\in\mathcal{N}^{-1}(\mathbf{y})}\left(1/\sum_{\mathbf{y}''\in\mathcal{N}(\mathbf{y}')} Q\left(\mathbf{x}|\mathbf{y}''\right)\right)$, which is the sum of the inhibition factors over all nodes $\mathbf{y}'$ that have node $\mathbf{y}$ in their neighbourhood. This scheme for introducing lateral inhibition is discussed in greater detail in [3]. The leakage introduced by $\Pr\left(\mathbf{y}|\mathbf{y}'\right)$ induces topographical ordering as usual.

In the limit $n \longrightarrow 1$ where D_1 is dominant, this network behaves like a topographic mapping network, except that the output layer splits up into a number of "domains" each of which is typically a lateral inhibition length in size, and each of which forms a separate topographic mapping. These domains are seamlessly joined together, so no domain boundaries are actually visible. In the limit $n \longrightarrow \infty$ where D_2 is dominant, this network approximates its input as a superposition of reference vectors $\sum_{\mathbf{y}=1}^{\mathbf{m}} \Pr\left(\mathbf{y}|\mathbf{x}\right)\mathbf{x}'\left(\mathbf{y}\right)$ (see (8)). Thus the network is capable of explaining the input in terms of multiple causes.

6 Conclusions

A single theoretical framework has been shown to describe a number of standard self-organising neural networks. This makes it easy to understand the relationship between these neural networks, and it provides a useful framework for analysing their properties.

REFERENCES

[1] Luttrell S P, *A Bayesian analysis of self-organising maps*, Neural Computation, Vol. 6(5) (1994), pp767-794.

[2] Luttrell S P, *Designing analysable networks*, Handbook of Neural Computation, OUP (1996).

[3] Luttrell S P, *Partitioned mixture distribution: an adaptive Bayesian network for low-level image processing*, IEE Proc. Vision Image Signal Processing, Vol. 141(4) (1994), pp251-260.

[4] Linde Y, Buzo A and Gray R M, *An algorithm for vector quantiser design*, IEEE Trans. COM, Vol. 28(1) (1980), pp84-95.

[5] Kohonen T, *Self organisation and associative memory*, Springer-Verlag (1984).

[6] Luttrell S P, *Derivation of a class of training algorithms*, IEEE Trans. NN, Vol. 1(2) (1990), pp229-232.

[7] Goodhill G J, *Correlations, competition, and optimality: modelling the development of topography and ocular dominance*, CSRP 226 (1992), Sussex University.

Acknowledgements

NEURAL NETWORK SUPERVISED TRAINING BASED ON A DIMENSION REDUCING METHOD

G.D. Magoulas, M.N. Vrahatis*, T.N. Grapsa* and G.S. Androulakis*

Department of Electrical and Computer Engineering, University of Patras, GR-261.10, Patras, Greece. Email: magoulas@ee-gw.ee.upatras.gr

** Department of Mathematics, University of Patras, GR-261.10 Patras, Greece. Email: vrahatis—grapsa—gsa@math.upatras.gr*

In this contribution a new method for supervised training is presented. This method is based on a recently proposed root finding procedure for the numerical solution of systems of non-linear algebraic and/or transcendental equations in $\mathbb{R}^n$. This new method reduces the dimensionality of the problem in such a way that it can lead to an iterative approximate formula for the computation of $n-1$ connection weights. The remaining connection weight is evaluated separately using the final approximations of the others. This reduced iterative formula generates a sequence of points in $\mathbb{R}^{n-1}$ which converges quadratically to the proper $n-1$ connection weights. Moreover, it requires neither a good initial guess for one connection weight nor accurate error function evaluations. The new method is applied on some test cases in order to evaluate its performance.

Subject classification: AMS(MOS) 65K10, 49D10, 68T05, 68G05.

Keywords: Numerical optimization methods, feed forward neural networks, supervised training, back-propagation of error, dimension-reducing method.

1 Introduction

Consider a feed forward neural network (FNN) with l layers, $l \in [1, L]$. The error is defined as $e_k(t) = d_k(t) - y_k^L(t)$, for $k = 1, 2, ..., K$, where $d_k(t)$ is the desired response at the kth neuron of the output layer at the input pattern t, $y_k^L(t)$ is the output at the kth neuron of the output layer L. If there is a fixed, finite set of input-output cases, the square error over the training set which contains T representative cases is:

$$E = \sum_{t=1}^{T} E(t) = \sum_{t=1}^{T} \sum_{k=1}^{K} e_k^2(t). \tag{1}$$

The most common supervised training algorithm for FNNs with sigmoidal non-linear neurons is the Back-Propagation (BP), [4]. The BP minimizes the error function E using the Steepest Descent (SD) with fixed step size and computes the gradient using the chain rule on the layers of the network. BP converges too slow and often yields suboptimal solutions. The quasi-Newton method (BFGS) [2], converges much faster than the BP but the storage and computational requirements of the Hessian for very large FNNs make its use impractical for most current machines. In this paper, we derive and apply a new training method for FNNs named Dimension Reducing Training Method (DRTM). DRTM is based on the methods studied in [3] and it incorporates the advantages of Newton and SOR algorithms (see [4]).

2 Description of the DRTM

Throughout this paper $\mathbb{R}^n$ is the n-dimensional real space of column weight vectors w with components $w_1, w_2, \ldots, w_n$; $(y; z)$ represents the column vector with components $y_1, y_2, \ldots, y_m, z_1, z_2, \ldots, z_k$; $\partial_i E(w)$ denotes the partial derivative of $E(w)$ with respect to the ith variable w_i; $g(w) = (g_1(w), \ldots, g_n(w))$ defines the gradient $\nabla E(w)$ of the objective function E at w while $H = [H_{ij}]$ defines the Hessian

$\nabla^2 E(w)$ of E at w; $\bar{\mathcal{A}}$ denotes the closure of the set $\mathcal{A}$ and $E(w_1, \ldots, w_{i-1}, \cdot, w_{i+1}, \ldots, w_n)$ defines the error function obtained by holding $w_1, \ldots, w_{i-1}, w_{i+1}, \ldots, w_n$ fixed.

The problem of training is treated as an optimization problem in the FNN's weight space (i.e., n–dimensional Euclidean space). In other words, we want to find the proper weights that satisfy the following system of equations :

$$g_i(w) = 0, \quad i = 1, \ldots, n\,. \tag{2}$$

In order to solve this system iteratively we want a sequence of weight vectors $\{w^p\}, p = 0, 1, \ldots$ which converges to the point $w^* = (w_1^*, \ldots, w_n^*) \in \mathcal{D} \subset \mathrm{I\!R}^n$ of the function E. First, we consider the sets $\mathcal{B}_i$, to be those connected components of $g_i^{-1}(0)$ containing w^* on which $\partial_n g_i \neq 0$, for $i = 1, \ldots, n$ respectively. Next, applying the Implicit Function Theorem (see [4, 3]) for each one of the components g_i we can find open neighborhoods $\mathcal{A}_1^* \subset \mathrm{I\!R}^{n-1}$ and $\mathcal{A}_{2,i}^* \subset \mathrm{I\!R}$ of the points $y^* = (w_1^*, \ldots, w_{n-1}^*)$ and w_n^* respectively, such that for any $y = (w_1, \ldots, w_{n-1}) \in \bar{\mathcal{A}}_1^*$ there exist unique mappings φ_i defined and continuous in $\mathcal{A}_1^*$ such that : $w_n = \varphi_i(y) \in \bar{\mathcal{A}}_{2,i}^*$, and $g_i(y; \varphi_i(y)) = 0, \quad i = 1, \ldots, n$. Moreover, the partial derivatives $\partial_j \varphi_i, j = 1, \ldots, n-1$ exist in $\mathcal{A}_1^*$ for each φ_i, they are continuous in $\bar{\mathcal{A}}_1^*$ and they are given by :

$$\partial_j \varphi_i(y) = -\frac{\partial_j g_i\big(y; \varphi_i(y)\big)}{\partial_n g_i\big(y; \varphi_i(y)\big)}, \quad i = 1, \ldots, n, \quad j = 1, \ldots, n-1\,. \tag{3}$$

Working exactly as in [3], we utilize Taylor's formula to expand $\varphi_i(y)$, about y^p. By straightforward calculations, utilizing approximate values for $g_i(\cdot)$ and $\partial_j g_i(\cdot) \equiv \partial_{ij}^2 E$ (see [5], where error estimates for these approximations can also be found) we obtain the following iterative scheme for the computation of the $n-1$ components of w^* :

$$y^{p+1} = y^p + A_p^{-1} V_p, \quad p = 0, 1, \ldots, \tag{4}$$

where $y^p = [w_i^p]$, $V_p = [v_i] = [w_n^{p,i} - w_n^{p,n}]$ and the elements of the matrix A_p are :

$$[a_{ij}] = \left[\frac{g_i(y^p + he_j; w_n^{p,i}) - g_i(y^p; w_n^{p,i})}{g_i(y^p; w_n^{p,i} + he_n) - g_i(y^p; w_n^{p,i})} - \frac{g_n(y^p + he_j; w_n^{p,n}) - g_n(y^p; w_n^{p,n})}{g_n(y^p; w_n^{p,n} + he_n) - g_n(y^p; w_n^{p,n})}\right], \tag{5}$$

with $w_n^{p,i} = \varphi_i(y^p)$, h a small quantity and e_j the j–th unit vector. After a desired number of iterations of (4), say $p = m$, the nth component of w^* can be approximated by means of the following relation :

$$w_n^{m+1} = w_n^{m,n} - \sum_{j=1}^{n-1} \left\{ (w_j^{m+1} - w_j^m) \cdot \frac{g_n(y^m + he_j; w_n^{m,n}) - g_n(y^m; w_n^{m,n})}{g_n(y^m; w_n^{m,n} + he_n) - g_n(y^m; w_n^{m,n})} \right\}. \tag{6}$$

Note that the iterative formula (4) uses the matrices A_p and V_p. The matrix A_p constitutes the reduced–Hessian of our network and its components incorporate components of the Hessian but are evaluated at different points. The matrix V_p uses only the points $w_n^{p,i}$ $(i = 1, \ldots, n-1)$ and $w_n^{p,n}$ instead of the gradient values employed in Newton's method. A proof for the convergence of (4) and (6) can be found in [6].

Relative procedures for obtaining w^* can be constructed by replacing w_n with any one of the components $w_1, \ldots, w_{n-1}$, for example w_{int}. The above described method

	FR		*PR*		*BFGS*		*DRTM*		
w^0	*IT*	*FE*	*IT*	*FE*	*IT*	*FE*	*IT*	*FE*	*ASG*
$(0.3, 0.4)$	F	F	F	F	F	F	5	20	100
$(-1, -2)$	F	F	F	F	14	274	7	28	140
$(-1, 10)$	F	F	F	F	14	285	7	28	140
$(0.2, 0.2)$	F	F	F	F	F	F	5	20	100
$(2, 1)$	F	F	F	F	13	298	5	20	100
$(0.3, 0.3)$	F	F	F	F	F	F	5	20	100
$(-1.2, 1.2)$	F	F	F	F	F	F	7	28	140

Table 1 Comparative results for Example 1.

does not require the expressions φ_i but only the values $w_n^{p,i}$ which are given by the solution of the one–dimensional equations $g_i(w_1^p, \ldots, w_{n-1}^p, \cdot) = 0$. So, by holding $y^p = (w_1^p, \ldots, w_{n-1}^p)$ fixed, we can solve the equations : $g_i(y^p; r_i^p) = 0, \quad i = 1, \ldots, n$, for an approximate solution r_i^p in the interval (a, b) with an accuracy D. In order to solve the one–dimensional equations, we employ a modified bisection method described in [3, 12] and given by the following formula :

$$w^{p+1} = w^p + \mathrm{sgn}\psi(w^p)\, q \,/\, 2^{p+1}, \qquad p = 0, 1, \ldots, \tag{7}$$

with $w^0 = a$, $q = \mathrm{sgn}\psi(a)\,(b-a)$ and where sgn defines the well known sign function. This method computes with certainty a root when $\mathrm{sgn}\psi(w^0)\,\mathrm{sgn}\psi(w^p) = -1$ (see [12]). It is evident from (7) that the only computable information required by this method is the algebraic signs of the function ψ.
A high–level description of the new algorithm can be found in [8].

3 Simulation Results

Here we present and compare the behavior of the DRTM with other popular methods on some artificially created but characteristic situations. For example, it is common in FNN training to take minimization steps that increase some weights by large amounts pushing the output of the neuron into saturation. Moreover, in various small and large scale neural network applications the error surface has flat and steep regions. It is well known that the BP is highly inefficient in locating minima in such surfaces. In the following examples, the gradient is evaluated using finite differences for the DRTM and analytically for all the other methods.

Example 1 *The objective function's surface has flat and steep regions*

$$E(w) = \sum_{i=1}^{10} g_i^2, \qquad g_i(w_1, w_2) = 2 + 2i - \left(e^{ix_1} + e^{ix_2}\right). \tag{8}$$

System (8), which is a well–known test case, *(Jennrich and Sampson Function)* (see [9]), has a global minimum at $w_1 = w_2 = 0.2578\ldots$. In Table 1 we present results obtained by applying the nonlinear conjugate gradient methods Fletcher–Reeves (FR) and Polak–Ribiere (PR) and the quasi–Newton Broyden–Fletcher–Goldfarb–Shanno (BFGS) method with the corresponding numerical results of DRTM. In this Table *IT* indicates the total number of iterations required to obtain w^* (iterations

BP			*DRTM*			
MN	*STD*	*SUC*	*MN*	*STD*	*SUC*	*MAS*
100.4	77.3	38.5	2.3	1.2	72.5	67.8

Table 2 Comparison of Back–propagation with DRTM for Example 2.

limit= 500); *FE* the total number of function evaluations (and derivatives) and *ASG* the total number of algebraic signs of the components of the gradient that are required for applying the iterative scheme (7). Because of the difficulty of the problem FR and PR failed to converge in all the cases (marked with an F in the table). The results are mixed with the BFGS method. Especially, when we are close to the minimum BFGS leaves the appropriate region moving to wrong direction in order to minimize the objective function.

Example 2 *The objective function's surface is oval shaped and bent.*

We can artificially create such a surface by training a single neuron with sigmoid non–linearity using the patterns $\{-6,1\}$, $\{-6.1,1\}$, $\{-4.1,1\}$, $\{-4,1\}$, $\{4,1\}$, $\{4.1,1\}$, $\{6,1\}$, $\{6.1,1\}$ for input and $\{0\}$, $\{0\}$, $\{0.97\}$, $\{0.99\}$, $\{0.01\}$, $\{0.03\}$, $\{1\}$, $\{1\}$ for output. The weights w_1, w_2 take values in the interval $[-3,3] \times [-7.5,7.5]$. The global minimum is located at the center of the surface and there are two valleys that lead to local minima. The step size for the BP was 0.05. The initial weights were formed by spanning the interval $[-3,3]$ in steps of 0.05 and the interval $[-7.5,7.5]$ in steps of 0.125.

The behavior of the methods is exhibited in Table 2, where *MN* indicates the mean number of iterations for simulations that reached the global minimum; *STD* the standard deviation of iterations; *SUC* the percentage of success in locating the global minimum and *MAS* the mean number of algebraic signs that are required for applying the iterative scheme (7). Note that for DRTM, since finite differences are used, two error function evaluations are required in each iteration. BP succeeds to locate the global minimum when initial weights take values in the intervals $w_1 \in [-0.8,1.5]$ and $w_2 \in [-2.5,2.5]$. On the other hand, DRTM is less affected by the initial weights. In this case we exploit the fact that we are able to isolate the weight vector component most responsible for unstable behavior by reducing the dimension of the problem. Therefore, DRTM is very fast and possesses high percentage of success.

4 Conclusion and Further Improvements

This paper describes a new training method for FNNs. Although the proposed method uses reduction to simpler one–dimensional equations, it converges quadratically to $n-1$ components of an optimal weight vector, while the remaining weight is evaluated separately using the final approximations of the others. Thus, it does not require a good initial estimate for one component of an optimal weight vector. Moreover, it is at the user's disposal to choose which will be the remaining weight, according to the problem. Since it uses the modified one–dimensional bisection method, it requires only that the algebraic signs of the function and gradient values be correct. It is also possible to use this method in training with block of

weights using different remaining weights. In this case, the method can lead to a network training and construction algorithm. This issue is currently under development and we hope to address it in a future communication.
Note that in general the matrix of our reduced system is not symmetric. It is possible to transform it to a symmetric one by using proper perturbations [6]. If the matrix is symmetric and positive definite the optimal weight vector minimizes the objective function. Furthermore, DRTM appears particularly useful when it is difficult to evaluate the gradient values accurately, as well as when the Hessian at the optimum is singular or ill–conditioned [8].

REFERENCES

[1] D. E. Rumelhart and J. L. McClelland eds., *Parallel Distributed Processing : Explorations in the Microstructure of Cognition*, Vol. 1, MIT Press, 1986, pp318–362.

[2] R. L. Watrous, *Learning algorithms for connectionist networks: applied gradient methods of non-linear optimization*, in Proc. IEEE Int. Conf. Neural Networks, San Diego, CA, Vol.2 (1987), pp619–627.

[3] T. N. Grapsa, M. N. Vrahatis, *A dimension–reducing method for solving systems of non–linear equations in* $\mathbb{R}^n$, Int. J. Computer Math., Vol.32 (1990), pp205–216.

[4] J. M. Ortega, W. C. Rheinboldt. *Iterative Solution of Non–linear Equations in Several Variables*, Academic Press, New York, (1970).

[5] J. E. Dennis, R. B. Schnabel, *Numerical methods for unconstrained optimization and non–linear equations*, Prentice–Hall, Englewood Cliffs, NJ, (1983).

[6] T. N. Grapsa, M. N. Vrahatis, *A dimension–reducing method for unconstrained optimization*, J. Comp. Appl. Math. Vol. 66 (1996), pp239–253.

[7] M. N. Vrahatis, *Solving systems of non–linear equations using the non zero value of the topological degree*, ACM Trans. Math. Software, Vol. 14 (1988), pp312–329.

[8] G. D. Magoulas, M. N. Vrahatis, T. N. Grapsa, G. S. Androulakis, *A dimension–reducing training method for feed–forward neural networks*, Tech. Rep. CSL–1095, Department of Electrical & Computer Engineering, University of Patras, (1995).

[9] B. J. Moré , B. S. Garbow, K. E. Hillstrom, *Testing unconstrained optimization*, ACM Trans. Math. Software, Vol. 7 (1981), pp17–41.

A TRAINING METHOD FOR DISCRETE MULTILAYER NEURAL NETWORKS

G.D. Magoulas, M.N. Vrahatis*, T.N. Grapsa* and G.S. Androulakis*

Department of Electrical and Computer Engineering, University of Patras, GR-261.10, Patras, Greece. Email: magoulas@ee-gw.ee.upatras.gr
** Department of Mathematics, University of Patras, GR-261.10 Patras, Greece. Email: vrahatis—grapsa—gsa@math.upatras.gr*

In this contribution a new training method is proposed for neural networks that are based on neurons whose output can be in a particular state. This method minimises the well known least square criterion by using information concerning only the signs of the error function and inaccurate gradient values. The algorithm is based on a modified one–dimensional bisection method and it treats supervised training in networks of neurons with discrete output states as a problem of minimisation based on imprecise values.

Subject classification: AMS(MOS) 65K10, 49D10, 68T05, 68G05.

Keywords: Numerical analysis, imprecise function and gradient values, hard–limiting threshold units, feed forward neural networks, supervised training, back–propagation of error.

1 Introduction

Consider a Discrete Multilayer Neural Network (DMNN) consisting of L layers, in which the first layer denotes the input, the last one, L, is the output, and the intermediate layers are the hidden layers. It is assumed that the (l-1)–th layer has N_{l-1} units. These units operate according to the following equations :

$$net_j^l = \sum_{i=1}^{N_{l-1}} w_{ij}^{l-1,l} y_i^{l-1} + \theta_j^l, \qquad y_j^l = \sigma^l\left(net_j^l\right), \tag{1}$$

where net_j^l is the net input to the jth unit at the lth layer, $w_{ij}^{l-1,l}$ is the connection weight from the ith unit at the $(l-1)$–th layer to the jth unit at the lth layer, y_i^l denotes the output of the ith unit belonging to the lth layer, θ_j^l denotes the threshold of the jth unit at the lth layer, and σ is the activation function. In this paper we consider units where $\sigma(net_i^l)$ is a discrete activation function. We especially focus on units with two output states, usually called binary or hard–limiting units [1], i.e. $\sigma^l(net_j^l) =$ "*true*", if $net_j^l \geq 0$, and "*false*" otherwise.

Although units with discrete activation function have been superseded to a large extent by the computationally more powerful units with analog activation function, still DMNNs are important in that they can handle many of the inherently binary tasks that neural networks are used for. Their internal representations are clearly interpretable, they are computationally simpler to understand than networks with sigmoid units and provide a starting point for the study of the neural network properties. Furthermore, when using hard–limiting units we can understand better the relationship between the size of the network and the complexity of the training [2]. In [3] it has been demonstrated that DMNNs with only one hidden layer, can create any decision region that can be expressed as a finite union of polyhedral sets when there is one unit in the input layer. Moreover, artificially created examples were given where these networks create non convex and disjoint decision regions.

Finally, discrete activation functions facilitate neural network implementations in digital hardware and are much less costly to fabricate.

The most common feed forward neural network (FNN) training algorithm, the back–propagation (BP) [4] that makes use of the gradient descent, cannot be applied directly to networks of units with discrete output states, since discrete activation functions (such as hardlimiters) are non–differentiable. However, various modifications of the gradient descent have been presented [5, 6, 7]. In [8] an approximation to gradient descent, the so–called pseudo–gradient training method, was proposed. This method uses the gradient of a sigmoid as a heuristic hint instead of the true gradient. Experimental results validated the effectiveness of this approach.

In this paper, we derive and apply a new training method for DMNNs that makes use of the gradient approximation introduced in [8]. Our method exploits the imprecise information regarding the error function and the approximated gradient, like the pseudo–gradient method does, but it has an improved convergence speed and has potential to train DMNNs in situations where, according to our experiments, the pseudo–gradient method fails to converge.

2 Problem Formulation and Proposed Solution

We consider units with two discrete output states and we shall use the convention f (or $-f$) for "false" and t (or $+t$) for "true", where f, t are real positive numbers and $f < t$, instead of the classical 0 and 1 (or -1, and $+1$). Real positive values prevent units from saturating, give to the logic "false" some power of influence over the next layer of the DMNN, and help the justification of the approximated gradient value which we shall employ.

First, let us define the error for a discrete unit as follows: $e_j(t) = d_j(t) - y_j^L(t)$, for $j = 1, 2, ..., N_L$, where $d_j(t)$ is the desired response at the jth neuron of the output layer at the input pattern t, $y_j^L(t)$ is the output at the kth neuron of the output layer L. For a fixed, finite set of input–output cases, the square error over the training set which contains T representative cases is:

$$E = \sum_{t=1}^{T} E(t) = \sum_{t=1}^{T} \sum_{j=1}^{N_L} e_j^2(t). \tag{2}$$

The idea of the pseudo–gradient was first introduced in training discrete recurrent neural networks [9, 10] and extended to DMNNs [8]. The method approximates the true gradient of the error function with respect to the weights, i.e. $\nabla E(w)$, by introducing an analog set of values for the outputs of the hidden layer units and the output layer units.

Thus, it is assumed that y_j^l in (1) can be written as $y_j^l = \tilde{\sigma}^l\left(s(net_j^l)\right)$, where $\tilde{\sigma}$(x)= "*true*" if x$\geq$ 0.5, and "*false*" otherwise, if $s(\cdot)$ is defined in $[0,1]$. If $s(\cdot)$ is defined in $[-1,1]$ then $\tilde{\sigma}$(x)= "*true*" if x$\geq$ 0, and "*false*" otherwise.

Using the chain rule, the pseudo–gradient is computed :

$$\frac{\widetilde{\partial E}}{\partial w_{ij}^{l-1,l}} = \widetilde{\delta}_j^l y_i^{l-1}, \tag{3}$$

where the back–propagating error signal $\tilde{\delta}$ for the output layer is $\widetilde{\delta_j^L} = \Big(d_j - s(net_j^L)\Big) \cdot s'(net_j^L)$ and for the hidden layers ($l \in [2, L-1]$) is $\widetilde{\delta_j^l} = s'(net_j^l)$

$\sum_n w_{jn}^{l,l+1} \widetilde{\delta_n^{l+1}}$. In these relations $s'(net_j^l)$ is the derivative of the analog activation function.

By using real positive values for "true" and "false" we ensure that the pseudo–gradient will not reduce to zero when the output is "false". Note also that we do not use σ' which is zero everywhere and non–existent at zero. Instead, we use s' which is always positive, so $\widetilde{\delta_j^l}$ gives an indication of the direction and magnitude of a step up or down as a function of net_j^l in the error surface E.

However, as pointed out in [8], the value of the pseudo–gradient is not accurate enough, so gradient descent based training in DMNNs is considerably slow when compared with BP training in FNNs.

In order to alleviate this problem we propose an alternative to the pseudo-gradient training method procedure. To be more specific, we propose to solve the one–dimensional equation :

$$E(w_1, \ldots, w_{i-1}^0, w_i^0, w_{i+1}^0, \ldots, w_n^0) - E(w_1^0, \ldots, w_{i-1}^0, w_i^0, w_{i+1}^0, \ldots, w_n^0) = 0,$$

for w_1 keeping all other components of the weight vector in their constant values. Now, if $\hat{w}_1$ is the solution of the above equation, then the point defined by the vector $(\hat{w}_1, w_2^0, \ldots, w_n^0)$ possesses the same error function value with the point w^0, so it belongs to the same contour line of w^0. Assuming that the error function curves up from w^* in all directions, we can claim that any point which belongs to the line with endpoints w^0 and $(\hat{w}_1, w_2^0, \ldots, w_n^0)$ possesses smaller error function value than these endpoints. With this fact in mind we can now choose such a point, say, for example $w_1^1 = w_1^0 + \gamma\,(\hat{w}_1 - w_1^0)$, $\gamma \in (0, 1)$, and solve the one–dimensional equation :

$$E(w_1^1, w_2, \ldots, w_{i-1}^0, w_i^0, w_{i+1}^0, \ldots, w_n^0) - E(w_1^1, w_2^0, \ldots, w_{i-1}^0, w_i^0, w_{i+1}^0, \ldots, w_n^0) = 0,$$

for w_2 keeping all other components in their constant values. If $\hat{w}_2$ is the solution of this equation then we can obtain a better approximation for this component by taking $w_2^1 = w_2^0 + \gamma\,(\hat{w}_2 - w_2^0)$, $\gamma \in (0, 1)$.

Continuing in a similar way with the remaining components of the weight vector we obtain the new vector $w^1 = (w_1^1, \ldots, w_n^1)$ and replace the initial vector w^0 by w^1. The procedure can then be repeated to compute w^2 and so on until the final estimated point is computed according to a predetermined accuracy. So, in general we want to find the parameter $\hat{x}$ (a weight or threshold) that satisfies :

$$E(x_1^{k+1}, \ldots, x_{i-1}^{k+1}, x, x_{i+1}^k, \ldots, x_n^k) - E(x_1^{k+1}, \ldots, x_{i-1}^{k+1}, x_i^k, x_{i+1}^k, \ldots, x_n^k) = 0,$$

by applying the modified bisection (see [12, 13]) in the interval (a_i, b_i) within accuracy d :

$$x_i^{p+1} = x_i^p + C\,\text{sgn}\,\big(E(z^p) - E(z^0)\big)\,/2^{p+1}, \quad p = 0, 1, \ldots, \lceil \log_2((b_i - a_i)\,d^{-1}) \rceil,$$

where the notation $\lceil\cdot\rceil$ refers to the smallest integer not less than the real number quoted and $z^0 = (x_1^{k+1}, \ldots, x_{i-1}^{k+1}, a_i, x_{i+1}^k, \ldots, x_n^k)$, $z^p = (x_1^{k+1}, \ldots, x_{i-1}^{k+1}, x_i^p, x_{i+1}^k, \ldots, x_n^k)$, $C = \text{sgn}E(z^0)(b_i - a_i)$, $a_i = \bar{x}_i^k - \frac{1}{2}\{1 + \text{sgn}\widetilde{\partial_i E(\bar{x}^k)}\}h_i$, $b_i = a_i + h_i$. If an iteration of the algorithm fails we switch to the pseudo–gradient training method. So, the justification of the new procedure is based on the heuristic justification of the pseudo–gradient which can be found in any one of [8, 9, 10]. A formal justification of the proposed procedure in case of differentiable objective functions can be found in [11].

	BP			New method				
	MN	*STD*	*MNE*	*MN*	*STD*	*MNE*	*MAS*	*SAS*
a)	561	550.4	0.0396	40.6	4.2	0.0000008	239.6	54.12
b)	18121	3048.7	0.49	28.5	13.43	0.45	20673	9310.9

Table 1 Experimental results a) XOR, b) $\sin x \cos 2x$.

3 Experimental Results

Here we present and compare the behaviour of the new training method with the BP [4] and the pseudo–gradient training method [8] for the XOR problem and training an 1–10–1 network to approximate the function $\sin x \cos 2x$ (Table 1). In all problems $\gamma = 0.5, d = 10^{-10}, \bar{h} = 10$ and no pseudo–gradient subprocedure has been applied with the proposed method in order to get more fair evaluation. *MN* indicates the mean number of iterations; *STD* the standard deviation of iterations; *MNE* the mean value of the error; *MAS* the mean number of algebraic signs required for the bisection scheme and *SAS* the standard deviation of the required algebraic signs. The results are for 10 simulation runs, for the same initial weights; the maximum number of iterations was set to 2000, the weights were initialised in the interval $[-10, 10]$ and the step size for BP was set to the standard value 0.75. For the XOR the thresholds were set as follows: "*true*" = 0.8 and "*false*" = 0.2. Under the same conditions the pseudo–gradient training needed more than 2000 iterations to converge. The frequency with which the algorithm became trapped in local minima seems to be about the same as for BP for binary tasks. We also used the new method in training DMNN to learn smooth functions. One hidden layer of hard–limiting units and one output unit with linear activation function was used in all our experiments. We did not manage to train DMNNs using the pseudo–gradient training method due to oscillations, although various step sizes and different discrete activation functions have been tried. With the new algorithm and discrete activation functions such as 0.5 for "*true*" and -0.5 for "*false*" DMNNs were trained as fast as, and often faster than, BP trained FNNs until $E \leq 0.5$ (over 21 input/output cases). After this error bound, the convergence speed was reduced due to saturation problems.

However, it is worth noticing the difference in the behaviour between BP and the new method. Back–propagation trained FNNs exhibit a greater tendency to fit closely data with higher variation than data with low variation. On the other hand, although DMNNs do not produce smooth functions, they learn the general trend of the data values and therefore might be more useful than FNNs when there is noise in the data and the error goal can be set so high that the network does not have to fit all the target values perfectly. Situations like this usually occur in system identification and control (see [14]).

4 Conclusion and Further Improvements

This paper describes a new training method for DMNNs. The method does not directly perform gradient evaluations. Since it uses the modified one–dimensional bisection method it requires only that the algebraic signs of the function and gradient values be correct; so it can be applied to problems with imprecise function and gradient values. The method can also be used in training with block of network parameters, for example train the entire network, then the weights to the output layer and the thresholds of the hidden units, etc. We have tested such configurations and the results were very promising, providing faster training.

REFERENCES

[1] W. McCullough, W. H. Pitts, *A logical calculus of the ideas imminent in nervous activity*, Bulletin Mathematical Biophysics, Vol. 5 (1943), pp115–133.

[2] S. E. Hampson, D. J. Volper, *Representing and learning boolean functions of multivalued features*, IEEE Trans. Systems, Man & Cybernetics, Vol. 20 (1990), pp67–80.

[3] G. J. Gibson, F. N. Cowan, *On the decision regions of multi-layer perceptrons*, Proc. IEEE, Vol. 78 (1990), pp1590–1594.

[4] D. E. Rumelhart and J. L. McClelland eds., *Parallel Distributed Processing : Explorations in the Microstructure of Cognition*, Vol. 1, MIT Press (1986), pp318–362.

[5] B. Widrow, R. Winter, *Neural nets for adaptive filtering and adaptive pattern recognition*, IEEE Computer (March 1988), pp25–39.

[6] D. J. Tom, *Training binary node feed forward neural networks by back-propagation of error*, Electronics Letters, Vol. 26 (1990), pp1745–1746.

[7] E. M. Gorwin, A. M. Logar, W. J. B. Oldham, *An iterative method for training multilayer networks with threshold functions*, IEEE Trans. Neural Networks, Vol. 5 (1994), pp507–508.

[8] R. Goodman, Z. Zeng, *A learning algorithm for multi-layer perceptrons with hard-limiting threshold units*, in: Proc. IEEE Neural Networks for Signal Processing (1994), pp219–228.

[9] Z. Zeng, R. Goodman, P. Smyth, *Learning finite state machines with self-clustering recurrent networks*, Neural Computation, Vol. 5 (1993), pp976–990.

[10] Z. Zeng, R. Goodman, P. Smyth, *Discrete recurrent neural networks for grammatical inference*, IEEE Trans. Neural Networks, Vol. 5 (1994), pp320–330.

[11] M. N. Vrahatis, G. S. Androulakis, G. E. Manoussakis, *A new unconstrained optimization method for imprecise function and gradient values*, J. Mathematical Analysis & Applications, Vol. 197 (1996), pp586–607.

[12] M. N. Vrahatis, *Solving systems of non-linear equations using the non zero value of the topological degree*, ACM Trans. Math. Software, Vol. 14 (1988), pp312–329.

[13] M. N. Vrahatis, *CHABIS: A mathematical software package for locating and evaluating roots of systems of non-linear equations*, ACM Trans. Math. Software, Vol. 14 (1988), pp330–336.

[14] H. J. Sira-Ramirez, S. H. Zak, *The adaptation of perceptrons with applications to inverse dynamics identification of unknown dynamic systems*, IEEE Trans. Systems, Man & Cybernetics, Vol. 21 (1991), pp634–643.

LOCAL MINIMAL REALISATIONS OF TRAINED HOPFIELD NETWORKS

S. Manchanda and G.G.R. Green*

Dept. of Chemical and Process Engineering,
University of Newcastle upon Tyne, Newcastle upon Tyne, NE1 7RU, UK.
** Dept. of Physiological Sciences, Email: gary.green@ncl.ac.uk*

A methodology for investigating the invariant structural characteristics of the different approximations produced by Hopfield networks is presented. The technique exploits the description of the dynamics of a network as a Generating series which relates the output of a network to the past history of inputs. Truncations of a Hopfield Generating series are approximations to unknown dynamics to a specified order. As a truncated series has finite Lie rank, a local minimal realisation can be formulated. This realisation has a dimension whose lower bound is determined by the relative order of the network and whose upper bound is determined by the order of truncation. The maximal dimension of the minimal realisation is *independent* of the number of nodes in the network.

Keywords: Hopfield networks, nonlinear dynamics, realisations, minimality.

1 Introduction

Trained recurrent networks are commonly used to provide models of an unknown nonlinear dynamic system. The representations are in the form of state-space models which are usually characterised as sets of nonlinear differential equations. However, different combinations of network weight parameters often produce comparable approximation capabilities. Thus a fundamental problem is the interpretation of these representations. One approach to this problem is to attempt to reduce the state-space model to a minimal form as this is the description to which all other representations are related by diffeo-morphisms.

In practice, network model building is concerned with producing a suitable approximation of the unknown dynamic system, thus what is required is a method for specifying the order of the approximation and for producing the corresponding minimal realisation which has the same approximation capability. The input-output behaviour of a trained network can be formulated as a formal power series in non-commutative variables. This formal power series, the Generating series [2], has a minimal realisation if its Lie rank is finite [1]. If the infinite Hopfield Generating series which, in general, is not of finite Lie rank can be truncated, it can be used to produce minimal realisations whose input-output behaviour match that of the network up to a specified arbitrary order. This is equivalent to producing the minimal realisation of the unknown dynamics to a specified order of approximation.

In this article the tools for constructing minimal realisations of truncated Generating series are applied to Hopfield recurrent networks. These tools were originally described by Fliess [1]. The approach was further developed by Jacob & Oussous [3].

2 Hopfield Networks and their Local Solutions

The Lie derivatives, A_0 and A_1, that define the state-space of the single-input ($m = 1$) single-output (SISO) Hopfield RNN are

$$A_0 = \sum_i^N(-\kappa_i x_i + \sum_j^N w_{ij}\sigma(x_j))\frac{\partial}{\partial x_i} \quad A_1 = \sum_i^N \gamma_i \frac{\partial}{\partial x_i}$$

where $\sigma(x_i)$ is the output of the ith node in a single layer of N hidden nodes, κ_i acts as a time constant of the *ith* node, w_{ij} is the weight between node i and j, and $\gamma_i u$ is the weighted input u into node i. It is assumed that the σ nonlinearity is the tanh function and that the output of the network is $y = h(x) = \sigma(x_1)$.
The Generating series solution of this specific linear analytic system is formed by the Peano-Baker iteration of the state-space differential equations. It can be shown to be [2]

$$y(t) = S = h_{|X_0} + \sum_{\nu \geq 0} \sum_{j_1,..,j_\nu=0}^{m} A_{j_1}A_{j_2}...A_{j_\nu}(h)_{|X_0} z_{j_\nu} \cdots z_{j_2} z_{j_1}$$

where S is a mapping between the free monoid Z^*, constructed from the alphabet set z_0, z_1, into $\mathbb{R}$ and the subscript $_{|X_0}$ means evaluated at the initial conditions of the state vector. Each word, $z_{j_1} z_{j_2} .. z_{j_k}$ corresponds to the iterated integral

$$\int_0^t u_{j_1}(\tau_1) \int_0^{\tau_1} u_{j_2}(\tau_2) \cdots \int_0^{\tau_{k-1}} u_{j_k}(\tau_k) d\tau_k \cdots d\tau_2 d\tau_1$$

defined recursively on its length,(u_0 is defined to be unity). The coefficient of the word $z_{j_1} z_{j_2} .. z_{j_k}$ is the iterated Lie derivative $A_{j_k} .. A_{j_2} A_{j_1}$ operating on the output h and evaluated at the initial conditions. The Generating series is a causal functional expansion about a point and is valid local to this position in state space, for a short time and for small input u.
Two systems are locally equivalent *if and only if* their Generating series match. In this framework *any training algorithm* for a recurrent network can be viewed as a method for adjusting the coefficients of words to produce this matching by altering the contribution of the weights, to each term, in the Generating series.

3 Network Minimal Realisations

The Generating series form of the Hopfield network is an infinite series. Truncation of this series produces an approximation of the local input-output behaviour of the network and therefore of the unknown system.
To produce the minimal realisation of this approximation depends upon identifying the structural characteristics of a *truncated* Generating series which does not include a constant term. This latter constraint can always be satisfied by considering the dynamics from a specific position in state space. The truncated Generating series of arbitrary order k can be expressed in terms of a Lie-Hankel matrix [3]. A Lie-Hankel matrix, LH_S, of a Generating series S is an (infinite) array whose rows are indexed by a totally ordered basis of the Lie algebra of Z, $L\langle Z\rangle$, and the columns are indexed by Z^*. The finiteness of the rank of this matrix determines whether a corresponding minimal state-space realisation exists, while the magnitude of the rank governs the dimension of the realisation [1].
As the basis of $L\langle Z\rangle$, the Lyndon basis (the specific Lie polynomials, P_i) can be chosen [3, 4].
For example, if the Generating series of a n state Hopfield network is truncated so that the length of the words ≤ 2, then the Lyndon words are the set $\{z_0, z_1, z_0 z_1\}$ and the corresponding Lie polynomials P_i are $\{z_0, z_1, [z_0, z_1]\}$ where $[z_0, z_1]$ is the Lie bracket of the words z_0, z_1 and is defined as $z_0 z_1 - z_1 z_0$. The Lie-Hankel matrix is shown in Table 1 whose elements are evaluated at a point in the state space of the Hopfield network. Similar analyses can be made for truncated Generating series

	ϵ	z_0	z_1
z_0	$A_0(h)$	$A_0^2(h)$	$A_1A_0(h)$
z_1	$A_1(h)$	$A_0A_1(h)$	$A_1^2(h)$
$[z_0, z_1]$	$A_1A_0(h) - A_0A_1(h)$	0	0

Table 1

order	rank
1	1
2	3
3	5
4	8

Table 2

of higher order. The maximum rank, as a function of truncation order is shown in Table 2.

The rank, and therefore the dimension of the minimal realisation, is not determined by the number of hidden nodes in the network as the elements of the Lie-Hankel matrix are defined for an arbitrary number of hidden nodes. The rank reduces if certain network weights result in either linear row interdependence or rows having zero entries. This latter condition can occur if the networks have relative order greater then unity as then particular terms in the Generating series are zero. The lower bound on the rank of the Lie-Hankel matrix is determined by the relative order of the network.

3.1 Construction of the Minimal Realisation

Lyndon words can be used to construct a basis set of polynomials Q_j. The basis set Q represents the local coordinates of the minimal state-space realisation. The set Q is used to reconstruct the truncated Generating series S. The series is expressed in terms of linear combinations and shuffle products of the elements Q_j of the basis set Q. Thus, for the truncated Hopfield network of relative order unity, the set Q consists of the elements $Q_1 = z_0$, $Q_2 = z_1$ and $Q_3 = z_0z_1$.

The truncated series is reconstructed from the basis set Q by using a modification of the algorithm proposed by Jacob & Oussous [3] to deal with Generating series with arbitrary coefficients of words. The algorithm iteratively searches for and identifies proper left factors of the truncated series.

The vector fields are reconstructed in terms of linear combinations and shuffle products of the elements of Q and translated into the state space coordinates q. Thus, in the length two example, the vector fields of the minimal realisation are

$$A_0 = \frac{\partial}{\partial q_1}, \; A_1 = \frac{\partial}{\partial q_2} + q_1 \frac{\partial}{\partial q_3}$$

The output function is given by

$$y = (A_0A_1(h) - A_1A_0(h))q_3 + \frac{1}{2}A_1^2(h)q_2^2 + A_1(h)q_2$$

$$+A_1A_0(h)q_1q_2+\frac{1}{2}A_0^2(h)q_1^2+A_0(h)q_1$$

4 Discussion

This article is concerned with local approximations to unknown nonlinear dynamics up to a specified order. The approximation order is in terms of the length of the Generating series that represents the input-output behaviour of a trained network. A trained recurrent network can closely approximate, in a local sense, an unknown dynamic when the network Generating series is similar to that of the unknown system. It should be noted that the unknown dynamic system may not necessarily be represented by a suitable global model and therefore one should seek local models in the first instance. The Generating series, like the Taylor series, is a *local* functional expansion.

In this article only an upper and lower bound on the rank of the Lie-Hankel matrix is described. The upper bound is determined by the length of the truncated Generating series and is directly related to the order of approximation of the unknown dynamics by the Hopfield network.

The rank determines the dimension of the minimal realisation. The dimension of the minimal realisation is *independent of the number of hidden nodes* in the Hopfield network. The network trajectory evolves locally on a submanifold of the Hopfield state-space.

The local minimal realisation of a truncated Generating series of a Hopfield network is a set of polynomial differential equations and an output which is polynomial in the states. The state-space dynamics are fixed and do not depend upon the position in the original Hopfield state space. The minimal state space dynamics are input driven, with zero initial conditions. The state space dynamics reflect the local influence of the system input. However, the output map is dependent upon the position in the Hopfield state space. These observations on the form of the local minimal realisations imply that any two networks which are used to approximate an unknown system have the same minimal state-space dynamics and differ only in the form of the output function.

Acknowledgements

We gratefully acknowledge support from the UK EPSRC and the Research Committee of the University of Newcastle upon Tyne, UK.

REFERENCES

[1] M. Fliess, *Realisation locale des systemes non lineaires, algebres de lie filtrees transitives et series generatrices non commutatives*, Invent. Math., Vol. 71 (1983), pp521–537.

[2] M. Fliess, M. Lamnabhi, and F. Lamnabhi-Lagarrigue, *An algebraic approach to nonlinear functional expansions*, IEEE Transactions on Circuits and Systems, Vol. 30 (1983) pp554–570.

[3] G. Jacob and N. Oussous, *Local and minimal realisation of nonlinear dynamical systems and lyndon words*, in: A. Isidori, editor, IFAC symposium: Nonlinear Control Systems Design (1989), pp155–160.

[4] G. Viennot. *Algebre de Lie libres et monoides libres. Lecture Notes in Mathematics*, Vol. 691 (1978), Springer-Verlag.

DATA DEPENDENT HYPERPARAMETER ASSIGNMENT

Glenn Marion and David Saad*

Department of Statistics and Modelling Science, Livingstone Tower, 26 Richmond Street, Glasgow G1 1XH, UK. Email: glenn@stams.strath.ac.uk

** Department of Computer Science and Mathematics, Aston University, The Aston Triangle, Birmingham B4 7ET, UK. Email: D.Saad@uk.ac.ed*

We show that in supervised learning from a particular data set Bayesian model selection, based on the evidence, does not optimise generalization performance even for a learnable linear problem. This is achieved by examining the finite size effects in hyperparameter assignment from the evidence procedure and its effect on generalisation. Using simulations we corroborate our analytic results and examine an alternative model selection criterion, namely cross-validation. This numerical study shows that in the learnable linear case for finite sized systems leave one out cross-validation estimates correlate more strongly with optimal performance than do those of the evidence.

1 Introduction

The problem of supervised learning, or learning from examples, has been much studied using the techniques of statistical physics (see *e.g.* [7]). A major advantage of such studies over the usual approach in the statistics community is that one can examine the situation where the fraction (α) of the number of examples (p) to the number of free parameters (N) is finite. This contrasts with the asymptotic (in α) treatments found in the statistics literature (see *e.g.* [6]). However, one draw back of the statistical physics approach is that it is based on the, so called, thermodynamic limit where one allows N and p to approach infinity whilst keeping α constant. A quantity is said to be *self averaging* if its variance over data sets of examples tends to zero in the thermodynamic limit. We show that in Bayesian model selection based on the evidence, conclusions drawn from the thermodynamic results are qualitatively at odds with the finite size behaviour.

In the supervised learning scenario one is presented with a set of data

$$\mathcal{D} = \{(y_t(\mathbf{x}^\mu), \mathbf{x}^\mu) : \mu = 1..p\}$$

consisting of p examples of an otherwise unknown *teacher* mapping denoted by the distribution $P(y_t \mid \mathbf{x})$. Furthermore, we assume that the N dimensional input space is sampled with probability $P(\mathbf{x})$. The learning task is to use this data $\mathcal{D}$ to set the N_s parameters $\mathbf{w}$ of some model (or student) such that it's output, $y_s(\mathbf{x})$, *generalizes* to examples not contained in the training data, $\mathcal{D}$. Often this is achieved by minimising a weighted sum, $\beta E_{\mathbf{w}}(\mathcal{D}) + \gamma C(\mathbf{w})$ of the quadratic error of the student on the training examples, $E_{\mathbf{w}}(\mathcal{D})$, and some *cost function*, $C(\mathbf{w})$, which penalises over complex models. Provided γ is non-zero this serves to alleviate the problem of *overfitting*. It is the setting of the, so-called, *hyperparameters* β and γ which we will examine in this presentation.

In terms of practical methods for hyperparameter assignment there are essentially two choices. Firstly one can attempt to estimate the generalisation error (*e.g.* by cross-validation [6]) and then optimise this measure with respect to the hyperparameters. However, such an approach can be computationally expensive. Secondly, one can optimise some other measure and hope that the resulting assignments produce low generalisation error. In particular, MacKay [6] advocates the *evidence* as such a measure. Model selection based on the evidence, in the case of a linear student and teacher, has been studied by Bruce and Saad [1] in the thermodynamic limit. Their results show that optimising the average, over all possible data sets $\mathcal{D}$, of the log evidence with respect to the hyperparameters optimises the average generalization error. An average case analysis of an unlearnable scenario can be found in [3] and shows that in general the evidence need not be optimal on average. In this paper we examine hyperparameter assignment from the evidence *based on an individual data set*, in the learnable linear case. In the next section we review the evidence framework and introduce the generalization error. In section 3, we show that the evidence procedure is unbiased and that the evidence and generalization error are self averaging. In section 4 we examine hyperparameter assignment from the evidence based on a particular data set. First order corrections to the performance measures show that in general the evidence procedure does not lead to optimal performance. Finally, we corroborate these conclusions using a numerical study which, furthermore, reveals that even leave one out cross-validation is a superior model selection criterion to the evidence in the learnable linear case for small systems.

2 Objective Functions

2.1 The Evidence

Since $E_{\mathbf{w}}(\mathcal{D})$ is the sum squared error then, if we assume that our data is corrupted by Gaussian noise with variance $1/2\beta$, the probability, or *likelihood* of the data($\mathcal{D}$) being produced given the model $\mathbf{w}$ and β is $P(\mathcal{D} \mid \beta, \mathbf{w}) \propto e^{-\beta E_{\mathbf{w}}(\mathcal{D})}$. The complexity cost can also be incorporated into this Bayesian scheme by assuming the *a priori* probability of a rule is weighted against 'complex' rules, $P(\mathbf{w} \mid \gamma) \propto e^{-\gamma C(\mathbf{w})}$. Multiplying the likelihood and the prior together we obtain the post training or student distribution, $P(\mathbf{w} \mid \mathcal{D}, \gamma, \beta) \propto e^{-\beta E_{\mathbf{w}}(\mathcal{D}) - \gamma C(\mathbf{w})}$. It is clear that the most probable model $\mathbf{w}^*$ is given by minimizing the composite cost function $\beta E_{\mathbf{w}}(\mathcal{D}) + \gamma C(\mathbf{w})$ with respect to $\mathbf{w}$.

The evidence, $P(\mathcal{D} \mid \gamma, \beta)$, is the normalisation constant for the post training distribution. That is, the probability of (or evidence for) the data set ($\mathcal{D}$) given the hyperparameters β and γ. Throughout this paper we refer to the *evidence procedure* as the process of fixing the hyperparameters to the values that simultaneously maximize the evidence for a given data set.

2.2 The Generalization Error

We will use the notation $\langle f(z) \rangle_P$ to denote the average of the quantity $f(z)$ over the distribution $P(z)$. However, we will use the short hand $\langle . \rangle_{\mathbf{w}}$ to mean the average over the post training distribution $P(\mathbf{w} \mid \mathcal{D}, \gamma, \beta)$. As our performance measure we choose the expected difference over the input dimension $P(\mathbf{x})$ between the average student and the average teacher. That is, the data dependent generalisation error, $\epsilon_g(\mathcal{D}) = \langle (\langle y_t(\mathbf{x}) \rangle_{P(y_t|\mathbf{x})} - \langle y_s(x) \rangle_{\mathbf{w}})^2 \rangle_{P(\mathbf{x})}$. If we were to *average over all possible data sets* of fixed size then this would correspond to the generalization error studied in [1].

3 Finite System Size

Since the student is linear with output $y(\mathbf{x}) = \mathbf{w}.\mathbf{x}/\sqrt{N}$, $N_s = N$. We also assume that the teacher mapping is linear, with weights $\mathbf{w}^o$, and corrupted by zero mean Gaussian noise of variance σ^2. Thus, $P(y_t \mid \mathbf{x}_\mu) \propto e^{-(y_t^\mu - \mathbf{w}^o.\mathbf{x}_\mu/\sqrt{N})^2/2\sigma^2}$. Further, we assume $P(\mathbf{x})$ is $\mathcal{N}(0, \sigma_x)$[1] and adopt weight decay as our regularization procedure, that is $C(\mathbf{w}) = \mathbf{w}^T\mathbf{w}$. In this case we can explicitly calculate the evidence, or rather the normalised log of the evidence $f(\mathcal{D}) = -1/N \ln(P(\mathcal{D} \mid \lambda, \beta)$, where we have introduced the weight decay parameter $\lambda = \gamma/\beta$. The generalisation error and the consistency can be calculated from $f(\mathcal{D})$ by averaging appropriate expressions over the input distribution $P(\mathbf{x})$. Details of these calculations will appear in a subsequent paper [4].

3.1 Consistency, Unbiasedness and Self Averaging

Firstly, we examine the *free energy*, $f(\mathcal{D})$, and the generalisation error in the limit of large amounts of data (*i.e.* as $p \to \infty$ with N fixed). Using the central limit theorem we can show that, in this limit, to first order the generalisation error is independent of the weight decay whilst f is optimised by $\lambda_{ev} = \lambda_0 \equiv \sigma^2/(\sigma_x^2\sigma_w^2)$ and $\beta_{ev} = \beta_0 \equiv 1/(2\sigma^2)$. As we shall see later in the context of large N this insensitivity of the generalisation error to the value of the weight decay is associated with a divergence in the variance of the optimal weight decay as the number of examples grows large. This asymptotic insensitivity to the weight decay is a reflection of the fact that our linear student is *mean square consistent.* We will thus focus on the following quantity when assessing the evidence procedure's performance,

$$\kappa_{\epsilon_g}(\lambda_{ev}) = \frac{\epsilon_g(\lambda_{ev}(\mathcal{D})) - \epsilon_g(\lambda_{opt}(\mathcal{D}))}{\epsilon_g(\lambda_{opt}(\mathcal{D}))} \quad . \tag{1}$$

Secondly, it can be shown that $\langle g_{ij}\rangle_{P(\{\mathbf{x}^\mu:\mu=1..p\})} \propto \delta_{ij}$, then the resulting average free energy, $f = \langle f(\mathcal{D})\rangle_{P(\mathcal{D})}$ is extremised by $\lambda = \lambda_0$ and $\beta = \beta_0$. Similarly, the average generalisation error is optimised by λ_0. This corresponds to the average case result obtained for the thermodynamic limit in [1] but is valid for all N and p. Thus, the particular conclusion, of the thermodynamic average case analysis, for the learnable linear scenario, that the evidence procedure optimises average performance is valid for all N and in this sense the procedure is unbiased.

Finally using results of [9] [2] one can show that the variance, over possible realisations of the data set, of the free energy, $f(\mathcal{D})$ is order $\mathcal{O}(1/N)$ as we approach the thermodynamic limit; it is a self averaging quantity. Similarly, it can also be shown that the generalization error is self averaging. This means that in the thermodynamic limit the behaviour exhibited by the system for any particular data set will correspond to the average case behaviour, that is the fluctuations around the average vanish. Thus, the average case analysis of [1] corresponds to the case for a *particular data set* because their results were obtained in the thermodynamic limit.

4 Data Dependent Hyperparameter Assignment

Having now established that the evidence procedure is unbiased and that the free energy and performance measures are self averaging we now wish to examine the system behaviour for particular data sets of finite size. This is clearly the regime

---

[1] Where $\mathrm{N}(\bar{\mathrm{x}}, \sigma)$ denotes a normal distribution with mean $\bar{\mathrm{x}}$ and variance σ^2.

[2] Alternatively one can show this result using diagrammatic methods.

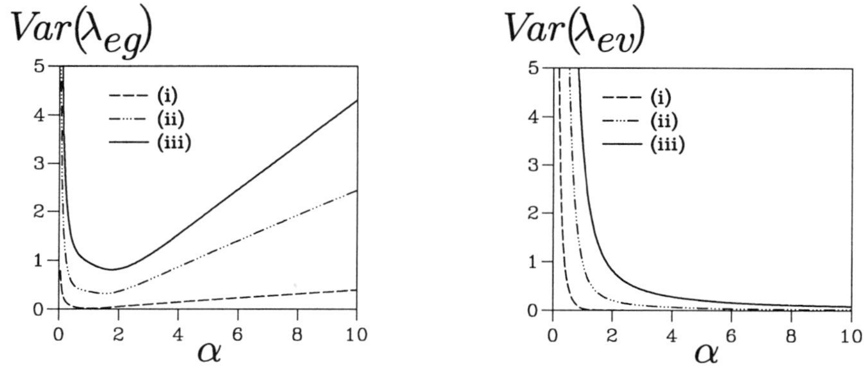

Figure 1 The variance in the optimal weight decay ($Var(\lambda_{eg})$) for various noise levels, (i) $\lambda_0 = 0.04$, (ii) $\lambda_0 = 0.25$ and (iii) $\lambda_0 = 4/9$ is shown in the left-hand graph. Notice the linear divergence in α which corresponds to our result in section 3.1 that, for sufficiently large p, the generalization error is independent of λ. The variance in the evidence optimal weight decay ($Var(\lambda_{ev})$) is shown, in the right-hand graph, for the same noise levels. The $\mathcal{O}(1/\alpha)$ decay of this quantity is a reflection of the fact that for large p $\lambda_{ev}(\mathcal{D}) = \lambda_0$.

of interest to *real world* applications since one is then in the business of optimising performance based on a particular data set. To obtain the hyperparameter assignments made by the evidence procedure we must simultaneously solve $\partial_\lambda f(\mathcal{D}) = 0$ and $\partial_\beta f(\mathcal{D}) = 0$, where $\partial_\theta f \equiv \partial f / \partial \theta$. We can linearize these equations, close to the thermodynamic limit, by expanding around $\lambda = \lambda_0$ and $\beta = \beta_0$. Similarly, we can also expand the true optimal weight decay about the thermodynamic limit value, λ_0.

We find that (co)-variances of these quantities are $\mathcal{O}(1/N)$. Figure 1 shows, to first order, the scaled variances [3] in the evidence optimal weight decay, $Var(\lambda_{ev})$ and that in the true optimal weight decay, $Var(\lambda_{opt})$. The asymptotic $\mathcal{O}(1/\alpha)$ decay of the former reflects the fact that, as discussed in section 3.1, $\lim_{\alpha \to \infty} \lambda_{ev}(\mathcal{D}) = \lambda_0$. Similarly, the divergence of the latter is indicative of the insensitivity of the generalization error to the weight decay for large α. The divergence of both curves for small α is order $\mathcal{O}(1/N\alpha)$ and reflects the break down of the thermodynamic limit when the number of examples p does not scale with the system size N,

Similarly we find that the average squared distance between the evidence assignment and the optimal, $< (\lambda_0(\mathcal{D}) - \lambda_{ev}(\mathcal{D}))^2 >_{P(\mathcal{D})}$, is order $\mathcal{O}(1/N)$. This distance is *non zero*, except for $\alpha > 1$ in the noiseless limit. Further, in the large α limit this distance diverges, revealing the inconsistency of the evidence weight decay assignment.

4.1 Effects on Performance

We now examine the effects on performance of this sub-optimal hyperparameter assignment. Firstly, to order $\mathcal{O}(1/\sqrt{N})$ the optimal performance, $\epsilon_g(\lambda_{opt}, \mathcal{D})$, and that resulting from use of the evidence procedure, $\epsilon_g(\lambda_{ev}, \mathcal{D})$ are the same. However,

[3] *i.e.* N times the true variances

to order $\mathcal{O}(1/N)$ they differ thus we can write the correlation between them, somewhat suggestively, as $1 - \mathcal{O}(1/N)$. Unfortunately, we are unable to calculate this correlation to $\mathcal{O}(1/N)$. Therefore, we examine $< \kappa_{\epsilon_g} >_{P(\mathcal{D})}$ which tends to $1/N$ in the limit of large α reflecting the inconsistency of the evidence weight decay assignments. In the limit of no noise for $\alpha > 1$ we find that $< \kappa_{\epsilon_g} >_{P(\mathcal{D})} = (\alpha+1)/N(\alpha-1)$ revealing that even for small noise levels the evidence procedure is sub-optimal.

4.2 Comparison with Cross-validation

Given, that the evidence procedure is sub-optimal it is natural to ask if another model selection criteria could do better. Here we compare the evidence procedure with leave-one-out cross-validation using simulations of a 1-dimensional system. That is we set the weight decay using the cross-validatory estimate and the evidence estimate and compare the resulting generalisation error to the optimal. The results, averaged over 1000 realisations of the data set for each value of p, are plotted in figure 2. These show that the evidence weight decay assignment results in sub-optimal performance with $\epsilon_g(\lambda_{ev}, \mathcal{D})$ not fully correlated with $\epsilon_g(\lambda_0, \mathcal{D})$. Moreover, the left-hand graph shows that the resulting error from the cross-validatory estimate correlates more strongly with the optimal generalisation error than does that resulting from the evidence estimate. In addition, the right-hand graph shows that the fractional increase in the generalisation error is considerably larger for the evidence procedure than for cross-validation.

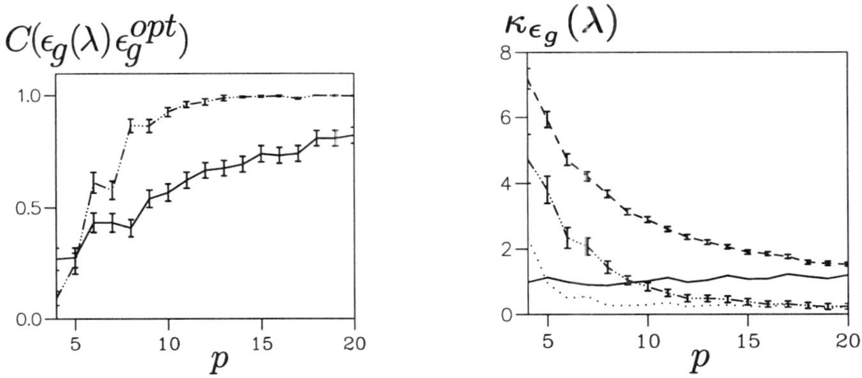

Figure 2 1-D simulation results: The left-hand graph shows the correlation between the optimal generalization error and those obtained using the evidence (solid) and cross-validation (chain) with $\lambda_0 = 1.0$. The right-hand graph shows the fractional increase in generalization error $\kappa_{\epsilon_g}(\lambda) = (\epsilon_g(\lambda) - \epsilon_g(\lambda_{opt}))/\epsilon_g(\lambda_{opt})$. λ is set by the evidence (dashed) and by cross-validation (chain) for $\lambda_0 = 1.0$. For $\lambda_0 = 0.01$ the evidence case is the solid curve cross-validation the dotted curve. In the latter case the error bars are not shown for the sake of clarity.

5 Conclusion

We have shown that, despite thermodynamic and average case results to the contrary, model selection based on the evidence does not optimise performance even in the learnable linear case. In addition, numerical studies indicate that for small systems cross-validation is closer, than the evidence procedure, to optimal performance. However, for large systems the evidence might still be a reasonable alternative to the computationally expensive cross-validation.

REFERENCES

[1] Bruce A D and Saad D, *Statistical mechanics of hypothesis evaluation.* J. of Phys. A: Math. Gen. Vol. 27 (1994), pp3355–3363.

[2] MacKay D J C, *Bayesian interpolation*, Neural Comp. Vol. 4 (1992), pp415–447.

[3] Marion G and Saad D, *A statistical mechanical analysis of a Bayesian inference scheme for an unrealizable rule.* J. of Phys. A: Math. Gen. Vol. 28 (1995), pp2159–2171.

[4] Marion G and Saad D, *Finite size effects in Bayesian model selection and generalization.* J. of Phys. A: Math. Gen. Vol. 29 (1996), pp5387–5404.

[5] Sollich P, *Finite-size effects in learning and generalization in linear perceptrons.* J. of Phys. A: Math. Gen. Vol. 27 (1994), pp7771–7784.

[6] Stone M, *An asymptotic equivalence of choice of model by cross-validation and Akaikes criterion*, J. Roy. Statist. Soc. Ser. B Vol. 39 (1977), pp44–47.

[7] Watkin T L H, Rau A, Biehl M, *The statistical mechanics of learning a rule.* Reviews of Modern Physics Vol. 65 (1993), pp499–556.

Acknowledgements

The authors wish to thank the Physics Department, University of Edinburgh where this work was conducted.

TRAINING RADIAL BASIS FUNCTION NETWORKS BY USING SEPARABLE AND ORTHOGONALIZED GAUSSIANS

J. C. Mason, I. J. Anderson, G. Rodriguez* and S. Seatzu*

School of Computing and Mathematics, University of Huddersfield, Queensgate, Huddersfield HD1 3DH, UK.

** Department of Mathematics, University of Cagliari, viale Merello 92, 09123 Cagliari, Italy.*

Radial basis function (RBF) networks have the great advantage that they may be determined rapidly by solving a linear least squares problem, assuming that good positions for the radial centres may be selected in advance. Here it is shown that, if there is some structure in the data, for example if the data lie on lines, then variables in Gaussian RBFs may be separated and a near-optimal least squares solution may be obtained rather efficiently. Second, it is shown that a system of Gaussian RBFs with structured or scattered centres may be orthogonalized over a continuum or discrete data set and thereafter the least squares solution is immediate. Keywords: Gaussians, orthogonalization, RBF, separability.

1 Introduction

Suppose that there are m input data $\mathbf{x}^{(1)}, \ldots, \mathbf{x}^{(m)}$, and that each datum $\mathbf{x}$ has d components $x_1, \ldots, x_d$. Suppose that we adopt a radial basis function network with the centres $\mathbf{w}^{(1)}, \ldots, \mathbf{w}^{(n)}$, given by $\mathbf{w}^{(i)} = \left(w_1^{(i)}, w_2^{(i)}, \ldots, w_d^{(i)}\right)'$, for $i = 1, \ldots, n$. The components, $w_j^{(i)}$ of the centres are "weights" in the network, between the input and hidden layer. Frequently good choices of centres may be made by clustering techniques [3], and so we assume $w_j^{(i)}$ to be fixed. Suppose that coefficients c_i, for $i = 1, \ldots, n$, are associated with radial basis (transfer) functions $\phi_i(r)$ applied to the argument r_i, where

$$r_i = \left[\sum_j \left(x_j - w_j^{(i)}\right)^2\right]^{1/2} = \left\|\mathbf{x} - \mathbf{w}^{(i)}\right\|_2 .$$

The coefficients $\{c_i\}$ are weights between the hidden and output layers, and the output function $f(\mathbf{x})$ is approximated by an RBF, $F(\mathbf{x})$, as follows,

$$f(\mathbf{x}) \approx F(\mathbf{x}) = \sum_{i=1}^{n} c_i \phi\left(\left\|\mathbf{x} - \mathbf{w}^{(i)}\right\|_2\right).$$

Frequently the RBFs $\{\phi_i(r)\}$ are taken to be the same function $\phi(r)$ for each i. In this paper we consider the basis function $\phi(r) = \exp(-r^2)$.

2 Separability of Gaussians

The Gaussian has some particular advantages in terms of (i) its separability and (ii) the simplicity of its inner product. In this section, we consider separability and in Section 3 we exploit the inner product in discussing orthogonalization.
If $\phi(r) = \exp(-r^2)$, then

$$\phi(\|\mathbf{x}\|) = \phi(x_1)\phi(x_2)\ldots\phi(x_d).$$

Thus the RBF is a product of d one-dimensional Gaussians.

2.1 Fast Approximation on a Mesh

Suppose that the 2-dimensional data $\mathbf{x} = (x_1, x_2)'$ and the corresponding centres $\mathbf{w} = (w_1, w_2)'$ are each placed on meshes

$$\begin{aligned} \mathbf{x}_{k,\ell} &= \left(x_1^{(k)}, x_2^{(\ell)}\right) \quad \text{for } k = 1, \ldots, m_x \text{ and } \ell = 1, \ldots, m_y, \\ \mathbf{w}_{i,j} &= \left(w_1^{(i)}, w_2^{(j)}\right) \quad \text{for } i = 1, \ldots, n_x \text{ and } j = 1, \ldots, n_y, \end{aligned}$$

where $n_x \le m_x$ and $n_y \le m_y$.

Here n_x and n_y are the numbers of different values for the two respective components of the centres, and m_x and m_y are the corresponding numbers of different values for the two components of the data. Then our RBF approximation on the data is

$$f(\mathbf{x}_{k,\ell}) = \sum_{i=1}^{n_x} \left(\sum_{j=1}^{n_y} c_{i,j} \phi(x_2^{(\ell)} - w_2^{(j)}) \right) \phi(x_1^{(k)} - w_1^{(i)}). \tag{1}$$

For each $\ell = 1, \ldots, m_y$, we obtain the (overdetermined) linear system,

$$f(\mathbf{x}_{k,\ell}) = \sum_{i=1}^{n_x} b_i^{(\ell)} \phi(x_1^{(k)} - w_1^{(i)}) \tag{2}$$

for $k = 1, \ldots, m_x$, where, for each $i = 1, \ldots, n_x$, we have the (overdetermined) system

$$b_i^{(\ell)} = \sum_{j=1}^{n_y} c_{i,j} \phi(x_2^{(\ell)} - w_2^{(j)}) \tag{3}$$

for $\ell = 1, \ldots, m_y$.

Using matrix notation, we may express the system of equations (2) as

$$A_x \mathbf{b}^{(\ell)} = \mathbf{f}^{(\ell)}$$

for $\ell = 1, 2, \ldots, m_y$, where A_x is a matrix whose (k, i)th element is $\phi(x_1^{(k)} - w_1^{(i)})$, $\mathbf{b}^{(\ell)}$ is a vector of the elements $b_i^{(\ell)}$ for $i = 1, 2, \ldots, n_x$, and $\mathbf{f}^{(\ell)}$ is a vector of the elements $f(\mathbf{x}_{k,\ell})$ for $k = 1, 2, \ldots, m_x$. We note that the matrix A_x is independent of ℓ and so it is only necessary to factorize it once.

Similarly, we may express the system (3) as

$$A_y \mathbf{c}^{(i)} = \mathbf{b}_i$$

for $i = 1, 2, \ldots, n_x$, Here, the matrix A_y is independent of i and so, again, it is only necessary to factorize this matrix once. Thus, the solution of (2) and (3) by QR factorization can be achieved in $\mathcal{O}(m_y n_x (m_x + n_y))$ operations. This is a great saving over the $\mathcal{O}(m_x m_y n_x^2 n_y^2)$ operations that would be required if the system (1) of $m_x m_y$ equations were solved by least squares without exploiting any structure.

2.2 Data on Lines

If the data are less structured than a mesh, but do form lines, then fast methods may be adopted. Consider lines of data, where the x_2 values are fixed but the x_1 values are scattered (in different positions on each line). The data abscissae may be written as $(x_1^{(k,\ell)}, x_2^{(\ell)})$, for $k = 1, \ldots, m_\ell$ and $\ell = 1, \ldots, m_y$, so the x_1 values now vary with both k and ℓ. Equations (2) and (3) are still valid, but with $x_1^{(k)}$ and m_x replaced by $x_1^{(k,\ell)}$ and m_ℓ. We may therefore still solve (2) and (3) in the least squares sense. However, the solution is no longer the true least squares solution of (1). Indeed the solution of (2) now involves a different matrix for each value of ℓ, and this also means that the solution is less efficient — $\mathcal{O}\left(m_x m_y n_x^2\right)$ operations are needed to solve (2), although only $\mathcal{O}\left(m_y n_y n_x\right)$ operations are still required for (3). The method we describe here is the Gaussian RBF analogue of the methods of Clenshaw and Hayes [2] for polynomial approximation and of Anderson, Cox and Mason [1] for spline approximation of data on lines.

3 Orthogonalized Gaussians

Gaussians can be orthogonalized in a number of ways. Suppose that for data $\{\mathbf{x}\} = \{(x_1, \ldots, x_d)'\}$, we have centres $\mathbf{w}^{(i)}$ for $i = 1, \ldots, n$, and Gaussian RBFs $\phi_i(\|\mathbf{x}\|) = \exp(-\|\mathbf{x} - \mathbf{w}^{(i)}\|^2)$ for $i = 1, \ldots, n$.

Then a general orthogonalization technique, based on the Gram-Schmidt procedure, is to form a new basis $\psi_1, \ldots, \psi_n$ as,

$$\psi_i = \sum_{k=1}^{i} d_k^{(i)} \phi_k \tag{4}$$

$$= \sum_{k=1}^{i} e_k^{(i)} \psi_k \tag{5}$$

for $i = 1, 2, \ldots, n$, where $e_k^{(i)}$ and $d_k^{(i)}$ are appropriate coefficients such that $d_i^{(i)} = 1$ and $e_i^{(i)} = 1$. The values of the remaining coefficients are determined by requiring the new basis functions, $\psi_1, \ldots, \psi_n$, to be orthogonal with respect to some specified inner product. Thus we have

$$< \psi_i, \psi_j >= 0 \qquad \text{for } i \neq j.$$

Let us define

$$t_{i,j} =< \phi_i, \phi_j >, \tag{6}$$

and

$$n_k =< \psi_k, \psi_k >,$$

the values of $t_{i,j}$ being constants that may be calculated once and for all, and the values of n_k being normalization constants. Then, by setting $< \psi_i, \psi_j >= 0$ where (without loss of generality) $i < j$ we deduce, using equations (4) and (5), that

$$e_i^{(j)} = \frac{-1}{n_i} \sum_{k=1}^{i} d_k^{(i)} t_{k,j}. \tag{7}$$

By taking inner products of both sides of equation (5) with themselves, we deduce that

$$n_1 = t_{1,1}, \qquad \text{and} \qquad n_i = t_{i,i} - \sum_{k=1}^{i-1} (e_k^{(i)})^2 n_k. \tag{8}$$

Expanding equation (5) using (4) and equating similar terms, we derive

$$d_i^{(j)} = \sum_{k=i}^{j-1} e_k^{(j)} d_i^{(k)}. \tag{9}$$

Equations (7)–(9) suffice to determine n_k, $e_i^{(j)}$ and $d_i^{(j)}$ for all $i < j$ given values of $t_{i,j}$.

3.1 Continuum

Let us adopt an inner product over $\mathbb{R}^d = (-\infty, \infty)^d$ and define

$$V = \int_{\mathbb{R}^d} \exp(-\|\mathbf{x}\|^2)\,\mathbf{dS} = \int_{\mathbb{R}^d} \exp(-\|\mathbf{x}-\mathbf{w}\|^2)\,\mathbf{dS},$$

for any fixed $\mathbf{w}$. Now $t_{i,j}$ is readily calculated by using the following formula (whose derivation follows from the cosine rule),

$$\|\mathbf{x}-\mathbf{w}^{(i)}\|^2 + \|\mathbf{x}-\mathbf{w}^{(j)}\|^2 = 2\|\mathbf{x}-\mathbf{w}_{ij}\|^2 + \frac{1}{2}\|\mathbf{w}^{(i)} - \mathbf{w}^{(j)}\|^2, \qquad (10)$$

where $\mathbf{w}_{ij} = \frac{1}{2}(\mathbf{w}^{(i)} + \mathbf{w}^{(j)})$.
Now equation (6) becomes,

$$\begin{aligned} t_{i,j} &= <\phi_i, \phi_j> \\ &= \int \exp(-\|\mathbf{x}-\mathbf{w}^{(i)}\|^2 - \|\mathbf{x}-\mathbf{w}^{(j)}\|^2)\,\mathbf{dS} \\ &= \exp(-\frac{1}{2}\|\mathbf{w}^{(i)} - \mathbf{w}^{(j)}\|^2) \int \exp(-2\|\mathbf{x}-\mathbf{w}_{ij}\|^2)\,\mathbf{dS} \\ &= (\sqrt{2})^{-d} V \left(\phi_i(\mathbf{w}^{(j)})\right)^{1/2}. \end{aligned}$$

Thus $t_{i,j}$ is immediately determined from $\{\mathbf{w}^{(i)}\}$ without sums or integrals (V being a scalar multiplier), and the orthogonalization procedure is particularly straightforward.
This inner product is the natural one to use for a continuum of data. Indeed the best least squares approximation to f of the form

$$F(\mathbf{x}) = \sum_{i=1}^{n} c_i \psi_i(\mathbf{x})$$

is defined by setting

$$c_i = < F, \psi_i > / n_i.$$

3.2 Scattered Discrete Data

We might also adopt this inner product for a discrete data set, since it has the advantage of being data independent. The snag is that we do not then obtain a diagonal system for determining a least squares approximation on the data set and must solve

$$[F, \psi_j] = \sum_{i=1}^{n} c_i [\psi_i, \psi_j]$$

for $i = 1, \ldots, n$, where $[F, \phi]$ denotes the inner product over the discrete data set. However, we would expect the matrix with entries $[\psi_i, \psi_j]$ to be "close to diagonal".
Alternatively, if we define a discrete inner product over the data $\{\mathbf{x}^{(k)}\}$

$$< f, g > = \sum_{\mathbf{x}^{(k)}} f(\mathbf{x}^{(k)}) g(\mathbf{x}^{(k)})$$

and write

$$S_{k,i} = \exp(-\|\mathbf{x}^{(k)} - \mathbf{w}^{(i)}\|^2) = \phi_i(\mathbf{x}^{(k)})$$

then

$$t_{i,j} = < \phi_i, \phi_j > = (S^{\mathrm{T}} S)_{i,j}$$

where S is the matrix of $S_{k,i}$. Thus we are effectively forming the components of the normal matrix. The calculation is similar to that of Section 3.1, except that $S^{\mathrm{T}}S$ is now used rather than S (hence requiring a more complicated calculation).

4 Results

The validity of the procedure of Section 3.2 has been successfully tested by using orthogonalized RBFs to recognize the ten digits 0,. . .,9 from their pixel patterns — we do not have sufficient space here to give details, but note that the procedure is very fast compared with using back propagation procedures and sigmodal approximations. We have also calculated condition numbers for a variety of RBF matrices which occur in data fitting, and there are apparent advantages for conditioning in using orthogonality on a continuum rather than on a discrete data set. However further work is needed to develop an orthogonalization algorithm which consistently improves conditioning compared with the use of a conventional Gaussian basis.

REFERENCES

[1] I. J. Anderson, M. G. Cox and J. C. Mason, *Tensor-product spline interpolation to data on or near a family of lines.* Numerical Algorithms, Vol. 5 (1993), pp193–204.

[2] C. W. Clenshaw and J. G. Hayes, *Curve and surface fitting.* J. Inst. Math. Appl., Vol. 1 (1965), pp164–183.

[3] J. D. Mason, R. J. Craddock, J. C. Mason, P. C Parks and K. Warwick, *Towards a stability and approximation theory for neuro-controllers.* Control 94. IEE Pub. 389 (1994), pp100–103.

ERROR BOUNDS FOR DENSITY ESTIMATION BY MIXTURES

Ronny Meir and Assaf J. Zeevi

Electrical Engineering Department, Technion, Haifa 32000, Israel.

We consider the problem of estimating a density function from a sequence of N independent and identically distributed observations $\mathbf{x}_i$ taking values in $\mathbb{R}^d$. The estimation procedure constructs a convex mixture of 'basis' densities and estimates the parameters using the maximum likelihood method. Viewing the error as a combination of two terms, the approximation error measuring the adequacy of the architecture, and the estimation error resulting from the finiteness of the sample size, we derive upper bounds to the total error, thus obtaining bounds for the rate of convergence. These results then allow us to derive explicit expressions relating the sample complexity and model complexity needed for learning.

1 Introduction

There have traditionally been two principal approaches to density estimation, namely the parametric approach which makes stringent assumptions about the density, and the nonparametric approach which is essentially distribution free. In recent years, a new approach to density estimation, often referred to as the method of sieves [2] has emerged. In this latter approach, one considers a family of parametric models, where each member of the family is assigned a 'complexity' index in addition to the parameters. In the process of estimating the density one usually sets out with a simple model (low complexity index) slowly increasing the complexity of the model as the need may be. This general strategy seems to exploit the benefits of both the parametric as well as the nonparametric approaches, namely fast convergence rates and universal approximation ability, while not suffering from the drawbacks of the other methods. In this paper we consider the representation of densities as convex combinations of 'basis' densities, thus permitting an interpretation as a mixture model. We split the problem into two separate issues, namely approximation and estimation, which are discussed at more length in section 2.

2 Statement of the Problem

The problem of density approximation by convex combinations of densities can be phrased as follows: we wish to approximate a class of density functions, by a convex combination of 'basis' densities. In this work we consider the class, $\mathcal{F}$, of compactly supported and continuous a.e density functions. We thus seek linear combinations of densities of the form

$$f_n^{\theta}(\mathbf{x}) = \sum_{i=1}^{n} \alpha_i \phi(\mathbf{x}; \boldsymbol{\theta}_i) \qquad (\alpha_i > 0 \quad \& \quad \sum_{i=1}^{n} \alpha_i = 1), \tag{1}$$

where $\phi(\mathbf{x}; \boldsymbol{\theta}_i)$ represent a family of densities, the members of which are parameterized by the parameter vectors $\{\boldsymbol{\theta}_i\}$. We denote the full set of parameters by $\boldsymbol{\theta}$, namely $\boldsymbol{\theta} = \{\{\alpha_i\}, \{\boldsymbol{\theta}_i\}\}$. In particular, we wish to find values n^* and $\boldsymbol{\theta}^*$ such that for any $\epsilon > 0$, $d(f, f^*) \leq \epsilon$, where f^* is the value of f_n^{θ} evaluated at $\boldsymbol{\theta} = \boldsymbol{\theta}^*$ and $n = n^*$. This objective can be attained by a specific choice of the basis densities ϕ, so that $\cup_{n=1}^{\infty} f_n^{\theta}$ is dense in $\mathcal{F}$ (see [2] for exact conditions). Here $d(f, g)$ represents some generic distance function between densities f and g, whose exact form will be specified in the next section. We note that in the usual formulation of mixture estimation, one usually considers a fixed value of n, assuming that the true density is a member of the class. In our formulation n is a parameter, whose magnitude will be bounded.

Another line of recent work is that of function approximation through linear combinations of non-linearly parameterized 'basis' functions (for example neural networks). The novel feature concerning the representation given in eq. (1), as compared with the function approximation literature, is that we demand the coefficients α_i to be nonnegative and sum to one, and moreover require the functions $\phi(\mathbf{x};\boldsymbol{\theta})$ to be densities, i.e. $\phi(\mathbf{x};\boldsymbol{\theta}) > 0$ and $\int \phi(\mathbf{x};\boldsymbol{\theta})d\mathbf{x} = 1$.

As discussed above, the establishment of the existence of a good approximating density f^* is only the first step in the estimation procedure. One still needs to consider an effective procedure, whereby the optimal function can be obtained, at least in the limit of an infinite amount of data. Assuming the estimation is based on the finite data set $\{\mathbf{x}_i\}_{i=1}^N$, and denoting the estimated density by $\hat{f}_{n,N}$,the minimal requirement (referred to as consistency) is that $\hat{f}_{n,N} \rightarrow f^*$ as $N \rightarrow \infty$, where the convergence takes place in some well defined probabilistic sense. Since we are interested in this paper in convergence rates, we will in fact make use of stronger results [4] which actually characterize the rates at which the above convergence takes place (see section 4).

In summary then, the basic issue we address in this work is related to the relationship between the approximation and estimation errors and (i) the dimension of the data, d, (ii) the sample size, N, and (iii) the complexity of the model class parameterized by n.

3 Preliminaries

In order to discuss approximation of densities we must define an appropriate distance measure, $d(f, g)$, between densities f and g. A commonly used measure of discrepancy between densities is the so-called Kullback-Leibler (KL) divergence, given by $d_{\mathrm{K}}(f||g) = \int f \log \frac{f}{g}$. As is obvious from the definition, the KL divergence is not a true distance function since it is not symmetric. To circumvent this problem one often resorts to an alternative definition of distance, namely the squared Hellinger distance $d_{\mathrm{H}}^2(f,g) = \int \left(\sqrt{f} - \sqrt{g}\right)^2$, which can be shown to be a true metric and is particularly useful for problems of density estimation.

Using the results of [2] concerning the method of sieves we conclude that under appropriate conditions on ϕ, the target density f belongs to the closure of the convex hull of the set of basis densities $\Phi = \{\phi(\cdot,\boldsymbol{\theta})\}$. The question arises, however, as to how many terms are needed in the convex combination in order to achieve an approximation error smaller than some arbitrary $\epsilon > 0$. The answer to this question can be obtained using a remarkable lemma of Maurey which is proved for example in [1].

4 Main Results

Using the results of Maurey referred to above, it can be shown that given any $\epsilon > 0$ one can construct a convex combination of densities, $\phi_c \in \Phi$, in such a way that the total error between an arbitrary density and the model is smaller than ϵ. We consider now the problem of estimating a density function from a sequence of d-dimensional samples, $\{\mathbf{x}_i\}$, $i = 1, 2, \ldots, N$, which will be assumed throughout to be independent and identically distributed according to $f(\mathbf{x})$. As in eq. (1) we let

n denote the number of components in the convex combination. The total number of parameters will be denoted by m, which in the problem studied here is $O(nd)$.
In the remainder of this section we consider the problem of estimating the parameters of the density through a specific estimation scheme, namely maximum likelihood, corresponding to the optimization problem, $\hat{\boldsymbol{\theta}}_{n,N} = \text{argmax}_{\boldsymbol{\theta}} L(\mathbf{x}^N;\boldsymbol{\theta})$ where $L(\mathbf{x}^N;\boldsymbol{\theta})$ is the likelihood function, $L(\mathbf{x}^N;\boldsymbol{\theta}) = \prod_k f_n^{\boldsymbol{\theta}}(\mathbf{x}_k)$, $\mathbf{x}^N = \{\mathbf{x}_i\}_{i=1}^N$ and $f_n^{\boldsymbol{\theta}}(\mathbf{x}) = \sum_{i=1}^n \alpha_i \phi(\mathbf{x};\boldsymbol{\theta}_i)$. We denote the value of $f_{n,N}^{\boldsymbol{\theta}}$ evaluated at the maximum likelihood estimate by $\hat{f}_{n,N}$. Now, for a fixed value of n, the finite mixture model, $f_n^{\boldsymbol{\theta}}$, may not be sufficient to approximate the density f, to the required accuracy. Thus, the model for finite n falls into the so called class of misspecified models [4] and the procedure of maximizing L should more properly be referred to as quasi maximum likelihood estimation. Thus, $\hat{\boldsymbol{\theta}}_{n,N}$ should be referred to as the quasi maximum likelihood estimator. Since the data are assumed to be i.i.d, it is clear from the strong law of large numbers that $\frac{1}{N}L(\mathbf{x}^N;\boldsymbol{\theta}) \to E\log f_n^{\boldsymbol{\theta}}(\mathbf{x})$ almost surely as $N \to \infty$, where the expectation is taken with respect to the true (but unkown) density, $f(\mathbf{x})$, generating the examples. From the trivial equality $E\log f_n^{\boldsymbol{\theta}}(\mathbf{x}) = -d_{\mathrm{K}}(f\|f_n^{\boldsymbol{\theta}}) + E\log f(\mathbf{x})$ we see that the maximum likelihood estimator $\hat{\boldsymbol{\theta}}_{n,N}$ is asymptotically given by $\boldsymbol{\theta}_n^*$, where $\boldsymbol{\theta}_n^* = \arg\min_{\boldsymbol{\theta}} d_{\mathrm{K}}(f\|f_n^{\boldsymbol{\theta}})$. For further discussion see [4].
Now, the quantity of interest in density estimation is the distance between the true density, f, and the density obtained from a finite sample of size N. Using the previous notation and the triangle inequalitiy for metric $d(\cdot,\cdot)$ we have $d(f,\hat{f}_{n,N}) \le d(f,f_n^*) + d(f_n^*,\hat{f}_{n,N})$. This inequality stands at the heart of the derivation which follows. We will show that the first term, namely the *approximation error*, is small. This demonstration utilizes Maurey's lemma as well as several inequalities. In order to evaluate the second term, the *estimation error*, we make use of the results of White [4] concerning the asymptotic distribution of the quasi maximum likelihood estimator $\hat{\boldsymbol{\theta}}_{n,N}$. The splitting of the error into two terms in the triangle inequality, is closely related to the expression of the mean squared error in regression as the sum of the bias (related to the approximation error) and the variance (akin to the estimation error).
As mentioned above, Maurey's lemma provides us with an existence proof, in the sense that there exists a parameter value $\boldsymbol{\theta}^0$ such that the error of the combination (1) is smaller than c/n. Since we are dealing here with a specific estimation scheme, namely maximum likelihood, which asymptotically approaches a particular parameter value $\boldsymbol{\theta}_n^*$, the question we ask, however, is whether the parameter $\boldsymbol{\theta}_n^*$ obtained through the maximum likelihood procedure also gives rise to an approximation error of the same order as that of $\boldsymbol{\theta}^0$. The answer to this question is affirmative, as we demonstrate in the next theorem, which is the first main result of this section.

Theorem 1 *(Approximation error) Given appropriate assumptions, the Hellinger distance between the true density f and the density f_n^* minimizing the Kullback-Leibler divergence, is bounded as follows: $d_{\mathrm{H}}^2(f,f_n^*) \le \epsilon + \frac{C_{\mathcal{F},\Phi}}{n}$ where $C_{\mathcal{F},\Phi}$ is a constant depending on the class of target densities $\mathcal{F}$ and the family of basis densities Φ and ϵ is an arbitrary precision constant.*

Proof (sketch) The proof follows by a series of inequalities relating the Kullback-Leibler divergence and the Hellinger distance. By bounding the KL divergence from above and below by the Hellinger distance and utilizing the fact that the maximum likelihood estimator minimizes the KL divergence we conclude the proof. □

We note that the arbitrary precision constant ϵ appearing in the theorem can be eliminated by restricting attention to densities belonging to the *information closure*, defined as $\bar{\mathcal{G}} = \{f \in \mathcal{F} \mid \inf_{g \in \mathcal{G}} d_{\mathrm{K}}(f\|g) = 0\}$, where $\mathcal{G} = \cup \mathcal{G}_n$ and $\mathcal{G}_n$ comprises all convex combinations of n terms as in (1). We will restrict ourselves in the sequel to this subspace. We stress that the main point of theorem 1 is the following. While Maurey's lemma guarantees the existence of a parameter value $\boldsymbol{\theta}^0$ and a corresponding function f_n^0 which lies within a distance of $O(1/n)$ from f, it is not clear apriori that f_n^*, evaluated at the quasi maximum likelihood estimate, $\boldsymbol{\theta}_n^*$, is also within the same distance from f. Theorem 1 establishes this fact.

Up to now we have been concerned with the first part of the triangle inequality. In order to bound the *estimation error* resulting from the maximum likelihood method, we need to consider now the second term in the same equation. To do so we will need to make use of a lemma of White [4], which characterizes the asymptotic distribution of the estimator $\hat{\boldsymbol{\theta}}_{n,N}$ obtained through the quasi maximum likelihood procedure. A quantity of interest, which will be used is $C(\boldsymbol{\theta}) = A(\boldsymbol{\theta})^{-1}B(\boldsymbol{\theta})A(\boldsymbol{\theta})^{-1}$ where $A(\boldsymbol{\theta}) = E\left[\nabla\nabla^T \log f_n^{\theta}(\mathbf{x})\right]$ and $B(\boldsymbol{\theta}) = E\left[\left(\nabla \log f_n^{\theta}(\mathbf{x})\right)\left(\nabla \log f_n^{\theta}(\mathbf{x})\right)^T\right]$ with the expectations taken with respect to the true density f, and the gradient operator ∇ represents differentiation with respect to $\boldsymbol{\theta}$. White's lemma then proceeds to give sufficient conditions so that the distribution of the quasi maximum likelihood estimator is asymptotically normal.

Finally, we will make use of the Fisher information matrix defined with respect to the density f_n^*, which we shall refer to as the pseudo-information matrix, given by $I^* = E^*[\nabla \log f_n^*(\mathbf{x}) \nabla \log f_n^*(\mathbf{x})^T]$. The expectation E^* is taken with respect to f^*, the density f_n^{θ} evaluated at $\boldsymbol{\theta} = \boldsymbol{\theta}^*$. Denoting expectations over the data (according to the true density f) by $E_{\mathcal{D}}[\cdot]$, we have:

Theorem 2 *(Error bound) For sample size N sufficiently large, and given appropriate smoothness assumptions (see [4]), the expected estimation error,*

$$E_{\mathcal{D}} d_{\mathrm{H}}^2(f, \hat{f}_{n,N}),$$

obtained from the quasi maximum likelihood estimator, $\hat{f}_{n,N}$, is bounded as follows: $E_{\mathcal{D}}\left[d_{\mathrm{H}}^2(f, \hat{f}_{n,N})\right] \leq O\left(C_{\mathcal{F},\Phi}/n\right) + O\left(m^*/N\right)$, where d denotes the data dimension, and $m^* = \mathrm{Tr}(C^* I^*)$ with C^* and I^* given above.

Proof (sketch) The initial step in the proof is to expand $d_H^2(f_n^*, \hat{f}_{n,N})$ to a first order Taylor series with remainder. Some simple algebraic manipulations yield an approximation in terms of the quasi maximum likelihood estimator and the pseudo information matrix. Taking expectation with respect to the data we obtain the bound $O\left(\frac{m^*}{N}\right)$ utilizing the asymptotic results of White (1982). The final derivation follows by the triangle inequality and the approximation bound. □

If we take $n, N \to \infty$ so that $(n/N) \to 0$ the matrix C^* converges to the inverse of the 'true' density Fisher information matrix, which we shall denote by $I^{-1}(\boldsymbol{\theta})$, and the pseudo-information matrix, I^*, converges to the Fisher information $I(\boldsymbol{\theta})$. This argument follows immediately from Theorem 2, which ensures the convergence of the misspecified model to the 'true', underlying density. Therefore their product converges to the identity matrix, with a dimension of the parameter vector $m = n(d+2)$. The bound on the estimation error will therefore be given asymptotically by $E_{\mathcal{D}}\left[d_{\mathrm{H}}^2(f, \hat{f}_{n,N})\right] \leq O\left(\frac{C_{\mathcal{F},\Phi}}{n}\right) + O\left(\frac{nd}{N}\right)$ which is valid in the limit ($N \to \infty$, $n \to \infty$, $\frac{n}{N} \to 0$). The optimal complexity index n may be obtained from the asymptotic convergence rate bound, and is given by $n_{\mathrm{opt}} = (C_{\mathcal{F},\Phi} N/d)^{1/2}$ where d is the dimension of the data in the sample space.

We remark that the parameter m^* may be interpreted as the *effective number* of parameters of the model, under the misspecification of finite n. This parameter correlates the misspecified model's generalized information matrix C^*, with the pseudo-information matrix related to the density f_n^*, so that the effect of misspecification results in a modification in the number of *effective* parameteres.

5 Discussion

We have considered in this paper the problem of estimating a density function over a compact domain X. Specifically, the problem is phrased in the language of mixture models, for which a great deal of theoretical and practical results are available. Moreover, one can immediately utilize the powerful EM algorithm for estimating the parameters. Finally, we comment that the method we used, namely combining approximation error bounds with White's framework for misspecified models, gave rise to lower estimation bounds than those obtained so far for function estimation. We believe that this result is not restricted to density estimation, and can be directly applied to function estimation using, for example, least-squares estimation.

REFERENCES

[1] A. R. Barron, *Universal Approximation Bounds for Superpositions of a Sigmoidal Function*, IEEE Trans. Inf. Theory, Vol. 39(3) (1993), pp930-945.

[2] S. Geman and C. Hwang, *Nonparametric density estimation by the method of sieves*, Ann. Statist., Vol. 13(2) (1982) pp435-475.

[3] M. I. Jordan and R. A. Jacobs, *Hierarchical mixtures of experts and the EM algorithm*, Neural Computation, Vol. 6 (1994), pp181-214.

[4] H. White, *Maximum Likelihood Estimation of Misspecified Models*, Econometrica, Vol. 50(1) (1982), pp1-25.

Acknowledgements

The authors thank Robert Adler, Paul Feigin and Allan Pinkus for helpful discussions.

ON SMOOTH ACTIVATION FUNCTIONS

H. N. Mhaskar

Department of Mathematics, California State University
Los Angeles, California, 90032, USA.

We had earlier constructed neural networks which are capable of providing optimal approximation rates for smooth target functions. The activation functions evaluated by the principal elements of these networks were infinitely many times differentiable. In this paper, we prove that the parameters of any network with these two properties must satisfy certain lower bounds. Our results can also be thought of as providing a rudimentary test for the hypothesis that the unknown target function belongs to a Sobolev class.

1 Introduction

The notion of a *generalized translation network* was introduced by Girosi, Jones and Poggio [4] (*generalized regularization networks* in their terminology). Let $1 \le d \le s$ be integers, and $\phi : \mathbb{R}^d \to \mathbb{R}$ be a fixed function. A generalized translation network with n *neurons* evaluates a function of the form

$$\sum_{k=1}^{n} a_k \phi(A_k \mathbf{x} - \mathbf{b}_k), \tag{1}$$

where $\mathbf{x} \in \mathbb{R}^s$, a_k's are real numbers, $\mathbf{b}_k$'s are vectors in $\mathbb{R}^d$, and A_k's are $d \times s$ real matrices. This mathematical model includes the traditional neural networks, where $d = 1$, as well as the radial basis function networks, where $d = s$, A_k's are all equal to the $s \times s$ identity matrix, and ϕ is a radial function. Girosi, Jones, and Poggio have discussed the importance of the more general networks for applications in computer graphics, robotics, control, image processing, etc., as well as emphasized the need for a theoretical investigation of the capabilities of these networks for function approximation.

One important reason for using generalized translation networks for function approximation is to obtain a concrete, trainable model for the typically unknown target function. Some of the features required of the model are the following. Of course, the model should approximate the target function within a given margin of error, utilizing as few neurons as possible. It is also desirable that the function evaluated by the model be smoother than the target function. Moreover, it is also expected that the parameters a_k A_k, $\mathbf{b}_k$ of the model remain bounded as the margin of error approaches zero. In this paper, we prove that these goals are incompatible with each other: the parameters of a model that evaluates a good approximation, with ϕ smoother than the target function, must tend to infinity as the margin of error tends to zero. In order to motivate this result further, we first review certain known "positive" results.

It is well known [1], [2], [5], [6] that an arbitrary continuous function of s variables can be approximated arbitrarily closely on an arbitrary compact subset of $\mathbb{R}^s$ by neural networks. A similar result was established in [8] for the case of generalized translation networks. A deeper problem in this context is to determine the number of neurons required to approximate all functions in a given function class within a given margin of error. Equivalently, one seeks to estimate the *degree of approximation* of the target function in terms of the number of neurons, n. Since the target function is typically not known in advance, it is customary to assume that it belongs to some known function class. A simple assumption is that the function possesses continuous derivatives up to order r, where $r \geq 1$ is some integer. It is well known [12] that for any function satisfying this condition, there is an algebraic polynomial of degree not exceeding m, which gives a uniform approximation to this function on $[-1,1]^s$ with an order of accuracy $\mathcal{O}(m^{-r})$. In terms of the number n of parameters involved, this order is $\mathcal{O}(n^{-r/s})$. According to a result of DeVore, Howard, and Micchelli [3], this is asymptotically the best order of approximation that can possibly be achieved for the entire class of target functions, using any "reasonable" approximation process involving n parameters. It is an open problem to determine whether the same degree of approximation can be achieved with generalized translation networks. One expects that the actual degree of approximation should depend upon certain growth and smoothness characteristics of the *activation function* ϕ.

This author and Micchelli investigated this problem in detail in [10], starting with the case when both the target function and the activation function are 2π-periodic. When ϕ is a 2π- periodic function, we were able to approximate the trigonometric monomials by generalized translation networks, with a bound on the accuracy of approximation in terms of the trigonometric degree of approximation of ϕ. This turned out to be a very fruitful idea, enabling us to establish a connection between the degree of approximation provided by generalized translation networks on one hand, and the degree of trigonometric polynomial approximation to the target function and to the activation function ϕ on the other hand. The general theorem was applied to the case when ϕ is not periodic, establishing degree of approximation theorems for a very wide class of activation functions. As far as we are aware, our estimates on the degree of approximation by radial basis functions were the first of their kind, in that the estimates were in terms of the number of function evaluations, rather than a scaling factor. These results were announced in [11]. In [10], we constructed networks to provide to an optimal recovery of functions, as well as networks to provide simultaneous approximation of a function and its derivatives. The idea was also applied in [9] to obtain certain *dimension-independent bounds.* Both in [9] and [10], we give explicit constructions of the networks. The results indicated that both the growth and smoothness of the activation function play a role in the complexity problem.

In [7], we concentrated on activation functions that are infinitely often differentiable in an open set, and for which there is at least one point in this open set at which none of the partial derivatives is zero. Using the ideas in the paper [6] of Leshno, Lin, Pinkus, and Schocken, we proved that generalized translation networks with such activation functions provide the optimal degree of approximation for all smooth functions. We also obtained estimates for the approximation of analytic functions. The activation functions to which our results are applicable include the squashing function, $(1+e^{-x})^{-1}$ when $d=1$, and the Gaussian function, the thin plate splines, and multiquadrics, when $1 \leq d \leq s$. We give explicit constructions, and the matrices A_k and "thresholds" $\mathbf{b}_k$ in the networks thus obtained are uniformly bounded, independently of the degree of approximation desired. Unfortunately, the coefficients a_k in the networks may grow exponentially fast as the desired degree of approximation tends to zero.

In this paper, we demonstrate that this phenomenon cannot be avoided if the activation function is a bounded analytic function in a poly-strip; the coefficients and the matrices cannot all be bounded independently of the desired degree of approximation. This fact persists even if ϕ satisfies less stringent conditions. In particular, all the special functions ϕ mentioned above necessarily have this drawback. For the sake of simplicity, we have presented our results in the context of uniform approximation. They are equally valid when the approximation is considered in an L^p space.

2 Main Results

Let $k, m \geq 1$ be integers, and B be a closed subcube of $\mathbb{R}^m$ (not necessarily compact). The class of all functions $f : \mathbb{R}^m \to \mathbb{R}$ having continuous and bounded partial derivatives of order up to (and including) k on B will be denoted by C_B^k. In this section, we prove that if the activation function $\phi \in C^\ell_{\mathbb{R}^d}$ for some integer $\ell \geq 1$, and the target function f is not infinitely often differentiable on $[-1,1]^s$, then the coefficients a_k in any generalized translation network of the form (1) that provides a uniform approximation of f on $[-1,1]^s$ must satisfy certain lower bounds. These lower bounds will be obtained in terms of the norms of the matrices A_k. If $\mathbf{x} = (x_1, \ldots, x_m) \in \mathbb{R}^m$, we define

$$|\mathbf{x}|_m := \max_{1 \leq j \leq m} |x_j|. \tag{2}$$

If $d, s \geq 1$ are integers, and A is a $d \times s$ matrix, we define its norm by

$$||A|| := \max_{|\mathbf{x}|_s \leq 1} |A\mathbf{x}|_d. \tag{3}$$

In the sequel, $c, c_1, \cdots$ will denote positive constants, which may depend upon fixed quantities, such as ϕ, d, and s, and other indicated parameters only.
We prove the following theorem.

Theorem 1 *Let $1 \leq d \leq s$, $\ell, r \geq 1$ be integers, and α, ϵ be positive real numbers. Suppose that $\phi \in C^\ell_{\mathbb{R}^d}$, $f : [-1,1]^s \to \mathbb{R}$, and $f \notin C^r_{[a,b]^s}$ for some $[a,b] \subset (-1,1)$. Suppose that for every integer $n \geq 1$, there exists a generalized translation network*

$$\mathcal{N}_n(\mathbf{x}) := \sum_{k=1}^{n} a_{k,n}\phi(A_{k,n}\mathbf{x} + \mathbf{b}_{k,n}), \tag{4}$$

such that

$$|f(\mathbf{x}) - \mathcal{N}_n(\mathbf{x})| \leq cn^{-\alpha}, \qquad \mathbf{x} \in [-1,1]^s, \tag{5}$$

where c is a positive constant that may depend upon f, ϕ, d, s, and α but is independent of n. Then there exists a subsequence Λ of integers and a positive constant c_1 depending on f, ϕ, d, s, α, and ϵ such that

$$\sum_{k=1}^{n} |a_{k,n}| \geq c_1 \left(\frac{n^{\alpha(1/(r+\epsilon)-1/\ell)}}{M_n}\right)^\ell, \qquad n \in \Lambda, \tag{6}$$

where

$$M_n := \max_{1 \leq k \leq n} ||A_{k,n}||. \tag{7}$$

We recall that one of the objectives of approximation is to obtain approximants which are smoother than the original function. The theorem is therefore most interesting if ϕ has more derivatives than f. In this case, if the matrices $A_{k,n}$ in the approximating networks are $o(n^{\alpha(1/(r+\epsilon)-1/\ell)})$, then the sum of the absolute values of the coefficients must tend to infinity. The smoother the activation function ϕ, the faster is this growth. Thus, the goals of smoothing and having bounded parameters are not compatible.

Another way to interpret this theorem is that if, for a function f, a sequence of approximating networks of the form (4) can be found to yield the order of approximation as in (5), but with the growth of the matrices $A_{k,n}$ and the coefficients $a_{k,n}$ controlled so that (6) is not satisfied, then f must have continuous partial derivatives of order at least r. Thus, for an infinitely many times differentiable activation function ϕ, we have a "converse theorem" : the existence of networks with properly controlled growth for the matrices and coefficients implies a smoothness of the target function, which is unknown to start with. We observe that in the case of the neural networks ($d = 1$) constructed in [10], the "weights" $A_{k,n}$ are $\mathcal{O}(n)$ and an upper estimate on the sum of the absolute values of the coefficients is also known. The networks of [10] can therefore be used to verify the accuracy of the starting hypothesis about the smoothness class to which the target function belongs.

The ideas behind the proof of Theorem 1 lead us to the following corollary, which gives sharper lower bounds than in (6) in the case when the activation function is analytic.

Corollary 2 *Let $\delta > 0$ be a real number, $\phi : \mathbb{R}^d \to \mathbb{R}$ have an extension to the poly-strip*

$$\{(z_1, \ldots, z_d) \ : \ |\Im m z_k| \le \delta, \quad k = 1, \ldots, d\}$$

as a bounded, analytic function. Then the estimate (6) can be replaced by

$$\sum_{k=1}^{n} |a_{k,n}| \ge c_1 m^{-r-\epsilon}\left(1 + \frac{\pi}{2M_n}\right)^{m/2}, \qquad n \in \Lambda, \tag{8}$$

where $m := c_2 n^{\alpha/(r+\epsilon)}$.

Proof of Theorem 1. Let $n, m \ge 1$ be integers. We observe that the function ϕ has continuous and bounded partial derivatives of order ℓ on $\mathbb{R}^d$. Therefore, the Jackson theorem for algebraic polynomial approximation [12], §5.3.11, shows that there exist polynomials $P_{k,n}$, each of coordinatewise degree at most m, such that

$$|\phi(A_{k,n}\mathbf{x} + \mathbf{b}_k) - P_{k,n}(\mathbf{x})| \le cM_n^\ell m^{-\ell}, \qquad \mathbf{x} \in [-1, 1]^s, k = 1, \ldots, n \tag{9}$$

Writing $Q_m := \sum_{k=1}^{n} a_{k,n} P_{k,n}$, we see that Q_m is a polynomial of coordinatewise degree at most m. Moreover, from (5) and (9), we obtain

$$|f(\mathbf{x}) - Q_m(\mathbf{x})| \le c\left\{n^{-\alpha} + M_n^\ell m^{-\ell}\sum_{k=1}^{n}|a_{k,n}|\right\}, \qquad \mathbf{x} \in [-1, 1]^s, \ m, n = 1, 2, \cdots. \tag{10}$$

If possible, let (6) be not true. Then, choosing n to be the smallest integer exceeding $m^{(r+\epsilon)/\alpha}$, we see that

$$|f(\mathbf{x}) - Q_m(\mathbf{x})| \le cm^{-(r+\epsilon)}, \qquad \mathbf{x} \in [-1, 1]^s$$

for all sufficiently large integer m. In view of the converse theorems for algebraic polynomial approximation, [12] §6.3.4, this implies that $f \in C^r_{[a,b]^s}$ for every $[a, b] \subset (-1, 1)$. This contradiction completes the proof of the theorem. □

The proof of Corollary 2.2 is similar, except that one uses Bernstein's estimates similar to [12] §5.4.1, instead of the Jackson-type estimates.

3 Conclusions

We have discussed our previous work on the degree of approximation by generalized translation networks. It is shown here that the goals of having a smooth approximation, and bounded coefficients and weights are incompatible when the target function to be approximated fails to have at least as many continuous partial derivatives as the activation function. Our theorem can also be thought of as providing a rudimentary test for the hypothesis that the unknown target function belongs to a Sobolev class.

REFERENCES

[1] C. K. Chui and X. Li, *Approximation by ridge functions and neural networks with one hidden layer*, J. Approx. Theory, Vol. 70 (1992), pp.131-141.

[2] G. Cybenko, *Approximation by superposition of sigmoidal functions*, Mathematics of Control, Signal and Systems, Vol. 2 (1989), pp.303-314.

[3] R. DeVore, R. Howard, and C. A. Micchelli, *Optimal nonlinear approximation*, Manuscripta Mathematica, Vol. 63 (1989), pp.469-478.

[4] F. Girosi, M. Jones, and T. Poggio, *Regularization theory and neural networks architectures*, Neural Computation, Vol. 7 (1995), pp.219-269.

[5] K. Hornik, M. Stinchcombe, and H. White, *Multilayer feedforward networks are universal approximators*, Neural Networks, Vol. 2 (1989), pp.359-366.

[6] M. Leshno, V. Lin, A. Pinkus, and S. Schocken, *Multilayer feedforward networks with a nonpolynomial activation function can approximate any function*, Neural Networks, Vol. 6 (1993), pp.861-867.

[7] H. N. Mhaskar, *Neural networks for optimal approximation of smooth and analytic functions*, Neural Computation, Vol.8 (1996), pp164–177.

[8] H. N. Mhaskar and C. A. Micchelli, *Approximation by superposition of a sigmoidal function and radial basis functions, Advances in Applied Mathematics*, Vol. 13 (1992), pp.350-373.

[9] H. N. Mhaskar and C. A. Micchelli, *Dimension independent bounds on the degree of approximation by neural networks*, IBM Journal of Research and Development, Vol. 38 (1994), pp.277-284.

[10] H. N. Mhaskar and C. A. Micchelli, *Degree of approximation by neural and translation networks with a single hidden layer, Advances in Applied Mathematics*, Vol. 16 (1995), pp.151-183.

[11] H. N. Mhaskar and C. A. Micchelli, *How to choose an activation function*, in NIPS*6 (J. D. Cowan, G. Tesauro, J. Alspector Eds.), Morgan Kaufmann, 1994, pp.319-326.

[12] A. F. Timan, *Theory of Approximation of Functions of a Real Variable*, Macmillan Co., New York, 1963.

Acknowledgements

This research was supported, in part, by National Science Foundation Grant DMS 9404513 and Air Force Office of Scientific Research Grant F49620-93-1-0150.

GENERALISATION AND REGULARISATION BY GAUSSIAN FILTER CONVOLUTION OF RADIAL BASIS FUNCTION NETWORKS

Christophe Molina and Mahesan Niranjan
Cambridge University Engineering Department, Trumpington Street Cambridge CB2 1PZ, UK. Email: cm3/niranjan@eng.cam.ac.uk

This paper proposes a new technique called *Regularisation by Convolution* to improve the generalisation of GaRBF networks. The technique is based on the convolution after training of GaRBF networks with gaussian filters and, consequently, is independent of the learning stage and algorithm. Moreover, it alleviates the need for retraining. The performance of *Regularisation by Convolution* in improving regression is illustrated for Wahba's problem.
Keywords: convolution product, neural networks, Gaussian filter, Gaussian radial basis functions, regularisation.

1 Introduction

Nowadays *generalisation* and *regularisation* are two of the most challenging topics in neural computation. By generalisation it is generally understood that, from a given training set consisting of input-output observations $\{\mathbf{x}_i, y_i\}$, $i = 1, \ldots, n$, of an underlying event F_*, such that $F_*(\mathbf{x}_i) = y_i$, it is desired to construct an estimated map F which, for a new test set of input observations $\{\mathbf{x}_j\}$ will provide a good prediction for the unobserved output observations $\{y_j\}$.
One way of achieving generalisation, known as *regularisation* or *smoothing*, is to find the mapping F by means of a neural network, subject to some constraints on the solution. One possible constraint is to limit the number of units in the neural network, or to employ pruning techniques during learning in order to limit the degree of freedom of F and thus avoid overfitting of the observations (see [1] for a survey). A second class of regularisation techniques involves the determination of a mapping F in the d-dimensional Hilbert space $\mathcal{H}$ of functions with continuous first derivatives and square integrable second derivatives which minimise,

$$MSE = \frac{1}{n} \cdot \sum_{i=1}^{n} (y_i - F(\mathbf{x}_i))^2 \tag{1}$$

subject to the regularisation condition

$$\int (F^{(2)}(\mathbf{x}))^2 d\mathbf{x} \leq \kappa \tag{2}$$

for different values of a regularisation parameter κ (see [2] and references contained therein). Equation (1) is known as the Mean Squared Error (MSE) of the training set and (2) as the regularisation constraint, which is equal to the energy of the second derivative of the mapping F. If κ is made large the F will just interpolate the training data and, conversely, if it is chosen very small then the mapping, although smooth, will not represent the underlying event F_*. A good regularisation is achieved by adapting κ to reach the convenient tradeoff between the fitting and the smoothness of the solution. Normally this is achieved by choosing different values for κ, training under these κ constraints, and testing the generalisation error results on a test set by cross-validation. Although this solution may generalise well, it is computationally expensive and needs retraining for each of the possible values of κ. Moreover, the final results may be biased by the capacity of the neural network or the training rule to escape from local minima. In this paper, we propose a new regularisation technique based on convolution after training a Gaussian Radial Basis Function (GaRBF) network with gaussian filters. This technique, which does not need retraining, consists in essence of the following steps:

- Training a GaRBF network with a large number of units.
- Convolve the network with gaussian filters of different widths and normalise the network so that the final L_1-norm of the convolved $F(\mathbf{x})$ remains the same (this implicitly leads to a reduction of the energy of the second derivative of $F(\mathbf{x})$).
- Verify the generalisation performance of the convolved GaRBF networks by cross-validation, and retain the best solution.

The paper is organised as follows: Section 2 presents the mathematical principles of this technique. Section 3 describes the main algorithm for regularisation and a binary technique for searching for the best gaussian filter. Section 4 gives an experimental evaluation of the regularisation technique on the regression of a synthetic problem.

2 GaRBF Network Convolution with Gaussian Filters

GaRBF networks are defined as a linear combination of Gaussian units. Let this be denoted by,

$$F(\mathbf{x}) = \sum_{i=1}^{N} \alpha_i f_i(\mathbf{x}) \tag{3}$$

where N is the number of GaRBF units of general expression, $f_i(\mathbf{x}) = e^{-\frac{(\mathbf{x}-\mu_i)^2}{\sigma_i^2}}$, and with amplitude $\alpha_i \in \Re$, centre $\mu_i \in \Re^d$ and width $\sigma_i \in \Re^+$.

Let $g(\mathbf{x}, \sigma)$ be a Gaussian filter given by, $g(\mathbf{x}, \sigma) = e^{-\frac{\mathbf{x}^2}{\sigma_j^2}}$, with σ_j as width. We first define the integral convolution in the Hilbert space $\mathcal{H}$ of these two functions, $f_i(\mathbf{x})$ and $g(\mathbf{x}, \sigma)$ as

$$h(\tau) = \int_{-\infty}^{\infty} f_i(\mathbf{x}) g(\tau - \mathbf{x}, \sigma) d\mathbf{x} \tag{4}$$

Since GaRBFs are bounded and absolutely integrable on $\mathcal{H}$, the computation of their convolution may more easily be done by means of the convolution property, $\mathcal{F}\{h\}(\omega) = \sqrt{2\pi}\mathcal{F}\{f_i\}\mathcal{F}\{g\}$, where $\mathcal{F}\{\cdot\}$ is the Fourier transform. Fourier transforms of f_i and g respectively are

$$\mathcal{F}\{f\}(\omega) = \sigma_i^d \sqrt{\pi^d}\, e^{-\left(\frac{\sigma_i^2 \omega^2}{4} + \sqrt{-1}\, \frac{4\mu_i \omega}{\sigma_i^2}\right)} \tag{5}$$

and,

$$\mathcal{F}\{g\}(\omega) = \sigma_j^d \sqrt{\pi^d}\, e^{-\frac{\sigma_j{}^2 w^2}{4}} \tag{6}$$

Finally, from the inverse Fourier transform of their product, a new GaRBF of same location but different amplitude and width is obtained,

$$h(\tau) = (\frac{\sigma_i^2 \sigma_j^2}{\sigma_i^2 + \sigma_j^2}\pi)^{\frac{d}{2}}\, e^{-\frac{(\tau-\mu_i)^2}{\sigma_i^2+\sigma_j^2}} \tag{7}$$

The integral convolution of a GaRBF network $F(\mathbf{x})$ as defined in (3) and a gaussian filter $g(\mathbf{x}, \sigma)$ is a straightforward consequence of equation (7), since,

$$\int_{-\infty}^{\infty} F(\mathbf{x}) \cdot g(\tau - \mathbf{x}, \sigma) d\mathbf{x} = \sum_{i=1}^{N} \alpha_i \int_{-\infty}^{\infty} f_i(\mathbf{x}) \cdot g(\tau - \mathbf{x}, \sigma) d\mathbf{x} \tag{8}$$

and is equal to a new GaRBF network with same number of units, located at the same positions but with different amplitude and width. In the particular context of *regularisation by convolution*, it is of great importance to keep the convolved function $h(\tau)$ as close as possible to the original $F(\mathbf{x})$ except at those points where high frequencies have been filtered. This may be achieved by requiring the L_1-norm of the GaRBF network to remain constant. A good alternative is to calculate the L_1-norm of the gaussian filter, as follows,

$$\int_{-\infty}^{\infty} e^{-\frac{\mathbf{x}^2}{\sigma_j^2}} dx = \sigma_j^d\, (\pi)^{\frac{d}{2}} \tag{9}$$

and then convolve the network with a normalised filter which leads to the same results as the normalisation of the GaRBF network. Thus, the L_1-normalised convolution $F(\mathbf{x}) \otimes g(\mathbf{x}, \sigma)$ of a GaRBF network $F(\mathbf{x})$ and a gaussian filter $g(\mathbf{x}, \sigma)$ which retains the same norm of the original network may then be stated as,

$$F(\mathbf{x}) \otimes g(\mathbf{x}, \sigma) \doteq \frac{\int_{-\infty}^{\infty} F(\mathbf{x}) g(\tau - \mathbf{x}, \sigma) d\mathbf{x}}{\sigma_j^d\, (\pi)^{\frac{d}{2}}} \tag{10}$$

3 The Regularising Technique

This section describes the regularising technique based on the convolution of GaRBF units with gaussian filters, developed in previous section. The technique is to be applied to a pre-trained GaRBF network as defined in equation (3), and uses the Root Mean Squared (RMS) error obtained on a cross-validation set after regularisation as a performance criterion. The best regularising gaussian filter is found by binary search under the assumption that the RMS error has no local minima in the search space. Reasonable bounds for the binary searching are easily obtained from the bounded space on which the underlying function F_* lies. Thus the minimal bound for the width filter is equal to zero and the maximal bound is equal to the maximal distance between two points of the bounded space $\mathcal{H}$.

The structure of the related regularisation algorithm and its initialisation is shown below as pseudo-code,

- **Initial parameters and data**
  - Neural Network : $F(\mathbf{x}) = \sum_{i=1}^{N} \alpha_i f_i(\mathbf{x})$
  - Cross Validation set : $CV = \{\mathbf{x}_j, y_j\}\ j = 1, \ldots, n$
  - Gaussian Filter : $g(\mathbf{x}, \sigma) = e^{-\mathbf{x}^2/\sigma^2}$
  - Bounds of Gaussian filter widths and their average:

    $\sigma_{min} = 0$

    $\sigma_{max} = \left(\max\left(\sum_{k=1}^{d}\left(x_i^k - x_j^k\right)^2\right)\right)^{1/2} \quad \forall \mathbf{x} \in CV$

    $\sigma_{avg} = (\sigma_{max} + \sigma_{min})/2$
  - RMS errors obtained on the CV data set after convolving $F(\mathbf{x})$ with $g(\mathbf{x}, \sigma_{min})$, $g(\mathbf{x}, \sigma_{avg})$ and $g(\mathbf{x}, \sigma_{max})$:

    RMS_{min}, RMS_{avg} and RMS_{max}
  - Stop threshold for the binary search : ϵ

- **Regularising Algorithm**

  Loop until $| RMS_{max} - RMS_{min} | < \epsilon$

  1. Calculate the RMS_1 and RMS_2 errors obtained after convolution of $F(\mathbf{x})$ with $g(\mathbf{x}, \sigma)$ for widths σ_1 and σ_2, where,

     $\sigma_1 = (\sigma_{min} + \sigma_{avg})/2$

     $\sigma_2 = (\sigma_{avg} + \sigma_{max})/2$
  2. If $RMS_1 < RMS_2$ then,

     $\sigma_{max} = \sigma_{avg}$ & $\sigma_{avg} = \sigma_1$

     $RMS_{max} = RMS_{avg}$ & $RMS_{avg} = RMS_1$

     else

     $\sigma_{min} = \sigma_{avg}$ & $\sigma_{avg} = \sigma_2$

     $RMS_{min} = RMS_{avg}$ & $RMS_{avg} = RMS_2$

  end loop

4 Numerical Results

In order to illustrate the performance of *Regularisation by Convolution*, we have applied the algorithm to *Wahba's synthetic problem* [2]. This problem consists of the regression of a noisy function generated synthetically according to the model, $F_*(x) = 4.26\left(e^{-2x} - 4e^{-x} + 3e^{-3x}\right) + \nu$, where ν is normally distributed random noise with zero mean and standard deviation 0.2. In the original problem, 100 noisy observations were generated and used as learning set for the training of a sigmoid feed-forward neural network. Wahba performed regularisation during training using equation (2). The κ value which provided the lowest RMS error was obtained

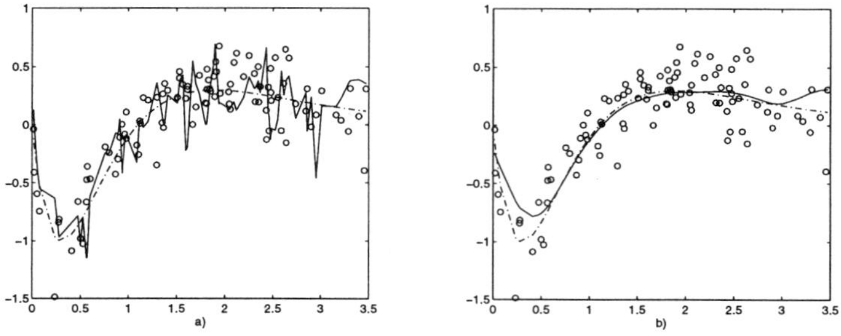

Figure 1 Original Wahba's function (dash-dot). Neural Network regression (solid). CV observations (circles). a) LRAN regression with RMS error equal to 0.3011 on the CV data set. b) The same LRAN after regularisation by convolution with the best Gaussian filter obtained by binary search ($\sigma_{avg} = 0.1709$) with RMS error equal to 0.2116.

by *leaving-one-out* cross-validation. Thus retraining was needed for each different choice of κ.

In our case we applied *Regularisation by Convolution* to the same problem after training a Limited Resource Allocating network (LRAN) by the *F-Projections* learning rule [3]. Training was only performed once, after which the network had learnt the underlying problem F_* with over-fitting of the noisy data as shown in Figure (1.a). The original training data was interpolated by a factor of ten to provide a sufficiently representative training set for the noisy problem, and a LRAN with 200 units (twice the number of training samples) was used to ensure learning with overfitting. We used an extra set of 100 samples as Cross-Validation set CV to calculate the best regularising filter. The stop threshold ϵ was fixed at 10^{-4}. Figure (1.b) illustrates the final result.

5 Summary

This paper has shown how a technique based on a convolution operator can be succesfully applied for regularising and then improving the performances on generalisation of Gaussian RBF networks. The advantage of this technique over other approaches is that it is independent of training processes and algorithms.

REFERENCES

[1] R. Reed, *Pruning algorithms-a survey*, IEEE Transactions on Neural Networks, Vol. 4 (September 1993), pp740–747.

[2] G. Wahba, *Generalisation and regularisation in nonlinear systems*, Tech. Rep. 921, Department of Statistics, University of Wisconsin, 1210 West Dayton ST. Madison, WI 53706, (1994).

[3] C. Molina and M. Niranjan, *Pruning with replacement on limited resource allocating networks by f-projections*, Neural Computation, Vol. 8 (1996), No. 4, pp855–868.

DYNAMICAL SYSTEM PREDICTION: A LIE ALGEBRAIC APPROACH FOR A NOVEL NEURAL ARCHITECTURE

Yves Moreau and Joos Vandewalle

Katholieke Universiteit Leuven, Dept. of Electrical Engineering, ESAT-SISTA

Kardinaal Mercierlaan 94, B-3001 Leuven (Heverlee), Belgium.

Email: moreau@esat.kuleuven.ac.be

In this paper we study the problem of the prediction of autonomous continuous-time dynamical systems from discrete-time measurements of the state variables. We show that the predictor of such a system needs to be an invertible map from the state-space into itself. The problem then becomes one of how to approximate invertible maps. We show that standard approximation schemes do not guarantee the property of invertibility. We therefore propose a new approximation scheme based on the composition of invertible basis functions which preserves invertibility. This approach can be cast in a Lie algebraic framework where the approximation is based on the use of the Baker-Campbell-Hausdorff formula. The method is implemented in a neural-like form. We also present a more general implementation which we call "MLP in dynamics space".

Keywords: System prediction, Lie algebras, Baker-Campbell-Hausdorff formula.

1 Introduction

We will study here the problem of the prediction of nonlinear dynamical systems from a set of sampled measurements of the state of the system. The nonlinear systems which we will consider are governed by a multidimensional ordinary differential equation. Although the dynamics of the system is continuous in time, the samples that we will use for prediction are the state variables measured at discrete time-intervals only. We are therefore led to postulate a discrete-time form for our prediction: $\hat{x}(k+1) = F(x(k))$. In the first section, we will show - using the fact that the underlying dynamics of the system is time-continuous - that the function F used for prediction should be invertible. The problem then becomes that of building an approximation scheme specifically designed for invertible maps. The main drawback of standard approximation schemes is that they are based on summing basis functions to build an approximation. However, this operation does not preserve invertibility. Using the operation of composition instead of addition, we are able to guarantee invertibility. We will thus build approximation schemes based on composition of invertible basis functions. In the second section, we will analyze those compositions within the framework of Lie algebra theory. Starting from a method from numerical analysis we will be able to derive a new approach to the prediction of nonlinear systems. In section three, this new method will be presented in a neural-like form and illustrated by an example. We will also present a general model for approximation which we call "MLP in dynamics space". Finally, we will conclude.

1.1 Invertibility of Dynamical Systems

The systems considered here are defined by an ordinary differential equation (ODE) on some n-dimensional manifold $\mathcal{M}$. We follow the differential geometric description of dynamical systems [2] and assume the standard smoothness assumptions. For each initial condition x_0, we can solve the initial value problem. We then collect all those solutions in one function $\Phi(x_0, t)$ which gives the solution of the ODE as a function of the initial condition:

$$\begin{cases} \dot{x} = f(x(t)) \\ \\ x(0) = x_0 \end{cases} \Rightarrow x(t) = \Phi(x_0, t) \tag{1}$$

Φ is called the flow of the dynamical system. The flow is a remarkable object which possesses the group property. We refer the reader to [4] for a general presentation of the group theoretic approach to dynamical systems. If we assume, for simplicity, that the flow is defined for all times, the group property writes as follows:

$$\begin{gathered} \Phi \; : \; \mathcal{M} \times \mathrm{IR} \to \mathcal{M} \\ \\ \Phi(x, t+s) = \Phi(\Phi(x,t), s), \quad \forall\, t, s \in \mathrm{IR} \end{gathered} \tag{2}$$

As we will see, this gives the flow the structure of a group. We define the time-t map as

$$\varphi^t(x_0) \equiv \Phi(x_0, t) \tag{3}$$

This map φ^t associates to any initial condition its image under the flow of the differential equation after a given time t. The map φ^t is a map from the manifold $\mathcal{M}$ into itself. Using the group property of the flow, we can deduce the properties of φ:

$$\begin{array}{ll} \varphi^t \circ \varphi^s(x_0) = \Phi(\Phi(x_0, s), t) = \Phi(x_0, t+s) = \varphi^{t+s}(x_0) & \textit{composition} \\ \varphi^0 = I \Leftarrow \varphi^0(x_0) = \Phi(x_0, 0) = x_0 = I(x_0) & \textit{identity} \\ \varphi^t \circ \varphi^{-t}(x0) = \Phi(x_0, 0) = x_0 = I(x_0) \Rightarrow \varphi^{-t} = (\varphi^t)^{-1} & \textit{inverse} \end{array} \tag{4}$$

Moreover, if f is C^r then φ is C^r. Hence, since φ is a smooth invertible map with a smooth inverse, φ is a diffeomorphism. Furthermore, the properties of φ show that $\{\varphi^t\}$ is a group. We therefore say that a flow $\Phi(x,t)$ is a one-parameter group of diffeomorphisms φ^t.

1.2 Dynamical System Prediction

Even if we assume that the underlying dynamics of the system is governed by an ODE, the system is generally observed only at discrete time-intervals. So, if we choose a sampling period Δt, we can assume a functional relationship between the current state and the next sample. The system becomes of the form:

$$x((k+1).\Delta t) = F(x(k.\Delta t)), \qquad x(k) \in \mathcal{M} \tag{5}$$

And, from what we have shown before, we see that F is a diffeomorphism as

$$F(.) = \varphi^{\Delta t}(.) \tag{6}$$

The following figure (Fig. 1) summarizes those observations. On the left we consider a square grid of initial conditions. We let each point of that grid follow its trajectory for a time-interval Δt. After this time, all the points of the grid have moved and the shape of the grid has changed. The diffeomorphism $\varphi^{\Delta t}$ is that transformation from the manifold (here, IR^2) into itself which maps the square grid on the left into the deformed grid on the right. One can see that this transformation is smooth and invertible, hence a diffeomorphism. So, the question of predicting a continuous-time system observed at discrete time-intervals becomes one of how we can approximate those diffeomorphisms which arise from the sampling of an ODE. The basic idea is that the set of all C^r diffeomorphisms is also a group. In a group, the natural operation is the composition of the elements of the group. While most

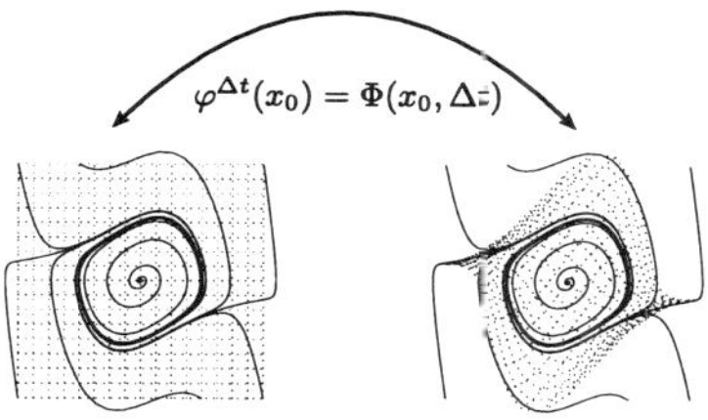

Figure 1 Diffeomorphic transformation of a square grid after one time-step.

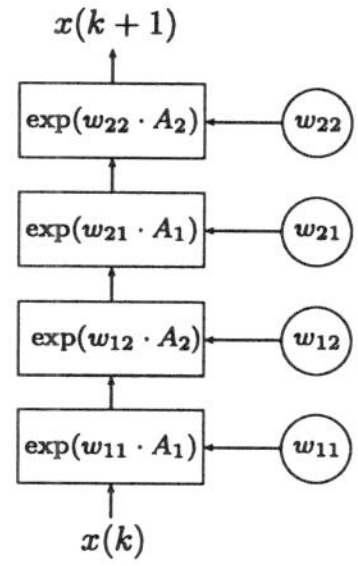

Figure 2 Implementation of the composition network.

standard approximation schemes are based on the summation of some basis functions, this operation does not preserve the property of being a diffeomorphism. On the other hand, composition does preserve this property, so we propose to build an approximation scheme based on composing basis functions instead of adding them.

2 Lie Algebra Theory

Lie algebra theory has a long history in physics, mostly in the areas of classical mechanics [1] and partial differential equations [8]. It is also an essential part of nonlinear system theory [5]. Our approach to system prediction can be best cast in this framework. A Lie algebra is a vector space where we define a supplementary operation: the bracket $[.,.]$ of two elements of the algebra. The bracket is an operation which is bilinear, antisymmetric and satisfies the Jacobi identity [8]. In the case where the Lie algebra is the vector space of all C^r vector fields, the time-t map φ^t plays a very important role. If the vector field is A, we define the *exponential map* as follows: $\exp(t.A) \equiv \varphi^t$. This notation is an extension of the case where the vector field is linear in space and where the solution is given by exponentiation of the matrix. The exponential is thus a mapping from the manifold into itself. And this map depends on the underlying vector field A and changes over time. From here on, the product of exponentials will denote the composition of the maps. One can then define the Lie bracket by

$$[A, B] = \left.\frac{\partial^2}{\partial s.\partial t}\right|_{t=s=0} \exp(-s.B).\exp(-t.A).\exp(s.B).\exp(t.A) \tag{7}$$

In the case where the manifold is $\mathbb{R}^n$, the bracket can be further particularized to

$$[A, B]_i = \sum_{i=1}^{n}\left(B_i.\frac{\partial A_j}{\partial x_i} - A_i.\frac{\partial B_j}{\partial x_i}\right) \tag{8}$$

2.1 The Baker-Campbell-Hausdorff Formula

The Baker-Campbell-Hausdorff (BCH) formula gives an expansion for the product of the exponentials of two elements of the Lie algebra, see [6]:

$$\exp(A).\exp(B) = \exp(A + B - \frac{1}{2}[A, B] + \frac{1}{12}([A, [A, B]] - [B, [B, A]]) + \ldots) \tag{9}$$

The problem of predicting a dynamical system with vector field X then becomes that of building an approximation for $\exp(\Delta t.X)$ as we have that $x(k+1) =$

$\exp(\Delta t.X)[x(k)]$. This problem has recently been the focus of much attention in the field of numerical analysis for the integration of Hamiltonian differential equations [6] [7]. Suppose that the vector field X is of the form $X = A + B$ where we can integrate A and B directly. We can use the BCH formula to produce a first-order approximation to the exponential map:

$$\text{BCH} : \exp(\Delta t.X) = \exp(\Delta t.A).\exp(\Delta t.B) + o(\Delta t^2) \tag{10}$$

This is the essence of the method as it shows that one can approximate an exponential map (that is the map arising from the solution of an ODE) by composing simpler maps. By repeated use of the BCH formula, we can show that the following leapfrog scheme is second-order.

$$\text{Leapfrog} : \exp(\Delta t.X) = \exp(\frac{\Delta t}{2}.A).\exp(\Delta t.B).\exp(\frac{\Delta t}{2}.A) + o(\Delta t^3) \tag{11}$$

Using this leapfrog scheme as a basis element for further leapfrog schemes, Yoshida [9] showed that it was possible to produce an approximation to $\exp(\Delta t.X)$ up to any order. Forest and Ruth [3] showed that approximations could be built for more than two vector fields. Combining the two we can state that it is possible to build an approximation to the solution of a linear combination of vector fields as a product of exponential maps:

$$\begin{array}{l} X = \sum_{i=1}^{m} a_i.A_i \\ \Rightarrow \exists w_{ij} : \exp(\Delta t.X) = \prod_{j=1}^{k} \prod_{i=1}^{m} \exp(w_{ij}.\Delta t.A_i) + o(\Delta t^{p+1}) \end{array} \tag{12}$$

3 Network Implementation

Such an approximation scheme can be easily implemented as a multilayer network as can be seen in the following figure (Fig. 2). The problem of predicting the system can now simply be solved by minimizing the prediction error of the model by tuning the weights w_{ij} using some gradient-based optimization technique.

3.1 Example

We will now present an example to illustrate how this method can be applied. We will do this by looking at the Van den Pol oscillator. This system can be written as a first-order system in state-space form which can be seen as a linear combination of two vector fields A_1, A_2 which can be solved analytically:

$$\begin{pmatrix} \dot{x} \\ \dot{y} \end{pmatrix} = \begin{pmatrix} y \\ -x \end{pmatrix} + \alpha.\begin{pmatrix} 0 \\ (1-x^2).y \end{pmatrix} = A_1 + \alpha.A_2 \tag{13}$$

One can then build a predictor according to the architecture just presented (Fig. 2), simply choosing an appropriate number of layers. One then finds the appropriate weights w_{ij} by minimizing the error on the training set. One interesting property of this method is that we are able to use the a priori knowledge we have about the system. Such a feature is uncommon in the field of system prediction using neural networks. This method allowed us to build a predictor for the Van der Pol oscillator in the case where the parameter α was unknown. We also produced a similar result for the Lorenz attractor.

3.2 MLP in Dynamics Space

If we decide to approximate the vector field of our system by a multi-layer perceptron, one can derive a composition network to implement this. The form of the vector field is

$$X(x) = \sum_{j=1}^{n} \vec{c}_j.\sigma(\vec{b}_j.x + b_{j_0}) = \sum_{j=1} A_j^{\vec{c}_j,\vec{b}_j}(x) \tag{14}$$

where $\sigma(x) =$ tanh(x) and $\vec{c}_j, \vec{b}_j \in \mathrm{IR}^{d+1}, j = 1, ..., n$.
But the differential equation $\dot{x} = \sigma(x)$ can be solved explicitly in the one-dimensional case. We can use this to explicitly integrate the multidimensional system $\dot{x} = A^{\vec{c},\vec{b}}(x)$ for any value of the parameters $\vec{c}_j, \vec{b}_j$. So, we can design a network of the following form:

$$\hat{x}(k+1) = F(x(k)) = \exp(w_k.A^{\vec{c}_k,\vec{b}_k}) \circ \ldots \circ \exp(w_1.A^{\vec{c}_1,\vec{b}_1})(x(k)) \tag{15}$$

We call this an "MLP in dynamics space" as the MLP is implicitly used to parametrize the vector field. Further work will be devoted to finding computationally efficient methods for the training of such a network.

4 Conclusions

We have studied the problem of predicting an autonomous continuous-time non-linear dynamical system from discrete-time measurements of its state. We showed that because the predictor must have the form of an invertible map, it is interesting to have an approximation scheme which has this property. This can be achieved by using compositions instead of additions in the approximation. The theory of Lie algebras provided the framework to develop such a method. We showed that this resulted in a multi-layer architecture and we illustrated it by a simple example. Further, the method was extended to some form of "MLP in dynamics space".

REFERENCES

[1] V.I. Arnold, *Mathematical methods of classical mechanics*, Springer-Verlag, New York (1989).

[2] D.R.J. Chillingworth, *Differential topology with a view to applications*, Pitman Publishing, London (1977).

[3] E. Forest, R. Ruth, *Fourth-order symplectic integration*, Physica D, Vol. 43 (1990) pp105–117.

[4] M.C. Irwin, *Smooth Dynamical Systems*, Academic Press, New York (1980).

[5] A. Isidori, *Nonlinear control theory*, Springer-Verlag, New York (1989).

[6] P.-V. Koseleff, *Calcul formel pour les méthodes de Lie en mécanique hamiltonienne*, Ph.D. thesis, Ecole Polytechnique, Paris (1993).

[7] R.I. McLachlan, *On the numerical integration of ordinary differential equations by symmetric composition methods*, SIAM J. Sci. Comput., Vol. 16(1) (1995), pp151–168.

[8] P.J Olver, *Applications of Lie groups to differential equations*, Springer-Verlag, New York (1985).

[9] H. Yoshida, *Construction of higher order symplectic integrators*, Phys. Lett. A, Vol. 150 (1990), pp262–269.

Acknowledgements

This research work was carried out at the ESAT laboratory of the Katholieke Universiteit Leuven, in the framework of the Concerted Action Project of the Flemish Community GOA-MIPS, and within the framework of the Belgian program on inter-university attraction poles (IUAP-17) initiated by the Belgian State, Prime Minister's Office for Science. The scientific responsibility rests with its authors. Yves Moreau is a research assistant of the N.F.W.O. (Belgian National Fund for Scientific Research).

STOCHASTIC NEURODYNAMICS AND THE SYSTEM SIZE EXPANSION

Toru Ohira and Jack D. Cowan*

Sony Computer Science Laboratory 3-14-13 Higashi-gotanda, Shinagawa, Tokyo 141, Japan. Email: ohira@csl.sony.co.jp

** Departments of Mathematics and Neurology, The University of Chicago, Chicago, IL 60637, USA. Email: cowan@synapse.uchicago.edu*

We present here a method for the study of stochastic neurodynamics in the master equation framework. Our aim is to obtain a statistical description of the dynamics of fluctuations and correlations of neural activity in large neural networks. We focus on a macroscopic description of the network via a master equation for the number of active neurons in the network. We present a systematic expansion of this equation using the "system size expansion". We obtain coupled dynamical equations for the average activity and of fluctuations around this average. These equations exhibit non–monotonic approaches to equilibrium, as seen in Monte Carlo simulations.

Keywords: stochastic neurodynamics, master equation, system size expansion.

1 Introduction

The correlated firing of neurons is considered to be an integral part of information processing in the brain[12, 2]. Experimentally, cross–correlations are used to study synaptic interactions between neurons and to probe for synchronous network activity. In theoretical studies of stochastic neural networks, understanding the dynamics of correlated neural activity requires one to go beyond the mean field approximation that neglects correlations in non– equilibrium states[8, 6]. In other words, we need to go beyond the simple mean–field approximation to study the effects of fluctuations about average firing activities.

Recently, we have analyzed stochastic neurodynamics using a master equation[5, 8]. A network comprising binary neurons with asynchronous stochastic dynamics is considered, and a master equation is written in "second quantized form" to take advantage of the theoretical tools that then become available for its analysis. A hierarchy of moment equations is obtained and a heuristic closure at the level of second moment equations is introduced. Another approach based on the master equation via path integrals, and the extension to neurons with a refractory state are discussed in [9, 10].

In this paper, we introduce another master equation based approach to go beyond the mean field approximation. We concentrate on the macroscopic behavior of a network of two–state neurons, and introduce a master equation for the number of active neurons in the network at time t. We use a more systematic expansion of the master equation than hitherto, the "system size expansion"[11]. The expansion parameter is the inverse of the total number of the neurons in the network. We truncate the expansion at second order and obtain an equation for fluctuations about the mean number of active neurons, which is itself coupled to the equation for the average number of active neurons at time t. These equations show non–monotonic approaches to equilibrium values near critical points, a feature which is not seen in the mean field approximation. Monte Carlo simulations of the master equation itself show qualitatively similar non–monotonic behavior.

2 Master Equation and the System Size Expansion

We first construct a master equation for a network comprising N binary elements with two states, "active" or firing and "quiescent" or non–firing. The transitions between these states are probabilistic and we assume that the transition rate from active to quiescent is a constant α for every neuron in the network. We do not make any special assumption about network connectivity, but assume that it is "homogeneous", i.e., all neurons are statistically equivalent with respect to their activities, which depend only on the proportion of active neurons in the network. More specifically, the transition rate from quiescent to active is given as a function ϕ of the number of active neurons in the network. Taking the firing time to be about $2ms$, we have $\alpha \approx 500s^{-1}$. For the transition rate from quiescent to active, the range of the function is $\approx 30 - 100s^{-1}$ reflecting empirically observed firing–rates of cortical neurons. With these assumptions, one can write a master equation as follows.

$$
\begin{aligned}
-\frac{\partial}{\partial t} P_N[n,\, t] &= \alpha(nP_N[n,\, t] - (n+1)P_N[(n+1),\, t]) \\
&+ \quad N(1-\frac{n}{N})\phi(\frac{n}{N})P_N[n\,\, t] - N(1-\frac{(n-1)}{N})\phi(\frac{n-1}{N})P_N[(n-1),\, t], \quad (1)
\end{aligned}
$$

where $P_N[n,\, t]$ is the probability that the number of active neurons is n at time t. (We absorbed the parameter representing total synaptic weight into the function ϕ.) This master equation can be deduced from the second quantized form cited earlier, which will be discussed elsewhere. The standard form of this equation can be rewritten by introducing the "step operator", defined by the following action on an arbitrary function of n:

$$
\mathcal{E}f(n) = f(n+1), \quad \mathcal{E}^{-1}f(n) = f(n-1) \qquad (2)
$$

In effect, $\mathcal{E}$ and $\mathcal{E}^{-1}$ shift n by one. Using such step operators, Eq. (1) becomes

$$
\frac{\partial}{\partial t} P_N[n,\, t] = (\mathcal{E}-1)r_n P_N[n,\, t] + (\mathcal{E}^{-1}-1)g_n P_N[n,\, t], \qquad (3)
$$

where $r_n = \alpha n$, and $g_n = (N-n)\phi(\frac{n}{N})$. This master equation is non–linear since g_n is a nonlinear function of n. Linear master equations, in which both r_n and g_n are linear functions of n, can be solved exactly. However, in general, non–linear master equations cannot be solved exactly, so in our case, we seek an approximate solution.

We now expand the master equation to obtain approximate equations for the stochastic dynamics of the network. We use the system size expansion, which is closely related to the Kramers–Moyal expansion, to obtain the "macroscopic equation" and time–dependent approximations to fluctuations about the solutions of such equation. In essence, this method is a way to expand master equations in powers of a small parameter, which is usually identified as the inverse size of the system. Here, we identify the system size with the total number of neurons in a network.

We make a change of variables in the master equation given in (3). We assume that fluctuations about the macroscopic value of n are of order $N^{(1/2)}$. In other words, we expect that $P_N(n,t)$ will have a maximum around the macroscopic value of n

with a width of order $N^{(1/2)}$. Hence, we set

$$n(t) = N\mu(t) + N^{\frac{1}{2}}\xi(t) \tag{4}$$

where μ satisfies the macroscopic equation and ξ is a new variable, whose distribution is equivalent to $P_N(n,t)$, i.e., $P_N(n,\ t) = \Pi(\xi,t)$. We expand the step operators as:

$$\mathcal{E} = 1 + N^{-\frac{1}{2}}\frac{\partial}{\partial\xi} + N^{-1}\frac{\partial^2}{\partial\xi^2}\ldots,\quad \mathcal{E}^{-1} = 1 - N^{-\frac{1}{2}}\frac{\partial}{\partial\xi} + N^{-1}\frac{\partial^2}{\partial\xi^2}\cdots \tag{5}$$

as $\mathcal{E}$ shifts ξ by $\xi + N^{(-1/2)}$. With this change of variables, the master equation is given as follows:

$$\frac{\partial}{\partial t}\Pi(\xi,t) - N^{\frac{1}{2}}\frac{\partial}{\partial t}\mu(t)\frac{\partial}{\partial\xi}\Pi(\xi,t) = N(N^{-\frac{1}{2}}\frac{\partial}{\partial\xi} + \frac{1}{2}N^{-1}\frac{\partial^2}{\partial\xi^2}\ldots)[\alpha(\mu + N^{-\frac{1}{2}}\xi)\Pi]$$
$$+N(-N^{-\frac{1}{2}}\tfrac{\partial}{\partial\xi} + \tfrac{1}{2}N^{-1}\tfrac{\partial^2}{\partial\xi^2}\ldots)[1-(\mu + N^{-\frac{1}{2}}\xi)][\phi(\mu + N^{-\frac{1}{2}}\xi)]\Pi(\xi,t) \tag{6}$$

Collecting terms, we obtain, to order $N^{(1/2)}$,

$$-\frac{\partial\mu}{\partial t} = \alpha\mu - (1-\mu)\phi(\mu) \tag{7}$$

This is the macroscopic equation, which can be obtained also by using a mean–filed approximation to the master equation. We make μ satisfy this equation so that terms of order $N^{(1/2)}$ vanish.

The next order is $N^{(0)}$, which gives a Fokker–Planck equation for the fluctuation ($\phi'(\mu) \equiv \frac{\partial}{\partial x}\phi(x)|_{x=\mu}$):

$$\frac{\partial}{\partial t}\Pi = -\frac{\partial}{\partial\xi}[-\alpha\xi - \xi\phi(\mu) + (1-\mu)\xi\phi'(\mu)]\Pi + \frac{1}{2}\frac{\partial^2}{\partial\xi^2}[\alpha\mu + (1-\mu)\phi(\mu)]\Pi \tag{8}$$

We note that this equation does not depend on the variable N justifying our assumption that fluctuations are of order $N^{(1/2)}$.

We now study the behavior of the equations obtained through the system size expansion to the second order. ¿From Eqs. (7) and (8), we obtain

$$\frac{d\chi}{dt} = -\alpha\chi + (1-\chi)\phi(\chi-\eta) + \eta(1-\chi+\eta)\phi'(\chi-\eta) \tag{9}$$

$$\frac{d\eta}{dt} = -\alpha\eta - \eta\phi(\chi-\eta) + \eta(1-\chi+\eta)\phi'(\chi-\eta) \tag{10}$$

where $\chi \equiv \frac{n}{N} = \mu + \eta$, and $\eta = N^{-\frac{1}{2}}\xi$. Equations (9) and (10) can be numerically integrated. Some examples are shown in Figure 1(B). For comparison, we plot solutions of the macroscopic equations with the same parameter sets in Figure 1(A). We observe a physically expected bifurcation into an active network state with decreasing α, for either approximation. However, different dynamics are seen as one approaches bifurcation points. In particular, the coupled–equations exhibit a non–monotonic approach to the limiting value. The validity of the system size expansion is limited to the region not close to the bifurcation point, as discussed in the last section. The point is that by incorporating higher order terms into the approximation, we can extend its validity to a domain closer to the bifurcation point and thereby better capture stochastic dynamical behavior of such networks. Monte Carlo simulations [3] of the two dimensional network based on (1) with 2500 neurons with periodic boundary conditions were performed. The connectivity is set up as follows: a neuron is connected to a specified number k of other neurons chosen randomly from the network. The strength of connection is given by the Poisson form:

$$w_{ij} = w_0 \frac{{r_{ij}}^s}{s!} e^{-r_{ij}} \tag{11}$$

where r_{ij} is the distance between two neurons, and w_0 and s are constants. We show in Figure 2 the average behavior of χ for (A) $k = 200$ ($k/N = 0.08$) and (B) $k = 15$m ($k/N = 0.006$). The non–monotonic dynamics is more noticeable in the low connectivity network. More quantitative comparisons between simulations and theory will be carried out in the future. The qualitative comparison shown here, however, indicate the need to model fluctuations of total activity near critical points in order to capture the dynamics of sparsely connected networks. This is consistent with our earlier investigations of a one–dimensional ring of neurons via a master equation.

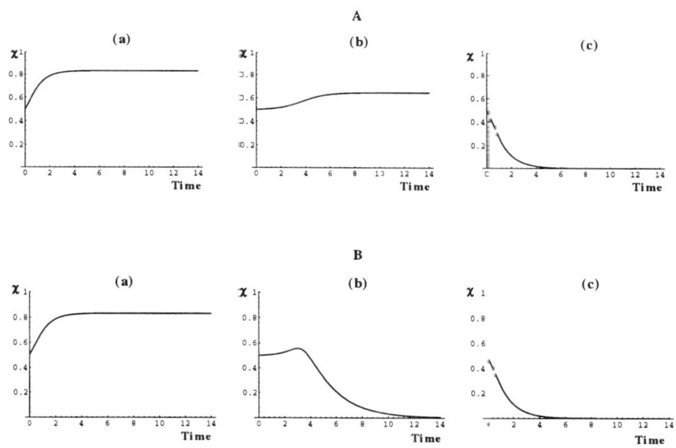

Figure 1 Comparison of solutions of (A) the macroscopic equation, and (B) (23) and (24). The parameters are set at $\beta = 15$ $\theta = 0.5$ and $\alpha =$ (a) 0.2, (b) 0.493, and (c) 0.9. The initial conditions are $\chi = 0.5$, and $\eta =$(A)0.01, and (B) 0.

3 Discussion

We have here outlined an application of the system size expansion to a master equation for stochastic neural network activity. It produced a dynamical equation for the fluctuations about mean activity levels, the solutions of which showed a non–monotonic approach to such levels near a critical point. This has been seen in model networks with low connectivity. Two issues raised by this approach require further comment: (1) In this work we have used the number of neurons in the network as a expansion parameter. Given the observation that the overall connectedness affects the stochastic dynamics a parameter representing the average connectivity per neuron may be better suited as an expansion parameter. We note that this parameter is typically small for biological neural networks. (2) There are many studies of Hebbian learning in neural networks[1, 4, 7]. In such studies attempts

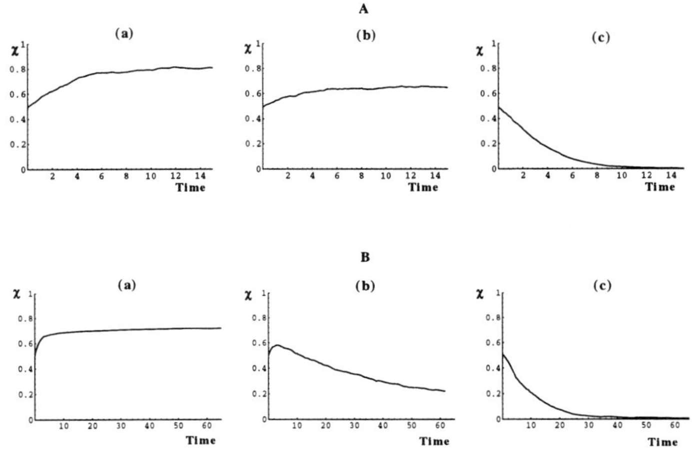

Figure 2 Comparisons of Monte Carlo simulations of the master equation with high ($k = 200$) and low ($k = 15$) connectivities per neuron. The parameters are set at $\beta = 15$, $\theta = 0.5$, $w_0 = 100.0$, $s = 3.0$, and for (A) $\alpha =$ (a) 0.05, (b) 0.1, and (c) 0.4, and for (B) $\alpha =$ (a) 0.001, (b) 0.05, and (c) 0.2. The initial condition is a random configuration.

have also been made to incorporate correlations of neural activities. It is of interest to see if we can formulate such attempts within the framework presented here.

REFERENCES

[1] S. Amari, K. Magiu, *Statistical neurodynamics of associative memory*, Neural Networks, Vol. 1 (1988), pp63–73.

[2] D. J. Amit, N. Brunel, M. V. Tsodyks, *Correlations of cortical Hebbian reverberations: theory versus experiment*, J. of Neuroscience, Vol. 14 (1994), pp6435–6445.

[3] K. Binder, *Introduction: Theory and "technical" aspects of Monte Carlo simulations*, Monte Carlo Methods in Statistical Physics, 2nd Ed., Springer-Verlag, Berlin (1986).

[4] A. C. C. Coolen, D. Sherrington, *Dynamics of fully connected attractor neural networks near saturation*, Phys. Rev. Lett., Vol. 71 (1994), pp3886–3889.

[5] J. D. Cowan, *Stochastic neurodynamics*, in: Advances in Neural Information Processing Systems 3, R. P. Lippman, J. E. Moody, and D. S. Toretzky, eds., Morgan Kaufmann Publishers, San Mateo (1991).

[6] I. Ginzburg, H. Sompolinsky, *Theory of correlation in stochastic neural networks*, Phys. Rev. E, Vol. 50 (1995), pp3171–3191.

[7] H. Nishimori, T. Ozeki, *Retrieval dynamics of associative memory of the Hopfield type*, J. Phys. A: Math. Gen., Vol. 26 (1993), pp859–871.

[8] T. Ohira, J. D. Cowan, *Master equation approach to stochastic neurodynamics*, Phys. Rev. E, Vol.48 (1993), pp2259–2266.

[9] T. Ohira, J. D. Cowan, *Feynman diagrams for stochastic neurodynamics* in: Proceedings of Fifth Australian Conference of Neural Networks, Brisbane (1994).

[10] Ohira, T., and Cowan, J. D., *Stochastic dynamics of three-state neural networks* in: Advances in Neural Information Processing Systems 7, G. Tesauro, D. S. Toretzky, T. K. Leen, eds., MIT Press, Cambridge (1995).

[11] N. G. van Kampen, *Stochastic Processes in Physics and Chemistry*. North-Holland, Amsterdam (1992).

[12] D. Wang, J. Buhmann, C. von der Malsburg, *Pattern segmentation in associative memory*, Neural Computation, Vol.2 (1990), pp94–106.

AN UPPER BOUND ON THE BAYESIAN ERROR BARS FOR GENERALIZED LINEAR REGRESSION

Cazhaow S. Qazaz, Christopher K. I. Williams and Christopher M. Bishop

Neural Computing Research Group, Dept. of Computer Science and Applied Mathematics, Aston University, Birmingham, UK. Email: ncrg@aston.ac.uk

In the Bayesian framework, predictions for a regression problem are expressed in terms of a distribution of output values. The mode of this distribution corresponds to the most probable output, while the uncertainty associated with the predictions can conveniently be expressed in terms of error bars given by the standard deviation of the output distribution. In this paper we consider the evaluation of error bars in the context of the class of generalized linear regression models. We provide insights into the dependence of the error bars on the location of the data points and we derive an upper bound on the true error bars in terms of the contributions from individual data points which are themselves easily evaluated.

1 Introduction

Many applications of neural networks are concerned with the prediction of one or more continuous output variables given the values of a number of input variables. As well as predictions for the outputs, it is also important to provide some measure of uncertainty associated with those predictions.

The Bayesian view of regression leads naturally to two contributions to the error bars. The first arises from the intrinsic noise on the target data, while the second comes from the uncertainty in the values of the model parameters as a consequence of having a finite training data set [1, 2]. There may also be a third contribution which arises if the true function is not contained within the space of models under consideration, although we shall not discuss this possibility further.

In this paper we focus attention on a class of universal non-linear approximators constructed from linear combinations of fixed non-linear basis functions, which we shall refer to as *generalized linear regression* models. We first review the Bayesian treatment of learning in such models, as well as the calculation of error bars [3]. Then, by considering the contributions arising from individual data points, we provide insight into the nature of the error bars and their dependence on the location of the data in input space. This in turn leads to the key result of the paper which is an upper bound on the true error bars expressed in terms of the single-data-point contributions. Our analysis is very general and is independent of the particular form of the basis functions.

2 Bayesian Error Bars

We are interested in the problem of predicting the value of a noisy output variable t given the value of an input vector $\boldsymbol{x}$. Throughout this paper we shall restrict attention to regression for a single variable t since all of the results can be extended in a straightforward way to multiple outputs. To set up the Bayesian formalism we begin by defining a model for the distribution of t conditional on $\boldsymbol{x}$. This is most commonly chosen to be a Gaussian function in which the mean is governed by the output $y(\boldsymbol{x}; \boldsymbol{w})$ of a network model, where $\boldsymbol{w}$ is a vector of adaptive parameters (weights and biases). Thus we have

$$p(t|\boldsymbol{x},\boldsymbol{w}) = \frac{1}{(2\pi\sigma_\nu^2)^{1/2}} \exp\left\{-\frac{(y(\boldsymbol{x};\boldsymbol{w})-t)^2}{2\sigma_\nu^2}\right\} \tag{1}$$

where σ_ν^2 is the variance of the distribution.

In the Bayesian framework, our state of knowledge of the weight values is expressed in terms of a distribution function over $\boldsymbol{w}$. This is initially set to some *prior* distribution, from which a corresponding *posterior* distribution can be computed using Bayes' theorem once we have observed the training data. A common choice of prior is a Gaussian distribution of the form

$$p(\boldsymbol{w}) = \frac{1}{(2\pi)^{M/2}} |\boldsymbol{S}|^{1/2} \exp\left\{-\frac{1}{2}\boldsymbol{w}^{\mathrm{T}}\boldsymbol{S}\boldsymbol{w}\right\} \tag{2}$$

where M is the total number of weight parameters, $\boldsymbol{S}$ is the inverse covariance matrix of the distribution, and $|\boldsymbol{S}|$ denotes the determinant of $\boldsymbol{S}$. Since the parameters in $\boldsymbol{S}$ control the distribution of other parameters they are often referred to as *hyperparameters*. The noise variance σ_ν^2 is commonly also called a hyperparameter since, in a Bayesian framework, it can be treated using similar techniques to $\boldsymbol{S}$. Here we shall assume that the values of σ_ν^2 and $\boldsymbol{S}$ are fixed and known.

The training data set D consists of N pairs of input vectors $\boldsymbol{x}^n$ and corresponding target values t^n where $n = 1, \ldots, N$. From this data set, together with the noise model (1), we can construct the *likelihood* function given by

$$p(D|\boldsymbol{w}) = \prod_{n=1}^{N} p(t^n|\boldsymbol{x}^n,\boldsymbol{w}) = \frac{1}{(2\pi\sigma_\nu^2)^{N/2}} \exp\left\{-\frac{1}{2\sigma_\nu^2}\sum_{n=1}^{N}\{y(\boldsymbol{x}^n;\boldsymbol{w})-t^n\}^2\right\} \tag{3}$$

We can then combine the likelihood function and the prior using Bayes' theorem to obtain the posterior distribution of weights given by $p(\boldsymbol{w}|D) = p(D|\boldsymbol{w})p(\boldsymbol{w})/p(D)$. The predictive distribution of t given a new input $\boldsymbol{x}$ can then be written in terms of the posterior distribution in the form

$$p(t|\boldsymbol{x},D) = \int p(t|\boldsymbol{x},\boldsymbol{w})p(\boldsymbol{w}|D)\,d\boldsymbol{w} \tag{4}$$

where $p(t|\boldsymbol{x},\boldsymbol{w})$ is given by (1).

Throughout this paper we consider a particular class of non-linear models of the form

$$y(\boldsymbol{x};\boldsymbol{w}) = \sum_{j=1}^{M} w_j\phi_j(\boldsymbol{x}) = \boldsymbol{\phi}^{\mathrm{T}}(\boldsymbol{x})\boldsymbol{w} \tag{5}$$

which we shall call generalized linear regression models. Here the $\phi_j(\boldsymbol{x})$ are a set of fixed non-linear basis functions, with generally one of the basis functions $\phi_1 = 1$ so that w_1 plays the role of a bias parameter. Such models possess universal approximation capabilities for reasonable choices of the $\phi_j(\boldsymbol{x})$, while having the advantage of being linear in the adaptive parameters $\boldsymbol{w}$.

Since (5) is linear in $\boldsymbol{w}$, both the noise model $p(t|\boldsymbol{x},\boldsymbol{w})$ and the posterior distribution $p(\boldsymbol{w}|D)$ will be Gaussian functions of $\boldsymbol{w}$. It therefore follows that, for a Gaussian prior of the form (2), the integral in (4) will be Gaussian and can be evaluated analytically to give a predictive distribution $p(t|\boldsymbol{x},D)$ which will be a Gaussian function of t. The mean of this distribution is given by $y(\boldsymbol{x};\boldsymbol{w}_{\mathrm{MP}})$ where $\boldsymbol{w}_{\mathrm{MP}}$ is found by minimizing the regularized error function

$$\frac{1}{2\sigma_\nu^2}\sum_{n=1}^{N}\{\boldsymbol{\phi}^{\mathrm{T}}(\boldsymbol{x}^n)\boldsymbol{w} - t^n\}^2 + \frac{1}{2}\boldsymbol{w}^{\mathrm{T}}\boldsymbol{S}\boldsymbol{w} \tag{6}$$

and is therefore given by the solution of the following linear equations

$$\boldsymbol{A}\boldsymbol{w}_{\mathrm{MP}} = \sigma_\nu^{-2}\boldsymbol{\Phi}^{\mathrm{T}}\boldsymbol{t} \tag{7}$$

where $\boldsymbol{t}$ is a column vector with elements t^n, $\boldsymbol{A}$ is the Hessian matrix given by

$$\boldsymbol{A} = \frac{1}{\sigma_\nu^2}\sum_{n=1}^{N}\boldsymbol{\phi}(\boldsymbol{x}^n)\boldsymbol{\phi}(\boldsymbol{x}^n)^{\mathrm{T}} + \boldsymbol{S} = \frac{1}{\sigma_\nu^2}\boldsymbol{\Phi}^{\mathrm{T}}\boldsymbol{\Phi} + \boldsymbol{S} \tag{8}$$

and $\boldsymbol{\Phi}$ is the $N \times M$ *design matrix* with elements $\Phi_{nj} = \phi_j(\boldsymbol{x}^n)$. Solving for $\boldsymbol{w}_{\mathrm{MP}}$ and substituting into (5) we obtain the following expression for the corresponding network output

$$y_{\mathrm{MP}}(\boldsymbol{x}) = \boldsymbol{\phi}^{\mathrm{T}}(\boldsymbol{x})\boldsymbol{w} = \sigma_\nu^{-2}\boldsymbol{\phi}^{\mathrm{T}}(\boldsymbol{x})\boldsymbol{A}^{-1}\boldsymbol{\Phi}^{\mathrm{T}}\boldsymbol{t} \tag{9}$$

The covariance matrix for the posterior distribution $p(\boldsymbol{w}|D)$ is given by the inverse of the Hessian matrix. Together with (4) this implies that the total variance of the output predictions is given by

$$\sigma^2(\boldsymbol{x}) = \sigma_\nu^2 + \sigma_w^2(\boldsymbol{x}) = \sigma_\nu^2 + \boldsymbol{\phi}^{\mathrm{T}}(\boldsymbol{x})\boldsymbol{A}^{-1}\boldsymbol{\phi}(\boldsymbol{x}) \tag{10}$$

Here the first term represents the intrinsic noise on the target data, while the second term arises from the uncertainty in the weight values as a consequence of having a finite data set.

3 An Upper Bound on the Error Bars

We first consider the behaviour of the error bars when the data set consists of a single data point. As well as providing important insights into the nature of the error bars, it also leads directly to an upper bound on the true error bars.

In the absence of data, the variance is given from (8) and (10) by

$$\sigma^2(\boldsymbol{x}) = \sigma_\nu^2 + \boldsymbol{\phi}^{\mathrm{T}}(\boldsymbol{x})\boldsymbol{S}^{-1}\boldsymbol{\phi}(\boldsymbol{x}) \tag{11}$$

where the second term, due to the prior, is typically much larger than the noise term σ_ν^2. If we now add a single data point located at $\boldsymbol{x}^0$ then the Hessian becomes $\boldsymbol{S}+\sigma_\nu^{-2}\boldsymbol{\phi}(\boldsymbol{x}^0)\boldsymbol{\phi}^{\mathrm{T}}(\boldsymbol{x}^0)$. To find the inverse of the Hessian we make use of the identity

$$\left(\boldsymbol{M} + \boldsymbol{v}\boldsymbol{v}^{\mathrm{T}}\right)^{-1} = \boldsymbol{M}^{-1} - \frac{(\boldsymbol{M}^{-1}\boldsymbol{v})\,(\boldsymbol{v}^{\mathrm{T}}\boldsymbol{M}^{-1})}{1 + \boldsymbol{v}^T\boldsymbol{M}^{-1}\boldsymbol{v}} \tag{12}$$

which is easily verified by multiplying both sides by $(\boldsymbol{M} + \boldsymbol{v}\boldsymbol{v}^{\mathrm{T}})$. The variance at an arbitrary point $\boldsymbol{x}$ for a single data point at $\boldsymbol{x}^0$ is then given by

$$\sigma^2(\boldsymbol{x}) = \sigma_\nu^2 + C(\boldsymbol{x},\boldsymbol{x}) - \frac{C(\boldsymbol{x},\boldsymbol{x}^0)^2}{\sigma_\nu^2 + C(\boldsymbol{x}^0,\boldsymbol{x}^0)} \tag{13}$$

where we have defined the *prior covariance function*

$$C(\boldsymbol{x},\boldsymbol{x}') = \boldsymbol{\phi}^{\mathrm{T}}(\boldsymbol{x})\boldsymbol{S}^{-1}\boldsymbol{\phi}(\boldsymbol{x}') \tag{14}$$

The first two terms on the right hand side of (13) represent the variance due to the prior alone, and we see that the effect of the additional data point is to reduce the variance from its prior value, as illustrated for a toy problem in Figure 1. From (13) we see that the length scale of this reduction is related to the prior covariance function $C(\boldsymbol{x},\boldsymbol{x}')$.

If we evaluate $\sigma^2(\boldsymbol{x})$ in (13) at the point $\boldsymbol{x}^0$ then we can show that the error bars satisfy the upper bound $\sigma^2(\boldsymbol{x}^0) \leq 2\sigma_\nu^2$. Since the noise level is typically much less than the prior variance level, we see that the error bars are pulled down very substantially in the neighbourhood of the data point. Again, this is illustrated in Figure 1.

We now extend this analysis to provide an upper bound on the error bars. Suppose we have a data set consisting of N data points (at arbitrary locations) and we add an extra data point at $\boldsymbol{x}^{N+1}$. Using (8) the Hessian $\boldsymbol{A}_{N+1}$ for the $N+1$ data points can be written in terms of the corresponding Hessian $\boldsymbol{A}_N$ for the original N data points in the form

$$\boldsymbol{A}_{N+1} = \boldsymbol{A}_N + \sigma_\nu^{-2}\boldsymbol{\phi}(\boldsymbol{x}^{N+1})\boldsymbol{\phi}^{\mathrm{T}}(\boldsymbol{x}^{N+1}) \tag{15}$$

Using the identity (12) we can now write the inverse of $\boldsymbol{A}_{N+1}$ in the form

$$\boldsymbol{A}_{N+1}^{-1} = \boldsymbol{A}_N^{-1} - \frac{\boldsymbol{A}_N^{-1}\boldsymbol{\phi}(\boldsymbol{x}^{N+1})\boldsymbol{\phi}^{\mathrm{T}}(\boldsymbol{x}^{N+1})\boldsymbol{A}_N^{-1}}{\sigma_\nu^2 + \boldsymbol{\phi}^{\mathrm{T}}(\boldsymbol{x}^{N+1})\boldsymbol{A}_N^{-1}\boldsymbol{\phi}(\boldsymbol{x}^{N+1})} \tag{16}$$

Substituting this result into (10) we obtain

$$\sigma_{N+1}^2(\boldsymbol{x}) = \sigma_N^2(\boldsymbol{x}) - \frac{\left[\boldsymbol{\phi}^{\mathrm{T}}(\boldsymbol{x}^{N+1})\boldsymbol{A}_N^{-1}\boldsymbol{\phi}(\boldsymbol{x})\right]^2}{\sigma_\nu^2 + \boldsymbol{\phi}^{\mathrm{T}}(\boldsymbol{x}^{N+1})\boldsymbol{A}_N^{-1}\boldsymbol{\phi}(\boldsymbol{x}^{N+1})} \tag{17}$$

From (8) we see that the Hessian $\boldsymbol{A}_N$ is positive definite, and hence its inverse will be positive definite. It therefore follows that the second term on the right hand side of (17) is negative, and so we obtain

$$\sigma_{N+1}^2(\boldsymbol{x}) \leq \sigma_N^2(\boldsymbol{x}) \tag{18}$$

This represents the intuitive result that the addition of an extra data point cannot lead to an increase in the magnitude of the error bars. Repeated application of this result shows that the error bars due to a set of data points will never be larger than the error bars due to any subset of those data points.

It can also be shown that the average change in the error bars resulting from the addition of an extra data point satisfies the bounds

$$\langle \Delta\sigma^2(\boldsymbol{x}) \rangle \equiv \frac{1}{N}\sum_{n=1}^{N}\left[\sigma_{N+1}^2(\boldsymbol{x}^n) - \sigma_N^2(\boldsymbol{x}^n)\right] \geq -\frac{\sigma_\nu^2}{N} \tag{19}$$

A further corollary of the result (18) is that, if we consider the error bars due to each of a set of N data points individually, then the *envelope* of those error bars constitutes an *upper bound* on the true error bars. This is illustrated with a toy problem in Figure 1. The contributions from the individual data points are easily evaluated using (13) and (14) since they depend only on the prior covariance function and do not require evaluation or inversion of the Hessian matrix.

4 Summary

In this paper we have explored the relationship between the magnitude of the Bayesian error bars and the distribution of data in input space. For the case of a single isolated data point we have shown that the error bar is pulled down close to the noise level, and that the length scale over which this effect occurs is characterized by the prior covariance function. From this result we have derived an upper bound on the error bars, expressed in terms of the contributions from individual data points.

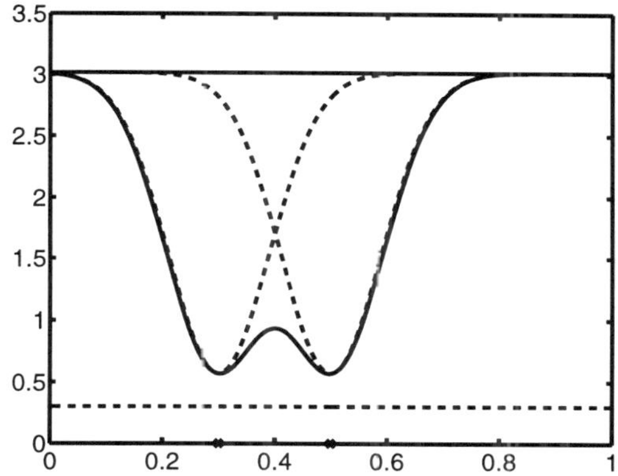

Figure 1 A simple example of error bars for a one-dimensional input space and a set of 30 equally spaced Gaussian basis functions with standard deviation 0.07. There are two data points at $x = 0.3$ and $x = 0.5$ as shown by the crosses. The solid curve at the top shows the variance $\sigma^2(x)$ due to the prior, the dashed curves show the variance resulting from taking one data point at a time, and the lower solid curve shows the variance due to the complete data set. The envelope of the dashed curves constitutes an upper bound on the true error bars, while the noise level (shown by the lower dashed curve) constitutes a lower bound.

REFERENCES

[1] C. M. Bishop. *Neural Networks for Pattern Recognition*. Oxford University Press, (1995).

[2] D. J. C. MacKay. Bayesian interpolation. *Neural Computing*, Vol. 4(3) (1992), pp415–447.

[3] C. K. I. Williams, C. Qazaz, C. M. Bishop, and H. Zhu. *On the relationship between Bayesian error bars and the input data density*, In Proceedings Fourth IEE International Conference on Artificial Neural Networks (1995), pp160–165, Cambridge, UK, IEE.

Acknowledgements

This work was supported by EPSRC grant GR/K51792 *Validation and verification of neural network systems.*

CAPACITY BOUNDS FOR STRUCTURED NEURAL NETWORK ARCHITECTURES

Peter Rieper, Sabine Kröner* and Reinhard Moratz**

FB Mathematik, Universität Hamburg, Bundesstr. 55, D-20146 Hamburg, Germany.

** Technische Informatik I, TU Hamburg-Harburg, Harburger Schloßstr. 20, D-21071 Hamburg, Germany. Email: Kroener@tu-harburg.d400.de*

*** AG Angewandte Informatik, Universität Bielefeld, Postfach 100131, D-33501 Bielefeld, Germany.*

In this paper an upper bound of the capacity or Vapnik-Chervonenkis dimension of structured multi-layer feedforward neural networks with shared weight vectors is derived. It mainly depends on the number of free network parameters analogous to the case of feedforward networks with independent weights. This means that weight sharing in a fixed neural architecture leads to a significant reduction of the upper bound of the capacity.

1 Introduction

Structured multi-layer feedforward neural networks gain more and more importance in speech- and image processing applications. Their characteristic is that a-priori knowledge about the task to be performed is already built into their architecture by use of nodes with shared weight vectors. Examples are time delay neural networks [10] and networks for invariant pattern recognition [4, 5]. One problem in the training of neural networks is the estimation of the number of training samples needed to achieve good generalization. In [1] is shown that for feedforward architectures this number is correlated with the capacity or Vapnik-Chervonenkis dimension of the architecture. So far an upper bound for the capacity has been derived for two-layer feedforward architectures with independent weights: it depends with $\mathcal{O}(\frac{w}{a} \cdot \ln \frac{q}{a})$ on the number w of connections in the architecture with q nodes and a output elements. In this paper we focus on the calculation of upper bounds for the capacity of structured multi-layer feedforward neural architectures. First we give some definitions and introduce a new general terminology for the description of structured neural networks. In section 3 we apply this terminology on structured feedforward architectures first with one layer then with multiple layers. We show that they can be transformed into equivalent conventional multi-layer feedforward architectures. By extending known estimations for the capacity we achieve upper bounds for the capacity of structured neural architectures which increase with the number of independent network parameters. This means that weight sharing in a fixed neural architecture leads to a significant reduction of the upper bound of the capacity. The capacity mainly depends on the number of free parameters analogous to the case with independent weights. At the end we comment the results.

2 Definitions

A *layered feedforward network architecture* $\mathcal{N}^r_{e,a}$ is a directed acyclic graph with a sequence of e input nodes, $r-1$ ($r \in \mathbb{N}$) intermediate (*hidden*) layers of nodes, and a final output layer with a nodes. Every node is connected only to nodes in the next layer. To every node k with indegree $n \in \mathbb{N}$ a triplet $(\boldsymbol{w}_k, s_k, f_k)$ is assigned, consisting of a weight vector $\boldsymbol{w}_k \in \mathbb{R}^n$, a threshold value $s_k \in \mathbb{R}$, and an activation

function f_k : $\mathrm{IR} \rightarrow \{0,1\}$. The activation function for all but the input nodes is the hard limiter function, and without loss of generality we choose $s = 0$ for the threshold values of all nodes. We define an architecture $\mathcal{N}^r_{e,a}$ with given triplets $(\boldsymbol{w}, s, f)$ for all nodes as a *net* $N^r_{e\ a}$. With the net itself a function F : $\mathrm{IR}^e \mapsto \{0,1\}^a$ is associated.
Let S be a fixed $(m \times e)$-input-matrix for $\mathcal{N}^r_{e,a}$. All nets $N^r_{e,a}$ that map S on the same $(m \times a)$-output-matrix T are grouped in a *net class* of $\mathcal{N}^r_{e,a}$ related to S. $\Delta(S)$ is the number of net classes of $\mathcal{N}^r_{e,a}$ related to S. The *growth function* $g(m)$ of an architecture $\mathcal{N}^r_{e,a}$ with m input vectors is the maximum number of net classes over all $(m \times e)$-input matrices S. Now we consider the nodes of the architecture $\mathcal{N}^r_{e,a}$ within one layer (except the input layer) with the same indegree $d \in \mathrm{IN}$. All nodes k whose components of their weight vectors $\boldsymbol{w}_k \in \mathrm{IR}^d$ can be permuted through a permutation π_k : $\mathrm{IR}^d \rightarrow \mathrm{IR}^d$ so that $\pi_k(\boldsymbol{w}_k) = \boldsymbol{w}\ \forall k$ for some vector $\boldsymbol{w} \in \mathrm{IR}^d$ are elements of the same *node class* $K_{\boldsymbol{w}}$. We call an architecture $\mathcal{N}^r_{e,a}$ *structured* if at least one node class has more than one element. Then the architecture with b node classes $K_{\boldsymbol{w}_i} (i = 1, \ldots, b)$ is denoted $\mathcal{N}^r_{e,a}(K_{\boldsymbol{w}_1}, \ldots, K_{\boldsymbol{w}_b})$.
The *Vapnik-Chervonenkis dimension* d_{VC} [9] of a feedforward architecture is defined by $d_{VC} := \sup\{m \in \mathrm{IN} \mid g(m) = 2^{ma}\}$. Let $Q := \left\{m \in \mathrm{IN} \;\middle|\; \frac{g(m)}{2^{ma}} \geq \frac{1}{2}\right\}$. Then $c := \sup Q$ for $Q \neq \emptyset$, or $c := 0$ for $Q = \emptyset$ is an upper bound for the Vapnik-Chervonenkis dimension and is also defined as capacity in [2, 7].

3 Upper Bounds for the Capacity

In this section is shown how structured architectures can be transformed into conventional architectures with independent weights. The upper bounds for the capacity of these conventional architectures then are applied to the structured architectures. A basic transformation needed in the following derivations is the transformation of structured one-layer architectures $\mathcal{N}(K_{\boldsymbol{w}_1}, \ldots, K_{\boldsymbol{w}_b})$ with input nodes of outdegree ≥ 1 and input vectors $\boldsymbol{x}_l$ into structured one-layer architectures $\mathcal{N}'(K_{\boldsymbol{w}_1}, \ldots, K_{\boldsymbol{w}_b})$ with input nodes of outdegree 1 only and dependent input vectors $\boldsymbol{x}_l{}'$ $(l = 1, \ldots, m)$: Every input node with outdegree $z > 1$ is replaced by z copies of that input node. The outgoing edges of the input node are assigned to the copies in such a way that every copy has outdegree 1. The elements of the input vectors are duplicated in the same way. By permuting the input nodes and the corresponding components of the input vectors we get the architecture $\mathcal{N}''(K_{\boldsymbol{w}_1}, \ldots, K_{\boldsymbol{w}_b})$ without any intersecting edges.

3.1 Structured One-layer Architectures

I) First we focus on structured one-layer architectures $\mathcal{N}^1_{e,a}(K_{\boldsymbol{w}})$ with a set $I := \{u_1, \ldots, u_e\}$ of e input nodes and the output layer $K := \{k_1, \ldots, k_a\}$. Let $K_{\boldsymbol{w}} := K$ be the only node class. All nodes in $K_{\boldsymbol{w}} = K$ have the same indegree $d \in \mathrm{IN}$.

Theorem 1 *Let a structured one-layer architecture $\mathcal{N}^1_{e,a}(K_{\boldsymbol{w}})$ with only one node class $K_{\boldsymbol{w}} = K$ be given. Suppose $d \in \mathrm{IN}$ as the indegree of all nodes in $K_{\boldsymbol{w}}$. The number of input nodes is $e \leq a \cdot d$. For m input vectors of length e an upper bound for the growth function $g(m)$ of the structured one-layer architecture $\mathcal{N}^1_{e,a}(K_{\boldsymbol{w}})$ is* *given by*

$$C(m{\cdot}a,d) := 2\cdot\sum_{i=0}^{d-1}\binom{m{\cdot}a-1}{i}\ .$$

Proof At first we examine structured one-layer architectures with outdegree 1 for every input node, equivalent to architectures $\mathcal{N}^1_{e,a}(K_{\boldsymbol{w}})$ with $e = a\cdot d$ input nodes. By permuting the input nodes and the corresponding components of the input vectors we get the architecture $\mathcal{N}''(K_{\boldsymbol{w}})$. Without loss of generality we consider the permutation π of the node class $K_{\boldsymbol{w}}$ as the identity function. Thus we have $\boldsymbol{w} = \boldsymbol{w}(k_1) = \ldots = \boldsymbol{w}(k_a) \in \mathrm{IR}^d$ for the a weight vectors (cf. Figure 1 a)). For m fixed input vectors $\boldsymbol{x}_l := (\boldsymbol{x}_l^1,\ldots,\boldsymbol{x}_l^a) \in \mathrm{IR}^{ad}$ ($\boldsymbol{x}_l^i \in \mathrm{IR}^d$, $l = 1,\ldots,m$, $i = 1,\ldots,a$) let S be an $(m \times a\cdot d)$-input matrix for $\mathcal{N}^1_{e,a}(K_{\boldsymbol{w}})$:

$$S := \begin{pmatrix} \boldsymbol{x}_1 \\ \vdots \\ \boldsymbol{x}_m \end{pmatrix} = \begin{pmatrix} \boldsymbol{x}_1^1 & \ldots & \boldsymbol{x}_1^a \\ \vdots & \ddots & \vdots \\ \boldsymbol{x}_m^1 & \ldots & \boldsymbol{x}_m^a \end{pmatrix} .$$

A given weight vector $\boldsymbol{w}_1 \in \mathrm{IR}^d$ defines a function $F_1 :\ \mathrm{IR}^{ad} \rightarrow \{0,1\}^a$ or a net

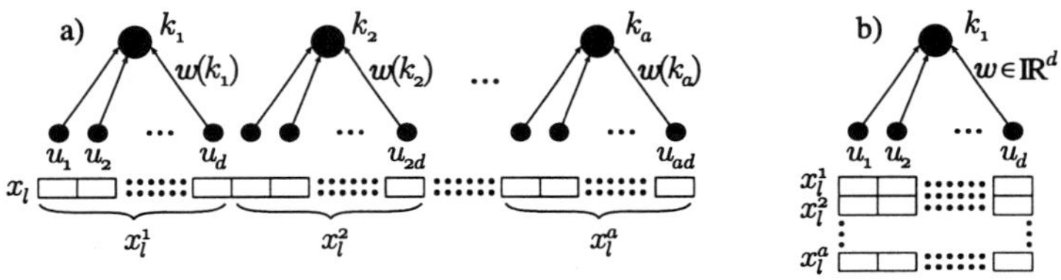

Figure 1 a) Structured architecture $\mathcal{N}(K_w)''$ with an input vector x_l ($l \in \{1,\ldots,m\}$). b) Architecture $\mathcal{N}^1_{d,1}$ with the corresponding a input vectors $x_l^1,\ldots,x_l^a$.

N_1, respectively. Let $\boldsymbol{w}_2$ be a weight vector that defines a function F_2 (a net N_2) different to F_1 on the input matrix S. Thus these two nets are elements of different net classes of $\mathcal{N}^1_{e,a}(K_{\boldsymbol{w}})$ related to the input matrix S. Now we consider the one-layer architecture $\mathcal{N}^1_{d,1}$, consisting of a single node with indegree d. By rearranging the m rows of the input matrix S for $\mathcal{N}''(K_{\boldsymbol{w}})$ to one column of the $m\cdot a$ input vectors $\boldsymbol{x}_l^i \in \mathrm{IR}^d$ ($l = 1,\ldots,m$, $i = 1,\ldots,a$) we derive the $(m\cdot a \times d)$-input matrix $\widetilde{S}$ for $\mathcal{N}^1_{d,1}$ (cf. Figure 1 b)):

$$\widetilde{S} := \begin{pmatrix} \boldsymbol{x}_1^1 \\ \boldsymbol{x}_1^2 \\ \vdots \\ \boldsymbol{x}_m^a \end{pmatrix} . \tag{1}$$

On $\mathcal{N}^1_{d,1}$ the weight vector $\boldsymbol{w}_1$ ($\boldsymbol{w}_2$) defines a function $\widetilde{F_1} :\ \mathrm{IR}^d \rightarrow \{0,1\}$ ($\widetilde{F_2} : \mathrm{IR}^d \rightarrow \{0,1\}$) or a net $\widetilde{N_1}$ ($\widetilde{N_2}$), respectively. Because of $F_1(\boldsymbol{x}_s) \neq F_2(\boldsymbol{x}_s)$ for at least one input vector $\boldsymbol{x}_s$ ($s \in \{1,\ldots,m\}$) and definition (1) the nets $\widetilde{N_1}$ and $\widetilde{N_2}$ are elements of different net classes of $\mathcal{N}^1_{d,1}$ related to the input matrix $\widetilde{S}$. Summarizing we get: if two nets of the architecture $\mathcal{N}^1_{e,a}(K_{\boldsymbol{w}})$ are different related to any input matrix

S we can define an input matrix $\widetilde{S}$ for $\mathcal{N}^1_{d,1}$ by (1), so that the corresponding nets are different, too. For the number of net classes this yields

$$\Delta(S) \leq \Delta(\widetilde{S}) . \tag{2}$$

With the results of [7] the growth function of the architecture $\mathcal{N}^1_{d,1}$ is given by $C(m \cdot a, d)$. From (2) also follows that this is an upper bound for the growth function of the structured one-layer architecture $\mathcal{N}''(K_{\boldsymbol{w}})$ or $\mathcal{N}^1_{ad,a}(K_{\boldsymbol{w}})$ respectively: $g(m) \leq C(m \cdot a, d)$. The inequation $g(m) \geq C(m \cdot a, d)$ can easily be verified in a similar way, so it yields $g(m) = C(m \cdot a, d)$ for the growth function of structured one-layer architectures $\mathcal{N}^1_{e,a}(K_{\boldsymbol{w}})$ with outdegree 1 for every input node.
Now we consider structured one-layer architectures $\mathcal{N}^1_{e,a}(K_{\boldsymbol{w}})$ with outdegree $z > 1$ for some input nodes. These architectures can be transformed into structured one-layer architectures $\mathcal{N}''(K_{\boldsymbol{w}})$ with $e = a \cdot d$ input nodes all with outdegree 1. But the input vectors of the input matrix for the transformed architecture $\mathcal{N}''(K_{\boldsymbol{w}})$ cannot be chosen totally independent. Thus, $C(m \cdot a, d)$ is an upper bound for the growth function of structured one-layer architectures $\mathcal{N}^1_{e,a}(K_{\boldsymbol{w}})$ with exactly one node class $K_{\boldsymbol{w}} = K$. □

Remark 1 *With [7] we find* $\frac{2 \cdot c}{a}$ *as an upper bound for the capacity of structured one-layer architectures* $\mathcal{N}^1_{e,a}(K_{\boldsymbol{w}})$ *with exactly one node class* $K_{\boldsymbol{w}}$.

II) Second we focus on structured one-layer architectures $\mathcal{N}^1_{e,a}(K_{\boldsymbol{w}_1}, \ldots, K_{\boldsymbol{w}_b})$ with b $(2 \leq b < a)$ node classes $K_{\boldsymbol{w}_1}, \ldots, K_{\boldsymbol{w}_b}$. These classes form the set K of the a output nodes: $K = K_{\boldsymbol{w}_1} \dot{\cup} \ldots \dot{\cup} K_{\boldsymbol{w}_b}$.

Theorem 2 *Assume a structured one-layer architecture* $\mathcal{N}^1_{e,a}(K_{\boldsymbol{w}_1}, \ldots, K_{\boldsymbol{w}_b})$ *with* $e \leq \sum_{i=1}^b \alpha_i \cdot d_i$ *input nodes,* $a = \sum_{i=1}^b \alpha_i$ *output nodes, and* $b \in \mathbb{N}$ $(2 \leq b \leq a)$ *node classes* $K_{\boldsymbol{w}_i}$ $(i = 1, \ldots, b)$. *Let* $\alpha_i := |K_{\boldsymbol{w}_i}|$ *be the sizes of the node classes* $K_{\boldsymbol{w}_i}$, *and* d_i *the indegrees of the nodes in* $K_{\boldsymbol{w}_i}$ $(i = 1, \ldots, b)$. *For* m *input vectors the product*

$$\prod_{i=1}^{b} C(m \cdot \alpha_i, d_i)$$

is an upper bound for the growth function of $\mathcal{N}^1_{e,a}(K_{\boldsymbol{w}_1}, \ldots, K_{\boldsymbol{w}_b})$.

Proof At first we examine structured one-layer architectures $\mathcal{N}^1_{e,a}(K_{\boldsymbol{w}_1}, \ldots, K_{\boldsymbol{w}_b})$ with $e = \sum_{i=1}^b \alpha_i \cdot d_i$ input nodes (all with outdegree 1) and an $(m \times e)$-input matrix S. The a nodes in the output layer K are permuted so that we get the ordered sequence $K = \{K_{\boldsymbol{w}_1}, \ldots, K_{\boldsymbol{w}_b}\}$ with $K_{\boldsymbol{w}_i} := \{k^i_1, \ldots, k^i_{\alpha_i}\}$ $(i = 1, \ldots, b)$. These permutations generate b structured one-layer sub architectures $\mathcal{N}^1_{e_i,\alpha_i}(K_{\boldsymbol{w}_i})$ with $e_i := \alpha_i \cdot d_i$ input nodes, α_i output nodes and $(m \times e_i)$-sub input matrices S^i $(i = 1, \ldots, b)$. With Theorem 1 we get $g_i(m) \leq C(m \cdot \alpha_i, d_i)$ for the growth functions $g_i(m)$ of these sub architectures. For the determination of the growth function $g(m)$ of $\mathcal{N}^1_{e,a}(K_{\boldsymbol{w}_1}, \ldots, K_{\boldsymbol{w}_b})$ the b input matrices S^i for the sub architectures can be chosen independently. Thus we get $g(m) = \prod_{i=1}^b g_i(m) \leq \prod_{i=1}^b C(m \cdot \alpha_i, d_i)$. The result for structured one-layer architectures $\mathcal{N}^1_{e,a}(K_{\boldsymbol{w}_1}, ..., K_{\boldsymbol{w}_b})$ with outdegree ≥ 1 for some input nodes, equivalent to $e < \sum_{i=1}^b \alpha_i \cdot d_i$ input nodes, follows in a similar way to Theorem 1. □

Theorem 3 *For the capacity of a structured one-layer architecture* $\mathcal{N}^1_{e,a}(K_{\boldsymbol{w}_1}, \ldots, K_{\boldsymbol{w}_b})$ *with* $b \in \mathbb{N}$ $(2 \leq b \leq a)$ *node classes* $K_{\boldsymbol{w}_i}$ $(i = 1, \ldots, b)$, *maximum indegree* $\widehat{d} \geq 2$ *for all nodes, maximum size* $\widehat{\alpha} := |K_{\boldsymbol{w}_i}|$ *of the node classes, and* $t := \frac{\widehat{\alpha} \cdot b}{a} \geq 2$ *we get*

$$c = \mathcal{O}\left(\frac{b \cdot \widehat{d}}{a} \cdot \ln t\right) .$$

Proof For the growth function $g(m)$ of the architecture $\mathcal{N}^1_{e,a}(K_{\boldsymbol{w}_1}, \ldots, K_{\boldsymbol{w}_b})$ we get with the above definitions and Theorem 2:

$$g(m) \leq \prod_{i=1}^{b} C(m \cdot \alpha_i, d_i) \leq \prod_{i=1}^{b} C(m \cdot \widehat{\alpha}, \widehat{d}) = C(m \cdot \widehat{\alpha}, \widehat{d})^b .$$

This yields an upper bound for the capacity: $c \leq \sup \left\{ m \in \mathbb{N} \;\middle|\; \frac{C(m \cdot \widehat{\alpha}, \widehat{d})^b}{2^{ma}} \geq \frac{1}{2} \right\}$.

With some estimations and $const := \frac{2 + 2 \cdot \ln(2)}{(\ln(2))^2}$ it follows:

$$m \leq const \cdot \frac{t \cdot \widehat{d}}{\widehat{\alpha}} \cdot \ln(t) .$$

For details and further information see [8]. □

3.2 Structured Multi-layer Architectures

Consider a structured r-layer architecture with e input nodes, a_j nodes in the hidden layers H^j $(j = 1, \ldots, r-1)$ and a nodes in the output layer K. Let the layers H^j be the disjoint union of the $b_j \leq a_j$ node classes $H_{\boldsymbol{w}^j_1}, \ldots, H_{\boldsymbol{w}^j_{b_j}}$ and the output layer the disjoint union of the node classes $K_{\boldsymbol{w}_i}$ $(i = 1, \ldots, b)$. The number of node classes is $\sum_{j=1}^{r-1} b_j + b =: \beta$. The structured architecture is denoted by $\mathcal{N}^r_{e,a}(H_{\boldsymbol{w}^1_1}, \ldots, K_{\boldsymbol{w}_b})$. A structured r-layer feedforward architecture $\mathcal{N}^r_{e,a}(H_{\boldsymbol{w}^1_1}, \ldots, K_{\boldsymbol{w}_b})$ can be regarded as a combination of r structured one-layer feedforward architectures since the output matrices of each layer are the input matrices for the following layer. Thus, we get an upper bound for the growth function $g(m)$ of $\mathcal{N}^r_{e,a}(H_{\boldsymbol{w}^1_1}, \ldots, K_{\boldsymbol{w}_b})$ by multiplying the growth functions of the r structured one-layer architectures (refer to Theorem 2):

$$g(m) \leq \prod_{j=1}^{r-1} \left(\prod_{i=1}^{b_j} C(m \cdot \alpha^j_i, d^j_i) \right) \cdot \prod_{i=1}^{b} C(m \cdot \alpha_i, d_i) . \tag{3}$$

With the maximum size $\widehat{\alpha} := \max\left\{\alpha_1, \ldots, \alpha_b, \alpha^1_1, \ldots, \alpha^{r-1}_{b_{r-1}}\right\}$ of the β node classes, and the maximum indegree $\widehat{d}$ of all nodes of the architecture $\mathcal{N}^r_{e,a}(H_{\boldsymbol{w}^1_1}, \ldots, K_{\boldsymbol{w}_b})$, $C(m \cdot \widehat{\alpha}, \widehat{d})^\beta$ is an upper bound for (3).

Theorem 4 *Let* $\mathcal{N}^r_{e,a}(H_{\boldsymbol{w}^1_1}, \ldots, K_{\boldsymbol{w}_b})$ *be a structured* r*-layer feedforward architecture with* $\beta \geq 2$ *node classes* $H_{\boldsymbol{w}^1_1}, \ldots, K_{\boldsymbol{w}_b}$, $\widehat{d} \geq 2$ *the maximum indegree of all nodes,* $\widehat{\alpha}$ *the maximum size of all* β *node classes, and* $\widehat{t} := \frac{\widehat{\alpha} \cdot \beta}{a} \geq 2$. *For the capacity of* $\mathcal{N}^r_{e,a}(H_{\boldsymbol{w}^1_1}, \ldots, K_{\boldsymbol{w}_b})$ *we get*

$$c = \mathcal{O}\left(\frac{\beta \cdot \widehat{d}}{a} \cdot \ln \widehat{t}\right) .$$

Proof Analogous to the proof of Theorem 3. □

An architecture $\mathcal{N}^r_{e,a}(H_{\boldsymbol{w}^1_1}, \ldots, K_{\boldsymbol{w}_b})$ with $\sum_{j=1}^{r-1} b_j + b = \sum_{j=1}^{r-1} a_j + a$ node classes is equivalent to an architecture $\mathcal{N}^r_{e,a}$ in which every node class has size 1. So the above upper bounds for the capacity hold good for conventional r-layer feedforward architectures, too.

4 Conclusion

By transforming architectures with shared weight vectors into equivalent conventional feedforward architectures and the extension of the definitions of the growth function and the capacity to multi-layer feedforward architectures we obtain estimations for the upper bounds of the capacity of structured multi-layer architectures. These upper bounds depend with $\mathcal{O}(\frac{p}{a} \cdot \ln \widehat{t})$ on the number p of free parameters in the structured neural architecture with maximum size $\widehat{\alpha}$ of the β node classes, $\widehat{t} := \frac{\widehat{\alpha} \cdot \beta}{a} \geq 2$, and a nodes in the output layer. So weight sharing in a fixed neural architecture leads to a reduction of the upper bound of the capacity. The amount of the reduction increases with the extent of the weight sharing. With $\widehat{\alpha} = 1$ the upper bounds hold good for conventional feedforward networks with independent weights, too. It is known that the generalization ability of a feedforward neural architecture improves within certain limits with a reduction of the capacity for a fixed number of training samples. As a consequence of our results a better generalization ability can be derived for structured neural architectures compared to the same unstructured ones. This is a theoretic justification for the generalization ability of structured neural architectures observed in experiments [5]. Further investigations focus on an improvement of the upper bounds, on the determination of capacity bounds for special structured architectures, and on the derivation of capacity bounds for structured architectures of nodes with continuous transfer functions [3, 6].

REFERENCES

[1] E. B. Baum, D. Haussler, *What Size Net gives Valid Generalization?*, Advances in Neural Information Processing Systems, D. Touretzky, (Ed.), Morgan Kaufmann, (1989).

[2] T. M. Cover, *Geometrical and Statistical Properties of Systems of Linear Inequalities with Applications in Pattern Recognition*, IEEE Trans. on Electronic Computers, Vol. 14 (1965), pp326-334.

[3] P. Koiran, E.D. Sontag, *Neural Networks with Quadratic VC Dimension*, NeuroCOLT Technical Report Series, NC-TR-95-044, London (1995).

[4] S. Kröner, R. Moratz, H. Burkhardt: *An adaptive invariant transform using neural network techniques*, Proc. of 7th Europ. Sig. Proc. Conf., Holt et al. (Eds.), Vol. III (1994), pp1489-1491, Edinburgh.

[5] Y. le Cun, *Generalization and Network Design Strategies*, Connectionism in Perspective, R. Pfeiffer et al. (Eds.), Elsevier Science Publishers B.V. North-Holland (1989), pp143-155.

[6] W. Maass, *Vapnik-Chervonenkis Dimension of Neural Nets*, Preprint, Techn. Univ. Graz, (1994).

[7] G. J. Mitchison, R. M. Durbin, *Bounds on the Learning Capacity of Some Multi-Layer Networks*, Biological Cybernetics, Vol. 60 No. 5 (1989), pp345-356.

[8] P. Rieper, *Zur Speicherfähigkeit vorwärtsgerichteter Architekturen künstlicher neuronaler Netze mit gekoppelten Knoten*, Diplomarbeit, Universität Hamburg, (1994).

[9] V. Vapnik, *Estimation of Dependences Based on Empirical Data*, Springer-Verlag, Berlin (1982).

[10] A. Waibel, *Modular Construction of Time-Delay Neural Networks for Speech Recognition*, Neural Computation, Vol.1 (1989), pp39-46.

ON-LINE LEARNING IN MULTILAYER NEURAL NETWORKS

David Saad and Sara A. Solla*

Dept. of Computer Science and Applied Mathematics, University of Aston, Birmingham B4 7ET, UK.

** CONNECT, The Niels Bohr Institute, Blegdamsvej 17, Copenhagen 2100, Denmark.*

We present an analytic solution to the problem of on-line gradient-descent learning for two-layer neural networks with an arbitrary number of hidden units in both teacher and student networks. The technique, demonstrated here for the case of adaptive input-to-hidden weights, becomes exact as the dimensionality of the input space increases.

Layered neural networks are of interest for their ability to implement input-output maps [1]. Classification and regression tasks formulated as a map from an N-dimensional input space $\boldsymbol{\xi}$ onto a scalar ζ are realized through a map $\zeta = f_{\mathbf{J}}(\boldsymbol{\xi})$, which can be modified through changes in the internal parameters $\{\mathbf{J}\}$ specifying the strength of the interneuron couplings. Learning refers to the modification of these couplings so as to bring the map $f_{\mathbf{J}}$ implemented by the network as close as possible to a desired map $\tilde{f}$. Information about the desired map is provided through independent examples $(\boldsymbol{\xi}^{\mu}, \zeta^{\mu})$, with $\zeta^{\mu} = \tilde{f}(\boldsymbol{\xi}^{\mu})$ for all μ. A recently introduced approach investigates *on-line learning* [2]. In this scenario the couplings are adjusted to minimize the error after the presentation of each example. The resulting changes in $\{\mathbf{J}\}$ are described as a dynamical evolution, with the number of examples playing the role of time. The average that accounts for the disorder introduced by the independent random selection of an example at each time step can be performed directly. The result is expressed in the form of dynamical equations for *order parameters* which describe correlations among the various nodes in the trained network as well as their degree of specialization towards the implementation of the desired task. Here we obtain *analytic* equations of motion for the order parameters in a general two-layer scenario: a student network composed of N input units, K hidden units, and a single linear output unit is trained to perform a task defined through a teacher network of similar architecture except that its number M of hidden units is not necessarily equal to K. Two-layer networks with an arbitrary number of hidden units have been shown to be universal approximators [1] for N-to-one dimensional maps. Our results thus describe the learning of tasks of arbitrary complexity (general M). The complexity of the student network is also arbitrary (general K, independent of M), providing a tool to investigate realizable ($K = M$), over-realizable ($K > M$), and unrealizable ($K < M$) learning scenarios. In this paper we limit our discussion to the case of the soft-committee machine [2], in which all the hidden units are connected to the output unit with positive couplings of unit strength, and only the input-to-hidden couplings are adaptive. Consider the student network: hidden unit i receives information from input unit r through the weight J_{ir}, and its activation under presentation of an input pattern $\boldsymbol{\xi} = (\xi_1, \ldots, \xi_N)$ is $x_i = \mathbf{J}_i \cdot \boldsymbol{\xi}$, with $\mathbf{J}_i = (J_{i1}, \ldots, J_{iN})$ defined as the vector of incoming weights onto the i-th hidden unit. The output of the student network is $\sigma(\mathbf{J}, \boldsymbol{\xi}) = \sum_{i=1}^{K} g\,(\mathbf{J}_i \cdot \boldsymbol{\xi})$, where g is the activation function of the hidden units, taken here to be the error function $g(x) \equiv \text{erf}(x/\sqrt{2})$, and $\mathbf{J} \equiv \{\mathbf{J}_i\}_{1 \le i \le K}$ is the set of input-to-hidden adaptive weights. Training examples are of the form $(\boldsymbol{\xi}^\mu, \zeta^\mu)$. The components of the independently drawn input vectors $\boldsymbol{\xi}^\mu$ are uncorrelated random variables with zero mean and unit variance. The corresponding output ζ^μ is given by a deterministic teacher whose internal structure is that of a network similar to the student except for a possible difference in the number M of hidden units. Hidden unit n in the teacher network receives input information through the weight vector $\mathbf{B}_n = (B_{n1}, \ldots, B_{nN})$, and its activation under presentation of the input pattern $\boldsymbol{\xi}^\mu$ is $y_n^\mu = \mathbf{B}_n \cdot \boldsymbol{\xi}^\mu$. The corresponding output is $\zeta^\mu = \sum_{n=1}^{M} g\,(\mathbf{B}_n \cdot \boldsymbol{\xi}^\mu)$. We will use indices $i, j, k, l \ldots$ to refer to units in the student network, and $n, m, \ldots$ for units in the teacher network. The error made by a student with weights $\mathbf{J}$ on a given input $\boldsymbol{\xi}$ is given by the quadratic deviation

$$\epsilon(\mathbf{J}, \boldsymbol{\xi}) \equiv \frac{1}{2}\,[\,\sigma(\mathbf{J}, \boldsymbol{\xi}) - \zeta\,]^2 = \frac{1}{2}\left[\,\sum_{i=1}^{K} g(x_i) - \sum_{n=1}^{M} g(y_n)\,\right]^2 . \tag{1}$$

Performance on a typical input defines the *generalization error* $\epsilon_g(\mathbf{J}) \equiv \;<\epsilon(\mathbf{J}, \boldsymbol{\xi})>_{\{\xi\}}$ through an average over all possible input vectors $\boldsymbol{\xi}$, to be performed implicitly through averages over the activations $\mathbf{x} = (x_1, \ldots, x_K)$ and $\mathbf{y} = (y_1, \ldots, y_M)$. Note that both $< x_i > = < y_n > = 0$, while the components of the covariance matrix $\mathcal{C}$ are given by overlaps among the weight vectors associated with the various hidden units: $< x_i\, x_k > \,=\, \mathbf{J}_i \cdot \mathbf{J}_k \equiv Q_{ik}$, $< x_i\, y_n > \,=\, \mathbf{J}_i \cdot \mathbf{B}_n \equiv R_{in}$, and $< y_n\, y_m > \,=\, \mathbf{B}_n \cdot \mathbf{B}_m \equiv T_{nm}$. The averages over $\mathbf{x}$ and $\mathbf{y}$ are performed using a joint probability distribution given by the multivariate Gaussian:

$$\mathcal{P}(\mathbf{x}, \mathbf{y}) = \frac{1}{\sqrt{(2\pi)^{K+M}|\mathcal{C}|}} \exp\left\{-\frac{1}{2}(\mathbf{x}, \mathbf{y})^T \mathcal{C}^{-1} (\mathbf{x}, \mathbf{y})\right\}\;, \text{ with } \mathcal{C} = \begin{bmatrix} Q & R \\ R^T & T \end{bmatrix} . \tag{2}$$

The averaging yields an expression for the generalization error in terms of the order parameters Q_{ik}, R_{in}, and T_{nm}. For $g(x) \equiv \text{erf}(x/\sqrt{2})$ the result is:

$$\begin{aligned} \epsilon_g(\mathbf{J}) \;=\; & \frac{1}{\pi}\left\{\sum_{ik} \arcsin \frac{Q_{ik}}{\sqrt{1+Q_{ii}}\,\sqrt{1+Q_{kk}}} + \sum_{nm} \arcsin \frac{T_{nm}}{\sqrt{1+T_{nn}}\,\sqrt{1+T_{mm}}}\right. \\ & \left. -2\sum_{in} \arcsin \frac{R_{in}}{\sqrt{1+Q_{ii}}\,\sqrt{1+T_{nn}}}\right\} . \end{aligned} \tag{3}$$

The parameters T_{nm} are characteristic of the task to be learned and remain fixed, while the overlaps Q_{ik} and R_{in} are determined by the student weights $\mathbf{J}$ and evolve during training. A gradient descent rule for the update of the student weights results in $\mathbf{J}_i^{\mu+1} = \mathbf{J}_i^\mu + \frac{\eta}{N}\,\delta_i^\mu\,\boldsymbol{\xi}^\mu$, where the learning rate η has been scaled with the input size N, and $\delta_i^\mu \equiv g'(x_i^\mu)\left[\sum_{n=1}^{M} g(y_n^\mu) - \sum_{j=1}^{K} g(x_j^\mu)\right]$ is defined in terms of both the activation function g and its derivative g'. The time evolution of the overlaps R_{in} and Q_{ik} can be explicitly written in terms of similar difference equations. The dependence on the current input $\boldsymbol{\xi}^\mu$ is only through the activations $\mathbf{x}$ and $\mathbf{y}$, and the corresponding averages can be performed using the joint probability distribution (2). In the thermodynamic limit $N \to \infty$ the normalized example number $\alpha = \mu/N$

can be interpreted as a continuous time variable, leading to the equations of motion:

$$\begin{aligned} \frac{dR_{in}}{d\alpha} &= \eta \left\{ \sum_m I_3(i,n,m) - \sum_j I_3(i,n,j) \right\} , \\ \frac{dQ_{ik}}{d\alpha} &= \eta \left\{ \sum_m I_3(i,k,m) - \sum_j I_3(i,k,j) \right\} + \\ & \eta \left\{ \sum_m I_3(k,i,m) - \sum_j I_3(k,i,j) \right\} + \\ & \eta^2 \left\{ \sum_{n,m} I_4(i,k,n,m) - 2\sum_{j,n} I_4(i,k,j,n) + \sum_{j,l} I_4(i,k,j,l) \right\} . \end{aligned} \quad (4)$$

The two multivariate Gaussian integrals: $I_3 \equiv < g'(u)\ v\ g(w) >$ and $I_4 \equiv < g'(u)\ g'(v)\ g(w)\ g(z) >$ represent averages over the probability distribution (2). The averages can be performed analytically for the choice $g(x) = \text{erf}(x/\sqrt{2})$. Arguments assigned to I_3 and I_4 are to be interpreted following our convention to distinguish student from teacher activations. For example, $I_3(i,n,j) \equiv < g'(x_i)\ y_n\ g(x_j) >$, and the average is performed using the three-dimensional covariance matrix C_3 which results from projecting the full covariance matrix $\mathcal{C}$ of Eq. (2) onto the relevant subspace. For $I_3(i,n,j)$ the corresponding matrix is:

$$C_3 = \begin{pmatrix} Q_{ii} & R_{in} & Q_{ij} \\ R_{in} & T_{nn} & R_{jn} \\ Q_{ij} & R_{jn} & Q_{jj} \end{pmatrix} .$$

I_3 is given in terms of the components of the C_3 covariance matrix by

$$I_3 = \frac{2}{\pi} \frac{1}{\sqrt{\Lambda_3}} \frac{C_{23}(1+C_{11}) - C_{12}C_{13}}{1+C_{11}} , \quad (5)$$

with $\Lambda_3 = (1+C_{11})(1+C_{33}) - C_{13}^2$. The expression for I_4 in terms of the components of the corresponding C_4 covariance matrix is

$$I_4 = \frac{4}{\pi^2} \frac{1}{\sqrt{\Lambda_4}} \arcsin\left(\frac{\Lambda_0}{\sqrt{\Lambda_1}\sqrt{\Lambda_2}} \right) , \quad (6)$$

where $\Lambda_4 = (1+C_{11})(1+C_{22}) - C_{12}^2$, and

$$\begin{aligned} \Lambda_0 &= \Lambda_4 C_{34} - C_{23}C_{24}(1+C_{11}) - C_{13}C_{14}(1+C_{22}) + C_{12}C_{13}C_{24} + C_{12}C_{14}C_{23} , \\ \Lambda_1 &= \Lambda_4(1+C_{33}) - C_{23}^2(1+C_{11}) - C_{13}^2(1+C_{22}) + 2C_{12}C_{13}C_{23} , \\ \Lambda_2 &= \Lambda_4(1+C_{44}) - C_{24}^2(1+C_{11}) - C_{14}^2(1+C_{22}) + 2C_{12}C_{14}C_{24} . \end{aligned}$$

These dynamical equations provide a novel tool for analyzing the learning process for a general soft-committee machine with an arbitrary number K of hidden units, trained to perform a task defined by a soft-committee teacher with M hidden units. This set of coupled first-order differential equations can be easily solved numerically, even for large values of K and M, providing valuable insight into the process of learning in multilayer networks, and allowing for the calculation of the time evolution of the generalization error [3]. In what follows we focus on learning a realizable task ($K = M$) defined through uncorrelated teacher vectors of unit length

($T_{nm} = \delta_{nm}$). The time evolution of the overlaps R_{in} and Q_{ik} follows from integrating the equations of motion (3) from initial conditions determined by a random initialization of the student vectors $\{\mathbf{J}_i\}_{1\leq i\leq K}$. Random initial norms Q_{ii} for the student vectors are taken here from a uniform distribution in the $[0, 0.5]$ interval. Overlaps Q_{ik} between independently chosen student vectors $\mathbf{J}_i$ and $\mathbf{J}_k$, or R_{in} between $\mathbf{J}_i$ and an unknown teacher vector $\mathbf{B}_n$ are small numbers, of order $1/\sqrt{N}$ for $N \gg K$, and taken here from a uniform distribution in the $[0, 10^{-12}]$ interval. We show in Fig. 1a-c the resulting evolution of the overlaps and generalization error for $K = 3$ and $\eta = 0.1$. This example illustrates the successive regimes of the learning process. The system quickly evolves into a symmetric subspace controlled by an unstable suboptimal solution which exhibits no differentiation among the various student hidden units. Trapping in the symmetric subspace prevents the specialization needed to achieve the optimal solution, and the generalization error remains finite, as shown by the plateau in Fig. 1c. The symmetric solution is unstable, and the perturbation introduced through the random initialization of the overlaps R_{in} eventually takes over: the student units become specialized and the matrix R of student-teacher overlaps tends towards the matrix T, except for a permutational symmetry associated with the arbitrary labeling of the student hidden units. The generalization error plateau is followed by a monotonic decrease towards zero once the specialization begins and the system evolves towards the optimal solution. Curves for the time evolution of the generalization error for different values of η shown in Fig. 1d for $K = 3$ identify trapping in the symmetric subspace as a small η phenomenon. We therefore consider the equations of motion (3) in the small η regime. The term proportional to η^2 is neglected and the resulting truncated equations of motion are used to investigate a phase characterized by students of similar norms: $Q_{ii} = Q$ for all $1 \leq i \leq K$, similar correlations among themselves: $Q_{ik} = C$ for all $i \neq k$, and similar correlations with the teacher vectors: $R_{in} = R$ for all $1 \leq i, n \leq K$. The resulting dynamical equations exhibit a fixed point solution at $Q^* = C^* = 1/(2K-1)$ and $R^* = \sqrt{Q^*/K} = 1/\sqrt{K(2K-1)}$. The corresponding generalization error is given by $\epsilon_g^* = (K/\pi)\left\{\pi/6 - K \arcsin\left((2K)^{-1}\right)\right\}$. A simple geometrical picture explains the relation $Q^* = C^* = K(R^*)^2$ at the symmetric fixed point. The learning process confines the student vectors $\{\mathbf{J}_i\}$ to the subspace $\mathcal{S}_B$ spanned by the set of teacher vectors $\{\mathbf{B}_n\}$. For $T_{nm} = \delta_{nm}$ the teacher vectors form an orthonormal set: $\mathbf{B}_n = \mathbf{e}_n$, with $\mathbf{e}_n \cdot \mathbf{e}_m = \delta_{nm}$ for $1 \leq n, m \leq K$, and provide an expansion for the weight vectors of the trained student: $\mathbf{J}_i^* = \sum_n R_{in}\mathbf{e}_n$. The student-teacher overlaps R_{in} are independent of i in the symmetric phase and independent of n for an isotropic teacher: $R_{in} = R^*$ for all $1 \leq i, n \leq K$. The expansion $\mathbf{J}_i^* = R^* \sum_n \mathbf{e}_n$ results in $Q^* = C^* = K(R^*)^2$. The length of the symmetric plateau is controlled by the degree of asymmetry in the initial conditions [2] and by the learning rate η. The small η analysis predicts trapping times inversely proportional to η, in quantitative agreement with the shrinking plateau of Fig. 1d. The increase in the height of the plateau with decreasing η is a second order effect [3], as the truncated equations of motion predict a unique value of $\epsilon_g^* = 0.0203$ at $K = 3$. Escape from the symmetric subspace signals the onset of hidden unit specialization. As shown in Fig. 1b, the process is driven by a breaking of the uniformity of the student-teacher correlations [3]: each student node becomes increasingly specialized to a specific teacher node, while its overlap with the remaining

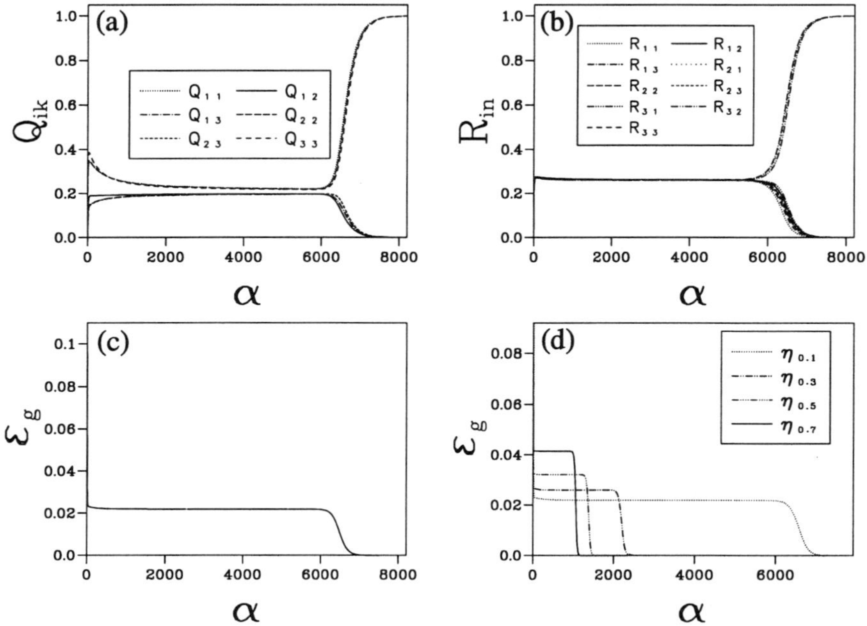

Figure 1 The overlaps and the generalization error as a function of α for a three-node student learning an isotropic teacher ($T_{nm} = \delta_{nm}$). Results for $\eta = 0.1$ are shown for (a) student-student overlaps Q_{ik}, (b) student-teacher overlaps R_{in}, and (c) the generalization error. The generalization error for different values of the learning rate η is shown in (d).

teacher nodes decreases and eventually decays to zero. We thus distinguish between a growing overlap R between a given student node and the teacher node it begins to imitate, and decaying secondary overlaps S between the same student node and the remaining teacher nodes. Further specialization involves the decay to zero of the student-student correlations C and the growth of the norms Q of the student vectors. The student nodes can be relabeled so as to bring the matrix of student-teacher overlaps to the form $R_{in} = R\delta_{in} + S(1-\delta_{in})$; the matrix of student-student overlaps is of the form $Q_{ik} = Q\delta_{ik} + C(1-\delta_{ik})$. The subsequent evolution of the system converges to an optimal solution with perfect generalization, characterized by a fixed point at $(R^*)^2 = Q^* = 1$ and $S^* = C^* = 0$, with $\epsilon_g^* = 0$. Linearization of the full equations of motion around the asymptotic fixed point results in four eigenvalues, of which only two control convergence. An initially slow mode is characterized by a negative eigenvalue that decreases monotonically with η, while an initially faster mode is characterized by an eigenvalue that eventually increases and becomes positive at $\eta_{max} = \pi/(\sqrt{3}K)$, to first order in $1/K$. Exponential convergence of R, S, C, and Q to their optimal values is guaranteed for all learning rates in the range $(0, \eta_{max})$; in this regime the generalization error decays exponentially to $\epsilon_g^* = 0$, with a rate controlled by the slowest decay mode.

REFERENCES

[1] G. Cybenko, *Approximation by superposition of sigmoidal functions*, Math. Control Signals and Systems Vol. 2 (1989), pp303–314.

[2] M. Biehl and H. Schwarze, *Learning by online gradient descent*, J. Phys. A Vol. 28 (1995), pp643–656.

[3] D. Saad and S. A. Solla, *Exact solution for on-line learning in multilayer neural networks*, Phys. Rev. Lett. Vol. 74 (1995), pp4337–4340.

[4] D. Saad and S. A. Solla, *On-line learning in soft committee machines*, Phys. Rev. E Vol 52 (1995), pp4225–4243.

Acknowledgements

Work supported by EU grant ERB CHRX-CT92-0063

SPONTANEOUS DYNAMICS AND ASSOCIATIVE LEARNING IN AN ASSYMETRIC RECURRENT RANDOM NEURAL NETWORK

M. Samuelides, B. Doyon*, B. Cessac and M. Quoy*****

Centre d'Etudes et de Recherches de Toulouse, 2 avenue Edouard Belin, BP 4025, 31055 Toulouse Cedex, France. Email: samuelid@cert.fr.
** Unité INSERM 230, Service de Neurologie, CHU Purpan, 31059 Toulouse Cédex, France.*
*** University of New-Mexico, Department of Electrical and Computer Engineering, Albuquerque, NM 87131, USA.*
**** Universität Bielefeld, BiBos, Postfach 100131, 33501 Bielefeld, Germany.*

Freeman's investigations on the olfactory bulb of the rabbit showed that its dynamics was chaotic, and that recognition of a learned pattern is linked to a dimension reduction of the dynamics on a much simpler attractor (near limit cycle). We adress here the question wether this behaviour is specific of this particular architecture or if this kind of behaviour observed is an important property of chaotic neural network using a Hebb- like learning rule. In this paper, we use a mean-field theoretical statement to determine the spontaneous dynamics of an assymetric recurrent neural network. In particular we determine the range of random weight matrix for which the network is chaotic. We are able to explain the various changes observed in the dynamical regime when sending static random patterns. We propose a Hebb-like learning rule to store a pattern as a limit cycle or strange attractor. We numerically show the dynamics reduction of a finite-size chaotic network during learning and recognition of a pattern. Though associative learning is actually performed the low storage capacity of the system leads to the consideration of more realistic architecture.

1 Introduction

Most part of studies on recurrent neural networks assume sufficient conditions of convergence. Relaxation to a stable network state is simply interpreted as a stored pattern. Models with symmetric synaptic connections have relaxation dynamics. Networks with asymmetric synaptic connections lose this convergence property and can have more complex dynamics. However, as pointed out by Hirsch, [8], it might be very interesting, from an engineering point of view, to investigate non convergent networks because their dynamical possibilities are much richer for a given number of units.

Moreover, the real brain is a highly dynamic system. Recent neurophysiological findings have focused attention on the rich temporal structures (oscillations) of neuronal processes [7, 6] which might play an important role in information processing. Chaotic behavior has been found out in the nervous system [2] and might be implicated in cognitive processes [9]. Freeman's paradigm [9] is that the basic dynamics of a neural system is chaotic and that a particular pattern is stored as an attractor of lower dimension than the initial chaotic one. The learning procedure thus leads to the creation of such an attractor. During the recognition process, first, the network explores a large region of its phase space through a chaotic dynamics.

When the stimulus is presented then the dynamics is reduced and the systems follows the lower dimensional attractor which has been created during the learning process. The question arises wether this paradigm which has been simulated in [11] using an artifical neural network is due to a very specific architecture or if it is a general phenomenum for recurrent network.
The first step to adress this problem was to determine the conditions for the existence of chaotic dynamics among the various architecture of recurrent neural networks. A theoretical major advance in that direction was achieved by Sompolinsky [10]. They established strong theoretical results concernig the occurence of chaos for fully connected assymetric random recurrent networks in the thermodynamic limit by using dynamical mean field theory. In their model, neurons are formal neurons with activation state in [-1,1] with a symmetric transfer function and no threshold. The authors show that the system exhibits chaotic dynamics. These results were extended by us in [5] to the case of diluted networks with discrete time dynamics. One can ask whether such results remain valid in a more general class of neural networks with no reversal symmetry i.e. with activation state in [0,1] and thresholds. The presence of thresholds is biologically interesting. Moreover, it allows to study the behaviour of the network when submitted to an external input. In this paper, we describe this model and report the main results about spontaneous dynamics in section 2. In section 3, we define a hebbian learning rule. We study the reduction of the dynamics during the learning process and the recognition of a learned stimuli. We then discuss the results and conclude (4).

2 Spontaneous Dynamics of Random Recurrent Networks with Thresholds

The neurons states are continuous variables x_i, $i = 1 \ldots N$. The network dynamics is given by:

$$i = 1 \ldots N: \quad x_i(t+1) = f\left[\sum_{j=1} N J_{ij} x_j(t) - \theta_i\right] \tag{1}$$

where J_{ij} is the synaptic weight between the neuron j and the neuron i . The J_{ij}'s are independant identically distributed random variables with expectation $E(J_{ij}) = \frac{\overline{J}}{N}$ and a variance $Var(J_{ij}) = \frac{J^2}{N}$. The thresholds (θ_i) are independant identically distributed gaussian random variables of expectation $E(\theta_i) = \overline{\theta}$ and variance $Var(\theta_i) = \sigma_\theta^2$. Our numerical studies are made with the sigmoidal function: $f(x) = \frac{1}{1+e^{2gx}}$ so that the neurons states $x_i(t)$ belong to [0,1]. Thus $x_i(t)$ may be seen as the mean firing rate of a neuron.
This kind of system is known to present the "propagation of chaos" property in the thermodynamic limit. This approach was initiated for neural networks by Amari, [1]. Though the denomination of "chaos" for this basic properties of vanishing finite-size correlations is quite confusing and has nothing to do with determinsitic chaos which will be considered afterwards, we shall keep it. Namely the intra-correlations between finite sets of neuron activation state and between neurons and weights vanish and each neuronal activation state process converges in law in the thermodynamic limit towards independant gaussian processes. This statement allow us to

derive mean field equations

$$\text{governing the limits for } N \to \infty \text{ of } \begin{cases} m_N(t) &= \frac{1}{N}\sum_{i=1}^{N} x_i(t) \\ q_N(t) &= \frac{1}{N}\sum_{i=1}^{N} x_i(t)^2 \end{cases} \tag{2}$$

These mean field equations are

$$\begin{cases} m(t+1) &= \int_{-\infty}^{\infty} \frac{dh}{\sqrt{2\pi}} e^{\frac{-h^2}{2}} f[h\sqrt{J^2 q(t) + \sigma\theta^2} + m(t)\overline{J} - \overline{\theta} \\ q(t+1) &= \int_{-\infty}^{\infty} \frac{dh}{\sqrt{2\pi}} e^{\frac{-h^2}{2}} f^2[h\sqrt{J^2 q(t) + \sigma\theta^2} + m(t)\overline{J} - \overline{\theta} \end{cases} \tag{3}$$

We shall now restrict ourselves for numerical studies to the case where $\overline{J} = 0$. The second mean-field equation is self-consistent and we are able to determine the critical surface in the space $\left(\frac{\overline{\theta}}{J}, gJ, \frac{\sigma_\theta}{J}\right)$ between a single stable fixed point and two stable fixed points (saddle-node bifurcation) . Consider a fixed point x^* of the system (1). Its components (x_i^*) are i.i.d. gaussian random variables, their moments are given by the previous mean-field equations. To determine the stability of x^* in (1), we compute the Jacobi matrix of the evolution operator

$$D(x^*) = 2gL(x^*)J \tag{4}$$

where $L(x^*)$ is the diagonal matrix of components $(x_i^* - x_i^{*2})$ and where J is the connection weight matrix . The spectral radius of this random matrix can be computed and this computation determines a stability boundary surface as shown below in figure 1. At the thermodynamic limit, it is possible to use the "propagation of chaos" property to compute the evolution of the quadratic distance between two trajectories of the system coming for arbitrary close initial conditions [3]. 0 is a fixed point for this recurrence and the critical condition for its destabilization is exactly the same than the previous condition for the first destabilization of the fixed point of the network. This proves, that at the thermodynamic limit, one observes a sharp transition between a fixed point regime and a chaotic regime. So in the bifurcation map of figure 1 there are four different regions: - region 1 : there is only one stable fixed point - region 2 : there are two stable fixed points (actually region 2 is a very small cusp) - region 3 : one stable fixed point and one strange attractor coexist. One may converge towards one or the other depending on the intial conditions. - region 4 : there is only one strange attractor Regions 2 and 3 shrink when $\sigma\theta$ increases. When $\sigma\theta = 0.2$, only regions 1 and 4 remain. For finite size systems, the destabilization and apparition of chaos boundaries are different. There exists an intermediate zone where the system is periodic or quasiperiodic. This corresponds to the quasiperiodicity route to chaos we observe in the system when gJ is increased [5, 4]. The simulations confirm with accuracy all these theoretical predictions for medium-sized networks (from 128 units up to 512 units), showing the progressive stretching of the transition zone where periodic and almost-periodic attractors take place.

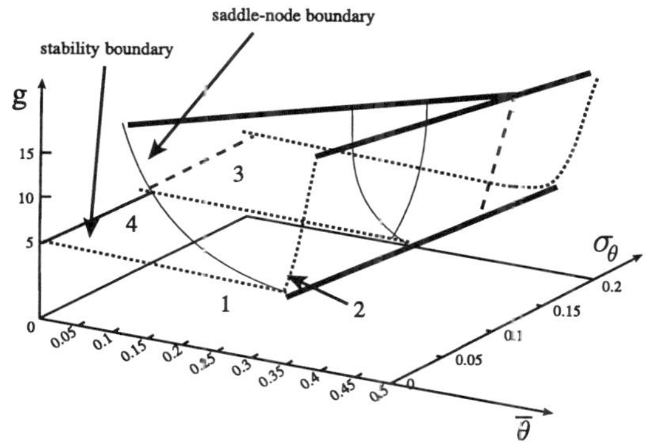

Figure 1 Saddle-node bifurcation surface and destabilization boundary in the $\left(\frac{\overline{\theta}}{J}, gJ, \frac{\sigma_\theta}{J}\right)$ space.

3 Learning and Retrieving Random Patterns.

3.1 Network Submitted to a Static Random Input

We study now the reaction of our network when submitted to an external input. The input is a vector of random gaussian variables I_i independent of θ_i's with a mean value $\overline{I}$ and a variance σ_I^2. We get

$$x_i(t+1) = f\left[\sum_{j=1}^{N} J_{ij}x_j(t) - \theta_i - I_i\right] \tag{5}$$

Hence the input is equivalent to a threshold. The global resulting threshold has a mean value $\overline{\theta} - \overline{I}$ and a variance. We can then interpret the presentation of an input as a change of the parameters of the system. Its effect can therefore be predicted from the bifurcation map.

If the configuration of the network stands in the chaotic region near the boundary of this region, then the presentation of an input will tend to reduce the dynamics of the system on a limit cycle by crossing the boundary, falling into the limit cycles and $T2$ torus area. The same input may lead to different answers by different networks with the same statistical parameters. This modification of the parameters by a pattern presentation creates a new system (with a different attractor).

3.2 Auto-associative Learning.

The learning procedure we define will enable us to associate a limit cycle or a strange attractor to a presented pattern. We modify the connection strength by a biologically motivated Hebb-like rule:

$$\text{if } x_j(t) > 0.5 \text{ then } J_{ij}(t+1) = J_{ij}(t) + \frac{\alpha}{N}\left[x_j(t) - 0.5\right]\left[x_i(t+1) - 0.5\right]$$
$$\text{else } J_{ij}(t+1) = J_{ij}(t)$$

We add the constraint that a weight cannot modify its sign. α is the learning rate. The learning procedure is implemented at each step when the network has reached the stationary regime.

In all our simulations the learning procedure reduces the fractal dimension of the chaotic attractors of the dynamics. Eventually the system follows an inverse quasi-periodicity route towards a fixed point. We have chosen to stop the procedure on a limit cycle, thus associating this cycle with the pattern learned.
In fact, one can speak of learning if the network has a selective response for the learned pattern, and if the learning procedure does not affect the dynamical behaviour when an other pattern is presented. On order to study this selectivity property, we make the following simulation. We learn one prototype pattern (ie. we iterate the learning dynamics upon reaching a limit cycle). Then we present 30 other random patterns (drawn randomly with the same statistics than the learned pattern), and we compare the attractors before, and after learning. For all patterns but one, the dynamics before learning were chaotic. For all these patterns, the dynamics were still chaotic after learning (the pattern whose response was periodic, had still a periodic attractor). Hence the network reduces its dynamics only for the learned prototype pattern.

3.3 Retrieval Property

In order to study the retrieval property of this associative learning process, we add noise to a pattern previously learned, and show how it affects the recognition. A pattern is a vector of gaussian random variables (for the simulations, each component has a mean zero and standard deviation 0.1). We add to each component a gaussian noise of mean zero and standard deviation 0.01, and 0.02, which thus corresponds to a level of noise of 10% and 20% on the pattern. We recall that the presentation of a noisy pattern changes the parameters of the system. So recognition has to be defined by some similarities between the attractors. In order to quantify the similarity between cycles, we compute their gravity center, their mean radius and winding (rotation) number and we define a crtierion of similarity based on these numerical indexes.
To estimate the recognition rate, we learn one prototype pattern. Then we present 30 noisy patterns (derived from the prototype one), and compute the similarity values. With a 10% level of noise recognition rate after 7 learning steps is 83%, with 20% noise it falls down to 27%.

4 Discussion and Conclusion

Our model reproduces the observations by Freeman concerning the dimension reduction of the system attractor by recognition of a learned pattern, in a model of the olfactory bulb [11]. The system does not need to wait until a fixed point is reached to perform recognition: relying on our experiments, convergence on an attractor is very fast. This gives an insight into the mechanism leading to such a phenomenon by the extraction of the few relevant parameters related to it.
However this model suffers severe drawbacks concerning the control of the learning process and the storage capacity. Moreover, the modifications supported by the weights during the learning process are difficult to interpret theoretically. These limitations suggest to introduce at the next step architectural and functional differentiation into the network (inhibitory and excitatory neurons, multiple layers, random geometric-dependant connectivity and time delays, modular architecture of chaotic oscillators).

Coding by dynamical attractors is also particularly suited for learning of temporal signals. For the moment, we only focused on the learning of static patterns. However, we performed with interesting results some preliminary simulations on presentation of temporals sequences. This could lead to connect different chaotic networks in order to perform recognition tasks using the synchronization processes highlighted by Gray [7].

REFERENCES

[1] Amari S.I., *Characteristics of random nets of analog neuron-like elements*, IEEE Trans.Syst.Man.Cyb, Vol. 2.5(1972), pp643–657.

[2] Babloyantz A., Nicolis C., Salazar J.M., *Evidence of chaotic dynamics of brain activity during the sleep cycle*, Phys. Lett. Vol. 111A (1985), pp152–156.

[3] Cessac B., *Increase in complexity in random neural networks*, J.PhysI, Vol. 5 (1995), pp409–432.

[4] Cessac B., Doyon B., Quoy M., Samuelides M., *Mean-field equations, bifurcation map and route to chaos* in: discrete time neural networks, Physica D, Vol. 74 (1994), pp24–44.

[5] Doyon B., Cessac B., Quoy M., Samuelides M., *Chaos in Neural Networks With Random Connectivity*, International Journal Of Bifurcation and Chaos, Vol. 3 (1993), No. 2, pp279–291.

[6] Eckhorn R., Bauer R., Jordan W., Brosch M., Kruse W., Munk M., Reitboeck H.J., *Coherent oscillations: A mechanism of feature linking in the visual cortex? Multiple electrode and correlation analysis in the cat*, Biol. Cybernet. Vol. 60 (1988), pp121–130.

[7] Gray C.M., Koenig P., Engel A.K., Singer W. *Oscillatory responses in cat visual cortex exhibit intercolumnar synchronisation which reflects global stimulus properties*, Nature Vol. 338 (1989), pp334–337.

[8] Hirsch .M.W., *Convergent Activation Dynamics in Continuous Time Networks*, Neural Networks Vol. 2 (1989), pp331–349.

[9] Skarda C.A., Freeman W.J., *How brains make chaos in order to make sense of the world*, Behav. Brain Sci. Vol. 10 (1987), pp161-195.

[10] Sompolinsky H., Crisanti A., Sommers H.J., *Chaos in random neural networks*, Phys. Rev. Lett. Vol. 61 (1988), pp259–262.

[11] Yao Y., Freeman W.J., *Model of biological pattern recognition with spatially chaotic dynamics*, Neural Networks Vol. 3 (1990), pp153–170.

Acknowledgements

This research has been supported by a grant from DRET (the National French Defense Agency) and by the COGNISCIENCE research program of the C.N.R.S.. M Quoy is supported by a Lavoisier grant of the French Foreign Office and B. Cessac by a Cognisciences grant of the C.N.R.S..

A STATISTICAL MECHANICS ANALYSIS OF GENETIC ALGORITHMS FOR SEARCH AND LEARNING

Jonathan L. Shapiro, Adam Prügel-Bennett* and Magnus Rattray

Department of Computer Science, University of Manchester, Manchester, M13 9PL, UK.

** NORDITA Blegdamsvej 17, DK-2100 Copenhagen O, Denmark.*

Statistical mechanics can be used to derive a set of equations describing the evolution of a genetic algorithm involving crossover, mutation and selection. This paper gives an introduction to this work. It is shown how the method can be applied to to very simple problems, for which the dynamics of the genetic algorithm can be reduced to a set of nonlinear coupled difference equations. Good results are obtained when the equations are truncated to four variables.

Keywords: Genetic Algorithms, Statistical Mechanics, Fitness Distributions.

1 Introduction

Genetic Algorithms (GA) are a class of search techniques which can be used to find solutions to hard problems. They have been applied in a range of domains: optimisation problems, machine learning, training neural networks or evolving neural network architectures, and many others. (For an introduction, see Goldberg [1].) They can be naturally applied to discrete problems for which other techniques are more difficult to use, and they parallelise well. Most importantly, they have been found to work in many applications.

Although GAs have been widely studied empirically, they are not well understood theoretically. Unlike gradient descent search and simulated annealing, genetic algorithms are not based on a well-understood process. The goal of the research described here is to develop a formalism which allows the study of genetic algorithm dynamics for problems of realistic size and finite population sizes. The problems we have studied are clearly toy problems; however, they contain some realistic aspects, and we hope their consideration will be a stepping stone to the study of more realistic problems.

2 The Statistical Mechanics Approach

Ideally, one would like to solve the dynamics of genetic algorithms exactly. This could be done, in principle, either by studying the stochastic equation directly, or by using a Markov Chain formulation to analyse the deterministic equation for the probability of being in a given population (see [2, 3]). However, it is very difficult to make progress in this way, because one must solve a high-dimensional, strongly interacting, nonlinear system which is extremely difficult to analyse.

In these exact approaches, the precise details of which individuals are in the population is considered. In our approach much less information is assumed to be known. We consider only statistical properties of the distribution of fitnesses in the population; from the distribution of fitnesses at one time, we predict the distribution of fitnesses at the next time step. Iterating this from the initial distribution, we propose to predict the fitness distribution for all times.

This distribution tells you want you want to know – for example the evolution of the best member of the population can be inferred. But is it possible, in principle, to predict the fitness at later times based on the fitness at earlier times?

The answer is no. Although it is possible to predict the effect of selection based solely on the fitness distribution, mutation and crossover depend upon the configurations of the strings in the population which cannot be inferred from their fitnesses. We use a statistical mechanics assumption to bridge this gap.

We characterise the distribution by its cumulants. Cumulants are statistical properties of a distribution which are like moments, but are more stable and robust. The first two cumulants are the mean and variance respectively. The third cumulant is related to the skewness; it measure asymmetry of the distribution about the mean. The fourth cumulant is related to the kurtosis; it measure whether the distribution falls off faster or more slowly than Gaussian.

3 Test Problems

The method has been applied to four problems. The simplest task, and one which will be used throughout this paper to illustrate the method, is the optimisation of a linear, spatially inhomogeneous function, *counting random numbers*. In this problem, each bit of the string contributes individually an arbitrary amount. The fitness is,

$$F[\boldsymbol{\tau}] = \sum_{i=1}^{N} J_i \tau_i .$$

Here $\boldsymbol{\tau}$ is a string of ± 1 of length N which the GA searches over. The J_i's are fixed random numbers.

Other problems to which the method has been applied include: the task of maximising the energy of a *spin-glass chain* [4, 5, 6], the *subset sum* problem [7] (an NP hard problem in the weak sense), and learning in an Ising perceptron [8]. For the first two problems, the dynamics can be solved, and the formalism predicts accurately the evolution of the genetic algorithm. The latter problem has been much more difficult to solve, however.

4 The Genetic Operators

We now discuss how our approach is applied to the study of three specific GA operators: selection, mutation, and crossover. We will use the *counting random numbers* task to illustrate how the calculations are done.

4.1 Selection

Selection is the operation whereby better members of the population are replicated and less good members are removed. The most frequently used method is to chose the members of the next population probabilistically using a weighting function $R(F^\alpha)$. We have studied Boltzmann selection

$$R(F) \propto \exp(\beta F)$$

where β is a parameter controlling the selection rate. Fitness proportional selection ($R(F) = F$), culling selection (choose the n best), and other forms can also be handled by the approach.

In an infinite population, the new distribution of fitness in terms of the old $\rho(F)$ would simply be $R(F)\rho(F)$ up to a normalisation factor. In a finite population, there will be fluctuations around this. The way to treat this is to draw P levels from ρ. The generating function for cumulants is

$$G(\gamma) = \left[\prod_{\alpha=1}^{P} \int_{-\infty}^{\infty} \rho(F^{\alpha}) dF^{\alpha}\right] \log \left[\sum_{\alpha=1}^{P} R(F^{\alpha}) \exp(-\gamma F^{\alpha})\right].$$

This problem is analogous to the Random Energy Model proposed and studied by Derrida [9], and can be computed by using the same methods developed for that problem.

For Boltzmann selection, the cumulant expansion for the distribution after selection in terms of selection before can be found as an expansion in the selection parameter β,

$$\begin{aligned} \kappa_1^s &= \kappa_1 + \beta\left(1 - \frac{1}{P}\right)\kappa_2 + \frac{\beta^2}{2}\left(1 - \frac{3}{P}\right)\kappa_3 + \frac{\beta^3}{3!}\left[\left(1 - \frac{7}{P}\right)\kappa_4 - \frac{6}{P}\kappa_2^2\right] + \cdots, \\ \kappa_2^s &= \left(1 - \frac{1}{P}\right)\kappa_2 + \beta\left(1 - \frac{3}{P}\right)\kappa_3 + \frac{\beta^2}{2}\left[\left(1 - \frac{7}{P}\right)\kappa_4 - \frac{6}{P}\kappa_2^2\right] + \cdots, \\ \kappa_3^s &= \left(1 - \frac{3}{P}\right)\kappa_3 + \beta\left[\left(1 - \frac{7}{P}\right)\kappa_4 - \frac{6}{P}\kappa_2^2\right] + \cdots. \end{aligned} \tag{1}$$

Or the cumulants can be found for arbitrary β numerically.

For many problems, the initial distribution will be nearly Gaussian. Selection introduces a negative third cumulant – the low-fitness tail is more occupied than the high-fitness one. An optimal amount of selection is indicated. The improvement of the mean increases with β initially, but saturates for large β. Selection also decreases the variance; this effect is small for small β but becomes important for increasing values. The trade-off between these two effects of selection — increase in mean but decrease in genetic diversity — are balanced for intermediate values of β. This has been discussed in earlier work [5, 6].

4.2 Mutation

Mutation causes small random changes to the individual bits of the string. Thus, it causes a local exploration, in common with many other search algorithms. It acts on each member of the population independently.

To study the effect of mutation, we introduce a set of mutation variables, m_i^{α}, one for each site of each string, which take the value 1 if the site is mutated, 0 otherwise. Let m be the mutation probability. In terms of these variables, the fitness after mutation is (for *counting random numbers*)

$$F = \sum_i J_i \left(1 - 2m_i^{\alpha}\right) \tau_i^{\alpha}. \tag{2}$$

Averaging over all variables gives the cumulants after mutation. This yields,

$$\begin{aligned} \kappa_1^m &= (1 - 2m)\kappa_1 \\ \kappa_2^m &= \kappa_2 + \left(1 - (1 - 2m)^2\right)(N - \kappa_2) \\ \kappa_3^m &= \kappa_3(1 - 2m)^3 - 2(1 - 2m)\left(1 - (1 - 2m)^2\right)\frac{1}{P_3}\sum_i J_i^3 \langle \tau_i \rangle \end{aligned} \tag{3}$$

where $< \tau >$ denotes population average. (The fourth cumulant can be calculated in a similar fashion).

The first two equations express obvious effects. Mutation brings the mean and variance back towards values of a random population — mean decreases to zero and the variance increases toward N. The equation for the third cumulant is more interesting. The first term decreases the third cumulant, but the second increases its magnitude if it is negative (which it typically is). This is the part which depends upon the configuration average.

4.3 Crossover

Crossover can be treated in a similar manner to mutation. Introduce a set of crossover variables, $\chi_i^{\alpha\beta}$ which are 1 if α crossed with β at site i and 0 otherwise, write equations for the cumulants in terms of these variables and average. One finds that both the mean and the variance remain unchanged. The third and higher cumulants are reduced and brought to natural values which depend upon configurational averages.

4.4 Using the Statistical Mechanics Ansatz to Infer Configurational Averages from Fitness Distribution Averages

In the previous section we showed that the effect of mutation on the cumulants depends upon the fitness distribution (i.e. on the cumulants) *and* upon properties of the configuration of the strings. As we have argued, one cannot, in principle, determine the configuration from the fitness distribution. We invoke a statistical mechanics ansatz. We assume that the string variables are free to fluctuate subject to the constraint that the cumulants are given. In other words, our assumption is that of all the configurations which have the same distribution of fitnesses, the more numerous ones are more likely to describe the actual one. This can be seen as a maximum entropy assumption. We use a simple statistical mechanics model to implement the proposed relationship between fitness statistics and configuration statistics. Details are presented in [6].

5 Discussion and Future Work

The equations for each of the genetic operators can be put together to predict the whole dynamics. Typical curves are shown in figure 1. The theoretical curves were produced by calculation of the initial distribution theoretically, and iterating the equations repeatedly. No experimental input was used. Although, the agreement between experiment and theory is not perfect, these results are as accurate as any approach of which we are aware.

This gives a picture of the role of crossover, for this simple problem. Selection improves the average fitness, but decreases variance and introduces a negative skewness. Mutation increases the variance, introducing genetic diversity; however, it also decreases the mean. Crossover has no effect on the first two cumulants. It reduces the magnitude of the skewness, however. This replaces some of the low-fitness tail with some high-fitness tail, which improves the best member of the population. Since, for this problem, crossover has no effect on the mean, there is no cost in doing this and crossover is helpful. For a realistic problem, however, crossover will introduce a deleterious effect to the mean; whether this effect dominates over the improvement due to the decrease of the third cumulant may determine whether the crossover operator is a useful one for the problem in question.

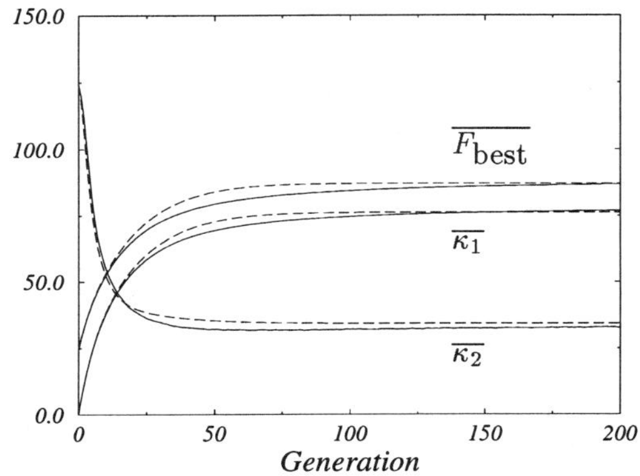

Figure 1 The solid curves show the evolution of the first two cumulants and the fitness of the best member of the population for $N = 127$, $P = 50$, $\beta = 0.1$ and $m = 1/2N$. The ground state is at $F_{best} \approx 101$. The dashed curve shows the theoretical prediction. The overscore indicates averaging over 10 000 runs. From reference [6].

REFERENCES

[1] David E. Goldberg, *Genetic Algorithms in Search, Optimization & Machine Learning*, Addison-Wesley, Reading, Mass. (1989).

[2] A Nix and Michael D. Vose, *Modelling genetic algorithms with Markov chains*, Annals of Mathematics and Artificial Intelligence, Vol. 5 (1991), pp79–88.

[3] Darrell Whitley. *An executable model of a simple genetic algorithm*, in: L. Darrel Whitley, ed., Foundations of Genetic Algorithms 2. Morgan Kaufmann, San Mateo (1993).

[4] A. Prügel-Bennett and J. L. Shapiro, *An analysis of genetic algorithms using statistical mechanics*, Phys. Rev. Letts., Vol. 72(9) (1994), pp1305–1309.

[5] J. L. Shapiro, A. Prügel-Bennett, and M. Rattray, *A statistical mechanical formulation of the dynamics of genetic algorithms*, Lecture Notes in Computer Science, No. 864 (1994), pp17–27.

[6] A. Prügel-Bennett and J. L. Shapiro, *Dynamics of genetic algorithms for simple random Ising systems*, Physica D, in press (1997).

[7] L. M. Rattray, *An analysis of a genetic algorithm with stabilizing selection*, Complex Systems Vol.9 (1995), pp213–234.

[8] L. M. Rattray and J. L. Shapiro, *The dynamics of a genetic algorithm for a simple learning problem*, Journal of Physics A, Vol.29(23) (1996), pp7451–7473.

[9] B. Derrida. *Random-energy model: An exactly solvable model of disordered systems*, Phys. Rev., Vol. B24 (1984), pp2613–2626.

VOLUMES OF ATTRACTION BASINS IN RANDOMLY CONNECTED BOOLEAN NETWORKS

Sergey A. Shumsky

P.N.Lebedev Physics Institute, Leninsky pr.53, Moscow, Russia.

The paper presents the distribution function of the volumes of attraction basins in phase portraits of Boolean networks with random interconnections for a special class of *uniform* nets, built from unbiased elements. The distribution density at large volumes tends to universal power law $\mathcal{F} \propto V^{-3/2}$.

1 Introduction

Randomly Connected Boolean Networks (RCBN) represent a wide class of connectionist models, which attempt to understand the behavior of systems, built from a large number of richly interconnected elements [1].

Since the early studies of Kauffman [2] RCBN became a classical model for studying the dynamical properties of random networks. The most intriguing feature of RCBN is the phase transition from the stochastic regime to the ordered behavior, first observed in simulations [2], and later explained analytically [3]-[5].

In the *chaotic phase* the phase trajectories are attracted by very long cycles, which lengths grow exponentially with the size of the system N [4]. Thus, even for not so large systems it is practically impossible to indicate these cycles, and their phase trajectories resemble random walks in the phase space.

On the contrary, in the *ordered phase* the short cycles dominate [4]. In fact, this paper will present a numerical evidence, that almost the whole system's phase space belongs to the attraction basins of the fixed points. The distribution of the volumes of these attraction basins is an important characteristic, since it gives the probabilities of different kinds of asymptotic behavior of the system.

So far, the distribution of attraction basins is known only for fully connected Boolean networks, namely the Random Map Model (RMM) [6], which represents the *chaotic* RCBN. The onset of the *ordered phase* implies, that the mean number of inputs per one element, K, does not exceed some critical value, which depends only on the type of the Boolean elements [5]. Thus, this phase takes place only in the case of extremely sparse interconnections: $K/N \to 0$ for $N \to \infty$.

In the present paper we calculate the distribution of attraction basins in the *ordered phase*, using the fact, that in sparsely connected networks there exists a correlation between the number of logical switchings at the consequent time steps, which is absent in the RMM. In Sec. 2 we formulate our model as the straightforward extention of the RMM, which takes into account the above correlation. Sec. 3 presents the solution for our problem found by means of the theory of branching processes. Sec. 4 presents the comparison of the theoretical predictions with the simulations results for the Izing neural networks. Sec. 5 gives some concluding remarks.

2 Model Description

The networks under consideration consist of N two-state automata receiving their inputs from the outputs (states) of other automata, connected with the given one. These connections are attached at random when the network is assembled and then fixed. The parallel dynamics is governed by the map:

$$\mathbf{x} \Rightarrow \phi(\mathbf{x}), \qquad (\mathbf{x}, \phi \in \{\pm 1\}^N). \tag{1}$$

Function $\phi(\mathbf{x})$ depends vacuously on some of its arguments.

In a phase portrait of a network there is a unique phase vector, begining at each phase state. However, there are no restrictions on the number of vectors coming to that state. Thus, any phase portrait represents a forest of the trees with their roots belonging to the attractor set. For the *ordered phase* this attractor set is represented mainly by fixed points.

We shall be interested in the statistical properties of this forest, namely by the distribution of volumes of the trees. These statistical properties, of course, should characterize not an individual map, but some ensemble of maps. The ensemble of RCBN contains all possible variants of interconnections among N automata, chosen at random from some infinite basic set of automata. We assume, that this set of automata is *unbiased*, that is, the statistical properties of phase vectors do not depend on the state point. Such ensembles will be further referred to as *uniform* ones.

Such is, for example, the RMM, where phase vector starting in any state may come to each state with equal probability. Since there are Ω such possibilities for each state point (where $\Omega = 2^N$ is the phase volume of a system), this ensemble consists of Ω^Ω maps, corresponding to all possible variants of fully connected Boolean networks.

In the absence of correlations between consequent vectors, one can characterize the uniform ensemble by only one statistical characteristic - the distribution of vectors lengths (in the Hamming sense), W_m, which is binomial:

$$W_m = \binom{N}{m} (1 - w_0)^m (w_0)^{N-m}, \tag{2}$$

with $w_0 = (1 + \nu_0)/2$ being the mean fraction of fixed points in the phase portraits of automata from the basic set [5]. For the RMM, for example, $\nu_0 = 0$ and $w_0 = 1/2$. But in the absence of *selfexcitable* automata in the basic automata set (i.e. those, that oscillate for the fixed values of their inputs), $\nu_0 \geq 0$. This leads to exponentially large number of fixed points:

$$\Omega_0 = \Omega W_0 = (1 + \nu_0)^N. \tag{3}$$

In general case there exists a correlation between the lengths of consequent vectors. This correlation is more pronounced in diluted networks. Indeed, recall, that the vector's length is the number of automata, which change state at the corresponding time step. In diluted networks the probability, that a given automaton will change state is proportional to the probability, that at least one of its inputs has changed its value. As a consequence, the mean number of automata switchings at the next step is proportional to that at the previous step.

To take this fact into account we introduce the conditional probability P_{ml} that in phase trajectories from a given ensemble vector with length m will be followed by vector of length l. This is a straightforward generalization of the RMM, for which $P_{ml} = W_l$.

Summarizing, we will deal with an ensemble of phase portraits (1) with the statistical characteristics of phase trajectories given by W_m and P_{ml}. We are interested, however, not in the characteristics of trajectories, but rather in that of random trees in phase portraits from our ensemble. Such is the mean number Π_{lm} of vectors with the length m, which precede the vector with the length l:

$$\Pi_{lm} = W_m P_{ml} / W_l, \quad (m = 1, \ldots, N; \quad l = 0, \ldots, N). \tag{4}$$

Zero-length vectors do not precede any state, and are thus excluded: $\Pi_{l0} \equiv 0$. The normalization condition $\sum_{l=0}^{N} P_{ml} = 1$ may be rewritten as:

$$\sum_{l=0}^{N} W_l \Pi_{lm} = W_m, \qquad (m = 1, \ldots, N). \tag{5}$$

To complete the description of random forest one needs not only the average number Π_{lm}, but the whole distribution function for the number of different vectors, preceding the given vector of length l. In the limit $\Omega \to \infty$ this distribution tends to a Poisson one with the generating function:

$$\boldsymbol{f}(\boldsymbol{s}) = \exp[\hat{\Pi}(\boldsymbol{s} - \mathbf{1})]. \tag{6}$$

The latter is a function of formal parameter $\boldsymbol{s}$:

$$f_l(s) = \sum_{m_1, \ldots, m_N} f_{l;m_1,\ldots,m_N} s_1^{m_1}, \ldots, s_N^{m_N},$$

with $f_{l;m_1,\ldots,m_N}$ being the probability, that a vector of length l is preceded by m_1 vectors of length 1, ..., m_N vectors of length N. In the following of this paper all running indexes range from 1 to N.

3 Distribution of the Basins Volumes

Now, when all the characteristics of random trees are determined, one can use the well known results of the theory of brunching processes. For the sake of clarity we will not supply the details here, relegating the involved calculations to a more extensive publication.

3.1 General Solution

The theory of brunching processes allows one to find the distribution of the volumes of random trees, provided the generating function $\boldsymbol{f}(\boldsymbol{s})$ is known [7]. For the one given by (6) the fraction of trees of volume V is:

$$\mathcal{F}(V) = \frac{\exp\left(-\sum_i k_i \delta_i^2/2\right)}{\sqrt{2\pi \sum_i k_i p_i^2}}, \tag{7}$$

where $\mathbf{k}$, $\mathbf{p}$ and $\boldsymbol{\delta}$ satisfy the saddle point equations:

$$\sum_j \pi_{ij} \delta_j = -\beta, \tag{8}$$

$$\sum_i (\overline{k}_i - k_i) \pi_{ij} = k_j \delta_j, \qquad \sum_j \pi_{ij} (\overline{p}_j - p_j) = p_i \delta_i. \tag{9}$$

Here $\overline{p}_i = -\delta_i/\beta = \sum_j {\pi^{-1}}_{ij}$, and matrix $\pi_{ij} \equiv \delta_{ij} - \Pi_{ij}$ has the eigenvalues $\gamma_i = 1 - \kappa_i$, being the relaxation decrements for the initial Markov process (κ_i are eigenvalues of matrixes $\hat{P}$ and $\hat{\Pi}$).

The solution of this system of equations reads:

$$k_i = \sum_a \frac{l_i^a k^a}{\lambda_a - \beta}, \qquad p_i = \sum_a \frac{r_i^a p^a}{\lambda_a - \beta}, \tag{10}$$

with λ_a, l_i^a and r_i^a being the eigenvalues, the left and the right eigenvectors of the generalized eigenvalue problem:

$$\sum_i l_i^a \pi_{ij} = \lambda_a \overline{p}_j l_j^a, \qquad \sum_j \pi_{ij} r_j^a = \lambda_a \overline{p}_i r_i^a. \tag{11}$$

Coefficients k^a and p^a in (10) represent the spectral expansion of the known vectors $\overline{k}_i = \sum_a l_i^a k^a/\lambda_a$, $\overline{p}_i = \sum_a r_i^a p^a/\lambda_a$. The Lagrange parameter β is found from the equation:

$$V = \sum_i k_i = \sum_a \frac{p^a k^a}{\lambda_a - \beta}. \tag{12}$$

Multiplication of the first equation of (9) on δ_j with subsequent summation over j gives: $\sum_j k_j \delta_j^2 = \beta(V - \overline{V})$, and one finally obtains:

$$\mathcal{F}(V) = \frac{\exp[-\beta(V-\overline{V})/2]}{\sqrt{2\pi \sum_i k_i p_i^2}} \tag{13}$$

3.2 Distribution of Basins Volumes

Distribution (13) is valid for a general branching process with different types of branches. Now we will make use of the specific feature of our branching process in random phase portraits. Namely, in this particular case the first eigenvalue λ_1 of the above generalized eigenvalue problem is much less than the others, and is so small, that the exponential factor in (13) is negligible: $\lambda_a = O\left(N^a(1-\nu_0)^N/\Omega\right)$ The exponential cut-off of the distribution (13) occurs at $\beta \to \lambda_1$, that is at $V \sim 1/\lambda_1$. Since $1/\lambda_1 \gg \Omega$, the exponential factor is negligible, and distribution (13) is represented by a power law.

For $\beta < \lambda_1$ one can leave β only in the term with $m = 1$ in (10), obtaining:

$$\mathcal{F}(V) \propto P_3(V)^{-1/2}, \tag{14}$$

with $P_3(V)$ being the polynomial of the third degree. For $V \gg \overline{V}$ the asymptotic scaling is: $\mathcal{F}(V) \propto V^{-3/2}$, the same as for the RMM.

4 Simulations

The above theoretical predictions were checked in the computer simulations of neural networks with random diluted asymmetric Izing interconnections. The networks consisted of N two state elements $x_i \in \{\pm 1\}$, connected with K randomly chosen other elements. The states of the elements were updated in parallel according to the rule:

$$x_i \to \text{sign}(h_i), \quad h_i = \textstyle\sum_j J_{ij} C_{ij} x_j \tag{15}$$

where $\hat{C}$ is the random interconnection matrix with K units and $N-K$ zeros in each row ($C_{ii} = 0$), and matrix $\hat{J}$ has the Izing components $J_{ij} = \pm 1$ with equal probabilities. For a given network these matrixes are fixed during the simulations. If h_i appears to be zero, the state of the i-th neuron is unchanged. The latter case may occur only for the even number of interconnections K. The *ordered* phase for such model takes place only for $K \leq 2$. Since the case $K = 1$ is degenerate, we considered networks with $K = 2$.

The first thing we examined was the fraction of phase space in the basins of fixed points. This quantity was estimated by tracing 10^3 random trajectories till they

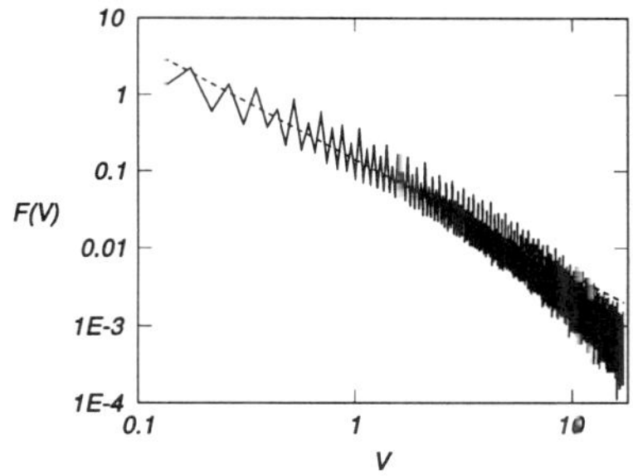

Figure 1 Distribution density of basins volumes in the ensemble of 25000 networks with $N = 11$ and $K = 2$

reached their attractors. The results showed that for sufficiently large $N > 25$ all phase trajectories converge to some fixed point.

To obtain the distribution of the basins we examined the whole phase space. Since the computational time grows exponentially with the size of the network, we chose the networks of relatively small size, $N = 11$ (the measured probability of convergence was 0.97). For $K = 2$, 25000 random networks were generated, and each phase portrait was examined point by point. Fig. 4 shows the obtained distribution of the volumes of the basins of fixed points. The dotted line on this plot represents the asymptotic power law $\mathcal{F} \propto V^{-3/2}$. The correspondence is good in a wide range of volumes, except the very tail of the distribution. The observed cutt-off of the power law is due to the finiteness of the state space, ignored by the branching process approach.

5 Conclusions

The paper presented the distribution of the attraction basins of randomly connected Boolean networks, which generalize the Kauffman *NK*-model. The obtained results may be useful, for example, for studying the relaxation processes in nonergodic systems. At finite temperature the volumes of basins play a similar role as the energy levels of the valleys in spin glasses.

REFERENCES

[1] J. Doyne Farmer, *A Rosetta stone for connectionism*, Physica D, Vol. 42 (1990), pp153–187.

[2] S. A. Kauffman, *Metabolic stability and epigenesis in randomly connected nets*, J. Theor. Biol., Vol. 22 (1969), pp437–467.

[3] B. Derrida and Y. Pomeau, *Random networks of automata: a simple annealed approximation* Europhys. Lett., Vol. 1 (1986), pp45–49.

[4] K. E. Kürten, *Critical phenomena in model neural networks* Phys. Lett. A, Vol. 129 (1988), pp157–160.

[5] S. A. Shumsky, *Phase portrait characteristics of random logical networks* J. Moscow Phys. Soc., Vol. 2 (1992), pp263–281.

[6] B. Derrida and H. Flyvbjery, *The random map model: a disordered model with deterministic dynamics*, J. Phys. France, Vol. 48 (1987), pp971–978.

[7] T. E. Harris, *The Theory of Branching Processes*. Springer-Verlag, Berlin (1963).

EVIDENTIAL REJECTION STRATEGY FOR NEURAL NETWORK CLASSIFIERS

A. Shustorovich

Business Imaging Systems, Eastman Kodak Company, Rochester, USA.

In this paper we present an approach to estimation of the confidences of competing classification decisions based on the Dempster-Shafer Theory of Evidence. It allows us to utilize information contained in the activations of all output nodes of a neural network, as opposed to just one or two highest, as it is usually done in current literature. On a test set of 8,000 ambiguous patterns, a rejection strategy based on this confidence measure achieves up to 30% reduction in error rates as compared to traditional schemes.

1 Introduction

Neural network classifiers usually have as many output nodes as there are competing classes. A trained network produces a high output activation of the node corresponding to the desired class and low activations of all the other nodes. In this type of encoding, the best guess corresponds to the output node with the highest activation. Our confidence in the chosen decision depends on the numeric value of the highest activation as well as on the difference between it and the others, especially the second highest. Depending on the desired level of reliability, a certain percentage of classification patterns can be rejected, and the obvious strategy is to reject patterns with lower confidence first. The rejection schemes most commonly used in literature are built around two common-sense ideas: the confidence increases with the value of the highest activation and with the gap between the two highest activations.

In some systems, only one of these values is used as the measure of confidence; in others, some ad-hoc combination of both. For example, Battiti and Colla [1] reject patterns with the highest activation (HA) below a fixed threshold, and also those with the difference between the highest and the second highest activation (DA) below a second fixed threshold. Martin et al. [5] use only DA in their Saccade System, whereas Gaborski [4] uses the ratio of the highest and the second highest activation (RA) as the preferred measure of confidence. Fogelman-Soulié et al. [3] propose a distance-based (DI) rejection criterion in addition to HA and DA schemes; namely they compare the Euclidean distance between the activation vector and the target activation vectors of all classes and reject the pattern if the smallest of these distances is greater than a fixed threshold. Bromley and Denker [2] mention experiments conducted by Yann Le Cun in support of their choice of the DA strategy.

Logically, one expects the two highest activations to provide almost all the information for the rejection decision, because usually ambiguities involve a choice between the right classification and, at most, one predominant alternative. Still, ideally, we would prefer a formula combining all the output activations into a single measure of confidence. Such formula can be derived if we view this problem as one of integration of information from different sources in the framework of the Dempster-Shafer Theory of Evidence [6]. We can treat the activation of each output node as the evidence in favor of the corresponding classification hypothesis and combine them into the measure of confidence of the final decision.

2 The Dempster-Shafer Theory of Evidence

The Dempster-Shafer Theory of Evidence is a tool for representing and combining measures of evidences. This theory is a generalization of Bayesian reasoning, but it is more flexible than Bayesian when our knowledge is incomplete, and, therefore, we have to deal with uncertainty. It allows us to represent only actual knowledge, without forcing us to make a conclusion when we are ignorant.

Let Θ be a set of mutually exhaustive and exclusive atomic hypotheses $\Theta = \{\theta_1, \ldots, \theta_N\}$. Θ is called the *frame of discernment*. Let 2^Θ denote the set of all subsets of Θ. A function $\mathbf{m}$ is called a *basic probability assignment* if

$$\mathbf{m} : 2^\Theta \rightarrow [0,1], \quad \mathbf{m}(\emptyset) = 0, \quad \text{and} \quad \sum_{A \subseteq \Theta} \mathbf{m}(A) = 1. \tag{1}$$

In the probability theory, a measure of *probability* analogous to the basic probability assignment is associated *only* with the atomic hypotheses θ_n. The probabilities of all other subsets are derived as sums of probabilities of its atomic components, and there is nothing left to express our measure of ignorance. In the Dempster-Shafer theory, $\mathbf{m}(A)$ represents the *belief* that is committed exactly to every (not necessarily atomic) subset A. It is useful to "...think of these portions of belief as semi-mobile 'probability masses', which can sometimes move from point to point but are restricted in that various of them are [...] confined to various subsets of Θ. In other words, $\mathbf{m}(A)$ measures the probability mass that is confined to A, but can move freely to every point of A" [6]. Now it is easier to understand why $\mathbf{m}(\Theta)$ represents our measure of ignorance: this portion of our total belief is not committed to any proper subset of Θ.

The simplest possible type of the basic probability assignment is a *simple evidence function*, that corresponds to the case in which all our belief is concentrated in only one subset $F \subseteq \Theta$, its *focal element*. If $F \neq \Theta$, then we can define $\mathbf{m}(F) = \mathrm{s}$, $\mathbf{m}(\Theta) = 1 - \mathrm{s}$, and $\mathbf{m}$ is 0 elsewhere. The *degree of support* s represents our belief in F, while $1 - \mathrm{s}$ represents our ignorance.

The Dempster-Shafer theory provides us with the rule for the combination of evidences from two sources. This combination $\mathbf{m} = \mathbf{m}_1 \oplus \mathbf{m}_2$ is called their *orthogonal sum:*

$$\mathbf{m}(A) = K \cdot \sum_{X \cap Y = A} \mathbf{m}_1(X) \cdot \mathbf{m}_2(Y) \text{ where } K^{-1} = \sum_{X \cap Y \neq \emptyset} \mathbf{m}_1(X) \cdot \mathbf{m}_2(Y). \tag{2}$$

The main idea expressed in this nonintuitive formula is actually rather simple: the portion of belief committed to the intersection of two subsets X and Y should be proportional to the product of $\mathbf{m}(X)$ and $\mathbf{m}(Y)$ (Figure 1). Only if this intersection is empty, do we have to exclude it from the sum and renormalize it. Obviously, this rule can be generalized to accommodate for more than two sources of information. Please refer to [6] for more detailed explanations.

3 Combination of Evidences as the Measure of Confidence

Consider a frame of discernment $\Theta = \{\theta_1, \ldots, \theta_N\}$, where θ_n is the hypothesis that a pattern belongs to class n. The activation of the n-th output node of a neural network, o_n, provides information in favor of the corresponding hypothesis θ_n. Our partial belief based on this information can be expressed as a simple evidence function

$$\mathbf{m}_n(\theta_n) = \phi_n, \qquad \mathbf{m}_n(\Theta) = 1 - \phi_n, \tag{3}$$

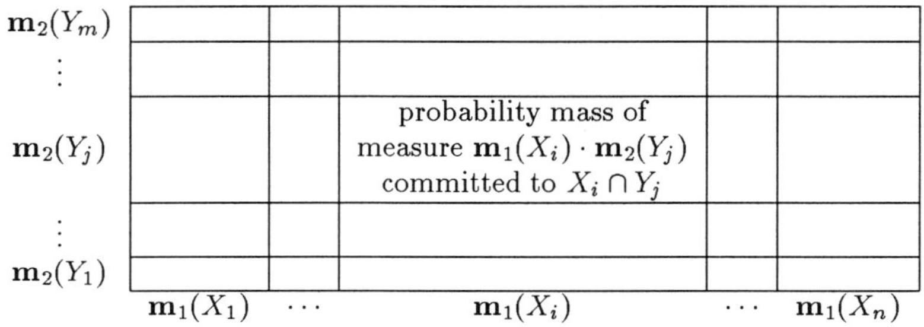

Figure 1 The Dempster combination rule.

where ϕ_n is a monotonic function of o_n. We shall discuss a specific form of this function later.

Now we have to combine these evidences into their orthogonal sum according to eqn. (2). Let us start with the case in which $N = 2$. The first simple evidence function $\mathbf{m}_1$, with its focal element θ_1, has the degree of support ϕ_1. Its only other nonzero value is $\mathbf{m}_1(\Theta) = 1 - \phi_1$. Similarly, θ_2 is the focal element of $\mathbf{m}_2$, with a degree of support of ϕ_2, and $\mathbf{m}_2(\Theta) = 1 - \phi_2$. When we produce the orthogonal sum $\mathbf{m} = \mathbf{m}_1 \oplus \mathbf{m}_2$, we have to compute beliefs for the total of four subsets of Θ: $\emptyset$, θ_1, θ_2, and Θ (Figure 2). The value $\mathbf{m}(\Theta)$ should be proportional to $\mathbf{m}_1(\Theta) \cdot \mathbf{m}_2(\Theta)$

$\mathbf{m}_2(\Theta) = 1 - \phi_2$	$\theta_1 : \phi_1 \cdot (1 - \phi_2)$	$\Theta : (1 - \phi_1) \cdot (1 - \phi_2)$
$\mathbf{m}_2(\theta_2) = \phi_2$	$\emptyset : \phi_1 \cdot \phi_2$	$\theta_2 : (1 - \phi_1) \cdot \phi_2$
	$\mathbf{m}_1(\theta_1) = \phi_1$	$\mathbf{m}_1(\Theta) = 1 - \phi_1$

Figure 2 Orthogonal sum of two simple evidence functions with atomic foci.

because this is the only way to obtain Θ as the intersection. Similarly, $\mathbf{m}(\theta_1)$ should be proportional to $\mathbf{m}_1(\theta_1) \cdot \mathbf{m}_2(\Theta)$, while $\mathbf{m}(\theta_2)$ should be proportional to $\mathbf{m}_2(\theta_2) \cdot \mathbf{m}_1(\Theta)$. The only way we can produce $\emptyset$ as an intersection of a subset with nonzero $\mathbf{m}_1$-evidence and another subset with nonzero $\mathbf{m}_2$-evidence is $\emptyset = \theta_1 \cap \theta_2$. The corresponding product, $\phi_1 \cdot \phi_2$, should be excluded from the normalization constant K. Finally,

$$\mathbf{m}(\theta_1) = K \cdot \phi_1 \cdot (1 - \phi_2) \quad , \qquad \mathbf{m}(\theta_2) = K \cdot \phi_2 \cdot (1 - \phi_1),$$
$$\mathbf{m}(\Theta) = K \cdot (1 - \phi_1) \cdot (1 - \phi_2) \quad , \qquad K = \frac{1}{1 - \phi_1 \cdot \phi_2} \tag{4}$$

It is obvious that if both $\phi_1 = 1$ and $\phi_2 = 1$, our formula cannot work because it involves division of $\frac{0}{0}$. However, this is quite appropriate, because it indicates that both $\mathbf{m}_1$ and $\mathbf{m}_2$ are absolutely confident and flatly contradict each other. In such a case, there is no hope of reconciling the differences. If only one of the two degrees of support equals 1, for example, $\phi_1 = 1$, then $\mathbf{m}(\theta_1) = 1$, $\mathbf{m}(\theta_2) = 0$, and $\mathbf{m}(\Theta) = 0$. In this case, $\mathbf{m}_2$ cannot influence the absolutely confident $\mathbf{m}_1$.

If neither of the degrees of support equals 1, we can denote $\alpha_n = \frac{\phi_n}{1-\phi_n}$ and transform eqn. (4) into a more convenient form:

$$\mathbf{m}(\theta_1) = \frac{\alpha_1}{1 + \alpha_1 + \alpha_2}, \quad \mathbf{m}(\theta_2) = \frac{\alpha_2}{1 + \alpha_1 + \alpha_2}, \quad \mathbf{m}(\Theta) = \frac{1}{1 + \alpha_1 + \alpha_2}. \tag{5}$$

Using mathemaical induction, one can prove that when we have to combine N simple evidence functions with atomic focal elements, their orthogonal sum becomes

$$\mathbf{m}(\theta_n) = \frac{\alpha_n}{1 + \sum_i \alpha_i}, \qquad \mathbf{m}(\Theta) = \frac{1}{1 + \sum_i \alpha_i}. \tag{6}$$

The combined evidence $\mathbf{m}(\theta_n)$ represents our share of belief (or confidence) associated with each of N competing classification decisions. Our formula has a number of intuitively attractive properties:

- the highest confidence corresponds to the highest activation,
- the confidence increases with the growth of the corresponding activation,
- the confidence decreases with the growth of any other activation.

Now we can rate all patterns according to the confidence of the best-guess classification and reject them in order of increasing confidence. We will call this rejection strategy "evidential".

4 The Experiment

We tested the proposed method on the handprint digits classification problem. A trained neural network classifier was used to generate sets of activations for two test files, both of approximately 25,000 characters. To accentuate the comparisons, unambiguous patterns (those with the highest activation above 0.9 and all other activations below 0.1) were excluded from the experiment. Indeed, one can argue that any responsible rejection strategy should accept such patterns, especially because many neural networks are trained with target activations of 0.9 and 0.1 (sometimes even 0.8 and 0.2) instead of 1 and 0. In addition, the error vs reject curves differ for different test sets depending on the quality of the data. The exclusion of unambiguous patterns allows us to normalize the curves to some extent.

We found approximately 6,500 ambiguous patterns in the first set, and approximately 8,000 in the second set. The first subset was used to select the best monotonic transformation of the activations into the support functions. Comparison of a large number of possible functions led to the choice of the $\lambda(x) = \log_2(1 + x)$ as the seed of a whole family of transformations λ^k, and finally we chose $\phi = \lambda^{15}$.

The evidential (EV) rejection strategy was then used on the second subset, and its results were compared to those achieved with the rejection scheme based on the highest activation (HA), the difference between the highest and the second highest activation (DA), the ratio of the highest and the second highest activation (RA), and the distance-based rejection criterion (DI) described above. Figure 3 presents the comparison of error vs reject graphs for all the five schemes studied. To compute data for each of the curves, all patterns are sorted according to the corresponding confidence measure. Then the patterns are rejected one by one, and the number of remaining misclassifications is counted. Their percent of the total number of the remaining patterns constitutes the error rate which is plotted against the percent reject. Obviously, there is no difference among the strategies at zero and hundred percent reject.

5 Conclusions

In this paper we demonstrated how the Dempster-Shafer Theory of Evidence can provide the framework for estimation of the confidences of competing classification

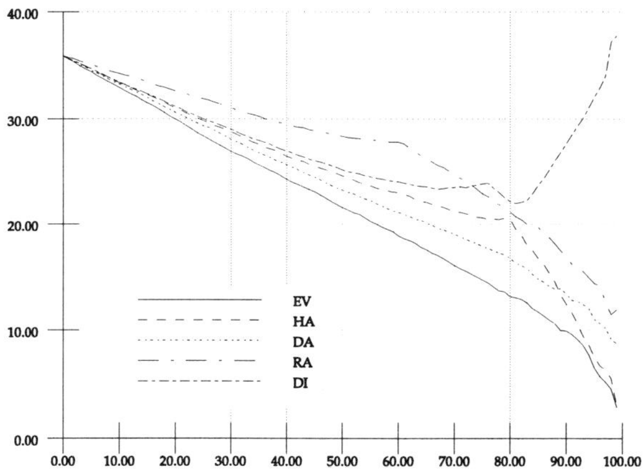

Figure 3 Percent error vs percent rejected for different strategies.

decisions. Although we worked with activations generated by a neural network, this approach can be applied if it is necessary to combine the outputs of any collection of single-class recognizers.

Our formula consistently utilizes all the output activations of a neural network classifier. Extensive experimentation allowed us to select a simple monotonic transformation of output activations as the basic probability assignment. The testing we conducted on the 8,000 strong set of ambiguous patterns confirmed that the evidential rejection strategy reduces the classification error up to 30%. It is necessary to mention here that the best choice of the monotonic transformation for the basic probability assignment depends on the concrete application.

Further work is needed, for we have not analyzed any information we can obtain from the distribution of output activation values for different classes. Another possible line of action is the analysis of the confusion matrix or, broader still, the joint distribution of activation pairs.

REFERENCES

[1] Battiti, R. and Colla, A.M., *Democracy in neural nets: voting schemes for classification*, Neural Networks Vol. 7 (4) (1994), pp691–707.

[2] Bromley, J. and Denker, J., *Improving rejection performance on handwritten digits by training with "rubbish"*, Neural Computation Vol. 5 (3) (1993), pp367–370.

[3] Fogelman-Soulié, F., Viennet, E., and Lamy, B., *Multi-modular neural network architectures: applications in optical character and human face recognition*, International Journal of Pattern Recognition and Artificial Intelligence Vol. 7 (4) (1993), pp721–755.

[4] Gaborski, R.S., *Neural network with back propagation controlled through an output confidence measure.* United States Patent 5,052,043 (1991).

[5] Martin, G., Mosfeq, R., Chapman, D., and Pittman, J., *Learning to see where and what: training a net to make saccades and recognize handwritten characters*, in: S.J. Hanson, J.D. Cowan, and C.L. Giles (Eds.), Advances in Neural Information Processing Systems, Vol. 5 (1993), pp441–447. San Mateo: Morgan Kaufmann.

[6] Shafer, G., *A Mathematical Theory of Evidence,* Princeton: MIT Press (1976).

DYNAMICS APPROXIMATION AND CHANGE POINT RETRIEVAL FROM A NEURAL NETWORK MODEL

J. Smid and P. Volf*

Department of Mathematics Morgan State University, Baltimore, MD 21239 USA.
Email: smid@ltpsun.gsfc.nasa.gov
** UTIA The Czech Academy of Sciences, Prague 8, CZ 180 00, Czech Republic. Email: volf@utia.cas.cz*

Discrete dynamical systems and nonlinear response models contaminated with random noise are considered. The objective of the paper is to propose a method of extraction of change–points of a mapping (system) from a neural network approximation. The method is based on the comparison of normalized Taylor series coefficients of the estimator and on the consistency of the estimator and its derivatives. The proposed algorithm is illustrated on a simple piecewise polynomial mapping.

1 Introduction

Consider real-valued variables y as output and x as input of a system. Their relation is modeled by a general piecewise smooth function $f : [0, d] \to \mathbb{R}$ in a model

$$y = f(x) + e, \tag{1}$$

where e stands for random noise. The analysis of the function $f(x)$ will be based on a sequence of observation data, x_i, y_i, generated by random variables $X_i, Y_i, i = 1, .., n$. We assume that random variables $e_i = Y_i - f(X_i)$, representing random noise entering the system, are mutually independent and identically distributed, with mean zero and finite variance σ^2. A discrete dynamical system

$$y_t = g(y_{t-h}) + e_t, \tag{2}$$

can be viewed as a system of the type (1) where we set $x_t = y_{t-h}$ and $y_t = g(x_t) + e_t$. Thus the estimation of the generator g of the equation (2) is transformed into a regression problem of the type (1).

Throughout the paper we will be mainly concerned with models (1) and (2). However, the proposed solution can be extended to the multivariable nonlinear function $y_i = f(x_{i1}, x_{i2}, ..., x_{ik}) + e_i$ and to autoregressive systems, dynamic regression and recursive response cases, e.g. $y_t = g(y_t, y_{t-h}, ..., y_{t-mh}) + e_t$.The present paper considers the use of a feedforward neural network approach. That is the spline network (as a representative of feedforward neural nets) will be used as the tool for estimation of the model functions.

2 Polynomial Splines and Feedforward Neural Networks

A neural network is a system of interconnected nonlinear units. The topology of connections between units can be complicated. In the simplest scenario a neural network model is no more than the sum of units. The nonlinear units are either localized (e.g. splines and radial basis functions) or their sums form localized functions (e.g. perceptrons). The local nature of the units has been exploited for classification/pattern recognition problems, e.g. in [4]. We will show usefulness of local processing units for the function change–point estimation problems.

2.1 Polynomial Spline Functions

A polynomial spline function $f(x)$ is a function that consists of polynomial pieces $f(x) = f_i(x) on [\lambda_i, \lambda_{i+1}], \quad (i = 0, ..., M)$ where f_i is a polynomial of degree k. The points $\lambda_0, \lambda_1, ..., \lambda_M$ at which the function $f(x)$ changes its character are termed break points or knots in the theory splines (other authors prefer "joints" or "nodes") The polynomial pieces are joined together with certain smoothness conditions. The smoothness conditions are $\lim_{x \to \lambda_i -} f^{(j)}(x) = \lim_{x \to \lambda_i +} f^{(j)}(x), \quad (j = 1, ..., k-1)$. In other words, a spline function of degree $k \geq 0$, having as break points the strictly increasing sequence $\lambda_j, (j = 0, 1, ..M+1;\ \lambda_0 = 0, \lambda_{M+1} = d)$, is a piecewice polynomial on intervals $[\lambda_j, \lambda_{j+1}]$ of degree k at most, with continuous derivatives up to order $k-1$ on $[0, d]$. It is known that a uniformly continuous function can be approximated by polynomial splines to arbitrary accuracy, see for instance de Boor [2]. This concept can be naturally extended to higher dimensions. The set of spline functions is endowed with the natural structure of a finite vector space. The dimension of the vector space of spline functions of degree k with M interior break points is $m = M + k + 1$. A neural network–like basis of the space of spline functions is the basis of B-splines. Each spline function can be written as a unique linear combination of basis functions.In this paper we shall use the basis of B-splines, which may be defined, for example, in a recursive way (cf. de Boor [2]). Let us define $\{\lambda_{-k} = \lambda_{-k+1} = ... = \lambda_0 = 0 < \lambda_1 < \lambda_2 < ... < \lambda_M < d = \lambda_{M+1} = ... = \lambda_m\}$ an extended set of $M + 2k + 2$ knots associated with the interval $[0, d]$. Each B-spline basis function (a unit in neural network terminology) $B_j^k(x)$ is completely described by a set of $k+2$ knots $\{\lambda_{j-k-1}, \lambda_{j-k}, ..., \lambda_j\}$. There are two important properties of these units [2], namely they are nonnegative, vanish everywhere except on a few contiguous subintervals $B_j^k(x) > 0$ if $\lambda_{j-k-1} \leq x \leq \lambda_j$, $B_j^k(x) = 0$ otherwise, and they define a partition of unity on $[0, d]$, $\sum_{j=1}^{m} B_j^k(x) = 1$ for all $x \epsilon [0, d]$. We shall mainly deal with cubic ($k = 3$) and quadratic ($k = 2$) B–splines because of their simplicity and importance in applications. Higher–degree splines are used whenever more smoothness is needed in the approximating function. For a chosen number m of units, the resulting polynomial spline is a function f_m from the set $\mathcal{S}_m^k = \{f_m : [0, d] \to \mathrm{I\!R} \mid f_m(x) = \sum_{j=1}^{m} w_j B_j^k(x)\}$.By $\mathcal{S}^k = \bigcup_m \mathcal{S}_m^k$ we denote the set of all univariate splines of degree k (order $k+1$). All these properties allow us to think of spline functions as neural networks. The numbers w_j are called weights (in statistics and neural network theory) or control points (in computer aided geometric design).

2.2 Feedforward Neural Networks

The virtue of neural networks in our approach is their capability to capture more information about the true system structure then, e.g. by polynomials. There is a number of methods for estimation of the network parameters. For example, incremental learning algorithms are described in Fahlman and Lebier [4] or Jones's approach in [5]. We will assume that neural network parameters have been estimated by one of the available learning algorithms. In the case of B–spline networks, the simplest approach computes the weights by the least squares method and, eventually, iterates the placement of knots in order to optimize it. Neural networks do not provide immediate insight into how the modeled mechanism works. This insight can be gained by solving an extraction problem. What we mean by an extraction problem for a neural net is how to extract the underlying structure of dependence in terms of a local polynomial regression model. This framework is useful when a simple explicit description (e.g. in terms of the low-degree polynomial regression) is required. Also this technique is more feasible than a 'direct' nonlinear polynomial regression for systems where the generator g is changing in time.

3 Extraction of a Piecewise Polynomial Model

Why we should use nets instead of polynomials? It is well known that the set of all polynomials is dense in the space of all continuous functions (Stone-Weierstrass theorem). However, for practical purposes approximation by a single polynomial may create polynomials of prohibitively high degree. These high degree polynomials most likely do not reflect the nature of underlying response function. A neural network may perform approximation tasks more efficiently. Important questions include how to extract the structure of the function f. When speaking about extraction of the underlying polynomial structure we envision a target function to be a polynomial or a piecewise polynomial. These functions admit a local approximation by a lower degree polynomial. This local approximation can be arbitrarily accurate provided that the interval over which we approximate is sufficiently small. This is true even across the break points of a piecewise polynomial. Polynomial extraction and diagnosis of the point of change is based on the consistency of the approximation and its derivatives, i.e. on their convergence to the target function and its derivatives.

It is well known that a smooth function f and its derivatives can be approximated to arbitrary accuracy by splines. This stems for example from the error bounds for polynomial splines and their derivatives established by Hall and Meyer [3], Marsden [6]. For cubic spline interpolants the error bound is

$$\|(f - f_m)^{(r)}\|_\infty \leq C_r \|f^{(4)}\| h^{4-r}, (r = 0, 1, 2, 3) \tag{3}$$

where h is the mesh gauge and C_r are constants. For noisy data the consistency of the functional need to be extended for the statistical estimators as well.

If we assume that the response function f is smooth and has bounded derivatives then it can be locally approximated to arbitrary accuracy by the Taylor polynomial of degree k. The Lagrange's remainder term of the Taylor expansion at the point a has the form

$$R_k = \frac{(x-a)^{k+1}}{(k+1)!} f^{(k+1)}((x-a)\theta + a),\ 0 \leq \theta \leq 1 \tag{4}$$

This is particularly true for $k = 2, 3$ when the mesh gauge $h = max_i|\lambda_{i+1} - \lambda_i|, i = 0, \ldots n-1$ is sufficiently small. It follows from the equations (3), (4) that good approximation of the smooth response function f implies good approximation of the coefficients of the local Taylor expansion of f. It means that one polynomial piece will be approximated by a spline having polynomial pieces with the same coefficients at a common point. If f is not smooth, i.e. it has a finite set of active break points, then good approximation by splines is still possible except for arbitrarily small neighborhoods around break points. In the neighborhood of a break point of f the polynomial piece of the spline approximation will reflect abrupt change of the function f. This approach can be generalized for noisy data. We will utilize the results of Stone [8] showing that a sequence of the optimal estimates $\hat{f}_{mn} \in \mathcal{S}_m$ of f from a noisy data set $(x_1, y_1), (x_2, y_2), .., (x_n, y_n)$ converges to f as m and n go to infinity, and that ,the same holds for derivatives $\hat{f}_{mn}^{(k)}$, $f^{(k)}$, for k not greater than the degree of estimating splines, provided $f^{(k)}$ is Lipschitz continuous.

4 Tests for Functional Change

A gradually changing response function will produce gradually changing normalized polynomial coefficients. By normalized coefficients we mean coefficients of polynomial pieces expanded about a common point. An abrupt change in response function will be reflected by an abrupt change in the normalized coefficients. To test for the points of change in the behavior of the neural network approximation $\hat{f}_{mn}$ the polynomial pieces, with coefficients $p_{ij}(\lambda_j)$ were recalculated about a common point $x = 0$. A set of new coefficients $p_{ij}(0, \lambda_j)$ was obtained and we call those coefficients normalized Taylor coefficients. The index i refers to the degree of the piece p_{ij} and j to the jth interval. The points with the same normalized coefficients indicate no change of the functional dependence.

For stationary functions/systems all normalized coefficients will be constant or almost constant (due to noise and approximation errors).

5 Large Sample Properties

To establish the consistency of the estimator $\hat{f}_{mn}$ and its derivatives we recall the results of Stone [8] who deals with optimal rates of convergence of response function estimator based on the spline functions $\hat{f}_{mn}(x) = \sum_{j=1}^{m} \hat{w}_j B_j^k(x)$. This representation is a very useful one because it casts the spline into a multiple linear regression context. If the set of knots is fixed, the estimator may be found as the least squares solution in parameters $w_j, j = 1, .., m$. Then the vector of weights $\hat{w} = (Z^T Z)^{-1} Z^T Y$, where $Y = (y_1, ..., y_n)^T$ and Z is a (n, m) matrix such that $z_{ij} = B_j^k(x_i)$. Let us denote $\mathcal{C}_p$ a set of all functions $f : [0, d] \rightarrow \mathbb{R}$ having continuous the pth derivatives, $\|.\|$ the L_2 norm on [0,d], and $E(.)$ the mean operator. For given sequences of numbers a_n, b_n, $b_n > 0$, by $a_n = O(b_n)$ we mean that sequence a_n/b_n is bounded. When A_n are random variables, $P\lim_{n\to\infty} A_n = 0$ means that for each $\varepsilon > 0$ $lim_{n\to\infty} P(|A_n| < \varepsilon) = 1$. For simplicity we assume that data points $x_1, ..., x_n$ and interior knots (break points) are uniformly distributed in the interval $[0, d]$. To assure good approximation of the response function we assume that we sampled more data points than the number of B-spline units, i.e. $m = O(n^\gamma)$, $\gamma \epsilon (0, 1)$.

Proposition 1 *Suppose f is from $\mathcal{C}_1$. Then $E\|\hat{f}_{mn} - f\|^2 = O(n^{\gamma-1}) + O(n^{-2\gamma})$. (This follows from the Lipschitz continuity of f). Suppose f is from $\mathcal{C}_p, p > 0$ and k is the degree of estimating spline. Let $\gamma = \frac{1}{2p+1}$. Then, for $l = 0, 1, .., min(k, p-1)$ it holds that $E\|\hat{f}_{mn}^{(l)} - f^{(l)}\|^2 = O(n^{-2r_l})$, where $r_l = \frac{p-l}{2p+1}$.*

The consistency of the derivatives gives supports diagnostics based on the Taylor expansion, especially for an analysis of the low-order derivatives. The procedure of the model retrieval is an iterative process combining techniques of estimation with methods of testing, i.e. of comparing the model with the actual behavior of the system.

6 Numerical Example of Estimation of 1-D Discrete Piecewise Quadratic Dynamical System

The algorithm has been applied on a time series of satellite data set, see reference [7]. Here, for the numerical illustration, let us consider a following simple example: A discrete dynamical system is defined by two quadratic maps: $f_n = 4f_{n-1} - 4f_{n-1}^2, f_{n-1} \leq 0.5$ and $f_n = 1.2 + 0.4f_{n-1} - 1.6f_{n-1}^2, f_{n-1} \geq 0.5$. This map

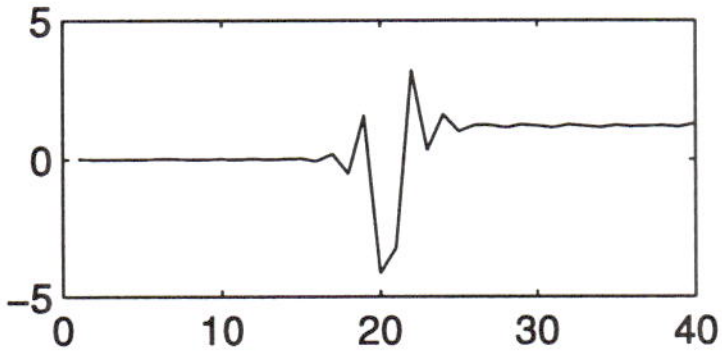

Figure 1 Constants at $x = 0$; $c_1 = 0$, $c_2 = 1.2$.

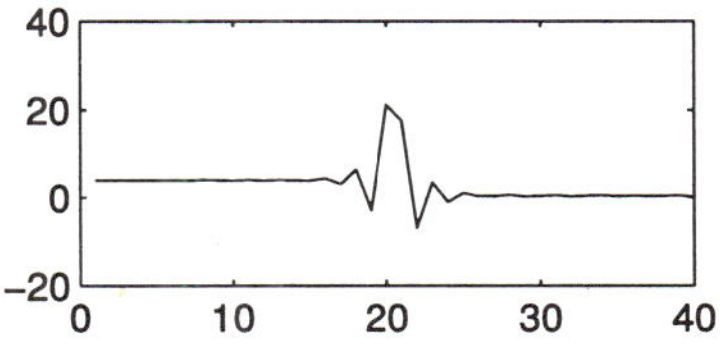

Figure 2 Lin. Coeff. at $x = 0$; $b_1 = 4$, $b_2 = 0.4$.

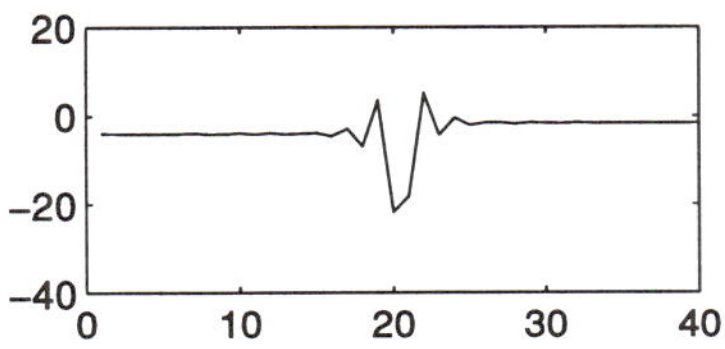

Figure 3 Qdr. Coeff. at $x = 0$; $a_1 = -4$, $a_2 = -1.6$.

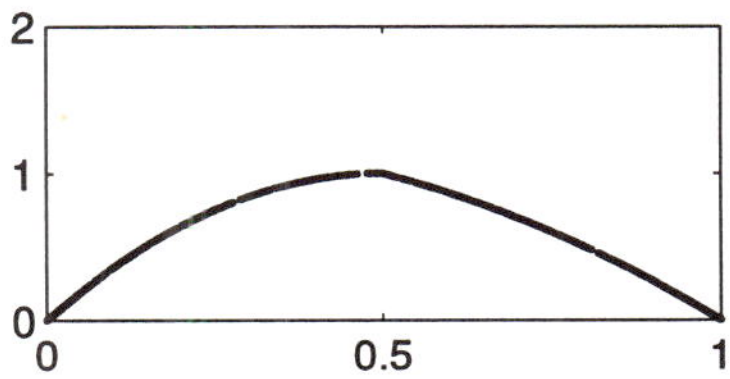

Figure 4 $y(n)$ vs. $y(n-1)$ for $n = 1$ to 800.

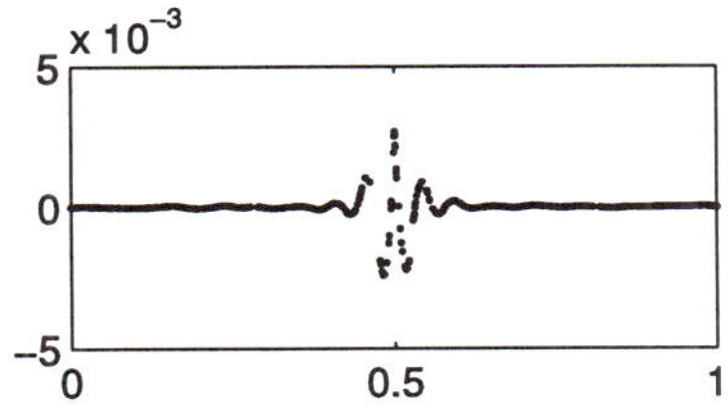

Figure 5 Spline fit error.

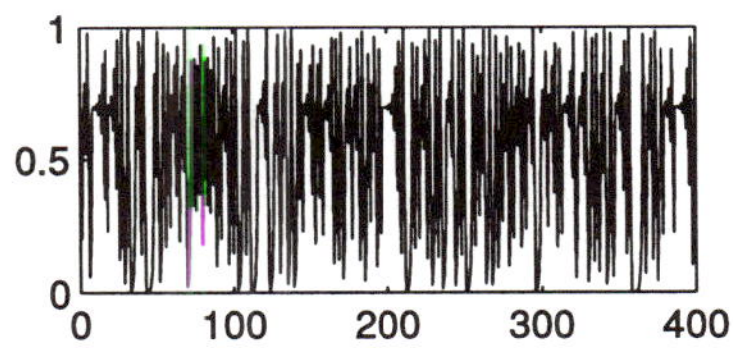

Figure 6 Quadratic Map time series.

is from the family of quadratic maps that is known to be chaotic and ergodic. The time series generated by this map cannot be predicted for many steps ahead but the generator of this series can be identified from the time series. We used a quadratic spline $\hat{f}_{mn}$ with 40 interior break points to identify sets of polynomial coefficients. Pieces of the spline $\hat{f}_{mn}$ are represented by local polynomials $a_j(x-\lambda_j)^2 + b_j(x-\lambda_j) + c_j, (j = 0, 1, \cdots, 39)$. Figures 1, 2 and 3 show polynomial coefficients $a_j(0), b_j(0), c_j(0)$. These coeffiecient were recalculated from the local coefficients at the common break point $\lambda_0 = 0$. Figure 4 shows the piecewise quadratic map. Figure 5 shows the error of the spline fit. Figure 6 shows 400 points of the chaotic time series generated by the piecewise quadratic map and additive gaussian noise $N(0, \sigma^2 = 0.0001)$. The dynamical problem then becomes the following approximation test: a domain is randomly partitioned into a finite number of subintervals. On each subinterval are generated data by a noisy polynomial. The aim of the analysis is to find those polynomials and/or to find all break points.

7 Concluding Remarks

We have proposed a method employing the B–splines network for estimation of an unknown response function from noisy data, and for extraction a potential piecewise polynomial submodel. It has been shown how the first terms of the Taylor expansion of the estimator, when expanded at different points of its domain, can be utilized for revealing the degree of the underlying polynomial model, and for the detection of changes in the model. This approach can be adapted for multidimensional and discrete dynamical systems (3) or (4). In these cases, we have to work with the partial derivatives. However, the multivariate case leads to the use of multivariate approximating functions. In such a situation, the estimation becomes less effective (a much greater amount of data is needed), even the theoretical rate of convergence is slower. Many authors (cf. Breiman[1], Stone[8]) recommend the use of additive approximations with low–dimensional components.

REFERENCES

[1] Breiman L., *Fitting additive models to regression data: diagnostics and alternative views*, Comp.Statistics and Data Analysis Vol. 15 (1993), pp13–46.

[2] de Boor C., *A Practical Guide to Splines*, Springer Verlag (1978).

[3] Hall C.A. and Meyer W.W., *Optimal error bounds for cubic spline interpolation*, Journal of Approximation Theory Vol. 16, No.2 (February 1976).

[4] Fahlman S.E. and Lebiere C., *The cascade correlation learning architecture*, Research Report CMU-CS-90-100 (1990).

[5] Kurkova V. and Smid J., *An incremental architecture algorithm for feedforward neural nets*, in: Computer Intensive Methods in Control and Signal Processing, Preprints of the European IEEE Workshop, Prague (1994).

[6] Marsden, M.J.(1974), *Quadratic Spline Interpolation*, Bulletin of the American Mathematical Society, Vol. 80, No.5 (September 1974).

[7] Smid J. and Volf P., *Dynamics retrieval and characterization from nonlinear time series*, Neural Network World, to appear (1995).

[8] Stone C.J., *Additive regression and other nonparametric models*, The Annals of Statistics Vol. 13 (1985), pp689–705.

Acknowledgements

This research is supported by NASA/GSFC under Grants NAG 5-2686, NCC 5-127 and by the Czech Academy of Science Grant No 275 408

QUERY LEARNING FOR MAXIMUM INFORMATION GAIN IN A MULTI-LAYER NEURAL NETWORK

Peter Sollich

Department of Physics, University of Edinburgh
Edinburgh EH9 3JZ, UK Email: P.Sollich@ed.ac.uk

In supervised learning, the redundancy contained in random examples can be avoided by learning from queries, where training examples are chosen to be maximally informative. Using the tools of statistical mechanics, we analyse query learning in a simple multi-layer network, namely, a large tree-committee machine. The generalization error is found to decrease exponentially with the number of training examples, providing a significant improvement over the slow algebraic decay for random examples. Implications for the connection between information gain and generalization error in multi-layer networks are discussed, and a computationally cheap algorithm for constructing approximate maximum information gain queries is suggested and analysed.

1 Introduction

In supervised learning of input-output mappings, the traditional approach has been to study generalization from random examples. However, random examples contain redundant information, and generalization performance can thus be improved by *query learning*, where each new training input is selected on the basis of the existing training data to be most 'useful' in some specified sense. Query learning corresponds closely to the well-founded statistical technique of (sequential) *optimal experimental design*. In particular, we consider in this paper queries which maximize the expected information gain, which are related to the criterion of (Bayes) D-optimality in optimal experimental design. The generalization performance achieved by maximum information gain queries is by now well understood for single-layer neural networks such as linear and binary perceptrons [1, 2, 3]. For multi-layer networks, which are much more widely used in practical applications, several heuristic algorithms for query learning have been proposed (see e.g., [4, 5]). While such heuristic approaches can demonstrate the power of query learning, they are hard to generalize to situations other than the ones for which they have been designed, and they cannot easily be compared with more traditional optimal experimental design methods. Furthermore, the existing analyses of such algorithms have been carried out within the framework of 'probably approximately correct' (PAC) learning, yielding worst case results which are not necessarily close to the potentially more relevant average case results. In this paper we therefore analyse the average generalization performance achieved by query learning in a multi-layer network, using the powerful tools of statistical mechanics. This is the first quantitative analysis of its kind that we are aware of.

2 The Model

We focus our analysis on one of the simplest multi-layer networks, namely, the tree-committee machine (TCM). A TCM is a two-layer neural network with N input units, K hidden units and one output unit. The 'receptive fields' of the individual hidden units do not overlap, and each hidden units calculates the sign of a linear combination (with real coefficients) of the N/K input components to which it is connected. The output unit then calculates the sign of the sum of all the hidden unit outputs. A TCM therefore effectively has all the weights from the hidden to the output layer fixed to one. Formally, the output y for a given input vector $\mathbf{x}$ is

$$y = \text{sgn}\left(\sum_{i=1}^{K} \sigma_i\right) \qquad \sigma_i = \text{sgn}\left(\mathbf{x}_i^{\mathrm{T}} \mathbf{w}_i\right) \tag{1}$$

where the σ_i are the outputs of the hidden units, $\mathbf{w}_i$ their weight vectors, and $\mathbf{x}^{\mathrm{T}} = (\mathbf{x}_1^{\mathrm{T}}, \ldots, \mathbf{x}_K^{\mathrm{T}})$ with $\mathbf{x}_i$ containing the N/K (real-valued) inputs to which hidden unit i is connected. The N (real) components of the K (N/K)-dimensional hidden unit weight vectors $\mathbf{w}_i$, which we denote collectively by $\mathbf{w}$, form the adjustable parameters of a TCM. Without loss of generality, we assume the weight vectors to be normalized to $\mathbf{w}_i^2 = N/K$. We shall restrict our analysis to the case where both the input space dimension and the number of hidden units are large ($N \to \infty$, $K \to \infty$), assuming that each hidden unit is connected to a large number of inputs, i.e., $N/K \gg 1$. As our training algorithm we take (zero temperature) Gibbs learning, which generates at random any TCM (in the following referred to as a 'student') which predicts all the training outputs in a given set of p training examples $\Theta^{(p)} = \{(\mathbf{x}^\mu, y^\mu), \mu = 1 \ldots p\}$ correctly. We take the problem to be perfectly learnable, which means that the outputs y^μ corresponding to the inputs $\mathbf{x}^\mu$ are generated by a 'teacher' TCM with the same architecture as the student but with different, unknown weights $\mathbf{w}^0$. It is further assumed that there is no noise on the training examples. For learning from random examples, the training inputs $\mathbf{x}^\mu$ are sampled randomly from a distribution $P_0(\mathbf{x})$. Since the output (1) of a TCM is independent of the length of the hidden unit input vectors $\mathbf{x}_i$, we assume this distribution $P_0(\mathbf{x})$ to be uniform over all vectors $\mathbf{x}^{\mathrm{T}} = (\mathbf{x}_1^{\mathrm{T}}, \ldots, \mathbf{x}_K^{\mathrm{T}})$ which obey the spherical constraints $\mathbf{x}_i^2 = N/K$. For query learning, the training inputs $\mathbf{x}^\mu$ are chosen to maximize the expected information gain of the student, as follows. The information gain is defined as the decrease in the entropy S in the parameter space of the student. The entropy for a training set $\Theta^{(p)}$ is given by

$$S(\Theta^{(p)}) = -\int d\mathbf{w} P(\mathbf{w}|\Theta^{(p)}) \ln P(\mathbf{w}|\Theta^{(p)}). \tag{2}$$

For the Gibbs learning algorithm considered here, $P(\mathbf{w}|\Theta^{(p)})$ is uniform on the 'version space', the space of all students which predict all training outputs correctly (and which satisfy the assumed spherical constraints on the weight vectors, $\mathbf{w}_i^2 = N/K$), and zero otherwise. Denoting the version space volume by $V(\Theta^{(p)})$, the entropy can thus simply be written as $S(\Theta^{(p)}) = \ln V(\Theta^{(p)})$. When a new training example $(\mathbf{x}^{p+1}, y^{p+1})$ is added to the existing training set, the information gain is $I = S(\Theta^{(p)}) - S(\Theta^{(N+1)})$. Since the new training output y^{p+1} is unknown, only the *expected* information gain, obtained by averaging over y^{p+1}, is available for selecting a maximally informative query $\mathbf{x}^{p+1}$. As derived in Ref. [2], the probability distribution of y^{p+1} given the input $\mathbf{x}^{p+1}$ and the existing training set $\Theta^{(p)}$ is $P(y^{p+1} = \pm 1|\mathbf{x}^{p+1}, \Theta^{(p)}) = v^\pm$, where $v^\pm = V(\Theta^{(N+1)})|_{y^{p+1}=\pm 1}/V(\Theta^{(p)})$. The expected information gain is therefore

$$\langle I \rangle_{P(y^{p+1}|\mathbf{x}^{p+1},\Theta^{(p)})} = -v^+ \ln v^+ - v^- \ln v^- \tag{3}$$

and attains its maximum value $\ln 2$ ($\equiv$ 1 bit) when $v^\pm = \frac{1}{2}$, i.e., when the new input $\mathbf{x}^{p+1}$ *bisects* the existing version space. This is intuitively reasonable, since $v^\pm = \frac{1}{2}$ corresponds to maximum uncertainty about the new output and hence to maximum information gain once this output is known.

Due to the complex geometry of the version space, the generation of queries which achieve exact bisection is in general computationally infeasible. The 'query by committee' algorithm proposed in Ref. [2] provides a solution to this problem by first sampling a 'committee' of $2k$ students from the Gibbs distribution $P(\mathbf{w}|\Theta^{(p)})$ and then using the fraction of committee members which predict +1 or -1 for the output y corresponding to an input $\mathbf{x}$ as an approximation to the true probability $P(y = \pm 1|\mathbf{x}, \Theta^{(p)}) = v^{\pm}$. The condition $v^{\pm} = \frac{1}{2}$ is then approximated by the requirement that exactly k of the committee members predict +1 and −1, respectively. An approximate maximum information gain query can thus be found by sampling (or *filtering*) inputs from a stream of random inputs until this condition is met. The procedure is then repeated for each new query. As $k \to \infty$, this algorithm approaches the exact bisection algorithm, and it is on this limit that we focus in the following.

3 Exact Maximum Information Gain Queries

The main quantity of interest in our analysis is the generalization error ϵ_g, defined as the probability that a given student TCM will predict the output of the teacher incorrectly for a random test input sampled from $P_0(\mathbf{x})$. It can be expressed in terms of the overlaps $R_i = \frac{K}{N}\mathbf{w}_i^T\mathbf{w}_i^0$ of the student and teacher hidden unit weight vectors $\mathbf{w}_i$ and $\mathbf{w}_i^0$ [6]. In the thermodynamic limit, the R_i are self-averaging, and can be obtained from a replica calculation of the average entropy S as a function of the normalized number of training examples, $\alpha = p/N$; details will be reported in a forthcoming publication [7]. The resulting average generalization error is plotted in Figure 1; for large α, one can show analytically that $\epsilon_g \propto \exp(-\alpha\frac{1}{2}\ln 2)$. This exponential decay of the generalization error ϵ_g with α provides a marked

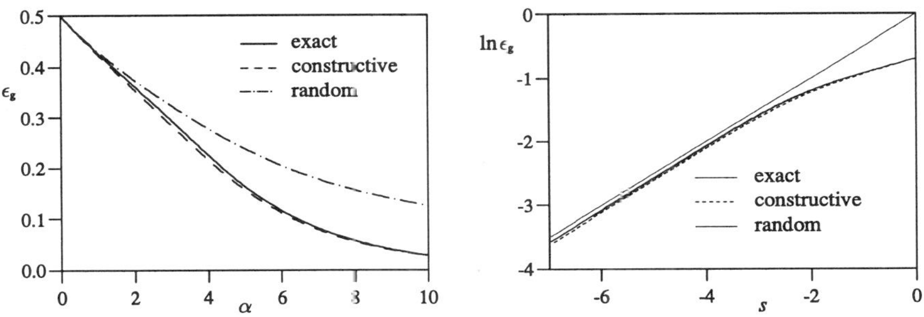

Figure 1 Left: Generalization error ϵ_g vs. (normalized) number of examples α, for *exact* maximum information gain queries (Section 3), queries selected by *constructive* algorithm (Section 4), and *random* examples. Right: $\ln \epsilon_g$ vs. (normalized) entropy s. For both queries and random examples, $\ln \epsilon_g \approx \frac{1}{2}s$ (thin full line) for large negative values of s (corresponding to large α).

improvement over the $\epsilon_g \propto 1/\alpha$ decay achieved by random examples [6]. The effect of maximum information gain queries is thus similar to what is observed for a binary perceptron learning from a binary perceptron teacher, but the decay constant c in $\epsilon_g \propto \exp(-c\alpha)$ is only half of that for the binary perceptron [2]. This means that asymptotically, twice as many examples are needed for a TCM as for a binary perceptron to achieve the same generalization performance, in agreement with the results for random examples [6]. Since maximum information gain queries lead to an entropy $s = -\alpha \ln 2$ in both networks, we can also conclude that the relation $s \approx \ln \epsilon_{\mathrm{g}}$ for the binary perceptron [2] has to be replaced by $s \approx \ln \epsilon_{\mathrm{g}}^2$ for the tree committee machine. Figure 1 shows that, as expected, this relation holds independently of whether one is learning from queries or from random examples.

4 Constructive Query Selection Algorithm

We now consider the practical realization of maximum information gain queries in the TCM. The query by committee approach, which in the limit $k \to \infty$ is an exact algorithm for selecting maximum information queries, filters queries from a stream of random inputs. This leads to an exponential increase of the query filtering time with the number of training examples that have already been learned [3]. As a cheap alternative we propose a simple algorithm for *constructing* queries, which is based on the assumption of an approximate decoupling of the entropies of the different hidden units, as follows. Each individual hidden unit of a TCM can be viewed as a binary perceptron. The distribution $P(\mathbf{w}_i|\Theta^{(p)})$ of its weight vector $\mathbf{w}_i$ given a set of training examples $\Theta^{(p)}$ has an entropy S_i associated with it, in analogy to the entropy (2) of the full weight distribution $P(\mathbf{w}|\Theta^{(p)})$. Our 'constructive algorithm' for selecting queries then consists in choosing, for each new query $\mathbf{x}^{\mu+1}$, the inputs $\mathbf{x}_i^{\mu+1}$ to the individual hidden units in such a way as to maximize the decrease in their entropies S_i. This can be achieved simply by choosing each $\mathbf{x}_i^{\mu+1}$ to be orthogonal to $\bar{\mathbf{w}}_i^{\mu} = \langle \mathbf{w}_i \rangle_{P(\mathbf{w}|\Theta^{(\mu)})}$ (and otherwise random, i.e., according to $P_0(\mathbf{x})$) [7], thus avoiding the cumbersome and time-consuming filtering from a random input stream. In practice, one would of course approximate $\bar{\mathbf{w}}_i^{\mu}$ by an average of $2k$ (say) samples from the Gibbs distribution $P(\mathbf{w}|\Theta^{(\mu)})$; these samples would have been needed anyway in the query by committee approach.

The generalization performance achieved by this constructive algorithm can again be calculated by the replica method; as shown in Figure 1, it is actually slightly superior to that of exact maximum information gain queries. The α-dependence of the entropy, $s = -\alpha \ln 2$, turns out to be the same as for maximum information gain queries; this indicates that the correlations between the individual hidden units become sufficiently small for $K \to \infty$, so that queries selected to minimize the individual hidden units' entropies also minimize the overall entropy of the TCM.

5 Conclusions

We have analysed query learning for maximum information gain in a large tree-committee machine (TCM). Or main result is the exponential decay of the generalization error ϵ_{g} with the normalized number of training examples α, which demonstrates that query learning *can* yield significant improvements over learning from random examples (for which $\epsilon_{\mathrm{g}} \propto 1/\alpha$ for large α) in multi-layer neural networks. The fact that the decay constant c in $\epsilon_{\mathrm{g}} \propto \exp(-c\alpha)$ differs from that calculated for single-layer nets such as the binary perceptron raises the question of how large c would be in more complex multi-layer networks. Combining the worst-case bound in [3] in terms of the VC-dimension with existing storage capacity bounds, one would estimate that c could be as small as $O(1/\ln K)$ for networks with a large number of hidden units K. This contrasts with our result $c \to$ const. for $K \to \infty$, and further work is clearly needed to establish whether there are realistic networks which saturate the lower bound $c = O(1/\ln K)$.

We have also analysed a computationally cheap algorithm for constructing (rather than filtering) approximate maximum information gain queries, and found that it actually achieves slightly better generalization performance than exact maximum information gain queries. This result is particularly encouraging considering the practical application of query learning in more complex multi-layer networks. For example, the proposed constructive algorithm can be modified for query learning in a fully-connected committee machine (where each hidden unit is connected to all the inputs), by simply choosing each new query to be orthogonal to the subspace spanned by the average weight vectors of *all* K hidden units. As long as K is much smaller than the input dimension N, and assuming that for large enough K the approximate decoupling of the hidden unit entropies still holds for fully connected networks, one would expect this algorithm to yield a good approximation to maximum information gain queries. The same conclusion may also hold for a *general* two-layer network with threshold units (where, in contrast to the committee machine, the hidden-to-output weights are free parameters), which can approximate a large class of input-output mappings. In summary, our results therefore suggest that the drastic improvements in generalization performance achieved by maximum information gain queries can be made available, in a computationally cheap manner, for realistic neural network learning problems.

REFERENCES

[1] P. Sollich, *Query construction, entropy, and generalization in neural network models*, Phys. Rev. E, Vol. 49 (1994), pp4637–4651.

[2] H. S. Seung, M. Opper, and H. Sompolinsky, *Query by committee*, in: Proc. 5th Workshop on Computational Learning Theory (COLT '92), ACM, New York, (1992), pp287–294.

[3] Y. Freund, H. S. Seung, E. Shamir, and N. Tishby, *Information, prediction, and query by committee*, in: Advances in Neural Information Processing Systems 5, S. J. Hanson, J. D. Cowan, and C. Lee Giles eds., Morgan Kaufmann, San Mateo, CA (1993), pp483–490.

[4] E. Baum, *Neural network algorithms that learn in polynomial time from examples and queries*, IEEE Trans. Neural Netw., Vol. 2 (1991), pp5–19.

[5] J.-N. Hwang, J. J. Choi, S. Oh, and R.J. Marks II, *Query-based learning applied to partially trained multilayer perceptrons*, IEEE Trans. Neural Netw., Vol. 2 (1991), pp131–136.

[6] H. Schwarze and J. Hertz, *Generalization in a large committee machine*, Europhys. Lett., Vol. 20 (1992), pp375–380.

[7] P. Sollich, *Learning from minimum entropy queries in a large committee machine*, Phys. Rev. E, Vol.53 (1996), ppR2060–R2063.

Acknowledgements

This work was partially supported by European Union grant no. ERB CHRX-CT92-0063.

SHIFT, ROTATION AND SCALE INVARIANT SIGNATURES FOR TWO-DIMENSIONAL CONTOURS, IN A NEURAL NETWORK ARCHITECTURE

David McG. Squire and Terry M. Caelli

School of Computing, Curtin University of Technology Perth, Western Australia, Australia. Email: squizz@cs.curtin.edu.au, tmc@cs.curtin.edu.au

A technique for obtaining shift, rotation and scale invariant signatures for two dimensional contours is proposed and demonstrated. An *invariance factor* is calculated at each point by comparing the orientation of the tangent vector with vector fields corresponding to the generators of Lie transformation groups for shift, rotation and scaling. The statistics of these invariance factors over the contour are used to produce an *invariance signature*. This operation is implemented in a Model-Based Neural Network (MBNN), in which the architecture and weights are parameterised by the constraints of the problem domain. The end result after constructing and training this system is the same as a traditional neural network: a collection of layers of nodes with weighted connections. The design and modeling process can be thought of as *compiling* an invariant classifier into a neural network. We contend that these invariance signatures, whilst not unique, are sufficient to characterise contours for many pattern recognition tasks.

1 Introduction

1.1 The Model-Based Approach to Building Neural Networks

The MBNN approach aims to retain the advantages of Traditional Neural Networks (TNNs), i.e. parallel data-processing, but to constrain the process by which the architecture of the network and the values of the weights are determined, so that the designer can use expert knowledge of the problem domain. MBNNs were introduced in [1]. In that paper we proposed networks in which the weights were functions of the relative positions of nodes, and several, possibly shared, parameters. This reduced the dimensionality of the space searched during training, and the size of the training set required, since the network was guaranteed to respond only to certain features. The resultant network was just a collection of nodes and weighted connections, exactly as in a TNN. The key notion was that neural networks with highly desirable properties could be produced by using expert knowledge to constrain the weight determination process. The MBNN approach departs from the TNN view in that the operation is not determined entirely by the training set supplied.

1.2 Model-Based Neural Networks and Invariant Pattern Recognition

That the parameters of TNNs are entirely learnt can be a limitation. To achieve good performance, the training set must be sufficiently large and varied to span the input space. Collecting this data and training the network can be very time-consuming. The MBNN formulation allows the creation of networks guaranteed to respond to particular features in, and to be invariant under certain transformations of, the input image. A data set containing various shifted, distorted or otherwise transformed versions of the input patterns, such has long been a common approach to invariant pattern recognition using neural networks [2], is not required. The concept of MBNNs is here extended to include modular networks. Each module has a well-defined functionality. The weights in each module can be arrived at by any technique at all: some may be set by the designer, others by training the module for a specific task. This approach allows the the network designer great flexibility. Separately trained modules can perform data processing tasks independent of the final classification of the input pattern.

2 Invariance Signatures

2.1 Functions Invariant With Respect To Lie Transformation Groups

We wish to determine the invariance of a function $F(x, y)$ with respect to a Lie transformation group.

$$\mathbf{G}(x,y) = \left[\begin{array}{cc} g_x(x,y) & g_y(x,y) \end{array}\right]^T \tag{1}$$

is the vector field corresponding to the generator of the group. F is constant with respect to the action of the generator if

$$\nabla F \cdot \mathbf{G}(x,y) = 0, \quad \text{i.e.} \quad \frac{\partial F}{\partial x} g_x + \frac{\partial F}{\partial y} g_y = 0. \tag{2}$$

Consider a contour parameterised by t on which F is constant:

$$F(x(t), y(t)) = C \;\; \forall \; t. \tag{3}$$

Since F is constant on the contour, we have:

$$\frac{dF}{dt} = \frac{\partial F}{\partial x}\frac{dx}{dt} + \frac{\partial F}{\partial y}\frac{dy}{dt} = 0, \quad \text{so that} \quad \frac{\frac{\partial F}{\partial x}}{\frac{\partial F}{\partial y}} = -\frac{dy}{dx}. \tag{4}$$

Thus the invariance condition given in equation 2, holds if

$$\frac{dy}{dx} = \frac{g_y}{g_x}. \tag{5}$$

2.2 Mapping Points from Image Space to Invariance Space

The tangent to the contour at each point is compared with the vector fields characterising given transformations. Both the tangent vector $\theta(x, y)$ and the vector fields $\mathbf{v_c}(x, y)$ are normalised everywhere. The measure of consistency with invariance class c at point (x, y) is:

$$\iota_c(x, y) = \left|\hat{\theta}(x,y) \cdot \mathbf{v_c}(x,y)\right|. \tag{6}$$

This operation maps points from the image to the interior of a unit hypercube in an n-dimensional *invariance space*:

$$\hat{\theta}(x,y) \longrightarrow \left[\begin{array}{ccc} \iota_{rot} & \iota_{dil} & \iota_{trans} \end{array}\right]^T. \tag{7}$$

The origin of the image space is chosen to be the centroid of the contour, so that the *invariance signature* is shift invariant. The vector field for rotation invariance is:

$$\mathbf{v_{rot}}(x,y) = \frac{1}{\sqrt{x^2+y^2}} \left[\begin{array}{cc} -y & x \end{array}\right]^T. \tag{8}$$

The vector field for dilation invariance is similar. For the translation invariance case, the vector field $\mathbf{v_{trans}}(x, y)$ is constant for all (x, y). The direction is that of the dominant eigenvector of the coordinate covariance matrix of the contour. The invariance signature of an image consists of histograms of the invariance measures for all the "on" points. It is invariant under rotations, dilations, translations and reflections of the image. This encoding is not unique, unlike some previous integral transform representations [3].

3 A Neural Network System For Computing Invariance Signatures

A MBNN was constructed to compute invariance signatures and classify input patterns on this basis. This MBNN, consisting of a system of modules, some hand-coded and some trained, is shown in Figure 1. Whilst this system appears complex,

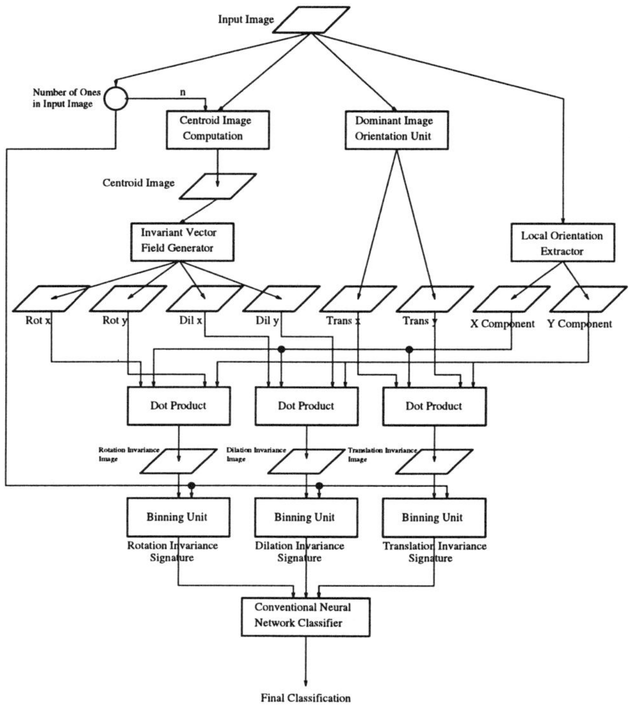

Figure 1 Invariance Signature-Based Contour Recognition System.

it retains the basic characteristics of a TNN[1]. Each node i computes the sum of its weighted inputs, $net_i = \sum_j w_{ij}x_j$. This is used as the input to the transfer function f, which is either linear, $f(net_j) = net_j$, or the standard sigmoid, $f(net_j) = \frac{1}{1+e^{-net_j}}$. The only departure from a TNN is that some of the weights are dynamic: the weight is calculated by a node higher up in the network. This allows the MBNN to compute dot products[2], and some nodes to act as gates. Since weights in any neural network implementation are just references to a stored value, this should not present any difficulty. There is insufficient space here to describe all the modules in the system. Descriptions of the *Local Orientation Extractor* and the *Binning Unit* are given as examples of the way the modules were constructed.

[1] with the exception of the *Dominant Image Orientation Unit*, for which a neural network solution is still being developed.

[2] The calculation of dot products is achieved by using the outputs of one layer as the *weights* on connections to another layer.

3.1 Local Orientation Extraction

A simple and robust estimate of the tangent vector at a point is the dominant eigenvector of the covariance matrix of a square window centred on that point. The vector magnitudes are weighted by the strength of the orientation. Let the eigenvalues be λ_1 and λ_2, $\lambda_1 \geq \lambda_2$. The corresponding unit eigenvectors are $\hat{\mathbf{e}}_1$ and $\hat{\mathbf{e}}_2$. The weighted tangent vector estimate $\mathbf{s}$ is:

$$\mathbf{s} = \begin{cases} \left(1 - \frac{\lambda_2}{\lambda_1}\right)\hat{\mathbf{e}}_1 & \lambda_1 \neq 0 \\ 0 & \lambda_1 = 0. \end{cases} \tag{9}$$

A TNN with a 3×3 input layer, 20 hidden nodes, and 2 output nodes was trained using backpropagation [4] to produce this output for all possible binary input images with a centre value of 1. Training was stopped after 6000000 iterations, when 96.89% of the training set variance was fitted. This problem is similar to edge extraction, except that edge extraction is usually performed on greyscale gradients rather than thin binary contours. Srinivasan *et al.* [5] have developed a neural network edge detector which produces a weighted vector output like that in equation 9. We intend to produce a more compact and accurate tangent estimator using a MBNN incorporating Gabor weighting functions, as used in [1].

3.2 The Binning Unit

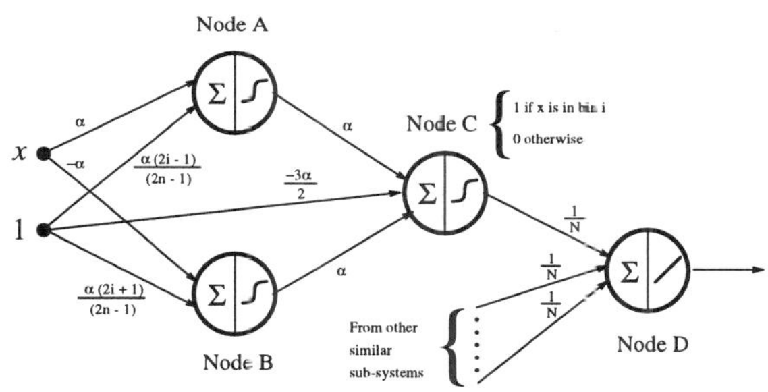

Figure 2 Neural Binning Subsystem.

The weights for the binning unit in figure 2 were determined by hand. There is a binning unit for each of the n bins in each invariance signature histogram. Each binning unit is connected to all nodes in the invariance image, and inputs to it are gated by the input image, so that only the N nodes corresponding to ones in the input image contribute. The bins have width $\frac{1}{n-1}$, since the first bin is centred on 0, and the last on 1 [3]. Nodes A and B only have an output of 1 when the input x is within bin i. This condition is met when:

$$\frac{2i-1}{2(n-1)} < x < \frac{2i+1}{2(n-1)}. \tag{10}$$

To detect this condition, the activations of nodes A and B are set to:

$$net_A = \alpha x - \frac{\alpha(2i-1)}{2(n-1)} \tag{11}$$

[3] A bin *ending* at 0 or 1 would miss contributions from the extrema since the edge of the neural bin is not vertical.

$$net_B \quad = \quad -\alpha x + \frac{\alpha(2i+1)}{2(n-1)} \qquad (12)$$

where α is a large number, causing the sigmoid to approximate a step function. Here, $\alpha = 1000$ was used. Node C acts as an AND gate. Node D sums the contributions to bin i from all N nodes.

4 Simulation Results

To demonstrate the feasibility of such an invariance signature-based classifier, a small simulation was done. The task was to classify an input pattern as one of the ten first letters of the alphabet. The training set contained four examples of each letter[4], each differently rotated or reflected[5], within an 18×18 input image. The test set contained three differently transformed examples of each letter. The final classification stage of the MBNN used a 9 node hidden layer and was trained using backpropagation. A TNN with an 18×18 input layer, 9 node hidden layer and 10 node output layer was also trained. After 1000 iterations, both correctly classified 100% of the training data. The MBNN correctly classified 76.66% of the test data, whereas the TNN did not correctly classify *any* of it. It is clear that the MBNN massively outperformed the TNN. Had the *Local Orientation Extractor* been ideal, the optimal performance on the training data would have been 80%, since “b” and “d” are identical under reflection in the font used.

5 Conclusion

Using the MBNN approach, neural networks can be constructed which are guaranteed to classify input contours using invariance signatures which are rotation, dilation, translation and reflection invariant. The resultant MBNN retains the useful properties of being composed of similar simple nodes joined by weighted connections, with inherently parallel computation. The MBNN approach is thus a useful technique for *compiling* a neural network, incorporating the designer’s expert knowledge.

REFERENCES

[1] Terry M. Caelli, David McG. Squire, and Tom P.J. Wild, *Model-based neural networks*, Neural Networks, Vol. 6 1993, pp613–625.

[2] K. Fukushima, S. Miyake, and T. Ito, *Neocognitron: A neural network model for a mechanism of visual pattern recognition*, IEEE Transactions on Systems, Man and Cybernetics, Vol. 13(5) (1983), pp826–834.

[3] Mario Ferraro and Terry M. Caelli, *Lie transform groups, integral transforms, and invariant pattern recognition*, Spatial Vision, Vol. 8(1) (1994), pp33–44.

[4] D.C. Plaut and G.E. Hinton, *Learning sets of filters using backpropagation*, Computer Speech and Language, Vol. 2 (1987), pp35–61.

[5] V. Srinivasan, P. Bhatia, and S. H. Ong, *Edge detection using a neural network*, Pattern Recognition, Vol. 27(12) (1994), pp1653–1662.

Acknowledgements

David Squire was funded by an Australian Postgraduate Award.

[4] More than one example of each letter was required since slightly different signatures were generated by different orientations, due to the residual error in the *Local Orientation Extractor*.

[5] all rotations were by multiples of $\frac{\pi}{2}$ radians.

FUNCTION APPROXIMATION BY THREE-LAYER ARTIFICIAL NEURAL NETWORKS

Shin Suzuki

Information Science Research Laboratory, NTT Basic Research Laboratories, 3-1 Morinosato-Wakamiya, Atsugi-Shi, Kanagawa Pref., 243-01 Japan.

Tel: +81 462 40 3574, Fax: +81 462 40 4721, Email: shin@idea.brl.ntt.jp

This paper presents *constructive* approximations by three-layer artificial neural networks with (1) trigonometric, (2) piecewise linear, and (3) sigmoidal hidden-layer units. These approximations provide (a) approximating-network equations, (b) specifications for the numbers of hidden-layer units, (c) approximation error estimations, and (d) saturations of the approximations.

Keywords: Constructive Approximation, Saturation.

1 Introduction

Previous studies on function approximation by artificial neural networks show only the existence of approximating networks by *non-constructive* methods[1][2] and thus contribute almost nothing to developing the networks and to specifying the properties of the approximations. This paper presents *constructive* approximations by networks with (1) trigonometric, (2) piecewise linear, and (3) sigmoidal hidden-layer units. These approximations provide (a) approximating-network equations, (b) specifications for the numbers of hidden-layer units, (c) approximation error estimations, and (d) saturations of the approximations.

2 Preliminaries

Let $\mathbb{N}$ and $\mathbb{R}$ be the set of natural and real numbers, and $\mathbb{N}_0 = \mathbb{N} \cup \{0\}$. Let $|\mathbf{r}| = \sum_{i=1}^{m} |r_i|$ for $\mathbf{r} = (r_i)_{i=1}^{m} \in \mathbb{N}_0^m$ and $\|\mathbf{t}\| = \left(\sum_{i=1}^{m} t_i^2\right)^{1/2}$ for $\mathbf{t} = (t_i)_{i=1}^{m} \in \mathbb{R}^m$. For $p \geq 1$, we denote by $L_{2\pi}^p(\mathbb{R}^m)$ the space of 2π-periodic on each $\mathbb{R}$ of $\mathbb{R}^m$ pth-order Lebesgue-integrable functions defined on $\mathbb{R}^m$ to $\mathbb{R}$ with $L_{2\pi}^p$-norm $\|f\|_{L_{2\pi}^p} = \left\{(2\pi)^{-m} \int_{-\pi}^{\pi} \cdots \int_{-\pi}^{\pi} |f(\mathbf{x})|^p d\mathbf{x}\right\}^{1/p}$ and by $C_{2\pi}(\mathbb{R}^m)$ the space of 2π-periodic continuous functions defined on $\mathbb{R}^m$ to $\mathbb{R}$ with $C_{2\pi}$-norm $\|f\|_{C_{2\pi}} = \sup\{|f(\mathbf{x})| \; ; \; |x_i| \leq \pi, \; i = 1, \ldots, m\}$. Let $\Psi = L_{2\pi}^p(\mathbb{R}^m)$ or $C_{2\pi}(\mathbb{R}^m)$ throughout this paper. For $f, g \in \Psi$, $\langle f(\mathbf{t}), g(\mathbf{t})\rangle = (2\pi)^{-m} \int_{-\pi}^{\pi} \cdots \int_{-\pi}^{\pi} f(\mathbf{t}) g(\mathbf{t}) d\mathbf{t}$ and the convolution $f * g(\mathbf{x}) = (2\pi)^{-m} \int_{-\pi}^{\pi} \cdots \int_{-\pi}^{\pi} f(\mathbf{t}) g(\mathbf{x} - \mathbf{t}) d\mathbf{t}$. Let the sigmoidal function $\mathrm{sig}(x) = \{1 + \exp(-x)\}^{-1}$. Let $f \in \Psi$ and $\delta \geq 0$. We introduce the modulus of continuity of f in Ψ $\omega_\Psi(f, \delta) = \sup\{\|f(\cdot + \mathbf{t}) - f(\cdot)\|_\Psi \; ; \; \mathbf{t} \in \mathbb{R}^m, \; \|\mathbf{t}\| \leq \delta\}$, where $\|f(\cdot + \mathbf{t}) - f(\cdot)\|_{L_{2\pi}^p} = \left\{(2\pi)^{-m} \int_{-\pi}^{\pi} \cdots \int_{-\pi}^{\pi} |f(\mathbf{x} + \mathbf{t}) - f(\mathbf{x})|^p d\mathbf{x}\right\}^{1/p}$ and

$$\|f(\cdot + \mathbf{t}) - f(\cdot)\|_{C_{2\pi}} = \sup\{|f(\mathbf{x} + \mathbf{t}) - f(\mathbf{x})| \; ; \; x_i| \leq \pi, \; i = 1, \ldots, m\}.$$

We say f satisfies a Lipschitz's condition with constant $M > 0$ and exponent $\nu > 0$ in Ψ, if

$$\|f(\cdot + \mathbf{t}) - f(\cdot)\|_\Psi \leq M \|\mathbf{t}\|^\nu$$

for $\mathbf{t} \in \mathbb{R}^m$. Let $\mathrm{Lip}_M(\Psi; \nu)$ be the set of functions satisfying this condition and Lipschitz's class of order ν $\mathrm{Lip}\,\nu = \cup\{\mathrm{Lip}_M(\Psi; \nu) \; ; \; M > 0\}$. We notice that if $f \in \Psi$ satisfies a Lipschitz's condition with constant M and exponent ν in Ψ, then $\omega_\Psi(f, \delta) \leq M\delta^\nu$.

3 Results

3.1 Constructive Approximations and approximation error estimations

Let $b_{\mathbf{r}}^{\lambda} = \prod_{i=1}^{m} \sin \frac{r_i+1}{\lambda+2}\pi$ for $\mathbf{r} = (r_i)_{i=1}^{m} \in \mathbb{N}_0^m$ and $B^{\lambda} = \left(\frac{2}{\lambda+2}\right)^m$ for $\lambda \in \mathbb{N}$ in this section.

Theorem 1 (trigonometric case) *Let* $\mathbf{f} = (f_i)_{i=1}^{n}$ *be a function defined on* $\mathbb{R}^m$ *to* $\mathbb{R}^n$ *such that* $f_i \in \Psi$. *For arbitrary parameter* $\lambda \in \mathbb{N}$, *a three-layer network with trigonometric hidden-layer units* $\mathbf{TN}[\mathbf{f}]^{\lambda} = \left(TN[f_i]^{\lambda}\right)_{i=1}^{n}$ *approximates to* $\mathbf{f}$ *with* Ψ*-norm, such that*

$$TN[f_i]^{\lambda}(\mathbf{x}) = \theta[f_i]^{\lambda} + \sum_{(\mathbf{p},\mathbf{q})}^{0\le p_i,\, q_i\le\lambda} \left\{\alpha[f_i]^{\lambda}(\mathbf{p},\mathbf{q})\cos(\mathbf{p}-\mathbf{q})\mathbf{x} + \beta[f_i]^{\lambda}(\mathbf{p},\mathbf{q})\sin(\mathbf{p}-\mathbf{q})\mathbf{x}\right\}, \tag{1}$$

where $\theta[f_i]^{\lambda} = \langle f_i(\mathbf{t}), 1\rangle$, $\alpha[f_i]^{\lambda}(\mathbf{p},\mathbf{q}) = 2B^{\lambda} b_{\mathbf{p}}^{\lambda} b_{\mathbf{q}}^{\lambda} \langle f_i(\mathbf{t}), \cos(\mathbf{p}-\mathbf{q})\mathbf{t}\rangle$, *and* $\beta[f_i]^{\lambda}(\mathbf{p},\mathbf{q}) = 2B^{\lambda} b_{\mathbf{p}}^{\lambda} b_{\mathbf{q}}^{\lambda} \langle f_i(\mathbf{t}), \sin(\mathbf{p}-\mathbf{q})\mathbf{t}\rangle$. *(The above summation is over combinations of* $\mathbf{p} = (p_i)_{i=1}^{m}$, $\mathbf{q} = (q_i)_{i=1}^{m} \in \mathbb{N}_0^m$ *such that* $\mathbf{p} \neq \mathbf{q}$, $0 \le p_i, q_i \le \lambda$, *i.e., if the summation is added in the case of* $(\mathbf{p},\mathbf{q})$, *it is not added in the case of* $(\mathbf{q},\mathbf{p})$. *This notation of the summation is used throughout this paper.) Then* $\mathbf{TN}[\mathbf{f}]^{\lambda}$ *has* $(2\lambda+1)^m - 1$ *hidden-layer units. Also the approximation error of each coordinate with* Ψ*-norm for* $i = 1,\ldots,n$ *is estimated by*

$$\left\|f_i - TN[f_i]^{\lambda}\right\|_{\Psi} \le \left(1 + \frac{\pi^2}{2}\sqrt{m}\right)\omega_{\Psi}\left(f_i,\, (\lambda+2)^{-1}\right). \tag{2}$$

The next corollary means that $\mathbf{TN}[\mathbf{f}]^{\lambda}$ can approximate $\mathbf{f}$ with any degree of accuracy if λ increases i.e., the number of hidden-layer units increases.

Corollary 1 $\left\|f_i - TN[f_i]^{\lambda}\right\|_{\Psi} \to 0$ *as* $\lambda \to \infty$ $(i = 1,\ldots,n)$.

Theorem 2 (piecewise linear case) *Let* $\mathbf{f} = (f_i)_{i=1}^{n}$ *be a function defined on* $\mathbb{R}^m$ *to* $\mathbb{R}^n$ *such that* $f_i \in L_{2\pi}^{p}(\mathbb{R}^m)$. *For two arbitrary independent parameters* $\lambda, \sigma \in \mathbb{N}$, *a three-layer network with piecewise linear hidden-layer units* $\mathbf{PN}[\mathbf{f}]^{\lambda,\sigma} = \left(PN[f_i]^{\lambda,\sigma}\right)_{i=1}^{n}$ *approximates to* $\mathbf{f}$ *with* $L_{2\pi}^{p}$*-norm, such that*

$$PN[f_i]^{\lambda,\sigma}(\mathbf{x}) = \theta[f_i]^{\lambda,\sigma} + \sum_{(\mathbf{p},\mathbf{q})}^{0\le p_i,\, q_i\le\lambda} \sum_{k=0}^{4|\mathbf{p}-\mathbf{q}|\sigma-1} \alpha[f_i]^{\lambda,\sigma}(\mathbf{p},\mathbf{q},k)\, PL_k^{\sigma}((\mathbf{p}-\mathbf{q})\mathbf{x}), \tag{3}$$

where

$$PL_k^{\sigma}(\mathbf{rx}) = \begin{cases} 0 \ \left(\mathbf{rx} \le -|\mathbf{r}|\pi + \frac{k\pi}{2\sigma}\right),\ 1 \ \left(\mathbf{rx} \ge -|\mathbf{r}|\pi + \frac{(k+1)\pi}{2\sigma}\right) \\ \frac{2\sigma}{\pi}\mathbf{rx} + 2|\mathbf{r}|\sigma - k \ \left(-|\mathbf{r}|\pi + \frac{k\pi}{2\sigma} < \mathbf{rx} < -|\mathbf{r}|\pi + \frac{(k+1)\pi}{2\sigma}\right) \end{cases},$$

$$\theta[f_i]^{\lambda,\sigma} = \langle f_i(\mathbf{t}), 1\rangle + 2B^{\lambda}\sin\frac{\pi}{4\sigma} \sum_{(\mathbf{p},\mathbf{q})}^{0\le p_i,\, q_i\le\lambda} (-1)^{|\mathbf{p}-\mathbf{q}|} b_{\mathbf{p}}^{\lambda} b_{\mathbf{q}}^{\lambda} \langle f_i(\mathbf{t}), \cos(\mathbf{p}-\mathbf{q})\mathbf{t}\rangle,$$

$$\alpha[f_i]^{\lambda,\sigma}(\mathbf{p},\mathbf{q},k) = 4(-1)^{|\mathbf{p}-\mathbf{q}|} B^{\lambda} b^{\lambda}_{\mathbf{p}} b^{\lambda}_{\mathbf{q}} \sin\frac{\pi}{4\sigma} \times$$
$$\left\{ \langle f_i(\mathbf{t}), \sin(\mathbf{p}-\mathbf{q})\mathbf{t}\rangle \cos\frac{(2k+1)\pi}{4\sigma} - \langle f_i(\mathbf{t}), \cos(\mathbf{p}-\mathbf{q})\mathbf{t}\rangle \sin\frac{(2k+1)\pi}{4\sigma} \right\},$$

Then $\mathbf{PN}[\mathbf{f}]^{\lambda,\sigma}$ *has* $2m\sigma\lambda(\lambda+1)(2\lambda+1)^{m-1}$ *hidden-layer units. Also the approximation error of each coordinate with* $L^p_{2\pi}$*-norm is estimated by*

$$\left\| f_i - PN[f_i]^{\lambda,\sigma} \right\|_{L^p_{2\pi}} \le \left(1 + \frac{\pi^2}{2}\sqrt{m}\right) \omega_{L^p_{2\pi}}\left(f_i, (\lambda+2)^{-1}\right) +$$
$$2\|f_i\|_{L^p_{2\pi}} \left\{ \left(\frac{8(\lambda+2)}{\pi^2}\right)^m - 1 \right\} \left\{ \frac{\pi\sqrt{m}}{(2\pi)^{m-1}\sigma} \left(\frac{4\sigma}{\pi} - \cot\frac{\pi}{4\sigma}\right) \right\}^{1/p}. \quad (4)$$

Theorem 3 (sigmoidal case) *Let* $\mathbf{f} = (f_i)_{i=1}^n$ *be a function defined on* $\mathbb{R}^m$ *to* $\mathbb{R}^n$ *such that* $f_i \in L^p_{2\pi}(\mathbb{R}^m)$. *For two arbitrary independent parameters* $\lambda, \sigma \in \mathbb{N}$, *a three-layer network with sigmoidal hidden-layer units* $\mathbf{SN}[\mathbf{f}]^{\lambda,\sigma} = \left(SN[f_i]^{\lambda,\sigma}\right)_{i=1}^n$ *approximates to* $\mathbf{f}$ *with* $L^p_{2\pi}$*-norm, such that*

$$SN[f_i]^{\lambda,\sigma}(\mathbf{x}) = \theta[f_i]^{\lambda,\sigma} +$$
$$\sum_{(\mathbf{p},\mathbf{q})}^{0\le p_i,q_i\le\lambda} \sum_{k=0}^{4|\mathbf{p}-\mathbf{q}|\sigma-1} \alpha[f_i]^{\lambda,\sigma}(\mathbf{p},\mathbf{q},k)\, SG^{\sigma}_k((\mathbf{p}-\mathbf{q})\mathbf{x}), \quad (5)$$

where $SG^{\sigma}_k(\mathbf{rx}) = \mathrm{sig}\left(\frac{8\sigma}{\pi}\mathbf{rx} + 8|\mathbf{r}|\sigma - 4k - 2\right)$, *and* $\theta[f_i]^{\lambda,\sigma}$ *and* $\alpha[f_i]^{\lambda,\sigma}(\mathbf{p},\mathbf{q},k)$ *are the same as in Theorem 2. Then* $\mathbf{SN}[\mathbf{f}]^{\lambda,\sigma}$ *has* $2m\sigma\lambda(\lambda+1)(2\lambda+1)^{m-1}$ *hidden-layer units. Also the approximation error of each coordinate with* $L^p_{2\pi}$*-norm is estimated by*

$$\left\| f_i - SN[f_i]^{\lambda,\sigma} \right\|_{L^p_{2\pi}} \le \left(1 + \frac{\pi^2}{2}\sqrt{m}\right) \omega_{L^p_{2\pi}}\left(f_i, (\lambda+2)^{-1}\right) +$$
$$2\|f_i\|_{L^p_{2\pi}} \left\{ \left(\frac{8(\lambda+2)}{\pi^2}\right)^m - 1 \right\} \left\{ \frac{\pi\sqrt{m}}{(2\pi)^{m-1}\sigma} \left(\log 2 - \frac{1}{2} + \frac{4\sigma}{\pi} - \cot\frac{\pi}{4\sigma}\right) \right\}^{1/p} \quad (6)$$

Remark 1 $\mathbf{PN}[\mathbf{f}]^{\lambda,\sigma}$ *and* $\mathbf{SN}[\mathbf{f}]^{\lambda,\sigma}$ *in Theorems 2 and 3 are based on* $\mathbf{TN}[\mathbf{f}]^{\lambda}$ *in Theorem 1. In fact, for any* $\lambda \in \mathbb{N}$, $\mathbf{PN}[\mathbf{f}]^{\lambda,\sigma}$ *and* $\mathbf{SN}[\mathbf{f}]^{\lambda,\sigma}$ *approach* $\mathbf{TN}[\mathbf{f}]^{\lambda}$ *as* σ *increases. Therefore they are almost determined by* λ *if* σ *is large enough for* λ.

For any $\lambda \in \mathbb{N}$, the second terms of the right-hand members of Inequalities (4) and (6) approach 0 as σ increases. Then, $\left\| f_i - PN[f_i]^{\lambda,\sigma} \right\|_{L^p_{2\pi}}$ and $\left\| f_i - SN[f_i]^{\lambda,\sigma} \right\|_{L^p_{2\pi}}$ are almost estimated by the first terms, which are the same as Inequality (2), when σ is large enough for λ. The following two corollaries give conditions on σ in terms of λ that the approximation errors approach 0, if λ increases. Under these conditions $\mathbf{PN}[\mathbf{f}]^{\lambda,\sigma}$ and $\mathbf{SN}[\mathbf{f}]^{\lambda,\sigma}$ can approximate $\mathbf{f}$ with any degree of accuracy, if the number of hidden-layer units increases.

Corollary 2 *If* σ *is a higher-order infinity than* $\lambda^{\frac{mp}{2}}$, *i.e.,* $\sigma = \sigma(\lambda) \to \infty$ *and* $\frac{\lambda^{\frac{mp}{2}}}{\sigma(\lambda)} \to 0$ *as* $\lambda \to \infty$, *then* $\left\| f_i - PN[f_i]^{\lambda,\sigma} \right\|_{L^p_{2\pi}} \to 0$ *as* $\lambda \to \infty \quad (i = 1, \ldots, n)$.

Corollary 3 *If σ is a higher-order infinity than λ^{mp}, i.e., $\sigma = \sigma(\lambda) \to \infty$ and $\frac{\lambda^{mp}}{\sigma(\lambda)} \to 0$ as $\lambda \to \infty$, then $\left\| f_i - SN\left[f_i\right]^{\lambda,\sigma} \right\|_{L^p_{2\pi}} \to 0$ as $\lambda \to \infty \quad (i = 1, \ldots, n)$.*

3.2 Saturation of Constructive Approximations

We denote $\theta_\lambda = o(\zeta_\lambda)$ $(\lambda \to \infty)$, if $\frac{\theta_\lambda}{\zeta_\lambda} \to 0$ as $\lambda \to \infty$ and $\theta_\lambda = O(\zeta_\lambda)$ $(\lambda \to \infty)$, if there exists a constant $M > 0$ such that $\left|\frac{\theta_\lambda}{\zeta_\lambda}\right| \leq M$ for large enough λ.

Definition 1 (Saturation of an approximation method) *A sequence of operators $\mathcal{U} = \{U_\lambda\}_{\lambda \in \mathbb{N}}$ in Ψ is called an approximation method in Ψ, if*

$$\lim_{\lambda \to \infty} \|U_\lambda(f) - f\|_\Psi = 0$$

for $f \in \Psi$. Let $\{\theta_\lambda\}_{\lambda \in \mathbb{N}}$ be a sequence of real numbers such that $\theta_\lambda \to 0$ as $\lambda \to \infty$. An approximation method $\mathcal{U}$ in Ψ is saturated with order θ_λ, if (S1) If $f \in \Psi$ and $\|U_\lambda(f) - f\|_\Psi = o(\theta_\lambda)$ $(\lambda \to \infty)$, then f is an identical element of $\mathcal{U}$, i.e., $U_\lambda(f) = f$ for $\lambda \in \mathbb{N}$ and (S2) The saturation class of $\mathcal{U}$ $S[\mathcal{U}] = \{ f \in \Psi \, ; \, \|U_\lambda(f) - f\|_\Psi = O(\theta_\lambda) \;\; (\lambda \to \infty)\}$ contains at least one element which is not an identical element of $\mathcal{U}$.

Theorem 4 (trigonometric case) *Approximation by $\mathcal{TN} = \left\{\mathbf{TN}^\lambda\right\}_{\lambda \in \mathbb{N}}$ in Theorem 1 is an approximation method saturated with order λ^{-2} in Ψ and its identical elements are just constant functions almost everywhere on $\mathbb{R}^m$. When $\Psi = C_{2\pi}(\mathbb{R}^m)$, the saturation class $S[\mathcal{TN}]$ is characterized as*

$$S[\mathcal{TN}] \supset \left\{ f \in \Psi \, ; \, \frac{\partial f}{\partial x_s} \in \text{Lip } 1, \; s = 1, \ldots, m \right\}$$

and, if $m = 1$, $S[\mathcal{TN}] = \left\{ f \in \Psi \, ; \, \frac{df}{dx} \in \text{Lip } 1 \right\}$.

Remark 2 (piecewise linear and sigmoidal cases) *Approximations by $\mathbf{PN}[\mathbf{f}]^{\lambda,\sigma}$ and $\mathbf{SN}[\mathbf{f}]^{\lambda,\sigma}$ in Theorems 2 and 3 are also saturated with order λ^{-2} in $L^p_{2\pi}(\mathbb{R}^m)$, if σ is large enough for λ. This is because, for any $\lambda \in \mathbb{N}$, $\mathbf{PN}[\mathbf{f}]^{\lambda,\sigma}$ and $\mathbf{SN}[\mathbf{f}]^{\lambda,\sigma}$ approach $\mathbf{TN}[\mathbf{f}]^\lambda$ as σ increases stated in Remark 1.*

3.3 Outline of the Proof

Multidimensional extension of approximation by the convolution operator and the multidimensional Fejér-Korovkin kernel, which are introduced in this study, provide a construction of an approximating network with trigonometric hidden-layer units, the approximation error estimation, and sturation of the approximation. Then, from the network and constructive approximation to multidimensional trigonometric functions by networks with piecewise linear and sigmoidal hidden-layer units, a constructions of approximating networks with piecewise linear and sigmoidal hidden-layer units, the approximation error estimations, and sturation of the approximations are derived.

4 Example

This is an example of an approximation to the function $\exp\left(-\left(x^2 + y^2\right)\right)$. Approximating networks are calculated at $\lambda = 2, 4, 6, 8, 10$ and $\sigma = 60$. The numbers of hidden-layer units are respectively 24, 80, 168, 288, 440 in the trigonometric case

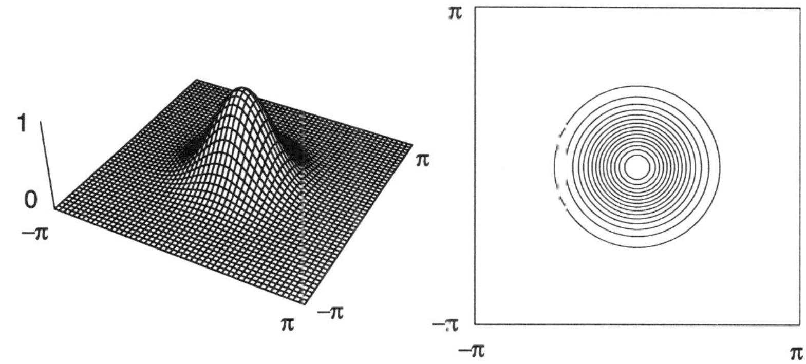

Figure 1 The approximated function.

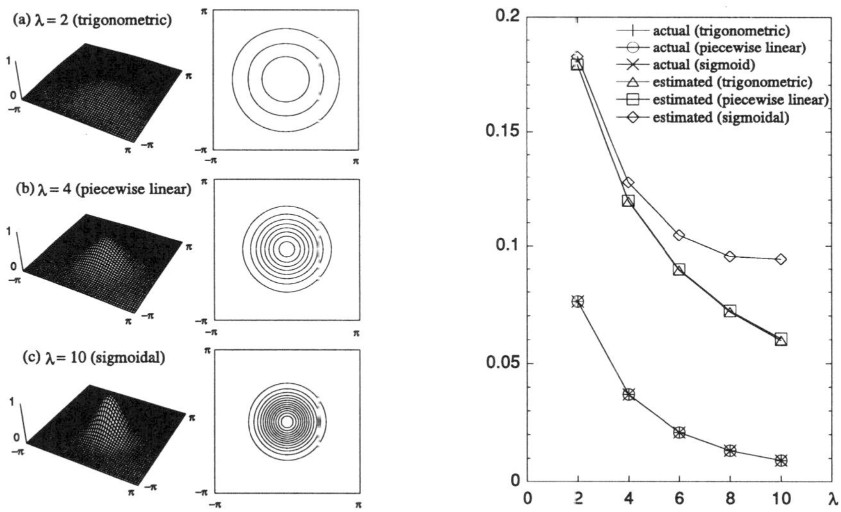

Figure 2 Approximating networks with three kinds of hidden layer units at $\sigma = 60$. (When λ is the same, the three kinds of networks have almost the same figures.)

and 7.2×10^3, 4.3×10^4, 1.3×10^5, 2.9×10^5, 5.5×10^5 in the piecewise linear and sigmoidal cases. The actual errors with $L^1_{2\pi}$-norm are numerically calculated from the left-hand members of Inequalities (2), (4), and (6), and the estimated errors are calculated from their left-hand members.

5 Conclusion

This paper presents constructive approximations by three-layer artificial neural networks with (1) trigonometric, (2) piecewise linear, and (3) sigmoidal hidden-layer units to 2π-periodic pth-order Lebesgue integrable functions defined on $\mathbb{R}^m$ to $\mathbb{R}^n$ for $p \geq 1$ with $L^p_{2\pi}$-norm. (In the case of (1), networks with trigonometric hidden-layer units can also approximate 2π-periodic continuous functions defined on $\mathrm{I\!R}^m$ to $\mathrm{I\!R}^n$ with $C_{2\pi}$-norm in the same time.) The approximations provide (a) approximating-network equations, (b) specifications for the numbers of hidden-layer units, (c) approximation error estimations, and (d) saturations of the approximations. These results can easily be applied to non-periodic functions defined on a bounded subset of $\mathrm{I\!R}^m$.

REFERENCES

[1] Cybenko, G., *Approximation by superpositions of sigmoidal function*, Mathematics of Control, Signals and System, Vol. 2(4) (1989), pp305–314.

[2] Hornik, K., *Approximation capabilities of multilayer feedforward networks*, Neural Networks, Vol. 4 (1991), pp251–257.

[3] Lorentz, George G., *Approximation of Functions*, Holt, Rinehart and Winston (1966).

[4] Davis, Philip J., *Interpolation and Approximation*, Dover (1975).

[5] Takenouchi, O. and Nishishiraho, T., *Kinji Riron (Approximation theory)*, in Japanese, Baifuukan (1986).

[6] DeVore, Roland A. and Lorentz, George G., *Constructive Approximation*, Springer-Verlag (1993).

[7] Suzuki, S., *Function Approximation by Three-Layer Artificial Neural Networks*, Proc. of 1993 Int. Symposium on Nonlinear Theory and its Applications, Vol. 4 (1993), pp1269–1272.

Acknowledgements

The author would like to thank Dr.Masaaki Honda, and other members of HONDA Research Group of Information Science Research Laboratory for many useful and helpful discussions.

NEURAL NETWORK VERSUS STATISTICAL CLUSTERING TECHNIQUES: A PILOT STUDY IN A PHONEME RECOGNITION TASK

G.Tambouratzis, T.Tambouratzis* and D.Tambouratzis

Dept. of Mathematics, Agricultural Univ.of Athens,
Iera Odos 75, Athens 118 55, Greece.
** Institute of Nuclear Technology - Radiation Protection,*
NRCPS "Demokritos", Aghia Paraskevi 153 10, Greece.

In this article, two neural network clustering techniques are compared to classical statistical techniques. This is achieved by examining the results obtained when applying each technique to a real-world phoneme recognition task. An analysis of the phoneme datasets exposes the clusters which exist in the pattern space. The study of the similarity of the patterns which are clustered together allows an objective evaluation of the clustering efficiency of these techniques. It also gives rise to a revealing comparison of the way each technique clusters the dataset.

1 Introduction

Clustering algorithms attempt to organise unclassified patterns into groups in such a way that patterns within each group are more similar than patterns belonging to different groups. In classical statistics, there exist a wide range of agglomerative and divisive clustering techniques [1], which use as distance measures either Euclidean-type distances or other metrics suitable for binary data. Recently, techniques based on neural networks have been developed and have been found well-suited to clustering large, high-dimensional pattern spaces. In this article, the clustering potential of two fundamentally different neural network models is studied and compared to that of statistical techniques. The network models are: (a) the Self-Organising Logic Neural Network (SOLNN) [2], which is based on the n-tuple sampling method and (b) the Harmony Theory Network (HTN) [3] which constitutes a derivative of the Hopfield network and a variant of the Boltzmann machine.
In an effort to evaluate the effectiveness of the two network models when discovering the clusters which exist in the pattern space, a comparison is made to a number of established statistical methods. This comparison is performed in a series of experiments which use real-world phoneme data. A number of phonemes is selected and used as prototypes. Various levels of noise are injected to the prototypes, resulting in different datasets, each consisting of well defined phoneme-classes. The varying levels of noise cause each dataset to have fundamentally different characteristics. The behaviour of the clustering techniques is then studied for each dataset.

2 Overview of the Clustering Techniques

The Self-Organising Logic Neural Network (SOLNN) shares the main structure of the discriminator network [4]. It is consequently based on the decomposition of the input pattern into tuples of n pixels and the comparison of these tuples to the corresponding tuples of training patterns. In the SOLNN model, the basic discriminator structure has been extended by allocating m bits to each tuple combination rather than a single one. This allows the network to store information concerning the frequency of occurrence of the corresponding tuple combination during learning and is instrumental to the SOLNN's ability to learn in the absence of external supervision. The SOLNN has been shown to successfully perform clustering tasks in an unsupervised manner [2,5]. The SOLNN model is characterised by the distribution constraint mechanism [5] which enables the user to determine the desired radius of the SOLNN clusters. This mechanism is similar to the vigilance parameter of Adaptive Resonance Theory (ART) [6].

The Harmony Theory Network (HTN) [3] consists of binary nodes arranged in exactly two layers. For this task, the lower layer encodes the features of the unclassified patterns and the upper layer encodes the candidate patterns of the clustering task. Each connection between a feature and a classified pattern specifies the positive or negative relation between them, i.e. whether or not the pattern contains the feature. No training is required to adapt the weights, which depend on the local connectivity of the HTN [3]. During clustering, each candidate pattern is input to the lower layer of the HTN; the activated nodes of the upper layer constitute the patterns to which the candidate pattern is clustered (also see [7] for a more detailed description). Both the required degree of similarity between clustered patterns and the desired number of clusters are monitored by the parameter k of Harmony Theory, which resembles the vigilance parameter of ART [6] and the radius of RBF (Radial-Basis Function) networks [8]. Its value is changed, in a uniform manner for all candidate patterns, in the search for optimal clustering results.

Hierarchical statistical clustering techniques [1] of the agglomerative type are used for clustering in this article. The techniques employed are (i) the single linkage, (ii) the complete linkage, (iii) the median cluster, (iv) the centroid cluster and (v) the average cluster.

3 Description of the Clustering Experiments

The data employed in the experiments are real-world phonemes which have been obtained from the dataset of the LVQ-PAK simulation package [9]. The phonemes in this package have been pre-processed so that each phoneme consists of 20 real-valued features. The selected phonemes (called prototypes) correspond to the letters "A", "O", "N", "I", "M", "U" and "S". Since both the SOLNN and the HTN networks require binary input patterns, the phonemes have been digitised, by encoding each real-valued feature into four bits via the thermometer-coding technique [10]. Consequently, the resulting prototypes are 80-dimensional binary patterns.

Each of the prototypes has been used to generate a number of noisy patterns by adding random noise of a certain level, namely 2.5, 5, 7.5 and 10%. A different dataset (experiment-dataset) is created for each level of noise. Every experiment-dataset consists of groups of noisy patterns whose centroids coincide with, or are situated very near to, the prototypes. The different levels of noise cause the experiment-datasets to occupy varying portions of the input space and the groups of noisy patterns to overlap to a different extent. The prototype and the noisy patterns for each level of noise constitute a phoneme class. An analysis of the phoneme classes in each experiment-dataset indicates that the patterns of each phoneme class are closer to other patterns of the same class than to patterns of other phoneme classes. As the noise level increases, each phoneme class occupies a larger portion of the pattern space and the distance between phonemes from different classes is reduced, while the probability of an overlap occurring between different classes in-

Phoneme Class	Average Distance within class	Minimum Distance within class	Maximum Distance within class	Minimum Distance between classes
A	16.11%	10.00%	20.00%	22.50% (A & O)
O	16.67%	10.00%	20.00%	22.50% (O & A)
N	16.22%	7.50%	20.00%	23.75% (N & O)
I	16.33%	10.00%	20.00%	20.00% (I & M)
M	16.22%	10.00%	20.00%	20.00% (M & I)
U	16.06%	10.00%	20.00%	23.75% (U & O)
S	16.22%	10.00%	20.00%	26.25% (S & I)

Table 1 Characteristics of the pattern space used for 10% noise level. Distances are calculated as percentages of the total number of pixels.

creases. The 10%-noise dataset is probably the most interesting one since, in that case, the minimum distance between two phonemes from different classes (more specifically classes "I" and "M") becomes equal to the maximum distance between patterns within any phoneme class. Due to this fact, it is expected to be the most difficult experiment-dataset to cluster successfully. Its characteristics are summarised in Table 1 to allow for a detailed evaluation of the clustering results.

The task consists of grouping the patterns of each experiment-dataset so that the phoneme classes are uncovered. The results obtained by each of the three clustering techniques are evaluated by taking into account the characteristics and topology of each experiment-dataset, i.e. the pixel-wise similarity between the patterns and the clusters in which they have been organised by each technique. This enables (i) a comparison of the way in which each technique operates for various data distributions and (ii) an evaluation of the effect that the relation between the maximum distance of patterns of the same phoneme class and the minimum distance of patterns of different phoneme classes has on clustering.

Additionally, a statistical analysis of the pattern space created by each experiment-dataset has been performed to investigate how effective the clustering techniques actually are. This investigation is based on the similarity between classes in the pattern space. The comparison of the two neural network techniques and the statistical methods, together with an in-depth analysis of the pattern space, provides an accurate insight to the capabilities and limitations of each of the techniques studied.

4 Experimental Results

The different clustering techniques are applied to the clustering task described in the previous paragraph. The results obtained are summarised in Table 2, where the following information is contained:

(i) the proportion of dataset phonemes that are correctly classified, that is of patterns assigned to a cluster representing their phoneme class;

(ii) the number of multi-phoneme clusters, that is clusters containing patterns from more than one phoneme class;

Noise Level	Criterion	SOLNN	HTN	Statistical
2.5%, 5%, 7.5%	Correct classification	100%	100%	100%
	Multi-phoneme clusters formed	0	0	0
	Phonemes in multi-phoneme cluster	1	1	1
	Number of created clusters	7	7	7
	Number of clusters per phoneme	1	1	1
10%	Correct classification	86%/100%	97%	100%
	Multi-phoneme clusters formed	4 / 0	1	0
	Phonemes in multi-phoneme cluster	4 / 1	2	1
	Number of created clusters	7 / 10	21	7
	Number of clusters per phoneme	4 / 2	4	1

Table 2 Comparative results of the three methods for the different noise levels. In the case of the SOLNN, for 10% noise, two sets of results are noted, the first corresponding to a 7-discriminator network and the second to a 10-discriminator network. In the case of statistical methods, the results are obtained using the Hamming distance metric.

(iii) the maximum number of phoneme classes contained in any multi-phoneme cluster;

(iv) the number of clusters created by each method;

(v) the maximum number of clusters to which patterns of any phoneme class are assigned.

As can be easily seen, the value of criterion (i) should ideally be equal to 100%, the value of criterion (ii) should be equal to 0, the value of criterion (iv) should be equal to 7, while the values of criteria (iii) and (v) should be equal to 1.

In the application of the SOLNN to the experiment-dataset, several network sizes ranging from 7 to 70 discriminators are simulated in order to investigate the effect of the network size on the SOLNN clustering performance. As has been shown [5], the SOLNN requires several iterations before settling to a clustering result, gradually separating each class. As the clustering task becomes more difficult, that is as the pattern classes become less clearly separated, the number of required iterations increases. For noise levels up to 7.5%, the SOLNN succeeds in separating all phoneme classes for all network sizes by creating a single group for each class. In the case of the 10% noise level, when the distance between the phoneme classes is considerably reduced, the SOLNN requires a larger number of iterations to settle to a clustering result. More specifically, the number of required iterations is of the order of 20, 50, 150 and 500 for noise levels of 2.5, 5, 7.5 and 10%, respectively. For high noise levels (10%), more than one cluster is generated for some phoneme classes. Misclassifications are occasionally observed, as some nodes have patterns assigned to them from more than one phoneme class. Such multi-phoneme clusters occur in particular when the number of nodes in the SOLNN is reduced. Characteristically, for a 10% level of noise, multi-phoneme clusters occur for a 7-node but not for a 10-node network. The formation of multi-phoneme clusters for the 7-node SOLNN (see

Table 2) is due to the fact that the network uses two nodes for the "U"-phoneme class, and is thus unable to form a cluster dedicated exclusively to the "O"-phoneme class. It is worth noting that multi-phoneme clusters consist of phonemes which have a relatively high degree of similarity. It has been reported [5] that for the optimal clustering to be achieved there need to be more nodes in the network than there are classes in the dataset. Indeed, this is confirmed by the results obtained with the 10-node SOLNN. Still, even for the 7-node system, the SOLNN succeeds in consistently clustering the majority of patterns in single-phoneme clusters.
For the HTN, each test pattern is input into the lower layer of the HTN. In contrast to the SOLNN, a single pass of activation-flow from the lower to the upper layer, at a pre-specified k value, reveals the patterns to which the test pattern becomes clustered. Optimum clustering with a HTN requires finding one (or more) value of k for which each test pattern becomes clustered with all the nodes of the upper layer representing patterns of the same phoneme class but with no nodes representing patterns of different phoneme classes. This has been established for noise levels up to 7.5% for k values around 0.650. The range of k values which result in the optimum clustering becomes narrower as the noise level increases. This can be explained by the fact that as the noise level rises (i) lower k values are required for grouping patterns of the same phoneme class, while at the same time, (ii) higher k values are required for patterns of different phoneme classes not to be grouped together. When the noise level reaches 10%, no value of k generating the optimum clustering can be found; some dataset patterns fail to be clustered with all the nodes of the upper layer representing patterns the same phoneme class, while they are clustered with nodes representing patterns of other phoneme classes. It is possible, however, to achieve a sub-optimum clustering by raising the value of k, whereas the problem of multi-phoneme clusters is avoided at the expense of multiple clusters for each phoneme class. As shown in Table 2, the sub-optimum clustering performed by the HTN for the 10% noise level is due to the network grouping together an "I" with an "M", which are the two phoneme patterns from different classes with the minimum distance. Due to the fact that this distance is equal to the maximum distance within any class (see Table 1), the structure of the pattern space justifies the sub-optimal clustering produced by the HTN.
For the statistical analysis, the five agglomerative clustering techniques mentioned in Section 2 have been used to cluster all patterns in the minimum possible number of groups, while avoiding the creation of any multi-phoneme clusters. Both the Hamming distance and the Euclidean distance were considered as distance measures. In the case of the Hamming distance in the 80-dimensional space, which in the case of binary patterns is equal to the square of the Euclidean distance, the seven phoneme classes are consistently separated by all statistical methods. When using the Euclidean distance metric, the seven phoneme classes are separated by all statistical methods for all noise levels except for the hierarchical average cluster method for the 10%-noise level dataset. In this case, for seven clusters, the phonemes "A", "O", "M" and "U" are grouped together, "N" and "S" form an independent cluster each, whilst "I" is split into four clusters. The minimum number of clusters, in order to avoid multi-phoneme clusters, is fourteen.

5 Conclusions

Both the neural network (SOLNN and HTN) and the statistical techniques have been found to perform the selected clustering task satisfactorily. For low noise levels, all techniques cluster the dataset successfully, by forming exclusively single-phoneme clusters. For higher noise levels, the statistical methods always generate the optimum clustering according to the Hamming distance metric, as witnessed by the study of the dataset structure. The quality of the clustering generated by the two neural network models is slightly inferior to that of the statistical techniques. This is indicated by the creation of multiple clusters for a few phoneme classes. However, the vast majority of clusters consist of patterns from a single phoneme class (see Table 2), thus producing successful clustering.

It is worth noting that the study of the Hamming distances between the different phoneme patterns in the dataset indicates that the clustering behaviour of all three techniques is justified. In particular, for the noise level of 10% when the most differences between the clustering results of the three methods are detected, the minimum distance between the phoneme classes is equal to the maximum distance between phonemes of the same class. This allows for more than one possible clustering results of almost the same quality.

REFERENCES

[1] Kaufman, L., Rousseeuw, P.J., *Finding Groups in Data*, Wiley, New York (1990).

[2] Tambouratzis, G., Tambouratzis, D., *Self-Organisation in Complex Pattern Spaces Using a Logic Neural Network*, Network: Computation in Neural Systems, Vol. 5 (1994), pp599–617.

[3] Smolensky, P., *Information processing in dynamical systems: foundations of Harmony Theory*, in: Rumelhart, D.E., McClelland, J.L. (eds.) Parallel Distributed Processing, Vol.1: Foundations, MIT Press, Cambridge MA. (1986), pp194–281.

[4] Aleksander, I., Morton, H., *An Introduction to Neural Computing*, Chapman and Hall, London, England (1990).

[5] Tambouratzis, G., *Optimising the Topology-Preservation Characteristics of a Discriminator-Based Logic Neural Network*, Pattern Recognition Letters, Vol. 15 (1994), pp1019–1028.

[6] Carpenter, G.A., Grossberg, S., *The ART of Adaptive Pattern Recognition by a Self-Organising Neural Network*, IEEE Computer (March 1988), pp77–88.

[7] Tambouratzis, T., Tambouratzis, D., *Optimal Training Pattern Selection Using a Cluster-Generating Artificial Neural Network*, in: Proceedings of the 1995 International Conference on Artificial Neural Networks and Genetic Algorithms, Mines d' Ales, France (April 1995), Springer-Verlag, pp472–475.

[8] Chen, S., Cowan, C.F.N., Grant, P.M., *Orthogonal Least Squares Learning Algorithm for Radial Basis Function Networks*, IEEE Transactions on Neural Networks, Vol. 2 (1991), pp302–309.

[9] Kohonen, T., Kangas, J., Laaksonen, J., Torkkola, K., *LVQ_PAK: The Learning Vector Quantisation Program Package*, (1992).

[10] Aleksander, I., Stonham, T.J., *Guide to Pattern Recognition using Random-Access Memories*, Computers and Digital Techniques, Vol. 2 (1979), pp29–40.

MULTISPECTRAL IMAGE ANALYSIS USING PULSED COUPLED NEURAL NETWORKS

Gregory L. Tarr, Xavier Clastres*, Laurent Freyss*, Manuel Samuelides*, Christopher Dehainaut and William Burckel

Phillips Laboratory, Kirtland Air Force Base Albuquerque, New Mexico, USA.

** Centre d'Etudes and Recherche de Toulouse, Toulouse, France.*

Pulsed oscillatory neural networks are examined for application to analysis and segmentation of multispectral imagery from the Satelite Pour l'Observation de la Terre (SPOT). These networks demonstrate a capacity to segment images with better performance against many of the resolution uncertainty effects caused by local area adaptive filtering. To enhance synchronous behavior, a reset mechanism is added in the model. Previous work suggests that a reset activation pulse is generated by sacatic motor commands. Consequently, an algorithm is developed, which behaves similar to adaptive histogram techniques. These techniques appear both biologically plausible and more effective than conventional techniques. Using the pulse time-of-arrival as the information carrier, the image is reduced to a time signal which allows an intelligent filtering using feedback.

1 Introduction

Histogram image analysis may play an important role in biological vision image processing. Structures of artificial neurons can be used to create histogram like signals quickly. In this paper, we will examine how algorithms based on fast histogram processing may offer advantages for computer vision systems.

In a biological vision system, the signals detected at the retina are passed to the LGN then to the Visual Cortex, where neighborhood preserving maps of the retina are repeated at least 15 times over the surface of the cortex. For every path forward, there are several neurological pathways in the reverse direction. Reverse direction transmission of information suggest feedback signals. Using appropiate feedback, the image processing can be controlled using recurrence. Pulses generated by dynamic neuronal models suggest a method for building recurrance into vision models.

1.1 Dynamic Neural Networks

Dynamic neural networks, first examined by Stephen Grossberg, Maas and others [3] were an attempt to construct models closer to their biological counterpart. In this model, the basic computational unit is not the usual static matrix multiplier with a non-linear transfer function between layers, but a leaky integrator with a pulsed oscillatory output. This work is sometimes refereed to as *Integrate and Fire Networks.*

To understand the role of synchrony in the cat visual cortex, Eckhorn devised a model which would replicate some of this behavior. The Eckhorn [1] dynamic model represents a visual neuron as a multi-input element with a single output. The output is made up of oscillatory electrical pulses in time. Three types of connections make up the input section: the feeding, the linking and the direct inputs. The direct input provides pixel information. The feeding inputs provide local information in the region of the direct inputs. The combination of the direct and feeding input provide texture information in a local region around the direct input. The linking field provides a global connection for all sub-regions in the image. The linking

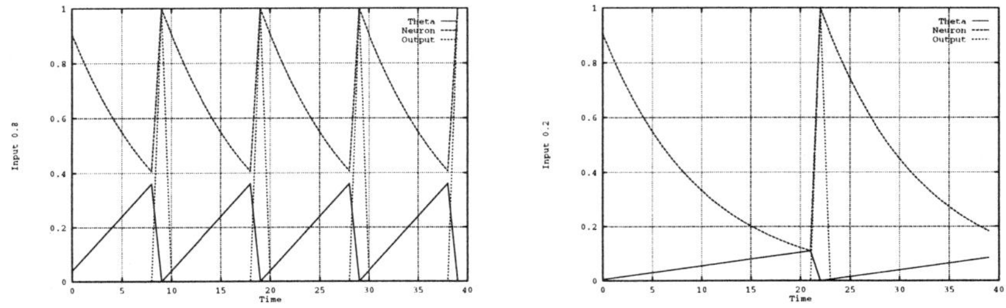

Figure 1 Behavior of a clean and noisy signal.

connections enforce synchrony between local regions. The information is extracted using correlation techniques.

Given these characteristics, several image processing functions are possible. In this paper we will explore only one, usually the most difficult: segmentation. If information in a particular part of the image is similar to information in another part of the image, they should have the same pulse repetition frequency as the feeding field, and the same phase after the linking fields. This information can easily be extracted using correlation filters.

For a single neuron, $U_j(t)$ is given by:

$$U_j(t) = (1 + \beta L_j(t))X_j(t) \tag{1}$$

$X_j(t)$, are the direct inputs to a neuron, $L_j(t)$ is the contribution from nearby neurons weighted by β the link coefficients. The spiking output, Y_j, is provided by a step function of a time dependent threshold $\theta_j(t)$ and the neuronal activity according to

$$Y_j = step[U_j(t) - \theta_j(t)] \tag{2}$$

$\theta_j(t)$ and $L_j(t)$ can have different decay constants α_θ and α_L. The dynamics of the linking field and threshold are given by

$$L_j(t) = \sum_k w_{k_j} e^{-t/\alpha_L} \cdot Y_k(t), \theta_j(t) = \theta_{max} e^{-(t-t_j)/\alpha_\theta} \tag{3}$$

where w_{k_j} is the connection weighting for the local field neurons. Sufficient neural activity combined with a decaying threshold lead to a spike output which resets the threshold to the maximum from which it decays again.

Built into this neuronal model are a number of characteristics common to biological vision: integrate and fire, latency and lateral interconnectivity. Figure 1 provides a means to visualize the firing behavior of a one dimensional signal in time. In the first graph, the input to the system is 0.8. The energy is integrated and plotted. The threshold, a decaying exponential relaxes from its initial maximum. This ensures a minimum pulse rate and a refractory period. When the two are equal, the neuron fires and both θ, the threshold, and $U_j(t)$ the neuron potential are reset. In the second graph, a lower energy input is used, which is characterized by a slower firing rate.

For large clusters of neurons, the group behavior can be characterized by the total firing rates over time. A signal based on the total number of neurons firing at a specific time could be used as a control signal for modification of the structure and appearance of the image. This is the basis for using pulse coupled neural networks to segment images.

In the following graphs, only the firing patterns are shown. A one dimensional signal is used to demonstrate the temporal encoding nature of the output signal. The first image, without using coupling between neurons shows, how the pulse frequency rate is related to the input strength.

In the second figure, coupling is added between adjacent neurons. The effect is to cluster neurons into separate time bins. By evaluating the behavior of the temporal signal, processing is performed on the actual image.

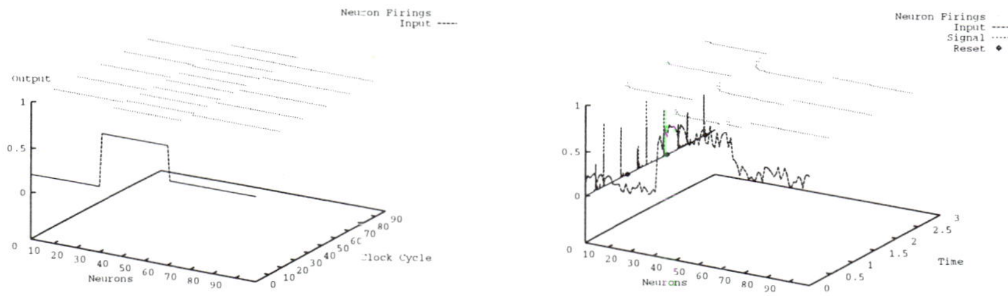

Figure 2

2 Pulse Coupled Neurons for Adaptive Histogram Analysis of Imagery

Most dynamic models of neural computation suggest that synchronization between regions is the primary information carrier. But if time of arrival is used as the information carrier, it demonstrates that mechanisms exist in the cellural architectures to perform histogram analysis and adaptive histogram analysis of images.

The following 32x32 image chips are taken for the SPOT satellite imagery and represent common problems in image segmentation.

Several variations of edge detection are currently used on these type of images, the most common being the Sobel and Canny operators. The difficulty lies in that the size of the window used for the operator affects the size of the detectable gradients, and the width of the edge. An improvement on the Sobel operator is the Canny edge detector, which effectively finds the center of the gradient and places an edge there. Its weakness, as with most convolution filter segmentation methods, is that overall resolution is usually reduced to the size of the filter window. This effect results in rounded and wide edges. In low resolution systems like SPOT, this loss of resolution is often unacceptable.

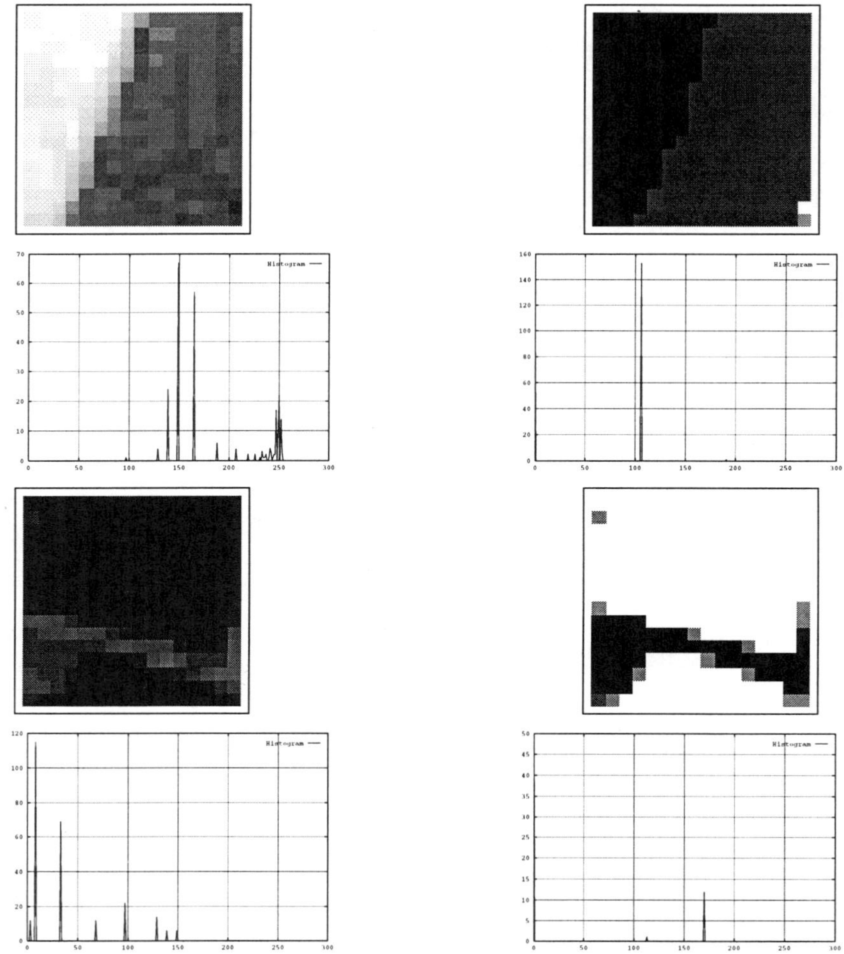

Figure 3

An important advantage of the pulsed coupled methods is that segmentation is possible for objects smaller than the window size. In the above image a road is detected having a width less than two pixels wide in some places. General threshold settings for the previous problem are not compatible with detection of features in the second image.

The adaptive nature of the algorithm allows pulses in the histogram to represent whole regions in the segmented image. The signal can be used to modify the image on the next cycle.

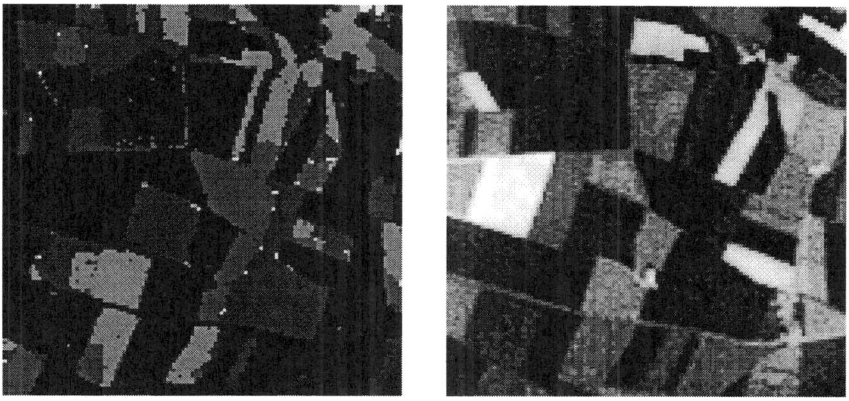

Figure 4

This image was segmented as part of a larger project to perform terrain categorization using a linear approximation to the Eckhorn model developed by Freyss. For a relatively complex image such as this, most of the common techniques perform relatively poorly. The advantage with this new technique is that there are almost no parameters to be set and no buried decisions being made by the operator.

3 Conclusions and Future Work

The model we developed demonstrates effective image segmentation over a wide variety of image class types. Although many of the results demonstrated here could be duplicated using standard techniques, these methods offer a simple modular approach to the image analysis, and are easily implemented in silicon devices.

Our work suggests that the group behavior of clusters of neurons provides a technique which encodes images into one dimensional signals in time. Using the temporal encoded group output as a control signal will add a large measure of robustness to a visual system.

An important aspect of this work is the new approach to image processing; that is expectation filtering for particular characteristics with feedback to enhance desired qualities in the signal. Donaho's [2] work on histogram equalization approximation for manufacturing processes could easily be implemented using this architecture.

REFERENCES

[1] R. Eckhorn H. Reitboeck M. Arndt P. Dicke, *Feature linking via synchronization among distributed assemblies simulations of results from cat visual cortex*, Neural Computation, Vol. 1(2) (1990), pp293-307.

[2] G.W. Donohoe and C. Jeong, *A combined analog-digital technique for normalizing video signals for the detection of moving objects*, in: Proceedings of the International Conference on Acoustics, Speech and Signal Processing (March 23-26).

[3] Stephen Grossberg, *Nonlinear neural networks: Principles, mechanisms, and architectures*, Neural Networks, Vol. 1 (1988), pp17–61.

REASONING NEURAL NETWORKS

Rua-Huan R. Tsaih

Department of Management Information Systems, National Chengchi University, Taipei, Taiwan, ROC.

The Reasoning Neural Network (RN) has a learning algorithm belonging to the weight-and-structure-change category, because it puts only one hidden node in the initial network structure, and will recruit and prune hidden nodes during the learning process. Empirical results show that learning of the RN is guaranteed to be completed, the number of required hidden nodes is reasonable, that the speed of learning is much faster than back propagation networks, and that the RN is able to develop good internal representation.

1 Introduction

Intuitively, human learning consists of cramming and reasoning at a high level of abstraction [5]. This observation has suggested a learning algorithm as shown in Figure 1. This learning algorithm belongs to the weight-and-structure-change category, because it puts only one hidden node initially, and will recruit and prune hidden nodes during the learning process. Our learning algorithm guarantees to achieve perfectly the goal of learning. There are some similar learning algorithms; however, most of them have more complex pruning strategies. [7, 4, 1, 2].

2 The RN's Network Architecture

The RN adopts the layered feedforward network structure. Let's suppose that the network has three layers with m input nodes at the bottom, p hidden nodes, and q output nodes at the top. Let $\mathbf{B}_c \in \{-1, 1\}^m$ be the cth given stimulus input, b_{cj} the stimulus value received in the jth input node when $\mathbf{B}_c$ is presented to the network, w_{ij} the weight of the connection between the jth input node and the ith hidden node, θ_i the negative of the threshold value of the ith hidden node, $\mathbf{w}_i \equiv (w_{i1}, w_{i2}, ..., w_{im})^t$ the vector of weights of the connections between all input nodes and the ith hidden node, where the superscript t indicates the transposition, $\mathbf{X}_i^t \equiv (\theta_i, \mathbf{w}_i^t)$, and $\mathbf{X}^t \equiv (\mathbf{X}_1^t, \mathbf{X}_2^t, ..., \mathbf{X}_p^t)$. Then, given the stimulus $\mathbf{B}_c$, the activation value of the ith hidden node is computed:

$$h(\mathbf{B}_c, \mathbf{X}_i) \equiv \tanh(\theta_i + \sum_{j=1}^{m} w_{ij} b_{cj}).$$

Let $\mathbf{h}(\mathbf{B}_c, \mathbf{X}) \equiv (h(\mathbf{B}_c, \mathbf{X}_1), h(\mathbf{B}_c, \mathbf{X}_2), \ldots, h(\mathbf{B}_c, \mathbf{X}_p))^t$ be the activation value vector of all hidden nodes when $\mathbf{B}_c$ is presented to the network, r_{li} the weight of the connection between the ith hidden node and the lth output node, $\mathbf{r}_l \equiv (r_{l1}, r_{l2}, ..., r_{lp})^t$ the vector of weights of the connections between all hidden nodes and the lth output node, s_l the negative of the threshold value of the lth output node, $\mathbf{Y}_l^t \equiv (s_l, \mathbf{r}_l^t)$, $\mathbf{Y}^t \equiv (\mathbf{Y}_1^t, \mathbf{Y}_2^t, ..., \mathbf{Y}_q^t)$, and $\mathbf{Z}^t \equiv (\mathbf{Y}^t, \mathbf{X}^t)$. The activation value of the lth output node is computed after $\mathbf{h}(\mathbf{B}_c, \mathbf{X})$:

$$O(\mathbf{B}_c, \mathbf{Y}_l, \mathbf{X}) \equiv \tanh(s_l + \sum_{i=1}^{p} r_{li} h(\mathbf{B}_c, \mathbf{X}_i)).$$

3 The Learning Algorithm

The block diagram of the learning algorithm is shown in Figure 1. There are four distinguished aspects of this learning algorithm: the linearly separating condition

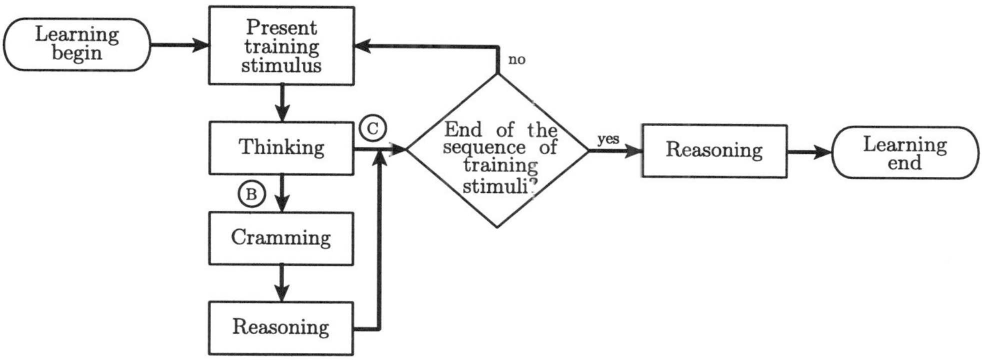

Figure 1 The block diagram of the learning algorithm. The details of the thinking box, the reasoning box and the cramming box are shown in Figure 2 and Figure 3.

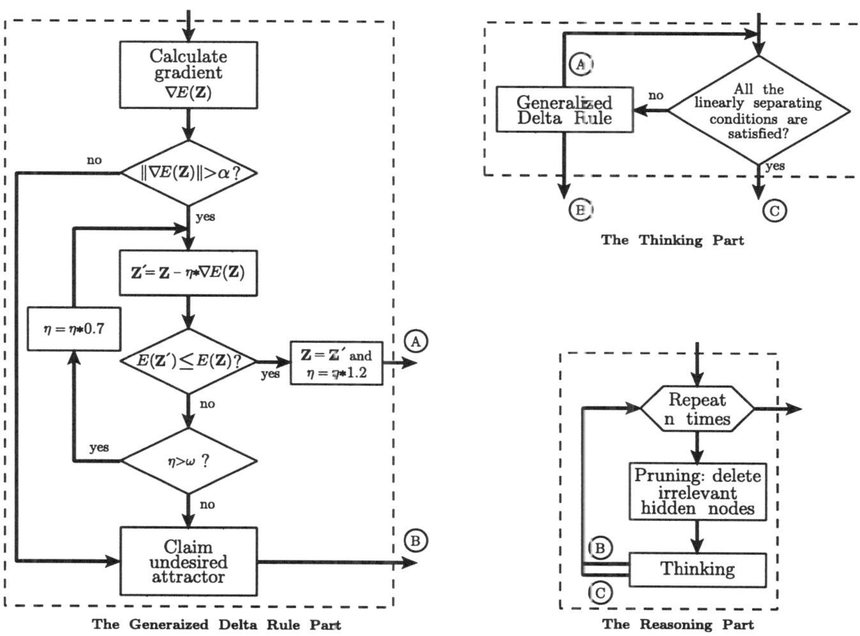

Figure 2 The Generalised Delta Rule part, the thinking part and the reasoning part. The values of given constants α and ω in the Generalised Delta Rule part are tiny.

(LSC), the thinking mechanism, the cramming mechanism; and the reasoning mechanism. These aspects are explained in the following.

With respect to each output node, the network is used as a classifier which learns to distinguish if the stimulus is a member of one class of stimuli, called class 1, or

$p+1 \to p$, then adds the new P^{th} hidden node with $\mathbf{w}_p = \mathbf{B}_k, \theta_p = 1 - m$, and $r_{lp} = 0$ for every $l \in L$, and, for every $l \notin L$

$$r_{lp} = \begin{cases} \max_{v \in K_{l2}(k-1)} \sum_{i=1}^{p-1} r_{li} h(\mathbf{B}_v, \mathbf{X}_i) - \sum_{i=1}^{p-1} r_{li} h(\mathbf{B}_k, \mathbf{X}_i) \text{ if } d_{kl} = 1.0 \\ \min_{u \in K_{l1}(k-1)} \sum_{i=1}^{p-1} r_{li} h(\mathbf{B}_u, \mathbf{X}_i) - \sum_{i=1}^{p-1} r_{li} h(\mathbf{B}_k, \mathbf{X}_i) \text{ if } d_{kl} = -1.0 \end{cases}$$

Figure 3 The Cramming part. Suppose that $l \in L$ if, before implementing the cramming mechanism, the LSC with respect to the lth output node is satisfied.

of a different class, called class 2, by being presented with exemplars of each class. With respect to the lth output node, let $K \equiv K_{l1} \cup K_{l2}$, where K_{l1} and K_{l2} are the sets of indices of all given training stimuli in classes 1 and 2, respectively; and let d_{cl} be the desired output value of the lth output node of the cth stimulus, with 1.0 and -1.0 being respectively the desired output values of classes 1 and 2. Learning seeks Z where, for all l,

$$d_{cl} O(\mathbf{B}_c, \mathbf{Y}_l, \mathbf{X}) \geq v \qquad \forall c \in K \tag{1}$$

and $0 < v < 1$. With respect to the lth output node, let the LSC be that

$$\min_{c \in K_{l1}} O(\mathbf{B}_c, \mathbf{Y}_l, \mathbf{X}) > \max_{c \in K_{l2}} O(\mathbf{B}_c, \mathbf{Y}_l, \mathbf{X}).$$

When the LSC with respect to the lth output node is satisfied, the requirement (1) with respect to the lth output node could be achieved by merely adjusting $\mathbf{Y}_l$ [5]. At the learning stage, the training stimuli are presented one by one. At the kth given stimulus, the objective function is defined as:

$$E(\mathbf{Z}) \equiv \sum_{c=1}^{k} \sum_{l=1}^{q} (O(\mathbf{B}_c, \mathbf{Y}_l, \mathbf{X}) - d_{cl})^2$$

and let $K(k) \equiv \{1, ..., k\}$ and $K(k) \equiv K_{l1}(k) \cup K_{l2}(k)$, where $K_{l1}(k)$ and $K_{l2}(k)$ are, respectively, the sets of indices of the first k training stimuli in classes 1 and 2, with respect to the lth output node. Then the thinking mechanism is implemented, in which the momentum version of the generalized delta rule (with automatic adjustment of learning rate) is adopted. Learning might converge to the bottom of a very shallow steep-sided valley [3], where the magnitude of the gradient will be tiny and the consecutive adaptive learning rates will also be tiny. Therefore, as shown in the generalized delta rule part of Figure 2, these two criteria are adopted to detect if the learning hits the neighborhood of an undesired attractor.

The desired solution is not required to render the requirement (1) satisfied or to be a stationary point in which $\nabla_z E(\mathbf{Z}) = 0$. Thus, the magnitude of $\|\nabla_z E(\mathbf{Z})\|$ before hitting the desired solution is not necessarily tiny and the learning time is rather less, compared with conventional stopping criteria (for example, small $E(\mathbf{Z})$ or $\|\nabla_z E(\mathbf{Z})\| = 0$).

The thinking mechanism does not guarantee that the LSC with respect to all output nodes will be satisfied. Two ideas could render the learning capable of escaping from the undesired attractor: add a hidden node and alter the objective function.

By adding a hidden node, the dimension of the weight space is increased; while altering the objective function will change its function surface on the weight space such that the trapped attractor could be no more an attractor. These two ideas are implemented in our learning algorithm via the cramming mechanism and that the objective function is altered by introducing a new training stimulus.

The cramming mechanism can be viewed as that, at first a new hidden node with the near threshold activation function is added, then the softening mechanism of [6] is used immediately to render the activation function of the new hidden node a tanh one. The Lemma in [6] shows that the mechanism of adding a new hidden node with the near threshold activation function and a finite value of the gain parameter can immediately render the LSC with respect to all output nodes satisfied, if the training set has no internal conflicts (different outputs for the same input).

However the number of required hidden nodes may be too many and the generalization ability of the network may be bad. Thus it is necessary to adopt the reasoning mechanism for the purpose of rendering the network more compact. The reasoning mechanism includes the thinking mechanism and the pruning mechanism of removing irrelevant hidden nodes. In a $\mathbf{Z}$, the ith hidden node is said to be irrelevant to the LSC with respect to the lth output node if the LSC is still satisfied with the same $\mathbf{Z}$ except $r_{li} = 0$; and a hidden node is irrelevant if it is irrelevant to the LSC with respect to all output nodes [5].

4 The Performance of the RN

We report three experiments. In each simulation, there are 100 testing cases, each with different input sequence of training stimuli. One experiment is the m-bits parity learning problem. In Figure 4a, the numbers of used hidden nodes during the 6-bits parity learning process are plotted. The variance of p is due to the different input sequence of training stimuli. Figure 4b shows the summary of the simulation results, and it shows that the average value p of the m-bits parity problems is merely a little bigger than m. However, it is surprising to see that the RN can solve the m-bits parity problems with less than m hidden nodes.

The output/hidden experiment is used to identify the relationship between the number of required hidden nodes and the number of used output nodes. The number of input nodes is fixed to be 8. The training stimuli and their input sequence are randomized; but the number of used output nodes is varied from 1 to 6. In Figure 4c, the simulation result of the "$m = 8$, $q = 3$, and $K = 100$" problem are plotted. Figure 4d shows the summary of the simulation results, and it shows that the relationship between the average value p of the RN and the value of q is rather a linear one.

One significant phenomenon of above simulations is that the value of q influences the value of p more significantly than the values of K and m do. Another interesting phenomenon is that if there is no correlation within current given training stimuli, the RN tends to cram them (in other words, memorize them individually) by using many more hidden nodes. But when there are correlation within the current given training stimuli, it seems that the RN will figure out a smart way to classify the given training stimuli by using less hidden nodes. In other words, the RN has the ability of developing a good internal representation for the given training stimuli.

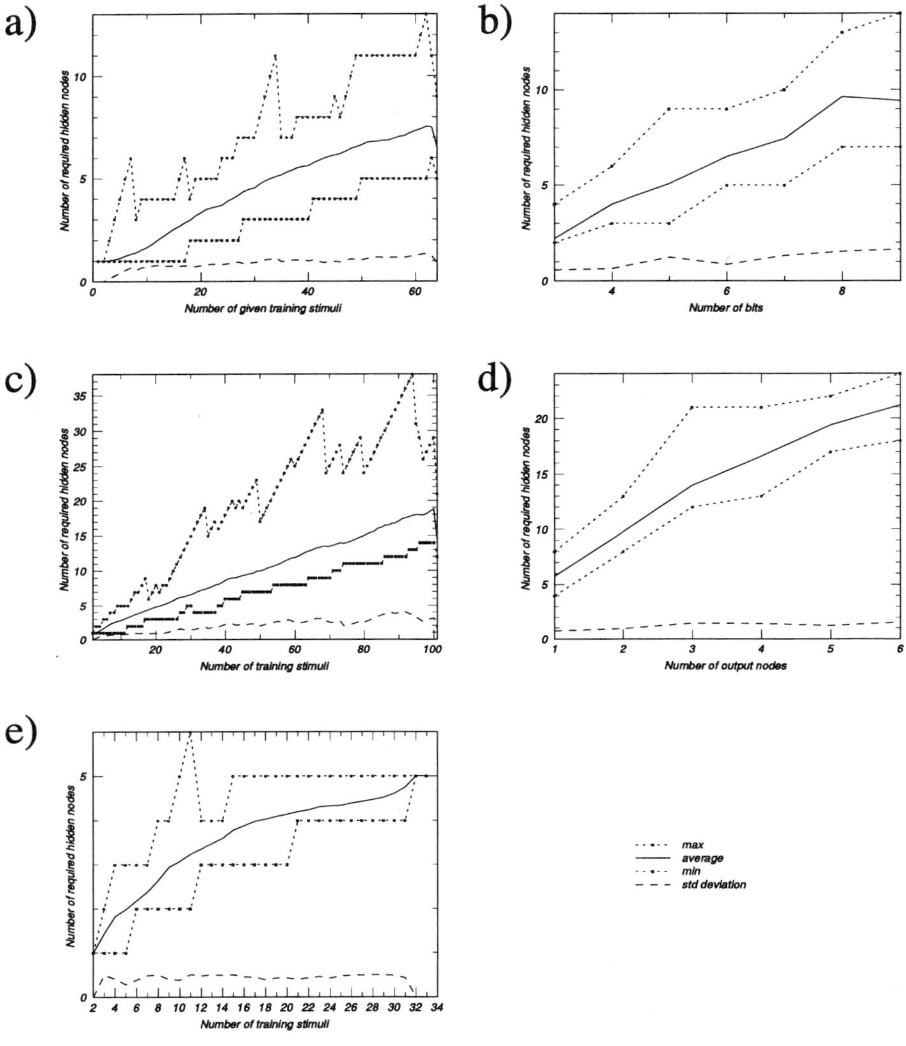

Figure 4 a) The simulation result of the 6-bits parity problem. b) The summary of simulation results of the m-bits parity problem. c) The simulation result of the "$m = 8$, $q = 3$, and $K = 100$" problem. d) The summary of simulation results of the output/hidden problems. e) The simulation result of the 5-p-5 problem.

The third experiment is the 5-p-5 problem (Figure 4e)), in which the training stimuli are the same as those of the 5-bits parity problem and the desired output vector is the same as the stimulus input vector. Somewhat surprisingly, as shown in Figure 5, each hidden node of one final RN has only one strong connection strength from input nodes, and each output node has only one strong connection strength from

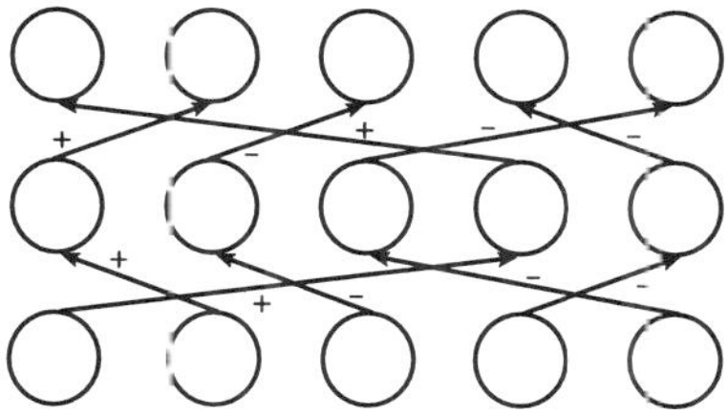

Figure 5 One final RNN of the 5-p-5 encoder problem, where we show only the connections with weights of large magnitude, and the signs of their weights. Note that the signs of two connected strongest connections are the same.

hidden nodes. In addition, different hidden nodes have strongest connections from different input nodes, different output nodes have strongest connections from a different hidden node, and the signs of connected strongest connections are the same. It seems that, after learning the full set of training stimuli, the RN had learned to use the hidden nodes to bypass the input stimulus, rather than to encode them.

5 Discussions and Future work

The empirical results show that the learning of the RN is much faster than the back propagation learning algorithm, and that the RN is able to develop good internal representation with good generalization. The RN has flexibility in its learning algorithm; different algorithms have been obtained by integrating the prime mechanisms in different way. These yield different simulation results: it seems that we should use different management in the RN for different application problems.

REFERENCES

[1] Fahlman, S. & C. Lebiere, *The Cascade-Correlation Learning Architecture*, in: Touretzky, D. (eds), Advances in Neural Information Processing Systems II, Denver (1989), San Mateo, Morgan Kaufmann.

[2] Frean, M., *The Upstart Algorithm: A Method for Constructing and Training Feedforward Neural Networks*, Neural Computation Vol. 2 (1990), pp198–209.

[3] McInerny, J., K. Hainer, S. Biafore, & R. Hecht-Nielsen,. *Back Propagation Error Surfaces Can Have Local Minima*, Proceedings of the International Joint Conference on Neural Networks (1989), Vol II, p627.

[4] Mézard, M & J. Nadal, *Learning in Feedforward Layered Networks: The Tiling Algorithm*, Journal of Physics Vol. A 22 (1989), pp2191–2204.

[5] Tsaih, R., *The Softening Learning Procedure*, Mathematical and Computer Modelling, Vol. 18 (1993), No. 8, pp61–64.

[6] Tsaih, R., *The Softening Learning Procedure for The Networks With Multiple Output Nodes*, MIS Review, Vol. 4 (1994), pp89–93, Taipei.

[7] Watanabe, E., & H. Shimizu, *Algorithm for Pruning Hidden nodes in Multi-Layered Neural Network for Binary Pattern Classification Problem*, Proceedings of the International Joint Conference on Neural Networks (1993), Vol I, pp327–330.

CAPACITY OF THE UPSTART ALGORITHM

Ansgar H. L. West* and David Saad
Neural Computing Research Group, Aston University, Aston Triangle, Birmingham B4 7ET, UK.
Email: A.H.L.West@aston.ac.uk, D.Saad@aston.ac.uk
** Also affiliated to: Department of Physics, University of Edinburgh, Mayfield Road, Edinburgh, EH9 3JZ, UK.*

The storage capacity of multilayer networks with overlapping receptive fields is investigated for a constructive algorithm within a one-step replica symmetry breaking (RSB) treatment. We find that the storage capacity increases logarithmically with the number of hidden units K without saturating the Mitchison-Durbin bound. The slope of the logarithmic increase decays exponentionally with the stability with which the patterns have been stored.

1 Introduction

Since the ground breaking work of Gardner [1] on the storage capacity of the perceptron, the replica technique of statistical mechanics has been successfully used to investigate many aspects of the performance of simple neural network models. However, progress for multilayer feedforward networks has been hampered by the inherent difficulties of the replica calculation. This is especially true for capacity calculations, where replica symmetric (RS) treatments [2] violate the upper Mitchison-Durbin bound [3] derived by information theory. Other efforts [4] break the symmetry of the hidden units explicitly prior to the actual calculation, but the resulting equations are approximations and difficult to solve for large networks. This paper avoids these problems by addressing the capacity of a class of networks with variable architecture produced by a constructive algorithm. In this case, results derived for simple binary perceptrons above their saturation limit [5] can be applied iteratively to yield the storage capacity of two-layer networks.

Constructive algorithms (e.g., [6, 8]) are based on the idea that in general it is *a priori* unknown how large a network must be to perform a certain classification task. It seems appealing therefore to start off with a simple network, e.g., a binary perceptron, and to increase its complexity only when needed. This procedure has the added advantage that the training time of the whole network is relatively short, since each training step consists of training the newly added hidden units only, whereas previously constructed weights are kept fixed. Although constructive algorithm seem therefore rather appealing, their properties are not well understood. The aim of this paper is to analyse the performance of one constructive algorithm, the upstart algorithm [8], in learning random dichotomies, usually referred to as the capacity problem.

The basic idea of the upstart algorithm is to start with a binary perceptron unit with possible outputs {1,0}. Further units are created only if the initial perceptron makes any errors on the training set. One unit may have to be created to correct WRONGLY ON errors (where the target was 0 but the actual output is 1) another to correct WRONGLY OFF errors (where the target was 1 but the output is 0). If these units still cause errors in the output of the network, more units are created in the next generation of the algorithm until all outputs are correct. Different versions of the upstart algorithm differ in the way new units are connected to the old units and to the output unit. The original upstart algorithm produces a hierarchical network where the number of hidden units tends to increase exponentionally with each generation. Other versions of the upstart algorithm[8] build a two-layer architecture and show only a linear increase of the number of units with each generation, which is in general easier to implement.

We have therefore analysed a non-hierarchical version of the upstart algorithm. Within a one-step replica symmetry breaking (RSB) treatment [9], networks constructed by the upstart algorithm show a logarithmic increase of the capacity with the number of nodes in agreement with the Mitchison-Durbin bound

$$(\alpha_c \propto \ln K / \ln 2)$$

, whereas the simpler RS treatment violates this bound. Furthermore, the algorithm does not saturate the Mitchison-Durbin bound for zero stability. We further find that the slope of the logarithmic increase of the capacity against network size decreases exponentionally with the stability.

2 Model Description and Framework

2.1 Definition of the Upstart Algorithm

The upstart algorithm first creates a binary perceptron (or unit) $\mathcal{D}_0$ which learns a synaptic weight vector $\boldsymbol{W} \in \mathrm{IR}^N$ and a threshold θ which minimize the error on a set of p input-output mappings $\boldsymbol{\xi}^\mu \in \{-1,1\}^N \to \zeta^\mu \in \{0,1\}$ $(\mu = 1,\ldots,p)$ from an N–dimensional binary input space to binary targets. The output of the binary perceptron is determined by

$$\sigma^\mu = \Theta\left(\frac{1}{\sqrt{N}}\boldsymbol{W}\cdot\boldsymbol{\xi}^\mu - \theta\right) = \Theta(h^\mu)$$

where $\Theta(x)$ is the Heavyside stepfunction, which is 1 for $x \geq 0$ and 0 otherwise, and h^μ is the activation of the perceptron. The error is defined as

$$E = \sum_\mu \Theta\left[\kappa - 2(\zeta^\mu - 1)h^\mu\right],$$

where κ is the stability with which we require the patterns to be stored. A suitable algorithm (e.g., [10]) will converge to a set of weights $\boldsymbol{W}$ which minimizes the above error. If the set of examples is not linearly separable with a minimum distance κ of all patterns to the hyperplane, the binary perceptron will not be able to classify all patterns correctly, i.e., $\sigma^\mu \neq \zeta^\mu$ for some μ's and the upstart algorithm has to create further daughter units an a hidden layer to realize the mapping. The upstart algorithm therefore creates a binary $\{0,1\}$ output unit $\mathcal{O}$ with threshold one and the initial perceptron $\mathcal{D}_0$ and all further daughter units to be built by the algorithm will form the hidden layer. The first perceptron is then connected to $\mathcal{O}$ with a $+1$ weight, i.e., $\mathcal{O}$ has initially the same outputs as $\mathcal{D}_0$.

The basic idea of the upstart algorithm is to create further daughter units $\mathcal{D}^+$ and $\mathcal{D}^-$ in the hidden layer to correct WRONGLY OFF and WRONGLY ON errors respectively. Consider, for example, the creation of the new hidden unit $\mathcal{D}^-$, which is connected with a large negative weight to $\mathcal{O}$, whose role is to inhibit $\mathcal{O}$. $\mathcal{D}^-$ should be active (1) for patterns for which $\mathcal{O}$ was WRONGLY ON and inactive (0) for patterns for which $\mathcal{O}$ was CORRECTLY ON. Similarly, $\mathcal{D}^-$ ought to be 0 if $\mathcal{O}$ was WRONGLY OFF, in order to avoid further inhibition of $\mathcal{O}$. However, we do not have to train $\mathcal{D}^-$ on patterns for which $\mathcal{O}$ was CORRECTLY OFF, since an active $\mathcal{D}^-$

would only reinforce $\mathcal{O}$'s already correct response. The resulting training sets and the targets of both daughter units are illustrated in Table 1. More formally we

	$\zeta = 1$	$\zeta = 0$
$\sigma = 1$	CORRECTLY ON $\mathcal{D}^+$ $*$ $\mathcal{D}^-$ 0	WRONGLY ON $\mathcal{D}^+$ 0 $\mathcal{D}^-$ 1
$\sigma = 0$	WRONGLY OFF $\mathcal{D}^+$ 1 $\mathcal{D}^-$ 0	CORRECTLY OFF $\mathcal{D}^+$ 0 $\mathcal{D}^-$ $*$

Table 1 The targets of the upstart II algorithm depending on the requested target ζ and the actual output σ of the output unit $\mathcal{O}$. The target "$*$" means that the pattern is not included in the training set of $\mathcal{D}^{\pm}$.

define the algorithm upstart II by the following steps which are applied recursively until the task is learned:

Step 0: Follow the above procedure for the original unit $\mathcal{D}_0$ and the creation of the output unit $\mathcal{O}$. Evaluate the number of WRONGLY OFF and WRONGLY ON errors.

Step 1: If the output unit $\mathcal{O}$ of the upstart network of i generations makes more WRONGLY OFF than WRONGLY ON errors, a new unit $\mathcal{D}^-_{i+1}$ is created and trained on the training set and targets given in Table 1. If there are more WRONGLY ON than WRONGLY OFF errors, a new unit $\mathcal{D}^+_{i+1}$ is created with training set and targets also given in Table 1. If both kind of errors occur equally, two units $\mathcal{D}^-_{i+1}$ and $\mathcal{D}^+_{i+1}$ are created with training sets and targets as above.

Step 2: The new units are trained on their training sets and their weights are frozen. The units $\mathcal{D}^+_{i+1}, \mathcal{D}^-_{i+1}$ are then connected with positive, negative weights to the output unit respectively. The modulus of the weights are adjusted so that $\mathcal{D}^{\pm}_{i+1}$ overrules any previous decisions if active. The total number of WRONGLY OFF and WRONGLY ON errors of the upstart network of generation $i + 1$ is then reevaluated. If the network still makes errors the algorithm goes back to Step 1.

The algorithm will eventually converge as a daughter unit will always be able to correct at least one of the previously misclassified patterns without upsetting any already correctly classified examples.

2.2 Statistical Mechanics Framework for Calculating the Capacity Limit

Since the upstart algorithm trains only perceptrons, we can apply knowledge of the capacity limit and of the error rate of perceptrons above saturation derived in a statistical mechanics framework to calculate the capacity limit of the upstart II algorithm for an arbitrary number of generations. Below, we briefly review this statistical mechanics calculation and refer the reader to [5] and to previous work [1] for a more detailed treatment.

In the capacity problem the aim is to find the maximum number p of random input-output mappings of binary N–dimensional input vectors $\boldsymbol{\xi}^\mu$ to targets $\zeta^\mu \in \{0,1\}$, which can be realized by a network on average. We assume that each component of the input vectors $\boldsymbol{\xi}^\mu$ is drawn independently with equal probability from $\{-1,1\}$. The distribution of targets is taken to be pattern independent with a possible bias b: $P(\zeta) = \frac{1}{2}(1+b)\delta(1-\zeta) + \frac{1}{2}(1-b)\delta(\zeta)$. We will here only consider an unbiased output distribution for the intial perceptron. The target distributions for daughter units however will in general be biased.

Each binary perceptron is trained stochastically and we only allow weight vector solutions with the minimal achievable error. The error rate, i.e., the number of errors divided by the total number of examples, is assumed to be self-averaging with respect to the randomness in the training set in the thermodynamic limit $N \to \infty$. In this limit the natural measure for the number of examples p is $\alpha = p/N$. With increasing α the weight space of possible solutions shrinks, leaving a unique solution at the capacity limit of the binary perceptron. Above the capacity limit many different weight space solutions with the same error are possible. In general the solution space will be disconnected as two solutions can possibly missclassify different patterns. As α diverges, the solution space becomes increasingly fragmented.

The replica trick is used to calculate the solution space and the minimal error rate averaged over the randomness of the training set. This involves the replication of the perceptron weight vector, each replica representing a different possible solution to the same storage problem. In order to make significant progress, one has further to assume some kind of structure in the replica space. Below the capacity limit, the connectedness of the solution space is reflected by the correctness of a replica symmetric (RS) ansatz. Above the capacity, the disconnectedness of the solution space breaks the RS to some degree. We have restricted ourselves to a one-step replica symmetry breaking (RSB) calculation, which is expected to be at least sufficient for small error rates. The form of the equations for the error rate resulting from the RS and one-step RSB calculations are quite cumbersome and will be reported elsewhere [5, 11]. For the perceptron, the error rate is a function of the output bias b and the load α only.

3 Results of the Upstart Algorithm

The capacity of an upstart network with K hidden units can now be calculated. The initial perceptron is trained with an example load of α and an unbiased output distribution $b = 0$. The saddlepoint equations and the WRONGLY ON and WRONGLY OFF error rates are calculated numerically. These error rates determine the load and bias for the unit(s) to be created in the next generation. Now its (their) error rates and the errors of the output unit can in turn be calculated by solving the saddlepoint equations. This is iterated until K units have been built. If the output unit still makes error, we are above the capacity limit of the upstart net with K hidden units and α has to be decreased. On the other hand, if the output unit makes no errors, α can be increased. The maximal α for which the output unit makes no errors defines the saturation point of the network. The capacity limit, defined here

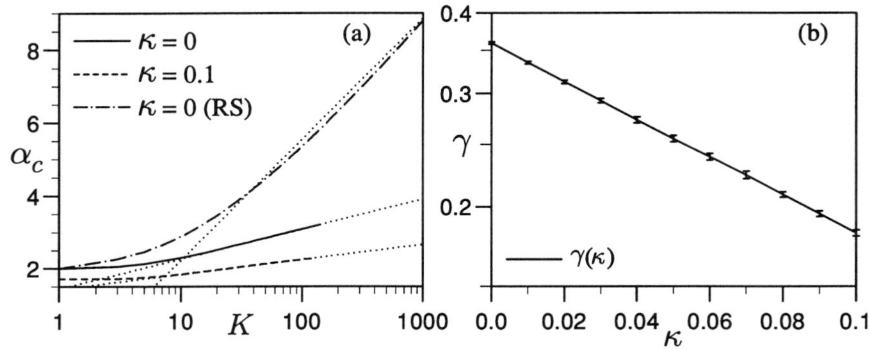

Figure 1 (a) Within the one-step RSB theory, the capacity α_c increases logarithmically with the number of hidden units K for large K for the stabilities $\kappa = 0$ (0.1), i.e., $\alpha_c \propto 0.3595\,(0.182) \ln K$ (see superimposed asymptotics). The RS theory violates the Mitchison-Durbin bound (third asymptotic: $\alpha_c \propto \ln K / \ln 2$) for $K \geq 180$. (b) The slope γ of the logarithmic increase of the capacity decreases exponentionally with the stability κ.

as the maximal number of examples per adjustable weight of the network, then becomes simply $\alpha_c(K) = \alpha/K$.

In Fig. 1a we present the storage capacity as a function of the number of hidden units for both a one-step RSB and a RS treatment at zero stability of the patterns ($\kappa = 0$). Whereas one-step RSB predicts a logarithmic increase $\alpha_c(K) \propto \ln(K)$ for large networks, in agreement with the Mitchison-Durbin bound, the results for the RS-theory violate this upper bound[1], i.e., the RS theory fails to predict the qualitative behaviour correctly.

In Fig. 1a we also show that the storage capacity still increases logarithmically with the number of units K for non-zero stability, but with a smaller slope γ. Fig. 1b shows the dependence of the slope γ as a function of the stability κ for one-step RSB. The maximal slope for zero stability $\gamma = 0.3595 \pm 0.0015$ does not saturate the Mitchison-Durbin bound $\gamma = 1/\ln 2 \approx 1.4427$, but is about four times lower. With increasing stabilities κ this slope decreases exponentionally $\gamma \propto \exp(-6.77 \pm 0.02\ \kappa)$.

4 Summary and Discussion

The objective of this work has been to calculate the storage capacity of multilayer networks created by the constructive upstart algorithm in a statistical mechanics framework using the replica method. We found that the RS-theory fails to predict the correct results even qualitatively. The one-step RSB theory yields qualitatively and quantitatively correct results over a wide range of network sizes and stabilities. In the one-step RSB treatment, a logarithmic increase with slope γ of the capacity of the upstart algorithm with the number of units K was found for all stabilities. The slope decreases exponentionally $[\gamma \propto \exp(-6.77\kappa)]$ with the stability κ. It would be interesting to investigate if this result carries over to other constructive algorithms or even to general two-layer networks.

[1]The violation occurs for $K \geq 180$ and the largest networks in the RS case were $K = 999$.

For zero stability the slope of this increase is around four times smaller than the upper bound $(1/\ln 2)$ predicted by information theory. We suggest that this indicates that the upstart algorithm uses its hidden units less effectively than a general two-layer network. We think this is due to the fact that the upstart algorithm uses the hidden units to overrule previous decisions, resulting in an exponential increase of the hidden layer to output unit weights. This is in contrast to general two-layer networks which usually have hidden-output weights of roughly the same order and can therefore explore a larger space of internal representations. For the upstart algorithm a large number of internal representations are equivalent and others cannot be implemented as they are related to erroneous outputs. However, it would be interesting to investigate how other constructive algorithms (e.g., [6]) perform in comparison. A systematic investigation of the storage capacity of constructive algorithms may ultimately lead to a better understanding, and thus possibly to novel, much improved algorithms.

REFERENCES

[1] E. Gardner, *The space of interactions in neural network models*, J. Phys. A Vol. 21 (1988), pp257–270.

[2] E. Barkai, D. Hansel and H. Sompolinsky, *Broken symmetries in multilayered perceptrons*, Phys. Rev. A Vol. 45 (1992), pp4146–4161.

[3] G. J. Mitchison and R. M. Durbin, *Bounds on the learning capacity of some multi-layer networks*, Biological Cybernetics Vol. 60 (1989), pp345–356.

[4] D. Saad, *Explicit symmetries and the capacity of multilayer neural networks*, J. Phys. A Vol. 27 (1994), pp2719–2734.

[5] A. H. L. West, and D. Saad, *Threshold induced phase transitions in perceptrons*, To appear in J. Phys. A (March 1997).

[6] M. Mézard and J.-P. Nadal, *Learning in feed-forward layered networks: the tiling algorithm*, J. Phys. A Vol. 22 (1989), pp2191–2203.

[7] J.-P. Nadal, *Study of a growth algorithm for a feed-forward network*, International Journal of Neural Systems, Vol.1 (1989), pp55–59.

[8] M. Frean, *The upstart algorithm: a method for constructing and training feed-forward neural networks*, Neural Computation Vol. 2 (1990), pp198–209.

[9] For an overview, see e.g., M. Mézard, G. Parisi and M. G. Virasoro, *Spin Glass Theory and Beyond*, World Scientific, Singapore (1987).

[10] M. Frean, *A thermal perceptron learning rule*, Neural Computation Vol. 4 (1992), pp946–957, and references therein.

[11] A. H. L. West and D. Saad, *Statistical mechanics of constructive algorithms*, in preparation (1997).

Acknowledgements

AHLW would like to acknowledge gratefully financial support by the EPSRC. This work has been supported by EU grant ERB CHRX-CT92-0063.

REGRESSION WITH GAUSSIAN PROCESSES

Christopher K. I. Williams
Neural Computing Research Group, Department of Computer Science and Applied Mathematics, Aston University, Birmingham B4 7ET, UK.
Email: c.k.i.williams@aston.ac.uk

The Bayesian analysis of neural networks is difficult because the prior over functions has a complex form, leading to implementations that either make approximations or use Monte Carlo integration techniques. In this paper I investigate the use of Gaussian process priors over functions, which permit the predictive Bayesian analysis to be carried out exactly using matrix operations. The method has been tested on two challenging problems and has produced excellent results.

1 Introduction

In the Bayesian approach to neural networks a prior distribution over the weights induces a prior distribution over functions. This prior is combined with a noise model, which specifies the probability of observing the targets $\boldsymbol{t}$ given function values $\boldsymbol{y}$, to yield a posterior over functions which can then be used for predictions. For neural networks the prior over functions has a complex form which means that implementations must either make approximations [4] or use Monte Carlo approaches to evaluating integrals [6].

As Neal [7] has argued, there is no reason to believe that, for real-world problems, neural network models should be limited to nets containing only a "small" number of hidden units. He has shown that it is sensible to consider a limit where the number of hidden units in a net tends to infinity, and that good predictions can be obtained from such models using the Bayesian machinery[1]. He has also shown that a large class of neural network models will converge to a Gaussian process prior over functions in the limit of an infinite number of hidden units.

Although infinite networks are one method of creating Gaussian processes, it is also possible (and computationally easier) to specify them directly using parametric forms for the mean and covariance functions. In this paper I investigate using Gaussian processes specified parametrically for regression problems[2], and demonstrate very good performance on the two test problems I have tried. The advantage of the Gaussian process formulation is that the integrations, which have to be approximated for neural nets, can be carried out exactly (using matrix operations) in this case. I also show that the parameters specifying the Gaussian process can be estimated from training data, and that this leads naturally to a form of "Automatic Relevance Determination" [4], [7].

2 Prediction with Gaussian Processes

A stochastic process is a collection of random variables $\{Y(\boldsymbol{x})|\boldsymbol{x} \in X\}$ indexed by a set X. Often X will be a space such as $\mathbb{R}^d$ for some dimension d, although it could be more general. The stochastic process is specified by giving the probability distribution for every finite subset of variables $Y(\boldsymbol{x}_1), \ldots, Y(\boldsymbol{x}_k)$ in a consistent manner. A Gaussian process is a stochastic process which can be fully specified by its mean function $\mu(\boldsymbol{x}) = E[Y(\boldsymbol{x})]$ and its covariance function $C(\boldsymbol{x}, \boldsymbol{x}') = E[(Y(\boldsymbol{x})-$

[1] Large networks cannot be successfully used with maximum likelihood training because of the overfitting problem.

[2] By regression problems I mean those concerned with the prediction of one or more real-valued outputs, as compared to classification problems.

$\mu(\boldsymbol{x}))(Y(\boldsymbol{x}')-\mu(\boldsymbol{x}'))]$; any finite set of points will have a joint multivariate Gaussian distribution.

Below I consider Gaussian processes which have $\mu(\boldsymbol{x}) \equiv 0$. This is the case for many neural network priors [7], and otherwise assumes that any known offset or trend in the data has been removed. A non-zero $\mu(\boldsymbol{x})$ can be incorporated into the framework, but leads to extra notational complexity.

Given a prior covariance function $C_P(\boldsymbol{x}, \boldsymbol{x}')$, a noise process $C_N(\boldsymbol{x}, \boldsymbol{x}')$ (with $C_N(\boldsymbol{x}, \boldsymbol{x}') = 0$ for $\boldsymbol{x} \neq \boldsymbol{x}'$) and data $\mathcal{D} = ((\boldsymbol{x}_1, t_1), (\boldsymbol{x}_2, t_2), \ldots, (\boldsymbol{x}_n, t_n))$, the prediction for the distribution of Y corresponding to a test point $\boldsymbol{x}$ is obtained simply by marginalizing the $(n+1)$-dimensional joint distribution to obtain the mean and variance

$$\hat{y}(\boldsymbol{x}) = \boldsymbol{k}_P^T(\boldsymbol{x})(K_P + K_N)^{-1}\boldsymbol{t} \tag{1}$$

$$\sigma_{\hat{y}}^2(\boldsymbol{x}) = C_P(\boldsymbol{x}, \boldsymbol{x}) + C_N(\boldsymbol{x}, \boldsymbol{x}) - \boldsymbol{k}_P^T(\boldsymbol{x})(K_P + K_N)^{-1}\boldsymbol{k}_P(\boldsymbol{x}) \tag{2}$$

where $[K_\alpha]_{ij} = C_\alpha(\boldsymbol{x}_i, \boldsymbol{x}_j)$ for $\alpha = P, N$, $\boldsymbol{k}_P(\boldsymbol{x}) = (C_P(\boldsymbol{x}, \boldsymbol{x}_1), \ldots, C_P(\boldsymbol{x}, \boldsymbol{x}_n))^T$ and $\boldsymbol{t} = (t_1, \ldots, t_n)^T$. $\sigma_{\hat{y}}^2(\boldsymbol{x})$ gives the "error bars" of the prediction. In the work below the noise process is assumed to have a variance σ_ν^2 independent of $\boldsymbol{x}$ so that $K_N = \sigma_\nu^2 I$.

The Gaussian process view provides a unifying framework for many regression methods. ARMA models used in time series analysis and spline smoothing (e.g. [10]) correspond to Gaussian process prediction with a particular choice of covariance function[3], as do generalized linear regression models ($y(\boldsymbol{x}) = \sum_i w_i \phi_i(\boldsymbol{x})$, with $\{\phi_i\}$ a fixed set of basis functions) for a Gaussian prior on the weights $\{w_i\}$. Gaussian processes have also been used in the geostatistics field (e.g. [3], [1]), and are known there as "kriging", but this literature has concentrated on the case where $\boldsymbol{x} \in \mathbb{R}^2$ or $\mathbb{R}^3$, rather than considering more general input spaces. Regularization networks (e.g. [8], [2]) provide a complementary view of Gaussian process prediction in terms of a Fourier space view, which shows how high-frequency components are damped out to obtain a smooth approximator.

2.1 Adapting Covariance Functions and ARD

Given a covariance function $C = C_P + C_N$, the log probability l of the training data is given by

$$l = -\frac{1}{2}\log\det K - \frac{1}{2}\boldsymbol{t}^T K^{-1}\boldsymbol{t} - \frac{n}{2}\log 2\pi \tag{3}$$

where $K = K_P + K_N$. If C has some adjustable parameters $\boldsymbol{\theta}$, then we can carry out a search in $\boldsymbol{\theta}$-space to maximize l; this is simply maximum likelihood estimation of $\boldsymbol{\theta}$ [4]. For example, in a d-dimensional input space we may choose

$$C(\boldsymbol{x}, \boldsymbol{x}') = v_0 \exp\left(-\sum_{i=1}^{d} \frac{w_i}{2}(x_i - x_i')^2\right) + v_1 \delta(\boldsymbol{x}, \boldsymbol{x}') \tag{4}$$

where v_0, v_1 and the $\{w_i\}$ are adjustable. In MacKay's terms [4] l is the log "evidence", with the parameter vector $\boldsymbol{\theta}$ roughly corresponding to his hyperparameters $\boldsymbol{\alpha}$ and β; in effect the weights have been exactly integrated out.

One reason for constructing a model with variable w's is to express the prior belief that some input variables might be irrelevant to the prediction task at hand, and

[3] Technically splines require generalized covariance functions.

[4] See section 4 for a discussion of the hierarchical Bayesian approach.

Method	No. of inputs	sum squared test error
Gaussian process	2	1.126
Gaussian process	6	1.138
MacKay	2	1.146
Neal	2	1.094
Neal	6	1.098

Table 1 Results on the robot arm task.

we would expect that the w's corresponding to the irrelevant variables would tend to zero as the model is fitted to data. This is closely related to the Automatic Relevance Determination (ARD) idea of MacKay and Neal [5], [7].

3 Experiments with Gaussian Process prediction

Prediction with Gaussian processes and maximum likelihood training of the covariance function has been tested on two problems : (i) a modified version of MacKay's robot arm problem and (ii) the Boston housing data set.
For both datasets I used a covariance function of the form given in equation 4 and a gradient-based search algorithm for exploring $\boldsymbol{\theta}$-space; the derivative vector $\partial l/\partial \boldsymbol{\theta}$ was fed to a conjugate gradient routine with a line-search[5].

3.1 The Robot Arm Problem

I consider a version of MacKay's robot arm problem introduced by Neal (1995). The standard robot arm problem is concerned with the mappings

$$y_1 = r_1 \cos x_1 + r_2 \cos(x_1 + x_2) \qquad y_2 = r_1 \sin x_1 + r_2 \sin(x_1 + x_2) \tag{5}$$

The data was generated by picking x_1 uniformly from [-1.932, -0.453] and [0.453, 1.932] and picking x_2 uniformly from [0.534, 3.142]. Neal added four further inputs, two of which were copies of x_1 and x_2 corrupted by additive Gaussian noise of standard deviation 0.02, and two further irrelevant Gaussian-noise inputs with zero mean and unit variance. Independent zero-mean Gaussian noise of variance 0.0025 was then added to the outputs y_1 and y_2. I used the same datasets as Neal and MacKay, with 200 examples in the training set and 200 in the test set.
The theory described in section 2 deals only with the prediction of a scalar quantity Y, so I constructed predictors for the two outputs separately, although a joint prediction is possible within the Gaussian process framework (see co-kriging, §3.2.3 in [1]). Two experiments were conducted, the first using only the two "true" inputs, and the second one using all six inputs. For each experiment ten random starting positions were tried. The log(v)'s and log(w)'s were all chosen uniformly from [-3.0, 0.0], and were adapted separately for the prediction of y_1 and y_2. The conjugate gradient search algorithm was allowed to run for 100 iterations, by which time the likelihood was changing very slowly. Results are reported for the run which gave the highest probability of the training data, although in fact all runs performed

[5] In fact the parameterization $\log \theta$ was used in the search to ensure that the v's and w's stayed positive.

Procedure used	ave. squared test error
Guessing overall mean	84.4
Best result in Quinlan (1993)	10.9
Gaussian process	8.6
Neal (Bayesian network with 2 hidden layers)	6.5

Table 2 Results on the Boston housing data task.

very similarly. The results are shown in Table 1 [6] and are encouraging, as they indicate that the Gaussian process approach is giving very similar performance to two well-respected techniques. All of the methods obtain a level of performance which is quite close to the theoretical minimum error level of 1.0. It is interesting to look at the values of the w's obtained after the optimization; for the y_2 task the values were 0.243, 0.237, 0.0650, 1.7×10^{-4}, 2.6×10^{-6}, 9.2×10^{-7}, and v_0 and v_1 were 7.920 and 0.0022 respectively. The w values show nicely that the first two inputs are the most important, followed by the corrupted inputs and then the irrelevant inputs.

3.2 Boston Housing Data

The Boston Housing data has been used by several authors as a real-world regression problem (the data is available from `ftp://lib.stat.cmu.edu/datasets`). For each of the 506 census tracts within the Boston metropolitan area (in 1970) the data gives 13 input variables, including per capita crime rate and nitric oxides concentration, and one output, the median housing price for that tract.

A ten-fold cross-validation method was used to evaluate the performance, as detailed in [9]). The dataset was divided into ten blocks of near-equal size and distribution of class values (I used the same partitions as in [9]). For each block in turn the parameters of the Gaussian process were trained on the remaining blocks and then used to make predictions for the hold-out block. For each of the ten experiments the input variables and targets were linearly transformed to have zero mean and unit variance, and five random start positions used, choosing the $\log(v)$'s and $\log(w)$'s uniformly from [-3.0,0.0]. In each case the search algorithm was run for 100 iterations. In each experiment the run with the highest evidence was used for prediction, and the test results were then averaged to give the entry in Table 2.

The fact that the Gaussian process result beats the best result obtained by Quinlan (who made a reasonably sophisticated application of existing techniques) is very encouraging. It was observed that different solutions were obtained from the random starting points, and this suggests that an hierarchical Bayesian approach, as used in Neal's neural net implementation and described in section 4, may be useful in further increasing performance.

[6] The bottom three lines of the table were obtained from [7]. The MacKay result is the test error for the net with highest "evidence".

4 Discussion

I have presented a Gaussian process framework for regression problems and have shown that it produces excellent results on the two test problems tried.

In section 2 I have described maximum likelihood training of the parameter vector $\boldsymbol{\theta}$. Obviously a hierarchical Bayesian analysis could be carried out for a model M using a prior $P(\boldsymbol{\theta}|M)$ to obtain a posterior $P(\boldsymbol{\theta}|\mathcal{D}, M)$. The predictive distribution for a test point and the "model evidence" $P(\mathcal{D}|M)$ are then obtained by averaging the conditional quantities over the posterior. Although these integrals would have to be performed numerically, there are typically far fewer parameters in $\boldsymbol{\theta}$ than weights and hyperparameters in a neural net, so that these integrations should be easier to carry out. Preliminary experiments in this direction with the Hybrid Monte Carlo method [7] are promising.

I have also conducted some experiments on the approximation of neural nets (with a finite number of hidden units) by Gaussian processes, although space limitations do not allow me to describe these here. Other directions currently under investigation include (i) the use of Gaussian processes for classification problems by softmaxing the outputs of k regression surfaces (for a k-class classification problem), and (ii) using non-stationary covariance functions, so that $C(\boldsymbol{x}, \boldsymbol{x}') \neq C(|\boldsymbol{x} - \boldsymbol{x}'|)$.

REFERENCES

[1] N. A. C. Cressie, *Statistics for Spatial Data*, Wiley (1993).

[2] F. Girosi, M. Jones, and T. Poggio, *Regularization Theory and Neural Networks Architectures*, Neural Computation, Vol. 7(2) (1995), pp219–269.

[3] A. G. Journel and Ch. J. Huijbregts, *Mining Geostatistics*, Academic Press (1978).

[4] D. J. C. MacKay, *A Practical Bayesian Framework for Backpropagation Networks*, Neural Computation, Vol. 4(3) (1992), pp448–472.

[5] D. J. C. MacKay, *Bayesian Methods for Backpropagation Networks*, In J. L. van Hemmen, E. Domany, and K. Schulten, editors, Models of Neural Networks II, Springer (1993).

[6] R. M. Neal, *Bayesian Learning via Stochastic Dynamics*, in: S. J. Hanson, J. D. Cowan, and C. L. Giles, eds., Neural Information Processing Systems, Vol. 5 (1993), pp475–482. Morgan Kaufmann, San Mateo, CA,.

[7] R. M. Neal, *Bayesian Learning for Neural Networks*, PhD thesis, Dept. of Computer Science, University of Toronto (1995).

[8] T. Poggio and F. Girosi, *Networks for approximation and learning*, Proceedings of IEEE, Vol. 78 (1990), pp1481–1497.

[9] J. R. Quinlan, *Combining Instance-Based and Model-Based Learning*, in: P. E. Utgoff, ed., Proc. ML'93, Morgan Kaufmann, San Mateo, CA (1993).

[10] G. Wahba, *Spline Models for Observational Data*, Society for Industrial and Applied Mathematics, CBMS-NSF Regional Conference series in applied mathematics (1990).

Acknowledgements

I thank Radford Neal and David MacKay for many useful discussions and for generously proving data used in this paper, Chris Bishop, Peter Dayan, Radford Neal and Huaiyu Zhu for comments on earlier drafts, George Lindfield for making his implementation of the scaled conjugate gradient search routine available and Carl Rasmussen for his C implementation which runs considerably faster than my MATLAB version. This work was supported by EPSRC grant GR/J75425.

STOCHASTIC FORWARD-PERTURBATION, ERROR SURFACE AND PROGRESSIVE LEARNING IN NEURAL NETWORKS

Li-Qun Xu

Intelligent Systems Research Group, BT Research Laboratories
Martlesham Heath, Ipswich, IP5 7RE, UK.

We address the issue of progressive learning of neural networks, focusing on the situation in which the environment or the training set for a learner is of fixed size.[1] We concentrate on the phenomenon of the change in *shape* of the error surface of a neural network (defined over the weight space) as a result of presenting it with a range of *intermediate* tasks during the course of learning, and a *goal-driven mechanism* is therefore proposed and analysed. The stochastic gradient smoothing algorithm (SGSA) [14, 16] is found to be effective in implementing this idea, experiments done demonstrate the usefulness of our approach towards progressive learning.

1 Active Learning: Non-fixed vs Fixed Data Set

The findings in cognitive science have shown that a learning process is normally a bidirectional process involving the interactive actions (information exchange) between a learner and its surrounding environment [3]. In active learning of neural networks, the *learner* is a neural network of specified configuration $\mathcal{A}$ parameterised by some connection weight vector $\mathbf{W} \in \mathbb{R}^N$, learning to perform a particular task such as function mapping [8], pattern classification [11] and robot control [13] among many others. The *environment* is characterised by a training data set of fixed or non-fixed size, or some exploratory space of certain underlying structures.

Current research on active learning of neural networks has been focusing on the design of various well-defined information and/or generalisation criteria [6, 8, 13, 9, 4] based on which the selection, can be made from among a set of available data examples, of a *new* data example, which, when added to the previous training set and learned, allow the trained network has the maximum accuracy of fit to the data and improved generalisation performance [10]. Notably, this strategy imposes no restrictions on the size of the data set.

However other approaches to active learning, given that the training data set is of fixed size, follow a slight different trend which essentially emphasises the principle of *progressive* learning [11]. This is usually achieved by letting the neural network learn a succession of varied subsets that represent, on one occasion, a different level of abstraction of the final complex task. Subsequently, the response of the learner to the changeable environment – the particular subsets engaged – is monitored, and the performance, in terms of model misspecification and network variance, thus far achieved will determine what aspects of the environment the learner is to face next time.

There are various ways whereby the whole environment can be decomposed : one can consider to divide the entire data set according to sample *size* from small to large [1], the *degree of difficulty* from low to high [5], [3], etc. This way of division of the entire data set is by and large based on the results of empirical studies and

[1] which is often the case in practical applications of neural networks, especially pattern recognition.

the understanding of individual experimenters to the tasks at hand. In this paper we propose an alternative way of performing progressive learning while freeing from the difficulties of artificially decomposing the environment. In the following section we introduce the view of progressive learning in terms of dealing with the change in shape of error surfaces. In section 3 we propose to use stochastic gradient smoothing algorithm (SGSA) to implement this idea. In section 4 experiments are conducted to demonstrate the usefulness of the approach for active learning of neural networks. The paper is concluded in section 5.

2 Progressive Learning – a Goal-driven Perspective

It would be instructive if we interpret the progressive way of learning an entire environment by a neural network based on the change in *shape* of its error surface vs connection weights : Given a neural network $\mathcal{A}$ specified by a connection weight vector $\mathbf{W} \in \mathrm{IR}^N$, a training set $\Theta^{(S)}$ of $|S|$ pairs of labelled examples, $\Theta^{(S)} = \{x_j, y_j\}_{j=1}^{|S|}$ describing the whole environment, an error function can then be expressed as,

$$f_{\Theta^{(S)}}(\mathbf{W}) \ : \ \mathrm{IR}^N \longrightarrow \mathrm{IR}^1, \tag{1}$$

the notation $\Theta^{(S)}$ in the equation is meant to show the fact that the shape of the error surface in the weight space $\mathbf{W} \in \mathrm{IR}^N$ is entirely determined by the training set. (Figure 1 (a) shows a two-dimensional profile of such an error surface when a final convergence has been reached.) Consequently, the strategy of using a varied

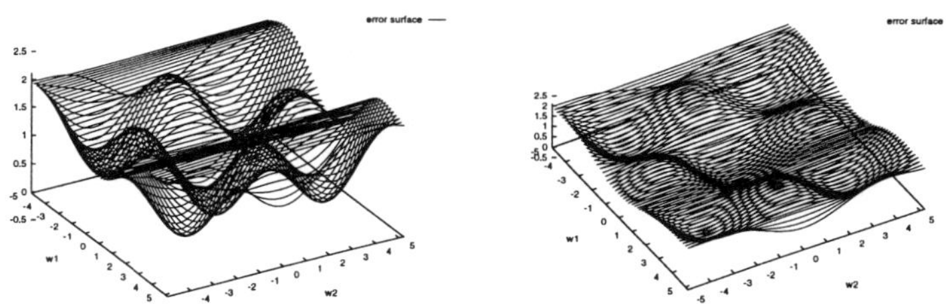

Figure 1 (a) A two-dimensional profile of an error surface with multiple valleys and ridges. (b) A smoothed version of case (a), retaining much of its main features while freeing from details – *steepness, roughness and ravine*. In between, there exist a range of *intermediate* error surfaces that may arise from either of the two mechanisms discussed below.

data subset in session k, $\Theta^{(s_k)}$, $s_k \subset S$, for the training of $\mathcal{A}$ will invariably lead to the change in shape of its error surface, or $f_{\Theta^{(s_k)}}(\mathbf{W})$, $s_k \subset S$. This is what we mean by the *data-driven mechanism* detailed in Figure 2 (a). With $\Theta^{(s_k)}$, $s_k \subset S$ being properly constructed, it is expected that the shape of the error surface will change from initially coarse and more or less smooth terrain to the final one bearing all the details but somehow with less regularities.

We are interested, however, in exploring the idea from an opposite perspective. In fact, we can manipulate the shape of the error surface by subjecting it to some mathematically smoothing operations to generate at our own disposal a sequence of *intermediate* error surfaces to achieve the same effects as that of previous strategy.

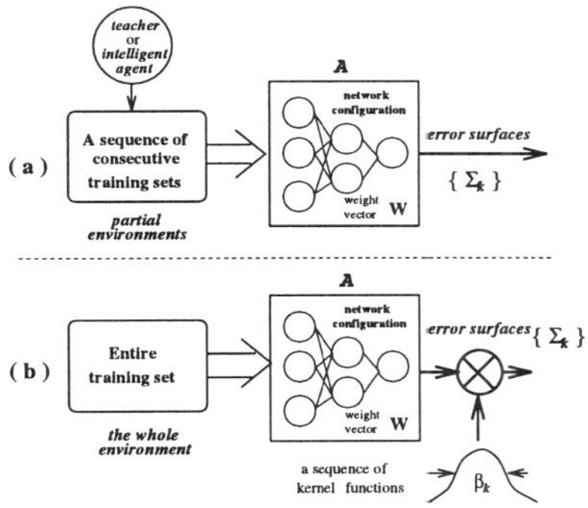

Figure 2 Two alternative mechanisms giving rise to a sequence of error surfaces $\{\Sigma_k\}$ (*intermediate* tasks), given a neural network, $\mathcal{A}$, specified by its weight vector $\mathbf{W} \in \mathbb{R}^N$: see Note (i) below.

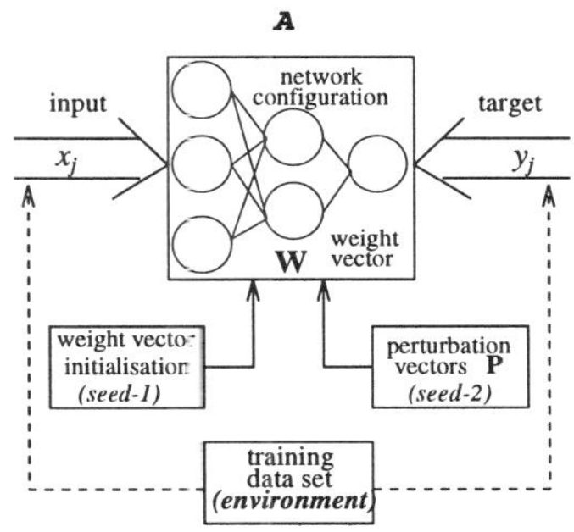

Figure 3 A model-free neural network learning paradigm for stochastic forward perturbation algorithms. See Note (ii) below.

Note (i): The *data-driven mechanism* (a) where $\{\Sigma_k \equiv f_{\Theta^{(s_k)}}(\mathbf{W}),\, s_k \subset S\}$. The learner is faced, each time, with a varied training set describing different details of the environment, and consequently has to learn a different error surface defined by the training (sub)set engaged By learning the preceding error surfaces, the weight vector $\mathbf{W} \in \mathbb{R}^N$ tends to be positioned in an advantageous location to facilitate the process of learning the following error surfaces; The *goal-driven mechanism* (b) where $\{\Sigma_k \equiv \tilde{f}_{\Theta^{(S)}}(\mathbf{W}, \beta_k), k = 1, 2, \cdots\}$. The learner in (b) is confronted with the entire training set $\Theta^{(S)}$, or the whole environment, though the actual task for the learner at a time is a simplified version of the error surface obtainable by convolving it with an appropriate N-dimensional kernel function (p.d.f.) of the same family but a varied "width" β_k. Consequently, this strategy also results in a sequence of error surfaces of different shapes. Note that in (b), the convolution operation is implicitly carried out in the course of learning by the SGSA.

Note (ii): The environment is given by the training data set $\Theta^{(S)} = \{x_j,\, y_j\}_{j=1}^{|S|}$. All the connection weights in $\mathcal{A}$ are arranged as a weight vector $\mathbf{W} \in \mathbb{R}^N$. In this paradigm an extra dimension of randomness characterised by the perturbation vectors $\mathbf{P}$ can be explored.

Figure 2 (b) illustrates this idea which we call *goal-driven mechanism*, where the *sequence of error surfaces* at the output end can be equally viewed as those ranging between Figure 1 (b), a smooth shallow surface with established prominent characteristics, and Figure 1 (a), a surface with all the details (and idiosyncrasies). It is from this viewpoint we argue that the stochastic forward-perturbation algorithms [15] – the category of learning algorithm that has its roots nurtured by the theory of stochastic approximation of nonlinear dynamical processes – can be employed to accomplish the task of progressive learning without caring about how to divide the training set.

3 Mathematical Analysis

As opposed to the back-propagation (BP) algorithm, the operations of updating the weight vector $\mathbf{W}$ by stochastic forward-perturbation algorithms generally follow an

F − P − F − G pattern (Figure 3) i.e. one *forward* propagation of the training set through $\mathcal{A}$ to measure as it currently stands error the function; one *perturbation* of the weight vector with some controllable noises $\mathbf{P} \in \mathrm{IR}^N$; and another *forward* propagation to measure the response of $\mathcal{A}$ due to the perturbation just introduced; based on these measurements a gradient estimation can be taken by employing some intuitive *difference* approximation or more subtle *correlation* methods. The estimated gradient can then be incorporated into stochastic approximation algorithms to update the weight vector.

In the following, the advanced algorithm called *stochastic gradient smoothing algorithm* [16] is employed. According to Figure 2 (b), the following smoothing operation has been invoked (Note that the data-dependent notation $\Theta^{(S)}$ has been dropped.)

$$\begin{aligned}\tilde{f}(\mathbf{W},\beta) &= f(\mathbf{W}) \otimes [\hat{G}(-\mathbf{W},\beta) + \hat{G}(\mathbf{W},\beta)] \\ &= \int_{\mathrm{IR}^N} \hat{G}(\mathbf{\Lambda},\beta)\, [f(\mathbf{W}+\mathbf{\Lambda}) + f(\mathbf{W}-\mathbf{\Lambda})] d\mathbf{\Lambda} \qquad (2)\end{aligned}$$

where the symbol '⊗' denotes the convolution operator. Following some mathematical manipulations, one stochastic gradient estimator ξ_k is shown as follows :

$$\xi_k \equiv \hat{\nabla}_w \tilde{f}(\hat{\mathbf{W}}_k,\beta_k) = \frac{1}{n_k}\frac{1}{2\beta_k}\sum_{i=1}^{n_k} \mathbf{\Lambda}_i\, \delta^{(i)} f(\hat{\mathbf{W}}_k) \qquad (3)$$

where $\mathbf{\Lambda}_i$ is a random (perturbation) vector generated from an independent Gaussian p.d.f. $G(\mathbf{\Lambda})$. The scalar β_k, referred to as the *smoothing factor*, determines the *width* of the underlying p.d.f. or the *perturbation strength* of the generated random vectors. Finally, the difference in the cost function due to the *ith* perturbation of $\hat{\mathbf{W}}_k$ is $\delta^{(i)} f(\hat{\mathbf{W}}_k)$. Based on the estimated gradient ξ_k, the weight vector $\hat{\mathbf{W}}_k$ is updated according to,

$$\mathbf{d}_k = \rho_k \cdot \xi_k + (1-\rho_k) \cdot \mathbf{d}_{k-1}, \qquad (4)$$

$$\hat{\mathbf{W}}_{k+1} = \hat{\mathbf{W}}_k - \eta_k \cdot \mathbf{d}_k \qquad (5)$$

where the *direction* vector $\mathbf{d}_k = (d_{k1}\ d_{k2}\ \cdots\ d_{kN})' \in \mathrm{IR}^N$ represents a running average over the current gradient estimate ξ_k and the previous direction vector $\mathbf{d}_{k-1}$. The other two important parameters appeared in the above formulas include η_k – the learning rate (or adaptive step size) and ρ_k – the accumulating factor. It is desirable that with the iteration $k \to \infty$, $\eta_k \to 0$, $\rho_k \to 1$. The parameters η_k and ρ_k are locally adaptable.

4 Experimental Results

A simulated two-class pattern classification problem, of which the details can be found in [7], is used to demonstrate our approach for active learning of neural networks. The distributions of these two classes (C_1 and C_0) are overlapped, and a complete separation of their examples is impossible even for an optimal classifier. In the experiments, the training set consists of 200 examples with 100 drawn from each class, while the test set contains 1000 examples with 500 belonging to each class. The neural network used for this task has a fully-connected three-layer 2 – 4 – 1 structure, amounting to 17 weights including biases. The single output of the trained network should ideally be for examples in C_1 a "1" and in C_0 a "0" when being shown the unseen data in the testing phase.

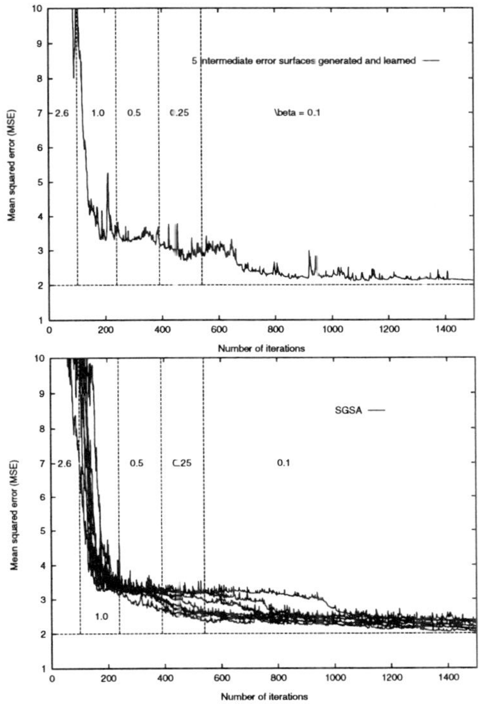

a)

b)

Figure 4 (a) A typical learning trajectory achieved by the SGSA. The vertical dashed lines mark the boundaries where a new *intermediate* error surface, characterised by a different value of β_k shown along the lines, is encountered by the learner. In this case, there are 4 intermediate error surfaces (where β_k assumes a value of 2.6, 1.0, 0.5 and 0.25 in order) to be learned before the learner faces the final task (where $\beta_k = 0.1$) which is approximate to the error surface imposed by the complete environment for which $\beta_k = 0$. (b) A set of 10 learning trajectories for the test problem by the SGSA with different initial weight vectors.

For the problem, 10 trials are performed, each starting with a different weight vector $\hat{\mathbf{W}}_0$ having random values ranging between ± 0.5. Figure 4 (a) shows a typical learning trajectory, the mean squared error vs number of iterations, achieved by the SGSA.

Table 1 summarises the average performance among ten trials for the SGSA, where E_{tr} denotes the mean squared error (MSE) for the training set; n_{tr} gives, up to the indicated iterations, the number of examples yet to be correctly learned in the training set (200 examples in total); n_{te} shows the generalisation performance measured by the number of examples that are still misclassified, up to the given training iterations, in the test set (1000 examples in total). An important result is that the generalisation performance given by the n_{te} tends to saturate rather than deteriorate with more iterations, as is not the case with the experiments using deterministic Quick-prop algorithm (an advanced version of the BP algorithm) [15].

ALGO.	Iter.	700	800	900	1000	1100	1200	1300	1400	1500
SGSA	E_{tr}	2.658	2.551	2.477	2.410	2.367	2.313	2.290	2.261	2.229
	n_{tr}	11.4	9.9	9.7	9.6	8.9	8.6	8.3	8.4	8.3
	n_{te}	66.9	66.0	64.6	62.2	62.1	62.5	63.2	61.9	61.9

Table 1 The average performance among 10 trials of the SGSA at selected iterations when applied to the simulated two-class pattern classification problem.

Thus the SGSA compares favourably with the Quick-prop in this regard. Figure 4 (b) describes the corresponding set of 10 learning trajectories obtained.

5 Summary

An alternative way has been explored for active learning of neural networks, focusing on the viewpoint of interpreting the error surface imposed by the whole training set (a certain task) in terms of a range of its intermediate versions, or a set of intermediate tasks. We analysed two different perspectives, called, respectively, *data-driven mechanism* and *goal-driven mechanism*, that give rise to such a range of error surfaces. We argued that the later approach could well be an effective way to control the amount of information about a complex environment at a time accessible to a learner, therefore fulfilling the same objective (of progressive learning) as the former without explicitly decomposing the environment in a hard fashion. The stochastic gradient smoothing algorithm (SGSA) was employed to implement this idea. Experiments have been conducted to support our claims. Further theoretical studies of this issue are needed.

REFERENCES

[1] C. Cachin, *Neural Networks*, Vol. 7(1) (1994).
[2] D.A. Cohn, Z. Ghahramani, Z., M.I. Jordan, in: [12].
[3] J.E. Elman, *Technical Report CRL-9101*, UCSD (1991).
[4] A. Krogh, J. Vedelsby, in [12].
[5] J. Ludik, I. Cloete, *Proc. of ESANN* (April 1994), Brussels.
[6] D.J.C. MacKay, *Neural Computation*, Vol. 4(4) (1992).
[7] L. Niles, H. Silverman et al., *Proc. of ICASSP'89*, Glasgow (1989).
[8] M. Plutowski, H. White, *Technical Report CS91-180*, UCSD (1991).
[9] P. Sollich, *Physical Review E*, Vol. 49 (1994).
[10] E.M. Strand, W.T. Jones, *Proc. of IJCNN* Vol. I, Baltimore (1992).
[11] N. Szilas, E. Ronco, *Proc. of ECCS'95*, Saint-Malo, France (1995).
[12] G. Tesauro, D.S. Touretzky, and T.K. Leen eds., *Advances in Neural Information Processing Systems 7*, MIT Press, Cambridge, MA (1995).
[13] S.B. Thrun, in D.A. White and D.A. Sofge (eds.), *Handbook of intelligent control: Neural, Fuzzy and Adaptive Approaches*, Van Nostrand Reinhold, Kentucky (1993).
[14] L.Q. Xu, T.J. Hall, *Proc. of ICANN'94*, Naples, Italy (1994).
[15] L.Q. Xu, *Proc. of EANN'95*, Helsinki, Finland (1995).
[16] L.Q. Xu, T.J. Hall, submitted to *Neural Networks*, (May 1995).

Acknowledgements

This research was conducted at the University of Abertay, Dundee, and was funded in part by a grant from the Nuffield Foundation.

DYNAMICAL STABILITY OF A HIGH-DIMENSIONAL SELF-ORGANIZING MAP

Howard Hua Yang

Lab for Information Representation, FRP, RIKEN, 2-1 Hirosawa, Wako-Shi, Saitama 351-01, Japan. Email: hhy@murasaki.riken.go.jp

The convergence and the convergence rate of one self-organization algorithm for the high-dimensional self-organizing map in the linearized Amari model are studied in the context of stochastic approximation. The conditions on the neighborhood function and the learning rate are given to guarantee the convergence. It is shown that the convergence of the algorithm can be accelerated by averaging.

Keywords: high-dimensional self-organizing map, neighborhood function, convergence, stochastic approximation, acceleration by averaging.

1 Introduction

The self-organizing neural networks were found in modeling some self-organized phenomena in nervous systems. The typical models are those given by Willshaw and von der Malsburg (1976)[14], Grossberg (1976)[8], Amari (1980)[1], and Kohonen (1982)[9]. These self-organization systems can alter their internal connections to represent the statistical features and topological relations in an input space.

The self-organizing maps (SOMs) are expressed by the weights of the self-organizing networks. They are very effective in modeling the topographic mapping among neural fields. Although the SOMs are widely used in neural modeling and applications, the theory of the SOMs is far from being complete. The question whether the self-organizing maps converge to the topological correct mappings is still open especially in the high dimensional case.

There are many models for the SOMs. Due to the space limit we only consider Amari's nerve field model[1, 2]. Another important SOM model is the feature map[9]. The stability of the feature map is discussed in [3, 6, 7, 10, 12].

The stability of the SOM in the nerve field model is analyzed in [1, 5, 13, 15]. The existing convergence results are most for the one-dimensional model. It is very difficult to analyze the stability of the SOM in any high dimension. The results in [5, 15] are only valid for some special cases of the linearized Amari model. We shall formulate the linearized Amari model in any high dimension and discuss not only the convergence but also the convergence rate of the self-organization algorithm for updating the weights. The approach used can also be used to analyze the stability of the feature map.

2 High-dimensional Self-organizing Maps

Let the K-dimensional grid $\mathcal{L}_K = \{0, 1, \cdots, N\}^K$ of $(N+1)^K$ neurons be the presynaptic field in the Amari model. A neuron in $\mathcal{L}_K$ is denoted by $J = (j_1, \cdots, j_K) \in \mathcal{L}_K$.

Let $\mathcal{W}_K$ be the space of all mappings $W = W(J) : \mathcal{L}_K \to \mathcal{C}_n \subseteq R^n$ where each $W(J)$ is a column vector in R^n. The weight vectors in $\mathcal{W}_K$ are labeled by the neurons in $\mathcal{L}_K$.

2.1 High Dimensional Topographic Map

Let us consider a system consisting of a presynaptic field $\mathcal{L}_K$ and a postsynaptic field $\mathcal{C}_n$. The neighborhood relation between each pair of neurons in $\mathcal{L}_K$ is determined by their relative positions in $\mathcal{L}_K$. A high dimensional topographic map is an ordered mapping in $\mathcal{W}_K$ under which the neighborhood relation in $\mathcal{L}_K$ is preserved in $\mathcal{C}_n$. To achieve a topographic map, we choose a random mapping in $\mathcal{W}_K$, then use the following algorithm to update the mapping recursively:

$$W_{t+1}(J) = \begin{cases} (1-\lambda_t)W_t(J) + \frac{\lambda_t}{c_t}\sum_{J'\in N_c(t)} W_t(J'), & J \in N_c(t) \bigcap \mathcal{L}_K^0 \\ W_t(J), & J \in \mathcal{L}_K^0 - N_c(t) \\ B(J) \text{ (boundary condition)}, & J \in \delta\mathcal{L}_K \end{cases} \quad (1)$$

where

λ_t is a learning rate, $\mathcal{L}_K^0 = \{1,\cdots,N-1\}^K$ the inner lattice of $\mathcal{L}_K$, $\delta\mathcal{L}_K = \mathcal{L}_K - \mathcal{L}_K^0$, $N_c(t) = \sigma_t(I_t)$ a neighborhood set, $I_t = (i_1(t),\cdots,i_K(t))$ a random stimulus process on $\mathcal{L}_K$, $\sigma_t(I)$ a neighborhood set around I such that $\sigma_t(I) \subseteq \mathcal{L}_K$ for each $I \in \mathcal{L}_K$ and t, and c_t the number of points in the set $N_c(t)$.

The equation (1) is a linearized version of the learning equation in [1]. It does not update the mapping on the boundary of $\mathcal{L}_K$. But the boundary condition will affect the map on $\mathcal{L}_K^0$ (the inner lattice) whenever the neighborhood set touches the boundary of the grid $\mathcal{L}_K$, and eventually shape the topographic map.
Let $h_t(I,J) = \mathbf{1}_{(J\in\sigma_t(I)\bigcap\mathcal{L}_K^0)}$ be the characteristic function of the set $\sigma_t(I)\bigcap\mathcal{L}_K^0$. The equation (1) can be rewritten as the following:

$$W_{t+1}(J) = W_t(J) - \lambda_t h_t(I_t,J)\{W_t(J) - \frac{1}{c_t}\sum_{J'\in\mathcal{L}_K^0} h_t(I_t,J')W_t(J')\}$$
$$+\frac{\lambda_t}{c_t}h_t(I_t,J)\sum_{J'\in\delta\mathcal{L}_K} h_t(I_t,J')B(J') \quad (2)$$

where $c_t = \sum_{J\in\mathcal{L}_K} h_t(I_t,J)$. Note from the definition of c_t, it is easy to show that $W_t(J)$ is bounded.
In the rest of this paper, we assume a general neighborhood function $h_t(I,J) \geq 0$ on $\mathcal{L}_K \times \mathcal{L}_K$ in (2). Let the neurons in $\mathcal{L}_K^0$ be arranged in the dictionary order $\{J_1, J_2, \cdots, J_m\}$ by their indexes in $\mathcal{L}_K^0$, where $J_1 = (1,\cdots,1)$, $J_2 = (1,\cdots,1,2)$, $\ldots$, $J_m = (N-1,\cdots,N-1)$ and $m = (N-1)^K$. Each mapping

$$W_t = (W_t(J_1),\cdots W_t(J_m))$$

is a $n \times m$ matrix. Using w_t^i to denote the transpose of the i-th row of W_t, we find the following vector form for (2):

$$w_{t+1}^i = w_t^i - \lambda_t U_t w_t^i + \frac{\lambda_t}{c_t}u_t u_t^T w_t^i + \lambda_t b_t^i \quad (3)$$

where $(\cdot)^T$ denotes the transpose, $u_t = (h_t(I_t,J_1), h_t(I_t,J_2),\cdots,h_t(I_t,J_m))^T$, $U_t = diag(u_t)$, $b_t^i = \frac{1}{c_t}u_t\sum_{J'\in\delta\mathcal{L}_K} h_t(I_t,J')B^i(J')$.
To analyze the convergence of the algorithm (2), we rewrite the system (3) as:

$$w_{t+1}^i = w_t^i - \lambda_t(Q_t w_t^i - b_t^i) = w_t^i - \lambda_t(\bar{Q}_t w_t^i - \bar{b}_t^i + \xi_t^i) \quad (4)$$

where $Q_t = U_t - \frac{1}{c_t}u_t u_t^T$, $\bar{Q}_t = E[Q_t]$, $\bar{b}_t^i = E[b_t^i]$, $\xi_t^i = (Q_t - \bar{Q}_t)w_t^i - (b_t^i - \bar{b}_t^i)$, and ξ_t^i is a martingale-difference process, i.e., $E[\xi_t^i|\mathcal{F}_{t-1}] = 0$ for $\mathcal{F}_t = \sigma(I_0,\cdots,I_t)$.
We need the following assumptions:

A1 $h_t(I,J) \to h(I,J)$ and $c_t \to c$ (a positive constant) as $t \to \infty$.

A2 I_t is a independent random sequence in $\mathcal{L}_K^0$ with the probability distribution $\{P(J_k)\}$.

Denote

$$u(I) = (h(I,J_1) \cdots, h(I,J_m))^T,$$

$$Q(I) = diag(u(I)) - \frac{1}{c}u(I)u(I)^T, \quad Q = \sum_{k=1}^{m} Q(J_k)P(J_k),$$

$$b^i(I) = \frac{1}{c}u(I) \sum_{J' \in \delta\mathcal{L}_K} h(I,J')B^i(J'), \quad b^i = \sum_{k=1}^{m} b^i(J_k)P(J_k)$$

From (4), we have

$$w_{t+1}^i = w_t^i - \lambda_t(Qw_t^i - b^i + \xi_t^i + \eta_t^i) \tag{5}$$

where $\eta_t^i = (\bar{Q}_t - Q)w_t^i - (\bar{b}_t^i - b^i) \to 0$ as $t \to \infty$ because of **A1**.
Let $m^i = Q^{-1}b^i$ be the stationary state of the system (5). The next theorem shows that W_t^T almost surely converges to $M = (m^1, \cdots, m^n)$.

Theorem 1 *Under the assumptions* **A1** *and* **A2**, *if* $Q > 0$ *(positive definite) and the learning rate* $\lambda_t > 0$ *satisfies the following conditions:*

$$\sum_t \lambda_t = \infty, \quad \sum_t \lambda_t^2 < \infty, \tag{6}$$

then for $i = 1, \cdots, n$, $w_t^i \to m^i$ *a.s. (almost sure convergence).*

Proof Let x_t be generated by the following equation: $x_{t+1} = x_t - \lambda_t(Q(x_t - m^i) + \xi_t^i)$. Let $h(x) = Q(x - m^i)$, then $(x - m^i)^T Qh(x) = (x - m^i)^T Q^T Q(x - m^i) > 0$, $\forall x \neq m^i$. Therefore, applying Gladyshev's Theorem (see Theorem 2.2 in [4]), we have $x_t \to m^i$, a.s.
Let $y_t = w_t^i - x_t$, then y_t satisfies $y_{t+1} = y_t - \lambda_t(Qy_t + \eta_t^i)$. Since $Q > 0$ and η_t^i tends to zero as t tends to infinity, y_t also tends to zero. Therefore, $w_t^i \to m^i$, a.s.
□
Note an example is given in [15] where $Q > 0$. When the first condition in (6) is not satisfied, the map may still converge but not to the desired stationary state.
We shall use an approach in [11] to discuss the convergence of $\overline{W}_t = \frac{1}{t}\sum_{s=0}^{t-1} W_t$ assuming that the learning rate satisfies one of the following conditions:

$$\lambda_t \equiv \lambda, \quad 0 < \lambda < 2(\min_i \mu_i(Q))^{-1}. \tag{7}$$

$$\lambda_t \downarrow 0, \quad \frac{\lambda_t - \lambda_{t+1}}{\lambda_t} = o(\lambda_t) \tag{8}$$

where $\{\mu_i(Q)\}$ are eigenvalues of Q. Note the learning rate $\lambda_t \propto t^{-\alpha}$ with $0 < \alpha < 1$ satisfies the condition (8).
The next theorem gives the convergence rate of the averaged weight $\overline{W}_t$. It also shows that $\overline{W}_t^T$ converges to M in mean square.

Theorem 2 *Let* $Q > 0$, *the learning rate satisfy (7) or (8), and the following conditions hold:*

A3 $\gamma > \frac{1}{2}$, $\bar{Q}_t - Q = O(t^{-\gamma})$, *and* $\bar{b}_t^i - b^i = O(t^{-\gamma})$;

A4 *for each* J, $\sup_t \sum_{k=1}^m |h_t(J_k, J) - \bar{h}_t(J)|^\beta P(J_k) < \infty$, *where* $\beta > 2$ *and* $\bar{h}_t(J) = \sum_{k=1}^m h_t(J_k, J)P(J_k)$;

A5 *for each* J *and* J', $\sup_t \sum_{k=1}^m |h_t(J_k, J)h_t(J_k, J') - \bar{h}_t(J, J')|^\beta P(J_k) < \infty$, *where* $\bar{h}_t(J, J') = \sum_{k=1}^m h_t(J_k, J)h_t(J_k, J')P(J_k) < \infty$;

A6 $lim_{t\to\infty} E[\xi_t^i(\xi_t^i)^T] = S^i > 0$.

Denote $V = Q^{-1}S^iQ^{-1}$. *Then for* $\bar{w}_t^i = \frac{1}{t}\sum_{s=0}^{t-1} w_t^i$, *we have*

$$\sqrt{t}(\bar{w}_t^i - m^i) \xrightarrow{\mathcal{D}} N(0, V)$$
$$lim_{t\to\infty} E[t(\bar{w}_t^i - m^i)(\bar{w}_t^i - m^i)^T] = V. \tag{9}$$

Proof From **A4** and **A5**, we have $\sup_t E[|Q_t - \bar{Q}_t|^\beta] < \infty$ and $\sup_t E[|b_t^i - \bar{b}_t^i|^\beta] < \infty$. Therefore,

$$\sup_t E[|\xi_t^i|^\beta] < \infty. \tag{10}$$

Because w_t^i is bounded, we have $\sup_t E[|\xi_t^i|^2|\mathcal{F}_{t-1}] < \infty$. From (10), we have

$$\lim_{C\to\infty} \overline{\lim}_{t\to\infty} E[|\xi_t^i|^2 \mathbf{1}_{(|\xi_t^i|>C)}|\mathcal{F}_{t-1}] = 0, \quad a.s.$$

So Assumptions 2.1-2.5 in [11] are satisfied. However, we cannot apply the results there directly due to the term η_t^i in the system (5). We can use the same approach in [11] to get the following:

$$\sqrt{t}\bar{\Delta}_t = \frac{1}{\sqrt{t}}\alpha_t\bar{\Delta}_0 - \frac{1}{\sqrt{t}}\sum_{s=1}^{t-1} Q^{-1}(\xi_s^i + \eta_s^i) - \frac{1}{\sqrt{t}}\sum_{s=1}^{t-1} V_s^t(\xi_s^i + \eta_s^i), \tag{11}$$

where $\bar{\Delta}_t = \bar{w}_t^i - m^i$, and $\bar{\Delta}_0 = w_0^i - m^i$, $\alpha_t = \alpha_1^t$, $V_j^t = \alpha_j^t - Q^{-1}$, with $\alpha_j^t = \lambda_j \sum_{i=j}^{t-1} \prod_{k=j+1}^i (I - \lambda_k Q)$, α_t and V_j^t are bounded, and $\lim_{t\to\infty} \frac{1}{t}\sum_{j=1}^{t-1} \|V_j^t\| = 0$. Noticing the assumption **A3** implies $\eta_t^i = O(t^{-\gamma})$,

$$\frac{1}{t}\sum_{s=1}^{t-1} \eta_s^i(\eta_s^i)^T \to 0, \quad \text{and} \quad \frac{1}{\sqrt{t}}\sum_{s=1}^{t-1} Q^{-1}\eta_s^i \to 0, \quad \text{ast} \to \infty,$$

we can apply the proofs in [11] to (11) and conclude that $\sqrt{t}(\bar{w}_t^i - m^i)$ is asymptotically normal with zero mean and the covariance matrix V, and (9) holds. □

Theorem 2 allows us to use a small constant learning rate or even the learning rate $\lambda_t \propto t^{-\alpha}$ with $0 < \alpha < \frac{1}{2}$ which tends to zero slower than $\frac{1}{\sqrt{t}}$. The assumption $\beta > 2$ in **A4** and **A5** can be relaxed to $\beta = 2$ if we only want to obtain (9).

Note we showed the convergence of the SOM but we did not show that the stationary states are the topographic mappings which preserves the topology. Based on the simulation results in [5, 13] we believe that the SOM converges to a topographic map, or a micro-structure consisting of several topographic sub-maps.

3 Conclusion

The convergence of the learning algorithm for updating the SOM is studied. The conditions on the neighborhood function and the learning rate have been found to guarantee the convergence. The learning algorithm can be accelerated by averaging the weight vectors in the training history. For the learning algorithm with averaging, the convergence rate has been found.

REFERENCES

[1] S.-I. Amari, *Topographic organization of nerve fields*, Bulletin of Mathematical Biology, Vol. 42 (1980), pp339–364.

[2] S.-I. Amari, *Field theory of self-organizing neural nets*, IEEE Trans. on Systems, Man and Cybernetics, Vol. 13(5) (September/October 1983), pp741–748.

[3] M. Budinich and J. G. Taylor, *On the ordering conditions for self-organising maps*, Neural Computation, Vol. 7(2) (March 1995).

[4] Han-Fu Chen, *Recursive Estimation and Control for Stochastic Systems*, John Wiley & Sons, Inc. (1985).

[5] M. Cottrell and J. C. Fort, *A stochastic model of retinotopy: A self organizing process*, Biological Cybernetics, Vol. 53 (1986), pp405–411.

[6] M. Cottrell, J. C. Fort, and G. Pages, *Two or three things that we know about the kohonen algorithm*, in: Proc. ESANN94 Conf., De Facto Ed., Brussels (April 1994).

[7] E. Erwin, K. Obermayer, and K. Schulten, *Self-organizing maps: Ordering, convergence properties and energy functions*, Biological Cybernetics, Vol. 67 (1992), pp47–55.

[8] S. Grossberg, *Adaptive pattern classification and universal recording: I. Parallel development and coding of neural feature detectors*, Biological Cybernetics, Vol. 22 (1976), pp121–134.

[9] T. Kohonen, *Self-organized formation of topologically correct feature maps*, Biological Cybernetics, Vol. 43 (1982), pp59–69.

[10] Z.-P. Lo and B. Bavarian, *On the Rate of Convergence in Topology Preserving Neural Networks*, Biological Cybernetics, Vol. 65 (1991), pp55–63.

[11] T. Polyak and A. B. Juditsky, *Acceleration of stochastic approximation by averaging*, SIAM Journal of Control and Optimization, Vol. 30(4) (July 1992), pp838–855,.

[12] H. Ritter and K. Schulten, *Convergence properties of kohonen's topology conserving maps: Fluctuations, stability, and dimension selection*, Biological Cybernetics, Vol. 60 (1988), pp59–71.

[13] A. Takeuchi and S.-I Amari, *Formation of topographic maps and columnar microstructures*, Biological Cybernetics, Vol. 35 (1979), pp63–72.

[14] D.J. Willshaw and C. von der Malsburg, *How patterned neural connections can be set up by self-organization*, Proceedings of the Royal Society of Longdon, Vol. B 194 (1976), pp431–445.

[15] Hua Yang and T. S. Dillon, *Convergence of self-organizing neural algorithms*, Neural Networks, Vol. 5 (1992), pp485–493.

MEASUREMENTS OF GENERALISATION BASED ON INFORMATION GEOMETRY

Huaiyu Zhu* and Richard Rohwer**

Neural Computing Research Group, Department of Computer Science and Applied Mathematics, Aston University, Birmingham B4 7ET, UK

** Current address: Santa Fe Institute, 1399 Hyde Park Road, Santa Fe, NM87501, USA. Email: zhuh@santafe.edu*

*** Current address: Prediction Co., 320 Aztec Street, SuiteB, Santa Fe, NM87501, USA.*

Neural networks are statistical models and learning rules are estimators. In this paper a theory for measuring generalisation is developed by combining Bayesian decision theory with information geometry. The performance of an estimator is measured by the information divergence between the true distribution and the estimate, averaged over the Bayesian posterior. This unifies the majority of error measures currently in use. The optimal estimators also reveal some intricate interrelationships among information geometry, Banach spaces and sufficient statistics.

1 Introduction

A neural network (deterministic or stochastic) can be regarded as a parameterised statistical model $P(y|x, w)$, where $x \in X$ is the input, $y \in Y$ is the output and $w \in W$ is the weight. In an environment with an input distribution $P(x)$, it is also equivalent to $P(z|w)$, where $z := [x, y] \in Z := X \times Y$ denotes the combined input and output as data [11]. Learning is the task of inferring w from z. It is a typical statistical inference problem in which a neural network model acts as a "likelihood function", a learning rule as an "estimator", the trained network as an "estimate" and the data set as a "sample". The set of probability measures on sample space Z forms a (possibly infinite dimensional) differential manifold $\mathcal{P}$ [2, 16]. A statistical model forms a finite-dimensional submanifold $\mathcal{Q}$, composed of representable distributions, parameterised by weights w acting as coordinates.

To infer w from z requires additional information about w. In a Bayesian framework such auxiliary information is represented by a prior $P(p)$, where p is the true but unknown distribution from which z is drawn. This is then combined with the likelihood function $P(z|p)$ to yield the posterior distribution $P(p|z)$ via the Bayes formula $P(p|z) = P(z|p)P(p)/P(z)$.

An estimator $\tau : Z \rightarrow \mathcal{Q}$ must, for each z, fix one $q \in \mathcal{Q}$ which in a sense approximate p. [1] This requires a measure of "divergence" $D(p, q)$ between $p, q \in \mathcal{P}$ defined independent of parameterisation. General studies on divergences between probability distributions are provided by the theory of information geometry (See [2, 3, 7] and further references therein). The main thesis of this paper is that generalisation error should be measured by the posterior expectation of the information divergence between true distribution and estimate. We shall show that this retains most of the mathematical simplicity of mean squared error theory while being generally applicable to any statistical inference problems.

[1] Some Bayesian methods give the entire posterior $P(p|z)$ instead of a point estimate q as the answer. They will be shown later to be a special case of the current framework.

2 Measurements of Generalisation

The most natural "information divergence" between two distribution $p, q \in \mathcal{P}$ is the δ-divergence defined as [2] [2]

$$D_\delta(p,q) := \frac{1}{\delta(1-\delta)}\left(1 - \int p^\delta q^{1-\delta}\right), \qquad \forall \delta \in (0,1). \tag{1}$$

The limits as δ tends to 0 and 1 are taken as definitions of D_0 and D_1, respectively. Following are some salient properties of the δ-divergences [2]:

$$D_\delta(p,q) = D_{1-\delta}(q,p) \geq 0. \qquad D_\delta(p,q) = 0 \iff p = q. \tag{2}$$

$$D_0(q,p) = D_1(p,q) = K(p,q) := \int p \log \frac{p}{q}. \tag{3}$$

$$D_{1/2}(p,q) = D_{1/2}(q,p) = 2\int \left(\sqrt{p} - \sqrt{q}\right)^2. \tag{4}$$

$$D_\delta(p, p+\Delta p) \approx \frac{1}{2}\int \frac{(\Delta p)^2}{p} \approx \frac{1}{2}\langle(\Delta \log p)^2\rangle. \tag{5}$$

The quantity $K(p,q)$ is the Kullback-Leibler divergence (cross entropy). The quantity $D_{1/2}(p,q)$ is the Hellinger distance. The quantity $\int(\Delta p)^2/p$ is usually called the χ^2 distance between two nearby distributions.

Armed with the δ-divergence, we now define the generalisation error

$$E_\delta(\tau) := \int_p P(p) \int_z P(z|p) D_\delta(p, \tau(z)), \qquad E_\delta(q|z) := \int_p P(p|z) D_\delta(p,q), \tag{6}$$

where p is the true distribution, τ is the learning rule, z is the data, and $q = \tau(z)$ is the estimate. A learning rule τ is called δ-optimal if it minimises $E_\delta(\tau)$. A probability distribution q is called a δ-optimal estimate, or simply a δ-estimate, from data z, if it minimises $E_\delta(q|z)$. The following theorem is a special case of a standard result from Bayesian decision theory.

Theorem 1 (Coherence) *A learning rule τ is δ-optimal if and only if for any data z, excluding a set of zero probability, the result of training $q = \tau(z)$ is a δ-estimate.*

Definition 2 (δ-coordinate) *Let $\mu := 1/\delta$, $\nu := 1/(1-\delta)$. Let L_μ be the Banach space of μth power integrable functions. Then L_μ and L_ν are dual to each other as Banach spaces. Let $p \in \mathcal{P}$. Its δ-coordinate is defined as $l_\delta(p) := p^\delta/\delta \in L_\mu$ for $\delta > 0$, and $l_0(p) := \log p$ [2]. Denote by $l_{1/\delta}$ the inverse of l_δ.*

Theorem 3 (δ-estimator in $\mathcal{P}$) *The δ-estimate $\widehat{q} \in \mathcal{P}$ is uniquely given [14] by $\widehat{q} \sim l_{1/\delta}(\int P(p|z) l_\delta(p))$.*

3 Divergence between Finite Positive Measures

One of the most useful properties of the least mean square estimate is the so called $MSE = VAR + BIAS^2$ relation, which also implies that, for a given linear space W, the LMS estimate of w within W is given by the projection of the posterior mean $\widehat{w}$ onto W. This is generalised to the following theorem [16], applying the generalised Pythagorean Theorem for δ-divergences [2].

---

[2]This is essentially Amari's α-divergence, where $\alpha \in [-1,1]$, re-parameterised by $\delta = (1-\alpha)/2 \in [0,1]$ for technical convenience, following [6].

Theorem 4 (Error decomposition in $\mathcal{Q}$) *Let $\mathcal{Q}$ be a δ-flat manifold. Let $P(p)$ be a prior on $\mathcal{Q}$. Then $\forall q \in \mathcal{Q}$, $\forall z \in Z$,*

$$E_\delta(q|z) = E_\delta(\widehat{p}|z) + D_\delta(\widehat{p}, q), \tag{7}$$

where $\widehat{p}$ is the δ-estimate in $\mathcal{Q}$.

To apply this theorem it is necessary to extend the definition of δ-divergence to $\widetilde{\mathcal{P}}$, the space of finite positive measures, which is δ-flat for any δ for a finite sample space Z [2], following suggestions in [2].

Definition 5 (δ-divergence on $\widetilde{\mathcal{P}}$) *The δ-divergence on $\widetilde{\mathcal{P}}$ is defined by*

$$D_\delta(p, q) := \frac{1}{\delta(1-\delta)} \int \left(\delta p + (1-\delta) q - p^\delta q^{1-\delta}\right) \tag{8}$$

This definition retains most of the important properties of δ-divergence on $\mathcal{P}$, and reduces to the original definition when restricted to $\mathcal{P}$. It has the additional advantage of being the integral of a positive measure, making it possible to attribute the divergence between two measures to their divergence over various events [16]. In particular, the generalised cross entropy is [16]

$$K(p, q) := \int \left(q - p + p \log \frac{p}{q}\right). \tag{9}$$

The δ-divergence defines a differential structure on $\widetilde{\mathcal{P}}$. The Riemannian geometry and the δ-affine connections can be obtained by the Eguchi relations [2, 7] The most important advantage of this definition is that the following important theorem is true and can be proved by pure algebraic manipulation [16].

Theorem 6 (Error Decomposition on $\widetilde{\mathcal{P}}$) *Let $P(p)$ be a distribution over $\widetilde{\mathcal{P}}$. Let $q \in \widetilde{\mathcal{P}}$. Then*

$$\langle D_\delta(p, q) \rangle = \langle D_\delta(p, \widehat{p}) \rangle + D_\delta(\widehat{p}, q), \tag{10}$$

where $\widehat{p}$ is the δ-average of p given by $\widehat{p}^\delta := \langle p^\delta \rangle$.

Theorem 7 (δ-estimator in $\widetilde{\mathcal{P}}$) *The δ-estimate $\widehat{p} = \tau_\delta(z)$ in $\widetilde{\mathcal{P}}$ is given by $\widehat{p}^\delta = \langle p^\delta \rangle_z$. In particular, the 1-estimate is the posterior marginal distribution $\widehat{p} = \langle p \rangle_z$.*

Theorem 8 (δ-estimator in $\mathcal{Q}$) *Let $\mathcal{Q}$ be an arbitrary submanifold of $\widetilde{\mathcal{P}}$. The δ-estimate $\widehat{q}$ in $\mathcal{Q}$ is given by the δ-projection of $\widehat{p}$ onto $\mathcal{Q}$, where $\widehat{p}$ is the δ-estimate in $\widetilde{\mathcal{P}}$.*

4 Examples and Applications to Neural Networks

Explicit formulas are derived for the optimal estimators for the multinomial [15] and normal distributions [14].

Example 1 *Let $m \in \mathbb{N}^n$, $p \in \mathcal{P} = \Delta^{n-1}$, $a \in \mathbb{R}^n_+$. Consider multinomial family of distributions $M(m|p)$ with a Dirichlet prior $D(p|a)$. The posterior is also a Dirichlet distribution $D(p|a+m)$. The δ-estimate $\widehat{p} \in \widetilde{\mathcal{P}}$ is given by $(\widehat{p}_i)^\delta = (a_i + m_i)_\delta / (|a+m|)_\delta$, where $|a| := \sum_i a_i$ and $(a)_b := \Gamma(a+b)/\Gamma(a)$. In particular, $\widehat{p}_i = (a_i + m_i)/|a+m|$ for $\delta = 1$, and $\widehat{p}_i = \exp\left(\Psi(a_i + m_i) - \Psi(|a+m|)\right)$ for $\delta = 0$, where Ψ is the the digamma function. The δ-estimate $\widehat{q} \in \mathcal{P}$ is given by normalising $\widehat{p}$.*

Example 2 *Let $z, \mu \in \mathbb{R}$, $h \in \mathbb{R}_+$, $a \in \mathbb{R}$, $n \in \mathbb{R}_+$. Consider the Gaussian family of distributions $f(z|\mu) = N(z - \mu|h)$, with fixed variance $\sigma^2 = 1/h$. Let the prior be another Gaussian $f(\mu) = N(\mu - a|nh)$, Then the posterior after seeing a sample z of size k, is also a Gaussian $f(\mu|z) = N(\mu - a_k|n_k h)$, where $n_k = n + k$, $a_k = (na + \sum z)/n_k$, which is also the posterior least squares estimate. The δ-estimate $\widehat{q} \in \mathcal{P}$ is given by the density $f(z'|\widehat{q}) = N\left(z' - a_k\middle|h/(1 + \delta/n_k)\right)$.*

The entities $|a|$ for the multinomial model and n for the Gaussian model are effective previous sample sizes, a fact known since Fisher's time. In a restricted model, the sample size might not be well reflected, and some ancillary statistics may be used for information recovery [2].

Example 3 *In some Bayesian methods, such as the Monte Carlo method [10], no estimator is explictly given. Instead, the posterior is directly used for sampling p. This produces a prediction distribution on test data which is the posterior marginal distribution. Therefore these methods are implicitly 1-estimators.*

Example 4 *Multilayer neural networks are usually not δ-convex for any δ, and there may exist local optima of $E_\delta(\cdot|z)$ on $\mathcal{Q}$. A practical learning rule is usually a gradient descent rule which moves w in the direction which reduces $E_\delta(q|z)$. The 1-divergence can be minimised by a supervised learning rule, the Boltzmann machine learning rule [1]. The 0-divergence can be minimised by a reinforcement learning rule, the simulated annealing reinforcement learning rule for stochastic networks[13].*

$$\mathrm{Min}_q K(p,q) \iff \Delta w \sim \langle \partial_w l_0(q)\rangle_p - angle \partial_w l_0(q)\rangle_q \tag{11}$$

$$\mathrm{Min}_q K(q,p) \iff \Delta w \sim \langle \partial_w l_0(q),\ l_0(p) - \lambda_0(q)\rangle_q \tag{12}$$

5 Conclusions

The problem of finding a measurement of generalisation is solved in the framework of Baysian decision theory, with machinery developed in the theory of information geometry.

By working in the Bayesian framework, this ensures that the measurement is internally coherent, in the sense that a learning rule is optimal if and only if it produces optimal estiamtes for almost all the data. By adopting an information geometric measurement of divergence between distributions, this ensures that the theory is independent of parameterisation. This resolves the controversy in [8, 12, 9].

To guarantee a unique and well-defined solution to the learning problem, it is necessary to generalise the concept of information divergence to the space of finite positive measures. This development reveals certain elegant relations between information geometry and the theory of Banach spaces, showing that the dually-affine geometries of statistical manifolds are in fact intricately related to the dual linear geometries of Banach spaces.

In a computational model, such as a classical statisitical model or a neural network, the optimal estimator is the projection of the ideal estimator to the model. This theory generalises the theory of linear Gaussian regression to general statistical estimation and function approximation problems. Further research may lead to Kalman filter type learning rules which are not restricted to linear and Gaussian models.

REFERENCES

[1] D. H. Ackley, G. E. Hinton, and T. J. Sejnowski, *A learning algorithm for Boltzmann machines*, Cog. Sci., Vol. 9 (1985), pp147–169.

[2] S. Amari, *Differential-Geometrical Methods in Statistics*, Vol. 28 of Springer Lecture Notes in Statistics. Springer-Verlag, New York 1985.

[3] S. Amari, *Differential geometrical theory of statistics*, In Amari et al. [4], Ch. 2, pp19–94.

[4] S. Amari, O. E. Barndoff-Nieldon, R. E. Kass, S. L. Lauritzen, and C. R. Rao, eds., *Differential Geometry in Statistical Inference*, Vol. 10 of IMS Lecture Notes Monograph. IMS, Hayward, CA (1987).

[5] S. J. Hanson, J. D. Cowan, and C. L. Giles, eds., *Advances in Neural Information Processing Systems*, Vol. 5 (1993), San Mateo, CA. Morgan Kaufmann.

[6] R. E. Kass, *Canonical parameterization and zero parameter effects curvature*, J. Roy. Stat. Soc., B, Vol. 46 (1984), pp86–92.

[7] S. L. Lauritzen, *Statistical manifolds*, in: Amari et al. [4], Ch. 4, pp163–216.

[8] D. J. C. MacKay, *Bayesian Methods for Adaptive Models*. PhD thesis, California Institute of Technology, Pasadena, CA (1992).

[9] D. J. C. MacKay, *Hyperparameters: Optimise, or integrate out?*, Technical report, Cambridge (1993).

[10] R. M. Neal, *Bayesian learning via stochastic dynamics*, in: Hanson et al. [5], pp475–482.

[11] H. White, *Learning in artificial neural networks: A statistical perspective*, Neural Computation, Vol. 1(4) (1989), pp425–464.

[12] D. H. Wolpert, *On the use of evidence in neural neworks*, In Hanson et al. [5], pp539–546.

[13] H. Zhu, *Neural Networks and Adaptive Computers: Theory and Methods of Stochastic Adaptive Computations*. PhD thesis, Dept. of Stat. & Comp. Math., Liverpool University (1993), `ftp://archive.cis.ohio-state.edu/pub/neuroprose/Thesis/zhu.thesis.ps.Z`.

[14] H. Zhu and R. Rohwer, *Bayesian invariant measurements of generalisation for continuous distributions*, Technical Report NCRG/4352, Dept. Comp. Sci. & Appl. Math., Aston University (August 1995), `ftp://cs.aston.ac.uk/neural/zhuh/continuous.ps.Z`.

[15] H. Zhu and R. Rohwer, *Bayesian invariant measurements of generalisation for discrete distributions*, Technical Report NCRG/4351, Dept. Comp. Sci. & Appl. Math., Aston University (August 1995), `ftp://cs.aston.ac.uk/neural/zhuh/discrete.ps.Z`.

[16] H. Zhu and R. Rohwer, *Information geometric measurements of generalisation*, Technical Report NCRG/4350, Dept. Comp. Sci. & Appl. Math., Aston University (August 1995), `ftp://cs.aston.ac.uk/neural/zhuh/generalisation.ps.Z`.

Acknowledgements

We are grateful to Prof. S. Amari for clarifying a point of information geometry. We would like to thank many people in the Neural Computing Research Group, especially C. Williams, for useful comments and practical help. This work was partially supported by EPSRC grant (GR/J17814).

TOWARDS AN ALGEBRAIC THEORY OF NEURAL NETWORKS: SEQUENTIAL COMPOSITION

R. Zimmer

Computer Science Department, Brunel University, Uxbridge, Middx. UB8 3PH, UK. Email: Robert.Zimmer@brunel.ac.uk

This paper marks a step towards an algebraic theory of neural networks. In it, a new notion of sequential composition for neural networks is defined, and some observations are made on the algebraic structure of the class of networks under this operation. The composition is shown to reflect a notion of composition of state spaces of the networks. The paper ends on a very brief exposition of the usefulness of similar composition theories for other models of computation.

1 What is an Algebraic Study?

The view of mathematics that underlies this work is one forged by Category Theory (see for example [1]). In Category Theory scrutiny is focused less on objects than on mappings between them. Thus the natural question is: "What are the mappings?". In this kind of study the answer tends to be: "Functions (or sometimes partial functions) that preserve the relevant operations." So before we can start looking at the category of neural networks we need to answer the question: "What are the relevant operations?"

For example, recall that a **group** is a set, G, with a binary operation (*), a constant (e), and a unary operation $()^{-1}$. To be a group, it is also necessary that these operations satisfy some equations to the effect that * is associative, e is a two-sided identity for * and $()^{-1}$ forms inverses, but these are the defining group operations. A **group homomorphism** is a function, ϕ, from one group to another satisfying

$$\phi(a * b) = \phi(a) * \phi(b), \qquad \phi(e) = e' \qquad \text{and} \qquad \phi(a)^{-1} = (\phi(a))^{-1}.$$

That is a group homomorphism is defined to be a function that preserves all of the defining operations of a group.

2 What are the Defining Operations of Neural Nets?

A synchronous neural net is a set of nodes each one of which computes a function; the input for the function at a node at a given time is the output of some nodes at the previous time step (the nodes that supply the input to the given node is fixed for all time and determined by the interconnection structure of the net). This structure is captured diagrammatically by drawing a circle for each node and an arrow from node N to node M if M acts as an input for N. For example, the following is a picture of a two-noded net each of whose nodes takes an input from node f, and g takes another input from itself:

Figure 1

The letters indicate that node on the left computes the function $f(n)$ and the node on the right computes function $g(n, m)$. So a neural net is a finite directed graph

each of whose nodes is labelled by a function. We will call the underlying unlabelled graph the **shape** of the net.
As well as the shape (the interconnection structure), there is a recursive computational structure generated by the network. In this example we get the two recursive functions:

$$f_{n+1} = f(f_n).$$
$$g_{n+1} = g(f_n, g_n).$$

where, for example, f_i denotes the state of the node labelled by f at time i. Once f and g are known, these equations entirely determine the dynamics of the system: that is, the sequence of values of the pair $< f_i, g_i >$.

3 The State Space of a Boolean Net

In this section we will restrict ourselves to nets whose nodes compute boolean functions. A **state** of such a net is a vector of 0's and 1's, representing the states of the nodes of the net. When we say that a net is in state vect, we mean that for all i, the ith node of the net has most recently computed the ith value of vect. Since the next state behaviour of a net is completely determined by the recursion equations, we can completely compute a graph of the possible states of the net. In the example above if f is *invert* and g is *and* then the state graph is given below:

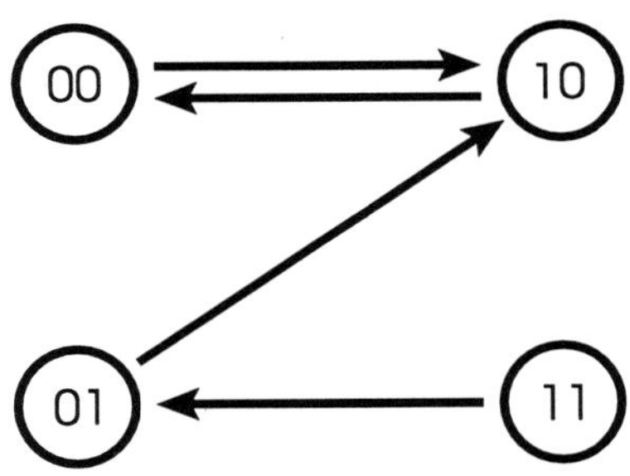

Figure 2

This exemplifies a mapping from boolean neural nets to state spaces and points to an algebraic relationship whose desirability can guide us in our setting out of our algebraic theory: we should ensure that the space of boolean neural networks is **fibred** over the space of boolean state spaces. For a detailed discussion of fibred categories see [2], for now it will suffice to give an informal definition.
Recall that a category is simply a collection of objects and maps between them. In essence, what it means for a category , **E**, to be a fibred over a category, **C**, is that there is a projection from **E** to **C** (the part of **E** that gets projected to a particular **C**-object C constitutes the **fibre** over C) such that: for every **C**-mapping $f : C \to C'$ and **E**-object, E, in the fibre over C, there is a unique lifting of f to a map starting at E and projecting onto f. The idea is that what happens in **E** gets reflected down to **C**, and, if we are lucky, what happens in **C** is liftable to **E**. This can hold for maps and operations. We want to ensure that the category of Neural Networks is in this relationship to the category of state spaces, and that the state space composition is liftable.

4 Composition in the State Space

We wish to define a notion of composition of nets that is a lifting of state space composition. The sequential composition of two graphs with the same nodes is quite well-known: an arc in the composite graph is an arc in the first graph followed by an arc in the second. Two nets with the same nodes automatically yield state graphs with the same nodes. Our first lifting of state-space composition will take advantage of this fact and only be defined for networks on the same (perhaps after renaming) nodes. We shall see that this lifting is all we need to explain the closure properties of state spaces under composition.

To continue with our example, consider the net given by the equations

$$\begin{aligned} f_{n+1} &= f_n * g_n \\ g_{n+1} &= \sim f_n. \end{aligned}$$

Notice that the shape of this net differs from the other. The shape is shown by:

Figure 3

The state space and the result of composing it with the graph above are pictured below:

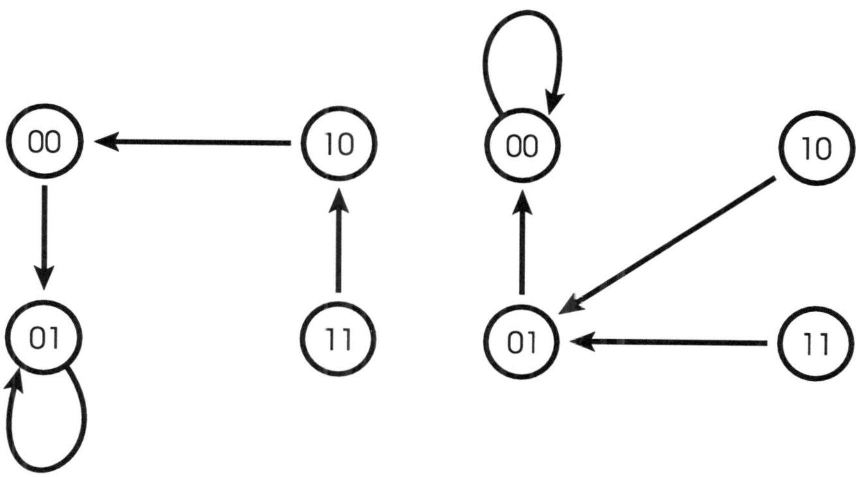

Figure 4

The observation that initiated this work is that the composite state space (and all others that can be similarly derived) is the state space of a neural network. That is, if SS denotes the function that sends a neural net to its state space, then for any two boolean nets, N and M, the composition $SS(N) * SS(M)$ turns out to be $SS(something)$. We will now describe an operation on the nets such that $SS(N) * SS(M) = SS(N * M)$.

5 Simple Composition of Nets

The first form of neural network composition is direct functional composition on the recursion equations. The concept is most readily understood in terms of an example. Thus, to continue the example above:

First Net $f_{n+1} =\sim f_n$ and $g_{n+1} = f_n * g_n$

Second Net $f_{n+1} = f_n * g_n$ and $g_{n+1} =\sim f_n$

The composition consists of the second net using the results of the first net:

Composite Net $f_{n+2} = f_{n+1} * g_{n+1} =\sim f_n * f_n * g_n = 0$

$g_{n+2} =\sim f_{n+1} =\sim\sim f_n = f_n$

Note that the composite net works with $n+2$ as one step, since its one step is a sequence of one step in each of two nets. With that rewriting in mind ($n+1$ for $n+2$), the equations for the composite net yield the composite state space above. And it is not hard to see that this will hold for any two boolean nets with the same set of nodes.

The set of nets with the same nodes is a monoid under this operation: the composition is associative and has an identity.

6 Two More Complex Notions of Sequential Composition

More interesting notions of composition allow us to compose nets with different nodes. The first of these compositions requires a function from the nodes of the second net to the nodes of the first. The composition is then very like the simple one except that instead of simply using the same names to say, for example,

$$f_{n+2} = f_{n+1} * g_{n+1} =\sim f_n * f_n * g_n$$

there is an extra dimension, say

$$f_{n+2} = f_{n+1} * g_{n+1}$$

in the second net and translate to

$$\phi(f)_{n+1} * \phi(g)_{n+1}$$

in the first net.

This is obviously more general (the simple version is just the special case in which f is the identity) and we believe it will lead to rich composition theories.

An even more general composition comes from taking the union of these compositions for all functions ϕ. This composition is related to the concept of **wreath product** for groups and automata (see [3]).

7 What use is a Composition Theory?

A proper composition theory can be used to explain how complex things can and do get built from simple ones. The theory can be used to break things down as well. For example, there could well be a set of primitive objects and a theorem that all objects can be built from them. A famous instance of such a theorem was given by Krohn and Rhodes:

Theorem [Krohn-Rhodes 4] *Given a finite monoid, M, M divides a wreath product of simple groups and switches each of which divides M.*

And an instance that we've been using is given by:

Theorem [5] *Given a finite concrete category, C, divides a wreath product of primitive minimal categories each of which divides C.*

This paper marks only the beginning of a composition theory of neural nets. The Krohn-Rhodes theorem has fostered a whole branch of algebra that has shed much light on automata and semigroups, while the other theorem has found application in various fields of computing. We would like our neural net composition to be useful in both of these fashions. The mathematics will consist of a study of the category of Networks as a fibred category and some projects that natural arise are: uncover a set of primitives, study the ordering determined by the decomposition, devise a homomorphism theorem, and extend the work to other operations, such as parallel composition. And to give some idea of the kinds of application we envisage, here are two applications of the categorical composition theory:

Designing Chips: We take an algebraic description of a chip design and use the decomposition to implement it using pre-defined primitive modules (see [6]).

Problem Solving: We turn difficult problems into sequences of problems that are more easily solved (see [7]).

We hope to find applications that are akin to these. The problem solving work automatically makes hierarchies of search spaces. Could we form similar neural network hierarchies? Moreover, if one wanted to design a net with a particular behaviour this might be a modular way to do it. And to finish with an interesting entirely open question: how can we apply a theory like this to nets as they are trained?

REFERENCES

[1] Saunders MacLane. *Categories for the Working Mathematician*, Graduate Texts in Mathematics 5, Springer-Verlag, Berlin (1971).

[2] John Gray, Fibred and Cofibred Categories, *Proceedings of The Conference on Categorical Algebra*, S. Eilenberg et al eds., Springer Verlag, Heidleberg (1965).

[3] Samuel Eilenberg, *Automata, Languages and Machines*, Vol. B (1976), Academic Press, New York.

[4] K. Krohn and J. Rhodes, *Algebraic Theory of Machines, I. Prime Decomposition Theorem for Finite Semigroups and Machines*, Trans. Amer. Soc. Vol. 116 (1965), pp450–464.

[5] Robert Zimmer, *Decomposing Categories*, to appear in Categorical Structures in Computer Science.

[6] R. Zimmer, A MacDonald and R Holte, *Automated Representation Changing for Problem Solving and Electronic CAD*, Applications of Artificial Intelligence 1993: Knowledge-Based Systems in Aerospace and Industry, Usama M. Fayad, Ramasmy Uthurusamy, eds., Proc. SPIE (1993), pp126–137.

[7] R. Holte, C. Druumond, R. Zimmer, Alan MacDonald, *Speeding Up Problem-Solving by Abstraction: A Graph-Oriented View*, to appear (1996).